TAKING A CASE TO THE EUR
OF HUMAN RIGI

TAKING A CASE TO THE EUROPEAN COURT OF HUMAN RIGHTS

FOURTH EDITION

PHILIP LEACH

*Professor of Human Rights Law, Middlesex
University, Solicitor
Director, European Human Rights Advocacy
Centre (EHRAC)
With a foreword by Tim Eicke*

OXFORD
UNIVERSITY PRESS

OXFORD
UNIVERSITY PRESS

Great Clarendon Street, Oxford, OX2 6DP,
United Kingdom

Oxford University Press is a department of the University of Oxford.
It furthers the University's objective of excellence in research, scholarship,
and education by publishing worldwide. Oxford is a registered trade mark of
Oxford University Press in the UK and in certain other countries

Third Edition published in 2011
Fourth Edition published in 2017

Impression: 1

Published in the United States of America by Oxford University Press
198 Madison Avenue, New York, NY 10016, United States of America

British Library Cataloguing in Publication Data
Data available

Library of Congress Control Number: 2017930946

ISBN 978–0–19–875541–8 (pbk)

Printed and bound by
CPI Group (UK) Ltd, Croydon, CR0 4YY

For Becky, Anna, Katy and Mary

In memory of Tahir Elçi, Kurdish human rights lawyer (1966–2015)

FOREWORD

This fourth edition of Philip Leach's 'indispensable guide to the Convention system', as Sir Nicolas Bratza described it in his Foreword to the second edition some ten years ago, is extremely timely; not only have there been significant changes (largely of procedure and practice) since the last edition but there continue to be significant challenges (some old and some new) confronting the Court and the Convention system as a whole. Building on Philip's more than twenty years' experience of practising before and interacting with the Strasbourg Court as well as other elements of the Convention system, this edition, like its predecessors, provides a thorough, accessible and, at the same time, practical and readable guide to making the most effective use of the Convention system.

When the last edition was published (2011) the Strasbourg Court was confronted by a significant backlog of nearly 160,000 pending cases which appeared to be increasing daily as the number of applications brought before it continued to rise. It was clear both to the Court itself and to the Contracting Parties that steps needed to be taken to address the challenges posed to the Court and the whole system of human rights protection under the Convention.

Significant reforms were initiated following the Brighton Conference in April 2012.[1] These included, inter alia, the adoption and opening for signature, in 2013, of Protocols 15 and 16 to the Convention as well as providing a mandate to the Steering Committee for Human Rights (CDDH) to conduct a detailed study on the 'longer-term future of the Convention system' (and, in doing so, to 'think out of the box') which was published in December 2015.[2] Importantly, the mandate, and the study ultimately published, expanded the focus from being only on the Court to considering the whole operation of the 'Convention system', to include matters such as application of the Convention by the domestic authorities and courts and the execution of the Court's judgments. Protocol 15, which requires ratification by all 47 Contracting Parties to the Convention to enter into force,[3] will, inter alia, make the following significant changes to the Convention itself:

- It will add an express reference to the principle of 'subsidiarity' and the doctrine of the 'margin of appreciation' to the Preamble of the Convention;
- It will reduce the time limit within which an application must be made to the Court from six to four months;
- It will amend the 'significant disadvantage' admissibility criterion to remove the provision preventing rejection of an application that has not been duly considered by a domestic tribunal; and
- It will remove the right of the parties to a case to object to relinquishment of jurisdiction over it by a Chamber in favour of the Grand Chamber.

---

[1] This edition of the Book summarises these developments, and looks ahead beyond them, towards the end of Chapter 1.
[2] See 1.58 (note 115).
[3] At the time of writing some 33 Contracting Parties to the Convention have ratified Protocol 15.

As indicated above, in parallel the Court itself also addressed the challenges arising out of the ever increasing backlog of cases. The first and perhaps most apparent change adopted by the Court was the strict application, with effect from 1 January 2014, of the revised Rule 47 of the Rules of Court under which, in order for an application to have been validly made and for the six-month time limit to stop running, applicants must now use the Court's new application form, with all fields completed and all necessary supporting documents appended, must make sure that they provide a signed authority if they are represented and must ensure that the application form is duly signed by them. Non-compliance has the consequence that (subject to very limited exceptions) the application will not be allocated to a judicial formation of the Court for decision. This major change in the Court's practice, fully dealt with in Chapters 2–3, has had the effect of freeing up large amounts of Registry time which had previously been taken up by processing incomplete submissions. In addition, it is also clear that a stronger emphasis is being placed on the principles of subsidiarity and the doctrine of the margin of appreciation, both of which, of course, have their origins and are deeply embedded in the Court's case law. These developments occurred independent of and in parallel with the discussions about Protocol 15 and reflecting the fact that the responsibility of enforcing Convention rights is shared with other parts of the Convention system including, in particular, domestic authorities and courts. Finally, it is worth mentioning that the Court also now pays greater attention to the need for an applicant to have exhausted domestic remedies in the sense that the complaints intended to be made before the Strasbourg Court should have been aired before domestic authorities, at least in substance and in compliance with the formal requirements laid down in domestic law.

These changes have had a significant effect on the backlog of pending cases; so much so that, as of 1 January 2016, the number of pending cases came down to just below 65,000 pending cases. That said the elimination of the backlog of manifestly inadmissible applications, the Court's focus on more complex and time-consuming applications as well as the higher volume of incoming applications at least in part as a result of the various crises confronting Contracting States has again resulted in an increase in the stock of pending cases. At the end of the year 2016, the number of pending applications was at nearly 80,000 (while, in the same year, some 53,000 applications were allocated to a judicial formation and the Court decided nearly 40,000 applications by decision or judgment).

In addition to the challenges arising out of the sheer number of cases being brought before it, the Strasbourg Court, like some national constitutional or supreme courts and other international dispute settlement mechanisms, also appears to be confronted with renewed challenges to its legitimacy if not its very existence and purpose as an integral part of the machinery designed to uphold the (international) rule of law in Europe and to provide for the 'collective enforcement' of the rights enshrined in the Convention; rights which the Preamble describes, reflecting the historic experiences which led to the adoption of the Convention, as 'the foundation of justice and peace in the world'.

In meeting these challenges, those who bring applications to and appear before the Strasbourg Court play an important if not vital role. The quality of the arguments advanced domestically and before this Court is essential in ensuring the protection of the rights protected under the Convention as well as enabling the Court's registry and its judicial formations to continue to process and decide the large number of applications before it and to fulfil the purpose for which it was created. This book, now in its fourth edition, continues to provide applicants and practitioners (those acting for applicants as well as government agents) with all the tools necessary to make the most of the Convention system, both in terms of procedure and substantive law. For that it is to be congratulated.

Tim Eicke
European Court of Human Rights
Strasbourg
March 2017

PREFACE

The Fourth Edition

Now in its fourth edition, this book is a guide to the law, practice and procedure of the European Court of Human Rights. My aim has been to provide an accessible and practical manual for practitioners, scholars and students interested in the Strasbourg system. The book gives step-by-step guidance on the process of litigating cases before the European Court, covering areas such as lodging the initial application, legal aid and costs, interim measures, case prioritisation, friendly settlements and unilateral declarations, third party interventions, pilot judgments and Grand Chamber referrals. It includes practical advice about drafting pleadings and conducting oral hearings. There is a focus on questions of redress and it incorporates the latest developments in the practice of the Committee of Ministers in supervising the implementation of European Court judgments.

This edition takes in a series of developments in the Court's practice and procedure since 2010, including: the introduction (in 2014) of the Court's mandatory application form; the possibility of electronic filing; the updated Court Rules and practice directions; a broadening of the Court's 'victim status' rule; a more expansive approach to 'interim measures' (as well as some states' apparent ambivalence towards such orders); the basis for invoking the 'no significant disadvantage' admissibility test and further applications of the exhaustion of domestic remedies rule, the six months' time limit and the *ratione temporis* criterion; the steep rise in the Court's use of unilateral declarations in striking cases out; the re-introduction of reasoned inadmissibility decisions; significant further developments in the Court's use of 'Article 46 judgments' and pilot judgments; and the Court's more extensive application of non-pecuniary measures of redress (including reinstatement to employment, disclosure of information and the protection of witnesses).

An expanded article-by-article commentary on the substantive law of the European Convention on Human Rights has been updated to February 2017. New issues covered by the recent case-law include cases of extraordinary or secret rendition, restrictions on *in vitro* fertilisation and surrogacy, cases arising from medical mistreatment, the spate of 'missing babies' in Serbia, the treatment of migrants travelling by sea (including collective expulsions) and structural deficiencies in asylum procedures.

The Court has issued judgments clarifying where an individual's deportation would amount to a flagrant denial of justice because of the real risk of the admission of evidence obtained by torture, and to what extent diplomatic assurances can be relied on in respect of the return of individuals to countries where they face a risk of ill-treatment.

There have also been new decisions concerning the failure to give legal recognition to same-sex partnerships, restrictions on the right to freedom of religion in the workplace, the right of conscientious objection to military service, the balancing of rights under Articles 8 and 10 and several cases concerning freedom of expression via the Internet.

There is additional jurisprudence on the right to receive information, the right to demonstrate peacefully and for political purposes, trade union rights and the duty to contain violent, homophobic counter-demonstrators. The Court's decisions have highlighted discrimination on the basis of gender, ethnicity, nationality, sexual orientation and disability (including discrimination against people with HIV).

There has been further application of the Convention standards to the right of access to a lawyer for suspects held in police custody, to detention on grounds of mental health, to the need to conduct reviews into the detention of life sentence prisoners, to deaths in custody, prison conditions (and the treatment of people with disabilities in detention) and the duty to prevent risks to life and to conduct effective investigations into fatal incidents and cases of ill-treatment. There is more case-law too on the use of lethal force by the police or security forces (including when 'off-duty'), on the specific duty to protect the victims of domestic violence and on the positive obligations which arise in countering cases of domestic servitude and human trafficking.

Recent years have seen a series of successful Article 18 applications (where actions by the authorities restricting rights under Article 5 of the Convention have been applied for ulterior purposes). The Court has made further decisions impacting on the right of access to court and in relation to disciplinary proceedings against judges. It has clarified the 'overall fairness' test (under Article 6), including where there is evidence that criminal proceedings were manifestly arbitrary, and it has refined its approach as to the fairness in criminal proceedings of admitting statements by absent witnesses.

Finally, there have been important developments in the case-law concerning states' extra-territorial jurisdiction, as well as detention during occupation or armed conflict, raising the tricky issue of the application of international humanitarian law concurrently with international human rights law.

The Wider Context

These are undoubtedly troubled times for the very notion of human rights. Globally, we see autocratic governments pushing back on the concept, fiercely protecting perceived ideas of national sovereignty and targeting 'traitorous' NGOs and human rights defenders with unjust and repressive laws. Europe is far from immune from these pressures. Legislation in Russia characterises human rights defenders as 'foreign agents' and their funders as 'undesirable organisations'. Amongst those in Europe who take on the burden of monitoring and reporting on human rights abuses, or of striving for accountability and redress, lives are at risk. The last edition of this book was dedicated to our colleague Natalia Estemirova (of the NGO *Memorial*), who was abducted and murdered in Grozny in 2009. She had been tireless in her determined pursuit of justice for victims of egregious human rights abuses in the North Caucasus—her own case is now pending before the Court. This edition of the book is dedicated to Tahir Elçi, the Kurdish human rights lawyer who was gunned down in Diyarbakir in November 2015. Tahir had been equally indefatigable in seeking to uphold human rights standards as a reality.

Elsewhere, human rights lawyers and activists are being jailed in a bid to keep them quiet— no more so than in Azerbaijan, as evidenced by the cases of Leyla and Arif Yunus, Intigam

Aliyev and Rasul Jafarov, all of whom were imprisoned in Baku in various periods between 2014 and 2016. In its 2016 judgment in the case brought by Rasul Jafarov (supported by the European Human Rights Advocacy Centre (EHRAC)), the European Court found, in terms, that Jafarov was prosecuted in order to silence and punish him for his human rights activities. For the first time, on that basis, the Court found a violation of Article 18 of the European Convention (in other words, he had been detained for ulterior purposes)—a decision that is emblematic of its time.

In parallel with these events, and apparently in ignorance (or defiance?) of them, some influential politicians and commentators in the UK, and in countries such as the Netherlands, Switzerland and Belgium, have consistently sought to denigrate the defence of human rights, and human rights institutions too. One of their regular targets has been the European Court of Human Rights, which, they say, is reaching out beyond its mandate to trample on the democratic will of national politicians and parliaments. While the Court is not a perfect institution, in my view such criticisms are unjustified and represent ill-informed (and in some instances downright malevolent) populist political opportunism. What is more, in the miasma of Euro-phobia stoked by such politicians and commentators, the distinctions between the roles of the European Union and the Council of Europe are seldom clearly drawn, and, after the Brexit referendum, it is far from clear what the future holds for the UK's participation in the Council of Europe, or indeed the European Court system. In any event, having practised at the European Court for more than twenty years now, I can say that the version of the Court which is portrayed by these commentators is simply not one that I recognise. I remain deeply impressed by the professionalism and integrity of those who work at the Court. It is an institution which, in practice, provides a genuine opportunity for accountability and redress to people in Europe who have been badly let down by their own authorities, be it the police, the prison or security services, the courts and many other bodies. It does so, often in highly politically contentious circumstances. It also frequently has to operate in the face of governmental obfuscation, demonstrated by the failure to disclose vital case documents, measures taken in defiance of the Court's interim measures orders, and the hindrance of applicants' right of access to the Court in various ways (in violation of Article 34 of the European Convention). While reading a large number of judgments and decisions for the purpose of writing this new edition, I was also struck by the extent to which some governments will habitually raise arguments (at the admissibility or the merits stages) that are so weak as to be obviously unsustainable. The Court being the Court responds to such points with respect—much more so than may really be deserved.

Having said all of that, of course one of the serious drawbacks of the Court continues to be the excessive length of time to process cases, caused, in the main, by the backlog of cases. Since the third edition of this book was published, the caseload of the Court peaked in 2011 at over 151,000 pending cases, but it has been decreasing since then—to a figure of about 65,000 in 2015 (although rising again to 84,000 by January 2017). That is a significant reduction, and the general direction of travel is very promising, but there are still two causal factors to grapple with in particular.

Firstly, the vast majority of cases continue to be declared inadmissible by the Court: in 2013 this figure was 92 per cent. In the calendar year of 2016, the Court declared 36,579 applications inadmissible (or struck them out) and delivered judgments on the merits in 1,926 applications. In the Court's view, the reason for this is that both applicants themselves and their legal advisors do not sufficiently understand the Court's admissibility criteria.[1] No one has yet been able to come up with an explanation for this—after all, the Court's admissibility criteria are, in the main, well-established and pretty clear. Nor are they so complicated as to be difficult to apply—at least in most cases.

The second big issue is the 'implementation crisis'—that in far too many cases, state authorities are failing to respond adequately to the Court's judgments, which require legislative amendments, changes in policy or practice or a much more significant domestic political investment to tackle large-scale systemic problems. As a consequence, the Committee of Ministers' caseload has continued to rise—to a high of just over 11,000 in 2012 and 2013.[2] At the end of 2015 there were still 10,652 cases pending at the Committee of Ministers. There has also been an increase in the number of cases pending for more than five years: by 2015, these amounted to 55 per cent of the pending cases.[3] In my view, the time has come for a thorough review and revision of the supervision process of the implementation of the Court's judgments, which should be both strengthened and opened up.

Contents

Chapter 1 provides an overview of the Convention system and the main institutions. The practice and procedure of the Court are explained in chapters 2 and 3, from lodging the initial application to the Court to the enforcement of judgments. These chapters include explanations of the Strasbourg legal aid system and the system for obtaining emergency relief (interim measures). Chapter 4 explains the Court's admissibility rules, which are a critical element in the Convention system—including the criterion concerning 'significant disadvantage'. Chapter 5 discusses the most important underlying principles of the Convention and chapter 6 provides an overview of the Convention case law, including Articles 1 to 14 of the European Convention, together with Protocol Nos. 1, 4, 6, 7, 12 and 13. Chapter 7 deals with derogation and reservation from the Convention. Chapter 8 explains the principles applied by the Court in awarding 'just satisfaction' (including compensation and costs). The book endeavours to set out the law and practice of the Court as at January 2017.

Note on Citation of Cases

The decisions and judgments of the European Court (and former Commission) of Human Rights are available on the Court's hudoc site. The case law referred to in this book has been cited so as to enable the decisions to be found on the hudoc site. The best way to do so is to search for the case using the case number (or alternatively, by the name).
Judgments are cited like this:

Al-Skeini and others v *UK*, No. 55721/07, 7.7.11.

---

[1] European Court of Human Rights, Practical Guide on Admissibility Criteria, 2014, p. 7.
[2] *Supervision of the execution of judgments of the European Court of Human Rights—Annual Report*, 2015, Council of Europe, March 2016, p. 56.
[3] *Supervision of the execution of judgments of the European Court of Human Rights—Annual Report*, 2015, Council of Europe, March 2016, p. 10.

Note that there may be two judgments on the merits of the case—where a chamber judgment is referred to the Grand Chamber. In addition to the judgment on the merits, there may be a separate 'just satisfaction' judgment. In the vast majority of cases, the decision on admissibility is now incorporated into the judgment itself.

Separate admissibility decisions (issued by the Court or the Commission) are cited like this:

Sarisülük v *Turkey*, No. 64126/13, dec. 25.3.14.

In addition, some older judgments include references to the 'Series A' reports (the Court's official law reports prior to 1996). For example:

Open Door and Dublin Well Woman v *Ireland*, Nos. 14234/88 and 14253/88, Series A, No. 246, 29.10.92.

The merits reports published by the (former) European Commission of Human Rights are cited like this:

Kröcher and Müller v *Switzerland*, No. 8463/78, Comm. Rep. 16.12.82.

In addition, some of the decisions of the European Commission refer to citations in the 'Decisions and Reports' series (published from 1974 to 1995). For example:

X v *Belgium*, No. 8988/80, dec. 10.3.81, DR 24.

CONTENTS

ACKNOWLEDGEMENTS

I am very grateful to Stephen Phillips (European Court Section Registrar) for kindly answering my procedural queries. My thanks to Aigerim Kamidola for updating the table of ratifications and to Kia Kyhl for her research assistance. I would also like to thank Tim Eicke for very kindly writing the foreword to this edition.

For being ever helpful and founts of unlimited knowledge: Michael O'Boyle (the former European Court Registrar), Karen Reid, Hasan Bakırcı, Olga Chernishova, Uğur Erdal, Gail Fitzpatrick (all at the Court Registry), plus Musa Khasanov and Pavlo Pushkar (Department for Execution of Judgments), Günter Schirmer (Department of Legal Affairs and Human Rights, Parliamentary Assembly) and Andrew Drzemczewski (formerly at the same Department).

Similarly, in Georgia, to my good friends Sopo Japaridze, Beso Bokhashvili, Kety Abashidze and Natia Katsitadze. The third edition of this book was published in Georgian in 2014 by the Georgian Bar Association, with the financial support of an EU-funded Project (*Support to the Reform of Criminal Justice System in Georgia*) and NORLAG. My thanks to them and to their translators.

This fourth edition would not have seen the light of day, were it not for my brilliant, inspiring colleagues at the European Human Rights Advocacy Centre (EHRAC) at Middlesex University. They are (or, in some cases, have been): Victoria Armfield, Jarlath Clifford, Tina Devadasan, Jo Evans, Jess Gavron, Vahe Grigoryan, Pamela Harling, Barbara Karch, Kate Levine, Oksana Popova, Ramute Remezaite, Sophie Rust, Jo Sawyer, Laure Trebosc and Sabrina Vashisht. To you all I say: sorry for my absences and what a wonderful samovar!

My gratitude also to our colleagues in EHRAC's partner organisations—too many to name individually, but especially *Memorial* (Russia), *Georgian Young Lawyers' Association*, the Ukrainian Helsinki Human Rights Union and human rights defenders in Armenia and Azerbaijan. How remarkable and inspirational they are—especially at a time when governmental repression of human rights defenders seems to know no bounds.

Thank you to Sam Knights (Matrix Chambers) and Professor Bill Bowring (Birkbeck College), not least in your capacities as chairs, respectively, of EHRAC's Advisory Board and International Steering Committee.

I would also want to take this opportunity to reiterate my thanks to EHRAC's funders for their committed support: the Oak Foundation, the Sigrid Rausing Trust, the MacArthur Foundation, the Open Society Institute, the European Commission, the National Endowment for Democracy, and, most recently, Avaaz.

At Middlesex University I would like to acknowledge my profound gratitude to the School of Law (and to Anna Kyprianou, Dean of the Business School and Pro-Vice Chancellor) for the incredibly supportive, engaging and collegiate milieu created by an inspirational bunch of international lawyers and human rights academics: Professor Joshua Castellino (Dean, School of Law), Dr Nadia Bernaz, Dr Anthony Cullen, Dr Elvira Dominguez-Redondo,

Dr Alice Donald, Dr Erica Howard, Anne-Katrin Speck, Dr David Keane, Lughaidh Kerin, Professor Laurent Pech and Professor Bill Schabas. And in the School of Law 'engine room', my thanks to Joanne Nunn, Yvette Tomkinson and Christiana Rose.

My thanks to Faye Mousley, Liana Green and Katie Hooper at Oxford University Press.

Once again, eternal gratitude to Candy Whittome and Marc Stephens for so generously allowing me unlimited access to their bolt-hole in Cromer, where much of this edition was written.

Finally, thank you to Becky, Anna, Katy and Mary—for their constant support.

Philip Leach
February 2017

TABLE OF CASES

TABLE OF INTERNATIONAL INSTRUMENTS

TABLE OF NATIONAL LEGISLATION

TABLE OF RULES OF COURT (14 NOVEMBER 2016)

1

INTRODUCTION—THE COUNCIL OF EUROPE AND THE EUROPEAN CONVENTION ON HUMAN RIGHTS

The Council of Europe: Origins and Principal Bodies

The European Convention on Human Rights[1] is a creation of the Council of Europe, which **1.01** was established immediately after World War II by the Statute of the Council of Europe 1949 with the aim of enhancing the cultural, social and political life of Europe and promoting human rights, democracy and the rule of law. The creation and early work of the Council of Europe (based in Strasbourg) was in part a reaction to the serious human rights violations encountered in Europe during World War II. There were originally ten member states of the Council of Europe and there are now 47 members.

The Council of Europe's primary decision-making bodies are the Committee of Ministers **1.02** and the Parliamentary Assembly.

---

[1] Convention for the Protection of Human Rights and Fundamental Freedoms, Rome, 4.11.50, European Treaty Series No. 5 (referred to in this book as the 'European Convention on Human Rights', the 'European Convention' or simply 'the Convention').

Committee of Ministers

1.03   The Committee of Ministers is made up of the Ministers for Foreign Affairs of each member state who meet twice a year, with Ministers' Deputies or permanent representatives acting on a day-to-day basis. It is the executive organ of the Council of Europe that issues its decisions in the form of treaties, declarations, resolutions, and recommendations. The Committee of Ministers is assisted by a Steering Committee for Human Rights that receive reports from Committees of Experts. The Committee of Ministers has the power to invite European states to become members of the Council of Europe, and it also has powers of suspension and termination. The Committee of Ministers supervises the enforcement of judgments of the European Court of Human Rights under Article 46 of the European Convention on Human Rights (see further, Enforcement of Judgments, 3.19, below). This function is primarily carried out through four regular meetings each year.

Parliamentary Assembly

1.04   The Parliamentary Assembly (PACE) is composed of groups of representatives from the national parliaments of member states (currently 648 members: 324 members and 324 substitutes). The size of the national delegation varies according to the population of the member state. Non-member states can be given special guest status, in order to facilitate the process of accession to the Council of Europe (the Belarusian parliament's status has been suspended since 1997) or observer status (currently the parliaments of Canada, Israel and Mexico). A series of specialist committees are appointed by the Assembly to work on particular issues. One such committee, the Committee on the Election of Judges to the European Court of Human Rights (operational since January 2015), examines candidates for the position of judge at the European Court prior to their election by the Parliamentary Assembly. The Parliamentary Assembly elects the judges of the European Court from a list of three candidates presented by each member state.[2] PACE also elects the Commissioner for Human Rights and the Secretary General and Deputy Secretary General of the Council of Europe. The Committee on Legal Affairs and Human Rights has a role (supplemental to that of the Committee of Ministers) in supervising the execution of the European Court's judgments.[3]

1.05   A third body, the Congress of Local and Regional Authorities of the Council of Europe was created in 1994 as a consultative body concerned with local self-government and comprises representatives (currently 648) from the local or regional authorities of the member states. The Congress has produced, for example, the European Charter of Local Self Government (1985).

Other human rights mechanisms within the Council of Europe

1.06   More than 200 conventions and agreements have been adopted under the auspices of the Council of Europe. Most significant in the human rights field have been the establishment

---

   [2] See: Committee on the Election of Judges to the European Court of Human Rights, Procedure for electing judges to the European Court of Human Rights, Information document prepared by the Secretariat, AS/Cdh/ Inf (2016) 01, Rev. 4, 22 June 2016.
   [3] PACE Resolution 1226 (2000), *Execution of Judgments of the European Court of Human Rights*, 28.9.00. The Committee's eighth report on the implementation of judgments was published in 2015: Committee on Legal Affairs and Human Rights, Implementation of judgments of the European Court of Human Rights, Report (Rapporteur: Mr Klaas de Vries, Netherlands, Socialist Group), Doc. 13864, 9 September 2015.

of the European Convention on Human Rights (1950), the European Social Charter (1961), the European Convention for the Prevention of Torture and Inhuman and Degrading Treatment or Punishment (1987), the European Commission against Racism and Intolerance (1993), the Framework Convention for the Protection of National Minorities (1994), the Convention on Action against Trafficking in Human Beings (2005) and the Convention on Preventing and Combating Violence against Women and Domestic Violence (2011). A selection of the main human rights mechanisms of the Council of Europe are introduced below.

The European Social Charter[4] came into force in 1965 and is in effect the counterpart to **1.07** the European Convention on Human Rights in the field of social and economic rights. Compliance with the Charter is monitored by the European Committee of Social Rights (ECSR) made up of 15 independent and impartial experts, together with the Governmental Committee (made up of representatives of the states) and the Committee of Ministers. The ECSR monitors annual national reports and receives collective complaints,[5] inter alia, from trade unions, employers' organisations and international non-governmental organisations (NGOs) with consultative status with the Council of Europe. Protocols were added to the Charter in 1988, 1991 and 1995 and in 1996 the revised Social Charter was opened for signature. It came into force in 1999 and is progressively replacing the first Charter.

The European Convention for the Prevention of Torture and Inhuman or Degrading **1.08** Treatment or Punishment[6] came into force in 1989 and has been ratified by the 47 member states of the Council of Europe. It established a proactive non-judicial system for monitoring compliance: the European Committee for the Prevention of Torture and Inhuman or Degrading Treatment or Punishment (CPT). The CPT comprises independent experts from various backgrounds (such as lawyers, doctors and prison experts) and has both a fact-finding and a reporting function. It makes periodic and ad hoc visits to places of detention (including, e.g. prisons, police stations, psychiatric hospitals and barracks). The CPT may interview detainees in private and has the power to communicate freely with anyone who has relevant information. Its reports are confidential and may only be published with the agreement of the contracting state, but where there is no agreement the CPT may issue its own public statement. Protocol No. 1 to the Torture Convention, which came into force on 1 March 2002, enables the Committee of Ministers to invite any non-member state of the Council of Europe to accede to the Convention. By September 2016, the CPT had made 397 visits and it had published 347 reports.[7]

The European Commission against Racism and Intolerance (ECRI) monitors states' legis- **1.09** lation and policies in relation to racism, racial discrimination, xenophobia, antisemitism and intolerance.[8] ECRI carries out an in-depth study into each state, before issuing specific proposals. Following a confidential dialogue with state liaison officers, ECRI's reports are published.

---

[4] Council of Europe Treaty Series, No. 35, 18.10.61.
[5] See further at: http://www.coe.int/en/web/turin-european-social-charter.
[6] Council of Europe Treaty Series, No. 126, 26.11.87.
[7] See, in particular, *The CPT Standards*, CPT/Inf/E (2002) 1- Rev. 2015 at: http://www.cpt.coe.int/en/documents/eng-standards.pdf.
[8] See Committee of Ministers' Resolution Res(2002)8 on the statute of the European Commission against Racism and Intolerance, 13 June 2002.

1.10   The Framework Convention for the Protection of National Minorities[9] came into force in 1998. It includes a periodic reporting process (within one year of the date of entry into force of the Convention, and then every five years) and is monitored by the Committee of Ministers assisted by an Advisory Committee of 18 independent experts in the field of national minorities. The Advisory Committee examines state reports and produces an opinion on the steps taken by the state. It may request additional information and may receive information from other sources, such as NGOs.

1.11   The Council of Europe Convention on Action against Trafficking in Human Beings came into force in 2008 and is primarily aimed at the protection of victims of trafficking and the safeguarding of their rights.[10] The implementation of the Convention is monitored by the Group of Experts of Action against Trafficking in Human Beings (GRETA) which has between ten and 15 members and the Committee of the Parties (comprising state representatives) which may make recommendations addressed to individual states on the basis of GRETA's reports.

1.12   The Convention on Preventing and Combating Violence against Women and Domestic Violence (the Istanbul Convention) entered into force on 1 August 2014 (CETS No. 210, 11.5.11). The implementation of the Istanbul Convention is monitored by an independent body, the Group of Experts on Action against Violence against Women and Domestic Violence (GREVIO). The GREVIO has between ten and 15 members and it publishes reports about legislative and other measures taken by states parties. The GREVIO may adopt recommendations and initiate a special inquiry procedure. The Committee of the Parties consists of state representatives, and, on the basis of reports published by the GREVIO, it can issue specific recommendations to the states parties.

Secretary General of the Council of Europe

1.13   The Secretary General of the Council of Europe is appointed by the Parliamentary Assembly on the recommendation of the Committee of Ministers for a period of five years. The Secretary General has a number of roles in relation to the European Convention on Human Rights, including conducting inquiries into states' domestic laws under Article 52 (see 1.15 below). Each state party is required to deposit its instrument of ratification of the Convention with the Secretary General,[11] and to notify the Secretary General if it denounces the Convention.[12] States must also notify the Secretary General of the application of the Convention to dependent territories[13] and the Secretary General must be informed of any steps taken in derogation from the Convention, as well as the reasons for doing so.[14]

1.14   The current Secretary General is Thorbjørn Jagland (a former Prime Minister and Foreign Minister of Norway) who was elected in 2009 and re-elected in 2014. The Secretary General has the power to appoint additional ad hoc bodies such as special representatives and advisory committees in particular fields. For example, the International Advisory Panel

---

[9] Council of Europe Treaty Series, No. 157, 1.2.95.
[10] Council of Europe Treaty Series, No. 197, 16.5.05.
[11] Article 59 of the European Convention on Human Rights.
[12] Article 58 of the European Convention on Human Rights (see 1.36 below).
[13] Article 56 of the European Convention on Human Rights.
[14] Article 15(3) of the European Convention on Human Rights. See further at 7.01 below.

on Ukraine was established by the Secretary General to oversee the investigations into the violent incidents which took place in Ukraine in 2013–2014.[15] In addition, there is a Special Advisor of the Secretary General for Ukraine—Regis Brillat was appointed to the post in May 2016. In January 2016 Tomáš Boček was appointed Special Representative of the Secretary General on Migration and Refugees. In September 2016 a new post of Special Representative of the Secretary General of the Council of Europe for Roma Issues was established, with Valeriu Nicolae, a Romanian Roma, being appointed.

Inquiries by the Secretary General

The Secretary General of the Council of Europe may institute inquiries under Article 52 **1.15** of the European Convention on Human Rights into the domestic implementation of the Convention standards. The member states are obliged to provide the Secretary General with an explanation as to how the Convention is implemented in national law, when requested to do so.

The power has only infrequently been invoked. The first five inquiries concerned all **1.16** the states parties to the Convention. For example, in 1988 the Secretary General asked member states to provide information about the implementation of the right to a fair trial under Article 6(1) (in relation to various disciplinary and regulatory matters) and Article 6(3) (in relation to criminal and regulatory offences). The Governments' replies were published in 1993.[16] The results of these inquiries may provide useful comparative material about the implementation of Convention principles, but there have been criticisms that the ambiguity of the questions has produced responses that are not comparable with one another.[17] Moreover, the responses of the Governments are not critically scrutinised by the Council of Europe. In December 1999 the Secretary General invoked Article 52 in relation to Chechnya[18] and in 2002 an inquiry was instituted in respect of Moldova's compliance with the European Convention following concerns about restrictions being placed on political parties in Moldova.[19] In 2006 an Article 52 inquiry was instigated by the Secretary General in relation to secret detentions and rendition flights in Europe.[20] In December 2015, the Secretary General opened an Article 52 inquiry into Azerbaijan's implementation of the European Convention, with particular reference to the case brought by activist and political blogger Ilgar Mammadov, and his ongoing imprisonment in Azerbaijan.[21]

---

[15] See: International Advisory Panel, Report of the International Advisory Panel on its review of the Maidan Investigations, 31 March 2015 and International Advisory Panel, Report of the International Advisory Panel on the Odesa events, 4 November 2015.

[16] H/SG (93) 1.

[17] H/SG (93) 1, p. 208.

[18] See: *Russian Federation: Information provided by the Secretary-General on the Situation of Democracy, Human Rights and the Rule of Law in the Chechen Republic*, SG/Inf(2001)22, 26 June 2001.

[19] *Report by the Secretary-General on the Use of his Powers under Article 52 of the European Convention on Human Rights in Respect of Moldova*, SG/Inf(2002)20, 6 May 2002. See, e.g. *Christian Democratic People's Party v Moldova*, No. 28793/02, 14.2.06.

[20] See SG/Inf(2006)5, 28 February 2006, available at: https://wcd.coe.int/wcd/ViewDoc.jsp?id=976731 &Site=COE.

[21] *Ilgar Mammadov v Azerbaijan*, No. 15172/13, 22.5.14 (violations of Articles 5(1)(c), 5(4), 6(2) and 18 in conjunction with Article 5). See: Council of Europe press release, Azerbaijan human rights inquiry–Secretary General launches inquiry into respect for human rights in Azerbaijan, 16 December 2015.

Commissioner for Human Rights

1.17   Created in 1999,[22] the role of the Commissioner for Human Rights is non-judicial and preventive. The Commissioner's functions include the promotion of the effective implementation of human rights standards by member states, the provision of advice and assistance to states, to national human rights institutions and to the Committee of Ministers and the Parliamentary Assembly. The first Commissioner, Alvaro Gil-Robles, was elected by the Parliamentary Assembly in September 1999 for a non-renewable six year term. The second Commissioner, Thomas Hammarberg, served from 2006 to 2012. The current Commissioner is Nils Muižnieks who took up office in April 2012. The Commissioner carries out country monitoring and thematic work and has developed a particular focus on the protection of human rights defenders. The Commissioner's publications include Opinions, Recommendations, Issue Papers and Annual Reports.

1.18   The changes to the system of the European Convention on Human Rights which were implemented in accordance with Protocol No. 14 to the European Convention (see 1.29 below) expressly enable the Commissioner for Human Rights to intervene in cases before the Chamber or Grand Chamber of the European Court of Human Rights as a third party.[23]

The European Programme for Human Rights Education for Legal Professionals (HELP)

1.19   The European Programme for Human Rights Education for Legal Professionals (HELP) supports the Council of Europe member states in implementing the European Convention on Human Rights at the national level. The HELP programme aims to support the capacity of judges, lawyers and prosecutors in each of the states to apply the Convention. This involves a network of national training institutions, an e-learning platform on human rights and a human rights training methodology for legal professionals.[24]

European Commission for Democracy through Law (the 'Venice Commission')

1.20   The European Commission for Democracy through Law (usually known as the 'Venice Commission') was established in 1990 as the Council of Europe's advisory body on constitutional matters.[25] It has 61 member states (including all of the Council of Europe states, and Algeria, Brazil, Chile, Costa Rica, Israel, Kazakhstan, the Republic of Korea, Kosovo, Kyrgyzstan, Mexico, Morocco, Peru, Tunisia and the USA). The Venice Commission is composed of senior legal academics, supreme or constitutional court judges and members of national parliaments who act as independent experts. Its primary task is to give legal advice to states (usually at their request) on laws that are important for the democratic functioning of institutions. Its publications include opinions (notably on legislation or draft laws and the extent of their compliance with Council of Europe standards) and thematic studies. The European Court frequently refers to Venice Commission reports, notably when

---

[22] Committee of Ministers Resolution (99)50 on the Council of Europe Commissioner for Human Rights, 7 May 1999.

[23] Article 36(3), as well as Article 36(2), of the European Convention. See, for example, *M.S.S.* v *Belgium and Greece*, No. 30696/09, 21.1.11; *Mamasakhlisi* v *Georgia and Russia*, No. 29999/04 (see CommDH(2007)18, 16 August 2007); *Centre for Legal Resources on behalf of Valentin Câmpeanu* v *Romania*, No. 47848/08, 17.7.14. See further at 2.125 below.

[24] See: www.coe.int/HELP.

[25] See http://www.venice.coe.int/.

required to assess the compatibility of domestic legislation (and/or its implementation) with the Convention.[26]

In *Bijelić* v *Montenegro and Serbia*,[27] the Venice Commission intervened as a third party in European Court proceedings which were originally communicated to the Government of the State Union of Serbia and Montenegro, after which Montenegro declared its independence in June 2006. In its submission the Commission argued that the Court should hold Montenegro responsible for the breaches of the applicants' Convention rights (the non-enforcement of a final eviction order) caused by its authorities between March 2004 and June 2006.   **1.21**

The European Convention on Human Rights

The European Convention on Human Rights was adopted on 4 November 1950 and came   **1.22**
into force on 3 September 1953. It was primarily intended to protect civil and political rights, rather than economic, social or cultural rights.[28] It represented a significant step in the enforcement of particular aspects of the 1948 United Nations Universal Declaration of Human Rights.

The Convention created a right of individual petition—the right of individuals and organi-   **1.23**
sations to challenge their Government through the Strasbourg process, by taking their case to the European Commission of Human Rights (established in 1954), and then to the European Court (established in 1959). The Court's judgments are binding on the state parties to the Convention. The substantive rights in the Convention have been supplemented by additional protocols to the Convention: Protocol No. 1,[29] Protocol No. 4,[30] Protocol No. 6,[31] Protocol No. 7,[32] Protocol No. 12[33] and Protocol No. 13.[34] To permit such a right of individual petition was in many ways revolutionary, given the strength of notions of independent sovereignty of the state at the time of the creation of the Convention system. In other ways, however, the process involved undeniably political aspects: the system was to be supervised by a political body, the Committee of Ministers; the European Commission initially had a majority of serving or former ministers, civil servants or MPs, rather than legal professionals; and the procedure before the Commission was kept confidential. The system has subsequently developed into an evidently legal process although some of the procedural changes (including Protocol No. 11—see below) have been significantly influenced by political considerations.[35]

---

[26] See, e.g. *Baka* v *Hungary*, No. 20261/12, 23.6.16.

[27] No. 11890/05, 28.4.09.

[28] But the Court acknowledges that there is no watertight division separating the sphere of social and economic rights from the field covered by the Convention—see *Sidabras and Džiautas* v *Lithuania*, Nos 55480/00 and 59330/00, 27.7.04, para. 47.

[29] Adopted 20.3.52 and came into force on 18.5.54 (European Treaty series No. 9).

[30] Adopted 16.9.63 and came into force on 2.5.68 (European Treaty series No. 46).

[31] Adopted 28.4.83 and came into force on 1.3.85 (European Treaty series No. 114).

[32] Adopted 22.11.84 and came into force on 1.11.88 (European Treaty series No. 117).

[33] Adopted 4.11.00 and came into force on 1.4.05 (European Treaty series No. 177).

[34] Adopted 3.5.02 and came into force on 1.7.03 (European Treaty Series No. 187).

[35] For example, the manner of appointment of European Court judges has been criticised for its 'ad hoc and often politicised processes': see *Judicial Independence: Law and Practice of Appointments to the European Court of Human Rights*, Interights, May 2003. See also: PACE, Recommendation 1429 (1999) National procedures for nominating candidates for election to the European Court of Human Rights, 24 September 1999; NP Engel,

1.24 The Convention represents the minimum human rights standards which could be agreed by European states more than 60 years ago. The concept of human rights has developed enormously in those 60 years, leaving the Convention in some respects inadequate to uphold human rights in the twenty-first century. Despite the additional protocols and the accepted notion of the Convention as a 'living instrument', there are significant omissions of rights in the Convention and many have argued that the restrictions on the Convention rights are too widely drawn. Nevertheless, the Convention has also been extraordinarily influential on the development of legislation and policy in the human rights field throughout Europe. The European Convention is considered to be one of the most successful human rights systems in the world, particularly because of its enforcement mechanisms and its membership: it was described by Rolv Ryssdal, the former President of the European Court, as 'the Basic Law of Europe'. However, the Court has been struggling for many years with a massive caseload, including a very high proportion of repeat violation (or 'clone') cases and a high number of applications that are declared inadmissible. The caseload of the Court in recent years is incomparable to the early years (see further: Current Trends and Future Reforms, at 1.54). In the 1960s the Court produced just ten judgments, 26 in the 1970s and 169 in the 1980s. This number had increased by the early 1990s to more than 50 judgments a year. This figure subsequently increased at a remarkable rate, so that in 2003, the Court produced a total of 703 judgments and in 2010 the Court published 2,607 judgments (as well as more than 38,500 admissibility or striking-out decisions). Another way of demonstrating the remarkable increase in 'output' is to compare the number of decisions (38,389) made by the Commission and Court in the 44 years up to 1998, with the number of decisions made by the post-1998 Court in its first five years (61,633).[36]

1.25 There was a rapid expansion of the Convention system in the 1990s when a number of central and eastern European states joined the Council of Europe and ratified the Convention: Bulgaria, Czech Republic and Slovakia (1992), Poland (1993), Romania and Slovenia (1994), Lithuania (1995), Albania, Andorra and Estonia (1996), Ukraine, Croatia, Moldova, 'the former Yugoslav Republic of Macedonia' and Latvia (1997), Russia (1998) and Georgia (1999). In 2002 the Convention was ratified by Armenia, Azerbaijan and Bosnia and Herzegovina. The latest ratifications have been by Serbia (2004), Monaco (2005) and Montenegro (2006). There are now 47 member states of the Council of Europe, all of which have ratified the Convention.

'More transparency and governmental loyalty for maintaining professional quality in the election of judges to the European Court of Human Rights' (2012) 32 Human Rights Law Journal, 448–455. If there is no real choice as between the candidates, or if there has not been a fair, transparent and consistent selection procedure, the Parliamentary Assembly will reject the State's list—see, e.g. PACE, Committee on Legal Affairs and Human Rights, Doc. No 11767, Nomination of candidates and election of judges to the European Court of Human Rights (Rapporteur Mr Christopher Chope), 1 December 2008, para. 8; and PACE, Bureau of the Assembly, Election of Judges to the European Court of Human Rights, Progress Report, Doc. 13813 Addendum II, 15 June 2015. One of the results of the Interlaken Conference (see below) was the creation of a Panel of Experts on the appointment of judges to the Court. See: Resolution CM/Res(2010)26 on the establishment of an Advisory Panel of Experts on Candidates for Election as Judge to the European Court of Human Rights, 10 November 2010.

[36] Explanatory Report to Protocol No. 14, to the Convention for the Protection of Human Rights and Fundamental Freedoms, amending the control system of the Convention, 13 May 2004, para. 5.

Protocol No. 11

The increased membership of the Council of Europe in the 1990s placed even greater **1.26** strains on the system which meant long delays in the processing of cases which were taking at least four to five years (in addition to the time taken to pursue domestic proceedings). Cases were initially processed by the European Commission of Human Rights, through first an admissibility stage and secondly, a merits stage. Only then would cases proceed to the European Court or to the Committee of Ministers for the final determination. In the 1980s various proposals were discussed[37] to simplify and speed up the system, culminating in Protocol No. 11.

As from 1 November 1998, Protocol No. 11[38] to the Convention was brought into **1.27** effect, abolishing the two-tier system of Commission and Court, and creating a single full-time permanent Court. Protocol No. 11 did not change the substantive provisions of the Convention or the admissibility criteria, but in addition to the abolition of the Commission, there were a number of other significant procedural changes, such as the creation of a re-hearing procedure before the Grand Chamber of the Court and the removal of the quasi-judicial role of the Committee of Ministers (which continues to supervise the enforcement of judgments).

Protocol No. 11 proved, however, to be insufficient in managing the ever-increasing flow **1.28** of cases to the Court. For example, by 2003, whilst the Court was able to make decisions in 1,500 cases per month, this was still considerably fewer than the 2,300 new cases that were being received each month.[39] Consequently, further changes to the European Court system were proposed and debated from 2001 to 2004, leading to the adoption by the Committee of Ministers of Protocol No. 14 to the Convention in May 2004 (discussed in further detail at 1.29 below).

Protocol No. 14

The ever-increasing workload of the Court, even since the changes implemented under **1.29** Protocol No. 11, reflected, at least in part, the expanding membership of the Council of Europe notably since the late 1990s. In February 2001, the Committee of Ministers' Deputies established an Evaluation Group,[40] which was tasked with making proposals 'on the means of guaranteeing the continued effectiveness of the European Court of Human Rights'. The Evaluation Group's report was published in September 2001 and made a series of proposals, some of which would require amendments to the Convention and some of which would not.[41] Between 2001 and 2004, a Council of Europe committee of government

---

[37] See *Reform of the Control System of the European Convention on Human Rights* (1993) 15 EHRR 321.

[38] *Protocol No. 11 to the Convention for the Protection of Human Rights and Fundamental Freedoms, Restructuring the Control Machinery Thereby*, Council of Europe, Doc. H (94) 5; (1994) 17 EHRR 501.

[39] Explanatory Report to Protocol No. 14 (note 36 above), para. 5.

[40] Comprising the President of the Court, Luzius Wildhaber, the Deputy General Secretary of the Council of Europe, Hans-Christian Krüger, and the Permanent Representative of Ireland to the Council of Europe, Justin Harman.

[41] *Report of the Evaluation Group to the Committee of Ministers on the European Court of Human Rights*, 27 September 2001, EG (Court) 2001, Strasbourg—available at: https://wcd.coe.int/wcd/ViewDoc.jsp?Ref=C M(2006)203&Sector=secCM&Language=lanEnglish&Ver=original&BackColorInternet=9999CC&BackC olorIntranet=FFBB55&BackColorLogged=FFAC75.

experts, the Steering Committee for Human Rights, debated various proposals, leading to the drafting of an additional protocol to the European Convention in 2004.

1.30 As a result of this process, Protocol No. 14 to the European Convention on Human Rights was adopted by the Committee of Ministers of the Council of Europe in May 2004.[42] However, it did not come into force until 1 June 2010, because of Russia's opposition to it.[43] The aim of Protocol No. 14 was to make various changes to the European Court system in order, in particular, to simplify and speed up the processing of individual applications.

1.31 The most significant, and most controversial, change to the system was the addition of a further admissibility criterion to Article 35 of the Convention. This new criterion incorporated a threefold test: a case may be declared inadmissible by the Court if it considers that:

  (i) the applicant has not suffered a significant disadvantage,

 (ii) unless respect for human rights requires an examination of the application on the merits, and

(iii) provided that no case may be rejected on this ground that has not been duly considered by a domestic tribunal.[44]

1.32 The proposal to amend the admissibility criteria was the subject of criticism from many quarters,[45] as being unnecessary, wrong in principle, ill-targeted and overly vague. The decisions of the Court in which it has subsequently applied the new criterion (grappling with its concepts of 'significant disadvantage' and 'respect for human rights') are discussed below in chapter 4. In practice, the application of the new criterion has had no discernible effect on the Court's backlog (which was the aim in introducing it) and it has not been applied by the Court so as to limit applicants' access to justice.

1.33 The other most significant changes to the European Court system as set down in Protocol No. 14 were as follows:

  • in certain cases a single judge may decide on inadmissible applications, although not in respect of their 'own' states;[46]

  • a simplified, summary procedure was introduced enabling a committee of three judges to decide on the admissibility and merits of an application where the underlying question in the case, concerning the interpretation or application of the Convention, is already

---

[42] Protocol No. 14 to the Convention for the Protection of Human Rights and Fundamental Freedoms, amending the control system of the Convention, Council of Europe Treaty Series, No. 194, 13 May 2004.

[43] Pending the final ratification of Protocol No. 14, in order to tackle the Court's excessive caseload, a new Protocol 14*bis* was adopted in May 2009 in Madrid. This protocol contained two procedural measures included in Protocol No. 14: the single-judge procedure and the new powers of the three-judge committees to deal with the merits of 'well-founded' cases. It entered into force in October 2009, and those procedures were then applied in respect of states which had ratified Protocol 14*bis*. Protocol 14*bis* ceased to have effect once Protocol No. 14 came into force on 1 June 2010. After much cajoling by the Council of Europe and its other member states, Russia finally ratified Protocol No. 14 in February 2010.

[44] Article 35(3) of the Convention. Note, however, that when it enters into force, Protocol No. 15 will delete this third element of the test: See Article 5 of Protocol No. 15. See the discussion of Protocol No. 15 below at 1.51.

[45] See the references in section 1.25 of the third edition of this book.

[46] Articles 26 and 27 of the Convention.

the subject of well-established case law of the Court (known as 'WECL' cases).[47] This procedure is accordingly intended to speed up the processing of 'repetitive violation' or 'clone' cases;

- a new procedure enables the Committee of Ministers to bring 'infringement' proceedings before the Court where a state refuses to comply with a judgment;[48]
- European Court judges are appointed for a single, nine-year term;[49]
- the Council of Europe Commissioner for Human Rights is entitled to intervene in cases as a third party;[50] and
- the European Union may accede to the European Convention.[51]

Territorial application

Member states may extend the application of the Convention and the right of individual petition to any of their territories for whose international relations they are responsible (Article 56). To do so, the Secretary-General of the Council of Europe must be notified, either on ratification of the Convention or at any later time. The Convention will be applied in such territories 'with due regard ... to local requirements' (Article 56(3)).[52] **1.34**

Exclusion of other means of dispute settlement

In ratifying the Convention, member states agree that they will not seek to use other methods of dispute resolution (treaties, conventions or declarations) in order to solve a dispute arising out of the interpretation or application of the Convention (Article 55).[53] **1.35**

Denunciation of the Convention

A member state may withdraw from the Council of Europe and the Convention system by the process of denunciation (Article 58). This may only be done from five years after the state becomes a party to the Convention and six months' notice must be given to the Secretary-General of the Council of Europe. Denunciation will take effect at the end of the six-month period, but the state will remain responsible for any violation of the Convention prior to that date. **1.36**

The European Court of Human Rights

The Convention as amended by Protocol No. 11 in 1998 established a new Court functioning on a permanent basis.[54] Applicants were provided with a mandatory right to complain directly to the Court. **1.37**

---

[47] Article 28(1)(b) of the Convention.
[48] Article 46(4) of the Convention.
[49] Article 23(1) of the Convention.
[50] Article 36(3) of the Convention (in addition to Article 36(2)).
[51] Article 59(2) of the Convention.
[52] See, e.g. *Py* v *France*, No. 66289/01, 11.1.05 (restrictions on the right to vote in elections for Congress in New Caledonia—no violation of Article 3 of Protocol No. 1).
[53] Article 55 would, however, allow a state to do so 'by special agreement'.
[54] Article 19 of the European Convention on Human Rights.

1.38 The main features of the European Court system, as amended by Protocol No. 14 in 2010, are outlined below:

- One judge is elected to the Court by the Parliamentary Assembly for each state party,[55] who holds office for nine years and may not be re-elected.[56]
- Each judge must retire at 70.[57] There is a power of dismissal where a two-thirds majority of the judges consider that the judge has ceased to fulfil the required conditions.[58]
- The Court is divided into five sections. The composition of the sections is intended to be balanced in terms of geography and gender and takes account of the different domestic legal systems.[59] The composition of the sections is fixed for three years.
- The Plenary Court is concerned with electing the President, Vice-Presidents, Presidents of Chambers, the Registrar and Deputy Registrar, and adopting rules.[60] It has no judicial role.
- The Court sits in a single-judge formation, in committees of three judges, in Chambers of seven judges or in a Grand Chamber of seventeen judges.[61] The judge elected in respect of the state concerned will sit in each case brought against that state which is decided by a Chamber or Grand Chamber (as an *ex officio* member of the Chamber, if he or she is not a member of the relevant section),[62] but the national judge will not necessarily sit in committee. When sitting in single-judge formation, the judge may not consider any application against the state in respect of which that judge has been elected.[63] A committee may declare a case inadmissible or it may declare a case admissible and at the same time issue a judgment on the merits, if the underlying question in the case, concerning the interpretation or the application of the Convention, is already the subject of well-established case law.[64]
- The Council of Europe Commissioner for Human Rights may submit written comments to the Court and take part in hearings.[65]
- The most important cases may be relinquished by a Chamber to a Grand Chamber of 17 judges provided that both parties consent to relinquishment.[66]

---

[55] Article 22 of the European Convention on Human Rights. Each state submits a list of three candidates. In order to do so, States are advised by a panel of experts on candidates for election as judges to the Court (which was set up by the Committee of Ministers in 2010), before they send their lists of candidates to the Assembly. The state lists of candidates are assessed by the Committee on the Election of Judges to the European Court of Human Rights which makes recommendation to the Assembly. The Assembly then elects the judge. On the procedure, see: Parliamentary Assembly, Committee on the Election of Judges to the European Court of Human Rights, Procedure for electing judges to the European Court of Human Rights–Information document prepared by the Secretariat, AS/Cdh/Inf (2016) 01 rev 4, 22 June 2016. See also the discussion at note 35 above.

[56] Article 23(1) of the European Convention on Human Rights.

[57] Article 23(2) of the European Convention on Human Rights. When it enters into force, Protocol No. 15 will abolish the 70 year age limit and replace it with the requirement that candidates for the post of judge be less than 65 years of age at the date by which the list of candidates has been requested by the Parliamentary Assembly. See Article 2 of Protocol No. 15.

[58] Article 23(4) of the European Convention on Human Rights.

[59] Rule 25(2). See A. Drzemczewski, *The Internal Organisation of the European Court of Human Rights: The Composition of Chambers and the Grand Chamber* [2000] EHRLR 233.

[60] Article 25 of the European Convention on Human Rights.

[61] Article 26(1) of the European Convention on Human Rights.

[62] Article 26(4) of the European Convention on Human Rights.

[63] Article 26(3) of the European Convention on Human Rights.

[64] Article 28(1) of the European Convention on Human Rights.

[65] Article 36(3) of the European Convention on Human Rights.

[66] Article 30 of the European Convention on Human Rights. Note, however, when it enters into force, that Protocol No. 15 will abolish the right of the parties to object to relinquishment. See the discussion of Protocol No. 15 below.

- The Grand Chamber is established for three years and is formed by rotation within two groups which alternate every nine months. The groups are intended to be geographically balanced and reflect the varying domestic legal systems of member states.
- Cases decided on the merits by a Chamber may be referred to a Grand Chamber if the case raises a serious question affecting the interpretation or application of the Convention, or a serious issue of general importance.[67] Requests for re-hearings are subject to screening by a panel of five judges. If a request is accepted by the panel, the national judge will sit again in the re-hearing.[68]
- Court judgments are binding on the state party concerned.[69]
- Supervision of the execution of judgments is carried out by the Committee of Ministers.[70]
- If the Committee of Ministers considers that a state refuses to abide by a Court judgment, it may refer the question to the Court as to whether that state has failed to fulfil its obligations under Article 46(1).[71]

The Court's expenditure is met by the Council of Europe (Article 50), whose budget is **1.39** financed by state contributions in accordance with scales based on population and GDP. The Court does not have a separate budget—its budget is part of the general budget of the Council of Europe. The Court's budget in 2016 was €71,165,500 (covering the salaries of judges and staff, IT, travel, translation and interpreting costs, publications, representational expenses, legal aid, and fact-finding missions etc).

The Court procedures are discussed more fully in chapters 2 and 3.

Advisory opinions

The Court may issue advisory opinions on legal questions concerning the interpretation **1.40** of the Convention, at the request of the Committee of Ministers (Article 47). In doing so, the Court is obliged to give reasons and judges may deliver separate opinions where there is disagreement (Article 49). However, this provision is very limited, as the Court's advisory opinions may not deal with the content or scope of the substantive Convention rights (Article 47(2)). Indeed, the Court's first decision under Article 47, delivered by the Grand Chamber in 2004,[72] concluded that the request for an advisory opinion did not come within its advisory competence. The request was made by the Committee of Ministers and concerned the Convention on Human Rights of the Commonwealth of Independent States (CIS). The Court was asked to decide whether the CIS Human Rights Commission could be regarded as 'another procedure of international investigation or settlement' within the meaning of Article 35(2)(b) of the Convention. The Grand Chamber concluded that the Court's competence was excluded by Article 47(2) as the issue was one that might have to be decided in future proceedings under the Convention. In an advisory opinion issued at the request of the Committee of Ministers in 2008 the Grand Chamber was asked to assess the composition of lists of candidates for election as judges of the European Court.[73] Due to the under-representation of female judges on the Court, the Parliamentary Assembly had

---

[67] Article 43 of the European Convention on Human Rights.
[68] Articles 43 and 26(5) of the European Convention on Human Rights.
[69] Article 46(1) of the European Convention on Human Rights.
[70] Article 46(2) of the European Convention on Human Rights.
[71] Article 46(4) of the European Convention on Human Rights.
[72] *Decision on the competence of the Court to give an advisory opinion*, 2.6.04.
[73] *Advisory Opinion—composition of lists of candidates for election as judges of European Court*, 12.2.08.

rejected an all-male list submitted by Malta in 2006. The Court held that the practice of the Parliamentary Assembly in refusing candidate lists solely on the basis of gender-related issues was incompatible with the Convention where the country concerned had taken all necessary and appropriate steps to ensure the list contained a candidate of the under-represented sex. A second advisory opinion was issued in 2010 in relation to the right of states to withdraw lists of candidates for the post of Judge at the Court.[74] See also the discussion below (at xx) about Protocol No. 16 which will (when it enters into force) allow the highest domestic courts and tribunals to request the Court to issue advisory opinions.

Individual applications

1.41 Article 34 of the Convention provides for the 'individual' application process, or more strictly, for applications to be brought by 'any person, non-governmental organisation or group of individuals' who claim to be victims of violations of their Convention rights. State bodies may not therefore bring applications under Article 34 (see also 4.25 below). However, states which have ratified the Convention may take cases to the European Court to challenge Convention violations allegedly perpetrated by another contracting state (this is discussed below at 1.42).

Inter-state cases

1.42 The inter-state process, as provided for by Article 33 of the Convention (formerly Article 24), has been remarkably under-used: there have just been 20 such cases.[75] This process provides Council of Europe States with an opportunity to police each other—for any contracting state to require another contracting state to account for its actions, or inactions, through the international legal mechanism of the European Court. The apparent reluctance of states to invoke this mechanism is not peculiar to the European system, however; it is also a feature of other regional human rights mechanisms, including the Inter-American and African systems, and reflects the broader realities of inter-state relations. Whilst civil society, in the form of human rights NGOs, have tried to cajole states into utilising Article 33 (in recent years, for example, to highlight the plight of the Kurds in Turkey or the Chechens in Russia), they clearly remain reluctant to do so.

1.43 When a government does, however, decide to invoke the inter-state process, the case is almost invariably of some considerable political importance. It is possible to discern three categories of inter-state case. The first category is where the applicant state represents, or is closely connected with, the individual victims, in the context of a particular political dispute, or other political differences, between states. Thus a series of cases has been brought to the European Commission and Court by the Government of Cyprus following Turkey's military operations in northern Cyprus in 1974 and as a response to its continuing occupation of that territory and its proclamation of the 'Turkish Republic of Northern Cyprus' in 1983, which is not recognised by the international community. As a result of these cases Turkey has been found to have perpetrated multiple Convention violations.[76] In a case decided in

---

[74] *Advisory Opinion (no. 2) on certain legal questions concerning the lists of candidates submitted with a view to the election of judges to the European Court of Human Rights,* 22.1.10.

[75] European Court of Human Rights, Inter-states applications. Available at: http://www.echr.coe.int/Documents/InterStates_applications_ENG.pdf.

[76] See, e.g. *Cyprus v Turkey,* Nos 6780/74 and 6950/75, Comm. Rep. 10.7.76 (violations of Articles 2, 3, 5, 8, 13, 14 and Article 1 of Protocol No. 1); *Cyprus v Turkey,* No. 8007/77, Comm. Rep. 4.10.83 (violations of Articles 5, 8 and Article 1 of Protocol No. 1).

2001, the Cypriot Government brought an application concerning the rights of missing persons and their relatives, the property rights of those who had been displaced, the rights of enclaved Greek Cypriots in northern Cyprus, and the rights of Turkish Cypriots and the gypsy community in northern Cyprus. The application resulted in the Court finding 14 separate violations of the Convention.[77] A feature of such cases within a context of a highly charged political dispute would appear to be that a state may withdraw its 'co-operation' with the Court, as for example when the Turkish Government failed to submit a final written pleading to the Court and even failed to appear at the hearing before the Grand Chamber in September 2000.[78] Cases such as *Ireland* v *UK*[79] would also fall into this first category. That case concerned the 'five techniques' of interrogation used by the British security forces in relation to detained IRA suspects (see below at 6.134). Georgia brought inter-state proceedings against Russia as a result of a series of arrests, detentions and deportations of Georgians in 2006–2007 (which followed the arrest in Tbilisi of a number of Russian service personnel on espionage charges). The Court found Russia to be responsible for an administrative practice of the detention and collective expulsion of Georgian nationals, in breach of Articles 3, 5(1) and Article 4 of Protocol No. 4 (as well as Articles 5(4) and 13).[80] Georgia has also brought inter-state proceedings against Russia relating to the 2008 armed conflict in South Ossetia,[81] and Ukraine has brought several cases against Russia in relation to occupation and conflict in Crimea and eastern Ukraine.[82]

A second category of inter-state applications can be illustrated by a case such as *Denmark* v **1.44** *Turkey*[83] in which the applicant state sought to obtain a remedy for one of its nationals whose rights had been violated by the respondent state. There, it was alleged that a Danish citizen was tortured by the Turkish police. The case was settled on the basis of an *ex gratia* payment, a statement of regret (albeit in respect only of 'the occurrence of occasional and individual cases of torture') and various undertakings, including that the Turkish police would participate in Council of Europe training, as well as a bilateral police training project funded by the Danish Government, and an agreement to co-operate with the Committee on the Prevention of Torture (CPT). The settlement also recorded changes in the Turkish Penal Code which were aimed at redefining and limiting torture and ill-treatment.

A third category reflects the potential for states to operate a more general 'policing' role, **1.45** such as the *Greek case*.[84] There, the Governments of Denmark, Norway, Sweden and the Netherlands brought two applications in 1967 alleging that the Greek Government had violated Articles 5, 6, 8, 9, 10, 11, 13 and 14 of the Convention as a result of a series of administrative and legislative measures that had been taken following the military coup d'état in April 1967, leading to mass internment, torture, trials before extraordinary courts martial and media censorship. This led to the Greek Government denouncing the Convention on

---

[77] *Cyprus* v *Turkey*, No. 25781/94, 10.5.01.

[78] *Ibid.*, para. 12.

[79] Series A, No. 25, 18.1.78.

[80] *Georgia* v *Russia* (I), No. 13255/07, 3.7.14.

[81] *Georgia* v *Russia* (II), No. 38263/08, dec. 13.12.11.

[82] These include *Ukraine* v *Russia*, No. 20958/14 and 43800/14, communicated 11.14; and *Ukraine* v *Russia* (IV), No. 42410/15, communicated 10.15.

[83] No. 34382/97, 5.4.00.

[84] *Denmark, Norway, Sweden and the Netherlands* v *Greece*, Nos 3321/67, 3322/67, 3323/67 and 3344/67, 5.11.69, *Yearbook of the European Convention on Human Rights*, Vol. 12, 1969.

12 December 1969, shortly before the Committee of Ministers found that there had been violations of ten Convention Articles.[85]

1.46 Unlike individual applications, in an inter-state case, a state may challenge a law *in abstracto*. This is because Article 33 (and the former Article 24) allows a contracting state to challenge 'any alleged breach' of the Convention by another contracting state, which includes a breach resulting from the 'mere existence' of a law which is incompatible with the Convention.[86] For example, in *Cyprus* v *Turkey*[87] the Court found Article 6 to have been violated by virtue of the existence of laws in the 'Turkish Republic of Northern Cyprus' which authorised the trial of civilians in military courts.[88]

1.47 The applicant state in an inter-state application may be entitled to claim compensation pursuant to Article 41 of the Convention. In *Cyprus* v *Turkey*[89] the Grand Chamber found that the Cypriot government was entitled to make a just satisfaction claim on behalf of 1,456 missing people and the Greek Cypriot residents of the Karpas peninsula.

Reform of the Court: Interlaken, Izmir, Brighton and Brussels

1.48 Since 2010 there have been a series of conferences to consider further reforms to the Convention system, leading to the adoption of Protocols 15 and 16 (discussed further below): Interlaken (2010), Izmir (2011), Brighton (2012) and Brussels (2015). In 2010 a Ministerial conference was held at Interlaken in Switzerland which resulted in the adoption of the Interlaken Declaration which incorporated an 'Action Plan' for reforms up to 2019.[90] This envisaged that between 2012 and 2015 the Committee of Ministers would assess to what extent the implementation of Protocol No. 14 and the Interlaken Action Plan had improved the situation of the Court. A further reform action plan was adopted in Brussels in 2015 which included particular emphasis on improving states' execution of European Court judgments.[91]

1.49 The accession of the European Union to the European Convention on Human Rights (as required by the Lisbon Treaty and as enabled by Protocol No. 14 to the European Convention) has been on the agenda for more than 30 years, in order to achieve a greater degree of harmonisation of the interpretation of human rights standards across the European continent, and in particular, so that the acts of the EU institutions become subject to scrutiny by the European Court of Human Rights. The Brussels Declaration reaffirmed the importance of the accession proposal;[92] however, the process was stalled at the end of 2014, when the Court of Justice of the European Union published its opinion on the draft agreement on accession.[93]

---

[85] Committee of Ministers Resolution DH(70)1, 15.4.70.

[86] *Ireland* v *UK*, Series A, No. 25, 18.1.78, para. 240.

[87] No. 25781/94, 10.5.01, para. 358.

[88] On this issue, see also *Incal* v *Turkey*, No. 22678/93, 9.6.98.

[89] No. 25781/94, 12.5.14.

[90] High Level Conference on the Future of the European Court of Human Rights, Interlaken Declaration, 19 February 2010.

[91] High-level Conference on the 'Implementation of the European Convention on Human Rights, our shared responsibility'——Brussels Declaration, 27 March 2015.

[92] *Ibid.*, para. 15.

[93] CJEU, Opinion No. 2/13, ECLI:EU:C:2014:2454. Dean Spielmann, the then President of the European Court suggested that 'the principal victims will be those citizens whom this opinion ... deprives of the right to

In response to the Brussels Declaration and other recent reform proposals, inadmissibility **1.50** decisions made by single judges now include reasons (since the final quarter of 2016).[94] However, the Court has declined two proposals from the states parties: to give reasons for a decision rejecting a request for referral of a case to the Grand Chamber; and to give reasons for granting interim measures.[95]

Protocol No. 15

Protocol No. 15 was adopted in 2013, but it has not, as yet, entered into force.[96] The **1.51** Protocol inserts a reference to the principle of subsidiarity and the doctrine of the margin of appreciation into the preamble to the Convention. Given that both principles have been applied by the Court for many years, it is pertinent to ask why it was necessary to add such references to the preamble.[97] The Protocol will also reduce the time within which an application must be lodged with the Court after a final national decision has been taken from six months to four months (see the discussion of the 'six months rule' in chapter 4). The Protocol will also abolish the right of either party to object to relinquishment of a case to the Grand Chamber pursuant to Article 30,[98] and delete the third element of the 'no significant disadvantage' admissibility criterion.[99]

Protocol No. 16

Protocol No. 16 was adopted in 2013, and it also has not yet entered into force.[100] It will **1.52** allow the highest domestic courts and tribunals in each Convention state to request the Court to give advisory opinions on questions of principle relating to the interpretation or application of the rights and freedoms defined in the Convention or the protocols. The aim of this provision is to reinforce implementation of the Convention at the national level, and also to promote dialogue between the European Court and national courts.[101]

The requesting court or tribunal may only seek an advisory opinion in the context of a case **1.53** pending before it.[102] The requesting court must give reasons for its request and also provide

---

have acts of the European Union subjected to the same external scrutiny as regards respect for human rights as that which applies to each member State'. See European Court of Human Rights, Annual Report 2014, p. 6.

[94] European Court of Human Rights, The Interlaken process and the Court (2016 Report), 1 September 2016, para. 15.

[95] *Ibid.*, paras. 16–21.

[96] Council of Europe Treaty Series, No. 213, 24.6.13.

[97] In the author's view, the reasons relate to criticisms from certain quarters, which were at their height at around the time of the Brighton conference (in 2012), to the effect that the Court was considered to be over-extending its remit. For a response to such criticisms, see, e.g. A. Donald and P. Leach, *Parliaments and the European Court of Human Rights*, Oxford University Press, 2016. The Court made clear its reservations in: European Court of Human Rights, Opinion of the Court on Draft Protocol No. 15 to the European Convention on Human Rights, 6 February 2013.

[98] Article 3 of Protocol No. 15. Relinquishment is discussed further in chapter 2.

[99] In other words, it will delete the following text from Article 35(3)(b): 'and provided that no case may be rejected on this ground which has not been duly considered by a domestic tribunal'. See Article 5 of Protocol No. 15. This admissibility criterion is discussed in detail in chapter 4.

[100] Council of Europe Treaty Series, No. 214, 2.10.13. Protocol No. 16 will enter into force when 10 States have signed and ratified it, but only in respect of the States in question (Article 8 of Protocol No. 16).

[101] See further: Council of Europe, Explanatory Report to Protocol No. 16 to the Convention for the Protection of Human Rights and Fundamental Freedoms, 2 October 2013; European Court of Human Rights, Reflection Paper on the Proposal to Extend the Court's Advisory Jurisdiction (undated).

[102] Article 1(2) of Protocol No. 16.

the relevant legal and factual background of the pending case.[103] Any request will be considered by a panel of five judges of the Grand Chamber, which will decide whether to accept it or not (giving reasons for any refusal). If the request is accepted, the advisory opinion will be delivered by the Grand Chamber.[104] As their name suggests, advisory opinions will not be binding.[105] Clearly, therefore, it will be up to the requesting court to decide on the effect of the advisory opinion on the domestic proceedings.[106]

Current trends and future reforms

1.54 Much progress has been made in reducing the Court's backlog of cases in recent years. This has been primarily due to the modernisation and streamlining of the Court's working methods, as well as the introduction of the single-judge procedure and the frequent application of the pilot judgment procedure.[107]

1.55 In 2011 more than 100,000 applications had been identified by the Court for allocation to a single-judge formation—by 2015 that number was down to 3,200 (achieved through the work of the Court's Filtering Section).[108] By 2015, the number of repetitive cases accounted for almost half of all pending cases (30,500 out of 64,850) and the Court aims to reduce this number in the coming years.[109] By 2015 there were 11,500 priority cases pending before the Court, 19,600 normal, non-repetitive cases, and the Court will also be looking to reduce these backlogs too.[110]

1.56 Although the total number of cases pending before the Court has been significantly reduced from the position in September 2011 (when there were more than 160,000 cases pending),[111] there will clearly continue to be pressures on the Court's caseload, from varying sources. As at January 2017, the number of pending cases before the Court was 84,300 (including 18,650 from Ukraine, 14,800 from Turkey, 9,750 from Hungary, 8,000 from Russia and 7,900 from Romania). The number of new applications to the Court rose considerably in 2015 and 2016, not least because of the number of prison condition cases from Hungary and Romania, and cases relating to the situation in Crimea and the Donbass region of Ukraine,[112] and the situation in Turkey, following the attempted *coup d'état* in July 2016.[113]

---

[103] Article 1(3) of Protocol No. 16.

[104] Articles 2(1) and 2(2) of Protocol No. 16.

[105] Article 5 of Protocol No. 16.

[106] The European Court has noted the need for requests for advisory opinions to be dealt with expeditiously (given that the domestic proceedings will be stayed in the meantime) and has expressed its concerns about the lack of clarity as to who is responsible for having relevant documents translated. See: European Court of Human Rights, Opinion of the Court on Draft Protocol No. 16 to the Convention extending its competence to give advisory opinions on the interpretation of the Convention, 6 May 2013.

[107] European Court of Human Rights, Annual Report 2015, p. 32 (Speech given by Mr Dean Spielmann, President of the European Court of Human Rights, on the occasion of the opening of the judicial year, 30 January 2015).

[108] European Court of Human Rights, Annual Report 2015, p. 5.

[109] *Ibid.*

[110] *Ibid.*

[111] European Court of Human Rights, Annual Report 2015, p. 31.

[112] European Court of Human Rights, The Interlaken process and the Court (2016 Report), 1 September 2016, para. 2.

[113] European Court of Human Rights, Annual Report 2016, p. 7.

The number of judgments produced by the Court has been decreasing since a high of 1,625   **1.57**
in 2009–in 2015 it published 823 judgments (and 993 in 2016). However, the number of
applications which the Court has examined has not necessarily decreased—the reduction in
the number of judgments reflects the fact that the Court will frequently join similar applications together.[114]

In December 2015 the Steering Committee for Human Rights published its report on the   **1.58**
long-term future of the Court.[115] The report identified three particular areas for further
inquiry: national procedures for selecting candidates for the post of judge and the procedure
for electing them to the Court; enhancing procedures for implementing judgments relating
to large-scale violations of human rights in contexts such as armed conflict or territorial dispute; and a comprehensive study of the Convention as part of European and international
law. The report also concluded that, aside from the issue relating to the appointment of
judges, changes were not required beyond the framework of the existing structures.

---

[114] European Court of Human Rights, Overview 1959–2015, p. 5.

[115] Steering Committee for Human Rights, CDDH report on the longer-term future of the system of
the European Convention on Human Rights, CDDH(2015)R84 Addendum I, 11 December 2015. See
also: European Court of Human Rights, Comment from the Court on the report of the CDDH on the longer-
term future of the Convention system, February 2016.

2

PRACTICE AND PROCEDURE OF
THE EUROPEAN COURT—THE
PRE-JUDGMENT PHASE

Lodging the Application with the Court

2.01 The European Court of Human Rights has its own application form which applicants must use in lodging their case with the Court. It was previously possible to instigate a case at the

Court simply by letter,[1] but that has not been possible since 1 January 2014 when the Court's new application process was introduced.

The application form should be sent to the Court at this address:　　　　　　　　　**2.02**

> The Registrar
> European Court of Human Rights
> Council of Europe
> F-67075 Strasbourg Cedex
> France

All applications to the Court must comply with the admissibility requirements contained **2.03** in Article 35 of the Convention, in particular the obligation to exhaust domestic remedies before applying to the Court, and the six-month time limit within which a case must be lodged with the Court. The admissibility rules are a critical part of the Convention system. In general, the admissibility rules are strictly applied by the Court and a very high proportion of cases do not pass the admissibility hurdle. For example, in 2016, 36,579 cases were declared inadmissible, or struck out, by the Court.[2] Therefore, it is essential for practitioners who intend to take European Court cases to be fully familiar with the admissibility requirements and to pay very close attention to them. The admissibility criteria are explained in more detail in chapter 4. In practice, the two most important admissibility rules are closely linked. They are set out in Article 35(1) of the Convention and they stipulate that the Court may only deal with a case after all domestic remedies have been exhausted (according to the generally recognised rules of international law) and within a period of six months from the date on which the final decision was taken. Therefore, the application must be submitted to the Court in compliance with the six-month time limit.

For some prospective applicants to the European Court, it may not be at all clear whether **2.04** a particular form of redress would amount to a 'domestic remedy' for the purposes of Article 35. This is discussed in more detail in chapter 4 on the admissibility rules. However, if there is any doubt about the effectiveness of a particular 'remedy', practitioners should consider lodging an application with the Court in order to protect their client's position. If an application is not lodged, there is a danger that the Government might argue that the applicant had pursued a remedy that was not 'effective' for the purposes of Article 35 and therefore that the application should be declared inadmissible as having been submitted after the expiry of the six-month period. For example, the UK Government successfully argued such a point in the case of *Raphaie* v *UK*[3] on the basis that the applicant had pursued an internal prison complaint which was not 'effective'. Accordingly, should practitioners ever be in doubt about the effectiveness of a remedy, they should carefully consider lodging an application with the Court *at the same time* as pursuing the remedy in question. The Court should then be kept informed about any significant developments in the domestic proceedings, and also once the domestic process has been completed.

---

[1]　As discussed in chapter 2 of the last edition of this book.
[2]　European Court of Human Rights, Annual Report 2016, p. 193.
[3]　No. 20035/92, dec. 2.12.93.

Completing the application form

2.05 A copy of the Court's application form can be downloaded directly from the Court's website.[4] The application form should be downloaded, completed, printed out and sent by post to the Court with the necessary documentation. The downloaded form contains a barcode which enables the applicant's details to be entered directly into the Court's database. Applicants are required to use this form (Rule 47(1)), unless the Court decides otherwise. It should preferably be typed, although the Court will accept handwritten applications, if legible.[5] Each application should set out the following (according to Rule 47(1)):

    (a) the name, date of birth, nationality and address of the applicant and, where the applicant is a legal person, the full name, date of incorporation or registration, the official registration number (if any) and the official address;

    (b) the name, address, telephone and fax numbers and e-mail address of the representative, if any;

    (c) where the applicant is represented, the dated and original signature of the applicant on the authority section of the application form; the original signature of the representative showing that he or she has agreed to act for the applicant must also be on the authority section of the application form;

    (d) the name of the Contracting Party or Parties against which the application is made;

    (e) a concise and legible statement of the facts;

    (f) a concise and legible statement of the alleged violation(s) of the Convention and the relevant arguments; and

    (g) a concise and legible statement confirming the applicant's compliance with the admissibility criteria laid down in Article 35(1) of the Convention.

2.06 The Rules require that the information referred to in Rule 47(1)(e) to (g) (as set out above) that is included in the application form 'should be sufficient to enable the Court to determine the nature and scope of the application without recourse to any other document' (Rule 47(2)(a)). This means that applicants must treat the application form as a self-standing document which meets these requirements.[6] Applicants may supplement the information by appending to the application form further information (to a maximum of 20 pages). This may include further information on the facts, and/or on the alleged violations of the Convention and the relevant arguments (Rule 47(2)(b)).[7]

2.07 The application form must be signed by the applicant or the applicant's representative (Rule 47(3.1)). The Court requires the original form with the original signature (not a photocopy). For that reason, there is no point in faxing an application to the Court.[8]

---

[4] http://www.echr.coe.int/Pages/home.aspx?p=applicants/forms&c=. See the Practice Direction on the Institution of Proceedings (1 January 2016). See also the Court's 'Notes for filling in the application form', ENG—2016/1 and 'Common Mistakes in Filling in the Application Form and How to Avoid Them', 1.1.16.

[5] Practice Direction: *Institution of Proceedings*, para. 10.

[6] See also 'Common Mistakes in Filling in the Application Form and How to Avoid Them', 1.1.16.

[7] Any additional information must also comply with the following: if typed, be set out in a font size of at least 12 pt in the body of the text and 10 pt in the footnotes; in the case of annexes, be set out in A4 page format with a margin of not less than 3.5 cm; have pages numbered consecutively; and be divided into numbered paragraphs (Practice Direction: *Institution of Proceedings* (1 January 2016), para. 5).

[8] Practice Direction: *Institution of Proceedings* (1 January 2016), para. 3; 'Common Mistakes in Filling in the Application Form and How to Avoid Them', 1.1.16, p. 2.

It is extremely important that applicants should also provide the Court with *copies* of any **2.08** relevant documents, particularly the decisions (judicial or otherwise) relating to the object of the application and those showing that the admissibility criteria have been satisfied (Rule 47(3.1)). Grounds of appeal may also be relevant, in order to show that the points raised before the Court have been canvassed, as far as possible, before the domestic courts. The documents submitted must be listed in order by date, numbered consecutively and be identified clearly (Rule 47(3.2)).[9] If one of the requisite documents is not available to the applicant and cannot therefore be submitted, a detailed explanation should be provided to the Court (with documentary evidence, where necessary). The Court's Practice Direction refers to the question of costs and a refusal of an authority to provide a decision as being reasons which could be relied on in this respect.

Failure to comply with the requirements set out in Rule 47(1)–(3) will result in the appli- **2.09** cation not being examined by the Court, unless (a) the applicant has provided an adequate explanation for the failure to comply;[10] (b) the application concerns a request for an interim measure; or (c) the Court otherwise directs of its own motion or at the request of an applicant (Rule 47(5.1)).[11] This has been interpreted very strictly by the Court. For example, in 2014, of the 52,758 applications which were submitted to the Court, 12,191 (23 per cent) failed to comply with Rule 47.[12]

There are particular requirements for cases involving multiple applicants.[13] If complaints **2.10** are lodged by more than one applicant whose applications are based on *different* facts, a separate application form should be filled in for each individual applicant. If there are more than five applicants, in addition to the application forms and documents, the Court should be provided with a table setting out the requisite identifying details for each applicant (the table can be downloaded from the Court's website).[14] If the representative in the case is a lawyer, the table should also be provided in electronic form (on a CD-ROM or memory stick). In cases of large groups of applicants, the Registry may require the text of submissions or documents to be provided to the Court by electronic or other means.

Applicants should indicate in the application form whether they have submitted their com- **2.11** plaints to any other procedure of international investigation or settlement (Rule 47(2)(b)). This might include complaints, for example, to the UN Human Rights Committee in relation to the obligations under the International Covenant on Civil and Political Rights. For further discussion of this condition, see chapter 4.

---

[9] Applicants are also required not to staple, bind or tape the documents.

[10] Examples of exceptions include the following: 'where prisoners or persons in detention have not had access to particular documents, where an alien in detention has difficulty understanding what is required; in respect of applications coming out of the region of Ukraine where there is an ongoing conflict with destruction of property and disruption of public services which affects availability of documents and information' (Report on the implementation of the revised rule on the lodging of new applications, February 2015, p. 2).

[11] Practice Direction: *Institution of Proceedings* (1 January 2016), para. 10. The Court has clarified that point (c) could encompass 'very exceptional cases where an application raises important issues of interpretation of the Court's case-law or of the Convention which are of a significance for the effective functioning of the Convention mechanism beyond the individual circumstances of the case' (Report on the implementation of the revised rule on the lodging of new applications, February 2015, p. 2).

[12] Report on the implementation of the revised rule on the lodging of new applications, February 2015, p. 1.

[13] Practice Direction: *Institution of Proceedings* (1 January 2016), paras. 14–16.

[14] See: http://www.echr.coe.int/Documents/Applicants_Table_ENG.pdf.

2.12   There is no requirement upon applicants to set out what the 'object' of the application is—in other words there is no requirement as such to set out what the applicant seeks in terms of redress (which is a change from the procedure prior to 2014). It is certainly not necessary to provide a detailed claim for compensation under Article 41 in the initial application—this is not required until after the communication of the case. However, applicants should consider including in the initial application an outline indication of what is sought under Article 41. This will usually encompass the following:

   (ii) a claim for compensation (pecuniary and/or non-pecuniary damages); and/or
   (iii) a claim for legal costs and expenses (including, where relevant, a claim for the legal costs of any domestic proceedings).

Exceptionally, it is also possible for an applicant to claim other non-monetary redress (which is discussed further in chapter 3).

2.13   Even though detailed damages claims are not required in the initial application, it is nevertheless wise to obtain all the information and evidence necessary to make an Article 41 claim at the beginning of the case, as European Court cases take several years to progress through the system, by which time it may be much more difficult to obtain the evidence needed to sustain a claim under Article 41 (see chapter 8).

2.14   The Court may in any case request an applicant to provide further information or documents within a particular time-limit (Rule 47(5.2)). Applicants are required to keep the Court informed of any change of address and of all circumstances relevant to the application (Rule 47(7)).

An applicant who already has an application pending before the Court is required to inform the Court Registry, and provide the application number.[15]

2.15   The date of introduction of the application (for the purposes of the six months time limit in Article 35(1)) is the date on which an application form satisfying the requirements of Rule 47 is sent to the Court (Rule 47(6)). The Rules also expressly stipulate that the date of dispatch will be the date of the postmark (although 'where it finds it justified', the Court may decide that a different date is to be considered as the date of introduction— Rule 47(6)(b)).[16]

2.16   It is highly advisable to submit an application form to the Court well in advance of the six months deadline. The reason for that is, if the application form is incorrectly filled out (as set out above) it will be rejected by the Court. Therefore, if the form has been sent at the last moment, there will be no time to re-submit an application form. If an application form is rejected as being incomplete, the Court does not retain any file or documents in respect of that application. Therefore, it is not open to the applicant simply to send in a letter with the missing information, or to submit a missing document. Instead, a complete new application

---

[15] Practice Direction: *Institution of Proceedings*, para. 11.
[16] This is illustrated by a case decided prior to the introduction in 2014 of the Court's application form. In *Kemevuako* v *Netherlands*, No. 65938/09, dec. 1.6.10 the applicant introduced his case by fax and was informed by the Registry that he was required to lodge a full application within eight weeks—by 4 March 2010. On that date he sent the application by fax, but did not post the application until 10 March, and it was received by the Court on 12 March. The application was therefore declared inadmissible as being out of time. See also, e.g. *Bulinwar OOD and Hrasnov* v *Bulgaria*, No. 66455/01, 12.4.07.

form (with all the relevant documents) will need to be submitted (which must be done within the relevant six months time limit).[17]

Court rules and practice directions

The Rules of Court originally entered into force on 1 November 1998 and have subsequently **2.17** been amended on several occasions.[18] The Rules incorporate seven Practice Directions issued under Rule 32: *Requests for Interim Measures, Institution of Proceedings, Written Pleadings, Just Satisfaction Claims, Secured Electronic Filing by Governments, Electronic Filing by Applicants* and *Requests for Anonymity*. The relevant Rules and Practice Directions are referred to throughout this chapter. Compliance with the Court's practice directions is *not* equated with compliance with the admissibility criteria.[19]

Languages

Although the official languages of the Court are English and French,[20] any communication **2.18** with the Court (including the application form and any other pleading) submitted on behalf of an applicant prior to the notification of the case to the respondent government, may be in any one of the official languages of one of the state parties (Rule 34(2)). After notification has been given, the parties must obtain the permission of the President of the Chamber to continue to use one of the official languages of one of the state parties, otherwise they will be required to use either English or French (Rule 34(3)). State parties, and third parties, are required to use either English or French unless the President of the Chamber allows otherwise (Rule 34(4)). If permission is granted for the state to use one of its official languages, it will also be required to provide a translation of its submissions into English or French. Witnesses, experts and others appearing before the Court may use their own language if they do not have sufficient knowledge of either English or French (Rule 34(6)).

Representation

There is no requirement that an application to the European Court should be submitted by **2.19** a lawyer (Rule 36(1)). Indeed, many applications to the Strasbourg Court are submitted directly by applicants. An application may also initially be submitted 'through a representative' (Rule 36(1))—not necessarily a legal representative.[21]

It is a requirement of the Court that following communication of a case to the respondent **2.20** government, an applicant should be represented by an advocate (unless exceptionally the

---

[17] *Malysh and Ivanin v Ukraine*, Nos. 40139/14 and 41418/14, dec. 9.9.14. See also 'Common Mistakes in Filling in the Application Form and How to Avoid Them', 1.1.16, p. 4.

[18] See: http://www.echr.coe.int/Documents/Rules_Court_ENG.pdf. At the time of writing the latest edition of the Rules was dated 14 November 2016. Rule 111 now provides that both states parties, and 'organisations with experience in representing applicants before the Court [and] ... relevant Bar associations' will be consulted about proposed amendments to the Rules.

[19] See: *Yüksel v Turkey*, No. 49756/09, dec. 1.10.13.

[20] Rule 34(1).

[21] The Court's guidance notes state as follows: 'Some applicants may choose not to, or may not be able to, take part in the proceedings themselves for reasons such as health or incapacity. They may be represented by a person without legal training, for example a parent representing a child, or a guardian or family member or partner representing someone whose practical or medical circumstances make it difficult to take part in the proceedings (e.g. an applicant who is in hospital or prison). The representative must indicate in what capacity he or she is representing the applicant or his or her relationship with the applicant, together with his or her identity and contact details.' See Notes for filling in the application form, ENG—2016/1, p. 4.

President of the Chamber decides otherwise—Rule 36(2)). An applicant's refusal to instruct a lawyer following a direction from the Court after the communication of the case may lead to the case being struck out.[22] The appointed lawyer should be authorised to practise in one of the European Convention states and also resident in one of the Convention states, otherwise the representative will have to obtain the approval of the President of the relevant Chamber (Rule 36(4)(a)).[23] Accordingly, advocates authorised to practise in a Convention state will not need the Court's permission to represent an applicant before the Court, but, for example, an academic lawyer not authorised to practise would need the Court's permission. Representatives are required to supply to the Court a power of attorney or written authority to act from the applicant (Rule 45(3)).

2.21 In exceptional circumstances, where the 'circumstances or the conduct' of the representative 'so warrant', the Court has the power to direct that the appointed lawyer may no longer represent or assist the applicant and that the applicant should seek alternative representation (Rule 36(4)(b)).[24]

2.22 As discussed below (at 2.83) a committee may declare a case admissible and at the same time issue a judgment on the merits, if the underlying question in the case, concerning the interpretation or the application of the Convention, is already the subject of well-established case law (Article 28). In those circumstances, the Court's practice is usually not to grant legal aid or to require that the applicant is represented by a lawyer.

Costs, Legal Aid and Fees

2.23 European Court cases usually take several years to progress through the system (if they pass through the admissibility stage) and some cases take longer. Whilst these delays can be extremely frustrating to applicants, in other respects the Convention system is more accessible and litigant-friendly than domestic court procedures.

The respondent government's costs

2.24 Significantly, there is no provision in the Convention for the respondent government's costs to be paid by the applicant in any circumstances.[25] Therefore, even if an applicant withdraws or settles a complaint before judgment or if an applicant is ultimately unsuccessful following a contested hearing before the Court, he or she cannot be required to pay the government's costs. This may be a significant factor in deciding whether European Court proceedings should be taken in the first place. Whereas many litigants in domestic proceedings will face the daunting prospect of having to pay some or all of the opponent's costs if they are unsuccessful (according to the usual rule that costs follow the event), there is no such risk in Strasbourg. This, it is suggested, is a very important element in making the Convention system relatively accessible to even the poorest of applicants.

---

[22] *Grimalyo* v *Ukraine*, No. 69364/01, dec. 7.2.06.

[23] As occurred in *Abdolkhani and Karimnia* v *Turkey*, No. 30471/08, 22.9.09.

[24] See, e.g. *Petrović* v *Serbia*, No. 56551/11 et al, 18.10.11; *Bekauri* v *Georgia*, No. 14102/02, dec. 10.4.12; *Martins Alves* v *Portugal*, No. 56297/11, dec. 21.1.14.

[25] Rule 43(4) provides that when an application has been struck out (see 2.165 below), the costs shall be at the discretion of the Court. In practice, the Court does not require the applicant to pay the government's costs.

The applicant's costs

An applicant's reasonable costs incurred can be recovered from the respondent government, **2.25** either as an element of a settlement or if costs are awarded by the Court to a successful applicant. Under Article 41 of the Convention, if the Court finds that there has been a violation of the Convention, it may award 'just satisfaction' to the applicant. As well as pecuniary and non-pecuniary damages, the Court may award the applicant legal costs and expenses under Article 41. The Court will only award costs to the extent that it is satisfied that they were actually and necessarily incurred and that the amount was reasonable. Therefore it is absolutely essential that practitioners should accurately record all costs and expenses incurred from the start of the case and, when the question of costs is ready to be considered, they should be able to provide the Court with a detailed bill of costs. Practitioners should therefore include in their client letter at the start of the case a reference to the client's liability to pay, which can later be produced to the Court, if necessary, to show that the applicant has actually incurred the costs in question. The recovery of the applicant's costs is dealt with in more detail below in chapter 8.

In some Council of Europe states it may be possible for applicants to enter into 'contingency **2.26** fee' agreements with their lawyers—where the client agrees to pay the lawyers' fees amounting to a specific percentage of any award of damages made by the Court to the applicant. Such agreements are not, however, binding on the Court.[26]

Court fees

There is no court fee payable at any stage by an applicant to the European Court. Applicants **2.27** to the European Court may therefore be able to instruct lawyers on a conditional fee basis and combined with the lack of court fees and the absence of any requirement to pay the government's costs, a Strasbourg case may not amount to the sort of stressful financial gamble that domestic litigation may represent.

Legal aid

Legal aid for European Court proceedings will only very rarely be available from domes- **2.28** tic sources.[27] However, a limited form of legal aid is available for Strasbourg proceedings from the European Court itself (see Rules 100–105). A small set fee is payable (by the European Court) in respect of each stage that a case reaches in the Court proceedings. The amounts are limited and are generally considered to represent a contribution to an applicant's costs. However, if legal aid is granted, it will also pay for reasonable travel expenses (for the applicant(s) and their lawyer) to Strasbourg for any hearing which is scheduled before the Court.

Legal aid cannot be applied for prior to starting European Court proceedings, or even on **2.29** the opening of a case. Legal aid can only be applied for if and when a case is communicated to the government to reply. If legal aid is granted at that stage, the applicant will then receive the appropriate set fee for lodging the initial application. Legal aid is dealt with in more detail below at 2.105.

---

[26] *Iatridis* v *Greece*, No. 31107/96, 19.10.00, para. 55.
[27] For example, the Legal Aid Act in Denmark allows free legal aid to be granted to applicants in respect of international human rights proceedings: see *Vasileva* v *Denmark*, No. 52792/99, 25.9.03, para. 50.

Getting Assistance

2.30 There are a number of human rights non-governmental organisations (NGOs) with substantial experience and expertise in bringing or advising on European Court applications. Practitioners might consider contacting these NGOs for advice or assistance on both the European Convention law and the procedure. A number of NGOs have also developed the practice of intervening in cases as a third party (which is discussed below at 2.120).

Opening of the Case File and Initial Stages

2.31 On receipt of a properly completed application form (which complies with Rule 47—see above), the Court will open a file and the application will be given a file number. It will be allocated to one of the Court's judicial formations: a single judge, committee or chamber (as discussed below).

The Court's practice is to provide barcode labels which should be affixed to the first page of any subsequent correspondence sent to the Court.

Time limits for pleadings

2.32 Unlike the six-month time limit for lodging an initial application, it is possible to obtain extensions of other time limits set by the Court in relation to the submission of pleadings and other steps required by the Court. Requests should be made in writing explaining the reasons for the further time needed, such as difficulties in obtaining information, the need to carry out further research or obtain further evidence and/or documentation. However, any written observations filed after the expiry of a time limit may not be included in the case file, unless the President of the Chamber decides otherwise (Rule 38(1)).[28] Therefore, time limits should be observed and requests for extensions of time limits should be made in good time.[29]

Form of authority (power of attorney)

2.33 In the Court's application form, the applicant is required to sign it in order to authorise the named representative to act on their behalf, and the lawyer (or other representative) is also required to sign the application form in order to indicate their acceptance of the instructions. In those circumstances, no separate power of attorney or form of authority is required by the Court.

2.34 A separate form of authority is only required if the applicant instructs a lawyer for the first time after lodging the application, or changes the lawyer. In those circumstances, the form can be downloaded from the Court's website.[30] The failure to submit a form of authority could lead to the case being struck out[31] or declared inadmissible.[32]

---

[28] A document whose 'certified date of dispatch' is on or before the time limit will be taken to comply with that time limit. However, if there is no such certified date, then the relevant date is the actual date of receipt at the Court Registry (Rule 38(2)).

[29] See the Practice Direction: *Written Pleadings*, paras. 19–21.

[30] http://www.echr.coe.int/Pages/home.aspx?p=applicants/forms&c=.

[31] See, e.g. *Yüksel Erdoğan and others* v *Turkey*, No. 57049/00, 15.2.07.

[32] *Post* v *Netherlands*, No. 21727/08, dec. 20.1.09.

Governments have been known to try to challenge the validity or authenticity of applicants' **2.35**
powers of attorney. However, the Court rightly takes a robust position, to the effect that neither the Convention nor the Rules set down any particular requirements as to the form of
the power of attorney: 'what is important for the Court is that the form of authority should
clearly indicate that the applicant has entrusted his or her representation before the Court to
a representative and that the representative has accepted that commission'.[33]

The Court Registry

The Court Registry comprises the Court Registrar, Deputy Registrars, Section Registrars, **2.36**
Deputy Section Registrars, Non-judicial Rapporteurs and the Juriconsult[34] (currently about
640 staff in total) (see Article 24 and Rules 15–18B). The Registry is staffed by teams of lawyers who administer the cases, draft the case correspondence and draft Court decisions for
consideration by the Judge Rapporteur or the single Judge.

Strategy

Practitioners are well advised to submit the strongest possible application at the outset of a **2.37**
Convention case, rather than rely on augmenting the applicant's case at each stage in reply to
the government's arguments. It is of course possible to develop an applicant's case in response
to the government's submissions as the case progresses, but it is extremely important to
remember that a case may be declared inadmissible by the Court at the initial stages, without
the case even being referred to the government. Under the Court's admissibility conditions,
cases can be declared inadmissible as being 'manifestly ill-founded'. This condition amounts,
in effect, to a preliminary test of the case on its merits (see chapter 4 as to the admissibility
rules). Convention applications are frequently declared inadmissible as being manifestly ill-
founded, accordingly the more authoritative and convincing an initial application, the less
likely it is to fall at this troublesome early hurdle.

Careful consideration should also be given to the scope of the applicant's case. There may be **2.38**
a number of Convention points which could be taken in any case. For example, in a criminal case, practitioners may want to consider each of the separate limbs of Article 5 (liberty
and security of the person) and Article 6 (fair trial), but they may also want to give consideration to Article 7 (no punishment without law), to Article 13 (effective remedy), Article
14/Protocol No. 12 (prohibition of discrimination) and even the extent of any interference
caused by the criminal proceedings with the rights under Articles 8 to 11. Consideration may
also have to be given to various provisions in Protocol No. 7: Article 2 (the right of appeal);
Article 3 (compensation for wrongful conviction) and Article 4 (the right not to be tried or
punished twice). If there are various different arguments that could be made, practitioners
will want to consider to what extent to focus on the main arguments and how far to rely on
the subsidiary points. Of course, if an alleged violation of an Article of the Convention is not
included at all in the initial application, it may be declared inadmissible for failing to comply
with the six-months rule. This will require an intelligent and considered approach, so that
all reasonably arguable points are included, but weak points, which may be distracting for
the Court, are not. The Court is tending to take a stricter line than previously, in that weak

---

[33] *Hirst Jamaa and others* v *Italy*, No. 27765/09, 23.2.12, para. 53.
[34] The role of the Juriconsult is to ensure the consistency of case-law and to provide information to the
Court. See Rule 18B.

points will simply not be communicated to the government. It is also quite possible that as the case develops, and in the light of the government's observations in reply, the subsidiary arguments may get weaker or stronger. Once the government's cards are also on the table, the applicant's representative may then decide that any remaining weak points can be dropped, without the applicant being penalised in any way.

Confidentiality

2.39 The Court operates on the general principle that information about proceedings before the Court should be in the public domain. Not only are 'statements of facts', admissibility decisions and Court judgments publicly available documents (on the Court's HUDOC system), but so too are all documents lodged with the Registry (see 2.72 below). The Court also publishes regular monthly bulletins about its caseload which include brief details of some of the cases which have only reached the stage of being communicated to the respondent government. Therefore an applicant's identity could be publicly available as early as communication of the case (or perhaps earlier if the Court issues a press release).

2.40 However, the President of the relevant Chamber of the Court may permit an applicant's anonymity (Rule 47(4)). Applicants who do not wish their identity to be disclosed in the proceedings should therefore write to the Court giving their full reasons for requesting anonymity, and explaining the impact that publication may have (see the Practice Direction: *Requests for Anonymity*). The request should be made when completing the application form or as soon as possible afterwards. If the application for confidentiality is successful, the applicant will be referred to by his or her initials[35] or by an 'anonymous' initial, such as X or Y.[36] Retroactive requests for anonymity in respect of cases published on the HUDOC website before 1 January 2010 can also be made to the Court. It is also the Court's frequent practice to protect the identity of other '*dramatis personae*', such as family members, police officers and other public officials, by referring to them by their initials.

Legal aid

2.41 Legal aid is not available at this stage, but if legal aid is subsequently granted, a limited set fee is recoverable for the preparation of the application (see the section on legal aid below at 2.105).

Urgent cases: interim measures

2.42 There is no injunctive process as such within the European Convention system. However, in urgent cases where the applicant's life is at risk or where there is a substantial risk of serious ill-treatment, the Court may apply 'interim measures' under Rule 39 (formerly Rule 36). The President (or acting President) of a Chamber of the Court (or the Chamber itself) may indicate to any of the parties any interim measures that they consider should be adopted in the interests of the parties or the proper conduct of the proceedings. The Court may also request information from the parties in connection with the implementation of any interim measure which it has indicated (Rule 39(3)). The request for interim measures may be made by a party (an individual applicant or a state party applicant), or by 'any other person concerned', such as a

---

[35] As, for example, the applicant in *M.S.S. v Belgium and Greece*, No. 30696/09, 21.1.11. However, not all such requests are successful. See, e.g. *Ponomaryovi v Bulgaria*, No. 5335/05, 21.6.11, para. 8.

[36] Practice Direction: *Institution of Proceedings*, para. 12.

relative of a person held in detention, or, exceptionally, the Secretary-General of the Council of Europe[37] (see 1.13 above). The Court may also make an interim measures indication of its own motion[38] (Rule 39(1)). Whilst interim measures are usually directed towards the respondent state, the Court may invoke Rule 39 in respect of the applicant, as it did in *Ilaşcu and others v Moldova and Russia,*[39] in order to urge one applicant, Mr Ivanţoc, to call off a hunger strike.

In considering requests for interim measures, the Court applies a threefold test: **2.43**

- there must be a threat of irreparable harm of a very serious nature; and
- the harm threatened must be imminent and irremediable; and
- there must be an arguable (prima facie) case.

The Court has emphasised that it issues interim measures

> only in truly exceptional cases and on the basis of a rigorous examination of all the relevant circumstances. In most of these cases, the applicants face a genuine threat to life and limb, with the ensuing real risk of grave, irreversible harm in breach of the core provisions of the Convention.[40]

Interim measures have most commonly been applied where an applicant is threatened with expulsion to a country where there is a danger of torture or death—the vast majority of cases relate to deportation or extradition proceedings.[41] For example, interim measures were sought by the applicants in the cases of *Soering* v *UK*[42] and *D* v *UK*.[43] In both cases interim measures were granted in order to prevent the removal of the applicants in circumstances in which their lives were at risk in the receiving country, albeit for rather different reasons. The applicant in *Soering* faced extradition to the United States and a death sentence for a murder charge and in *D*, the applicant, who was in the advanced stages of AIDS, was threatened with removal to his country of birth, St Kitts, where, he argued, medical treatment for his condition would be totally inadequate. Rule 39 has also been invoked by the Court, for example, in *Hilal* v *UK*[44] to prevent the applicant's expulsion to Tanzania, in *Kalantari* v *Germany,*[45] *Amrollahi* v *Denmark*[46] and *S.F. and others* v *Sweden*[47] to prevent, in each case, the applicant's expulsion to Iran, in *N* v *Finland*[48] to prevent the applicant's expulsion to the Democratic Republic of Congo, in *Sufi and Elmi* v *UK*[49] to prevent the applicants' removal to Somalia, and in *Shamayev and others* v *Georgia and Russia*[50] to prevent the extradition of

---

[37] See, e.g. *Denmark, Norway, Sweden and the Netherlands v Greece,* Nos. 3321/67, 3322/67, 3323/67 and 3344/67, 5.11.69, *Yearbook of the European Convention on Human Rights,* Vol. 13, 1969.

[38] See, e.g. *Denmark, Norway and Sweden v Greece,* No. 4448/67, dec. 26.5.70, *Yearbook of the European Convention on Human Rights,* Vol. 13, 1970.

[39] No. 48787/99, 8.7.04, para. 11.

[40] *Amirov v Russia,* No. 51857/13, 27.11.14, para. 67.

[41] *Mamatkulov and Askarov v Turkey,* Nos. 46827/99 and 46951/99, 4.2.05, para. 104.

[42] No. 14038/88, Series A, No. 161, 7.7.89.

[43] No. 30240/96, 2.5.97. See also *Bensaid v UK,* No. 44599/98, 6.2.01, para. 4.

[44] No. 45276/99, 6.3.01, para. 5.

[45] No. 51342/99, 11.10.01.

[46] No. 56811/00, 11.7.02, para. 5.

[47] No. 52077/10, 15.5.12.

[48] No. 38885/02, 26.7.05.

[49] Nos. 8319/07 and 11449/07, 28.6.11.

[50] No. 36378/02, 12.4.05 (and see ECHR press release: 10.10.02). Five applicants were nevertheless handed over to the Russian authorities, after the Georgian authorities had been notified by telephone of the Rule 39 indication, but prior to their receipt of written notification (see paras. 5–12). The measures were subsequently

11 Chechens from Georgia to Russia. During the course of the case of *Chahal* v *UK*,[51] which concerned the proposed deportation on national security grounds of an alleged Sikh militant, the European Commission of Human Rights invoked the interim measures procedure in requesting the Government not to deport the applicant. When the case went before the Court, the Government undertook to provide the Court with at least two weeks' notice of any intended deportation. Requests for interim measures in respect of the removal of applicants to other European Convention signatory states are not usually granted, on the basis that it is assumed that the state will comply with its Convention obligations, unless there is clear evidence to suggest otherwise.[52] In *M.S.S.* v *Belgium and Greece*[53] an interim measures application was rejected in respect of the applicant's transfer from Belgium to Greece, but the Court subsequently applied Rule 39 to indicate to the Greek Government that the applicant should not be deported to Afghanistan, pending the outcome of the Strasbourg proceedings.

2.44 As a Chamber judgment does not immediately come into force (see Article 44(2)) the Court may order that a Rule 39 indication should continue in force until the judgment becomes binding (or is referred to the Grand Chamber under Article 43).[54]

2.45 Although most interim measures decisions relate to expulsion cases, Rule 39 has been applied in an increasingly wide range of situations. For example, in *Öcalan* v *Turkey*,[55] concerning the prosecution of the leader of the Kurdish Workers' Party (PKK), the Court requested the Government to ensure compliance with Article 6 in relation to the criminal proceedings against the applicant in the State Security Court and also to ensure that the applicant was able effectively to exercise his right of application to the European Court through lawyers of his own choosing. Subsequently, the Turkish Government was asked by the Court under Rule 39 to confirm specific points about the applicant's trial (which the Government refused to answer, arguing that such questions went beyond the scope of the Rule). The Court further requested that the Turkish Government should take all necessary steps to ensure that the death penalty (which had been passed by the State Security Court in Turkey) was not carried out.[56] In *Shamayev and others* v *Georgia and Russia* the Court applied Rule 39 in order, inter alia, to ensure that the applicant Chechens (who had been extradited to Russia) could have access to their lawyers.[57]

2.46 The Court may also indicate interim measures in exceptional circumstances to protect the health of vulnerable detainees.[58] In *Aleksanyan* v *Russia*[59] the Court invoked Rule 39 to order

---

lifted following undertakings by the Russian Government to guarantee unhindered access for the applicants to appropriate medical treatment, legal advice and the Court itself, and that the applicants would not face capital punishment and that their health and safety would be protected (ECHR press release: 26.11.02).

[51] No. 22414/93, 15.11.96.

[52] See, e.g. *A.G.* v *Sweden*, No. 27776/95, dec. 26.10.95 (proposed expulsion of Kurds to Turkey). But there are exceptions: see, e.g. *Shamayev and others* v *Georgia and Russia*, No. 36378/02, 12.4.05 (Rule 39 applied in order to prevent the extradition of a group of Chechens from Georgia to Russia).

[53] No. 30696/09, 21.1.11.

[54] See, e.g. *Klein* v *Russia*, No. 24268/08, 1.4.10, paras. 76–7.

[55] No. 46221/99, 12.5.05.

[56] Press Release, European Court of Human Rights, 30.11.99; *Öcalan* v *Turkey*, No. 46221/99, 12.5.05.

[57] No. 36378/02, 12.4.05, para. 24. But the Rule 39 indication was not in fact complied with by the Russian authorities—see paras. 228–9 and 310. See also *Shtukaturov* v *Russia*, No. 44009/05, 27.3.08 (Government requested to allow the applicant to meet his lawyer in the psychiatric hospital where he was detained); *D.B.* v *Turkey*, No. 33526/08, 13.7.10 (Rule 39 invoked to allow lawyer to visit applicant asylum-seeker in detention).

[58] See, e.g. *Patane* v *Italy*, No. 11488/85, dec. 3.12.86; *Ilijkov* v *Bulgaria*, No. 33977/96, dec. 20.10.97; *Makharadze and Sikharulidze* v *Georgia*, No. 35254/07, 22.11.11.

[59] No. 46468/06, 22.12.08.

the authorities immediately to ensure that the applicant detainee received treatment in a specialist AIDS hospital (and to provide a copy of his medical file) and subsequently that he should be examined by a mixed medical commission including his own doctors. Similarly, in *Amirov v Russia*[60] the Court stipulated that the applicant, a paraplegic who had been paralysed following an assassination attempt, should be immediately examined by independent medical experts to determine whether the medical treatment he was receiving in the detention facility was adequate and whether his condition was compatible with detention or required his admission to hospital. In *Popov v Russia*,[61] the Court applied Rule 39 to indicate to the Government that the applicant was not to be required to perform physical labour or physical exercise in prison, and that there should be an independent medical examination of the applicant in a specialised uro-oncological institution. In *Tehrani and others v Turkey*,[62] the Court ordered the respondent Government to allow an applicant to be examined by a psychiatrist in a fully equipped state hospital, in order that his mental state could be diagnosed. As a result of the application of Rule 39 in *Grori v Albania*,[63] the applicant, who was suffering from multiple sclerosis, was transferred from prison to a civilian hospital. Interim measures were also invoked by the Court in *Paladi v Moldova*,[64] in order that the applicant, who was seriously ill, should *not* be transferred from a neurological centre to a prison hospital.

Exceptionally, the Court has invoked Rule 39 in order to *obtain* pertinent evidence in circumstances where the state authorities appear to be unable or unwilling to do so. The case of *Diri v Turkey*[65] concerned the applicant's allegations that he had been subject to *falaka* (the beating of the soles of the feet) whilst in prison: Mr Diri claimed that he was beaten because during the daily prison rollcall he refused to stand up and shout his name. The doctors who examined Mr Diri found no signs of ill-treatment on his body, which resulted in a decision by the public prosecutor not to take any action. However, soon after that decision the Court applied Rule 39 to require that a magnetic resonance imaging (MRI) scan and a bone scintigraphy scan be carried out. The bone scintigraphy revealed signs of trauma in his feet and a subsequent expert forensic report commissioned by Mr Diri's lawyer found that the results of the scan were consistent with his allegations of *falaka*. In its judgment, the Court concluded that Mr Diri had been subjected to torture.   **2.47**

Rule 39 may also be applied to guarantee applicants' protection more generally: in *R.R. v Hungary*[66] the Government was required to ensure the personal security of the first applicant, his wife and children. The first applicant had been active in a Serbian drug-trafficking mafia group. Having admitted various offences he secretly gave evidence to the authorities about the gang's activities, and, as a result, he, his wife and children were put on a witness protection scheme. His family members successfully invoked Article 2 when they were subsequently excluded from the witness protection scheme because the first applicant had breached its terms. Furthermore, the Court applied both Rule 39 and Article 46 in requiring the authorities to continue to ensure their adequate protection (including proper   **2.48**

---

[60] No. 51857/13, 27.11.14. However, the authorities' failure to comply with the Rule 39 order led to the Court finding a violation of Article 34. There was a similar Rule 39 stipulation (and Article 34 violation) in *Kondrulin v Russia*, No. 12987/15, 20.9.16.

[61] No. 26853/04, 13.7.06.

[62] Nos. 32940/08, 41626/08, 43616/08, 13.4.10.

[63] No. 25336/04, 7.7.09.

[64] No. 39806/05, 10.3.09.

[65] No. 68351/01, 31.7.07.

[66] No. 19400/11, 4.12.12.

cover identities if necessary) until it was established that the threat had ceased.[67] The Court invoked the interim measures procedure in *Shabazova* v *Russia*[68] in response to the disappearance in 2005 of Mahmut Magomadov, an expert working for the NGO, the International Protection Centre. It was alleged that Mr Magomadov was kidnapped by unknown men in Grozny. The Government was required to confirm whether Mr Magomadov had been detained by a state authority and, if so, to confirm the legal basis for such detention.

2.49 In *Evans* v *UK*[69] the applicant complained that the domestic law permitted her former partner to withdraw his consent to the storage and use by her of embryos created jointly by them. The Court applied Rule 39 in requiring the Government to ensure that the embryos were preserved pending the resolution of the case.

2.50 The interim measures procedure may be invoked to prevent housing evictions, as occurred in *Yordanova* v *Bulgaria*[70] which concerned the proposed eviction of members of a Roma community. The Court applied Rule 39 to prevent the applicants from being evicted from their homes, and pending the authorities' provision of information about the arrangements made to secure housing for the children, elderly, disabled and other vulnerable individuals.

Rule 39 has also been invoked by the Court in the context of inter-state armed conflict, to call on the parties to comply with their Convention rights, notably Articles 2 and 3.[71]

In a groundbreaking decision in 2017 in the case of *Rustavi 2 Broadcasting Company* v *Georgia*,[72] the Court applied Rule 39 in a case concerning media ownership and allegations of governmental interference with the media.[73] On 2 March 2017 the Georgian Supreme Court made a decision ordering the ownership of the Rustavi 2 television company to be transferred back to its former co-owner. On the following day, the European Court applied interim measures to indicate to the Government that the enforcement of the Supreme Court judgment should be suspended. It also stipulated that the authorities should abstain from interfering with the applicant's company's editorial policy 'in any manner'. This represents a significant change in the Court's approach to its interim measures remit, as discussed and illustrated above.

2.51 Interim measures have, historically, been relatively rarely sought and rarely granted. By 1989 there had been 182 requests for interim measures in cases concerning expulsion, which had been granted in only 31 cases.[74] Between 1974 and 2002 there were a total of 2,219 requests for interim measures, of which only 321 were granted (14.5 per cent). In February 2011 the President of the Court noted an 'alarming rise' in interim measures requests, as a result of a 4,000 per cent increase between 2006 and 2010 (4,786 applications in 2010). The President also commented on the fact that a large number of such requests are incomplete and do not contain sufficient information to enable the Court to make a proper assessment of the risks

---

[67] These stipulations were included in the operative provisions of the judgment.

[68] No. 4023/05, dec. 2.4.09. For an earlier case in which the Court applied Rule 39, see *Bitiyeva and X* v *Russia*, Nos. 57953/00 and 37392/03, 21.6.07, para. 63.

[69] No. 6339/05, 10.4.07.

[70] No. 25446/06, 24.4.12.

[71] *Georgia* v *Russia (II)*, No. 38263/08, dec. 13.12.11, para. 5; *Interim measure granted by European Court in inter-State case brought by Ukraine against Russia*, European Court press release, 13.3.14.

[72] No. 16812/17. Letter from European Court to applicant's representatives, 3 March 2017.

[73] See, e.g. Parliamentary Assembly of the Council of Europe, *Attacks against journalists and media freedom in Europe*, Report, Committee on Culture, Science, Education and Media (Rapporteur: Mr Volodymyr Ariev, Ukraine, Group of the European People's Party), 8 December 2016.

[74] *Cruz Varas* v *Sweden*, No. 15576/89, 20.3.91, para. 55.

to the applicants.[75] In the period from 2012 to 2015, there were 6,951 interim measures requests, of which 588 were granted (about 8 per cent). The number of interim measures requests granted since 2012 were: 103 (5 per cent) in 2012; 108 (7 per cent) in 2013; 216 (11 per cent) in 2014; 161 (11 per cent) in 2015,[76] and 129 (6 per cent) in 2016.[77]

The procedure

The procedure is set out in the Court's Practice Direction on *Requests for Interim Measures*.[78] **2.52** An applicant seeking interim measures should send their request in urgent cases by fax or by post.[79] The Practice Direction states that requests should *not* be sent by standard post (because of the delay involved) or by email. The request should be clearly headed 'Rule 39-Urgent'. Full contact details (including address, telephone and email) of the applicant or applicant's representative should be provided. In extradition or deportation cases, the applicant's address or place of detention should be provided, together with details of the expected date and time of their removal and any official case-reference number.

The request should, where possible, be written in one of the official languages of the Convention **2.53** states (although this is not obligatory). There is no prescribed format, as such, but it is essential that adequate reasons are given. The Practice Direction states: 'The applicant must in particular specify in detail the grounds on which his or her particular fears are based and the nature of the alleged risks and the Convention provisions alleged to have been violated.'

The Practice Direction advises that requests should be made in good time: as soon as possible **2.54** after the final domestic decision. This is extremely important—in practice the Court will simply be unable to deal with applications that are made at too short notice. In extradition or deportation cases, where steps may be taken immediately following the final decision, the Practice Direction states that the interim measures request should be submitted without waiting for that decision.[80]

The Court's decision is made by a chamber, a section President or by a duty judge (Rule 39(1) **2.55** and (4)). The Court has the power to take a decision on the admissibility of the case at the same time as considering the request for interim measures.[81] Where a request for interim measures is refused, the Court will ask the applicant whether s/he wants to pursue the application. If interim measures are granted, the applicants must keep the Court regularly and promptly informed about the state of any continuing domestic proceedings, otherwise the case may be struck out of the Court's list of cases.[82]

---

[75] Governments, applicants and their lawyers urged to co-operate fully with European Court, following 'alarming rise' in requests to suspend deportation, Press Release, European Court of Human Rights, 11.2.11.

[76] Of that total, 2,930 requests were considered to be 'out of scope' and 3,433 were rejected. See: European Court of Human Rights, Rule 39 requests granted and refused in 2012, 2013, 2014 and 2015 by respondent state, available at: http://www.echr.coe.int/Documents/Stats_art_39_01_ENG.pdf. During this four-year period, the most number of requests were made in relation to the UK: 2,524 requests, of which just 20 were granted (less than 1 per cent). 170 of the 199 requests made against both Ukraine and Russia (together) were granted (85 per cent).

[77] European Court of Human Rights, Analysis of Statistics 2016, January 2017, p. 5.

[78] Issued on 5 March 2003 and amended in 2009 and 2011. See also the President's statement made in February 2011 commenting on the incompleteness of many requests for interim measures (n. 75 above).

[79] Practice Direction: *Requests for Interim Measures*, section II.

[80] Practice Direction: *Requests for Interim Measures*, section III. Applicants in extradition and expulsion cases must first pursue any domestic avenues which are capable of suspending removal, before applying to the Court for interim measures. See Practice Direction: *Requests for Interim Measures*, section IV.

[81] Practice Direction: *Requests for Interim Measures*, section I.

[82] Practice Direction: *Requests for Interim Measures*, section V.

2.56 At the same time as submitting a request for interim measures to the Court, it may also be advisable for the applicant's representative to notify the government agent directly that such a request is being made.[83] This may help to ensure that the respondent state is in a position to act quickly if the Court grants the request for interim measures.

2.57 It is critical that the applicant's representative should lodge all relevant supporting documents, including domestic court documents and also any documents needed to establish the extent of the risk to the applicant's life or of ill-treatment. These may include both documents about the general situation in the relevant country, such as reports of UN Rapporteurs, Amnesty International, Human Rights Watch and other NGOs, but more importantly, there will need to be sufficient evidence of the particular risks arising in the applicant's specific situation. If the request is granted, the government is informed immediately by the Court. The Court may request information from the parties 'on any matter connected with the implementation' of any interim measure (Rule 39(3)). Notice of any interim measures may also be sent to the Committee of Ministers (Rule 39(2)). It may be advisable for the applicant's representative to take steps also to inform the appropriate *national* authority directly of the Court's decision to apply interim measures.

Enforceability and compliance

2.58 Interim measures indications are binding on states parties.[84] However, that was not always the case. The enforceability of an interim measures request was considered by the Court in a case where the respondent government did not comply with the request of the European Commission of Human Rights not to expel the applicants to their native Chile: *Cruz Varas v Sweden*.[85] The applicants, a married couple and their young son, had sought political asylum and refugee status in Sweden because of the first applicant's political activity against the Pinochet regime in Chile. He alleged that he had been tortured. Their requests were refused by the Swedish authorities. An application was lodged on their behalf with the European Commission on 5 October 1989. At 9.10 am the Swedish Government was informed by telephone that the Commission had indicated that the applicants should not be deported. Nevertheless, Mr Cruz Varas was deported at 4.40 pm later that day. The European Court subsequently had to decide whether the Government's failure to comply with the Commission's request had violated the duty not to hinder the effective exercise of the right of individual petition (then under Article 25, now Article 34 of the Convention). It found that the Rule could not create a binding obligation on Convention states.[86] By just ten votes to nine, the Court held that the failure to comply with the interim measures request did not violate the Swedish Government's obligation not to hinder European Convention applications.

2.59 However, this decision was in effect overturned by the Grand Chamber judgment in 2005 in *Mamatkulov and Askarov v Turkey*.[87] There, the Court found a violation of Article 34 arising

---

[83] In *Al-Moayad v Germany*, No. 35865/03, dec. 20.2.07 the applicant was extradited to the United States after the applicant had submitted a Rule 39 application to the Court, but before it had ruled on it. Therefore the Government was not found to have failed to comply with an interim measures indication. It was disputed between the parties whether or not the Government had been informed of the Rule 39 application by the applicant's lawyer.

[84] Practice Direction: *Requests for Interim Measures*.

[85] No. 15576/89, 20.3.91.

[86] *Cruz Varas v Sweden*, No. 15576/89, 20.3.91, paras. 94–103.

[87] Nos. 46827/99 and 46951/99, 4.2.05.

from the Turkish Government's failure to comply with an interim measures request not to extradite the applicant Uzbek nationals to Uzbekistan where they were wanted for an alleged terrorist attack on the President, and where they may have faced the death penalty. The Court gave its indication on 18 March 1999. However, the Turkish Cabinet issued a decree for their extradition on the following day and on 27 March 1999 the applicants were handed over to the Uzbek authorities. This was justified by the Turkish Government on the basis that it had received assurances from the Uzbek Government that the applicants would not be tortured or be subject to the death penalty. The applicants were subsequently convicted and sentenced to terms of imprisonment, but the applicants' representatives were unable to make contact with them and, in view of that, the Court found that there had been a violation of their right of individual application to the Court under Article 34.[88] The Grand Chamber emphasised that, in interpreting Article 34:

> ... the Court must have regard to the special character of the Convention as a treaty for the collective enforcement of human rights and fundamental freedoms. Unlike international treaties of the classic kind, the Convention comprises more than mere reciprocal engagements between Contracting States. It creates, over and above a network of mutual, bilateral undertakings, objective obligations which, in the words of the Preamble, benefit from a 'collective enforcement'.[89]

2.60 Having reviewed the interim measures procedure in the light of developments in other regional and international human rights mechanisms,[90] the Court held that, as a result of Article 34:

> ... Contracting States undertake to refrain from any act or omission that may hinder the effective exercise of an individual applicant's right of application. A failure by a Contracting State to comply with interim measures is to be regarded as preventing the Court from effectively examining the applicant's complaint and as hindering the effective exercise of his or her right and, accordingly, as a violation of Article 34.[91]

2.61 Thus the Grand Chamber judgment in *Mamatkulov and Askarov* establishes that there is an *obligation* on states to comply with an interim measures indication. This could be interpreted as meaning that a failure to comply with a Rule 39 indication will *necessarily* result in a violation of the right of effective application under Article 34, or that Article 34 will only be breached if the authorities of a contracting state are deemed to have failed to have taken all the steps which could reasonably have been taken in order to comply with interim measures indicated by the Court.[92] Interim measures must also be complied with as a matter of urgency.[93]

---

[88] See also *Kamaliyevy* v *Russia*, No. 52812/07, 3.6.10.

[89] *Mamatkulov and Askarov* v *Turkey*, Nos. 46827/99 and 46951/99, 4.2.05, para. 100.

[90] Notably, the judgment of the International Court of Justice in *LaGrand (Germany* v *United States of America)*, 27 June 2001.

[91] *Mamatkulov and Askarov* v *Turkey*, Nos. 46827/99 and 46951/99, 4.2.05, para. 128.

[92] The conclusion that Article 34 is automatically violated was, however, challenged by Judge Cabral Barreto in his concurring opinion, and by the joint partly dissenting opinion of Judges Caflisch, Türmen and Kovler. See also the earlier decision in *Conka and Others* v *Belgium*, No. 51564/99, dec. 13.3.01, where the Court found no violation of Article 34 following the applicants' deportation to Slovakia. The judgment in *Shtukaturov* v *Russia*, No. 44009/05, 27.3.08 reiterates the binding nature of a Rule 39 indication (para. 144). See also *Paladi* v *Moldova*, No. 39806/05, 10.3.09, para. 88 (but see the dissenting opinions in that case).

[93] *Paladi* v *Moldova*, No. 39806/05, 10.3.09, para. 98; *Grori* v *Albania*, No. 25336/04, 7.7.09, para. 190. In *Hamidovic* v *Italy*, No. 31956/05, dec. 13.9.11. an inadvertent delay in complying with a Rule 39 indication, which did not have irreversible consequences, was not found to violate Article 34.

2.62   In spite of the Court's clear stance on the binding nature of the interim measures obligation, there has been a worrying increase in the rate of states' non-compliance in recent years.[94] One of the starkest examples of this took place in *Trabelsi v Belgium*[95] in which the Belgian authorities decided to extradite the applicant to the United States, in spite of a long-standing Rule 39 order not to do so, which the Court held breached Article 34. The Court rejected each of the Government's arguments seeking to justify its actions, finding that it had

> deliberately and irreversibly lowered the level of protection of the rights set out in Article 3 of the Convention which the applicant had endeavoured to uphold by lodging his application with the Court. The extradition has, at the very least, rendered any finding of a violation of the Convention otiose, as the applicant has been removed to a country which is not a Party to that instrument, where he alleged that he would be exposed to treatment contrary to the Convention.[96]

2.63   The failure of the Georgian authorities to comply with a Rule 39 indication not to extradite the applicants to Russia was held, in *Shamayev and others v Georgia and Russia*[97] to violate Article 34. It was noted that the four applicants who were extradited were then held in isolation and were denied access to their lawyers. There have also been a number of cases concerning the forcible transfer of individuals from Russia to Central Asia (in spite of a Rule 39 indication), in circumstances where the applicants were abducted by unidentified individuals, but the Court has concluded that the transfer could not have happened without either the passive or active involvement of the Russian authorities.[98] In *Aoulmi v France*,[99] the failure of the authorities to comply with a Rule 39 indication not to deport the applicant to Algeria violated Article 34, as was the conclusion in *Ben Khemais v Italy*,[100] because of the authorities' failure to comply with an interim measures indication that the applicant should not be deported to Tunisia. In *Aleksanyan v Russia*[101] the authorities were found to have violated Article 34 because of their failure to comply with two interim measures indications: that the applicant detainee should be taken to a specialist AIDS hospital for treatment and that he should be examined by a mixed medical commission including doctors whom he had selected. Interim measures were invoked by the Court in *Paladi v*

---

[94] In *Cruz Varas v Sweden*, No. 15576/89, 20.3.91 the Court had commented that there had been almost total compliance with interim measures indications. But more recently, see, e.g. *Concerns over repeated Italian expulsions*—Statement by Thorbjørn Jagland, Secretary General of the Council of Europe, Press release—403(2010), 19.5.10. See also *Labsi v Slovakia*, No. 33809/08, 15.5.12; *Rrapo v Albania*, No. 58555/10, 25.9.12.

[95] No. 140/10, 4.9.14.

[96] *Ibid.*, para. 150.

[97] No. 36378/02, 12.4.05.

[98] *Savriddin Dzhurayev v Russia*, No. 71386/10, 25.4.13. In that case, in applying Article 46 (see chapter 3), the Court stipulated that the Russian authorities should ensure suitable general measures including the establishment of a system for investigating every breach of the Court's interim measures indications. See also *Abdulkhakov v Russia*, No. 14743/11, 2.10.12; *Nizomkhon Dzhurayev v Russia*, No. 31890/11, 3.10.13.

[99] No. 50278/99, 17.1.06.

[100] No. 246/07, 24.2.09. See also: *Mannai v Italy*, No. 9961/10, 27.3.12.

[101] No. 46468/06, 22.12.08. See also *Makharadze and Sikharulidze v Georgia*, No. 35254/07, 22.11.11 (failure to transfer prisoner suffering from tuberculosis to specialist medical institution—violation of Article 34); *Salakhov and Islyamova v Ukraine*, No. 28005/08, 14.3.13 (three days' delay in complying with Rule 39 order for the immediate transfer of HIV-positive prisoner to hospital—violation of Article 34); *Amirov v Russia*, No. 51857/13, 27.11.14 (failure to comply with Rule 39 order that applicant detainee should be immediately examined by independent medical experts—violation of Article 34).

Moldova,[102] in order that the applicant, who was seriously ill, should *not* be transferred from a neurological centre back to prison. As a result of delays and a failure to comply, the Grand Chamber found a violation of Article 34 by a 9–8 majority.[103] The Court was highly critical of the Russian Government's failure to comply with an interim measures order in *Kondrulin v Russia*[104] whose purpose was to ensure that the applicant detainee (who had cancer) received the requisite medical treatment. The Court concluded that

> … in view of the vital role played by interim measures in the Convention system, they must be strictly complied with by the State concerned. The Court therefore cannot conceive of allowing authorities to circumvent an interim measure … by replacing expert medical opinion with their own assessment of an applicant's situation. However, that is exactly what the Government have done in the present case. In so doing, the State has frustrated the purpose of the interim measure, which was to enable the Court, on the basis of relevant, independent medical opinion, to effectively respond to and, if need be, prevent the possible continued exposure of the applicant to physical and mental suffering in violation of the guarantees of Article 3…[105]

2.64 There was a violation of Article 34 in the case of *Al-Saadoon and Mufdhi v UK*[106] which concerned the applicants' detention by the British armed forces in southern Iraq in 2003, on suspicion of murdering two British soldiers. On 30 December 2008, pursuant to Rule 39, the UK Government was informed that the applicants should not be removed or transferred from its custody. However, on the following day they were nevertheless handed over to the Iraqi authorities: 'the Government took the view that, exceptionally, it could not comply with the measure indicated by the Court'. This led the Court to find a violation of Article 3 because of the risk that they would face the death penalty, and it reiterated that a state could not enter into an agreement with another state that breached its Convention obligations. The Court concluded that the 'objective impediment' claimed by the UK Government (the absence of any course of action consistent with respect for Iraqi sovereignty other than the transfer of the applicants) was 'of the respondent State's own making'. The Court was also not satisfied that the United Kingdom had taken any steps to comply with the Rule 39 indication—for example, there was no binding assurance from the Iraqi authorities that the death penalty would not be used. Accordingly, the Court found a violation of Article 34. Invoking Article 46 (see chapter 3), the Court found that in order to comply with its Article 3 obligations, the Government should take all possible steps to obtain an assurance from the Iraqi authorities that the applicants would not be subjected to the death penalty. In *D.B. v Turkey*,[107] the Government's failure to comply with an interim measures indication in order for the applicant asylum-seeker to be visited by his lawyer whilst in detention led to the finding of a violation of Article 34.

The Court may also draw adverse inferences from a state's refusal to implement interim measures.[108]

---

[102] No. 39806/05, 10.3.09.
[103] See also *Grori v Albania*, No. 25336/04, 7.7.09 (delay of 17 days in transferring applicant from prison to hospital—violation of Article 34).
[104] No. 12987/15, 20.9.16.
[105] *Ibid.*, para. 47.
[106] No. 61498/08, dec. 30.6.09.
[107] No. 33526/08, 13.7.10.
[108] *Aleksanyan v Russia*, No. 46468/06, 22.12.08, para. 155.

Expediting cases: the Court's priority policy

2.65   Formerly, the standard procedure of the Court was to deal with cases in the order in which they were lodged with the Court. Of course, once registered, the time which cases take to progress through the Court system may vary enormously, depending upon the particular circumstances of the case and the 'route' it takes through the Court. The Court can give notification of the introduction of urgent cases to the respondent government, by any available means (Rule 40).[109] The Court may also give priority to particular cases, under Rule 41. Rule 41 was amended in 2009 to specify that the Court will consider the importance and urgency of the issues raised in a case in deciding the order in which it is to be dealt with. In November 2010 the Court, for the first time, published the criteria which it will apply[110] which comprise seven categories:

> Category I—**Urgent** applications (in particular risk to life or health of the applicant, other circumstances linked to the personal or family situation of the applicant, particularly where the well-being of a child is at issue, application of Rule 39 of the Rules of Court).

> Category II—Applications raising questions capable of having an **impact on the effectiveness of the Convention system** (in particular a structural or endemic situation that the Court has not yet examined, pilot-judgment procedure) or applications raising an **important question of general interest** (in particular a serious question capable of having major implications for domestic legal systems or for the European system), inter-State cases.

> Category III—Applications which on their face raise as main complaints issues under **Articles 2, 3, 4 or 5(1)** of the Convention ('core rights'), irrespective of whether they are repetitive, and which have given rise to direct threats to the physical integrity and dignity of human beings.

> Category IV—Potentially well-founded applications based on other Articles.

> Category V—Applications raising issues already dealt with in a pilot/leading judgment ('repetitive cases').

> Category VI—Applications identified as giving rise to a problem of admissibility.

> Category VII—Applications which are manifestly inadmissible.

2.66   The Court's policy indicates that in principle a case in a higher category will be examined before a case in a lower category, but that a Chamber or President may decide that an individual case should be treated differently. If a party seeks expedition, full reasons should be given to the Court at the earliest possible stage in the proceedings, with reference to any relevant categories of the Court's priority policy. The essence of the policy is to concentrate more resources on the most important cases—those within the top three categories.[111] The application of the Court's priority policy to a particular case does not guarantee that it will be processed within a particular time, but it clearly does enable the Court to process cases in a matter of days, as occurred for example in cases concerning the protests in central Kiev at the end of 2013.[112]

---

[109] See, e.g. *Shamayev and others* v *Georgia and Russia,* No. 36378/02, 12.4.05, para. 6.

[110] Available on the Court's website at: http://www.echr.coe.int/Documents/Priority_policy_ENG.pdf.

[111] By the end of 2016, there were 19,870 cases in the top three categories pending with the Court. See: European Court of Human Rights, Analysis of Statistics 2016, January 2017, p. 5.

[112] *Sirenko* v *Ukraine*, No. 9078/14 (lodged on 28 January 2014 and communicated on 1 February 2014); *Derevyanko* v *Ukraine*, No. 7684/14 (lodged on 23 January 2014 and communicated on 20 February 2014).

The decisions discussed below are cases in which priority was granted by the Court, before **2.67** its new priority criteria were published in 2010. For example, the case of *Papon* v *France* was expedited by the Court because of the advanced age and ill-health of the applicant in prison. The case was lodged on 12 January 2001 and on 23 January the Court asked the respondent government to submit information and comments about the applicant's prison conditions and regime.[113] One month after the application in *Siddik Aslan* v *Turkey* was lodged with the Court, it was given priority treatment as it concerned the alleged killings of the applicants' relatives by the security forces and Rule 41 was applied in particular because of the possibility of vital evidence being destroyed due to the decomposition of the bodies.[114]

One case that was given priority by the (former) Court was *Soering* v *UK*,[115] which was **2.68** processed by the Court within 12 months from the application being lodged to the judgment of the Court. *Soering* concerned the applicant's threatened extradition from the United Kingdom to face a capital murder charge in the United States, which clearly required expedition by the European Court.

Another case given priority by the Convention system was the case of *D* v *UK*[116] concerning **2.69** the removal of the applicant, who was suffering from the advanced stages of AIDS, from the United Kingdom to St Kitts. It was dealt with by the former Commission and Court within 15 months.

Rule 41 was applied to give priority to the application in *Mouisel* v *France*, which con- **2.70** cerned the continuing detention of a prisoner suffering from cancer. The case was lodged in October 2000 and a decision was made to accord it priority in April 2001. The case was declared admissible in March 2002 and judgment was handed down in November 2002.[117] However, the case which has been dealt with most quickly by the European Court was *Pretty* v *UK*[118] in which the terminally ill applicant sought, unsuccessfully, a right to assisted suicide. The case was turned around by the European Court in less than four months: it was first lodged with the Court in December 2001 and judgment was given on 29 April 2002.

Joinder of cases

The Court may order the joinder of cases (Rule 42—former Rule 43), which it will do where **2.71** cases raise identical or very similar points.[119] Applicants should consider applying for joinder with other cases if they raise the same issues and if it is considered that to do so would strengthen the case. For example, the joinder of similar cases may underline to the Court that the issue raised is not just a one-off problem, but is likely to lead to repeated Convention violations. The Court can order joinder at the request of the parties or of its own motion. The Court can also order cases to be conducted simultaneously, whether or not joinder is ordered (Rule 42(2)).

---

[113] See European Court press release, 23.1.01.
[114] No. 75307/01, 18.10.05, para. 81.
[115] No. 14038/88, 7.7.89, Series A, No. 161.
[116] No. 30240/96, 2.5.97.
[117] *Mouisel* v *France*, No. 67263/01, 14.11.02.
[118] No. 2346/02, 29.4.02.
[119] See, e.g. *Schwabe and M.G.* v *Germany*, Nos. 8080/08 and 8577/08, 1.12.11.

Public access to documents

2.72 All documents lodged with the Court in relation to an application (except those related to friendly settlement negotiations) are accessible to the public, unless the President of the Chamber decides otherwise.[120] The President may decide to restrict public access either at his or her own motion, or at the request of one of the parties or 'any other person concerned' (Rule 33(1)). The President may exclude public access in the interest of morals, public order or national security in a democratic society, where the interests of juveniles or the protection of the private life of the parties so require, or to the extent strictly necessary in the opinion of the President in special circumstances where publicity would prejudice the interests of justice (Rule 33(2)). If a party seeks confidentiality for a particular document, reasons must be provided and it must be specified whether it is requested that all or part of the document should be made inaccessible (Rule 33(3)).[121]

2.73 The extent of public access was a change to the Convention system brought about by Protocol No. 11 in November 1998. Under the old system, the European Commission of Human Rights applied strict rules of confidentiality to proceedings. The Court's public access rules now allow applicants or their representatives to apply for copies of specified documents, including government submissions, in any case before the Court (the documents can then be inspected at the Court by appointment). This may be extremely useful where there are cases similar to a proposed application which are already registered with the Court. The Court publishes summaries of selected cases in its monthly *Information Notes*, which include cases which have been communicated to the respondent government. In addition, in 2016 the Court introduced a new 'State of Proceedings' public search engine which shows what stage has been reached in the proceedings concerning an application.[122]

Immunity of applicants and their representatives

2.74 The 1996 *European Agreement relating to persons participating in proceedings of the European Court of Human Rights*[123] sets out various immunities available to those involved in European Court proceedings. The Agreement applies to anyone taking part in Court proceedings, including the parties, their representatives and advisers and witnesses and experts (Article 1). The Agreement establishes immunity in respect of oral or written statements and documents made or submitted to the Court, but it would not apply to statements made outside the Court (Article 2).

2.75 Governments are obliged to respect the right of applicants and their representatives to correspond freely with the Court and there are particular provisions protecting the rights of people in detention (Article 3 of the Agreement). These provisions to a great extent overlap with the obligations that the Court has read into both Article 8 of the Convention

---

[120] Article 40(2) of the European Convention on Human Rights. See also: http://www.echr.coe.int/Documents/Practical_arrangements_ENG.pdf.

[121] For example, at the Russian Government's request, the Court classified as confidential all the documents in the case file relating to *Shamayev and others* v *Georgia and Russia* (No. 36378/02, 12.4.05, para. 21).

[122] Available on the Court's website: http://app.echr.coe.int/SOP/index.aspx?lg=en.

[123] European Treaty Series, No. 161. It was adopted on 5.3.96 and came into force on 1.1.99.

(the right to respect for correspondence) and Article 34 (the duty not to hinder the right of individual petition). Parties and their representatives are to be permitted free movement in order to attend Court proceedings (Article 4 of the Agreement). However, the Court is obliged to waive immunity where it would otherwise impede the course of justice (Article 5 of the Agreement). In *Albertsson* v *Sweden*[124] the Court rejected a request by the applicant to waive immunity (in the course of domestic proceedings for slander) in respect of written submissions made to the Court alleging that the applicant had criminal convictions for offences involving dishonesty. The Court emphasised 'the need to ensure free and open communication in its proceedings and to protect those who plead before it from being sued or prosecuted for their statements'. The Court will waive immunity 'only in exceptional circumstances', for example where statements are made which are 'manifestly excessive or plainly irrelevant'.

Withdrawal of judges

Rule 28(2) of the Court Rules requires the withdrawal of judges in the following circumstances: **2.76**

(a) he or she has a personal interest in the case, including a spousal, parental or other close family, personal or professional relationship, or a subordinate relationship, with any of the parties;
(b) he or she has previously acted in the case, whether as the Agent, advocate or adviser of a party or of a person having an interest in the case, or as a member of another national or international tribunal or commission of inquiry, or in any other capacity;
(c) he or she, being an ad hoc judge or a former elected judge continuing to sit by virtue of Rule 26(3), engages in any political or administrative activity or any professional activity which is incompatible with his or her independence or impartiality;
(d) he or she has expressed opinions publicly, through the communications media, in writing, through his or her public actions or otherwise, that are objectively capable of adversely affecting his or her impartiality;
(e) for any other reason, his or her independence or impartiality may legitimately be called into doubt.

In situations where there is any 'doubt' about whether such criteria apply, the Rules require the chamber to decide the matter by a vote (taken in the absence of the judge in question).[125] In *Cyprus* v *Turkey*,[126] for example, three Court judges (two Turkish and one Cypriot) were withdrawn following challenges by the state parties. No reasons were given for their withdrawal. It is possible for applicants to invoke Rule 28(2). For example, in *Vardanyan and Nanushyan* v *Armenia*[127] the applicants challenged the appointment of an (Armenian) ad hoc judge on various grounds. As a result, the chamber deliberated and decided (pursuant to Rule 28(4)) that the appointed ad hoc judge could not sit on the case, and the judge was replaced with another judge.[128]

---

[124] No. 41102/07, dec. 6.7.10.
[125] Rule 28(4).
[126] No. 25781/94, 10.5.01.
[127] No. 8001/07.
[128] European Court's letter to applicants' representative, 27 September 2016.

Procedure before a Single Judge, Committee or Chamber

The Judge Rapporteur

2.77 Applications made under Article 34 (other than those dealt with by the single judge formation—see 2.79 below) are assigned by the President of the particular section to one of the Court judges, known as a 'Judge Rapporteur', whose function is to examine the case (Rule 49). The identity of the Judge Rapporteur is not disclosed.

2.78 The Judge Rapporteur may ask the parties to provide further information, documents or other relevant material, within a specified time. The Judge Rapporteur will decide whether the application should be considered by a single-judge formation, by a committee or by a Chamber. Convention cases which appear on their face not to satisfy the admissibility requirements are referred by the Judge Rapporteur to a single judge or to a committee which fulfil the role within the Convention system of disposing of the weakest cases.

Admissibility decided by a single judge

2.79 In accordance with the changes introduced by Protocol No. 14 (see chapter 1), a single judge may declare an application inadmissible or strike it out of the Court's list of cases (which decision is final) (Article 27; Rules 27A and 52A). The Court's practice was that the applicant was informed by letter of any such decision(providing the name of the judge who made the decision and very brief reasons) In response to the Brussels Declaration (see chapter 1) and other recent reform proposals, inadmissibility decisions made by single judges are now made in a formal judicial decision which includes reasons (since the final quarter of 2016).[129] In addition to the possibility of declaring the case inadmissible, the case may be struck out, for example, if the matter is resolved or if the applicant withdraws the application (see the section on striking out at 2.165 below). Such decisions by a single judge are taken 'without further examination'—in other words, without having been communicated to the respondent government.

2.80 Single judges may be assisted by a 'non-judicial rapporteur' (Rule 27A(4)). The judge may not consider any application against the state in respect of which that judge has been elected (Article 26(3); Rule 52A(2)). If the single judge does not take such a decision, the application will then be dealt with either by a Committee or a Chamber.

Admissibility decided by a Committee

2.81 A Committee of three judges may declare a case inadmissible (or strike it out of the list) provided that the Committee is unanimous (Article 28; Rule 53). Such a decision may be made without, or following, communication of the case to the respondent government. The judge elected in respect of the respondent state may be invited to take part in the deliberations of the Committee.

2.82 If an inadmissibility decision is made by a Committee without communicating the case, applicants are informed of the Committee's decision by letter (Rule 53(5)). The Court's practice has been to issue a letter in a standard format which provides no reasons relating to the

---

[129] European Court of Human Rights, The Interlaken process and the Court (2016 Report), 1 September 2016, para. 15.

particular case other than a formulaic response referring to the admissibility criteria under Article 35, but, as with single judge decisions (see above), the practice was changed following the 2015 Brussels conference, so that there is now a formal judicial decision which includes reasons. The decision of a Committee is final.[130]

If a Committee cannot reach a unanimous decision as to the inadmissibility of an application then it passes to a Chamber for consideration.

Judgment by a Committee in 'manifestly well-founded' cases

In accordance with the changes introduced under Protocol No. 14 to the Convention (see 1.29 above), a Committee may declare a case admissible and at the same time issue a judgment on the merits, if the underlying question in the case, concerning the interpretation or the application of the Convention, is already the subject of well-established case law (Article 28(1)(b); Rule 53(2)). This provision introduced a simplified and swifter procedure to deal with 'manifestly well-founded cases' (sometimes described as 'clone' or 'repetitive violation' or 'WECL' (i.e. well-established case law) cases). The 'WECL' procedure will be applied for example in respect of issues such as conditions of detention, length of proceedings, the non-enforcement of domestic decisions, and the excessive length of proceedings. In these cases, the time-limit for any governmental observations is usually 16 weeks, and applicants will not generally be invited to submit just satisfaction claims as awards are made in accordance with the method of calculation adopted in the relevant leading or pilot judgment. Governments are encouraged to settle such cases wherever possible, failing which default (summary) judgments are adopted by the Court. **2.83**

Admissibility decided by a Chamber

If a decision is not made by a single judge under Article 27, or by a Committee under Article 28, a Chamber of seven judges will decide on the admissibility and merits of the application (Article 29; Rule 54). **2.84**

The Chamber may decide to declare the case inadmissible or to strike it out of the list. In those circumstances, the Chamber produces a reasoned decision explaining the grounds for doing so. As with other inadmissibility decisions, there is no right of appeal against an inadmissibility decision made by a Chamber. **2.85**

Alternatively, the President of the Chamber may seek further information or documents from the parties, or may invite further written observations, or may give notice to the respondent government of the application (commonly known as communication of the case). **2.86**

Before taking a decision on admissibility, the Chamber may decide to hold an oral hearing (see 2.181 below), but this is increasingly rare in practice. If such a hearing is held, it will usually also incorporate consideration of the merits of the case (Rule 53(5)). **2.87**

Reopening inadmissible cases

There is no right of appeal against an inadmissibility decision, whether by a single judge, a Committee or a Chamber. Nevertheless, the Court has found that, in exceptional **2.88**

---

[130] Article 28; Rule 53(4).

circumstances, it may reopen a case which has previously been declared inadmissible. This power is exercised 'in the interests of justice'. The relevant test applied by the Court is that there has been a 'manifest error of fact or in the assessment of the relevant admissibility requirements'. This has been confirmed in the Court's case law as an 'inherent power'—there is no provision for it in either the Convention or the Court's Rules.[131]

2.89 In *Appietto* v *France*,[132] the applicant complained about the unfairness of administrative proceedings, invoking Articles 6(1), 13 and 14 of the Convention. The case was initially declared inadmissible by a Committee on the basis that the applicant had failed to exhaust domestic remedies, and that a complaint about the unreasonable length of proceedings had been lodged outside the six-month time limit. The applicant then wrote to the Court, insisting that the complaint about the length of proceedings had been introduced to the Court within the requisite time period. Having reviewed, and been satisfied, that that was indeed the case, the Court made the decision to reopen the case.[133] A similar decision was made in *Grzegorz Hulewicz* v *Poland (No. 2)*.[134]

2.90 The case of *Storck* v *Germany* was also reopened, but the decision provides little guidance as to the reasons. It was first declared inadmissible by a Committee in October 2002. Following the receipt of several letters by the applicant, the case was reopened in January 2003, and was declared admissible by the third section in October 2004, in spite of the respondent Government's objection to the reopening of the case.[135] However, the Committee decision does not set out any reasoning, and the section decision does not record what the applicant had said in her letters.

Undoubtedly, this is a power that the Court will only be willing to exercise in the most exceptional of cases.

Communication of a case to the respondent government

2.91 If there are no clear reasons for declaring an application inadmissible, the President of the Chamber will communicate the case to the respondent government and ask the government to submit its written observations—usually within 16 weeks (and then invite the applicant to submit observations in reply—normally within six weeks) (Rule 54(2)(b)). If an application concerns 'well-established case law' (see 2.83 above), the Court's practice is *not* to expect to receive observations from the government—with a view to discouraging an adversarial approach in such cases where there is a clear violation of the Convention, and with a view to resolving or settling the case.

2.92 When a case is communicated to the respondent government, the Court's usual practice has been to produce a reasonably detailed 'statement of facts' and to ask the parties to reply to specific questions within a stipulated time. The statement of facts includes a summary of the relevant facts, the steps that the applicant has taken to exhaust domestic remedies,

---

[131] *Storck* v *Germany*, No. 61603/00, dec. 26.10.04. See also the decision of the European Commission of Human Rights in *V.S. and T.H.* v *Czech Republic*, No. 26347/95, dec. 10.9.96.

[132] No. 56927/00, dec. 26.2.02.

[133] See, in contrast, *Des Fours Walderode* v *Czech Republic*, No. 40057/98, dec. 18.5.04 (the Court examined the applicant's challenges to the Court's admissibility decision of 4.3.03, but rejected them and confirmed the previous decision). A similar decision was made in *Harrach* v *Czech Republic*, No. 77532/01, dec. 18.5.04.

[134] No. 6544/05, 19.1.10, para. 47.

[135] No. 61603/00, dec. 26.10.04.

a summary of the relevant domestic law and practice and a summary of the applicant's Convention complaints. The government may obtain extensions of time in order to lodge its observations, in the same way that the applicant can. At the same time, copies of the statement of facts and the list of questions are sent to the applicant who is notified that the case has been communicated and is informed of the time limit given to the government to reply. In March 2016, the Court began to change its procedure on communication (on a trial basis) in order to speed up the processing of cases. Thus, in cases concerning certain states, instead of a detailed statement of facts, the parties will receive a briefer indication of the subject matter of the case, together with the questions which the parties should answer.[136]

The Court's factual summary and list of questions will be the first indication for the applicant **2.93** of the Court's initial view of the case. If the Court's list of questions to the government omits any aspects of the applicant's case then it is likely that those elements of the case are considered to be weak (and therefore not matters which the Court considers merit a response from the government). On the other hand, the Court may ask the government specific questions in relation to a particular Article of the Convention which may give a good indication of the Court's thinking as to the crux of the case.

Following communication of a case, the Court may require any unrepresented applicant to **2.94** obtain representation from an advocate who is authorised to practise in any of the state parties to the Convention, or who is otherwise approved by the President (Rule 36(2)).

When deciding to communicate a case to the respondent state, the standard practice of the **2.95** Court is now to examine both the admissibility and merits of the application at the same time (Rule 54A(1)). Accordingly, the parties will be invited at that stage to lodge submissions dealing with just satisfaction and friendly settlement (see further 2.96). Exceptionally, the Court may decide initially only to examine the admissibility of the application.

Applicant's observations in reply

As the observations in reply will usually be the applicant's final submissions to the Court, **2.96** they should encapsulate the totality of the applicant's case and, in general, should follow the order of the original application: the facts; followed by the relevant law; followed by the arguments as to why the Convention has been violated. As with other pleadings, the format of the observations should comply with the rules set out in the Practice Direction on *Written Pleadings* (see 2.102). Specifically in respect of parties' pleadings following communication, the Practice Direction states[137] that they should include:

- any comments on the facts of the case; and
- legal arguments relating to both the admissibility and merits of the case.

However, there are additional provisos set out in the Practice Direction as regards both the **2.97** submissions on the facts and the legal arguments. If a party does not contest the facts as set out in the statement of facts prepared by the Registry, it should limit its observations to a brief

---

[136] See: European Court of Human Rights, The Interlaken process and the Court (2016 Report), 1 September 2016, paras. 9–11; European Court of Human Rights, Annual Report 2016, p. 16. The states in question are Albania, Bulgaria, Germany, Greece, Hungary, Iceland, Italy, Romania, Russia, Spain, the former Yugoslav Republic of Macedonia and Turkey.
[137] Practice Direction: *Written Pleadings*, para. 14.

statement to that effect. If a party contests only part of the facts as set out by the Registry, or wishes to supplement them, it should limit its observations to those specific points. If a party objects to the facts or part of the facts as presented by the other party, it should state clearly which facts are uncontested and limit its observations to the points in dispute. Furthermore, as to the legal arguments, if specific questions on a factual or legal point were put to a party, it should (without prejudice to Rule 55—as to pleas of inadmissibility) limit its arguments to such questions. If a pleading replies to arguments of the other party, the submissions should refer to the specific arguments in the order prescribed in the Practice Direction.

2.98   It should always be borne in mind that the European Convention system is primarily a written rather than an oral procedure. Some advocates may be used to supplementing written submissions with lengthy oral arguments in domestic proceedings, but the European Court permits no such luxury. The vast majority of European Court cases will not include an oral hearing. If any Court hearing is held at all, it usually takes less than half a day from start to finish: see below at 2.181. Accordingly, the applicant's observations in reply should always be written with this in mind.

2.99   It is usual for the Court to stipulate that any just satisfaction claims (details of any claims for compensation and/or costs—under Article 41) should be included as part of the applicant's observations in reply (see also Rule 60(2)). A failure to submit such a claim is likely to mean that no award is made (Rule 60(3)).[138] Compensation claims (see chapter 8) can include both pecuniary and non-pecuniary losses. In either case, the applicant should include sufficient documentary evidence of the losses incurred. In many cases, the Court has refused to award compensation simply because the applicant has failed to substantiate their claims adequately or even at all. Pecuniary claims may include, for example, documentary proof of loss of earnings or other income. Non-pecuniary items may include claims for suffering and distress caused by the Convention violation in question, which should, if relevant, be supported by medical reports. In relation to both pecuniary and non-pecuniary claims, it may be advisable to submit a detailed statement from the applicant setting out the extent of the loss incurred. The submissions on compensation, whether in the form of a statement or otherwise, should also aim to establish clearly the link between the violation and the resulting loss. For example, it may be necessary to establish that, but for the Convention violation in question, the applicant would have been expected to earn a certain level of salary. In that situation, the applicant should provide the Court with information about the salaries payable in the sorts of positions that the applicant would have attained.

2.100   Costs schedules should be as detailed as possible, including supporting documentation, failing which the applicant risks not being awarded some, or even all, of the costs. The Court will only award costs on provision of proof that they have been actually and necessarily incurred and provided that the amount of costs is reasonable. Practitioners are therefore advised to submit to the Court detailed bills of costs which set out each aspect of the work carried out, the relevant dates, the time taken and the hourly rate being charged. Practitioners should be able to satisfy the Court that the applicant has actually incurred the costs in question, for example by being able to produce a client letter referring to the client's liability to pay. In *Öztürk* v *Germany*[139] the applicant's costs claim was rejected by the Court, inter alia, because

---

[138]   See, e.g. *Ambruosi* v *Italy*, No. 31227/96, 19.10.00.
[139]   No. 8544/79, Series A, No. 73, 21.2.84.

there was nothing to show that he had paid, or was bound to pay, the sums in question.[140] Any reasonably incurred expenses can also be claimed under Article 41. These may include necessary travel costs (including the costs of attending a hearing in Strasbourg), telephone, photocopying, postage and couriers, translation and other fees.

The claim for costs and expenses can also include sums incurred in attempting to secure **2.101** redress for the violation of the Convention through the domestic legal system. As with costs incurred during the European Court procedure, any claim for domestic court costs should be fully itemised.

Any claim by an applicant under Article 41 will be sent by the Court to the respondent government for its observations in reply (Rule 60(4)). Awards of just satisfaction under Article 41 are considered in more detail in chapter 8.

Practice direction: *Written Pleadings*

The main points of the Practice Direction are as follows: **2.102**

- Time limits for the filing of pleadings must be complied with—extensions of time limits may be sought (if made in good time, and before the expiry of the time limit), with reasons being given.
- Pleadings may be lodged with the Court by post or fax, but not by email (although note the possibility of electronic filing as set out below).
- Three copies of all pleadings (plus any annexed documents) should be lodged with the Court (or one copy sent by fax, followed by three copies sent by post). Secret documents should be filed by registered post.
- Any pleading exceeding 30 pages should be accompanied by a short summary.
- Each document annexed to a pleading should be listed in a separate annex.

The Practice Direction provides the following guidance as to the format of pleadings, which should include the case name and application number, together with a title (such as 'Reply to the government's observations on admissibility'). They should also normally:

- be in A4 page format (with at least a 3.5 cm margin);
- be typed;
- have all numbers expressed as figures;
- be divided into numbered paragraphs;
- have consecutive page numbering;
- provide a reference for each document or piece of evidence mentioned;
- be divided into sections headed: *Facts, Domestic Law [and Practice], Complaints, Law,* and include any answer to a question from the Court or from another party under a separate heading.

The Court's practice also enables electronic filing of pleadings by governments, or appli- **2.103** cants, through a secured server, which is subject to two separate Practice Directions, *Secured Electronic Filing by Governments* (issued in 2008) and *Electronic Filing by Applicants* (issued in 2014).

---

[140] *Ibid.*, para. 9. See also *Dudgeon v UK*, No. 7525/76, 22.10.81, paras. 21–2.

Electronic filing

2.104 Respondent governments may use the Court's secured server for electronic filing (Practice Direction: *Secured Electronic Filing by Governments*). Since 2015 it has also been possible for some applicants to file pleadings electronically after the communication of a case to the respondent government, through the Court's Electronic Communications Service (eComms) (Practice Direction: *Electronic Filing by Applicants*). Applicants must file such documents in pdf format (preferably searchable pdf format). The Court's practice is to contact the applicants and/or their representatives in particular cases in order to initiate electronic communications.

Legal aid

2.105 Free legal aid is available from the European Court to cover representatives' fees and travel, subsistence and other expenses necessarily incurred by applicants (exceptionally, including legal entities) or their representatives (Rules 100–105). Legal aid may be granted once observations on the admissibility of an application have been received from the respondent state (or once the time limit for doing so has expired) (Rule 100(1)). The applicant is sent, on request, the Court's Declaration of Applicant's Means form, which should be completed (and returned to the Court within four weeks) in order to provide details of income and capital assets, and any financial commitments in respect of dependants, or any other financial obligations. The assessment of financial means is then carried out by the appropriate *domestic* body (Rule 102(1)). Once certified by the appropriate domestic authority, the form should be lodged with the European Court. The respondent state may be asked to comment on it in writing (Rule 102(2)).

2.106 The test which the Court applies (under Rule 101) in considering requests for legal aid is twofold:

(1) that it is necessary for the proper conduct of the case; and
(2) that the applicant has insufficient means to meet all or part of the costs entailed.

2.107 In practice, if the domestic authority certifies a client's financial eligibility, then it is very likely that legal aid will be granted by the Court, unless there are any other particular reasons for the Court not to do so. However, it is important to remember that even if a client would not be financially eligible for legal aid in domestic proceedings, he or she may nevertheless be granted legal aid by the European Court. So it is worth applying to the Court, if you consider that the applicant cannot realistically afford to pay all *or* part of the costs which will be incurred. The extent to which the income of other members of the applicant's family is taken into account is a matter of discretion for the Court. A grant of legal aid can be revoked or varied by the Court at any time if it is satisfied that the conditions of eligibility are no longer fulfilled (Rule 105).

2.108 The grant of legal aid is retrospective and there is a set scale of fees for each stage of the proceedings. Applicants are *not* required by the European Court to pay contributions, as may happen in domestic proceedings.

2.109 Offers of legal aid are sent to the lawyer at each stage of the proceedings and should be signed and returned by the lawyer. Monies are paid by bank transfer. The scale of legal aid fees is modest, and so legal aid should be considered as a contribution to an applicant's costs and expenses, rather than representing payment for the work done, however reasonable. Nevertheless, legal aid should always be applied for where possible, in particular because it will pay for the reasonable expenses incurred at any Court hearings, which can be considerable. If the Court decides to hold a hearing on the admissibility and/or the merits of an application (as to Court hearings, see below at 2.112 and 2.181), Strasbourg legal aid will pay for the applicant's and the applicant's lawyer's reasonable travel and subsistence expenses (Rule 103(2)). This will cover, for example, the costs of flights to Strasbourg and hotel costs for one night in Strasbourg.

Legal aid may cover the costs of more than one lawyer (Rule 103(1)). However, the usual **2.110** practice of the Court is to offer legal aid for only one lawyer, unless there are exceptional circumstances.

For applicants who are authorised to represent themselves and who are, exceptionally, **2.111** granted legal aid, the practice of the Court is to pay their reasonable expenses, but not to pay them the equivalent of 'fees' for work done.

Admissibility hearings

It is possible for a Chamber to hold a hearing to decide on the admissibility of an applica- **2.112** tion (Rule 54(5)). Admissibility hearings used to be fairly common, but the Court's practice now is to hold admissibility hearings very rarely, in view of the considerable backlog of cases pending before the Court. The decision to hold a hearing can be taken by the Chamber of its own motion, or at the request of a party. If an applicant has particular reason to believe that he or she has a greater chance of success at a hearing on admissibility, rather than admissibility being decided on the papers, written reasons should be submitted to the Court as to the need for a hearing. In advance of the admissibility hearing, the parties may be asked specific questions by the Court, in order to assist in focusing the argument. Hearings on admissibility will usually only take place if the case raises difficult or new issues.

If a hearing on admissibility is held, then the parties will usually also be asked to address **2.113** issues arising relating to the merits of the case (Rule 54(5)). The procedure adopted by the Court for oral hearings is discussed below. The usual order of oral pleading in admissibility hearings is for the government to open and the applicant to reply (in merits hearings, the applicant opens—see 2.181 below).

Decisions on admissibility by a Chamber

Following communication of an application to the respondent government and consider- **2.114** ation of the parties' written submissions (and oral submissions, where relevant), the Chamber will publish its decision on admissibility. It is the usual practice now for a decision on admissibility and merits to be taken together (see 2.117); however, a decision on admissibility may be taken separately (Article 29(1)).

Where a separate admissibility decision is issued, it will contain the following sections: **2.115**

- the facts: the particular circumstances of the case and the relevant domestic law and practice;
- complaints: a summary of the applicant's Convention complaints; and
- the law: a summary of the parties' submissions and the Court's findings.

The admissibility decision also includes the names of the seven judges making up the Chamber, together with the Section Registrar. Admissibility decisions may be made unanimously or by a majority (Rule 56(1)). In majority decisions, there are no published dissenting decisions (unlike the position for Court judgments) and the names of the dissenting judges are not revealed. There is no right of appeal against a finding of inadmissibility.

2.116 An application may be declared admissible/inadmissible in part, in which case the application proceeds in respect of the admitted aspects only.

Admissibility and merits dealt with together

2.117 In order to achieve greater efficiency, it has become the Court's standard procedure to decide the question of the admissibility and merits of an application at the same time (under Article 29(1)).[141] In accordance with Rule 54A(1), the Court will usually make a decision when communicating a case to the respondent government to examine both the admissibility and merits at the same time. Accordingly, the parties will be invited at that stage to lodge submissions dealing with just satisfaction and friendly settlement. As noted above at 2.83, the changes brought about by Protocol No. 14 also enable committees to decide on both the admissibility and merits of 'manifestly well-founded' cases.

Relinquishment to a Grand Chamber

2.118 In cases that are considered to raise important issues, a Chamber may relinquish its jurisdiction to a Grand Chamber of 17 judges (under Article 30; Rule 72). A case can be relinquished to the Grand Chamber at any time before a Chamber has given its judgment. This might happen in one of two situations:

(1) where a case raises a serious question affecting the interpretation of the Convention (or the protocols); or
(2) where a judgment might be inconsistent with earlier jurisprudence.

2.119 Such cases will therefore be considered by the broadest composition of judges. It is possible, however, for one party to the case to 'object' to relinquishment. The parties will be given one month from notification of the Chamber's intention to relinquish jurisdiction to lodge any 'duly reasoned objection', in accordance with Rule 72(4). What is not clear, however, is whether a party's objection should amount to an automatic 'veto' which prevents relinquishment.[142] The Court's current practice appears to accept that this Rule does provide a veto. In *Öcalan v Turkey*,[143] for example, in its Chamber judgment the Court merely stated that the Government objected to relinquishment and 'as a consequence' the case remained before the Chamber, without referring to the nature of the Government's objections.[144] It is suggested, however, that the requirement for a 'duly reasoned' objection entitles the Court to make an assessment of the reasons given and then to decide whether or not to relinquish the case to the Grand Chamber: parties should not therefore be allowed an automatic right of veto. The

---

[141] See, e.g. *Ferrazzini v Italy*, No. 44759/98, 12.7.01; *Kleyn and others v Netherlands*, Nos. 39343/98, 39651/98, 43147/98 and 46664/99, 6.5.03, para. 10.

[142] Note, however, that when it enters into force, Protocol No. 15 will abolish the right of the parties to object to relinquishment. See the discussion of Protocol No. 15 in chapter 1.

[143] No. 46221/99, 12.3.03 (Chamber judgment), para. 6.

[144] After the Chamber issued its judgment the Government successfully requested the referral of the case to the Grand Chamber under Article 43.

current practice might permit a party to object to relinquishment, but then subsequently seek referral to the Grand Chamber under Article 43 if there are objections to the Chamber's decision on the merits.

Third Party Intervention

The European Court operates a well-established and important system for interven- **2.120** tion in cases by third parties. Under Article 36 of the Convention, the Court may permit Convention states to intervene. Under Article 36(1), a state is entitled to intervene to submit written comments and/or take part in hearings where one of its nationals is an applicant.[145] Furthermore, Article 36 also permits 'any person concerned' (which might include a state, or an individual, or an organisation) to intervene if it is considered to be 'in the interest of the proper administration of justice'. Once the Court has given the respondent state notice of an application, a third party may be given permission by the Court to submit written comments or, in exceptional cases, to take part in hearings[146] (Article 36(2); Rule 44(3)).

Any third party seeking to intervene should write to the President of the Chamber for per- **2.121** mission to do so within 12 weeks[147] of notice of the application having been given to the respondent state (Rule 44(3)(b)). The request for leave must be 'duly reasoned'. If the request is granted, the Court will almost invariably set out certain conditions for intervening. These conditions are likely to include a maximum length for the written submissions (commonly ten to 15 pages), a specified time limit for lodging the submissions (usually within three to six weeks) and, importantly, conditions as to the matters which can be covered by the intervention. It is usual for the Court to indicate that the intervention should not comment on the particular facts or merits of the case (as those are matters for the parties).

It is therefore suggested that a letter seeking permission to intervene should set out details **2.122** about the intervener (including any relevant expertise and experience) and outline the issues which the intervener proposes to address in its submissions. The written submissions are sent to the parties to the case who will be entitled to submit observations in reply, or, where appropriate, to reply at any hearing. Those observations in reply will be sent to the intervener, but there will usually be no opportunity for the intervener to submit any further comments.

---

[145] Rule 44(1). See, for example, *Scozzari & Giunta* v *Italy*, Nos. 39221/98 and 41963/98, 13.7.00, para. 8. However, there is no such right of state intervention where a case concerns an applicant's fear of being returned to the relevant state, where it is alleged that they may be subject to treatment contrary to Articles 2 or 3 of the Convention. See: *I* v *Sweden*, No. 61204/09, 5.9.13.

[146] See, for example, *Opuz* v *Turkey*, No. 33401/02, 9.6.09 (Interights was given leave to make submissions at the oral hearing); *Schalk and Kopf* v *Austria*, No. 30141/04, 24.6.10 (leave to appear at the oral hearing granted collectively to FIDH, ICJ, the AIRE Centre and ILGA-Europe); *M.S.S.* v *Belgium and Greece*, No. 30696/09, 21.1.11 (leave granted to the Netherlands and UK Governments, the Commissioner for Human Rights and the UNHCR); *Hirst Jamaa and others* v *Italy*, No. 27765/09, 23.2.12 (oral intervention by the UNHCR); *Avotiņš* v *Latvia*, No. 17502/07, 23.5.16 (the European Commission was represented at the hearing before the Grand Chamber).

[147] Under Rule 44(3)(b), another time limit may be fixed by the President of the Chamber 'for exceptional reasons'. Time limits may also be extended 'if sufficient cause is shown' (Rule 44(4)(b)). In Grand Chamber cases, the 12-week time limit will run from the date when the parties were notified of the decision of the Chamber to relinquish jurisdiction to the Grand Chamber, or, as appropriate, from the date when the parties were notified of the decision of the panel to accept a request for referral to the Grand Chamber (Rule 44(4)(a)).

2.123 For the Court, the third party intervention process may assist in clarifying the context in which a particular policy or practice has been adopted by a Convention state. Frequently, the Court is assisted through this process by having relevant comparative international law materials before it which have been submitted by human rights organisations with particular experience and expertise in that area. For applicants, it may be of considerable assistance to have a respected human rights organisation making submissions which in effect support their position (although of course this will not always be the case).

2.124 Requests for permission to lodge third party interventions will usually be made in relation to the merits stage of the proceedings. It is also possible to be granted permission to lodge a third party intervention for the purposes of deciding admissibility. For example, *TI v UK*[148] concerned the removal to Germany of an asylum-seeker, a Sri Lankan national who had applied for asylum in Germany and then in the United Kingdom, who had previously been tortured in Sri Lanka. The Court accepted written observations submitted both by the German Government and the United Nations High Commissioner for Refugees.

2.125 The Council of Europe Commissioner for Human Rights may also submit written comments to the Court and take part in hearings[149] in any case before a Chamber or Grand Chamber (Article 36(3); Rule 44(2)). The Commissioner for Human Rights was previously entitled to seek leave to intervene as a 'person concerned', but Article 36(3) now expressly gives the Commissioner the right to do so, without needing the leave of the President of the Court. The current Commissioner for Human Rights, Nils Muižnieks (who was elected in 2012) has been very active in submitting such interventions.[150]

2.126 In recent years it has been a regular practice of human rights organisations and other bodies to seek and obtain leave from the Court to submit written comments in cases concerning significant points of law, practice or policy. Interventions have often considered the comparative situation under other international human rights provisions (such as the International Covenant on Civil and Political Rights), in other European Convention states or according to the domestic constitutions from both Convention and non-Convention states.[151] It is also reasonably common now for states to intervene as third parties.[152]

---

[148] No. 43844/98, dec. 7.3.00.

[149] See, e.g. *Centre for Legal Resources on behalf of Valentin Câmpeanu v Romania*, No. 47848/08, 17.7.14.

[150] He has intervened notably in cases concerning human rights defenders and journalists. See, for example, *Hilal Mammadov v Azerbaijan*, No. 81553/12, 4.2.16; *Intigam Aliyev v Azerbaijan*, No. 68762/14 (pending); *Anar Mammadli v Azerbaijan*, No. 47145/14 (pending); *Rasul Jafarov v Azerbaijan*, No. 69981/14, 17.3.16; *Leyla Yunusova and Arif Yunusov v Azerbaijan*, No. 68817/14 (pending); *Khadija Ismayilova v Azerbaijan*, No. 30778/15 (pending); and *Svetlana Estemirova v Russia*, No. 42705/11 (pending). Copies of the Commissioner's interventions are available on the website: http://www.coe.int/en/web/commissioner/third-party-interventions.

[151] See, by way of example: *M.S.S. v Belgium and Greece*, No. 30696/09, 21.1.11 (interveners: Netherlands, UK, AIRE Centre, Amnesty International, Commissioner for Human Rights, the Office of the United Nations High Commissioner for Refugees (UNHCR) and the Greek Helsinki Monitor); *R.R. v Poland*, No. 27617/04, 26.5.11 (interveners: United Nations Special Rapporteur on the Right of Everyone to the Enjoyment of the Highest Attainable Standard of Physical and Mental Health, the International Federation of Gynaecology and Obstetrics, and the International Reproductive and Sexual Health Law Programme, University of Toronto). See also the examples set out from para. 2.125 of the last edition of this book.

[152] See, e.g. *Lautsi and others v Italy*, No. 30814/06, 18.3.11 (in which ten governments intervened, as well as various civil society organisations).

Establishing the Facts

In accordance with Article 38 of the Convention, in order to adjudicate on an application, **2.127** the Court *may* examine witnesses and carry out on-the-spot investigations (see below),[153] although this is rare in practice. In most cases, the Court is able to establish the facts from the documentary evidence before it. In view of the Convention requirement to exhaust domestic remedies prior to bringing an application to the European Court, in many cases the significant facts are no longer in dispute, following the decisions of the domestic courts.

The Court has consistently emphasised that it is reluctant (without very good reason) to **2.128** question findings of fact made by domestic courts: 'where domestic proceedings have taken place, it is not the Court's task to substitute its own assessment of the facts for that of the domestic courts'.[154] Furthermore, while the Court is not bound by findings of the domestic courts, it will require 'cogent elements to lead it to depart from the findings of fact reached by those courts'.[155] The Court has also stated that it is 'sensitive to the subsidiary nature of its role and must be cautious in taking on the role of a first instance tribunal of fact, where this is not rendered unavoidable by the circumstances of a particular case'.[156] However, where allegations are made under Articles 2 and 3 of the Convention the Court has stated that it must apply a 'particularly thorough scrutiny' even if certain domestic proceedings and investigations have already taken place.[157]

The Convention requires that the respondent state should provide 'all necessary facilities' for **2.129** any investigation (in whatever form it takes) carried out by the Court in order to establish the facts (Article 38—formerly Article 38(1)(a)) (see further at 5.65 below) and the state may be specifically criticised by the Court under this provision if it fails to do so.[158] The Court has frequently acknowledged that the state's non-disclosure of key case documents may severely hamper its ability to assess and analyse the facts in a particular case.[159]

A failure to provide information or documentary evidence (or a delay in doing so)[160] may **2.130** lead the Court to draw inferences as to the well-foundedness of the allegations (particularly where it is only the state which has access to information which could corroborate or refute the applicant's allegations).[161] For example, the Court drew such inferences in *Aktaş v Turkey*,[162] a case concerning the death of the applicant's brother in custody, for three reasons: the Government had failed to trace the doctor who had pronounced the applicant

---

[153] See, e.g. the *Greek Case* (1969) 12 YB 1 (*Denmark, Norway, Sweden and the Netherlands v Greece*, Nos. 3321/67, 3322/67, 3323/67 and 3344/67, 5.11.69, *Yearbook of the European Convention on Human Rights*, Vol. 13, 1969); the *Cyprus v Turkey* cases, Nos. 6780/74 and 6950/75, 10.7.76 (1975); *Ireland v UK*, 18.1.78, Series A, No. 25; *France, Norway, Denmark, Sweden and the Netherlands v Turkey*, Nos. 9940–9944/82, 7.12.85.

[154] See, e.g. *Klaas v Germany*, 22.11.93, para. 29.

[155] *Ibid.*, para. 30.

[156] See, e.g. *Tanlı v Turkey*, No. 26129/95, 10.4.01, para. 110; *Bitiyeva and X v Russia*, Nos. 57953/00 and 37392/03, 21.6.07, para. 130.

[157] *Ribitsch v Austria*, No. 18896/91, Series A, No. 336, 4.12.95, para. 32; *Avşar v Turkey*, No. 25657/94, 10.7.01, para. 283; *Aktaş v Turkey*, No. 24351/94, 24.4.03, para. 271.

[158] See, e.g. *Tanrikulu v Turkey*, No. 26763/94, 8.7.99, paras. 71 and 98.

[159] See, e.g. *Kerimova and others v Russia*, No. 17170/04 et al, 3.5.11, para. 243.

[160] *Orhan v Turkey*, No. 25656/94, 18.6.02.

[161] See also Rule 44C. See, e.g. *Timurtaş v Turkey*, No. 23531/94, 13.6.00, paras. 66–7.

[162] No. 24351/94, 24.4.03.

dead; the fact that the Government objected to the hearing of 11 witnesses in the presence of the applicant, his family and his representatives; and that photographs said to be of the applicant's brother's body were only provided to the Court during the hearing of witnesses. The Turkish Government was accordingly found to have failed to meet its obligations under Article 38(1)(a) in *Aktaş*. Similar findings were made by the Court in *Trubnikov* v *Russia*[163] because of the Government's refusal to disclose the medical file concerning the applicant's son who had committed suicide in prison. In *Abdulkhakov* v *Russia*,[164] the applicant claimed to have been abducted in Moscow and transferred into detention in Tajikistan. The Court noted that the applicant provided detailed descriptions of his kidnapping and transfer; however, there was no evidence that the authorities had made any efforts to locate and question witnesses who may have been able to confirm or disprove the applicant's account. Given the information provided by the applicant, the Court found that it would have been possible to establish which flight he had been on, and to question the flight attendants and passengers. Accordingly, the Court concluded that the applicant had made a prima facie case, and the Government had failed to refute his allegations or to provide a convincing explanation as to how he arrived in Tajikistan.

2.131   An Annex to the Rules of the Court (Rules A1 to A8) regulates the practice and procedure relevant to establishing the facts. In order to clarify the facts, the Court may adopt 'any investigative measure', including requesting documentary evidence and hearing any person as a witness or expert (or in any other capacity) (Rule A1(1)). The Chamber may appoint any number of judges to conduct an inquiry, carry out an on-the-spot investigation or take evidence in any other way. This usually happens after a case has been declared admissible (although the Rules provide for it also to happen before admissibility in exceptional cases— Rule A1(3)). It can also appoint external experts to assist the Court's delegation (Rule A1(3)) and third parties may also be granted leave to participate in any investigative measure (Rule A1(6)). Both the respondent government and the applicant must assist the Court in its measures for taking evidence (Rule A2(1)). If measures are taken, such as obtaining an expert's report, at the request of a state party, the Court Rules provide that the costs are borne by the party in question, unless the Court decides otherwise (Rule A5(6)). In other situations, the Court will decide whether the costs are to be paid by the Council of Europe, or by an applicant or third party at whose request or on whose behalf the person appears. Costs are taxed by the President of the Chamber. In practice, however, the applicant is rarely, if ever, required to pay the experts' or witnesses' costs.

2.132   The relevance, weight and cogency of any evidence submitted to the Court will be fundamental to the Court's assessment of it. For example, in the case of *El-Masri* v *former Yugoslav Republic of Macedonia*,[165] concerning the 'extraordinary rendition' of the applicant by the authorities into the custody of the CIA, the Court noted that the applicant's allegations were contested by the Government on all counts. However, the Court found his description of the events in question to be detailed, specific and consistent throughout (ultimately finding violations of Articles 3, 5, 8 and 13 in his case). There are no strict rules as to what *type* of evidence may be put before the Court (see further at 5.51 below). Accordingly, applicants and their

---

[163] No. 49790/99, 5.7.05.
[164] No. 14743/11, 2.10.12.
[165] No. 39630/09, 13.12.12.

advisers should be alive to the possibility of adducing various types of evidence to the Court, such as photographic and video or audio evidence. For example, in *Scozzari and Giunta v Italy* the Court reviewed video and audio recordings of contact visits with children,[166] and in *Giuliani and Gaggio v Italy*,[167] the Court was shown film of demonstrations surrounding the G8 summit in Genoa in 2001, which led to a fatal shooting of a demonstrator by a member of the *carabiniere*. In the *El-Masri* case (referred to above) the Court's assessment of the evidence incorporated flight logs, scientific testing of the applicant's hair follicles, geological records confirming the applicant's recollection of minor earthquakes during his detention in Afghanistan, the applicant's sketches of the layout of the prison where he was detained, a statement from the former Minister of Interior confirming the applicant's detention and rendition at the request of the U.S. authorities, and the Marty Report into secret rendition (produced by the Parliamentary Assembly in 2006[168]). This body of evidence was sufficient to establish a prima facie case, and therefore the burden of proof shifted to the government, which was then found to have failed to provide a satisfactory and convincing explanation as to how the events at issue occurred.

The Court is regularly referred to, and frequently places reliance upon, reports produced by **2.133** inter-governmental institutions and human rights NGOs. For example, in cases concerning the poor condition of prisons, the Court is likely to be influenced by up-to-date reports of the European Committee for the Prevention of Torture and Inhuman or Degrading Treatment or Punishment (CPT) (another Council of Europe institution—see 1.08 above). For example, in *Dougoz v Greece*[169] the Court took account of CPT reports on conditions in a police headquarters and a detention centre, in finding a violation of Article 3, and in *Peers v Greece* the Court took note of a CPT report on Koridallos prison.[170]

The Court does not take a restrictive view about the submission to it of *new* evidence: **2.134**

> The Court is in principle not prevented from taking into account any additional information and fresh arguments in determining the merits of a complaint, if it considers them relevant. New information may, for example, be of value in confirming or refuting the assessment that has been made by the Contracting State. Such 'new' material takes the form either of further particulars as to the facts underlying the complaints declared admissible or of legal argument relating to those facts.[171]

In *KA v Finland*,[172] concerning the taking of the applicant's children into public care in **2.135** 1992, the Government submitted to the European Court further evidence (including a civil servant's notes created between 1992 and 1996) in seeking to justify the measures that had been taken. The Court, however, found that as this information had not been available to the domestic decision-making bodies and the parties, it was not relevant to its decision as to whether Article 8 of the Convention had been violated.

---

[166] Nos. 39221/98 and 41966/98, 13.7.00, paras. 10, 94 and 176.
[167] No. 23458/02, 24.3.11.
[168] Parliamentary Assembly of the Council of Europe, Report, Committee on Legal Affairs and Human Rights (Rapporteur: Dick Marty), *Alleged secret detentions and unlawful inter-State transfers of detainees involving Council of Europe member States*, Doc. 10957, 12 June 2006.
[169] No. 40907/98, 6.3.01.
[170] No. 28524/95, 19.4.01, para. 61.
[171] *KA v Finland*, No. 22751/95, 14.1.03, para. 89.
[172] No. 22751/95, 14.1.03.

Fact-finding hearings and on-the-spot investigations[173]

2.136   Notwithstanding the Court's cautious approach to fact-finding (as described above), where there are, nevertheless, fundamental factual disputes between the parties that cannot be resolved by considering the documents before it, the Court is able to carry out hearings to establish the facts, by hearing evidence from witnesses, and to mount on-the-spot investigations. This is a function that was formerly carried out by the European Commission of Human Rights.

2.137   For example, in the case of *Ireland* v *UK*,[174] concerning the arrest and detention of IRA suspects by the British security forces, 119 witnesses were heard by the European Commission. Prior to the Court's judgment in *Cyprus* v *Turkey*,[175] the European Commission heard evidence in Strasbourg, Nicosia and London, and Commission delegates also visited a border crossing point, a court building and Greek Cypriot villages in northern Cyprus. In *Poltoratskiy* v *Ukraine*,[176] the Commission heard evidence in Kiev and visited the Ivano-Frankivsk prison in order to assess the treatment of prisoners on death row. In *Balyemez* v *Turkey*[177] and other cases concerning long-term hunger strikers, the Court arranged for medical experts to examine the applicants in prison.

2.138   The requirement for each respondent state to provide 'all necessary facilities' for any investigation carried out by the Court in order to establish the facts (Article 38), as noted above, applies equally to the Court's fact-finding hearings and on-the-spot investigations. Furthermore, Rule A2 requires the state to provide the Court delegation with 'the facilities and co-operation necessary for the proper conduct of the proceedings'. The state is also obliged to ensure freedom of movement and adequate security for the Court delegation and all applicants, witnesses and experts, and 'to take steps to ensure that no adverse consequences are suffered by any person or organisation on account of any evidence given, or of any assistance provided, to the delegation' (Rule A2(2)) (see also 2.74 above). The state is therefore obliged to co-operate fully with the Court in the conduct of investigations. Nevertheless, it is not unusual for problems to arise. In *Shamayev and others* v *Georgia and Russia*,[178] the Court's delegation was refused access to five extradited applicants who were being held within the jurisdiction of the Stavropol Regional Court, which led the Court to remind the Government of its obligations under both former Article 38(1) and Article 34 of the Convention, and to reiterate that:

> the issue of access to the applicants is a matter of international law—in particular the European Convention on Human Rights, which, under Russian law, takes precedence over domestic law—and, therefore, falls to be decided solely by the European Court of Human Rights.[179]

---

[173] For an extensive analysis of the Court's fact-finding hearings and on-the-spot investigations, see: P. Leach, C. Paraskeva and G. Uzelac, *International Human Rights and Fact-Finding—An analysis of the fact-finding missions conducted by the European Commission and Court of Human Rights*, Human Rights and Social Justice Research Institute, London Metropolitan University, February 2009. See also: Michael O'Boyle and Natalia Brady, Investigatory Powers of the European Court of Human Rights [2013] 4 E.H.R.L.R. 478.

[174] Series A, No. 25, 18.1.78.

[175] No. 25781/94, 10.5.01.

[176] No. 38812/97, 29.4.03.

[177] No. 32495/03, 21.12.05. See European Court Press Release, 6.9.04.

[178] No. 36378/02, 12.4.05.

[179] European Court Press Release, 24.10.03. The Russian Government was also required to pay the costs incurred by the Court in setting up a fact-finding visit to Russia, which had to be cancelled.

Furthermore, a failure to ensure that witnesses attend the Court's hearings may therefore lead the Court to draw inferences as to the well-foundedness of the allegations.[180] In *Kaja* v *Greece*,[181] the Court carried out an on-the-spot investigation in order to ascertain the conditions of the police detention centre in Larissa—it noted that the detention centre had been meticulously cleaned and freshly repainted prior to the mission.

In a series of cases brought by individuals against Turkey from the mid-1990s, the former **2.139** Commission and the Court held fact-finding hearings in Strasbourg and in Turkey in order to adjudicate on fundamental factual differences between the parties. The cases against Turkey concerned gross violations, including village destruction, extrajudicial killings and torture occurring in the south-east of Turkey, which had been declared a state of emergency region. In many of these cases there was a failure by the domestic authorities to carry out any form of effective investigation into the allegations and accordingly there was no finding of fact by any domestic courts.

The Strasbourg organs have acknowledged their own limitations in establishing the facts in **2.140** this way.[182] Witnesses cannot be compelled to attend and respondent governments cannot be ordered to produce particular documents. There may also be problems in assessing evidence obtained orally through interpreters and the Commission and Court will of course not have direct familiarity with the particular conditions in the region in question.

There are some judges and Court Registry staff who would not be inclined to hold fact- **2.141** finding hearings due to considerations of cost and delay. Hearings can take up to a week and involve at least five or six Court officials (usually three[183] judges, a registrar and lawyer(s)) plus interpreters. In spite of such concerns, the new Court (i.e. since 1998) has held a number of fact-finding hearings and/or on-the-spot investigations in cases where a sufficiently strong prima facie case has been made out by the applicant. In cases particularly concerning alleged gross Convention violations and in which there have been no domestic findings of fact, it is suggested that the Court's fact-finding role is an absolutely essential element of the European Convention process, without which victims of serious violations of their rights will find it extremely difficult to obtain redress in Strasbourg.[184]

In addition to the Turkish cases,[185] the Court has held fact-finding hearings and/or mis- **2.142** sions in a number of other contracting states. For example, in *Valašinas*, Court delegates took evidence in Lithuania and visited a prison.[186] In 2003 a delegation of four judges took evidence from 43 witnesses in Chişinău and Tiraspol in Moldova in the case of *Ilaşcu and Others* v *Moldova and Russia*,[187] in which the applicant Moldovans complained of

---

[180] See, e.g. *Aktaş* v *Turkey*, No. 24351/94, 24.4.03; *Tangiyeva* v *Russia*, No. 57935/00, 29.11.07.

[181] No. 32927/03, 27.7.06, para. 47.

[182] See, e.g. *Mehmet Emin Akdeniz and others* v *Turkey*, No. 23594/94, Comm. Rep. 10.9.99, para. 384.

[183] Occasionally four judges: see, e.g. *Adalı* v *Turkey*, No. 38187/97, European Court Press Release, 23.6.03; sometimes two judges: see *N* v *Finland*, No. 38885/02, European Court Press Release, 19.3.04; sometimes five judges: see *Georgia* v *Russia (No. 1)*, No. 13255/07; European Court Press Release, 4.2.11.

[184] These issues are discussed more fully in P. Leach, C. Paraskeva and G. Uzelac, *International Human Rights and Fact-Finding—An analysis of the fact-finding missions conducted by the European Commission and Court of Human Rights*, Human Rights and Social Justice Research Institute, London Metropolitan University, February 2009.

[185] See also, e.g. *Yöyler* v *Turkey*, No. 26973/95, 24.7.03; *Ipek* v *Turkey*, No. 25760/94, 17.2.04; *Tanış and others* v *Turkey*, No. 65899/01, European Court Press Release, 30.4.03.

[186] *Valašinas* v *Lithuania*, No. 44558/98, 24.7.01.

[187] *Ilaşcu, Lesco, Ivantoc and Petrov-Popa* v *Moldova and Russia*, No. 48787/99, dec. 8.7.04.

various Convention violations in the Russian-occupied area of Transdniestria. The hearings took place in various locations: at the OSCE Mission to Moldova; in a prison; and at the headquarters of the 'Operative Group of Russian Forces in the Transdniestrian Region of the Republic of Moldova' in Tiraspol. In addition to hearing the applicants, the judges took evidence from politicians and officials from Moldova, representatives of the prison service in Tiraspol and Russian army officers.[188] The Court has also carried out missions to investigate conditions of detention in Greece,[189] Turkey[190] (both at the pre-admissibility stage), Croatia[191] and Ukraine.[192] In *N v Finland*,[193] in which the applicant alleged that he would face inhuman treatment if deported to the Democratic Republic of Congo, a delegation of two judges heard evidence in Helsinki. In 2011 five judges of the Court heard evidence in Strasbourg from 21 witnesses in the inter-state case of *Georgia v Russia (No. 1)* concerning the arrest, detention and collective expulsion of Georgian nationals from Russia in 2006.[194]

2.143   In *Hugh Jordan v UK*,[195] however, the Court declined to carry out a fact-finding hearing because various domestic proceedings (a civil action and inquest) were still pending. The Court distinguished that case from the Turkish cases where the Court *had* undertaken fact-finding even though domestic proceedings were still pending,[196] on the basis that the proceedings in question in Turkey had been criminal and they had terminated at least at first instance and it had been an essential part of the applicants' arguments in those cases that the defects in the investigations had been such as to render the criminal proceedings ineffective.[197]

2.144   There is no doubt that both fact-finding hearings and on-the-spot investigations can be extremely significant in influencing the Court's evaluation of pre-existing evidence, as well as producing further compelling evidence. In *Peers v Greece*,[198] Commission delegates took evidence from the applicant and three witnesses in Koridallos prison (one inmate and two prison officials). They inspected the prison segregation unit where they found that 'the general atmosphere was repulsive' and they compared the applicant's cell to a 'medieval oubliette'.[199]

2.145   The Court has expressed its concerns about the inevitable lapse of time between the events at issue and the Court's fact-finding process. For example, in *Ipek v Turkey*,[200] the Court stated that 'the passage of time takes a toll on a witness's capacity to recall events in detail and with

---

188   Press release, European Court of Human Rights, 18.3.03.
189   *Kaja v Greece*, No. 32927/03, 27.7.06.
190   *Tekin Yildiz v Turkey*, No. 22913/04, 10.11.05. This case was one of a group of 53 similar cases in which the applicants had been imprisoned because of their membership of terrorist organisations. Their prison sentences had been suspended on medical grounds, as they were suffering from Wernicke-Korsakoff Syndrome as a result of their prolonged hunger strikes in prison.
191   *Cenbauer v Croatia*, No. 73786/01, 9.3.06.
192   *Druzenko and others v Ukraine*, Nos. 17674/02 & 39081/02, 15.1.07.
193   No. 38885/02, 26.7.05.
194   *Georgia v Russia (I)*, No. 13255/07, 3.7.14.
195   No. 24746/94, 4.5.01.
196   See, e.g. *Salman v Turkey*, No. 21986/93, 27.6.00.
197   No. 24746/94, 4.5.01, para. 111.
198   No. 28524/95, 19.4.01.
199   *Ibid.*, para. 53.
200   No. 25760/94, 17.2.04, para. 116.

accuracy … the witnesses testifying before the Delegates were asked to recollect incidents which occurred many years previously'.

The Court has also stated that its decision as to whether to hold a fact-finding hearing may **2.146** be influenced by the time which has elapsed since the incident in question. For example, in *Tanlı* v *Turkey* the Court stated that the length of time which had passed since the death of the applicant's son (in 1994) was a factor in deciding that a fact-finding investigation would not assist in resolving the issues.[201] This rationale of course risks prejudicing applicants in that they may in effect be penalised by delays in the progress of their case over which they have no control and which are entirely a consequence of the unacceptably long backlog within the Court system itself. In the particular case of *Tanlı*, concerning the death of the applicant's son whilst in custody of the security services, the decision not to hold a fact-finding hearing probably did not prejudice the applicant's position substantially as the Court was able to find the state responsible for the death, under Article 2, as no plausible explanation was forthcoming from the Government. However, in other cases that do not allow for this shifting of the burden of proof in relation to alleged victims of ill-treatment in custody, a decision not to hold a fact-finding hearing, based on delay, may be extremely detrimental to applicants' efforts to prove their cases beyond reasonable doubt, as the Court requires.[202]

A feature of the fact-finding process that undoubtedly reduces its effectiveness is the absence **2.147** of any power to compel a witness to attend and give evidence to the Court. This problem was alluded to in *Denizci and others* v *Cyprus*, a case in which 28 witnesses were summoned to give evidence and five failed to appear.[203] In *Ipek* v *Turkey*,[204] a case concerning the 'disappearance' of the applicant's two sons, the Court was critical of the fact that two witnesses summoned by the Government failed to appear. The Court delegates were informed on the day that he was due to give evidence that a village *muhtar* had refused to give evidence. The Court then asked the Government to obtain a sworn affidavit from him confirming that he had declined to give evidence of his own free will. In his affidavit he stated that he had not appeared because he had no knowledge of the incident in question, which the Court stated did not justify his refusal to give evidence. The refusal of a key public prosecutor to give evidence to Commission delegates was the subject of the Court's 'strong disapproval' in *Nuray Şen* v *Turkey* (*No. 2*).[205]

Nevertheless, the failure of a key witness to provide evidence to the Court's delegation may **2.148** be a factor in the Court's reaching a particular factual conclusion in the absence of such evidence. For example, in *Elçi and others* v *Turkey*,[206] which concerned the detention and ill-treatment of the applicant lawyers, various prosecutors gave evidence to the effect that the chief public prosecutor had been ultimately responsible for the applicants' arrests. The Court noted, however, that the chief public prosecutor had not given evidence and had not even been proposed by the Government as a witness.[207] Accordingly, the Court found that there

---

[201] No. 26129/95, 10.4.01, para. 7.
[202] See also U. Erdal, 'Burden and Standard of Proof in Proceedings under the European Convention' (2001) 26 *EL Rev. Human Rights Survey* 68.
[203] Nos. 25316–25321/94 and 27207/95, 23.5.01, para. 315. See also, e.g. *Aktaş* v *Turkey*, No. 24351/94, 24.4.03.
[204] No. 25760/94, 17.2.04, para. 116.
[205] No. 25354/94, 30.3.04, para. 156.
[206] Nos. 23145/93 and 25091/94, 13.11.03.
[207] *Ibid.*, para. 680.

was no clear picture as to the prior authorisation for the arrests, which was one of the factors which led the Court to find that Article 5(1) of the Convention had been breached. The failure to produce key witnesses may also result in findings that the government has failed to comply with its obligations under Article 38 (former Article 38(1)(a)) of the Convention to furnish all necessary facilities to the Court in its task of establishing the facts, and in the Court drawing certain inferences (see further 5.65 below).

Fact-finding hearings: the procedure

2.149   In exceptional cases where the applicant considers it necessary for the Court to hold a fact-finding hearing, the applicant's representative should write to the Court to set out the reasons why the applicant believes the Court should hear witnesses. It may also be beneficial to send the Court a list of suggested witnesses. This list should include not only witnesses who may support the applicant's version of events, but also 'state witnesses' such as, depending upon the context of the case, public prosecutors, police officers and prison officials. It is not unknown for a respondent government to provide a minimal list of suggested witnesses, which may even omit key 'state' witnesses whom the government would prefer not to be questioned. Therefore it is essential that the applicant's representative includes a full list of state witnesses. If the name of a particular official is unknown, then they can of course be identified to the Court by their position or title (such as public prosecutor of a named town). For each witness, a summary should be provided as to the evidence that that witness is expected to give (where you already have witness statements), or at least the areas that the witness is expected to cover (if you have no witness statements). By providing such a list the applicant's representative will be attempting to demonstrate that such a hearing would be highly beneficial to the Court in reaching a judgment in the case. The applicant's representative will want to demonstrate that key witnesses are available to give evidence and that their evidence could be important in establishing a violation of the Convention. In cases concerning fatalities, for example, where state officials are implicated by the applicant, the Court may decide to hold a fact-finding hearing if it considers there is a reasonable chance of establishing through such a process whether the state is responsible for the victim's death under Article 2, or not. If, however, the only likely outcome is a finding that there was a failure by the state adequately to investigate a fatal incident, then it is unlikely that a fact-finding hearing would be held.

2.150   The Court will subsequently inform the parties of its decision to take evidence (and may provide provisional dates). If not already provided, the Court will require a brief outline or statement of the evidence which it is anticipated each witness will give. The Court will provide a provisional list of witnesses after considering proposals from the parties as to the witnesses to be called. The Court may request the parties' representatives to attend a pre-hearing in Strasbourg in order to finalise the list of witnesses (see Rule A4(2)). This hearing usually takes place before the delegation of judges who will conduct the full hearing (together with the section registrar and lawyers in attendance). At the pre-hearing the parties may be asked to confirm whether witnesses are still willing and able to attend the fact-finding hearing and there may be questions for the parties as to the evidence that witnesses are expected to provide.

2.151   The Court will subsequently provide a provisional timetable for the hearings and its list of witnesses and it will also provide witness summonses to be served via the parties. The Court provides interpreters who will interpret from the national language into English and/or French, and vice versa. If witnesses are expected to give their evidence in a non-national language then the Court should be given prior notice (this has been the case, for example, with some witnesses in fact-finding hearings in Turkey giving evidence in Kurdish). The Court will require reasons to be given if any witness summonsed does not attend. The hearings are usually conducted by a delegation of three judges, with the Section Registrar and a Court Registry lawyer in attendance. The President of the delegation of judges will preside over the hearing. The President may lead in questioning witnesses, or other judges may be requested to do so. For an 'applicant's witness', the applicant's representative will then be given the opportunity to question the witness, followed by the government (with a 'state witness' the government precedes the applicant). However, Court delegations have varied in the procedure they follow. Some have extensively questioned the witnesses before the parties' representatives were given the chance to do so, others did not. Accordingly, it is suggested that representatives should be fully prepared, if necessary, to question each witness in full. It has usually not been the Court's practice to prepare, or to require the parties to prepare, 'core bundles' of documents. This can cause problems when witnesses are requested to review particular documents and it is suggested that this is a practice that the Court should review. It may be helpful for the parties to try to agree a list of documents with the Court, prior to the hearing.

2.152 Parties' representatives should give consideration as to the manner of presentation of particular types of evidence such as maps, photographs and video film. The Court will need prior notice if special facilities are required such as equipment for showing video film. In *Yöyler v Turkey*,[208] for example, which concerned an attack on a village by the security forces, the applicant requested in advance overhead projector facilities in order to project the applicant's hand-drawn map of his village which witnesses then used to identify houses that were burned.

2.153 Applicants' representatives should be ready to expect further disclosure of documents by the respondent government immediately before, during or after the hearing. This would appear to be a reasonably common practice, even though full disclosure should have been given prior to the hearing. Parties' representatives should be alive to requesting further disclosure of 'new' documents that are identified by the witnesses during the hearing.

2.154 Following the fact-finding hearing, the Court will provide transcripts of the hearing for the parties to check and propose corrections of any errors (Rule A8). The Court may require further documentary evidence from the parties, arising from the oral evidence.

Friendly Settlement

2.155 The friendly settlement procedure (Articles 37 and 39 and Rule 62) provides the respondent government and the applicant with an opportunity to resolve a dispute. The Court will write to the parties asking for any proposals as to settlement. The case is struck off the Court's list of cases if settlement is agreed (Article 39(3)). This may happen at any stage of the proceedings (Articles 37(1) and 39(1)). Greater emphasis is now being placed on the friendly settlement procedure, notably as a means of resolving repetitive applications (or 'clone cases') but also

---

[208] No. 26973/95, 24.7.03.

more generally. As they are very closely linked, this section should be read in conjunction with the sections below on striking out and unilateral declarations.

2.156   At the same time as a case is communicated to the respondent government, the Court will write to the parties to inform them that the Court is at the parties' disposal for the purpose of securing a friendly settlement and inviting proposals from either party (Article 39(1) and Rule 62). The Court will usually set a time limit for any proposals. However, the time limit may be extended (the Court is keen for cases to be resolved and so is likely to grant more time if a settlement is a real possibility).

2.157   Prior to the implementation of Protocol 11, the European Commission's practice was to try to encourage the friendly settlement process by giving an indication on a confidential basis of the Commission's provisional view as to whether or not there had been a Convention violation. The Court has not continued this practice, but if the parties indicate that they are interested in reaching a settlement, it may be prepared to put forward proposals as to settlement.

2.158   The Court's role in the friendly settlement procedure has previously often been little more than a post box. If proposals were made by either party, they would be sent on to the other party for comment. However, if no such proposals were put forward, the Court would usually take no further action to encourage settlement. However, it is more common now for the Court actively to become involved in facilitating settlement in a more proactive way, and it may consider striking out an application if an applicant is considered 'unreasonably' to have refused friendly settlement proposals (see Striking Out, below at 2.165). For example, where financial negotiations run into difficulties, the Court may be prepared to suggest what would represent a reasonable sum for settlement of the case. Rule 62 permits the Court to take any steps that appear necessary to facilitate settlement, which may include arranging a meeting between the parties. In *Köksal v Netherlands*,[209] for example, which concerned the alleged torture and death of the applicants' son and father in police custody, the Court Registry brought the parties together for a meeting in The Hague. The case was settled on the payment of 140,000 Netherlands guilders and with the Dutch Government expressing its 'deepest regret' at the man's death, although it was also said that that statement 'does not constitute an acknowledgement from the side of the Government that the Netherlands have violated the European Convention on Human Rights'.[210] The Court's practice as regards applications concerning 'well-established case law' (see 2.83 above) is now to be rather more proactive: in order to encourage the resolution of such cases, the Court may of its own motion send settlement proposals to the parties.

2.159   Friendly settlement negotiations are confidential and are without prejudice to the parties' arguments in the contentious proceedings (Rule 62(2)). Therefore, the details of the negotiations cannot be referred to or relied on in the substantive proceedings, or in any other contentious proceedings. In *R.R. v Poland*[211] when the Government tried to argue that the applicant had lost her 'victim status' because she had refused to accept the Government's friendly settlement offer, this point was reiterated and the Government's argument rejected.

---

[209]   No. 31725/96, 20.3.01.
[210]   *Ibid.*, para. 14.
[211]   No. 27617/04, 26.5.11.

Breaching this confidentiality could lead to an application being declared inadmissible on grounds of abuse of the right of application (see section 4.168 below).[212]

From the respondent government's perspective, the friendly settlement procedure may offer **2.160** an opportunity to conclude cases that it considers are likely to be successful at the Court, if pursued. A government may be willing to settle a case where the particular problem has been identified (either as a result of the case being brought or even before the application was made) and has been, or is being, resolved. If a government proposes to revise a particular procedure or introduce new legislation to deal with an issue raised by a Convention application, then it is possible that it will be prepared to settle the case and therefore avoid a Court judgment finding a Convention violation. It may well be prepared to offer a sum of money and costs to the applicant to settle the case, in addition to the substantive changes being made. More problematically, governments may seek to avoid issues raising clear Convention violations by 'paying off' individual applicants. Of course, if an applicant is prepared to settle a case on payment of a certain sum, it is possible for a case to be settled without any attempt by the government to deal with the substantive issue in question.

For the applicant, the friendly settlement procedure *may* represent an opportunity to achieve **2.161** more than would be obtained from a Court judgment itself (other than a finding of a violation). Whilst a Court judgment may provide the applicant with a declaration of a finding of a violation and payment of 'just satisfaction' (see chapter 8), it is important to remember that as a procedure of *settlement*, the applicant can of course attempt to negotiate for any form of redress, including compensation and costs, but also to obtain government commitments to revise policy or practice or to introduce new legislation. Any settlement might also include a requirement that steps be taken by the government within a specified time, in which case the applicant may be able to obtain a remedy well in advance of a Court judgment, were the case to proceed. The government may be willing to pay higher rates of compensation (and costs) in settlement than would be likely to be granted by the Court. For some applicants, however, the achievement of obtaining a successful Court judgment may itself be very important and a strong disincentive to settle.

The Court will be willing to facilitate settlement of cases as this will mean a reduction in the **2.162** Court's still substantial backlog of cases. If terms are agreed, both parties should write to the Court to confirm the terms of the settlement agreement and request that the case be struck out of the Court's list of cases. The Court will publish a decision or judgment (if concluded post-admissibility) recording the facts of the case and the terms agreed between the parties and formally striking the case out of the list (Articles 37 and 39). Settlements therefore have a higher 'visibility' than was previously the case prior to the implementation of Protocol No. 11. This in itself may be an important factor when advising on settlement negotiations.

However, the Court's role in agreed friendly settlements is not merely to 'rubber-stamp' the **2.163** decision. In accordance with Article 37(1) of the Convention, in the process of assessing whether to strike applications out, the Court will continue the examination of the case 'if respect for human rights as defined in the Convention and the protocols thereto so requires'. The factors affecting this decision will include the importance of the issue raised by the case,

---

[212] See, e.g. *Hadrabová and Others* v *Czech Republic*, No. 42165/02 and 466/03, dec. 25.9.07; *Popov* v *Moldova*, No. 74153/01, 18.1.05; *Miroļubovs* v *Latvia*, No. 798/05, 15.9.09.

the terms of settlement proposed by the parties and whether the issue has previously been considered by the Court. Thus, a friendly settlement that had been agreed between the parties in *Ukrainian Media Group* v *Ukraine*[213] was rejected by the Court because of the gravity of the alleged interferences with the applicant company's right to freedom of expression. The applicant had published articles in its daily newspaper which were critical of two politicians, both of whom were presidential candidates. The politicians brought civil proceedings that resulted in the applicant being ordered to pay them compensation and publish an apology. It is suggested that the broader context of the case—international concern over restrictions on media freedom in Ukraine—was also an important factor in the Court's decision not to accept the settlement. The Court went on to find a violation of Article 10. The Court may also decline to confirm a friendly settlement agreement if, for example, it is not satisfied that the applicant has unambiguously consented to its terms.[214]

2.164   Article 37(2) enables the Court to restore a case to its list if the terms of a friendly settlement are not subsequently complied with. In *Katić* v *Serbia*[215] the applicants' complaint about the length of civil proceedings was settled on the basis of a payment by the state of €6,000. As the applicants were mentally disabled and had been deprived of their legal capacity, the monies were ordered to be paid into a bank account opened on behalf of the applicants and managed by an interim guardian. The sum had been paid into the account, but as only €400 had subsequently been spent on the applicants' subsistence, the Court ordered the restoration of the case to the list, granted it priority status and restarted friendly settlement negotiations.

Striking Out (and Unilateral Declarations)

2.165   In addition to the resolution of cases through the friendly settlement procedure, the Court may strike out a case at any stage in the proceedings where it considers that any of the following three situations applies (Article 37(1); Rule 43):

(1) the applicant does not intend to pursue his or her application; or
(2) the matter has been resolved; or
(3) for any other reason established by the Court it is no longer justified to consider the examination of the application.

2.166   In any of these situations, the Court may not, however, strike the case out if 'respect for human rights' requires that the case should continue. The rationale is that

> Although the primary purpose of the Convention system is to provide individual relief, its mission is also to determine issues on public-policy grounds in the common interest, thereby raising the general standards of protection of human rights and extending human rights jurisprudence throughout the community of the Convention States ...[216]

In *Tyrer* v *UK*,[217] for example, a case concerning corporal punishment of a child, the Court refused to strike out the case even though the applicant wished to withdraw, as the case

---

[213] No. 72713/01, 29.3.05.
[214] See, e.g. *Paladi v Moldova*, No. 39806/05, 10.7.07, paras. 51–3 (the case was subsequently referred to the Grand Chamber).
[215] No. 13920/04, dec. 7.7.09.
[216] *Konstantin Markin* v *Russia*, No. 30078/06, 22.3.12, para. 89.
[217] No. 5856/72, 25.4.78.

was considered to raise questions of a general character affecting the observance of the Convention which required further examination. The case of *Gagiu v Romania*[218] concerned the medical treatment of the applicant in prison. After his death, the Government requested that the case be struck out under Article 37(1), but the Court refused to do so, having regard to the fact that he had no family, and the nature of the complaints that he had submitted prior to his death.[219] One of the applicants in *Tehrani and others v Turkey*,[220] informed the Court that he wished to withdraw his case and then requested that he be deported to Iran, where he stated his life would be in danger. In view of doubts about the applicant's mental state, this request was rejected. The case of *F.G. v Sweden*[221] concerned the proposed deportation of the applicant to Iran. By the time the case came before the Grand Chamber the deportation order had become statute-barred, but the Court rejected the Government's request for the case to be struck out as it raised important issues which went beyond the applicant's case. It would also appear that the Court may decide not to strike out a case if it raises an important question of Convention law which has not yet been decided.[222] In *K.A.S. v UK*,[223] the Court stated that it should consider 'when the continued examination of an application would contribute to elucidating, safeguarding and developing the standards of protection under the Convention' or whether a case raised 'a new issue of concern or when there is a paucity of case-law on a particular subject', but it also found that it should be slow to find that such circumstances exist where a case 'has been the subject of careful and detailed examination by the domestic courts'.

Cases may be partially struck off, for example, where there is agreement between the parties **2.167** as to the resolution of part of the case, without prejudice to the remainder of the application.[224] Cases struck off the list may be restored if the Court considers that there are exceptional circumstances for doing so (Article 37(2) and Rule 43(5))—see, for example, *Acar v Turkey*,[225] referred to below. Where a case is struck out by the Court, the costs are at the discretion of the Court. The Court accordingly has a discretion to award an applicant's costs (under Rule 43(4)), as the Grand Chamber did, for example, in *Pisano v Italy*.[226] In practice, the Court will not award costs against an applicant.

Any case to be struck out following the admissibility decision will be struck out by way of a judgment (Rule 43(3)) that is then sent on to the Committee of Ministers to supervise the execution of any relevant undertakings (under Article 46(2)).[227]

---

[218] No. 63258/00, 24.2.09.

[219] In contrast, see *Léger v France*, No. 19324/02, 30.3.09 (and the dissenting opinion of Judge Spielmann joined by Judges Bratza, Gyulumyan and Jebens arguing that, in spite of the applicant's death, the case should not have been struck out on the basis that the Court should have taken the opportunity to consider the important issues under Article 5 raised by the case).

[220] Nos. 32940/08, 41626/08, 43616/08, 13.4.10.

[221] No. 43611/11, 23.3.16. See also *Paposhvili v Belgium*, No. 41738/10, 13.12.16.

[222] *Djokaba Lambi Longa v Netherlands*, No. 33917/12, dec. 9.10.12.

[223] No. 38844/12, dec. 4.6.13.

[224] See, e.g. *Cēsnieks v Latvia*, No. 45175/04, dec. 13.3.12; *De Tommaso v Italy*, No. 43395/09, 23.2.17.

[225] No. 26307/95, 6.5.03. See also *Aleksentseva and 28 others v Russia*, No. 75025/01, dec. 23.3.06.

[226] No. 3673/97, 24.10.02. See also *Sisojeva and others v Latvia*, No. 60654/00, 8.1.07, paras. 130–4; *Pilato v Italy*, No. 18995/06, dec. 2.9.08; *Youssef v Netherlands*, No. 11936/08, dec. 27.9.11.

[227] The number of such undertakings included within friendly settlements has generally been rising: 6 in 2010, 21 in 2011, 54 in 2012, 45 in 2013, 98 in 2014 and 59 in 2015. See: *Supervision of the execution of judgments of the European Court of Human Rights—Annual Report*, 2015, Council of Europe, March 2016, p. 84.

Non-pursuit of application (Article 37(1)(a))

2.168   The first Article 37(1) category is clear and the Court will usually provide the applicant with a number of opportunities to reply to the Court's letters over a period of time, before striking the case out. For example, in *Peltonen v Finland*[228] the case was struck out in September 2000, after there had been no response from the applicant since March 2000. In *Yakan v Turkey*[229] the applicant had repeatedly failed to respond to the Court's letters (which included letters sent by registered post) since March 1999. On this basis the Court struck out a series of cases against Georgia, arising from the armed conflict relating to South Ossetia in 2008.[230] This provision requires that contact between applicants and their representatives is maintained throughout the proceedings, otherwise cases will be susceptible to being struck out.[231]

Resolution of the matter (Article 37(1)(b))

2.169   The second category covers cases which are considered to have been 'resolved'. This will require an assessment as to whether the circumstances complained of by an applicant still obtain, and also whether the effects of a possible violation of the Convention as a result of those circumstances have been redressed.[232] For example, Article 37(1)(b) was applied in *Xiaolin v Hungary*[233] after the Hungarian Government had rejected the request of the Chinese Government to extradite the applicant. Similarly, *Abdouni v France*[234] was struck out on this basis once the prohibition order which had been issued against the applicant Algerian national was subsequently annulled. In *Pisano v Italy*,[235] the applicant complained under Article 6 about the unfairness of criminal proceedings brought against him, but the case was struck out by the Grand Chamber as having been resolved, following the applicant's acquittal at a later retrial. In the subsequent proceedings, a key witness had been heard (the failure to hear the witness had been one of the applicant's main complaints) and the applicant's conviction had been quashed. In *Balikçi v Turkey*[236] disciplinary action had been taken against the applicant civil servant on account of his participation in industrial action protesting about the absence of trade union rights for civil servants. However, the Turkish Constitution had subsequently been amended to recognise such rights, there had been further amendments to the domestic law on trade union rights for civil servants in compliance with the European Convention, and the applicant had received the benefit of an amnesty law, which resulted in his reprimand being removed from his record. Furthermore, the applicant had continued to work for his employer, without suffering prejudice. In those circumstances, the Court found that the matter had been resolved and struck the case out under Article 37(1)(b). The Grand Chamber invoked this provision in striking out the case of *Sisojeva and others*

---

[228] No. 27323/95, 28.9.00.

[229] No. 43362/98, 19.9.00.

[230] *1,549 cases against Georgia concerning the Georgia-Russia conflict of August 2008 struck out by the European Court of Human Rights*, European Court of Human Rights, Press release, 10.1.11.

[231] *V.M. and others v Belgium*, No. 60125/11, 17.11.16, paras. 35–41.

[232] See, e.g. *El Majjaoui & Stichting Touba Moskee v Netherlands*, No. 25525/03, 20.12.07, para. 30 (a case which was struck out by a majority of the Grand Chamber as having been resolved, with three judges dissenting).

[233] No. 58073/00, 8.3.01.

[234] No. 37838/97, 27.2.01.

[235] No. 3673/97, 24.10.02.

[236] No. 26481/95, 6.1.04.

v *Latvia*.[237] The applicants had taken up residence in Latvia as Soviet nationals, but had become stateless after the break-up of the Soviet Union. They brought domestic proceedings to challenge the revocation of their residency status, and lodged an application in Strasbourg relying on Article 8. It was struck out on the basis that the applicants were not at imminent risk of deportation and they had failed to respond over a period of years to the immigration authorities which had explained the procedure they needed to follow in order to regularise their residency in Latvia. The Court may be called on to apply Article 37(1)(b) in cases which challenge whether national authorities have resolved systemic violations or not.[238] For example, in *Association of Real Property Owners in Łódź* v *Poland*,[239] the Court examined the legislative changes introduced following the pilot judgment in *Hutten-Czapska* v *Poland*,[240] relating to legislative restrictions on the rights of landlords to charge rent for their properties and to recover property maintenance costs. In those circumstances, as well as considering the position of the individual applicant, the Court will also assess the adequacy of the remedial action taken in order to implement the general measures aimed at resolving the systemic defects identified in the pilot judgment. In that case, the introduction of a statutory damages scheme meant that the matter was considered to have been resolved.

In contrast, a case will not be considered to have been 'resolved' within the meaning of Article **2.170** 37(1)(b) where a provision of criminal law, under which the applicant was prosecuted and convicted, has been subsequently repealed, leaving the applicant's conviction unaffected.[241] In *Konstantin Markin* v *Russia*[242] the Court rejected the Government's request to strike the case out as having been resolved. The case concerned discrimination in the domestic law against male military personnel in relation to entitlement to parental leave. The applicant had in fact been granted a period of parental leave on an exceptional basis, but the legislation in question remained in force and the Court considered that the case raised an important question of general interest which it had not yet examined.

Continued examination of an application no longer justified (Article 37(1)(c))

The third category is, however, rather more difficult to define with any real precision. It **2.171** allows the Court an extensive discretion to strike out cases which do not justify continued examination 'for any other reason'. This has included cases in which the applicants are considered not to have pursued their domestic cases with sufficient diligence.[243] In *Léger* v *France*[244] the Grand Chamber invoked Article 37(1)(c) in striking out a case in which the applicant had died, and a request that the application be continued had been made by a person who was neither an heir nor a close relative, nor had she established any legitimate interest in the case.

---

[237] No. 60654/00, 8.1.07. See also *Chevanova* v *Latvia*, No. 58822/00, 7.12.07 and *Kaftailova* v *Latvia*, No. 59643/00, 7.12.07.

[238] See also: *Wolkenberg and others* v *Poland*, No. 50003/99, dec. 4.12.07 and *E.G. and 175 other Bug River applications* v *Poland*, No. 50425/99, dec. 23.9.08 (both relating to the pilot judgment in *Broniowski* v *Poland*, No. 31443/96, 22.6.04).

[239] No. 3485/02, dec. 8.3.11.

[240] No. 35014/97, 19.6.06.

[241] *L and V* v *Austria*, Nos. 39392/98 and 39829/98, 9.1.03.

[242] No. 30078/06, 22.3.12.

[243] See, e.g. *Goryachev* v *Russia*, No. 34886/06, dec. 9.4.13.

[244] No. 19324/02, 30.3.09.

2.172 Other cases struck out under Article 37(1)(c) suggest that there is a good deal of overlap with Article 37(1)(b). In *Kalantari v Germany*[245] the previous decision to expel the applicant to Iran was revoked and accordingly the case was struck out under Article 37(1)(c) on the basis that its examination was no longer necessary. In reaching this decision, the Court contrasted the case with the decision in *Ahmed v Austria*[246] where the Court refused to strike out the case as the authorities had merely decided to stay the execution of the applicant's deportation order (to Somalia), which otherwise remained valid. In *Victor Emmanuel of Savoy v Italy*,[247] the applicant was the son of the last King of Italy who complained of being banned by law from entering or living in Italy. The case was struck out after the domestic law was amended and the applicant was permitted to return to Italy. In *JM v UK*,[248] the applicant was a rape victim whom the domestic law permitted to be extensively cross-examined in court by her attacker. The application was struck out under Article 37(1)(c) following the agreement by the state to pay £6,000 in damages, plus legal costs. Furthermore, legislation had been introduced in 1999[249] which restricted a defendant's ability to cross-examine a victim of an alleged crime personally.

Unilateral declarations

2.173 In 2001 Article 37(1)(c) was invoked by the Court to justify striking out a series of cases against Turkey concerning alleged gross human rights violations: *Akman v Turkey*[250] (a fatal shooting by the security forces), *Haran v Turkey*,[251] *Toğçu v Turkey*,[252] and *TA v Turkey*[253] (each of which were 'disappearance' cases). In each case, settlement terms had been discussed between the parties, but terms could not be agreed. The Government then submitted to the Court a 'unilateral' statement of terms on the basis of which it sought the striking out of the cases under Article 37. The applicants in each case opposed striking out on the basis that the terms put forward by the Government failed to resolve the case or otherwise justify its discontinuance. Nevertheless, in a series of Chamber judgments, these cases were struck out. The Grand Chamber of the Court subsequently took steps to clarify the Court's powers and the relevant procedures. The 'disappearance' case of *TA* was referred to the Grand Chamber which, in its judgment in *Acar v Turkey*[254] in 2003, in effect 'overturned' the Chamber's decision to strike out the case, which was restored to the list under Article 37(2).[255] The Court found that it may, depending upon the circumstances of a case, be appropriate to strike a case out under Article 37(1)(c) as a result of a respondent state's unilateral declaration, even where this is objected to by the applicant.[256] The following factors were identified as potentially being relevant:[257]

---

[245] No. 51342/99, 11.10.01.

[246] No. 25964/94, 17.12.96.

[247] No. 53360/99, 24.4.03.

[248] No. 41518/98, dec. 28.9.00.

[249] Youth Justice and Criminal Evidence Act 1999.

[250] No. 37453/97, 26.6.01.

[251] No. 25754/94, 26.3.02.

[252] No. 27601/95, 9.4.02.

[253] No. 26307/95, 9.4.02.

[254] No. 26307/95, 6.5.03.

[255] In its subsequent judgment on the merits (8.4.04) the Court found a violation of Article 2 as a result of the inadequacies in the investigation into the 'disappearance'.

[256] See, e.g. *Van Houten v Netherlands,* No. 25149/03, 29.9.05.

[257] *Acar v Turkey,* No. 26307/95, 6.5.03, paras. 75–7. See also: European Court of Human Rights, Unilateral declarations: policy and practice, September 2012.

- the nature of the complaints made;
- whether the issues raised are comparable to issues already determined by the Court in previous cases;
- the nature and scope of any measures taken by the respondent government in the context of the execution of judgments delivered by the Court in any such previous cases;
- the impact of those measures on the case at issue;
- whether the facts are in dispute between the parties, and, if so, to what extent, and what prima facie evidentiary value is to be attributed to the parties' submissions on the facts;
- whether the Court itself has already taken evidence in the case for the purposes of establishing disputed facts;
- whether in its unilateral declaration the respondent government has made any admissions in relation to the alleged violations of the Convention and, if so, the scope of such admissions and the manner in which it intends to provide redress[258] to the applicant.

The Grand Chamber decided in *Acar* not to strike out the case because the facts were to a **2.174** large extent in dispute between the parties, the Government had rejected any admission of responsibility or liability[259] and the Government's unilateral declaration did not adequately address the applicant's grievances under the Convention. Perhaps most significant, however, was the omission of an undertaking to carry out a Convention-complaint investigation into the 'disappearance'. Accordingly, the 'respect for human rights' test, under Article 37(1), required the examination of the case on its merits. In their joint concurring opinion, Judges Bratza, Tulkens and Vajić expressed the view that the use of the striking out procedure 'must remain an exceptional one and, in any event, cannot be used to circumvent the applicant's opposition to a friendly settlement'. Subsequently, the Court has shown itself to be willing to reject unilateral declarations, as a result of the 'respect for human rights' test, or otherwise because a case raises an issue which is yet to be decided.[260] The Court is likely to be highly reluctant to accept unilateral declarations in relation to systemic issues, the resolution of which is not covered by the proposed declaration. That was the outcome in the pilot judgment in *Gerasimov and others* v *Russia*[261] which concerned the failure to implement domestic court judgments ordering the state to provide housing or other services in kind. Although the Government had acknowledged Convention violations in the individual cases, and offered to pay compensation, it had made no undertaking to address the wider issue, which still affected large numbers of people. Similarly, in *Tahirov* v *Azerbaijan*,[262] a case which concerned the arbitrary refusal to register an independent candidate for parliamentary elections, the Court rejected the Government's unilateral declaration notably because there had been numerous complaints of various electoral irregularities after elections in Azerbaijan,

---

[258] As regards redress, the Court has stipulated that the use of the term 'ex gratia' in relation to compensation is regarded as being 'at odds with a clear acknowledgment of a violation'. Where an applicant is considered to have unjustifiably refused a friendly settlement, the Court may accept a 10 per cent reduction in the basic sum as derived from the scales as developed from its caselaw. See: European Court of Human Rights, Unilateral declarations: policy and practice, September 2012, p. 1.

[259] Similarly, in *Prencipe* v *Monaco*, No. 43376/06, 16.7.09 the Court rejected the Government's request for a unilateral declaration striking out the case as the Government had made no acknowledgement that the Convention had been violated.

[260] See, e.g. *De Tommaso* v *Italy*, No. 43395/09, 23.2.17.

[261] No. 29920/05 et al, 1.7.14.

[262] No. 31953/11, 11.6.15. See also *Annagi Hajibeyli* v *Azerbaijan*, No. 2204/11, 22.10.15.

and the terms proposed by the Government failed to deal with the systemic or structural issues arising.

2.175 In *Rantsev v Cyprus and Russia*,[263] which concerned the death of the applicant's daughter in Cyprus, the Court rejected a request made by the Cypriot Government to strike out the case on the basis of a unilateral declaration which acknowledged violations of Articles 2, 3, 4 and 5(1) and offered a global sum of compensation of €37,300. In doing so, the Court took account of the serious nature of the allegations of human trafficking which arose in the case, and the paucity of the case law under Article 4 in relation to trafficking. Therefore, 'respect for human rights' required the continuation of the examination of the case. Similarly, the respondent state's unilateral declaration was rejected by the Court in *Vyerentsov v Ukraine*[264] applying the 'respect for human rights' test, because the issues raised in the case, concerning the adequacy of the legislative framework regulating the right to peaceful assembly, had not previously been considered in respect of Ukraine. The applicant in *Hakimi v Belgium*[265] sought the reopening of criminal proceedings against him. When the Government submitted a unilateral declaration in the course of the Strasbourg proceedings, it was rejected by the Court because it was unclear whether under Belgian law proceedings could be reopened following a unilateral declaration, as opposed to a Court judgment. It went on to find a breach of the right of access to court pursuant to Article 6(1) and found that the most appropriate form of redress would be the reopening of the proceedings. The Court refused to accept the Government's unilateral declaration in *Topčić-Rosenberg v Croatia*:[266] whereas there was an admission of a violation of Article 14 with Article 8 (in a case concerning the refusal to pay maternity leave to an adoptive mother), the just satisfaction offered was considered to be insufficient.

2.176 Since the *Acar* judgment, the use of 'unilateral declarations' has been codified (Rule 62A) and they have become a common feature of the Strasbourg system.[267] The usual procedure is that a unilateral declaration may only be submitted after the applicant has refused the terms of a friendly settlement proposal, although 'exceptional circumstances' may justify the submission of a unilateral declaration without a prior attempt at friendly settlement.[268]

The cases of *Kalanyos and others v Romania*[269] and *Gergely v Romania*[270] concerned the burning of Roma houses by the local populace, their poor living conditions and the authorities' failure to prevent the attack and to carry out an adequate investigation. The cases were struck out in response to unilateral declarations in which the Government accepted that there had been violations of Articles 3, 6, 8, 13 and 14 of the Convention and undertook to pay each

---

[263] No. 25965/04, 7.1.10.

[264] No. 20372/11, 11.4.13.

[265] No. 665/08, 29.6.10. See also *Rozhin v Russia*, No. 50098/07, 6.12.11 (re civil proceedings).

[266] No. 19391/11, 14.11.13.

[267] For example, there were 30 unilateral declarations in 2007, compared with 692 in 2011 (see: Unilateral declarations: policy and practice, September 2012, p. 1). There were 2,970 and 1,767 unilateral declarations in 2015 and 2016, respectively (see: European Court of Human Rights, Analysis of Statistics 2016, January 2017, p. 4). A unilateral declaration can also be invoked during the course of reserved Article 41 proceedings. See *Megadat.com SRL v Moldova*, No. 21151/04, 17.5.11. See further: Dominika Bychawska-Siniarska, Unilateral Declarations: The Need for Greater Control [2012] 6 E.H.R.L.R. 673.

[268] Rule 62A. See also *Telegraaf Media Nederland Landelijke Media B.V. and van der Graaf v Netherlands*, No. 33847/11, dec. 30.8.16.

[269] No. 57884/00, 26.4.07.

[270] No. 57885/00, 26.4.07.

of the applicants damages of €30,000 to €36,500, plus costs and expenses. The Government also undertook to adopt a series of general measures relating to the judicial system, to educational, social and housing programmes and aimed at fighting discrimination against the Roma in the area concerned, and stimulating their participation in the economic, social, educational, cultural and political life of the local community. The Court rejected the applicants' objections to the striking out, in particular in view of the previous judgment concerning these issues in *Moldovan v Romania (No. 2)*.[271] The Court accepted the Government's unilateral declaration in *Union of Jehovah's Witnesses of Georgia and others v Georgia*,[272] a case concerning the failure to register the applicant religious organisations. The Government had accepted that Articles 9 and 11 had been breached and offered commensurate compensation, and the relevant legislation had been amended.

It is important to emphasise that if the Court strikes out a case pursuant to a unilateral **2.177** declaration, the Court still has the power to restore the case to its list under Article 37(2) of the Convention.[273] In *Žarković and others v Croatia*[274] the Court stated that its decision to strike out the case (complaints under Articles 2 and 14 of the Convention concerning the lack of an effective investigation into a killing) following a unilateral declaration was without prejudice to the Government's 'continuing obligation to conduct an investigation in compliance with the requirements of the Convention'. In *Jeronovičs v Latvia*[275] the applicant complained that after his application under Article 3 alleging ill-treatment by the police had been struck out by the Court pursuant to a unilateral declaration (in which the Government acknowledged a breach of Article 3), the authorities had simply paid out compensation, without also conducting an effective investigation. The Grand Chamber held that, even in the absence of any express provision in the unilateral declaration to carry out such an investigation, the state had a continuing obligation to conduct an investigation in compliance with the requirements of the Convention, which had been violated.[276] Of course, where a respondent government includes in the terms of a unilateral declaration, an undertaking, for example, to carry out an effective investigation,[277] the applicant will have the right to seek the restoration of the case to the Court's list if no such investigation is in fact subsequently carried out.

Submissions Post-admissibility

It is no longer common for the Court to issue a separate decision on the admissibility of a **2.178** case, before it goes on to consider the merits. If a separate decision on admissibility is issued the parties will then be invited by the Court to lodge final written submissions.

---

[271] Nos. 41138/98 and 64320/01, 12.7.05.

[272] No. 72874/01, dec. 21.4.15.

[273] As it did in *Aleksentseva and others v Russia*, No. 75025/01, dec. 23.3.06 (restoration ordered due to the Government's failure to pay compensation). Note, however, that the Committee of Ministers does *not* have the power to supervise the fulfillment of undertakings in unilateral declarations.

[274] No. 75187/12, dec. 9.6.15.

[275] No. 44898/10, 5.7.16.

[276] The decision was reached by a majority of ten votes to seven. The seven dissenting judges (Judges Silvis, Villiger, Hirvelä, Mahoney, Wojtyczek, Kjølbro and Briede) argued that no obligation to investigate arose from the unilateral declaration.

[277] See, e.g. *Tedliashvili and others v Georgia*, No. 64987/14, dec. 24.11.15.

2.179 As to format and strategy, see the section on the applicant's Observations in reply at 2.96 above. As with other pleadings, the format of the submissions should comply with the rules set out in the Practice Direction on *Written Pleadings* (see 2.102 above). Specifically in respect of parties' pleadings post-admissibility, the Practice Direction states[278] that they should include:

- a short statement confirming a party's position on the facts of the case as established in the decision on admissibility;
- legal arguments relating to the merits of the case; and
- a reply to any specific questions on a factual or legal point put by the Court.

These submissions may differ from the original application in a number of ways. Any issues already found to be inadmissible can no longer be pursued. The applicant's submissions will of course also take into account the responses made by the government to the applicant's arguments. An applicant may have decided not to pursue particular arguments (even if they were declared admissible) in the light of the government's observations in reply, or an applicant may seek to emphasise the principal arguments over and above any subsidiary points. As discussed above, it should always be borne in mind that the European Convention system is primarily a written rather than an oral procedure.

The Court is not precluded at this stage from taking into account any new information, evidence or fresh arguments,[279] although the scope of the case is of course determined by the admissibility decision.

2.180 Details of any compensation and/or costs that are being claimed (under Article 41) should be included with the submissions (unless the President of the Chamber directs otherwise) (Rule 60).[280] A failure to submit such a claim is likely to mean that no award is made (Rule 60(3)).[281] See also the comments on making a just satisfaction claim in the section on the applicant's observations in reply at 2.96 above. The claim for costs and expenses can include sums incurred in attempting to secure redress for the violation of the Convention through the domestic legal system. Any claim by an applicant under Article 41 will be sent by the Court to the respondent government for its observations in reply (Rule 60(4)). Awards of just satisfaction under Article 41 are considered in more detail in chapter 8.

Oral Hearing

2.181 The practice of the Court of holding a hearing on the admissibility and/or merits of a case is now very much the exception rather than the rule (Rule 59(3)). Although it is the Court's practice to ask the parties whether they want the Court to hold an oral hearing, in any event the vast majority of cases are decided without a hearing. The Court is more likely to hold a hearing if further clarification is needed on the facts of the case or the relevant domestic law or practice. It is suggested that the legal or political importance of a case may also be relevant

---

[278] Practice Direction: *Written Pleadings*, para. 15.
[279] See, e.g. *K and T v Finland*, No. 25702/94, 12.7.01.
[280] Practice Direction: *Written Pleadings*, para. 15(b) also requires applicants to comply with the Practice Direction on filing just satisfaction claims.
[281] See, e.g. *Ambruosi v Italy*, No. 31227/96, 19.10.00.

factors in assessing the need for a hearing. The Registrar will usually issue a press release about the case prior to the hearing and a second press release is usually issued on the day of the hearing. A schedule of forthcoming hearings is included on the Court's website. Since 2007 the Court has also published webcasts of hearings on its website (from 2.30 pm on the day of the hearing).

If the Court decides to hold an oral hearing on the merits, when writing to inform the parties **2.182** of its decision it may list various questions for the parties to answer at the hearing. The Court may also set a date, prior to the hearing, by which time any additional documents must be submitted to the Court. Prior to the hearing, the applicant's representative will be asked to provide a copy of the oral submissions to the Court for the purposes of the Court's interpreters. It is not compulsory to do so, but it is advisable if at all possible, as it will facilitate the simultaneous interpretation of the oral submissions. If the text of the proposed submissions cannot be sent in advance, then at least a summary of the main points should be sent. Of course, advocates are not bound by any text sent in advance, but are free to alter their submissions as they consider fit.

The parties are also asked by the Court to provide, prior to the hearing, the names of all those **2.183** who will attend the hearing including legal representatives, advisers and applicants. The Court Rules require that an applicant must be represented at hearings by an advocate who is authorised to practise in any of the state parties to the Convention or other representative approved by the Court (Rule 36(3)). The President may allow applicants to present their own cases,[282] but this is in practice extremely rare. Where an applicant is represented by an advocate at the hearing, the Court may also permit the applicant her/himself to make oral submissions.[283] The Court may permit several representatives to speak on behalf of the parties (subject to the overall time limits).

The hearings are usually conducted in one of the Court's official languages (English or **2.184** French), but the President may allow the use of an official language of one of the state parties. Prior notice will have to be given to the Court if a party wishes to address the Court in a language other than English or French.

The conduct of hearings will be directed by the President of the relevant Chamber (Rule 64). **2.185** However, hearings usually take no more than two hours in total, either from 9.00 to 11.00 am or from 2.30 to 4.30 pm. Only exceptionally will the parties be allowed further time. Applicants are usually given 30 minutes to put their primary oral arguments.[284] The respondent government is then given 30 minutes in which to respond (in admissibility hearings the government will usually open and the applicant will reply). These times should be strictly adhered to and it is essential that advocates keep to their allotted maximum of 30 minutes, otherwise they may be stopped by the President (whether or not their submissions have been completed) or their time for replying to the other party may be reduced. The President will usually convene a short informal meeting prior to the hearing to remind the parties about the need to keep to the allotted times and to discuss any other particular arrangements for the

---

[282] See, e.g. *Wloch* v *Poland*, No. 27785/95, 19.10.00.

[283] See, e.g. *Hartman* v *Czech Republic*, No. 53341/99, 10.7.03; *Gorzelik and others* v *Poland*, No. 44158/98, 17.2.04.

[284] Exceptionally, this has been increased to 45 minutes (as was the case before the Chamber in *Öcalan* v *Turkey*, No. 46221/99, 12.3.03).

hearing. For example, there may be discussion concerning the admission to the Court file of any documents filed late by the parties.

2.186 Clearly, the presentation of oral submissions in the context of a European Convention application is in a number of respects quite different from advocacy in the domestic courts. The procedure is primarily written, concluded in some cases by a very short hearing before the Court. In 30 minutes, the representatives will be required to complement the written submissions already lodged with the final oral submissions on behalf of the parties. The submissions will be simultaneously interpreted and a number of the judges will be listening to the interpreters, rather than the advocates. Advocates are therefore advised to speak clearly and not too quickly. The parties can expect the Judge Rapporteur to have an in-depth knowledge of the case, however this cannot necessarily be assumed of all of the judges. Given the very limited time, it is not necessary to dwell on the facts of the case (unless there are particular factual disputes). It is not of course necessary to argue every point in issue, provided that each point has been included in the written submissions already lodged with the Court. It is usual for oral submissions to concentrate on the primary matters of dispute between the parties. If the Court has provided the parties with specific questions in advance of the hearing, then those questions should of course be the focus of the oral submissions (although they need not necessarily be limited to answering the Court's specific questions). Given the strict time limits, it is quite common for advocates to prepare written speeches that they have timed, in order to ensure that the 30 minutes are not exceeded. After the parties have each made their 30-minute submissions, the Court may ask questions of the representatives. The questions are often directed specifically at one of the parties, although this will not always be the case. Any of the judges may ask questions (Rule 64(2)) and they may be fired at the parties in quick succession. The parties are provided at the Court with a sheet indicating the names of the judges in the order that they are sitting in the Court, which will assist in identifying which judge has asked which question. If the Court does have questions, there may be a short adjournment (of ten to 15 minutes) for the parties to consider their responses (but this may not always be the case). The parties may remain in the Court Chamber, or may be directed to meeting rooms below the Court during the adjournment.

2.187 Following the adjournment, each party will usually have about ten minutes to answer the Court's questions and to reply to the other side, with the applicant opening and the government responding.

2.188 The Court's hearings take place in public, unless there are exceptional circumstances for the hearing to be held in private (Article 40 and Rule 63). For example, in *Scozzari and Giunta v Italy*[285] a private hearing was held in a case concerning access to children. Any party or any other person concerned may request that a hearing take place in private. Reasons should be given for the request and it should be specified whether all or just part of the hearing should be held in private (Rule 63(3)). The Court can exclude both the press and the public from all or part of a hearing for any of the following reasons (Rule 63(2)):[286]

(1) in the interests of morals; or
(2) in the interests of public order; or

---

[285] Nos. 39221/98 and 41963/98, 13.7.00, para. 9. See also, e.g. *Z v Finland*, No. 22009/93, 25.2.97.
[286] See, for example, *Daoudi v France*, No. 19576/08, 3.12.09.

(3) in the interests of national security in a democratic society; or

(4) where the interests of juveniles so require; or

(5) where the protection of the private life of the parties so require; or

(6) to the extent strictly necessary in the opinion of the Chamber in special circumstances where publicity would prejudice the interests of justice.

If a party fails to appear for a hearing without showing sufficient cause, the Court may never- **2.189** theless proceed with the hearing in the absence of the party, provided that the Court is satisfied that to do so would be consistent with the proper administration of justice (Rule 65).[287]

The Court may make a verbatim record of the hearing (Rule 70). The proceedings are **2.190** recorded on tape, but a verbatim record is not prepared unless the Court decides to do so. The verbatim record will include:

(1) the composition of the Court;

(2) a list of those appearing before the Court (including agents, advocates, advisers and third parties);

(3) the text of the submissions made, questions put and replies given;

(4) the text of any ruling delivered during the hearing.

If one is prepared, the verbatim record will be sent to the parties for them to correct within a specified time limit (although they may not correct the sense of what was said). The Court deliberates in private and its deliberations remain secret (Rule 22). Any decisions made by the Court are made by a majority of the judges. If there is a tie, a fresh vote is taken, and if there is still a tie, the President has the casting vote (Rule 23(1)). Votes are taken by a show of hands and the President may take a roll-call vote, in reverse order of precedence (Rule 23(3)).

---

[287] See, e.g. *Cyprus* v *Turkey*, No. 25781/94, 10.5.01, para. 12.

3

PRACTICE AND PROCEDURE OF THE EUROPEAN COURT—JUDGMENT AND ENFORCEMENT

Delivery of Judgment

3.01 The Court's reasoned judgment is usually published several months after the submission of final written observations (or after any oral hearing). Notice will also be posted in advance on the Court's website. The Court's legal aid does not cover the attendance of the applicant or the applicant's representatives at the judgment, which is not required or expected by the Court. It is therefore usual for the applicant not to be represented at the delivery of the judgment.

3.02 Grand Chamber judgments are read out (in summary) at a public hearing by the President of the Grand Chamber or a judge delegated by the President. There is rarely a public hearing in respect of Chamber judgments, which are sent directly to the parties. Judgments adopted by Committees are sent to the parties (without there being a hearing). Once judgment is handed down, the Court will issue a press release summarising the judgment. The press release will be posted on the Court's website immediately. The judgment itself will also be posted on the website on the day judgment is given. The parties are sent the judgment by post by the Registrar who also sends copies to the Committee of Ministers, the Secretary-General of the Council of Europe, any third party and any person directly concerned (Rule 77).

3.03 Judgments are drafted in one of the two official languages of the Court (English or French), although the most important judgments are produced in both languages (Rule 76). As to which language is used, this would seem to depend on the preference of the particular

Registry lawyer dealing with the case. Judgments are written in a standard format, in accordance with Rule 74(1). All judgments will contain the following:

(1) the names of the President and the other judges constituting the Chamber or the Committee concerned, and the name of the Registrar or Deputy Registrar;
(2) the dates on which it was adopted and delivered;
(3) a description of the parties;
(4) the names of the agents, advocates or advisers of the parties;
(5) an account of the procedure followed;
(6) the facts of the case;
(7) a summary of the submissions of the parties;
(8) the reasons in point of law;
(9) the operative provisions;
(10) the decision, if any, in respect of costs;
(11) the number of judges constituting the majority;
(12) where appropriate, a statement as to which text is authentic.

In respect of Chamber or Grand Chamber judgments, judges may append their separate opinion, dissenting from or concurring with the majority judgment (Article 45(2) and Rule 74(2)), or they may include a bare statement of dissent. Judgments in repetitive violation ('clone') cases tend to be much more concise than other judgments (as to the summary of the facts and the submissions etc).

3.04 The Court's primary remedy is a declaration that there has been a violation of one or more Convention rights. Where the Court finds that there has been a violation of the Convention, the judgment may include an award for 'just satisfaction' under Article 41 (previously under Article 50, prior to November 1998), if the question of compensation is ready for decision. This may include compensation for both pecuniary and non-pecuniary losses and legal costs and expenses. The Court can, and usually does, direct that interest at a prescribed rate is to be payable on any sums not paid within a specified time (usually three months). There is no provision in the Convention for costs to be awarded against an applicant.

3.05 If the Article 41 claim is not ready for decision, awards for just satisfaction may be reserved in order for the Court to receive further submissions (Rule 75). In those circumstances, the Court will subsequently fix the procedure for adjudication of the just satisfaction claim. The Court will usually be composed of the same judges in order to consider the Article 41 claim, but this may not necessarily be the case (Rule 75(2)). If an Article 41 claim is subsequently agreed between the parties, the Court will strike the case out of the list, provided it is satisfied that the agreement is equitable (Rule 75(4)). Levels of Article 41 awards are discussed further in chapter 8.

3.06 As there is provision for referral of the judgment of a Chamber to the Grand Chamber (see below at 3.08), the judgment of a Chamber is not immediately final. The judgment of a Chamber will only become final when one of three conditions is satisfied (Article 44(2)):

(1) when the parties declare that they will not request that the case be referred to the Grand Chamber; or

(2) three months after the date of the judgment, if reference of the case to the Grand Chamber has not been requested; or

(3) when the panel of the Grand Chamber rejects the request to refer the case.

The judgment of a Grand Chamber is final (Article 44(1)). Once final, judgments have binding force (Article 46(1)).

3.07 Any clerical errors, errors in calculation or 'obvious mistakes' made in the Court's judgments can be rectified, but the parties should notify the Court of any such errors within one month of the delivery of the judgment (Rule 81). The Court can also rectify clerical errors of its own motion.

Referral to the Grand Chamber

3.08 There is no right of appeal, as such, from a chamber judgment, but there is a right to request a re-hearing before the Grand Chamber (under Article 43; Rule 73). Within three months of a Chamber giving judgment,[1] in exceptional cases, any party may ask for the case to be referred to the Grand Chamber for a final judgment. The party seeking referral should specify its reasons. The request is considered by a panel of five judges from the Grand Chamber (Rule 73(2)). The panel's role is to decide whether the case involves any of the following:

(1) a serious question affecting the interpretation of the Convention; or

(2) a serious question affecting its application (for example, if it necessitates a substantial change to national law or practice); or

(3) a serious issue of general importance (for example, a substantial political issue or an important issue of policy) (Article 43(2)).

If a request is refused, the panel need not give reasons, but if it is accepted, the Grand Chamber will decide any such referral by means of a judgment (Article 43(3)).

3.09 The introduction of a re-hearing process (through the Protocol No. 11 changes in 1998) represented a political compromise by the Convention member states and it is an unusual feature of an international court in that it allows a full re-hearing of a case before the same (albeit differently constituted) court. The fact that a national judge who votes in the Chamber decision will also, in practice, sit and vote in a referral to the Grand Chamber has been the subject of judicial criticism.[2] However, it is the Court's usual practice that the President of the Chamber which delivered the first judgment will not also sit on the Grand Chamber.

3.10 It is clear from the text of Article 43 itself that the procedure is only relevant to 'exceptional cases', and therefore the panel of five judges only rarely allows such referrals. Indeed in 2016 the panel received 151 requests, but accepted only 14 cases.[3]

---

[1] But as regards the situation of multiple applicants in one case, see *Kovačić and others* v *Slovenia*, No. 44574/98 et seq., 3.10.08, paras. 197–200.

[2] See the partly dissenting opinion of Judge Costa in *Kyprianou* v *Cyprus*, No. 73797/01, 15.12.05 and the concurring opinion of Sir Nicolas Bratza in *Dickson* v *UK*, No. 44362/04, 4.12.07. See also the concurring opinion of Judge Myjer in *Sanoma Uitgevers B.V.* v *Netherlands*, No. 38224/03, 14.9.10.

[3] *Annual Report 2016 of the European Court of Human Rights*, Council of Europe, pp. 183–4. The figures for 2014 were 18 referrals from 176 requests and in 2015 there were 15 referrals from 135 requests.

Once a panel accepts a case for re-hearing under this procedure, there is no mechanism **3.11** allowing the Court to review the panel's decision—the case will then have to be considered by the Grand Chamber which will decide the case by means of a judgment. Once a case is referred to it, the Grand Chamber may utilise the full range of judicial powers conferred on the Court, which may include the finding of a friendly settlement (Article 39) or a striking out (Article 37).[4] In *K and T* v *Finland*[5] the Court was called on to clarify the scope of a case once it has been referred to the Grand Chamber, in response to submissions from the Finnish Government to the effect that the Court should only re-examine those issues where Article 8 had been found to be violated. However, the Grand Chamber resolved that once a case is referred to it under Article 43, the whole case (as declared admissible) is to be considered afresh.[6] In the case of *Refah Partisi (the Welfare Party) and others* v *Turkey*[7] the Grand Chamber found that this meant that the applicants were entitled to submit arguments that the interference in question (the dissolution of a political party) had not been in accordance with domestic law even though the applicants had conceded the point before the Chamber, on the basis that they had included such arguments in their original applications. However, the Court stated that it did not exclude the possibility of estoppel 'where one of the parties breaks good faith through a radical change of position'.[8] In *Öcalan* v *Turkey*,[9] in considering the applicant's complaints about the conditions of his detention, under Article 3, the Grand Chamber included events that had occurred since its Chamber judgment, as they were directly related to the complaints which had been declared admissible.

Interpretation of Judgment

Within a year of the delivery of a judgment, either party may request the interpretation of **3.12** the operative provisions of a judgment (Rule 79). The original Chamber will usually decide such requests, but not if the original Chamber cannot be constituted. The request can be refused by the Chamber if there is no reason to warrant considering it. Otherwise, the other party will be asked to comment on the request within a specified time limit. If the request is granted, the question will be decided by way of a judgment. In exercising its inherent jurisdiction to consider interpretation, the Court will go no further than to clarify the meaning and scope which it intended to give to a previous decision.[10] Requests for interpretation concerning the attachment of sums awarded by way of just satisfaction by the Court have been rejected as being beyond the scope of 'interpretation'.[11]

---

[4] *Pisano* v *Italy*, No. 36732/97, 24.10.02, paras. 26–9.

[5] No. 25702/94, 12.7.01.

[6] *Ibid.*, para. 140. See also: *Göç* v *Turkey*, No. 36590/97, 19.10.00; *Perna* v *Italy*, No. 48898/99, 6.5.03; *Pisano* v *Italy*, No. 36732/97, 24.10.02; *Nachova and others* v *Bulgaria*, Nos. 43577/98 and 43579/98, 6.7.05; *D.H. and Others* v *Czech Republic*, No. 57325/00, 13.11.07; *Sanoma Uitgevers B.V.* v *Netherlands*, No. 38224/03, 14.9.10. In the preliminary judgment in *Acar* v *Turkey*, No. 26307/95, 6.5.03, the Grand Chamber limited its scope to considering the Chamber's decision to strike out the case under Article 37(2). The Government's request to strike out the case was rejected and in its subsequent judgment on the merits (8.4.04), the Court found a violation of Article 2.

[7] Nos. 41340/98, 41342/98, 41343/98 and 41344/98, 13.2.03.

[8] *Ibid.*, para. 56.

[9] No. 46221/99, 12.5.05, para. 190.

[10] See, e.g. *Ringeisen* v *Austria (No. 3)*, Series A, No. 16, 23.6.73, para. 13; *Allenet de Ribemont* v *France*, Series A, No. 308, 26.6.96, para. 17.

[11] See, e.g. *Allenet de Ribemont* v *France*, Series A, No. 308, 26.6.96.

Revision of Judgment

3.13 Parties may seek a revision of a judgment if a decisive new fact is discovered (Rule 80). The revision of judgments is considered to be an 'exceptional procedure',[12] not least because it calls into question the finality of judgments. The conditions for seeking revision are as follows:

(1) a fact has been discovered which might by its nature have a decisive influence; and
(2) when the judgment was delivered the fact was unknown to the Court; and
(3) when the judgment was delivered the fact could not reasonably have been known to the requesting party.

The request must be made not later than six months after the fact became known to the party. The request should identify the relevant judgment, show that the necessary conditions have been complied with and include all supporting documents (Rule 80(2)). The original Chamber will usually decide such requests, but not if the original Chamber cannot be constituted. The request can be refused by the Chamber if there is no reason to warrant considering it. Otherwise, the other party will be asked to comment on the request within a specified time limit. If the request is granted, the question will be decided by way of a judgment.

3.14 An example of the revision process is the case of *Pardo* v *France*,[13] which concerned the Court's original 1993 judgment. The applicant had complained of various violations including his right to a fair trial under Article 6(1), and in particular that he had not had the opportunity of an oral hearing despite the fact that the President of the Court of Appeal had announced that there would be such a hearing at a later date. The Court found no violation of Article 6(1) in its 1993 judgment because the applicant had failed to produce sufficient evidence of his version of events. When the applicant obtained copies of certain key documents, which had been retained in the domestic court case-file, he applied for revision of the original judgment in 1995. In reconsidering the position, the Court in 1996 found that the documents revealed that the applicant's version of events had been correct and it could not exclude the possibility that the documents might by their nature have had a decisive influence on the proceedings. Therefore, by five votes to four, the request for revision was found to be admissible and was referred to the Chamber that gave the original judgment. However, in its subsequent judgment in *Pardo*,[14] the Court dismissed the request for revision on the basis that the new documents did not cast doubt on the original decision of the Court in 1993.

3.15 Rule 80 has frequently been applied in circumstances where an applicant dies during the course of the proceedings, but this does not come to light until after the judgment is issued. It was applied, for example, in *Pupillo* v *Italy*[15] to award damages to the original applicant's heir, after the Court was notified shortly after its principal judgment that the applicant had died just before the judgment was published.[16]

---

[12] *Pardo* v *France*, No. 13416/87, 10.7.96.
[13] No. 13416/87, 10.7.96. See also *McGinley and Egan* v *UK*, Nos. 21825/93 and 25414/94, 28.1.00.
[14] No. 13416/87, 29.4.97.
[15] No. 41803/98, 18.12.01.
[16] See also *Guerrera and Fusco* v *Italy*, No. 40601/98, 31.7.03; *Lutz* v *France*, No. 49531/99, 25.11.03; *Bajrami* v *Albania*, No. 35853/04, 18.12.07; *Wypukoł-Piętka* v *Poland*, No. 3441/02, 8.6.10; *Dzhabrailovy* v *Russia*, No. 68860/10, 4.2.16; *Kavaklıoğlu and others* v *Turkey*, No. 15397/02, 14.6.16.

By contrast, however, in *EP v Italy*[17] the Court granted the Government's request for revision of the judgment in respect of just satisfaction under Article 41. In the original Chamber judgment,[18] the Court had found a violation of Article 6(1) (length of proceedings) and of Article 8 (interruption of contact between mother and daughter). However, the applicant had died just two months before that judgment had been published. The original judgment was amended to state that no amount of compensation for non-pecuniary damage was awarded as the Court had not been informed as to whom it could legitimately award the monies due. Furthermore, no award as to costs or expenses was to be made as the applicant's lawyer had failed to provide the Court with information that had been requested. In *Manushaqe Puto and others v Albania*,[19] the Court's original 2012 judgment was revised in 2014 after it came to light that in one of the applications the applicant's brother had died in 2009 (less than a month after the case was lodged), although the Court had not been informed. Therefore, 'in the interest of the good administration of justice' the Court halved the damages awarded in that application (reducing it to €680,000). In *Stoicescu v Romania*,[20] the Court accepted the Government's claim for revision of a previous judgment and declared the case inadmissible. The applicant had successfully brought an action in respect of the nationalisation of property that had belonged to his aunt, but it was subsequently discovered that he had lost his status as heir in domestic proceedings. **3.16**

Rule 80 may be applicable where there have been errors within the Court, such as those caused by IT defects. In *Damir Sibgatullin v Russia*[21] in 2012 the Court had found a violation of Article 38 (see 5.65) because of the Government's apparent failure to disclose certain witness statements which had been requested by the Court. However, in its revised judgment in 2014,[22] the Court accepted that the statements had in fact been uploaded to the Court's secure server, but that due to a technical glitch they were not traceable. Therefore, the Court revoked its earlier finding as regards Article 38. **3.17**

The Irish Government has recently made a request for the revision of the 1978 judgment in *Ireland v UK*[23] (concerning the use of the 'five interrogation techniques' by the British army in Northern Ireland) on the basis that new evidence had come to light (unearthed at the national archives in Kew) which had not been known to the Court. The Irish Government is seeking the Court's re-classification of the treatment as torture, and indeed one of the Court's questions to the parties is whether they 'consider that the documents produced by the Irish Government, on which the revision request is based, amount to facts which might by their nature have had a decisive influence on the conclusion whether the "five techniques of deep interrogation" amounted to "torture"'? **3.18**

---

[17] No. 31127/96, 3.5.01. See also *Gabay v Turkey*, No. 70829/01, 27.6.06 (case struck out due to applicant's death during the proceedings—no relative expressed a wish to continue the proceedings); *Eremiášová and Pechová v Czech Republic*, No. 23944/04, 20.6.13 (judgment revised due to death of one of the two applicants—struck out in respect of applicant who had died).

[18] No. 31127/96, 16.11.99.

[19] No. 604/07 et al, 4.11.14.

[20] No. 31551/96, 21.9.04.

[21] No. 1413/05, 24.4.12.

[22] No. 1413/05, 28.5.14.

[23] No. 5310/71, 18.1.78. The request was communicated on 22.3.16.

Enforcement of Judgments

Remedies

3.19 It is extremely important that applicants are clearly advised at the outset of the proceedings as to what the European Court may and may not do, in terms of providing remedies in respect of violations of the Convention. The effect of a judgment in which the Court has found a violation of the Convention is to impose a legal obligation on the respondent state to put an end to the breach and to make reparation for its consequences in such a way as to restore as far as possible the situation existing before the breach (*restitutio in integrum*). Therefore, if *restitutio in integrum* is possible, then it is for the state to carry it out, as the Court has no power to effect restitution.[24] If *restitutio in integrum* is in practice impossible, the respondent state is free to choose the means for complying with a judgment,[25] provided that those means are compatible with the conclusions set out in the Court's judgment.[26]

3.20 The Court has clarified its position by explaining that:[27]

> A judgment in which the Court finds a breach imposes on the respondent state a legal obligation not just to pay those concerned the sums awarded by way of just satisfaction, but also to choose, subject to supervision by the Committee of Ministers, the general and/or, if appropriate, individual measures to be adopted in their domestic legal order to put an end to the violation found by the Court and to redress so far as possible the effects.

3.21 The Court has also stated in relation to just satisfaction that:[28]

> Under Article 41 of the Convention the purposes of awarding sums by way of just satisfaction is to provide reparation solely for damage suffered by those concerned to the extent that such events constitute a consequence of the violation that cannot otherwise be remedied.

3.22 European Court judgments are therefore 'essentially declaratory in nature'.[29] In a case in which the applicant has successfully established that the Convention has been violated, the Court will issue a declaration that the Convention has been violated and it may also award compensation and costs. It will not, however, quash decisions of the domestic authorities or courts (including convictions),[30] strike down domestic legislation, *require* a state to alter its legislation[31] or otherwise require a respondent government to take particular measures within the national legal system (such as ordering the transfer of prisoners to the jurisdiction of another Convention state[32] or order repayment of fines). This reflects the fact that the European Court is adjudicating on breaches of international law. Nevertheless, the Court may in certain circumstances be willing to go further than issuing a declaration and awarding compensation, as is discussed in the following sections.

---

[24] See, e.g. *Iatridis* v *Greece*, No. 31107/96, 19.10.00.

[25] See, e.g. *Selçuk and Asker* v *Turkey*, Nos. 23184/94 and 23185/94, 24.4.98, para. 125.

[26] See, e.g. *Scozzari and Giunta* v *Italy*, Nos. 39221/98 and 41963/98, 13.7.00.

[27] *Scozzari and Giunta* v *Italy*, Nos. 39221/98 and 41963/98, 13.7.00, para. 249.

[28] *Ibid.*, para. 250.

[29] See, e.g. *Assanidze* v *Georgia*, No. 71503/01, 8.4.04, para. 202.

[30] See, e.g. *Schmautzer* v *Austria*, No. 15523/89, Series A, No. 328-A, 23.10.95, paras. 42–4; *Lyons and others* v *UK*, No. 15227/03, dec. 8.7.03.

[31] See, e.g. *Lundevall* v *Sweden*, No. 38629/97, 12.11.02, para. 44.

[32] Nos. 39221/98 and 41963/98, 13.7.00.

Systemic Convention violations and the 'pilot judgment procedure'

In addition to the Court's 'traditional' approach to redress (as outlined above from section **3.23** 3.19), the Court has been increasingly inclined in recent years to make more general reference in its judgments to obligations which it considers arise from the Convention and its jurisprudence. For example, in *Scozzari and Giunta* v *Italy*,[33] which concerned parental visits to children, the Court stated[34] that 'the relevant authorities, in this case the Youth Court, have a duty to exercise constant vigilance, particularly as regards action taken by the Social Services, to ensure the latter's conduct does not defeat the authorities' decisions'. In *Görgülü* v *Germany*,[35] the Court stated that, as a consequence of the violation of the applicant's Article 8 rights ensuing from the refusal of access and custody rights in relation to his son, the obligation on the state to abide by the judgment in accordance with Article 46 meant 'making it possible for the applicant to at least have access to his child'.

The Court may also make proposals as to 'general measures' which could be taken to alle- **3.24** viate a particular situation highlighted by a case before it. For example, the case of *Tan* v *Turkey*[36] concerned the inadequacies in the domestic law as to the monitoring of prisoners' correspondence. Applying Article 41, the Court stated that bringing the domestic law into conformity with Article 8 would be an appropriate way to put a stop to this type of violation. In two cases concerning applicants who were displaced from their homes during the Nagorno-Karabakh conflict between Armenia and Azerbaijan in the early 1990s, and who had subsequently been unable to return, the Court found continuing violations of Article 1 of Protocol No. 1, as well as Article 8.[37] As regards the question of redress, the Grand Chamber stipulated that:

> At the present stage, and pending a comprehensive peace agreement, it would appear particularly important to establish a property claims mechanism, which should be easily accessible and provide procedures operating with flexible evidentiary standards, allowing the applicants and others in their situation to have their property rights restored and to obtain compensation for the loss of their enjoyment.[38]

Where a Convention state fails to take adequate action to amend legislation that has been **3.25** found to breach the Convention, the Court has been increasingly willing to comment on that fact in subsequent judgments on the same point. For example, in *Messina* v *Italy (No. 2)*, which concerned legislation relating to the monitoring of prisoners' correspondence (an issue which had already been found to violate Article 8), the Court commented as follows:

> The Court has already held that section 18, which does not lay down rules on either the period of validity of the measures for monitoring prisoners' correspondence or the reasons which may warrant them, does not indicate with sufficient clarity the scope and manner of exercise of the discretion conferred on the public authorities in the relevant sphere …
>
> … The Court emphasises that to date neither the amendment of section 35 of the Prison Administration Act mentioned by the Government … nor the bill presented to the Senate by

---

[33] Nos. 39221/98 and 41963/98, 13.7.00.
[34] *Ibid.*, para. 181.
[35] No. 74969/01, 26.2.04, para. 64.
[36] No. 9469/03, 3.7.07.
[37] *Chiragov and others* v *Armenia*, No. 13216/05, 16.6.15; *Sargsyan* v *Azerbaijan*, No. 40167/06, 16.6.15.
[38] *Chiragov and others* v *Armenia*, No. 13216/05, 16.6.15, para. 199; *Sargsyan* v *Azerbaijan*, No. 40167/06, 16.6.15, para. 238.

the Minister of Justice on 23 July 1999 which was intended to change the applicable law to bring it into line with the Court's judgments in the Calogero Diana and Domenichini cases … seem to have been adopted. Moreover, several other applications which likewise concern the monitoring of prisoners' correspondence are pending before the Court.[39]

3.26 The Court has also taken steps to highlight the problem of the length of proceedings in cases emanating from Italy. The Court has found that the accumulation of breaches of the reasonable time requirement in Italian cases has resulted in a practice incompatible with the Convention, and that this accumulation amounts to an aggravating circumstance in finding a violation of Article 6(1) of the Convention.[40]

3.27 Such developments reflected the increasingly overwhelming burden on the Court created by 'clone' cases (i.e. similar repeat violations) and the Court's impatience with states that fail to remedy laws which already violate the Convention. In a Resolution adopted in 2004 the Committee of Ministers urged the Court to take further steps to assist states by identifying underlying problems. The Resolution invited the Court:[41]

> as far as possible, to identify, in its judgments finding a violation of the Convention, what it considers to be an underlying systemic problem and the source of this problem, in particular when it is likely to give rise to numerous applications, so as to assist states in finding the appropriate solution and the Committee of Ministers in supervising the execution of judgments …

3.28 The Committee of Ministers has also urged states in this context to reassess the effectiveness of domestic remedies, and in particular to: 'review, following Court judgments which point to structural or general deficiencies in national law or practice, the effectiveness of the existing domestic remedies and, where necessary, set up effective remedies, in order to avoid repetitive cases being brought before the Court'.[42]

3.29 The Committee of Ministers furthermore sought to improve its process for the supervision of the enforcement of judgments, by urging the Ministers' Deputies to: 'take specific and effective measures to improve and accelerate the execution of the Court's judgments, notably those revealing an underlying systemic problem'.[43]

Pilot judgments[44]

3.30 As a result of these various impetuses, since 2004 the Court has developed a markedly more rigorous approach in seeking to tackle systemic violations of the Convention and reduce its

---

[39] No. 25498/94, 28.8.00, paras. 81–2.

[40] *Bottazzi v Italy*, No. 34884/97, 28.7.99, para. 22 (the Grand Chamber referred to more than 1,400 European Commission reports resulting in a Committee of Ministers' resolution finding Italy in violation of Article 6(1) for the same reason). See also, for example, *Mennitto v Italy*, No. 33804/96, 5.10.00.

[41] Resolution Res(2004)3 of the Committee of Ministers on judgments revealing an underlying systemic problem, 12 May 2004.

[42] Recommendation Rec(2004)6 of the Committee of Ministers to Member States on the improvement of domestic remedies, 12 May 2004. See also Recommendation Rec(2004)5 of the Committee of Ministers to Member States on the verification of the compatibility of draft laws, existing laws and administrative practice with the standards laid down in the European Convention on Human Rights, 12 May 2004.

[43] *Ensuring the effectiveness of the implementation of the European Convention on Human Rights at national and European levels*, Declaration of the Committee of Ministers, 12 May 2004.

[44] See also P. Leach, H. Hardman, S. Stephenson and B. Blitz, *Responding to Systemic Human Rights Violations—An analysis of pilot judgments of the European Court of Human Rights and their impact at national level*, Intersentia, 2010.

burden of repetitive cases, through its use of the 'pilot judgment procedure' and by invoking Article 46 of the Convention. The first judgment in which the Court responded to these resolutions and recommendations of the Committee of Ministers was the 'pilot judgment' in *Broniowski v Poland*[45] in which the Grand Chamber found a violation of Article 1 of Protocol No. 1 as a result of the failure to compensate the applicant for property which he and his family had lost (which was now in Lviv, Ukraine) after being repatriated to Poland following World War II (a group of similar cases are known collectively as the 'Bug River cases'). The Court stated that it was 'inherent in the Court's findings that the violation of the applicant's right guaranteed by Article 1 of Protocol No. 1 originated in a widespread problem that resulted from a malfunctioning of Polish legislation and administrative practice and which has affected and remains capable of affecting a large number of persons'.[46] The Court acknowledged that 80,000 people were affected by the systemic problem[47] and that 167 related applications were pending before the Court: 'this is not only an aggravating factor as regards the state's responsibility under the Convention for an existing or past state of affairs, but also represents a threat to the future effectiveness of the Convention machinery'.[48] Thus the Court stated that general measures were required at a national level in order to remedy the systemic defect and provide individual redress. The Court subsequently decided to adjourn all pending and future applications that raised the same issues, until measures were taken at a national level in order to implement the *Broniowski* judgment.[49] The pilot judgment procedure was then closed in respect of the Bug River cases in September 2008, following the introduction of new domestic legislation.[50]

By the end of 2009, the Court had issued six pilot judgments: two concerning Poland **3.31** (*Broniowski v Poland*[51] and *Hutten-Czapska v Poland*[52]), three relating to states of the former Soviet Union (*Burdov (No. 2) v Russia*,[53] *Olaru and others v Moldova*,[54] and *Yuriy Nikolayevich Ivanov v Ukraine*[55]) and the other was *Suljagić v Bosnia and Herzegovina*.[56] In each case the right to property (Article 1 of Protocol No. 1) was found to have been violated. The right to a fair hearing (Article 6(1)) was breached in three cases, and the right to an effective domestic remedy (Article 13) was violated in two cases. In each of the pilot

---

[45] No. 31443/96, 22.6.04.

[46] *Ibid.*, para. 189.

[47] Relating to an area known as the 'territories beyond the Bug River', following the fixing of Poland's eastern border along the Bug River, after World War II.

[48] No. 31443/96, 22.6.04, para. 193.

[49] See *'Bug River' Cases Adjourned*, European Court Press Release, 31.8.04.

[50] E.G. v *Poland (and 175 other Bug River applications)*, No. 50425/99, dec. 23.9.08. See also *Wolkenberg and others* v *Poland*, No. 50003/99, dec. 4.12.07 and *Witkowska-Tobola* v *Poland*, No. 11208/02, dec. 4.12.07.

[51] No. 31443/96, 22.6.04.

[52] No. 35014/97, 19.6.06.

[53] No. 33509/04, 15.1.09. As to the new domestic remedy introduced after *Burdov (No. 2)*, see *Nagovitsyn and Nalgiyev v Russia*, Nos. 27451/09 and 60650/09, dec. 23.9.10; *Fakhretdinov v Russia*, Nos. 26716/09, 67576/09 and 7698/10, dec. 23.9.10. In *Ilyushkin and others v Russia*, No. 5734/08, 17.4.12, the Court found that the new legislation applied only to the non-enforcement of judgments establishing pecuniary obligations and not to those imposing obligations in kind. The applicants were former service personnel who had secured domestic judgments requiring the provision of housing to them. The Court found violations of Article 13, 6(1) and Article 1 of Protocol No. 1. See also the subsequent pilot judgment in *Gerasimov and others v Russia*, No. 29920/05 et al, 1.7.14 (relating to housing awards and other awards in kind).

[54] Nos. 476/07, 22539/05, 17911/08 and 13136/07, 28.7.09.

[55] No. 40450/04, 15.10.09.

[56] No. 27912/02, 3.11.09.

judgments against Russia, Ukraine and Moldova, the Court found a violation of Article 6 on account of the systemic failure to execute domestic court judgments. In *Hutten-Czapska* the Polish state was found not to have given effective protection to landlords' rights.[57] In *Suljagić* v *Bosnia and Herzegovina* the Court found a systemic violation of Article 1 of Protocol No. 1 to the Convention as a result of the Government's failure adequately to reimburse applicants for foreign currency savings deposited in national banks in the former Yugoslavia before 1991. The Court accordingly stipulated in the operative provisions of the judgment that Government bonds should be issued and outstanding instalments be issued within six months.[58]

3.32 These six cases all share the following features, which it is suggested are the criteria that define a 'full' pilot judgment:[59]

(1) the explicit application by the Court of the pilot judgment procedure; and
(2) the identification by the Court of a systemic violation of the Convention; and
(3) general measures are stipulated in the operative part of the judgment in order that the respondent state should resolve the systemic issue (that may be subject to specific time limits).

3.33 A pilot judgment *may* also adjourn all other cases arising from the same systemic issue, either for a particular period of time, or, more generally, pending the resolution of the issue by the state (as was in fact the case for each of these six judgments). However, other cases will not be adjourned where the circumstances of the case effectively preclude further delays (such as cases concerning poor prison conditions).[60]

3.34 The Court subsequently issued an Information Note on the pilot judgment procedure,[61] and a factsheet[62] and it also issued a new Rule on the pilot judgment procedure—Rule 61 of the Rules of Court—which came into force in April 2011. Rule 61 provides that before initiating the pilot judgment procedure, the Court will consult the parties as to whether the case results from a structural or systemic problem or other similar dysfunction, and as to the suitability of the procedure.[63] Rule 61 stipulates, inter alia, that:

- pilot cases will be granted priority treatment (in accordance with Rule 41);
- the Court will identify both the nature of the structural or systemic problem and the type of remedial measures that the respondent state is required to take;
- the Court may impose time limits within which the remedial measures must be adopted; and

---

[57] The pilot judgment procedure was closed in relation to this issue in March 2011. See: *Association of Real Property Owners in Łódź* v *Poland*, No. 3485/02, dec. 8.3.11.

[58] See also *Ališić and others* v *Bosnia and Herzegovina, Croatia, Serbia, Slovenia and former Yugoslav Republic of Macedonia*, No. 60642/08, 16.7.14.

[59] A distinction is drawn here with 'quasi-pilot judgments' (or 'Article 46 judgments') which are discussed below. Only very rarely in 'quasi-pilot' judgments does the Court also prescribe general measures in the operative part of the judgment (two examples being *Lukenda* v *Slovenia*, No. 23032/02, 6.10.05 and *Xenides-Arestis* v *Turkey*, No. 46347/99, 22.12.05).

[60] See, e.g. *Varga and others* v *Hungary*, No. 14097/12, 10.3.15.

[61] Available at http://www.echr.coe.int/Documents/Pilot_judgment_procedure_ENG.pdf.

[62] Available at http://www.echr.coe.int/Documents/FS_Pilot_judgments_ENG.pdf.

[63] This does not, however, give the parties a right of veto. For example, the Court applied the pilot judgment procedure in *W.D.* v *Belgium* (No. 73548/13, 6.9.16) in spite of the Government's objections.

- the Court may adjourn the examination of all similar applications (but the Court may at any time examine an adjourned application 'where the interests of the proper administration of justice so require').[64]

Since 2009, further pilot judgments have also been issued in respect of a range of states, **3.35** including Germany, Greece, Romania, the United Kingdom, Bulgaria, Hungary, Poland and Belgium. In *Rumpf v Germany*[65] the Court issued a pilot judgment in respect of cases concerning the excessive length of civil proceedings, which had already been the subject of numerous previous European Court judgments. It required the Government to introduce an effective domestic remedy for length of proceedings cases 'without delay', and at the latest within a year.[66] A similar problem in relation to the length of administrative, criminal and civil proceedings in Greece has been found in three pilot judgments.[67] In 2011 the Court issued a pilot judgment as regards the length of criminal proceedings in Bulgaria, having already handed down more than 80 such judgments, and having 200 similar cases pending.[68] It required the introduction of remedies (within a year) which were capable of both expediting the process and providing redress for past delays. A similar decision was made in respect of Turkey in the *Ümmühan Kaplan* judgment in 2012,[69] and, in 2015, as regards Hungarian civil proceedings in *Gazsó v Hungary*.[70] When the pilot judgment in *Rutkowski and others v Poland*[71] was issued in 2015 there were another 650 cases pending before the Court concerning the length of both civil and criminal proceedings in Poland. This issue had been the subject of the *Kudła v Poland* judgment in 2000,[72] which had led to legislative amendments in 2004, but the cases forming part of the *Rutkowski* judgment showed that the domestic remedies still remained deficient. The Court stipulated that the authorities should therefore ensure the implementation of comprehensive, large-scale legislative and administrative actions, involving authorities at various levels, and they were given two years in which to do so.

---

[64] For example, in January 2012, as a result of the failure of the Ukrainian Government to introduce general measures following the pilot judgment in *Yuriy Nikolayevich Ivanov v Ukraine* (No. 40450/04, 15.10.09)—concerning the non-enforcement of domestic judgments—the Court decided to resume consideration of such applications. See: *Court decides to resume examination of applications concerning non-enforcement of domestic decisions in Ukraine*, European Court press release, 29.2.12.

[65] No. 46344/06, 2.9.10. See also *Sürmeli v Germany*, No. 75529/01, 8.6.06.

[66] The remedy which was subsequently introduced (Protracted Court Proceedings and Criminal Investigations Act) entered into force in December 2011 and was found by the Court to be an effective domestic remedy which would need to be utilised before applying to the Court (see *Taron v Germany*, No. 53126/07, dec. 29.5.12).

[67] *Vassilios Athanasiou and others v Greece*, No. 50973/08, 21.12.10 (administrative proceedings); *Michelioudakis v Greece*, No. 54447/10, 3.4.12 (criminal proceedings); *Glykantzi v Greece*, No. 40150/09, 30.10.12 (civil proceedings).

[68] *Dimitrov and Hamanov v Bulgaria*, No. 48059/07 & 2708/09, 10.5.11 (see para. 125 as to the requisite elements of an effective remedy). See also the pilot judgment in *Finger v Bulgaria*, No. 37346/05, 10.5.11 (as regards civil proceedings) and the subsequent admissibility decisions in *Balakchiev and others v Bulgaria*, No. 65187/10 and *Valcheva and Abrashev v Bulgaria*, No. 6194/11 and 34887/11, dec. 18.6.13.

[69] *Ümmühan Kaplan v Turkey*, No. 24240/07, 20.3.12. See also the subsequent admissibility decisions of *Turgut and others v Turkey*, No. 4860/09, dec. 26.3.13 and *Demiroğlu and others v Turkey*, No. 56125/10, dec. 4.6.13.

[70] No. 48322/12, 16.7.15.

[71] No. 72287/10 et al, 7.7.15.

[72] No. 30210/96, 26.10.00.

3.36   The systemic problem in Romania which was the subject of a pilot judgment in *Maria Atanasiu and others* v *Romania*[73] was the applicants' inability to obtain restitution of their nationalised properties or to secure compensation. In *Manushaqe Puto and others* v *Albania*,[74] the systemic failure to ensure the enforcement of court decisions concerning compensation for property owners was the subject of a pilot judgment. As successive UK Governments had failed to amend the domestic law in response to the judgment in *Hirst* v *UK (No. 2)*,[75] concerning the blanket ban on convicted prisoners from voting whilst in prison, the Court issued a pilot judgment in 2010 in the case of *Greens and M. T.* v *UK*.[76] Noting that there were 2,500 similar pending cases, the Court also stipulated that the Government was required to bring forward proposals to amend the legislation within six months of the judgment becoming final.

3.37   The case of *Kurić and others* v *Slovenia*[77] concerned the position of the 'erased'—former citizens of Yugoslavia whose names were taken off the register of permanent residents and who therefore became de facto stateless after Slovenian independence. Having found that people in the applicants' position had not been awarded proper financial redress for the years during which they were in a position of vulnerability and legal insecurity, the Grand Chamber applied the pilot judgment procedure and directed the Government to set up an ad hoc domestic compensation scheme (within one year).

3.38   The unacceptable state of prisons has resulted in several pilot judgments, including cases against Italy,[78] Bulgaria[79] and Hungary,[80] as well as a 'quasi-pilot' judgment concerning Moldova.[81] Applying Article 46 in *Ananyev and others* v *Russia*,[82] the respondent Government was required to introduce a combination of effective remedies (both preventive and compensatory)—and to produce a binding time frame to do so, within six months of the judgment. Furthermore, within 12 months, redress was to be provided to all victims of the inhuman or degrading conditions of detention in Russian remand prisons who had applications pending before the European Court.

3.39   In *W.D.* v *Belgium*[83] the Court identified a structural deficiency in the Belgian psychiatric detention system, and urged the Government to take action to reduce the number of offenders with mental disorders who were detained in prison psychiatric wings without being given appropriate treatment.

---

[73] Nos. 30767/05 and 33800/06, 12.10.10. See also *Viaşu* v *Romania*, No. 75951/01, 9.12.08; *Faimblat* v *Romania*, No. 23066/02, 13.1.09; *Katz* v *Romania*, No. 29739/03, 20.1.09. In *Preda and others* v *Romania*, No. 9584/02 et al, 29.4.14 the Court considered the new law which had been introduced in 2013 in response to the pilot judgment in *Maria Atanasiu*, finding it only partially effective.

[74] No. 604/07, 31.7.12.

[75] No. 74025/01, 6.10.05.

[76] Nos. 60041/08 and 60054/08, 23.11.10. See also *Firth and others* v *UK*, No. 47784/09 et al, 12.8.14.

[77] No. 26828/06, 26.6.12. See also the subsequent judgment on just satisfaction issued on 12.3.14. In *Anastasov and others v Slovenia*, No. 65020/13, dec. 18.10.16 the Court closed the pilot judgment procedure on the basis of the adequacy of the compensation scheme which had subsequently been established.

[78] *Torreggiani and others* v *Italy*, No. 43517/09, 8.1.13. See also *Stella and others* v *Italy*, Nos. 49169/09 et al, dec. 16.9.14.

[79] *Neshkov and others* v *Bulgaria*, No. 36925/10, 27.1.15.

[80] *Varga and others* v *Hungary*, No. 14097/12, 10.3.15.

[81] *Shishanov* v *Moldova*, No. 11353/06, 15.9.15.

[82] Nos. 42525/07 and 60800/08, 10.1.12.

[83] No. 73548/13, 6.9.16 (violations of Articles 3, 5(1) and (4) and 13, combined with Article 3).

Article 46 ('quasi-pilot') judgments

In addition to 'pilot judgments', the Court's increasingly frequent practice is to invoke Article **3.40**
46 in highlighting systemic or structural problems which have been the source of repeated
Convention violations. They usually stop short however of including binding obligations
in the operative provisions of the judgments, and for that reason they can be distinguished
from 'full' pilot judgments.[84] In these decisions the Court refers to the legal obligation under
Article 46 to introduce general and/or individual measures in the domestic legal system in
order to end the violations and provide redress.

In a number of cases the Court has found that there was a structural problem that amounted **3.41**
to a practice that was incompatible with the Convention, for example relating to over-
crowding in Polish prisons and remand centres,[85] and the excessive length of pre-trial detention in Poland.[86]

The Court has also identified widespread and systemic problems relating to pre-trial deten- **3.42**
tion in Turkey. These cases have concerned both the length of pre-trial detention under
Article 5(3) (in almost all of the decisions the domestic courts ordered the applicants' detention pending trial using identical, stereotypical terms) and the absence of any remedy in
Turkish law within the meaning of Article 5(4) by which challenges can be made to the lawfulness of pre-trial detention. As these problems were found to have originated from the malfunctioning of the Turkish criminal justice system and the state of the Turkish legislation, the
Court stipulated that general measures were required to reform the system.[87] The Court has
also invoked Article 46 in stipulating general measures in order to protect the health of pre-
trial detainees in Turkey.[88] Similar problems concerning compliance with Article 5 were also
identified in *Kharchenko* v *Ukraine*,[89] with the Court calling for the urgent implementation

---

[84] Only rarely in 'quasi-pilot' judgments does the Court also prescribe general measures in the operative part
of the judgment (e.g. *Lukenda* v *Slovenia*, No. 23032/02, 6.10.05 and *Xenides-Arestis* v *Turkey*, No. 46347/99,
22.12.05). In neither of these judgments, however, did the Court state expressly that it was applying the pilot
judgment procedure. Other examples include: *Šekerović and Pašalić* v *Bosnia and Herzegovina*, Nos. 5920/04
and 67396/09, 8.3.11, in which the Court ordered that the relevant domestic legislation be amended in order
to resolve systemic discrimination in the pension system; *Zorica Jovanović* v *Serbia*, No. 21794/08, 26.3.13,
in which the Court required that the authorities establish an effective mechanism of redress to provide credible information to parents of babies who had died or gone missing from Serbian hospitals in the 1970s to
the 1990s; *M.C. and others* v *Italy*, No. 5376/11, 3.9.13, in which the authorities were required to guarantee
the payment of appropriate compensation to individuals who had been contaminated by HIV, hepatitis B or
hepatitis C following blood transfusions; *Vlad and others* v *Romania*, Nos. 40756/06, 41508/07 and 50806/
07, 26.11.13, in which the Romanian authorities were required to establish an appropriate system of redress
for length of proceedings cases. The Court's practice has not always been clear or consistent. For example, the
judgment in *Doğan and others* v *Turkey*, Nos. 8803–8811/02, 8813/02 and 8815–8819/02, 29.6.04 (concerning the applicants' forced evictions from their homes) was not defined by the Court as a pilot judgment, but in
the later admissibility decision in *İçyer* v *Turkey*, No. 18888/02, dec. 12.1.06 the Court referred to *Doğan* as a
'pilot judgment' (paras. 73 and 94).
[85] *Orchowski* v *Poland*, No. 17885/04, 22.10.09 and *Norbert Sikorski* v *Poland*, No. 17599/05, 22.10.09.
The subsequent admissibility decisions of *Łatak* v *Poland*, No. 52070/08, dec. 12.10.10 and *Łomiński* v *Poland*,
No. 33502/09, dec. 12.10.10 describe both *Orchowski* and *Norbert Sikorski* as 'pilot judgments' although in
neither case did the operative provisions include any express obligation to implement particular measures
within the domestic system.
[86] *Kauczor* v *Poland*, No. 45219/06, 3.2.09.
[87] *Cahit Demirel* v *Turkey*, No. 18623/03, 7.7.09.
[88] *Gülay Çetin* v *Turkey*, No. 44084/10, 5.3.13.
[89] No. 40107/02, 10.2.11. See also *Chanyev* v *Ukraine*, No. 46193/13, 9.10.14; *Ignatov* v *Ukraine*, No.
40583/15, 15.12.16.

of reforms to Ukraine's legislation and administrative practice. Systemic problems relating to the ill-treatment of criminal suspects in police custody were identified in *Kaverzin v Ukraine*.[90] In *Vasilescu v Belgium*[91] Article 46 was applied to require the adoption of general measures in order to guarantee prisoners conditions of detention compatible with Article 3, and to provide them with a suitable domestic remedy. The Court has also invoked Article 46 in relation to the length of legal proceedings in Slovenia, noting 'the persistent backlog in the Slovenian courts',[92] and to require the Serbian authorities to ensure that pensions are paid to insured people in Kosovo.[93]

3.43 The Court has frequently invoked Article 46 having identified a flaw in domestic legislation, and in order to recommend that it be amended, under the supervision of the Committee of Ministers. Such cases have concerned, for example, the following issues:

- the excessive length of pre-trial detention;[94]
- an effective remedy to challenge detention pending trial and to claim compensation;[95]
- the detention of juveniles;[96]
- the right to a fair trial within a reasonable time;[97]
- the right to a hearing for prisoners charged with disciplinary measures;[98]
- the practice of holding trials *in absentia*;[99]
- the system of review of whole life sentences;[100]
- the absence of a prosecuting party in cases relating to administrative offences;[101]
- the system for disciplining judges;[102]
- the inadequacy of compensation for expropriated property;[103]
- shortcomings in the law regulating the restitution of agricultural land;[104]
- the rights of leaseholders in relation to 'ground-lease' contracts;[105]
- a rent control scheme imposing low level rents on landlords;[106]
- restrictions as regards compensation for the transfer of allotment land and in letting out the land at a rent reasonably related to its value;[107]

---

[90] No. 23893/03, 15.5.12.

[91] No. 64682/12, 25.11.14. See also *Bamouhammad v Belgium*, No. 47687/13, 17.11.15.

[92] *Lukenda v Slovenia*, No. 23032/02, 6.10.05 (at the time of the judgment there were 500 length of proceedings cases pending against Slovenia at the European Court).

[93] *Grudić v Serbia*, No. 31925/08, 17.4.12.

[94] *Zherebin v Russia*, No. 51445/09, 24.3.16.

[95] *Altınok v Turkey*, No. 31610/08, 29.11.11.

[96] *Grabowski v Poland*, No. 57722/12, 30.6.15.

[97] *Vlad and others v Romania*, Nos. 40756/06, 41508/07 and 50806/07, 26.11.13; *Barta and Drajkó v Hungary*, No. 35729/12, 17.12.13; *Luli and others v Albania*, No. 64480/09 et al, 1.4.14.

[98] *Gülmez v Turkey*, No. 16330/02, 20.5.08.

[99] *Sejdovic v Italy*, No. 56581/00, 10.11.04 and 1.3.06 (and see, originally, *Colozza v Italy*, No. 9024/80, 12.2.85); *R.R. v Italy*, No. 42191/02, 9.6.05.

[100] *László Magyar v Hungary*, No. 73593/10, 20.5.14; *Harakchiev and Tolumov v Bulgaria*, Nos. 15018/11 and 61199/12, 8.7.14.

[101] *Karelin v Russia*, No. 926/08, 20.9.16.

[102] *Oleksandr Volkov v Ukraine*, No. 21722/11, 9.1.13.

[103] *Scordino v Italy (No. 1)*, No. 36813/97, 29.7.04 & 29.3.06; *Scordino v Italy (No. 3)*, No. 43662/98, 17.5.05 and 6.3.07; *Guiso-Gallisay v Italy*, No. 58858/00, 21.10.08; *Driza v Albania*, No. 33771/02, 13.11.07; *Ramadhi and 5 others v Albania*, No. 38222/02, 13.11.07.

[104] *Mutishev and others v Bulgaria*, No. 18967/03, 28.2.12.

[105] *Lindheim and others v Norway*, Nos. 13221/08 and 2139/10, 12.6.12.

[106] *Bittó and others v Slovakia*, No. 30255/09, 28.1.14.

[107] *Urbárska obec Trenčianske Biskupice v Slovakia*, No. 74258/01, 27.11.07.

- changes in the law to ensure that leadership conflicts in religious communities are resolved by the religious community concerned and that disputes about the civil consequences of such conflicts are decided by the courts;[108]
- the introduction of additional safeguards in deportation cases;[109]
- structural malfunctioning within the health service, requiring changes to the rules governing forensic medical expert reports;[110]
- an effective mechanism of redress to provide credible information to parents of babies who had died or gone missing from Serbian hospitals in the 1970s to the 1990s;[111]
- discriminatory legislation relating to the naming of children;[112]
- the establishment of a right of direct access to a court for a person who has been partially deprived of legal capacity,[113] and the right of independent representation for people with mental health disabilities;[114]
- the right to civilian service, as an alternative for conscientious objectors to military service;[115]
- a legislative lacuna concerning freedom of assembly;[116]
- the investigation of ill-treatment by the police;[117]
- the regulation of the use of tear gas during demonstrations,[118] and as regards the policing of demonstrations more generally,[119] and the judicial scrutiny of demonstrations;[120]
- the payment of appropriate compensation to individuals who had been contaminated by HIV, hepatitis B or hepatitis C following blood transfusions;[121]
- discriminatory constitutional provisions concerning the right to stand for election;[122]
- the implementation of domestic court judgments against the state;[123] and
- the amendment of a settlement plan to ensure compliance with domestic court judgments ordering the payment of war damages.[124]

It is reasonably common for the Court to state that 'to bring the relevant domestic law **3.44** into compliance with the Convention would constitute an appropriate form of redress by which to put an end to the violation in question'. It has done so, for example, in relation to the law in Turkey banning the publication of statements of terrorist organisations,[125] the

---

[108] *Holy Synod of the Bulgarian Orthodox Church (Metropolitan Inokentiy) and others* v Bulgaria, Nos. 41203 and 35677/04, 22.1.09

[109] *M and others* v Bulgaria, No. 41416/08, 26.7.11; *Auad* v Bulgaria, No. 46390/10, 11.10.11.

[110] *Aydoğdu* v Turkey, No. 40448/06, 30.8.16.

[111] *Zorica Jovanović* v Serbia, No. 21794/08, 26.3.13.

[112] *Cusan and Fazzo* v Italy, No. 77/07, 7.1.14.

[113] *Stanev* v Bulgaria, No. 36760/06, 17.1.12.

[114] *Centre for Legal Resources on behalf of Valentin Câmpeanu* v Romania, No. 47848/08, 17.7.14.

[115] *Erçep* v Turkey, No. 43965/04, 22.11.11.

[116] *Vyerentsov* v Ukraine, No. 20372/11, 11.4.13.

[117] *Cestaro* v Italy, No. 6884/11, 7.4.15.

[118] *Abdullah Yaşa and others* v Turkey, No. 44827/08, 16.7.13; *Ataykaya* v Turkey, No. 50275/08, 22.7.14.

[119] *İzci* v Turkey, No. 42606/05, 23.7.13.

[120] *Süleyman Çelebi and others* v Turkey, No. 37273/10 et al, 24.5.16.

[121] *M.C. and others* v Italy, No. 5376/11, 3.9.13.

[122] *Zornić* v Bosnia and Herzegovina, No. 3681/06, 15.7.14.

[123] *Foundation Hostel for Students of the Reformed Church and Stanomirescu* v Romania, Nos. 2699/03 and 43597/07, 7.1.14.

[124] *Đurić and others* v Bosnia and Herzegovina, Nos. 79867/12 et al, 20.1.15. See also *Čolić and others* v Bosnia and Herzegovina, Nos. 1218/07 et al, 10.11.09.

[125] *Gözel and Özer* v Turkey, Nos. 43453/04 and 31098/05, 6.7.10.

Moldovan law regulating broadcasting (to prevent governmental interference),[126] and to ensure that the Turkish educational system respected parents' convictions (in relation to religious instruction).[127]

3.45 The Court may be more prescriptive in indicating the type of general or individual measure that could be taken in order to put an end to a situation in question. The Court has identified a number of systemic problems relating to the procedure for the expropriation of land in Turkey. In *Sarica and Dilaver v Turkey*,[128] the Court applied Article 46 in stating that the authorities would need to take measures to prevent the unlawful occupation of immovable property, and to adopt provisions to hold to account those responsible for unlawful expropriations. Furthermore, in *Yetiş and others v Turkey*[129] the Court recommended the incorporation into the Turkish legal system of a mechanism to take account of depreciation in the value of compensation for expropriation resulting from the length of proceedings and/or inflation. A structural problem with the Maltese housing legislation was identified in *Ghigo v Malta*[130] in respect of restrictions on rent obtained by property owners. The Court advocated the introduction of a mechanism in domestic law which maintained a fair balance between the interests of landlords, including their entitlement to derive profit from their property, and the wider interests of the community, which included the availability of sufficient accommodation for the less well-off. Having found in *Yordanova v Bulgaria*[131] that the proposed eviction of members of a Roma community violated Article 8, the Court applied Article 46 to stipulate both general measures (legislative reform) and individual measures (the repeal or suspension of the eviction order). As a result of the inadequacies of schooling for Roma children, the Court found a violation of Article 14 in conjunction with Article 2 of Protocol No. 1 in *Sampani and others v Greece*,[132] and, applying Article 46, it recommended that the applicants should be enrolled at another state school (or at alternative educational institutions for those who had already reached the age of majority).

3.46 Where an applicant is no longer within the jurisdiction of the respondent state, the Court has acknowledged that it may be more difficult for it to take remedial measures; however, it is not exempt from doing so, and indeed the Court has explicitly stipulated that the state is still required 'to find out and use in good faith such legal, diplomatic and/or practical means as may be necessary to secure to the maximum possible extent the applicant's right which the Court has found to have been violated'.[133] In the case of *Al-Saadoon and Mufdhi v UK*,[134] which concerned the applicants' detention by the British armed forces in southern Iraq in 2003, and their subsequent transfer to the Iraqi authorities, the Court found that the respondent Government's compliance with Article 3 would mean taking all possible steps to obtain an assurance from the Iraqi authorities that they would not be subjected to the death

---

[126] *Manole and others v Moldova*, No. 13936/02, 17.9.09.

[127] *Hasan and Eylem Zengin v Turkey*, No. 1448/04, 9.10.07; *Mansur Yalçın and others v Turkey*, No. 21163/11, 16.9.14.

[128] No. 11765/05, 27.5.10.

[129] No. 40349/056, 6.7.10.

[130] No. 31122/05, 17.7.08.

[131] No. 25446/06, 24.4.12.

[132] No. 59608/09, 11.12.12.

[133] *Savriddin Dzhurayev v Russia*, No. 71386/10, 25.4.13, para. 253.

[134] No. 61498/08, 2.3.10.

penalty.[135] In *Hirst Jamaa and others* v *Italy*,[136] the Grand Chamber found that the transfer back to Libya of migrants whose boats were intercepted on the high seas violated Article 3 because of their exposure to a risk of being ill-treated in Libya, and of being arbitrarily repatriated to the countries of origin—Somalia and Eritrea. It therefore stipulated that the Italian Government should take all possible steps to obtain assurances from the Libyan authorities that the applicants would not be treated incompatibly with Article 3, or arbitrarily repatriated. Following the forcible transfer of the applicant in *Savriddin Dzhurayev* v *Russia*[137] to Tajikistan (in breach of a Rule 39 order), the Court found that it was still possible for the Russian authorities to take tangible measures with a view to protecting the applicant against the risks to his life and health, including carrying out an effective investigation into the incident. In view of the evidence of repeated abductions of individuals from Russia and their forcible transfer to countries in Central Asia 'by deliberate circumvention of due process', the Court went on to stipulate general measures including the establishment of an effective mechanism to protect individuals from kidnapping and forced removal, and a system for investigating every breach of the Court's interim measures indications.

The case of *Klaus and Iouri Kiladze* v *Georgia*[138] highlighted a 'legislative void' which prevented **3.47** victims of political repression in the Soviet era from obtaining compensation. The Court invoked Article 46 in also holding that the authorities were required to act swiftly to adopt legislative, administrative and budgetary measures in order to plug the gap. In *Poghosyan* v *Georgia*[139] the Court identified a systemic problem in Georgia concerning the failure to provide adequate medical care to prisoners infected with viral hepatitis C, and other diseases. In applying Article 46, the Court proposed that the authorities should take legislative and administrative steps to prevent the transmission of viral hepatitis C in prisons, to introduce screening arrangements and to ensure timely and effective treatment. Having highlighted the serious and the structural nature of the problem of overcrowding and inadequate living and sanitary conditions in Polish detention facilities in *Sławomir Musiał* v *Poland*,[140] the Court held that the Government must secure 'at the earliest possible date' adequate conditions for the applicant's detention, including the requisite psychiatric treatment and constant medical supervision. *Amirov* v *Russia*[141] concerned the inadequate medical treatment received by the applicant in prison, a paraplegic who used a wheelchair and who suffered from a range of illnesses affecting his nervous, urinary, muscular and endocrine systems. Applying Article 46, the Court ordered his admission to a specialised medical facility.

The Court invoked Article 46 in *Dybeku* v *Albania*[142] in urging the Albanian authorities **3.48** to take the necessary measures as a matter of urgency to secure appropriate conditions of

---

[135] See also *Al Nashiri* v *Poland*, No. 28761/11, 24.7.14 (the Polish Government was required to obtain similar assurances from the US Government in respect of the applicant's 'extraordinary rendition').

[136] No. 27765/09, 23.2.12.

[137] No. 71386/10, 25.4.13. See also *Mamazhonov* v *Russia*, No. 17239/13, 23.10.14. See further *Kim* v *Russia*, No. 44260/13, 17.7.14 (general measures requiring a mechanism allowing individuals to institute proceedings for the examination of the lawfulness of their detention pending removal; individual measures ordered to prevent the applicant from being re-arrested and put in detention for offences resulting from his status as a stateless person).

[138] No. 7975/06, 2.2.10.

[139] No. 9870/07, 24.2.09.

[140] No. 28300/06, 20.1.09. See also *Szafrański* v *Poland*, No. 17249/12, 15.12.15 (insufficient separation of sanitary facilities from remainder of prison cell—violation of Article 3).

[141] No. 51857/13, 27.11.14.

[142] No. 41153/06, 18.12.07.

detention and adequate medical treatment for prisoners who were in need of special care because of their poor state of health. Having found violations of Articles 3 and 13 in *M.S.S. v Belgium and Greece*,[143] as a result of the applicant asylum-seeker's living conditions and treatment in Greece, the Court applied Article 46 in stipulating that the authorities should examine his asylum request without delay. The case of *M.D. and others v Malta*[144] concerned the applicants' automatic deprivation of their parental rights following their criminal conviction for ill-treatment of their children, which the Court found violated Articles 6(1) and 8. Invoking Article 46, the Court stipulated that the first applicant should be given the opportunity to request a review by an independent and impartial tribunal of the forfeiture of her parental rights, and also proposed that the Government should take general measures to ensure that people affected by a care order are provided with a right of access to court.

3.49 In *Sinan Isik v Turkey*,[145] the Court found that the requirement to state a person's religion on their identity card violated Article 9 of the Convention, and indicated that the deletion of the 'religion' box on identity cards would be an appropriate form of reparation to put an end to the breach in question.

3.50 In a significant development in 2012, the Court applied Article 46 in the case of *Aslakhanova and others v Russia*[146] having found for the first time that the incidents of enforced disappearances in the North Caucasus region of Russia amounted to a systemic problem. The Court's focus was on the scale of disappearances in Chechnya and Ingushetia between 1999 and 2006, but also took account of similar cases outside that period, and in other regions, such as Dagestan. Although the Court was 'not in a position' to order the 'exact' general and individual measures to be implemented, nevertheless it was 'compelled to provide some guidance on certain measures that must be taken, as a matter of urgency, by the Russian authorities to address the issue of the systemic failure to investigate disappearances in the Northern Caucasus'. As regards the victims' families, aside from the payment of substantial compensation, the Court focused on a recurring recommendation, namely the creation of a single, high-level body with the role of solving disappearances in the region, which would maintain a database of all disappearances. It also underlined the need for adequate resources to carry out forensic and scientific work on the ground, including the following: the location and exhumation of burial sites; the collection, storage and identification of remains; and systematic matching through up-to-date genetic databanks.

3.51 The Court also set out a second group of measures required, relating to the ineffectiveness of the criminal investigation. In the light of its many previous decisions concerning disappearances in the region, the Court was in a position to explain what steps were required in order for such investigations to be effective, including the identification of the lead agencies and commanding officers of special operations aimed at identifying and capturing suspected illegal insurgents. More specifically, the Court called on the Russian authorities to ensure access to records of the passage of service vehicles through security roadblocks, which it noted was a recurrent problem, and for investigators to be given unhindered access to any relevant

---

[143] No. 30696/09, 21.1.11. See also: *O'Rourke v UK*, No. 39022/97, dec. 26.6.01; *Larioshina v Russia*, No. 56869/00, dec. 23.4.02; *Budina v Russia*, No. 45603/05, dec. 18.6.09.

[144] No. 64791/10, 17.7.12.

[145] No. 21924/05, 2.2.10.

[146] Nos. 2944/06, 332/08 and 42509/10, 18.12.12. See also *Yandiyev and others v Russia*, Nos. 34541/06, 43811/06 and 1578/07, 10.10.13.

data held by the military and security agencies. The Court further urged the authorities to permit families access to the relevant case files where an investigation has been suspended for failure to identify the suspects (with possible exceptions relating to confidentiality or secrecy). Finally, the Court required the government to address the statute of limitations, underlining that the termination of investigations into abductions solely because the statutory time-limit had expired was in violation of Article 2.

Redress: Non-pecuniary Individual Measures Ordered by the Court

In exceptional cases, the Court is able to go further than merely providing declaratory **3.52** relief and compensation. In various areas discussed below the Court has been prepared to order the state to take individual measures other than compensating the victim. These areas are:

- restitution in property cases;
- the release of a person unlawfully detained;
- maintaining effective family contact;
- reinstatement to former occupation;
- disclosure of information;
- criminal investigations;
- the protection of witnesses; and
- rehearings in criminal proceedings.

Restitution in property cases

In relation to restitution in property cases, the Court has for some years proved willing to **3.53** break out beyond the boundaries of declaratory relief. In a number of property cases, notably those concerning the nationalisation of property, where applicants have successfully complained of violations of Article 1 of Protocol No. 1 to the Convention, the Court has required the state to return the property, failing which it would be obliged to compensate the applicant.[147] This is discussed in more detail in chapter 8, below.

In *Karanović* v *Bosnia and Herzegovina*,[148] the Court found a violation of Article 6 because **3.54** of the failure to implement a decision of the Human Rights Chamber[149] in relation to the applicant's right to a pension, resulting from systemic discrimination affecting pensioners living in Bosnia and Herzegovina who were internally displaced in the Republika Srpska during the conflict in the mid-1990s. Applying Article 46, the Court ordered the state to implement the Human Rights Chamber's decision and transfer the applicant to the pension fund in Bosnia.

Release of a person unlawfully detained

The applicant in *Assanidze* v *Georgia*[150] remained in detention in the Ajarian autonomous **3.55** province of Georgia three years after the Georgian Supreme Court had acquitted him and

---

[147] See, e.g. *Papamichalopoulos and others* v *Greece*, No. 14556/89, Series A, No. 330-B, 31.10.95; *Brumarescu* v *Romania*, No. 28342/95, 23.1.01; *Bozcaada Kimisis Teodoku Rum Ortodoks Kilisesi Vakfi* v *Turkey (no. 2)*, Nos. 37639/03, 37655/03, 26736/04 and 42670/04, 3.3.09.

[148] No. 39462/03, 20.11.07. In the subsequent judgment in *Šekerović and Pašalić* v *Bosnia and Herzegovina*, Nos. 5920/04 and 67396/09, 8.3.11, the Court applied Article 46 to require that legislative amendments be introduced.

[149] A domestic body established in accordance with the 1995 Dayton Peace Agreement.

[150] No. 71403/01, 8.4.04.

ordered his release. The Georgian Government had taken both legal and political steps to ensure his release, but without success. The Grand Chamber held that the applicant's continuing detention was arbitrary and in violation of both Articles 5(1) and 6(1). In what was an exceptional case and, in view of its urgency, the Court ordered the respondent state to 'secure the applicant's release at the earliest possible date'. The Court's reasoning for taking such an unprecedented step was rather limited: that 'by its very nature, the violation found in the instant case does not leave any real choice as to the measures required to remedy it'. A similar decision was made by the Grand Chamber in *Ilaşcu and others* v *Moldova and Russia*,[151] in which the Court held, inter alia, that three applicants had been, and continued to be, unlawfully detained in the 'Moldavian Republic of Transdniestria', a region of Moldova which declared its independence in 1991 but which has not been recognised by the international community. They had been convicted by the 'Supreme court of the Moldavian Republic of Transdniestria' which had been set up by an entity which was illegal under international law. The Court reasoned as follows:

> The Court ... considers that any continuation of the unlawful and arbitrary detention of the three applicants would necessarily entail a serious prolongation of the violation of Article 5 found by the Court and a breach of the respondent states' obligation under Article 46(1) of the Convention to abide by the Court's judgment.

> Regard being had to the grounds on which they have been found by the Court to be in violation of the Convention ... the respondent states must take every measure to put an end to the arbitrary detention of the applicants still detained and to secure their immediate release.

3.56 Two of the applicants in the case lodged a further application with the Court in 2005, as they remained in detention in Transdniestria in spite of the Court's judgment. That application was communicated by the Court to the respondent governments in 2006,[152] and they were eventually released in June 2007.[153]

3.57 The case of *Tehrani and others* v *Turkey*,[154] concerned the detention of the four Iranian applicants in Turkey because of their involvement with the People's Mojahedin Organisation of Iran (PMOI). Having found a violation of Article 5(1) (in addition to violations of Articles 3, 5(4) and 13), and in view of the 'urgent need' to put an end to it, the Court also ordered the respondent Government to secure the release of two applicants still being held at an accommodation centre and also stipulated that it should not re-detain the other two applicants who had previously been released. In *Del Río Prada* v *Spain*[155] the Grand Chamber found violations of Article 5(1) and Article 7 because the date of the applicant's release from prison was delayed (from 2008 to 2017) when the case law relating to the remission of sentences was amended while she was in prison - such a change had been unforeseeable. Accordingly, the Court ordered the state to ensure her release at the earliest possible date. In *Yakışan* v *Turkey*[156] the Court found that holding the applicant on remand for more than 11 years

---

[151] No. 48787/99, 8.7.04.

[152] See: Information Note No. 84 on the case-law of the Court, March 2006, p. 32.

[153] Interim Resolution CM/ResDH(2007)106 concerning the judgment of the European Court of Human Rights of 8 July 2004 (Grand Chamber) in the case of Ilaşcu and others against Moldova and the Russian Federation, 12 July 2007.

[154] Nos. 32940/08, 41626/08, 43616/08, 13.4.10.

[155] No. 42750/09, 21.10.13.

[156] No. 11339/03, 6.3.07, para. 49 (but the Court did not invoke Article 46 and did not include such a provision in the operative part of the judgment).

violated Article 5(3) and that the length of criminal proceedings against him (13 years and still pending) violated Article 6(1). Under Article 41 the Court stated that an appropriate way of putting an end to the violation would be to try the applicant as quickly as possible, or to release him pending trial. In *Stanev* v *Bulgaria*,[157] the Grand Chamber found various violations of Articles 5 and 6 as a result of the applicant's detention for more than eight years, without his consent, in a social care home for people with mental disorders. Invoking Articles 46 and 41 together, the Court stipulated that

> ... the authorities should ascertain whether he wishes to remain in the home in question. Nothing in this judgment should be seen as an obstacle to his continued placement in the Pastra social care home or any other home for people with mental disorders if it is established that he consents to the placement. However, should the applicant object to such placement, the authorities should re-examine his situation without delay in the light of the findings of this judgment.[158]

Fatullayev v *Azerbaijan*[159] concerned criminal proceedings brought against the applicant newspaper editor as a result of his articles on the Nagorno-Karabakh war and concerning Azerbaijan's position relating to US–Iranian relations. As a consequence, he was sentenced to periods of imprisonment of 2½ years and 8½ years (see the discussion of the case at 6.612 below). Not only did the Court find the interferences with the applicant's freedom of expression not to be justified under Article 10(2), but also that there was no justification for imposing prison sentences on him. Invoking Article 46, the Court accordingly ordered the respondent government to secure his immediate release. This represents an important extension of the Court's practice, as this order was made in the context of a case concerning media freedom under Article 10 of the Convention; there was no finding of a violation of Article 5.

In *Aleksanyan* v *Russia*,[160] the Court found several violations of the Convention relating to **3.58** the applicant's detention, in particular that his serious illnesses (he was HIV-positive) could not be adequately treated in his remand prison, and also that his detention did not serve any meaningful purpose under Article 5. The Court concluded that his continuing detention was unacceptable and accordingly ordered the Government to introduce other, reasonable, less stringent measures of restraint, in accordance with Russian law. The case of *L.M. and others* v *Russia*[161] concerned the proposed deportation of the applicants to Syria, which was held to violate Articles 2 and 3. Having also found their continuing detention to be unlawful, and in breach of Article 5(1)(f), the Court ordered their immediate release (under Article 46).

Maintaining effective family contact

The applicant father in *Gluhaković* v *Croatia*[162] complained that in practice he was not able **3.59** to maintain contact with his daughter because the courts had failed to take account of his work schedule. Although he worked in Italy, he was granted contact at counselling centres in Croatia, at a fixed time each week, which made it impossible in practice for him to attend,

---

[157] No. 36760/06, 17.1.12.

[158] *Ibid.*, para. 257. This was not, however, stipulated in the operative provisions of the judgment. See also: *L.B.* v *Belgium*, No. 22831/08, 2.10.12 (applicant prisoner not provided with appropriate psychiatric care; pursuant to Article 41, the Court indicated that the applicant's transfer to a suitable institution would constitute the most appropriate means of remedying the violation).

[159] No. 40984/07, 22.4.10.

[160] No. 46468/06, 22.12.08.

[161] Nos. 40081/14, 40088/14 and 40127/14, 15.10.15.

[162] No. 21188/09, 12.4.11.

and as a result he had lost contact with his daughter for several years. Having found a violation of Article 8, the Court went on to stipulate (in the operative provisions of the judgment) that the authorities were required to ensure effective contact with his daughter at a time which was compatible with his work schedule and on suitable premises.

Reinstatement to former occupation

3.60 In *Oleksandr Volkov* v *Ukraine*,[163] the Court found a number of breaches of Article 6(1) (and a breach of Article 8) because of the unfairness of the proceedings relating to the applicant's dismissal as a Supreme Court judge. In addition to identifying 'serious systemic problems as regards the functioning of the Ukrainian judiciary' and calling for legislative reform, the Court also invoked Article 46 in order to secure the applicant's reinstatement as a Supreme Court judge 'at the earliest possible date' (in the operative provisions of the judgment).[164] The Court issued this stipulation having expressly found that there were no prospects that the applicant would receive a fair hearing were his case to be re-opened.

Disclosure of information

3.61 In *Youth Initiative for Human Rights* v *Serbia*,[165] having found a violation of Article 10, as a result of the refusal of the Serbian intelligence agency to disclose information to the applicant NGO about the number of people who had been the subject of electronic surveillance, the Court stipulated, in the operative provisions of the judgment, that the state should ensure that the agency provide the information within three months.

Criminal investigations

3.62 In a number of cases in which it was alleged that the authorities had violated their obligations under the European Convention by failing to carry out an adequate or effective investigation of criminal offences, applicants have sought from the Court a declaration that the respondent state should carry out such an investigation. In general, the Court has proved reluctant to do so, preferring to leave to the Committee of Ministers questions as to what practically may be required in order to comply with each judgment. However, as set out below, the Court's position has evolved recently, such that it may be willing to make such a direction for an effective criminal investigation to be carried out.

3.63 In *Finucane* v *UK*,[166] the Court found a violation of Article 2 as a result of numerous inadequacies in the way in which the investigation into the murder of the Northern Ireland solicitor Patrick Finucane was carried out. The Court refused to require the UK Government to mount a fresh investigation into the death, on the basis that it was not 'appropriate to do so in the present case', a formula which left open the possibility in a more 'appropriate' case. Its reasoning was as follows:[167]

> It cannot be assumed in such cases that a future investigation can usefully be carried out or provide any redress, either to the victim's family or by way of providing transparency

---

[163] No. 21722/11, 9.1.13.
[164] Mr Volkov was subsequently reinstated to his post of judge at the Supreme Court in February 2015. See: Committee of Ministers, Decision of the Deputies, *Oleksandr Volkov* v *Ukraine*, Case No. 22, 1222nd meeting—12 March 2015.
[165] No. 48135/06, 25.6.13.
[166] No. 29178/95, 1.7.03.
[167] *Ibid.*, para. 89.

and accountability to the wider public. The lapse of time, the effect on evidence and the availability of witnesses, may inevitably render such an investigation an unsatisfactory or inconclusive exercise, which fails to establish important facts or put to rest doubts and suspicions.

The Court has usually rejected such requests in other right to life cases.[168] However, such a **3.64** stance appears to conflict with the position taken by the court in *Acar* v *Turkey*,[169] in which the Grand Chamber in effect 'overturned' the decision of the Chamber to strike out the case as a result of the Turkish Government's unilateral declaration. The Grand Chamber reasoned[170] that:

> ... in cases concerning persons who have disappeared or have been killed by unknown perpetrators and where there is prima facie evidence in the case-file supporting allegations that the domestic investigation fell short of what is necessary under the Convention, a unilateral declaration should at the very least contain an admission to that effect, combined with an undertaking by the respondent government to conduct, under the supervision of the Committee of Ministers in the context of the latter's duties under Article 46(2) of the Convention, an investigation that is in full compliance with the requirements of the Convention as defined by the Court in previous similar cases.

The 2010 judgment in *Abuyeva and others* v *Russia*,[171] concerned a series of fatalities caused **3.65** by the shelling of the village of Katr-Yurt in Chechnya in 2000 by the Russian armed forces. The decision followed the *Isayeva* judgment in 2005 relating to the same incident.[172] The Court noted 'with great dismay' in *Abuyeva* that an effective investigation had still not been carried out into the attack. The Court found that the Government had 'manifestly disregarded the specific findings of a binding judgment concerning the ineffectiveness of the investigation' and it also appeared that an effective investigation into the case was still possible. Therefore, although the state's compliance with the judgment was to be assessed by the Committee of Ministers, the Court considered it 'inevitable that a new, independent, investigation should take place'.[173] A third judgment on the Katr-Yurt attack was issued in 2015—*Abakarova* v *Russia*,[174] in which the Court found that, as regards the investigation of the incident, none of the issues identified in the *Abuyeva* judgment had been resolved. Noting the particular vulnerability of the applicant (a child who had lost all her family), the Court concluded that

> ... the inadequacy of the investigation into the deaths and injuries of dozens of civilians, including the deaths of the applicant's family, was not the result of objective difficulties that can be attributed to the passage of time or the loss of evidence, but rather the result of the investigating authorities' sheer unwillingness to establish the truth and punish those responsible.[175]

---

[168] *Orhan* v *Turkey*, No. 25656/94, 18.6.02; *Varnava and others* v *Turkey*, No. 16064/90, 18.9.09 (but see the concurring opinion of Judge Spielmann, joined by Judges Ziemele and Kalaydjeva); *Kukayev* v *Russia*, No. 29361/02, 15.11.07; *Medova* v *Russia*, No. 25385/04, 15.1.09 (but see the partly dissenting opinion of Judge Spielmann).

[169] No. 26307/95, 6.5.03.

[170] *Ibid.*, para. 84.

[171] No. 27065/05, 2.12.10.

[172] *Isayeva* v *Russia*, No. 57950/00, 24.2.05.

[173] *Abuyeva and others* v *Russia*, No. 27065/05, 2.12.10, para. 243.

[174] No. 16664/07, 15.10.15.

[175] *Ibid.*, para. 98.

In applying Article 46, the Court accordingly concluded that the situation required actions over and above those set out in *Abuyeva*: a variety of individual and general measures 'aimed at drawing lessons from the past, raising awareness of the applicable legal and operational standards and at deterring new violations of a similar nature'.

3.66 The Court went on to stipulate that the appropriate measures could include the following:

- recourse to non-judicial means of collecting information and establishing the truth about the events;
- public acknowledgement and condemnation of a serious violation of the right to life in the course of a security operation;
- assessing the adequacy of the national legal instruments relating to large-scale security operations and the mechanisms governing military-civilian cooperation in such situations; and
- greater dissemination of information and better training for military and security personnel in order to ensure strict compliance with the relevant legal standards, including human rights and international humanitarian law.

As regards the applicant in *Abakarova*, the Court required the authorities to

> ... take all steps necessary to safeguard the legitimate interests of the applicant, starting by taking into account in all future proceedings the information concerning her family members' deaths, and ensuring that she is fully informed of all relevant procedural steps and is provided with the necessary information and legal advice in sufficiently good time to be able to effectively participate in these proceedings, including commissioning any further expert reports.[176]

Finally, as a measure separate from the criminal investigation, the Court required the Government to set up a reparations mechanism not only for the applicant, but also for the other victims of the attack.[177]

3.67 The case of *Association '21 December 1989' and others v Romania*[178] concerned the inadequacy of the investigations into the crackdown on anti-government protests in Romania in December 1989, shortly before President Nicolae Ceaușescu was overthrown. The Court found a number of serious failings in the investigation, and, applying Article 46, stipulated that the authorities should provide an appropriate remedy to ensure that an effective investigation should be carried out, and which would not be affected by the application of any statutory limitation period. Furthermore, applying Article 41, the Court also found that the authorities should take necessary measures to expedite the investigations into the murder of the applicants' son. These stipulations were not, however, set out in the operative provisions of the judgment. The Court took a new line in *Nihayet Arıcı and others v Turkey*[179] which concerned the killing of two civilians by the Turkish army, near the Iraqi border. The Government was found to have violated Article 2, on both substantive and procedural grounds. The authorities' investigation into the killings was still pending after more

---

[176] *Ibid.*, para. 113.
[177] The applicant was also awarded €12,600 in pecuniary damages and €300,000 in non-pecuniary damages.
[178] No. 33810/07, 24.5.11.
[179] Nos. 24604/04 and 16855/05, 23.10.12. There was a similar direction in *Benzer and others v Turkey*, No. 23502/06, 12.11.13. See also: *İzci v Turkey*, No. 42606/05, 23.7.13; *Ataykaya v Turkey*, No. 50275/08, 22.7.14; *Aydoğdu v Turkey*, No. 40448/06, 30.8.16.

than 13 years. Applying Article 46, the Court stipulated that the investigation should be concluded without delay, and this direction was included in the operative provisions of the judgment. The Court went notably further in its judgment in *McCaughey and others* v *UK*[180] which concerned the shooting of the applicants' relatives by the security forces in Northern Ireland (in 1990). Having found a violation of Article 2 as a result of the excessive investigative delays, it also noted that delays in such inquests in Northern Ireland remained a 'serious and pervasive problem'. Accordingly, it made the following direction, under Article 46, in the operative provisions of the judgment:

> that the Government must take, as a matter of some priority, all necessary and appropriate measures to ensure, in the present case and in similar cases concerning killings by the security forces in Northern Ireland where inquests are pending, that the procedural requirements of Article 2 of the Convention are complied with expeditiously.

The protection of witnesses

The Court applied both Article 46 and Rule 39 in *R.R.* v *Hungary*[181] in requiring the authori-   **3.68**
ties to continue to ensure the adequate protection of an informant's family members (including proper cover identities if necessary) until it was established that the threat to them had ceased.[182] The first applicant had been active in a Serbian drug-trafficking mafia group. Having admitted various offences he secretly gave evidence to the authorities about the gang's activities, and as a result he, his wife and children were put on a witness protection scheme. His family members successfully invoked Article 2 when they were subsequently excluded from the witness protection scheme because the first applicant had breached its terms.

Reopening of domestic proceedings following a finding of a violation of the Convention

Whilst the Court will only rarely *require* a state to hold a re-hearing in the domestic pro-   **3.69**
ceedings following a finding of a violation of the Convention in the course of those proceedings,[183] there has been increasing pressure on states to do so. The Committee of Ministers has recognised that in certain cases the re-examination of a case by the domestic authorities or the reopening of proceedings will be the most efficient means of achieving *restitutio in integrum*. A Committee of Ministers Recommendation in 2000[184] urged Convention states to

---

[180] No. 43098/09, 16.7.13.

[181] No. 19400/11, 4.12.12.

[182] These stipulations were included in the operative provisions of the judgment.

[183] The Court has held that it does not have jurisdiction to order the reopening of proceedings—see, e.g. *Verein Gegen Tierfabriken Schweiz (VgT)* v *Switzerland (no. 2)*, No. 32772/02, 30.6.09, para. 89. However, in *Lungoci* v *Romania*, No. 62710/00, 26.1.06 the Court included in its operative provisions a direction to the state to ensure that, if the applicant so desired, the proceedings (civil proceedings to recover possession of property) were reopened within six months of the judgment becoming final. In *Vladimir Romanov* v *Russia*, No. 41461/02, 24.7.08 Judges Spielmann and Malinverni argued that such a direction should have been made (as regards the criminal proceedings in issue in that case) and should be included in the operative provisions of judgments where states had made provision for proceedings to be reopened. See also generally: *Fischer* v *Austria*, No. 27569/02, dec. 6.5.03 (following a finding of a violation of Article 4 of Protocol No. 7); *Lyons and others* v *UK*, No. 15227/03, dec. 8.7.03 (following a finding of a violation of Article 6).

[184] Committee of Ministers Recommendation No. R(2000)2 of 19.1.00. See, for example, the concurring opinion of Judge Ress in *Sigurðsson* v *Iceland*, No. 39731/98, 10.4.03, arguing for the reopening of domestic proceedings before the Supreme Court after a finding by the European Court of a violation of Article 6(1) because of the justified complaint about the lack of objective impartiality in those proceedings.

ensure that it is possible to re-examine or reopen cases where the European Court has found a violation of the Convention. As a result, many Convention states have now established means by which domestic proceedings can be reopened following a European Court finding of a violation of the Convention.[185] Where the domestic legal system does not allow for the reopening of proceedings in such circumstances, the Court will urge the state to take steps to ensure that the applicants can be adequately redressed.[186]

3.70 It has become common practice for the Court itself to emphasise this point in judgments relating to domestic criminal proceedings. In a series of cases against Turkey in 2003 finding that the applicants had been convicted by a court that was not independent and impartial within the meaning of Article 6(1), the Court sought to emphasise that the most appropriate form of redress in such circumstances would in principle be for them to be retried by an independent and impartial court at an early date.[187] A similar recommendation that criminal proceedings be reopened or the applicant be retried was made in *Somogyi v Italy*[188] following a finding that there had been a potential violation of the applicant's right to participate in his trial. It is suggested that there is no reason why such recommendations should not be made in all cases where there has been a violation of Article 6 in the course of criminal proceedings resulting in an unsafe conviction. More recently, the Court has taken a more interventionist approach, by stipulating the measures to be taken by the state in the operative provisions of its judgments.[189] In *Scoppola v Italy (No. 2)*[190] the Grand Chamber held that, in view of its finding of a violation of Articles 6 and 7 as a result of the imposition of a sentence of life imprisonment, the state was required to ensure that the applicant's sentence was replaced with a penalty that was consistent with the principles enunciated in the judgment. Having found that criminal appeal proceedings had been unfair, a four-three majority in *Maksimov v Azerbaijan*[191] held that the state must take all measures to reopen the proceedings. Finding the domestic court's reasoning for convicting the applicant of murder and sentencing him

---

[185] See Committee of Ministers Recommendation No. R(2000)2, 19.1.00, Explanatory Memorandum, para. 3.

[186] See, e.g. *Karanović v Bosnia and Herzegovina*, No. 39462/03, 20.11.07; *Laska and Lika v Albania*, Nos. 12315/04 and 17605/04, 20.4.10.

[187] *Akkaş v Turkey*, No. 52665/99; *Çakar v Turkey*, No. 42741/98; *Çavuş and Bulut v Turkey*, Nos. 41580/98 and 42439/98; *Dalgiç v Turkey*, No. 51416/99; *Eren v Turkey*, No. 46106/99; *Ergül and Engin v Turkey*, No. 52744/99; *Gençel v Turkey*, No. 53431/99; *Hayrettin Barbaros Yılmaz v Turkey*, No. 50743/99; *Mesut Erdoğan v Turkey*, No. 53895/00; *Özyol v Turkey*, No. 48617/99; *Peker v Turkey*, No. 53014/99; *Şimşek v Turkey*, No. 50118/99; *Süvariogullari and others v Turkey*, No. 50119/99, and *Tutmaz and others v Turkey*, No. 51053/99, all 23.10.03. See also *Öcalan v Turkey*, No. 46221/99, 12.5.05, para. 210. Following the *Öcalan* judgment, the applicant's case was reassessed by the Assize Court in Istanbul which dismissed his request to be retried, concluding that even without the violations found by the European Court, his sentence would not have been any different. The Committee of Ministers then found that Turkey had fulfilled its obligations under Article 46 and closed its examination of the execution of the judgment. A subsequent application to the Court complaining of the non-execution of the judgment was dismissed by the Court on the basis that it could not encroach upon the powers of the Committee of Ministers (*Öcalan v Turkey*, No. 5980/07, dec. 6.7.10).

[188] No. 67972/01, 18.5.04. See also, e.g. *Stoichkov v Bulgaria*, No. 9808/02, 24.3.05; *Claes and Others v Belgium*, Nos. 46825/99, 47132/99, 47502/99, 49010/99, 49104/99, 49195/99 and 49716/99, 2.6.05; *Abbasov v Azerbaijan*, No. 24271/05, 17.1.08; *Pishchalnikov v Russia*, No. 7025/04, 24.9.09; *Aleksandr Zaichenko v Russia*, No. 39660/02, 18.2.10; *A. T. v Luxembourg*, No. 30460/13, 9.4.15.

[189] See also the joint concurring opinion of Judges Spielmann and Malinverni in *Vladimir Romanov v Russia*, No. 41461/02, 24.7.08.

[190] No. 10249/03, 17.9.09 (operative provision 6(a)).

[191] No. 38228/05, 8.10.09 (operative provision 3).

to 40 years' imprisonment to be inadequate in *Ajdarić* v *Croatia*,[192] the Court unanimously ordered the reopening of the proceedings within six months. In *Grand Stevens and others* v *Italy*,[193] having found a violation of Article 4 of Protocol No. 7 (the prohibition of double jeopardy), the Court ordered the state to ensure that the second set of proceedings brought against the applicants was 'closed as rapidly as possible and without adverse consequences for the applicants'.[194]

The Court is less likely to make recommendations advocating re-hearings in civil cases, **3.71** because of the difficulties this may cause to the other (non-state) parties to the proceedings. However, decisions to similar effect have been made in cases concerning the denial of access to court in respect of civil proceedings.[195] For example, in *Lawyer Partners A.S.* v *Slovakia*,[196] a domestic court's refusal to allow the applicant company to file a large number of civil claims electronically (as envisaged by the domestic law) was found to breach the right of access to court under Article 6. The Court stated that the most appropriate form of redress in such circumstances would be for the domestic court to register the claims as having been lodged on the original date of their submission and then to process them 'in keeping with all the requirements of a fair trial'.

In *Henryk Urban and Ryszard Urban* v *Poland*,[197] the Court found that the use of an 'asses- **3.72** sor' in the District Court breached the requirement of an independent tribunal because the assessor could be removed at any point by the Minister of Justice. The Court held, however, that the decision did not entail an obligation to reopen all proceedings in which assessors had participated at the first-instance level. In doing so, the Court noted that the Polish Constitutional Court had already identified the structural problem, which had then been rectified by Parliament, and also that the Constitutional Court had found that it would be disproportionate and contrary to legal certainty to allow challenges to final rulings given by assessors. The Constitutional Court had further found there to be no automatic correlation between the structural deficiency and the validity of each and every ruling made by assessors in individual cases.

Examination of measures taken by a respondent state to remedy a violation found by the Court

The assessment of the adequacy of measures taken by a state in response to a judgment find- **3.73** ing a violation of the Convention will ordinarily fall within the remit of the Committee of Ministers under Article 46(2),[198] which is discussed at 3.77 below.

---

[192] No. 20883/09, 13.12.11 (including the proviso: 'should the applicant so request').
[193] No. 18640/10 et al, 4.3.14.
[194] *Ibid.*, para. 237.
[195] See, e.g. *Cudak* v *Lithuania*, No. 15869/02, 23.3.10. In their concurring opinion in that case, Judges Malinverni, Casadevall, Cabral Barreto, Zagrebelsky and Popović, argued that this point should have been included in the operative provisions of the judgment. Another example is *Vulakh and others* v *Russia*, No. 33468/03, 10.1.12 (re-opening of civil proceedings, following breach of Article 6(2) arising from related criminal proceedings).
[196] No. 54252/07, 16.6.09. See also *Lungoci* v *Romania*, No. 62710/00, 26.1.06 and *Yanakiev* v *Bulgaria*, No. 40476/98, 10.8.06; *Jehovah's Witnesses of Moscow* v *Russia*, No. 302/02, 10.6.10.
[197] No. 23614/08, 30.11.10.
[198] See, e.g. *Haase and others* v *Germany*, No. 34499/04, dec. 12.2.08; *Hulki Güneş* v *Turkey*, No. 17210/09, dec. 2.7.13.

3.74 However, a further application *can* be made to the Court where it raises a new issue that was not decided by the previous judgment.[199] Thus the Court will consider whether or not the second application relates essentially to the same person, the same facts and the same complaints. For example, in the case of *Verein Gegen Tierfabriken Schweiz (VgT) v Switzerland (No. 2)*,[200] the applicant animal rights association complained about the continued prohibition on the broadcasting of its advertisement in spite of the European Court's earlier judgment finding a violation of its right to freedom of expression.[201] The Swiss Government sought to argue that the case should be declared inadmissible *ratione materiae*, on the basis that the execution of the Court's judgments fell solely within the jurisdiction of the Committee of Ministers. However, the applicant had reapplied to the Federal Court requesting that it review its earlier judgment in the light of the Strasbourg judgment, and the Federal Court had dismissed the application, invoking further grounds. This refusal was accordingly considered (by the majority) to constitute relevant new information capable of giving rise to a fresh violation of Article 10, and indeed the Grand Chamber went on to find a violation of Article 10 (by 11 votes to six).

3.75 The case of *Emre v Switzerland (No. 2)*[202] also concerned the follow-up to an earlier Strasbourg judgment[203] which had found that the permanent exclusion of the applicant, a Turkish national, had breached Article 8. When the applicant subsequently applied to the Federal Court for a review of his case, it annulled an earlier judgment, but he was still excluded for a period of ten years. As the Federal Court was found to have failed sufficiently to examine the detailed conditions set out in the earlier Strasbourg judgment, the Court found a violation of Article 8 taken together with Article 46. The applicant in *Bochan v Ukraine (No. 2)*[204] had successfully secured a European Court judgment in 2007[205] finding a violation of Article 6(1) as regards the unfairness of domestic litigation relating to ownership of land. When she subsequently lodged an 'exceptional appeal' based on the Strasbourg decision, the Supreme Court dismissed her application, finding that the original decisions had been well-founded. The 'new issue' in her second Strasbourg application therefore concerned the manner in which the Supreme Court had reached its decision in the appeal proceedings. The European Court found a violation of Article 6(1) in its second judgment on the basis that the Supreme Court's decision had been grossly arbitrary because of its misrepresentation of the European Court's findings in its first judgment.

3.76 In *Ivanţoc and others v Moldova and Russia*[206] the applicants complained about their continuing detention after the date of the European Court judgment in *Ilaşcu and others v Moldova and Russia*,[207] in which the Court had found their detention to be arbitrary and

---

[199] See, e.g. *Wasserman v Russia (No. 2)*, No. 21071/05, 10.4.08. However, there was held to be no such new issue in *Egmez v Cyprus*, No. 12214/07, dec. 18.9.12 (where there had been a re-investigation of the applicant's ill-treatment). See also *House of Macedonian Civilisation and others v Greece*, No. 1295/10, 9.7.15.

[200] No. 32772/02, 30.6.09. For a further example, see *Sidabras and others v Lithuania*, Nos. 50421/08 and 56213/08, 23.6.15. See, by contrast, *Steck-Risch and others v Liechtenstein*, No. 29061/08, dec. 11.5.10 (refusal to reopen civil proceedings following finding of a violation of Article 6—inadmissible).

[201] The earlier judgment was *Vgt Verein Gegen Tierfabriken v Switzerland*, No. 24699/94, 28.6.01.

[202] No. 5056/10, 11.10.11.

[203] No. 42034/04, 22.5.08.

[204] No. 22251/08, 5.2.15.

[205] No. 7577/02, 3.5.07.

[206] No. 23687/05, 15.11.11.

[207] No. 48787/99, 8.7.04.

unlawful, in violation of Article 5, and ordered their release. The Court found that it had jurisdiction (as regards Russia, but not Moldova) to consider the claim as regards the period of detention from the date of the *Ilaşcu* judgment (July 2004) until their release in June 2007. It went on to find aggravated violations of Articles 3 and 5 because of the failure to comply with the Court's earlier direction to release the applicants (as well as breaches of Articles 8 and 13).

Supervision of the enforcement of judgments: the role of the Committee of Ministers

Judgments are transmitted to the Committee of Ministers which supervises their execution (Article 46(2)). In practice, the respondent government will be asked to report to the Committee of Ministers on any measures taken in response to a judgment of the Court. Firstly, the Committee of Ministers will be concerned to ensure that any just satisfaction awarded by the Court has been paid, and with any other specific measures for the benefit of the applicant (the 'individual measures'), including, for example, to end any continuing unlawful situation. Secondly, the Committee of Ministers will at the same time be concerned with broader measures which are intended to prevent further similar violations (the 'general measures'). These may entail, for example, legislative, administrative or policy changes. The Committee of Ministers is also responsible for supervising the execution of friendly settlement decisions and judgments. **3.77**

Information on the state of execution of the cases pending before the Committee can be found on the Committee's website,[208] which now incorporates the HUDOC-EXEC search engine which was launched in January 2017.[209] Useful information can also be found in the Committee of Ministers' annual reports (which have been published since 2007). **3.78**

By way of example, 'individual measures' have included the following: **3.79**

- the reopening of domestic proceedings;[210]
- the lifting of an injunction;[211]
- an acquittal;[212]
- the cancellation of a criminal record;[213]
- release from custody;[214]
- the withdrawal of an arrest warrant;[215]
- the requirement to carry out an effective investigation into a disappearance and death;[216]

---

[208] See: http://www.coe.int/en/web/cm/execution-judgments.

[209] See: http://hudoc.exec.coe.int/eng#{%22EXECDocumentTypeCollection%22:[%22CEC%22]}.

[210] See, e.g. *Unterpertinger* v *Austria*: Committee of Ministers Resolution DH(89)002, 18.1.89; *Jersild* v *Denmark*: Committee of Ministers Resolution DH(95)212, 11.9.95; *Sadak, Zana, Dicle and Doğan* v *Turkey*: Committee of Ministers Interim Resolution ResDH(2002)59, 30.4.02.

[211] See, e.g. *Open Door and Dublin Well Woman* v *Ireland*: Committee of Ministers Resolution DH(96)368, 25.6.96.

[212] See, e.g. *Barberà, Messegué and Jabardo* v *Spain*: Committee of Ministers Resolution DH(94)84, 16.11.94.

[213] See, e.g. *Marijnissen* v *Netherlands*: Committee of Ministers Resolution DH(85)004, 25.2.85.

[214] See, e.g. *Van Mechelen and others* v *Netherlands*: Committee of Ministers Resolution DH(99)124, 19.2.99; *Sadak, Zana, Dicle and Doğan* v *Turkey*: Committee of Ministers Interim Resolution ResDH(2004)31, 2.4.04.

[215] See, e.g. Decisions of the Committee of Ministers concerning the *Ülke* case, 1144th (DH) meeting, 4–6 June 2012, CM/Del/Dec(2012)1144 of 6 June 2012.

[216] See, e.g. Interim Resolution CM/ResDH(2008)35 on the execution of the judgment of the European Court of Human Rights in the case Gongadze against Ukraine, 5 June 2008.

- the reinstatement of a judge;[217]
- the revocation of a decision to expel;[218]
- the recognition of a church.[219]

3.80 'General measures' have included the following:[220]

- the introduction of new legislation;[221]
- consequential changes in the case law of the domestic courts;[222]
- in those countries where there is clear evidence that the European Convention on Human Rights and the judgments of the European Court receive direct effect (within the constitutional powers of the judicial bodies concerned) the publication and dissemination of the judgment will usually be enough to convince the Committee of Ministers that the necessary changes in the case law will take place;[223]
- instructions issued to relevant domestic authorities;[224]
- education and/or training of public officials.[225]

3.81 As to the payment of just satisfaction, the practice is to give states three months within which to confirm that payment has been made to the applicant. The applicant is then given two months within which to contest what the government has said, failing which that aspect of the case will be closed. In any event, as to the payment of just satisfaction and the taking of 'individual measures', the applicant is entitled to write to the secretariat of the Committee of Ministers to submit any complaints they may have as to the adequacy of the measures proposed, or taken (including whether or not any damages and/or costs awarded have been paid) (Rule 9 of the Committee of Ministers' Rules relating to Article 46(2)[226]).

3.82 Communications concerning just satisfaction should be sent by post to:

Council of Europe
DGI—Directorate General of Human Rights and Rule of Law
Just Satisfaction Section

---

[217] Decisions adopted at the 1222nd (DH) meeting (11–12 March 2015), Case No. 22 (Oleksandr Volkov), 12 March 2015.

[218] See, e.g. *D* v *UK*: Committee of Ministers Resolution DH(98)10, 18.2.98.

[219] See, e.g. *Metropolitan Church of Bessarabia and others* v *Moldova*; Final Resolution ResDH(2010)008).

[220] See also: *General measures adopted to prevent new violations of the European Convention on Human Rights—Stock-taking of measures reported to the Committee of Ministers in its control of execution of the judgments and decisions under the Convention*, H/Exec (2006)1.

[221] See, e.g. *Pauwels* v *Belgium*: Committee of Ministers Interim Resolution DH(96)676, 15.11.96 (a bill to reform military tribunals).

[222] See, e.g. *Beaumartin* v *France*: Committee of Ministers Resolution DH(95)254, 20.11.95.

[223] See, e.g. the Norwegian Supreme Court's press release following the European Court judgment in *Bergens Tidende* v *Norway*: Committee of Ministers Resolution ResDH(2002)69, 11.7.02.

[224] See, e.g. *Assenov* v *Bulgaria*: Committee of Ministers Resolution ResDH(2000)109, 2.10.00; *Saunders* v *UK*: Committee of Ministers Interim Resolution DH(2000)27, 14.2.00.

[225] See, e.g. *Yagiz* v *Turkey*: Committee of Ministers Resolution DH(99)20, 18.1.99; Interim Resolution CM/ResDH(2007)107 concerning the judgments of the European Court of Human Rights in the case of Velikova and seven other cases against Bulgaria relating in particular to the ill-treatment inflicted by police forces, including three deaths, and the lack of an effective investigation, 17 October 2007.

[226] Committee of Ministers, Rules of the Committee of Ministers for the supervision of the execution of judgments and of the terms of friendly settlements, 10 May 2006. See *Supervision of the execution of judgments of the European Court of Human Rights—Annual Report*, 2015, Council of Europe, March 2016.

Department for the Execution of Judgments of the ECHR
F-67075 Strasbourg Cedex
or by fax: +33(0)3 88 41 27 93
or by email: dghl_execution_just_satisfaction@coe.int/

The Committee of Ministers has published a memorandum setting out its practice in rela- **3.83**
tion to monitoring sums awarded by way of just satisfaction, and suggesting solutions to
practical problems that may hinder payments being made.[227]

The Committee of Ministers holds four regular meetings a year in order to deal specifically **3.84**
with matters related to the supervision of European Court judgments. Furthermore, urgent
cases can also be considered at other 'ordinary' meetings, if necessary. In recent years there
has been a steady increase in the Committee of Ministers' caseload, reflecting in part the
rise in the Court's caseload—from a figure of 7,238 pending cases in 2008, the numbers
increased to a high of just over 11,000 in 2012 and 2013.[228] There has also been an increase
in the number of cases which have been pending with the Committee of Ministers for more
than five years: by 2015, these amounted to 55 per cent of the pending cases.[229] The failure
of states parties to take their implementation obligations seriously is demonstrated simply
by the remarkably few action plans or action reports (see 3.86 below) which are submitted,
in spite of the large backlog of pending cases: for example, 236 action plans and 350 action
reports in 2015.[230]

The slow rate and negligence in execution have continually been acknowledged.[231] These **3.85**
problems have necessitated a series of changes to the Committee of Ministers' working practices.[232] At the beginning of 2011 a new twin-track system for the supervision of the execution of judgments was introduced.[233] Under this system, most cases will be examined under

---

[227] *Monitoring of the payment of sums awarded by way of just satisfaction: an overview of the Committee of Ministers' present practice—Memorandum prepared by the Department for the Execution of Judgments of the European Court of Human Rights* (DG-HL), CM/Inf/DH(2008)7 final, 15 January 2009.

[228] What is more, prior to that period, the numbers had risen from 709 in 1996 to 5,523 in 2006. *Supervision of the execution of judgments of the European Court of Human Rights—Annual Report*, 2015, Council of Europe, March 2016, p. 56. There were 10,904 cases pending in 2014 and 10,652 in 2015.

[229] *Supervision of the execution of judgments of the European Court of Human Rights—Annual Report*, 2015, Council of Europe, March 2016, p. 10.

[230] *Supervision of the execution of judgments of the European Court of Human Rights—Annual Report*, 2015, Council of Europe, March 2016, p. 73. The figures for 2014 were 266 and 481.

[231] See, e.g. *Supervision of the execution of judgments of the European Court of Human Rights—Annual Report*, 2015, Council of Europe, March 2016, p. 10; Committee on Legal Affairs and Human Rights, Implementation of judgments of the European Court of Human Rights, Report (Rapporteur: Mr Klaas de Vries, Netherlands, Socialist Group), Doc. 13864, 9 September 2015; High-level Conference on the 'Implementation of the European Convention on Human Rights, our shared responsibility'—Brussels Declaration, 27 March 2015 (section C).

[232] See further: Supervision of the execution of judgments of the European Court of Human Rights: pro-cedure and working methods for the Committee of Ministers' Human Rights meetings, GR-H(2016)2-final, 30 March 2016. For a summary of the procedures, see: *Supervision of the execution of judgments of the European Court of Human Rights—Annual Report*, 2015, Council of Europe, March 2016.

[233] See: *Supervision of the execution of the judgments and decisions of the European Court of Human Rights: implementation of the Interlaken Action Plan*, CM/Inf/DH(2010)45 final, 7 December 2010 and *Supervision of the execution of judgments and decisions of the European Court of Human Rights: implementation of the Interlaken Action Plan–Modalities for a twin-track supervision system*, CM/Inf/DH(2010)37E, 6 September 2010. The new procedure applies to all cases that became final after 1 January 2011. Transitional provisions apply to cases that were pending before the Committee of Ministers prior to that date.

a 'standard procedure'. Cases which will be subject to an 'enhanced procedure' are those falling into the following categories:

- judgments requiring urgent individual measures;
- pilot judgments;[234]
- judgments disclosing major structural and/or complex problems as identified by the Court and/or the Committee of Ministers;
- inter-state cases.

The Committee of Ministers may also decide to examine any case under the enhanced procedure at the request of a member state or the Secretariat.

3.86 Under both the standard and enhanced supervision procedures, states are required to provide an 'action plan' or 'action report'[235] on the case 'as soon as possible and in any case at the latest within six months from the date upon which the judgment became final'. An 'action plan' sets out the measures which a state intends to take to implement a judgment of the Court. An 'action report' describes the measures which have been taken by a state to implement a judgment and also explains why no measures, or no further measures, are necessary. The Committee's involvement in the standard procedure is limited to verifying whether or not action plans or action reports have indeed been submitted by states.

3.87 Where the state and the Secretariat are agreed on the content of an action report, the case will be submitted to the Committee of Ministers in order for it to be closed, at the next Human Rights meeting (or in any event within six months of the presentation of the action report). Action plans will be subject to a preliminary assessment by the Secretariat as to both the measures envisaged and the timetable proposed and contact will be made with the national authorities 'if further information and clarifications are necessary'.

3.88 When a state informs the Secretariat that it considers that all measures have been taken and that it has complied with its obligation under Article 46 of the Convention, the action plan is turned into an action report. The Secretariat will then make a 'conclusive assessment' of it (within six months). If the state and the Secretariat agree on the measures adopted or implemented, the Secretariat will propose that the Committee of Ministers adopts a final resolution closing the examination of the case.

3.89 If a case is subject to the enhanced procedure, it is envisaged that the Secretariat will engage in 'more intensive and pro-active cooperation' with the state. This may involve:

- assistance in the preparation and/or implementation of action plans; or
- expert assistance as regards the type of measures to be taken; or
- bilateral or multilateral co-operation programmes (such as seminars or round-tables).

Enhanced procedure cases may also be the subject of a debate, at the request of any state or the secretariat, or they can be the subject of a narrative decision, without the need for a debate.

---

[234] See also Rule 4 of the Committee of Ministers' Rules relating to Article 46(2).

[235] See also: Action Plans–Action Reports, Definitions and objectives—Memorandum prepared by the Department for the Execution of Judgments of the European Court of Human Rights, CM/Inf/DH(2009)29rev, 3 June 2009.

Cases may be transferred between the two procedures. For example, a case will be transferred from the standard to the enhanced procedure if there is serious delay in the implementation of an action plan.

The case will remain on the agenda of the Committee of Ministers until the respondent **3.90** government has reported that the necessary action has been taken and the Committee of Ministers is satisfied with the sufficiency of those measures. Any information and documents provided by the state to the Committee of Ministers in this context will be accessible to the public (unless the Committee decides otherwise).[236] A summary of the information available before each meeting, and the Committee of Ministers' evaluation of it, are usually included in the annotated agenda of the meeting. The decision taken by the Committee of Ministers on the basis of this information, and any new information submitted at the meeting, are also published. The documents are made available on the Committee of Ministers' website after the meeting.

The Committee of Ministers may take various steps in order to assist execution of the judg- **3.91** ment, such as declarations by the Chair, press releases, holding 'high level' meetings, issuing decisions adopted as the result of a debate and issuing interim resolutions.[237] When the Committee of Ministers considers that the information submitted by the respondent state about the execution measures taken demonstrates compliance with a judgment, it will adopt a resolution stating that it has completed its task under Article 46(2) of the Convention.[238] Interim and final resolutions are published on the Committee of Ministers' website and they can also be found on the Court's HUDOC site. If there is a justifiable delay in the execution of a judgment, the Committee of Ministers will adopt an interim resolution which will note what interim measures have rapidly been adopted to limit, as far as possible, the number of new violations and will indicate a timetable for further reforms needed in order to resolve the problem in question.

If, however, there are problems with the execution of a judgment (or where there is uncer- **3.92** tainty), the Committee of Ministers may issue further more strongly worded resolutions that urge the respondent state to take the steps necessary to comply with the judgment in question.[239] Where there are continuing systemic problems, the Committee of Ministers may issue a series of resolutions calling for further action to be taken by the authorities, as has been the case, for example, with applications concerning the excessive length of proceedings before the civil and administrative courts in Italy.[240] Having first closed its examination of the matter in 1995, on the basis of various reforms reported by the Italian Government, the Committee of Ministers reopened the issue in 1997 because of the continuing high volume of cases coming to the Court. In 1999 the Committee of Ministers adopted an

---

[236] Rule 8 of the Committee of Ministers' Rules relating to Article 46(2).

[237] *Supervision of the execution of judgments of the European Court of Human Rights—Annual report,* 2009, Council of Europe, April 2010, p. 21.

[238] See, e.g. *Assenov* v *Bulgaria*: Committee of Ministers Resolution ResDH(2000)109, 2.10.00.

[239] See, e.g. Committee of Ministers Interim Resolution ResDH(2001)79, 26.6.01 (re *Matthews* v *UK*); Committee of Ministers Interim Resolution ResDH(2004) 39, 2.6.04 (re *A* v *UK*); Committee of Ministers Interim resolution CM/ResDH(2014)185, Execution of the judgments of the European Court of Human Rights in the cases Varnava, Xenides-Arestis and 32 other cases against Turkey, 25.9.14.

[240] Committee of Ministers Resolution DH(97)336, 11.7.97; Committee of Ministers Interim Resolution DH(99)436, 15.7.99; Committee of Ministers Interim Resolution DH(99)437, 15.7.99; Committee of Ministers Interim Resolution ResDH(2000)135, 25.10.00.

interim resolution that recalled that there had been a very high number of such cases since the end of the 1980s, and that in spite of various measures taken by the Italian authorities, the number of violations of Article 6(1) resulting from the systemic problem had not decreased. Therefore the interim resolution referred to the major problems still persisting, urged the Italian authorities to take further steps, and decided to review the position again within one year.[241] In order to ensure that Italy adequately reviewed the efficiency of its judicial system, the Committee of Ministers called upon Italy to maintain reform as a high priority, and in 2000 set up a system of yearly reports to be submitted to it on the progress achieved.[242] However, this problem is still ongoing.[243] The non-enforcement of domestic judicial decisions in Ukraine has similarly been the subject of repeated interim resolutions by the Committee of Ministers, but there has been little or no tangible progress since 2004.[244] As regards the UK's ban on prisoners voting, in 2014 the Committee of Ministers expressed 'profound concern and disappointment' that the Government had not introduced a bill to parliament in order to resolve the matter (as recommended by the Joint Committee on Human Rights).[245]

3.93 In the 1990s and 2000s the European Court found serious violations of the Convention (especially of Articles 2 and 3 of the Convention) which were perpetrated by the security forces in south-east Turkey.[246] These decisions led to unprecedented resolutions by the Committee of Ministers from 1999. The first resolution[247] referred to 13 judgments in which the Court had found violations of Articles 2, 3, 6, 8, 13 and Article 1 of Protocol No. 1 and noted that: 'the principal problems at the origin of the violations found remain, notably in the territory subject to a state of emergency, and, in particular, that investigations relating to these violations, when they have taken place, have as yet not given concrete and satisfactory results'. The resolution called upon the Turkish authorities to reorganise and improve the training of the security forces, rapidly to complete the proposed reforms of the system of criminal proceedings against members of the security forces and to reform the prosecutor's office 'in order to ensure that prosecutors will in the future have the independence and necessary means to ensure the identification and punishment of agents of the security forces who abuse their powers so as to violate human rights'. The second resolution[248] in 2002 referred to 42 judgments and decisions finding that Turkey was responsible for numerous breaches of the Convention, including killings, torture, the destruction of property and the absence of effective domestic remedies. The resolution took note of various steps that had been taken by the Turkish authorities, including constitutional and legislative amendments, the issuing of instructions and the progressive lifting of the state of emergency. However, the resolution also expressed concern at the further complaints of alleged torture and ill-treatment and called for additional training (of police, *gendarmerie*, prosecutors and judges) and reform

---

[241] Committee of Ministers Interim Resolution DH(99)437, 15.7.99.

[242] See Committee of Ministers Interim Resolution ResDH(2000)135, 25.10.00.

[243] See, e.g. Decisions of the Committee of Ministers concerning the Ceteroni group of cases, 1172nd DH meeting, 4–6 June 2013, CM/Del/OJ/DH(2013)1172/14, 3 June 2013.

[244] Decisions adopted at the 1214th (DH) meeting (2–4 December 2014), Case No. 26 (Zhovner group), 4 December 2014.

[245] Decision adopted at the 1208th meeting (23–25 September 2014), Case No. 25, 25 September 2014.

[246] As to repeated findings of violations of Article 10 by Turkey, see Committee of Ministers Interim Resolution ResDH(2001)106 and Committee of Ministers Interim Resolution ResDH(2004)38, 2.6.04.

[247] Committee of Ministers Interim Resolution DH(99)434, 9.6.99.

[248] Committee of Ministers Interim Resolution ResDH(2002)98, 10.7.02.

measures to be taken.[249] A comparable process has been undertaken in relation to egregious violations of the Convention committed by the Russian security forces in Chechnya (notably between 1999 and 2006), including disappearances, unlawful killings, unacknowledged detentions, torture and ill-treatment and the destruction of property.[250]

The Committee of Ministers may also issue strongly worded narrative decisions or resolutions where problems of enforcement arise in individual cases. For example, following the judgment in *Socialist Party and others* v *Turkey*, the Committee of Ministers issued resolutions insisting that the authorities should take action without delay to erase all the consequences resulting from the Party Chairman's criminal conviction (which had been confirmed *after* the European Court judgment).[251] In the judgment in *Scozzari and Giunta* v *Italy*, the Court, inter alia, found a violation of Article 8 because of the placement of the first applicant's children with a particular community, following their having been taken into public care. The Committee of Ministers subsequently issued an interim resolution[252] that noted that the children remained in the community in question and encouraged the resolution of their placement in the light of an approach by the Belgian authorities to the Italian authorities raising the possibility of their placement in Belgium (in view of the first applicant's residence in Belgium). In the light of further delays, a second interim resolution,[253] inter alia, invited the Italian authorities 'rapidly to take concrete and effective measures in order to prevent that the children be irreversibly separated from their mother'. The case of *Al-Saadoon and Mufdhi* v *UK*[254] concerned the applicants' detention by the British armed forces in southern Iraq in 2003, where the United Kingdom was an occupying power. They were held in British detention facilities before being handed over to the Iraqi authorities in 2008. In 2010 the Committee expressed its 'deep concern' that the applicants were faced with the risk of the death penalty and the Iraqi authorities had not given any assurances to the United Kingdom that the death penalty would not be applied and called upon the United Kingdom to take all further possible steps to obtain such assurances.[255] The Grand Chamber judgment in *Sejdić and Finci* v *Bosnia and Herzegovina*[256] found the rules regarding the right to stand for election to the House of Peoples and the Presidency of Bosnia and Herzegovina to be discriminatory (see 6.730 below). In a Decision taken in December 2010 the Committee 'deeply regretted' that the 2010 elections had taken place in contravention of the judgment,

3.94

---

[249] See also: Interim Resolution CM/ResDH(2008)69 on the execution of the judgments of the European Court of Human Rights of cases concerning the Actions of the security forces in Turkey—Progress achieved and outstanding issues, 18 September 2008; and 'Bati group of cases against Turkey—68 cases concerning the lack of effective investigations in respect of the actions of the Turkish security forces', 1120th (DH) meeting, 13–14 September 2011, CM/Del/OJ/DH(2011)1120list5 of 17 June 2011.

[250] See, e.g. *Actions of the security forces in the Chechen Republic of the Russian Federation: general measures to comply with the judgments of the European Court of Human Rights*, CM/Inf/DH(2008)33, 11 September 2008 and CM/Inf/DH(2010)26, 27 May 2010; Committee of Ministers Interim Resolution CM/ResDH(2015)45 Execution of the judgments of the European Court of Human Rights in 221 cases against the Russian Federation concerning actions of the security forces in the Chechen Republic of the Russian Federation, 12 March 2015.

[251] Committee of Ministers Interim Resolution DH(99)245, 4.3.99; Committee of Ministers Interim Resolution DH(99)529, 28.7.99.

[252] Committee of Ministers Interim Resolution ResDH(2001)65, 29.5.01.

[253] Committee of Ministers Interim Resolution ResDH(2001)151, 3.10.01.

[254] No. 61498/08, 2.3.10.

[255] CM/Del/Dec(2010)1100, 6 December 2010. Subsequently, at the Committee of Ministers' 108th meeting, on 10 March 2011, it was noted that the Iraqi President of the Public Prosecution service had stated by letter that the charges against the applicants carried a maximum penalty of 15 years' imprisonment.

[256] No. 27996/06, 22.12.09.

deplored the fact that no political consensus has been reached, and 'strongly urged' the authorities and political leaders to bring the Constitution and Electoral Code into line with the judgment.[257] The Committee of Ministers has also deplored the expulsion of individuals from Italy to Tunisia in breach of interim measures indications issued by the Court,[258] and in 2014 it expressed its 'grave concern' that no tangible progress had been made in relation to domestic investigations into allegations of torture by the police in Russia.[259] In 2016 the Committee of Ministers' interim resolution in the case of *Ilgar Mammadov* v *Azerbaijan*[260] deeply deplored the fact that the applicant had still not been released and noted that it was 'intolerable that, in a State subject to the rule of law, a person should continue to be deprived of his liberty on the basis of proceedings engaged, in breach of the Convention, with a view to punishing him for having criticised the government'.[261]

3.95 Problems arising from a state's failure to comply with a judgment may to lead to a very strongly worded interim resolution recalling the unconditional nature of the obligation to comply with the Court's judgments, stressing that compliance is a condition of membership of the Council of Europe, and possibly even calling upon member states to take all actions they deem appropriate in order to assist in ensuring execution. The failure to pay just satisfaction awarded by the Court was the subject of a Committee of Ministers' resolution in 1996 following the 1994 judgment in *Stran Greek Refineries and Stratis Andreadis* v *Greece*.[262] A subsequent resolution confirmed that the Greek Government had paid the sum owing to the applicants (of more than $30 million) in January 1997.[263] Similarly the Turkish Government's failure to pay the damages awarded in the 1998 judgment in *Loizidou* v *Turkey* was the subject of several Committee of Ministers' resolutions which were increasingly strongly worded, inter alia, 'very deeply deploring' Turkey's failure to comply with the judgment.[264] The monies awarded by the Court in *Loizidou* were eventually paid by the Turkish Government (together with interest) in December 2003.[265]

3.96 The Rules of the Committee of Ministers do not expressly permit the applicant to send communications addressing the question of 'general measures' (as opposed to just satisfaction or 'individual measures'), but nor is this expressly excluded by the Rules. Accordingly, it is suggested that the applicant's representative should consider writing to the Department for Execution of Judgments of the European Court of Human Rights if there are any 'general measures' that they consider should be carried out by the state as a consequence of the Court's judgment. Whilst the applicant strictly may not be regarded as having locus standi to petition the Committee of Ministers as to 'general measures', it may be important that the secretariat is aware of the views of the applicants and/or their representatives. It may also

---

[257] CM/Del/Dec(2010)1100, 6 December 2010.

[258] Interim Resolution CM/ResDH(2010)83, Execution of the judgments of the European Court of Human Rights, Ben Khemais against Italy, 3 June 2010.

[259] Decisions adopted at the 1201st (DH) meeting, Cases No. 16 (Mikheyev group), 5 June 2014.

[260] No. 15172/13, 22.5.14.

[261] Interim Resolution CM/ResDH(2016)144, Execution of the judgment of the European Court of Human Rights, Ilgar Mammadov against Azerbaijan, 8 June 2016.

[262] Committee of Ministers Interim Resolution DH(96)251, 15.5.96.

[263] Committee of Ministers Final Resolution DH(97)184, 20.3.97.

[264] Committee of Ministers Interim Resolution DH(99)680, 6.10.99; Committee of Ministers Interim Resolution DH (2000) 105, 24.7.00; Committee of Ministers Interim Resolution DH(2001)80, 26.6.01; Committee of Ministers Interim Resolution ResDH(2003)174, 12.11.03.

[265] Committee of Ministers Resolution ResDH(2003)190, 2.12.03.

be effective for the applicant's representative to write directly to other Council of Europe member states' agents in order to urge them to take a particular stance on 'general measures' (within the context of the Committee of Ministers' supervision role).

The Rules of the Committee of Ministers were amended in 2006 to provide that the **3.97** Committee of Ministers may consider communications from NGOs or national human rights institutions as regards the execution of judgments (Rule 9(2)).[266] This provision therefore entitles civil society organisations to raise any issue in relation to execution with the Committee of Ministers. This was an important change, in that it enhances civil society participation in the process of deciding how states should respond to judgments of the European Court. As well as being an important tool for NGOs, it is also important in practice that the secretariat of the Committee of Ministers receives information from civil society in order to assist it in considering and assessing government submissions. However, the low numbers of civil society 'Rule 9 submissions' (just 81 in 2015) indicate that this mechanism is still not being fully utilised.[267]

Only in the most exceptional cases, such as *Loizidou* v *Turkey*, have there been very serious **3.98** problems with the enforcement of European Court judgments. Following the Court's judgment in *Ilaşcu and others* v *Moldova and Russia*,[268] in July 2004, the Russian Foreign Ministry was quoted as stating that 'Moscow expresses its surprise over the controversy and the obviously political bias of the European Court of Human Rights in Strasbourg'.[269] In the light of difficulties illustrated by such cases, and in order to improve its capacity to meet future challenges, two further procedures have been added to strengthen the Committee of Ministers' armoury, in accordance with Protocol No. 14 (see chapter 1): interpretation proceedings and infringement proceedings.

Interpretation proceedings

Disagreements may arise as to the interpretation of judgments. Accordingly, if the Committee **3.99** of Ministers (by a majority of two-thirds) considers that the supervision of the execution of a final judgment is hindered by a problem of interpretation of the judgment, it may refer the matter to the Court for a ruling on the question of interpretation (Article 46(3); Rules 79 and 91–93). A request for interpretation must be made within a year of the delivery of the judgment (Rule 79(1)). The request should specify 'fully and precisely the nature and source of the question of interpretation that has hindered execution of the judgment' in question and include information about any execution proceedings before the Committee of Ministers (Rule 91).

---

[266] See, generally, Lucja Miara and Victoria Prais, 'The Role of Civil Society in the Execution of Judgments of the European Court of Human Rights' [2012] 5 E.H.R.L.R. 528. Rule 9 was amended in January 2017 to enable the Committee of Ministers to consider submissions on the execution of judgments from both international intergovernmental organisations with a human rights remit, and also from bodies given leave to intervene as a third party in the proceedings before the Court. See: Ministers' Deputies, Decisions, CM/Del/Dec(2017)1275/4.1, 18 January 2017.

[267] *Supervision of the execution of judgments of the European Court of Human Rights—Annual Report*, 2015, Council of Europe, March 2016, p. 74. There were 80 in 2014, 81 in 2013 and 47 in both 2011 and 2012. A new independent body, the European Implementation Network (EIN) has been established to support civil society engagement with the implementation of European Court judgments. See: http://european-implementation.net/.

[268] No. 48787/99, 8.7.04.

[269] *The Moscow Times*, 9.7.04.

Infringement proceedings

3.100   If the Committee of Ministers (by a majority of two-thirds) considers that a state refuses to abide by a Court judgment, it may refer the question to the Court as to whether that state has failed to fulfil its obligations under Article 46(1) of the European Convention (Article 46(4); Rules 94–99). Any request must be reasoned and must include information about the execution proceedings before the Committee of Ministers, and any relevant documents (Rule 95).

3.101   In practice, this procedure is likely to be invoked only in the most exceptional cases.[270] The Grand Chamber of the Court will consider any such referral (Article 31(b)) and may hold a hearing in order to do so (Rule 98). If the Court finds a violation of Article 46(1) the case will be referred to the Committee of Ministers for consideration of the measures to be taken.

3.102   Regrettably, there is no express sanction available if the European Court finds that a state has indeed failed to fulfil its obligations under Article 46(1) and in a politically controversial case, it is possible that states may use this opportunity of a second public forum to attempt to re-argue their position. This new process provides the Committee of Ministers with a further sanction to address non-compliance, short of recourse to Article 8 of the Council of Europe's Statute, which provides for the suspension of voting rights in the Committee of Ministers or expulsion from the Council of Europe. However, at the time of writing, the infringement proceedings mechanism had never once been invoked.[271]

Other means of securing the enforcement of judgments

3.103   The Parliamentary Assembly of the Council of Europe (PACE) also has a role in the supervision of the enforcement of European Court judgments.[272] In practice, this is carried out by the Committee on Legal Affairs and Human Rights in a process which is supplementary to that of the Committee of Ministers.[273] The Committee on Legal Affairs and Human Rights will focus on cases which raise important implementation issues and judgments concerning violations of a particularly serious nature. Being a committee of the Parliamentary Assembly, its emphasis has been to take advantage of the possibilities for dialogue with national legislators, including holding hearings.[274] It also undertakes country visits (for example, in 2009–2010 to Bulgaria, Ukraine, Greece, Italy, Moldova, Romania, Russia and Turkey, and in 2014 to Turkey, Italy and Poland). The Committee will seek explanations from national delegates for a government's failure to comply with a judgment and it will make recommendations to

---

[270]   Explanatory Report to Protocol No. 14, para. 100.

[271]   See: Committee on Legal Affairs and Human Rights, Implementation of judgments of the European Court of Human Rights, Report (Rapporteur: Mr Klaas de Vries, Netherlands, Socialist Group), Doc. 13864, 9 September 2015, para. 34. This report argues that given the 'very worrying' situation as regards the levels of non-implementation of the Court's judgments, 'it is perhaps time for the Committee of Ministers to make use of the procedures set up in Article 46 paragraphs 3, 4 and 5 of the Convention and in particular the "infringement procedure". As long as they have not been used, it is impossible to assess their efficiency' (para. 49).

[272]   See PACE Resolution 1226(2000), *Execution of judgments of the European Court of Human Rights*, 28.9.00.

[273]   In 2015, the Committee established a Sub-committee on the implementation of judgments of the European Court of Human Rights whose role is to focus on implementation (e.g. by disseminating good practice, addressing particular problems of non-implementation, and holding hearings).

[274]   In 2012–2013 it held hearings with parliamentary delegations from Bulgaria, Greece, Italy, the Republic of Moldova, Poland, Romania, the Russian Federation, Turkey, Ukraine and the United Kingdom. See: Committee on Legal Affairs and Human Rights, Implementation of judgments of the European Court of Human Rights, Report (Rapporteur: Mr Klaas de Vries, Netherlands, Socialist Group), Doc. 13864, 9 September 2015, para. 1.

the Committee of Ministers. This in turn may elicit a formal response from the Committee of Ministers.[275] It has published eight reports on the implementation of judgments since 2000.[276] It is therefore possible for applicants and/or their representatives to engage in this process by communicating with the Committee on Legal Affairs and Human Rights and/or with national delegates within PACE. Parliamentarians may also assist in putting pressure on the Committee of Ministers and the respondent state in specific cases through oral and written questions and other initiatives.

The Commissioner for Human Rights of the Council of Europe (see 1.17 above) may meet **3.104** with state officials to discuss systemic problems highlighted in European Court judgments, or to discuss follow-up in the more politically controversial cases (the Commissioner does not, however, have the power to intervene as such in the execution of individual cases).[277] Furthermore, the Secretary-General of the Council of Europe may take up matters on enforcement, but this is only likely to happen in the most exceptional cases (such as *Loizidou* v *Turkey*).[278]

There may be further potential leverage in respect of states seeking access to the European **3.105** Union, as accession agreements may include specific undertakings to comply with the European Convention on Human Rights.[279] Similarly, leverage may be exerted in respect of existing EU member states, as respect for the European Convention on Human Rights is among the essential principles to be observed by other member states, and a failure to comply with European Court judgments may therefore by actionable as a question of EU undertakings.

It may also be advisable for an applicant to take the matter up directly with the govern- **3.106** ment, and to seek the assistance of appropriate NGOs, and the media, in drawing public attention to systemic problems. National parliaments may have an important role in the implementation of European Court judgments, as exemplified by the Joint Committee on Human Rights in the United Kingdom.[280] Whether or not applicants will succeed in push-ing through changes of policy or practice will depend upon the extent to which they can establish that the Convention violation identified in their case reveals a general problem with the relevant system or practice, rather than a one-off incident.

If the execution measures proposed by the respondent state do not correspond to those **3.107** desired by the applicant, and if the questions arising from it are of some complexity (for

---

[275] See, e.g. *Written Question No. 428 to the Chair of the Committee of Ministers by Mr Jurgens: 'Execution of the European Court's judgments by Turkey'*, CM/AS(2003)Quest428 final, 5.9.03.

[276] The eighth report was published in 2015: Committee on Legal Affairs and Human Rights, Implementation of judgments of the European Court of Human Rights, Report (Rapporteur: Mr Klaas de Vries, Netherlands, Socialist Group), Doc. 13864, 9 September 2015.

[277] See, however: Commissioner for Human Rights, Non-implementation of the Court's judgments: our shared responsibility, 23 August 2016. On the issue of prisoner voting rights in the UK, see: Memorandum by Nils Muižnieks, Council of Europe Commissioner for Human Rights, to the Joint Committee on the Draft Voting Eligibility (Prisoners) Bill, CommDH(2013)23, 17 October 2013.

[278] No. 15318/89, 18.12.96.

[279] See, e.g. *Council Decision of 8 March 2001 on the principles, priorities, intermediate objectives and condi-tions contained in the Accession Partnership with the Republic of Turkey* (2001/235/EC).

[280] See, e.g. Enhancing Parliament's role in relation to human rights judgments, Human Rights Joint Committee—Fifteenth Report, session 2009–2010, 9 March 2010. See further, A. Donald and P. Leach, *Parliaments and the European Court of Human Rights*, Oxford University Press, 2016.

example, as regards the correct interpretation of the Court's judgment), an applicant could consider lodging a new complaint with the Court (see also section 3.73–3.76 above). Whereas the Committee of Ministers is well equipped to put considerable pressure on recalcitrant states in clear cases, its composition and procedures create problems when it comes to solving difficult questions of law, especially where the respondent state opposes the measures sought. Applicants should therefore consider pursuing additional cases before the Court where execution raises such difficult problems of interpretation. If the problem is evident at an early stage, applicants might also consider the possibility of submitting a request to the Court for the interpretation of the judgment (see 3.99 above). If the applicant seizes the Court with the matter, the Committee of Ministers will usually postpone its own examination of the relevant execution question until the Court has given its decision. In this context it is important to bear in mind that the Court's examination will usually primarily concern the question as to whether the new situation violates a substantive article of the Convention, whereas the Committee of Ministers' examination addresses the question as to whether the state has achieved *restitutio in integrum*. These are two different perspectives which should be borne in mind by applicants when they plead questions linked with execution. In *Mehemi v France (No. 2)*,[281] the applicant, an Algerian national, had been permanently excluded from France following his conviction for drug-trafficking. In its judgment of 6 September 1997, the European Court had found that to expel the applicant permanently to a country with which he had no ties violated Article 8. The applicant subsequently brought a further case, following the domestic court's decision to give effect to the European Court's judgment by merely reducing the exclusion order to ten years, complaining under Article 8 only about the continuing effects of the expulsion and challenging the conditions imposed on his residence in France after his return. The Chamber of the Court in this judgment stated that while it had no jurisdiction to supervise the execution of a judgment,[282] there was nothing to prevent it from examining a subsequent complaint raising a new issue that had not been decided in the first judgment (although on the facts there was no further violation of Article 8, or of Article 2 of Protocol No. 4). See also the section on 'Examination of measures taken by a respondent state to remedy a violation found by the Court', at 3.73 above.

---

[281] No. 53470/99, 10.4.03.
[282] See, also, e.g. *Komanický v Slovakia*, No. 13677/03, dec. 1.3.05.

[Handwritten table:]

relevant provisions	
Jurisdiction	admissibility / standing
4.142	4.04 4.17 4.35
4.146	4.05 4.25 4.43
4.148	4.10 4.27 4.48
4.157	4.12

4

STANDING AND ADMISSIBILITY CRITERIA

Introduction

The European Court's 'standing' and admissibility criteria are set out in Articles 34 and 35 of the Convention, which provide as follows: **4.01**

Article 34 **4.02**

The Court may receive applications from any person, non-governmental organisation or group of individuals claiming to be the victim of a violation by one of the High Contracting Parties of the rights set forth in the Convention or the Protocols thereto. The High Contracting Parties undertake not to hinder in any way the effective exercise of this right.

Article 35

1. The Court may only deal with the matter after all domestic remedies have been exhausted, according to the generally recognised rules of international law, and within a period of six months from the date on which the final decision was taken.
2. The Court shall not deal with any application submitted under Article 34 that
   (a) is anonymous; or
   (b) is substantially the same as a matter that has already been examined by the Court or has already been submitted to another procedure of international investigation or settlement and contains no relevant new information.
3. The Court shall declare inadmissible any individual application submitted under Article 34 if it considers that:
   (a) the application is incompatible with the provisions of the Convention or the Protocols thereto, manifestly ill-founded, or an abuse of the right of individual application; or
   (b) the applicant has not suffered a significant disadvantage, unless respect for human rights as defined in the Convention and the Protocols thereto requires an examination of the application on the merits and provided that no case may be rejected on this ground which has not been duly considered by a domestic tribunal.
4. The Court shall reject any application which it considers inadmissible under this Article. It may do so at any stage of the proceedings.

4.03 The admissibility rules are a critical aspect of the European Convention system, not least because a very high proportion of cases are declared inadmissible. For example, in 2016 36,579 cases were found to be inadmissible (or struck off), compared with 1,926 judgments published.[1] Article 34 (formerly Article 25) sets out the requirements relating to standing. Article 35 (formerly Article 26) sets out the admissibility criteria, the most important of which in practice are the requirement to exhaust effective domestic remedies and to submit an application to the Court within six months of the final decision in the domestic proceedings.[2] The Court now publishes its own admissibility guide, which is available on its website.[3]

4.04 This chapter will discuss the following aspects of Articles 34 and 35:

- Capacity and standing—who may petition the Court?
- Who can claim to be a victim?
- Exhaustion of domestic remedies
- Six-month time limit
- No significant disadvantage
- Anonymous applications
- Applications substantially the same as a matter already examined by the Court
- Applications already submitted to another procedure of international investigation or settlement
- Incompatibility with the provisions of the Convention
- Manifestly ill-founded
- Abuse of the right of application.

---

[1] *Annual Report 2016 of the European Court of Human Rights,* Council of Europe, p. 193. The equivalent figures in 2015 were 43,133 decisions and 2,441 judgments.

[2] Compliance with the Court's practice directions is *not* equated with compliance with the admissibility criteria. See: *Yüksel* v *Turkey,* No. 49756/09, dec. 1.10.13.

[3] Practical Guide on Admissibility Criteria, available at: http://www.echr.coe.int/Documents/Admissibility_guide_ENG.pdf.

The obligation on governments not to hinder the right of application (in Article 34) is considered below at 5.54.

Capacity and Standing—Who May Petition the Court?

The European Court rules relating to capacity and standing are not restrictive, although they **4.05** are inextricably linked to the requirement that an applicant must claim to be the victim of a violation of one or more Convention rights (which is discussed below at 4.27). The Court does not consider itself bound by domestic criteria relating to locus standi, on the basis that such rules may serve a different purpose to that of Article 34 of the Convention.[4]

Article 34 states that the Court may receive applications from 'any person, non- **4.06** governmental organisation or group of individuals …'. Accordingly, individuals, groups of individuals, NGOs,[5] companies (even if dissolved),[6] shareholders, trusts, professional associations, trade unions, political parties and religious organisations may all submit applications to the Court. Depending on the nature of the Convention violation alleged, a company itself may bring an application under the Convention, as may the chairperson and managing director of the company[7] and as may individual shareholders in exceptional circumstances.[8]

However, certain rights by definition can only be claimed by individuals and cannot extend **4.07** to organisations, such as freedom of thought, conscience and religion,[9] the right to education[10] and the right not to be subjected to degrading treatment or punishment.[11]

Nationality and residence

Nationality and place of residence are irrelevant to the right to complain to the Court of **4.08** violations of the Convention, reflecting the obligation in Article 1 for the parties to secure Convention rights to everyone within their jurisdiction (see also below at 6.01). The test applied is whether or not the applicant can claim to be a victim of a violation of his or her Convention rights.

Legal capacity

Lack of legal capacity will not generally affect the right of petition. The Court may allow **4.09** a person lacking legal capacity under domestic law to conduct Convention proceedings in their own right.[12] For example, in the case of *Winterwerp* v *Netherlands*[13] an application was

---

[4] *Scozzari and Giunta* v *Italy*, Nos. 39221/98 and 41963/98, 13.7.00, para. 139.

[5] An NGO cannot be an applicant if it cannot itself claim to be a victim of a Convention violation. See, e.g. *Conka and others* v *Belgium*, No. 51564/99, dec. 13.3.01 (the *Ligue des Droits de L'homme* could not claim to be a victim of violations experienced by the applicant family). For exceptional situations see 4.11 below.

[6] *Pine Valley Developments Ltd* v *Ireland*, No. 12742/87, Series A, No. 222, 29.11.91.

[7] *Kaplan* v *UK*, No. 7598/76, dec. 17.7.80.

[8] *Agrotexim and others* v *Greece*, No. 14807/89, Series A, No. 330, 24.10.95; *G.J.* v *Luxembourg*, No. 21156/93, 26.10.00; *Credit and Industrial Bank* v *Czech Republic*, No. 29010/95, 21.10.03.

[9] *X and Church of Scientology* v *Sweden* (1979) 16 DR 68.

[10] *Ingrid Jordebo Foundation & Christian Schools and Ingrid Jordebo* v *Sweden*, No. 11533/85, (1987) 51 DR 125.

[11] *Kontakt-Information-Therapie and Hengen* v *Austria*, No. 11921/86, (1988) 57 DR 81.

[12] *Zehentner* v *Austria*, No. 20082/02, 16.7.09, para. 39.

[13] Series A, No. 33, 24.10.79.

brought by a man who had suffered severe brain damage in an accident and who had been compulsorily detained under the Dutch mental health legislation. Similarly, the applicant in *Van der Leer* v *Netherlands*[14] sought to challenge her compulsory detention in a psychiatric hospital. In *Zehentner* v *Austria*[15] the applicant lacked legal capacity under domestic law, as she suffered from paranoid psychosis. She herself lodged an application with the Court. Her guardian subsequently wrote to the Court to say that she had not approved the application and did not wish to pursue it. The applicant, however, stated that she wished the Court to proceed with her case and that she did not want her guardian to represent her. The Court allowed her to present her own case. Where, however, applicants are represented before the Court by a relative or other person, the Court will require evidence of their authority to represent the applicant.

Standing to represent another

4.10 The Court has accepted that a close relative may bring an application on behalf of a 'victim' of an alleged violation of the Convention, particularly having regard to the vulnerability of the victim[16] or the poor state of the victim's health.[17]

Furthermore, the Court may permit a person to bring proceedings on behalf of another person (such as a child), even though they may not be entitled to do so under domestic law[18] (see also 4.12 Children, and 4.17 Death of victim or applicant, below).

In these circumstances, the applicant should lodge with the Court a letter from the victim confirming the applicant relative's authority to bring the case.[19]

4.11 In *Centre for Legal Resources on behalf of Valentin Câmpeanu* v *Romania*[20] the Grand Chamber exceptionally found that the applicant NGO (CLR) did have standing to bring an Article 2 application on behalf of Valentin Câmpeanu who had died in an orphanage aged 18, having been HIV-positive and having had severe mental disability. The Court took account of the fact that Mr Câmpeanu had had no next-of-kin and that CLR had initiated domestic legal proceedings on his behalf, without any objections from the relevant domestic authorities. Furthermore, no guardian or other form of representative had been appointed by the state authorities. The Court therefore concluded that '[t]o find otherwise would amount to preventing such serious allegations of a violation of the Convention from being examined at an international level, with the risk that the respondent State might escape accountability under the Convention as a result of its own failure to appoint a legal representative to act on his behalf as it was required to do under

---

[14] No. 11509/85, Series A, No. 170, 21.2.90.

[15] No. 20082/02, 16.7.09.

[16] See, e.g. *Y.F.* v *Turkey*, No. 24209/94, 22.7.03, para. 3.

[17] *Ilhan* v *Turkey*, No. 22277/93, 27.6.00, paras. 53–5.

[18] See, e.g. *Nielsen* v *Denmark*, No. 10929/84, 28.11.88, paras. 56–7; *Scozzari and Giunta* v *Italy*, Nos. 39221/98 and 41963/98, 13.7.00, para. 138.

[19] *Ilhan* v *Turkey*, No. 22277/93, 27.6.00, para. 53.

[20] No. 47848/08, 17.7.14. See also *Bulgarian Helsinki Committee* v *Bulgaria*, Nos. 35653/12 and 66172/12, dec. 28.6.16 (applicant NGO not considered to have victim status—inadmissible). In *Lambert and others* v *France*, No. 46043/14, 5.6.15, the Court drew a distinction between the right of the relatives of a man in a 'vegetative state' to bring Articles 2 and 3 complaints on his behalf (which was not allowed) and their right to bring such complaints on their own behalf (which was allowed). See further: Constantin Cojocariu, Handicapping Rules: The Overly Restrictive Application of Admissibility Criteria by the European Court of Human Rights to Complaints Concerning Disabled People [2011] 6 E.H.R.L.R. 686.

national law'.[21] The case of *Kondrulin v Russia*[22] concerned the inadequate medical care of the applicant detainee. When the applicant died of cancer during the course of the case, the NGO, AGORA, which had been representing him, applied to take his place in the proceedings. This request was granted by the Court on the basis that the applicant had died in custody leaving no known relatives, and that AGORA's lawyers had been representing him in the domestic proceedings, without any objection from the national authorities.

Children

Children may be applicants in cases before the European Court, both in conjunction with adult 'victims' arising from the same complaint and in their own right. For example, in *Marckx v Belgium*,[23] an unmarried mother and her young daughter complained of the illegitimacy laws in Belgium, including in relation to the bequeathing and inheritance of property. The case of *A v UK*[24] concerned the severe ill-treatment of the applicant child by his stepfather and the failure of the state to provide the child with protection from ill-treatment. The cases of *T and V v UK*[25] concerned the criminal proceedings brought against the applicants when they were aged 11, in relation to the abduction and murder of a two-year-old boy committed when they were ten years old. **4.12**

Children may also be represented by a parent (as in *Campbell and Cosans v UK*[26] where the applicants complained on their children's behalf of the risk of corporal punishment in school) or other family member.[27] This will depend on whether there is any potential conflict of interest[28] or for any reason the parent or other relative does not have legal standing in domestic law to do so. The Court will also consider whether the children would otherwise be deprived of the effective protection of their Convention rights.[29] **4.13**

In *Hokkanen v Finland*[30] an application was brought by a father in respect of a child custody dispute with the child's maternal grandparents. The applicant father also lodged an application on behalf of his daughter, but that aspect of the case was declared inadmissible as it was found that he was no longer the child's custodian at the relevant time. But in *Scozzari and Giunta v Italy*,[31] the Grand Chamber acknowledged that where there is a conflict over a minor's interests between a natural parent and a person appointed by the authorities to act as a child's guardian, there could be a risk that certain issues may not be brought to the Court's attention. Therefore it was held in that case that the applicant, as the natural mother, had standing to represent her children, even though she had been deprived of parental rights.[32] **4.14**

---

[21] *Centre for Legal Resources on behalf of Valentin Câmpeanu v Romania*, No. 47848/08, 17.7.14, para. 112. There was a similar finding in *Association for the Defence of Human Rights in Romania—Helsinki Committee on behalf of Ionel Garcea v Romania*, No. 2959/11, 24.3.15.

[22] No. 12987/15, 20.9.16.

[23] Series A, No. 31, 13.6.79.

[24] Nos. 24724/94 and 24888/94, 16.12.99.

[25] No. 25599/94, 23.9.98. See also *SC v UK*, No. 60958/00, 15.6.04.

[26] Nos. 7511/76 and 7743/76, 16.5.80.

[27] See, e.g. *N. Ts. and others v Georgia*, No. 71776/12, 2.2.16 (Article 8 complaint brought on behalf of three boys by their aunt).

[28] See *P., C. and S. v UK*, No. 56547/00, dec. 11.12.01.

[29] See, e.g. *N. Ts. and others v Georgia*, No. 71776/12, 2.2.16.

[30] No. 19823/92, Series A, No. 299-A, 23.9.94.

[31] Nos. 39221/98 and 41963/98, 13.7.00. See also *Siebert v Germany*, No. 59008/00, dec. 9.6.05.

[32] *Scozzari and Giunta v Italy*, Nos. 39221/98 and 41963/98, 13.7.00, para. 138. See also *A.K. and L. v Croatia*, No. 37956/11, 8.1.13.

Nevertheless, the Court has also held that in cases arising out of disputes over access between parents, it is the parent with custody who is entitled to act in order to safeguard the child's interests and therefore in such situations being a natural parent may not be sufficient in order to be able to bring an application on behalf of a child.[33]

4.15 Children may also be represented at the Court by others, such as a legal representative, provided that the representative produces proof of authority to act. For example, in *SD, DP and T* v *UK*,[34] which concerned delay in care proceedings, the application was brought by a solicitor on behalf of the three children, supported by a letter of authority from the guardian ad litem appointed by the court to safeguard the interests of the children in the domestic proceedings. This was challenged by the Government, which argued that neither the solicitor nor the guardian ad litem had authority to act on the children's behalf in the proceedings under the European Convention. However, the Commission rejected the Government's objections, emphasising that it would not take a restrictive or technical approach to such questions, as children generally relied on others to represent their interests, and required specific protection of their interests which had to be both practical and effective. No conflicts of interest were found to arise and on the facts there was no alternative means of representation.

4.16 If children reach the age of majority during the course of pending European Court proceedings, they will be asked to confirm whether they wish to continue the application.[35]

Death of victim or applicant

Applications brought on behalf of people who have died

4.17 The Court will not accept applications in the name of a deceased person. However, it is well established that an application can be brought on behalf of the deceased by a close relative or heir,[36] where they are considered to have a sufficient or legitimate interest, or where there is a wider general interest which justifies the continuation of the case.[37]

4.18 This principle has frequently been applied where the application relates to the circumstances of the death. For example, the case of *McCann and others* v *UK*,[38] concerning the fatal shooting of three members of the IRA in Gibraltar by British soldiers, was brought by members of the victims' families who were representatives of the estates of the deceased. In *Keenan* v *UK*,[39] following her son's suicide in prison, the applicant complained of the

---

[33] *Sahin* v *Germany*, No. 30943/96, dec. 12.12.00; *Petersen* v *Germany*, No. 31178/96, dec. 6.12.01; *Wildgruber* v *Germany*, No. 32817/02, dec. 16.10.06; *Eberhard and M.* v *Slovenia*, Nos. 8673/05 & 9733/05, 1.12.09.

[34] No. 23715/94, 20.5.96. See also *Giusto and Bornacin* v *Italy*, No. 38972/06, dec. 15.5.07; *Šneersone and Kampanella* v *Italy*, No. 14737/09, 12.7.11. See, by contrast, *Moretti and Benedetti* v *Italy*, No. 16318/07, 27.4.10; *Kruškić and others* v *Croatia*, No. 10140/13, dec. 25.11.14.

[35] See, e.g. *Lautsi and others* v *Italy*, No. 30814/06, 18.3.11, para. 1; *Raw and others* v *France*, No. 10131/11, 7.3.13, para. 53.

[36] But see *Thevenon* v *France*, No. 2476/02, dec. 28.2.06. This may include unmarried partners: *Finogenov and others* v *Russia*, Nos. 18299/03 and 27311/03, 20.12.11, para. 205.

[37] See, e.g. *Micallef* v *Malta*, No. 17056/06, 15.10.09. This principle may still be applied even if domestic inheritance proceedings are still pending: *Malhous* v *Czech Republic*, No. 33071/96, dec. 13.12.00. As regards an application concerning Article 3, an applicant seeking to bring a case on behalf of a relative who had subsequently died will need to demonstrate either a strong moral interest or other compelling reasons, such as an important general interest: see *Kaburov* v *Bulgaria*, No. 9035/06, dec. 19.6.12. See also *Boacă and others* v *Romania*, No. 40355/11, 12.1.16; *Karpylenko* v *Ukraine*, No. 15509/12, 11.2.16.

[38] No. 18984/91, Series A, No. 324, 27.9.95.

[39] No. 27229/95, 6.9.99.

prison authorities' failure to take adequate steps to safeguard her son's life. It is *not* necessary for an applicant in such cases to have to establish financial dependency or pecuniary loss. In *Keenan*, the applicant's son had been over 18 when he died and he had no dependants, which effectively ruled out domestic proceedings or bereavement damages. The absence of any pecuniary loss did not prevent Mrs Keenan from making an application to the European Commission of Human Rights and indeed the very fact that she could not bring domestic proceedings in respect of her son's death led to a finding by the Commission of a violation of the right to an effective remedy under Article 13. Where the standing of an applicant to bring Convention proceedings in respect of a deceased relative has been challenged, the Strasbourg institutions have underlined the objective and purpose of the Convention as being to provide practical and effective safeguards. Accordingly, in *Yaşa* v *Turkey*[40] the Court held that the applicant, as the deceased's nephew, could legitimately claim to be a victim of an act as tragic as the murder of his uncle. It did not matter that there might have been closer relatives who could have brought proceedings on behalf of the deceased. It may be the case that the Convention rights of the deceased's relative have also been violated and therefore an application should be brought in the applicant's own right, as well as on behalf of the deceased. For example, in *Kurt* v *Turkey*[41] the applicant complained of her son's disappearance in south-east Turkey, invoking Articles 2, 3, 5, 13, 14 and 18 in respect of her son, and Article 3 in respect of herself, because of the anguish and distress caused by her son's continued disappearance which she argued amounted to inhuman treatment. On the facts of the case, the Court found violations of Articles 5 and 13 in respect of the applicant's son, and a violation of Article 3 in relation to the applicant. *Gradinar* v *Moldova*[42] concerned the fairness of criminal proceedings for murder brought against the applicant's husband. He was originally acquitted but on appeal his retrial was ordered. In the meantime he had been shot dead, but the domestic law allowed the applicant to have the case considered by the courts and to exercise her own civil rights as the victim's widow (to seek compensation and an apology). The applicant accordingly was found to have standing to bring an application to the Strasbourg Court.

However in *Sanles Sanles* v *Spain*,[43] the applicant lodged a case with the Court on behalf of **4.19** her brother-in-law who had committed suicide. Her brother-in-law had been a tetraplegic following an accident and had sought through domestic proceedings a right to die a painless death without rendering those assisting him liable to prosecution. After he died (assisted by unidentified persons), the applicant unsuccessfully sought to continue the domestic proceedings on his behalf. The European Court found that the applicant had not been directly affected by the alleged violations of the Convention and could not therefore claim to have been a victim. In *Fairfield* v *UK*,[44] an application was brought by the daughter and executors of Harry Hammond, an evangelical Christian who had sought to challenge his conviction under Articles 9 and 10 of the Convention. Mr Hammond had died whilst the domestic proceedings were still pending and the Divisional Court had granted the executors permission to continue the appeal. However, the European Court declared the case inadmissible, finding that the applicants did not have the requisite standing under Article 34.

---

[40] No. 22495/93, 2.9.98.
[41] No. 24276/94, 25.5.98.
[42] No. 7170/02, 8.4.08. See also *Nölkenbockhoff* v *Germany*, No. 10300/83, 25.8.87.
[43] No. 48335/99, dec. 9.11.00.
[44] No. 24790/04, dec. 8.3.05.

The death of an applicant whilst the case is pending before the European Court

4.20   If an applicant dies while a case is pending before the Court, the case can usually be continued by the applicant's close relatives or heirs, if that person has a legitimate interest,[45] or if
the Court is satisfied that the complaint is of general importance. For example, the parents of
a haemophiliac who had contracted HIV could continue an application brought in respect
of the length of domestic proceedings for compensation following the applicant's death.[46]
In *Laskey, Jaggard and Brown v UK*,[47] a case concerning criminal proceedings for assault
brought in relation to sadomasochistic activities, there was no objection to the father of the
first applicant continuing with the proceedings following the first applicant's death.

4.21   In *Lukanov v Bulgaria*,[48] a case concerning the arrest and prosecution of a former Prime
Minister of Bulgaria, it was not disputed that the applicant's widow and two children could
continue with the application after Mr Lukanov was shot dead outside his home. However,
the right of the widow and children of the applicant to continue proceedings was disputed in
Ahmet Sadik v Greece.[49] The applicant was a newspaper publisher and parliamentary election
candidate who was prosecuted for publishing false and defamatory information about other
election candidates and for inciting the Muslim population to disturb the peace. He died
after the European Commission of Human Rights had published its report on the merits
and his widow and two children sought to continue the case. The Government argued that
an application concerning an Article 10 violation could not be transferred to the applicant's
heirs, but the Court held that his heirs had a legitimate moral interest in obtaining a ruling
that the applicant's conviction infringed Article 10, as well as having a pecuniary interest in
the case.

4.22   However, an executor may not have standing to bring an application. For example, in *Scherer
v Switzerland*,[50] the application was struck out where, rather than any close relative, an executor proposed to continue the proceedings (for pecuniary reasons only) and the Court considered there to be no public policy reasons to pursue the case. It was a relevant consideration
in striking the case out that the domestic law in question had been substantially changed
since the events in question. In *S. G. v France*,[51] concerning the unfairness of civil proceedings, the applicant died during the course of the proceedings and her estate was inherited
by a residuary legatee, *La Fondation de France*, which was found to have no legitimate interest in continuing the proceedings and the case was accordingly struck out. An 'interest' in
obtaining compensation under Article 41 was not considered sufficient. In *Léger v France*[52]

---

[45]   See, e.g. *Jecius v Lithuania*, No. 34578/97, 31.7.00; *Ergezen v Turkey*, No. 73359/10, 8.4.14. This may
include a *de facto* partner (see, e.g. *Koryak v Russia*, No. 24677/10, 13.11.12; *Ivko v Russia*, No. 30575/08,
15.12.15). The cousin of a deceased applicant was *not* permitted to pursue an application in *Kurić and others v
Slovenia*, No. 26828/06, 13.7.10 (chamber judgment). The applicant's lawyer will not have a sufficient interest to pursue the application: see, e.g. *Sevgi Erdoğan v Turkey*, No. 28492/95, 29.4.03 (but, exceptionally, see
Kondrulin v Russia, No. 12987/15, 20.9.16 and the other cases discussed at 4.11 above).

[46]   *X v France*, 31.3.92, No. 9993/82. See also *Hristozov and others v Bulgaria*, Nos. 47039/11 and 358/12,
13.11.12 (complaints under Articles 2 and 6 brought by relatives of cancer sufferers).

[47]   No. 21627/93, 19.2.97.

[48]   No. 21915/93, 20.3.97.

[49]   *Ahmet Sadik v Greece*, No. 18877/91, 15.11.96.

[50]   No. 17116/90, 25.3.94.

[51]   No. 40669/98, 18.9.01. See also *Thevenon v France*, No. 2476/02, dec. 28.2.06 (application brought by
universal legatee struck out).

[52]   No. 19324/02, 30.3.09.

the Grand Chamber struck out a case in which the applicant had died, and a request that the application be continued had been made by a person who was neither an heir nor a close relative, nor who had established any legitimate interest.

Exceptionally, the Court may allow a case to proceed even where the applicant has died and **4.23** there are no relatives or heirs who wish to pursue the application. The applicant in *Karner v Austria*[53] died during the course of the Convention proceedings and despite the absence of an heir to pursue the case, the Court rejected the Government's application for the case to be struck out under Article 37, in view of the general importance of the issue raised by the case (the right of a homosexual man to succeed to his partner's tenancy) for all Convention states. The Court stated that:[54]

> As a rule, and in particular in cases which primarily involve pecuniary, and, for this reason, transferable claims, the existence of other persons to whom that claim is transferred is an important criterion, but cannot be the only one … human-rights cases before the Court generally also have a moral dimension, which must be taken into account when considering whether the examination of an application after the applicant's death should be continued. All the more so, if the main issue raised by the case transcends the person and the interests of the applicant …

Furthermore:[55]

> Although the primary purpose of the Convention system is to provide individual relief, its mission is also to determine issues on public-policy grounds in the common interest, thereby raising the general standards of protection of human rights and extending human-rights jurisprudence throughout the community of Convention States.

As regards NGOs exceptionally being allowed to bring cases in the place of deceased **4.24** applicants, see *Centre for Legal Resources on behalf of Valentin Câmpeanu v Romania*[56] and *Kondrulin v Russia*[57] and the other cases discussed at 4.11 above.

Public corporations

Public bodies, such as local authorities, cannot make applications to the European Court, as **4.25** Article 34 only permits a 'person, non-governmental organisation or group of individuals' to petition the Court. This rule excludes any 'decentralised authorit[y] that exercise[s] public functions'.[58] Various state bodies, such as a Spanish city council and a Swiss local government commune, have been thwarted from petitioning Strasbourg for this reason.[59] There was a similar result in *Transpetrol A.S. v Slovakia*[60] on the basis that the applicant, a joint stock

---

[53] No. 40016/98, 24.7.03.
[54] *Ibid.*, para. 25.
[55] *Ibid.*, para. 26.
[56] No. 47848/08, 17.7.14.
[57] No. 12987/15, 20.9.16.
[58] *Danderyds Kommun v Sweden*, No. 52559/99, dec. 7.6.01.
[59] See *Ayuntamiento de M v Spain*, No. 15090/89, dec. 7.1.91, 68 DR 209; *Rothenthurm Commune v Switzerland*, No. 13252/87, dec. 14.12.88, 59 DR 251. See also *16 Austrian Communes and some of their councillors v Austria*, No. 5765/77, dec. 31.5.74; *The Province of Bari, Sorrentino and Messeni Nemagna v Italy*, No. 41877/98, dec. 15.9.98; *The Municipal Section of Antilly v France*, No. 45129/98, ECHR 1999-VIII, and *Ayuntamiento de Mula v Spain*, No. 55346/00, dec. 1.2.01; *Döşemealtı, Belediyesi v Turkey*, No. 50108/06, dec. 23.3.10; *Demirbaş and others v Turkey*, No. 1093/08 et al., dec. 9.11.10.
[60] No. 28502/08, dec. 15.11.11.

company in which the Government had a majority shareholding, was considered to have interests that were concurrent with those of the Government.

4.26   The national broadcasting company Radio France has been found by the Court *not* to be a governmental organisation that is precluded from bringing an application under the Convention, in view of its independent regulation and its position as a broadcaster, which is comparable to that of private radio stations.[61]

Who Can Claim to be a Victim?

4.27   In accordance with Article 34, an applicant must claim to be the *victim* of a violation of one or more Convention rights.[62] The Court will only consider the particular circumstances of each case and will not permit abstract challenges (*actio popularis*),[63] nor will the Court admit hypothetical breaches. This may lead to all or part of Convention applications being rejected. For example, in *Buckley* v *UK*[64] the applicant, who was a gypsy, complained that she was prevented from living in caravans on her own land with her family and from following a life as a traveller. The applicant also complained to the Court about the domestic law provisions which criminalised the use of gypsy caravans in certain circumstances. However, the Court found that as measures had been taken against the applicant under neither statute, those particular complaints could not be considered.

4.28   The test applied by the Court is that applicants must show that they have been personally or directly affected by the alleged Convention violation. The Court has also stipulated that in order for an applicant to be able to claim to be a victim of a violation of the Convention, there must be a sufficiently direct link between the applicant and the harm that they consider they have sustained as a result of the alleged violation. This requirement was in issue in *Brudnicka and others* v *Poland*.[65] There, the applicants were the relatives of sailors who had died when a ferry sank. The causes of the accident were investigated by several maritime disputes divisions, which found that the crew had been negligent. The Government argued that the applicants did not have 'victim status' as individual crew members had not been named by the maritime chambers. However, the Court rejected that position, finding that the status of victim was not conditional solely on a finding that an applicant's reputation

---

[61] *Radio France and others* v *France*, No. 53984/00, dec. 23.9.03. In *Österreichischer Rundfunk* v *Austria*, No. 35841/02, 7.12.06, the applicant public broadcaster was considered to qualify as a 'non-governmental organisation' in view of its editorial independence and institutional autonomy. See also *Islamic Republic of Iran Shipping Lines* v *Turkey*, No. 40998/98, 13.12.07; *Unédic* v *France*, No. 20153/04, 18.12.08; *Mackay and BBC Scotland* v *UK*, No. 10734/05, 7.12.10.

[62] See, e.g. *Senator Lines GmbH* v *15 Member States of the European Union*, No. 56672/00, dec. 10.3.04.

[63] See, e.g. *Burden* v *UK*, No. 13378/05, 29.4.08, para. 33. See also, e.g. *Lindsay and others* v *UK*, No. 31699/96, dec. 17.1.97 (application claiming to represent more than one million people in Northern Ireland declared inadmissible *ratione personae* with the provisions of the Convention); *Skender* v *former Yugoslav Republic of Macedonia*, No. 62059/00, dec. 10.3.05 (provision of primary schooling in Turkish: the applicant's daughter could not claim to be a 'victim' as she had in fact been receiving her education in the Turkish language); *Ada Rossi and others* v *Italy*, No. 55185/08, dec. 16.12.08 (complaint by severely disabled persons, and representative associations, concerning domestic court decision permitting artificial nutrition and hydration of coma victim to be discontinued); *Hubert Caron and others* v *France*, No. 48629/08, dec. 29.6.10 (conviction for destroying fields of genetically modified crops).

[64] No. 20348/92, 25.9.96.

[65] No. 54723/00, 3.3.05.

had been harmed, and that the applicability of the Convention did not depend on estab-lishing whether each individual crew member was at fault. The case of *Dilipak v Turkey*[66] concerned the prosecution of a journalist for denigrating the armed forces, after writing an article critical of various commanding officers' interventions into Government policy. The Government argued that as the criminal proceedings had been discontinued, the applicant did not have 'victim status'. However, this was rejected by the Court on the basis of the 'chill-ing effect' of the applicant remaining at risk of being found guilty and punished: the criminal proceedings had been pending for six and a half years.

There are numerous examples of Convention applications in which the applicants have been **4.29** found to have failed the victim status test,[67] in which case the application will be declared inadmissible *ratione personae*. For example, in *Fédération Chrétienne des Témoins de Jéhovah de France v France*,[68] the applicant, a national association representing Jehovah's Witnesses, sought to complain about a parliamentary report on sects which it claimed provoked a policy of repression and a law to prevent and repress sects. The case was declared inadmissible on the basis that the applicant could not claim to have been directly affected by the measure in question. Similarly, the applicants in *Ouardiri v Switzerland*[69] and *Ligue des musulmans de Suisse and others v Switzerland*[70] were found not to have 'victim status'. They sought to oppose a proposed ban on the building of minarets, but the cases were considered to be akin to *actio popularis* as the measure had not begun to be implemented and there was nothing to suggest it would have any practical effects on the applicants. In *Magee v UK*,[71] the applicant bar-rister complained of the requirement to take an oath of allegiance for applicants to become Queen's Counsel, which he argued amounted to a violation of Articles 9, 10, 13 and 14 of the Convention. However, the case was declared inadmissible on the basis that as his application to become a Queen's Counsel had been turned down, he could not claim to be a victim of a violation under Article 34. In a case relating to common law developments restricting the use of 'discovered' documents which had been read out in court,[72] the applicants were journalists and a newspaper company who argued that their sources of information had been adversely affected because recipients of such information would be unwilling to allow journalists to see the information, and that the risk of contempt proceedings had a 'chilling effect' on their right to freedom of expression. However, the applicants were not considered to be victims because they had not themselves been restrained or fettered. In order to satisfy the 'victim' test, the detriment complained of had to be of a less indirect and remote nature.

Agrotexim and others v Greece[73] concerned the alleged unlawful interference by the muni- **4.30** cipal authorities with various rights of a brewery company, the shareholders of which were the applicants. The Court held the application to be incompatible *ratione personae* with the

---

[66] No. 29680/05, 15.9.15.

[67] See, e.g. *SEGI v Germany and others*, Nos. 6422/02 and 9916/02, dec. 23.5.02; see also *Akdeniz v Turkey*, No. 20877/10, dec. 11.3.14 (application by internet user concerning measures blocking access to internet music providers—inadmissible).

[68] No. 53430/99, dec. 6.11.01. See also, e.g. *Vatan v Russia*, No. 47978/99, 7.10.04; *Stichting Mothers of Srebrenica and others v Netherlands*, No. 65542/12, dec. 11.6.13; *Vallianatos and others v Greece*, Nos. 29381/09 and 32684/09, 7.11.13.

[69] No. 65840/09, dec. 28.6.11.

[70] No. 66274/09, dec. 28.6.11.

[71] No. 24892/95, dec. 6.4.95.

[72] *Leigh, Guardian Newspapers Ltd and Observer Ltd v UK*, No. 10039/82, dec. 11.5.84.

[73] No. 14807/89, Series A, No. 330, 24.10.95. See also, e.g. *Pokis v Latvia*, No. 528/02, dec. 5.10.06.

Convention as the applicant shareholder companies were not 'victims'. The brewery company itself could have brought the application (despite being in liquidation): piercing the 'corporate veil' would only be exceptionally justified where it was established that it was impossible for the company itself to apply under the Convention.[74] In *Capital Bank AD v Bulgaria*[75] the Court allowed an application to be brought by the chairman, vice-chairman and shareholders of a bank which was in liquidation (and where therefore it should usually have been brought by the liquidators). The Court also declined a subsequent request by the Government to have the case struck out on the basis that the bank had been liquidated. It emphasised that cases before the Court generally also had a 'moral dimension', which should be taken into account when considering whether to continue to pursue them even after an applicant had ceased to exist.[76] This would particularly be the position where the issue raised by the case transcended the person and the interests of the applicant. The Court has emphasised, however, that the right of application under Article 34 is not a transferable proprietary right.[77]

4.31 The victim test may rule out some applicants in a case, but not others.[78] In *Ahmed and others v UK*,[79] a complaint made by the union UNISON concerning the restrictions on the political activities of local government officers was declared inadmissible. The European Commission of Human Rights found that the regulations in question did not affect the rights of the union as such (under Articles 10 or 11) and therefore UNISON could not claim to be a victim of a violation of the Convention. However, applications brought by individual local government officers who were affected by the regulations were declared admissible. Therefore, if there are doubts about an applicant organisation's victim status, it is advisable to include at least one individual victim as an applicant.

4.32 Where potential applicants settle domestic proceedings prior to bringing European Court proceedings it may mean that they will no longer be able to claim to be victims of a Convention violation. This was held to be the position by the Grand Chamber in *Calvelli and Ciglio v Italy*.[80] There, the applicants' baby had died two days after birth. As a result, they brought civil proceedings for compensation, but they subsequently settled the domestic case (for 95 million lira) before their application to the European Court was lodged. See also 'Loss of victim status' at 4.48 below.

4.33 The Strasbourg institutions have allowed a degree of flexibility in certain circumstances in defining what is meant by a 'victim'. For example, in *Gorraiz Lizarraga and others v Spain*,[81] the applicants were campaigners against the flooding of their village, prior to the construction of a dam. Domestic proceedings had been brought by a local association (of which the applicants were the chairperson and a member) that had been set up in order to lobby

---

[74] See also *Pană and others v Romania*, No. 3240/03, dec. 15.11.11. In *Centro Europa 7 S.r.l. and Di Stefano v Italy*, No. 38433/09, 7.6.12 the applicant's company statutory representative was found not to have 'victim status' in respect of the failure to allocate radio frequencies to the applicant company, a licensed television broadcaster.

[75] No. 49429/99, 24.11.05.

[76] See also *OAO Neftyanaya kompaniya YUKOS v Russia*, No. 14902/04, dec. 29.1.09.

[77] *Nassau Verzekering Maatschappij N.V. v Netherlands*, No. 57602/09, dec. 4.10.11.

[78] See, e.g. *Bowman and the Society for the Protection of the Unborn Child v UK*, No. 24839/94, 4.12.95.

[79] No. 22954/93, 12.9.95. See also, e.g. *Purcell and others v Ireland*, No. 15404/89, 16.4.91.

[80] No. 32967/96, 17.1.02.

[81] No. 62543/00, 27.4.04.

against the dam's construction. Even though the applicants had not themselves been a party to the proceedings, the Court found that they could nevertheless still claim to be 'victims' in respect of a claim of a violation of Article 6 on the basis that the association had been set up for the specific purpose of defending its members' interests before the courts and that those members were directly affected by the dam project. In *Aksu* v *Turkey*[82] the applicant (who was of Roma origin) complained that a book about gypsies and a dictionary were insulting to the Roma community. Although he was not personally targeted by the publications, he was found to have victim status as he 'could … have felt offended by the remarks concerning the ethnic group to which he belonged' and he had been able to take domestic proceedings on the issue, which had been considered at two levels of jurisdiction. The case of *Cengiz and others* v *Turkey*[83] concerned the wholesale blocking of the YouTube website by an Ankara court, on the basis that selected pages of the site had infringed the prohibition on insulting the memory of Kemal Atatürk. An application was brought to Strasbourg by a group of individual users of the YouTube website. Although they had not been party to the proceedings in which the domestic court had made its decision, the Court accepted that the applicants could legitimately claim that the blocking order had affected their right to receive and impart information or ideas.

Where there is any doubt about an individual's 'victim' status, practitioners should consider **4.34** carefully whether their clients fall into any of the categories set out below at 4.35 (potential victims) or 4.43 (indirect victims).

Potential victims

Article 34 may permit an applicant to complain that the law itself violates their Convention **4.35** rights, even if there has been no specific measure implemented against them. However, potential victims of Convention violations must satisfy the Court that there is a real personal risk of being directly affected by the violation.[84]

Those considered to be at risk have fallen into various categories, including those at risk **4.36** of criminal prosecution. The cases of *Dudgeon* v *UK*,[85] *Norris* v *Ireland*,[86] and *Modinos* v *Cyprus*[87] all concerned domestic legislation criminalising homosexual acts. In *Dudgeon*, the applicant complained that he was liable to prosecution because of his homosexual conduct and complained of the fear, suffering and psychological distress caused by the very existence of the laws in question. He had been questioned by the police about his homosexual activities and his house had been searched, but criminal proceedings had not been brought against him. Nevertheless, the Court accepted that the very existence of the legislation continuously and directly affected his private life. It was also relevant that the law in question was not a 'dead letter'. A similar decision was reached by the Commission on the applicant's status as a 'victim' in *Sutherland* v *UK*,[88] which concerned the fixing of the minimum age for lawful

---

[82] Nos. 4149/04 and 41029/04, 15.3.12.
[83] Nos. 48226/10 and 14027/11, 1.12.15.
[84] See, e.g. *Open Door and Dublin Well Woman* v *Ireland*, Nos. 14234/88 and 14253/88, Series A, No. 246, 29.10.92, para. 44 and *Johnston and others* v *Ireland*, No. 9697/82, Series A, No. 112, 18.12.86, para. 42; *Burden* v *UK*, No. 13378/05, 29.4.08, para. 34.
[85] No. 7525/76, Series A, No. 45, 23.9.81.
[86] No. 10581/83, Series A, No. 142, 26.10.88.
[87] No. 15070/89, Series A, No. 259, 22.4.93.
[88] No. 25186/94, 1.7.97.

homosexual activities at 18 rather than 16. Before he reached the age of 18, the existence of the legislation directly affected the applicant's private life, even though he had not even been threatened with prosecution. In *ADT* v *UK*,[89] the applicant was prosecuted and convicted for gross indecency. This was held to violate Article 8, but so too was the maintenance in force of legislation criminalising homosexual acts between men in private. The applicant in *S.A.S.* v *France*[90] was a Muslim woman who wished to wear a full-face veil. She was considered to have the status of a 'victim' as she faced the possibility of prosecution under a 2010 law prohibiting anyone concealing their face in public places.

4.37 Those who fall into a particular group within society which might be affected by a particular measure or omission may also be considered as potential victims. In *Balmer-Schafroth* v *Switzerland*[91] the Government argued that the applicants, who were residents living close to a nuclear power station, could not claim to be victims of a decision to extend the power station's operating licence because the consequences of the violations of which they complained were too remote to affect them directly and personally. However, the Court rejected those arguments, as the applicants' objections had been found admissible by the Swiss Federal Council and because there could be a Convention violation even in the absence of prejudice (which is relevant only in the context of Article 41 awards). In *John Shelley* v *UK*,[92] the applicant complained that the authorities were failing to take preventive steps in respect of known risks through the spread of viruses in prison. Although he did not claim to have been directly affected himself, the Court accepted the applicant's victim status as he was detained in prison where there was a significantly higher risk of infection of HIV and HCV, and therefore could claim to be affected by the health policy.

4.38 The case of *Open Door and Dublin Well Woman* v *Ireland*[93] concerned an injunction imposed by the Irish courts preventing the dissemination of information to pregnant women on abortion facilities outside Ireland. The Government raised objections about the victim status of two of the applicants who joined the application as women of child-bearing age, but who were not pregnant. The Court held that the two applicants belonged to a class of women of child-bearing age that might be adversely affected by the restrictions imposed by the injunction. Therefore, they ran the risk of being directly prejudiced by the measure complained of. The applicant in *Michaud* v *France*[94] was a French lawyer who objected to rules introduced by the National Bar Council requiring the reporting of suspected money-laundering. Although the rules had not been invoked against the applicant, as they applied to all French lawyers, he was considered to belong to a class of people who risked being directly affected by them. In *Burden* v *UK*,[95] the applicant sisters, who lived together, complained (under Article 14 taken together with Article 1 of Protocol No. 1) that, when either of them died, the survivor would be required to pay inheritance tax on the dead sister's share of the family home (unlike the survivor of a married couple or a homosexual relationship registered under the Civil Partnership Act 2004). The Grand Chamber accepted that given

---

[89] No. 35765/97, 31.7.00.
[90] No. 43835/11, 1.7.14.
[91] No. 22110/93, 26.8.97.
[92] No. 23800/06, dec. 4.1.08.
[93] Nos. 14234/88 and 14253/88, Series A, No. 246, 29.10.92.
[94] No. 12323/11, 6.12.12.
[95] No. 13378/05, 29.4.08.

their ages, the nature of their wills and the value of their property, the applicants had established a real risk that one of them would be required to pay substantial inheritance tax on the property inherited from her sister, and they could therefore claim to be victims of the alleged discriminatory treatment.

In *Campbell and Cosans* v *UK*[96] the Government argued that a complaint brought by parents on behalf of children who might be subjected to corporal punishment if they did not behave properly, could not satisfy the victim test. However, the European Commission of Human Rights found that the threat of a potential use of corporal punishment as a means of discipline meant that the children had the requisite direct and immediate personal interest.

4.39

Potential violations of the Convention will also arise in cases concerning specific measures which, if implemented, would breach the Convention. This often arises in the context of immigration or extradition cases. The case of *Soering* v *UK*[97] concerned the decision to extradite the applicant to the United States where he faced capital murder charges in Virginia and a possible death sentence. Therefore, if he were sentenced to death, he would be exposed to the 'death row phenomenon', which he claimed would violate Article 3. In those circumstances, the Court found that the responsibility of the state would be engaged where there were substantial grounds for believing that, if extradited, the applicant faced a real risk of being subjected to torture or inhuman or degrading treatment or punishment. That had to be the case, in order to ensure the effectiveness of the Article 3 safeguards, given the serious and irreparable nature of the suffering which the applicant faced. There have been many examples of applicants complaining of prospective violations in deportation cases.[98] In *Chahal* v *UK*[99] the applicant complained that his deportation to India would violate his rights under Article 3 because as a Sikh political activist he risked being subjected to torture. The state's responsibility will be engaged where there are substantial grounds for believing that the applicant, if expelled, would face a real risk of inhuman or degrading treatment contrary to Article 3. In *D* v *UK*[100] the applicant, who was suffering from the advanced stages of the AIDS virus, complained of a violation of Article 3 were he to be removed to St Kitts, where he was born, because the lack of adequate medical treatment would expose him to inhuman and degrading treatment.

4.40

Nevertheless, applicants will be required to wait for the final decision in any domestic proceedings and to exhaust available and effective avenues of appeal before their complaints will be admitted by the Court. The applicants in *Vijayanathan and Pusparajah* v *France*[101] were found not to be 'victims' of a violation of the Convention where they had been ordered to leave French territory. As Sri Lankan citizens of Tamil origin, they claimed they would be at risk of torture were they to be returned to Sri Lanka. It was decisive that the direction to leave was not in itself enforceable, that no expulsion order had been made and were such an order to be made the applicants would have had a right of appeal.

4.41

---

[96] Nos. 7511/76 and 7743/76, 16.5.80.
[97] No. 14038/88, Series A, No. 161, 7.7.89.
[98] See, e.g. *N* v *Finland*, No. 38885/02, 26.7.05; *Nnyanzi* v *UK*, No. 21878/06, 8.4.08.
[99] No. 22414/93, 15.11.96. The principle established in *Chahal* was confirmed by the Grand Chamber in *Saadi* v *Italy*, No. 37201/06, 28.2.08.
[100] No. 30240/96, 2.5.97.
[101] Nos. 17550/90 and 17825/91, Series A, No. 241-B, 27.8.92.

4.42 The extent of the secrecy of legislation or measures taken by public authorities may have a bearing on the question of victim status. In *Klass and others v Germany*,[102] the applicant lawyers complained about the domestic law in Germany relating to secret surveillance, even though they had no evidence that they had been under surveillance themselves. The Court found that the applicants should not be prevented from claiming to be victims of the alleged violation where, because of the secrecy of the measures in question, it was not possible to prove any specific implementation against the applicants. The NGOs, Liberty, British Irish Rights Watch and the Irish Council for Civil Liberties, successfully complained to the Court about the alleged interception of their communications in the 1990s by the British Ministry of Defence. The Court accepted that the existence of powers under the Interception of Communications Act 1985, particularly those allowing the examination, use and storage of intercepted communications, constituted an interference with the Article 8 rights of the applicant NGOs, since they were persons to whom the powers might have been applied.[103] Accordingly, applicants may in certain circumstances legitimately complain to the Court of being a victim of a violation because of the mere existence of secret surveillance measures.[104] In assessing such cases, the Court will consider the scope of the legislation permitting secret surveillance to assess whether applicants could be affected by it, either because they belong to a group of persons targeted by the legislation or because the legislation directly affects all users of communication services. The Court will also take account of the availability of national remedies and will adjust the degree of scrutiny depending on the effectiveness of such remedies.[105]

Indirect victims

4.43 An individual who is not directly affected by a particular measure or omission may nevertheless have been 'indirectly' affected by the violation of the Convention rights of another person. This may often be the case in respect of close family connections, but it could also include other third parties. For example, family members of a person who is subject to a deportation decision might claim to be victims of a Convention violation. The case of *Chahal v UK*[106] concerned the proposed deportation of Mr Chahal, a Sikh separatist leader, on grounds that he posed a threat to national security. Not only did Mr Chahal himself bring proceedings under the Convention, but so too did his wife and children, arguing that his deportation would violate their right to respect for family life under Article 8. In *Kurt v Turkey*[107] the applicant complained of the disappearance of her son who had last been seen in the custody of the security forces. She successfully invoked Articles 5 and 13 in respect of her son, but she also obtained a finding of a violation of Article 3 in respect of her own anguish and distress, which she had suffered over a prolonged period.

4.44 The case of *Abdulaziz, Cabales and Balkandali v UK*[108] concerned the 1971 Immigration Act and Rules that prevented the applicants' husbands from remaining with them or joining

---

[102] Series A, No. 28, 6.9.78. See also, e.g. *Case of the Association for European Integration and Human Rights and Ekimdzhiev v Bulgaria*, No. 62540/00, 28.6.07.

[103] *Liberty and Others v UK*, No. 58243/00, 1.7.08.

[104] See also, e.g. *Virginia Matthews v UK*, No. 28576/95, 16.10.96: allegation that applicant peace campaigner's telephone calls had been intercepted.

[105] *Roman Zakharov v Russia*, No. 47143/06, 4.12.15, para. 171.

[106] No. 22414/93, 15.11.96.

[107] No. 24276/94, 25.5.98.

[108] Nos. 9214/80, 9473/81 and 9474/81, 28.5.85.

them in the United Kingdom. The case was brought by the wives who were lawfully and permanently settled in the United Kingdom and the Court found a violation of Article 8 taken together with Article 14 (as victims of sex discrimination) and of Article 13.

Absence of requirement of 'prejudice'

There is no need for a 'victim' to have suffered 'prejudice' or 'detriment', which is relevant **4.45** only in relation to awards of 'just satisfaction' under Article 41 of the Convention.[109] Article 41 awards are discussed in chapter 8. For example, in *De Jong, Baljet and Van Den Brink* v *Netherlands*[110] the Government objected to Mr Van den Brink's victim status because of the alleged lack of detriment to him. He was a military conscript who had refused to obey orders on grounds of conscientious objection and was therefore arrested and held in custody. The Government argued that he could not claim to be a 'victim' as his time spent in custody on remand was deducted from the sentence imposed upon him. However, the Court held that he had been directly affected by the decision in issue and that the deduction from sentence could not deprive the applicant of his victim status. A similar decision was made in *CC* v *UK*,[111] where the applicant complained of automatic pre-trial detention. The European Commission of Human Rights found that the deduction of the period of pre-trial detention from his sentence did not remove his victim status as it did not constitute an acknowledgement that the Convention had been violated.

In *Eckle* v *Germany*,[112] which concerned the length of criminal proceedings for fraud brought **4.46** against the applicant, the Court held that the mitigation of sentence and the discontinuance of the proceedings granted because of their excessive length, did not in principle deprive the applicant of his victim status. They were matters to be taken into consideration in assessing the extent of the damage he had suffered.

The position may be different, however, where the national authorities have acknowledged, **4.47** either expressly or in substance, that there has been a violation of the Convention and where redress has then been provided to the victim.[113] This is discussed further below at 4.48.

Loss of victim status

Any applicant to the European Court must (pursuant to Article 34 of the Convention) claim **4.48** to be the *victim* of a violation of the Convention (see 4.27 above). Applicants may, however, lose their status as 'victims' for the purposes of Article 34.[114] In *Eckle* v *Germany*,[115] the Court laid down the following test as to when an applicant will be considered to have lost their 'victim status':

(1) where the national authorities have acknowledged that there has been a breach of the Convention, either expressly, or in substance; and
(2) where the applicant has been provided with redress.

---

[109] See, e.g. *Balmer-Schafroth* v *Switzerland*, No. 22110/93, 26.8.97, para. 26 and *Amuur* v *France*, No. 19776/92, 25.6.96, para. 36.

[110] Nos. 8805/79, 8806/79 and 9242/81, Series A, No. 77, 22.5.84.

[111] No. 32819/96, dec. 1.2.97.

[112] No. 8130/78, Series A, No. 51, 15.7.82.

[113] *Ibid.*, para. 66.

[114] For a summary of the relevant principles, see: *Scordino* v *Italy (No. 1)*, No. 36813/97, 29.3.06.

[115] No. 8130/78, Series A, No. 51, 15.7.82, para. 66. See also, e.g. *Christian Democratic People's Party* v *Moldova*, No. 28793/02, dec. 22.3.05.

4.49 There are accordingly two issues raised in the relevant case-law: the adequacy of the 'acknowledgement' by the authorities and the sufficiency of the redress provided to the applicant.[116] The adequacy of any redress will be assessed by the Court in the light of all of the circumstances of the case, and may include, for example, an assessment as to whether the amount of any compensation awarded in the course of domestic proceedings is commensurate with the nature of the damage complained of.[117] An applicant's victim status may therefore be affected by settlement of the domestic proceedings, or acquittal in criminal proceedings,[118] a successful appeal or discontinuation of the domestic proceedings. For example, in *Caraher v UK*,[119] the applicant alleged violations of Articles 2 and 13 arising from the fatal shooting of her husband by British soldiers in Northern Ireland. Two soldiers were prosecuted for the shooting, but were acquitted. The application was introduced in Strasbourg in 1994. In 1998 the applicant settled a High Court action against the Ministry of Defence for aggravated damages in respect of the death of her husband on receipt of £50,000 in full and final settlement of all claims. The application to the European Court was subsequently declared inadmissible as the Court found that the applicant could no longer claim to be a victim of a violation of the Convention, having settled the civil proceedings.[120] However, an award of damages from a statutory compensation scheme may not remove an applicant's victim status. In *ZW v UK*,[121] the applicant complained under Article 3 of the Convention that she has been subjected to inhuman and degrading treatment arising from the failure of the local authority to monitor her foster placement and protect her from physical and sexual abuse by her foster-parents. Unlike the position in the *Caraher* case, the payment to the claimant was not made by the body which had allegedly caused the Convention violation, but rather came from the statutory Criminal Injuries Compensation Scheme and was not related to any alleged failings by the local authority in question. See also, 'Who can claim to be a victim' at 4.27 above.

---

[116] For example, in *O'Keeffe v Ireland*, No. 35810/09, 28.1.14 (a case concerning the state's failure to protect the applicant from being sexually abused by a teacher in primary school), the Court rejected the government's arguments that the applicant had lost her victim status, as there had neither been acknowledgement of a violation of the Convention by the state, nor was she likely to receive adequate redress.

[117] See, e.g. *R.R. v Poland*, No. 27617/04, 26.5.11. See also *Mironovas and others v Lithuania*, No. 40828/12 et al., 8.12.15 (very low levels of compensation awarded by domestic courts in relation to poor prison conditions—applicants had not lost their victim status).

[118] See, e.g. *Bouglame v Belgium*, No. 16147/08, dec. 2.3.10. However, a defendant's acquittal may not always exclude that person from claiming to be a victim of a violation of the procedural guarantees of Article 6. See, e.g. *Heaney and McGuinness v Ireland*, No. 34720/97, 21.12.00, paras. 43–6; *Quinn v Ireland*, No. 36887/97, 21.12.00, paras. 43–6.

[119] No. 24520/94, dec. 11.1.00. But contrast that decision with *Nikolova and Velichkova v Bulgaria*, No. 7888/03, 20.12.07. See also *McCaughey and others v UK*, No. 43098/09, 16.7.13 (in view of the applicants' pending civil action, their complaints under Article 2 (except for complaint about investigative delay) found to be inadmissible, as being premature on the ground that domestic remedies had not yet been exhausted).

[120] See also *Hay v UK*, No. 41894/98, dec. 17.10.00; *Murillo Saldias and others v Spain*, No. 76973/01, dec. 28.11.06; *Chagos Islanders v UK*, No. 35622/04, dec. 11.12.12.

[121] No. 34962/97, dec. 27.11.01. See also, by contrast, *Şandru and others v Romania*, No. 22465/03, 8.12.09 (compensation awards which did not result from a friendly settlement between the parties and where the authorities had not acknowledged any deficiencies in the investigation—no loss of victim status).

Case examples: victim status retained

Applying the *Eckle* test in the case of *Lüdi* v *Switzerland*,[122] the Court rejected the **4.50**
Government's arguments that the applicant was no longer a victim of a Convention violation because his sentence had been reduced by the Court of Appeal. The Court found that
rather than acknowledging that the use of an undercover agent in the criminal proceedings
against the applicant had violated the Convention, the authorities had expressly decided that
it had been compatible with the Convention's obligations.

In the case of *Moustaquim* v *Belgium*,[123] the applicant's deportation order had been sus- **4.51**
pended for a trial period of two years and he was allowed to remain in Belgium. However,
the authorities had not made reparation for the consequences of living under threat of
deportation for more than five years. Therefore, the Court rejected the Government's submissions that the case had become 'devoid of purpose'. *Kurić and others* v *Slovenia*[124] concerned the position of the 'erased'—former citizens of Yugoslavia who complained they had
been arbitrarily deprived of the possibility of acquiring Slovenian citizenship, and whose
names were taken off the register of permanent residents, and who became de facto stateless
after Slovenian independence. The Government argued that six applicants, who had subsequently been granted permanent residence permits, had lost their victim status. However,
that argument was rejected by the Court, which found that they had not received appropriate or sufficient redress, taking account of the insecurity and legal uncertainty to which
they had been subjected for nearly 20 years, the gravity of the consequences of the 'erasure'
and the fact that compensation claims were still pending. There was a similar outcome in
Nada v *Switzerland*[125] which concerned a travel ban imposed on the applicant resulting
from legislation implementing UN Security Council resolutions. Although the ban was
later rescinded, this did not amount to an acknowledgement of a Convention violation
(even implicitly), and no redress had been provided (in respect of a six year period when the
ban had remained in force). The applicant in *Burdov* v *Russia*[126] successfully brought proceedings for compensation, after having been exposed to radiation when called up to work
on the aftermath of the Chernobyl disaster. However, crucially, those proceedings were not
in fact implemented until 2001, when the outstanding sum was paid to the applicant by
the authorities. In those circumstances, the applicant could still claim to be a victim of a
Convention violation as there had been no acknowledgement of the alleged violations and
the redress he had received was inadequate. In *Pisano* v *Italy*,[127] the applicant complained
under Article 6 about the unfairness of the criminal proceedings brought against him,
notably because of the failure to call a particular witness. The Grand Chamber held that,
even though he was subsequently acquitted during a retrial, the applicant could still claim
to be a 'victim' of a Convention violation because the domestic authorities had not found
a violation of the Convention as regards the failure to examine the witness during the initial trial (although it struck the case out as having been resolved, under Article 37(1)(b)).
In *Posokhov* v *Russia*,[128] whilst the applicant's criminal conviction had subsequently been

---

[122] No. 12433/86, Series A, No. 238, 15.6.92.
[123] No. 12313/86, Series A, No. 193, 18.2.91.
[124] No. 26828/06, 26.6.12.
[125] No. 10593/08, 12.9.12.
[126] No. 59498/00, 7.5.02. See also *Prodan* v *Moldova*, No. 49806/99, 18.5.09.
[127] No. 36732/97, 24.10.02.
[128] No. 63486/00, 4.3.03.

erased, the authorities had failed to acknowledge expressly the Convention violation arising from the involvement of lay judges in the applicant's case. Similarly, in *Osmani and others v former Yugoslav Republic of Macedonia*,[129] the fact that the applicant was not required to serve all of his sentence following his criminal conviction, as a result of an amnesty, did not amount to an acknowledgement of a Convention violation. Where the 'redress' provided to the applicant is in the form of compensation, the sum awarded by the domestic authorities 'must bear a reasonable relationship to the sum awarded by the [European] Court in similar cases'.[130] In *Sakhnovskiy v Russia*[131] the Grand Chamber sought to resolve inconsistencies in the Court's case law as to the application of the 'loss of victim status' test in respect of criminal proceedings in Russian cases. In one line of cases the Court had simply accepted the reopening of criminal proceedings as a form of redress in itself, without considering the subsequent course of such proceedings. However, the Court was concerned about the number of cases in which the authorities had reopened proceedings following the communication of the case in Strasbourg, which it considered could be open to abuse. Therefore, in *Sakhnovskiy* the Grand Chamber clarified that in order to decide whether or not applicants had retained their victim status the Court will consider the proceedings as a whole, including the proceedings that follow the reopening. In *Mosley v UK*,[132] although the applicant had successfully brought domestic proceedings for breach of privacy, and had been awarded damages, he was still considered to have retained his victim status as regards his additional complaint about the adequacy of the relevant domestic law, which could not have been remedied by an award of damages.

4.52   The effectiveness of investigations will be critical in cases relating to Articles 2 and 3 of the Convention.[133] The case of *Nikolova and Velichkova v Bulgaria*[134] concerned the death of the first applicant's husband (the second applicant's father) of a brain haemorrhage following his detention by the police. Two police officers were convicted of causing the death of Mr Nikolov using intentional grievous bodily harm and they were sentenced to a three-year suspended prison sentence. The applicants were awarded compensation, to be paid by the police officers. Even so, the Court rejected the Government's arguments that, as a consequence, the applicants had lost their victim status, as the criminal proceedings against the police officers had lasted seven years, they received only the minimum sentence (which was suspended) and were never in fact disciplined. As a result the Court considered that the authorities had fostered the officers' 'sense of impunity' and had failed to provide appropriate redress to the applicants (and the Court found both a substantive and procedural violation of Article 2). In *Gäfgen v Germany*,[135] the applicant complained of a violation of Article 3 because he was threatened in police detention with the use of 'intolerable pain' so

---

[129]   No. 50841/99, dec. 11.10.01.

[130]   See, e.g. *Scordino and others v Italy*, No. 36813/97, dec. 27.3.03 (compensation for excessive length of proceedings awarded by the Court of Appeal was about a tenth of sums awarded by the European Court in similar cases); *Kudić v Bosnia and Herzegovina*, No. 28971/05, 9.12.08 (insufficient pecuniary damages for non-enforcement of final judgment); *Mučibabić v Serbia*, No. 34661/07, 12.7.16 (insufficient compensation relating to death of applicant's son).

[131]   No. 21272/03, 2.11.10. See also *Yefimenko v Russia*, No. 152/04, 12.2.13 (re violation of Article 5(1)(a)).

[132]   No. 48009/08, 10.4.11.

[133]   See, e.g. *Mučibabić v Serbia*, No. 34661/07, 12.7.16 (insufficient scope of review by Constitutional Court relating to death of applicant's son).

[134]   No. 7888/03, 20.12.07.

[135]   No. 22978/05, 1.6.10.

that he should disclose the whereabouts of a boy whom he had abducted and murdered. Whilst the domestic courts had expressly acknowledged that his interrogation had violated Article 3, and the police officers were found guilty of coercion and incitement to coercion, the Court found that the applicant had not lost his victim status because the two officers were subjected only to modest and suspended fines (60 and 90 daily payments of €60 and €120, respectively). The Court was also critical of the fact that one officer was subsequently appointed as chief of a police authority, and that the applicant's proceedings for compensation had been unresolved for three years.[136] In *Çamdereli* v *Turkey*[137] the applicant received a modest payment of compensation after she was beaten by a gendarme. However, criminal proceedings against the gendarme had been suspended and the charges dropped. Accordingly, the authorities were found to have failed to have provided adequate redress and the applicant retained her victim status.

Case examples: victim status lost

The case of *Göktepe* v *Turkey*[138] concerned the death of a journalist after the police intervened during a demonstration following a funeral. In contrast to *Nikolova and Velichkova*, a swift domestic investigation had established that his death had been caused by blows inflicted by the police. A number of police officers were prosecuted for unintentional homicide, and five officers were convicted (two years and two months after the incident) and given prison sentences of seven and a half years. Furthermore, the applicants received pecuniary and non-pecuniary compensation in respect of the death of their relative. Accordingly, they were no longer considered to be 'victims' of a violation of the Convention. In *Beck* v *Norway*[139] criminal proceedings brought against the applicant exceeded the reasonable time requirement under Article 6(1). However, the city court had expressly upheld the applicant's complaint of a violation of Article 6(1) and the applicant was deemed to have received adequate redress, as his sentence of imprisonment was considerably reduced. In those circumstances, the applicant could no longer claim to be a 'victim'. A similar decision was made in *Bako* v *Slovakia*,[140] a case concerning the length of civil proceedings, where the Constitutional Court had acknowledged the violation and awarded the applicant a sum of compensation that was not unreasonable. The presumption of innocence was in issue in the case of *Arrigo and Vella* v *Malta*,[141] as a result of prejudicial comment made by the Prime Minister whilst criminal proceedings were pending against the applicant judges. The

4.53

---

[136] The Court left open the question whether measures of restitution were also required relating to the continuing impact of the prohibited method of investigation on the trial (notably the exclusion of evidence obtained in violation of Article 3). See also on this point the joint partly concurring opinion of Judges Tulkens, Ziemele and Bianku.

[137] No. 28433/02, 17.7.08. See also, e.g. *Vladimir Romanov* v *Russia*, No. 41461/02, 24.7.08; *Ciorap* v *Moldova (No. 2)*, No. 7481/06, 20.7.10; *Razzakov* v *Russia*, No. 57519/09, 5.2.15.

[138] No. 64731/01, dec. 26.4.05. See also *Floarea Pop* v *Romania*, No. 631/01, 6.4.10.

[139] No. 26390/95, 26.6.01. See also *Morby* v *Luxembourg*, No. 27156/02, dec. 13.11.03. But contrast these decisions with *Jensen* v *Denmark*, No. 48470/99, dec. 20.9.01 (where the domestic court expressly rejected the applicant's claim that proceedings had exceeded a reasonable time under Article 6(1) of the Convention—the applicant could therefore still claim to be a 'victim' of a violation).

[140] No. 60227/00, dec. 15.3.05. See also *Kalajzic* v *Croatia*, No. 15382/04, dec. 8.9.06. But contrast those decisions with *Tomašić* v *Croatia,* No. 21753/02, 19.10.06 (compensation awarded by Constitutional Court amounted to about 15 per cent of awards made by European Court in equivalent circumstances—no loss of victim status); *Gräßer* v *Germany*, No. 66491/01, 5.10.06 (Federal Constitutional Court acknowledged violation of Article 6(1) but had no power to speed up proceedings or order compensation).

[141] No. 6569/04, dec. 10.5.05.

case was declared inadmissible as the applicants could no longer claim to be 'victims' of a Convention violation, because the Constitutional Court had acknowledged the breach of the applicants' Article 6(2) rights and had provided redress by requiring that its decision was brought to the attention of the court hearing the criminal charges pending against the applicants. In *Akkoç* v *Turkey*[142] the applicant teacher received a disciplinary sanction of one year's suspension from promotion, resulting from a statement she had made to the press. This decision was subsequently quashed with retrospective effect by the administrative court. Even though the process took more than five and a half years and the applicant was not awarded any compensation, she was considered no longer to be a victim of a violation of her rights under Article 10. The case of *M.A.* v *UK*[143] concerned the applicant's successive attempts, as a non-resident father, to gain contact with his daughter. The High Court had acknowledged a series of failings in the domestic system and made recommendations for future changes required. The applicant had not sought compensation in the domestic proceedings, but he did receive a public apology from the High Court for the systemic failures. Therefore, the violation of the applicant's Convention rights had been acknowledged in substance and he had received sufficient redress.

4.54 Where interferences with rights are caused by 'incidental errors' rather than being deliberate and systematic, a formal apology may remove the applicant's victim status. For example, an apology for interference with prisoners' correspondence, and an assurance that steps would be taken to prevent it happening again, have been found to do so.[144] In *Grant* v *UK*,[145] a case concerning the rights of transsexuals, following on from the judgment in *Christine Goodwin* v *UK*,[146] the Court was required to assess when the applicant's victim status began and ended. It found that from the date of the *Goodwin* judgment there was no longer any justification for failing to recognise the change of gender of post-operative transsexuals. The applicant's victim status ended when the Gender Recognition Act 2004 came into force (providing the applicant with the means to obtain the legal recognition previously denied).

When Inadmissibility Arguments can be Raised and Decided

4.55 The Court may declare an application inadmissible at any stage of the proceedings (Article 35(4)).[147] An admissibility issue may be considered by the Court of its own motion, even though the point has not been made by the respondent government.[148] It may uphold a respondent government's arguments that the applicants had failed to exhaust appropriate domestic remedies at the merits stage of the case, even though the case was previously declared admissible.[149] This was the case in *McGinley and Egan*,[150] concerning access to records relating to the applicants' participation in nuclear tests on Christmas Island in

---

[142] Nos. 22947/93 and 22948/93, 10.10.00.

[143] No. 35242/04, dec. 26.4.05.

[144] See *Faulkner* v *UK*, No. 37471/97, dec. 18.9.01; *Armstrong* v *UK*, No. 48521/99, dec. 25.9.01.

[145] No. 32570/03, 23.5.06.

[146] No. 28957/95, 11.7.02.

[147] See, e.g. *Sammut and Visa Investments Limited* v *Malta*, No. 27023/03, dec. 16.10.07, para. 56.

[148] See, e.g. *Walker* v *UK*, No. 34979/97, dec. 25.1.00 (six months' time limit); *The Professional Trades Union for Prison, Correctional and Secure Psychiatric Workers (POA) and others* v *UK*, No. 59253/11, dec. 21.5.13 (application already submitted to another procedure of international investigation or settlement).

[149] See, e.g. *Aytekin* v *Turkey*, No. 22880/93, 23.9.98; *Azinas* v *Cyprus*, No. 56679/00, 28.4.04.

[150] Nos. 21825/93 and 23414/94, 9.6.98.

1958. In its judgment in that case, the Court accepted the Government's arguments that the failure to utilise a procedure available before the Pensions Appeal Tribunal to obtain disclosure of relevant documents meant that it could not be said that the state had prevented the applicants from gaining access to the documents, or that the state had falsely denied the existence of relevant documents. The Commission, however, had found that the applicants would not have had a feasible means of obtaining the records, because of the Minister's power to refuse access to documents under the Pensions Appeal Tribunal procedure, on national security grounds.

However, the respondent government will be estopped from raising new admissibil- **4.56** ity arguments at the merits stage, if those arguments were not previously raised at the admissibility stage (as required by Rule 55),[151] unless there are developments after the admissibility decision which are relevant to the question of admissibility amounting to special circumstances warranting its re-examination,[152] or further information comes to light,[153] such as a reversal of domestic case law or the introduction by the applicant of a new complaint. In *McGonnell* v *UK*,[154] the Government argued before the Court that the applicant had failed to exhaust domestic remedies in relation to his complaint that the domestic proceedings had not been independent or impartial, as he had failed to appeal to the Court of Appeal. The Court found that the Government was estopped from relying on such arguments which had not been raised before the European Commission. In *N.C.* v *Italy*,[155] the Government raised objections, after the admissibility stage, concerning the applicant's alleged failure to exhaust domestic remedies. The case was declared admissible in December 1998, and the Government's objection was based on the applicant's failure to lodge a claim for compensation with the domestic courts following his acquittal, which became final in October 1999. Accordingly, the Court acknowledged that this point could not have been raised on admissibility. However, noting that the objection was not lodged by the Government until January 2002 (after a delay of two years and two months) the Grand Chamber held that the Government was estopped from raising its objection because of the unreasonable delay. The case of *Al-Skeini and others* v *UK*[156] concerned the deaths of the applicants' relatives during the British Army's occupation of Iraq in 2003. When the Government sought to argue before the Grand Chamber that their deaths were not attributable to the UK armed forces, the Court found that it was estopped from raising that argument, which had not previously been made before the domestic courts.

As regards estoppel, the Court makes a distinction between points of admissibility and **4.57** issues of jurisdiction. Therefore, a government may not be estopped from raising a new issue at the merits stage which goes to the Court's temporal jurisdiction.[157]

---

[151] See, e.g. *Artico* v *Italy*, Series A, No. 37, 13.5.80, paras. 27–8; *Pine Valley Developments Ltd* v *Ireland*, No. 12742/87, Series A, No. 222, 29.11.91, para. 45; *Akkoç* v *Turkey*, Nos. 22947/93 and 22948/93, 10.10.00; *Svinarenko and Slyadnev* v *Russia*, Nos. 32541/08 and 43441/08, 17.7.14, paras. 77–83.

[152] *Stankov and the United Macedonian Organisation Ilinden* v *Bulgaria*, Nos. 29221/95 and 29225/95, 2.10.01, para. 54.

[153] See, e.g. *Haralambidis and others* v *Greece*, No. 36706/97, 29.3.01.

[154] No. 28488/95, 8.2.02.

[155] No. 24952/94, 18.12.02.

[156] No. 55721/07, 7.7.11.

[157] *Blečić* v *Croatia*, No. 59532/00, 8.3.06, paras. 63–9.

[handwritten margin notes, top:] relevant provisions → exhaustion | no significant disadvantage: 4.129 (also 8.33)

[handwritten left margin:] 4.58 4.64 4.91 4.68 4.98

[handwritten:] 6 month: 4.104 4.122 4.116

Exhaustion of Domestic Remedies

Introduction

4.58 By far the most important admissibility rules, in practice, are the requirement to exhaust domestic remedies and to lodge an application with the European Court within six months from the date when the final decision was taken. The rules are closely linked, as the time limit for lodging an application will depend upon the extent of the domestic remedies available. Respondent governments will frequently raise, wherever possible, any objection that domestic remedies have not been exhausted; therefore this is an area where practitioners need to be very clear about their client's position.

4.59 The rationale for the domestic remedies rule is the principle that the domestic authorities should always be given the opportunity to put right a Convention violation before the matter is to be considered by the European Court. The rule is based on the assumption, reflected in Article 13, that there is in the domestic system an effective remedy available in respect of the alleged breach, whether or not the Convention is incorporated into national law.[158] The assessment as to whether domestic remedies have been exhausted will usually be carried out with reference to the date when the case was lodged at the European Court. However, this is not an inflexible rule. In *Wizerkaniuk v Poland*,[159] for example, the Government argued that the applicant had not exhausted domestic remedies as he did not wait for the outcome of his Constitutional Court complaint before lodging in Strasbourg. His complaint was subsequently dismissed and the Court, taking account of the principle of subsidiarity, rejected the Government's argument.

Burden of proof

4.60 Applicants are required to set out in their application the steps taken to exhaust domestic remedies. The burden of proof is then on the respondent government to raise non-exhaustion,[160] by pointing to a domestic remedy which in the circumstances of the particular case should have, but which had not, been invoked. The government must satisfy the Court that the remedy was an effective one available both in theory and in practice at the relevant time.[161] This will mean a remedy that was accessible, that was capable of providing redress in respect of the applicant's complaint and offered reasonable prospects of success.

4.61 The Court will require the respondent state to provide examples of any alleged remedy having been successfully utilised by litigants in a similar position to that of the applicant.[162]

---

[158] See, e.g. *Akdivar v Turkey*, No. 21893/93, 16.9.96, para. 65. See also Recommendation Rec(2004)6 of the Committee of Ministers to Member States on the improvement of domestic remedies.

[159] No. 18990/05, 5.7.11.

[160] *De Wilde, Ooms and Versyp v Belgium*, Series A, No. 12, 18.6.71, para. 60; *Deweer v Belgium*, Series A, No. 35, 27.2.80, para. 26.

[161] See, e.g. *Bosphorus Hava Yollari Turizm Ve Ticaret AS v Ireland*, No. 45036/98, dec. 13.9.01; *Selim v Cyprus*, No. 47293/99, dec. 18.9.01; *Benzan v Croatia*, No. 62912/00, dec. 16.5.02; *Apostol v Georgia*, No. 40765/02, 28.11.06.

[162] See, e.g. *Kangasluoma v Finland*, No. 48339/99, 20.1.04; *M.M. v UK*, No. 24029/07, 13.11.12; *Wegrzynowski and Smolczewski v Poland*, No. 33846/07, 16.7.13; *Vallianatos and others v Greece*, Nos. 29381/09 and 32684/09, 7.11.13. As regards areas of new or developing domestic law, the Court may be willing to accept that as a reason for the absence of any settled law in relation to domestic remedies–see *Gherghina v Romania*, No. 42219/07, dec. 9.7.15, para. 100.

For example, in *Apostol* v *Georgia*,[163] the respondent government failed to satisfy the Court that an individual constitutional complaint in Georgia incorporated an effective mechanism to provide redress for the non-enforcement of domestic court judgments. In *Rodić and 3 others* v *Bosnia and Herzegovina*[164] the Government was not able to satisfy the Court that a petition to a prison inspector would have offered reasonable prospects of success in relation to complaints of assault. In *Hajduová* v *Slovakia*,[165] a case concerning domestic violence, the Court found that the Government had failed to show, 'with reference to demonstrably established consistent case law in cases similar to the applicant's' that an action for protection of personal integrity would have amounted to an effective remedy. In reaching that decision, the Court took account of the particular vulnerability of victims of domestic violence.

If the government raises an available remedy that in its view should have been utilised, the **4.62** applicant must either show why the remedy was in fact exhausted, or why the purported remedy is not adequate or effective or that there were special reasons absolving the applicant from invoking the remedy (see below at 4.98).

A respondent government whose submissions in relation to domestic remedies are incon- **4.63** sistent with its arguments in the domestic proceedings will be given short shrift by the Court. For example, in *Kolompar* v *Belgium*,[166] the Government was prevented from arguing that the applicant had failed to exhaust domestic remedies where, in the domestic proceedings, as the defendant, the state had contested the domestic court's jurisdiction in those proceedings.

An applicant should raise in domestic proceedings the substance of the complaint to be **4.64** made to the Court[167] on the basis that the domestic courts should have the opportunity to decide on a claim before it is considered by the European Court. In *Guzzardi* v *Italy*,[168] the applicant, a suspected mafioso, complained about his three-year confinement on the island of Asinara. He argued that there had been violations of various articles, but he did not refer to Article 5(1), which the European Commission of Human Rights itself raised and considered and which was the only article found by the Commission and Court to have been violated. It is therefore not strictly necessary to specify which article, or even which right, is being invoked, provided that the applicant has in substance raised the issue in question.[169] It is certainly preferable specifically to invoke the Convention in domestic proceedings, but it is not absolutely necessary to do so. In *Ahmet Sadik* v *Greece*,[170] the applicant was found by the Court not to have exhausted domestic remedies as he had at no stage relied on Article 10, or on equivalent arguments, in the domestic courts, even though Article 10 was directly applicable in Greek law. The applicant in *Azinas* v *Cyprus*,[171] was found by the Grand Chamber (at

---

[163] No. 40765/02, 28.11.06.

[164] No. 22893/05, 27.5.08, para. 58.

[165] No. 2660/03, 30.11.10. See also *Mikolajova* v *Slovakia*, No. 4479/03, 18.1.11.

[166] No. 11613/85, Series A, No. 235-C, 24.9.92, para. 31. See also *Pine Valley Developments Ltd* v *Ireland*, No. 12742/87, Series A, No. 222, 29.11.91, para. 47.

[167] See, e.g. *Glasenapp* v *Germany*, No. 9228/80, Series A, No. 104, 28.8.86, paras. 42–6. However, it may not be strictly necessary for the applicant to have been a party to the proceedings, provided that her/his claims were in substance brought to the attention of the courts (see, e.g. *P., C. & S* v *UK*, No. 56547/00, 11.12.01).

[168] Series A, No. 39, 6.1.80.

[169] See, e.g. *L.L.* v *France*, No. 7508/02, 10.10.06.

[170] No. 18877/91, 15.11.96.

[171] No. 56679/00, 28.4.04.

the 'merits stage') not to have exhausted domestic remedies because he had failed to invoke Article 1 of Protocol No. 1 before the Supreme Court, even though it was directly applicable in the Cypriot legal system. The Grand Chamber reached a similar conclusion in *Vučković and others v Serbia*,[172] a case brought by former Yugoslav army reservists who claimed they had been the victims of discrimination as they had not received per diem allowances in respect of their military service. Although they had instigated civil claims, they had not also invoked the specific domestic law provisions relating to discrimination and failed to do so in the course of an appeal to the Constitutional Court. Therefore, the Court upheld the Government's objection that they had failed to exhaust domestic remedies.

Compliance with domestic procedural rules

4.65   In raising the issue expressly or in substance in domestic proceedings, an applicant will be required to have complied with the formal and procedural rules, including time limits, in the domestic law and to have invoked any procedural means that might have prevented a breach of the Convention.[173] Domestic remedies will accordingly not be considered exhausted if an applicant has not pursued a remedy because the time limits or other procedural rules have not been complied with.[174] In *Barberà, Messegué and Jabardo v Spain*,[175] the failure during the trial to raise allegations of a judge's hostility towards some defendants and witnesses, meant that the applicants were found not to have exhausted domestic remedies.

Flexibility of the rule

4.66   The Court has said that the rule in Article 35 should be applied with 'some degree of flexibility and without excessive formalism'.[176] This flexibility reflects the fact that the rule is being applied in the context of a system intended to protect human rights.[177] Therefore the exhaustion of domestic remedies rule is not absolute, nor is it applied automatically (see also Special circumstances, at 4.85 below).[178] The circumstances of each case are always considered, including the general context in which the formal remedies operate and the personal circumstances of the applicant. The Court will then examine, in all the circumstances of the case, whether applicants have done everything that could reasonably be expected of them to exhaust domestic remedies.[179]

Premature applications

4.67   If a case is declared inadmissible for failure to exhaust domestic remedies, because the application is lodged prematurely with the Court (before the domestic remedies have been allowed to run their course), then it will be open to the applicants to submit a fresh application once domestic remedies have in fact been exhausted.[180] See also the discussion of 'doubtful remedies' at 4.116 below.

---

[172] No. 17153/11 et al., 25.3.14.
[173] *Cardot v France*, No. 11069/84, 19.3.91, para. 34.
[174] See, e.g. *Gäfgen v Germany*, No. 22978/05, 1.6.10, para. 143.
[175] Nos. 10588/83, 10589/83 and 10590/83, 6.12.88, Series A, No. 146.
[176] See, e.g. *Guzzardi v Italy*, Series A, No. 39, 6.1.80, para. 72; *Cardot v France*, No. 11069/84, 19.3.91, para. 34; *Demopoulos and others v Turkey*, No. 46113/99 et al., dec. 1.3.10, para. 70.
[177] *Akdivar v Turkey*, No. 21893/93, 16.9.96, para. 69.
[178] See, e.g. *Kozacıoğlu v Turkey*, No. 2334/03, 19.2.09, para. 40.
[179] See, e.g. *Yaşa v Turkey*, No. 22495/93, 2.9.98, para. 77.
[180] See, e.g. *Sarisülük v Turkey*, No. 64126/13, dec. 25.3.14.

Availability, effectiveness and sufficiency of remedies

Whilst Article 35(1) states that the Court may only deal with a matter after all domestic **4.68** remedies have been exhausted, an applicant is only required to pursue remedies that are available, effective and sufficient. In the case of *Uzun* v *Turkey*[181] the Court had to consider the introduction in Turkey in 2012 of a new remedy before the Constitutional Court, which has jurisdiction to examine individual applications concerning breaches of rights under the European Convention, after other ordinary remedies have been exhausted. The Court found that the new remedy was accessible to individual applicants, that the Constitutional Court had sufficient jurisdiction to adjudicate on human rights complaints and the necessary means to ensure their implementation. Accordingly, individuals would be expected to utilise the new mechanism before lodging applications with the European Court.

Availability of remedies

For a domestic remedy to be *available*, the applicant must be able to initiate the proceedings **4.69** directly (without being reliant upon a public body or official).[182] Where, for example, as in Italy, individuals are not entitled to apply directly to the Constitutional Court to challenge a law's constitutionality (cases must be referred by other courts), this cannot amount to a remedy which has to be exhausted.[183] The unavailability of legal aid may affect the accessibility of a remedy, depending upon the applicant's financial resources, the complexity of the remedy and whether or not legal representation is compulsory in domestic proceedings.[184] The Court has accepted that where a domestic remedy has been established as a result of progressive interpretation by the courts, there should be a reasonable period of time (which will vary according to the circumstances) within which to allow the public to become effectively aware of the decision in question.[185]

The European Court will not be satisfied with respondent governments raising the exist- **4.70** ence of remedies which are only theoretically available. In this respect, the Court may require the government to produce examples of the claimed remedy having been successfully utilised. For example, in *De Jong, Baljet and van den Brink* v *Netherlands*,[186] the applicant servicemen who were conscientious objectors complained about their detention for refusing to obey military orders. The respondent Government argued that the applicants had not exhausted domestic remedies because they could have brought a claim in the civil courts. However, that argument was rejected by the Court as there was not a single example of a detained serviceman having sued for damages and it was therefore not certain whether such a remedy was in fact available.[187] Similarly, in *Van Oosterwijck* v

---

[181] No. 10755/13, dec. 30.4.13. See also *Koçintar* v *Turkey*, No. 77429/12, dec. 1.7.14.

[182] See, for example, *Lepojić* v *Serbia*, No. 13909/05, 6.11.07 (as regards a 'request for protection of legality' which could only be filed by the public prosecutor); *Akçiçek* v *Turkey*, No. 40965/10, dec. 18.10.11 (an appeal procedure which was applied at the discretion of the principal public prosecutor at the court of cassation). See also the discussion below on the accessibility of a remedy before the Constitutional Court in Croatia in respect of length of proceedings cases.

[183] See, e.g. *Immobiliare Saffi* v *Italy*, No. 22774/93, 28.7.99, para. 42. See also: *Iordachi and others* v *Moldova*, No. 25198/02, dec. 5.4.05; *Tănase* v *Moldova*, No. 7/08, 27.4.10.

[184] See *Airey* v *Ireland*, Series A, No. 32, 9.10.79; *Faulkner* v *UK*, No. 30308/96, Comm. Rep. 1.12.98.

[185] *Depauw* v *Belgium*, No. 2115/04, dec. 15.5.07; *Provide S.R.L.* v *Italy*, No. 62155/00, dec. 5.7.07; *Vinčić and Others* v *Serbia*, No. 44698/06 et seq., dec. 1.12.09.

[186] Nos. 8805/79, 8806/79, 9242/81, Series A, No. 77, 22.5.84.

[187] See also *Dulaş* v *Turkey*, No. 25801/94, 30.1.01, para. 46 (no example of compensation having been awarded in response to complaints of property having been deliberately destroyed by the security forces).

Belgium,[188] it was held in relation to one form of redress raised by the Government, that in the absence of any decided domestic cases, the applicant could not be blamed for failing to bring such an action.

4.71   In *Krombach* v *France*[189] the opportunity for the applicant, who had been tried *in absentia*, to opt for a retrial, was not considered to be an available remedy, as its availability depended on the applicant's arrest, which would not be a voluntary act. In *Conka* v *Belgium*,[190] which concerned the expulsion of a group of Slovakian Roma asylum-seekers, the Court identified several factors leading to a finding that domestic remedies were not in fact available to the applicants:

- information about a potential remedy was handed out at a police station, but was written in tiny characters in a language which the applicants did not understand;
- only one interpreter was available for a large group of Romany families, and accordingly there was little prospect of their being able to contact a lawyer from the police station;
- the authorities failed to offer the applicants any legal assistance at the police station or the detention centre; and
- decisively, a lawyer was only informed of the applicants' position at 10.30 pm on a Friday evening and the applicants were expelled on the following Tuesday, and so an appeal (to the committals division) could not have been heard in time.

4.72   The Court reached a similar decision in *Rahimi* v *Greece*,[191] concerning the extent of redress available to the applicant (an unaccompanied minor asylum-seeker who spoke Farsi) to complain about his detention. The applicant was not given information about the procedure for complaining to the chief of police, he had no legal representation and was only given information in Arabic.

4.73   In *Kucheruk* v *Ukraine*, in assessing the extent to which the detained applicant could have complained to the prison authorities about his medical treatment, the Court took account of his mental condition, which was such as 'to impair substantially his ability to communicate with the outside world'.[192]

4.74   Where a state establishes a new form of domestic redress which has retrospective effect, a question may arise as to the position of applicants who had lodged their cases in Strasbourg before the new redress had been available. The Court's default stance is that the assessment of whether domestic remedies have been exhausted is normally carried out with reference to the date on which the application was lodged with the Court. However, the Court is increasingly recognising exceptions to this principle, meaning that applicants with cases pending in Strasbourg may be required to revert back to the domestic system if a relevant new domestic remedy has subsequently been created. That was the finding, for example, in *Shibendra Dev* v *Sweden*[193] where the Swedish Supreme Court introduced a new remedy in 2013 with retrospective effect (to 2009) in relation to 'double jeopardy' (in response to the Grand Chamber judgment in *Zolotukhin* v *Russia*[194]). Similar decisions have been made in

---

188 No. 7654/76, 6.11.80.
189 No. 29731/96, 13.2.01, para. 67.
190 No. 51564/99, 5.2.02, paras. 43–6.
191 No. 8687/08, 5.4.11.
192 No. 2570/04, 6.9.07.
193 No. 7362/10, dec. 21.10.14.
194 No. 14939/03, 10.2.09.

particular as regards new remedies relating to the excessive length of legal proceedings, which is discussed further at 4.91 below.

However, the foreseeability of domestic law changes may be relevant here. In *Yavuz Selim* **4.75** *Güler v Turkey*[195] the applicant military officer complained about a military sanction imposed on him. At the time his application was lodged in Strasbourg, it was clear under the domestic law that the Military Administrative High Court did not have jurisdiction to consider such a claim. Subsequently, that court decided to the contrary, but the European Court held that as the applicant could not reasonably have foreseen that this remedy would be available, it was not one that he was required to exhaust.

Effectiveness and sufficiency of remedies

A remedy will be considered *effective* and *sufficient* if it may provide redress for the applicant **4.76** in respect of the alleged Convention violation.[196] This includes not only judicial remedies, but also any administrative domestic remedy which may provide redress in the circumstances of the particular case.[197] It will often be important to analyse very carefully the nature of redress that is available, to consider whether it is *effective* and *sufficient*—in terms of ensuring that the right in question is actually secured, and not only that an applicant is compensated. For example, in *Gherghina v Romania*,[198] a case concerning a disabled student's inability to access university buildings, the Grand Chamber underlined that for remedies to be considered effective:

> … they must have been capable, primarily, of preventing or putting a swift end to the alleged violations and, secondarily, of affording adequate redress for any violation that had already occurred. If the only remedies available to litigants are of a compensatory nature and can lead solely to a retrospective award of pecuniary compensation, the rights which the respondent State has undertaken to safeguard by virtue of Article 2 of Protocol No. 1–which requires any State that has set up higher-education institutions to ensure effective access to them …—are at risk of becoming illusory.[199]

The opportunity to request an authority to reconsider a decision it has already taken does **4.77** not generally constitute a sufficient remedy.[200] Applicants will also not be required to have pursued remedies that are purely discretionary. In *Buckley v UK*,[201] the European Commission rejected the Government's arguments that the applicant had not exhausted domestic remedies because she had not applied to the Secretary of State to exercise power under the Caravan Sites Act 1968 to direct a local authority to provide caravan sites. The Commission found that the Secretary of State had a very wide discretion and had only acted under the relevant provision of the 1968 Act in five cases. Similarly in *Temple v UK*,[202] the applicant was not required to apply to the Secretary of State under the Employment Act

---

[195] No. 76476/12, 15.12.15.

[196] For example, in Russia, a constitutional complaint is not considered to be an effective remedy in relation to an alleged violation resulting from the erroneous application or interpretation of a statutory provision which is not unconstitutional. See *Sergey Smirnov v Russia*, No. 14085/04, dec. 6.7.06.

[197] See, e.g. *Rodić and 3 others v Bosnia and Herzegovina*, No. 22893/05, 27.5.08, paras. 57–8 (petition to prison inspector together with constitutional appeal).

[198] No. 42219/07, dec. 9.7.15.

[199] *Ibid.*, para. 91.

[200] *B v UK*, No. 18711/91.

[201] No. 20348/92, dec. 3.3.94.

[202] No. 10530/83, dec. 16.5.85.

1982 for compensation in respect of his dismissal as a railway shunter, as such a procedure was essentially discretionary and amounted to an application for an *ex gratia* payment. There was no legal entitlement to compensation even if the statutory eligibility criteria were satisfied. In *Devlin v UK*,[203] the applicant alleged that he was not given an appointment within the civil service in Northern Ireland because of religious discrimination. The applicant was not required to have made a complaint to the Parliamentary Ombudsman, as the Ombudsman had no power to render a binding decision granting redress, and also could not affect the implementation of a certificate issued by the Government in the domestic proceedings that asserted that the applicant had not been appointed in order to safeguard national security and protect public safety. A similar decision as regards the Lithuanian Parliamentary Ombudsman was made in *Mironovas and others v Lithuania*,[204] because the Ombudsman could not issue binding orders to the prison service to improve the conditions for prisoners, and it had not been shown that the Ombudsman's recommendations could provide relief within a reasonably short time period. In cases of doubt about the effectiveness of a domestic remedy, including an appeal process (see below), for the purposes of the European Court's exhaustion of domestic remedies test, the remedy should be pursued.[205] Thus the application in *Mogos and Krifka v Germany*,[206] concerning the expulsion of stateless persons of Romanian origin, was declared inadmissible because of the failure to pursue the case before the Federal Constitutional Court—it was not sufficient that the applicants' legal representatives believed such an action had no prospects of success. This has been found to be particularly the case in common law systems, where the courts extend and develop principles through case law: 'it is generally incumbent on an aggrieved individual to allow the domestic courts the opportunity to develop existing rights by way of interpretation'.[207] The failure to bring proceedings for breach of confidence led to a finding of a failure to exhaust domestic remedies in *Earl and Countess Spencer v UK*,[208] which concerned the publication in the tabloids of information about the Princess of Wales which was said to have been obtained from her close friends. The Court's stance on the effectiveness of a particular remedy may of course change over time. For example, in *Ignats v Latvia*[209] the Court overturned its previous decisions to the effect that administrative court proceedings did not offer an accessible remedy to detainees (in the light of subsequent evidence about the effectiveness of such proceedings). There was a comparable decision in *Benmouna and others v France*[210] in which the Court found that the relatives of a man who had appeared to have committed suicide in police custody could have brought an action under the Judicature Act to establish state responsibility (in effect, overturning previous decisions finding such a cause of action to be ineffective[211]). Given recent domestic court decisions, the Court was satisfied that it had acquired a sufficient degree of legal certainty.

---

[203] No. 29545/95, dec. 11.4.02.

[204] No. 40828/12 et al., 8.12.15.

[205] See, e.g. *Ignats v Latvia*, No. 38494/05, dec. 24.9.13; *Gherghina v Romania*, No. 42219/07, dec. 9.7.15, para. 106.

[206] No. 78084/01, dec. 27.3.03.

[207] *Earl and Countess Spencer v UK*, Nos. 28851/95 and 18852/95, dec. 16.1.98. See also *D v Ireland*, No. 26499/02, dec. 27.6.06.

[208] Nos. 28851/95 and 18852/95, dec. 16.1.98.

[209] No. 38494/05, dec. 24.9.13.

[210] No. 51097/13, dec. 15.9.15.

[211] See, e.g. *Saoud v France*, No. 9375/02, 9.10.07.

In *D* v *Ireland*,[212] which concerned a complaint about the lack of abortion services in respect **4.78** of lethal foetal abnormality, the applicant was found to have failed to exhaust available domestic remedies as she did not bring a constitutional complaint—in spite of the uncertainties as to the likelihood of its success. By contrast, in *Kozak* v *Poland*,[213] the respondent Government was unsuccessful in arguing that the applicant had failed to exhaust domestic remedies by not lodging a constitutional complaint. The case concerned the homosexual applicant's inability to succeed to the tenancy of a flat following his partner's death. In rejecting the Government's argument, the Court noted a 'continuing and established interpretation' by the Polish domestic courts to the effect that the phrase 'a person living with a tenant in *de facto* marital cohabitation' was construed as applying only to heterosexual relationships. The Court also took account of the 'general legal and political context relating to same-sex relationships in Poland'. There was a similar conclusion in *Kurić and others* v *Slovenia*,[214] which concerned the position of the 'erased'—former citizens of Yugoslavia who complained they had been arbitrarily deprived of the possibility of acquiring Slovenian citizenship. The Government argued that six applicants had not exhausted domestic remedies, because of their failure to appeal to the Constitutional Court. However, the Court held that they were dispensed from taking such action in view of the domestic authorities' failure, over several years, to comply with two earlier Constitutional Court judgments which had found the 'erasure' to be unlawful and which had ordered the adoption of various general measures. The case of *McFarlane* v *Ireland*[215] illustrates the difficulties in interpretation that can arise as to the question of the effectiveness of remedies. There, a majority of the Grand Chamber found a violation of Article 13 because of the absence of an effective remedy to claim damages for delays in criminal proceedings. The majority Court found that it was too uncertain whether, as argued by the Government, an action for damages for a breach of the constitutional right to reasonable expedition would have amounted to an effective remedy. However, five dissenting judges[216] argued that the case should have been declared inadmissible because the applicants had failed to test the effectiveness of such an action for damages.

In general, applicants will be required to pursue processes of appeal available in the course **4.79** of domestic remedies, if such an appeal process would or might provide a remedy for the alleged Convention violation.[217] For example, the application in *Epözdemir* v *Turkey*[218] was declared inadmissible because of the applicant's failure to appeal against the decision of the public prosecutor not to prosecute the village guards who were allegedly responsible for the death of her husband: it was not established that an appeal to an Assize Court would have been devoid of success.

However, it is not necessary for applicants to pursue a potential form of redress or an **4.80** appeal process that would not in fact provide a remedy,[219] for example where it is clear on settled legal opinion, or in view of the consistent practice of the domestic courts, that

---

[212] No. 26499/02, dec. 27.6.06. See, by contrast, *A, B & C* v *Ireland*, No. 25579/05, 16.12.10.
[213] No. 13102/02, 2.3.10.
[214] No. 26828/06, 26.6.12.
[215] No. 31333/06, 10.9.10.
[216] Judges Gyulumyan, Ziemele, Bianku and Power, and, separately, Lopez-Guerra.
[217] See, e.g. *Civet* v *France*, No. 29340/95, 28.9.99.
[218] No. 57039/00, dec. 31.1.02.
[219] See, e.g. *Hilton* v *UK*, No. 5613/72, dec. 5.3.76, (1976) 4 DR 177; *Csikós* v *Hungary*, No. 37251/04, 5.12.06.

it has no prospects of success.[220] In that situation, the applicant will have to satisfy the court that there were no such prospects of success and practitioners should consider filing with the Court an expert legal opinion to that effect. In *McFeeley v UK*,[221] a case concerning the conditions for prisoners in the Maze Prison in Northern Ireland, the European Commission found that an order of certiorari could not have provided an effective remedy because of serious doubts as to whether the remedy would have been open to the applicants according to 'settled legal opinion' and whilst it could have been sufficient to redress the applicants' Article 6 complaints, it would not have provided redress for their complaints under Article 3. Where an applicant complains that their proposed removal from a state would lead to a risk of treatment contrary to Article 3, the Court has held that appeal processes which do not have suspensive effect are not considered 'effective' within the meaning of Article 35(1).[222] The question as to whether a domestic remedy may offer reasonable prospects of success is likely to require a close analysis of relevant decisions made by domestic bodies. The applicants in *Sufi and Elmi v UK*[223] contested orders for their deportation to Somalia, after having been convicted of serious criminal offences. The Court rejected the Government's arguments that the applicants had failed to exhaust domestic remedies as they had not made fresh asylum claims in view of the changing circumstances in Mogadishu. Having reviewed relevant decisions of the Asylum and Immigration Tribunal, the Court was satisfied that it did not in fact offer a reasonable likelihood of success.

4.81 Where an applicant seeks to challenge the state of the law itself, there are unlikely to be any effective domestic remedies available. For example, in *Iordachi and others v Moldova*[224] the applicants were members of the NGO 'Lawyers for Human Rights' who complained that they were liable to be under state surveillance (although they did not allege that there had been any particular instances). Noting that the applicants complained that the law did not contain sufficient safeguards to prevent abuse by the authorities, the Court found that there were no effective remedies. Only the Moldovan Parliament could change the law, and only the Constitutional Court could declare laws unconstitutional (but to which individuals and organisations had no direct access). Conversely, the limited remit of a body such as a constitutional court will mean that it does not offer an effective remedy for certain applicants. For example, the Court has held that a complaint to the Polish Constitutional Court will only be considered effective where it is argued that the violation in question resulted from the direct application of a legal provision which is challenged as being unconstitutional.[225] Where relevant, applicants may be required to bring domestic proceedings based on EU law, including allowing for the possibility of the domestic court requesting a preliminary ruling from the Court of Justice of the European Union (CJEU) as regards the compatibility of the domestic law with EU law, given that such a ruling by

---

[220] See, e.g. *De Wilde, Ooms and Versyp v Belgium*, Series A, No. 12, 18.6.71, para. 62; *Salah Sheekh v Netherlands*, No. 1948/04, 11.1.07, para. 123; *Chapman v Belgium*, No. 39619/06, dec. 5.3.13, paras. 32–3; *Tarantino and others v Italy*, Nos. 25851/09, 29284/09 and 64090/09, 2.4.13, para. 41.

[221] No. 8317/78, dec. 15.5.80.

[222] See, e.g. *X v Germany*, No. 7216/75, dec. 20.5.76; DR 5, p.137; *M v France*, No. 10078/82, dec. 13.12.84, DR 41, p. 103; *Sultani v France*, No. 45223/05, 20.9.07, para. 50. See also chapter 6 (section 6.692) as to remedies with suspensive effect and Article 13.

[223] Nos. 8319/07 and 11449/07, 28.6.11.

[224] No. 25198/02, dec. 5.4.05.

[225] See, e.g. *R.R. v Poland*, No. 27617/04, 26.5.11.

the CJEU is binding on the referring national court as to the interpretation of the EU law rule in question.[226]

The length of domestic proceedings will be a factor in the consideration of their effective- **4.82** ness.[227] For example, the case of *Tanlı v Turkey*[228] concerned the killing of the applicant's son in police custody. Criminal proceedings had been instituted but were still pending one year and eight months after the death of the applicant's son. In view of the serious nature of the crime involved, the European Commission of Human Rights found that the criminal proceedings were an ineffective remedy. Delay in the availability of a remedy may mean that it need not be utilised by the applicant. In *Reed v UK*,[229] the applicant complained of being assaulted in prison, invoking Article 3. The Government argued that he had failed to exhaust domestic remedies because he had not brought a civil action for damages. However, the applicant had been first required to allow the prison authorities to investigate his complaints and he was denied access to a lawyer for more than two years. In those circumstances, the applicant was not barred for non-exhaustion of domestic remedies, even where the remedy subsequently became available after the two-year period, as in principle a remedy should have been immediately available to every aggrieved person, particularly in cases of alleged maltreatment. At issue in *Bellizzi v Malta*[230] was whether the applicants were required to lodge a fresh set of constitutional court proceedings to challenge an earlier decision of the same court to reject their case. Although the Court noted that such an application was possible, after ten years of litigation it found that the applicants were not required to utilise this process because it was a cumbersome and lengthy procedure.

If there are a number of possible domestic remedies, an applicant will not be required to **4.83** have exhausted them all, or even to have utilised more than one if they would not achieve anything more.[231] In other words, an applicant is entitled to choose 'one feasible domestic remedy over another'.[232] The Court has held that an applicant cannot be criticised for not having had recourse to legal remedies which would have been directed essentially to the same end and would in any case not have offered better chances of success.[233]

Exhaustion of domestic remedies may take place after an application has been introduced **4.84** with the Court, but such remedies must have been exhausted before the admissibility decision is made.[234]

---

[226] See, e.g. *Laurus Invest Hungary Kft and others v Hungary*, No. 23265/13 et al., dec. 8.9.15 (in which the Court held that an action based on Article 56 of the Treaty on the Functioning of the European Union (TFEU) offered a reasonable prospect of success for the applicants to have their claims adjudicated on the merits and obtain damages).

[227] This will especially be the case where the violation in issue necessarily requires a swift judicial response in order to be effective, such as interference in an instantaneous political demonstration: *Patyi v Hungary*, No. 35127/08, 17.1.12, para. 23.

[228] No. 26129/94, dec. 5.3.96.

[229] No. 7630/76, dec. 6.12.79.

[230] No. 46575/09, 21.6.11.

[231] See, e.g. *Bosphorus Hava Yollari Turizm Ve Ticaret AS v Ireland*, No. 45036/98, dec. 13.9.01; *Moreira Barbosa v Portugal*, No. 65681/01, dec. 29.4.04; *Jeličić v Bosnia and Herzegovina*, No. 41183/02, dec. 15.11.05; *Boicenco v Moldova*, No. 41088/05, 11.7.06; *Mikolajova v Slovakia*, No. 4479/03, 18.1.11; *Hristovi v Bulgaria*, No. 42697/05, 11.10.11.

[232] See, e.g. *O'Keeffe v Ireland*, No. 35810/09, 28.1.14, para. 111.

[233] *A v France*, No. 14838/89, Series A, No. 277-B, 23.11.93.

[234] *Luberti v Italy*, No. 9019/80, dec. 7.7.81, 27 DR 181.

4.85 A civil action for damages in respect of the death of the applicant's relative at the hands of an unidentified person was not considered to be an effective remedy where the claimant in such an action was required to identify the person believed to have committed the tort.[235] In the same circumstances, an administrative law action was found not be a sufficient remedy, where damages could be awarded against the state on a strict liability basis. The Court has also held that in arguable cases concerning killing, torture or the destruction of property by the state, an award of damages will not in itself satisfy the obligation to provide an effective remedy under Article 13 of the Convention, which also requires a thorough and effective investigation that is capable of leading to the identification and punishment of those responsible.[236] The case of *Güvenç v Turkey*[237] concerned the death of a man caused by an electrical fault in a water pump in a fountain in the gardens of a mosque. The applicants raised Article 2, and also Article 6, due to the length of criminal proceedings brought against a municipal employee who was responsible for the maintenance of the fountain. The case was declared inadmissible because the applicants had not lodged a claim for compensation with the administrative courts–the Court noted that such proceedings were *not* dependent on the outcome of the criminal proceedings, and that the administrative or civil courts were not bound by criminal law considerations when ruling on a person's liability.[238] In the case of *Eremiášová and Pechová v Czech Republic*,[239] which concerned the death of the applicant's relative in police custody, the Government identified four potential legal remedies, including a constitutional appeal, which it suggested could have been utilised. However, the Court found that the practice of the Constitutional Court suggested that it was highly improbable that it would have quashed the prosecutor's decision in the case. The applicants had raised serious issues about the alleged lack of independence, impartiality, and inadequacy of the investigation into their relative's death, but the Court was not persuaded that it was likely that the Constitutional Court would have adequately addressed such issues. Furthermore, the other three potential remedies only offered the prospect of an award of damages, which was insufficient in the context of proceedings relating to Article 2.

4.86 Clearly a failure by the authorities to investigate serious allegations is likely to obviate the need for the victims to take up additional potential avenues of redress. In *Elçi and others v Turkey*,[240] the applicant lawyers made a series of complaints about their ill-treatment in custody, to a public prosecutor, a judge and to the State Security Court. As, however, none of the authorities investigated the allegations, the Court found that it was not necessary for the applicants to have attempted to pursue other theoretically available administrative or civil law remedies. In *Egmez v Cyprus*[241] it was held to be sufficient for the applicant to raise his complaint of police ill-treatment with the ombudsman. According to the Court, proceedings should then have been brought against the police officers allegedly involved.[242]

---

[235] *Yaşa v Turkey*, No. 22495/93, 2.9.98, para. 73.

[236] *Ibid.*, para. 74. See also, e.g. *Khashiyev and Akayeva v Russia*, Nos. 57942/00 and 57945/00, 24.2.05, para. 121; *Branko Tomašic and others v Croatia*, No. 46598/06, 15.1.09, para. 42; *Kerimova and others v Russia*, No. 17170/04 et al., 3.5.11, para. 215; *Mocanu and others v Romania*, Nos. 10865/09, 32431/08 and 45886/07, 17.09.14, para. 234.

[237] No. 43036/08, dec. 21.5.13.

[238] The position in Turkish law contrasted with French law which applied the principle that civil proceedings must await the outcome of criminal proceedings—see *Perez v France*, No. 47287/99, 12.2.04.

[239] No. 23944/04, 16.2.12.

[240] Nos. 23145/93 and 25091/94, 13.11.03, paras. 606–8.

[241] No. 30873/96, 21.12.00.

[242] *Ibid.*, para. 72.

It is quite possible for the Court to change its view as to the adequacy, or otherwise, of par-   **4.87**
ticular remedies, in the light of their application in practice. For example, in *Kaverzin* v
Ukraine,[243] the Court changed its position as regards the effectiveness of remedies relating
to allegations of ill-treatment by the police and of ineffective investigations. Although in
a series of cases the Court had found that applying to a prosecutor, and then if necessary
appealing to the courts, in principle provided effective remedies, in *Kaverzin* the Court
concluded that such remedies had not in practice proved to be capable of providing redress
(as they often resulted in lengthy and repeated re-examinations of complaints by the prosecutors and the courts, but without any meaningful effect). Following the Court's pilot
judgment relating to overcrowding in Italian prisons (*Torreggiani and others* v *Italy*[244]), the
Court was required to assess the adequacy of the consequential legislative changes introduced. In *Stella and others* v *Italy*[245] the Court found that the combination of both preventive and compensatory measures for prison overcrowding provided effective domestic
remedies which had to be pursued by applicants before they could consider applying to the
European Court.

The Court has also confirmed that in relation to cases concerning the lawfulness of deten-   **4.88**
tion, it will not be necessary for an applicant to bring an action for damages in order to
exhaust domestic remedies. This recognises that the right to have the lawfulness of detention
examined by a court and the right to obtain compensation for a deprivation of liberty that is
incompatible with Article 5 are distinct rights.[246] The applicant in *Demir* v *Turkey*[247] sought
to complain about the legality of his pre-trial detention. He did so after he had been convicted, and therefore at a point when his pre-trial detention had ended. The Court reiterated
that, to be effective, a remedy in respect of the length of pre-trial detention must provide
for the possibility of release from detention. However, after the period of pre-trial detention
had ended, a remedy would be deemed effective if it allowed for both the recognition of the
unreasonable nature of the length of the detention, and also an award of compensation.
As the applicant had failed to utilise a remedy newly available under the Code of Criminal
Procedure, his application was declared inadmissible.

If an applicant is able to establish that there has been a 'pattern of violations' over a period   **4.89**
of time, this is likely to affect the Court's consideration of the effectiveness of potential
remedies. In *Özturk* v *Turkey*,[248] the applicant publisher was the subject of 19 sets of criminal proceedings, relating to articles and publications concerning the Kurdish situation. The
Court found that the application was not primarily concerned with individual acts or events,
but with a consistent pattern of actions taken over a relatively long period of time and that
were aimed at preventing the applicant's company from publishing. It was held that there
was no remedy that would have been effective in changing the general situation, of which
the applicant complained, and it was therefore irrelevant that in one case the applicant had
not appealed against a conviction.

---

[243] No. 23893/03, 15.5.12.
[244] No. 43517/09, 8.1.13.
[245] No. 49169/09 et al., dec. 16.9.14.
[246] See, for example, *Wloch* v *Poland*, No. 27785/95, 19.10.00, para. 90; *Schwabe and M.G.* v *Germany*, Nos.
8080/08 and 8577/08, 1.12.11, para. 49.
[247] No. 51770/07, dec. 16.10.12.
[248] No. 29365/95, dec. 27.5.03.

4.90   The Court has confirmed that in relation to the United Kingdom, a declaration of incompatibility under the Human Rights Act 1998 does not provide an applicant with an effective remedy.[249] This is because such a declaration is not binding on the parties to the proceedings in which it is made, and it provides the appropriate minister merely with a power, rather than a duty, to amend the offending legislation so as to make it compatible with the Convention.[250]

Domestic remedies relating to the excessive length of proceedings[251] or the failure to implement domestic judgments

4.91   In cases concerning the undue length of proceedings, a remedy will be considered effective either if it can lead to the expedition of the proceedings, or if it provides adequate redress for delays that have already occurred,[252] for example, through the payment of compensation.[253] However, the Court has underlined, given the prevalence of this problem in many states, that prevention, by expediting the proceedings, is of course much the better option.[254] Nevertheless, where length of proceedings violations *already* exist, a remedy to expedite proceedings may not be considered in itself adequate to redress the situation.[255]

4.92   Where states subsequently establish new remedies to deal with this issue that have retroactive effect, these remedies will have to be pursued, if they are found to be effective.[256] This obligation may apply even to cases that were lodged at the European Court before the domestic remedy in question became effective.[257] In Italy the 'Pinto Act' was introduced

---

[249] *Hobbs* v *UK*, No. 63684/00, dec. 18.6.02. See also *Walker* v *UK*, No. 37212/02, dec. 16.3.04; *Pearson* v *UK*, No. 8374/03, dec. 27.4.04; *B and L* v *UK*, No. 36536/02, dec. 29.6.04; *Burden* v UK, No. 13378/05, 29.4.08.

[250] In *Burden* v *UK*, No. 13378/05, 29.4.08, the Grand Chamber acknowledged the UK Government's argument that in all the cases where declarations of incompatibility had become final, steps had been taken to amend the legislative provision in question. Accordingly, the Grand Chamber concluded that 'it cannot be excluded that at some time in the future the practice of giving effect to the national courts' declarations of incompatibility by amendment of the legislation is so certain as to indicate that section 4 of the Human Rights Act is to be interpreted as imposing a binding obligation'. Therefore, in such circumstances, applicants would be required first to exhaust that remedy before applying to the European Court (except where an effective remedy necessitated the award of damages in respect of past loss or damage caused by the alleged Convention violation).

[251] See also: Recommendation CM/Rec(2010)3 of the Committee of Ministers to member states on effective remedies for excessive length of proceedings, 24 February 2010.

[252] *Sürmeli* v *Germany*, No. 75529/01, 8.6.06, para. 99.

[253] See, e.g. *Vidaković* v *Serbia*, No. 16231/07, dec. 24.5.11.

[254] *Scordino* v *Italy (No. 1)*, No. 36813/97, 29.3.06, para. 183; *Sürmeli* v *Germany*, No. 75529/01, 8.6.06, para. 100.

[255] *Scordino* v *Italy (No. 1)*, No. 36813/97, 29.3.06, para. 185.

[256] See, e.g. *Holzinger* v *Austria*, No. 23459/94, 30.1.01 (where proceedings lasted from 1988 to 1993 and a new remedy was established in 1990—s. 91 Courts Act); *Basic* v *Austria*, No. 29800/96, 30.1.01 (Article 132 of the Federal Constitution); *Krasuski* v *Poland*, No. 61444/00, 14.6.05 (the 2004 'Kudla Law'); *Techniki Olympiaki A.E.* v *Greece*, No. 40547/10, dec. 1.10.13 (Law no. 4055/2012) (and as to Law No. 4239/2014, see *Xynos* v *Greece*, No. 30226/09, 9.10.14).

[257] See, e.g. *Grzinčič* v *Slovenia*, No. 26867/02, 3.5.07; *Nagovitsyn and Nalgiyev* v *Russia*, Nos. 27451/09 and 60650/09, dec. 23.9.10; *Fakhretdinov* v *Russia*, Nos. 26716/09, 67576/09 and 7698/10, dec. 23.9.10; *Ahlskog* v *Finland*, No. 5238/07, dec. 9.11.10; *Balan* v *Moldova*, No. 44746/08, dec. 24.1.12; *Turgut and others* v *Turkey*, No. 4860/09, dec. 26.3.13; *Balakchiev and others* v *Bulgaria*, No.65187/10 and *Valcheva and Abrashev* v *Bulgaria*, Nos. 6194/11 and 34887/11, decs. 18.6.13; *Savickas and others* v *Lithuania*, No. 66365/09 et al., dec. 15.10.13. As to domestic remedies in Slovenia, see also *Korenjak* v *Slovenia*, No. 463/03, dec. 15.5.07; *Branko Žunič* v *Slovenia*, No. 24342/04, dec. 18.10.07 and *Robert Lesjak* v *Slovenia*, No. 33946/03, 21.7.09 (no effective remedy in respect of the length of Supreme Court proceedings). However, the passage of time will be a relevant factor—see *Reynolds* v *UK*, No. 2694/08, 13.3.12 (as regards a complaint under Articles 2 and 13).

in 2001 in order to provide a remedy at the Court of Appeal in respect of unduly lengthy legal proceedings, including in relation to cases already lodged in Strasbourg. Accordingly, applicants are required to invoke this procedure, in order to exhaust domestic remedies (although applicants can still apply to Strasbourg if the Pinto proceedings themselves are overly prolonged or do not provide adequate redress, as has repeatedly been found to be the case).[258] The Court has also recognised that case law developments in France have established that the domestic law[259] provides a remedy for an alleged violation of the right to have a case heard within a reasonable time (whether the domestic proceedings have ended or not). Thus the Court held that by September 1999, this remedy had the requisite degree of legal certainty to make it obligatory for applicants to pursue in order to comply with the domestic remedies rule.[260] In Portugal, too, the Court has found that there has been an effective remedy in respect of the excessive length of judicial proceedings since at least October 1999.[261] In respect of cases concerning the length of proceedings in Croatia, the Court initially rejected arguments that in order to exhaust domestic remedies, applicants were obliged to invoke a Constitutional Court procedure,[262] as such a mechanism was not available as of right, but depended upon the discretion of the Court itself. Furthermore, there were doubts about its effectiveness, as the Government failed to produce any examples of applicants successfully invoking such a procedure.[263] However, once the domestic law was amended in 2002 to establish a mechanism that was available to applicants in length of proceedings cases,[264] the European Court then declared cases inadmissible if the new remedy had not been utilised.[265] Nevertheless, in *Šoć v Croatia*,[266] although the applicant had not invoked the new mechanism, the case was not declared inadmissible as the domestic proceedings in question had already been concluded, and the practice of the Constitutional

---

[258] See, e.g. *Brusco* v *Italy*, No. 69789/01, dec. 6.9.01; *Daddi* v *Italy*, No. 15476/09, dec. 2.6.09. But see *Mascolo* v *Italy*, No. 68792/01, dec. 16.10.03; *Scordino and others* v *Italy*, No. 36813/97, dec. 27.3.03 (inadequate compensation awarded by the Court of Appeal for the excessive length of proceedings meant that the applicants could still claim to be 'victims' of a Convention violation); *Di Sante* v *Italy*, No. 56079/00, dec. 24.6.04; *Sgattoni* v *Italy*, No. 77132/01, 6.10.05; *Cocchiarella* v *Italy*, No. 64886/01, 29.3.06; *Della Cave and Corrado* v *Italy*, No. 14626/03, 5.6.07 (Pinto proceedings found to be ineffective both because of delay and inadequate compensation). See also, *Simaldone* v *Italy*, No. 22644/03, 31.3.09 (a case in which the Court expressly commented on the problem of delay in the payment of Pinto compensation). The judgment in *Gaglione and others* v *Italy*, No. 45867/07, 21.12.10 concerned the delays in paying compensation in 475 Pinto law cases, which the Court described as a 'widespread problem' given the 3,900 similar cases which were then pending before the Court. See further *Olivieri and others* v *Italy*, No. 17708/12 et al., 25.2.16 (ineffectiveness of Pinto remedy–violation of Article 13).

[259] Article L. 781–1, Code of Judicial Organisation.

[260] See *Giummarra and others* v *France*, No. 61166/00, dec. 12.6.01; *Mifsud* v *France*, No. 57220/00, dec. 11.9.02 (Grand Chamber).

[261] *Paulino Tomas* v *Portugal*, No. 58698/00 and *Gouveia Da Silva Torrado* v *Portugal*, No. 65305/01, dec. 22.5.03. But see also *Martins Castro and Alves Correia de Castro* v *Portugal*, No. 33729/06, 10.6.08 (inability to obtain compensation for non-pecuniary damage) and *Valada Matos das Neves* v *Portugal*, No. 73798/13, 29.10.15 (applicants not required to have pursued a domestic remedy which had not acquired the requisite degree of legal certainty at the time they had lodged their case in Strasbourg).

[262] Under s. 59(4), Constitutional Court Act.

[263] *Horvat* v *Croatia*, No. 51585/99, 26.7.01.

[264] Under s. 63, Constitutional Court Act.

[265] *Slaviček* v *Croatia*, No. 20862/02, dec. 4.7.02; *Nogolica* v *Croatia*, No. 77784/01, 5.9.02. See also *Sukobljevic* v *Croatia*, No. 5129/03, 2.11.06.

[266] No. 47863/99, 9.5.03. But in *Vidas* v *Croatia*, No. 40383/04, 3.7.08 the Court found a violation of Article 13 where the applicant's complaint to the Constitutional Court itself took more than three years to resolve. See also *Kaić and others* v *Croatia*, No. 22014/04, 17.7.08 (both insufficient compensation and delay led to a finding of a violation of Article 13).

Court was only to consider cases that were still proceeding. Similarly in Slovakia, applicants are required to invoke the Constitutional Court complaint procedure in respect of excessively long domestic proceedings before submitting applications to the European Court.[267] Following the *Kudla* judgment,[268] new legislation was introduced in Poland in September 2004 in order to provide a domestic remedy for length of proceedings cases. Under the new legislation the appellate courts may find a violation of Article 6, instruct the lower court to accelerate proceedings and award damages of up to about €2,250.[269] Accordingly, complaints from applicants who have not exhausted this new procedure will be declared inadmissible.[270] Developments in the case-law of the Serbian Constitutional Court relating to the non-enforcement of domestic court judgments against socially-owned companies led to a Court finding in *Marinković* v *Serbia*[271] that an appeal to the Constitutional Court was an effective domestic remedy which had to be exhausted.[272]

4.93 At issue in *Parizov* v *former Yugoslav Republic of Macedonia*,[273] was a 2006 law that had introduced a right of compensation in respect of the excessive length of proceedings. However, the applicant was not required to have utilised the law because of the lack of precision in various of its provisions, and 12 months after its introduction there had been no domestic court decisions clarifying it. However, in 2011 the Court found that the defects had been resolved by amendments to the law introduced in 2008, which meant that it provided an effective remedy.[274] In *Hartman* v *Czech Republic*,[275] the Court concluded in 2003 that there was no available effective remedy in respect of length of proceedings cases in the Czech Republic. Firstly, an appeal to a higher authority was not 'available' as it did not give applicants the right to require the exercise of the state's supervisory powers. Secondly, whilst the Constitutional Court could order that proceedings be continued forthwith, it could not impose any sanction for failure to comply,[276] nor could it award compensation for any delays. However, the compensatory remedy introduced into Czech domestic law in 2006 will have to be pursued in order for a complaint to pass the Strasbourg admissibility test.[277]

---

[267] *Andrášik and others* v *Slovakia*, Nos. 59784/00, 60237/00, 60242/00, 60679/00, 60680/00, 69563/01 and 60226/00, dec. 22.10.02 (a complaint under Article 127 of the Constitution, which has been available since January 2002). But for refinements on this position, see also: *Bako* v *Slovakia*, No. 60227/00, 15.3.05; *Obluk* v *Slovakia*, No. 69484/01, 20.6.06; *Mazurek* v *Slovakia*, No. 16970/05, dec. 3.3.09; *Ištván and Ištvánová* v *Slovakia*, No. 30189/07, 12.6.12 (re prior use of a remedy under the Courts Act).

[268] No. 30210/96, 26.10.00.

[269] See European Court press release, 30.9.04.

[270] *Charzyński* v *Poland*, No. 15212/03, dec. 1.3.05. See also: *Krasuski* v *Poland*, No. 61444/00, 14.6.05. However, in *Ratajczyk* v *Poland*, No. 11215/02, dec. 31.5.05 the domestic proceedings had finished three years before the new procedure had come into force and therefore it was not available to the applicant: declared admissible.

[271] No. 5353/11, dec. 29.1.13.

[272] But only as regards socially-owned companies which were undergoing insolvency proceedings or which no longer existed—*not* in respect of companies which were still undergoing a process of restructuring (because of the limitations in the Constitutional Court's awards of compensation in such cases).

[273] No. 14258/03, 7.2.08.

[274] *Adži-Spirkoska and others* v *former Yugoslav Republic of Macedonia*, Nos. 38914/05 and 17879/05, dec. 3.11.11.

[275] No. 53341/99, 10.7.03, paras. 66–9.

[276] The Court contrasted the position of both the Swiss Federal Court (see *Boxer Asbestos S.A.* v *Switzerland*, No. 20874/92, dec. 9.3.00) and the Spanish Constitutional Court (see *Gonzalez Marin* v *Spain*, No. 39521/98, dec. 5.10.99).

[277] *Vokurka* v *Czech Republic*, No. 40552/02, dec. 16.10.07.

In *Sürmeli* v *Germany*,[278] the Court held that a complaint to the German Federal Consti- **4.94** tutional Court as regards the length of proceedings was ineffective as it could neither set deadlines for the lower court, nor order other measures to speed up the proceedings, nor award compensation.

Domestic remedies in de facto regimes/occupation and situations of armed conflict

Difficult questions have been raised about the extent of the need to exhaust domestic rem- **4.95** edies in situations where states are in *de facto* (but not *de jure*) control of territory claimed by another state. In *Cyprus* v *Turkey*[279] the applicant Government argued that as the Turkish Republic of Northern Cyprus (TRNC) had not been recognised by the international community, it was not necessary for 'victims' of Convention violations to exhaust remedies created by the TRNC authorities, and that the law of the Republic of Cyprus should be considered instead. However, this argument was rejected by a majority of the Court (by ten votes to seven) who found that in principle the TRNC remedies should still be exhausted unless their inexistence or ineffectiveness could be proved.[280] The majority argued that it was in the interests of the inhabitants of the territory in question to seek the protection of such organs, and in their view their decision did not have the effect of legitimising the TRNC regime. Judge Palm dissenting (joined by five other judges) argued that as a consequence of the decision of the majority, the Court might recognise as legally valid both the decisions of the TRNC courts and (implicitly) the provisions of the constitution which instituted it. This risked undermining the position of the international community. In the subsequent case of *Demopoulos and others* v *Turkey*[281] the Grand Chamber was called upon to assess the effectiveness of the Immovable Property Commission (IPC) (a body set up in the TRNC), in order to decide whether it was a domestic remedy which had to be exhausted by Greek Cypriots with property claims arising from the Turkish occupation of the north of Cyprus since 1974.[282] The difficulties discerned by the Court are clear from this passage:[283]

> ... the Court finds itself faced with cases burdened with a political, historical and factual complexity flowing from a problem that should have been resolved by all parties assuming full responsibility for finding a solution on a political level. This reality, as well as the passage of time and the continuing evolution of the broader political dispute must inform the Court's interpretation and application of the Convention which cannot, if it is to be coherent and meaningful, be either static or blind to concrete factual circumstances.

Noting that 433 cases had been taken before the IPC, which had ordered compensation, restitution and exchange of property, the Court rejected a series of challenges to its effectiveness, independence, impartiality and accessibility, and declared the series of cases inadmissible for failure to exhaust domestic remedies.

There was a rather different outcome in *Ilaşcu, Lesco, Ivantoc and Petrov-Popa* v *Moldova and* **4.96** *Russia*[284] in which the applicant Moldovans complained of various Convention violations

---

[278] No. 75529/01, 8.6.06. However, since 2011 the Court has recognised the effectiveness of a newly introduced domestic remedy (see *Taron* v *Germany*, No. 53126/07, dec. 25.9.12).

[279] No. 25781/94, 10.5.01.

[280] *Ibid.*, para. 98. See also *Djavit An* v *Turkey*, No. 20652/92, 20.2.03.

[281] No. 46113/99 et al., dec. 1.3.10.

[282] The IPC was subject to a 2005 law which had been enacted following the Court's judgment in *Xenides-Arestis* v *Turkey*, No. 64347/99, 22.12.05.

[283] *Demopoulos and others* v *Turkey*, No. 46113/99 et al., dec. 1.3.10, para. 85.

[284] No. 48787/99, dec. 4.7.01.

in the Russian-occupied area of Transdniestria, a region of Moldova that declared its independence in 1991. Russia argued that the applicants could have applied to the Supreme Court of Russia, but the European Court found that as the Russian Government had denied all the allegations that its armed forces, or other officials, had taken part in the applicants' arrest, imprisonment or conviction, it would be contradictory to expect the applicants to have approached the Russian authorities. In two cases concerning applicants who were displaced from their homes during the Nagorno-Karabakh conflict between Armenia and Azerbaijan in the early 1990s, the Court found that the remedies referred to by the Governments did not address the specific situation of the dispossession of property as a result of armed conflict.[285] In respect of Armenia, the Court also noted a similar 'denial of responsibility' point,[286] and in relation to Azerbaijan, as regards applicants who were now living in Armenia, it took account of the fact that there were no diplomatic relations between the two countries, the borders were closed and there was no viable postal service.[287]

4.97   In the context of armed conflict in Chechnya, the Court was prepared to accept that for a period between January and November 2000, because of the disruption to the Chechen judicial system, there were no domestic remedies available.[288]

See also Special circumstances, at 4.98 below.

Special circumstances

4.98   There may, exceptionally, be 'special circumstances' absolving the applicant from exhausting domestic remedies, or which are otherwise relevant to the application of the 'six months rule' (discussed below). 'Special circumstances' will *not* include lack of legal knowledge of the Convention, negligent advice by lawyers, or the applicant's depressive state. However, the Court has accepted that an applicant's mental health may have a bearing on their ability to engage with domestic remedies. For example, in *Premininy v Russia*[289] the Court found there was 'clear and conclusive evidence' that the applicant's poor mental health (when he was held in detention as a criminal suspect) meant that he could not reasonably have been expected to use the national channels of redress. The applicant in *M.S. v Croatia (no. 2)*[290] had not brought a Constitutional Court complaint to challenge her confinement in a psychiatric hospital. However, the Court found that she was not required to do so because of her vulnerability, taking account of her serious mental disorder, her inability to pay for a private lawyer and that she had not in practice been assisted by her assigned legal aid lawyer.

4.99   In the case of *Akdivar v Turkey*,[291] concerning the burning of houses by security forces in south-east Turkey, the Court held that the failure of the national authorities to investigate or offer assistance in circumstances where serious allegations of misconduct or the infliction of

---

[285] *Chiragov and others v Armenia*, No. 13216/05, 16.6.15, paras. 118–19; *Sargsyan v Azerbaijan*, No. 40167/06, 16.6.15, paras. 118–19.

[286] *Chiragov and others v Armenia*, No. 13216/05, 16.6.15, para. 119.

[287] *Sargsyan v Azerbaijan*, No. 40167/06, 16.6.15, para. 117.

[288] *Chitayev and Chitayev v Russia*, No. 59334/00, 18.1.07, para. 143.

[289] No. 44973/04, 10.2.11.

[290] No. 75450/12, 19.2.15.

[291] No. 21893/93, 16.9.96. See also *Benzer and others v Turkey*, No. 23502/06, 12.11.13 (discussed below at 4.115).

harm by state agents were made, might constitute 'special circumstances'. The burden then shifts back to the government to show what has been done in response to the scale and seriousness of the matters in issue. The *Akdivar* case also confirmed that the exhaustion rule is inapplicable where an 'administrative practice' has been shown to exist (that is, the repetition of acts incompatible with the Convention and with the official tolerance of state authorities), such that it would be futile or ineffective to attempt to bring proceedings.[292] In 2007 Georgia brought inter-state proceedings against Russia as a result of a series of arrests, detentions and deportations of Georgians in 2006–2007 (which followed the arrest in Tbilisi of a number of Russian service personnel on espionage charges). The Court found Russia to be responsible for an administrative practice of the detention and collective expulsion of Georgian nationals.[293] As a result, the Court dismissed the Russian Government's objection on the grounds of the non-exhaustion of domestic remedies.

4.100 In *Ayder and others* v *Turkey*,[294] which concerned widescale destruction of property in southeast Turkey, special circumstances were found to have arisen absolving the applicants from pursuing administrative remedies: there had been an unqualified undertaking by a senior public official that damage assessment reports would be prepared and all property owners would be compensated for the damage sustained. Another relevant factor is the insecurity or vulnerability which applicants might face in such circumstances.[295]

4.101 In *Opuz* v *Turkey*,[296] the Court found a violation of Article 14 taken together with Articles 2 and 3 because of the authorities' failure to respond adequately to domestic violence. The case concerned an escalating series of violent attacks on the applicant and her mother by the applicant's husband, culminating in his fatally shooting the applicant's mother. There were in that case special circumstances absolving the applicant from her obligation to exhaust domestic remedies, because of the ineffectiveness of the domestic law in providing equal protection of the law to her and her mother.

4.102 'Special circumstances' were also found to be applicable in a case concerning prison conditions in Netherlands Antilles: *AB* v *Netherlands*.[297] There, the Court accepted that the Government had provided various court decisions that demonstrated the existence of a remedy before the civil courts, which the applicant had not invoked. The Court noted that the situation in the prisons was, and continued to be, characterised by significant, serious structural problems. In considering the application of Article 35, the Court stated that it was required to take account not only of the existence of the potential remedy within the domestic legal system, but also 'the general legal and political context in which it operates, as well as the personal circumstances of the applicant'. Taking into account relevant findings of the European Committee for the Prevention of Torture (CPT) and the fact that the authorities had failed for more than a year to comply with injunctions to repair the serious structural

---

[292] *Ibid.*, paras. 66–7. See also *Thiermann and others* v *Norway*, No. 18712/03, dec. 8.3.07 (no 'special circumstances' to absolve applicants from exhausting domestic remedies in respect of their treatment as 'war children' born out of the Nazi '*Lebensborn*' scheme, and no evidence of an administrative practice).

[293] *Georgia* v *Russia* (I), No. 13255/07, 3.7.14.

[294] No. 23656/94, 8.1.04.

[295] See, e.g. *Dulaş* v *Turkey*, No. 25801/94, 30.1.01, paras. 47–8; *Selçuk and Asker* v *Turkey*, Nos. 23184/94 and 23185/94, 24.4.98, paras. 70–1.

[296] No. 33401/02, 9.6.09.

[297] No. 3738/97, 29.1.02.

shortcomings in relation to elementary hygienic and humanitarian issues, the Court concluded as follows:[298]

> In the absence of convincing explanations from the Government for their failure to take
> the necessary measures within a reasonable time to repair the structural problems ... and to
> observe the aforementioned court orders, there were special circumstances at the material
> time which dispensed the applicant from the obligation to exhaust the remedy suggested by
> the Government.

4.103 In *Öcalan* v *Turkey*,[299] there were 'special circumstances' absolving the applicant from utilising potential domestic remedies concerning the legality of his detention in police custody.
He could not in practice have sought redress because he was held in total isolation, he had no
legal training and had no possibility of consulting a lawyer. The Court also rejected sugges-
tions that the applicant's lawyers could have sought redress without consulting him. 'Special
circumstances' were also acknowledged in *Güveç* v *Turkey*,[300] absolving the applicant from
complaining about his detention, given that he was only fifteen years old, he had serious
health problems and did not receive adequate legal representation.

Six-Month Time Limit

General principles

4.104 According to Article 35(1), the Court may only deal with a matter that has been submitted
within six months of the final decision taken in the domestic proceedings.[301]

The time limit is intended to promote legal certainty, to provide the authorities with a degree
of protection from uncertainty, and to ensure that past decisions are not continually open to
challenge.[302] It is also intended to ensure that cases are processed within a reasonable time,
and it increases the likelihood of evidence being available that might otherwise disappear.
As the six months rule has a value in itself of promoting legal certainty it therefore cannot be
waived by respondent governments.[303]

4.105 The Court considers that the six months rule allows a prospective applicant time to consider
whether to lodge an application and, if so, to decide on the specific complaints and arguments to be raised.

4.106 Time runs from the day after the date of the final decision in the domestic proceedings that
the applicant is required to invoke under the exhaustion of domestic remedies rule.[304] This
will usually mean the date when judgment is given. But if judgment is not given publicly,
time will run from the date when the applicant or their representative is informed of the
decision.[305] This will mean that time will start to run when the applicant's representative

---

[298] *Ibid.*, para. 73.
[299] No. 46221/99, 12.3.03, paras. 71–2 and endorsed by the Grand Chamber, 12.5.05, para. 70.
[300] No. 70337/01, 20.1.09.
[301] When it enters into force, Protocol No. 15 will reduce this time limit to four months (see further chapter 1).
[302] See, e.g. *Kozak* v *Poland*, No. 13102/02, 2.3.10, para. 63.
[303] See, e.g. *Walker* v *UK*, No. 24979/97, dec. 25.1.00.
[304] See, e.g. *Otto* v *Germany*, No. 21425/06, dec. 10.11.09.
[305] See, e.g. *KCM* v *Netherlands*, No. 21034/92, dec. 9.1.95, 80 DR 87; *Karataş* v *Turkey*, No. 33179/96, 9.7.02; *Rudnichenko* v *Ukraine*, No. 2775/07, 11.7.13.

receives notification of a decision, even if the applicant is not informed until later.[306] Where a decision is not served on the parties, but is merely added to the case file at the court registry, the applicants may be deemed to have been notified and the six months will start to run from that point.[307] The six months rule is strictly applied—even if the period expires on a weekend or holiday it must be complied with.[308]

If reasons for a decision follow after the date when the decision itself was made public or notified **4.107** to the applicant, the time will only start to run from the later date if the reasons given for the decision are relevant to the Convention application.[309]

In *Worm* v *Austria*,[310] the applicant journalist had been prosecuted for publishing an article that **4.108** was considered capable of influencing the outcome of criminal proceedings relating to a former Minister. The Government challenged the admissibility of the application as it had not been lodged within six months of the date when the operative provisions and the relevant reasons were read out by the Court of Appeal. The applicant was not, however, provided with a written copy of the judgment until more than five months later. The Court held that time only started to run after receipt of the written judgment, which contained more than nine pages of detailed legal reasoning.

If there are no applicable domestic remedies, an application should be lodged at the Court **4.109** within six months of the incident or decision complained of, or within six months of the applicant's date of knowledge of the incident or decision.[311] This will be the Court's approach where it is clear from the outset that no effective remedy was available to the applicant.

Similarly, where a complaint is made about the absence of an adequate remedy against a particu- **4.110** lar act which is alleged to be in breach of the Convention, the six months will run from the date when the act took place.[312]

Where there has been a series of events that the applicant proposes to raise with the European **4.111** Court, the safest course is to lodge an application within six months of the first incident. However, if the events are linked, it may be possible to lodge within six months of the final event in the series. For example, in *Opuz* v *Turkey*,[313] the Court considered recurring acts of violence by the applicant's husband towards both the applicant and her mother to be a 'chain of connected events', rather than separate episodes (see also 'continuing breaches' at 4.122 and '*ratione temporis*' at 4.148 below).

The Court's inconsistent approach in applying the six months rule as regards non-consecutive **4.112** periods of pre-trial detention was clarified by the Grand Chamber in its 2012 judgment in

---

[306] See, e.g. *Andorka and Vavra* v *Hungary*, Nos. 25694/03 & 28338/03, dec. 12.9.06.
[307] See, e.g. *Yavuz and others* v *Turkey*, No. 48064/99, dec. 1.2.05.
[308] See, e.g. *Kadiķis* v *Latvia*, No. 62393/00, dec. 25.9.03; *Otto* v *Germany*, No. 21425/06, dec. 10.11.09; *Büyükdere and others* v *Turkey*, Nos. 6162/04, 6297/04, 6304/04, 6305/04, 6149/04, 9724/04 and 9733/04, 8.6.10; *Sabri Güneş* v *Turkey*, No. 27396/06, 29.6.12.
[309] *Worm* v *Austria*, No. 22714/93, 29.8.97.
[310] No. 22714/93, 29.8.97.
[311] See, e.g. *X* v *UK*, No. 7379/76, dec. 10.12.76, 8 DR 211; *Scotts of Greenock Ltd* v *UK*, No. 9599/81, dec. 11.3.85, 42 DR 33; *Hazar and Others* v *Turkey*, Nos. 62566/00 et seq., dec. 10.1.02; *Ünal Tekeli* v *Turkey*, No. 29865/96, 16.11.04.
[312] See, e.g. *Papon* v *France*, No. 64666/01, 7.6.01; *Slivenko and others* v *Latvia*, No. 48321/99, 23.1.02.
[313] No. 33401/02, 9.6.09, para. 111.

Idalov v *Russia*.[314] Previously, the Court had first applied the *Neumeister*[315] approach: assessing the six months rule in relation to each period of detention. Subsequently, the Court followed a 'global approach', calculating the multiple periods as a whole and not separately assessing the six months rule.[316] For example, in *Solmaz* v *Turkey*[317] the Court held that consecutive detention periods imposed on an individual should be regarded as a whole, so that the six-month period should only start to run from the end of the last period of pre-trial detention. In some cases, however, the Court had then reverted back to the *Neumeister* approach.[318] Accordingly, in *Idalov* the Court sought to clarify the position, by, in essence, confirming the *Neumeister* approach: where an accused's pre-trial detention is broken into several non-consecutive periods and where applicants are free to lodge complaints about pre-trial detention while they are at liberty, the non-consecutive periods of detention should not be assessed as a whole, but separately.

4.113　In relation to a reference to the CJEU,[319] the six months time limit runs from the domestic court's application of the ruling of the CJEU, rather than from the date of the decision of the CJEU itself.[320]

4.114　The six-month time limit can only be satisfied by the lodging with the European Court of a completed application form which (strictly) complies with the requirements set out in Rule 47 of the Court Rules.[321] The Court's application form was introduced in January 2014—prior to that it had been possible to lodge a case at the Court with an introductory letter, but that is no longer possible. The Rule 47 requirements, and the application process in general, are set out in chapter 2.

4.115　It is only in exceptional cases that the six-month time limit might be suspended, or that considerable delays in applying to the Court may be considered acceptable. For example, an applicant who introduced an application concerning the killing of her daughter and her husband lodged medical evidence setting out her medical and psychiatric treatment. The European Commission accepted that for a certain time following her daughter's death, the applicant was unable to lodge an application because of the state of her health. Nevertheless the application was still declared inadmissible as being two years too late.[322] In *Benzer and others* v *Turkey*,[323] a case concerning the deaths of the applicants' relatives caused by the bombing of their village in south-east Turkey in 1994, the Court rejected the Government's complaint relating to the fact that the applicants' case had only been lodged 12 years after the incident. The Court found reasonable the applicants' argument that in an atmosphere of fear, where serious human rights violations were not being investigated, it was not possible to make a complaint about their villages having been bombed by military planes. The Court took account of the fact that the applicants had to abandon

---

[314] No. 5826/03, 22.5.12.
[315] *Neumeister* v *Austria*, Series A, No. 8, 27.6.68.
[316] As exemplified by *Kemmache* v *France (No. 1 and No. 2)*, Series A, No. 218, 27.11.91.
[317] No. 27561/02, 16.1.07, para. 36.
[318] As it did, e.g. in *Bordikov* v *Russia*, No. 921/03, 8.10.09.
[319] Under Article 267 of the Treaty on the Functioning of the European Union (TFEU).
[320] *Bosphorus Hava Yollari Turizm Ve Ticaret AS* v *Ireland*, No. 45036/98, dec. 13.9.01.
[321] See, e.g. *Allan* v *UK*, No. 48539/99, dec. 28.8.01; *Sergey Kuznetsov* v *Russia*, No. 10877/04, 23.10.08, para. 27; *Kozak* v *Poland*, No. 13102/02, 2.3.10, para. 64.
[322] *H* v *UK and Ireland*, No. 9833/82, dec. 7.3.85, 42 DR 53.
[323] No. 23502/06, 12.11.13.

their villages and move to other parts of the country, and also noted that there would have been difficulties securing probative evidence. Furthermore, the delays had not created any particular obstacles for the authorities in establishing the facts. Similarly, in *Mocanu and others v Romania*,[324] the Court found that one applicant's vulnerability and feeling of powerlessness, as a victim of mass abuses committed by the security forces (during the repression of large-scale demonstrations against the Romanian Government in 1990), provided a plausible and acceptable explanation for delaying for several years before bringing a criminal complaint about his attack.

Doubtful remedies

If an applicant pursues a remedy that proves to be ineffective, the six months may run from **4.116** the final decision in the effective remedy pursued (or from the date of the incident itself, if there were no effective remedies). For some prospective applicants to the European Court, it may not be at all clear whether a particular form of redress would amount to a 'domestic remedy' for the purposes of Article 35. In those circumstances, there is a danger that the government might argue that the applicant had pursued a remedy that was not 'effective' for the purposes of Article 35 and therefore that the application should be declared inadmissible as having been submitted after the expiry of the six months period.[325] For example, in *Berdzenishvili v Russia*,[326] the applicant's criminal conviction was confirmed by a judgment of the Supreme Court. He then applied for 'supervisory review' of the judgment and lodged an application with the European Court only after his supervisory review complaint had been rejected. The Court found that as the supervisory review procedure did not amount to an effective remedy, his application should have been lodged within six months of the Supreme Court judgment.[327]

The UK Government successfully argued such a point in the case of *Raphaie v UK*,[328] on **4.117** the basis that the applicant had pursued an internal prison complaint which was not 'effective'. Where there is real doubt as to the availability or effectiveness of domestic remedies, the Court may be more flexible in applying the six months rule. The Court will, in general, not require an applicant to lodge a complaint before the position in relation to the matter

---

[324] Nos. 10865/09, 32431/08 and 45886/07, 17.9.14.

[325] See, e.g. *Prystavska v Ukraine*, No. 21287/02, dec. 17.12.02; *Tucka v UK*, No. 34586/10, dec. 18.1.11 (an application to the Criminal Cases Review Commission did not constitute an effective remedy—inadmissible); *Kashlan v Russia*, No.60189/15, dec. 19.4.16 (new cassation appeal procedure in criminal proceedings did not constitute an effective remedy—inadmissible).

[326] No. 31697/03, dec. 29.1.04.

[327] See also *Martynets v Russia*, No. 29612/09, dec. 5.11.09 (supervisory review under Code of Civil Procedure as amended in 2007). The Court makes a limited exception, however, where a request to reopen proceedings is successful. In cases where proceedings *are* reopened or a final decision is reviewed, the running of the six-month period will be interrupted, but *only* in relation to the Convention issues which formed the basis of the review or reopening and were examined by the extraordinary appeal body. See, e.g. *Sapeyan v Armenia*, No. 35738/03, 13.1.09. Since the reforms introduced in Russia in 2003, the process of supervisory review before the Supreme Commercial Court *will* be considered to amount to an effective remedy—see *Kovaleva and others v Russia*, No. 6025/09, dec. 25.6.09. See further *Abramyan and Yakubovskiye v Russia*, Nos. 38951/13 and 59611/13, dec. 12.5.15 (new cassation appeal procedure introduced in 2012 constituted an effective remedy which had to be exhausted—inadmissible); *Sakhanov v Russia*, No. 16559/16, dec. 18.10.16 (failure to use new cassation appeal procedure in commercial proceedings—inadmissible); *Chigirinova v Russia*, No. 28448/16, dec. 13.12.16 (failure to use new cassation appeal procedure introduced in Code of Administrative Procedure—inadmissible).

[328] No. 2000/92, dec. 2.12.93.

in question has been settled at the domestic level.[329] If an applicant pursues an apparently existing remedy and only subsequently becomes aware of circumstances that render the remedy ineffective, the six months may only start to run from the date when the applicant first became aware, or ought to have become aware, of the circumstances that made the remedy ineffective.[330]

4.118 The case of *Keenan* v *UK*,[331] concerned the applicant's son's suicide in prison and the failure of the prison authorities to safeguard his life, given his history of threatening to kill himself in custody. The Government argued that the applicant had failed to comply with the six months rule as there had been no effective domestic remedies and the complaint should therefore have been lodged within six months of the applicant's son's death. The applicant had had a potential remedy under the Law Reform (Miscellaneous Provisions) Act 1934. She applied for and was granted legal aid. She obtained the opinion of a consultant psychiatrist and then obtained counsel's opinion. Counsel advised that there were no effective domestic remedies available to her. An application to the European Commission of Human Rights was lodged within six months of that advice. The Commission found that it was not until she had received counsel's advice that she could reasonably have known that there were no domestic remedies and accordingly the six months only ran from the date of that advice.[332] The position might be different, however, if there were any evidence of abuse or delay by an applicant or an applicant's lawyer. It may be that in reaching this decision the Commission was influenced by the gravity of the case. *Edwards* v *UK*[333] concerned the death of the applicants' son who was kicked and stamped to death by his cell-mate whilst being held on remand in Chelmsford Prison in 1994. His parents were advised in 1996 that any civil proceedings would have been uneconomic and they only lodged their Strasbourg application in 1998 after a non-statutory inquiry had published its findings. Nevertheless, the Court rejected the Government's arguments that the case had been lodged out of time, taking into account the difficulties for the applicants in obtaining information about their son's death in prison and finding it reasonable for them to have awaited the outcome of the inquiry. The case of *Kerimova and others* v *Russia*[334] concerned an aerial attack on a town in Chechnya which resulted in the deaths of the applicants' relatives. The Government argued that their applications should have been lodged within six months of the decision to discontinue the domestic criminal investigation. However, that point was rejected by the Court on the basis that it had not been shown that the applicants, or their legal representatives,

---

[329] See, e.g. *Brecknell* v *UK*, No. 32457/04, dec. 6.3.07; *Scotts of Greenock Ltd* v *UK*, No. 9599/81, dec. 11.3.85, 42 DR 33.

[330] See, e.g. *Laçin* v *Turkey*, No. 23654/94, dec. 15.5.95, 81 DR 76; *Paul and Audrey Edwards* v *UK*, No. 46477/99, 7.6.01; *Yüksel Erdoğan and others* v *Turkey*, No. 57049/00, 15.2.07; *Kerimova and others* v *Russia*, No. 17170/04 et al., 3.5.11; *Chapman* v *Belgium*, No. 39619/06, dec. 5.3.13.

[331] No. 27229/95, dec. 22.5.98.

[332] See also *Younger* v *UK*, No. 57420/00, dec. 7.1.03.

[333] No. 46477/99, dec. 7.6.01. See also *Finucane* v *UK*, No. 29178/95, dec. 2.7.02 (complaint admissible when lodged within six months of announcement of decision not to prosecute anyone in respect of the applicant's husband's murder). But cf. *Lizette Dennis and others* v *UK*, No. 76573/01, dec. 2.7.02—case brought by relatives of the victims of the *Marchioness/Bowbelle* collision in 1989. The applicants were not entitled to await the report of a judicial inquiry in 2001 before lodging in Strasbourg.

[334] No. 17170/04 et al., 3.5.11. See also *Amuyeva and others* v *Russia*, No. 17321/06, 25.11.10; *Gakayeva and others* v *Russia*, No. 51534/08, 10.10.13; *Petimat Ismailova and others* v *Russia*, No. 25088/11 et al., 18.9.14; *Sultygov and others* v *Russia*, No. 42575/07 et al., 9.10.14; *Tagayeva and others* v *Russia*, No. 26562/07, dec. 9.6.15, para. 498.

had been informed of the decision at the time (or soon afterwards), and because once they became aware of the decision the lawyers made various unsuccessful attempts to obtain a copy of it (in order to consider appealing against it). It was only when the lawyers were later informed by letter that the case file had been classified as secret that they could then have realised the futility of their efforts to obtain a copy of the decision, and therefore that was the point when the six months period was considered to have begun.

The case of *El-Masri* v *former Yugoslav Republic of Macedonia*[335] concerned the 'extraordinary **4.119** rendition' of the applicant by the Macedonian authorities into the custody of the CIA. The Government argued that the applicant's criminal complaint had been lodged too late, and also that it had been an ineffective process, meaning that he should have lodged his application to the European Court much earlier than he did. These arguments were rejected by the Court which found, firstly, that the four year delay in lodging a criminal complaint was acceptable, taking account of the sensitivity of the issue and the evidence that European governments had denied their involvement in rendition. Accordingly, it was reasonable for the applicant to 'wait for developments that could have resolved crucial factual or legal issues'.[336] Secondly, although the applicant's criminal complaint was rejected in December 2008, the six months time limit only started to run once the applicant had been informed about it.

The applicants in *Fernandez-Molina Gonzalez and 370 other applications* v *Spain*[337] had all **4.120** been victims of very serious food poisoning that gave rise to a condition known as 'toxic syndrome', following their consumption of rapeseed oil. As a result, criminal proceedings were brought in the *Audiencia Nacional* against the individuals and companies responsible, which resulted in a judgment in 1989, inter alia, providing for compensation to be paid to the victims. Following problems of enforcement, the applicants' subsequent *amparo* appeals to the Constitutional Court were dismissed by decisions made in 2000 and 2001. Before the European Court, the Government argued that the applications should have been submitted within six months of the decision of the *Audiencia Nacional*, on the basis that the right to enjoyment of possessions was not protected by the *amparo* remedy. However, the Court rejected these arguments as taking too formalistic an approach to the six months time limit, and finding that it was more in keeping with the spirit and purpose of the Convention to take an overall view of the complaints raised by the applicants, in deciding the appropriate time limit. The applicant priest in *Ahtinen* v *Finland*[338] objected to his transfer to another parish 100 km away. There was no ordinary appeal available against a decision of the Cathedral Chapter, but the applicant pursued an extraordinary appeal to the Supreme Administrative Court. The Government argued that his European Court application should have been lodged within six months of the decision by the Cathedral Chapter. Noting that Article 35 did not require recourse to extraordinary remedies, the Court nevertheless dismissed the Government's objection as the extraordinary appeal had been the only judicial remedy open to the applicant, and which he had speedily pursued. He had then lodged his Strasbourg application within two months of the decision of the Supreme Administrative Court. Therefore, his application was not out of time. In *Roseiro Bento* v *Portugal*,[339] the

---

[335] No. 39630/09, 13.12.12.
[336] *Ibid.*, para. 142.
[337] No. 64359/01 and 370 other applications, dec. 8.10.02.
[338] No. 48907/99, dec. 31.5.05.
[339] No. 29288/02, dec. 30.11.04.

applicant invoked Article 10 after being prosecuted for proffering insults during his time in office as a mayor. As regards admissibility, the Court found that the applicant was entitled to lodge his case in Strasbourg after having pursued doubtful remedies relating to the Constitutional Court:

> The Court considers that the applicant cannot be criticised for having sought relief in the higher courts by attempting to argue in the Court of Appeal that a new statutory provision on which the Constitutional Court had yet to give a public ruling was unconstitutional. His decision to appeal to the Constitutional Court was also comprehensible as at that juncture the Constitutional Court's case-law on the subject consisted of a single decision and was not therefore entirely settled in Portuguese law. The Court notes in that connection that if the Constitutional Court had held the relevant legislation to be unconstitutional, the Court of Appeal would have been obliged to examine the applicant's other grounds of appeal, including the alleged violation of his freedom of expression.

In *Ünal Tekeli* v *Turkey*, the applicant complained that, as a married woman, she was prevented from using her maiden name in official documents. The Government argued that as her complaint flowed from the domestic law itself, she should have lodged her case with the Court within six months of her marriage. However, although acknowledging the Civil Code to be the source of the problem, the Court rejected the Government's position because of the possibility that the applicant might have been able to secure some form of redress:[340]

> ... the Court notes that in the proceedings before them the domestic courts could have directly applied the provisions of the Convention, which forms an integral part of the domestic law by virtue of Article 90 of the Constitution, or raised an objection that Article 153 of the Civil Code was unconstitutional ... and, lastly, they could have granted the applicant's request. Consequently, even if it is accepted that the remedy offered only a remote prospect of success, as alleged here, it was not a futile step. Accordingly, it had the effect at least of postponing the beginning of the six-month period ...

4.121 Care should be taken to ensure that if an applicant pursues domestic remedies or appeals, those remedies would be capable of providing redress for every complaint to be made to the European Court.[341] This may arise, for example, in a criminal case where the applicant wishes to complain about aspects of their detention, as well as the fairness of the proceedings. However, if the applicant's appeal against conviction would have no bearing on the question of the lawfulness of the pre-trial detention, then the question of the detention must be considered carefully and a Convention application lodged within six months of the end of the period of the detention at the latest (or within six months of the final decision in any domestic remedy relating to the detention). For example, in *Surriye Ali* v *UK*,[342] the applicant complained under Article 6 about the fairness of the criminal proceedings against her and also under Article 5 about the lawfulness of her initial detention. The application concerning both aspects of the case was not lodged until after judgment was handed down by the Court of Appeal, but the applicant's Article 5 complaint was found to be out of time as the appeal proceedings were not capable of affecting the position in relation to the detention.

---

[340] No. 29865/96, 16.11.04.
[341] See, e.g. *Lines* v *UK*, 24519/94, dec. 17.1.97.
[342] No. 25605/94, dec. 28.2.96.

Continuing breaches of the Convention ≠ *disappearances → continuing breach*

4.122 Where the matter which the applicant complains about is continuing (such as a period of detention), the time limit will not start to run until the breach ceases to have a continuing effect.[343] Where there is a continuing violation, an application could be lodged with the European Court several years after the violation first started.[344] However, great care should of course be taken to ascertain that the violation is a continuing one, rather than a one-off decision. There will be a continuing breach, for example, where the applicant complains of the continued existence of particular laws, as in *Dudgeon* v *UK*,[345] which concerned the existence in Northern Ireland of laws which made homosexual acts between consenting adult males criminal offences. In *Almeida Garrett and others* v *Portugal*,[346] the Court found that the expropriation and nationalisation of the applicants' land in the mid-1970s (prior to the date of entry into force of the Convention in respect of Portugal) had been an instantaneous act, but that the complaint of the failure to pay compensation was a continuing one (which led to a finding of a violation of Article 1 of Protocol No. 1). The applicants in *Potomska and Potomski* v *Poland*[347] successfully complained about their continuing inability to develop their property (as it was listed as a historic monument, being formerly a Jewish cemetery). In *Roche* v *UK*,[348] the Court found that the applicant's complaint under Articles 8 and 10 of the Convention in respect of the state's refusal to provide him with information concerning chemical weapons testing carried out on him as a serving soldier in the 1960s amounted to a continuing situation. The applicant in *Paksas* v *Lithuania*[349] was a former president of Lithuania who had been impeached, and who was prevented from standing for public office by a decision of the Constitutional Court which imposed a lifetime ban on anyone who had been removed from office as president for a gross violation of the Constitution or a breach of the constitutional oath. His complaint was accordingly found to relate to a continuing state of affairs, in respect of which there was no domestic remedy.

4.123 The Court also recognises that the repetition of the same events may be considered as a 'continuing situation' even though they are not strictly continuous. Examples include the repeated transfer of prisoners in similar conditions[350] and the regular confinement of suspects in a metal cage in the courtroom.[351]

---

[343] See, e.g. *Jecius* v *Lithuania*, No. 34578/97, 31.7.00, para. 44; *Riener* v *Bulgaria*, No. 46343/99, 23.5.06, para. 101; *Daróczy* v *Hungary*, No. 44375/05, 1.7.08, para. 18; *Kurić and others* v *Slovenia*, No. 26828/06, 26.6.12, para. 339.

[344] See, e.g. *De Becker* v *Belgium*, No. 214/56, Series B, No. 4, 27.3.62 (concerning a statutory provision which created a continuing restriction on the applicant journalist's freedom of expression by preventing him publishing). However, there was no continuing violation in *Prince Hans-Adam II of Liechtenstein* v *Germany*, No. 42527/98, 12.7.01 as regards the expropriation of a painting by the authorities of former Czechoslovakia in 1946.

[345] No. 7525/76, Series A, No. 45, 23.9.81.

[346] Nos. 29813/96 and 30229/96, 11.1.00. In contrast, see, e.g. *Von Maltzan and others* v *Germany*, Nos. 71916/01, 71917/01 and 10260/02, dec. 2.3.05 (no question of the continuing violation of the Convention in relation to property expropriated during the Soviet occupation between 1945 and 1949) and *Preussische Treuhand GmbH & CO. Kg A. A.* v *Poland*, No. 47550/06, dec. 7.10.08 (no continuing violation of the Convention as regards the expropriation of private property of ethnic Germans, located on territories entrusted to Poland after World War II).

[347] No. 33949/05, 29.3.11.

[348] No. 32555/96, dec. 23.5.02.

[349] No. 34932/04, 6.1.11.

[350] *Fetisov and others* v *Russia*, No. 43710/07 et al., 17.1.12.

[351] *Svinarenko and Slyadnev* v *Russia*, Nos. 32541/08 and 43441/08, 17.7.14.

4.124   There was a violation of the applicant's rights under Article 8 because of the non-enforcement of his right of access to his daughter in the case of *Hokkanen* v *Finland*.[352] The case was introduced in 1992 and the Court found that the violation arising from the non-enforcement of access had continued until September 1993 when the Court of Appeal decided that the applicant's access to his daughter could not be enforced against her wishes.

4.125   However, in *Posti and Rahko* v *Finland*,[353] the Court held that restrictions placed on the applicants' fishing rights over a period of years did not constitute a continuing situation as those restrictions resulted from specific events on specific dates, namely the issuing of decrees. The applicants in *Hingitaq 53* v *Denmark*[354] complained about the restrictions of Inuit access to hunting and fishing as a result of the establishment of the Thule Air Base in 1951, and the relocation of the population from their settlement in 1953. The Court rejected their arguments that the alleged violations were continuing, finding that they were instantaneous acts, and declared that aspect of the case to be incompatible *ratione temporis* with the Convention. In *Veeber* v *Estonia (No. 1)*,[355] the Court found that a police search of the applicant's company premises and seizure of the applicant's documents did not give rise to any possible continuing situation of a violation of Article 8. That aspect of the case, which had occurred prior to the entry into force of the Convention in respect of Estonia, was accordingly found to be inadmissible *ratione temporis*.

4.126   Special consideration has been given to the phenomenon of enforced disappearances.[356] The case of *Varnava and others* v *Turkey*,[357] concerned disappearances of Greek Cypriots in northern Cyprus following Turkey's invasion of Cyprus in 1974. Noting that not all continuing situations are the same, the Grand Chamber held that applicants must not delay unduly in bringing a complaint before the Court about the ineffectiveness of an investigation into a case of disappearance:

> … applications can be rejected as out of time in disappearance cases where there has been excessive or unexplained delay on the part of applicants once they have, or should have, become aware that no investigation has been instigated or that the investigation has lapsed into inaction or become ineffective and, in any of those eventualities, there is no immediate, realistic prospect of an effective investigation being provided in the future.[358]

4.127   In *Varnava* the applications were introduced in 1990, 15 years after the applicants' relatives had disappeared, and three years after Turkey had accepted the right of petition to the Court. Such a delay was, however, considered to be reasonable, given the exceptional situation of international conflict, that no normal investigative procedures had been available, and that the applicants had been entitled to await the outcome of initiatives taken by their Government and the United Nations (which had established a Committee on Missing Persons).[359]

---

[352] No. 19823/92, Series A, No. 299-A, 23.9.94.

[353] No. 27824/95, 24.9.02.

[354] No. 18584/04, dec.12.1.06.

[355] No. 37571/97, 7.11.02.

[356] See, e.g. *Palić* v *Bosnia and Herzegovina*, No. 4704/04, 15.2.11.

[357] No. 16064/90, 18.9.09. See also: *Er and others* v *Turkey*, No. 23016/04, 31.7.12 (application lodged nine years after disappearance of applicants' relative while domestic investigation still under way: Government's preliminary objection dismissed).

[358] *Ibid.*, para. 165.

[359] See, by contrast, the subsequent inadmissibility decisions in *Orphanou and others* v *Turkey*, Nos. 43422/04 et al., dec. 1.12.09; *Karefyllides and others* v *Turkey*, No. 45503/99, dec. 1.12.09; *Charalambous and others* v *Turkey*, Nos. 46744/07 et al., dec. 1.6.10.

The case of *Zorica Jovanović* v *Serbia*,[360] concerned the circumstances of the death (or disappearance) of the applicant's new-born baby in hospital in 1983. As it related to the failure of the authorities to provide credible information about the fate of the applicant's son, it was considered to be a continuing situation. As regards the application of the six months rule, the Court held that the applicant was entitled to wait for the results of a report by a parliamentary working group into the phenomenon of 'missing babies' (who had gone missing from Serbian hospitals from the 1970s to the 1990s)—only by then would it have become obvious that no redress would be forthcoming. The case of *Palić* v *Bosnia and Herzegovina*[361] concerned the disappearance in 1995 of the applicant's husband, a military commander, during the war in Bosnia. Although the case was not lodged until 2004, the Court found that at that date it was still realistic to expect that an effective investigation would be carried out, in the light of the various steps which were being taken by the authorities, including the setting up of a Missing Persons Institute, the creation of the Court of Bosnia and Herzegovina in 2002 and its war crimes sections (in 2005) and the adoption of a National War Crimes Strategy (in 2008).

The Court discerned similarities between the situation in *Varnava* and the cases of *Chiragov* **4.128** *and others* v *Armenia*[362] and *Sargsyan* v *Azerbaijan*[363] which concerned the applicants' loss of their homes and property after they fled from the fighting during the armed conflict in the Nagorno-Karabakh region in 1992. Both types of case concerned complaints about continuing violations in a complex post-conflict situation. It was considered reasonable for the applicants in the Nagorno-Karabakh cases to await the outcome of political processes such as peace talks and negotiations that might offer the only realistic hope of a solution. In post-conflict situations, the Court acknowledged that generous time frames were required in order to allow the situation to settle and to enable the applicants to collect information on the chances of obtaining a solution at the domestic level. By applying to the Court within about three years (*Chiragov*) and about four years (*Sargsyan*) after the respective states had ratified the Convention, the applicants were found to have acted without undue delay.[364]

No Significant Disadvantage

Under Protocol No. 14 to the Convention (see 1.29 above), a further admissibility criter- **4.129** ion was added to Article 35 of the Convention, with effect from 1 June 2010 (Article 35(3) (b)).[365] This new criterion incorporates a threefold test: a case may be declared inadmissible by the Court if it considers that:

(1) the applicant has not suffered a 'significant disadvantage';[366]
(2) unless respect for human rights as defined in the Convention and the Protocols thereto requires an examination of the application on the merits;

---

[360] No. 21794/08, 26.3.13.
[361] No. 4704/04, 15.2.11.
[362] No. 13216/05, dec. 14.12.11.
[363] No. 40167/06, dec. 14.12.11.
[364] See, by contrast, *Sokolov and others* v *Serbia*, No. 30859/10 et al., dec. 14.1.14.
[365] It is not applicable to cases declared admissible before that date: *Vistiņš and Perepjolkins* v *Latvia*, No. 71243/01, 25.10.12, para. 66.
[366] In the French, *'préjudice important'*.

(3) provided that no case may be rejected on this ground that has not been duly considered by a domestic tribunal.[367]

4.130 In essence, this criterion reflects the principle that 'a violation of a right, however real from a purely legal point of view, should attain a minimum level of severity to warrant consideration by an international court'.[368] The introduction of this new admissibility provision into the Convention was not uncontroversial, on the basis of the risk that it might pose to the right of individual petition, its vagueness and the extent to which it added anything new.[369]

4.131 The assessment of the 'minimum threshold' (as regards the extent of the 'disadvantage' suffered by an applicant) will depend on the circumstances of the case—the Court will take account of the nature of the right allegedly breached, the seriousness of the impact of the alleged violation on the exercise of the right and the potential consequences of the violation on the applicant's personal situation.[370] Clearly, where a case is considered to raise an 'important matter of principle', it will not be declared inadmissible on this basis.[371] The Court will consider both the applicant's subjective perceptions[372] and also what is objectively at stake in a particular case.[373] 'Significant disadvantage' may be based, for example, on the financial impact of the matter in dispute or the importance of the case for the applicant. The Court invoked this provision, for example, in declaring inadmissible the application of *Kiousi* v *Greece*[374] in relation to a pecuniary damages claim of €500, the case of *Ionescu* v *Romania*[375] which concerned a contractual claim for €90, the case of *Korolev* v *Russia*,[376] in which the applicant complained of a failure by a state body to pay a judgment debt worth 22½ Russian rubles (less than one euro), and the case of *Rinck* v *France*,[377] that concerned a fine of €150

---

[367] Note, however, that when it enters into force, Protocol No. 15 will delete this third element of the test: See Article 5 of Protocol No. 15 and the discussion of Protocol No. 15 in chapter 1.

[368] *Korolev* v *Russia*, No. 25551/05, dec. 1.7.10.

[369] See, e.g. P. Leach, 'Access to the European Court of Human Rights–From a Legal Entitlement to a Lottery?' (2006) 27 HRLJ 11. The 'triviality' of a case had provided grounds for rejecting cases prior to the advent of Protocol No. 14. For example, in *Bock* v *Germany*, No. 22051/07, dec. 19.1.10 the Court declared inadmissible, as being an abuse of the right of petition, an application concerning legal proceedings relating to the reimbursement of just under €8, noting the triviality of the facts and the pettiness of the amount involved. In their joint dissenting opinion in *Micallef* v *Malta*, No. 17056/06, 15.10.09 Judges Costas, Jungwiert, Kovler and Fura argued, even prior to Protocol No. 14 having come into force, that the applicant had not incurred a significant disadvantage in proceedings which concerned a 'trivial dispute between neighbours'.

[370] *Giusti* v *Italy*, No. 13175/03, 18.10.11, para. 34.

[371] See, e.g. *Vartic* v *Romania (No. 2)*, No. 14150/08, 17.12.13 (complaint by detainee that he was not provided with a vegetarian diet as required by his Buddhist convictions).

[372] See, e.g. *Shefer* v *Russia*, No. 45175/04, dec. 13.3.12.

[373] See, e.g. *Ladygin* v *Russia*, No. 31956/05, dec. 13.9.11. See also *Hebat Aslan and Firas Aslan* v *Turkey*, No. 15048/09, 28.10.14 (court proceedings relating to the legality of the applicants' detention—Government objection based on 'no significant disadvantage' rejected); *C.P.* v *UK*, No. 300/11, dec. 6.9.16 (complaint about pupil's temporary suspension from school considered to be 'essentially procedural'—no significant disadvantage).

[374] No. 52036/09, dec. 20.9.11.

[375] No. 36659/04, dec. 1.6.10. See, by contrast, *Sancho Cruz and 14 others* v *Portugal*, No. 8851/07 et al., 18.1.11 (expropriation of property) and *Gaglione and others* v *Italy*, No. 45867/07 et al., 21.12.10 (length of proceedings).

[376] No. 25551/05, dec. 1.7.10. See also *Vasilchenko* v *Russia*, No. 34784/02, 23.9.10; *Cecchetti* v *San Marino*, No. 40174/08, dec. 9.4.13.

[377] No. 18774/09, dec. 19.10.10. See also *Gaftoniuc* v *Romania*, No. 30934/05, dec. 22.2.11 (failure to receive payment of court fees equivalent to €25–no significant disadvantage); *Ştefănescu* v *Romania*, No. 11774/04, dec. 12.4.11 (claim for non-pecuniary damages equivalent to €125–no significant disadvantage); *Boelens and others* v *Belgium*, No. 20007/09, dec. 11.9.12 (€50 fine for refusing to participate in organisation of elections—no significant disadvantage).

for a road traffic offence, costs of €22 and the deduction of one point from the applicant's driving licence. However, the Court accepted in *Korolev* that, in principle, even modest pecuniary damage could be 'significant' in view of personal circumstances (or the economic conditions in a region or country) and also that a Convention violation could cause 'significant disadvantage' without affecting pecuniary interests. In *Giuran v Romania*,[378] the Court rejected the Government's argument that the applicant had not suffered a significant disadvantage. Legal proceedings brought by the applicant concerned the theft from his home of items worth €350. In addition to the value of the goods, the Court also took account of the applicant's position as someone who was retired, the sentimental value attached to the stolen items, and that a question of principle was in issue—the applicant's right to his possessions and his home. There was a similar outcome in *Eon v France*[379] which concerned the applicant's conviction for insulting the French President (for which he received a suspended fine of €30). The Court took account of the subjective importance of the case for the applicant, and, objectively, that it related to the question whether insulting the head of State should remain a criminal offence.

4.132 The applicant in *Gagliano Giorgi v Italy*[380] complained under Article 6 about unduly long criminal proceedings against him. He was convicted of forgery, but a second charge of bribery was time-barred, because of the excessive length of the proceedings. As this meant a reduction in the applicant's sentence, he was found not to have suffered a 'significant disadvantage'. There was also no such disadvantage in *Zwinkels v Netherlands*[381] where the applicant's complaint concerned the fact that work inspectors had entered his private garage without his permission. The applicant in *Galović v Croatia*[382] complained about the length of legal proceedings relating to a court order for her eviction from her flat. However, as the length of proceedings had benefited her, by postponing her eviction, the applicant was considered not to have suffered a significant disadvantage.

4.133 As to whether 'respect for human rights' requires an examination of an application on the merits, the Court will consider, for example, if the relevant law has changed (therefore making the decision of 'historical interest' only), whether similar issues have already been resolved in other cases before the Court or whether a systemic issue arising in a particular state has already been considered by the Court or Committee of Ministers.[383]

4.134 The purpose of the second 'safeguard clause' (due consideration by a domestic tribunal) is to ensure that every case receives a judicial examination whether at the national level or at the European level—'to avoid a denial of justice'.[384] The case of *Dudek v Germany*[385]

---

[378] No. 24360/04, 21.6.11.

[379] No. 26118/10, 14.3.13. See, by contrast, *Sylka v Poland*, No. 19219/07, dec. 3.6.14 (a freedom of expression case with no wider public ramifications—no significant disadvantage).

[380] No. 23563/07, 6.3.12.

[381] No. 16593/10, dec. 9.10.12.

[382] No. 54388/09, dec. 5.3.13.

[383] *Ionescu v Romania*, No. 36659/04, dec. 1.6.10 and *Korolev v Russia*, No. 25551/05, dec. 1.7.10. See also *Holub v Czech Republic*, No. 24880/05, dec. 14.12.10 and *Bratři Zátkové, a.s. v Czech Republic*, No. 20862/06, dec. 8.2.11; *Juhas Ðurić v Serbia*, No. 48155/06, 7.6.11; *Nicoleta Gheorghe v Romania*, No. 23470/05, 3.4.12. The phrase also appears in Article 37 and is considered above at 2.155 (friendly settlement) and 2.165 (striking out).

[384] *Korolev v Russia*, No. 25551/05, dec. 1.7.10. See also *Holub v Czech Republic*, No. 24880/05, dec. 14.12.10 and *Bratři Zátkové, a.s. v Czech Republic*, No. 20862/06, dec. 8.2.11.

[385] No. 12977/09, dec. 23.11.10.

concerned the length of proceedings in relation to claims ranging from €71 to €312. However, the Court was precluded from applying the 'significant disadvantage' criterion as there was no domestic remedy available in Germany in relation to length of proceedings cases, and accordingly the case had not been 'duly considered by a domestic tribunal'. Nevertheless, the Court still declared the application inadmissible on the basis that its pettiness amounted to an abuse of the right of application (relying on the precedent of *Bock* v *Germany*).[386] The requirement for due consideration by a domestic tribunal does not apply as regards allegations of Convention violations by last instance judicial bodies.[387]

Anonymous Applications

4.135 Every application to the European Court must identify the applicant (Article 35(2)(a)). Any application that does not do so may be declared inadmissible on this ground alone.[388]

4.136 In some cases applicants may have very good reasons for not wishing to have their identities disclosed. In such cases, the applicant's details (including name, address, date of birth, nationality and occupation) will have to be set out in the application form, but the applicant can request confidentiality. There is a section on confidentiality in chapter 2 (2.39). If the applicant's request for confidentiality is accepted by the Court, the applicant will be identified in the case reports by their initials or simply by a letter.

Applications Substantially the Same as a Matter That Has Already Been Examined by the Court

4.137 An application that is substantially the same as a matter that has already been examined by the Court and that contains no relevant new information will be declared inadmissible by the Court (Article 35(2)(b)). For example, repeated applications from the same applicant concerning the same matter will be declared inadmissible on this ground, unless relevant new information has come to light. However, the exception concerning 'relevant new information' is important. For example, an applicant whose petition has previously been declared inadmissible for non-exhaustion of domestic remedies may resubmit the case to the European Court after having exhausted effective domestic remedies. There may also be new factual information, or new developments in domestic proceedings, which may justify a further application, such as the increased length of domestic proceedings.[389] However, additional legal arguments will not amount to 'relevant new information'.[390]

---

[386] No. 22051/07, dec. 19.1.10—see note 369 above.
[387] *Galović* v *Croatia*, No.54388/09, dec. 5.3.13.
[388] See, e.g. *'Blondje'* v *Netherlands*, No. 7245/09, dec. 15.9.09.
[389] See, e.g. *X* v *UK*, No. 8233/78, dec. 3.10.79, 17 DR 122; *Vallan* v *Italy*, No. 9621/81, dec. 13.10.83, 33 DR 217.
[390] *X* v *UK*, No. 8206/78, dec. 10.7.81, 25 DR 147.

Applications Already Submitted to Another Procedure of International Investigation or Settlement

The Court may not consider any application that has already been submitted[391] to another **4.138** procedure of international investigation or settlement, and that contains no relevant new information (Article 35(2)(b)). For example, a previous petition to the Human Rights Committee under the International Covenant on Civil and Political Rights would prevent an applicant also complaining to the European Court (even where an application was made to the Human Rights Committee to defer its decision until the European Commission had decided on admissibility),[392] as would an application to the ILO Committee on Freedom of Association.[393] But to be inadmissible on this ground, the contents of the applications would have to be essentially the same[394] and submitted by the same applicant.[395] In *Pauger* v *Austria*[396] the applicant complained of a violation of Article 6 because of the lack of a public hearing in proceedings concerning the discriminatory provision of a survivor's pension. A previous decision of the UN Human Rights Committee brought by the same applicant on the same facts did not, however, preclude an application to Strasbourg, because the petition to the Human Rights Committee concerned discrimination, whereas the European Convention application concerned the fairness of the proceedings.[397] In *Peraldi* v *France*[398] the Court found that a prior complaint to the UN Working Party on Arbitrary Detention would preclude an application to the European Court. It was decisive that the Working Group could accept individual applications, its proceedings were adversarial, and its decisions were reasoned, notified to the parties and published in its reports. Furthermore, its recommendations were determinative of state liability, were capable of bringing the violations in question to an end and were also subject to a monitoring procedure. For those reasons, the Court found that there were many similarities with the UN Human Rights Committee. However, in *Malsagova and others* v *Russia*,[399] a case concerning the applicants' relative's enforced disappearance in Chechnya,

---

[391] The Court has clarified that the key issue is not in fact the 'submission' of the petition as such, but whether or not a 'decision' has been taken. On that basis in *National Union of Rail, Maritime and Transport Workers* v *UK*, No. 31045/10, 8.4.14 the Court rejected the Government's objection that the applicant had made a similar complaint to the ILO Committee on Freedom of Association, as the complaint had subsequently been withdrawn before any decision had been made.

[392] *Cacerrada Fornieles and Cabeza Mato* v *Spain*, No. 17512/90, dec. 6.7.92, 73 DR 214; see also the separate opinion of Judges Zupančič and Borrego Borrego in *Folgerø and others* v *Norway*, No. 15472/02, 29.6.07.

[393] *Fédération hellénique des syndicats des employés du secteur bancaire* v *Greece*, No. 72808/10, dec. 6.12.11.

[394] See, e.g. *OAO Neftyanaya Kompaniya Yukos* v *Russia*, No. 14902/04, 20.9.11, paras. 523–6; *Savda* v *Turkey*, No. 42730/05, 12.6.12, paras. 68–70.

[395] See, e.g. No. 11603/85, (1987) 50 DR 228, where the Commission decided that an application brought by individuals was not the same as a complaint lodged with the International Labour Organisation (ILO) by the Trades Union Congress. See also *The Professional Trades Union for Prison, Correctional and Secure Psychiatric Workers (POA) and others* v *UK*, No. 59253/11, dec. 21.5.13 (prior complaint to the ILO's Committee on Freedom of Association by the applicant union, meant that its application to the European Court, and that of two of its officers (because of their close association with the proceedings), was inadmissible).

[396] No. 16717/90, 28.5.97.

[397] See also *Smirnova* v *Russia*, Nos. 46133/99 and 48183/99, dec. 3.10.02 (prior application to UN Human Rights Committee did not rule out an application to the European Court because it concerned a much wider factual basis).

[398] No. 2096/05, dec. 7.4.09. See also *Gürdeniz* v *Turkey*, No. 59715/10, dec. 18.3.14.

[399] No. 27244/03, dec. 6.3.08.

the Court rejected the Government's argument that the complaint should be declared inadmissible because a prior complaint had been submitted to the UN Working Group on Enforced or Involuntary Disappearances. Firstly, the complaint to the working group had been submitted by the NGO Human Rights Watch, not the applicant, and secondly, the Court found that the Working Group was not 'a procedure of international investigation or settlement' as it did not investigate disappearances, or provide relatives with a legal means of redress, and nor was it capable of attributing responsibility for the deaths of missing persons or making findings as to the causes.

4.139 The fact that a case has been examined by the European Committee for the Prevention of Torture (CPT) would not prevent an application to the European Court,[400] nor would a complaint to the European Commission,[401] a complaint under the UN's 1503 procedure,[402] or inter-state talks conducted within the OSCE.[403] In response to a request from the Committee of Ministers for an Advisory Opinion under Article 47, the Court declined to decide whether the Human Rights Commission established by the Convention on Human Rights of the Commonwealth of Independent States would amount to 'another procedure of international investigation or settlement' within the meaning of Article 35(2)(b) (as to advisory opinions, see 1.40 above).[404]

4.140 In *Jeličić v Bosnia and Herzegovina*,[405] the Court was required to consider whether the Human Rights Chamber in Bosnia was an 'international' body within the meaning of Article 35(2)(b). It did so by assessing the Chamber's composition, its competence, its place in the existing legal system and its funding. It concluded that although the Chamber was set up by an international treaty (the 1995 Dayton Agreement) it was to be considered a domestic remedy within the meaning of Article 35(1) as it formed part of the domestic legal system (its mandate did not cover obligations between states). Article 35(2)(b) will not preclude an individual application in relation to a matter that has previously been considered in the course of an inter-state application (as the applications will not have been introduced by the same persons).[406]

Incompatibility with the Provisions of the Convention

4.141 Article 35(3)(a) requires the Court to declare inadmissible any application that it considers 'incompatible with the provisions of the Convention or the Protocols thereto ...'. The concept of incompatibility with the Convention has four aspects to it:

- incompatibility of an application because of the limits of the state's jurisdiction (known as '*ratione loci*');

---

[400] Explanatory Report to the Convention for the Prevention of Torture and Inhuman or Degrading Treatment or Punishment, CPT/Inf/C(89)1[EN], para. 92.

[401] *Karoussiotis v Portugal*, No. 23205/08, 1.2.11; *Shaw v Hungary*, No. 6457/09, 26.7.11.

[402] *Celniku v Greece*, No. 21449/04, 5.7.07, para. 40.

[403] *Chiragov and others v Armenia*, No. 13216/05, dec. 14.12.11.

[404] Decision on the Competence of the Court to give an Advisory Opinion, 2 June 2004.

[405] No. 41183/02, dec. 15.11.05.

[406] *Varnava and others v Turkey*, No. 16064/90, 18.9.09, para. 118. See also *Georgia v Russia (II)*, No. 38263/08, dec. 13.12.11, para 79. The issue had been left open in *Donnelly and others v UK*, Nos. 5577/72–5583/72, dec. 5.4.73, Yearbook 16, p. 212 (applying former Article 27(1)(b)).

- incompatibility of an application because of the limits as to what the Convention rights cover (known as '*ratione materiae*');
- incompatibility of an application because of the limits in time as to the state's obligations under the Convention (known as '*ratione temporis*');
- incompatibility of an application because of the limits as to who may bring Convention applications and as to who may be respondents (known as '*ratione personae*').

These four categories are explained in more detail below.

Jurisdiction: *ratione loci*

The alleged violation of the Convention must have occurred within the respondent state's **4.142** *jurisdiction*. This is primarily a territorial question, but not exclusively so, as the Court will exceptionally permit other bases of the jurisdictional competence of a state, where the state exercises 'effective control' over the territory in question or where 'through the consent, invitation or acquiescence of the Government of that territory, [the state] exercises all or some of the public powers normally to be exercised by that Government'.[407] The jurisdiction of a state includes a 'dependent territory' if the state has made a declaration under Article 56 that the Convention applies to the territory.[408]

For example, in the *Cyprus* v *Turkey* cases, Turkey has been found to be responsible for **4.143** its armed forces in Cyprus. The Turkish armed forces in Cyprus were considered to have brought any persons or property there within the jurisdiction of Turkey, 'to the extent that they exercise control over such persons or property'.[409]

It is generally not possible to complain under the European Convention about the decisions **4.144** of an international organisation, but the transfer of state power to an international organisation does not necessarily exclude the state's responsibility, as otherwise the Convention guarantees could easily be excluded or limited. In cases concerning the applicants' secondment to the European Space Agency,[410] the Court has underlined the principle that where states establish international organisations and give them powers and immunities, there may be implications for human rights, and it would be incompatible with the purpose and objectives of the Convention if contracting states were thereby absolved from their responsibility under the Convention.

The case of *Bosphorus Hava Yollari Turizm Ve Ticaret AS* v *Ireland*[411] concerned the impound- **4.145** ing of the applicant's leased aircraft in Ireland, as a result of a directly effective EC Regulation implementing UN sanctions in respect of the then Federal Republic of Yugoslavia.[412] As the measures had been taken by the Irish authorities in its territory, following a decision by the Minister of Transport, the Court found that the applicant company fell within the

---

[407] See the discussion of jurisdiction, in relation to Article 1, at 6.01–6.23.

[408] See, e.g. *Quark Fishing Limited* v *UK*, No. 15305/06, dec. 19.9.06 (no declaration under Article 56 in relation to the South Georgia and the South Sandwich Islands—inadmissible); *Chagos Islanders* v *UK*, No. 35622/04, dec. 11.12.12.

[409] See, e.g. *Cyprus* v *Turkey*, Nos. 6780/74 and 6950/75, 10.7.76, para. 83; *Cyprus* v *Turkey*, No. 25781/94, 10.5.01. See also Article 1 at 6.01 below.

[410] *Beer and Regan* v *Germany*, No. 28934/95, 18.2.99; *Waite and Kennedy* v *Germany*, No. 26083/94, 18.2.99.

[411] No. 45036/98, 30.6.05.

[412] EC Regulation 990/93 implementing UNSC Resolution 820(1993).

jurisdiction of the respondent state, and therefore its complaint was compatible *ratione loci, personae* and *materiae* with the Convention (see further at 6.775, below).

Ratione materiae

4.146 Complaints about rights that are not protected by the Convention will be declared inadmissible on this ground, including rights clearly not covered by the Convention at all, and rights that are found not to fall within the scope of Convention articles, for example if an activity is not considered to be part of your 'private life' under Article 8.[413] In *Botta v Italy*[414] the applicant complained of the Government's failure to take measures to remedy the omissions of private bathing organisations that had the effect of preventing disabled people from getting access to the beach and the sea. The Court held that this did not fall within the scope of Article 8, particularly because the case concerned access to the beach away from the applicant's normal place of residence during holidays.

4.147 However, it is very important to keep in mind the principle that the Convention is to be interpreted as a 'living instrument'.[415] Accordingly, the Court is obliged to interpret the Convention in the light of present day conditions, and not by assessing what the drafters of the Convention had intended by a particular provision. Practitioners should be aware of the possibilities of particular provisions being 'developed' to fall into line with present day situations. For example, it is arguably questionable whether those who drafted the Convention had envisaged that Article 8 would protect an applicant's home from the effects of a nearby privately-owned waste treatment plant. However, in *Lopez Ostra v Spain*,[416] the Court held that Article 8 was violated in such circumstances. Similarly, in *Guerra and others v Italy*,[417] Article 8 was found to have been breached because of the failure to provide the local population with information relating to the safety risks of a nearby chemical factory.

Ratione temporis

4.148 Complaints against a state that had not ratified the Convention or accepted the right of individual petition at the relevant date will be declared inadmissible on this ground.

4.149 Where the events complained of started before the entry into force of the Convention and continued afterwards, only the latter part can be the subject of a complaint, although the Court may take facts into account that have occurred before the entry into force of the Convention.[418] For example, *Zana v Turkey*,[419] concerned the length of criminal proceedings that had started before Turkey had accepted the right of individual petition. In assessing the reasonableness of the length of the proceedings, the Court

---

[413] See, e.g. *Baytüre v Turkey*, No. 3270/09, dec. 12.3.13 (complaint under Article 8 about paralysis caused by vaccine—incompatible *ratione materiae*).

[414] No. 21439/93, 24.2.98.

[415] See, e.g. *Selmouni v France* No. 25803/94, 28.7.99, para. 101.

[416] No. 16798/90, Series A, No. 303-C, 9.12.94.

[417] No. 14967/89, 19.2.98.

[418] See, e.g. *Kerojärvi v Finland*, No. 17506/90, Series A, No. 328, 19.7.95; *Trzaska v Poland*, No. 25792/94, 11.7.00; *Haroutyounian v Armenia*, No. 36549/03, 28.6.07; *Teren Aksakal v Turkey*, No. 51967/99, 11.9.07; *Kurić and others v Slovenia*, No. 26828/06, 26.6.12.

[419] No. 18954/91, 25.11.97.

took into account that at that date the proceedings had already lasted two years and five months.

In *Hokkanen* v *Finland*,[420] concerning rights of custody and access over the applicant's **4.150** daughter, domestic proceedings had begun in 1986. However, the Convention did not enter into force in relation to Finland until 1990. Therefore, the Court could only consider whether there had been a violation of the Convention arising out of the facts occurring after 1990, when the Convention entered into force. However, the Court took into account the background of events prior to 1990, particularly the large number of court actions brought by the applicant, the fact that all decisions in his favour had been effectively resisted by the grandparents and that the embittered relationship between the applicant and the child's grandparents did not favour a co-operative approach to resolving the dispute.

Difficult questions can arise where the events in issue 'straddle' the date of entry into force **4.151** of the Convention. In *Sovtransavto Holding* v *Ukraine*,[421] the applicant Russian transport company complained of measures taken to reduce its shareholding in a Ukrainian public company, such that it lost control of the company. The Government argued that the events in question occurred before Ukraine had ratified the Convention, on 11 September 1997. However, the Court accepted that the measures in question had been carried out over a three-stage process, with the final stage taking place after Ukraine had ratified the Convention. This sequence of events was held to create a continuing situation and the application was not therefore inadmissible *ratione temporis*. The Court went on to examine the complaint in respect of the third stage, although it also took into account the prior events.

The applicants in *Chiragov and others* v *Armenia*[422] and *Sargsyan* v *Azerbaijan*[423] complained **4.152** of having lost their homes and property after they fled from the fighting during the armed conflict in the Nagorno-Karabakh region in 1992. Although their displacement in 1992 was considered to result from an instantaneous act falling outside the Court's competence *ratione temporis*, their subsequent lack of access to their homes and property amounted to a continuing situation, which the Court had had competence to examine since 2002 when both states had ratified the Convention. In *Aćimović* v *Croatia*[424] the applicant complained about the destruction of his cottage by the Croatian army prior to the date of entry into force of the Convention (5 November 1997). The Court reiterated that the destruction of property is an instantaneous act that does not create any continuing situation. The applicant also complained about a legislative amendment introduced in 1999 that stayed all similar proceedings arising out of actions of the Croatian army during the 'Homeland War'. Nevertheless, the Court declared the case inadmissible *ratione temporis*, finding that 'although the legislative interference took place after the Convention entered into force in respect of Croatia it was so closely related to the events that gave rise to the applicant's claim that divorcing the two would amount to giving retroactive effect to the Convention which would be contrary

---

[420] No. 19823/92, Series A, No. 299-A, 23.9.94, see especially para. 53. See also, e.g. *Lukanov v Bulgaria*, No. 21915/93, 20.3.97, para. 40.
[421] No. 48553/99, 25.7.02.
[422] No. 13216/05, dec. 14.12.11.
[423] No. 40167/06, dec. 14.12.11.
[424] No. 61237/00, dec. 7.11.02.

to general principles of international law'. The Grand Chamber followed this reasoning in its judgment in *Blečić* v *Croatia*:[425]

> … in cases where the interference pre-dates ratification while the refusal to remedy it postdates ratification, to retain the date of the latter act in determining the Court's temporal jurisdiction would result in the Convention being binding for that State in relation to a fact that had taken place before the Convention came into force in respect of that State.

4.153　*Blečić* concerned the termination of the applicant's specially protected tenancy, which under Croatian law occurred when a court judgment to such effect became *res judicata*. The decision to terminate the tenancy was made by the Municipal Court in 1994. It was then overturned by the County Court, but the County Court's judgment was reversed by the Supreme Court in 1996. It was at that moment that the applicant lost her tenancy. As the date of Croatia's ratification of the Convention was 5 November 1997, the interference was held to fall outside the Court's temporal jurisdiction. This was not affected by a subsequent judgment of the Constitutional Court in 1999 (dismissing the applicant's constitutional complaint). Accordingly, the application was found (by 11 votes to six)[426] to be incompatible *ratione temporis* with the Convention.

4.154　The Grand Chamber in *Blečić* held that in order to adjudicate upon the Court's temporal jurisdiction, it is essential in each case to identify the precise time of the alleged interference, and that, to do so, the Court must take account of both the facts of the case and the scope of the Convention right alleged to have been violated. This principle was applied by the Grand Chamber in the case of *Šilih* v *Slovenia*,[427] which concerned the death of the applicants' son in prison, as a result of an anaphylactic shock. Having reviewed relevant Article 2 case law, the Court found that, in addition to the substantive aspect of Article 2, the procedural obligation to carry out an effective investigation under Article 2 had evolved into a separate and autonomous duty. Therefore, it was considered to be a 'detachable obligation' that was capable of binding the state even when the death took place before the date of entry into force of the Convention.[428] However, the Court emphasised that in such circumstances the Court's temporal jurisdiction is not 'open-ended': only procedural acts or omissions which occur after the date will fall within the Court's jurisdiction. Furthermore, there must be a 'genuine connection' between the death and the entry into force of the Convention; thus, a 'significant proportion' of the procedural steps required by Article 2 should have been carried out after the date in question. The Court has also clarified that 'a connection which is not "genuine" may nonetheless be sufficient to establish the Court's jurisdiction if it is needed to ensure that the guarantees and the underlying values of the Convention are protected in a real and effective way'.[429]

4.155　Applying these principles to the facts of *Šilih*, the Court held the procedural aspect of Article 2 to fall within its jurisdiction because, although the death of the applicants' son

---

[425]　No. 59532/00, 8.3.06. See also *Meltex Ltd* v *Armenia*, No. 37780/02, dec. 27.5.08.

[426]　The dissenting judges argued that the judgment terminating the applicant's tenancy only became irreversible as a result of the Constitutional Court decision.

[427]　No. 71463/01, 9.4.09.

[428]　See also *Tuna* v *Turkey*, No. 22339/03, 19.1.10 (re Articles 2 and 3); *Yatsenko* v *Ukraine*, No. 75345/01, 16.2.12 (re Article 3). The Court's decision in *Šilih* can be contrasted with cases such as *Moldovan and others and Rostaş and others* v *Romania*, Nos. 41138/98 and 64320/01, dec. 13.3.01.

[429]　*Janowiec and others* v *Russia*, Nos. 55508/07 and 29520/09, 21.10.13, para. 141.

occurred just over a year before the entry into force of the Convention in respect of Slovenia (in June 1994), all the criminal and civil proceedings (except for the preliminary investigation) were carried out after that date.[430] *Janowiec and others v Russia*,[431] concerned the investigation of the murder of more than 21,000 Polish soldiers and officials by the Soviet secret police in 1940. Investigations into the murders had been conducted between 1990 and 2004. As Russia had only ratified the European Convention in 1998, 58 years after the executions, the Grand Chamber found no 'genuine connection' between the two events. A significant number of procedural steps had been undertaken by the authorities in the early 1990s, but there was no evidence of any real investigative steps having been carried out after 1998. The Court also took account of the fact that the events in question (which might have triggered the obligation to investigate) took place more than ten years before the Convention came into existence. Accordingly, the Government's objection on the basis of *ratione temporis* was upheld.

4.156 In *Varnava and others v Turkey*,[432] the Grand Chamber drew a distinction between the investigation of killings and disappearances:

> A disappearance is a distinct phenomenon, characterised by an ongoing situation of uncertainty and unaccountability in which there is a lack of information or even a deliberate concealment and obfuscation of what has occurred…This situation is very often drawn out over time, prolonging the torment of the victim's relatives. It cannot therefore be said that a disappearance is, simply, an 'instantaneous' act or event; the additional distinctive element of subsequent failure to account for the whereabouts and fate of the missing person gives rise to a continuing situation. Thus, the procedural obligation will, potentially, persist as long as the fate of the person is unaccounted for; the ongoing failure to provide the requisite investigation will be regarded as a continuing violation …[433]

Where the act complained of has occurred prior to the date of entry into force of the Convention, careful consideration should therefore be given as to whether there might be a continuing breach of the Convention (see 4.122 above). For example, the case of *Zorica Jovanović v Serbia*,[434] concerned the circumstances of the death of the applicant's newborn baby in hospital. The baby had apparently died (or gone missing) in 1983, and the Convention only came into force as regards Serbia in 2004, but as the application related to the failure of the authorities to provide credible information about the fate of the applicant's son, it was considered to be a continuing situation.

Ratione personae

4.157 This condition will in general exclude complaints that are not directed against the state (or any emanation of the state, such as a public authority, state-owned company,[435] court or tribunal), but against a private individual or entity, or an international organisation or

---

[430] See also *Şandru and others v Romania*, No. 22465/03, 8.12.09; *Association '21 December 1989' and others v Romania*, No. 33810/07, 24.5.11; *Jelić v Croatia*, No. 57856/11, 12.6.14.

[431] Nos. 55508/07 and 29520/09, 21.10.13; see also *Mocanu and others v Romania*, Nos. 10865/09, 32431/08 and 45886/07, 17.9.14.

[432] No. 16064/90, 18.9.09.

[433] *Ibid.*, para. 148.

[434] No. 21794/08, 26.3.13.

[435] See, e.g. *Mykhaylenky and others v Ukraine*, Nos. 35091/02, 35196/02, 35201/02, 35204/02, 35945/02, 35949/02, 35953/02, 36800/02, 38296/02 and 42814/02, 30.11.04.

tribunal. For example, the Court has found that the acts or omissions of bodies established by resolutions of the UN Security Council for the administration of Kosovo (KFOR and UNMIK),[436] the decisions of the High Representative for Bosnia and Herzegovina (whose authority derived from UN Security Council Resolutions),[437] and the acts or omissions of the International Criminal Tribunal for the former Yugoslavia (ICTY) (established under the UN Charter as a subsidiary organisation of the Security Council),[438] and of the International Criminal Court[439] could not be attributed to the respondent Convention states.[440]

4.158 In *Boivin v France, Belgium and 32 member states of the Council of Europe*,[441] the applicant complained about his dismissal from the European Organisation for the Safety of Air Navigation (Eurocontrol), whose decisions were upheld by the ILO's Administrative Tribunal (ILOAT). His application was declared inadmissible *ratione personae* as the applicant had not been under the jurisdiction of the respondent states for the purposes of Article 1 of the Convention. The applicant association in the case of *Cooperatieve Producentenorganisatie Van De Nederlandse Kokkelvisserij U.A.* v *Netherlands*[442] had obtained a licence to carry out cockle fishing in an area protected by environmental legislation. During subsequent domestic proceedings instigated by environmental NGOs, the domestic tribunal sought a preliminary ruling from the Court of Justice of the European Communities (CJEU). The applicant association complained in Strasbourg that it had been denied the right to respond to the Opinion of the Advocate General during the proceedings before the CJEU. The Strasbourg Court declared inadmissible *ratione personae* the complaint against the European Community, as an intergovernmental entity with a separate legal personality. As to the question of the responsibility of the Netherlands, however, the Court distinguished the case from *Boivin* on the basis that the proceedings concerned an intervention by the CJEU which had been sought by a domestic court in proceedings pending before it. Where a state party to the European Convention transfers sovereign power to an international or supranational organisation such as the EU, this is considered to be justified by the Strasbourg Court provided that the organisation in question is considered to protect fundamental rights (both substantively and procedurally) to an extent that is at least equivalent to that provided by the Convention. If such equivalent protection is considered to be provided by the organisation, it is presumed that a state has not breached its obligations under the Convention simply by implementing its legal obligations flowing from membership of that organisation (although such a presumption can be rebutted). In the *Bosphorus* case (see 4.145 and 6.775) the Court found that this rebuttable

---

[436] *Behrami* v *France*, No. 71412/01 *& Saramati* v *France, Germany and Norway*, No. 78166/01, dec. 2.5.07; *Kasumaj* v Greece, No. 6974/05, dec. 5.7.07; *Azemi* v *Serbia*, No. 11209/09, dec. 5.11.13.

[437] *Berić and others* v *Bosnia and Herzegovina*, No. 36357/04 et al., dec. 16.10.07.

[438] *Galić* v *Netherlands*, No. 22617/07, dec. 9.6.09 and *Blagojević* v *Netherlands*, No. 49032/07, dec. 9.6.09.

[439] *Djokaba Lambi Longa* v *Netherlands*, No. 33917/12, dec. 9.10.12.

[440] Such a point was raised unsuccessfully in *Nada* v *Switzerland*, No. 10593/08, 12.9.12 which concerned a travel ban imposed on the applicant resulting from legislation implementing UN Security Council resolutions. The Court noted that *Behrami and Saramati* concerned the acts and omissions of the Kosovo Force (KFOR) which were directly attributable to the UN, whereas *Nada* concerned a measure implemented at national level, by an ordinance of the Federal Council.

[441] No. 73250/01, dec. 9.9.08. See also *Connolly* v *15 Member States of the European Union*, No. 73274/01, dec. 9.12.08; *La société Etablissement Biret et CIE S.A.* v *15 Member States of the European Union*, No. 13762/04, dec. 9.12.08; *Beygo* v *46 member States of the Council of Europe*, No. 36099/06, dec. 16.6.09; *Lopez Cifuentes* v *Spain*, No. 18754/06, dec. 7.7.09 (re International Olive Council).

[442] No. 13645/05, dec. 20.1.09.

presumption applies to the EU.[443] In the *Cooperatieve* case the Court accordingly assessed whether the procedure before the CJEU was accompanied by guarantees that ensured equivalent protection of the applicant's rights. It answered this question positively, as there had been the possibility of reopening the oral proceedings before the Advocate General. The applicant association was therefore found not to have rebutted the presumption, and the application against the Netherlands was declared manifestly ill-founded.[444] The applicant in *Gasparini* v *Italy and Belgium*[445] complained that NATO's internal labour dispute resolution system did not protect fundamental rights in a manner that was equivalent to that provided by the European Convention. For the Court, this meant assessing whether the respondent states, at the time they joined NATO and transferred some of their sovereign powers to it, had been in a position to decide that NATO's internal dispute resolution mechanism did not flagrantly breach the Convention. The Court reviewed the applicant's complaints about the lack of a public hearing and alleged bias within the NATO Appeals Board and held that the states had correctly considered that such proceedings would provide a fair hearing. The case was accordingly adjudged to be manifestly ill-founded.

In some situations, however, the state's responsibility is not engaged because of a particular **4.159** executive or legislative *act* that affects individuals, but because legislation is 'activated' as a result of the actions of private individuals.[446]

The Court has emphasised that the state cannot absolve itself from responsibility by delegat- **4.160** ing its obligations to private bodies or individuals. In *Costello-Roberts* v *UK*[447] the Court applied this principle in a case relating to corporal punishment in a private school. The Court found that the state has an obligation to provide children with their right to education, including responsibility for a school's disciplinary system; the right to education applies equally to pupils in independent schools as well as those in state schools. In *Woś* v *Poland*,[448] the respondent state's responsibility *ratione personae* was established in respect of the Polish-German Reconciliation Foundation, a private law body established under international agreements in order to compensate victims of Nazi persecution. Although the state did not exert a direct influence over individual decisions, its role had been crucial in establishing the overall framework within which the Foundation operated. The applicant in *Buzescu* v *Romania*[449] complained about decisions made by a bar association, the Romanian Union of Lawyers. The state's responsibility was found to be engaged as the association was legally constituted and had administrative and rule-making powers. It exercised a form of control

---

[443] See also *Michaud* v *France*, No. 12323/11, 6.12.12 in which the Court found that application of the presumption of equivalent protection in the legal system of the EU is subject to two conditions: (i) the absence of any margin of manoeuvre on the part of the domestic authorities; and (ii) the deployment of the full potential of the supervisory mechanism provided for by the EU. In *Michaud* the Court held that the presumption of equivalent protection was not applicable, as (a) the case concerned the implementation of a Directive (not a Regulation) and (b) the *Conseil d'Etat* did not refer the case to the CJEU for a preliminary ruling. See also *Avotiņš* v *Latvia*, No. 17502/07, 23.5.16 (presumption of equivalent protection applicable as regards enforcement of Cypriot domestic court judgment—no violation of Article 6).

[444] See also, as regards the European Patent Convention: *Lenzing AG* v *Germany*, No. 39025/97, dec. 9.9.98 and *Rambus Inc.* v *Germany*, No. 40382/04, dec. 16.6.09.

[445] No. 10750/03, dec. 12.5.09.

[446] See, e.g. *J.A. Pye (Oxford) Ltd and J.A. Pye (Oxford) Land Ltd* v *UK*, No. 44302/02, 30.8.07, para. 57.

[447] No. 13134/87, Series A, No. 247-C, 25.3.93.

[448] No. 22860/02, dec. 1.3.05.

[449] No. 61302/00, 24.5.05.

over issues such as registration with the bar and its decisions were subject to the jurisdiction of the administrative courts. Furthermore, under domestic law the association was classified as a public authority which performed administrative acts and fulfilled a public service role.

4.161 There may also be exceptions to the *ratione personae* criterion where the state is found to be responsible for the alleged breach, by, for example, failing to take appropriate measures to protect an individual against the actions of others. For example, the case of *Young, James and Webster* v *UK*[450] concerned former British Rail employees who had been dismissed for failing to comply with the closed shop agreement. The Court found the state to be responsible for the domestic law that made the treatment of the applicants lawful.

4.162 The responsibility of the state in cases concerning ill-treatment by private individuals may also be incurred under the Convention by virtue of the combined obligations under Articles 1 and 3. Article 1 requires the state to secure to everyone within its jurisdiction the rights and freedoms set out in the Convention. The state must therefore take the necessary steps to prevent individuals being subjected to inhuman and degrading treatment or punishment, even by private individuals. This will require that there is effective deterrence to prevent ill-treatment, in particular, of children and other vulnerable people, such as those with mental health problems. *A* v *UK*[451] concerned the applicant nine-year-old child's ill-treatment by his stepfather. The stepfather was prosecuted for assault occasioning actual bodily harm for beating the child with a garden cane, but was acquitted. The applicant complained, inter alia, of a violation of Article 3. The Court found that as it was a defence to a charge of assault that the treatment in question amounted to 'reasonable chastisement', the law did not provide adequate protection against the ill-treatment of the applicant, in violation of Article 3. This was accepted before the Court by the UK Government. In *X and Y* v *Netherlands*,[452] the applicant complained that it was impossible to bring criminal proceedings against the perpetrator of a sexual assault on his daughter, because her mental illness meant that it was not possible to determine her wishes, as was required by the domestic law at the time. The Court found a violation of Article 8 as the criminal code failed to protect the victim.

4.163 In *Gustafsson* v *Sweden*,[453] the applicant restaurant owner complained of action taken by various unions representing employees, after he refused to allow collective bargaining, invoking, inter alia, Article 11 and Article 1 of Protocol No. 1, on the basis that the state had failed to protect the applicant against industrial action. The Court held that Article 11 was applicable, although it had not been violated, and that Article 1 of Protocol No. 1 did not apply as the case concerned contractual relationships between the applicant and his suppliers or deliverers. In *Wilson, the NUJ and others* v *UK*,[454] the Court found a violation of Article 11 because the domestic law allowed an employer to de-recognise trade unions for collective bargaining purposes and it also permitted offers to be made of more favourable conditions of employment to employees who agreed not to be represented by the unions. The Court held that as it was possible for an employer effectively to undermine or frustrate a trade union's ability to seek the protection of its members' interests, and by permitting employers to use

---

[450] Nos. 7601/76 and 7806/77, Series A, No. 44, 26.6.81.
[451] No. 25599/94, 23.9.98.
[452] No. 8978/80, Series A, No. 91, 26.3.85.
[453] No. 15573/89, 25.4.96.
[454] Nos. 30668/96, 30671/96 and 30678/96, 2.7.02.

financial incentives to induce employees to surrender important union rights, there was a failure to comply with the positive obligations inherent in Article 11. The state's responsibility was also found to be engaged in *Vgt Verein Gegen Tierfabriken* v *Switzerland*[455] where the domestic law made lawful the refusal of a private television company, on political grounds, to broadcast the applicant's television advertisement concerning treatment of animals in the food industry.

Complaints against a state that has not ratified the Convention or the relevant Protocol will **4.164** be excluded by this condition. Issues may also arise in relation to state dissolution or succession. The applicants in *Bijelić* v *Montenegro and Serbia*[456] originally complained against the Government of the State Union of Serbia and Montenegro about the failure to enforce a court eviction order. While the European Court proceedings were pending, Montenegro declared its independence—in 2006. The Court applied the principle that fundamental rights protected by international human rights treaties belong to individuals living in the territory of a state party, regardless of any subsequent dissolution or succession. Therefore, as the Convention had entered into force in respect of the State Union of Serbia and Montenegro with effect from March 2004, it was deemed to have been continuously in force in relation to Montenegro since 2004. The proceedings in question had solely fallen within the competence of the Montenegrin authorities, and so the application as regards Serbia was declared incompatible *ratione personae*.

Finally, an application from a person (or organisation) who could not properly claim to be **4.165** a 'victim' of a Convention violation would be declared inadmissible *ratione personae*.[457] The definition of a 'victim' is discussed at section 4.27 above. See also the discussion about the application of Article 1 at 6.01 below.

Manifestly Ill-founded

An application may be declared inadmissible as being 'manifestly ill-founded' (Article 35(3) **4.166** (a)) if, on a preliminary investigation, the application does not disclose prima facie grounds that there has been a breach of the Convention—for example, where the applicant fails to adduce any evidence in support of the application, or if the facts complained of clearly fall within the limitations or restrictions on the Convention rights. For example, an applicant would need to produce sufficient evidence of ill-treatment, failing which the application would be declared inadmissible as being manifestly ill-founded.

In practice, this requirement amounts to a preliminary merits test and a large number of **4.167** cases are declared inadmissible on this ground. It is in effect a filtering mechanism, intended to root out the weakest cases. This is perhaps an inevitable part of the Strasbourg system, given the very large number of cases that the Court has to deal with. However, it is something of a misnomer, as applications can still be declared 'manifestly ill-founded' even after the

---

[455] No. 24699/94, 28.6.01, para. 47.

[456] No. 11890/05, 28.4.09.

[457] See, e.g. *A and B* v *UK*, No. 25599/94, dec. 9.9.96: father of child beaten by stepfather could not claim to be a direct or indirect victim, unlike the child himself who clearly was a victim; *Ada Rossi and others* v *Italy*, No. 55185/08, dec. 16.12.08 (complaint by severely disabled persons, and representative associations, concerning domestic court decision permitting artificial nutrition and hydration of coma victim to be discontinued).

Court has decided that the case was worthy of being communicated to the respondent government, and only in the light of the government's submissions.[458] Furthermore, such decisions do not require unanimity, but can be made by a majority of the Chamber of the Court.

Abuse of the Right of Application

4.168 Under Article 35(3)(a), the Court will declare inadmissible any application which it considers an abuse of the right of application.[459] Vexatious petitions[460] or petitions written in offensive language[461] will be declared inadmissible on this ground. Deliberately concealing relevant information from the Court, or falsifying documents, are likely to lead to a declaration of inadmissibility on this ground.[462] Disclosing information about, or documents relating to, friendly settlement proceedings before the Court may also be characterised as an abuse of the right of application.[463] In *Drozd v Poland*,[464] the application was struck off the Commission's list of cases following publication in a newspaper (of which the applicant was on the editorial board) of correspondence from the European Commission of Human Rights, in breach of the Commission's confidentiality rules. Furthermore, an application will be rejected as being abusive if it is 'knowingly based on untrue facts'[465] or which deliberately omits significant facts.[466] In *Bock v Germany*[467] the Court declared inadmissible, as being an abuse of the right of petition, an application concerning legal proceedings relating to the reimbursement of just under €8, noting the triviality of the facts and the pettiness of the amount involved (see also the discussion of the 'significant disadvantage' admissibility criterion at 4.129 above).

4.169 In *Akdivar v Turkey*,[468] which concerned the destruction of homes by the security forces in south-east Turkey, the respondent government sought to argue that the case amounted to an abuse of the right of petition. It was argued that the failure of the applicants to pursue domestic remedies was part of the general policy of the Workers' Party of Kurdistan (PKK) to denigrate Turkey and its judicial institutions. This argument was rejected by the Court on the basis that the Commission had in fact substantially upheld the applicants' complaints.

---

[458] See, e.g. *Mentzen v Latvia*, No. 71074/01, dec. 7.12.04.

[459] See also the examples of cases listed at *S.A.S. v France*, No. 43835/11, 1.7.14, para. 67.

[460] See, e.g. *M v UK*, No. 13284/87, dec. 15.10.87, 54 DR 214: a series of 'ill-founded and querulous complaints'.

[461] See, e.g. *Duringer and others v France*, Nos. 61164/00 and 18589/02, dec. 4.2.03; *Di Salvo v Italy*, No. 16098/05, dec. 11.1.07.

[462] See, e.g. *F v Spain*, No. 13524/88, dec. 12.4.91, 69 DR 185: where the applicant was found not to have deliberately concealed certain domestic proceedings in progress; *Foxley v UK*, No. 33274/96, dec. 12.10.99; *Jian v Romania*, No. 46640/99, dec. 30.3.04; *Kerechashvili v Georgia*, No. 5667/02, dec. 2.5.06; *Bagheri and Maliki v Netherlands*, No. 30164/06, dec. 15.5.07; *Hadrabová and others v Czech Republic*, No. 42165/02 and 466/03, dec. 25.9.07; *Predescu v Romania*, No. 21447/03, 2.12.08; *Bekauri v Georgia*, No. 14102/02, dec. 10.4.12; *Martins Alves v Portugal*, No. 56297/11, dec. 21.1.14; *Gross v Switzerland*, No. 67810/10, 30.9.14 (a Grand Chamber finding that the case was inadmissible as an abuse of application—by nine votes to eight).

[463] See, e.g. *Hadrabová and others v Czech Republic*, Nos. 42165/02 and 466/03, dec. 25.9.07; *Popov v Moldova*, No. 74153/01, 18.1.05; *Miroļubovs v Latvia*, No. 798/05, 15.9.09; *Mandil v France*, No. 67037/09, dec. 13.12.11.

[464] No. 25403/94, dec. 5.3.96.

[465] *Varbanov v Bulgaria*, No. 31365/96, 5.10.00.

[466] *Al-Nashif v Bulgaria*, No. 50963/99, 20.6.02, para. 89.

[467] No. 22051/07, dec. 19.1.10. See also: *Vasylenko v Ukraine*, No. 25129/03, dec. 18.10.11.

[468] No. 21893/93, 16.9.96.

Article 35(3) will *not* exclude 'political' applications or those made for purposes of gaining **4.170** publicity. In *McFeeley* v *UK*,[469] the applicants complained about the conditions in the Maze Prison in Northern Ireland. The Government argued that the application was an abuse of the right of petition as it was inspired by motives of publicity and propaganda and was intended to pressurise the Government into reintroducing the special category status. The European Commission rejected these arguments, finding that a complaint of abuse might be upheld if an application were clearly unsupported by the evidence or outside the scope of the Convention.

In *Georgian Labour Party* v *Georgia*,[470] the Court reprimanded the chairman of the applicant **4.171** party for statements he had made to the media, 'vexing manifestations of irresponsibility and a frivolous attitude towards the Court', some of which were found to have come close to contempt of court, but the application was not struck out as an abuse of process. However, the case of *Milan Řehák* v *Czech Republic*[471] was struck out as abuse of the right of application in view of defamatory allegations made against Court judges and members of the Court Registry. A finding of abuse of application may also result from negligence by an applicant's representative—for example, for failing repeatedly to submit observations to the Court or the failure to inform the Court of key developments in the case.[472]

---

[469] No. 8317/78, dec. 15.5.80.
[470] No. 9103/04, dec. 22.5.07. See also *Chernitsyn* v *Russia*, No. 5964/02, 6.4.06.
[471] No. 67208/01, dec. 18.5.04.
[472] See, e.g. *Bekauri* v *Georgia*, No. 14102/02, 10.4.12.

5

UNDERLYING CONVENTION PRINCIPLES

Introduction

5.01 This chapter highlights key principles that permeate the Convention and its case law. Some of the principles, such as legality and proportionality, are fundamental to the substantive Convention law, whereas others are issues of interpretation. The principles outlined below have application in a variety of substantive Convention articles and in a variety of contexts. They are illustrated further in chapter 6 on the substantive Convention rights.

Subsidiarity

5.02 The European Convention system for the protection of human rights is intended to be subsidiary to national systems safeguarding human rights. This is reflected in the requirement to exhaust effective domestic remedies before applying to the Court: 'States are dispensed from answering before an international body for their acts before they have had an opportunity to put matters right through their own legal system.'[1] The principle is also linked to the right

---

[1] See, e.g. *Akdivar* v *Turkey*, No. 21893/93, 16.9.96, para. 65.

in Article 13 to an 'effective remedy' in the domestic system, whether or not the Convention has been incorporated into national law.

The Interlaken Declaration, adopted by a Ministerial conference in 2010, (see chapter 1)   **5.03**
emphasised the 'subsidiary nature of the supervisory mechanism established by the Convention and notably the fundamental role which national authorities, i.e. governments, courts and parliaments, must play in guaranteeing and protecting human rights at the national level'.[2] When it enters into force, Protocol No. 15 to the European Convention will insert a reference to the principle of subsidiarity (and the doctrine of the margin of appreciation) into the preamble to the Convention.[3]

The concept of the margin of appreciation (see 5.11 below) is a further aspect of this prin-   **5.04**
ciple of subsidiarity.

A Democratic Society

The concept of a democratic society is said to prevail throughout the Convention[4] and is   **5.05**
acknowledged as a fundamental feature of the European public order: 'democracy … appears to be the only political model contemplated by the Convention and, accordingly, the only one compatible with it'.[5] It is referred to in the preamble to the Convention and it is a requirement that any restriction on the rights conferred by Articles 8–11 must be 'necessary in a democratic society'.

The Court will therefore be particularly concerned to uphold rights that touch on this con-   **5.06**
cept. For example, freedom of political debate has been held to be at the very core of the concept of a democratic society, but it is also relevant to press freedom generally and may be a relevant consideration in cases concerning the rights to freedom of peaceful assembly, to freedom of thought, conscience and religion, and to the right to vote. The principles of democracy and pluralism form the touchstone of such Convention rights:[6]

> … sweeping measures of a preventive nature to suppress freedom of assembly and expression other than in cases of incitement to violence or rejection of democratic principles—however shocking and unacceptable certain views or words used may appear to the authorities, and however illegitimate the demands made may be—do a disservice to democracy and often even endanger it.

Legal Certainty

The principle of the rule of law is referred to in the preamble to the Convention and in the   **5.07**
Statute of the Council of Europe and was an important impetus in setting up the Convention

---

[2] High Level Conference on the Future of the European Court of Human Rights, Interlaken Declaration, 19 February 2010. Available at: http://www.eda.admin.ch/etc/medialib/downloads/edazen/topics/europa/euroc.Par.0133.File.tmp/final_en.pdf.
[3] Council of Europe Treaty Series, No. 213, 24.6.13. Protocol No. 15 was adopted in 2013, but it has not, as yet, entered into force.
[4] *Oberschlick* v *Austria*, No. 11662/85, Series A, No. 204, 23.5.91, para. 58.
[5] *United Communist Party of Turkey and others* v *Turkey*, No. 19392/92, 30.1.98, para. 45.
[6] *Association of Citizens Radko & Paunkovski* v *former Yugoslav Republic of Macedonia*, No. 74651/01, 15.1.09.

system.[7] The rule of law is also said to be inherent in all articles of the Convention, and entails a duty on the state and all public authorities to comply with judicial orders or decisions against it.[8]

5.08 The principle of legal certainty is accordingly inherent throughout the law of the Convention.[9] For example, Articles 8–11, and Article 2 of Protocol No. 4, require any interference with rights to be 'in accordance with the law' or 'prescribed by law' (see below at 6.442). Under Article 5, any detention must be lawful and 'in accordance with a procedure prescribed by law', referring to both procedural and substantive legality. Article 7 requires certainty of the criminal law.

5.09 This means that the legal basis for any interference with Convention rights must be adequately accessible and formulated with sufficient precision to enable a person to regulate their conduct: a person 'must be able—if need be with appropriate advice—to foresee, to a degree that is reasonable in the circumstances, the consequences which a given action may entail'.[10] The requirement for legality therefore not only requires a specific legal rule or regime authorising the interference, but also relates to the *quality* of the particular domestic legal provision. Where the domestic law confers a discretion, it should also indicate the scope of that discretion.[11] The Convention recognises that of course absolute certainty in the law is not, however, attainable. So, for example, incremental common law developments are acceptable under the Convention.[12] The degree of 'certainty' required in the law will differ depending upon the nature of the right being exercised and the nature of the interference.

Proportionality

5.10 Articles 8–11 only permit interferences with the substantive rights to the extent that they are 'necessary in a democratic society' in pursuit of particular legitimate aims—in other words, a test of proportionality. The concept of proportionality is also a fundamental constituent element of other Convention rights, such as the prohibition of discrimination (Article 14 and Protocol No. 12), the right to peaceful enjoyment of possessions (Article 1 of Protocol No. 1), the right to free elections (Article 3 of Protocol No. 1) and freedom of movement (Article 2 of Protocol No. 4). The principle of proportionality requires there to be a 'pressing social need' for the measure or interference in question and also that it is *proportionate* to the aim being pursued. In assessing the proportionality of a particular measure, the Court will consider whether there is an alternative means of protecting the relevant public interest without an interference at all, or by means which are less intrusive. The Court will assess whether the reasons for the interference are 'relevant' and 'sufficient' to justify it. It is a further requirement that the decision-making process leading to the measure of interference should be fair. The existence of effective controls on measures taken by the authorities is also a relevant factor in assessing proportionality.

---

[7] See, e.g. *Golder* v *UK*, Series A, No. 18, 21.2.75, para. 34.

[8] *Hornsby* v *Greece*, No. 18357/91, 19.3.97, paras. 40–1.

[9] See, e.g. *Marckx* v *Belgium*, Series A, No. 31, 13.6.79, para. 58.

[10] *Sunday Times* v *UK* (*No. 1*), Series A, No. 30, 26.4.79, para. 49.

[11] *Silver* v *UK*, Nos. 5947/72, 6205/73, 7052/75, 7061/75, 7107/75, 7113/75 and 7136/75, Series A, No. 61, 25.3.83, paras. 88–9.

[12] See, e.g. *SW and CR* v *UK*, No. 20166/92, Series A, No. 355-B, 22.11.95.

In assessing proportionality, the state is allowed a certain discretion or 'margin of appreciation' (see below at 5.11).

Margin of Appreciation

In considering the proportionality of a particular interference with a Convention right, the **5.11** Court will apply the 'margin of appreciation' concept: that state authorities are in principle in a better position than the European Court to give an opinion on the necessity of a restriction. In addition to its application within the concept of proportionality in Articles 8–11, the margin of appreciation is also relevant in other contexts, for example, to Article 5 (e.g. in deciding whether an individual should be detained as being of 'unsound mind'),[13] Article 6 (e.g. in considering limitations on the right of access to court),[14] Article 14 (in assessing to what extent differences in otherwise similar situations justify a different treatment in law),[15] Article 15 (in assessing the existence of a public emergency), Article 1 of Protocol No. 1 (e.g. in considering the extent of the right of the authorities to enforce laws so as to control the use of property),[16] Article 2 of Protocol No. 1 (e.g. in considering the impact of the display of crucifixes in state schools on the right to education)[17] and Article 3 of Protocol No. 1 (e.g. in assessing limitations on the right to vote and stand for elections).[18]

Depending upon the context, the breadth of the state's margin of appreciation will vary. For **5.12** example, the state has a wide margin of appreciation in relation to contentious societal issues such as laws relating to abortion,[19] important public health issues such as a state's approach to home births,[20] in relation to the justification for interferences with property (under Article 1 of Protocol No. 1) and in assessing the existence of a public emergency (under Article 15), but it is narrow in respect of steps taken to maintain the authority and impartiality of the judiciary (under Article 10). A relevant factor as regards the breadth of the state's margin of appreciation is the existence, or not, of a consensus within the member states of the Council of Europe—either as to the relative importance of the interest at stake or as to the best means of protecting it.[21] When it enters into force, Protocol No. 15 to the European Convention will insert a reference to the doctrine of the margin of appreciation (and the principle of subsidiarity) into the preamble to the Convention.[22]

The Convention as a 'Living Instrument'

The Convention is regarded as a 'living instrument' and therefore the role of the Court is **5.13** to interpret the Convention in the light of present day conditions and situations, rather

---

[13] See, e.g. *Luberti v Italy*, Series A, No. 75, 23.2.84, para. 27.
[14] See, e.g. *Osman v UK*, No. 23452/94, 28.2.98, para. 147.
[15] See, e.g. *Petrovic v Austria*, No. 20458/92, 27.3.98, para. 38.
[16] See, e.g. *Chassagnou and others v France*, Nos. 25088/94, 28331/95 and 28443/95, 29.4.99, para. 75.
[17] *Lautsi and others v Italy*, No. 30814/06, 18.3.11, paras. 68–77.
[18] See, e.g. *Gitonas v Greece*, No. 18747/91, 1.7.97, para. 39.
[19] See, e.g. *A, B & C v Ireland*, No. 25579/05, 16.12.10.
[20] *Dubská and Krejzová v Czech Republic*, Nos. 28859/11 and 28473/12, 15.11.16.
[21] See, e.g. *Parrillo v Italy*, No. 46470/11, 27.8.15, para. 169.
[22] Council of Europe Treaty Series, No. 213, 24.6.13. Protocol No. 15 was adopted in 2013, but it has not, as yet, entered into force.

than to try to assess what was intended by the drafters of the Convention (in the late 1940s). It therefore applies a dynamic, rather than historical approach. This principle was applied, for example, in *Matthews* v *UK*[23] in assessing whether Article 3 of Protocol No. 1 was applicable to the European Parliament even though that body was not envisaged by the drafters of the Convention. In *Selmouni* v *France*,[24] the Court took the 'living instrument' principle into account in assessing the severity of the ill-treatment suffered by the applicant in police custody and found that acts which in the past had been classified as 'inhuman and degrading treatment', rather than torture could be classified differently in the future. The Court was influenced by the increasingly high standard being required in protecting human rights. Another example is the judgment in *Stafford* v *UK*[25] in which the Grand Chamber of the Court overturned the 1994 decision in *Wynne* v *UK*[26] in the light of subsequent domestic law developments, in finding that mandatory life sentences no longer constituted imprisonment for life. The Court therefore went on to consider whether there was a sufficient causal connection between the original conviction of the applicant for murder and the later decision to recall him because of a risk of non-violent offending. Applying the 'living instrument' principle, the Court has also found that the essential elements of the right of association as regards trade unions are subject to evolution, depending on developments in labour relations.[27] In addition to the Court's substantive case-law, the living instrument principle also applies to procedural provisions.[28]

Absence of Doctrine of Precedent

5.14 There is no formal doctrine of precedent as such within the Convention system. The Court does not consider itself to be bound by its previous judgments, although 'it is in the interests of legal certainty, foreseeability and equality before the law that it should not depart, without good reason, from precedents laid down in previous cases'.[29]

Practical and Effective Rights

5.15 The provisions of the Convention are to be interpreted and applied so as to make the safeguards in the Convention 'practical and effective', not 'theoretical or illusory'. For example, the applicant in *Matthews* v *UK*[30] complained that as a resident of Gibraltar she had no right to vote in the elections for the European Parliament. Applying this principle of practical and effective rights, the Court found that European legislation affected the population of Gibraltar in the same way as domestic legislation. Therefore, there was no reason why the United Kingdom should not be required to secure the right to vote under Article 3 of

---

[23] No. 24883/94, 18.2.99.
[24] No. 25803/94, 28.7.99: see especially para. 101.
[25] No. 46295/99, 28.5.02.
[26] No. 15484/89, 18.7.94.
[27] *Demir and Baykara* v *Turkey*, No. 34503/97, 12.11.08, para. 146.
[28] *Loizidou* v *Turkey*, No. 15318/89, 23.3.95, para. 71.
[29] See, e.g. *Beard* v *UK*, No. 24882/94, 18.1.01, para. 81; *Scoppola* v *Italy (No. 2)*, No. 10249/03, 17.9.09, para. 104.
[30] No. 24883/94, 18.2.99.

Protocol No. 1 in relation to European legislation. The applicant in *Siliadin* v *France*[31] was a Togolese national who had been forced to work as a 'maid of all work' for several years since her arrival in France at the age of 15. She was accordingly found to have been required to perform forced labour and held in servitude—the Court concluded that Article 4 had been violated as the domestic law was of insufficient scope and had failed to provide the applicant with practical and effective protection.

There is a link here with the Court's acknowledgement that the application of the rule requir-   **5.16**
ing the exhaustion of domestic remedies should make due allowance for its application in the context of machinery for the protection of human rights.[32] Therefore, the rule should be applied flexibly. Applicants are not required to exhaust theoretical remedies: only domestic remedies which are sufficiently certain in practice need be utilised. This is discussed further in chapter 4.

Autonomous Concepts

A number of terms used in the Convention, such as the meaning of a 'civil right' or 'criminal   **5.17**
charge' under Article 6, the meaning of 'association' under Article 11 and the notion of a 'possession' under Article 1 of Protocol No. 1, are autonomous concepts. This means that the classification under national law will be a factor in the Court's determination as to whether the Convention is applicable, but it will not be decisive.

Positive Obligations

The Convention is to a great extent concerned with limits on interferences with rights by   **5.18**
public authorities. However, there are a number of areas where it is established that there are positive obligations on the state to take action to prevent Convention violations. For example, the cases concerning the recognition of transsexuals, such as *Goodwin* v *UK*[33] are about the extent to which the state has failed to comply with a positive obligation to ensure that their right to respect for their private lives is upheld, by allowing alteration of their birth certificates. In that sort of context, in order to decide whether there is a positive obligation, the Court will try to take account of the fair balance to be struck between the general inter-est of the community and the interests of the individual. Another example is Article 2. The obligation on states in Article 2(1) to protect everyone's right to life has been interpreted as creating a positive duty to safeguard lives. In *Osman* v *UK*,[34] for example, the Court found a positive obligation to take preventive operational measures to protect those whose lives were at risk from criminal attack.

The extent of the positive duties on the state will vary as between different Articles of the   **5.19**
Convention. For example, in the case of *Budayeva and others* v *Russia*[35] which concerned a death, injuries and the destruction of property caused by mudslides, the Court emphasised

---

[31] No. 73316/01, 26.7.05, para. 148.
[32] See, e.g. *Akdivar* v *Turkey*, No. 21893/93, 16.9.96, para. 69.
[33] No. 28957/95, 11.7.02. See also *Sheffield and Horsham* v *UK*, No 22985/93 and 23390/94, 30.7.98.
[34] No. 23452/94, 28.20.98: see especially para. 115.
[35] Nos. 15339/02, 21166/02, 20058/02, 11673/02 and 15343/02, 20.3.08.

that the positive obligations arising as regards the protection of life and the protection of property were not the same:

> ... for the purposes of the present case a distinction must be drawn between the positive obligations under Article 2 of the Convention and those under Article 1 of Protocol No. 1 to the Convention. While the fundamental importance of the right to life requires that the scope of the positive obligations under Article 2 includes a duty to do everything within the authorities' power in the sphere of disaster relief for the protection of that right, the obligation to protect the right to the peaceful enjoyment of possessions, which is not absolute, cannot extend further than what is reasonable in the circumstances. Accordingly, the authorities enjoy a wider margin of appreciation in deciding what measures to take in order to protect individuals' possessions from weather hazards than in deciding on the measures needed to protect lives.

5.20 In *Nachova and others* v *Bulgaria*, the Court emphasised that strict obligations are placed on the state when investigating racist violence:

> ... where there is suspicion that racial attitudes induced a violent act it is particularly important that the official investigation is pursued with vigour and impartiality, having regard to the need to reassert continuously society's condemnation of racism and ethnic hatred and to maintain the confidence of minorities in the ability of the authorities to protect them from the threat of racist violence. Compliance with the State's positive obligations under Article 2 of the Convention requires that the domestic legal system must demonstrate its capacity to enforce criminal law against those who unlawfully took the life of another, irrespective of the victim's racial or ethnic origin.[36]

5.21 In *MC* v *Bulgaria*[37] the Court found that Bulgarian law did not comply with the state's positive obligations because of the practice of prosecuting rape perpetrators only where there was evidence of significant physical resistance, and as a result of various inadequacies in the manner in which the investigation of the offence was carried out. Furthermore, Article 4 encompasses specific positive obligations on states to penalise and prosecute effectively acts of slavery, servitude or forced or compulsory labour and to combat trafficking.[38]

5.22 A positive obligation may arise in cases solely concerning private individuals or entities. For example, the right to peaceful assembly under Article 11 imposes on the authorities a general duty not to interfere with peaceful assemblies, but it may also require positive measures to protect demonstrators from counter-demonstrators.[39]

Therefore, the state may be liable in certain circumstances for Convention violations by non-state bodies. Similarly, the contracting out of services by public authorities to private companies may not relieve the state of its duties under the Convention.[40]

Restrictions on Rights

5.23 The Court has emphasised that inherent in the whole of the Convention is the fair balance to be struck between the general interest of the community and the interests of the individual.[41]

---

[36] *Nachova and others* v *Bulgaria*, Nos. 43577/98 and 43579/98, 26.2.04, para. 157 (and endorsed by the Grand Chamber in its judgment of 6.7.05 (para. 160)).
[37] No. 39272/98, 4.12.03.
[38] See: *Siliadin* v *France*, Nos. 73316/01, 26.7.05 and *Rantsev* v *Cyprus and Russia*, No. 25965/04, 7.1.10.
[39] See, e.g. *Ezelin* v *France*, No. 11800/85, Series A, No. 202, 26.4.91.
[40] See, e.g. *Di Sarno and others* v *Italy*, No. 30765/08, 10.1.12, para. 110.
[41] See, e.g. *James* v *UK*, No 8793/79 Series A, No. 98, 21.2.86.

The aim to achieve such a balance is clearly evident in Articles 8–11, which include second paragraphs setting out the circumstances in which the right to respect for the private life or the right to freedom of expression etc. can be restricted (see chapter 6). However, the balance of rights is reflected throughout the Convention, for example, in the circumstances set out in Article 2 as to when deprivation of life may be permitted and the right of the authorities to enforce laws to control the use of property 'in accordance with the general interest' or to deprive a person of their possessions where it is in 'the public interest', under Article 1 of Protocol No. 1.

5.24 There are specific Convention provisions concerning restrictions in Article 16 (restrictions on the political activity of aliens) and in Article 18 (limitation on the use of restrictions in rights), which are considered below.

Restrictions on the political activity of aliens

5.25 Article 16 states that: 'Nothing in Articles 10, 11 and 14 shall be regarded as preventing the High Contracting Parties from imposing restrictions on the political activity of aliens.'

5.26 In spite of the obligation on states enshrined in Article 1 to ensure that 'everyone within their jurisdiction' receives the protection of the Convention, Article 16 provides that in relation to the rights of freedom of expression, freedom of assembly and association and the prohibition of discrimination, states cannot be prevented from imposing restrictions on the political activity of aliens. There is no equivalent provision in the International Covenant on Civil and Political Rights.

5.27 Article 16 has, however, been interpreted so as to diminish its importance. *Piermont* v *France*[42] concerned a German MEP who was invited to French Polynesia by the French Polynesian Liberation Front prior to parliamentary elections. Whilst in French Polynesia, the applicant denounced nuclear testing in the Pacific and as a result she was subsequently expelled and/or excluded from that territory and from New Caledonia. She argued that there had been violations of Article 2 of Protocol No. 4 (freedom of movement), Article 10 and Article 14 (taken together with Article 10). She claimed she had been discriminated against on grounds of national origin. In relation to her claim under Article 10, the French Government invoked Article 16, arguing that she could not rely on her status either as an MEP or as a European citizen. However, the Court decided that Article 16 could not be raised against her because she was a national of a member state of the European Union and an MEP, and found a violation of Article 10, by five votes to four. The four dissenting judges argued the reference to 'aliens' was unambiguous and had no express exceptions. Nevertheless, they also argued that Article 16 could not permit any restriction at all on the political activity of aliens, but that such restrictions would have to be limited. Article 16 was raised by the Swiss Government in *Perinçek* v *Switzerland*,[43] a case concerning the criminal prosecution of the applicant, a Turkish national, for denying the Armenian genocide. However, the Grand Chamber found that Article 16 was not applicable, as it was only capable of authorising restrictions on 'activities' that directly affect the political process.

---

[42] Nos. 15773/89 and 15774/89, Series A, No. 314, 27.4.95.
[43] No. 27510/08, 15.10.15.

Limitations on the use of restrictions on rights

5.28 Article 18 states that: 'The restrictions permitted under this Convention to the said rights and freedoms shall not be applied for any purpose other than those for which they have been prescribed.'

5.29 Under Article 18, the Court may examine the reasons for a restrictive measure and if in fact the measure complained of was taken for reasons other than those invoked, then there may be a Convention violation. Article 18 is therefore linked to the underlying Convention concept of 'lawfulness' and, in particular, the prevention of arbitrary measures. Article 18 must be invoked with another Convention right,[44] but there can be a violation of Article 18 (taken together with another Convention right), even if there is no violation of the other right taken alone. The Court may examine compliance of restrictions with Article 18 even if the point is not raised by an applicant.[45]

5.30 The Court imposes a 'very exacting standard of proof' on anyone wishing to establish a violation of Article 18:

> ... an applicant alleging that his rights and freedoms were limited for an improper reason must convincingly show that the real aim of the authorities was not the same as that proclaimed (or as can be reasonably inferred from the context). A mere suspicion that the authorities used their powers for some other purpose than those defined in the Convention is not sufficient to prove that Article 18 was breached.

Therefore in practice, it may often be very difficult to provide sufficient evidence to satisfy the Court of a violation of Article 18. In *Khodorkovskiy v Russia*[46] the complaints brought under Article 18 by Mikhail Khodorkovskiy, the former board member and major shareholder of the Yukos oil company, that his arrest, detention and prosecution were politically motivated, were rejected by the Court. Whilst acknowledging that 'certain suspicions' were raised in his case, the Court did not have adequate proof to establish, as the applicant argued, that in his case the whole legal machinery had been misused *ab initio*. Article 18 was also raised unsuccessfully by the applicant oil company in *OAO Neftyanaya Kompaniya Yukos v Russia*,[47] which concerned the prosecution and enforcement of tax proceedings against the applicant, leading to the imposition of massive fines, its insolvency and liquidation, various aspects of which were found to breach Article 1 of Protocol No. 1, Articles 6(1) and 6(3) (discussed further below at 6.792).

---

[44] *Mudayevy v Russia*, No. 33105/05, 8.4.10, para. 127.

[45] See, e.g. *McFeeley v UK*, No. 8317/78, dec. 15.5.80, (1978) 20 DR 44.

[46] *Khodorkovskiy v Russia*, No. 5829/04, 31.5.11, paras. 255–6. See also *Khodorkovskiy and Lebedev v Russia*, Nos. 11082/06 and 13772/05, 25.7.13 (finding no violation of Article 18, the Court concluded that 'the accusations against the applicants were serious, that the case against them had a "healthy core", and that even if there was a mixed intent behind their prosecution, this did not grant them immunity from answering the accusations') (para. 908). In *Navalnyy and Ofitserov v Russia*, Nos. 46632/13 and 28671/14, 23.2.16 the majority of the Court declared the applicants' complaint under Article 18 together with Articles 6 and 7 inadmissible on the basis that 'the provisions of [those] Articles, in so far as relevant to the present case, do not contain any express or implied restrictions that may form the subject of the Court's examination under Article 18'. This view was challenged in a joint partly dissenting opinion, by Judges Nicolaou, Keller and Dedov, who argued that the Court should also have considered the merits of the applicants' complaint under Article 18 together with Article 6, arguing persuasively that Article 6 incorporates inherent restrictions and that there is no reason why Article 18 should not apply in conjunction with Article 6, as well as with Article 5.

[47] No. 14902/04, 20.9.11, paras. 663–6.

In spite of the evidential difficulties in establishing a breach of Article 18, there have been a **5.31**
number of high profile political cases in which violations of Article 18 have been found. The
applicant in *Gusinskiy* v *Russia*,[48] a former chairman of the board and majority shareholder
in a media company, was charged with fraud. The Court found a violation of Article 18,
in conjunction with Article 5, on the basis that the applicant had been detained not only
because of a reasonable suspicion of his involvement in an offence (and therefore in order
for him to be taken before a competent legal authority), but also in order to intimidate the
applicant into transferring his shares to a state-controlled company. The Court concluded
that 'it is not the purpose of such public-law matters as criminal proceedings and detention
on remand to be used as part of commercial bargaining strategies'.[49] The case of *Lutsenko* v
Ukraine[50] concerned the detention of Yuriy Lutsenko, the leader of an opposition political
party (and a former Minister of the Interior) in the course of criminal proceedings brought
against him for unlawfully arranging work-related benefits for his former driver. The Court
found that the applicant's detention was arbitrary and violated Article 5(1) and that it also
breached the spirit of the Convention.[51] The Court noted that the prosecuting authorities
had stated that the applicant's communication with the media was one of the grounds for his
arrest and accused him of distorting public opinion about crimes he had committed, of dis-
crediting the prosecuting authorities and of trying to influence the outcome of his upcoming
trial. For the Court, this clearly demonstrated the prosecuting authorities' wish to punish the
applicant for publicly disagreeing with the accusations made against him and for asserting
his innocence. Therefore, it concluded that the restriction of the applicant's liberty (under
Article 5(1)(c)) was applied not only for the purpose of bringing him before the competent
legal authority on reasonable suspicion of having committed an offence, but also for other
reasons, which violated Article 18 in conjunction with Article 5. The former Prime Minister
of Ukraine, Yuliya Tymoshenko, also successfully raised a complaint of a violation of Article
5 together with Article 18 in relation to criminal proceedings brought against her for alleged
excess of authority and abuse of office. In *Tymoshenko* v *Ukraine*,[52] she argued that her pre-
trial detention had been used by the authorities to exclude her from political life and to prevent her from standing in the 2012 Ukrainian parliamentary elections. Noting similarities
with the *Lutsenko* case, the Court found that the actual purpose of her detention had been to
punish her for her perceived hindering of the proceedings and her contemptuous behaviour
towards the court. The case of *Ilgar Mammadov* v *Azerbaijan*[53] concerned the detention and
prosecution of a prominent opposition politician and blogger who was accused of instigating a riot. The Court found that there had been no 'reasonable suspicion' to justify his arrest,
and accordingly the authorities had failed to demonstrate that they had acted in good faith.
Indeed, the Court noted that his arrest was linked to his publication of several blog posts
about the causes of the riots. The Court therefore concluded that the purpose of the measures
taken 'was to silence or punish the applicant for criticising the Government and attempting to disseminate what he believed was the true information that the Government were

---

[48] No. 70276/01, 19.5.04.
[49] *Ibid.*, para. 76. See also *Cebotari* v *Moldova*, No. 35615/06, 13.11.07 (violation of Article 18 in conjunction with Article 5).
[50] No. 6492/11, 3.7.12.
[51] All told, the Court found two violations of both Articles 5(1) and 5(3), as well as violations of
Articles 5(2) and 5(4).
[52] No. 49872/11, 30.4.13.
[53] No. 15172/13, 22.5.14. There was also a breach of Article 5(4).

trying to hide' and that there was a breach of Article 18 of the Convention taken together with Article 5. *Merabishvili v Georgia*[54] related to the prosecution for abuse of office (and other offences), and pre-trial detention, of a leading opposition politician (and former Prime Minister and Minister of the Interior). The Court noted that various international observers had expressed concerns about the possible use of criminal proceedings against him for an improper, hidden political agenda. It also found as credible and convincing his account that he was taken from his prison cell late one night to a meeting with the Chief Public Prosecutor and the head of the prison authority who tried to persuade him to provide evidence about an investigation into the death of the former prime minister and a case relating to the former president. The Court concluded that the applicant's pre-trial detention had been used not only for the purpose of bringing him before the competent legal authority on reasonable suspicion of the offences with which he had been charged, but also as a means of exerting moral pressure on him. There was therefore a violation of Article 18 together with Article 5(1).[55] The one case to date in which a human rights defender has successfully raised Article 18 (also in conjunction with Article 5) is *Rasul Jafarov v Azerbaijan*.[56] There, the applicant was arrested in 2014 in the course of criminal proceedings for alleged irregularities in the financial activities of several NGOs. He was also banned from travelling, his bank accounts were frozen and he was detained until his conviction and imprisonment in 2015. The Court noted the increasingly restrictive legislative regulation of NGO activities and funding, and that numerous statements had been made by high-ranking officials and articles published in the pro-government media, in which NGOs and their leaders had been accused of being traitors and foreign agents, and were harshly criticised for contributing to a negative image of the country abroad by reporting on the human rights situation in the country. Furthermore, other high-profile human rights defenders had similarly been arrested and charged with serious criminal offences entailing heavy custodial sentences, as part of a wider crackdown. Therefore, the Court concluded that the actual purpose of the measures taken against the applicant had been to silence and punish him for his human rights activities.

5.32 Article 18 was raised in the context of gross human rights violations perpetrated by the security forces in south-east Turkey, but the Court repeatedly found no violation in such cases. For example, in *Kurt v Turkey*,[57] a 'disappearance' case, the applicant argued that the authorities had acted outside the framework of domestic legislation in relation to detention, but the Court found the complaint under Article 18 unsubstantiated. An Article 18 claim also did not succeed in *Rai, Allmond and 'Negotiate Now' v UK*[58] in which the applicants complained about the refusal to allow them to hold a rally in Trafalgar Square, in central London, in order to promote peace negotiations in Northern Ireland. Article 18 was invoked in relation to a policy to ban demonstrations in Trafalgar Square which were not 'uncontroversial'. However, in declaring the case inadmissible, the European Commission of Human Rights found that there was no indication that the restriction was applied for a purpose not prescribed by the provisions of the Convention.

---

[54] No. 72508/13, 14.6.16 (referred to the Grand Chamber which held a hearing on the case on 8 March 2017). See also *Ugulava v Georgia*, No. 5432/15 (communicated 28.9.15)—a case concerning criminal proceedings brought against the former Mayor of Tbilisi.

[55] There was also a violation of Article 5(3), but no separate violation of Article 5(1).

[56] No. 69981/14, 17.3.16. There were also violations of Articles 5(1) and 5(4).

[57] No. 24276/94, 25.5.98: see especially paras. 148–52.

[58] No. 25522/94, dec. 6.4.95.

Prohibition of Abuse of Rights

Article 17 states that: **5.33**

> Nothing in this Convention may be interpreted as implying for any state, group or person any
> right to engage in any activity or perform any act aimed at the destruction of any of the rights
> and freedoms set forth herein or at their limitation to a greater extent than is provided for in
> the Convention.

Article 17 is intended to make it impossible for groups or individuals to derive from the   **5.34**
Convention a right to do anything aimed at destroying any of the Convention rights and
freedoms.[59] Article 17 applies only to an extent strictly proportionate to the seriousness and
duration of the threat.[60]

Individuals or groups should not therefore use their Convention rights to undermine dem-   **5.35**
ocracy or democratic institutions. The Court has explained that the objective of Article 17
is to prevent individuals or groups 'with totalitarian aims' from exploiting the Convention,
and has underlined that it is only applicable exceptionally, 'in extreme cases'.[61] For example,
in *Retimag AG v Germany*,[62] Article 17 was invoked by the European Commission in dismissing an application by the communist party in Germany (concerning its dissolution), as
its objective of establishing a communist society through the dictatorship of the proletariat
was considered to be incompatible with the Convention. The Court applied Article 17 in
Hizb Ut-Tahrir and others v Germany,[63] in declaring inadmissible an application concerning the proscription of the applicant organisation. As the Federal Administrative Court in
Germany had found that *Hizb Ut-Tahrir* denied the State of Israel's right to exist, and called
for its violent destruction and for the banishment and killing of its inhabitants, it could not
benefit from the protection of Article 11.

In *Glimmerveen and Hagenbeek v Netherlands*[64] the applicants complained of being con-   **5.36**
victed of possessing leaflets inciting racial discrimination and of being prevented from taking
part in municipal elections. They claimed violations of Article 10 and Article 3 of Protocol
No. 1. However, the Commission found that such conduct amounted to an 'activity' within
the meaning of Article 17 which was contrary to the text and spirit of the Convention.

Similarly, *Kuhnen v Germany*[65] concerned the conviction of a journalist for publishing   **5.37**
pamphlets advocating the reinstitution of national socialism and racial discrimination. The
Commission found that Article 10 may not be invoked in a sense contrary to Article 17. In
Garaudy v France,[66] the Court declared inadmissible a complaint brought under Article 10
by the author of a book, *The Founding Myths of Modern Israel*, who had been prosecuted,

---

[59] *Lawless v Ireland*, Series A, No. 3, 1.7.61.
[60] *De Becker v Belgium* (1962) Series, B No. 4, Comm. Rep., para. 279.
[61] *Paksas v Lithuania*, No. 34932/04, 6.1.11, para. 87. See also *Vona v Hungary*, No. 35943/10, 9.7.13 (not
established that applicant association's activities were intended to justify or propagate an ideology of oppression
serving 'totalitarian groups'–respondent Government's objection on basis of Article 17 dismissed).
[62] No. 712/60, (1962) 4 YB 38.
[63] No. 31098/08, dec. 12.6.12.
[64] (1979) 18 DR 187. See also *Féret v Belgium*, No. 15615/07, 16.7.09 (conviction of president of extreme
right wing party for publishing leaflets inciting racial hatred—no violation of Article 10, by four votes to three).
[65] (1988) 56 DR 205.
[66] No. 65831/01, dec. 7.7.03.

convicted and imprisoned for disputing the existence of crimes against humanity, public defamation of the Jewish community, and incitement to discrimination and racial hatred. The Court found that the applicant's book ran counter to the fundamental values of the Convention, and that in view of Article 17, he could not rely on Article 10 of the Convention.[67] A similar decision was made in the case of *Norwood* v *UK*[68] in which the applicant, a regional organiser of the British National Party, was prosecuted and convicted for displaying a poster in the window of his flat with a photograph of the Twin Towers in flame and the words 'Islam out of Britain—Protect the British People'. His complaint under Article 10 was declared inadmissible because such a general attack on all Muslims in the United Kingdom, linking them as a whole with a grave act of terrorism, was incompatible with the Convention. This decision can be contrasted with *Leroy* v *France*,[69] which concerned convictions for condoning terrorism as a result of the publication in a newspaper of a cartoonist's sketch of the attack on the Twin Towers, together with a parody of an advertising slogan: 'We have all dreamt of it. Hamas did it.' There, the Court rejected the Government's reliance on Article 17 on the basis that the underlying message which the applicants had sought to convey was not the negation of fundamental rights and although the publication had been found by the domestic courts to condone terrorism, it could not be interpreted as an unequivocal attempt to justify terrorist acts.

5.38   In *Lawless* v *Ireland*,[70] the applicant member of the IRA complained of his arbitrary detention. The Irish Government sought to invoke Article 17 in arguing that as an active member of the IRA his activities fell within the scope of the Article and therefore he could not rely on Articles 5, 6 or 7 or any other Convention right. However, the Court found that Article 17 did not deprive the applicant of the protection of Articles 5 or 6, as he had not relied on the Convention in order to justify or perform acts contrary to the Convention, but had complained of being deprived of the Article 5 and 6 guarantees.[71]

5.39   The Court has rejected attempts by the Turkish Government to invoke Article 17 in a series of cases brought following the dissolution of political parties in Turkey. For example, the United Communist Party of Turkey was dissolved in 1991 by the Constitutional Court for allegedly acting to the detriment of the unity of the Turkish nation. The Court held that Article 17 was not brought into play because there was no evidence that the party relied on the Convention to engage in activity or perform acts aimed at the destruction of any of the rights and freedoms in the Convention.[72] Article 17 was also found to be inapplicable in *Orban and others* v *France*[73] which concerned the conviction of the publishers of a book for

---

[67] See also *WP and others* v *Poland*, No. 42264/98, dec. 2.9.04 (members of the 'National and Patriotic Association of Polish victims of Bolshevism and Zionism' were found to be unable to rely on Article 11 because of the application of Article 17, in view of their racism and anti-semitism); *Ivanov* v *Russia*, No. 35222/04, dec. 20.2.07 (conviction for publications inciting hatred towards the Jewish people); *M'Bala M'Bala* v *France*, No. 25239/13, dec. 20.10.15 (criminal conviction of comedian known as Dieudonné, for expression of negationist and anti-Semitic views during performance—pursuant to Article 17, not entitled to rely on Article 10—inadmissible).

[68] No. 23131/03, dec. 16.11.04.

[69] No. 36109/03, 2.10.08 (the case was declared admissible, but the Court found no violation of Article 10).

[70] Series A, No. 3, 1.7.61.

[71] See also *Varela Geis* v *Spain*, No. 61005/09, 5.3.13.

[72] *United Communist Party of Turkey and others* v *Turkey*, No. 19392/92, 30.1.98, para. 60. See also, *Socialist Party and others* v *Turkey*, No. 21237/93, 25.5.98, para. 53; *Freedom and Democracy Party (Özdep)* v *Turkey*, No. 23885/94, 8.12.99, para. 47.

[73] No. 20985/05, 15.1.09.

condoning war crimes. The book was written by a former member of the special services who described acts of torture and summary executions in Algeria. The Court held that although the subject matter of the book was sensitive and controversial, it was a matter of public interest, and by publishing it the applicants had not used their right to freedom of expression for purposes that were contrary to the Convention (and Article 10 was found to have been violated).

Interpretation of the Scope of Substantive Rights

In general, the scope of the substantive Convention rights should not be restrictively interpreted. It is a well-established principle that in assessing the scope of a Convention right 'it is necessary to seek the interpretation that is most appropriate in order to realise the aim and achieve the object of the treaty, and not that which would restrict to the greatest possible degree the obligations undertaken by the parties'.[74]   **5.40**

Irrelevance of a State's Resources

Socio-economic problems or lack of resources cannot justify a state's failure to comply with its obligations under the Convention. Thus a state may not cite lack of funds as justification for failing to honour a judgment.[75] In *Poltoratskiy* v *Ukraine*,[76] in which the Court found a violation of Article 3 due to the conditions in which the applicant was held in prison on 'death row', it was stated that: **5.41**

> The Court has also borne in mind, when considering the material conditions in which the applicant was detained and the activities offered to him, that Ukraine encountered serious socio-economic problems in the course of its systemic transition and that prior to the summer of 1998 the prison authorities were both struggling under difficult economic conditions and occupied with the implementation of new national legislation and related regulations. However, the Court observes that lack of resources cannot in principle justify prison conditions which are so poor as to reach the threshold of treatment contrary to Article 3 of the Convention. Moreover, the economic problems faced by Ukraine cannot in any event explain or excuse the particular conditions of detention which it has found … to be unacceptable in the present case.

In *Burdov* v *Russia*,[77] there had been delays in the payment of an award of compensation (in respect of the applicant's exposure to radioactive emissions). The Court emphasised that financial difficulties experienced by the state could not justify failing to honour a judgment debt.   **5.42**

However, in *Broniowski* v *Poland*,[78] a case concerning the failure of the Polish state to compensate the applicant for property abandoned after World War II, the Court found that both the large number of potential claimants (80,000), and the total value of their claims, were factors that had to be taken into account in assessing whether the authorities   **5.43**

---

[74] See, e.g. *Wemhoff* v *Germany*, Series A, No. 7, 27.7.68, para. 8.
[75] See, e.g. *Prodan* v *Moldova*, No. 49806/99, 18.5.04, para. 53.
[76] No. 38812/97, 29.4.03, para. 148. See further at 6.104.
[77] No. 59498/00, 7.5.02. See also *Timofeyev* v *Russia*, No. 58263/00, 23.10.03.
[78] No. 31443/96, 22.6.04.

had struck a 'fair balance' between the rights of the claimants and the wider rights of the community.

Interpretation in Accordance with the Vienna Convention

5.44 In interpreting the Convention, the Court must take into account the Vienna Convention on the Law of Treaties (23 May 1969).[79] This means that the Court will assess the 'ordinary meaning' of the particular term in question and that it will also seek to take into account the object and purpose of the Convention.[80]

Interpretation in Accordance with International Law

5.45 In the light of Article 31(3)(c) of the Vienna Convention (see 5.44 above), which requires that account is to be taken of 'any relevant rules of international law applicable in the relations between the parties', the Court has emphasised that it must take rules of international law into account: 'the Convention should so far as possible be interpreted in harmony with other rules of international law of which it forms part'.[81] This principle was applied by the Court in *Al-Adsani v UK*[82] in upholding measures taken by the state reflecting 'generally recognised rules of international law' on state immunity. The Court accepted that the prohibition of torture had achieved the status of a peremptory norm in international law (or *jus cogens*) but it did not find any firm basis for concluding that, as a matter of international law, a state no longer enjoyed immunity from civil suit in the courts of another state where acts of torture were alleged.

5.46 The Court will frequently invoke human rights-related treaties, declarations, recommendations and case law from varied sources, including the Council of Europe,[83] the European Union,[84] UN Conventions and other standards[85] and UN Human Rights Committee

---

[79] See, e.g. *Bankovic v Belgium and others*, No. 52207/99, dec. 12.12.01, paras. 55–6.

[80] See, e.g. *East African Asians v UK*, Nos. 4403/70–4419/70, 4422/70, 4434/70, 4443/70, 4476/70–4478/70, 4486/70, 4501/70 and 4526/70–4530/70, 14.12.73, para. 188; *Stoll v Switzerland*, No. 69698/01, 10.12.07, paras. 59–62; *Saadi v UK*, No. 13229/03, 29.1.08, para. 62.

[81] See, e.g. *Loizidou v Turkey*, No. 15318/89, 18.12.96, para. 43; *Bankovic v Belgium and others*, No. 52207/99, dec. 12.12.01, para. 57.

[82] No. 35763/97, 21.11.01.

[83] See, e.g. *Poltoratskiy v Ukraine*, No. 38812/97, 29.4.03 (resolutions of the Parliamentary Assembly concerning the death penalty, and reports of the European Committee for the Prevention of Torture and Inhuman and Degrading Treatment or Punishment (CPT)); *Koua Poirrez v France*, No. 40892/98, 30.9.03, para. 39 (Committee of Ministers Recommendation No. R(92) 6, adopted on 9 April 1992 aimed at the adoption of a policy and measures adapted to the needs of persons with disabilities); *Sidabras and Džiautas v Lithuania*, Nos. 55480/00 and 59330/00, 27.7.04 (European Social Charter); *Demir and Baykara v Turkey*, No. 34503/97, 12.11.08 (European Social Charter); *Muñoz Díaz v Spain*, No. 49151/07, 8.12.09 (Framework Convention for the Protection of National Minorities); *Tănase v Moldova*, No. 7/08, 27.4.10 (European Convention on Nationality).

[84] See, e.g. *Scoppola v Italy (No. 2)*, No. 10249/03, 17.9.09 (EU Charter of Fundamental Rights).

[85] See, e.g. *A v UK*, No. 25599/94, 23.9.98, para. 22 (Articles 19 and 37, UN Convention on the Rights of the Child); *Finucane v UK*, No. 29178/95, 1.7.03 (The 'Minnesota Protocol'—Model Protocol for a legal investigation of extra-legal, arbitrary and summary executions, contained in the UN Manual on the Effective Prevention and Investigation of Extra-legal, Arbitrary and Summary Executions); *Doğan and others v Turkey*, Nos. 8803–8811/02, 8813/02 and 8815–8819/02, 29.6.04 (UN Guiding Principles on Internal Displacement, E/CN.4/1998/53/Add.2, 11 February 1998); *Siliadin v France*, No. 73316/01, 26.7.05 (e.g. ILO Forced Labour Convention).

case-law, other regional human rights mechanisms (such as the American Convention on Human Rights)[86] and relevant domestic case law both from within Council of Europe states and from other jurisdictions.[87]

The Court will take particular note where the respondent state is itself bound by other **5.47** international law principles or human rights norms which are relevant to the case in issue. For example, in cases concerning child abduction, the Court will assess the nature of the state's positive obligations under Article 8 of the European Convention in the light of the Hague Convention,[88] in particular where the state is a party to that Convention.[89] However, in its Grand Chamber judgment in *Demir and Baykara* v *Turkey*,[90] the Court confirmed that it could also take account of treaties or conventions that had not been ratified by a respondent state:

> it is not necessary for the respondent State to have ratified the entire collection of instruments that are applicable in respect of the precise subject matter of the case concerned. It will be suffi-cient for the Court that the relevant international instruments denote a continuous evolution in the norms and principles applied in international law or in the domestic law of the majority of member States of the Council of Europe and show, in a precise area, that there is common ground in modern societies.

Interpretation in the Light of the *Travaux Préparatoires*

In interpreting the Convention, the Court may consider the *travaux préparatoires*—the pre- **5.48** paratory documents related to the drafting of the Convention.[91] However, such a means of interpretation may conflict with the principle of the Convention as a 'living instru-ment' (see above at 5.13) which is more likely to prevail. The Court may also consider the meaning of the text of the Convention in French, which may have different nuances to the English text.[92]

---

[86] See, e.g. *Iorgov* v *Bulgaria*, No. 40653/98, 11.3.04, para. 52 (Human Rights Committee decisions concerning prolonged detention on death row) and *Timurtaş* v *Turkey*, No. 33274/96, 13.6.00, paras. 79–80 (referring to, e.g. *Velásquez Rodriguez case*, 29.7.88, Series C, No. 4). See also: European Court of Human Rights, Research Report—References to the Inter-American Court of Human Rights and Inter-American instruments in the case-law of the European Court of Human Rights, Council of Europe, 2016.

[87] See, e.g. *Appleby and others* v *UK*, No. 44306/98, 6.5.03 (case law from the United States and Canadian courts concerning freedom of speech within privately owned public spaces); *Hirst* v *UK* (*No. 2*), No. 74025/01, 30.3.04 (Chamber judgment) and 6.10.05 (Grand Chamber judgment) (Canadian Supreme Court judgment in *Sauvé* v *the Attorney General of Canada* (*No. 2*), 31.10.02 concerning the disenfranchisement of prisoners).

[88] The Hague Convention of 25 October 1980 on the Civil Aspects of International Child Abduction.

[89] See, e.g. *Ignaccolo-Zenide* v *Romania*, No. 31679/96, 25.1.00; *Sylvester* v *Austria*, Nos. 36812/97 and 40104/98, 24.4.03.

[90] No. 34503/97, 12.11.08, para. 86.

[91] *The Collected Edition of the Travaux Préparatoires of the European Convention on Human Rights*, Council of Europe. They are available on the European Court website: http://www.echr.coe.int/Documents/Library_TravPrep_Table_ENG.pdf. See, e.g. *Young, James and Webster* v *UK*, Nos. 7601/76 and 7807/77, Series A, No. 44, 26.6.81, paras. 51–3 (whether Article 11 guarantees a right not to be compelled to join a union); *Witold Litwa* v *Poland*, No. 26629/95, 4.4.00, para. 63; *Bankovic* v *Belgium and others*, No. 52207/99, dec. 12.12.01, paras. 58, 63 and 65; *Kononov* v *Latvia*, No. 36376/04, 17.5.10, para. 186.

[92] See, e.g. *Marckx* v *Belgium*, Series A, No. 31, 13.6.79, para. 63.

Issues Considered by the Court of its Own Motion

5.49   The Court is not bound by the Convention violations pleaded by the parties. As the Court is master of the characterisation to be given in law to the facts of a case, it may consider and apply Articles of the Convention not raised by the applicant (applying the principle of *jura novit curia*).[93] The Court has full jurisdiction within the scope of a case as determined by the admissibility decision and may deal with any issue of fact or law arising. The Court is also not restricted to considering cases on the basis of material submitted to it, but may, if necessary, assess a case in the light of material obtained *proprio motu*.[94]

Inability to Consider Cases in the Abstract

5.50   The Court will not admit applications which are theoretical or in the abstract (this is discussed further in chapter 4). The Court's role is not primarily to assess whether legislation or policies in general violate the Convention,[95] but to assess in concrete cases whether the application of such laws or policies has breached the Convention. In doing so, it will however take account of the 'general context' in which the application arises.[96]

Rules of Evidence and Burden of Proof

5.51   The Court is not bound by strict rules of evidence, and may rely on all forms of evidence.[97] The standard of proof applied by the Court is that of 'proof beyond reasonable doubt', although this is not interpreted as the same high degree of probability as in domestic criminal trials: reflecting the fact that the Court's role is to rule on state responsibility under international law and not to establish individual criminal liability. It has also reiterated that proof may follow from the co-existence of sufficiently strong, clear and concordant inferences or of similar unrebutted presumptions of fact.[98]

5.52   Furthermore, the Court has stated that it will allow a degree of flexibility:

> there are no procedural barriers to the admissibility of evidence or pre-determined formulae for its assessment. It adopts the conclusions that are, in its view, supported by the free evaluation of all evidence, including such inferences as may flow from the facts and the parties' submissions.[99]

---

[93] See, e.g. *Guerra and others* v *Italy*, No. 14967/89, 19.2.98, para. 44; *Pentiacova and others* v *Moldova*, No. 14462/03, dec. 4.1.05 (applicants sought to withdraw complaint under Article 8 which was nevertheless considered by the Court—and declared inadmissible); *Põder and others* v *Estonia*, No. 67723/01, dec. 26.4.05 (Article 1 of Protocol No. 1 was applied, even though it had not been raised by the applicants); *Şerife Yiğit* v *Turkey*, No. 3976/05, 2.11.10 (Article 14 and Article 1 of Protocol No. 1 considered, although not raised by the parties); *M.M.* v *UK*, No. 24029/07, 13.11.12 (Article 7 raised by applicant in relation to retention and disclosure of caution—Article 8 applied by the Court and found to have been violated).

[94] See, e.g. *Cruz Varas* v *Sweden*, No. 15576/89, 20.3.91, para. 25.

[95] See, e.g. *McCann* v *UK*, No. 18984/91, Series A, No. 324, 27.9.95, para. 153.

[96] See, e.g. *Young, James and Webster* v *UK*, Nos. 7601/76 and 7807/77, Series A, No. 44, 26.6.81, para. 53. See also the discussion of the Court's evolving approach to systemic violations, in chapter 3.

[97] *Lawless* v *UK*, No. 352/57, Series A, No. 3, 1.7.61, para. 209.

[98] See, e.g. *Ireland* v *UK*, No. 5310/71, 18.1.78, para. 161.

[99] See, e.g. *Nachova and others* v *Bulgaria*, Nos. 43577/98 and 43579/98, 6.7.05, para. 147.

See also 2.127 above, Establishing the Facts.

Waiver of Convention Rights

The Court has accepted that applicants may waive their rights under the Convention, but it **5.53** has emphasised that any waiver must be 'made in an unequivocal manner and must not run counter to any important public interest'.[100] For example, in *Nagula v Estonia*,[101] the Russian applicant's complaint under Article 8 about the refusal to extend his residence permit was declared inadmissible as he was already found to have voluntarily settled permanently in Russia. As a former member of the Soviet armed forces, his resettlement was agreed under the auspices of a treaty between Estonia and Russia concerning the withdrawal of troops, and accordingly the Court found that the applicant's waiver did not breach any important public interest.

The Effective Exercise of the Right of Application

As well as setting out the rules of 'standing' (see chapter 4), Article 34 (formerly Article 25) **5.54** establishes a duty on Convention states not to hinder the effective exercise of the right to apply to the European Court. The Court has frequently emphasised that it is of the utmost importance for the effective operation of the system of individual petition that applicants or potential applicants should be able to communicate freely with the Court. Article 34 states that:

> The Court may receive applications from any person, non-governmental organisation or group of individuals claiming to be the victim of a violation by one of the High Contracting Parties of the rights set forth in the Convention or the protocols thereto. The High Contracting Parties undertake not to hinder in any way the effective exercise of this right.

Where a state prevents the effective right of application, the Court may find a violation of **5.55** Article 34. Accordingly, if there is any evidence at any stage of a Convention application that the applicant's effective right of application is being restricted, then the matter should immediately be drawn to the Court's attention by lodging relevant evidence, including statements. The applicant's representative may plead a violation of Article 34 (albeit as a procedural, not a substantive right)[102] and may request that the Court takes the matter up with the respondent government. The right of application may be affected in a number of ways, including interception of the applicant's and/or the applicant's representative's communications[103] (post, telephone, email etc), or intimidation of the applicant, the applicant's family or potential witnesses.[104] There is no requirement on a complainant to prove any detriment, as such, caused by a breach of Article 34:

---

[100] See *Håkansson and Sturesson v Sweden*, No. 11855/85, 12.2.90, Series A No. 171-A, para. 66 (Article 6(1)); *Nagula v Estonia*, No. 39203/02, dec. 25.10.05.

[101] No. 39203/02, dec. 25.10.05.

[102] Therefore, issues of admissibility do not arise: see, e.g. *Savitskyy v Ukraine*, No. 38773/05, 26.7.12, para. 154.

[103] See, e.g. *Foxley v UK*, No. 33274/96, 20.6.00 (interception of applicant's mail by Receiver and Trustee in Bankruptcy led to finding of a violation of Article 8, and that it was not necessary to consider Article 34); *Poleshchuk v Russia*, No. 60776/00, 7.10.04.

[104] See, e.g. *Novinskiy v Russia*, No. 11982/02, 10.2.09.

... a failure by the respondent Government to comply with their procedural obligation under Article 34 of the Convention does not necessarily require that the alleged interference should have actually restricted, or had any appreciable impact on, the exercise of the right of individual petition. The Contracting Party's procedural obligation must be enforced irrespective of the eventual outcome of the proceedings and in such a manner as to avoid any actual or potential chilling effect on the applicants or their representatives.[105]

5.56 There are also positive obligations inherent in Article 34, such as the requirement to provide applicants with copies of documents necessary for the examination of their applications.[106] There was a violation of this provision in *Vasiliy Ivashchenko v Ukraine*[107] because of the authorities' failure to provide the applicant prisoner with a copy of his case-file. Furthermore, in view of the evidence of a systemic problem in Ukraine, the Court invoked Article 46 in directing the government to take legislative and administrative measures to ensure that detainees are given effective access to the documents they need in order to substantiate their complaints before the Court.

5.57 Under Article 34, applicants must not be subjected to any form of pressure from the authorities to modify or withdraw their complaints. The provision also rules out 'any act or omission which, by destroying or removing the subject matter of an application, would make it pointless or otherwise prevent the Court from considering it under its normal procedure'.[108] 'Pressure' includes direct coercion and flagrant acts of intimidation (of applicants, potential applicants, their families and legal representatives), but also any improper indirect acts or contacts designed to dissuade or discourage applicants from pursuing a Convention remedy. The questioning of applicants about their applications to the Court is considered to be a form of illicit and unacceptable pressure.[109] The Court has emphasised that if a government believes that in a particular case the right of individual petition is being abused, rather than question the applicant, it should inform the Court about its concerns.[110] In assessing the degree of interference, the Court will take account of the vulnerability of the complainant and his or her susceptibility to influence exerted by the authorities, including any legitimate fear of reprisals.

5.58 A number of complaints of intimidation have been upheld in the Kurdish cases against Turkey. There was a violation of Article 25 (now Article 34) in *Akdivar v Turkey*[111] where the applicants were directly asked about their petitions to Strasbourg and were presented with statements to sign declaring that no such applications had been brought (two applicants' interviews were filmed).[112] The applicant in *Kurt v Turkey*[113] alleged that she had been

---

[105] *Annagi Hajibeyli v Azerbaijan*, No. 2204/11, 22.10.15, para. 77.

[106] See, e.g. *Naydyon v Ukraine*, No. 16474/03, 14.10.10; *Savitskky v Ukraine*, No. 38773/05, 26.7.12.

[107] No. 760/03, 26.7.12.

[108] *Mamatkulov and Askarov v Turkey*, Nos. 46827/99 and 46951/99, 4.2.05, para. 102.

[109] *Assenov and others v Bulgaria*, No. 24760/94, 28.10.98. This principle has often been violated—see, e.g. *Akdivar and others v Turkey*, No. 21893/96, 16.9.96, para. 105; *Kurt v Turkey*, No. 24276/94, 25.5.98, para. 160; *Tanrikulu v Turkey*, No. 26763/94, 8.7.99, para. 130; *Orhan v Turkey*, No. 25656/94, 18.6.02; *Lopata v Russia*, No. 72250/01, 13.7.10.

[110] *Orhan v Turkey*, No. 25656/94, 18.6.02, para. 409; *Sisojeva and others v Latvia*, No. 60654/00, 15.1.07, para. 120; *Konstantin Markin v Russia*, No. 30078/06, 22.3.12, para. 160.

[111] No. 21893/93, 16.9.96.

[112] See also, *Bilgin v Turkey*, No. 23819/94, 16.11.00, paras. 130–6; *Dulas v Turkey*, No. 25801/94, 30.1.01, paras. 76–82; *Akdeniz v Turkey*, No. 23954/91, 31.5.01, paras. 115–21; *Orhan v Turkey*, No. 25656/94, 18.6.02, paras. 401–11.

[113] No. 24276/94, 25.5.98.

pressurised by the authorities to withdraw her application to the European Commission of Human Rights. She also complained that steps had been taken to bring criminal proceedings against her lawyer in relation to the allegations in the application to the European Commission.[114] The Court found that statements she had made repudiating all petitions in her name were not drafted on the initiative of the applicant (e.g. she was taken to the notary's office by a soldier and was not required to pay the notary's fee for drawing up a statement). The Court found there had therefore been improper pressure in violation of former Article 25.

The case of *Oferta Plus S.R.L.* v *Moldova*[115] concerned the non-implementation of a domestic judgment in the applicant company's favour against the Moldovan Ministry of Finance. Criminal proceedings for embezzlement had subsequently been instigated against the applicant company's chief executive. On the basis of the available evidence the Court held that there were sufficiently strong grounds to draw an inference that the proceedings were aimed at discouraging the company from pursuing its Strasbourg case. Furthermore, the chief executive was unable to have unimpeded access to his lawyer whilst in detention. On both counts there was accordingly a violation of Article 34. In *Fedotova* v *Russia*,[116] the Court found a violation of Article 34 as a result of police inquiries concerning the payment of taxes by the applicant's translator and representative in relation to her claim for just satisfaction in the Strasbourg proceedings, which, it found, could have been interpreted by the applicant as an attempt to intimidate her. In *Ryabov* v *Russia*[117] the various steps which were taken by the authorities to enquire about the financial arrangements between the applicant and his lawyer (after a just satisfaction claim had been submitted in the course of proceedings in Strasbourg) were found to have no basis in law. The Court concluded that the authorities had specifically targeted the applicant's representative in order to prevent her from participating in the Strasbourg proceedings, in violation of Article 34. **5.59**

In a number of cases where complaints of intimidation have been made, the Court has not been satisfied that there was sufficient evidence.[118] **5.60**

Article 34 has frequently been invoked by applicants detained in state custody.[119] In *Ilaşcu and others* v *Moldova and Russia*,[120] the applicants complained of various Convention violations in the 'Moldavian Republic of Transdniestria', a region of Moldova which declared its independence in 1991 but which has not been recognised by the international community. The Court found a violation of Article 34 as a result of threats and intimidation made by the Transdniestrian prison authorities against the applicants while they were held in detention. The Court also expressed great concern over a diplomatic note sent by the **5.61**

---

[114] See also *Şarli* v *Turkey*, No. 24490/94, 22.5.01, paras. 81–6, where the Court found a violation of former Article 25 due to criminal proceedings brought against the applicant's lawyer as a result of the applicant's petition to the European Court. The charges including submitting an application with the intention of degrading the state and making pro-PKK propaganda.

[115] No. 14385/04, 19.12.06.

[116] No. 73225/01, 13.4.06.

[117] No. 3896/04, 31.1.08.

[118] See, e.g. *Aksoy* v *Turkey*, No. 21987/93, 18.12.96, para. 106 and *Aydin* v *Turkey*, No. 23178/94, 28.6.97, para. 117; *Berktay* v *Turkey*, No. 22493/93, 1.3.01, para. 209.

[119] See, e.g. *Popov* v *Russia*, No. 26853/04, 13.7.06; *L.M. and others* v *Russia*, Nos. 40081/14, 40088/14 and 40127/14, 15.10.15.

[120] No. 48787/99, 8.7.04.

Russian Government to the Moldovan Government requesting the Moldovan Government to withdraw the observations they had submitted to the Court which had implied Russian responsibility for the alleged violations as a consequence of the Russian military presence in Transdniestria. The Moldovan Government did indeed modify their observations, as requested, which led the Court to conclude as follows:[121]

> such conduct on the part of the Government of the Russian Federation represented a negation of the common heritage of political traditions, ideals, freedom and the rule of law mentioned in the Preamble to the Convention and were capable of seriously hindering its examination of an application lodged in exercise of the right of individual petition and thereby interfering with the right guaranteed by Article 34 of the Convention itself.

5.62   The applicant in *Boicenco* v *Moldova*[122] had alleged severe police brutality and his representatives requested permission for him to be examined by an independent doctor while he was detained in prison and a psychiatric hospital, in order to ascertain his medical condition. The authorities' refusal was held to violate Article 34. It was an important factor in the case that the applicant's lawyers had informed the authorities that they and a doctor needed to see the applicant, and his medical file, for the purpose of proceedings before the European Court. There was a violation of Article 34 in *Shtukaturov* v *Russia*[123] not only because the applicant was prevented from having access to his lawyer during a period of more than six months when he was detained in a psychiatric hospital, but also because of the authorities' failure to comply with a Rule 39 indication by the Court, to allow the applicant access to his lawyer.[124] In *Sergey Antonov* v *Ukraine*[125] the applicant was a prisoner with HIV who had complained about the inadequacy of his medical treatment in prison. The Government produced a handwritten note signed by the applicant stating that he had no complaints about the prison medical staff, but the Court upheld his complaint that he had been intimidated into making a statement which would undermine his application to the Court. Hence, Article 34 was breached. Surveillance of, or interference with, correspondence or case files may violate Article 34, as occurred in *Annagi Hajibeyli* v *Azerbaijan*[126] where the applicant's lawyer's office was searched and his European Court case file seized and held for 76 days, for which there was found to be no justification. In *Cotlet* v *Romania*,[127] Article 34 was violated because of interferences with the applicant prisoner's correspondence with the European Commission and Court of Human Rights (the post was delayed; his letters were opened; and he was not provided with adequate writing materials) and because of the threat that he might be transferred to another prison because of his application to Strasbourg. Similarly, in *Gagiu* v *Romania*,[128] there was a breach of Article 34 because the prison authorities failed to

---

[121]   *Ibid.*, para. 481.

[122]   No. 41088/05, 11.7.06.

[123]   No. 44009/05, 27.3.08. See also *Rasul Jafarov* v *Azerbaijan*, No. 69981/14, 17.3.16 (applicant in detention prevented from seeing his lawyer whose domestic licence to practise had been suspended—violation of Article 34).

[124]   See also *D.B.* v *Turkey*, No. 33526/08, 13.7.10.

[125]   No. 40512/13, 22.10.15.

[126]   No. 2204/11, 22.10.15.

[127]   No. 38565/97, 3.6.03 (there was also a violation of Article 8). See also *Nurmagomedov* v *Russia*, No. 30138/02, 7.6.07; *Yefimenko* v *Russia*, No. 152/04, 12.2.13.

[128]   No. 63258/00, 24.2.09. See also *Naydyon* v *Ukraine*, No. 16474/03, 14.10.10. See, by contrast, *Yepishin* v *Russia*, No. 591/07, dec. 27.6.13 (prison's refusal to pay postage for prisoner to send letters to European Court—no violation of Article 34).

provide the applicant with the materials and documents he needed to be able to correspond with the Court and made several attempts to persuade him from doing so. Where the prison authorities lost 900 pages of papers, as part of a prisoner's application to the European Court, this was found to violate his Article 34 rights.[129]

Threats relating to the instigation of criminal or disciplinary proceedings made against lawyers **5.63** may also infringe Article 34. In *McShane v UK*[130] the Royal Ulster Constabulary (RUC) lodged a complaint with the Law Society about the applicant's lawyer in the course of inquest proceedings. It was alleged that the lawyer had breached an undertaking of confidentiality as a result of the alleged disclosure of information contained in witness statements to the applicant's representative for use in proceedings before the European Court of Human Rights. Even though the complaint was dismissed as unfounded by the Law Society, the Court found a violation of Article 34 because such complaints could have a 'chilling effect' on the exercise of the right of individual application. In *Colibaba v Moldova*,[131] Article 34 was found to have been violated as a result of a letter sent by the Prosecutor-General to the applicant's lawyer warning him that a criminal investigation would be instigated as a result of his allegedly improper complaint to 'international organisations' which, the European Court found, could have had a chilling effect on his intention to pursue an application before the Court. There was a violation of Article 34 in *Khodorkovskiy and Lebedev v Russia*[132] because of the pressure exerted by the authorities on the applicants' lawyers: there were several attempts to have them disbarred; they were subjected to administrative and financial checks; and two foreign lawyers were denied visas. The Court expressly found that such measures had been intended to intimidate the lawyers.

The Grand Chamber has now established that if a state fails to comply with an interim **5.64** measures indication under Rule 39, this may give rise to a violation of Article 34[133] (this is discussed at 2.42 above).

Duty to furnish all necessary facilities (Article 38—former Article 38(1)(a))

There is a further obligation on states under Article 38 to 'furnish all necessary facilities' **5.65** in relation to the Court's examination of a case and its establishment of the facts (formerly Article 38(1)(a)) (see further at 2.127 above). This provision has primarily been invoked where states fail to disclose documents that are relevant to the case, but violations of Article 38 may also be caused by the failure of a respondent state to provide adequate responses to the Court's questions.[134] The Court has underlined that states may not hide behind deficiencies in their domestic laws to justify non-disclosure, but are obliged to put in place such procedures as are needed to ensure that there is unhindered communication and exchange of documents with the Court.[135]

---

[129] *Buldakov v Russia*, No. 23294/07, 19.7.11.
[130] No. 43290/98, 28.5.02.
[131] No. 29089/06, 23.10.07.
[132] Nos. 11082/06 and 13772/05, 25.7.13.
[133] *Mamatkulov and Askarov v Turkey*, Nos. 46827/99 and 46951/99, 4.2.05. See also *Aoulmi v France*, No. 50278/99, 17.1.06; *Ben Khemais v Italy*, No. 246/07, 24.2.09; *Mannai v Italy*, No. 9961/10, 27.3.12; *Salakhov and Islyamova v Ukraine*, No. 28005/08, 14.3.13.
[134] *Nizomkhon Dzhurayev v Russia*, No. 31890/11, 3.10.13.
[135] *Nolan and K. v Russia*, No. 2512/04, 12.2.09, para. 56.

5.66 In *Tanrikulu* v *Turkey*,[136] for example, the Court found it to be 'a matter for grave concern' that the respondent state had failed to disclose certain documentary evidence or to ensure the attendance at oral fact-finding hearings of two public prosecutors. Such failings by the respondent government may lead the Court to draw inferences as to the well-foundedness of the allegations (particularly where only the Government has access to information capable of corroborating or refuting the applicant's allegations).[137] In *Orhan* v *Turkey*[138] the Court was critical of Turkey's failure to provide records relating to security force operations, and the failure to secure the attendance at the European Court fact-finding hearing of a particular commander of military operations or the officer in charge of a military establishment where it was believed the applicant's relatives had been held. Accordingly, Turkey was found to have fallen short of its obligations under Article 38(1)(a). A similar decision was made by the Court in *Tekdağ* v *Turkey*[139] because of the witholding of large parts of the investigation file from the Court. The Turkish Government was also criticised by the Court in *Ahmet Özkan* v *Turkey*[140] for its 'passive attitude in producing documents that were in their possession and which were unquestionably of fundamental importance for elucidating disputed facts, and [its] failure to submit these documents of their own motion at a much earlier stage in the proceedings'. In *Nevmerzhitsky* v *Ukraine*,[141] the Court highlighted the Government's failure to provide information and a medical report relating to the force feeding of the applicant during his pre-trial detention, concluding that Article 38(1)(a) had not been complied with. *Enukidze and Girgvliani* v *Georgia*[142] concerned the abduction and death of the applicants' son at the hands of Ministry of Interior officials: the Court identified myriad failings in the investigation of the case. It also found a violation of Article 38 on account of the Government's failure to submit the complete case files, including crucial CCTV images.

5.67 The failure to produce a single document, if considered by the Court to be particularly critical, may result in a finding of non-compliance with Article 38.[143] That was the case in *Janowiec and others* v *Russia*,[144] which concerned the investigation of the murder of more than 21,000 Polish soldiers and officials by the Soviet secret police in 1940. The refusal by the Russian Government to provide the Court with a copy of the decision made in 2004 to discontinue the investigation (on the basis that it was classified under domestic law) was found to breach Article 38. The Court noted that there had been no domestic judicial review of the justification for the report's secret classification, and reiterated that according to the Vienna Convention,[145] the provisions of internal law cannot be invoked by a state in order to justify its non-compliance with an international treaty.[146] Article 38 was also breached by Russia in the inter-state proceedings brought by Georgia relating to the detention and expulsion of

---

[136] No. 26763/94, 8.7.99.
[137] See, e.g. *Timurtaş* v *Turkey*, No. 23531/94, 13.6.00, paras. 66–7; *Taş* v *Turkey*, No. 24396/94, 14.11.00, paras. 54 and 66.
[138] No. 25656/94, 18.6.02, paras. 266–74.
[139] No. 27699/95, 15.1.04. See also: *Acar* v *Turkey*, No. 26307/95, 8.4.04 (failure to provide case file and video).
[140] No. 21689/93, 6.4.04, para. 481.
[141] No. 54825/00, 5.4.05.
[142] No. 25091/07, 26.4.11.
[143] See, e.g. *Dedovskiy* v *Russia*, No. 7178/03, 15.5.08; *Nolan and K.* v *Russia*, No. 2512/04, 12.2.09.
[144] Nos. 55508/07 and 29520/09, 21.10.13.
[145] Article 27 of the Vienna Convention on the Law of Treaties (23 May 1969).
[146] See also *Al Nashiri* v *Poland*, No. 28761/11, 24.7.14, para. 366 and *Husayn (Abu Zubaydah)* v *Poland*, No. 7511/13, 24.7.14, para. 358.

Georgian nationals, because of its refusal to disclose to the Court two government circulars, which were said to be classified.[147] There was a breach of Article 38 in *Benzer and others* v *Turkey*,[148] a case concerning the deaths of the applicants' relatives caused by the bombing of their village in south-east Turkey in 1994. The applicants obtained and submitted to the Court a copy of the relevant flight log; however, the Government provided no explanation for its failure to disclose the document.

The conduct of the Russian authorities in *Shamayev and others* v *Georgia and Russia*[149] was **5.68** found not to comply with Article 38(1)(a) as they had obstructed the Court's proposed fact-finding mission and denied it access to the applicants detained in prison in Russia. There was also a violation of Article 34 because the applicants were prevented from having contact with their lawyers. The Court has frequently found a failure to comply with Article 38(1)(a) because of the respondent government's non-disclosure of case documents requested by the Court in the course of litigation concerning Chechnya.[150] In the 'extraordinary rendition' cases of *Al Nashiri* v *Poland*,[151] and *Husayn (Abu Zubaydah)* v *Poland*,[152] the Polish authorities' failure to provide disclosure of documents sought by the Court was found to breach Article 38, notwithstanding the Government's claims of confidentiality and secrecy. This also meant that the Court was entitled to draw inferences from the Government's conduct.

---

[147] *Georgia* v *Russia (I)*, No. 13255/07, 3.7.14.
[148] No. 23502/06, 12.11.13.
[149] No. 36378/02, 12.4.05, para. 504.
[150] See, for example, *Imakayeva* v *Russia*, No. 7615/02, 9.11.06; *Baysayeva* v *Russia*, No. 74237/01, 5.4.07; *Akhmadova and Sadulayeva* v *Russia*, No. 40464/02, 10.5.07; *Bitiyeva and X* v *Russia*, Nos. 57953/00 and 37392/03, 21.6.07; *Kukayev* v *Russia*, No. 29361/02, 15.11.07; *Khamila Isayeva* v *Russia*, No. 6846/02, 15.11.07; *Medova* v *Russia*, No. 25385/04, 15.1.09.
[151] No. 28761/11, 24.7.14.
[152] No. 7511/13, 24.7.14.

6

THE SUBSTANTIVE RIGHTS OF
THE EUROPEAN CONVENTION

Article 1: Obligation to Respect Human Rights

6.01 Article 1 states:

> The High Contracting Parties shall secure to everyone within their jurisdiction the rights and freedoms defined in section 1 of this Convention.

Article 1 of the Convention establishes states' overriding obligation to ensure that everyone within their jurisdiction enjoys the rights and freedoms set out in section 1 of the Convention, namely the rights (and limitations on those rights) contained in Articles 2 to 18. Therefore, the state is required to uphold those Articles, regardless of an individual's nationality, residence[1] or any other characteristic. The sole condition is jurisdiction. Article 1 makes no distinction as to the type of rule or measure concerned, and does not exclude any part of a state's jurisdiction from scrutiny under the Convention.[2] The 'jurisdiction' of each contracting state is considered to be 'primarily territorial'.[3] However, in exceptional cases, acts by Convention states 'performed, or producing effects, outside their territories' can constitute an exercise of jurisdiction by them within the meaning of Article 1 of the Convention.[4]

Extra-territorial jurisdiction

6.02 In the leading judgment on the question of extra-territorial jurisdiction, *Al-Skeini and others* v *UK*,[5] (relating to the British Army's occupation of parts of Iraq in 2003) the Grand Chamber reiterated that two such situations had been acknowledged by the Court:

  (i) state agent authority and control; and
  (ii) effective control over an area.

State agent authority and control

6.03 The first category includes acts of diplomatic and consular agents on foreign territory, and also situations where one contracting state, 'through the consent, invitation or acquiescence of the Government of that territory, ... exercises all or some of the public powers normally to be exercised by that Government', including executive and judicial functions carried out on the territory of another state, with its agreement. Jurisdiction may also be applicable under this category where state agents operating outside its territory detain, or otherwise use force against an individual. In such situations, the Court has underlined that the finding of

---

[1] See, e.g. *D* v *UK*, No. 30240/96, 2.5.97; *Amuur* v *France*, No. 19776/92, 25.6.96.

[2] *United Communist Party of Turkey and others* v *Turkey*, No. 19392/92, 30.1.98, para. 29.

[3] *Banković* v *Belgium and others*, No. 52207/99, dec. 12.12.01, para. 59; *Al-Skeini and others* v *UK*, No. 55721/07, 7.7.11, para. 131. See also *Khan* v *UK*, No. 11987/11, dec. 28.1.14 (immigrant applicant who voluntarily returned to his country of origin—no territorial jurisdiction).

[4] *Banković* v *Belgium and others*, No. 52207/99, dec. 12.12.01, para. 67. Under Article 56 of the Convention, states may extend the application of the Convention to territories for whose international relations they have responsibility. See *Chagos Islanders* v *UK*, No. 35622/04, dec. 11.12.12 in which the Court did not accept the applicants' arguments that (in the light of *Al-Skeini*) any possible basis of jurisdiction under Article 1 must take precedence over Article 56.

[5] No. 55721/07, 7.7.11. Prior to that, the leading decision in this area had been *Bankovic* v *Belgium and others*, No. 52207/99, dec. 12.12.01 which concerned the NATO bombing of the RTS broadcasting centre in Belgrade in 1999. Other relevant cases include: *Cyprus* v *Turkey*, Nos. 6780/74 and 6950/75, 10.7.76; *Reinette* v *France*, No. 14009/88, dec. 2.10.89, (1989) 63 DR 189; *Loizidou* v *Turkey*, No. 15318/89, 18.12.96; *Wille* v *Liechtenstein*, No. 28396/95, 27.5.97 and *Issa and others* v *Turkey*, No. 31821/96, dec. 30.5.00.

jurisdiction is not simply a result of control being exercised by the state over the buildings, aircraft or ship in which the individuals were held:

> What is decisive in such cases is the exercise of physical power and control over the person in question.[6]

In its judgment in *Öcalan v Turkey*[7] the Grand Chamber found that the arrest of the leader of the Kurdish Workers' Party (PKK) by Turkish security agents in an aircraft in the international zone of Nairobi airport immediately brought the applicant within the effective control, and therefore the 'jurisdiction', of the state of Turkey. The Court noted that the applicant was then physically forced to return to Turkey by Turkish officials, under whose authority and control he remained once he was back in Turkey.[8] The case of *Al-Saadoon and Mufdhi v UK*[9] concerned the applicants' detention by the British army in southern Iraq in 2003, where the UK was an occupying power. They were held in British detention facilities before being handed over to the Iraqi authorities in 2008. The Court concluded that, as the British army enjoyed *de facto*, and subsequently also, *de jure*, control over the detention centres in question, the applicants were within the UK's jurisdiction. In the subsequent case of *Al-Skeini and others v UK*,[10] the Court also found that the UK had 'assumed authority and responsibility for the maintenance of security in south-east Iraq' in 2003, and accordingly, through its soldiers engaged in security operations, it exercised authority and control over those individuals who were killed during the security operations, thereby establishing a jurisdictional link. The case of *Jaloud v Netherlands*[11] concerned the death of Azhar Sabah Jaloud when a vehicle in which he was a passenger was fired upon while passing through a checkpoint manned by personnel under the command and direct supervision of a Dutch army officer, in south-eastern Iraq in 2004. The Grand Chamber found that the case fell within the jurisdiction of the Netherlands, operating within the limits of its mission as part of the Stabilization Force in Iraq, and for the purpose of asserting authority and control over people passing through the checkpoint.

Effective control over an area

The second category of extra-territorial jurisdiction is where a state exercises effective control of an area outside its national territory, whether through its armed forces or a 'subordinate local administration'. In that situation, the controlling state is obliged to secure the 'entire range of substantive [Convention] rights' within the area which it controls. The determination of 'effective control' is a question of fact in each case, but the Court will primarily assess this on account of the strength of the state's military presence (although the extent of its military, economic or political support for any local subordinate administration will also be relevant). Jurisdiction may therefore be applicable outside the territory covered by the Council of Europe member states (the '*espace juridique*').[12]

6.04

6.05

---

[6] *Al-Skeini and others v UK*, No. 55721/07, 7.7.11, para. 136. See also *Hassan v UK*, No. 29750/09, 16.9.14, paras. 76–80. Jurisdiction is applicable even during the active hostilities phase of an international armed conflict (*Hassan*, paras. 76–7).

[7] No. 46221/99, 12.5.05, para. 91.

[8] See also *Belozorov v Russia and Ukraine*, No. 43611/02, 15.10.15 (applicant arrested and his home searched in Crimea (Ukraine), by Ukrainian and Russian police officers—until he boarded a plane for Moscow, the events fell within the sole jurisdiction of Ukraine, as Ukrainian police officers were in control of the operation).

[9] No. 61498/08, 2.3.10.

[10] No. 55721/07, 7.7.11.

[11] No. 47708/08, 20.11.14.

[12] *Al-Skeini and others v UK*, No. 55721/07, 7.7.11, paras. 138–42. The Court has also previously recognised that 'effective control' may be exercised 'temporarily': see *Issa and others v Turkey*, No. 31821/96, 16.11.04, para.

6.06   In the inter-state case of *Cyprus* v *Turkey*[13] the Court found that as Turkey had effective overall control of northern Cyprus, its responsibility was not confined to the acts of its own soldiers or officials, but was also engaged by the acts of the local administration that survived by virtue of Turkish military and other support.

6.07   In *Ilaşcu and others* v *Moldova and Russia*,[14] the applicants complained of various Convention violations in the 'Moldavian Republic of Transdniestria', a region of Moldova which declared its independence in 1991 but which has not been recognised by the international community. The question of Moldovan responsibility is discussed below (at 6.12), but the Court also found that the responsibility of the Russian Government was engaged, in respect of:

> the unlawful acts committed by the Transdniestrian separatists, regard being had to the military and political support it gave them to help them set up the separatist regime and the participation of its military personnel in the fighting. In acting thus the authorities of the Russian Federation contributed both militarily and politically to the creation of a separatist regime in the region of Transdniestria, which is part of the territory of the Republic of Moldova.[15]

Other factors that led the Court to conclude that Russia's responsibility was engaged included the continuing Russian military presence in the region, and its financial support. Thus, the 'Moldavian Republic of Transdniestria' remained 'under the effective authority, or at the very least under the decisive influence, of the Russian Federation, and in any event ... it survive[d] by virtue of the military, economic, financial and political support given to it by the Russian Federation'.[16] The applicants in *Catan and others* v *Moldova and Russia*[17] were Moldovans who lived in Transdniestria and who were pupils at three Moldovan-language schools and their parents. Invoking Article 2 of Protocol No. 1 (the right to education), they complained about the closure of their schools and their harassment by the separatist Transdniestrian authorities. As regards Russia,[18] the Court acknowledged that there was no evidence of any direct involvement of Russian agents in the actions taken against the applicants' schools, and that the numbers of Russian troops in Transdniestria were significantly reduced. However, on the available evidence, and relying on its findings in *Ilaşcu*, the Court found that Russia exercised effective control over the 'Moldavian Republic of Transdniestria' during the relevant period (2002–2004), in view of its military, economic and political support.

6.08   In *Chiragov and others* v *Armenia*,[19] the applicants had been displaced from their homes and land in the region of Nagorno-Karabakh during armed conflict between Armenia and Azerbaijan in the early 1990s. The Armenian Government argued that it was not responsible

---

74 (Turkish armed forces carrying out military operations in northern Iraq). Like *Banković*, the case of *Marković and others* v *Italy* (No. 1398/03, 14.12.06) was brought by relatives of victims of the NATO bombing of the RTS broadcasting centre in Belgrade in 1999. Their claims in the Italian courts had been dismissed and the Grand Chamber found that accordingly a 'jurisdictional link' existed: if civil proceedings are brought in the domestic courts of a state, the state is required by Article 1 to secure in those proceedings respect for the rights protected by Article 6. There was, however, no violation of Article 6 taken together with Article 1 (see below at 6.319).

   [13]   No. 25781/94, 10.5.01, para. 77. See also *Djavit An* v *Turkey*, No. 20652/92, 20.2.03, paras. 18–23.
   [14]   No. 48787/99, 8.7.04.
   [15]   *Ibid.*, para. 382. A similar conclusion was reached in *Ivanţoc and others* v *Moldova and Russia*, No. 23687/05, 15.11.11 and in *Mozer* v *Moldova and Russia*, No. 11138/10, 23.2.16.
   [16]   *Ibid.*, para. 392.
   [17]   Nos. 43370/04, 8252/05 & 18454/06, 19.10.12.
   [18]   Like the *Ilaşcu* case, these matters were held to fall within the jurisdiction of both states. For the position of Moldova, the same reasons were relied on as in *Ilaşcu*.
   [19]   No. 13216/05, 16.6.15.

for the actions of the autonomous 'Nagorno-Karabakh Republic'. However, in light of the available evidence, the Court concluded that Armenia exercised effective control over the Nagorno-Karabakh territory in view of its military, political, financial and other support: 'Armenia … has had a significant and decisive influence over the [Nagorno-Karabakh Republic], … the two entities are highly integrated in virtually all important matters and … this situation persists to this day.'[20]

By contrast, in *Bankovic* v *Belgium and others*[21] the respondent Council of Europe/NATO states were found to have been acting outside their 'jurisdiction' when carrying out a NATO bombing raid on the *RTS* broadcasting centre in Belgrade during the Kosovo conflict in 1999, as they were not considered to be in effective control of the territory in question. **6.09**

Other forms of exercise of extra-territorial jurisdiction

Other examples of the application of extra-territorial jurisdiction include acts on board vessels registered in, or flying the flag of, the state.[22] The participation of a state in the defence of legal proceedings against it in another state does not equate to an exercise of extra-territorial jurisdiction.[23] **6.10**

Jurisdiction normally exercised throughout a state's territory

The case of *Assanidze* v *Georgia*[24] concerned the applicant's continuing detention in the Ajarian Autonomous Republic in violation of Georgian law. The central Government had taken legal and political steps to secure the applicant's release by the local Ajarian authorities, but to no avail. The Grand Chamber found the Ajarian Autonomous Republic to be an integral part of the territory of Georgia and subject to its competence and control. Thus while the Court was able to conclude that the unlawful detention was directly imputable to the Ajarian authorities, it was the Georgian state that was solely responsible under the Convention. **6.11**

Whilst 'jurisdiction' is presumed to be exercised normally throughout a state's territory, the Court has confirmed that this presumption may exceptionally be limited, particularly where a state is prevented from exercising its authority in part of its territory. The Court has acknowledged that this may result from military occupation by the armed forces of another state which effectively controls the territory concerned, from acts of war or rebellion, or the acts of a foreign state supporting the installation of a separatist state.[25] However, even in such a situation, the state may still have jurisdiction, because the state will be required to exercise its positive obligations: both in relation to measures needed to re-establish control over the **6.12**

---

[20] *Chiragov and others* v *Armenia*, No. 13216/05, 16.6.15, para. 186.

[21] No. 52207/99, dec. 12.12.01. In declaring the case inadmissible on grounds of 'jurisdiction', the Court in *Bankovic* did not need to decide whether the respondent states could be held liable under the European Convention for acts carried out by NATO. A similar issue arose, concerning the acts and omissions of UNMIK and KFOR (which were held *not* to be attributable to the respondent Convention states) in *Behrami* v *France*, No. 71412/01 and *Saramati* v *France, Germany and Norway*, No. 78166/01, dec. 2.5.07 which is discussed at 4.157 above in the section on *ratione personae*.

[22] *Bankovic* v *Belgium and others*, No. 52207/99, dec. 12.12.01, para. 73. See *Medvedyev and others* v *France*, No. 3394/03, 29.3.10 (crew of merchant ship intercepted and boarded by French warship were within France's jurisdiction for the purposes of Article 1); *Hirst Jamaa and others* v *Italy*, No. 27765/09, 23.2.12 (migrants intercepted on the high seas by boats of the Italian armed forces).

[23] See: *McElhinney* v *Ireland and UK*, No. 31253/96, 9.2.00; *Kalogeropoulou and others* v *Greece and Germany*, No. 59021/00, dec. 12.12.02; *Manoilescu and Dobrescu* v *Romania*, No. 60861/00, dec. 3.3.05.

[24] No. 71503/01, 8.4.04.

[25] *Ilaşcu and others* v *Moldova and Russia*, No. 48787/99, 8.7.04, para. 312.

territory in question, and measures to ensure respect for the applicant's individual rights (which may require undertaking judicial, political or administrative measures).[26] In *Ilaşcu and others v Moldova and Russia*[27] (discussed above) the Moldovan Government asserted that it was not in control of the region of Transdniestria. This was a point which the Court accepted, nevertheless the applicants were considered to come within the jurisdiction of the Republic of Moldova for the purposes of Article 1 and the Court found that the Moldovan authorities had failed to take sufficient steps to secure the applicants' release from detention since 2001. Therefore, the Court concluded that the Moldovan Government's responsibility was engaged under the Convention, for failing to comply with its positive obligations.[28]

6.13 The case of *Sargsyan v Azerbaijan*[29] concerned the applicants' forcible displacement in 1992 during the armed conflict between Azerbaijan and Armenia over the Nagorno-Karabakh territory. The applicants had lived in a village which was within Azerbaijani territory, but its status and exact location were disputed—it was situated on the front line between the Azerbaijani forces and those of the 'Nagorno-Karabakh Republic'. The Azerbaijani Government sought to argue that the '*Ilaşcu* exception' applied—in other words, that the limitation of the territorial state's responsibility in respect of parts of its territory which are occupied or under the effective control of another entity could also be applied to 'disputed areas'. However, this argument was explicitly rejected by the Court which concluded that Azerbaijan had jurisdiction as the territorial state and 'full responsibility under the Convention'.[30]

6.14 The case of *El-Masri v former Yugoslav Republic of Macedonia*[31] concerned the 'extraordinary rendition' of the applicant by the Macedonian authorities into the custody of the CIA. One of the issues which arose there was whether the applicant's ill-treatment by CIA agents at Skopje airport was imputable to the respondent state. This question was answered in the affirmative by the Court because the treatment was carried out in the presence of Macedonian officials, and within its jurisdiction.[32]

6.15 In *Boumediene and others v Bosnia and Herzegovina*,[33] the Court declared inadmissible a complaint brought by a group of Algerians who, before the Convention entered into force with respect to Bosnia and Herzegovina, were handed over to the US authorities and taken to Guantánamo Bay on suspicion of planning a terrorist attack. On the facts, the Court found that the authorities of Bosnia and Herzegovina had taken all possible steps to protect the applicants' rights, as had been required by the domestic courts (without considering whether they would have had an obligation under the Convention to intervene vis-à-vis the US authorities on behalf of the applicants even in the absence of domestic court decisions requiring such steps to be taken). In *Stephens v Malta (No. 1)*[34] the applicant was arrested and

---

[26] *Ibid.*, paras. 333–9.

[27] No. 48787/99, 8.7.04.

[28] See also *Ivanţoc and others v Moldova and Russia*, No. 23687/05, 15.11.11 and *Mozer v Moldova and Russia*, No. 11138/10, 23.2.16 in both of which cases the Court found that Moldova had jurisdiction under Article 1, but also that the Moldovan authorities had subsequently complied with their positive obligations in order to seek to secure the applicants' Convention rights.

[29] No. 40167/06, 16.6.15.

[30] *Ibid.*, para. 150.

[31] No. 39630/09, 13.12.12.

[32] *Ibid.*, para. 206. See also *Al Nashiri v Poland*, No. 28761/11, 24.7.14 and *Husayn (Abu Zubaydah) v Poland*, No. 7511/13, 24.7.14.

[33] Nos. 38703/06, 40123/06, 43301/06, 43302/06, 2131/07 and 2141/07, dec. 18.11.08.

[34] No. 11956/07, 21.4.09.

detained in Spain under a warrant issued by a Maltese court seeking his extradition, which was subsequently found to be issued *ultra vires*. The Maltese Government's responsibility under Article 5 (not Spain's) was held to be engaged because the applicant's deprivation of liberty had its sole origin in the measures taken by the Maltese authorities.

Attribution

It may sometimes be argued that particular acts or omissions are not *attributable* to the particular respondent state, and therefore that the case does not fall within that state's jurisdiction. The cases of *Behrami and Behrami* v *France* and *Saramati* v *France, Germany and Norway*[35] concerned complaints of Convention violations which occurred in Kosovo while it was a territory administered by the UN (through UNMIK[36]) and subject to a security force under UN auspices (KFOR—which was made up of multinational brigades), both of which were established under a resolution of the UN Security Council. *Behrami* concerned the death of the applicant's son, one of a group of children who had come across an undetonated cluster bomb, for which the applicant blamed the negligence of French KFOR troops. The applicant in *Saramati* complained about his extra-judicial detention by KFOR. The Grand Chamber concluded, however, that the relevant acts or omissions in these cases were attributable to the UN (acting through KFOR and UNMIK), rather than to the individual respondent states, on the basis that KFOR was exercising powers lawfully delegated by the UN Security Council and that UNMIK was a subsidiary organisation of the UN. Therefore, the applications were held to be incompatible *ratione personae* with the provisions of the Convention.[37]   **6.16**

The UK raised the question of attribution in *Al-Jedda* v *UK*,[38] arguing that the applicant's detention in Iraq (by the British armed forces) was attributable to the UN rather than to the UK. However, the Grand Chamber rejected this submission, finding that the role of the UN in Iraq in 2004 was quite different to its position in Kosovo in 1999. It noted that there had been no UN Security Council resolution in force when the UK had entered Iraq in 2003 (with the US and other coalition partners). Subsequent resolutions did not assign a security role to the UN, and the US and UK continued to exercise powers of government (through the Coalition Provisional Authority). The applicant was detained in a detention facility in Basra City, controlled exclusively by British armed forces, and he was therefore considered to be within the authority and control of the UK.   **6.17**

Other points on jurisdiction

The case of *Bosphorus Hava Yollari Turizm Ve Ticaret AS* v *Ireland*[39] concerned the impounding of the applicant's leased aircraft in Ireland, as a result of a directly effective EC Regulation implementing UN sanctions in respect of the then Federal Republic of Yugoslavia.[40] As the measures had been taken by the Irish authorities in its territory, following a decision by the Minister of Transport, the Court found that the applicant company fell within the jurisdiction of the respondent state.   **6.18**

---

[35] Nos. 71412/01 and 78166/01, dec. 2.5.07.
[36] The United Nations Interim Administration Mission in Kosovo.
[37] See also the discussion about the related concept of inadmissibility *ratione personae* (at 4.157).
[38] No. 27021/08, 7.7.11.
[39] No. 45036/98, 30.6.05.
[40] EC Regulation 990/93 implementing UNSC Resolution 820(1993).

6.19 As discussed above, liability under the Convention will normally arise in respect of an individual who is 'within the jurisdiction' of a Convention state, in that they are physically present on its territory. However, there are exceptions to this principle, as was found to be the case in *Galić v Netherlands*.[41] There, the fact that the International Criminal Tribunal for the former Yugoslavia (ICTY) was situated in the Netherlands was not sufficient to attribute the applicant's complaints about proceedings before the ICTY to the Netherlands.

inadmissability jurisdiction

6.20 An applicant who complains to the European Court about a matter which is found not to be within the respondent state's jurisdiction will have their application declared inadmissible under Article 35(3)(a). This is discussed further in chapter 4—see the discussion of the *ratione personae* admissibility condition at 4.157 above.

6.21 It is an important aspect of the Convention system that it does not specify how each contracting state is to ensure that the Convention is upheld. That is a matter for each state party. Article 1 does not, for example, necessarily require incorporation of the Convention into the domestic law of the state.

6.22 Because Article 1 itself defines the overriding obligation on state parties to ensure observance of the Convention's substantive rights, it cannot be the subject of a separate breach of the Convention. Accordingly, the European Commission of Human Rights rejected the Cypriot Government's arguments that Article 1 had been breached in *Cyprus v Turkey*.[42] Nevertheless, Article 1 may be invoked by the Court in conjunction with the other substantive rights and is linked to the fundamental principle that the Convention is to be interpreted in order to guarantee rights that are practical and effective, rather than theoretical or illusory[43] (see also above at 5.15). Article 1 is frequently referred to by the Court to strengthen the extent of the substantive rights. For example, Article 1 has been invoked in conjunction with the obligation to protect the right to life under Article 2, and to justify the finding that Article 2 requires some form of effective official investigation when individuals have been killed as a result of the use of force.[44]

6.23 It may also be invoked by the Court when the extent of the state's positive obligations are in question[45] (see also above at 5.18). For example, in *A v UK*,[46] Article 1 was referred to by the Court in finding that the respondent government could be liable under Article 3 of the Convention for its failure to ensure that the law adequately protected a young child from being beaten by his stepfather. The Court held that Article 1, taken together with Article 3, requires the state to take measures designed to ensure that individuals within its jurisdiction are not subjected to torture or inhuman or degrading treatment or punishment, including ill-treatment carried out by private individuals.[47] Consequently, the state

---

[41] No. 22617/07, dec. 9.6.09 (discussed further at 4.157 above).
[42] Nos. 6780/74 and 6950/75, 10.7.76.
[43] See, e.g. *Soering v UK*, No. 14038/88, Series A, No. 161, 7.7.89, para. 87.
[44] See, e.g. *McCann v UK*, No. 18984/91, Series A, No. 324, 27.9.95, para. 161; *Tanrikulu v Turkey*, No. 26763/94, 8.7.99, para. 101; *Akkoç v Turkey*, Nos. 22947/93 and 22948/93, 10.10.00, para. 97.
[45] See, e.g. *Vgt Verein Gegen Tierfabriken v Switzerland*, No. 24699/94, 28.6.01, paras. 45–7—application of Article 1 and Article 10 in a case concerning 'political advertising' on television.
[46] No. 25599/94, 23.9.98.
[47] See also *Z and others v UK*, No. 29392/95, 10.5.01, para. 73.

must ensure that there is effective deterrence to prevent such treatment of children and other vulnerable people.

Article 2: The Right to Life

Article 2 states: **6.24**

1. Everyone's right to life shall be protected by law. No one shall be deprived of his life intentionally save in the execution of a sentence of a court following his conviction of a crime for which this penalty is provided by law.
2. Deprivation of life shall not be regarded as inflicted in contravention of this Article when it results from the use of force which is no more than absolutely necessary:
   (a) in defence of any person from unlawful violence;
   (b) in order to effect a lawful arrest or to prevent the escape of a person lawfully detained;
   (c) in action lawfully taken for the purpose of quelling a riot or insurrection.

The protection of the right to life is regarded as one of the most fundamental of the   **6.25**
Convention rights; it 'enshrines one of the basic values of the democratic societies making up the Council of Europe'.[48] Deprivations of life are therefore subject to 'the most careful scrutiny' by the Court.[49] Under Article 15 of the Convention, there can be no derogation from Article 2 (other than in respect of deaths resulting from lawful acts of war). Article 2 comprises both positive and negative aspects: a positive duty to protect life and a negative obligation to refrain from the unlawful taking of life. The positive duty arises from a reading of Article 2 in conjunction with Article 1 of the Convention, and imposes, inter alia, an obligation to carry out an effective official investigation when an individual has been killed as a result of the use of force or other fatal incident.

Article 2 relates both to intentional and unintentional killings. Article 2(2) sets out an   **6.26**
exhaustive list of the circumstances in which it is permissible to use force (no more than is *absolutely necessary*) that may result, as the unintended outcome of the use of force, in the deprivation of life,[50] as well as regulating the intentional taking of life.

The use of force has to be strictly proportionate to the relevant Article 2(2) aim. This will   **6.27**
require consideration of the nature of the aim pursued, the nature of the risk to life inherent in the particular case and the extent of the risk that loss of life might be caused.

The scope of Article 2 is discussed further below in the following contexts: police opera-   **6.28**
tions and the use of lethal force (6.29); operations by military and security forces (6.40); deaths in custody (6.49); enforced disappearances (6.59); self-inflicted deaths in state custody and state institutions (6.61); death penalty and deportations creating a risk to life (6.65); victims of crime—the duties of prevention and investigation (6.67); the duty to protect life: environmental cases; hazards and accidents (6.97) and health care, abortion, euthanasia and assisted suicide (6.101).

---

[48] See, e.g. *McCann* v *UK*, No. 18984/91, Series A, No. 324, 27.9.95, para. 147.
[49] See, e.g. *Gül* v *Turkey*, No. 22676/93, 14.12.00, para. 78.
[50] *Stewart* v *UK*, No. 10044/82, dec. 10.7.84, 39 DR 162, pp 169–71.

Police operations and the use of lethal force

6.29 The use of lethal force by the police or security forces will be the subject of close scrutiny by the Court, both in respect of the broad legal framework and the planning and conduct of the particular operation in question. Policing operations must accordingly be sufficiently regulated by the domestic law, incorporating a system of adequate and effective safeguards against arbitrariness and the abuse of force. This obligation was found to be breached in *Makaratzis* v *Greece*[51] (discussed below at 6.38) because the applicable legislation regulating the use of firearms in Greece dated back to World War II. Although the Court was also highly critical of the chaotic way in which the police had used their firearms, the focus of the majority of the Grand Chamber was on the state of the domestic law. This was described by the Court as being 'obsolete and incomplete' because it failed to provide the police with clear guidelines and criteria governing the use of force in peacetime.[52] Similarly, the Court found a violation of Article 2 in *Soare and others* v *Romania*[53] (concerning the shooting of a Roma man by the police) because there were insufficient provisions in the domestic law regulating the use of weapons during police operations and there were no guidelines on the planning and management of operations.

6.30 The planning and control of a police operation must minimise the risk of loss of life.[54] In the leading case of *McCann and others* v *UK*,[55] concerning the fatal shooting by the British security services of three members of an IRA Active Service Unit in Gibraltar, the Court emphasised that in judging whether the force used was 'absolutely necessary', it should apply a stricter and more compelling test than that applied in considering whether state action is 'necessary in a democratic society'.[56] The Court rejected arguments that the incompatibility with Article 2 of national law and practice (as to the training and instruction of state agents) in itself violated the Convention, and that the inquest proceedings were inadequate. It also found that the soldiers had honestly and reasonably (albeit mistakenly) believed that it was necessary to shoot the suspects in order to prevent them from detonating a bomb and causing serious loss of life. However, by ten votes to nine the Court held that Article 2 had been violated as a result of the failures in the conduct and planning of the operation. The Court focused on the decision not to prevent the suspects from travelling into Gibraltar, the authorities' failure to make sufficient allowances for the possibility that their intelligence assessments might, at least in part, have been wrong, and the automatic recourse to lethal force when the soldiers opened fire. The Court was again split by the narrowest of margins in *Andronicou and Constantinou* v *Cyprus*,[57] which reflects the difficulties inherent in assessing police operations. There, the Court found no violation of the right to life (by five votes to four) arising from the fatal shooting by the police of a man and his fiancée whom he had taken hostage in his flat. They were shot dead when the police stormed the flat following

---

[51] No. 50385/99, 20.12.04.

[52] *Ibid.*, para. 70. But see also the concurring opinion of Judges Costas, Bratza, Lorenzen and Vajić (arguing that it was the conduct of the operation, not the legal framework, which should have led to the finding of a violation of Article 2). See also the Joint partly dissenting opinion of Judges Rozakis, Tulkens, Zupančič, Gyulumyan, Ziemele, Kalaydjieva and Karakaş in *Giuliani and Gaggio* v *Italy*, No. 23458/02, 24.3.11.

[53] No. 24329/02, 22.2.11.

[54] See, e.g. *Nachova and others* v *Bulgaria*, Nos. 43577/98 and 43579/98, 6.7.05, para. 103.

[55] No. 18984/91, Series A, No. 324, 27.9.95.

[56] *Ibid.*, para. 149.

[57] No. 25052/94, 9.10.97.

several hours of negotiation. The Court held that the use of lethal force had not exceeded what was 'absolutely necessary' and found that the rescue operation had been adequately planned and organised. The test applied in such situations is that the operations should minimise to the greatest extent possible any risk to the lives of those involved. However, there was a substantive violation of Article 2 in *Shchiborshch and Kuzmina v Russia*[58] because of inadequacies in the planning and conduct of a police operation, when the police were asked to assist in the hospitalisation of a man suffering from a psychiatric disorder. As he was in a delirious state the man believed the police to be burglars, threatened them with a knife and barricaded himself in his kitchen. After failed negotiations, the police stormed the kitchen. The man was seriously injured and later died in hospital. The Court found there was insufficient evidence to establish that he was killed directly as a result of the police use of force, but the Court was critical of various aspects of the operation: the police officers had no special training to deal with mental health patients; they should have been accompanied by qualified medical personnel and they delayed in calling for emergency psychiatric assistance; they used force as if dealing with any armed offender; and the storming of the kitchen was not properly planned.

The case of *Gül v Turkey*[59] was distinguished from *Andronicou*, where the applicant's husband **6.31** was shot dead by police officers as he answered their knock at his door in the early hours of the morning: 'the reaction … of opening fire with automatic weapons on an unseen target in a residential block inhabited by innocent civilians, women and children was … grossly disproportionate'. By contrast, in *Ahmet Özkan and others v Turkey*,[60] the decision of the Turkish security forces to open intensive fire on a village, in response to shots fired at them, was found to be 'absolutely necessary' in order to protect life. However, their failure then to check whether there were any civilian casualties violated the obligation under Article 2 to protect life. The case of *Celniku v Greece*[61] concerned the fatal wounding of a man during an attempted arrest by an off-duty police officer. The officer's gun was only discharged because the victim kicked his hand, which was holding a firearm that then went off. The Court therefore found that the use of force was not imputable to the state. Nevertheless, Article 2 was found to have been violated because the authorities had been negligent in conducting the operation and had not taken appropriate care to ensure that any risk to those present at the scene of the incident was kept to a minimum. The applicant in *Trévalec v Belgium*[62] was a reporter who had obtained permission from the police to film the operation of a unit responding to criminal gang activity. He was shot and seriously injured when police officers were apprehending suspects and they mistook his camera for a weapon. The officers had believed in good faith that their lives were at risk and had used their weapon in self-defence, believing they were acting lawfully. Nevertheless, Article 2 was found to be violated because the officers at the incident had not been specifically informed of the applicant's presence, and also in view of the fact that the applicant had not been given any safety instructions and

---

[58] No. 5269/08, 16.1.14 (there was also a separate violation of Article 2 because of the failure to investigate the planning and control of the operation).

[59] No. 22676/93, 14.12.00, para. 82.

[60] No. 21689/93, 6.4.04. See also *Perk and others v Turkey*, No. 50739/99, 28.3.06 (police stormed flat, killing occupants, knowing suspects were armed and believing that they planned to carry out terrorist attack—no violation).

[61] No. 21449/04, 5.7.07.

[62] No. 30812/07, 14.6.11.

had not been told to remain on the sidelines at the scene. The central facts of a case will often be hotly disputed by the parties, and in *Soare and others* v *Romania*[63] (discussed at 6.29) the Court emphasised that as the applicant had established a prima facie case, it was then for the Government to provide a plausible explanation for the injury caused by a shot fired at close range. However, the inadequacies in the investigation, including the failure to ascertain whether or not the applicant had been armed with a knife and whether he had stabbed the police officer, meant that the authorities had failed to demonstrate that the potentially lethal force used against the applicant had not gone beyond the bounds of what was absolutely necessary.

6.32 The use of lethal force for the purposes of self-defence and to effect an arrest was found not to be disproportionate in *Yüksel Erdoğan and others* v *Turkey*,[64] a case concerning the shooting by the police of the applicants' relatives in a café in central Istanbul. The police were responding to information that the men were armed. The Court accepted the domestic court findings that the police had ordered the deceased to surrender and gave the necessary warnings before shooting—and that the police only started shooting after having been fired at. There was no violation of Article 2 in *Bubbins* v *UK*,[65] a case concerning the fatal shooting of the applicant's brother following a two-hour siege of his flat. It was later discovered that the gun which he had been holding was a replica. The Court acknowledged that the police officer who had fired the fatal shot had honestly believed at the time that his life was in danger and that it was necessary to open fire in order to protect himself and his colleagues. The use of force was 'highly regrettable', but not disproportionate (and nor were there any significant deficiencies in the planning and control of the police operation). There was also no violation of Article 2 in *Giuliani and Gaggio* v *Italy*,[66] a case that concerned the fatal shooting of demonstrator Carlo Giuliani by a member of the *carabiniere* during clashes at the G8 summit in Genoa in 2001. The Court found that the officer had honestly believed that his life was in real and imminent danger during a violent attack on his jeep by demonstrators, and that he used his pistol as a means of defence against the attack. The use of force was accordingly not found to be disproportionate.[67]

6.33 There was a rather different outcome in *Aydan* v *Turkey*,[68] where a man was fatally wounded by shots fired by a gendarme officer from a military jeep while he was waiting for a bus, close to a demonstration. The national courts found that the officer should not be given a criminal penalty since he had exceeded the limits of self-defence while in an excusable state of emotion, fear or panic. However, the European Court distinguished that situation from a case in which an officer resorted to lethal force due to an honest belief which was considered to be valid at the time but which subsequently turned out to be mistaken. The Court found

---

[63] No. 24329/02, 22.2.11.

[64] No. 57049/00, 15.2.07. See also *Camekan* v *Turkey*, No. 54241/08, 28.1.14 (use of force had not exceeded what was absolutely necessary in order to ensure the defence of an individual against violence and in particular to proceed with a lawful arrest—no violation of Article 2 (by 4 votes to 3)).

[65] No. 50196/99, 17.3.05. See also *Huohvanainen* v *Finland*, No. 57389/00, 13.3.07.

[66] No. 23458/02, 24.3.11.

[67] Seven judges, dissenting, argued that there had been substantive violations of Article 2 as a result of (1) deficiencies in the domestic legislative framework, and (2) failures in the organisation and planning of the police operation, and also that there was a procedural violation of Article 2 as a result of inadequacies in the investigation.

[68] No. 16281/10, 12.3.13.

that the use of force was not absolutely necessary (in violation of Article 2) as it had not been sufficiently established that the danger created by the demonstrators' attack had been extremely violent, and therefore it could not be concluded that the gendarme officer had acted in the honest belief that his own life (or the lives of his colleagues) had been in danger. There were also separate findings of a violation of Article 2 due to the failure to impose a criminal penalty on the gendarme officer and the ineffective investigation. In *Ataykaya* v *Turkey*[69] the applicant's son got caught up in a demonstration and he was killed when he was hit on the head by a tear gas canister fired by a member of the security forces. As those facts were not disputed, the burden was on the Government to show that the use of force had been no more than was absolutely necessary. The Court then went on to consider the adequacy of the investigation, finding various deficiencies, including the failure to identify and question the individual who had fired the tear gas grenade, the failure to obtain an expert report as to the firing of the tear gas and delays in the progression of the investigation. Therefore, as there had been 'no serious investigation', the Government had not shown that the use of force had been absolutely necessary and proportionate. Furthermore, it was also not established that the preparation and supervision of the operation had reduced the risk to life to a minimum, and the authorities had not put in place an appropriate legislative and administrative framework. Accordingly there were both substantive and procedural violations of Article 2. In *Brady* v *UK*[70] the applicant's father was shot dead by the police during a robbery. Having been tipped off, the police were waiting at the scene (a working men's club) and police officers gave evidence at an inquest that the man had been shot after making a threatening movement with an object in his right hand (which turned out to be a small torch). In declaring the application inadmissible, the Court found that the use of lethal force had been absolutely necessary for the purpose of defending the police from unlawful violence within the meaning of Article 2(2)(a).

In *Kelly* v *UK*,[71] the applicant's son was shot dead by soldiers whilst he was joyriding and driving through a roadblock in Belfast. In rejecting the application as manifestly ill-founded, the European Commission of Human Rights accepted that the soldiers' actions were intended to effect a lawful arrest (Article 2(2)(b)) of people who were reasonably believed to be terrorists and that their use of force was justified (when assessed 'against the background of the events in Northern Ireland'). However, in *Nachova and others* v *Bulgaria*,[72] the Grand Chamber found Article 2 to have been violated as a result of the fatal shooting of two Roma men by the military police during an attempt to arrest them for going absent without leave from compulsory military service. Firstly, the legal framework was 'fundamentally deficient' as the relevant regulations on the use of firearms by the military police were not published and contained no clear safeguards to prevent the arbitrary deprivation of life. It was of 'grave concern' to the Court that they 'effectively permitted lethal force to be used when arresting a member of the armed forces for even the most minor offence'.[73] Furthermore, as the arresting officers were instructed to use all available means to make an arrest, the Court found that the planning and control of the operation 'betrayed a deplorable disregard for the pre-eminence

6.34

---

[69] No. 50275/08, 22.7.14.
[70] No. 55151/00, dec. 3.4.01.
[71] No. 17579/90, dec. 31.1.93, 74 DR 139.
[72] Nos. 43577/98 and 43579/98, 6.7.05. This case is discussed further below at 6.78 and in relation to Article 14.
[73] *Ibid.*, para. 99.

of the right to life'.[74] The Court also found that the arresting officers must have been aware that neither man was armed nor had previously used violence or posed any threat to anyone else. This led to an unequivocal statement by the Court, that: 'recourse to potentially deadly force cannot be considered as "absolutely necessary" where it is known that the person to be arrested poses no threat to life or limb and is not suspected of having committed a violent offence'.[75] Finally, the officer who shot the men was found to have used grossly excessive force. In *Putintseva* v *Russia*,[76] a military conscript was shot and killed while attempting to escape as he was being escorted back to his detention unit to complete a disciplinary sentence he had received for being absent without leave. As with *Nachova*, Article 2 was violated because the relevant legal framework was 'fundamentally deficient'—applying a test as to whether the use of force was 'legitimate' rather than whether it was 'absolutely necessary'. Under the domestic law, it was lawful to shoot any fugitive who did not surrender immediately in response to an oral warning or the firing of a warning shot in the air. Furthermore, the use of firearms to prevent the conscript from escaping had breached Article 2, as he had not been armed and he had not represented a danger to anyone else, and there had been other means available to prevent his escape. He was known to have had psychological difficulties, but the sergeant who had escorted and shot him had received no clear guidance in order to minimise the risk to life.

6.35　The case of *Alikaj and others* v *Italy*[77] concerned the fatal shooting by the police of a young man after he had been stopped in his car (with three friends) on the motorway for speeding. When he ran away, one police officer tried to pursue him in slippery conditions in the dark without a torch, eventually firing a shot which hit the victim in the heart. The man had not been armed and there was no reason to believe the young men presented a danger or had committed violent crimes. Accordingly, the use of force was not considered 'absolutely necessary'. There was a substantive violation of Article 2 in *Haász and Szabó* v *Hungary*,[78] where the actions of two police officers themselves created a situation in which they unnecessarily used potentially lethal force. Responding to a call about a suspicious car which was parked up at night time, the officers stopped in front of the car to block it and ran towards the car. Inside the car were two women who had decided to spend the night in the car after an excursion. Seeing the men running towards them, they attempted to drive off and the officer fired at the car (without injuring the occupants). The Court noted that neither of the occupants was wanted by the police, nor posed any known danger, and it found that they could not have known that the two men running towards them were police officers, as they were in plain clothes, had no insignia and drove an unmarked car. The officers were found to have failed to minimise the risk of the events turning into a life-threatening situation culminating in the use of firearms.

6.36　In *Saoud* v *France*[79] the Court held that the use of force by police officers was justified in order to arrest a young man who suffered from schizophrenia, and to ensure the physical safety of his mother and sisters. However, following his arrest he was pinned to the ground by police

---

[74]　*Ibid.*, paras. 103–5.
[75]　*Ibid.*, para. 107.
[76]　No. 33498/04, 10.5.12.
[77]　No. 47357/08, 29.3.11.
[78]　Nos. 11327/14 and 11613/14, 13.10.15.
[79]　No. 9375/02, 9.10.07.

officers for 35 minutes and he died of a cardiac arrest. No medical examination of the man had been carried out and the authorities had not issued precise instructions about the use of such a restraint technique. Accordingly, there was a violation of Article 2. There was no substantive violation of Article 2 in *Scavuzzo-Hager and others v Switzerland*[80] in circumstances where a disturbed man died after having been arrested by the police. The authorities later established that he had died as a result of an excessive intake of drugs. There was no liability under Article 2(2)(b) of the Convention as the Court found that it had been impossible for the arresting officers to know that the man was so vulnerable that the slightest impact on his body could lead to fatal complications. There was also no breach of the positive obligation to protect life. The police officers had acted appropriately in immediately calling for an ambulance and placing the unconscious man in the lateral safety position.

6.37 The use of force may be justified under Article 2(2)(c), in cases where the action is taken 'for the purpose of quelling a riot or insurrection'. This provision was breached in *Şimşek and others v Turkey*,[81] where police opened fire on demonstrators in Istanbul, causing a number of deaths and multiple injuries. The evidence established that, in order to disperse the crowd, police officers shot directly at the demonstrators without first having recourse to less life-threatening methods, such as tear gas, water cannons or rubber bullets. The Court was also critical of the police for acting 'in the grip of panic' and for the absence of any centralised policing command, and was critical of the authorities for failing to provide the police with equipment such as tear gas, plastic bullets or water cannon. In *Stewart v UK*,[82] the accidental fatal shooting of a 13-year-old boy by a British soldier in Belfast was found by the Commission not to violate Article 2 on the basis that the use of plastic bullets had been justified in the circumstances to quell a riot and that the death had occurred because, as the soldier fired, aiming at the legs of a person leading the riot, he was hit by missiles and his aim was deflected.

6.38 Article 2 may apply, exceptionally, even though the use of force does not in fact have lethal consequences. This will depend upon an assessment of the extent to which life was put at risk, by considering, inter alia, the degree and type of force used and the intention or aim behind the use of force.[83] In *Makaratzis v Greece*,[84] the police opened fire on a car that went through a red light, and several police road blocks, in the centre of Athens, seriously injuring the applicant, who was driving. The applicant was chased by a large number of police officers using revolvers, pistols and submachine-guns. The Court accepted that the police did not intend to kill the applicant but, irrespective of that, the police officers' excessive use of firearms had put his life at risk, and accordingly the case fell within the scope of Article 2.

---

[80] No. 41773/98, 7.2.06.

[81] Nos. 35072/97 and 37194/97, 26.7.05. See also *Evrim Öktem v Turkey*, No. 9207/03, 4.11.08.

[82] No. 10044/82, dec. 10.7.84, 39 DR 162.

[83] See, e.g. *Ilhan v Turkey*, No. 22277/93, 27.6.00, para. 75; *Berktay v Turkey*, No. 22493/93, 1.3.01, paras. 153–4; *Green v UK*, No. 28079/94, dec. 19.5.05; *Evrim Öktem v Turkey*, No. 9207/03, 4.11.08; *Denis Vasilyev v Russia*, No. 32704/04, 17.12.09; *Soare and others v Romania*, No. 24329/02, 22.2.11; *Peker v Turkey (No. 2)*, No. 42136/06, 12.4.11 (prisoner injured by gunshot wound to his leg—three dissenting judges argued that the Court should have applied Article 3, not Article 2); *Trévalec v Belgium*, No. 30812/07, 14.6.11; *Sašo Gorgiev v former Yugoslav Republic of Macedonia*, No. 49382/06, 19.4.12; *Atiman v Turkey*, No. 62279/09, 23.9.14; *Haász and Szabó v Hungary*, Nos. 11327/14 and 11613/14, 13.10.15.

[84] No. 50385/99, 20.12.04.

6.39 There have been divergent decisions as to the state's responsibility for acts perpetrated by state officials when off-duty, which requires the Court to assess the 'totality of the circumstances and consider the nature and circumstances of the conduct in question'.[85] The case of *Enukidze and Girgvliani v Georgia*[86] concerned the death of the applicants' son at the hands of Ministry of Interior officials (in the aftermath of a private birthday celebration). A majority of the Court concluded (by four votes to three) that the state could not in those circumstances be held responsible for a substantive violation of Article 2, as the officials were not considered to have been acting in the course of their official duties.[87] The three dissenting judges argued, however, that the killing was attributable to Georgia, on the basis that the victim had been severely beaten by senior police officers. In contrast, the state was found responsible under Article 2 in *Gorovenky and Bugara v Ukraine*,[88] where an off-duty police officer became involved in a quarrel and opened fire with his service weapon, killing his victim: there was a failure to vet adequately an officer who had a history of alcohol abuse, indiscipline and violence; he had been issued with a gun in breach of domestic regulations; and no checks had been made to ensure its safe storage when the officer was off-duty. A similar conclusion was reached in *Sašo Gorgiev v former Yugoslav Republic of Macedonia*,[89] where a police reservist officer accidentally shot and seriously injured the applicant, while on unauthorised leave of absence and when under the influence of alcohol. The Government was held to have violated Article 2 because the Court was not satisfied that there were rigorous safeguards to prevent the improper use of service weapons, or that an appropriate assessment was made of the reservist officer's fitness to be recruited and to be armed.

Operations by the military and security forces

6.40 Operations by the military and security forces will also be subject to very similar obligations under the Convention as operations conducted by the police (see 6.29 above).[90] From the mid-1990s the Court—and the former Commission—considered a series of applications arising from the activities of the security forces which led to fatalities in south-east Turkey. For example, in *Oğur v Turkey*,[91] the Court found a violation of Article 2 arising from the planning and execution of an operation of the Turkish security forces which led to Musa Oğur's shooting, and a separate violation of Article 2 resulting from the ineffective investigations following the incident carried out by the national authorities[92] (as to the requirement to investigate, see also below at 6.49 on deaths in custody). In *Ergi v Turkey*,[93] the Court again found violations of Article 2 on account of defects in the planning and conduct of a security forces operation and the lack of an adequate and effective investigation.[94] However, in a number of cases, including *Ergi*,[95] the Strasbourg institutions found that there was an

---

[85] *Sašo Gorgiev v former Yugoslav Republic of Macedonia*, No. 49382/06, 19.4.12, para. 48.

[86] No. 25091/07, 26.4.11.

[87] The Court did, however, find numerous failings in the investigation, resulting in a violation of the procedural aspect of Article 2 (see section 6.75 below).

[88] Nos. 36146/05 and 42418/05, 12.1.12.

[89] No. 49382/06, 19.4.12.

[90] See also the discussion of the Court's application of international humanitarian law (the law of armed conflict) at 6.48 and in relation to the case of *Hassan v UK*, No. 29750/09, 16.9.14 at 6.225.

[91] No. 21594/93, 20.5.99.

[92] *Ibid.*, paras. 71–84. See also *Demiray v Turkey*, No. 27308/95, 9.11.00; *Mansuroğlu v Turkey*, No. 43443/98, 26.2.08.

[93] No. 23818/94, 28.7.98.

[94] *Ibid.*, paras. 68–86.

[95] *Ibid.*, paras. 77 and 78.

insufficient factual and evidential basis on which to conclude beyond reasonable doubt that the victims had been intentionally killed by state agents.[96] Accordingly, in *Ergi*, the Court found no further substantive violation of Article 2 arising from the alleged unlawful killing of the applicant's sister.

As with the situation of individuals taken into state custody (see 6.49 below), where a person **6.41** is found injured or dead in an area within the exclusive control of the authorities of the state, the burden will be on the Government to provide a satisfactory and convincing explanation of how the events in question occurred (the rationale being that in such situations only the authorities will have knowledge of the facts).[97]

Since 2005 the Court has also adjudicated upon a large number of cases against Russia arising **6.42** from the conflict in Chechnya. Violations of the right to life[98] have frequently been found in those cases as a consequence of extra-judicial executions,[99] enforced 'disappearances',[100] deaths caused by aerial or artillery bombardment[101] and deaths caused by landmines.[102] Not only has the Court found the Russian Government responsible for a substantive violation of the right to life in many of the cases (i.e. that the authorities were themselves responsible for the fatality in question), but also the Court has commonly found that the investigations carried out were so inadequate as to breach the procedural obligation under Article 2.[103] For example, in the case of *Isayeva, Yusupova and Bazayeva v Russia*,[104] Article 2 was violated as a result of the aerial bombardment by the Russian air force of a convoy of civilian cars leaving Grozny in 1999. In view of the excessively disproportionate force used (12 non-guided air-to-ground missiles were fired) the Court concluded that the operation was not planned and executed with the requisite care for the lives of the civilian population. Similarly, there was a violation of Article 2 in *Isayeva v Russia*,[105] as a result of the aerial and artillery bombardment of the village of Katyr-Yurt in February 2000. The Court severely criticised the Russian

---

[96] See the partly dissenting opinion of Judge Bonello in *Yilmaz v Turkey*, No. 35875/97, 29.7.04, in which he argued for the finding of a 'substantive' violation of Article 2, rather than merely a 'procedural' breach. Whilst the majority of the chamber found that the state had failed to conduct a prompt and adequate investigation into the killing of the applicant's wife, it found that the applicant had failed to produce proof beyond reasonable doubt that the state was responsible for the murder. According to Judge Bonello, this was tantamount to 'visiting the failings of the state … on the victim of those failings'.

[97] *Akkum and others v Turkey*, No. 21894/93, 24.3.05, para. 211.

[98] Findings of violations of Articles 3, 5 and 13 have also been common in these cases.

[99] See, e.g. *Khashiyev and Akayeva v Russia*, Nos. 57942/00 and 57945/00, 24.2.05; *Estamirov v Russia*, No. 60272/00, 12.10.06; *Luluyev and others v Russia*, No. 69480/01, 9.11.06; *Bitiyeva and X v Russia*, Nos. 57953/00 and 37392/03, 21.6.07; *Musayev and others v Russia*, Nos. 57941/00, 58699/00 and 60403/00, 26.7.07.

[100] See, e.g. *Bazorkina v Russia*, No. 69481/01, 27.7.06; *Imakayeva v Russia*, No. 7615/02, 9.11.06; *Malika Dzhamayeva and others v Russia*, No. 26980/06, 21.12.10; *Aslakhanova and others v Russia*, No. 2944/06, 18.12.12; *Turluyeva v Russia*, No. 63638/09, 20.6.13; *Yandiyev and others v Russia*, Nos. 34541/06, 43811/06 and 1578/07, 10.10.13.

[101] See, e.g. *Isayeva v Russia*, No. 57950/00, 24.2.05; *Isayeva, Yusupova and Bazayeva v Russia*, Nos. 57947/00, 57948/00, 57949/00, 24.2.05; *Abuyeva and others v Russia*, No. 27065/05, 2.12.10; *Esmukhambetov and others v Russia*, No. 23445/03, 29.3.11; *Kerimova and others v Russia*, No. 17170/04 et al, 3.5.11; *Abdulkhanov and others v Russia*, No. 22782/06, 3.10.13; *Abakarova v Russia*, No. 16664/07, 15.10.15. As regards aerial bombing in south-east Turkey, see also *Benzer and others v Turkey*, No. 23502/06, 12.11.13.

[102] *Albekov and others v Russia*, No. 68216/01, 9.10.08.

[103] For an analysis of the Chechen judgments, see: P Leach, *The Chechen Conflict: Analysing the Oversight of the European Court of Human Rights* [2008] EHRLR 732–61.

[104] Nos. 57947/00, 57948/00, 57949/00, 24.2.05.

[105] No. 57950/00, 24.2.05. See also *Abuyeva and others v Russia*, No. 27065/05, 2.12.10 and *Abakarova v Russia*, No. 16664/07, 15.10.15 which concerned the same incident.

authorities for the massive use of indiscriminate weaponry (including heavy, free-falling, high-explosion aviation bombs with a damage radius of more than 1,000 metres):

> … using this kind of weapon in a populated area, outside wartime and without prior evacuation of the civilians, is impossible to reconcile with the degree of caution expected from a law-enforcement body in a democratic society.[106]

6.43 The case of *Finogenov and others* v *Russia*[107] related to a large-scale operation mounted to rescue some 900 hostages taken captive in a Moscow theatre and held for three days by an armed Chechen terrorist group. The Russian security forces pumped an unidentified narcotic drug into the theatre, before storming it and killing most of the hostage-takers. However, 125 hostages also died in the operation or shortly afterwards. The Court explicitly recognised that the magnitude of the incident was truly exceptional and that 'difficult and agonising decisions' had to be made by the authorities. Neither the decision to storm the building, nor the use of the gas was found to be contrary to Article 2. However, Article 2 was violated due to the inadequate planning of the operation, which was flawed for many reasons: the lack of centralised coordination of the various services involved; poor communication exchange about the victims' conditions; the medics' lack of clear priorities; the failure to provide medical assistance during the transportation of victims in buses; and the lack of a clear plan for the distribution of victims to the different hospitals. There were also failings in the implementation of the rescue operation, including the absence of toxicologists, the insufficiency of quantities of the antidote to the gas and the lack of guidance as to how to deal with hostages who had been exposed to the gas. Furthermore, the investigation into the operation was also held to be manifestly incomplete, in breach of the procedural obligation under Article 2.[108]

6.44 At issue in *Kavaklıoğlu and others* v *Turkey*[109] was a major operation conducted by the security forces at Ulucanlar Prison in 1999, which left ten prisoners dead and seventy injured, and fifteen members of the security forces injured. The Court accepted that the steps taken had had the aim of protecting prison staff, and subsequently of quelling an insurrection, under Article 2(2)(a) and 2(2)(c). However, the use of force was not considered absolutely necessary for a number of reasons: the authorities had lost control of the prison for some time; areas of the prison had not been searched in spite of the authorities' knowledge that weapons were being stored by prisoners; there had been sufficient time to plan the operation—the security forces were not acting spontaneously; about 250 gendarme conscripts had been deployed and there was no evidence that they were sufficiently qualified to take part; the regulatory framework applicable to the operation did not impose adequate safeguards; the supervision of the operation had been so rudimentary and imprecise as to have made the use of lethal force virtually inevitable; and there was nothing to suggest that the authorities had actually assessed the nature of the threat posed by the prisoners and made a distinction between lethal and non-lethal methods. Furthermore, once a group of key prisoners had been isolated, it appeared that the security forces had not been prepared to use non-lethal methods, such as the controlled use of tear gas, and no negotiations had been attempted.

---

[106] *Ibid.*, para. 191.

[107] Nos. 18299/03 and 27311/03, 20.12.11. See also *Tagayeva and others* v *Russia*, No. 26562/07, 13.4.17 (concerning the hostage-taking at a school in Beslan, North Ossetia, in September 2004).

[108] The inadequacies in the investigation included the failure to establish crucial facts (including the formula of the gas) or to interview key witnesses, and its lack of independence.

[109] No. 15397/02, 6.10.15.

The laying of landmines by the authorities will create positive obligations under Article 2 to **6.45** take adequate steps to protect the lives, for example, of nearby inhabitants.[110] Simply erecting barbed wire and notices around a mined area was found to be insufficient in the case of *Paşa and Erkan Erol v Turkey*[111] where the land was regularly used by local villagers as pasture for grazing animals. A nine-year-old boy tending sheep had entered the area and lost a leg caused by an exploding mine.

Operations by the military and security forces will be subject to the Article 2 procedural **6.46** requirement to carry out an effective investigation into fatalities. The case of *Jaloud v Netherlands*[112] concerned the death of Azhar Sabah Jaloud when a vehicle in which he was a passenger was fired upon while passing through a checkpoint manned by personnel under the command and direct supervision of a Dutch army officer, in south-eastern Iraq in 2004. The Grand Chamber found a procedural violation of Article 2 because of several inadequacies in the investigation of the incident by the Royal Military Constabulary (a branch of the Netherlands armed forces) which impaired its effectiveness:

(i) The military court did not make a full assessment of the proportionality of the use of force at the checkpoint (and did not have access to the official record of the questioning of members of the Iraqi Civil Defence Corps who manned the checkpoint);

(ii) There was a delay of six hours before the Dutch officer who had fired at the car was questioned (and no steps were taken to reduce the risk of collusion);

(iii) There was a failure to include in the investigation file a list of the names of Iraqi personnel who had fired their weapons, and the number of rounds fired;

(iv) There were several failings in relation to the autopsy carried out; and

(v) The bullet fragments were not properly stored and examined.

In *Musayev and others v Russia*,[113] which concerned extra-judicial killings by Russian service- **6.47** men in Novye Aldy in Grozny in February 2000, the Court decried that:

notwithstanding the domestic and international public outcry caused by the cold-blooded execution of more than 50 civilians, almost six years after the tragic events in Novye Aldy no meaningful result whatsoever has been achieved in the task of identifying and prosecuting the individuals who had committed the crimes.

In relation to cases concerning the actions of state security forces or armed forces in **6.48** conflict situations the Court's usual practice has been not to refer directly to international humanitarian law (which is regarded as the *lex specialis* in relation to armed conflict and which applies concurrently with international human rights law), although it has engaged with humanitarian law concepts such as the need to carry out military operations in a way that minimises incidental civilian losses and the prohibition of the use of indiscriminate weaponry.[114] However, in the Grand Chamber judgment in *Varnava and*

---

[110] See also *Oruk v Turkey*, No. 33647/04, 4.2.14 (failure to supervise and secure firing range containing unexploded ordnance—violation of Article 2).

[111] No. 5138/99, 12.12.06. However, see, by contrast, *Dönmez and others v Turkey*, No. 20349/08, dec. 17.6.14 and see also *Akdemir and Evin v Turkey*, Nos. 58255/08 and 29275/09, 17.3.15 (compensation awarded by domestic court in respect of deaths caused by ordnance belonging to army—inadmissible re Article 2).

[112] No. 47708/08, 20.11.14.

[113] Nos. 57941/00, 58699/00 and 60403/00, 26.7.07, para. 164.

[114] *Isayeva, Yusupova and Bazayeva v Russia*, Nos. 57947/00, 57948/00, 57949/00, 24.2.05, paras. 177, 195, 197 and 199; *Isayeva v Russia*, No. 57950/00, 24.2.05, paras. 176, 187, 189–91. See also the discussion

others v *Turkey*,[115] concerning disappearances of Greek Cypriots in northern Cyprus following Turkey's invasion of Cyprus in 1974, the Court emphasised that Article 2 must be interpreted in light of the general principles of international law, including the rules of international humanitarian law. It accordingly held that:

> ... in a zone of international conflict contracting states are under obligation to protect the lives of those not, or no longer, engaged in hostilities. This would also extend to the provision of medical assistance to the wounded; where combatants have died, or succumbed to wounds, the need for accountability would necessitate proper disposal of remains and require the authorities to collect and provide information about the identity and fate of those concerned, or permit bodies such as the ICRC to do so.[116]

Deaths in custody

6.49 Article 2 imposes a positive obligation upon the authorities to ensure that the law adequately protects the right to life, and an obligation to enforce the law. Article 2 should also be considered in conjunction with Article 13 which, because of the fundamental importance of the right to protection of life, imposes stricter requirements in relation to the investigation of fatal incidents.[117] This will require in the context of a death in custody that there is a thorough and effective official investigation into the circumstances in which the death occurred,[118] and that those responsible are held accountable (whether by prosecution or otherwise). It will also require that the complainant has effective access to the investigatory procedure and that the procedure is capable of leading to the identification and punishment of the offenders.[119]

6.50 Ordinarily, the burden is on the applicant to establish a violation of the Convention. However, the burden shifts to the state where death has occurred during custody. In those circumstances, the burden of proof is on the authorities to provide a 'satisfactory and convincing explanation' or a 'plausible explanation' for the events leading to a detainee's death[120] and to keep appropriate records. In *Salman* v *Turkey*,[121] the Court described the obligation in this way:

> Persons in custody are in a vulnerable position and the authorities are under a duty to protect them. Consequently, where an individual is taken into police custody in good health and is found to be injured on release, it is incumbent on the State to provide a plausible explanation of how those injuries were caused ... The obligation on the authorities to account for the treatment of an individual in custody is particularly stringent where that individual dies.

---

of the Court's explicit application of international humanitarian law in the case of *Hassan* v *UK*, No. 29750/09, 16.9.14 at 6.225.

[115] No. 16064/90, 18.9.09.

[116] *Ibid.*, para. 185.

[117] See, e.g. *Kaya* v *Turkey*, No. 22729/93, 19.2.98, para. 107; *Yaşa* v *Turkey*, No. 22495/93, 2.9.98, paras. 114–15.

[118] See, e.g. *Fonseca Mendes* v *Spain*, No. 43991/02, dec. 1.2.05 (domestic investigation into circumstances of death in police custody considered to be effective).

[119] See, e.g. *Aksoy* v *Turkey*, No. 21987/93, 18.12.96, para. 98; *Kaya* v *Turkey*, No. 22729/93, para. 107; *Aydin* v *Turkey*, No. 23178/94, 28.6.97, para. 103; *Yaşa* v *Turkey*, No. 22495/93, 2.9.98; *Tanrikulu* v *Turkey*, No. 26763/94, 8.7.99, para. 117.

[120] See, e.g. *Velikova* v *Bulgaria*, No. 41488/98, 18.5.00, para. 70; *Salman* v *Turkey*, No. 21986/93, 27.6.00; *Tanlı* v *Turkey*, No. 26129/95, 10.4.01, para. 141; *Orak* v *Turkey*, No. 31889/96, 14.2.02.

[121] No. 21986/93, 27.6.00.

Where the events in issue are wholly, or in large part, within the exclusive knowledge of the authorities, as in the case of persons within their control in custody, strong presumptions of fact will arise in respect of injuries and death occurring during that detention. Indeed, the burden of proof may be regarded as resting on the authorities to provide a satisfactory and convincing explanation.[122]

In applying this test, the Court will frequently be required to assess whether the investigation carried out by the domestic authorities was *capable* of establishing the facts in question. For example, the applicant in *Peker v Turkey (No. 2)*[123] was shot in the leg during a security services operation in a prison. The Court was critical of the authorities' failure to carry out various rudimentary steps such as searching for the bullet, the weapon and the spent cartridge, and locating any eyewitnesses, and in view, also, of nearly a five year delay in completing the investigation, concluded that Article 2 had been breached.   **6.51**

In *Tanlı v Turkey*[124] a healthy 22-year-old man died within a short period of being taken into custody. The Government claimed that he had died from natural causes, but this was never established and consequently the Court found that the Government had failed to provide any plausible or satisfactory explanation for his death (and laid particular emphasis on the failings during the first post-mortem).   **6.52**

In very grave cases, the obligation on the Government to provide a plausible explanation may be considered to be 'particularly stringent.' This was the position in *Mojsiejew v Poland*,[125] where the Court found a violation of Article 2 as a result of the death of the applicant's son in a sobering-up centre. He died from asphyxiation after having been immobilised with belts and left alone without medical supervision. The Court has also held that when people with disabilities are kept in detention, the authorities must demonstrate particular care in meeting their special needs.[126] The case of *Nencheva and others v Bulgaria*[127] concerned the deaths of fifteen children and young adults in a home for children suffering from severe mental disabilities, over a three-month period. Finding a violation of the positive obligations under Article 2, the Court took account of the fact that the children had had insufficient food, medicines, clothes and bed linen and that their rooms had been inadequately heated in the winter. The authorities at various levels had been made aware of the risks, and had failed to respond to the warnings issued by the manager of the home about the conditions. There was also a separate breach of Article 2 because of the dilatory and inadequate investigation which was carried out into the deaths.   **6.53**

The standard that the Court requires in assessing evidence of a Convention violation is proof beyond reasonable doubt. This test may be satisfied by 'the co-existence of sufficiently strong, clear and concordant inferences or of similar unrebutted presumptions of fact'.[128] *Anguelova v Bulgaria*[129] concerned the death in police custody of a 17-year-old   **6.54**

---

[122] *Ibid.*, paras. 99 and 100. See also *Velikova v Bulgaria*, No. 41488/98, 18.5.00.

[123] No. 42136/06, 12.4.11.

[124] No. 26129/95, 10.4.01. See, by contrast, *Douglas-Williams v UK*, No. 56413/00, dec. 8.1.02 (use of force by the police not shown to be excessive or disproportionate).

[125] No. 11818/02, 24.3.09, para. 63.

[126] See, e.g. *Jasinskis v Latvia*, No. 45744/08, 21.12.10, para. 59.

[127] No. 48609/06, 18.6.13. See also *Centre for Legal Resources on behalf of Valentin Câmpeanu v Romania*, No. 47848/08, 17.7.14.

[128] See, e.g. *Salman v Turkey*, No. 21986/93, 27.6.00, para. 100.

[129] No. 38361/97, 13.6.02.

Roma man, after suffering a fractured skull. He had been arrested by the police on suspicion of theft. There was conflicting medical evidence as to the cause of death, but the Court attached significant weight to the fact that the police behaved suspiciously, for example, by delaying contact with the doctor and by manipulating detention records. The Government's version of events, that the man had been injured by a fall before being arrested, was rejected by the Court as being implausible. There was a separate violation of Article 2 in *Anguelova* arising from the failure to provide timely medical care, which was found to have contributed decisively to the man's death. It was particularly significant for the Court that the case file did not indicate any disapproval of the man's inadequate treatment. The case of *Ognyanova and Choban v Bulgaria*[130] concerned the death of a Roma man as a result of his falling from a third floor window of a police station, following his arrest on suspicion of burglary. The Court could not establish whether he had jumped or been pushed, but found it 'highly improbable' that he had tried to escape. Article 2 was found to be violated because the authorities had failed to provide a plausible explanation for his death. The case of *Taïs v France*[131] concerned the death of a man (who had AIDS) in a sobering-up cell overnight in a police station. The substantive aspect of Article 2 was found to have been violated for two reasons. First, the authorities had failed to provide a convincing explanation for his death (or for the injuries found on his body) and, secondly, as a result of the lack of care and supervision for the man in spite of his evident physical and mental distress.

6.55   Where a prisoner's life is known to be at risk because of their poor health, the positive obligations imposed by Article 2 will require the authorities to do 'everything reasonably possible in the circumstances, in good faith and in a timely manner', to try to save the person's life.[132] In *Tarariyeva v Russia*,[133] the authorities were found to have failed to protect the applicant's son's right to life in view of a catalogue of failings in his medical treatment in various prisons. He suffered from a number of chronic illnesses and died after two years in custody, the causes of which also included defective and delayed surgery. The inadequacies in the ensuing investigation were also found to violate Article 2, as it was too slow, limited in scope and incomplete. There was a similar conclusion in *Dzieciak v Poland*,[134] as a result of the inadequacies in the medical care of the applicant's husband, who suffered from heart disease, during a period of four years in pre-trial detention, and which led to his death. The Court was particularly critical of the lack of co-operation between state authorities, the failure to transport him to hospital for scheduled operations, the failure to provide adequate and prompt information to the trial court about his state of health, the failure to ensure his access to doctors during the final days of his life and the failure to take account of his health in the course of automatic extensions of his term of detention. The case of *Makharadze and Sikharulidze v Georgia*[135] concerned a prisoner's death from multi-drug-resistant tuberculosis. His treatment was found to be inadequate, and in violation of Article 2, because of the cumulative effects of a series of failings: delays in carrying out laboratory tests in order to provide an accurate diagnosis of the condition; several

---

[130] No. 46317/99, 23.2.06.
[131] No. 39922/03, 1.6.06.
[132] See, e.g. *Salakhov and Islyamova v Ukraine*, No. 28005/08, 14.3.13, para. 181.
[133] No. 4353/03, 14.12.06.
[134] No. 77766/01, 9.12.08.
[135] No. 35254/07, 22.11.11.

months' delay in providing the requisite drugs, due to a national shortage; the inadequate expertise of the medical staff; not seeking recourse to other specialised medical facilities; the courts' failure to consider his conditional release pending medical treatment; and the failure to carry out an adequate enquiry into the cause of death. The death of the HIV positive applicant in *Salakhov and Islyamova v Ukraine*[136] resulted in a finding of a violation of Article 2 because he was denied urgent hospitalisation, he remained detained without justification while he was in a critical health condition, and because he was continuously handcuffed, which further exacerbated his condition. There was also a separate finding of a procedural violation of Article 2 because of the failure to investigate his death effectively, an issue which the Court found reflected a wider public interest: 'the knowledge of the facts and of possible errors committed in the course of medical care are essential to enable the institutions and medical staff concerned to remedy potential deficiencies and prevent similar errors'.[137]

The positive duty to protect the right to life of detainees under Article 2 also requires that   **6.56** they are adequately protected against attack from others held in custody. This duty was found to have been breached in *Paul and Audrey Edwards v UK*.[138] The applicants' son, Christopher Edwards, was kicked and stamped to death whilst being detained on remand, by his cell-mate, a dangerous and mentally ill man, Richard Linford. The Court found that information had been available to show that the cell-mate was a real and serious risk to others, but such information was not brought to the attention of the prison authorities: there was a series of shortcomings in the transmission of this information by the registrar, the police, the prosecution and the magistrates' court. The Court was also critical of the brief and cursory examination of Linford carried out in the prison by an inadequately trained screening health worker and of numerous failings in the way Christopher Edwards was treated, from the time of his arrest, through to the allocation of his cell and the failure to repair a defective cell-call button.

Where detainees are taken out of police or security forces premises, but where they   **6.57** still remain in state custody, then of course the burden will remain on the government to provide a plausible explanation for a detainee's death. In *Demiray v Turkey*,[139] the Government's case was that the applicant's husband had been taken by gendarmes to the site of an arms cache where he had been killed by a booby-trapped grenade planted by the PKK. The Court was unable to establish what had happened, but found Article 2 to have been violated (albeit by four votes to three) on the basis that the state had failed to take measures that, judged reasonably, might have been expected to safeguard against the risk incurred. For the dissenting judges, however, this decision placed too great a burden on the state.

Article 2 may exceptionally be invoked even where the use of force on a person does not in   **6.58** fact prove lethal. The degree and type of force used and the aim behind the use of force will be relevant factors in assessing compliance with Article 2.[140]

---

[136] No. 28005/08, 14.3.13.
[137] *Ibid.*, para. 193.
[138] No. 46477/99, 14.3.02.
[139] No. 27308/95, 21.11.00, para. 46. See also *Özalp and others v Turkey*, No. 32457/96, 8.4.04.
[140] *Ilhan v Turkey*, No. 22277/93, 27.6.00, paras. 75–6; *Berktay v Turkey*, No. 22493/93, 1.3.01, paras. 153–4. See also the discussion at 6.38 above.

Enforced disappearances

6.59 The Court initially assessed cases of enforced 'disappearance', primarily under Article 5, rather than Articles 2 or 3. In *Kurt* v *Turkey*,[141] the applicant's son had been last seen surrounded by soldiers and had not been seen for four and a half years. In considering whether there arose a positive obligation under Article 2 to carry out an effective investigation into the circumstances of the alleged unlawful killing, the Court applied a test as to whether there was 'concrete evidence' that could establish beyond reasonable doubt that the applicant's son had been killed by the authorities. In *Kurt* there was no such evidence and accordingly the Court found that the case was to be assessed in relation to Article 5, rather than Article 2.

6.60 However, in *Timurtaş* v *Turkey*,[142] the Court found a violation of Article 2 in relation to the disappearance of the applicant's son who had been taken into detention by the security forces and nothing further had been heard of him for six and a half years. Finding that the period of time was a relevant factor, although not decisive, the Court was satisfied that the applicant's son could be presumed dead. Similar findings have been made in a series of cases against Turkey, and against Russia, arising out of the conflict in Chechnya.[143] In finding the state responsible for the presumed death of the applicant's son in *Taş* v *Turkey*,[144] the Court drew 'very strong inferences' from the lack of any documentary evidence as to where he had been held and from the Government's inability to provide a plausible explanation as to what had happened to him. The failure competently to investigate a 'disappearance' may also violate Article 2 (see also 6.75, below), as was the case in *Taş* where the investigation was held to be neither prompt, nor adequate nor effective.[145] In *Tanış and others* v *Turkey* the Court noted that

> [t]he apathy displayed by the investigating authorities poignantly bears out the importance attached to the prompt judicial intervention required by Article 5 §§ 3 and 4 of the Convention which may lead to the detection and prevention of life-threatening measures in violation of the fundamental guarantees contained in Article 2.[146]

In the fourth inter-state application of *Cyprus* v *Turkey*,[147] and in the Grand Chamber judgment of *Varnava and others* v *Turkey*,[148] the Court found a *continuing* violation of Article 2 because of the failure of the authorities to conduct an effective investigation to clarify the

---

[141] No. 24276/94, 25.5.98.

[142] No. 23531/94, 13.6.00.

[143] See e.g. *Tanış and others* v *Turkey*, No. 65899/01, 2.8.05 ('disappearance' of two men for more than 4 years); *Imakayeva* v *Russia*, No. 7615/02, 9.11.06 (victims missing for more than four years and more than five and a half years, respectively); *Bazorkina* v *Russia*, No. 69481/01, 27.7.06 (applicant's son missing for more than six years); *Çiçek* v *Turkey*, No. 25704/94, 27.2.01 ('disappearance' of applicant's sons for six and a half years); *Bilgin* v *Turkey*, No. 25659/94, 17.7.01('disappearance' of applicant's brother for more than six and a half years); *Akdeniz* v *Turkey*, No. 3954/94, 31.5.01 (11 men presumed dead, following their detention by security forces, after having been missing for over seven years); *Orhan* v *Turkey*, No. 25656/94, 18.6.02 ('disappearance' over almost eight years); *Ipek* v *Turkey*, No. 25760/94, 17.2.04 ('disappearance' of almost nine and a half years).

[144] No. 24396/94, 14.11.00, para. 66.

[145] See also *Akdeniz* v *Turkey*, No. 3954/94, 31.5.01; *Bazorkina* v *Russia*, No. 69481/01, 27.7.06.

[146] No. 65899/01, 2.8.05, para. 208.

[147] No. 25781/94, 10.5.01, para. 136.

[148] No. 16064/90, 18.9.09. By contrast, in *Gürtekin and others* v *Cyprus*, Nos. 60441/13, 68206/13 and 68667/13, dec. 11.3.14 the Court declared inadmissible a complaint about the ineffectiveness of the investigation into the deaths of the applicants' relatives during inter-communal violence in the 1960s, following the recent discovery of their bodies—there was nothing to show that the investigations had not met the Article 2 standards.

whereabouts and fate of Greek Cypriot missing persons who had disappeared in life-threatening circumstances. By contrast, in *Palić* v *Bosnia and Herzegovina*,[149] the investigation into the disappearance of the applicant's husband, a military commander, during the war in Bosnia and Herzegovina in 1995 was considered to comply with Article 2. His mortal remains had been located, the authorities were considered to have carried out an independent and effective criminal investigation into his disappearance and death (which included the issuing of international arrest warrants against two suspects), and the applicant had received substantial compensation.[150]

Self-inflicted deaths in state custody and state institutions

The authorities have an obligation under Article 2 to take appropriate steps to safeguard the lives of detainees under their control, even where death or injury is self-inflicted or occurs as a result of suicide or attempted suicide. The Court has applied the *Osman* criteria (see 6.68 below) to the self-inflicted deaths of detainees (including in relation to military conscripts).[151] The relevant test to be applied is therefore whether the authorities knew, or ought to have known, that there was a real and immediate risk to the detainee's life, and, if so, whether they did all that could reasonably have been expected of them to prevent that risk.[152] In *Keenan* v *UK*,[153] there was found to have been no violation of Article 2 as a result of the suicide of the applicant's son in prison. The Court found that on the whole the prison authorities had responded reasonably—placing him under hospital care and under watch when he appeared suicidal, and providing daily medical supervision. The fact that an alarm buzzer had been deactivated was described as 'unfortunate,' but this was not considered to have contributed to the death. The Court also found no violation of Article 2 in *Trubnikov* v *Russia*,[154] a case concerning the applicant's son's suicide in prison, as it concluded on the facts that, in spite of a history of self-harm, the authorities could not reasonably have foreseen that he would hang himself. However, Article 2 was found to have been violated in *Renolde* v *France*,[155] which concerned the suicide of a mentally disturbed prisoner in a disciplinary cell. The Court found that the authorities had been aware that he was suffering from psychotic disorders capable of causing him to commit acts of self-harm, and therefore he required careful monitoring. Nevertheless, the authorities had failed to consider whether he should be admitted to a psychiatric hospital (as had been the case in *Keenan*), they provided medication to him twice a week but without providing supervision to ensure that he actually took it, and he had been subjected to a disciplinary sanction of 45 days' detention in a punishment cell, without consideration of his mental state.[156] The detention of a young man with mental

6.61

---

[149] No. 4704/04, 15.2.11.

[150] But see also the joint partly dissenting opinion of Judges Bratza and Vehabović who considered in particular that the extent of the delays in the investigations were unacceptable.

[151] *Ataman* v *Turkey*, No. 46252/99, 27.4.06.

[152] *Keenan* v *UK*, No. 27229/95, 3.4.01, para. 93.

[153] *Ibid.* See also *Tanrıbilir* v *Turkey*, No. 21422/93, 16.11.00; *Younger* v *UK*, No. 57420/00, dec. 7.1.03; *A and others* v *Turkey*, No. 30015/96, 27.7.04.

[154] No. 49790/99, 5.7.05. See also *Robineau* v *France*, No. 58497/11, dec. 3.9.13 (suicide of detainee in police custody—no grounds to believe authorities had known, or should have known, that the man might commit suicide—inadmissible).

[155] No. 5608/05, 16.10.08. See also *Jasińska* v *Poland*, No. 28326/05, 1.6.10 (suicide of prisoner through overdose). But in contrast, see *Marro and others* v *Italy*, No. 29100/07, dec. 8.4.14 (death of prisoner from drugs overdose—authorities not aware of particular risk—inadmissible).

[156] His detention was found to constitute inhuman and degrading treatment, in violation of Article 3.

health problems in the ordinary section of a prison, rather than in the psychiatric wing, as had been stipulated, was found in *De Donder and De Clippel* v *Belgium*[157] to have contributed to his risk of committing suicide—he subsequently hanged himself. Other factors leading to a finding of a violation of Article 2 were his placement in a punishment cell and the authorities' failure to treat him with sufficient regard for his mental condition. There was also a violation of Article 2 in *Ataman* v *Turkey*[158] as a result of the death of a military conscript who had apparently killed himself. The authorities were found to have failed to have taken the necessary steps to protect a young man known to have psychological troubles, and in particular to prevent his access to lethal weapons. The case of *Eremiášová and Pechová* v *Czech Republic*[159] concerned the death of the applicant's relative in police custody, who killed himself while apparently attempting to escape by jumping out of a window. The Court held that as the authorities were aware of a risk that he might abscond, Article 2 was breached because of the failure to have placed bars on the windows to the toilets in the police station. There was a violation of both Articles 2 and 3 in *Lykova* v *Russia*.[160] Several hours after being taken to a police station on suspicion of theft, the applicant's son died when he threw himself out of a fifth floor window. The Court found that he had been tortured by the police, as he had been subjected to humiliating and intense ill-treatment in order to extract a confession during detention which had been unrecorded. As regards Article 2, the Court found that it was not necessary to establish whether the authorities had had information about the applicant that he might be driven to suicide. His vulnerability had been caused by the police's ill-treatment of him. No satisfactory explanation for the death had been put forward by the authorities and accordingly the state was to be held responsible for the applicant's son's fatal fall.

6.62 There was no violation of Article 2 in *Horoz* v *Turkey*[161] in circumstances where the applicant's son died in prison as a result of a hunger strike. The authorities had been administering appropriate medical treatment, and it was not possible to establish a causal link between the authorities' refusal to release him and his death.

6.63 The case of *Mikayil Mammadov* v *Azerbaijan*[162] concerned the applicant's wife's suicide during a police operation to evict their family. On the facts of the case there was no substantive violation of Article 2, but the Court described the extent of the positive obligation arising in this way:

> … in a situation where an individual threatens to take his or her own life in plain view of State agents and, moreover, where this threat is an emotional reaction directly induced by the State agents' actions or demands, the latter should treat this threat with the utmost seriousness as constituting an imminent risk to that individual's life, regardless of how unexpected that threat might have been.… if the State agents become aware of such a threat a sufficient time in advance, a positive obligation arises under Article 2 requiring them to prevent this threat from materialising, by any means which are reasonable and feasible in the circumstances.[163]

---

[157] No. 8595/06, 6.12.11.

[158] No. 46252/99, 27.4.06. As regards deaths of military conscripts, see also *Abdullah Yılmaz* v *Turkey*, No. 21899/02, 17.6.08; *Beker* v *Turkey*, No. 27866/03, 24.3.09; *Lütfi Demirci and others* v *Turkey*, No. 28809/05, 2.3.10; *Mosendz* v *Ukraine*, No. 52013/08, 17.1.13.

[159] No. 23944/04, 16.2.12. See also *Keller* v *Russia*, No. 26824/04, 17.10.13.

[160] No. 68736/11, 22.12.15.

[161] No. 1639/03, 31.3.09. See also *Rappaz* v *Switzerland*, No. 73175/10, dec. 26.3.13 (decision to force-feed prisoner on hunger strike—inadmissible).

[162] No. 4762/05, 17.12.09.

[163] *Ibid.*, para. 115.

There was, however, a procedural violation of Article 2 in *Mikayil Mammadov*, primarily **6.64** because the ensuing investigation was limited only to considering whether state agents were responsible for inciting the applicant's wife to commit suicide. The inquiry failed also to assess whether the police officers became aware of the suicide threat and whether they then took all adequate and possible steps to protect the applicant's wife's life.

See also 6.49 above (deaths in custody).

[handwritten: ≠ no death penalty in Europe!]

Death penalty and deportations creating a risk to life

As originally drafted, Article 2(1) of the Convention would permit the death penalty, but **6.65** Protocol No. 6 to the Convention (which entered into force on 1 March 1985) has the effect of abolishing the death penalty in peacetime and Protocol No. 13 (which came into force on 1 July 2003) abolishes the death penalty in all circumstances, including during wartime (see further at 6.714, below).[164] Furthermore, the Court stated in its 2003 judgment in *Öcalan v Turkey*[165] that in the light of recent developments in Europe (the area encompassed by the Council of Europe states had become a zone free of capital punishment) 'it can be said that capital punishment in peacetime has come to be regarded as an unacceptable, if not inhuman, form of punishment which is no longer permissible under Article 2'.

Even if the death penalty were permissible, its implementation where the defendant has **6.66** not received a fair trial will violate Article 2.[166] In *Bader and Kanbor v Sweden*[167] the Court held that the expulsion of the applicant to Syria, where he had been sentenced to death in absentia, would violate Articles 2 and 3 of the Convention. The Court found that the applicant's trial had been manifestly unfair and noted that the death penalty was in fact carried out in Syria. In the 'extraordinary rendition' case of *Al Nashiri v Poland*,[168] the Court found a violation of Articles 2 and 3, taken together with Article 1 of Protocol No. 6 to the Convention: as a result of the applicant's transfer from Poland, there was a substantial and foreseeable risk that he could be subjected to the death penalty following a trial before a US military commission (in the course of which he risked being subjected to a 'flagrant denial of justice').

[handwritten: ≠ deportation p a country w/ a death penalty!]

If the state authorities propose to deport an individual to another country, where, for any reason, there are substantial grounds for believing they face a real risk to their life, they may invoke Article 2 (and indeed the interim measures procedure—see 2.42 above). For example, in *L.M. and others v Russia*,[169] two Syrians and a stateless Palestinian who had lived in Syria successfully challenged their proposed expulsion to Syria, in view of the on-going conflict there and the evidence of a humanitarian crisis, the extent of the suffering of civilians and the massive violations of human rights and humanitarian law by all the parties to the conflict. Accordingly, the Court concluded that the forced return of the applicants to

---

[164] See, e.g. *Shamayev and others v Georgia and Russia*, No. 36378/02, 12.4.05, para. 333 (at the time of writing, Russia had ratified neither Protocol No. 6 nor Protocol No. 13, and neither Armenia nor Azerbaijan had ratified Protocol No. 13).

[165] No. 46221/99, 12.3.03, para. 196 (Chamber) and 15.5.05, para. 163 (Grand Chamber).

[166] *Öcalan v Turkey*, No. 46221/99, 12.5.05, para. 166.

[167] No. 13284/04, 8.11.05. See by contrast *Saoudi v Spain*, No. 22871/06, dec.18.9.06.

[168] No. 28761/11, 24.7.14. See also the discussion of *Al-Saadoon and Mufdhi v UK*, No. 61498/08, 2.3.10 at 6.163 below.

[169] Nos. 40081/14, 40088/14 and 40127/14, 15.10.15.

Syria would violate Article 2 and/or Article 3.Expulsion cases are discussed in more detail in relation to Article 3 at 6.164 below.

Victims of crime—the duties of prevention and investigation

6.67 The positive duty arising from Article 2 of the Convention may impose obligations both to prevent fatalities from occurring (where the authorities had notice of a particular situation and failed to act reasonably to prevent it) and to carry out an effective investigation into a fatal incident.

The duty of prevention

6.68 In the seminal case of *Osman v UK*[170] the Court considered the extent of the positive obliga-tion on the state under Article 2 in the circumstances of a fatal shooting by a teacher of the father of a former pupil, with whom he had developed an obsession. In the context of the duty on the authorities to prevent and suppress offences, the Court found that it must be established that the authorities knew or ought to have known at the time of the existence of a real and immediate risk to the life of an identified individual from the criminal acts of a third party, and that they failed to take measures within the scope of their powers which, judged reasonably, might have been expected to avoid that risk.[171] This formulation (the 'Osman test') has subsequently been applied in a very wide range of circumstances where risks to life have arisen (as discussed throughout the sections on Article 2). The Court did emphasise in *Osman* that this positive obligation should not be interpreted to impose an impossible or dis-proportionate burden on the authorities. On the facts of the *Osman* case, the Court found no violation of Article 2 on the basis that the applicants had failed to point to any decisive stage in the sequence of events leading up to the shooting when it could be said that the police knew or ought to have known of a real and immediate risk to the lives of the Osman family.

6.69 Applying the *Osman* test in *Van Colle v UK*,[172] the Court found no violation of Article 2 aris-ing from the murder of a prosecution witness, Mr Van Colle, by a former employee accused of theft. The accused was a petty offender whose record did not show a propensity to serious violence, and Mr Van Colle was not the only, or even the main, witness in the case. There was therefore no reason to fear for his life. Subsequent threatening phonecalls received by Mr Van Colle were not considered to have changed that position. The Court contrasted the position as regards the 'risk factors' with that of cases such as *Kontrová* (discussed below). Although the Court acknowledged there was an escalating situation of intimidation of a number of witnesses, it concluded that there was no decisive stage in the sequence of events leading up to the shooting of Mr Van Colle when the police knew or ought to have known of a real and immediate risk to his life. The applicant in *R.R. v Hungary*[173] had been active in a Serbian drug-trafficking mafia group. Having admitted various offences he secretly gave evidence to the authorities about the gang's activities, and as a result he, his wife and children were put on a witness protection scheme. The case concerned the risk to his family when they were subsequently taken off the scheme because the applicant in prison breached the terms of the

---

[170] No. 23452/94, 28.2.98.
[171] *Ibid.*, para. 116.
[172] No. 7678/09, 13.11.12. The Court rejected an argument that the *Osman* test should be adapted by low-ering the threshold for state responsibility when the state has itself created the risk to the deceased (for example, by calling them as witnesses in criminal proceedings).
[173] No. 19400/11, 4.12.12.

scheme. Noting that the applicant's family had been excluded from the scheme for reasons unrelated to the level of risk that they faced, the Court found that the authorities had therefore potentially exposed the applicant's wife and their children to life-threatening vengeance from criminal circles, in breach of Article 2.

Article 2 was starkly violated in the case of *Dink* v *Turkey*,[174] which concerned the murder **6.70** of the journalist Hrant Dink. He had written extensively about Turkish–Armenian relations and as a consequence had been prosecuted and had been the victim of threats by extremist Turkish nationalists, before he was shot dead in 2007. The Court found not only that the Turkish security forces had known of the intense hostility towards the applicant from within the ultra-nationalist community, but also that the police and the gendarmerie had been informed about the likelihood of an assassination attempt, and even the identity of the suspected instigators. Nevertheless, the authorities were found to have failed to take the requisite steps to protect Hrant Dink's life (it did not matter that he had not requested police protection). Applying the *Osman* test in the context of south-east Turkey, the Court found a violation of Article 2 in *Mahmut Kaya* v *Turkey*,[175] because of the ineffectiveness of the criminal law protection in the region in relation to the actions of the security forces which meant that there had been a failure to prevent a real and immediate risk to life of a doctor who was suspected of giving assistance to wounded members of the PKK.[176] The positive obligations on the state under Article 2 were breached in *Turluyeva* v *Russia*[177] (which concerned the disappearance of the applicant's son in Chechnya in 2009) because of the authorities' failure to protect the life of an individual who had been seen having been detained by state agents. As the applicant had immediately complained to the authorities about her son's disappearance, the Court found that, given the prevalence of disappearances in the Chechen region, the authorities had been aware that he had been the victim of unlawful deprivation of liberty in a life-threatening situation. However, the state had failed to take requisite steps such as the immediate inspection of the premises in question, the collection of individual traces that could have been left by the missing person, the questioning of the servicemen involved, or the collection of CCTV records.

Increasing numbers of domestic violence cases are coming before the Court. In *Kontrová* v **6.71** *Slovakia*[178] the police failed to respond adequately to the applicant's criminal complaint and emergency phone calls concerning her husband's abusive behaviour: they failed to register the complaint, record the calls, open an investigation or instigate criminal proceedings. The Court accordingly found a violation of Article 2 after her husband shot dead their two children, which the Supreme Court found to be a direct consequence of the police failings. There was a violation of Article 2 in *Branko Tomašic and others* v *Croatia*,[179] in which a man acted on his earlier threats to kill his partner and their infant daughter. He had been jailed for five months because of death threats he had made, and was ordered to have compulsory

---

[174] No. 2668/07, 14.9.10. See, by contrast, *Selahattin Demirtaş* v *Turkey*, No. 15028/09, 23.6.15.

[175] No. 22535/93, 28.3.00.

[176] See also, *Akkoç* v *Turkey*, Nos. 22947/93 and 22948/93, 10.10.00.

[177] No. 63638/09, 20.6.13. See also, e.g. *Koku* v *Turkey*, No. 27305/95, 31.5.05; *Osmanoğlu* v *Turkey*, No. 48804/99, 24.1.08; *Medova* v *Russia*, No. 25385/04, 15.1.09.

[178] No. 7510/04, 31.5.07. See also *E.S. and others* v *Slovakia*, No. 8227/04, 15.9.09 (state failed to provide adequate protection for wife and children against violent and abusive husband/father—violations of Articles 3 and 8).

[179] No. 46598/06, 15.1.09.

psychiatric treatment in prison. Shortly after his release, he shot dead the woman and child, before committing suicide. The authorities had been aware of the seriousness of the threats, but failed in their positive obligations primarily because of the inadequacies in the psychiatric treatment: it was deemed to be too short; it was unclear whether in fact it had been properly administered; there was no risk assessment immediately prior to his release; and the domestic law had not allowed for compulsory psychiatric treatment to be continued beyond a term of imprisonment. In *Opuz* v *Turkey*, the Court acknowledged the particular gravity of domestic violence:

> It is a general problem which concerns all member States and which does not always surface since it often takes place within personal relationships or closed circuits and it is not only women who are affected. The Court acknowledges that men may also be the victims of domestic violence and, indeed, that children, too, are often casualties of the phenomenon, whether directly or indirectly.[180]

6.72 In *Opuz* both the applicant and her mother had been the victims of sustained violent assaults by the applicant's husband, culminating in her mother being shot and killed by him. In view of the history of escalating violence by the applicant's husband, of which the authorities had been notified, the Court concluded that they could have foreseen a lethal attack. Criminal proceedings had been instigated against the applicant's husband, but the Government argued that each time the prosecuting authorities brought such proceedings they had to be terminated, in accordance with the domestic law, because the applicant and her mother withdrew their complaints. As, in those circumstances, the prosecuting authorities were prevented by law from pursuing the criminal proceedings (because the acts in question had not resulted in sickness or unfitness for work for ten days or more), the Court found that the legislative framework was insufficient to meet the state's positive obligations to establish and apply effectively a system punishing all forms of domestic violence. Furthermore, the state was also found to have failed to comply with its positive obligation to take preventive operational measures to protect an individual whose life was at risk. This was compounded by a criminal investigation which was insufficiently prompt. There was accordingly a violation of Article 2 in respect of the applicant's mother (and a violation of Article 3 in respect of the applicant herself, and a violation of Article 14 taken together with both Articles—see section 6.700 below).

6.73 The limits of the 'Osman test' were explored further in *Mastromatteo* v *Italy*[181] where the applicant complained under Article 2 about the killing of his son by two men who had been released on prison leave. The applicant's son had been shot by the men as they tried to make their getaway after having robbed a bank. The Grand Chamber found that the Italian system for integrating prisoners back into society did not raise an issue under Article 2, and that on the facts of the case the authorities acted reasonably in releasing the two men: there had been nothing to suggest that their release would create a real and immediate threat to life, still less

---

[180] No. 33401/02, 9.6.09, para. 132. See also *Civek* v *Turkey*, No. 55354/11, 23.2.16 (authorities' failure to protect life of domestic violence victim—violation of Article 2); *Halime Kılıç* v *Turkey*, No. 63034/11, 28.6.16 (authorities' insufficient consideration of risk of fatal injuries from domestic violence—violation of Article 2). See further the comparable cases considered in respect of Article 3 at 6.124 and Article 8 at 6.485, and the Grand Chamber judgment in *Rohlena* v *Czech Republic*, No. 59552/08, 27.1.15 (discussed below in relation to Article 7)—especially para. 71.

[181] No. 37703/97, 24.10.02. See also *Choreftakis and Choreftaki* v *Greece*, No. 46846/08, 17.1.12 (killing by convicted murderer following his release on licence—no violation of Article 2 (by four votes to three)).

any particular threat to the applicant's son. That decision can be contrasted with *Maiorano and others* v *Italy*,[182] which concerned the decision to grant day release to a man who had been convicted and sentenced to life imprisonment for abduction, rape and murder. During his day release he murdered two women, for which he was given another life sentence. The authorities were aware that he had been breaching the conditions of his day release and had also been told by an informer that he was planning a murder and other serious offences. Therefore, even though at the time of his release it would not have been possible to have identified the two victims, the authorities were nevertheless found to have breached the duty of care under Article 2. There was also a separate procedural violation of Article 2. Although criminal proceedings were brought against the perpetrator, leading to a further life sentence and the payment of damages, there had been a failure to secure the full accountability of the state officials involved. Disciplinary proceedings had led to the judges involved being reprimanded by the National Council of the Judiciary, but these proceedings were considered to be defective by the Court as the Council had not considered a critical aspect of the case—namely, that neither the information provided by the informant nor the information from a police investigation had been utilised in order to consider whether the order for day release should have been revoked.

In addition to the established line of cases concerning risks to 'identifiable individuals', **6.74** the Court has also recognised that a more general duty of protection may arise in certain circumstances. For example, in *Bljakaj and others* v *Croatia*[183] the Court stipulated that the authorities had an 'obligation to afford general protection to society against potential violent acts of an apparently mentally disturbed person'. There, the person in question had shot dead his wife's lawyer (who had acted in divorce proceedings) and the Court identified a series of police failures in dealing with objective indications that the man was mentally disturbed. The case of *Kayak* v *Turkey*[184] concerned the fatal stabbing of a schoolboy by an older pupil, which resulted in a finding of a violation of Article 2. The Court underlined the primary duty on school authorities to protect pupils against any form of violence to which they might be subjected while under the school's supervision, and, on the facts of the case, there were found to have been particular failings of supervision on the school premises.

The duty to investigate

Article 2 requires the state authorities to ensure that an investigation into a fatality meets the **6.75** following criteria:[185]

- it is independent (the people responsible for carrying out the investigation should be independent from those implicated in the events); and
- it is effective (that is, capable of ascertaining the circumstances in which the incident took place and of leading to a determination of whether the force used was or was not justified in the circumstances and to the identification and punishment of those responsible). The Court has also stipulated that 'any deficiency in the investigation which undermines its capability of establishing the circumstances of the case or the person responsible is liable to

---

[182] No. 28634/06, 15.12.09.
[183] No. 74448/12, 18.9.14.
[184] No. 60444/08, 10.7.12.
[185] For a recent reiteration of these criteria by the Grand Chamber, see *Armani Da Silva* v *UK*, No. 5878/08, 30.3.16, paras. 231–40.

fall foul of the required standard of effectiveness[186] and that its conclusions must be based on thorough, objective and impartial analysis of all relevant elements; and

- it is accessible to the victim's family to the extent necessary to safeguard their legitimate interests; and
- there must be a sufficient element of public scrutiny of the investigation; and
- it is carried out promptly and with reasonable expedition.

6.76 The extent and nature of the duty to investigate fatal incidents was initially established by the Court, notably, in a series of cases concerning south-east Turkey in the 1990s, in which the Strasbourg organs found that the authorities had failed to investigate allegations of wrongdoing by the security forces, which led to findings that the procedural obligation under Article 2 had been violated. In *Tanrikulu* v *Turkey*,[187] for example, the Court found a violation of Article 2 arising from the failure of the Turkish authorities to carry out an effective investigation into the circumstances surrounding the shooting of the applicant's husband. Various problems with the criminal law system in Turkey were identified by the Court. Firstly, the investigation of offences allegedly committed by state officials was not the responsibility of the public prosecutor, but of 'administrative councils'. These councils were made up of civil servants who were subordinate to a governor who was also responsible for the security forces whose conduct was in question. The administrative councils were accordingly found neither to be independent nor effective. Moreover, investigations were often carried out by gendarmes who were linked hierarchically to the security force units allegedly involved. Secondly, the Court made a series of findings of the inadequacy of investigations into incidents involving the security forces, where the public prosecutor often failed to pursue complaints competently. Thirdly, by often attributing responsibility for such incidents to the PKK, jurisdiction was passed to the state security courts, which have themselves been found not to be independent due to the participation of a military judge.[188] These factors meant that there was a lack of accountability for the security forces which the Court found to be incompatible with the rule of law.[189] In the 2011 judgment in *Al-Skeini and others* v *UK*[190] concerning the British armed forces' occupation of parts of southern Iraq in 2003, the Grand Chamber reiterated that the procedural obligation under Article 2 also applies in difficult security conditions, and during armed conflict (acknowledging, at the same time, that in such circumstances there may inevitably be constraints on the effectiveness of investigations).

6.77 The Georgian authorities were the subject of excoriating criticism in the Court's judgment in *Enukidze and Girgvliani* v *Georgia*[191] which concerned the abduction and death of the applicants' son at the hands of Ministry of Interior officials. The Court identified a catalogue of failings in the investigation of the case, concluding that it 'manifestly lacked the

---

[186] See, e.g. *Ramsahai and others* v *Netherlands*, No. 52391/99, 15.5.07, para. 324 and *Putintseva* v *Russia*, No. 33498/04, 10.5.12, para. 51. Having reviewed the circumstances of the *Putintseva* case, the Court concluded that the authorities had carried out a thorough, impartial and careful examination into the killing of the applicant's son (paras. 52–8) and therefore there was no procedural violation of Article 2.

[187] No. 26763/94, 8.7.99.

[188] *Incal* v *Turkey*, No. 22678/93, 9.6.98.

[189] *Akkoç* v *Turkey*, Nos. 22947/93 and 22948/93, 10.10.00, paras. 87–92.

[190] No. 55721/07, 7.7.11, para. 164.

[191] No. 25091/07, 26.4.11.

requisite independence, impartiality, objectivity and thoroughness' and finding that different branches of state had acted in concert to prevent justice being done.

In the case of *Nachova and others* v *Bulgaria*, the Court emphasised that stricter obligations will arise in investigating racist violence:[192]   **6.78**

> ... where there is suspicion that racial attitudes induced a violent act it is particularly important that the official investigation is pursued with vigour and impartiality, having regard to the need to reassert continuously society's condemnation of racism and ethnic hatred and to maintain the confidence of minorities in the ability of the authorities to protect them from the threat of racist violence. Compliance with the state's positive obligations under Article 2 of the Convention requires that the domestic legal system must demonstrate its capacity to enforce criminal law against those who unlawfully took the life of another, irrespective of the victim's racial or ethnic origin.

Furthermore, the state is obliged to 'do what is reasonable in the circumstances to collect and secure the evidence, explore all practical means of discovering the truth and deliver fully reasoned, impartial and objective decisions, without omitting suspicious facts that may be indicative of racially induced violence'.[193] In view of the serious omissions and inadequacies in the investigation in *Nachova*, and in view of similar findings in *Velikova*[194] and *Anguelova*,[195] the Court found serious doubts about the objectivity and impartiality of the investigators and prosecutors involved.   **6.79**

The case of *Association '21 December 1989' and others* v *Romania*[196] concerned the inadequacy of the investigations into the crackdown on anti-government protests in Romania in December 1989, shortly before President Nicolae Ceauşescu was overthrown. The Court found a series of failings in the investigations (including excessive delays, a lack of independence and the failure to provide information to the victims' families). The Court emphasised that a speedy resolution of the investigation was significant for Romanian society as a whole, and reiterated 'the importance of the right of victims and their families and heirs to know the truth about the circumstances surrounding events involving a massive violation of rights as fundamental as that of the right to life'.[197]   **6.80**

The duty to investigate fatalities applies not only to cases concerning deaths at the hands of state officials, but also to any case in which the authorities are informed of a fatal incident.[198] It also has been said that the duty to investigate is an obligation of means, not of result.[199]   **6.81**

---

[192] Nos. 43577/98 and 43579/98, 26.2.04, para. 157 (endorsed by the Grand Chamber in its judgment of 6.7.05, para. 160). See also *Menson and others* v *UK*, No. 47916/99, dec. 6.5.03; *Angelova and Iliev* v *Bulgaria*, No. 55523/00, 26.7.07; *Soare and others* v *Romania*, No. 24329/02, 22.2.11 (police shooting of Roma man— no violation of Article 14 taken together with Article 2 (by four votes to three)). As to the application of these principles vis-à-vis Article 3, see *Bekos and Koutropoulos* v *Greece*, No. 15250/02, 13.12.05 (see 6.126 below).

[193] Nos. 43577/98 and 43579/98, 26.2.04, para. 159 (endorsed by the Grand Chamber in its judgment of 6.7.05, para. 160).

[194] No. 41488/98, 18.5.00.

[195] No. 38361/97, 13.6.02.

[196] No. 33810/07, 24.5.11. See also *Mocanu and others* v *Romania*, Nos. 10865/09, 45886/07 and 32431/08, 17.9.14.

[197] *Association '21 December 1989' and others* v *Romania*, No. 33810/07, 24.5.11, para. 144.

[198] See, e.g. *Ergi* v *Turkey*, No. 23818/94, 28.7.98, para. 82, and *Yaşa* v *Turkey*, No. 22495/93, 2.9.98, para. 100; *Tanrikulu* v *Turkey*, No. 26763/94, 8.7.99, para. 103; *Demiray* v *Turkey*, No. 27308/95, 27.11.00, para. 50.

[199] See, e.g. *Avşar* v *Turkey*, No. 25657/94, 10.7.01, para. 404.

The authorities must therefore take reasonable steps to secure relevant evidence (including eyewitness testimony and forensic evidence, and an autopsy must be carried out, as appropriate) in order that the investigation is *capable* of identifying and punishing the perpetrators. Therefore, failure to pursue an obvious line of inquiry in the course of an investigation may lead to a finding of a violation of Article 2.[200]

6.82　Those responsible for the investigation must be independent of those implicated—both in terms of hierarchical and institutional independence, but also 'practical independence'.[201] The case of *Ramsahai and others v Netherlands*[202] concerned the fatal shooting by the police of the applicants' relative. Officers from the same police force as those involved in the incident took various essential steps at the beginning of the investigation, prior to the involvement of the state Criminal Investigation Department 15½ hours after the death. The Grand Chamber of the Court accordingly found a procedural violation of Article 2 because the police investigation was not sufficiently independent. There was a procedural violation of Article 2 in *Al-Skeini and others v UK*,[203] as the bodies tasked with investigating fatalities allegedly caused by British soldiers during the UK's occupation of southern Iraq in 2003 were not independent of the military chain of command. The Court was also critical of the delays in the investigations, the failure to interview certain Iraqi witnesses and the narrow focus of the criminal proceedings brought against soldiers accused of being responsible for one of the deaths.

6.83　Once the authorities have been notified of a fatality, or it has otherwise come to their attention, they will be obliged to investigate, without the next of kin necessarily having to lodge a formal complaint as such.[204] The investigating authorities must also act reasonably promptly.[205] The Court has held that 'where an expert medical examination is of crucial importance in determining the circumstances of a death, significant shortcomings in the conduct of that examination may amount to serious failings capable of undermining the effectiveness of the domestic investigation'.[206] See further below at 6.89, Specific failings in investigations.

6.84　The case of *Armani Da Silva v UK*[207] concerned the fatal shooting by the police of a man who had been mistakenly identified as a suspect in the London transport suicide bombings in July 2005, and who therefore the police believed was a suicide bomber who might detonate a bomb at any time. In relation to the duty to investigate under Article 2, the applicant (the victim's cousin) made two specific complaints: firstly, that the investigating authorities were unable to assess whether the use of force was justified because they were precluded from considering whether the two firing officers' honest belief that the use of force was necessary was also a reasonable one; and, secondly, that deficiencies in the criminal justice system undermined

---

[200]　See, e.g. *Kolevi v Bulgaria*, No. 1108/02, 5.11.09, para. 201.

[201]　*Ogur v Turkey*, No. 21954/93, 20.5.99, paras. 91–2. See also, e.g. *Celniku v Greece*, No. 21449/04, 5.7.07; *Jasinskis v Latvia*, No. 45744/08, 21.12.10; *Enukidze and Girgvliani v Georgia*, No. 25091/07, 26.4.11; *Mustafa Tunç and Fecire Tunç v Turkey*, No. 24014/05, 14.4.15.

[202]　No. 52391/99, 15.5.07.

[203]　No. 55721/07, 7.7.11, para. 164. By contrast, see *Mustafa Tunç and Fecire Tunç v Turkey*, No. 24014/05, 14.4.15 (involvement of military prosecutors in investigation into death of soldier, and review by military court—no violation of Article 2).

[204]　*Ilhan v Turkey*, No. 22277/93, 27.6.00, para. 63.

[205]　See, e.g. *Yaşa v Turkey*, No. 22495/93, 2.9.98, paras. 102–4.

[206]　*Giuliani and Gaggio v Italy*, No. 23458/02, 24.3.11, para. 316.

[207]　No. 5878/08, 30.3.16.

the investigation's ability to lead to the punishment of those responsible. As regards the use of force, the Court reiterated that the relevant test was whether the person had an honest and genuine belief that the use of force was necessary, which would involve considering whether the belief was subjectively reasonable, on the basis of the circumstances pertaining at the relevant time. The Court concluded that the domestic law test was equivalent to this formulation, and that the independent investigating authorities had appropriately examined the subjective reasonableness of the officers' belief. As to the adequacy of the investigation more generally, the only issue raised was the decision not to prosecute individual police officers. The Court held that there were no deficiencies arising from the role of the Crown Prosecution Service or as a result of the threshold evidential test applied in deciding whether or not to prosecute, and it was noted that a decision not to prosecute could be challenged by way of judicial review. As a result, a 13-4 majority of the Court found no breach of Article 2.[208]

Instigating criminal proceedings, which are then pursued effectively, will usually be sufficient to meet the Article 2 requirement to investigate a fatality. The Court has found that:[209] **6.85**

> The obligation comes into play, primarily, in the aftermath of a violent or suspicious death and in the normal course of events, a criminal trial, with an adversarial procedure before an independent and impartial judge, must be regarded as furnishing the strongest safeguards of an effective procedure for the finding of facts and the attribution of criminal responsibility.

Clearly, where suspects are tried, convicted and sentenced for a killing, it will not usually be possible to claim that the procedure has not proved capable of identifying and punishing the perpetrators. However, if there are substantial shortcomings in the prosecution or sentencing then issues may arise under Article 2. For example, in *Avşar* v *Turkey*,[210] there was a violation of Article 2 due to the inadequacies of an investigation, even though six 'village guards' had been convicted of killing the applicant's brother. The reason for this was that the authorities had nevertheless failed to address a crucial issue which had arisen, namely the role of a seventh man, a member of the security forces. There was a violation of Article 2 in *Jelić* v *Croatia*,[211] concerning the investigation into the kidnapping and killing of an ethnic Serb in the early 1990s. Although a military officer with command responsibility had been prosecuted and found guilty, the investigation was deficient primarily because of the failure to follow up leads relating to the direct perpetrators. In *Opuz* v *Turkey*,[212] although the applicant's husband was tried and convicted of murdering the applicant's mother, the criminal proceedings were considered to be insufficiently prompt as they were still pending, after more than **6.86**

---

[208] In their dissenting opinion, Judges Karakaş, Wojtyczek and Dedov argued, inter alia, that the use of force test incorporated an objective element as well as a subjective one.

[209] *Brecknell* v *UK*, No. 32457/04, 27.11.07, para. 66.

[210] No. 25657/94, 10.7.01. See also *Kamil Uzun* v *Turkey*, No. 37410/97, 10.5.07 (procedural violation of Article 2 notwithstanding a conviction for abuse of authority); *Feyzi Yıldırım* v *Turkey*, No. 40074/98, 19.7.07 (procedural violation of Article 2 notwithstanding officer's conviction for 'ill-treatment'); *Mojsiejew* v *Poland*, No. 11818/02, 24.3.09, para. 61 (death of applicant's son in sobering-up centre—concurrent criminal proceedings against centre's employees would not absolve state from its Convention obligations); *Agache and others* v *Romania*, No. 2712/02, 20.10.09 (four persons convicted but did not serve their sentences as no steps were taken to extradite them—procedural violation of Article 2); *Makuchyan and Minasyan* v *Azerbaijan and Hungary*, No. 17247/13, communicated 12.1.16 (presidential pardon and release of convicted murderer following his transfer to Azerbaijan to serve remainder of sentence imposed in Hungary).

[211] No. 57856/11, 12.6.14.

[212] No. 33401/02, 9.6.09. See also *Kitanovska Stanojkovic and others* v *former Yugoslav Republic of Macedonia*, No. 2319/14, 13.10.16 (delayed enforcement of prison sentence imposed on perpetrator of attack—violation of Article 2).

six years, before the Court of Cassation. In *McBride v UK*,[213] two British army soldiers, who had been convicted of murder for shooting the applicant's son, were imprisoned for six years, before being allowed to rejoin the army. The Court rejected the applicant's arguments that the soldiers should also have been discharged from the army. In *Brecknell v UK*,[214] the Court considered the nature and extent of the investigative obligation where new evidence subsequently comes to light: 'the State authorities must be sensitive to any information or material which has the potential either to undermine the conclusions of an earlier investigation or to allow an earlier inconclusive investigation to be pursued further'.[215] As to what steps need to be taken, the authorities are entitled to take account of the lapse of time and the prospects of success of a prosecution. *Brecknell* concerned the murder of the applicant's husband by loyalist paramilitaries in Northern Ireland. The Court found that where plausible allegations were made years later of security force collusion in systematic targeting of innocent civilians, the authorities were obliged to verify the reliability of the information and assess whether a full investigation was required. Article 2 was violated because the allegations were initially investigated by the police force (the Royal Ulster Constabulary) that was itself implicated. Deaths in state custody will be the subject of particular scrutiny by the Court:[216]

> ... where a positive obligation to safeguard the life of persons in custody is at stake, the system required by Article 2 must provide for an independent and impartial official investigation that satisfies certain minimum standards as to effectiveness. Thereby, the competent authorities must act with exemplary diligence and promptness and must of their own motion initiate investigations which would be capable of, firstly, ascertaining the circumstances in which the incident took place and any shortcomings in the operation of the regulatory system and, secondly, identifying the State officials or authorities involved. The requirement of public scrutiny is also relevant in this context...

6.87   A series of cases emanating from Northern Ireland have exposed various inadequacies in the inquest system in relation to killings by the security forces[217] (see also 6.89 below). In *McCaughey and others v UK*[218] the Court found a violation of Article 2 because of the excessive delays in concluding an inquest into the deaths of the applicants' relatives in 1990 (members of an IRA active service unit who had been shot dead by the British Army). The inquest hearing had not started until 21 years after their deaths. The Court noted there were protracted disputes over disclosure, inordinately long periods of inactivity and various legal actions and initiatives which appeared to be necessary to drive the inquest process forward. As a result of the pervasive problem in Northern Ireland, the Court directed the UK Government to take 'all necessary and appropriate measures to ensure, in the present case and in similar cases concerning killings by the security forces in Northern Ireland where inquests are pending, that the procedural requirements of Article 2 of the Convention are complied with expeditiously'.[219] In *Harrison and others v UK*[220] the Court rejected as

---

[213] No. 1396/06, dec. 9.5.06.

[214] No. 32457/04, 27.11.07. See also: *McCartney v UK*, No. 34575/04, *McGrath*, No. 34651/04, *O'Dowd v UK*, No. 34622/04 and *Reavey v UK*, No. 34640/04 (all 27.11.07).

[215] *Ibid.*, para. 70.

[216] See, e.g. *Trubnikov v Russia*, No. 49790/99, 5.7.05, para. 88.

[217] *Jordan v UK*, No. 24746/94, 4.5.01; *McKerr v UK*, No. 28883/95, 4.5.01; *Kelly v UK*, No. 30054/96, 4.5.01; *Shanaghan v UK*, No. 37715/97, 4.5.01; *McShane v UK*, No. 43290/98, 28.5.02.

[218] No. 43098/09, 16.7.13.

[219] See also the discussion of this case at 3.67 above.

[220] No. 44301/13, dec. 25.3.14. See also *Williams v UK*, No. 32567/06, dec. 17.2.09.

inadmissible a complaint about the ineffectiveness of the investigations into the death of 96 football supporters in Sheffield in 1989. The Court noted that the flawed nature of the original inquests had recently been recognised by the Hillsborough Independent Panel, the Government and the High Court in the light of newly disclosed information. It also accepted that the findings of the Independent Panel constituted new evidence (relating, inter alia, to the inadequacy of the emergency response) which cast doubt on the effectiveness of the original inquest and criminal investigations, and accordingly the authorities were under an obligation, pursuant to Article 2, to take further investigative measures. As extensive further investigatory measures were underway, the application was deemed to be premature.

In *Paul and Audrey Edwards* v *UK*[221] the Court was required to consider whether a private, **6.88** non-statutory inquiry was compliant with Article 2 in respect of the killing of a remand prisoner by his cell-mate.[222] The inquiry heard a large number of witnesses and produced a 388-page report, which the Court described as a 'meticulous document'. It found numerous defects leading up to the killing of the applicants' son and made a series of recommendations for reform. Nevertheless, the inquiry violated Article 2 because it lacked the powers to compel witnesses to attend to give evidence. It also lacked sufficient public scrutiny: the Court found that the nature of the case required the 'widest exposure possible', yet the inquiry sat in private and the applicants themselves were only able to attend the inquiry for the three days when they gave evidence. The applicants were unrepresented and were unable to question the witnesses; accordingly they were not involved in the process to the extent necessary to safeguard their interests. Article 2 was found to have been violated in *Trubnikov* v *Russia*.[223] There, an initial investigation by a prison governor into an inmate's suicide was not sufficiently independent and its scope was too limited. A subsequent investigation only took place three years after the incident and completely excluded the applicant and his family.

Specific failings in investigations

Set out below are examples of the Court's findings as to the inadequacies of specific aspects **6.89** of the criminal investigation process.

The incident scene:

- failure to visit the site;[224]   **6.90**
- failure to collect or preserve evidence at the scene;[225]
- no photographs taken[226]—of weapons at location;[227]

---

[221] No. 46477/99, 14.3.02.

[222] There was no inquest and as the defendant pleaded guilty to manslaughter there were no criminal proceedings involving the examination of witnesses.

[223] No. 49790/99, 5.7.05.

[224] *Demiray* v *Turkey*, No. 27308/95, 21.11.00; *Ipek* v *Turkey*, No. 25760/94, 17.2.04; *Nihayet Arıcı and others* v *Turkey*, Nos. 24604/04 and 16855/05, 23.10.12 .

[225] *Nachova and others* v *Bulgaria*, Nos. 43577/98 and 43579/98, 26.2.04, para. 132; *Nuray Şen* v *Turkey* (*No. 2*), No. 25354/94, 30.3.04; *Yüksel Erdoğan and others* v *Turkey*, No. 57049/00, 15.2.07; *Udayeva and Yusupova* v *Russia*, No. 36542/05, 21.12.10; *Benzer and others* v *Turkey*, No. 23502/06, 12.11.13.

[226] *Önen* v *Turkey*, No. 22876/93, 14.5.02; *Yüksel Erdoğan and others* v *Turkey*, No. 57049/00, 15.2.07.

[227] *Gül* v *Turkey*, No. 22676/93, 14.12.00.

- no or inadequate sketch map;[228]
- failure to take measurements;[229]
- failure to carry out reconstruction of events;[230]
- failure to record or number empty cartridges found, or to record their location;[231]
- no attempt to determine bullet's trajectory;[232]
- failure to commission and/or delays in carrying out ballistics examination;[233]
- no or inadequate ballistics report;[234]
- failure to find spent bullets;[235]
- improper recording of alleged finding of two guns and spent cartridge;[236]
- failure to examine victim's body[237] or carry out forensic tests of victim's body or clothes;[238]
- no testing of traces of victim's hands to link him to gun fired;[239]
- failure to test officers' hands for gunshot residue;[240]
- failure to recover firearms used by police;[241]
- no testing of guns for fingerprints;[242]
- lack of report on police officer's weapon and ammunition;[243]
- failure to track down military vehicle identified by number-plate.[244]

Post-mortem and autopsy:

6.91
- failure of autopsy to fully record injuries or other data;[245]
- post-mortem defective in fundamental aspects (an autopsy should provide 'a complete and accurate record of possible signs of ill-treatment and injury and an objective analysis of clinical findings, including the cause of death');[246]

---

[228] *Önen v Turkey*, No. 22876/93, 14.5.02; *Nachova and others v Bulgaria*, Nos. 43577/98 and 43579/98, 6.7.05; *Perk and others v Turkey*, No. 50739/99, 28.3.06; *Yüksel Erdoğan and others v Turkey*, No. 57049/00, 15.2.07.

[229] *Nachova and others v Bulgaria*, Nos. 43577/98 and 43579/98, 6.7.05.

[230] *Ibid.*; *Perk and others v Turkey*, No. 50739/99, 28.3.06; *Ramsahai and others v Netherlands*, No. 52391/99, 15.5.07; *Abik v Turkey*, No. 34783/07, 16.7.13; *Makbule Kaymaz and others v Turkey*, No. 651/10, 25.2.14. But, by contrast, see *Camekan v Turkey*, No. 54241/08, 28.1.14.

[231] *Önen v Turkey*, No. 22876/93, 14.5.02.

[232] *Ramsahai and others v Netherlands*, No. 52391/99, 15.5.07.

[233] *Nuray Şen v Turkey (No. 2)*, No. 25354/94, 30.3.04; *Zengin v Turkey*, No. 46928/99, 28.10.04; *Nagmetov v Russia*, No. 35589/08, 5.11.15 Grand Chamber judgment of 30.3.17.

[234] *Fatma Kaçar v Turkey*, No. 35838/97, 15.7.05; *Şimşek and others v Turkey*, Nos. 35072/97 and 37194/97, 26.7.05; *Nihayet Arıcı and others v Turkey*, Nos. 24604/04 and 16855/05, 23.10.12.

[235] *Gül v Turkey*, No. 22676/93, 14.12.00; *Nuray Şen v Turkey (No. 2)*, No. 25354/94, 30.3.04; *Makaratzis v Greece*, No. 50385/99, 20.12.04; *Şimşek and others v Turkey*, Nos. 35072/97 and 37194/97, 26.7.05.

[236] *Gül v Turkey*, No. 22676/93, 14.12.00.

[237] *Mojsiejew v Poland*, No. 11818/02, 24.3.09; *Benzer and others v Turkey*, No. 23502/06, 12.11.13.

[238] *Nuray Şen v Turkey (No. 2)*, No. 25354/94, 30.3.04; *Estamirov v Russia*, No. 60272/00, 12.10.06; *Udayeva and Yusupova v Russia*, No. 36542/05, 21.12.10.

[239] *Gül v Turkey*, No. 22676/93, 14.12.00.

[240] *Ramsahai and others v Netherlands*, No. 52391/99, 15.5.07.

[241] *Makaratzis v Greece*, No. 50385/99, 20.12.04, para. 76.

[242] *Gül v Turkey*, No. 22676/93, 14.12.00. *Yüksel Erdoğan and others v Turkey*, No. 57049/00, 15.2.07; *Makbule Kaymaz and others v Turkey*, No. 651/10, 25.2.14.

[243] *Ramsahai and others v Netherlands*, No. 52391/99, 15.5.07.

[244] *Luluyev and others v Russia*, No. 69480/01, 9.11.06.

[245] *Anguelova v Bulgaria*, No. 38361/97, 13.6.02; *Tepe v Turkey*, No. 27244/95, 9.5.03; *Kakoulli v Turkey*, No. 38595/97, 22.11.05.

[246] *Tanlı v Turkey*, No. 26129/95, 10.4.01, para. 149.

- autopsy did not include drawings or photographs showing entry and exit wounds of fatal bullet;[247]
- autopsy performed by general practitioner.[248]

Treatment of witnesses:

- insufficient evidence obtained from eye-witnesses or other key witnesses;[249]   **6.92**
- only one witness statement taken by public prosecutor;[250]
- inadequate questioning of police/security forces/military officers/state officials;[251]
- failure to resolve conflicting testimony;[252]
- taking only the briefest of statements;[253]
- delays in taking statements;[254]
- failure to show photos of suspect to the applicant, or to carry out a formal confrontation;[255]
- questioning carried out by officials from a body implicated in the incident in question.[256]

General investigation:

- delay in gendarmerie alerting competent authority of a death in custody;[257]   **6.93**
- delay in instigating official investigation;[258]
- failure to obtain, or delay in obtaining, forensic medical report;[259]
- failure to ask security forces adequately to account for their actions[260] or assumption that the security forces were not responsible;[261]
- no prompt or effective investigation of allegations of collusion by the security forces;[262]
- inadequate steps taken to reduce risk of collusion between police officers;[263]

---

[247] *Ramsahai and others* v *Netherlands*, No. 52391/99, 15.5.07.

[248] *Demiray* v *Turkey*, No. 27308/95, 21.11.00.

[249] *Önen* v *Turkey*, No. 22876/93, 14.5.02; *Orhan* v *Turkey*, No. 25656/94, 18.6.02; *Tepe* v *Turkey*, No. 27244/95, 9.5.03; *Tekdağ* v *Turkey*, No. 27699/95, 15.1.04; *Ipek* v *Turkey*, No. 25760/94, 17.2.04; *Nuray Şen* v *Turkey (No. 2)*, No. 25354/94, 30.3.04; *Ahmet Özkan and others* v *Turkey*, No. 21689/93, 6.4.04; *Tahsin Acar* v *Turkey*, No. 26307/95, 8.4.04; *Özalp and others* v *Turkey*, No. 32457/96, 8.4.04; *Estamirov* v *Russia*, No. 60272/00, 12.10.06; *Rantsev* v *Cyprus and Russia*, No. 25965/04, 7.1.10; *Enukidze and Girgvliani* v *Georgia*, No. 25091/07, 26.4.11.

[250] *Fatma Kaçar* v *Turkey*, No. 35838/97, 15.7.05.

[251] *Önen* v *Turkey*, No. 22876/93, 14.5.02; *Anguelova* v *Bulgaria*, No. 38361/97, 13.6.02; *Demiray* v *Turkey*, No. 27308/95, 21.11.00; *Aktaş* v *Turkey*, No. 24351/94, 24.4.03; *Ahmet Özkan and others* v *Turkey*, No. 21689/93, 6.4.04; *Özalp and others* v *Turkey*, No. 32457/96, 8.4.04; *Makaratzis* v *Greece*, No. 50385/99, 20.12.04; *Rantsev* v *Cyprus and Russia*, No. 25965/04, 7.1.10; *Amuyeva and others* v *Russia*, No. 17321/06, 25.11.10; *Udayeva and Yusupova* v *Russia*, No. 36542/05, 21.12.10; *Nihayet Arıcı and others* v *Turkey*, Nos. 24604/04 and 16855/05, 23.10.12; *Benzer and others* v *Turkey*, No. 23502/06, 12.11.13.

[252] *Rantsev* v *Cyprus and Russia*, No. 25965/04, 7.1.10.

[253] *Orhan* v *Turkey*, No. 25656/94, 18.6.02.

[254] *Orak* v *Turkey*, No. 31889/96, 14.2.02; *Orhan* v *Turkey*, No. 25656/94, 18.6.02; *Ramsahai and others* v *Netherlands*, No. 52391/99, 15.5.07; *Makbule Kaymaz and others* v *Turkey*, No. 651/10, 25.2.14; *Mezhiyeva* v *Russia*, No. 44297/06, 16.4.15.

[255] *Önen* v *Turkey*, No. 22876/93, 14.5.02.

[256] *Aktaş* v *Turkey*, No. 24351/94, 24.4.03.

[257] *Ibid.*

[258] *Çiçek* v *Turkey*, No. 25704/94, 27.2.01; *Estamirov* v *Russia*, No. 60272/00, 12.10.06; *Luluyev and others* v *Russia*, No. 69480/01, 9.11.06; *Šilih* v *Slovenia*, No. 71463/01, 9.4.09.

[259] *Soare and others* v *Romania*, No. 24329/02, 22.2.11; *Kerimova and others* v *Russia*, No. 17170/04 et al, 3.5.11

[260] *Ipek* v *Turkey*, No. 25760/94, 17.2.04.

[261] *Önen* v *Turkey*, No. 22876/93, 14.5.02; *Ahmet Özkan and others* v *Turkey*, No. 21689/93, 6.4.04.

[262] *Shanaghan* v *UK*, No. 37715/97, 4.5.01.

[263] *Makbule Kaymaz and others* v *Turkey*, No. 651/10, 25.2.14.

- lack of independence of investigating officers from those implicated;[264]
- failure of police and public prosecutors adequately to co-ordinate investigation;[265]
- investigation not carried out with reasonable expedition;[266]
- investigation lacked requisite objectivity and thoroughness;[267]
- short and cursory investigation[268] or relevant information ignored;[269]
- investigation of limited scope and/or short duration;[270]
- failure to obtain important evidence or documentation,[271] or to investigate crucial documents adequately;[272]
- failure to look beyond what was stated on the face of custody records;[273]
- failure to examine whether there existed a causal link between detainee's death and his treatment in custody;[274]
- investigation carried out by 'Administrative Council', which was not independent from the security forces under investigation;[275]
- investigation under control of the very officials whom the victim and victim's relatives had accused;[276]
- failure to obtain photographs of missing people;[277]
- failure of public scrutiny and/or accountability or to inform or involve next-of-kin;[278]

---

[264] *Jordan* v *UK*, No. 24746/94, 4.5.01; *McKerr* v *UK*, No. 28883/95, 4.5.01; *Kelly* v *UK*, No. 30054/96, 4.5.01; *Shanaghan* v *UK*, No. 37715/97, 4.5.01; *McShane* v *UK*, No. 43290/98, 28.5.02; *Aktaş* v *Turkey*, No. 24351/94, 24.4.03; *Finucane* v *UK*, No. 29178/95, 1.7.03; *Ipek* v *Turkey*, No. 25760/94, 17.2.04; *Akpınar and Altun* v *Turkey*, No. 56760/00, 27.2.07; *Ramsahai and others* v *Netherlands*, No. 52391/99, 15.5.07; *Şandru and others* v *Romania*, No. 22465/03, 8.12.09; *Jasinskis* v *Latvia*, No. 45744/08, 21.12.10; *Soare and others* v *Romania*, No. 24329/02, 22.2.11; *Alikaj and others* v *Italy*, No. 47357/08, 29.3.11; *Enukidze and Girgvliani* v *Georgia*, No. 25091/07, 26.4.11; *Association '21 December 1989' and others* v *Romania*, No. 33810/07, 24.5.11; *Benzer and others* v *Turkey*, No. 23502/06, 12.11.13; *Mocanu and others* v *Romania*, Nos. 10865/09, 32431/08 and 45886/07, 17.9.14.

[265] *Tepe* v *Turkey*, No. 27244/95, 9.5.03; *Tekdağ* v *Turkey*, No. 27699/95, 15.1.04; *Nuray Şen* v *Turkey (No. 2)*, No. 25354/94, 30.3.04; *Tahsin Acar* v *Turkey*, No. 26307/95, 8.4.04; *Buldan* v *Turkey*, No. 28298/95, 20.4.04.

[266] *McKerr* v *UK*, No. 28883/95 4.5.01; *McShane* v *UK*, No. 43290/98, 28.5.02; *Tahsin Acar* v *Turkey*, No. 26307/95, 8.4.04; *Buldan* v *Turkey*, No. 28298/95, 20.4.04; *Fatma Kaçar* v *Turkey*, No. 35838/97, 15.7.05; *Şimşek and others* v *Turkey*, Nos. 35072/97 and 37194/97, 26.7.05; *Agache and others* v *Romania*, No. 2712/02, 20.10.09; *Şandru and others* v *Romania*, No. 22465/03, 8.12.09; *Kerimova and others* v *Russia*, No. 17170/04 et al, 3.5.11; *Tashukhadzhiyev* v *Russia*, No. 33251/04, 25.10.11; *Nihayet Arıcı and others* v *Turkey*, Nos. 24604/04 and 16855/05, 23.10.12; *Mocanu and others* v *Romania*, Nos. 10865/09, 32431/08 and 45886/07, 17.9.14; *Mezhiyeva* v *Russia*, No. 44297/06, 16.4.15.

[267] *Anguelova* v *Bulgaria*, No. 38361/97, 13.6.02.

[268] *Orhan* v *Turkey*, No. 25656/94, 18.6.02.

[269] *Çiçek* v *Turkey*, No. 25704/94, 27.2.01.

[270] *Akkoç* v *Turkey*, Nos. 22947/93 and 22948/93, 10.10.00; *Tekdağ* v *Turkey*, No. 27699/95, 15.1.04; *Ipek* v *Turkey*, No. 25760/94, 17.2.04; *Buldan* v *Turkey*, No. 28298/95, 20.4.04; *Şimşek and others* v *Turkey*, Nos. 35072/97 and 37194/97, 26.7.05; *Kerimova and others* v *Russia*, No. 17170/04 et al, 3.5.11.

[271] *Tahsin Acar* v *Turkey*, No. 26307/95, 8.4.04; *Buldan* v *Turkey*, No. 28298/95, 20.4.04.

[272] *Benzer and others* v *Turkey*, No. 23502/06, 12.11.13.

[273] *Orhan* v *Turkey*, No. 25656/94, 18.6.02; *Ipek* v *Turkey*, No. 25760/94, 17.2.04.

[274] *Ahmet Özkan and others* v *Turkey*, No. 21689/93, 6.4.04.

[275] *Orhan* v *Turkey*, No. 25656/94, 18.6.02; *Aktaş* v *Turkey*, No. 24351/94, 24.4.03; *Ipek* v *Turkey*, No. 25760/94, 17.2.04; *Özalp and Others* v *Turkey*, No. 32457/96, 8.4.04.

[276] *Kolevi* v *Bulgaria*, No. 1108/02, 5.11.09.

[277] *Orhan* v *Turkey*, No. 25656/94, 18.6.02.

[278] *Orhan* v *Turkey*, No. 25656/94, 18.6.02. *Fatma Kaçar* v *Turkey*, No. 35838/97, 15.7.05; *Estamirov* v *Russia*, No. 60272/00, 12.10.06; *Luluyev and others* v *Russia*, No. 69480/01, 9.11.06; *Enukidze and Girgvliani* v *Georgia*, No. 25091/07, 26.4.11; *Kerimova and others* v *Russia*, No. 17170/04 et al, 3.5.11; *Mocanu and others* v *Romania*, Nos. 10865/09, 32431/08 and 45886/07, 17.9.14; *Mezhiyeva* v *Russia*, No. 44297/06, 16.4.15.

- failure to make connections between killings that may have been linked;[279]
- lack of accountability of officers for their weapons.[280]

Inquest and inquiry procedures:

- failure to commence promptly and/or not sufficiently expedited;[281]   **6.94**
- key witnesses could not be required to attend to give evidence;[282]
- failure to provide legal aid to victim's family;[283]
- inability of victim's family to take part in the inquest[284] or the inquiry to establish cause of death;[285]
- non-disclosure of witness statements to victim's family;[286]
- use of public interest immunity certificates which prevented the inquest investigating relevant matters;[287]
- inquest procedure did not allow any verdict or findings which could play an effective role in securing a prosecution;[288]
- scope of inquest too narrow;[289]
- lack of public scrutiny.[290]

Prosecuting authorities:

- failure of public prosecutor to take statements from those involved (including the   **6.95** applicant);[291]
- failure of public prosecutor to inspect custody records or places of detention;[292]
- public prosecutor did not doubt the 'official version' of the death or accepted police officers' accounts without question;[293]
- prosecutor ignored significant facts, thus effectively shielding police officer from prosecution;[294]

---

[279] *Ekinci* v *Turkey*, No. 27602/95, 16.7.02.

[280] *Gül* v *Turkey*, No. 22676/93, 14.12.00.

[281] *Jordan* v *UK*, No. 24746/94, 4.5.01; *McKerr* v *UK*, No. 28883/95, 4.5.01; *Kelly* v *UK*, No. 30054/96, 4.5.01; *Shanaghan* v *UK*, No. 37715/97, 4.5.01; *McShane* v *UK*, No. 43290/98, 28.5.02; *Finucane* v *UK*, No. 29178/95, 1.7.03; *McCaughey and others* v *UK*, No. 43098/09, 16.7.13.

[282] *Jordan* v *UK*, No. 24746/94, 4.5.01; *McKerr* v *UK*, No. 28883/95, 4.5.01; *Kelly* v *UK*, No. 30054/96, 4.5.01; *McShane* v *UK*, No. 43290/98, 28.5.02; *Paul and Audrey Edwards* v *UK*, No. 46477/99, 14.3.02.

[283] *Jordan* v *UK*, No. 24746/94, 4.5.01; *Rantsev* v *Cyprus and Russia*, No. 25965/04, 7.1.10.

[284] *Rantsev* v *Cyprus and Russia*, No. 25965/04, 7.1.10.

[285] *Slimani* v *France*, No. 57671/00, 27.7.04.

[286] *Jordan* v *UK*, No. 24746/94, 4.5.01; *McKerr* v *UK*, No. 28883/95, 4.5.01; *Kelly* v *UK*, No. 30054/96, 4.5.01; *Shanaghan* v *UK*, No. 37715/97, 4.5.01.

[287] *McKerr* v *UK*, No. 28883/95, 4.5.01.

[288] *Jordan* v *UK*, No. 24746/94, 4.5.01; *McKerr* v *UK*, No. 28883/95, 4.5.01; *Kelly* v *UK*, No. 30054/96, 4.5.01; *Shanaghan* v *UK*, No. 37715/97, 4.5.01; *McShane* v *UK*, No. 43290/98, 28.5.02.

[289] *Shanaghan* v *UK*, No. 37715/97, 4.5.01; *Finucane* v *UK*, No. 29178/95, 1.7.03 (in both cases, preventing investigation of allegations of collusion by the security forces).

[290] *Paul and Audrey Edwards* v *UK*, No. 46477/99, 14.3.02; *Finucane* v *UK*, No. 29178/95, 1.7.03; *Benzer and others* v *Turkey*, No. 23502/06, 12.11.13.

[291] *Gül* v *Turkey*, No. 22676/93, 14.12.00; *Ipek* v *Turkey*, No. 25760/94, 17.2.04.

[292] *Çiçek* v *Turkey*, No. 25704/94, 27.2.01.

[293] *Orak* v *Turkey*, No. 31889/96, 14.2.02; *Şimşek and others* v *Turkey*, Nos. 35072/97 and 37194/97, 26.7.05.

[294] *Nachova and others* v *Bulgaria*, Nos. 43577/98 and 43579/98, 6.7.05, para. 116.

- prosecuting authorities' investigation amounted to little more than a defence of police officers concerned;[295]
- NCOs forced to give false statements to investigators;[296]
- failure to bring criminal proceedings against senior gendarmerie officers or police officers (and absence of judicial explanation for the omission);[297]
- public prosecutor reaching hasty conclusions on scant evidence;[298]
- lack of public scrutiny (and failure to provide information to victims' family) of the reasons for the prosecuting authority's decision not to prosecute any police officers;[299]
- domestic court's refusal to allow victim's family sufficient time and facilities to study case materials;[300]
- delays in instituting or conducting criminal proceedings[301] (leading to charges against perpetrators becoming time-barred).[302]

Other aspects:

6.96
- inadequate reasoning of domestic courts in acquitting police officers;[303]
- undue leniency in sentencing perpetrators;[304]
- persons convicted did not serve their sentences.[305]

The duty to protect life: environmental cases; hazards and accidents

6.97 The obligation on the state to protect life under Article 2 may be invoked in cases concerning environmental and other hazards that risk endangering life. In considering what positive steps should be taken under Article 2, the Court will assess whether 'the state did all that could have been required of it to prevent ... life from being avoidably put at risk'.[306] Article 2 may impose an obligation to provide information and advice and to monitor the health of individuals considered to be at risk or to introduce regulations.[307] Article 2 may therefore be in issue even where there has been no death.[308] However, cases of severe environmental pollution are likely to raise issues

---

[295] *Dink* v *Turkey*, No. 2668/07, 14.9.10.

[296] *Ibid.*

[297] *Ibid.*

[298] *Demiray* v *Turkey*, No. 27308/95, 21.11.00.

[299] *Jordan* v *UK*, No. 24746/94, 4.5.01; *McKerr* v *UK*, No. 28883/95, 4.5.01; *Kelly* v *UK*, No. 30054/96, 4.5.01; *Shanaghan* v *UK*, No. 37715/97, 4.5.01; *Finucane* v *UK*, No. 29178/95, 1.7.03.

[300] *Enukidze and Girgvliani* v *Georgia*, No. 25091/07, 26.4.11.

[301] *Mojsiejew* v *Poland*, No. 11818/02, 24.3.09; *Šilih* v *Slovenia*, No. 71463/01, 9.4.09; *Kerimova and others* v *Russia*, No. 17170/04 et al, 3.5.11; *Association '21 December 1989' and others* v *Romania*, No. 33810/07, 24.5.11; *Camekan* v *Turkey*, No. 54241/08, 28.1.14.

[302] *Alikaj and others* v *Italy*, No. 47357/08, 29.3.11.

[303] *Gül* v *Turkey*, No. 22676/93, 14.12.00.

[304] *Şimşek and others* v *Turkey*, Nos. 35072/97 and 37194/97, 26.7.05; *Enukidze and Girgvliani* v *Georgia*, No. 25091/07, 26.4.11.

[305] *Agache and others* v *Romania*, No. 2712/02, 20.10.09.

[306] *LCB* v *UK*, No. 23413/94, 9.6.98, para. 36.

[307] *Ibid.*, para. 38. As to regulations, see *Öneryildiz* v *Turkey*, No. 48939/99, 30.11.04, para. 90. The case of *Vilnes and others* v *Norway*, Nos. 52806/09 and 22703/10, 5.12.13 concerned the risks to which North Sea divers had been exposed from the 1960s to the 1990s. The Court found no violation of Article 2, but it did find a violation of Article 8 because of the inadequacy of the availability of information about the risks involved.

[308] See, e.g. *Budayeva and others* v *Russia*, Nos. 15339/02, 21166/02, 20058/02, 11673/02 and 15343/02, 20.3.08, para. 146.

under Article 8, rather than Article 2 (see below at 6.527, and, for example, *Guerra and others* v *Italy*).[309]

In *Öneryildiz* v *Turkey*[310] the applicant, whose house had been built in a shanty town on the edge of a rubbish tip, lost nine members of his family in a methane gas explosion that destroyed 11 houses. The Grand Chamber, in finding a violation of Article 2 (unanimously),[311] found a causal link between the accident and the negligence of the various responsible local authorities. Those authorities had known, or should have known, that the inhabitants of the slum areas had been faced with a real threat (of a methane gas explosion) and they had failed to remedy the situation by doing all that could reasonably have been expected of them. The Court was also critical of the authorities' failure to inform the inhabitants of the risks in question. Whilst administrative and criminal proceedings had been brought following the incident, those proceedings did not consider the possibility of a breach of the right to life and resulted in negligible fines for the two mayors. There was a substantive violation of Article 2 in *Budayeva and others* v *Russia*[312] because of the authorities' failure to implement land-planning and emergency relief policies in an area where there was a foreseeable risk to the lives of residents from mudslides. The Court found a causal link between those failings and the death of Vladimir Budayev and injuries sustained by the first and the second applicants and by members of their family. There was also a procedural violation of Article 2 as the question of state responsibility for the accident was never examined by any judicial or administrative authority. The case of *M. Özel and others* v *Turkey*[313] concerned the deaths of the applicants' relatives during an earthquake. The substantive Article 2 complaint was declared inadmissible as being out of time, but the Court found a procedural violation of Article 2. Criminal proceedings were brought against the developers of buildings which collapsed and the individuals directly involved in their construction, but the Court was critical of the delays which had resulted in several cases being time-barred. Furthermore, the applicants' civil proceedings took between eight and 12 years to be concluded and only resulted in minimal damages awards.

6.98

There was a breach of Article 2 in *Brincat and others* v *Malta*[314] arising from employees' exposure to asbestos in the workplace (a ship repair yard) over many years. On the available evidence, the Court found that the Government knew or ought to have known of the dangers arising from exposure to asbestos by the early 1970s. However, regulations relating to safety in the workplace were only introduced in 1987, and these were considered to provide inadequate protection against the risks of working near asbestos. The Court was also critical of the failure to provide sufficient information about the risks, or to undertake suitable studies.

6.99

In *Kalender* v *Turkey*[315] the authorities were found to be liable under Article 2 as a result of the deaths of the applicants' relatives during a rail accident, due to the extent and seriousness of the failure to implement safety regulations. The breaches included an absence of

---

[309] No. 14967/89, 19.2.98.
[310] No. 48939/99, 30.11.04.
[311] The Grand Chamber also found a breach of the procedural aspect of Article 2, by 15 votes to two.
[312] Nos. 15339/02, 21166/02, 20058/02, 11673/02 and 15343/02, 20.3.08.
[313] Nos. 14350/05, 15245/05 and 16051/05, 17.11.15.
[314] No. 60908/11 et al, 24.7.14.
[315] No. 4314/02, 15.12.09. See, by contrast, *Cavit Tınarlıoğlu* v *Turkey*, No. 3648/04, 2.2.16 (swimmer injured by motor boat—no violation of Article 2).

platforms at the station, the fact that the train stopped on a central track, forcing passengers to cross another track, and the lack of information and assistance provided to passengers. Although criminal proceedings were brought against the train driver (who was acquitted) no such proceedings were instigated against the railway company, as the criminal court had requested, and accordingly there was also a procedural violation of Article 2. The Article 2 duty of protection also requires the authorities to take reasonable measures to ensure the safety of individuals in public places. There was a breach of this duty in *Banel* v *Lithuania*[316] where the applicant's 13-year-old son died when he was struck by the balcony of a derelict building that fell on him. The municipal authorities were found to have known about the state of the derelict buildings, but had failed to care for them properly. It was also noted that the delays in the ensuing investigation led to the criminal inquiry being terminated because of the statute of limitations.

6.100 There was no violation of Article 2 in *Berü* v *Turkey*[317] which concerned a fatal attack on a nine-year-old girl by stray dogs, as the authorities were not considered to have been aware of any risk to life.

Health care, abortion, euthanasia and assisted suicide

6.101 Article 2 may give rise to arguments about the extent of the obligation to take adequate measures to protect life in the context of medical care.[318] Given the difficulties about the allocation of limited financial resources for health care, it is suggested that only in exceptional cases would the Court find a violation of Article 2 arising from failures in medical care (aside from the position of those detained in state custody which is discussed above).[319] However, discriminatory treatment in the provision of medical care may violate Article 2, as was acknowledged by the Court in *Cyprus* v *Turkey*[320] in stating that an issue may arise under Article 2 'where it is shown that the authorities of a contracting state put an individual's life at risk through the denial of health care which they have undertaken to make available to the population generally'. However, there was no violation of Article 2 in *Nitecki* v *Poland*[321] where the authorities paid only 70 per cent of the cost of life-saving drugs prescribed to the applicant, with the applicant being expected to pay the remainder.

6.102 In *Powell* v *UK*,[322] the Court stated that:

> It cannot be excluded that the acts and omissions of the authorities in the field of health care policy may in certain circumstances engage their responsibility under the positive limb of Article 2. However, where a contracting state has made adequate provision for securing high professional standards among health professionals and the protection of the lives of the patients, it cannot accept that matters such as errors of judgement on the part of a health professional or negligent co-ordination among health professionals, in the treatment of a

---

[316] No. 14326/11, 18.6.13. See also *Cevrioğlu* v *Turkey*, No. 69546/12, 4.10.16 (death of child on construction site—failure of state to enforce inspection system—violation of Article 2).

[317] No. 47304/07, 11.1.11.

[318] See, e.g. *Association X* v *UK*, No. 7154/75, (1978) 14 DR 31.

[319] See, e.g. *Lopes de Sousa Fernandes* v *Portugal*, No. 56080/13, 15.12.15 (applicant's husband's death following treatment in hospital—failings in public hospital service resulted in state's failure to protect his physical integrity—violation of Article 2) (case referred to Grand Chamber 2.5.16).

[320] No. 25781/94, 10.5.01, para. 219.

[321] No. 65653/01, dec. 21.3.02. See also *Budina* v *Russia*, No. 45603/05, dec. 18.6.09 (complaint under Article 3 concerning alleged inadequacy of old age pension—inadmissible).

[322] No. 45305/99, dec. 4.5.00.

particular patient are sufficient of themselves to call a contracting state to account from the standpoint of its positive obligations under Article 2 of the Convention to protect life.

In *Lambert and others* v *France*,[323] the relatives of a man in a persistent vegetative state caused   **6.103**
by very serious head injuries incurred in a car accident, sought to challenge the proposed withdrawal of hydration and nutrition. In finding that the withdrawal of treatment would not violate Article 2 (by 12 votes to five), the Grand Chamber took account of the fact that there was a suitably clear and precise legislative framework to regulate the decisions taken by doctors in such cases, that there had been a lengthy and meticulous decision-making process in his particular case, and that the applicants had had an effective judicial remedy, involving an in-depth medical and ethical assessment of the case.

The positive obligations created by Article 2 impose both preventive and investigative duties   **6.104**
in the public and private health sphere. In *Calvelli and Ciglio* v *Italy*,[324] the Court confirmed that states are required to make regulations compelling hospitals (both public and private) to adopt measures for the protection of patients' lives and to ensure that the cause of death of patients in the care of the medical profession can be determined by an 'effective, independent judicial system', so that anyone responsible may be made accountable. There was a violation of the positive obligations under Article 2 in *Mehmet Şentürk and Bekir Şentürk* v *Turkey*[325] where a pregnant woman (who was in need of immediate surgery) was denied an operation because she was unable to pay the medical fees. As a result, she was transferred to another hospital and she died during the journey. The domestic investigations had established that her death had been caused both by errors of judgement made by health professionals and also the failure to provide treatment because of her inability to pay the requisite fees. Accordingly, a 'flagrant malfunctioning of the hospital departments' meant that the authorities had failed to protect her physical integrity. There was also a separate procedural violation of Article 2 due to the delays, and other shortcomings, in the ensuing criminal proceedings brought against various health professionals.

In relation to the investigation of cases of medical negligence, a criminal law remedy may   **6.105**
not necessarily be required, as *Calvelli and Ciglio* confirmed that civil law proceedings may be sufficient, provided that such proceedings are capable of establishing any liability of the medical professionals involved and of providing appropriate civil redress, such as damages.[326] On the facts of *Calvelli and Ciglio*, by accepting compensation in settling civil proceedings relating to the death of their baby, the applicants were found to have denied themselves access to the best means of finding out the extent of the responsibility of the doctor concerned. It was the limited extent of the available redress which led to a finding of a violation of Article 2 in *Oyal* v *Turkey*.[327] As a new-born baby, the first applicant had contracted the

---

[323] No. 46043/14, 5.6.15.

[324] No. 32967/96, 17.1.02.

[325] No.13423/09, 9.4.13. See also *Asiye Genç* v *Turkey*, No. 24109/07, 27.1.15 (death of new-born baby after being refused admission to public hospitals—violation of Article 2); *Aydoğdu* v *Turkey*, No. 40448/06, 30.8.16 (negligent hospital treatment of premature baby, leading to life-endangering denial of medical care—violation of Article 2).

[326] *Calvelli and Ciglio* v *Italy*, No. 32967/96, 17.1.02, para. 51. But see the strong dissenting judgment of Judges Rozakis, Bonello and Stráznická who argued that 'criminal proceedings are, par excellence, the most suitable remedy for satisfying the procedural requirements of Article 2'. See also, e.g. *Codarcea* v *Romania*, No. 31675/04, 2.6.09 as regards the equivalent obligation in relation to protection of the right to physical integrity under Article 8.

[327] No. 4864/05, 23.3.10.

HIV virus because of a blood transfusion carried out in hospital. The family had had access to the civil and administrative courts that had established the liability of those responsible for the infection of the first applicant, and had received an award of damages. However, this was insufficient for the purposes of Article 2 as it only covered one year's treatment and medication for the first applicant. It was also decisive that the administrative proceedings assessing the extent of responsibility of the Ministry of Health took more than nine years.

6.106 Article 2 was found to have been violated in *Dodov v Bulgaria*,[328] because the domestic legal system failed to provide an adequate and timely response to the disappearance of the applicant's mother from a state-run nursing home. She had been suffering from Alzheimer's disease and needed constant supervision, but had been left alone for a few minutes during a visit to a dermatologist and in that time had disappeared. She had never been seen again. The ensuing criminal investigation suffered from serious delays, no disciplinary measures were taken against the nursing home staff and civil proceedings were still continuing after more than ten years. The procedural obligation under Article 2 was violated in *Byrzykowski v Poland*,[329] which concerned the death of the applicant's wife in child birth. Both the criminal and disciplinary proceedings that then ensued had been discontinued or stayed, and then resumed, on several occasions. They were still pending at the time of the European Court's judgment, in which it was held that in practice there had been no effective investigation into the death. In *Eugenia Lazăr v Romania*[330] the criminal investigation into the applicant's son's death in hospital, from a respiratory arrest, was found wanting in terms of both its length (four years and five months) and its effectiveness. The main shortcomings identified in the investigation were the lack of co-operation between the forensic medical experts (such that no coherent explanation of the cause of death had been provided) and the investigating bodies, and the lack of reasons in the experts' opinions.

6.107 In *D v UK*,[331] it was undisputed that the applicant's removal to St Kitts would hasten his death, because he was terminally ill with AIDS and the medical treatment he needed was unavailable there. The Court found that the issues under Article 2 were indistinguishable from those raised under Article 3, which was held to have been violated. In *Barrett v UK*[332] the European Commission of Human Rights recognised that the provision for alcohol consumption at a naval base, combined with the failure to take any steps to control drinking to excess and inadequate care and treatment, would raise issues under Article 2.

6.108 In *Vo v France*[333] the Grand Chamber held that, in the absence of a European consensus on the scientific and legal definition of the beginning of life, the issue of when the right to life begins falls within states' margin of appreciation. In *Boso v Italy*,[334] the applicant's complaint about the voluntary termination of his wife's pregnancy, in spite of his opposition, was declared inadmissible by the Court. Under the relevant domestic legislation, an abortion

---

[328] No. 59548/00, 17.1.08.
[329] No. 11562/05, 27.6.06.
[330] No. 32146/05, 16.2.10.
[331] No. 30240/96, 2.5.97.
[332] No. 30402/96, dec. 9.4.97.
[333] No. 53924/00, 7.3.06. See also, e.g. *Paton v UK*, No. 8416/78, dec. 13.5.80; *Open Door and Dublin Well Woman v Ireland*, Nos. 14234/88 and 14253/88, Series A, No. 246, 29.10.92; *Evans v UK*, No. 6339/05, 10.4.07; *A, B and C v Ireland*, No. 25579/05, 16.12.10; *Şentürk and Bekir Şentürk v Turkey*, No.13423/09, 9.4.13.
[334] No. 50490/99, dec. 5.9.02.

could be carried out in order to protect the woman's health, which was found to strike a fair balance between the need to ensure protection of the foetus and the woman's interests.

Similarly, there has been no substantive decision about euthanasia in the context of Article **6.109** 2, or of competing interests under Articles 3 or 8. In *Pretty v UK*,[335] the applicant, who was suffering from an incurable degenerative disease, alleged that Article 2 was violated because of the Director of Public Prosecution's failure to confirm that he would not prosecute her husband if he were to assist her suicide, and because English law made assisted suicide a criminal offence. However, whilst the Court was prepared to accept that Article 8 may be concerned with notions of the quality of life, it found that 'Article 2 cannot, without a distortion of language, be interpreted as conferring the diametrically opposite rights, namely a right to die'.[336]

Article 3: Prohibition of Torture and Inhuman or Degrading Treatment or Punishment [non derogable]

Article 3 states: **6.110**

No one shall be subjected to torture or to inhuman or degrading treatment or punishment.

The absolute prohibition on torture and inhuman or degrading treatment or punishment enshrined in Article 3 is so fundamental that it has no limitations or exceptions whatsoever and it may not be subject to derogation under Article 15 of the Convention.[337]

For any treatment to violate Article 3, it must be of a minimum level of severity, which **6.111** depends upon all the circumstances of the case, such as the duration of the treatment, its physical or mental effects, and, in some cases, the sex, age and state of health of the victim.[338] In many Convention cases, concerning a wide variety of circumstances, no violation of this Article has been found simply because the treatment in question is not considered to be sufficiently severe.[339] In less severe cases, consideration should be given to the right to respect for physical and moral integrity under Article 8[340] (see below at 6.450 and 6.482).

Sufficient evidence of a detainee's ill-treatment must be produced. For example, there **6.112** was found to be insufficient evidence in *Assenov and others v Bulgaria*[341] to confirm that the applicant had been beaten in police custody with truncheons. Similarly, the applicant in *Klaas v Germany*[342] alleged that injuries sustained during the course of her arrest by the police violated Article 3 (the fact of the arrest had not been disputed in the course

---

[335] No. 2346/02, 29.4.02. See also *Nicklinson and Lamb v UK*, Nos. 2478/15 and 1787/15, dec. 23.6.15.

[336] *Pretty v UK*, No. 2346/02, 29.4.02, para. 39.

[337] Under Article 15(2) no derogation is permitted from Articles 2 (except in respect of deaths resulting from lawful acts of war), 3, 4(1) or 7.

[338] *Ireland v UK*, No.5310/71 18.1.78, para. 162. See, e.g. *Toteva v Bulgaria*, No. 42027/98, 19.5.04 (account taken of applicant's age—67); *Menesheva v Russia*, No. 59261/00, 9.3.06 (19-year-old woman confronted by several policemen). In *Đorđević v Croatia*, No. 41526/10, 24.7.12, the Court found that persistent and violent harassment of a disabled person by local children reached the Article 3 severity threshold.

[339] See, e.g. *Fedotov v Russia*, No. 5140/02, 25.10.09, para. 65.

[340] See, e.g. *Wainwright v UK*, No. 12350/04, 26.9.06 (strip-searching of visitors to prison—violation of Article 8, but no violation of Article 3).

[341] No. 24760/94, 28.10.98. See also, e.g. *Hristovi v Bulgaria*, No. 42697/05, 11.10.11, paras. 70–9.

[342] No. 15473/89, 22.9.93.

of domestic proceedings). The Court found no violation because there was no further evidence that could lead it to depart from the findings of the domestic court that the applicant could have injured herself while resisting arrest and that the arresting officers had not used excessive force.[343] Where relevant, the Court will take account of patterns of alleged ill-treatment.[344]

6.113 The standard of proof required by the Court in assessing allegations of ill-treatment is 'beyond reasonable doubt', although this has rightly been the subject of criticism in cases of ill-treatment of detainees where the only available evidence may be in the hands of the authorities[345] (see also above at 6.49 re deaths in custody). In expulsion cases, however, the Court applies a test of whether there are substantial grounds of a real risk of treatment contrary to Article 3 (see below at 6.164).

A threat of treatment that violates Article 3 would also itself amount to a breach of that provision, provided the threat is sufficiently real and immediate.[346]

6.114 The absolute nature of Article 3 means that there can be no 'balancing exercise' of competing rights, as such. For example, in *M.S.S. v Belgium and Greece*[347] the applicant, who had claimed asylum in Greece, complained that the conditions in which he was held at Athens airport were inhuman and degrading. The Court acknowledged the pressures on states created by increasing numbers of migrants and asylum-seekers, but emphasized that this could not absolve Greece from its obligations under Article 3 and rejected the Government's argument that it should take such difficulties into account when assessing the applicant's complaint.

Definitions

6.115 The Court has applied the following definitions:

Torture: deliberate inhuman treatment causing very serious and cruel suffering.[348]
Noting the definition of torture in the UN Convention against Torture and other Cruel, Inhuman or Degrading Treatment or Punishment, the Court has found that there is also a purposive element to torture: the pain or suffering is inflicted for the purpose, inter alia, of obtaining information, inflicting punishment or intimidating.[349]

Inhuman treatment or punishment: intense physical or mental suffering.[350]
Inhuman treatment or punishment has been found to include treatment that was premeditated, applied for hours at a stretch and caused either actual bodily injury or intense physical or mental suffering.[351]

---

[343] See also *Mogos* v *Romania*, No. 20420/02, 13.10.05; *Mehdiyev* v *Azerbaijan*, No. 59075/09, 18.6.15.

[344] *Taraburca* v *Moldova*, No. 18919/10, 6.12.11 (where the Court took account of the background of systematic and large-scale ill-treatment of detainees by the Moldovan police in the aftermath of demonstrations against the 2009 general elections).

[345] See, e.g. the dissenting judgment of Bonello J in *Veznedaroğlu* v *Turkey*, No. 32357/96, 11.4.00.

[346] *Campbell and Cosans* v *UK*, Series A, No. 48, 25.2.82, para. 26.

[347] No. 30696/09, 21.1.11.

[348] *Ireland* v *UK*, Series A, No. 25, 18.1.78, para. 167.

[349] See, e.g. *Akkoç* v *Turkey*, Nos. 22947/93 and 22948/93, 10.10.00, para. 115.

[350] *Ireland* v *UK*, Series A, No. 25, 18.1.78, para. 167.

[351] See, e.g. *Kudla* v *Poland*, No. 30210/96, 26.10.00.

Degrading treatment or punishment: treatment which arouses in the victim feelings of fear, anguish and inferiority capable of humiliation and debasement and possibly breaking physical or moral resistance.[352]

The Court may have regard to 'whether its object is to humiliate and debase the person concerned and whether, as far as the consequences are concerned, it adversely affected his or her personality in a manner incompatible with Article 3'[353] or whether it drives the victim to act against his will or conscience.[354] Nevertheless, a positive intention to humiliate or debase is not a prerequisite for a finding of a violation of Article 3.[355] It is sufficient if the victim is humiliated in his or her own eyes.[356]

When analysing such definitions, the gradually evolving nature of the Convention should **6.116** always be taken into account. In a significant decision in 1999 in the case of *Selmouni* v *France*,[357] the Court found that, because of the need to interpret the Convention as a 'living instrument', acts which had previously been classified as inhuman and degrading treatment rather than torture, could be classified differently in future:

> … the increasingly high standard being required in the area of the protection of human rights and fundamental liberties correspondingly and inevitably requires greater firmness in assessing breaches of the fundamental values of democratic societies.

In 2015, the Grand Chamber found in the case of *Bouyid* v *Belgium*[358] (see 6.133) that Article 3 had been breached because the applicants, two brothers, had been slapped once in the face by police officers (in separate incidents), which was held to constitute degrading treatment. The Court has also found that extreme material poverty may engage state responsibility under Article 3, for example, where an applicant who is dependent on state support suffers serious deprivations that are considered to be incompatible with human dignity. In *M.S.S.* v *Belgium and Greece*,[359] the Grand Chamber found a violation of Article 3 because of the living conditions experienced by the applicant asylum-seeker in Greece. He had been forced to live on the street for several months, with no resources or access to sanitary facilities, and without any means of providing for his essential needs.

The requirements of Article 3 are discussed further below under the following headings: **6.117** positive obligations: the duty of prevention (6.118); positive obligations: the duty to investigate (6.121); policing and the use of force against detainees (6.129); conditions of detention and sentencing (6.144); death penalty (6.161); immigration, asylum and extradition (6.164); discrimination (6.181); child care (6.184); corporal punishment and military service (6.186); and medical treatment (6.189).

---

[352] *Ireland* v *UK*, Series A, No. 25, 18.1.78, para. 167. The Court has held that for an authority or agency to force someone, by whatever means, to work or continue to work as a prostitute would amount to inhuman or degrading treatment (*Tremblay* v *France*, No. 37194/02, 11.9.07).

[353] See, e.g. *Raninen* v *Finland*, No. 20972/92, 16.12.97, para. 55.

[354] *The Greek Case*, Nos. 3321–3/67, 3344/67, 5.11.69, (1969) 12 Yearbook 1.

[355] *V* v *UK*, No. 24888/94, 16.12.99, para. 71.

[356] *Tyrer* v *UK*, Series A, No. 26, 25.4.78, para. 23; *Smith and Grady* v *UK*, Nos. 33985/96 and 33986/96, 27.9.99, para. 120.

[357] No. 25803/94, 28.7.99.

[358] No. 23380/09, 28.9.15.

[359] No. 30696/09, 21.1.11. See also: *O'Rourke* v *UK*, No. 39022/97, dec. 26.6.01; *Larioshina* v *Russia*, No. 56869/00, dec. 23.4.02; *Budina* v *Russia*, No. 45603/05, dec. 18.6.09; *Rahimi* v *Greece*, No. 8687/08, 5.4.11.

§2 positive obligations!.

Positive obligations: the duty of prevention

6.118 Article 3 (taken together with Article 1) imposes on states a number of positive obligations, with the aim of preventing and providing redress for ill-treatment,[360] whether inflicted by state officials or by private individuals.[361] This therefore encompasses cases of domestic violence.[362] States are under an obligation to take 'reasonable steps' to prevent ill-treatment of which the authorities knew or ought to have known, as is discussed below, for example, in relation to child protection at 6.184 (see also the similar obligation arising in relation to the right to life, at 6.68 above). The Court has underlined the particular need to protect children from ill-treatment, especially in the context of their primary education. There was a violation of Article 3 on this basis in *O'Keeffe v Ireland*.[363] The applicant complained of having been the victim of sexual abuse by a primary school teacher in the 1970s, when she attended a National School (such schools were state-funded, but were owned and managed by the Catholic Church). The Grand Chamber found that the authorities had been aware of the sexual abuse of children by adults at the time (through the high numbers of criminal prosecutions), and yet the state had continued to entrust the management of primary education to the National Schools (which were non-state bodies), and had failed to establish a suitable mechanism of effective control against the risks of such abuse occurring.

6.119 By way of further example, there was a violation of Article 3 in the case of *97 members of the Gldani Congregation of Jehovah's Witnesses and 4 others v Georgia*,[364] which concerned an organised, sustained attack on the applicant Jehovah's Witnesses by members of a group of Orthodox extremists. The authorities failed to meet their positive obligations under Article 3 as the police refused to intervene promptly at the scene of the incident to protect the applicants (and a number of children) from ill-treatment and the applicants were then faced with total indifference by the relevant authorities. In *Identoba and others v Georgia*[365] the Court found a violation of Article 3, in conjunction with Article 14, because of the authorities' failure to protect demonstrators from homophobic violence. The applicant LGBT activists held a demonstration (of about 30 people) in Tbilisi to mark the International Day against Homophobia. The participants in the demonstration were insulted, threatened and assaulted by a larger group of counter-demonstrators who were members of two religious groups. Despite having been warned by the organisers of the likelihood of trouble, there was only a limited police presence, and the police officers had allowed the tension to degenerate into physical violence, before intervening to arrest some of the applicants, rather than restraining the counter-demonstrators. The Court also found the ensuing investigation to be ineffective, and in particular the failure to assess the homophobic motives of the counter-demonstrators.

---

[360] See, e.g. *A v UK*, No. 25599/94, 23.9.98.

[361] See, e.g. *Beganović v Croatia*, No. 46423/06, 25.6.09; *Denis Vasilyev v Russia*, No. 32704/04, 17.12.09. There is, for example, a positive obligation on the authorities to control discipline within schools in order to prevent violations of Articles 3 or 8 (*Đurđević v Croatia*, No. 52442/09, 19.7.11).

[362] See, e.g. *Valiulienė v Lithuania*, No. 33234/07, 26.3.13.

[363] No. 35810/09, 28.1.14.

[364] No. 71156/01, 3.5.07.

[365] No. 73235/12, 12.5.15 (there was also a violation of Article 11 taken together with Article 14). See also *M.C. and A.C. v Romania*, No. 12060/12, 12.4.16 (failure to take into account possible discriminatory motives in investigation of homophobic attack on LGBT rally—violation of Article 14 together with Article 3). As well as Article 3, Article 8 may be engaged in relation to the adequacy of the state's response to demonstrations - see, e.g. *Király and Dömötör v Hungary*, No. 10851/13, 17.1.17 (violation of Article 8 due to authorities' inadequate response to anti-Roma demonstration).

By contrast, there was no violation of Article 3 positive obligations in *P.F. and E.F. v UK*[366] in which the applicants complained about inadequate police protection from sectarian violence and disorder in Northern Ireland. The case concerned loyalist demonstrations in Belfast that severely disrupted pupils' access to a Catholic primary school. The police had sought to act as a shield between the demonstrators and the parents and children, but had also been mindful of the danger of causing an escalation, or displacement, of the violence. Taking into account the complex nature of operational decisions, and in view of the volatile situation in which they had been operating, the Court concluded that the police had taken all reasonable steps to protect the applicants, and declared the application inadmissible.

The duty to prevent ill-treatment will require the authorities to prevent attacks on people **6.120** detained by the state by other inmates. For example, in *Premininy v Russia*[367] the Court was highly critical of the authorities' inadequate response to a series of attacks by the applicant's cellmates, finding that the prison administration 'failed to detect, prevent or monitor, and respond promptly, diligently and effectively to the systematic inhuman and degrading treatment to which he had been subjected by his cellmates'.

Positive obligations: the duty to investigate

Article 3 also imposes an obligation on states to carry out an effective official investigation **6.121** into an allegation of serious ill-treatment, which is *capable* of leading to the identification and punishment of those responsible.[368] The investigation must be independent,[369] impartial, subject to public scrutiny, and the authorities must act diligently and promptly.[370] There must also be effective access for the complainant to the investigation procedure (which may require the provision of free legal representation).[371] In some cases, the Court may find a series of failings in the investigation, as it did, for example, in *Virabyan v Armenia*,[372] where, as a result, the domestic investigation into the applicant's allegations of ill-treatment in police custody was held to be 'ineffective, inadequate and fundamentally flawed'.

Given the difficulties of establishing allegations of ill-treatment in custody, an effective investigation in those circumstances will require that the authorities take reasonable steps to secure the evidence concerning the incident, including forensic evidence.[373] In situations where it is disputed how particular injuries were caused, the failure of the authorities to carry out an effective investigation into an incident may lead the Court to find a substantive violation of Article 3. For example, that was the case in *Stoica v Romania*,[374] where the inadequacies in the investigation into the cause of serious injuries suffered by a 14-year-old Roma boy led

---

[366] No. 28326/09, dec. 23.11.10.
[367] No. 44973/04, 10.2.11, para. 90. See also *D.F. v Latvia*, No. 11160/07, 29.10.13.
[368] *Assenov and others v Bulgaria*, No. 24760/94, 28.10.98, para. 102; *Sakik and others v Turkey*, No. 31866/96, 10.10.00, para. 62.
[369] See, e.g. *Yazgül Yılmaz v Turkey*, No. 36369/06, 1.2.11, paras. 61–3.
[370] See, e.g. *Isayeva and others v Russia*, Nos. 57947/00, 57948/00 and 57949/00, 24.2.05, paras. 208–13; *Premininy v Russia*, No. 44973/04, 10.2.11, paras. 108–14.
[371] *Savitskyy v Ukraine*, No. 38773/05, 26.7.12, para. 117 (applicant severely disabled and without any legal education).
[372] No. 40094/05, 2.10.12. As regards the numerous cases relating to the failure of the Russian authorities to investigate credible allegations of torture at the hands of the police, see, e.g. *Lyapin v Russia*, No. 46956/09, 24.7.14 (and the cases listed at para. 133 of that judgment).
[373] See, e.g. *Mammadov (Jajaloglu) v Azerbaijan*, No. 34445/04, 11.1.07, para. 74.
[374] No. 42722/02, 4.3.08.

the Court to find a find a substantive violation of Article 3 on the basis that the Government had not satisfactorily established that the applicant's injuries were caused otherwise than by the treatment inflicted on him by police officers. If law enforcement officers are permitted to carry out their duties without being identifiable (for example, by using balaclavas or not wearing distinctive signs on their clothing) the Court may conclude that the authorities have deliberately created a situation of impunity.[375] The Court has been highly critical of intimidating police raids in Bulgaria carried out by masked officers who were not subsequently identified and questioned, thereby effectively providing immunity from prosecution, a situation which it has held to be incompatible with Article 3.[376] The authorities were found to have failed to comply with their positive obligations under Article 3 in *Iribarren Pinillos* v *Spain*,[377] because of the inadequacies in the investigation of the applicant's serious injuries which were caused by a smoke bomb fired by the riot police during violent clashes in Pamplona. They were found to have failed to carry out a proper assessment of the damage he had sustained. Article 3 was breached in *Okkalı* v *Turkey*[378] because an investigation into police ill-treatment of a 12-year-old boy led to minimal, suspended sentences for the police officers involved. The Court found that 'the judges exercised their discretion more in order to minimise the consequences of an extremely serious unlawful act than to show that such acts could in no way be tolerated'. There was a similar outcome in *Zontul* v *Greece*,[379] which concerned the rape with a truncheon of a migrant on a boat after it was boarded by the Greek coastguard. The perpetrator was sentenced to a six-month suspended prison term, which was later commuted to a fine of €792. The Court accordingly found that the leniency of the penalty was manifestly disproportionate, in violation of Article 3, in view of the seriousness of the treatment inflicted on the applicant (which was found to be an act of torture). A further factor was the applicant's effective exclusion from participation in the criminal proceedings as a civil party.

In *Savin* v *Ukraine*[380] the inadequacies of the investigations carried out into a case of police torture were so evident that the Court found a situation of virtual total impunity for torture or ill-treatment by law-enforcement agencies. In *Karabet and others* v *Ukraine*[381] the Court found a violation of the procedural aspect of Article 3 because of multiple failings in the investigation into a special forces operation taken against prisoners who had led a hunger strike. The investigation was ineffective (factors included: inadequate medical examinations and the prosecution's passive and formalistic approach), not independent (it was carried out by the local prosecutor who also supervised the penal institutions), insufficiently prompt and lacked the requisite public scrutiny.

---

[375] See *Dedovskiy* v *Russia*, No. 7178/03, 15.5.08, para. 91.

[376] See, e.g. *Rashid* v *Bulgaria*, No. 47905/99, 18.1.07; *Vachkovi* v *Bulgaria*, No. 2747/02, 8.7.10; *Hristovi* v *Bulgaria*, No. 42697/05, 11.10.11 (in which the Court also highlighted the lacuna in the domestic criminal law as to the psychological (as opposed to physical) effects of an intimidating police raid—para. 95). Similar concerns have been expressed as regards police raids in Slovakia and Poland. See: *Kučera* v *Slovakia*, No.48666/99, 17.7.07; *Rachwalski and Ferenc* v *Poland*, No. 47709/99, 28.7.09; *Miroslaw Garlicki* v *Poland*, No. 36921/07, 14.6.11. As regards Article 2, see also *Ataykaya* v *Turkey*, No. 50275/08, 22.7.14.

[377] No. 36777/03, 8.1.09.

[378] No. 52067/99, 17.10.06. See also *Ali and Ayşe Duran* v *Turkey*, No. 42942/02, 8.4.08; *Atalay* v *Turkey*, No. 1249/03, 18.9.08.

[379] No. 12294/07, 17.1.12.

[380] No. 34725/08, 16.2.12.

[381] Nos. 38906/07 and 52025/07, 17.1.13. There was also a separate finding that the ill-treatment meted out amounted to torture.

In *Beganović* v *Croatia*,[382] the Court reaffirmed that where violence inflicted by private indi- **6.122** viduals crosses the minimum level of severity for Article 3 to be applicable, the authorities are required to ensure the implementation of adequate criminal-law mechanisms. The state's positive obligations were not met by the steps taken following a serious attack on the applicant, notably as criminal proceedings became time-barred due to delays caused by the authorities. Article 3 was violated in *Denis Vasilyev* v *Russia*[383] where the police found a young man lying on the ground unconscious, but then failed to take the requisite measures to prevent further harm to him, as they were called away to another incident. They did not examine the man in order to assess the gravity of his condition or the assistance he needed, nor did they call an ambulance or ask for any other medical assistance.

The Court has also held that states have a positive obligation inherent in Articles 3 and **6.123** 8 'to enact criminal-law provisions effectively punishing rape and to apply them in practice through effective investigation and prosecution'.[384] In *MC* v *Bulgaria*[385] the Court found that Bulgarian law did not comply with the state's positive obligations because of the practice of prosecuting alleged perpetrators of rape only where there was evidence of significant physical resistance. Article 3 was also breached as a result of various inadequacies in the manner in which the investigation of the offence was carried out.[386] The state's positive obligation to investigate and prosecute cases of sexual abuse effectively was violated in *Y.* v *Slovenia*[387] where criminal proceedings brought against a man accused of sexually assaulting the applicant (when aged 14) took more than seven years.

Victims of domestic violence are also owed effective protection by the state, pursuant to **6.124** Article 3 (as well as Articles 2, 8 and 14),[388] which will require both an effective investigation and commensurate prosecution.[389] There was a violation of Article 3 in *Valiulienė* v *Lithuania*[390] where the applicant had complained of having been beaten by her partner, and the prosecution of the case became time-barred, as a result of delays and flaws in the investigation of the case, for which the state authorities were responsible. The case of *Eremia* v *Moldova*[391] concerned the failure of the authorities to take adequate measures to protect the applicant and her teenage daughters from domestic violence perpetrated by the applicant's husband, a police officer, who frequently beat his wife in the presence of

---

[382] No. 46423/06, 25.6.09.

[383] No. 32704/04, 17.12.09 (the Court found five separate violations of Article 3 in the case due to the inadequate responses of the police, hospital and investigating authorities, and a violation of Article 13).

[384] *MC* v *Bulgaria*, No. 39272/98, 4.12.03, para. 153. Article 8 may impose a broader obligation on States to adopt adequate positive measures in the sphere of criminal-law protection to protect individuals against acts of violence by other individuals—see *Sandra Janković* v *Croatia*, No. 38478/05, 5.3.09 (discussed below at 6.484).

[385] No. 39272/98, 4.12.03.

[386] See also *S.Z.* v *Bulgaria*, No. 29263/12, 3.3.15 (delayed and ineffective investigation of rape case, in which the Court identified a systemic problem as regards the ineffectiveness of investigations in Bulgaria).

[387] No. 41107/10, 28.5.15. There was also a violation of Article 8 because of the failure to protect the applicant's personal integrity during the cross-examination process.

[388] See, e.g. *E.S. and others* v *Slovakia*, No. 8227/04, 15.9.09. See also the domestic violence (Article 2) cases discussed at 6.71 above.

[389] See, e.g. *M. and M.* v *Croatia*, No. 10161/13, 3.9.15 (authorities only prosecuted one in a series of violent acts committed by a father against his daughter—delays in investigation—violation of Article 3); *M.G.* v *Turkey*, No. 646/10, 22.3.16 (delays caused by, and passivity of, prosecuting authorities—civil law protections against domestic violence not available to applicant once divorced—violation of Article 3).

[390] No. 33234/07, 26.3.13.

[391] No. 3564/11, 28.5.13.

their daughters. The Court concluded that the decision to suspend an investigation into the husband's violent behaviour had had the effect of shielding him from criminal liability, rather than deterring him from committing further violence, and had resulted in his virtual impunity. Accordingly, the authorities were found to have breached their positive obligations under Article 3. The Court also found a violation of Article 14, together with Article 3, on the basis that the effect of the authorities' inaction had been to repeatedly condone such violence and reflected a discriminatory attitude towards the first applicant as a woman.[392]

6.125   Certain forms of harassment may also result in positive obligations engaging the authorities, even where the criminal law cannot be utilized. That was the case in *Đorđević v Croatia*[393] which concerned persistent and violent harassment of a mentally and physically disabled person by local children. The Court acknowledged that in that situation, individual acts might not as such amount to criminal offences, but a series of incidents of harassment may still be incompatible with Article 3. Furthermore, in the particular case, the children causing the harassment were under the age of criminal responsibility. The relevant test is whether the authorities were or should have been aware of the situation of harassment, and if so, whether they took all reasonable steps in the circumstances to protect the victim. There was a violation of Article 3 in *Đorđević* because no serious attempt was made to assess the true nature of the situation, and due to the failure to take adequate and comprehensive measures in response, with both the police and social services being criticised.

6.126   Article 3 also imposes a duty to investigate the existence of a possible link between racist attitudes and an act of violence.[394] There was a finding of a violation of Article 14 taken together with Article 3 in *Bekos and Koutropoulos v Greece*,[395] a case concerning assaults on two Roma men during their arrest by the police. Despite plausible information that the alleged assaults had been racially motivated (it was claimed that they were racially verbally abused), the authorities failed to examine this question.[396] There is a similar obligation as regards alleged political motivations for a person's ill-treatment:

> when investigating violent incidents State authorities have the additional duty to take all reasonable steps to unmask any political motive and to establish whether or not intolerance towards a dissenting political opinion may have played a role in the events. Failing to do so and treating politically induced violence and brutality on an equal footing with cases that have no political overtones would be to turn a blind eye to the specific nature of acts that are particularly destructive of fundamental rights.[397]

6.127   The Court has acknowledged that a broader 'right to the truth' may be relevant to its assessment of investigatory processes in some situations. For example, in the case of *El-Masri v*

---

[392] There was also a violation of Article 8 (due to the failure to protect the psychological well-being of the daughters).

[393] No. 41526/10, 24.7.12.

[394] As regards the duty under Article 8 to investigate incidents of racial abuse, see *R.B. v Hungary*, No. 64602/12, 12.4.16.

[395] No. 15250/02, 13.12.05.

[396] See also, e.g. *Stoica v Romania*, No. 42722/02, 4.3.08; *B.S. v Spain*, No. 47159/08, 24.7.12; *Abdu v Bulgaria*, No. 26827/08, 11.3.14; *Sakir v Greece*, No. 48475/09, 24.3.16 (flawed investigation into attack on Afghan migrant).

[397] *Virabyan v Armenia*, No. 40094/05, 2.10.12, para. 218 (violation of Article 14 taken together with Article 3).

former Yugoslav Republic of Macedonia,[398] concerning the practice of 'extraordinary rendition', the Court underlined

> ... the great importance of the present case not only for the applicant and his family, but also for other victims of similar crimes and the general public, who had the right to know what had happened.[399]

In the later rendition case of *Nasr and Ghali* v *Italy*[400] the Court found that there had been an effective investigation into the first applicant's allegations of ill-treatment which had led to the convictions of 26 US nationals and two Italians. Indeed, the Court paid tribute to the high calibre of the work of the Italian investigators, judges and prosecutors. However, the convictions of the Italians were quashed on grounds of state secrecy, and only one of the US citizens was made the subject of an extradition request (which was ineffective in any event) and three of them had been pardoned by the Italian President. Accordingly, there was a violation of Article 3 because the investigation had not led to the punishment of those responsible.

The obligation to carry out an effective investigation will be supplemented by Article **6.128** 13, which requires an effective *remedy*, entailing effective access for the complainant to the investigatory process and the payment of compensation where appropriate.[401] In a series of cases brought against Turkey from the mid-1990s, the Court found violations of Article 13 arising from the failure to investigate allegations of torture or ill-treatment in custody.[402] However, in *Al-Adsani* v *UK*,[403] the Court found that the United Kingdom was not under a duty to provide a civil remedy in respect of torture carried out by the authorities of another state in that state (and therefore outside the jurisdiction of the United Kingdom).

Policing and the use of force against detainees

A criminal suspect may be susceptible to ill-treatment during an arrest,[404] as well as whilst **6.129** subsequently in detention.[405] However, where suspects forcibly resist arrest, the burden on the state to show that the use of force was not excessive may be less stringent.[406]

Where an individual is taken into custody in good health, but is found to be injured at the **6.130** time of release, the obligation lies on the state to explain credibly and convincingly how the

---

[398] No. 39630/09, 13.12.12.

[399] *Ibid.*, para. 191. See also the joint concurring opinion of Judges Tulkens, Spielmann, Sicilianos and Keller (arguing for the recognition of the right to truth as an aspect of Article 13).

[400] No. 44883/09, 23.2.16.

[401] As to the distinction between the procedural obligation under Article 3 and Article 13, see the Grand Chamber judgment in *Ilhan* v *Turkey*, No. 22777/93, 27.6.00 and the separate opinion of Judge Bratza in *Poltoratskiy* v *Ukraine*, No. 38812/97, 29.4.03.

[402] See, e.g. *Aksoy* v *Turkey*, No. 21987/93, 18.12.96; *Aydin* v *Turkey*, No. 23178/94, 28.6.97; *Kaya* v *Turkey*, No. 22535/93, 28.3.00, para. 96.

[403] No. 35763/97, 21.11.01, para. 40.

[404] As alleged in *Rehbock* v *Slovenia*, No. 29462/95, 28.11.00, and in *Berktay* v *Turkey*, No. 22493/93, 1.3.01. See also *RL and M-JD* v *France*, No. 44568/98, 19.5.04 (violation of Article 3 by four votes to three).

[405] See, e.g. *Ribitsch* v *Austria*, No. 18896/91, Series A, No. 336, 4.12.95.

[406] See e.g. *Berlinski* v *Poland*, Nos. 27715/95 and 3009/96, 20.6.02, para. 62—the use of force was made necessary by the applicants' own conduct and was therefore not excessive. By contrast, see *Dembele* v *Switzerland*, No. 74010/11, 24.9.13 (use of force (batons) clearly disproportionate where applicant suffered fractured collarbone—violation of Article 3).

injuries occurred.[407] Furthermore, in such circumstances, the acquittal of those alleged to have been responsible for the ill-treatment, will not absolve the state of responsibility under the Convention.[408]

6.131　In assessing allegations of ill-treatment, the Court will take into account the particular vulnerability of a person detained in custody. The Court has endorsed the view of the European Committee for the Prevention of Torture (CPT) as to the importance of the proper medical examination of persons in custody:

> such examinations must be carried out by a properly qualified doctor, without any police officer being present and the report of the examination must include not only the details of any injuries found, but the explanations given by the patient as to how they occurred and the opinion of the doctor as to whether the injuries are consistent with those explanations.[409]

6.132　In *Algür v Turkey*,[410] the failings relating to medical examinations of a 22-year-old student, who was held in police custody for 14 days, were important factors in the Court's finding of a violation of Article 3: that she was not permitted to see a doctor of her choosing; that two medical reports which were drawn up were totally contradictory; and that contrary to the prison doctor's instructions, no additional medical examination was carried out in order to establish the causes of the injuries observed on her body.

6.133　The Court has consistently emphasised that the use of physical force against detainees, which has not been made strictly necessary by the individual's own conduct, diminishes human dignity and in principle infringes Article 3.[411] The Grand Chamber reiterated this principle in the case of *Bouyid v Belgium*[412] in which the Court found that Article 3 had been breached because the applicants, two brothers, had been slapped once in the face by police officers (in separate incidents). In finding that the treatment constituted degrading treatment, the Court emphasised that a 'slap inflicted by a law-enforcement officer on an individual who is entirely under his control constitutes a serious attack on the individual's dignity'. The Court took particular account of the fact that the applicants were slapped in the face, and also that one of them was a minor (aged 17) at the time.

6.134　The protections provided by Article 3 as to the physical integrity of individuals cannot be limited even in the context of the fight against terrorism or crime.[413] In the case of *Ireland v UK*[414] the Court assessed five interrogation techniques (wall-standing, hooding, subjection to noise, sleep deprivation and deprivation of food and drink) used during the detention of

---

[407] *Tomasi v France*, No. 12850/87, Series A, No. 241-A, 27.8.92, paras. 108–11; *Ribitsch v Austria*, No. 18896/91, Series A, No. 336, 4.12.95, para. 34; *Selmouni v France*, No. 25803/94, 28.7.99, para. 87; *Satik v Turkey*, No. 31866/96, 10.10.00, para. 54; *Tekin v Turkey*, No. 41556/98, 9.6.98, paras. 52–3, *Rehbock v Slovenia*, No. 29462/95, 28.11.00, para. 76; *Orak v Turkey*, No. 31889/96, 14.2.02; *Virabyan v Armenia*, No. 40094/05, 2.10.12, para. 151; *Ghedir and others v France*, No. 20579/12, 16.7.15, para. 112. But contrast these cases with *Klaas v Germany*, No. 15473/89, 22.9.93, where the domestic courts found that the applicant could have injured herself while resisting arrest and that the arresting officers had not used excessive force.

[408] See, e.g. *Ayşe Tepe v Turkey*, No. 29422/95, 22.7.03; *Çolak and Filizer v Turkey*, Nos. 32578/96 and 32579/96, 8.1.04.

[409] *Akkoç v Turkey*, Nos. 22947/93 and 22948/93, 10.10.00, para. 118.

[410] No. 32574/96, 22.10.02. See also *Ayşe Tepe v Turkey*, No. 29422/95, 22.7.03.

[411] *Ribitsch v Austria*, No. 18896/91, Series A, No. 336, 4.12.95, paras. 36 and 38.

[412] No. 23380/09, 28.9.15.

[413] *Tomasi v France*, No. 12850/87, 27.8.92; *Assenov and others v Bulgaria*, No. 24760/94, 28.10.98, para. 93.

[414] Series A, No. 25, 18.1.78.

five IRA suspects as against the obligations imposed by Article 3. Used in combination and for hours at a time, such treatment, causing at least intense physical and mental suffering and leading to acute psychiatric disturbances, was held to be inhuman and degrading treatment in violation of Article 3, but was not considered to amount to torture.[415] However, severe beatings of the body and feet, and other treatment including electric shocks and the use of a vice, inflicted by the Athens security police on political detainees in order to extract information, was found to amount to torture and inhuman treatment in breach of Article 3.[416]

In a series of cases brought against Turkey, arising from the actions of the security forces, the Court found the treatment of detainees by the Turkish authorities to be in violation of the prohibition against torture in Article 3.[417] For example, the applicant in *Aydin* v *Turkey*[418] was found to have been raped, beaten, kept blindfolded, paraded naked and pummelled with high pressure water whilst being spun around in a tyre. The Court found that, whilst detained in a police station for 24 hours, the first applicant in *Maslova and Nalbandov* v *Russia*[419] had been repeatedly raped and subjected to other forms of ill-treatment, including beatings, suffocation and electrocution, amounting to torture: 'rape of a detainee by an official of the State must be considered to be an especially grave and abhorrent form of ill-treatment given the ease with which the offender can exploit the vulnerability and weakened resistance of his victim'.[420] **6.135**

In *Aksoy* v *Turkey*[421] the applicant was found to have been subjected to 'Palestinian hanging', that is, he was stripped naked, with his arms tied together behind his back, and suspended by his arms, leading to paralysis. This treatment was found to have been administered with the aim of obtaining admissions or information.[422] In *Selmouni* v *France*,[423] the applicant was subjected to prolonged assaults by police officers over several days, which included being beaten, dragged by his hair, being urinated over and threatened with a blowlamp and a syringe. This treatment, taken as a whole, was considered to amount to torture in violation of Article 3. There was a finding of torture in *Savin* v *Ukraine*[424] where the applicant was so badly beaten about the head by police (after having been summoned as a witness) that he was disabled—with sensory and motor impairment and a convulsive disorder. In *Akkoç* v *Turkey*,[425] in addition to the physical ill-treatment of the applicant (electric shocks, hot and cold water treatment and blows to the head), the Court took into account threats made of **6.136**

---

[415] The Irish Government has recently made a request (under Rule 80—see chapter 3) for the revision of the 1978 judgment in *Ireland* v *UK* on the basis that new evidence had come to light (unearthed at the national archives in Kew) which had not been known to the Court. The Irish Government is seeking the Court's re-classification of the treatment as torture. The case was communicated on 22.3.16.

[416] *Greek Case*, Nos. 3321–3/67, 3344/67, 5.11.69, (1969) 12 Yearbook 1.

[417] See, e.g. *Elçi and others* v *Turkey*, Nos. 23145/93 and 25091/94, 13.11.03; *Bati and others* v *Turkey*, Nos. 33097/96 and 57834/00, 3.6.04.

[418] No. 23178/94, 28.6.97.

[419] No. 839/02, 24.1.08.

[420] *Ibid.*, para. 107. See also *Zontul* v *Greece*, No. 12294/07, 17.1.12 (migrant on boat boarded by Greek coastguard raped with a truncheon—torture).

[421] No. 21987/93, 18.12.96. See also, *Tekin* v *Turkey*, No. 22496/93, 9.6.98, paras. 48–54 (applicant held in a cold and dark cell, blindfolded and wounded and bruised during interrogation was found to have been subjected to inhuman and degrading treatment).

[422] See also *Aktaş* v *Turkey*, No. 24351/94, 24.4.03.

[423] No. 25803/94, 28.7.99.

[424] No. 34725/08, 16.2.12.

[425] Nos. 22947/93 and 22948/93, 10.10.00.

ill-treatment to the applicant's children, in finding that she had been the victim of torture. In *Mammadov (Jajaloglu) v Azerbaijan*[426] the application of *falaka* (beating of the soles of the feet) by police officers, in order to obtain admissions or information from the applicant was held to amount to torture. The applicant in *Mikheyev v Russia*[427] was found to have been subjected to torture whilst held in police custody, on suspicion of rape and murder. He claimed that he was tortured to make him corroborate a confession, that police officers administered electric shocks to his ears, and that he was threatened that he would be severely beaten and that an electric current would be applied to his genitals. The Court found that it was difficult to establish what had actually happened (not least because of the ineffective investigation and the refusal to disclose materials from the case file), but nevertheless concluded that he had been seriously ill-treated by police officers, with the aim of extracting a confession or information about the offences of which he was suspected. That caused him such severe physical and mental suffering that he then attempted suicide, by jumping out of the window, which caused his general and permanent physical disability.

6.137 Similar treatment has been meted out to detainees in Chechnya. There was a finding of torture in *Chitayev and Chitayev v Russia*,[428] a case in which the applicants complained of a catalogue of ill-treatment: electric shocks; being beaten, threatened and strangled; being forced to stand continually in a stretched position, with feet and hands spread wide apart; being beaten with rubber truncheons and plastic bottles filled with water; being strangled with adhesive tape, with a cellophane bag and a gas mask; having parts of their skin torn away with pliers; and having fingers and toes squashed with mallets. The Court made a finding of torture in *Sheydayev v Russia*[429] in circumstances where the medical report of injuries incurred by the applicant in police detention was not challenged by the domestic authorities or by the Government. The beating of prisoners in a correctional colony by a special squad using rubber truncheons was found to constitute torture in *Dedovskiy v Russia*.[430] The Court took account of the fact that the use of violence had been unjustified, retaliatory and gratuitous. The case of *Karabet and others v Ukraine*[431] concerned a special forces operation mounted against prisoners who had led a peaceful hunger strike. The Court found that the level of violence used was brutal, gratuitous and grossly disproportionate and had been carried out in retaliation against the prisoners' protest and in order to punish them. It therefore constituted torture. There was a finding of torture in *Kaverzin v Ukraine*,[432] where the applicant lost his sight as a result of injuries deliberately inflicted on him by the police, and also in *Virabyan v Armenia*,[433] in which the applicant's testicles were repeatedly kicked and punched and hit with metal objects by police officers, resulting in one testicle having to be removed. The case

---

[426] No. 34445/04, 11.1.07.
[427] No. 77617/01, 26.1.06. See also *Lyapin v Russia*, No. 46956/09, 24.7.14; *Razzakov v Russia*, No. 57519/09, 5.2.15 ('abhorrent acts of physical and psychological violence during a prolonged period of time'—torture).
[428] No. 59334/00, 18.1.07. See also, e.g. *Musayev and others v Russia*, Nos. 57941/00, 58699/00 and 60403/00, 26.7.07; *Gisayev v Russia*, No. 14811/04, 20.1.11.
[429] No. 65859/01, 7.12.06.
[430] No. 7178/03, 15.5.08. See also *Vladimir Romanov v Russia*, No. 41461/02, 24.7.08.
[431] Nos. 38906/07 and 52025/07, 17.1.13.
[432] No. 23893/03, 15.5.12. See also *Savitskyy v Ukraine*, No. 38773/05, 26.7.12 (applicant left disabled as a result of injuries inflicted by police—torture).
[433] No. 40094/05, 2.10.12. There was also a separate finding of a procedural violation of Article 3 because the domestic investigation into the applicant's allegations of ill-treatment was held to be 'ineffective, inadequate and fundamentally flawed'.

of *Cestaro* v *Italy*[434] concerned an operation involving 500 police officers against demonstrators at a G8 summit in Genoa. The police stormed a school used as a night shelter by the demonstrators who were systematically beaten up. The beating of the 62-year-old applicant caused him multiple fractures and left him with permanent weakness in his right arm and right leg. Such a totally gratuitous use of force was held to constitute torture.

The Court in *Al-Adsani* v *UK* accepted that repeated beatings of a detainee over several days, **6.138** in order to obtain a confession, could be categorised as torture.[435] However, in *Egmez* v *Cyprus*,[436] whilst the Court accepted that police officers had intentionally beaten the applicant, the Court found that an intention to extract a confession was not proven, and therefore the treatment could be categorised as being inhuman, but not torture. Holding a group of 11 men in the open for at least a week, most of whom were bound, and subjecting them to beatings, was found to amount to inhuman and degrading treatment in *Akdeniz* v *Turkey*.[437] Where ill-treatment is meted out by fellow detainees, the state may still be liable under Article 3 as a result of the application of positive obligations, and accordingly the state will be obliged to monitor vulnerable detainees.[438]

A series of judgments since 2012 have concerned the practice of 'extraordinary rendi- **6.139** tion': the unacknowledged detention of terrorist suspects by various European states in the early 2000s and their transfer into the custody of the US authorities. The applicant in *El-Masri* v *former Yugoslav Republic of Macedonia*[439] established that he had been arrested, held incommunicado, questioned and ill-treated, and that he was then handed over at Skopje Airport to CIA agents who had transferred him to a secret detention facility in Afghanistan (run by the CIA), where he had been ill-treated for four months. There were several violations of Article 3: he was detained incommunicado in a hotel for 23 days where he was interrogated in a foreign language and threatened with a gun (inhuman and degrading treatment); at Skopje airport, he was beaten, stripped, sodomised, shackled and hooded, transferred to a CIA aircraft, chained down and tranquilised (torture): and his transfer into US custody which exposed him to a real risk of ill-treatment and to conditions of detention contrary to Article 3. The applicants in *Al Nashiri* v *Poland*[440] and *Husayn (Abu Zubaydah)* v *Poland*[441] made similar complaints about their arrest in Poland (at the instigation of the CIA and with the Polish authorities' knowledge) and their subsequent transfer to the US naval base at Guantánamo Bay. Their treatment by the CIA included being subjected to mock executions (with a pistol and a power drill), threatened and being held in stress positions. Such measures were applied 'in a premeditated and organised manner, on the basis of a formalised, clinical procedure', and were designed to elicit information or confessions or to obtain intelligence and 'to psychologically "dislocate" the detainee, maximize his feeling of

---

[434] No. 6884/11, 7.4.15. There was also a procedural violation of Article 3 due to the inadequacy of the ensuing investigation.

[435] No. 35763/97, 21.11.01, para. 58.

[436] No. 30873/96, 21.12.00.

[437] No. 23954/94, 31.5.01, para. 98. See also *Ahmet Özkan and others* v *Turkey*, No. 21689/93, 6.4.04 (villagers rounded up into village square and made to lie face down on the ground; forcing villagers to walk long distance in adverse weather conditions and conditions in which villagers were held, leading to many contracting frostbite; failure to investigate allegations of ill-treatment).

[438] See, e.g. *Pantea* v *Romania*, No. 33343/96, 3.6.03.

[439] No. 39630/09, 13.12.12.

[440] No. 28761/11, 24.7.14.

[441] No. 7511/13, 24.7.14.

vulnerability and helplessness, and reduce or eliminate his will to resist'. Accordingly, it was held to constitute torture. Poland was found to be responsible for breaching Article 3 as it 'facilitated the whole process, created the conditions for it to happen and made no attempt to prevent it from occurring'. The first applicant in *Nasr and Ghali v Italy*[442] was abducted in Milan and then handed over to CIA agents and taken to Egypt where he was subjected to violent interrogation by the Egyptian intelligence services. The Court was satisfied that the Italian authorities had known, or ought to have known, that the operation would expose the applicant to a real risk of treatment proscribed by Article 3. However, they had failed to ensure that he was not subjected to acts of torture or to inhuman or degrading treatment or punishment.

6.140 Central to the case of *Gäfgen v Germany*,[443] was the threat made by the police to use torture against the applicant who had been arrested for abducting an 11-year-old boy (the applicant had in fact already suffocated the boy and hidden his corpse, but this was unknown to the police at the time). In an attempt to save the boy's life, he was threatened by police officers with 'intolerable pain' if he refused to disclose the boy's whereabouts. As a result, the applicant told the police where he had hidden the body. The interrogation under threat of ill-treatment lasted for about ten minutes, and the Court found that this would have caused him considerable fear, anguish and mental suffering, although there was no evidence of any long-term effects. The threat was premeditated and was made with the intention of extracting information. Accordingly, the treatment was found by the Grand Chamber to constitute inhuman treatment, in violation of Article 3, but it did not amount to torture. Recognising that the police were motivated by the desire to save the boy's life, the Court nevertheless reiterated the absolute nature of the prohibition of treatment violating Article 3:[444]

> ... the prohibition on ill-treatment of a person applies irrespective of the conduct of the victim or the motivation of the authorities. Torture, inhuman or degrading treatment cannot be inflicted even in circumstances where the life of an individual is at risk.... Article 3, which has been framed in unambiguous terms, recognises that every human being has an absolute, inalienable right not to be subjected to torture or to inhuman or degrading treatment under any circumstances, even the most difficult. The philosophical basis underpinning the absolute nature of the right under Article 3 does not allow for any exceptions or justifying factors or balancing of interests, irrespective of the conduct of the person concerned and the nature of the offence at issue.

6.141 The use of handcuffs may in certain circumstances breach Article 3, where, for example, their use during public hearings is unwarranted.[445] In the case of *Kaj Raninen v Finland*,[446] the applicant, who objected to military service, was handcuffed by military police for two hours and appeared in public handcuffed in the presence of his support group. The European Commission of Human Rights found that the use of force had not been strictly necessary as a result of the applicant's conduct, nor of any other legitimate consideration, diminishing his human dignity and amounting to degrading treatment in violation of Article 3. The Court,

---

[442] No. 44883/09, 23.2.16.
[443] No. 22978/05, 1.6.10.
[444] *Ibid.*, para. 107.
[445] See, e.g. *Gorodnichev v Russia*, No. 52058/99, 24.5.07.
[446] No. 20972/92, Comm. Rep. 24.1.96.

however, unanimously found no violation of Article 3 because it was not convinced that the incident had adversely affected the applicant's mental state or that the handcuffing had been aimed at debasing or humiliating him.[447] However, in *Erdoğan Yağız v Turkey*[448] the arrest and handcuffing of the applicant, a doctor, amounted to degrading treatment in breach of Article 3. He was handcuffed at his place of work in front of his patients and in the area where he lived, which, according to the psychiatric evidence, irreversibly affected his mental state. The handcuffing or shackling of detainees who are ill or otherwise vulnerable, or who are pregnant, will violate Article 3 because it is considered to be disproportionate to the requirements of security and implies an unjustifiable humiliation.[449] The handcuffing of a seriously ill prisoner in *Mouisel v France*[450] was considered to be a disproportionate response to any security risk involved. The Court has also acknowledged that artificially depriving prisoners of their sight by blindfolding them for lengthy periods spread over several days may, when combined with other ill-treatment, subject them to strong psychological and physical pressure.[451] Police strip-searching of suspects on arrest may violate Article 3[452] (see also 6.155 below). The use of tear gas by the police,[453] or of electrical discharge weapons (tasers)[454] may breach Article 3. In *Çiloğlu and others v Turkey*,[455] the use of pepper spray against demonstrators was found, on the facts, not to violate Article 3, but there was a breach of this provision in *Tali v Estonia*[456] as a result of the use of pepper spray within the confines of a prison. Together with the use of physical force, handcuffs, a telescopic baton and a restraint bed, the Court found that the cumulative effect of such measures against the applicant amounted to inhuman and degrading treatment. In *Gutsanovi v Bulgaria*,[457] a police operation to arrest a local politician at his home, carried out by armed, masked men at dawn, was found to be degrading, in breach of Article 3, notably because of the detrimental psychological effects on his wife and young daughters.

Article 3 may be violated by oppressive conditions at a public hearing, as was the case in **6.142** *Ramishvili and Kokhreidze v Georgia*.[458] There, the applicants were well-known co-founders and shareholders of a television channel who were accused of extortion. During televised proceedings they were detained in what appeared to be a metal cage, in the presence of

---

[447] *Raninen v Finland*, No. 20972/92, 16.12.97. See also *Portmann v Switzerland*, No. 38455/06, 11.10.10 (use of hood, handcuffs and leg shackles to restrain dangerous suspect for two hours—no violation of Article 3).

[448] No. 27473/02, 6.3.07.

[449] See, e.g. *Korneykova and Korneykov v Ukraine*, No. 56660/12, 24.3.16.

[450] No. 67263/01, 14.11.02. See also *Henaf v France*, No. 65436/01, 7.11.03; *Tarariyeva v Russia*, No. 4353/03, 14.12.06; *Filiz Uyan v Turkey*, No. 7446/03, 8.1.09 (refusal to remove handcuffs from prisoner referred to hospital for scan, and presence of male guards in the consultation room—violation of Article 3, by four votes to three); *Salakhov and Islyamova v Ukraine*, No. 28005/08, 14.3.13; *Ilievska v former Yugoslav Republic of Macedonia*, No. 20136/11, 7.5.15. In contrast, see *Naumenko v Ukraine*, No. 42023/98, 10.2.04.

[451] *Salman v Turkey*, No. 21986/93, 27.6.00, para. 132; *Öcalan v Turkey*, No. 46221/99, 12.5.05, para. 183.

[452] See, e.g. *Wieser v Austria*, No. 2293/03, 22.2.07.

[453] *Ali Güneş v Turkey*, No. 9829/07, 10.4.12 (police sprayed tear gas into detainee's face—violation of Article 3); *Abdullah Yaşa and others v Turkey*, No. 44827/08, 16.7.13 (thirteen-year-old struck in face by tear gas canister during demonstration—violation of Article 3). As regards fatalities caused by tear gas, see *Ataykaya v Turkey*, No. 50275/08, 22.7.14 (a case relating to the same demonstration which was the subject of the *Abdullah Yaşa* case referred to above) and *Nagmetov v Russia*, No. 35589/08, 5.11.15 and Grand Chamber of 30.3.17.

[454] *Anzhelo Georgiev and others v Bulgaria*, No. 51284/09, 30.9.14.

[455] No. 73333/01, 6.3.07.

[456] No. 66393/10, 13.2.14.

[457] No. 34529/10, 15.10.13.

[458] No. 1704/06, 27.1.09 (as a result of the courtroom conditions there was also a violation of Article 5(4)).

heavily armed guards in black hood-like masks. Such harsh and hostile conditions were found to be humiliating for the applicants. There was a violation of Article 3 in *Ashot Harutyunyan v Armenia*[459] because the applicant was kept in a metal cage (of about three square metres) during 12 public hearings in the course of criminal appeal proceedings, which was humiliating and could not be justified by 'security considerations.' In *Svinarenko and Slyadnev v Russia*[460]the Grand Chamber found that the applicant defendants' confinement in a cage in the courtroom during their jury trial for robberies with violence (surrounded by armed guards), which lasted more than a year, amounted to degrading treatment in breach of Article 3. It also found that the use of cages in that way could never be justified under Article 3: holding a person in a metal cage during a trial constitutes in itself an affront to human dignity.

6.143 The mental anguish and distress caused by the 'disappearance' of a close relative may give rise to a violation of Article 3, as was the case in *Kurt v Turkey*,[461] where the applicant was found to have suffered anguish for a long period of time over the disappearance of her son and in view of the complacency of the authorities in response to her complaints.[462] The mutilation or decapitation of corpses has also given rise to violations of Article 3.[463] In *Benzer and others v Turkey*,[464] the Court found a violation of Article 3 where the applicants witnessed the violent deaths of their relatives during aerial bombing raids of their villages by the Turkish armed forces. They then had to collect the bodies and they themselves were deprived of shelter because of the destruction of their homes. Furthermore, in a series of cases against Turkey, the security forces have been found responsible for destroying the homes and possessions of the applicants, resulting in findings of grave and unjustified violations of both Article 8 and Article 1 of Protocol No. 1. In a number of these cases where the applicants and/or their close relatives witnessed this destruction, the Court has also characterised such practices as inhuman treatment in violation of Article 3.[465] A similar conclusion was reached by the Court in *Esmukhambetov and others v Russia*,[466] where one of the applicants witnessed the killing of his wife and two young sons in the course of an indiscriminate bombing attack on his village by Russian federal fighter aircraft.

---

[459] No. 34334/04, 15.6.10 (but the use of the cage was not found to violate Articles 6(1) or 6(2)). See also *Khodorkovskiy v Russia*, No. 5829/04, 31.5.11; *Piruzyan v Armenia*, No. 33376/07, 26.6.12; *Khodorkovskiy and Lebedev v Russia*, Nos. 11082/06 and 13772/05, 25.7.13.

[460] Nos. 32541/08 and 43441/08, 17.7.14. See also, e.g. *Korneykova and Korneykov v Ukraine*, No. 56660/12, 24.3.16 (applicant detained in metal cage during court hearings, when she was pregnant, and later as a nursing mother—violation of Article 3); *Yaroslav Belousov v Russia*, Nos. 2653/13 and 60980/14, 4.10.16 (defendants held in overcrowded glass cabin in court room—degrading treatment—violation of Articles 3 and 6).

[461] No. 24276/94, 25.5.98.

[462] See also *Çakıcı v Turkey*, No. 23657/94, 8.7.99, paras. 98–9; *Taş v Turkey*, No. 24396/94, paras. 79–80; *Çiçek v Turkey*, No. 25704/94, 27.2.01, paras. 170–4; *Cyprus v Turkey*, No. 25781/94, 10.5.01, paras. 154–8 (continuing violation of Article 3); *Orhan v Turkey*, No. 25656/94, 18.6.02, paras. 356–60; *Ipek v Turkey*, No. 25760/94, 17.2.04, paras. 178–83; *Tanış and others v Turkey*, No. 65899/01, 2.8.05, paras. 217–21; *Bazorkina v Russia*, No. 69481/01, 27.7.06, paras. 139–42; *Varnava and others v Turkey*, No. 16064/90, 18.9.09, paras. 200–2; *Nasr and Ghali v Italy*, No. 44883/09, 23.2.16 (paras. 314–20). See, by contrast, *Janowiec and others v Russia*, Nos. 55508/07 and 29520/09, 21.10.13.

[463] *Akkum and others v Turkey*, No. 21894/93, 24.3.05; *Akpınar and Altun v Turkey*, No. 56760/00, 27.2.07; *Khadzhialiyev and others v Russia*, No. 3013/04, 6.11.08. See also *Kanlıbaş v Turkey*, No. 32444/96, 8.12.05.

[464] No. 23502/06, 12.11.13.

[465] See, e.g. *Selçuk and Asker v Turkey*, Nos. 23184/94 and 23185/94, 24.4.98; *Yöyler v Turkey*, No. 26973/95, 24.7.03; *Ayder and others v Turkey*, No. 23656/94, 8.1.04 (the Court in *Ayder* found that it was not necessary also to deal with a complaint of collective punishment, allegedly in violation of Article 3).

[466] No. 23445/03, 29.3.11.

Conditions of detention and sentencing

The conditions in which detainees[467] are held (whether on remand or following conviction) may **6.144** also violate Article 3, depending upon the particular circumstances. The Court has found[468] that:

> … the state must ensure that a person is detained in conditions which are compatible with respect for his human dignity, that the manner and method of the execution of the measure do not subject him to distress or hardship of an intensity exceeding the unavoidable level of suffering inherent in detention and that, given the practical demands of imprisonment, his health and well-being are adequately secured by, among other things, providing him with the requisite medical assistance.

Relevant factors will include the standards of the provision of living space,[469] heating, venti- **6.145** lation,[470] lighting, food and water,[471] medical treatment, toilets, facilities for sleeping and for recreation and the means of contact with others not in detention,[472] as well as the length of time during which the detainee was exposed to the conditions complained of.[473] The Court will assess the cumulative effects of any such conditions. For example, *Dougoz* v *Greece*[474] concerned the conditions at a police headquarters and a detention centre where a Syrian national was held pending deportation. The unacceptable state of prisons as a whole has led to several pilot judgments, including cases against Russia,[475] Italy,[476] Bulgaria[477] and Hungary[478] (see the discussion of pilot judgments at 3.30 above). As regards prison over-crowding, the Court will assess three issues in particular: (i) whether each detainee has an individual sleeping place in the cell; (ii) whether each detainee has at least three square metres of floor space; and (iii) whether the overall surface of the cell is such as to allow detainees to move freely between the furniture items.[479]

In *Ilaşcu and others* v *Moldova and Russia*,[480] the Court held that the cumulative treatment of **6.146** two of the applicants in custody in the 'Moldovan Republic of Transdniestria' amounted to

---

[467] These principles also apply to individuals deemed to be deprived of their liberty in social care institutions. See, e.g. *Stanev* v *Bulgaria*, No. 36760/06, 17.1.12.

[468] *Aerts* v *Belgium*, No. 25357/94, 30.7.98, para. 64; *Kudla* v *Poland*, No. 30210/96, 26.10.00, para. 94.

[469] See, e.g. *Sulejmanovic* v *Italy*, No. 22635/03, 16.7.09.

[470] See, e.g. *Florea* v *Romania*, No. 37186/03, 14.9.10 and *Elefteriadis* v *Romania*, No. 38427/05, 25.1.11 (re passive smoking). See also *Plathey* v *France*, No. 48337/09, 10.11.11 (prisoner held in foul-smelling cell for 28 days—violation of Article 3).

[471] For example, in *Soare and others* v *Romania*, No. 24329/02, 22.2.11, holding the applicants in a police station overnight for questioning, without food and water was considered to be degrading, in violation of Article 3.

[472] See, e.g. the *Greek Case*, Nos. 3321–3/67, 3344/67, 5.11.69, (1969) 12 Yearbook 1. There was, however, no violation on the facts in *Assenov and others* v *Bulgaria*, No. 24760/94, 28.10.98.

[473] See, e.g. *Sakkapoulos* v *Greece*, No. 61828/00, 15.1.04; *Kaja* v *Greece*, No. 32927/03, 27.7.06. In *MM* v *UK*, No. 58374/00, dec. 8.1.02, the Court was critical of the detention by the police of a 12-year-old for eight hours in a 'hostile and intimidating environment' (a juvenile justice centre 72 km away) as being cause for concern, but found that the treatment was not sufficiently severe to raise an issue under Article 3.

[474] No. 40907/98, 6.3.01.

[475] *Ananyev and others* v *Russia*, Nos. 42525/07 and 60800/08, 10.1.12.

[476] *Torreggiani and others* v *Italy*, No. 43517/09, 8.1.13.

[477] *Neshkov and others* v *Bulgaria*, 36925/10, 27.1.15.

[478] *Varga and others* v *Hungary*, No. 14097/12, 10.3.15.

[479] *Ananyev and others* v *Russia*, Nos. 42525/07 and 60800/08, 10.1.12, para. 148. See also, e.g. *Muršić* v *Croatia*, No. 7334/13, 20.10.16. In *Muršić*, the Grand Chamber held that 'a strong presumption of a violation of Article 3 arises when the personal space available to a detainee falls below 3 sq. m in multi-occupancy accommodation' (para. 324).

[480] No. 48787/99, 8.7.04.

torture. Notably, the applicants were held for several years in solitary confinement and were denied adequate medical care, contact and food. The two other applicants were subjected to inhuman and degrading treatment as a result of their treatment in custody. Taking account of reports of the Committee for the Prevention of Torture,[481] the Court found degrading treatment in violation of Article 3 as a result, in particular, of the serious over-crowding, the absence of sleeping facilities and the inordinate length of the detention. The applicant in *Peers* v *Greece*[482] complained of cell overcrowding, of the absence of ventila-tion and excessive temperatures. He was also practically confined to his bed in his cell for a considerable part of each day. Taken together, such conditions were held to amount to degrading treatment.

6.147 The appalling state of Russian prisons was evident from the Court's judgment in *Kalashnikov* v *Russia*[483] in which the applicant was detained on remand in a cell with dimensions of between 17 and 21 square metres, which was designed for eight inmates, but which usually held between 18 and 24 prisoners.[484] Inmates were forced to sleep in turn on bunks in eight hour shifts. Thus the Court found that the cell was continuously and severely overcrowded. Lights were continually on in the cell, causing sleep deprivation and the cell was inadequately ventilated and infested with vermin. Inmates were confined to the cell for all but one or two hours a day and the toilet in the cell was not separated from the living area. The applicant was detained on various occasions with people suffering from syphilis and tuberculosis and he himself contracted various recurring skin diseases and fungal infections. The Court acknowl-edged that such degrading conditions must have caused the applicant mental suffering, undermining his human dignity and arousing feelings of humiliation and debasement. In *Poltoratskiy* v *Ukraine*,[485] the Court found a violation of Article 3 as a result of the conditions in which the applicant was held in prison on death row, which included overcrowded cells, the cell light being kept on, being locked up for 24 hours a day, the absence of any natural light in the cell, the poor sanitary facilities, and restrictions on the applicant's contact with his family. These conditions were found to have caused the applicant 'considerable mental suffering', thus diminishing his human dignity. The Court reiterated that the state's socio-economic problems and lack of resources could not justify such prison conditions. However, in *Iorgov* v *Bulgaria*[486] and *GB* v *Bulgaria*[487] the applicants could not claim a violation of Article 3 as a result of the 'death row phenomenon' in circumstances where a moratorium on executions had been maintained in Bulgaria. Nevertheless, Article 3 was violated in both

---

[481] See, generally, *The CPT Standards*, CPT/Inf/E(2002) 1, Rev. 2015: http://www.cpt.coe.int/en/docs-standards.htm.

[482] No. 28524/95, 19.4.01.

[483] No. 47095/99, 15.7.02. See also, e.g. *Mayzit* v *Russia*, No. 63378/00, 20.1.05; *Novoselov* v *Russia*, No. 66460/01, 2.6.05; *Mamedova* v *Russia*, No. 7064/05, 1.6.06; *Ananyev and others* v *Russia*, Nos. 42525/07 and 60800/08, 10.1.12. As regards prison conditions in Latvia, see, e.g. *Kadiķis* v *Latvia*, No. 62393/00, 4.5.06.

[484] The Court noted that the Committee for the Prevention of Torture (CPT) had set seven square metres per prisoner as an approximate desirable guideline for a detention cell.

[485] No. 38812/97, 29.4.03. See also the following judgments of the same date: *Kuznetsov* v *Ukraine*, No. 39042/97, 29.4.03; *Nazarenko* v *Ukraine*, No. 39483/98, 29.4.03; *Dankevich* v *Ukraine*, No. 40679/98, 29.4.03; *Aliev* v *Ukraine*, No. 41220/98, 29.4.03, and *Khokhlich* v *Ukraine*, No. 41707/98, 29.4.03. As regards prison conditions in Ukraine see, also, e.g.: *Nevmerzhitsky* v *Ukraine*, No. 54825/00, 5.4.05; *Melnik* v *Ukraine*, No. 72286/01, 28.3.06.

[486] No. 40653/98, 11.3.04. As regards prison conditions in Bulgaria, see also *Harakchiev and Tolumov* v *Bulgaria*, Nos. 15018/11 and 61199/12, 8.7.14.

[487] No. 42346/98, 11.3.04.

cases because of the stringent detention conditions: they were kept alone in their cells for 23 hours a day and were allowed only minimal contact with others over a period of several years.

Excessive periods of detention in police or court cells may also breach the standards required **6.148** by Article 3. That was the case in *Fedotov v Russia*,[488] as a result of the applicant's detention in a police cell for 22 hours without access to a toilet, or to any food or drink. Detention in transit zones or holding cells of airports, or in removal centres, may raise issues under Article 3, as was the case in *Riad and Idiab v Belgium*.[489] There, the detention of the applicant Palestinians in the transit zone of Brussels airport for more than ten days was found to constitute inhuman and degrading treatment. The Court noted that there was no outdoor area for fresh air or physical exercise, no internal catering facilities, and no radio or television to maintain contact with the outside world. The Court found that theirs was not an isolated case, which lent support to the applicants' allegation that the aim of the Belgian authorities in abandoning them in the transit zone had been to force them to leave the country of their own accord. Article 3 was violated in *S.D. v Greece*[490] where the applicant was detained in a holding centre at a border post for more than two months without being allowed outdoors and without access to a telephone, blankets, clean sheets or sufficient toiletries.

Also relevant to the assessment of conditions of detention will be the particular circum- **6.149** stances or characteristics of the detainee, such as age or disability. The Court has acknowledged that the detention of an elderly person may raise an issue under Article 3,[491] as may the detention of a minor together with adults.[492]

The Court has emphasised that special care must be taken to ensure that detention conditions correspond to a person's individual needs resulting from disability.[493] In *Price v UK*,[494] the disabled applicant (who was four-limb deficient due to Thalidomide) was committed by a court to immediate imprisonment for contempt of court, but the prison authorities were clearly unable to cope. The Court found that 'to detain a severely disabled person in conditions where she is dangerously cold, risks developing sores because her bed is too hard or unreachable, and is unable to go to the toilet or keep clean without the greatest of difficulty' amounted to degrading treatment.[495]

There was a similar finding in *Grimailovs v Latvia*[496] where the applicant, who was paraplegic **6.150** and wheelchair bound, was held for almost two and a half years in a regular prison which was not adapted for people in wheelchairs. Various parts of the prison remained inaccessible to him, including the canteen, toilets, sauna, library, shop, gym, meeting room and telephone

---

[488] No. 5140/02, 25.10.09. See also *Moiseyev v Russia*, No. 62936/00, 9.10.08 (applicant detained in court cells on more then 150 days).

[489] Nos. 29787/03 and 29810/03, 24.1.08. See also *Shchebet v Russia*, No. 16074/07, 12.6.08 (34 days' detention in airport holding cell).

[490] No. 53541/07, 11.6.09.

[491] *Papon v France*, No. 64666/01, dec. 7.6.01; *Sawoniuk v UK*, No. 63716/00, dec. 29.5.01.

[492] *Güveç v Turkey*, No. 70337/01, 20.1.09.

[493] See, e.g. *Jasinskis v Latvia*, No. 45744/08, 21.12.10, para. 59.

[494] No. 33394/96, 10.7.01.

[495] *Ibid.*, para. 30. See also *Arutyunyan v Russia*, No. 48977/09, 10.1.12; *Zarzycki v Poland*, No. 15351/03, 12.3.13; *Topekhin v Russia*, No. 78774/13, 10.5.16.

[496] No. 6087/03, 25.6.13. See also: *D.G. v Poland*, No. 45705/07, 12.2.13; *Semikhvostov v Russia*, No. 2689/12, 6.2.14; *Helhal v France*, No. 10401/12, 19.2.15. See, by contrast, *Todorov v Bulgaria*, No. 8321/11, dec.12.2.13 and *Ürfi Çetinkaya v Turkey*, No. 19866/04, 23.7.13.

room. He could not properly wash or use the toilet, and had to rely on other inmates to assist him with daily routines and movement around the prison. There was a breach of Article 3 in *Amirov v Russia*[497] as a result of the inadequate medical treatment of the applicant in prison, a paraplegic who used a wheelchair and who suffered from a range of illnesses affecting his nervous, urinary, muscular and endocrine systems. As a result he had been exposed to prolonged mental and physical suffering which diminished his human dignity. The case of *Z.H. v Hungary*[498] concerned the arrest of a young man who was innately deaf and dumb, had medium-grade intellectual disability and was illiterate. He could communicate with a type of sign language which was only intelligible to his mother. He was detained on remand for nearly three months on a charge of mugging and complained of the conditions of his detention. The Court found that his treatment was inhuman and degrading due to his inevitable feelings of isolation and helplessness, his inability to understand his situation, and because he had been separated from his mother, who was the only person with whom he could effectively communicate. The authorities' failure to provide adequate medical treatment to a juvenile who was suffering from ADHD led to a finding of a breach of Article 3 in *Blokhin v Russia*.[499] There was a violation of Article 3 in the case of *Farbtuhs v Latvia*,[500] relating to the detention of the applicant following his conviction for crimes against humanity and genocide. The applicant was in his 80s, suffered from various debilitating illnesses and was a paraplegic. The detention conditions were found to be unsuited to his state of health, and consequently amounted to degrading treatment. In *Slyusarev v Russia*[501] the failure to provide glasses to a detainee suffering from myopia was found to constitute degrading treatment in violation of Article 3.

6.151 The transportation of prisoners in poor conditions may give rise to issues under Article 3, such as repeated use of cramped prison vans over excessive periods of time,[502] or transporting a seriously ill prisoner in a standard-issue prison van.[503] (See further Medical treatment at 6.189 below.)

6.152 To separate a mother from her baby in prison is likely to lead to a finding of a violation of Article 3. Such a complaint in *Togher v UK*[504] was declared admissible, but was subsequently settled by the UK Government on payment of £10,000 compensation, plus costs.

6.153 According to the Court, if applied, solitary confinement should be an exceptional and temporary measure.[505] It will not necessarily breach Article 3; this will depend 'on the particular conditions, the stringency of the measure, its duration, the objective pursued and its effects on the person concerned'.[506] The Court draws a distinction between 'complete sensory

---

[497] No. 51857/13, 27.11.14. See also the cases relating to Russia referred to at para. 90 of that judgment.
[498] No. 28973/11, 8.11.12.
[499] No. 47152/06, 23.3.16.
[500] No. 4672/02, 2.12.04. See also *Hüseyin Yıldırım v Turkey*, No. 2778/02, 3.5.07; *Flaminzeanu v Romania*, No. 56664/08, 12.4.11.
[501] No. 60333/00, 20.4.10.
[502] *Moiseyev v Russia*, No. 62936/00, 9.10.08. See also *Yakovenko v Ukraine*, No. 15825/06, 25.10.07.
[503] See, e.g. *Tarariyeva v Russia*, No. 4353/03, 14.12.06.
[504] No. 28555/95, Comm. Rep. 25.10.99.
[505] *Csüllög v Hungary*, No. 30042/08, 7.6.11, para. 34.
[506] *Rohde v Denmark*, No. 69332/01, 21.7.05, para. 93 (in that case, on the facts, solitary confinement of just over 11 months did not breach Article 3). See also *Khodorkovskiy and Lebedev v Russia*, Nos. 11082/06 and 13772/05, 25.7.13. See, by contrast, *Csüllög v Hungary*, No. 30042/08, 7.6.11 (violation of Article 3 where solitary confinement was combined with various restrictive measures which could not be justified

isolation' and partial or relative isolation (for example through restrictions on contact with other prisoners or family members).[507] The effects of solitary confinement on mental health have been noted by the Court.[508] Whilst removal of a prisoner's right of association with other prisoners may be justified, a more extreme regime of isolation is unlikely to be acceptable. The Court has found[509] that:

> complete sensory isolation, coupled with total social isolation, can destroy the personality and constitutes a form of inhuman treatment which cannot be justified by the requirements of security or any other reason.

In *Nevmerzhitsky v Ukraine*,[510] the Court found that the force-feeding of the applicant whilst in pre-trial detention—involving the use of handcuffs, a mouth-widener and the insertion of a rubber tube—amounted to torture. Although the applicant was on hunger strike, the Government failed to establish that force-feeding had been a medical necessity. Forcefully administering emetics to the applicant using a nasogastric tube, in order to recover drugs that he had swallowed, was found to constitute inhuman and degrading treatment in breach of Article 3 by a ten–seven majority of the Grand Chamber in *Jalloh v Germany*.[511] Its aim had been to obtain evidence of an offence, rather than being required for medical reasons. The handcuffing of a detainee with a serious mental health illness for a period of seven days, without any psychiatric justification, was found to amount to inhuman and degrading treatment in *Kucheruk v Ukraine*.[512] Forcing a suspect detained on remand to wear a balaclava whenever he left his cell, for a period of 13 months, was found to breach Article 3 in *Petyo Petkov v Bulgaria*,[513] and in *Kashavelov v Bulgaria*[514] the systematic handcuffing of a life prisoner whenever he left his cell (over a period of 13 years) constituted degrading treatment. The prolonged use of a restraint bed has also been found to violate Article 3.[515] In *Lindström and Mässeli v Finland*[516] the Court found no violation of Article 3 (by five votes to two) as a result of the requirement for prisoners in isolation to wear 'closed overalls' sealed with plastic strips.

6.154

---

by security reasons, including a ban on the applicant possessing a watch or teabags and a restriction on the number of books kept in his cell). The Grand Chamber found no violation of Article 3 (by 12 votes to 5) in *Ramirez Sanchez v France*, No. 59450/00, 4.7.06 (the applicant, who was considered to be 'one of the world's most dangerous terrorists' was held in solitary confinement for more than eight years). Detention in solitary confinement for an unnecessarily protracted period was found to violate Article 3 in *Mathew v Netherlands*, No. 24919/03, 29.9.05.

[507] See, e.g. *Sotiropoulou v Greece*, No. 40225/02, dec. 18.1.07.

[508] *Ibid.*

[509] *Van der Ven v Netherlands*, No. 50901/99, 4.2.03, para. 51. See also, e.g. *Bastone v Italy*, No. 59638/00, dec. 18.1.05 (complaint about a special prison regime imposed on applicant charged with homicide linked to the Mafia—inadmissible re Articles 3 and 8).

[510] No. 54825/00, 5.4.05. See also *Ciorap v Moldova*, No. 12066/02, 19.6.07 (a finding of torture on a similar basis). See, in contrast, *Pandjikidzé v Georgia*, No. 30323/02, dec. 20.6.06 (hunger striker who was not force-fed—inadmissible); *Rappaz v Switzerland*, No. 73175/10, dec. 26.3.13 (decision taken to force-feed prisoner on hunger strike which was not implemented—inadmissible).

[511] No. 54810/00, 11.7.06. See, by contrast, *Bogumil v Portugal*, No. 35228/03, 7.10.08 (operation carried out on person who had swallowed cocaine justified as medical necessity).

[512] No. 2570/04, 6.9.07. See also the cases concerning the use of handcuffs referred to in the section above on 'Policing and the use of force against detainees' (6.129).

[513] No. 32130/03, 7.1.10.

[514] No. 891/05, 20.1.11. See also *Kaverzin v Ukraine*, No. 23893/03, 15.5.12.

[515] *Julin v Estonia*, No. 16563/08, 29.5.12 (restraint for almost nine hours).

[516] No. 24630/10, 14.1.14. There was, however, a violation of Article 8 as their use had no proper legal basis.

6.155 An intimate body search may amount to degrading treatment, if the particular circumstances are such that the Article 3 threshold has been reached.[517] The Court has accepted that strip-searches may be necessary to ensure prison security or prevent disorder or crime, but they must be carried out in an appropriate way. For example in *Valasinas* v *Lithuania*,[518] a body search of the applicant was degrading in violation of Article 3 because he was obliged to strip naked in the presence of a woman, and his sexual organs were then examined with bare hands. Article 3 was also found to have been violated in *Wiktorko* v *Poland*[519] where the applicant, a woman, was forcibly stripped naked at a sobering-up centre by a woman and two men, and was then placed in restraining belts for ten hours overnight. In *El Shennawy* v *France*,[520] repeated, filmed strip searches were held to breach Article 3. A systematic regime of weekly strip-searches, which included anal inspections, over a period of years, was found to amount to inhuman or degrading treatment in both *Van der Ven* v *Netherlands*[521] and *Lorsé* v *Netherlands*.[522] Detainees held on remand should be treated so as to respect the presumption of innocence. The Court in *Iwanczuk* v *Poland*[523] confirmed that this has application not only to procedural rights, but also to the legal regime governing detention, including the manner of treatment by prison guards. Accordingly, forcing the applicant in *Iwanczuk* to strip naked in front of a group of prison guards, as well as a failure adequately to investigate allegations that they insulted him, was found to be degrading. In *Wainwright* v *UK*,[524] the strip-searching of the applicants who were visiting their close relative in prison was not found to violate Article 3, but it was nevertheless found to be disproportionate, and in violation of Article 8. The shaving of a prisoner's head may amount to degrading treatment in violation of Article 3, depending on its aim, the context in which it is carried out and the personal circumstances of the prisoner.[525] In *Khider* v *France*,[526] the applicant was found to have been subjected to inhuman and degrading treatment because of the cumulative effects of repeated transfers between prisons, his lengthy detention in solitary confinement and frequent full body searches. To leave an inmate in a security cell without his clothes for seven days was held to be inhuman and degrading treatment in *Hellig* v *Germany*.[527] There was a violation of Article 3 in *Piechowicz* v *Poland*,[528] because of the applicant's treatment as a 'dangerous detainee' over a period of two years and nine months, which involved his confinement in a solitary cell in a high-security prison ward, constant monitoring of his cell by CCTV, the wearing of 'joined shackles' when he was moved, his segregation from the prison community, limitations on family contact and routine strip-searching.

---

[517] There was, however, no breach in *McFeeley* v *UK*, No. 8317/78, dec. 15.5.80, (1980) 20 DR 44.
[518] No. 44558/98, 24.7.01, para. 117.
[519] No. 14612/02, 31.3.09.
[520] No. 51246/08, 20.1.11.
[521] No. 50901/99, 4.2.03.
[522] No. 52750/99, 4.2.03. See also *Salah* v *Netherlands*, No. 8196/02, 6.7.06; *Baybaşın* v *Netherlands*, No. 13600/02, 6.7.06; *Frérot* v *France*, No. 70204/01, 12.6.07.
[523] No. 25196/94, 15.11.01, para. 53.
[524] No. 12350/04, 26.9.06.
[525] *Yankov* v *Bulgaria*, No. 39084/97, 11.12.03, para. 114.
[526] No. 39364/05, 9.7.09. As regards repeated prison transfers, see also *Bamouhammad* v *Belgium*, No. 47687/13, 17.11.15 (violations of Articles 3 and 13). However, frequent transfers of a prisoner were not found to violate Article 3 in *Payet* v *France*, No. 19606/08, 20.1.11.
[527] No. 20999/05, 7.7.11.
[528] No. 20071/07, 17.4.12.

The failure to investigate effectively allegations of ill-treatment in prison may violate Article **6.156**
3, as was the case in *Indelicato v Italy*[529] where the Court was critical of the authorities' very
lengthy delays and of negligence in attempting to identify those responsible.

The failure to protect the well-being of prisoners, for example, who may be the subject of **6.157**
ethnically-motivated violence, may breach Article 3. This was the case in *Rodić and 3 others*
v Bosnia and Herzegovina[530] where the applicants were Serb and Croat prisoners who had
been convicted of war crimes against Bosniacs and who were detained in ordinary cell blocks
within a prison with a 90 per cent Bosniac population.

Sentencing

The Court has found that issues concerning the appropriateness of a sentence will generally **6.158**
fall outside the scope of the Convention, although in very exceptional cases a grossly disproportionate sentence could amount to ill-treatment contrary to Article 3.[531]

The Court has held that the imposition of a sentence of life imprisonment on an adult **6.159**
offender is not in itself incompatible with Article 3, but that the imposition of an irreducible life sentence (one where there is no prospect of release) may raise an issue under
Article 3. This test was applied by the Grand Chamber in *Kafkaris v Cyprus*[532] in which it
was held that in Cyprus life sentences were both *de jure* and *de facto* reducible, and accordingly there was no violation of Article 3 (by ten votes to seven). Five dissenting judges,
and Sir Nicolas Bratza in his concurring judgment, argued that the Court should clearly
affirm that the imposition of an irreducible life sentence, even for an adult offender, is in
principle inconsistent with Article 3 of the Convention. This was indeed the conclusion
reached by the Grand Chamber in its subsequent judgment in *Vinter and others v UK*.[533]
There must accordingly be a review process 'which allows the domestic authorities to consider whether any changes in the life prisoner are so significant, and such progress towards
rehabilitation has been made in the course of the sentence, as to mean that continued
detention can no longer be justified on legitimate penological grounds'.[534] Furthermore,
the Court found that international standards required that such a review should take place
within 25 years of the imposition of a life sentence, and periodically after that. There
was a violation of Article 3 in *Vinter* because, under the domestic law, release from a sentence of imprisonment for life was only possible in the event of terminal illness or serious

---

[529] No. 31143/96, 18.10.01. See also *Poltoratskiy v Ukraine*, No. 38812/97, 29.4.03.

[530] No. 22893/05, 27.5.08. See also *J.L. v Latvia*, No. 23893/06, 17.4.12 (inter-prisoner violence in reprisal
for cooperating with the police—violation of Article 3).

[531] *Harkins and Edwards v UK*, Nos. 9146/07 and 32650/07, 17.1.12, para. 133; *Wilcox and Hurford v UK*,
Nos. 43759/10 and 43771/12, dec. 8.1.13, para. 74; *Vinter and others v UK*, Nos. 66069/09, 130/10 and 3896/
10, 9.7.13, para. 102.

[532] No. 21906/04, 12.2.08. See also *Iorgov (II) v Bulgaria*, No. 36295/02, 2.9.10; *Garagin v Italy*, No.
33290/07, dec. 29.4.08. See further *Léger v France*, No. 19324/02, 11.4.06 and 30.3.09 (case struck out by
Grand Chamber following applicant's death); *Schuchter v Italy*, No. 68476/10, dec. 11.10.11; *Harkins and
Edwards v UK*, Nos. 9146/07 and 32650/07, 17.1.12; *Babar Ahmad and others v UK*, Nos. 24027/07, 11949/
08 and 36742/08, 10.4.12.

[533] Nos. 66069/09, 130/10 and 3896/10, 9.7.13. See also *Törköly v Hungary*, No. 4413/06, dec. 5.4.11;
László Magyar v Hungary, No. 73593/10, 20.5.14; *T.P. and A.T. v Hungary*, Nos. 37871/14 and 73986/14,
4.10.16. See, by contrast, *Bodein v France*, No. 40014/10, 13.11.14 (life imprisonment with possibility of
review after 30 years' imprisonment—no violation of Article 3).

[534] *Vinter and others v UK*, Nos. 66069/09, 130/10 and 3896/10, 9.7.13, para. 119.

incapacitation—such 'highly restrictive conditions' were not considered sufficient for the purposes of Article 3.[535]

6.160   There was also a violation of Article 3 for similar reasons in *Harakchiev and Tolumov* v *Bulgaria*.[536] Whole life regimes had been introduced in Bulgaria in 1998 when the death penalty was abolished. In 2006 the Bulgarian President was given a discretionary power of clemency to commute all life sentences, including those imposed without commutation. Therefore, the Court found that sentences were *de jure* reducible (since 2006), but not *de facto*, as the way the President used the power of clemency was opaque and lacked adequate safeguards. Even after reforms introduced in 2012 which clarified the presidential power of clemency, there was still a breach of Article 3 because the applicant's prison regime was so stringent (including solitary confinement), coupled with a lack of consistent periodical assessment of his progress towards rehabilitation, that he still did not have a genuine opportunity to reform.

Death penalty

6.161   In its 2003 Chamber judgment in *Öcalan* v *Turkey*[537] the Court accepted that, in the light of recent developments in Europe, it could be argued that the *implementation* of the death penalty could be regarded as inhuman and degrading treatment contrary to Article 3. However, the case was subsequently referred to the Grand Chamber, by which time Turkey had abolished the death penalty (and ratified Protocol No. 6 to the Convention), so the issue no longer arose.[538] In any event the *imposition* of the death sentence on the applicant following an unfair trial amounted to inhuman treatment in violation of Article 3. The Court concluded as follows:

> … to impose a death sentence on a person after an unfair trial is to subject that person wrongfully to the fear that he will be executed. The fear and uncertainty as to the future generated by a sentence of death, in circumstances where there exists a real possibility that the sentence will be enforced, must give rise to a significant degree of human anguish. Such anguish cannot be dissociated from the unfairness of the proceedings underlying the sentence which, given that human life is at stake, becomes unlawful under the Convention.[539]

6.162   In *Ilaşcu and others* v *Moldova and Russia*,[540] the Court held that the death sentence imposed on the first applicant, together with the conditions in which he was held (including strict isolation for eight years) and the treatment he suffered during his detention (which included mock executions), in the 'Moldavian Republic of Transdniestria', were particularly serious and cruel and accordingly were acts of torture within the meaning of Article 3 of the Convention.

---

[535]   There was no violation of Article 3 in the later case of *Hutchinson* v *UK*, No. 57592/08, 17.1.17, after the Court of Appeal had clarified that the Home Secretary was obliged to apply the power of release compatibly with Article 3.

[536]   Nos. 15018/11 and 61199/12, 8.7.14. See also *Murray* v *Netherlands*, No. 10511/10, 26.4.16 (*de facto* irreducibility of life sentence imposed on prisoner suffering from mental illness (in Netherlands Antilles)— violation of Article 3).

[537]   No. 46221/99, 12.3.03.

[538]   No. 46221/99, 12.5.05, paras. 151–5.

[539]   *Ibid.*, para. 169. However, Judges Costa, Caflisch, Türmen and Borrego Borrego dissented on this point. See also 6.170 below concerning 'death row syndrome'.

[540]   No. 48787/99, 8.7.04.

The case of *Al-Saadoon and Mufdhi v UK*[541] concerned the applicants' detention by the **6.163** British armed forces in southern Iraq in 2003, where the United Kingdom was an occupying power. Suspected of murdering two British soldiers, they were held in British detention facilities before their case was referred to the Iraqi authorities in 2005 and they themselves were handed over to the Iraqi authorities in 2008. In response to the UK's arguments that they had been obliged to respect Iraqi sovereignty and transfer the applicants, who were Iraqi nationals held on Iraqi territory, to the custody of the Iraqi courts when requested to do so, the Court reiterated that it was not open to a contracting state to enter into an agreement with another state that conflicted with its obligations under the Convention. The Court also noted that no request had been made to the Iraqi authorities for a binding assurance that the applicants would not be at risk of capital punishment. Therefore, in handing over the applicants, the Court held that the UK had failed to take proper account of its obligations under Articles 2 and 3, and Article 1 of Protocol No. 13, as there had been substantial grounds for believing that they would face a real risk of being sentenced to death and executed.[542] Accordingly, the applicants were found to have been subjected to the fear of execution, causing them psychological suffering of a nature and degree which constituted inhuman treatment, in violation of Article 3.[543] Invoking Article 46, the Court found that in order to comply with its Article 3 obligations, the UK Government should take all possible steps to obtain an assurance from the Iraqi authorities that the applicants would not be subjected to the death penalty.[544]

Immigration, asylum and extradition

The Court has frequently reiterated that a state is entitled to control the entry, residence and **6.164** expulsion of aliens; there is no right under the Convention to political asylum. However, a state may be found to be liable under Article 3 where an individual is to be deported or extradited to a country where there are substantial grounds for believing that they will face a real risk of treatment contrary to Article 3.[545] To that extent, therefore, Article 3 has a certain extra-territorial application. The assessment of the risk is a 'rigorous' one[546] and it will be carried out by the Court primarily with reference to the facts which were known, or which ought to have been known, at the time of the expulsion. The Court will make its assessment

---

[541] No. 61498/08, 2.3.10.

[542] The death penalty had been reintroduced into the Iraqi Penal Code in 2004 in respect of certain offences, including murder. See also *A.L. (X.W.) v Russia*, No. 44095/14, 29.10.15 (proposed deportation to China—risk that applicant would face death penalty—deportation would violate Articles 2 and 3).

[543] The Court held that it was unnecessary also to decide whether there had been violations of Article 2 and Article 1 of Protocol No. 13.

[544] At the Committee of Ministers' meeting on 10 March 2011, it was noted that the Iraqi President of the Public Prosecution service had stated by letter that the charges against the applicants carried a maximum penalty of 15 years' imprisonment.

[545] See, e.g. *Ahmed v Austria*, No. 25964/94, 17.12.96, paras. 38–9; *Hilal v UK*, No. 45276/99, 6.3.01, para. 59; *Thampibillai v Netherlands*, No. 61350/00, 17.2.04, para. 59; *Venkadajalasarma v Netherlands*, No. 58510/00, 17.2.04, para. 61; *Saadi v Italy*, No. 37201/06, 28.2.08, para. 146; *Ismoilov and others v Russia*, No. 2947/06, 24.4.08, para. 126; *NA v UK*, No. 25904/07, 17.7.08, para. 109; *Sufi and Elmi v UK*, Nos. 8319/07 and 11449/07, 28.6.11, para. 212; *Abdulkhakov v Russia*, No. 14743/11, 2.10.12, para. 132; *I v Sweden*, No. 61204/09, 5.9.13, para. 55. In *Babar Ahmad and others v UK*, No. 24027/07, 10.4.12 the Court explicitly confirmed that such a condition applies equally to extradition and other types of removal from the territory of a state and also that it applies without distinction between the various forms of ill-treatment which are proscribed by Article 3 (para. 176).

[546] See, e.g. *Chahal v UK*, No. 22414/93, 15.11.96, para. 96; *Sufi and Elmi v UK*, Nos. 8319/07 and 11449/07, 28.6.11, para. 214.

both in light of the general situation in the country or region concerned, and also taking account of the applicant's personal circumstances.[547] If the existence of such a risk is established, there will necessarily be a violation of Article 3, whether the risk is created by a general situation of violence, or the applicant's personal situation, or by a combination of both factors.[548] Where the applicant has not yet been expelled, the Court will make the assessment on the basis of the facts available at the time when the Court considers the case—this may mean taking account of information that has become available since the final decision taken by the domestic authorities.[549] In order to make its assessment, the Court is able to consider all the material put before it and also to obtain additional material of its own motion. The Court acknowledges the evidential difficulties that may arise in such cases:[550]

> ... direct documentary evidence proving that an applicant himself or herself is wanted for any reason by the authorities of the country of origin may well be difficult to obtain ... It is nevertheless incumbent on persons who allege that their expulsion would amount to a breach of Article 3 to adduce, to the greatest extent practically possible, material and information allowing the authorities of the Contracting State concerned, as well as the Court, to assess the risk a removal may entail.

6.165 The Court has also stipulated that 'requesting an applicant to produce "indisputable" evidence of a risk of ill-treatment in the requesting country would be tantamount to asking him to prove the existence of a future event, which is impossible, and would place a clearly disproportionate burden on him'.[551]

6.166 Where an assessment of the risk faced by an applicant has been made by a domestic court, the European Court's starting point is to defer to the national authorities where cases are 'borderline', provided that 'they have addressed all relevant aspects of the case and have given a reasonable interpretation of evidence and facts'.[552] The Court will assess whether the domestic courts have carried out an 'independent and rigorous scrutiny' of the applicant's claims as regards the risk of ill-treatment, failing which it will proceed to conduct its own analysis.[553]

6.167 In *N* v *Finland*,[554] an asylum case brought by a former member of the 'inner circle' of the President of the Democratic Republic of Congo, the Court sent a two-judge delegation to hear evidence in Finland (see also 6.174). Many cases are rejected simply because there is insufficient evidence of the extent of the risk of ill-treatment to the applicants.[555] In an exceptional situation, where an applicant can establish that they are a member of a group which is systematically exposed to a practice of ill-treatment, the Court has accepted that

---

[547] *Vilvarajah and others* v *UK*, Nos. 13163–5/87, 13447–8/87, 30.10.91, Series A, No. 215, para. 108.

[548] *NA* v *UK*, No. 25904/07, 17.7.08, paras. 115–16.

[549] See, e.g. *Chahal* v *UK*, No. 22414/93, 15.11.96, para. 86; *Vilvarajah and others* v *UK*, Nos. 13163–5/87, 13447–8/87, 30.10.91, Series A, No. 215, para. 107; *HLR* v *France*, No. 24573/94, 29.4.97; *J.K. and others* v *Sweden*, No. 59166/12, 23.8.16.

[550] See, e.g. *Said* v *Netherlands*, No. 2345/02, 5.7.05, para. 49 (deserter from Eritrean army—violation of Article 3).

[551] See, e.g. *Azimov* v *Russia*, No. 67474/11, 18.4.13, para. 128.

[552] *Ibid.*, para. 143. In that case, concerning the applicant's deportation to Tajikistan, the Court found the domestic court's analysis to be 'deficient in many respects'.

[553] See, e.g. *Savriddin Dzhurayev* v *Russia*, No. 71386/10, 25.4.13, para. 165.

[554] No. 38885/02, 26.7.05.

[555] See, e.g. *Katani and others* v *Germany*, No. 67679/01, dec. 31.5.01 (deportation of six Georgian families belonging to the Yezidi religious minority—inadmissible); *Elezaj* v *Sweden*, No. 17654/05, dec. 20.9.07 (deportation to Albania and risk from blood feud—inadmissible).

Article 3 will be applicable and that the applicant need not then 'show the existence of further special distinguishing features if to do so would render illusory the protection offered by Article 3'.[556] The case of *F.G.* v *Sweden*[557] concerned the proposed deportation of the applicant to Iran. The applicant had not initially relied on his conversion to Christianity as a ground for asylum, which he had considered to be a private matter. However, the Swedish authorities had been made aware of it and their failure, of their own motion, to assess this issue resulted in the Grand Chamber's finding that Articles 2 and 3 would be violated were he to be deported without such an assessment being made.

Article 3 may apply not only where the risk in question is created by public authorities in the receiving country, but also by private organisations or individuals, in circumstances where the risk is real and the authorities in the receiving state are not able to provide appropriate protection.[558] For example, in *J.K. and others* v *Sweden*[559] the Grand Chamber concluded (by ten votes to seven) that the applicants faced a real risk of treatment contrary to Article 3 were they to be deported to Iraq, because they had been targeted by al-Qaeda for having had business relationships, in particular, with the US armed forces. There had been attempts on the first applicant's life, and his relatives had also been kidnapped and attacked. Furthermore, there were shortcomings in both the capacity and the integrity of the Iraqi security and legal system, such that the Court was not convinced that the authorities would be able adequately to protect the applicants, as members of a targeted group. Moreover, internal relocation was not a realistic option. **6.168**

The Court has recognised the difficulties experienced by states on the external borders of the European Union as a result of increasing numbers of migrants and asylum-seekers—notably migration by sea. The applicants in *Hirsi Jamaa and others* v *Italy*[560] were Somali and Eritrean nationals on board three boats travelling from Libya to Italy, which were intercepted and boarded by the Italian revenue police and coastguard. They were then transferred onto Italian military ships and returned to Tripoli. Consequently, the Court found that there was a risk of ill-treatment not only in Libya, but also in their countries of origin. **6.169**

Where a state proposes to deport or extradite a person, their anticipated detention conditions in the receiving state may raise issues under Article 3. In *Soering* v *UK*[561] the Court held that there would be a violation of Article 3 if the applicant were deported to the United States on capital murder charges, where he faced exposure to the 'death-row phenomenon'. The Court found that the responsibility of the state would be engaged where there were substantial grounds for believing that, if extradited, the applicant faced a real risk of being subjected to torture or inhuman or degrading treatment or punishment. However, there will be no violation of Article 3 if sufficient guarantees are received from the state seeking extradition that the death penalty would not be sought or imposed.[562] The Court held that Article 3 did **6.170**

---

[556] See. e.g. *NA* v *UK*, No. 25904/07, 17.7.08, para. 117; *Abdolkhani and Karimnia* v *Turkey*, No. 30471/08, 22.9.09, para. 75. See also *Tehrani and others* v *Turkey*, Nos. 32940/08, 41626/08, 43616/08, 13.4.10.

[557] No. 43611/11, 23.3.16.

[558] *HLR* v *France*, No. 24573/94, 29.4.97, *Reports* 1997-III, paras. 40–1. Accordingly, where no complaint has been made to the authorities, an application is likely to be declared inadmissible—see *A.M. and others* v *Sweden*, No. 38813/06, dec. 16.6.09.

[559] No. 59166/12, 23.8.16.

[560] No. 27765/09, 23.2.12.

[561] No. 14038/88, Series A, No. 161, 7.7.89.

[562] *Nivette* v *France*, No. 44190/98, dec. 14.12.00; *Einhorn* v *France*, No. 71555/01, dec. 16.10.01; *Al-Moayad* v *Germany*, No. 35865/03, dec. 20.2.07.

not generally prohibit the death penalty itself (see 6.161 above), but the prospect of six to eight years on death row gave rise to a breach of Article 3. The applicants in *Babar Ahmad and others* v *UK*[563] were indicted on various charges of terrorism in the US and sought to challenge their extradition due to the highly restrictive conditions of the 'super-max' prisons. In spite of the regime's strict controls on contact between inmates, and with staff, there was no violation of Article 3 because of the opportunities for regular telephone calls, social visits and correspondence with their families, as well as the in-cell availability of television, radio, newspapers and books.

6.171 However, there was a different outcome in the related case of *Aswat* v *UK*,[564] primarily because of the applicant's serious mental disorder. The applicant in *Aswat* was suffering from paranoid schizophrenia and was being detained in a high-security psychiatric hospital in the UK. In light of the uncertainty as to where he would be detained if he were extradicted to the US, or for how long, and the possibility that he might be exposed to a highly restrictive regime (such as a 'super-max' prison) with long periods of social isolation, the Court found that there was a real risk that the applicant's extradition—to a different, and potentially more hostile, prison environment—would result in a significant deterioration in his mental and physical health, in violation of Article 3. There was also a breach of Article 3 in *Trabelsi* v *Belgium*[565] because of the applicant's extradition to the US on terrorism charges, where, if convicted, he faced the risk of an irreducible life sentence (as defined by the 2013 judgment in *Vinter and others* v *UK*[566]—discussed above at 6.159).

6.172 In *Chahal* v *UK*[567] the applicant complained that his deportation to India on national security grounds would violate his rights under Article 3 because, as a Sikh political activist, he risked being subjected to torture. In an important passage in that case, the Court affirmed that it was inappropriate to apply any balancing act in such circumstances: Article 3 provides absolute protection and the activities of the individual, 'however undesirable or dangerous', cannot be a material consideration. There was therefore no need for the Court to assess the threat that Mr Chahal allegedly posed to national security. That principle was reaffirmed in 2008 by the Grand Chamber in *Saadi* v *Italy*,[568] expressly rejecting submissions from the UK Government, as a third party intervenor, which sought to dilute the absolute protection provided by Article 3. According to the Court, it was a misconception to talk of 'balancing' the risk of harm if the person were sent back against the dangerousness that the person represented to the community if they were not: those were concepts which had to be assessed independently. The Court has also been consistently clear that 'diplomatic assurances' from the receiving state that an individual will not be subjected to ill-treatment, even if made in good faith, cannot be relied upon *per se*.[569] If such assurances are given, the Court will assess

---

[563] No. 24027/07, 10.4.12.

[564] No. 17299/12, 16.4.13.

[565] No. 140/10, 4.9.14.

[566] Nos. 66069/09, 130/10 and 3896/10, 9.7.13.

[567] No. 22414/93, 15.11.96.

[568] No. 37201/06, 28.2.08, paras. 138–41. See also *Ismoilov and others* v *Russia*, No. 2947/06, 24.4.08; *Ben Khemais* v *Italy*, No. 246/07, 24.2.09; *Abdolkhani and Karimnia* v *Turkey*, No. 30471/08, 22.9.09; *M.S.S.* v *Belgium and Greece*, No. 30696/09, 21.1.11, para. 223; *Auad* v *Bulgaria*, No. 46390/10, 11.10.11.

[569] See: *Chahal* v *UK*, No. 22414/93, 15.11.96, para. 105; joint partly dissenting opinion of Judges Bratza, Bonello and Hedigan in *Mamatkulov and Askarov* v *Turkey*, Nos. 46827/99 and 46951/99, 4.2.05; *Ryabikin* v *Russia*, No. 8320/04, 19.6.08, para. 119; *Klein* v *Russia*, No. 24268/08, 1.4.10, para. 55; *Abdulkhakov* v *Russia*, No. 14743/11, 2.10.12, para. 150; *Azimov* v *Russia*, No. 67474/11, 18.4.13, para. 133.

whether they provide a sufficient guarantee that the applicant would in practice be protected against the risk of treatment prohibited by the Convention.[570] In *Othman (Abu Qatada) v UK*[571] the Court reviewed the factors which it had found to be relevant in assessing diplomatic assurances. They are as follows:

(i) whether the terms of the assurances have been disclosed to the Court;

(ii) whether they are specific or are general and vague;

(iii) who has given the assurances and whether that person can bind the receiving state;

(iv) if the assurances have been issued by the central government of the receiving state, whether local authorities can be expected to abide by them;

(v) whether the assurances concern treatment which is legal or illegal in the receiving state;

(vi) whether they have been given by a contracting state;

(vii) the length and strength of bilateral relations between the sending and receiving states, including the receiving state's record in abiding by similar assurances;

(viii) whether compliance with the assurances can be objectively verified through diplomatic or other monitoring mechanisms, including providing unfettered access to the applicant's lawyers;

(ix) whether there is an effective system of protection against torture in the receiving state, including whether it is willing to cooperate with international monitoring mechanisms (including international human rights NGOs), and whether it is willing to investigate allegations of torture and to punish those responsible;

(x) whether the applicant has previously been ill-treated in the receiving state; and

(xi) whether the reliability of the assurances has been examined by the domestic courts of the sending/contracting state.

The parties accepted in the *Othman* case that there would be a real risk of ill-treatment of the applicant, as a 'high profile Islamist', if he were returned to Jordan without the diplomatic assurances which had been made. However, the Court found that there would be no risk of a violation of Article 3 were the applicant deported to Jordan, in view of the 'memorandum of understanding' which that country had agreed with the UK Government (which included monitoring by a human rights NGO). Nevertheless, the Court held that the applicant's deportation would still violate Article 6 because of the real risk of evidence obtained by torture of third parties being admitted at his retrial in Jordan (see further 6.340 below).

The Court has had to deal with a number of cases of 'secret rendition' by various states, on which it has made its position very clear:

> any extra-judicial transfer or extraordinary rendition, by its deliberate circumvention of due process, is an absolute negation of the rule of law and the values protected by the Convention.[572]

In *Savriddin Dzhurayev v Russia*,[573] the applicant was kidnapped in Moscow by unidentified persons who detained him in an unknown location before transferring him by aircraft to **6.173**

---

[570] *Saadi v Italy*, No. 37201/06, 28.2.08, para. 148; *Ismoilov and others v Russia*, No. 2947/06, 24.4.08, para. 127; *Soldatenko v Ukraine*, No. 2440/07, 23.10.08, paras. 73–4.

[571] No. 8139/09, 17.1.12, para. 189.

[572] See, e.g. *Abdulkhakov v Russia*, No. 14743/11, 2.10.12, para. 156 (applicant's transfer from Russia to Tajikistan, and from where he faced removal to Uzbekistan).

[573] No. 71386/10, 25.4.13. See also, amongst other cases, *Nizomkhon Dzhurayev v Russia*, No. 31890/11, 3.10.13; *Mamazhonov v Russia*, No. 17239/13, 23.10.14.

Tajikistan. The Court found that his forcible return to Tajikistan exposed him to a real risk of treatment contrary to Article 3 (as someone who was the subject of criminal proceedings in Tajikistan for being involved with the 'Islamic Movement of Uzbekistan'). The relevant authorities had immediately been informed about his abduction, and about the risk he faced, and were asked to take steps to protect him—their failure to take any action to avert the risk meant that the state was held to have breached its positive obligations under Article 3. The Court went on to find further violations of Article 3 on the basis that his forcible transfer to Tajikistan (via Domodedovo airport in Moscow) could not have happened without the knowledge and either passive or active involvement of the Russian authorities, and in view of the failure to carry out an effective investigation into the case.

6.174 The Court held in *Shamayev and others* v *Georgia and Russia*[574] that the extradition of one of the Chechen applicants from Georgia to Russia would breach Article 3, because of the risk that ill-treatment would be inflicted upon him. He and the other applicants had been detained after crossing the Russian–Georgian border; they were armed and some were injured. The Russian Government alleged that they were 'Chechen terrorists'. In its assessment under Article 3, the Court took account of the following: that five extradited applicants had been held in solitary confinement in the North Caucasus, without access to lawyers; the evidence that detainees held in 'filtration camps' in the North Caucasus were ill-treated; that the Russian authorities were hampering the international monitoring of prisoners; and that Chechens who had lodged applications at the European Court had been subjected to persecution and murder. The Court found a separate violation of the prohibition of inhuman treatment under Article 3 in *Shamayev* as a result of irregularities in the procedure for the enforcement of extradition orders against four applicants by the Georgian authorities, and because some of the applicants were injured by the special forces, and they were not provided with the appropriate medical treatment. The case of *N* v *Finland*[575] concerned an asylum application brought by a former member of the special protection force of the President of the Democratic Republic of Congo (DRC). The Court held that his expulsion to the DRC would violate Article 3, taking into account his particular role as informant and infiltrator, such that his situation could be worse than other former supporters of the President.

6.175 The Court has held that states are not precluded by Article 3 from relying on an 'internal flight alternative,' but in order to do so, certain guarantees have to be in place: the person to be expelled must be able to travel to the area concerned, gain admittance and settle there, failing which an issue might arise under Article 3.[576] In *Hilal* v *UK*,[577] in which the politically active applicant complained of the risk of ill-treatment in Zanzibar, in the light of the prevailing conditions in Tanzania, the Court rejected the Government's reliance on the 'internal flight' option, on the basis of which the Government had sought to argue that if he risked ill-treatment in Zanzibar, he would be safer in mainland Tanzania. In *Salah Sheekh* v

---

[574] No. 36378/02, 12.4.05. See also *M.G.* v *Bulgaria*, No. 59297/12, 25.3.14 (proposed extradition of Chechen suspected of belonging to terrorist group—extradition would violate Article 3).

[575] No. 38885/02, 26.7.05.

[576] See, e.g. *Salah Sheekh* v *Netherlands*, No. 1948/04, 11.1.07; *M.Y.H. and others* v *Sweden*, No. 50859/10, 27.6.13 (proposed deportation of Christian family to Iraq—no violation); *D.N.M.* v *Sweden*, No. 28379/11, 27.6.13; *S.A.* v *Sweden*, No. 66523/10, 27.6.13 (both cases concerned the risks faced by Sunni Muslims of honour-related crimes if deported to Iraq—no violation).

[577] No. 45276/99, 6.3.01.

Netherlands,[578] the Court did not accept the Government's proposal that the applicant could be returned to the 'relatively safe' areas of Somalia. The Court found a real risk of Article 3 ill-treatment in *Sufi and Elmi v UK*[579] if the applicants were returned to Somalia, both because of the intensity of the violence generally in Mogadishu, and also in view of the dire humanitarian conditions of internally displaced person (IDP) camps in southern and central Somalia.

The Court has also found that removal to an intermediary country does not absolve the state **6.176** from its responsibility to ensure that the applicant is not, as a result of its decision to expel, exposed to treatment contrary to Article 3. Thus, states cannot automatically rely, for example, on the provisions of the Dublin Regulation[580] concerning the attribution of responsibility between European countries for deciding asylum claims.[581] In *K.R.S. v UK*,[582] the Iranian applicant had applied for asylum in the United Kingdom but had travelled through Greece, which accepted responsibility for his asylum claim. The Court held that the UK's responsibility could not be engaged by removing the applicant to Greece under the Dublin Regulation, in spite of the UNHCR's recommendation that parties to the Regulation refrain from returning asylum-seekers to Greece. The Court found that the evidence established that Greece did not at that time remove people to Iran, that Greece was bound by the European Convention and that, if necessary, a Rule 39 application could be made against Greece. However, in *M.S.S. v Belgium and Greece*[583] the Grand Chamber found that the applicant's expulsion from Belgium to Greece was in violation of Article 3 (in circumstances where he had an arguable claim that his removal to Afghanistan would violate either Article 2 or Article 3 of the Convention). The Court concluded that at the time of his transfer the Belgian authorities knew, or ought to have known, that he had no guarantee that his asylum application would be seriously examined by the Greek authorities. Nevertheless, they failed to verify how the Greek authorities applied their asylum legislation in practice, and had they done so, they would have established that the risks the applicant faced were real and individual enough to fall within the scope of Article 3.

Applying a similar analysis in *Tarakhel v Switzerland*,[584] the Grand Chamber found that the **6.177** expulsion of an Afghan asylum-seeker family to Italy under the Dublin II Regulation would violate Article 3, taking particular account of the special protection which was required to be

---

[578] No. 1948/04, 11.1.07.

[579] Nos. 8319/07 and 11449/07, 28.6.11. See, by contrast, *K.A.B. v Sweden*, No. 886/11, 5.9.13 (proposed expulsion of asylum-seeker to Mogadishu following improvements in general situation there—no violation of Article 3) and *R.H. v Sweden*, No. 4601/14, 10.9.15 (proposed deportation of young Somali woman to Mogadishu— no violation of Article 3).

[580] Council Regulation (EU) No 604/2013 of 26 June 2013 (the Dublin III Regulation—previously, the Dublin II Regulation), which superseded the Dublin Convention (the Convention determining the State responsible for examining applications for asylum lodged in one of the Member States of the European Communities, 15 June 1990).

[581] See, e.g. *T.I. v UK*, No. 43844/98, dec. 7.3.00 (as regards the Dublin Convention); *K.R.S. v UK*, No. 32733/08, dec. 2.12.08 (as regards the Dublin Regulation).

[582] No. 32733/08, dec. 2.12.08.

[583] No. 30696/09, 21.1.11. See, by contrast, *Mohammed Hussein and others v Netherlands and Italy*, No. 27725/10, dec. 2.4.13 (proposed removal of Somali asylum-seeker to Italy under Dublin II Regulation— inadmissible); *Mohammed v Austria*, No. 2283/12, 6.6.13 (proposed removal of Sudanese asylum-seeker from Austria to Hungary—no violation of Article 3).

[584] No. 29217/12, 4.11.14. See, by contrast, *A.M.E. v Netherlands*, No. 51428/10, dec. 13.1.15 (proposed removal of young man with no dependents to Italy under Dublin II Regulation—inadmissible).

given to child asylum seekers. The family had landed on the Italian coast in 2011 before travelling on to Austria, and then Switzerland, where their application for asylum was refused on the basis that it should be dealt with by the Italian authorities. As regards the reception arrangements for asylum seekers in Italy, the Court noted the evidence of various failings, including delays in the identification procedure, the inadequate capacity of the reception facilities and the deteriorating living conditions (although it was not comparable to the situation in Greece at the time of the *M.S.S.* judgment). As regards the particular situation of the applicant family, the Swiss authorities had failed to obtain sufficient assurances from the Italian authorities that, if they were returned to Italy, the applicants would be taken charge of in a manner adapted to the age of the children.

6.178 Article 3 may be engaged even where the source of the risk of the proscribed treatment in the receiving country arises from factors which cannot engage (either directly or indirectly) the responsibility of the public authorities of that country, or which in themselves do not infringe Article 3. In *D v UK*[585] the applicant, who was suffering from the advanced stages of the AIDS virus, successfully argued that there would be a violation of Article 3 were he to be removed to St Kitts, where he was born, because the lack of adequate medical treatment would expose him to inhuman and degrading treatment. The Court emphasised that the decision was made 'in the very exceptional circumstances' of the case and 'given the compelling humanitarian considerations at stake'.[586] On the facts of the case of *Bensaid* v *UK*,[587] in contrast, the Court found no violation of Article 3 were the applicant (who was a schizophrenic with a psychotic disorder) to be expelled to Algeria. In 2008, in its judgment in *N v UK*,[588] the Grand Chamber reviewed the application of Article 3 in circumstances where an applicant is suffering from serious physical or mental illness, concluding that the high threshold set in the case of *D v UK* should be maintained:[589]

> Aliens who are subject to expulsion cannot in principle claim any entitlement to remain in the territory of a Contracting State in order to continue to benefit from medical, social or other forms of assistance and services provided by the expelling State. The fact that the applicant's circumstances, including his life expectancy, would be significantly reduced if he were to be removed from the Contracting State is not sufficient in itself to give rise to breach of Article 3. The decision to remove an alien who is suffering from a serious mental or physical illness to a country where the facilities for the treatment of that illness are inferior to those available in the Contracting State may raise an issue under Article 3, but only in a very exceptional case, where the humanitarian grounds against the removal are compelling.

In *Paposhvili* v *Belgium* in 2016 the Grand Chamber further clarified that the 'very exceptional cases' refer to 'situations involving the removal of a seriously ill person in which substantial grounds have been shown for believing that he or she, although not at imminent risk of dying, would face a real risk, on account of the absence of appropriate treatment in

---

[585] No. 30240/96, 2.5.97.

[586] *Ibid.*, para. 54. See, in contrast, *Amegnigan* v *Netherlands*, No. 25629/04, dec. 25.11.04.

[587] No. 44599/98, 6.2.01. See also *Karagoz* v *France*, No. 47531/99, dec. 15.11.01 (deportation to Turkey of applicant undergoing continuous medical treatment—declared inadmissible); *Arcila Henao* v *Netherlands*, No. 13669/03, dec. 24.6.03 (expulsion to Colombia of an HIV-positive drug offender—declared inadmissible); *Tatar* v *Switzerland*, No. 65692/12, 14.4.15 (proposed removal of mentally-ill person—no violation of Article 3).

[588] No. 26565/05, 27.5.08.

[589] *N v UK*, No. 26565/05, 27.5.08, para. 42. See also *Yoh-Ekale Mwanje* v *Belgium*, No. 10486/10, 20.12.11.

the receiving country or the lack of access to such treatment, of being exposed to a serious, rapid and irreversible decline in his or her state of health resulting in intense suffering or to a significant reduction in life expectancy'.[590] In that case, the Court found that the applicant's deportation to Georgia would violate Article 3 because he was suffering from a life-threatening leukaemia condition, and the medical treatment he was receiving in Belgium (which would enable him to undergo a donor transplant) would not be available in Georgia.

In *Collins and Akaziebie* v *Sweden*[591] it was undisputed that subjecting a woman to female **6.179** genital mutilation would amount to ill-treatment contrary to Article 3, although on the facts of the case the applicants failed to establish that they faced a 'real and concrete risk' of being subjected to such treatment. The Court found that Article 3 would be violated if the applicant in *N* v *Sweden*[592] were deported to Afghanistan. She had filed for divorce from her husband, and had admitted to an extra-marital relationship, and the Court acknowledged that women were particularly at risk of ill-treatment in Afghanistan if they were considered not to conform to stereotypical gender roles. It concluded on the facts that she risked reprisals from her husband, their families and from Afghan society.

Article 3 may arise in relation to inadequacies in the treatment of children. For example, **6.180** in *Mubilanzila Mayeka and Kaniki Mitunga* v *Belgium*[593] the Court held that Article 3 had been violated by holding an unaccompanied five-year-old child (who was found to be an illegal alien) in an adult immigration centre for two months. Such a situation also violated the mother's rights under Article 3 because of the distress and anxiety caused to her. Furthermore, the child's subsequent deportation to the DRC breached both the mother's and child's Article 3 rights because of the failure to provide adequate preparation, supervision and safeguards for her deportation. No adult was assigned to travel with the child and arrangements were not made for her to be met, leading the Court to criticise the 'total lack of humanity' shown. Similarly, the detention of children in a transit centre for over a month in *Muskhadzhiyeva and others* v *Belgium*[594] was found to breach Article 3. The children (aged seven months, three and a half years, five and seven years) had fled with their mother from Chechnya, had applied for asylum and were found to be exhibiting serious psychological and psychosomatic symptoms.

See also below at 6.509 in relation to immigration and asylum issues under Article 8, and at 6.181 in relation to discrimination.

Discrimination

Discriminatory treatment may in itself amount to degrading treatment, whether the discrimination is based on race or on other grounds. Whether Article 3 is engaged will depend **6.181**

---

[590] No. 41738/10, 13.12.16, para. 183.

[591] No. 23944/05, dec. 8.3.07. See also *Izevbekhai and others v Ireland*, No. 43408/08, dec. 17.5.11; *Omeredo v Austria*, No. 8969/10, dec. 20.9.11.

[592] No. 23505/09, 20.7.10.

[593] No. 13178/03, 12.10.06 (Article 8 was also violated as a result of both the detention and the deportation). See also *Rahimi v Greece*, No. 8687/08, 5.4.11 (detention of unaccompanied minor asylum-seeker—violation of Article 3); *Popov v France*, Nos. 39472/07 and 39474/07, 19.1.12.

[594] No. 41442/07, 19.1.10. See also *Kanagaratnam v Belgium*, No. 15297/09, 13.12.11 and *A.B. and others v France*, No. 11593/12, *R.K. and others v France*, No. 68264/14, *R.C. and V.C. v France*, No. 76491/14, *R.M. and others v France*, No. 33201/11, *A.M. and others v France*, No. 24587/12, 12.7.16 (administrative detention of minors pending expulsion—inhuman and degrading treatment—violation of Article 3).

upon the application of the Court's 'severity' test (see above at 6.115). In the *East African Asians* case,[595] the European Commission of Human Rights reiterated that 'a special importance should be attached to discrimination based on race; that publicly to single out a group of persons for differential treatment on the basis of race might, in certain circumstances, constitute a special form of affront to human dignity...'. In that case the Commission found that there had been degrading treatment in violation of Article 3 because of the application of immigration legislation that prevented British passport holders in East Africa from obtaining rights of residence in the UK.

6.182   The discriminatory treatment by the Turkish authorities of the Karpas Greek Cypriot community in northern Cyprus led to a finding of degrading treatment in the inter-state case of *Cyprus* v *Turkey*.[596] On the basis, the Court found, of their ethnic origin, race and religion, the community was isolated and their movements restricted and controlled such that they had no prospect of renewing or developing their community: 'the conditions under which that population is condemned to live are debasing and violate the very notion of respect for the human dignity of its members'.[597] Article 3 was found to have been violated in *Moldovan and others* v *Romania*,[598] a series of cases brought by Roma agricultural workers whose homes had been burnt by a mob, with the acquiescence of the police. The Court held that in view of the appalling living conditions which the applicants had experienced for ten years (an overcrowded and insanitary environment), coupled with the authorities' racially discriminatory attitude towards them (as evidenced by decisions of the local courts and remarks made by the mayor), they had been the victims of degrading treatment.[599]

6.183   In *Smith and Grady* v *UK*,[600] which concerned the armed forces' ban on homosexuals, the Court held that it 'would not exclude that treatment which is grounded upon a predisposed bias on the part of a heterosexual majority against a homosexual minority ... could, in principle, fall within the scope of Article 3'.

Child care

6.184   The Court has found that the protection of children (who, it is acknowledged are not capable of looking after themselves because of their age and vulnerability) requires not merely that the criminal law provides protection against treatment prohibited by Article 3, but also that in appropriate circumstances there will be implied a positive obligation on the authorities to take preventive measures to protect a child who is at risk from another individual.[601] There will be a positive obligation on, for example, a local authority to take such steps that could reasonably be expected of it to avoid a real and immediate risk of ill-treatment contrary to Article 3 of which the authority was aware or ought to have been aware. However, in

---

[595] Nos. 4403/70–4419/70, 4422/70, 4434/70, 4443/70, 4476/70–4478/70, 4486/70, 4501/70 and 4526/70–4530/70, 14.12.73. The case was never referred to the Court and the Committee of Ministers did not agree on its resolution. See also *Abdulaziz, Cabales and Balkandali* v *UK*, Nos. 9473–4/81, Series A, No. 94, 28.5.85; and *Hilton* v *UK*, No. 5613/72, dec. 5.3.76, (1976) 4 DR 177, re racial harassment.

[596] No. 25781/94, 10.5.01.

[597] *Ibid.*, para. 309.

[598] Nos. 41138/98 and 64320/01, 12.7.05 (judgment No. 2).

[599] There were also violations of Articles 8 and 6, and of Article 14 taken together with both Articles 8 and 6.

[600] Nos. 33985/96 and 33986/96, 27.9.99—see especially paras. 117–23.

[601] *Z and others* v *UK*, No. 29392/95, 10.5.01.

assessing the extent of the obligation on local authorities, any competing interests of parents or other family members under Article 8 will be relevant.

In *Z and others* v *UK*[602] the Court unanimously found a violation of Article 3 arising from the **6.185** failure of the local authority to take action in respect of the serious ill-treatment and neglect caused to four siblings by their parents over a period of more than four and a half years. This included under-nourishment, insanitary living conditions and physical abuse, causing behavioural disturbances and developmental delays, and such treatment was found to have reached the level of severity prohibited by Article 3. A similar decision was reached in *E and others* v *UK*,[603] in respect of four siblings who had alleged physical and sexual abuse by their stepfather over many years. There, the Court concluded that:[604]

> the pattern of lack of investigation, communication and co-operation by the relevant authorities must be regarded as having had a significant influence on the course of events and that proper and effective management of their responsibilities might, judged reasonably, have been expected to avoid, or at least, minimise the risk or the damage suffered.

In *M. and C.* v *Romania*,[605] the Court found violations of both Articles 3 and 8 on account of the failure of the domestic authorities to ensure adequate protection of the applicant's son from alleged acts of sexual abuse perpetrated by his father. While acknowledging the complexity of such investigations, the Court was critical of the prosecutors' failure to test the credibility of particular witnesses, to verify the surrounding circumstances of the case or to carry out a thorough investigation, in addition to noting the significant delays involved. As to the positive obligations on the state to protect schoolchildren from ill-treatment, see the discussion of *O'Keeffe* v *Ireland*[606] at 6.118 above.

Corporal punishment and military service

Corporal punishment will violate Article 3 if the minimum threshold is reached, whether it **6.186** is administered by the judicial system[607] or in state[608] or private[609] schools.

In *Costello-Roberts* v *UK*[610] there was no violation of Article 3 where a seven-year-old boy **6.187** had been slippered three times on the buttocks. Relevant factors included the fact that the punishment had been administered in private and there was no evidence of any severe or long-lasting effects. The state may also be found to be responsible for the failure of the law to protect children against the ill-treatment of others, including those acting in a 'private' capacity. The case of *A* v *UK*[611] concerned the applicant nine-year-old child's ill-treatment by his stepfather. The stepfather was prosecuted for assault occasioning actual bodily harm

---

[602] No. 29392/95, 10.5.01. By contrast, see *DP and JC* v *UK*, No. 38719/97, 10.10.02 (no violation of Article 3 as it was not established that the local authority ought to have known about the sexual abuse of the applicants by a friend of their mother's, but there was a violation of Article 13 because of the absence of an effective remedy in respect of allegations that the local authority had failed to take action to prevent the applicants' ill-treatment).

[603] No. 33218/96, 26.11.02.

[604] *Ibid.*, para. 100.

[605] No. 29032/04, 27.9.11.

[606] No. 35810/09, 28.1.14.

[607] *Tyrer* v *UK*, Series A, No. 26, 25.4.78.

[608] *Campbell and Cosans* v *UK*, Series A, No. 48, 25.2.82.

[609] *Costello-Roberts* v *UK*, No. 13134/87, Series A, No. 247-C, 25.3.93.

[610] *Ibid.*

[611] No. 25599/94, 23.9.98.

for beating the child with a garden cane, but was acquitted. The applicant complained of a violation of Article 3. The Court noted that, according to the domestic law, it was a defence to a charge of assault that the treatment in question amounted to 'reasonable chastisement' and despite the fact that the treatment was sufficiently severe to fall within the scope of Article 3, the jury acquitted the stepfather. Therefore, the Court found that the domestic law did not provide adequate protection against the ill-treatment of the applicant, in violation of Article 3.

6.188   The Court has spelled out the particular obligations on the state as regards military service:

> … a duty to ensure that a person performs military service in conditions which are compat-
> ible with respect for his human dignity, that the procedures and methods of military training
> do not subject him to distress or suffering of an intensity exceeding the unavoidable level of
> hardship inherent in military discipline and that, given the practical demands of such service,
> his health and well-being are adequately secured by, among other things, providing him with
> the medical assistance he requires.[612]

In *Taştan* v *Turkey*,[613] the Court held that requiring a 71-year-old man to perform military service amounted to degrading treatment, in violation of Article 3. After participating for a month in training intended for 20-year-olds he had been hospitalised. It was found to have been a distressing experience that had affected his dignity. In *Chember* v *Russia*[614] requiring the applicant, who was known to have a knee condition, to perform an excessive level of physical exercise during his national service, was found to constitute inhuman punishment. He had been exercised to the point of collapse, causing him long-term health damage. There was a violation of Article 3 in *Placì* v *Italy*[615] because of the military authorities' failure to ensure the well-being of a conscript in the army with mental health conditions.

Medical treatment

6.189   Failings in the provision of medical treatment may raise issues under Article 3 (see also in relation to the right to life: Health care, abortion, euthanasia and assisted suicide, at 6.101 and Conditions of detention and sentencing, at 6.144 above). This was the case, for example, in *Denis Vasilyev* v *Russia*[616] where the Court found a violation of Article 3 due to a hospital's medical negligence, as the seriously injured applicant had been left unattended for 32 hours, before emergency brain surgery was carried out. In *R.R.* v *Poland*[617] the applicant, a pregnant woman, complained about her lack of access to pre-natal genetic tests following an ultrasound scan which revealed a possible foetal malformation—even though the domestic law clearly entitled her to have such tests. This also meant that she was unable to have an abortion on the grounds of foetal abnormality. Finding that the applicant had been in a position of great vulnerability and was deeply distressed, but had been 'shabbily treated' and 'humiliated' by her doctors, the Court found violations of both Articles 3 and 8. In *P. and S.* v *Poland*,[618] the Court was highly critical of the deplorable treatment of a pregnant

---

[612] *Chember* v *Russia*, No. 7188/03, 3.7.08, para. 50.

[613] No. 63748/00, 4.3.08.

[614] No. 7188/03, 3.7.08. See also *Lyalyakin* v *Russia*, No. 31305/09, 12.3.15 (young conscript required to line up on parade ground in military briefs—degrading treatment).

[615] No. 48754/11, 21.1.14. See, by contrast, *Baklanov* v *Ukraine*, No. 44425/08, 24.10.13.

[616] No. 32704/04, 17.12.09 (the Court found five separate violations of Article 3 in the case due to the inadequate responses of the police, hospital and investigating authorities, and a violation of Article 13).

[617] No. 27617/04, 26.5.11.

[618] No. 57375/08, 30.10.12. There were also violations of Article 8 and Article 5(1).

14-year-old girl who was seeking an abortion after being raped. The Court found that the authorities' approach had been marred by procrastination, confusion and lack of proper and objective counselling and information. The Court noted that information about the case was released to the media by the hospital and that a criminal investigation was instituted against the girl herself on charges of unlawful sexual intercourse. There was accordingly a violation of Article 3.

In *V.C. v Slovakia*,[619] the Court found a violation of Article 3 due to the sterilisation of a 20-year-old Roma woman in hospital without her informed consent (during the delivery of her child by caesarean section). The Court underlined that **6.190**

> sterilisation constitutes a major interference with a person's reproductive health status. As it concerns one of the essential bodily functions of human beings, it bears on manifold aspects of the individual's personal integrity including his or her physical and mental well-being and emotional, spiritual and family life.[620]

In this case, the sterilisation procedure was found to have grossly interfered with the applicant's physical integrity and to have deprived her of her reproductive capability. There was also a separate violation of Article 8 because of the state's failure to comply with its positive obligation to establish effective legal safeguards to protect the reproductive health of women of Roma origin, who were considered to be at particular risk. In *Bataliny v Russia*[621] there was a violation of Article 3 where the applicant was subjected to forced psychiatric treatment, in the absence of evidence to establish the medical necessity for the treatment, and also because, without his consent, he was made to take part in scientific research into a new anti-psychotic drug.

In *Pretty v UK*,[622] the Court found that there was no positive obligation under Article 3 requiring the state to give an undertaking not to prosecute the applicant's husband were he to assist the terminally ill applicant to commit suicide. **6.191**

In *D v UK*[623] the lack of adequate medical treatment in St Kitts for an applicant suffering from the AIDS virus, led to a finding of a violation of Article 3 were he to be removed to St Kitts. **6.192**

Medical treatment of detainees

The failure to provide adequate medical treatment to persons deprived of their liberty may violate Article 3 in certain circumstances.[624] However, the Court has held that Article 3 does not require that every detained prisoner is entitled to receive medical treatment at the same level 'as the best civilian clinics'.[625] The standard of health care should be 'compatible with the human dignity' of a detainee, but should also take into account 'the practical demands **6.193**

---

[619] No. 18968/07, 8.11.11—see also *K.H. and others v Slovakia*, No. 32881/04, 28.4.09 referred to at 6.535 below.
[620] *V.C. v Slovakia,* No. 18968/07, 8.11.11, para. 106.
[621] No. 10060/07, 23.7.15. There were also breaches of Articles 5(1)(e) and 5(4), and a separate violation of Article 3 because of the applicant's ill-treatment in the psychiatric hospital.
[622] No. 2346/02, 29.4.02.
[623] No. 30240/96, 2.5.97.
[624] See, e.g. *Hurtado v Switzerland,* No. 17549/90, Series A, No. 280-A, 28.1.94; *Ilhan v Turkey,* No. 22277/93, 27.6.00, para. 87; *Nevmerzhitsky v Ukraine,* No. 54825/00, 5.4.05, paras. 100–6; *Melnik v Ukraine,* No. 72286/01, 28.3.06, paras. 104–6; *Hummatov v Azerbaijan,* Nos. 9852/03 and 13413/04, 29.11.07.
[625] See, e.g. *Aleksanyan v Russia,* No. 46468/06, 22.12.08, para. 139.

of imprisonment'.626 The availability of resources is also a relevant factor (for example as to whether expensive treatment such as anti-retroviral drugs can be administered).627 The extent of the available evidence is likely to be central to the Court's findings in this area— and the Court will draw adverse inferences from a failure by the state authorities to disclose detainees' medical documents.628 Where detainees have pre-existing conditions, the Court has acknowledged that it may not be possible to ascertain to what extent symptoms at the relevant time resulted from the conditions of detention imposed by the authorities. However, this is not determinative as to whether the authorities have failed to fulfil their obligations under Article 3.629 Therefore, proof of the actual effects of the conditions of detention may not be a major factor. For example, treatment of a mentally ill person may be incompatible with the standards imposed by Article 3 in the protection of fundamental human dignity, even though that person may not be able to point to any specific ill-effects.630 The applicant in *Boicenco* v *Moldova*631 alleged he had been the victim of severe police brutality and the Court found three distinct violations of Article 3—on the basis of his ill-treatment, his inadequate medical care in detention and the failure to investigate his complaint. The Court further held that there was a violation of Article 34 (prohibition of hindrance to the right of individual petition) because of the authorities' refusal to allow his legal representatives or his doctor to see him. It also found that the continuing denial of access amounted to an aggravated breach of Article 3 and stressed the urgent need for the Government to ensure that there was such access.

6.194 By way of example, there was a failure to provide the requisite medical care to the detained applicants in *Khudobin* v *Russia*632 (HIV-positive applicant who suffered from several other chronic diseases, as well as mental illnesses), *Aleksanyan* v *Russia*633 (failure to transfer HIV-positive applicant to specialist hospital), *Gagiu* v *Romania*634 (applicant suffering from various illnesses including chronic hepatitis), *Gorodnichev* v *Russia*635 (applicant suffering from tuberculosis), *Kotsaftis* v *Greece*636 (applicant suffering from cirrhosis of the liver caused by Hepatitis B virus), *Kaprykowski* v *Poland*637 (applicant suffering from epilepsy, encephalopathy and dementia), *G.* v *France*638 (applicant with schizophrenic type of psychotic disorder),

---

626 *Aleksanyan* v *Russia*, No. 46468/06, 22.12.08, para. 140. See also, e.g. *V.D.* v *Romania*, No. 7078/02, 16.2.10 (failure to provide dentures to a toothless, impecunious detainee—violation of Article 3).

627 *Aleksanyan* v *Russia*, No. 46468/06, 22.12.08, para. 148.

628 See, e.g. *Salakhov and Islyamova* v *Ukraine*, No. 28005/08, 14.3.13, para. 138.

629 *Keenan* v *UK*, No. 27229/95, 3.4.01, paras. 112–13.

630 *Ibid.*, para. 113.

631 No. 41088/05, 11.7.06. See also *Paladi* v *Moldova*, No. 39806/05, 10.3.09.

632 No. 59696/00, 26.10.06. See also *Yakovenko* v *Ukraine*, No. 15825/06, 25.10.07 (applicant suffering from HIV and tuberculosis infections); *Yoh-Ekale Mwanje* v *Belgium*, No. 10486/10, 20.12.11 (detainee with advanced stage of HIV infection); *Salakhov and Islyamova* v *Ukraine*, No. 28005/08, 14.3.13 (prisoner who was HIV positive); *Martzaklis and others* v *Greece*, No. 20378/13, 9.7.15 (HIV-positive prisoners held in poor physical and sanitary conditions and without adequate treatment—violation of Article 3 on its own and taken together with Article 14).

633 No. 46468/06, 22.12.08.

634 No. 63258/00, 24.2.09. See also *Poghosyan* v *Georgia*, No. 9870/07, 24.2.09.

635 No. 52058/99, 24.5.07. See also *Ivko* v *Russia*, No. 30575/08, 15.12.15.

636 No. 39780/06, 12.6.08.

637 No. 23052/05, 3.2.09 (a case in which the Court dismissed out of hand the Government's argument that the fact that the inmates with whom the applicant shared his cell knew how to react to his seizures could be considered adequate conditions of detention).

638 No. 27244/09, 23.2.12.

Grori v *Albania*[639] (applicant suffering from multiple sclerosis), and in *Raffray Taddei* v *France*[640] (applicant suffering from anorexia).

In certain situations, the psychological impact on close relatives in witnessing such suffering   **6.195**
may violate Article 3. That was the case in *Salakhov and Islyamova* v *Ukraine*.[641] There, the
mother of a man who was HIV positive and who died in prison was herself found to have
been the victim of inhuman treatment, because of her extensive efforts to alleviate his suffering and the 'cynical, indifferent and cruel attitude'[642] shown by the authorities towards her.
The case of *Elberte* v *Latvia*[643] concerned the removal of tissue from the applicant's deceased
husband's body without her knowledge or consent, following his death in a car accident.
The Court found that the applicant had had to face a long period of uncertainty, anguish
and distress in not knowing what organs or tissue had been removed from her husband's
body, and in what manner and for what purpose this had been done. It transpired that tissue
removal had been carried out over a nine-year period (in relation to nearly 500 people) as
part of a state-approved agreement with a pharmaceutical company abroad. The Court also
took account of the lack of clarity in the regulatory framework and that no one had been
prosecuted in connection with the tissue removals. Accordingly, the applicant's suffering was
found to amount to degrading treatment contrary to Article 3.

The Court has found that prisoners with serious mental disorders may require special meas-   **6.196**
ures to ensure that they receive humane treatment for their condition, regardless of the
seriousness of the offence of which they had been convicted,[644] and that Article 3 may be
breached because of their detention in establishments which are not suitable for the incar-
ceration of the mentally ill.[645] In *McGlinchey and others* v *UK*[646] there were a number of
failings in the treatment of the applicant's mother, a heroin addict who died in prison after
having been jailed for theft for four months. There were inadequate facilities to measure
her weight loss (following uncontrolled vomiting), gaps in the monitoring of her condition
over a weekend and the failure to take further steps such as admitting her to hospital or
obtaining more expert assistance in controlling the vomiting. Article 3 was found to have
been violated in *Keenan* v *UK*[647] because of the 'significant defects in the medical care provided to a mentally ill person known to be a suicide risk'. In those circumstances, imposing
seven days' segregation in a punishment block and prescribing an additional 28 days on
the sentence was held to amount to inhuman and degrading treatment and punishment.
The Court was also critical of the authorities' failure to refer Mark Keenan to a psychiatrist
and of the lack of medical notes, which undermined the effectiveness of any monitoring or supervision.[648] In *Renolde* v *France*[649] the imposition of a disciplinary sanction of

---

[639] No. 25336/04, 7.7.09.

[640] No. 36435/07, 21.12.10.

[641] No. 28005/08, 14.3.13.

[642] *Ibid.*, para. 204.

[643] No. 61243/08, 13.1.15.

[644] *Riviere* v *France*, No. 33834/03, 11.7.06. See also *Dybeku* v *Albania*, No. 41153/06, 18.12.07.

[645] See, e.g. *Sławomir Musiał* v *Poland*, No. 28300/06, 20.1.09; *Claes* v *Belgium*, No. 43418/09, 10.1.13.

[646] No. 50390/99, 29.4.03.

[647] No. 27229/95, 3.4.01. But contrast *Keenan* with the decision in *Kudla* v *Poland*, No. 30210/96, 26.10.00.

[648] In contrast, there was no violation of Article 3 arising from the alleged inadequacy of monitoring of a
prisoner held in pre-trial solitary confinement in *Rohde* v *Denmark*, No. 69332/01, 21.7.05 (by four votes to
three).

[649] No. 5608/05, 16.10.08.

45 days' detention in a punishment cell on a mentally disturbed prisoner (who later committed suicide) was found to constitute inhuman and degrading treatment in violation of Article 3.[650] In *Rivière* v *France*, the applicant had been sentenced to life imprisonment for murder and developed a psychiatric condition in prison. The failure to transfer him to hospital or to provide adequate medical care caused him hardship and distress at a level that was found to breach Article 3.[651]

6.197 In *Mouisel* v *France*,[652] the Court stated that Article 3 cannot be construed as laying down a general obligation to release detainees on health grounds, but reiterated[653] the

> right of all prisoners to conditions of detention which are compatible with human dignity, so as to ensure that the manner and method of execution of the measures imposed do not subject them to distress or hardship of an intensity exceeding the unavoidable level of suffering inherent in detention.

The continued detention of the applicant who was suffering from cancer, was found, in *Mouisel*, to have caused 'particularly acute hardship' which was held to amount to inhuman and degrading treatment in violation of Article 3.[654] The detention of the applicant in *Tekin Yildiz* v *Turkey*[655] was found to amount to inhuman and degrading treatment in violation of Article 3, as he had developed Wernicke-Korsakoff syndrome, and thus his state of health had been consistently found to be incompatible with detention. The Court also found that Article 3 would be violated if the applicant were sent back to prison without there being a significant improvement in his medical condition. In *Gelfmann* v *France*,[656] however, the continued imprisonment of the applicant, who had suffered from AIDS for 20 years, was found, on the facts, not to breach Article 3.

Article 4: Prohibition of Slavery and Forced Labour

6.198 Article 4 states:

1. No one shall be held in slavery or servitude.
2. No one shall be required to perform forced or compulsory labour.
3. For the purposes of this Article the term 'forced or compulsory labour' shall not include:
    (a) any work required to be done in the ordinary course of detention imposed according to the provisions of Article 5 of this Convention or during conditional release from such detention;
    (b) any service of a military character or, in case of conscientious objectors in countries where they are recognised, service exacted instead of compulsory military service;
    (c) any service exacted in case of an emergency or calamity threatening the life or well-being of the community;
    (d) any work or service which forms part of normal civic obligations.

---

[650] There was also a separate finding of a violation of Article 2 (see 6.61 above).

[651] *Rivière* v *France*, No. 33834/03, 11.7.06. See also *Kucheruk* v *Ukraine*, No. 2570/04, 6.9.07 (applicant suffering from schizophrenia and acute personality disorder).

[652] No. 67263/01, 14.11.02. See, by contrast, *Matencio* v *France*, No. 58749/00, 15.1.04.

[653] *Ibid.*, para. 40.

[654] See also *Gülay Çetin* v *Turkey*, No. 44084/10, 5.3.13.

[655] No. 22913/04, 10.11.05.

[656] No. 25875/03, 14.12.04. See also *Reggiani Martinelli* v *Italy*, No. 22682/02, dec. 16.6.05 (continued imprisonment of applicant suffering from a cerebral disease—inadmissible under Article 3).

In 2005 the European Court acknowledged that 'domestic slavery' persists in Europe and **6.199** concerns thousands of people, the majority of whom are women'.[657] Article 4 prohibits slavery and servitude absolutely and prohibits forced or compulsory labour subject to the exceptions set out in Article 4(3). The trafficking of human beings also falls within the scope of Article 4.[658] According to Article 15 there can never be any derogation from Article 4(1). In the case of *Siliadin* v *France*, the Court held that the provision incorporates positive obligations on the state, for example to adopt criminal law provisions penalising the practices referred to in Article 4 and to apply them in practice.[659] Furthermore, the obligation to investigate will arise where there is 'credible suspicion' of treatment contrary to Article 4.[660]

In *Siliadin* the Court adopted the definition of slavery in the 1927 Slavery Convention: 'the **6.200** status or condition of a person over whom any or all of the powers attaching to the right of ownership are exercised'.[661] In *Ould Barar* v *Sweden*,[662] the Court found that the expulsion of a person to a country where there was an officially recognised regime of slavery might raise an issue under Article 3. The applicant, a Mauritanian national, applied for asylum in Sweden, claiming he had left his country to escape slavery. He stated that he had to report once a year to his father's master and carry out various minor tasks. The Swedish Government acknowledged that although slavery was prohibited in Mauritanian law, it appeared that slavery still existed. On the facts, the Court found there was, however, no indication of ill-treatment.

The term 'servitude' has been defined by the Court as 'an obligation to provide one's services **6.201** that is imposed by the use of coercion' (and is linked with the concept of 'slavery', as defined above).[663] The Court has characterised servitude as an 'aggravated' form of forced or compulsory labour: the distinguishing feature being the victim's feeling that their condition is permanent and that the situation is unlikely to change.[664] In *Van Droogenbroeck* v *Belgium*[665] the applicant, a persistent criminal offender who was put at the 'disposal of the state' for ten years after his prison sentence expired, was found by the European Commission of Human Rights not to have been held in servitude, as there had been no violation of Article 5(1) in his case and he was found not to have been subjected to a 'particularly serious' form of 'denial of freedom'.

Forced labour involves 'physical or mental constraint', while compulsory labour has been **6.202** defined as 'work exacted under the menace of any penalty and also performed against the will of the person concerned, that is work for which he has not offered himself voluntarily'.[666] It can include paid work.[667] However, the Court has specified that not all work exacted from an

---

[657] *Siliadin* v *France*, No. 73316/01, 26.7.05, para. 111.
[658] *Rantsev* v *Cyprus and Russia*, No. 25965/04, 7.1.10, para. 282.
[659] No. 73316/01, 26.7.05, paras. 89 and 112.
[660] *C.N.* v *UK*, No. 4239/08, 13.11.12, para. 71.
[661] No. 73316/01, 26.7.05, para. 122.
[662] No. 42367/98, dec. 16.1.99.
[663] *Siliadin* v *France*, No. 73316/01, 26.7.05, para. 124.
[664] *C.N. and V.* v *France*, No. 67724/09, 11.10.12, para. 91.
[665] Series A, No. 50, 24.6.82.
[666] *Van der Mussele* v *Belgium*, No. 8919/80, Series A, No. 70, 23.11.83, para. 34. As to the definition of 'forced or compulsory labour' the Court takes account of the definition of that term in ILO Convention No. 29 (see, e.g. *Graziani-Weiss* v *Austria*, No. 31950/06, 18.10.11, para. 36). A 'penalty' is deemed to include threats of a psychological nature, such as threats to denounce victims to the police or immigration authorities: *C.N. and V.* v *France*, No. 67724/09, 11.10.12, para. 77.
[667] *Van der Mussele* v *Belgium*, No. 8919/80, Series A, No. 70, 23.11.83, para. 40.

individual under threat of a 'penalty' can be considered to be 'forced or compulsory labour', as this will depend on various factors such as the type and amount of work involved:

> These factors help distinguish between 'forced labour' and a helping hand which can reasonably be expected of other family members or people sharing accommodation.[668]

Van der Mussele v *Belgium*[669] concerned the obligation on pupil advocates to act without payment when required. The consequence for failing to act pro bono was striking off the role of pupils which was considered to be sufficiently serious enough to amount to a penalty. However, the obligation was found not to amount to 'forced labour' as: the services carried out were not outside the usual ambit of an advocate; there were compensatory advantages arising from the applicant's membership of the profession; the services also contributed to his professional training; the obligation ensured that his client obtained legal representation and was therefore 'founded on a conception of social solidarity'; and Mr Van der Mussele was not considered to have suffered a disproportionate burden, having provided only 17 to 18 hours of work.[670]

6.203   The applicant in *Siliadin* v *France*[671] was a Togolese national who had been forced to work as a 'maid of all work' for several years since her arrival in France at the age of 15. She was required to carry out household duties and care for children from 7 am to 10 pm every day, without being paid. She had neither a work nor a residence permit and no longer had a passport. The Court found that the applicant was not held in slavery, as no one exercised a genuine right of legal ownership over her. However, she was found to have been both required to perform forced labour and held in servitude. As to the former, the fact that she was a child was a particularly important factor, and that she was unlawfully living in a foreign country, in fear of being arrested by the police, and had no real choice other than to do the work she was told to do. The finding as to servitude was made in the light of her forced labour for 15 hours a day, seven days a week. Furthermore, she was found to have had no resources, no freedom of movement or free time and to have been vulnerable and isolated. The applicant's 'employers' were prosecuted under provisions criminalising the exploitation of individuals through labour and the subjection of working and living conditions that are incompatible with human dignity. However, they were acquitted on appeal. The European Court found Article 4 to have been violated as the domestic law was of insufficient scope and had failed to provide the applicant with practical and effective protection. A violation of Article 4 was also found in *C.N.* v *UK*[672] as a result of the domestic servitude of the applicant, a Ugandan national, who had worked as a live-in carer for an elderly Iraqi couple. Noting that the facts were similar to the *Siliadin* case, the Court found that the legislation in force in the UK at the relevant time was inadequate to provide practical and effective protection against treatment falling within the scope of Article 4,[673] and that the domestic investigation had been

---

[668]   *C.N. and V.* v *France*, No. 67724/09, 11.10.12, para. 74.

[669]   No. 8919/80, Series A, No. 70, 23.11.83.

[670]   See also *Steindel* v *Germany*, No. 29878/07, dec. 14.9.10 (requirement for opthalmologists to participate in emergency service scheme—inadmissible); *Graziani-Weiss* v *Austria*, No. 31950/06, 18.10.11 (obligation on lawyer to act as unpaid guardian to mentally ill person—no violation of Article 4 or of Article 4 taken together with Article 14).

[671]   No. 73316/01, 26.7.05.

[672]   No. 4239/08, 13.11.12.

[673]   Subsequently, in 2010, new legislation came into force specifically criminalising slavery, servitude and forced or compulsory labour (Section 71 of the Coroners and Justice Act 2009).

overly focused on the possible offence of trafficking for exploitation, rather than domestic servitude, which was a specific and distinct offence.

There was a similar outcome in *C.N. and V. v France*[674] which concerned the treatment of two **6.204** sisters (French nationals), who were born in Burundi and arrived in France at the respective ages of 16 and 10. They were then required to carry out household and domestic chores for their aunt, her husband and their seven children. Once the authorities were alerted to the situation, an investigation was initiated, and the aunt and uncle were prosecuted for subjecting vulnerable persons to working and living conditions that were incompatible with human dignity. However, they were acquitted by the court of appeal. The Court found that the elder sister (but not her younger sister) was subjected to 'forced and compulsory labour' as she did not go to school, and she was responsible for all the household chores, which involved working long hours for seven days a week, with no pay. This work was carried out under the 'menace of a penalty', as her aunt regularly threatened to send her back to Burundi. The Court also found that she was subjected to 'servitude', on the basis that she considered her situation (which had lasted four years) was permanent and could not be changed. However, her younger sister was not considered to be a victim of either servitude or forced labour, as she was allowed to go to school and do her homework after school, before working. The Court concluded that the French authorities had breached their positive obligations under Article 4 for failing to establish a legislative and administrative framework to combat servitude and forced labour effectively (as the domestic legal regime was the same as it had been in *Siliadin*).

The leading judgment on human trafficking, *Rantsev v Cyprus and Russia*,[675] highlighted the **6.205** serious problems in Cyprus (since the 1970s) involving young women, frequently from the countries of the former Soviet Union, being forced to work in the sex industry. The applicant's daughter, Oxana Rantseva, had died a few days after arriving in Cyprus on a 'cabaret-artiste' visa. The Court held in *Rantsev* that national laws must be adequate to ensure the practical and effective protection of the rights of victims or potential victims of trafficking. As well as criminal law provisions punishing traffickers, Article 4 also requires measures of control over businesses that are often used as a cover for human trafficking, and that immigration rules should address the encouragement, facilitation or tolerance of trafficking. Applying the '*Osman* criteria' (see 6.67 above), the Court further held that specific operational steps will be required where the authorities 'were aware, or ought to have been aware, of circumstances giving rise to a credible suspicion that an identified individual had been, or was at real and immediate risk of being, trafficked or exploited within the meaning of Article 3(a) of the Palermo Protocol and Article 4(a) of the Anti-Trafficking Convention'. Where such circumstances arise, the authorities will be required to take appropriate measures within the scope of their powers to remove the individual from that situation or risk. Article 4 also includes a procedural obligation to investigate situations of potential trafficking, which is equivalent to the duties arising under Articles 2 and 3 of the European Convention. In cross-border trafficking cases, states will be required to co-operate effectively with other states.[676] Although the broad legislative framework in Cyprus was found to be acceptable, Article 4 was violated

---

[674] No. 67724/09, 11.10.12.
[675] No. 25965/04, 7.1.10. See also *M. and others v Italy and Bulgaria*, No. 40020/03, 31.7.12 (allegation of trafficking of young Bulgarian girl in Italy not supported by sufficient evidence—inadmissible).
[676] *Rantsev v Cyprus and Russia*, No. 25965/04, 7.1.10, paras. 286–9.

because of inadequacies in the immigration system which failed to provide practical and effective protection against trafficking and exploitation. As to the specific circumstances of the case, the Court concluded that there had been sufficient indicators available to the police authorities, against the general backdrop of trafficking issues in Cyprus, for them to have been aware of circumstances giving rise to a credible suspicion that Ms Rantseva was, or was at real and immediate risk of being, a victim of trafficking or exploitation. Therefore, a positive obligation arose to take the necessary operational measures to protect Ms Rantseva. However, the police failed to question Ms Rantseva or to carry out the most basic investigatory steps, in further violation of Article 4. Russia was also held to be in violation of Article 4 for failing to investigate the 'recruitment' of Ms Rantseva and other victims of trafficking in Russia. There was also a violation of Article 4 in *L.E.* v *Greece*[677] because of the authorities' inadequate responses to a criminal complaint of human trafficking. The applicant complained that after arriving in Greece her passport had been confiscated by the individual who had helped her travel there (for a debt pledge) and that he had forced her into prostitution. Although the domestic legislation itself was considered to provide the applicant with sufficient protection, the operational measures taken were deemed inadequate. Procrastination by the police in obtaining the requisite evidence meant that there was a nine month delay in the applicant being formally recognised as a victim of trafficking. There were also delays in the criminal investigation against the alleged traffickers and other specific shortcomings as to how it was conducted.

6.206 Article 4(3) has the effect of excluding various forms of labour from the prohibition on forced or compulsory labour: work during detention (or during conditional release); military service[678] or work in lieu of military service (as to the possibility of invoking Article 9 in respect of conscientious objection to military service, see 6.568 below); emergency work; and work carried out as part of civic obligations. In *Chitos* v *Greece*[679] the Court clarified that Article 4(3)(b) only exempts compulsory military service, and not work carried out by regular soldiers. It went on to find a violation of Article 4(2) where the applicant, a regular soldier (and a medical officer) who wanted to leave the army, had been required immediately to pay more than €100,000 in order to buy back his remaining years of service.

6.207 It does not violate Article 4 to require work in prison[680] (even without being affiliated to the old age pension system[681]). There will also be no breach of Article 4 where a prisoner is forced to work in detention and the conviction is subsequently quashed or where there was no opportunity to challenge the legality of detention, in violation of Article 5(4).[682] In *De Wilde, Ooms and Versyp* v *Belgium*,[683] the work imposed on the applicants, who had given

---

[677] No. 71545/12, 21.1.16. See, by contrast, *J. and others* v *Austria*, No. 58216/12, 17.1.17 (prosecutor's decision not to pursue investigation into alleged human trafficking offences committed abroad by non-nationals—no violation of Article 4).

[678] However, in *Taştan* v *Turkey*, No. 63748/00, 4.3.08 the Court held that requiring a 71-year-old man to perform military service amounted to degrading treatment, in violation of Article 3.

[679] No. 51637/12, 4.6.15.

[680] See, e.g. *Floroiu* v *Romania*, No. 15303/10, dec. 12.3.13 (prisoner's sentence reduced in return for work done in prison—inadmissible). See also *Meier* v *Switzerland*, No. 10109/14, 9.2.16 (obligation on prisoner to work after reaching retirement age—no violation of Article 4).

[681] *Stummer* v *Austria*, No. 37452/02, 7.7.11.

[682] *De Wilde, Ooms and Versyp* v *Belgium*, Series A, No. 12, 18.6.71, para. 89.

[683] Series A, No. 12, 18.6.71.

themselves up voluntarily to the police and who were detained under vagrancy laws, was found not to exceed the ordinary limits under Article 4(3)(a) because it was aimed at their rehabilitation and because there were similar laws in other Council of Europe states.

6.208 The term 'normal civic obligations' has been found to include jury service[684] and compulsory work for the fire service (or a fine or compulsory financial levy in lieu of such service). However, an obligation to work for the fire service, which applied to men but not women, was found in *Schmidt* v *Germany*[685] to violate Article 14 in conjunction with Article 4(3)(d). Similarly, the fact that the Maltese authorities in practice required many more men than women to carry out jury service was also found to breach the same provisions in *Zarb Adami* v *Malta*.[686]

Article 5: Right to Liberty and Security of the Person

6.209 Article 5 states:

1. Everyone has the right to liberty and security of person. No one shall be deprived of his liberty save in the following cases and in accordance with a procedure prescribed by law:
   (a) the lawful detention of a person after conviction by a competent court;
   (b) the lawful arrest or detention of a person for non-compliance with the lawful order of a court or in order to secure the fulfilment of any obligation prescribed by law;
   (c) the lawful arrest or detention of a person effected for the purpose of bringing him before the competent legal authority on reasonable suspicion of having committed an offence or when it is reasonably considered necessary to prevent his committing an offence or fleeing after having done so;
   (d) the detention of a minor by lawful order for the purpose of educational supervision or his lawful detention for the purpose of bringing him before the competent legal authority;
   (e) the lawful detention of persons for the prevention of the spreading of infectious diseases, of persons of unsound mind, alcoholics or drug addicts or vagrants;
   (f) the lawful arrest or detention of a person to prevent his effecting an unauthorised entry into the country or of a person against whom action is being taken with a view to deportation or extradition.
2. Everyone who is arrested shall be informed promptly, in a language which he understands, of the reasons for his arrest and of any charge against him.
3. Everyone arrested or detained in accordance with the provisions of paragraph 1(c) of this article shall be brought promptly before a judge or other officer authorised by law to exercise judicial power and shall be entitled to trial within a reasonable time or to release pending trial. Release may be conditioned by guarantees to appear for trial.
4. Everyone who is deprived of his liberty by arrest or detention shall be entitled to take proceedings by which the lawfulness of his detention shall be decided speedily by a court and his release ordered if the detention is not lawful.
5. Everyone who has been the victim of arrest or detention in contravention of the provisions of this article shall have an enforceable right to compensation.

---

[684] *Zarb Adami* v *Malta*, No. 17209/02, 20.6.06, para. 47.

[685] No. 13580/88, Series A, No. 291-B, 18.7.94.

[686] No. 17209/02, 20.6.06. But see the concerns expressed by Judges Bratza and Garlicki in their concurring opinions as to how the case could be said to fall within the ambit of Article 4 given that jury service was a 'normal civic obligation' and was therefore excluded from the definition of 'forced or compulsory labour' under Article 4(3).

6.210 Article 5 of the Convention is aimed at preventing arbitrary detention and has been one of the most frequently invoked Convention Articles (second only to Article 6).[687] Article 5 requires that every arrest or detention is lawful (both procedurally and substantively) and that it has in fact been carried out for one of the six specified reasons in sub-paragraphs 5(1) (a) to (f), which amounts to an exhaustive list of circumstances.[688] Only a narrow interpretation of these exceptions will be consistent with the aims of Article 5.[689] It is possible that a detention may fall within the scope of more than one sub-paragraph of Article 5(1).[690]

6.211 There are also a number of procedural rights under Article 5. Anyone arrested must be promptly given the reasons for their arrest, they must be taken promptly before the judicial authorities (if arrested on reasonable suspicion of an offence) and they must be entitled to challenge their detention in court. There must also be a right to compensation whenever any of these requirements has been breached.

6.212 Article 5 incorporates positive obligations on the state to protect interferences with liberty by private persons or entities. Thus the authorities are required to take measures 'providing effective protection of vulnerable persons, including reasonable steps to prevent a deprivation of liberty of which the authorities have or ought to have knowledge'.[691] The question of the imputability of the state for the deprivation of liberty in a private psychiatric hospital was in issue in *Storck* v *Germany*.[692] The state's responsibility was found to be engaged for three reasons: a public authority had been involved in the applicant's placement in the clinic (the police took her back after she had escaped); the domestic courts had failed to interpret the relevant domestic law within the spirit of Article 5 of the Convention; and the state breached its positive obligation to protect the applicant, in failing to exercise any supervision of the lawfulness of the applicant's detention.

Deprivation of liberty

6.213 One of the first issues to consider in an apparent case of arrest or detention is whether it in fact amounted to a 'deprivation of liberty'. Article 5 is *not* concerned with mere restrictions of freedom of movement,[693] as opposed to arrest or detention. Relevant factors that are taken into account in this respect include the nature, duration, effects and manner of execution of

---

[687] European Court of Human Rights, *Overview—1959–2015*, p. 6.
[688] *Engel and others* v *Netherlands*, Series A, No. 22, 8.6.76, para. 57.
[689] *Conka* v *Belgium*, No. 51564/99, 5.2.02, para. 41.
[690] See, e.g. *Brand* v *Netherlands*, No. 49902/99, 11.5.04, para. 58.
[691] See, e.g. *Storck* v *Germany*, No. 61603/00, 16.6.05, para. 102.
[692] *Ibid.*
[693] *Engel and others* v *Netherlands*, Series A, No. 22, 8.6.76, para. 58. See also *Guzzardi* v *Italy*, Series A, No. 39, 6.1.80, para. 93 (where the Court held that the difference between deprivation of and restriction upon liberty was one of degree or intensity, and not one of nature or substance) and *De Tommaso* v *Italy*, No. 43395/09, 23.2.17. See also *Riera Blume and others* v *Spain*, No. 37680/97, 14.10.99, paras. 28–30, where the Court found the applicants (who were allegedly members of a sect) to have been deprived of their liberty after having been taken by Catalan police to a hotel and confined by their families for ten days and allegedly subjected to a 'deprogramming' process. In *Nada* v *Switzerland*, No. 10593/08, 12.9.12 a travel ban was imposed on the applicant resulting from legislation implementing UN Security Council resolutions. He lived in Campione d'Italia, a tiny Italian enclave surrounded by a Swiss canton, and was prevented from entering or transiting through Switzerland. This was held not to amount to a 'deprivation of liberty'. See also: *Gahramanov* v *Azerbaijan*, No. 26291/06, dec. 15.10.13 (airport security checks lasting a few hours—no deprivation of liberty—inadmissible); *Kasparov* v *Russia*, No. 53659/07, 11.10.16 (applicant detained for five hours by airport police – violations of Articles 5(1) and 11). As to the right to freedom of movement, see 6.836 below.

the measure in question.[694] In *Khodorkovskiy v Russia*[695] the Government's suggestion that the applicant had been 'subjected to attachment', rather than arrested, was held to be irrelevant since he had in any event been deprived of his liberty for many hours, in order to be taken in for questioning. The Court will review a domestic court's findings of fact but is not bound by its legal conclusions as to whether or not applicants were deprived of their liberty.[696] In *Lavents v Latvia*,[697] the placing of the applicant under house arrest for 11 months was found to amount to a 'deprivation of liberty' under Article 5. In *Amuur v France*,[698] the Court held that holding the applicant asylum-seekers for 20 days in an airport transit zone amounted to a deprivation of liberty, even though they were technically free to return to their country of origin. An important factor in the Court's decision was the lack of legal or social assistance provided to the applicants. In *Khlaifia and others v Italy*,[699] which concerned the authorities' interception at sea of applicants who were travelling in 'rudimentary vessels' from Tunisia to Italy, the Court found that they were deprived of their liberty both at the migrants' reception centre where they were taken to initially, and when they were subsequently accommodated in ships moored at Palermo.

Article 5 can be relied on in relation to any 'deprivation of liberty', even if the detention **6.214** lasts only for a short period.[700] Being stopped and searched by the police for a few minutes may therefore amount to a deprivation of liberty.[701] However, the practice by the police of 'kettling' demonstrators (for more than seven hours) was found not to deprive them of their liberty in *Austin and others v UK* (by a majority of 14 to three).[702] In reaching this decision, the Court took account of the particular context—that the measure had been imposed by the police to isolate and contain a large crowd in central London, in volatile and dangerous conditions.

The Grand Chamber has found that there may be a deprivation of liberty as a result of a **6.215** person being summoned to a police station.[703] In *M.A. v Cyprus*,[704] the Court found that there had been a deprivation of liberty where the police mounted a large-scale operation

---

[694] See, e.g. *HM v Switzerland*, No. 39187/98, 26.2.02, para. 42. In *Austin and others v UK*, Nos. 39692/09, 40713/09 and 41008/09, 15.3.12 the Court held that that the requirement to take account of the 'type' and 'manner of implementation' of the measure in question means that it may also take account of the specific context and circumstances surrounding the case in question (para. 59).

[695] No. 5829/04, 31.5.11.

[696] See, e.g. *Storck v Germany*, No. 61603/00, 16.6.05, para. 72.

[697] No. 58442/00, 28.11.02. See also *Dacosta Silva v Spain* No. 69966/01, 2.11.06 and *Buzadji v Moldova*, No. 23755/07, 5.7.16 (house arrest constituted a deprivation of liberty even where the applicant himself requested it).

[698] No. 19776/92, 25.6.96. See also *Shamsa v Poland*, Nos. 45355/99 and 45357/99, 7.11.03; *Riad and Idiab v Belgium*, Nos. 29787/03 and 29810/03, 24.1.08; *Nolan and K. v Russia*, No. 2512/04, 12.2.09. But in contrast see *Mahdid and Haddar v Austria*, No. 74762/01, dec. 8.12.05.

[699] No. 16483/12, 15.12.16.

[700] See, e.g. *X v Austria*, No. 8278/78, dec. 13.12.79, 18 DR 154 (1979); *X and Y v Sweden*, No. 7376/76, dec. 7.10.76, (1977) 7 DR 123; *Rantsev v Cyprus and Russia*, No. 25965/04, 7.1.10, para. 317; *Ostendorf v Germany*, No. 15998/08, 7.3.13, para. 64.

[701] *Foka v Turkey*, No. 28940/95, 24.6.08, paras. 74–9; *Gillan and Quinton v UK*, No. 4158/05, 12.1.10, para. 57; *Shimovolos v Russia*, No. 30194/09, 21.6.11, paras. 49–50.

[702] Nos. 39692/09, 40713/09 and 41008/09, 15.3.12. A compelling joint dissenting opinion of Judges Tulkens, Spielmann and Garlicki argued highly persuasively that there *had* been a deprivation of liberty.

[703] *Creangă v Romania*, No. 29226/03, 23.2.12. See also *Krupko and others v Russia*, No. 26587/07, 26.6.14.

[704] No. 41872/10, 23.7.13. There was a violation of Article 5(1) because the Government could identify no legal basis for the detention. There were also separate findings of a breach of Article 5(1) in relation to two other periods of detention.

(involving 250 police officers) to remove a group of protestors in Nicosia at 3 a.m., and then put them on buses to be taken to the police headquarters. The Court noted that the aim of the operation had been to identify protesters who were staying in the country unlawfully, in order to deport them—there was therefore an element of coercion to the operation. Article 5 will be in issue even where a person gives himself or herself up to be taken into detention.[705]

6.216 As the Grand Chamber recognised in *Stanev* v *Bulgaria*,[706] the question whether vulnerable people resident in different forms of social care institutions are 'deprived of their liberty' may be difficult to discern. In *HM* v *Switzerland*,[707] where the elderly applicant had been placed in a foster home on account of neglect, there was no deprivation of liberty as the purpose of the placement was to provide medical care, satisfactory living conditions and hygiene, and she did not object to her placement there. There was similarly no deprivation of liberty in *Nielsen* v *Denmark*[708] where a 12-year-old boy was placed in a psychiatric hospital ward at his mother's request for five and a half months, as the applicant was found to be in need of medical treatment and the restrictions placed on him were not much greater than would have been applied in an ordinary hospital. By contrast, the autistic applicant in *HL* v *UK*,[709] who was detained as an 'informal patient' in a psychiatric institution, was found to be subjected to 'deprivation of liberty', as he remained under continuous supervision and was not free to leave. A similar conclusion was reached in *Storck* v *Germany*.[710] There, the applicant had been detained (at the age of 18) in a psychiatric hospital, in a locked ward under constant supervision. The question as to whether she had consented to this treatment was disputed. However, her lack of consent was established by the fact that she had tried to escape on several occasions and when she once managed to so so, she was shackled and brought back to the clinic by the police. Accordingly, she was held to have been deprived of her liberty. The applicant in *Stanev* v *Bulgaria*[711] had been placed under partial guardianship against his will and was admitted to a social care home for people with mental disorders. The Court concluded that he had been deprived of his liberty on account of a series of factors, notably the authorities' involvement in his placement in the home, the restrictive rules on leave of absence, the duration of the placement (over eight years) and his lack of consent.

Lawfulness of detention

6.217 The requirement that any deprivation of liberty must be in accordance with a procedure prescribed by law means not only that there must be compliance with domestic substantive and procedural rules,[712] but also that the domestic law provides clearly defined pre-conditions

---

[705] *De Wilde, Ooms and Versyp* v *Belgium*, Series A, No. 12, 18.6.71, para. 65.
[706] No. 36760/06, 17.1.12.
[707] No. 39187/98, 26.2.02.
[708] No. 10929/84, Series A, No. 144, 28.11.88.
[709] No. 45508/99, 5.10.04.
[710] No. 61603/00, 16.6.05. See also, e.g. *D.D.* v *Lithuania*, No. 13469/06, 14.2.12.
[711] No. 36760/06, 17.1.12.
[712] See, e.g. *Butkevicius* v *Lithuania*, No. 48297/99, 26.3.02 (violation of Article 5(1) where there was no judicial order authorising the applicant's pre-trial detention for specific periods, and there was no other lawful basis for the detention); *Anguelova* v *Bulgaria*, No. 38361/97, 13.6.02 (the detention of the applicant's son was unlawful because it was not based on a written order, as was required by domestic law—Article 5(1) was also breached because of the lack of a proper record of the detention); *Rakevich* v *Russia*, No. 58973/00, 28.10.03 (order for psychiatric detention in breach of Article 5(1)(e) because of a failure to comply with the five-day domestic law time limit within which a hospital's request for a detention order should be considered by a judge); *Pezone* v *Italy*, No. 42098/98, 18.12.03 (applicant's detention was unlawful because of an error in the calculation of the length of his sentence); *De Donder and De Clippel* v *Belgium*, No. 8595/06, 6.12.11

for detention and its application is foreseeable.[713] Legal certainty is particularly important in the context of detention. The rationale here is that prospective detainees should be protected from arbitrary action.[714] Thus the failure to release a detainee after the period of their detention has expired is likely to violate Article 5(1)[715] (although the Court is prepared to allow the authorities a degree of leeway as regards short delays[716]). The applicant in *Assanidze v Georgia*[717] was kept in detention despite his acquittal by the Supreme Court of Georgia which also ordered his immediate release. The Grand Chamber accordingly found his continuing detention to have no judicial basis and to be arbitrary. In *Fedotov v Russia*[718] the applicant's arrest took place after the cancellation of his arrest warrant, thus breaching both the domestic law and the Convention. In *John v Greece*,[719] the applicant, a Nigerian national who had no residence permit, was arrested on his arrival at Athens airport and remanded in custody pending expulsion. When the maximum three-month period of detention expired, his release was ordered, but before he left the police station he was arrested again, and his detention was prolonged and a new expulsion order was issued. The Court found that this amounted to an attempt to circumvent the domestic law time limits, in violation of Article 5(1). The applicant's deprivation of liberty in *Kandzhov v Bulgaria*,[720] for committing offences of insult and hooliganism during a political demonstration, was found not be be lawful and in breach of Article 5(1). According to the domestic law, charges of 'insult' could not warrant being detained. He had been accused of hooliganism on the basis that he had gathered signatures calling for the resignation of the Minister of Justice and displayed posters describing him as a 'top idiot'; however, the Supreme Court found that such actions did not amount to the constituent elements of the offence of hooliganism.

Nevertheless, an error in a detention order will not *necessarily* mean that the underlying detention is unlawful for the purposes of Article 5(1). Thus the Court distinguishes between *ex facie* invalid detention orders (arising from a 'gross and obvious irregularity', for example an order made by a court beyond its jurisdiction) and detention orders which are prima facie valid unless they are overturned by a higher court.[721] However, such distinctions can be

6.218

(applicant with mental health disorder detained in ordinary section of prison, in spite of relevant legislation and public prosecutor's direction both requiring his detention in psychiatric facility); *Stanev v Bulgaria*, No. 36760/06, 17.1.12 (domestic law envisaged placement in a social care home as a protective measure, not a coercive one; the decision of the applicant's guardian to place him in social care without his consent was invalid under domestic law—violation of Article 5); *Creangă v Romania*, No. 29226/03, 23.2.12 (failure to follow statutory procedure for detention of suspect—violation of Article 5(1)); *Velinov v former Yugoslav Republic of Macedonia*, No. 16880/08, 19.9.13 (applicant imprisoned for non-payment of fine which he had in fact paid—violation of Article 5(1)).

[713] See, e.g. *Baranowski v Poland*, No. 28358/95, 28.3.00, para. 52; *Jecius v Lithuania*, No. 34578/97, 31.7.00, para. 56; *Ümit Bilgiç v Turkey*, No. 22398/05, 3.9.13, para. 94. See also *Ciobanu v Romania and Italy*, No. 4509/08, 9.7.13 (lack of clarity in Romanian law led to refusal to deduct period spent under house arrest overseas from length of prison sentence—violation of Article 5(1)).

[714] See, e.g. *Winterwerp v Netherlands*, Series A, No. 33, 24.10.79, (1979–80), para. 45; *Bozano v France*, No. 9990/82, Series A, No. 111, 18.12.86, para. 54; *Lexa v Slovakia*, No. 54334/00, 23.9.08, para. 118.

[715] See, e.g. *K.-F. v Germany*, No. 25629/94, 27.11.97.

[716] See, e.g. *Ignatenko v Moldova*, No. 36988/07, 8.2.11.

[717] No. 71503/01, 8.4.04. See also *Svipsta v Latvia*, No. 66820/01, 9.3.06 (continued detention on remand after expiry of order).

[718] No. 5140/02, 25.10.09.

[719] No. 199/05, 10.5.07.

[720] No. 68294/01, 6.11.08.

[721] See, e.g. *Dinç and Çakır v Turkey*, No. 66066/09, 9.7.13.

problematic to discern. In *Mooren v Germany*[722] the Grand Chamber of the Court found by a majority of nine votes to eight that the applicant's detention was lawful and not in violation of Article 5(1). The Court of Appeal had found that the applicant's detention order did not comply with the domestic law as it did not describe in sufficient detail the facts and evidence establishing the grounds for his arrest, but the defect was not so serious as to render it null and void. The domestic courts had also concurred that the substantive conditions for the applicant's detention were met (a strong suspicion of his involvement in tax evasion). The majority in Strasbourg therefore concluded that there had been no 'gross and obvious irregularity'. Moreover, the Court of Appeal's decision was considerd to have been sufficiently foreseeable not to violate the principle of legal certainty, and the district court had issued a new, reasoned, detention order within 15 days of the Court of Appeal's decision to remit the case—a period of time which did not mean that the applicant's detention was arbitrary.[723]

6.219 Article 5 also requires that there must be conformity with the *purposes* of the restrictions permitted under the relevant sub-paragraph of the Article.[724] Therefore an arrest will violate Article 5 if it is not in fact made for its ostensible purpose. For example, in *Bozano v France*,[725] the applicant's detention breached Article 5(1) when, after the French courts had declined to order his extradition, he was served with a deportation order and forcibly taken by French police to the Swiss border and expelled. Such action was held to amount to a 'disguised form of extradition' designed to circumvent a domestic court ruling.[726] The case of *Iskandarov v Russia*[727] concerned the abduction and de facto extradition of the applicant, a Tajik opposition leader, by plane from Russia to Tajikistan. Despite the Government's denial of responsibility, the Court found that his transfer had been carried out by state agents; and it was 'deeply regrettable that such opaque methods were employed'. The Court concluded that the applicant's detention had been carried out in pursuance of an unlawful removal designed to circumvent the Russian Prosecutor-General's Office's earlier dismissal of an extradition request, in violation of Article 5(1). In *Giorgi Nikolaishvili v Georgia*,[728] the applicant voluntarily attended a prosecutor's office after 'wanted' posters of him had been displayed by the police, and his lawyer had been informed that he was being sought as a witness in a murder case (in which his brother was the main suspect). However, he was arrested at the prosecutor's office for an unrelated firearms offence. The Court held that Article 5(1) had been breached as it was a ruse which had misled the applicant and also as his arrest had been carried out to create additional leverage in relation to the murder case against his brother. The applicant in *Gusinskiy v Russia*,[729] a former chairman of the board and majority shareholder in

---

[722] No. 11364/03, 9.7.09.

[723] The eight dissenting judges argued on the contrary that there had been a violation of Article 5(1) because of the 'serious irregularities' in the order for the applicant's detention and on the basis that the domestic law did not sufficiently guarantee the right to liberty.

[724] *Winterwerp v Netherlands*, Series A, No. 33, 24.10.79, para. 39.

[725] No. 9990/82, Series A, No. 111, 18.12.86. See also *Khodorkovskiy v Russia*, No. 5829/04, 31.5.11, para. 142.

[726] *Bozano v France*, No. 9990/82, Series A, No. 111, 18.12.86, para. 60.

[727] No. 17185/05, 23.9.10. See also *Savriddin Dzhurayev v Russia*, No. 71386/10, 25.4.13; *Belozorov v Russia and Ukraine*, No. 43611/02, 15.10.15.

[728] No. 37048/04, 13.1.09. See, by contrast, *Adamov v Switzerland*, No. 3052/06, 21.6.11 (arrest of former Russian Minister with a view to extradition—no violation of Article 5(1)).

[729] No. 70276/01, 19.5.04. See also *Lutsenko v Ukraine*, No. 6492/11, 3.7.12 (discussed at 5.31 above) concerning the arbitrary detention of the applicant (the leader of an opposition political party) in which the Court found two violations of both Articles 5(1) and 5(3), as well as violations of Articles 5(2) and 5(4), and a violation of Article 18 taken together with Article 5.

a media company, was remanded in custody before being charged, this being permitted in 'exceptional circumstances' under the code of criminal procedure. However, this term was undefined and accordingly the law was found not to be sufficiently prescribed. The Court also found a violation of Article 18, in conjunction with Article 5, on the basis that the applicant had been detained not only because of a reasonable suspicion of his involvement in an offence (and therefore in order for him to be taken before a competent legal authority), but also in order to intimidate the applicant into transferring certain shares to a state-controlled company. There was a violation of Article 5(1) in *Tymoshenko v Ukraine*,[730] because the pretrial detention of the applicant (a former Prime Minister) was arbitrary and unlawful: not only was her detention ordered for an indefinite period of time, but also the main justification for it was her alleged hindrance of the proceedings and her contemptuous behaviour towards the court (which would not have justified detention under Article 5(1)(c)).

The obligation to comply with the law procedurally meant that the failure of the courts to **6.220** hear a voluntary psychiatric patient before she was ordered to be confined compulsorily in hospital for six months (despite the domestic law requiring such a hearing) violated Article 5(1) in *Van der Leer v Netherlands*.[731] *Benham v UK*[732] concerned the applicant's imprisonment by the magistrates' court for failing to pay the community charge. The lawfulness of the detention under the domestic law depended on whether or not the magistrates had acted within their jurisdiction. However, the domestic courts had not subsequently had to decide this issue, because the relevant question on appeal was whether or not they had acted in bad faith, rather than whether they had acted within their jurisdiction. The European Court accordingly found that it had not been established that the order for detention was invalid and there was therefore no violation of Article 5(1).

Difficult questions may arise where a Council of Europe state acts extra-territorially to detain **6.221** criminal suspects in another state. The Court has confirmed that the Convention does not rule out, as such, co-operation between states through extradition treaties or in deportation proceedings,[733] and the fact that a suspect is handed over by one state to another does not necessarily make the detention unlawful under Article 5.[734] The Court will determine such a question by assessing whether the state acted in a manner that was 'inconsistent with the sovereignty of the host state' and therefore contrary to international law.[735] To find a violation, the Court must be satisfied of this beyond reasonable doubt. The lawfulness of the arrest of the leader of the Kurdish Workers' Party (PKK) by Turkish security officials in the international zone of Nairobi airport was analysed in *Öcalan v Turkey*.[736] The Court there rejected arguments that the Turkish authorities had violated Kenyan sovereignty, finding that there had in fact been co-operation between the two states (albeit in the absence of any formal extradition treaty). Accordingly, as the arrest complied with Turkish law, and, as there

---

[730] No. 49872/11, 30.4.13. There were also violations of Article 5(4) and 5(5), as well as Article 5 taken together with Article 18 (see 5.31 above).

[731] No. 11509/85, Series A, No. 170, 21.2.90.

[732] No. 19380/92, 10.6.96.

[733] *Stocke v Germany*, No. 11755/85, Series A, No. 199, 12.10.89.

[734] See, e.g. *Freda v Italy*, No. 8916/80, dec. 7.10.80, (DR) 21; *Klaus Altmann (Barbie) v France*, No. 10689/83, dec. 4.7.84, (DR) 37; *Reinette v France*, No. 14009/88, dec. 2.10.89, (DR) 63; *Öcalan v Turkey*, No. 46221/99, 12.5.05.

[735] *Öcalan v Turkey*, No. 46221/99, 12.5.05, para. 90.

[736] No. 46221/99, 12.5.05.

was no violation of international law, the applicant's arrest was deemed to have been carried out in accordance with a 'procedure prescribed by law' in compliance with Article 5(1)(c).

6.222 The applicants in *Medvedyev and others* v *France*,[737] were crew members on a Cambodian merchant ship which was intercepted by a French warship, because it was suspected to be carrying drugs. The ship was boarded and the crew were confined to their cabins while it was escorted to France, which was found to constitute a deprivation of liberty. As to the question of the lawfulness of the measures taken, the Court noted that under public international law, in cases concerning drug trafficking on the high seas, it is the 'flag state' that has jurisdiction (i.e., in this case, Cambodia, not France). Furthermore, the fact that Cambodia had consented in a diplomatic note to the intervention of the French authorities, also did not provide a sufficient legal basis. While the diplomatic note provided authorisation to intercept, inspect and take legal action against the ship, it did not give authority to take any action against the crew. Moreover, the ad hoc nature of the agreement by way of the diplomatic note was also not considered to be sufficiently foreseeable. Therefore, the Court found that the lack of a legal basis of the requisite quality for such measures meant that there was a violation of Article 5(1) (albeit by ten votes to seven).

6.223 Any significant delay in executing a decision to release a detainee is likely to lead to a finding of a violation of Article 5(1) as the continuing detention will not fall within any of the Article 5(1) sub-paragraphs.[738]

Article 5 together with Article 18

6.224 Where detention may have been imposed for purposes which are ulterior to the authority's ostensible reasons, applicants may raise Article 18 together with Article 5. Article 18 prevents restrictions of the Convention rights being applied for any purpose other than those for which they have been prescribed. In recent years the Court has increasingly found violations of these two provisions, in cases which can be broadly characterised as amounting to 'political prosecutions'. These cases are discussed further in section 5.28 above.

Detention during occupation or armed conflict

6.225 The question of the legality of the detention of individuals by occupying powers, or in situations of armed conflict, may be complex, not least because of the relevance of other branches or sources of law, other than international human rights law,[739] as exemplified by cases relating to the occupation of southern Iraq from 2003. The case of *Al-Jedda* v *UK*[740] concerned the applicant's detention in Iraq by British armed forces, as he was suspected of having committed various terrorist-related offences. He was interned without charge for more than three years, for 'imperative reasons of security'. The UK Government acknowledged that his detention did not fall within any of the exceptions in sub-paragraphs 5(1) (a) to (f) of the Convention, but argued that Article 5(1) had not been breached because its duties under Article 5 had been displaced by the obligations created by the relevant United Nations Security Council Resolution (UNSCR 1546). However, this argument was

---

[737] No. 3394/03, 29.3.10.
[738] See, e.g. *Quinn* v *France*, No. 18580/91, 22.3.95 (a one-hour delay); *Mancini* v *Italy*, No. 44955/98, 2.8.01 (a three-day delay—the Court was divided by four votes to three in favour of a violation).
[739] As to the concurrent application of international humanitarian law generally, see also 6.48 above.
[740] No. 27021/08, 7.7.11.

rejected by the Grand Chamber which found that although UNSCR 1546 authorised the Multinational Force to maintain security in Iraq, it did not require (or authorise) the use of indefinite internment without charge or judicial guarantees. Nor was there any other legal basis to 'disapply' the provisions of Article 5(1). There was therefore a violation of Article 5(1). The subsequent case of *Hassan v UK*[741] concerned the British army's arrest of Tarek Hassan in Basrah in Iraq in 2003 on suspicion of being a combatant. In adjudicating on his complaint under Article 5 of the Convention, the Grand Chamber was required to resolve the apparently inconsistent results of having to apply two bodies of international law which were applicable concurrently: human rights law and international humanitarian law. The Court noted that the peacetime powers of detention under Articles 5(1)(a) to (f) were not congruent with powers to arrest a combatant during an armed conflict (under the Third and Fourth Geneva Conventions). Reiterating that the European Convention had to be interpreted in harmony with other rules of international law, the Court found that in situations of international armed conflict, the European Convention safeguards continued to apply, although they would be interpreted against the background of the provisions of international humanitarian law. On that basis, the grounds of permitted deprivation of liberty set out in Articles 5(1)(a) to (f) should be 'accommodated, as far as possible, with the taking of prisoners of war and the detention of civilians who pose a risk to security under the Third and Fourth Geneva Conventions'. Accordingly, as Tarek Hassan's capture and detention were consistent with powers of detention under the Third and Fourth Geneva Conventions, and were not arbitrary, there was also no violation of Article 5 of the European Convention.[742]

Unacknowledged detention *most grave violation!*

Unacknowledged detention by the state has been found to be a 'complete negation' of the **6.226** Article 5 guarantees and accordingly a 'most grave violation'.[743] Therefore the failure to record a detention in official custody records has been found to be a particularly serious omission: 'the recording of accurate and reliable holding data provides an indispensable safeguard against arbitrary detention, the absence of which enables those responsible for the act of deprivation of liberty to escape accountability for the fate of the detainee'.[744] In *Çiçek v Turkey*,[745] the Court was highly critical of the gendarmes' practice (which was unlawful under domestic law) of their treatment of detainees during the period between the initial detention and their being formally placed into custody, which lasted up to 24 hours, and was not logged and during which time detainees were interrogated. The Court has also condemned the use of detention centres in Chechnya which had no official legal status, finding it:[746]

> inconceivable that in a State subject to the rule of law a person could be deprived of his or her liberty in a detention facility over which for a significant period of time no responsible

---

[741] No. 29750/09, 16.9.14.

[742] The Grand Chamber reached this decision by 13 votes to four. See the partly dissenting opinion of Judge Spano, joined by Judges Nicolaou, Bianku and Kalaydjieva, which compellingly disputes the majority's attempts to 'reconcile the irreconcilable'.

[743] *Kurt v Turkey*, No. 24276/94, 25.5.98, paras. 122–5; *Çakıcı v Turkey*, No. 23657/94, 8.7.99, para. 104; *Taş v Turkey*, No. 24396/94, 14.11.00, para. 84; *Çiçek v Turkey*, No. 25704/94, 27.2.01, para. 164; *Akdeniz v Turkey*, No. 23954/94, 31.5.01, para. 106; *Orhan v Turkey*, No. 25656/94, 18.6.02, para. 369.

[744] *Kurt v Turkey*, No. 24276/94, 25.5.98, para. 125; *Taş v Turkey*, No. 24396/94, 14.11.00, para. 85; *Ahmet Özkan and others v Turkey*, No. 21689/93, 6.4.04, para. 371; *Kaplanova v Russia*, No. 7653/02, 29.4.08, para. 122.

[745] No. 25704/94, 27.2.01, para. 166.

[746] *Bitiyeva and X v Russia*, Nos. 57953/00 and 37392/03, 21.6.07, para. 118.

authority was exercised by a competent State institution. This situation fosters impunity for all kinds of abuses and is absolutely incompatible with the responsibility of the authorities to account for individuals under their control.

6.227　In a series of cases concerning the practice of 'extraordinary rendition' of terrorist suspects, by various European states in the early 2000s, into the custody of the US authorities, the Court has found violations of Article 5. For example, in *El-Masri v former Yugoslav Republic of Macedonia*[747] the Court held that the Macedonian authorities failed to comply with their positive obligation to protect the applicant from being detained in contravention of Article 5, and also that they actively facilitated his detention in Afghanistan by handing him over to the CIA. Furthermore, his abduction and detention was found to amount to 'enforced disappearance'. The Government was found to be responsible for violating Article 5 during the entire period of his captivity.

6.228　There are increasing numbers of cases in which states collude in the ad hoc deportation of an individual from one state to the other, in which the Court finds that this process involves the applicant's unacknowledged detention (see also the discussion of these cases at 6.173).[748]

Article 5(1)(a): detention following conviction

6.229　Article 5(1)(a) permits detention after conviction by a competent court. This provision will be breached where a court lacks the power to order detention, or where, for example, a person is detained in prison beyond the lawfully required period due to the failure to apply the law on remission of sentences.[749] A conviction has been defined as a finding of guilt and the imposition of a penalty.[750] To be a 'competent court', the body in question must be independent of the parties and of the executive, it must have the power to order release and it should provide appropriate guarantees in the circumstances of the detention in question.[751] Furthermore, the composition of a court must be sufficiently established by law: there was a breach of Article 5(1)(a) for these reasons in *Yefimenko v Russia*,[752] where the applicant was convicted by a court which included two lay judges who had not received authority to sit as lay judges.

6.230　Article 5(1)(a) requires that there must be a sufficient causal connection between the conviction and the detention, which must result from, and depend upon, or occur by virtue of, a conviction.[753] In *Stafford v UK*[754] the applicant was sentenced to mandatory life imprisonment for murder. It was argued successfully that his detention after his recall on life licence had ceased to be justified by the original sentence. In ordering his recall, the Minister

---

[747]　No. 39630/09, 13.12.12 (there were also violations of Articles 3, 8 and 13). See also *Al Nashiri v Poland*, No. 28761/11, 24.7.14; *Husayn (Abu Zubaydah) v Poland*, No. 7511/13, 24.7.14 and *Nasr and Ghali v Italy*, No. 44883/09, 23.2.16.

[748]　See, e.g. *Belozorov v Russia and Ukraine*, No. 43611/02, 15.10.15.

[749]　See, e.g. *Grava v Italy*, No. 43522/98, 10.7.03.

[750]　See, e.g. *X v UK* (1982) 4 EHRR 188, para. 39.

[751]　*De Wilde, Ooms and Versyp v Belgium*, Series A, No. 12, 18.6.71; *Ilaşcu and others v Moldova and Russia*, No. 48787/99, 8.7.04, para. 462.

[752]　No. 152/04, 12.2.13.

[753]　*Weeks v UK*, No. 9787/82, Series A, No. 114, 2.3.87; *B v Austria*, No. 11968/86, Series A, No. 175, 28.3.90.

[754]　No. 46295/99, 28.5.02.

had relied on the risk of his non-violent offending and therefore the Grand Chamber found an insufficient causal connection, as required by Article 5(1)(a), with the original conviction.[755] This decision overturned the previous Court judgment in *Wynne v UK*[756] that a mandatory life sentence constituted punishment for life. In *M v Germany*[757] the applicant's initial placement in preventive detention, following his conviction for attempted murder and robbery in 1986, was found to comply with Article 5(1)(a). However, his continued detention beyond the ten-year maximum period allowed was found to breach Article 5(1) as there was not a sufficient causal connection between the applicant's original conviction by the sentencing court and his continuing deprivation of liberty beyond the ten-year period (which had only been made possible by a subsequent change in the law in 1998). The applicants in *James, Wells and Lee v UK*[758] were each sentenced to indeterminate sentences for public protection. After the expiry of their tariff periods they required a direction from the Parole Board in order for them to be released. However, while in prison they were not given the opportunity to complete instructional courses which the Parole Board considered to be necessary for their rehabilitation. Therefore, their detention was held to be arbitrary and in violation of Article 5(1). There was no violation of Article 5(1) in *De Schepper v Belgium*[759] where the applicant, after having been repeatedly sentenced for acts of paedophilia, in accordance with the Social Protection Act, was placed 'at the Government's disposal' for a period of ten years after serving his sentence (which meant that he could be released under certain conditions or could be made subject to preventive detention). When his sentence expired, his preventive detention was ordered. Placing the applicant 'at the Government's disposal' was not considered to be arbitrary as it was a condition set by the criminal court at the time of conviction, in order to protect society from a dangerous offender. The authorities had also sought to provide treatment to the applicant adapted to his condition. They had not, however, been successful and so there remained an obligation to find an institution that would be able to treat the applicant's case. There was also no violation of Article 5(1) in *Radu v Germany*[760] as a result of the applicant's continued detention in a psychiatric hospital after the expiry of his prison term. His detention in a psychiatric hospital had been imposed (in 1995) by the Regional Court which had found him guilty of homicide. It found that the applicant suffered from a serious personality disorder and that it was expected he might kill again. In the course of the review proceedings (in 2006) the domestic courts again found that the applicant suffered from a personality disorder, and that he was to be detained for his dangerousness, as it was likely that he would kill again. The Court accordingly found that the decision not to release the applicant was based on grounds that were consistent with the aims of the original sentencing court, and, therefore,

---

[755] But see, by contrast, *Waite v UK*, No. 53236/99, 10.12.02; *Lynch and Whelan v Ireland*, Nos. 70495/10 and 74565/10, dec. 8.7.14.

[756] No. 15484/89, 18.7.94.

[757] No. 19359/04, 17.12.09 (Article 7 was also breached). See also *Haidn v Germany*, No. 6587/04, 13.1.11; *Jendrowiak v Germany*, No. 30060/04, 14.4.11; *Schmitz v Germany*, No. 30493/04, 9.6.11; *Mork v Germany*, Nos. 31047/04 and 43386/08, 9.6.11; *O.H. v Germany*, No. 4646/08, 24.11.11; *Glien v Germany*, No. 7345/12, 28.11.13. There were two reasons for finding a violation of Article 5(1) in *H.W. v Germany*, No. 17167/11, 19.9.13. First, an order for the applicant's continued preventive detention was only made 27 days after the expiry of the relevant statutory time limit. Secondly, the domestic courts had relied on an out of date expert medical report.

[758] No. 25119/09 et al, 18.9.12.

[759] No. 27428/07, 13.10.09.

[760] No. 20084/07, 16.5.13.

there was a sufficient causal connection between his conviction in 1995 and his continuing detention in a psychiatric hospital.

6.231 In stipulating that detention under Article 5(1)(a) is permissible 'after conviction by a competent court', this does not require verification that *all* the requirements of the right to a fair trial under Article 6 have been met. However, the Court has held that Article 5(1)(a) will be breached where there has been a 'flagrant denial of justice'.[761] On this basis, the provision was found to have been violated in *Stoichkov v Bulgaria*,[762] because the applicant was tried in absentia, there was no evidence that he had expressly or impliedly waived his right to appear, and yet his subsequent application to have the proceedings reopened was refused (essentially because the case file had been destroyed). This provision was violated in *Dacosta Silva v Spain*[763] because of the imposition on a member of the Civil Guard by his superior of six days' house arrest for being absent from his barracks without leave. The penalty was immediately enforceable and was imposed by an officer who was not independent from the Civil Guard's hierarchy. Accordingly, the proceedings had not had the requisite judicial safeguards.

6.232 The Court has acknowledged that the transfer of a prisoner to another country could raise an issue under Article 5(1)(a), but only where the person faced a 'flagrantly longer' de facto sentence in the administering state.[764]

Article 5(1)(b): detention for non-compliance with a court order or to secure compliance with a legal obligation

6.233 The first limb of Article 5(1)(b) permits detention for failing to comply with the lawful order of a court,[765] which would allow, for example, an arrest for being in contempt of court or for failing to comply with a court injunction.

6.234 The second limb, which provides for detention to secure the fulfilment of an obligation prescribed by law, only concerns cases where the law permits the detention of a person to compel him or her to fulfil a 'specific and concrete obligation'.[766] The Court has confirmed that 'there must be an unfulfilled obligation incumbent on the person concerned and the arrest and detention must be for the purpose of securing its fulfilment and not punitive in character'.[767] A detention, however, cannot be justified under Article 5(1)(b) on the basis of a general duty of obedience to the law. The distinction between these two situations was considered by the European Commission of Human Rights in the case of *McVeigh, O'Neill and Evans v UK*[768] in the context of the UK's Prevention of Terrorism legislation. The applicants were arrested in Liverpool on arrival from Ireland, and were detained for about 45 hours,

---

[761] *Ilaşcu and others v Moldova and Russia*, No. 48787/99, 8.7.04, para. 461; *Wilcox and Hurford v UK*, Nos. 43759/10 and 43771/12, dec. 8.1.13, paras. 94–98.

[762] No. 9808/02, 24.3.05.

[763] No. 69966/01, 2.11.06.

[764] *Veermäe v Finland*, No. 38704/03, dec. 15.3.05; *Szabó v Sweden*, No. 28578/03, dec. 27.6.06.

[765] This term requires both that the person in question is aware of the order, and is given the chance to comply with it, and also that s/he has sufficient protection against a potentially arbitrary deprivation of liberty (*Beiere v Latvia*, No. 30954/05, 29.11.11).

[766] *Engel and others v Netherlands*, Series A, No. 22, 8.6.76, para. 69. See also, e.g. *Schwabe and M.G. v Germany*, Nos. 8080/08 and 8577/08, 1.12.11, para. 82.

[767] *Nowicka v Poland*, No. 30218/96, 3.12.02.

[768] Nos. 8022/77, 8025/77 and 8027/77, 18.3.81.

searched, questioned, photographed and had their fingerprints taken. They were, however, not charged with any offences. Even though there had been no specific prior breach of a legal duty, the European Commission found no violation of Article 5(1)(b). The domestic legislation imposed a requirement to 'submit to examination' which the Commission found to be a sufficiently specific and concrete obligation. The Commission did emphasise, however, that the decision was made in the context of measures taken to combat terrorism and specifically noted that the obligation to submit to examination only arose in limited circumstances and had a limited purpose. In *Ostendorf v Germany*,[769] the detention of a suspected football hooligan for four hours, to prevent his taking part in a brawl, was found to fall within the second limb of Article 5(1)(b). The Court underlined that the notion of an 'obligation' under Article 5(1)(b) must be very closely circumscribed—it found that the 'obligation' at issue in the case (to keep the peace by not committing a criminal offence) could only be considered to be 'specific and concrete' if the place and time of the commission of the offence and its potential victims had been sufficiently specified. This test was met as the applicant had been arrested in order to prevent a brawl during, or shortly after, a football match in Frankfurt. Furthermore, he had been warned that the police intended to prevent a brawl, and he was therefore under a specific obligation not to take part.

The Court has also emphasised (in relation to both limbs of Article 5(1)(b)) that a balance should be struck between the importance in a democratic society of securing the immediate fulfilment of the obligation in question, and the importance of the right to liberty.[770] Factors relevant to this assessment will include the following: the nature of the obligation arising from the relevant legislation, including its underlying object and purpose; the person being detained and the particular circumstances leading to the detention; and the length of the detention.[771] In *Vasileva v Denmark*,[772] for example, the applicant was detained after having been accused of travelling on a bus without a valid ticket: her detention was assessed under Article 5(1)(b) because it followed her refusal to comply with a specific and concrete domestic law obligation, namely to disclose her personal data. Her initial detention by the police was found to be justified, but the 67-year-old applicant was then held for a disproportionate period of 13½ hours, in violation of Article 5(1)(b). The applicant businessman in *Khodorkovskiy v Russia*[773] was served with a witness summons when he was in eastern Russia on a three-day business trip, and was required to return to Moscow within 21 hours. The applicant did not do so, but the Court found, however, that that did not justify the authorities forcibly bringing him to Moscow the following morning, on the basis that, in the particular context of the investigation, they could have waited. The Court was also critical that he was arrested by armed officers 'like a dangerous criminal', and that the facts of the case showed that the investigator's real intention had been to charge the applicant as a defendant. Accordingly, Article 5(1)(b) was breached. **6.235**

There was a violation of Article 5(1) in *Nowicka v Poland*,[774] where the applicant was detained as a result of a court order that she should submit to a psychiatric examination imposed in the **6.236**

---

769 No. 15998/08, 7.3.13.
770 See, e.g. *Paradis and others v Germany*, No. 4065/04, dec. 4.9.07 (first limb).
771 *Vasileva v Denmark*, No. 52792/99, 25.9.03.
772 No. 52792/99, 25.9.03.
773 No. 5829/04, 31.5.11.
774 No. 30218/96, 3.12.02. See also *Petukhova v Russia*, No. 28796/07, 2.5.13 (unlawful court order for applicant to submit to psychiatric examination—violation of Article 5(1)).

context of a private prosecution arising out of a neighbours' dispute. It was the fact that in order to carry out two such examinations the applicant was unjustifiably detained for a total period of 83 days, which led to the finding that detention was not in compliance with Article 5(1)(b).[775] In *Paradis and others* v *Germany*[776] the applicant complained about her coercive detention—imposed as a result of her failure to comply with an order to return her three children to her husband in Canada (under the Hague Convention on the Civil Aspects of International Child Abduction). Given the positive obligation on the state under the Hague Convention to take all necessary steps to reunite abducted children with the other parent, and as previous attempts to return the children had failed because of the applicants' explicit refusal, the detention order was not considered disproportionate and the application was declared inadmissible. The applicant in *Gatt* v *Malta*[777] was detained for a period of more than five and a half years for failing to comply with a court order to pay €23,300 as a result of his breaching a curfew imposed as a bail condition. The Court dismissed the Government's reliance on both limbs of Article 5(1)(b) as grounds for the applicant's detention, finding it to be disproportionate and in violation of Article 5(1).

Article 5(1)(c): arrest on reasonable suspicion of an offence

6.237 Article 5(1)(c) permits an arrest for the purpose of bringing a person before the competent legal authorities (1) on reasonable suspicion of having committed an offence; or (2) where it is reasonably considered necessary to prevent an offence; or (3) where it is reasonably considered necessary to prevent a person fleeing after having committed an offence.

The meaning of 'offence'

6.238 The approach of the Strasbourg institutions to this question has been to consider in the first place whether or not the provision defining the offence forms part of the domestic criminal law. However, the notion of an offence is an autonomous Convention concept and depends not only upon the domestic classification, but also upon the 'very nature of the offence' and the degree of severity of the penalty.[778] *Steel and others* v *UK*[779] concerned the arrest of the applicants on reasonable suspicion of their having committed a breach of the peace. The applicants had been involved in various protests or demonstrations at a grouse shoot, at the site of motorway building works and outside a fighter helicopter sales conference. Although breach of the peace is not a criminal offence according to domestic law, it was found by the Court to be an 'offence' in Convention terms, taking into account the public nature of the duty to keep the peace, the available power of arrest, and the power to imprison anyone who refuses to be bound over to keep the peace. The Court rejected arguments in that case that the concept of breach of the peace was too vague and ambiguous to comply with the requirement of lawfulness under Article 5.[780] However, in *Hashman and Harrup* v *UK*,[781] where the

---

[775] In contrast, there was no violation of Article 5(1)(b) in respect of shorter periods of detention in *B* v *France*, No. 10179/82, dec. 13.5.87; DR 52, p. 111 (one and four hours); *Reyntjens* v *Belgium*, No. 16810/90, dec. 9.9.92; DR 73, p. 136 (two and a half hours).

[776] No. 4065/04, dec. 4.9.07.

[777] No. 28221/08, 27.7.10.

[778] *Schmautzer* v *Austria*, No. 15523/89, Series A, No. 328-A, 23.10.95, para. 27.

[779] No. 24838/94, 23.9.98.

[780] See also *Öztürk* v *Germany*, No. 8544/79, Series A, No. 73, 21.2.84, para. 53. The Court in *Steel*, above, was, however, critical of the vagueness of the binding over order, particularly the requirement to be 'of good behaviour'.

[781] No. 25594/94, 25.11.99.

applicant hunt saboteurs had been bound over to keep the peace and not to behave *contra bonos mores*, the Court held that the term *contra bonos mores* was so generally defined that it failed the 'prescribed by law' test (see above at 6.217).

6.239 What amounts to an 'offence' has also been considered in relation to the definition of terrorism in UK legislation as 'the use of violence for political ends', which includes 'the use of violence for the purpose of putting the public or any section of the public in fear'. In *Ireland* v *UK*[782] such a definition was said by the Court to be 'well in keeping with the idea of an offence'. This position was confirmed by the Court in *Brogan and others* v *UK*.[783]

6.240 The second limb of Article 5(1)(c) only permits detention to prevent the commission of a concrete and specific offence. It does not provide a general preventive power of detention.[784] There was accordingly a violation of Article 5(1) in *Shimovolos* v *Russia*,[785] where the applicant, a human rights activist, had been listed on a 'surveillance database' and was detained by police purportedly to prevent him from committing offences 'of an extremist nature'. The Court concluded that the basis of the police's 'suspicion' was simply the fact that he was a member of human rights organisations. Therefore, his arrest had no legitimate purpose and was arbitrary. There was also a violation of Article 5(1) in *Schwabe and M.G.* v *Germany*,[786] where the applicants were arrested for preventive purposes as they made their way to demonstrate against a G8 summit. Noting that the domestic courts had appeared to take different views as to the offences which the applicants were considered to be about to commit, and that the applicants were detained for a period of 5½ days for preventive purposes, the Court concluded that their detention could not have been reasonably considered necessary to prevent them from committing a sufficiently concrete and specific offence. The Court has reiterated that the detention of an individual in order to prevent the person from committing an offence must also be 'effected for the purpose of bringing him before the competent legal authority'. Thus, in *Ostendorf* v *Germany*,[787] the detention of a suspected football hooligan for four hours, to prevent his taking part in a brawl, did not fall within the second limb of Article 5(1)(c) because the aim of his detention had, from the outset, been purely preventive (and he was to be released once the risk had passed). However, his detention did fall within the second limb of Article 5(1)(b) ('in order to secure the fulfilment of any obligation prescribed by law')—see above at 6.234.

Reasonable suspicion

6.241 An arrest on reasonable suspicion of having committed an offence will not necessarily violate Article 5 if the detainee is not subsequently charged or taken before a court, provided that the arrest had been made for that *purpose*.[788] This requirement applies to each of the circumstances in which an arrest may be lawful under Article 5(1)(c).[789] There is no requirement

---

[782] *Ireland* v *UK*, Series A, No. 25, 18.1.78.

[783] Nos. 11209/84, 11266/84, and 11365/85, Series A, No. 145-B, 29.11.88.

[784] But see *Eriksen* v *Norway*, No. 17391/90, 27.5.97. See also *Ječius* v *Lithuania*, No. 34578/97, 31.7.00, where four state bodies gave three different versions as to the applicability of the criminal law in question to the applicant's case.

[785] No. 30194/09, 21.6.11.

[786] Nos. 8080/08 and 8577/08, 1.12.11.

[787] No. 15998/08, 7.3.13.

[788] See, e.g. *Brogan and others* v *UK*, Nos. 11209/84, 11266/84 and 11365/85, Series A, No. 145-B, 29.11.88, para. 53; *Murray* v *UK*, No. 18731/91, 28.10.94, para. 55; *O'Hara* v *UK*, No. 37555/97, 16.10.01, para. 36.

[789] *Lawless* v *Ireland (No. 3)*, Series A, No. 3, 1.7.61, para. 14.

that the police should have obtained sufficient evidence to bring charges, either at the point of arrest, or while a person is in custody. The legality of continued detention depends upon the reasonable suspicion of the detainee persisting.[790]

6.242   The concept of 'reasonable suspicion' was defined by the Court in *Fox, Campbell and Hartley v UK*[791] as meaning 'the existence of facts or information which would satisfy an objective observer that the person concerned may have committed the offence'.[792] What is regarded as 'reasonable' will depend upon all the relevant circumstances. The case of *Ilgar Mammadov v Azerbaijan*[793] concerned the arrest of a prominent opposition politician and blogger who was accused of instigating a riot. The Court noted that the applicant was charged with 'organising' a riot that had already started the day before his visit to the town in question and which had initially been caused by a local incident. Furthermore, the prosecution documents contained no witness statements or other information establishing the applicant's involvement. The Court was critical of the 'vague and general references' by both the prosecution and the courts to unspecified 'case material'. Accordingly, the Court found there was no basis to arrest him on 'reasonable suspicion' that he had committed any offence, in violation of Article 5(1)(c).

6.243   The Court found in *Fox, Campbell and Hartley* that in the context of dealing with 'terrorist-type' offences in Northern Ireland, the reasonableness of the suspicion justifying such arrests could not always be judged according to the same standards as are applied in dealing with 'conventional crime'. However, the Court stressed that the exigencies of dealing with terrorism could not justify stretching the notion of 'reasonableness' to the point where the essence of the safeguard was impaired. Where, as in that case, the domestic law did not require 'reasonable suspicion' as such (but only 'honest suspicion'), the Court would have to have at least some facts or information capable of satisfying it that the arrested person had been reasonably suspected of having committed an offence.[794] Such evidence was not available (previous convictions for terrorist offences not being sufficient) and the Court found a violation of Article 5(1). In *Murray v UK*[795] the Court found that a material factor as to the level of suspicion required was the length of the deprivation of liberty at risk (limited to a maximum of four hours in *Murray*). No breach of Article 5(1)(c) was found in that case as the Court was satisfied that there was sufficient evidence to provide a 'plausible and objective basis' for a suspicion that the applicant may have been involved in collecting funds for the IRA.[796]

6.244   In *O'Hara v UK*,[797] the applicant, who was a prominent member of the Sinn Fein political party, was arrested on suspicion of murder. The arresting officer gave evidence that he had been given information by a superior officer relating to the applicant at a prior briefing. The applicant complained that no further information about this briefing was forthcoming during the domestic proceedings; however, the Court found that this was a consequence of the

---

[790] *Stögmüller v Austria*, Series A, No. 9, 10.11.69, para. 4.
[791] Nos. 12244/86, 12245/86 and 12383/86, 30.8.90.
[792] See also *O'Hara v UK*, No. 37555/97, 16.10.01, para. 34; *Stepuleac v Moldova*, No. 8207/06, 6.11.07, para. 73.
[793] No. 15172/13, 22.5.14. There was also a breach of Article 5(4).
[794] Contrast that case with *O'Hara v UK*, No. 37555/97, 16.10.01, para. 28, where the Court noted that the domestic law required both honest and reasonable suspicion.
[795] No. 14310/88, 28.10.94.
[796] *Ibid.*, para. 63.
[797] No. 37555/97, 16.10.01.

way in which the applicant pursued his domestic case (such as failing to take steps to have other officers involved in the arrest called to give evidence). The Court stated[798] that:

> There may … be a fine line between those cases where the suspicion grounding the arrest is not sufficiently founded on objective facts, and those which are. Whether the requisite standard is satisfied and whether the guarantee against arbitrary arrest laid down by Article 5(1)(c) is thereby satisfied depends on the particular circumstances of each case.

6.245 In *O'Hara* the respondent Government's case was that the applicant's arrest arose from suspicion of his involvement in a specific incident of murder which was based on information provided by four informers. The Court accepted that the applicant had argued 'with some force' that police officers should not be able to hide behind references to anonymous informers in order to justify abuse of their power of arrest.[799] The arrest of the applicant lawyers in *Elçi and others* v *Turkey*[800] was found not to have been carried out in accordance with the domestic law for a variety of reasons: there was confusion and inconsistency between various witnesses (heard by the European Court) as to the requirements of the domestic law; the legal position in relation to the investigation of offences alleged to have been committed by lawyers lacked clarity and was uncertain; it was unclear what steps had been taken to obtain the prior approval of a prosecutor for the arrests; and there was no documentation recording either the request for authorisation of the applicants' detention or the authority given by the chief prosecutor to detain the applicants. The Court in *Elçi* also emphasised[801] the importance of lawyers remaining free of harassment by the state:

> The Court would emphasise the central role of the legal profession in the administration of justice and the maintenance of the rule of law. The freedom of lawyers to practise their profession without undue hindrance is an essential component of a democratic society and a necessary prerequisite for the effective enforcement of the provisions of the Convention, in particular the guarantees of fair trial and the right to personal security. Persecution or harassment of members of the legal profession thus strikes at the very heart of the Convention system. For this reason, allegations of such persecution in whatever form, but particularly large scale arrests and detention of lawyers and searching of lawyers' offices, will be subject to especially strict scrutiny by the Court.

6.246 The requirement in Article 5(1)(c) to make an arrest only for the purpose of bringing a person before the competent legal authority should also be read in conjunction with Article 5(3) (see below at 6.266).

6.247 The third limb of Article 5(1)(c) requires reasonable grounds for believing that an offence has been committed. Accordingly, there is a substantial degree of overlap with the first limb.

Article 5(1)(d): detention of minors

6.248 Article 5(1)(d) permits the detention of minors (persons under 18) either by lawful order for the purpose of educational supervision, or lawful detention for the purpose of bringing them before the competent legal authority. The Court has found that the phrase 'educational supervision' must not be equated rigidly with notions of classroom teaching: in the context of local authority care this phrase must include many aspects of the exercise by a local authority

---

[798] *Ibid.*, para. 41.
[799] *Ibid.*, para. 43.
[800] Nos. 23145/93 and 25091/94, 13.11.03.
[801] *Elçi and others* v *Turkey*, Nos. 23145/93 and 25091/94, 13.11.03, para. 669.

of parental rights for the benefit and protection of the minor.[802] Furthermore, detention for educational supervision must take place in an appropriate facility with the resources to meet the necessary educational objectives and security requirements.[803]

6.249 In *Bouamar* v *Belgium*[804] the applicant minor, who was suspected of various offences, was repeatedly detained in a remand prison on nine occasions on the interim orders of a juvenile court. The Court found that Article 5(1)(d) did not prevent an 'interim custody' measure as a preliminary to a regime of supervised education, but such a regime had to be applied speedily following imprisonment. There was a violation of Article 5(1) in *Bouamar* because of the failure to implement such a regime. In *DG* v *Ireland*,[805] the applicant was a minor, with a criminal history, who was considered to have a personality disorder and to be a danger to himself and others. It was decided that he should be placed in a high-support therapeutic unit for 16- to 18-year-olds, but as there were no secure educational facilities available in Ireland, the High Court decided that he should be detained for three weeks in a prison, St Patrick's Institution, as the 'least offensive' of the various 'inappropriate' options available to it. This prison was found not to constitute 'educational supervision': it was a penal institution and the educational and other recreation services were entirely voluntary. Nor could it be said that it was an 'interim custody' measure for the purpose of an educational supervisory regime (which was followed 'speedily' by the application of such a regime), as the High Court orders were not based on any specific proposal for his secure and supervised education. His detention was accordingly found to be incompatible with Article 5(1)(d) of the Convention. In *Blokhin* v *Russia*[806] the decision of a court to detain a twelve-year-old applicant in a temporary detention centre for the purpose of 'correcting his behaviour' was found to breach Article 5(1). Such a period of detention could not exceed 30 days and the Court doubted that any meaningful educational supervision, to change a child's behaviour and provide appropriate treatment and rehabilitation, could be provided during such a period.

6.250 In *Mubilanzila Mayeka and Kaniki Mitunga* v *Belgium*[807] the Court held that Article 5(1) was violated by holding an unaccompanied five-year-old child (an illegal alien) in an adult immigration centre for two months. The conditions of the centre were not adapted to her position of 'extreme vulnerability' and the relevant law made no particular provision for minors.

Article 5(1)(e): detention of persons for the prevention of the spreading of infectious diseases, of persons of unsound mind, alcoholics or drug addicts or vagrants

6.251 Article 5(1)(e) provides for the lawful detention, for the prevention of the spreading of infectious diseases, of persons of unsound mind, alcoholics or drug addicts or vagrants. The Court

---

[802] See, e.g. *Koniarska* v *UK*, No. 33670/96, dec. 12.10.00 (17-year-old sent to specialised residential facility for seriously disturbed children—declared inadmissible).

[803] See, e.g. *Blokhin* v *Russia*, No. 47152/06, 23.3.16, para. 167. See also *D.L.* v *Bulgaria*, No. 7472/14, 19.5.16 (13-year-old girl placed in closed boarding school owing to antisocial behaviour and risk she would engage in prostitution—no violation of Article 5(1)).

[804] No. 9106/80, Series A, No. 129, 29.2.87.

[805] No. 39474/98, 16.5.02.

[806] No. 47152/06, 23.3.16.

[807] No. 13178/03, 12.10.06 (Article 8 was also violated as a result of both the detention and the deportation). See also *Muskhadzhiyeva and others* v *Belgium*, No. 41442/07, 19.1.10; and *Kanagaratnam* v *Belgium*, No. 15297/09, 13.12.11.

has emphasised that the justification for the detention of persons in such categories may be both for their own interests, and because of the danger to public safety.[808] This may therefore justify the detention under Article 5(1)(e) of a person with a psychopathic personality disorder, even where such a condition is not susceptible to medical treatment.[809]

In *Enhorn v Sweden*,[810] the applicant complained that he had been subject to compulsory **6.252** isolation orders and involuntary placements in hospital, as a person infected with HIV, after having transmitted the virus to another man as a result of sexual activity. In its judgment in *Enhorn*, the Court established[811] that the essential criteria when assessing the lawfulness of the detention of a person 'for the prevention of the spreading of infectious diseases' are as follows:

> … whether the spreading of the infectious disease is dangerous to public health or safety, and whether detention of the person infected is the last resort in order to prevent the spreading of the disease, because less severe measures have been considered and found to be insufficient to safeguard the public interest.

The Court found a violation of Article 5(1) in *Enhorn* on the basis that the applicant's com- **6.253** pulsory isolation had not in fact been a measure of last resort in order to prevent him from spreading the HIV virus—because less severe measures had not been considered. It was also relevant that the order for the applicant's compulsory isolation had been extended for nearly seven years, and that accordingly he had been involuntarily confined in hospital for a total of about a year and a half. As a result, the Swedish authorities had not balanced fairly the need to stop the virus spreading, as against the applicant's right to liberty.

The term 'unsound mind' has not been defined by the Strasbourg organs, as its meaning is **6.254** considered to be continually evolving, but there must be objective expert medical evidence of unsound mind of the person concerned at the relevant time (other than in emergencies).[812] Accordingly, detention pursuant to the order of a prosecutor, without obtaining a medical opinion, will violate this provision (even if the purpose of the detention is to obtain such an opinion).[813] The disorder must also be such that it requires compulsory confinement[814] and the detention can only continue to be justified by the persistence of the disorder.[815] The Court has held that the lawfulness of the detention under Article 5(1)(e) will also depend upon detention in a hospital, clinic or other appropriate authorised institution, but subject to that, it has no bearing on the appropriateness of the treatment or conditions.[816] In *Glien v Germany*[817] the applicant mental health patient was subject to preventive detention. The

---

[808] See, e.g. *Witold Litwa v Poland*, No. 26629/95, 4.4.00, para. 60.

[809] *Hutchison Reid v UK*, No. 50272/99, 20.2.03.

[810] No. 56529/00, 25.1.05.

[811] *Ibid.*, para. 44.

[812] See, e.g. *Herz v Germany*, No. 44672/98, 12.6.03; *Rakevich v Russia*, No. 58973/00, 28.10.03; *Constancia v Netherlands*, No. 73560/12, dec. 3.3.15.

[813] *Varbanov v Bulgaria*, No. 31365/96, 5.10.00; *Filip v Romania*, No. 41124/02, 14.12.06; *C.B. v Romania*, No. 21207/03, 20.4.10.

[814] See, e.g. *Shtukaturov v Russia*, No. 44009/05, 27.3.08. See also *Juncal v UK*, No. 32357/09, dec. 17.9.13 (order for confinement made as a result of finding of unfitness to plead (which was different to the Article 5(1)(e) test, but Article 5(1) requirements still met)—inadmissible).

[815] See *Winterwerp v Netherlands*, Series A, No. 33, 24.10.79, para. 39.

[816] *Ashingdane v UK*, No. 8225/78, Series A, No. 93, 28.5.85, para. 44; *De Donder and De Clippel v Belgium*, No. 8595/06, 6.12.11, para. 106.

[817] No. 7345/12, 28.11.13. See, by contrast, *Bergmann v Germany*, No. 23279/14, 7.1.16 (preventive detention of mental health patient in purpose-built centre providing appropriate medical care—no violation of

Court found a violation of Article 5(1) because he was detained on a prison wing, without an appropriate therapeutic environment (and he could have been transferred to a psychiatric hospital or other suitable institution).

6.255 *Stanev v Bulgaria*[818] concerned the detention of the applicant in a social care home for people with mental disorders, without his consent. The Grand Chamber found that none of the Article 5(1)(e) criteria had been met: there was no recent medical assessment; there was insufficient evidence to justify his detention; and there were deficiencies in the assessment of whether the disorders warranting the applicant's confinement still persisted. In *HL v UK*[819] the Court found that the system of detaining 'informal patients' in psychiatric institutions did not incorporate sufficient procedural safeguards in order to prevent arbitrary deprivations of liberty, in violation of Article 5(1). A similar finding was made in *X v Finland*,[820] not as regards the initial decision to subject the applicant to involuntary treatment in a mental hospital, but in relation to the *continuation* of such treatment: there was no opportunity for an independent psychiatric review, and the patients themselves could not instigate a periodic review of the continuing need for involuntary treatment. In *Johnson v UK*,[821] the release of the applicant, who had been detained under the Mental Health Act 1983, was ordered by the Mental Health Review Tribunal, conditional upon his living in a supervised hostel. However, his release was delayed because of the unavailability of a suitable hostel, which the Court found amounted to a violation of Article 5(1) as in the circumstances the onus was on the state to provide suitable accommodation.[822] In *Mocarska v Poland*[823] a delay of eight months in the admission of the applicant to a psychiatric hospital, during which period she was held in an ordinary remand centre, was found to violate Article 5(1). There must also be adequate procedural safeguards to prevent arbitrary detention. On that basis there was a violation of Article 5(1)(e) in *M.S. v Croatia (No. 2)*[824] because of the applicant's ineffective legal representation in proceedings concerning her detention in a psychiatric hospital. She was assigned a legal aid lawyer who failed to meet with her, and who therefore could not effectively represent her position before the court.

Admission to a psychiatric institution may also engage issues under Article 8.[825]

6.256 In *Witold Litwa v Poland*,[826] the Court held that the term 'alcoholics' should be interpreted in the light of the object and purpose of Article 5 and therefore the Article permits the detention of persons in a clinical state of 'alcoholism' as well as persons who are not medically

---

Article 5); *Petschulies v Germany*, No. 6281/13, 2.6.16 (preventive detention of violent mental health patient in purpose-built centre offering appropriate medical care— no violation of Article 5(1)). See also the discussion of *M. v Germany* at 6.230 above.

[818] No. 36760/06, 17.1.12.
[819] No. 45508/99, 5.10.04.
[820] No. 34806/04, 3.7.12.
[821] No. 22520/93, 24.10.97.
[822] See also *Brand v Netherlands*, No. 49902/99, 11.5.04; *Morsink v Netherlands*, No. 48865/99, 11.5.04; *RL and M-JD v France*, No. 44568/98, 19.5.04; *L.B. v Belgium*, No. 22831/08, 2.10.12. In contrast, see *Kolanis v UK*, No. 517/02, 21.6.05 (no violation arising from deferral of discharge from psychiatric hospital).
[823] No. 26917/05, 6.11.07.
[824] No. 75450/12, 19.2.15.
[825] See, e.g. *B v Romania (No. 2)*, No. 1285/03, 19.2.13.
[826] No. 26629/95, 4.4.00.

diagnosed as alcoholics but whose conduct and behaviour under the influence of alcohol poses a threat to public order or themselves. Furthermore, in order for the detention of an intoxicated person to be considered lawful, the authorities must also show that their detention was the 'last resort to safeguard the individual or the public interest', where less severe measures had been considered and found insufficient.[827] In *Hilda Hafsteinsdóttir* v *Iceland*[828] the Court found a violation of Article 5(1) because the domestic law was not sufficiently precise and accessible as to the discretion of the police to arrest a person for disorderly conduct resulting from the use of alcohol.

'Vagrancy' has not been defined, but in *De Wilde, Ooms and Versyp* v *Belgium*[829] the Court accepted that the then Belgian definition ('persons who have no fixed abode, no means of subsistence and no regular trade or profession') fell within the ambit of Article 5(1)(e) of the Convention.   **6.257**

Article 5(1)(f): detention relating to immigration, deportation or extradition

Article 5(1)(f) permits the lawful arrest or detention of persons to prevent their effecting an   **6.258** unauthorised entry into the country, or of a person against whom action is being taken with a view to deportation or extradition. The first limb of this provision permits the detention of a person who wishes to effect entry to a country, and who needs, but does not yet have, authorisation to do so, thus enabling the state to detain asylum-seekers or other immigrants prior to the grant of authorisation to enter. This was the finding of an eleven-six majority of the Grand Chamber in the case of *Saadi* v *UK*.[830] There, the Court found no violation of Article 5(1)(f) as regards the detention of an Iraqi Kurd in a reception centre for seven days, following his arrival at Heathrow airport where he claimed asylum. The applicant's detention was found to have complied with domestic law, the authorities were found to have acted in good faith in detaining him, he had been held in suitable conditions and the purpose of the deprivation of liberty had been to enable the authorities quickly and efficiently to determine his claim to asylum.[831] Both the length and conditions of detention will be relevant to the assessment of the legality of detention under the first limb of Article 5(1)(f),[832] nevertheless, Article 5(1)(f) does not lay down maximum time-limits for detention pending

---

[827] *Kharin* v *Russia*, No. 37345/03, 3.2.11, para. 40 (the Court found no violation of Article 5(1) in this case by four votes to three—see the strongly argued joint dissenting opinion of Judges Rozakis, Spielmann and Jebens).

[828] No. 40905/98, 8.6.04.

[829] Series A, No. 12, 18.6.71, especially para. 68; see also *Guzzardi* v *Italy*, Series A, No. 39, 6.1.80, para. 98.

[830] No. 13229/03, 29.1.08. The majority of the Grand Chamber expressly rejected the argument that Article 5(1)(f) only permits detention of a person who is shown to be trying to evade entry restrictions.

[831] The six dissenting judges (Judges Rozakis, Tulkens, Kovler, Hajiyev, Spielmann, and Hirvelä) referred to the principle that asylum-seekers who have presented a claim for international protection are considered to be lawfully within the territory of a state and emphasised that the applicant had expressly been given permission to enter the UK. They were critical that the majority judgment treated all categories of non-nationals in the same way, including illegal immigrants, and those liable to be deported or who had committed offences. They argued forcefully that the authorities should be required to satisfy themselves that detention had been ordered exclusively in pursuit of one of the Article 5(1) aims—in this case, to prevent the applicant's effecting unauthorised entry into the country. Such a test had not been met in the present case, as the applicant had not entered or attempted to enter the country unlawfully. In their view, the applicant's detention pursued a 'purely bureaucratic and administrative goal', which did not serve to prevent his unauthorised entry into the country.

[832] See, e.g. *Suso Musa* v *Malta*, No. 42337/12, 23.7.13 (detention of asylum-seeker for more than six months, and in inappropriate conditions—violation of Article 5(1)).

deportation.[833] The failure to consider the specific situation of children (separately from their parents) may also raise issues under Article 5(1)(f).[834]

6.259 Any arrest or detention must be lawful according to domestic law and not arbitrary.[835] Applying this principle, the domestic legal systems relating to detention with a view to extradition in several states has been found to be insufficiently precise or foreseeable, leading to a violation of Article 5(1).[836] There was a violation of this Article in the case of *Bozano* v *France*[837] following the applicant's forcible removal at night by French police officers to the Swiss border where he was taken into Swiss police custody. In *Conka* v *Belgium*[838] the Court was critical of a notice that was sent by Belgian police to a group of Slovakian Roma inviting them to attend a police station in order to pursue their asylum applications. In fact, on arrival they were served with an order to leave Belgium and for their removal to Slovakia. The Court found[839] that the wording of the notice was deliberately chosen to ensure the greatest compliance: 'a conscious decision by the authorities to facilitate or improve the effectiveness of a planned operation for the expulsion of aliens by misleading them about the purpose of a notice so as to make it easier to deprive them of their liberty is not compatible with Article 5'. There was a violation of Article 5(1)(f) in *Azimov* v *Russia*,[840] where the applicant was detained with a view to his expulsion to Tajikistan: the Court finding that the authorities' real purpose had been to keep him in prison with a view to extradition, after the relevant maximum legal period had expired. The applicant had been in detention with a view to extradition for one year before he was the subject of an order for his detention pending expulsion, which lasted for more than 17 months. The case of *Khlaifia and others* v *Italy*[841] concerned the authorities' interception at sea of applicants who were travelling in 'rudimentary vessels' from Tunisia to Italy. There was a violation of Article 5(1) because of the ambiguity in the domestic law regulating their detention in a migrants' reception centre.

6.260 Article 5(1)(f) does not require that the detention be reasonably considered necessary, for example, to prevent the commission of an offence or to prevent a person fleeing. In fact, all that is required is that 'action is being taken with a view to deportation' and it is irrelevant whether the underlying decision to expel can be justified under national or Convention law.[842] However, detention under Article 5(1)(f) does require deportation proceedings to

---

[833] See, e.g. *J.N.* v *UK*, No. 37289/12, 19.5.16, para. 90.

[834] See, e.g. *Popov* v *France*, Nos. 39472/07 and 39474/07, 19.1.12.

[835] See, e.g. *Dougoz* v *Greece*, No. 40907/98, 6.3.01, para. 57; *Garabayev* v *Russia*, No. 38411/02, 7.6.07; *S.D.* v *Greece*, No. 53541/07, 11.6.09; *Rahimi* v *Greece*, No. 8687/08, 5.4.11.

[836] *Nasrulloyev* v *Russia*, No. 656/06, 11.10.07; *Ismoilov and others* v *Russia*, No. 2947/06, 24.4.08; *Ryabikin* v *Russia*, No. 8320/04, 19.6.08; *Abdulkhakov* v *Russia*, No. 14743/11, 2.10.12; *Kim* v *Russia*, No. 44260/13, 17.7.14; *Soldatenko* v *Ukraine*, No. 2440/07, 23.10.08. See also *Abdolkhani and Karimnia* v *Turkey*, No. 30471/08, 22.9.09; *Toniolo* v *San Marino and Italy*, No. 44853/10, 26.6.12.

[837] No. 9990/82, Series A, No. 111, 18.12.86.

[838] No. 51564/99, 5.2.02.

[839] *Ibid.*, para. 42.

[840] No. 67474/11, 18.4.13.

[841] No. 16483/12, 15.12.16. There were also violations of Articles 5(2), 5(4) and 13 (taken together with Article 3).

[842] *Chahal* v *UK*, No. 22414/93, 15.11.96, para. 112. In *S.P.* v *Belgium*, No. 12572/08, dec. 14.6.11 the Court found that its application of interim measures did not render the applicant's detention unlawful under domestic law: although the deportation proceedings against the applicant were suspended, action was still 'being taken' with a view to his deportation.

be in progress and to be prosecuted with due diligence.[843] The assessment of the reasonableness of the length of the proceedings will depend upon the particular circumstances of the case: for example, the Court has found to be excessive cases involving delays of one year and six months pending extradition[844] and of three months pending deportation.[845] In *Chahal* v *UK*[846] the continued detention of the applicant, pending deportation, for more than three and a half years was found 'to give rise to serious concern', but was not held to violate this Article, in view of the complexity and the exceptional circumstances of the proceedings.[847] However, Article 5 was found to have been violated in *A and others* v *UK*,[848] in relation to applicants who were detained under the Anti-Terrorism, Crime and Security Act 2001 (legislation introduced following the terrorist attacks on the United States on 11 September 2001) on suspicion of being involved in international terrorism. The applicants were foreign nationals whom the UK Government would have deported had it been possible to find a state to receive them where they would not face a real risk of being subjected to treatment contrary to Article 3 of the Convention. The authorities considered their detention was necessary because their presence in the country was a threat to national security. Nevertheless, as the authorities had accepted that they could not be deported or removed 'for the time being', Article 5 was breached because, as regards nine of the applicants, it could not be said that they were persons against whom action was being taken with a view to deportation or extradition. The Government sought to rely on its derogation under Article 15, but, in tandem with the House of Lords judgment in the case, the Court found that while there had indeed been an emergency threatening the life of the nation, it concluded that the measures taken were disproportionate as they discriminated unjustifiably between nationals and non-nationals (see further at section 7.13 below).

Exceptionally, Article 5 will be violated where an applicant is removed to a state where they face a 'real risk of a flagrant breach' of Article 5[849] (similarly to the 'flagrant denial of justice' test under Article 6—see 6.392). **6.261**

Article 5(2): reasons for arrest

Article 5(2) requires reasons to be given promptly following any arrest or detention (see also below at 6.393 re provision of information on charge), including detention of a mental patient.[850] This has been interpreted by the Court as meaning that any arrested person 'must **6.262**

---

[843] *Quinn* v *France*, No. 18580/91, 22.3.95, para. 48. See also *RAF* v *Spain*, No. 53652/00, 17.6.03; *Leaf* v *Italy*, No. 72794/01, dec. 27.11.03; *Auad* v *Bulgaria*, No. 46390/10, 11.10.11; *Suso Musa* v *Malta*, No. 42337/12, 23.7.13. The Court has stipulated that particular expedition is required where extradition is sought in order to try the person concerned (as opposed to extradition requested for the purpose of enforcing a sentence). See *Gallardo Sanchez* v *Italy*, No. 11620/07, 24.3.15, para. 42. There was a violation of Article 5(1) in *J.N.* v *UK*, No. 37289/12, 19.5.16 because, for a period of more than a year, the applicant's deportation was not pursued with due diligence.

[844] *Gallardo Sanchez* v *Italy*, No. 11620/07, 24.3.15.

[845] *Tabesh* v *Greece*, No. 8256/07, 26.11.09.

[846] No. 22414/93, 15.11.96.

[847] The Commission, however, had unanimously found a violation of Article 5(1): No. 22414/93, Comm. Rep. 27.6.95. In *Ntumba Kabongo*, No. 52467/99, dec. 2.6.05 a period of 10 months, while the procedure for the applicant's expulsion had been pending, was not unreasonable, given her repeated refusals to board an aircraft. Article 5(1)(f) was violated in *Mikolenko* v *Estonia*, No. 10664/05, 8.10.09 (applicant detained with a view to expulsion for nearly four years).

[848] No. 3455/05, 19.2.09.

[849] *Othman (Abu Qatada)* v *UK*, No. 8139/09, 17.1.12, para. 233.

[850] *Van der Leer* v *Netherlands*, No. 11509/85, Series A, No. 170, 21.2.90, paras. 27–9.

be told, in simple, non-technical language that he can understand, the essential legal and factual grounds for his arrest, so as to be able, if he sees fit, to apply to a court to challenge its lawfulness' in accordance with Article 5(4).[851] Written reasons are not required.

6.263 All of the requisite information need not be provided by the arresting officer at the moment of arrest.[852] The applicants in *Fox, Campbell and Hartley v UK*[853] were told on being taken into custody that they had been arrested (under section 11 of the Northern Ireland (Emergency Provisions) Act 1978) on suspicion of being terrorists. That was found to be insufficient to meet the requirements of Article 5(2), but their subsequent interrogation by the police as to their suspected involvement in specific criminal offences and as to their membership of proscribed organisations was found to satisfy the Article. The fact that the questioning took place several hours after the applicants' arrests was nevertheless found to comply with the obligation to act promptly (the applicant was found to have been notified within six hours and 20 minutes of arrest). In *O'Hara v UK*,[854] notification during interview within six to eight hours of arrest was found to comply with the requirement of promptness. Similarly, in *Murray v UK*[855] the reasons for the applicant's arrest were sufficiently brought to her attention during her subsequent interview. It should be noted that each of these cases was decided in the context of investigations into terrorism and it is suggested that these periods may not be sufficiently prompt in cases that are not related to terrorism. A delay of four days before Russian detainees were provided with information about their detention by the Georgian authorities was held to be incompatible with Article 5(2) in *Shamayev and others v Georgia and Russia*.[856] The Court also took account of the fact that the information provided to the applicants was incomplete, that the applicants did not have access to lawyers or interpreters, and that their lawyers were denied access to the case files.

6.264 In *HB v Switzerland*[857] there was no violation of Article 5(2) in respect of the arrest of the applicant for forgery and the improper use of company funds. The applicant's specialised knowledge of the financial situation of the company, of which he was a manager and board member, was relevant to the assessment of compliance with the obligation to provide adequate reasons for the arrest.

6.265 Particular issues are likely to arise in relation to the arrest of individuals with certain disabilities. There was a violation of Article 5(2) in *Z.H. v Hungary*[858] which concerned the arrest of a young man who was innately deaf and dumb, had medium-grade intellectual disability and was illiterate. He could communicate with a type of sign language which was only intelligible to his mother. He was questioned in the police station in the presence of an official sign language interpreter, but he could not understand official sign language. The Court was also critical of the authorities' failure to ensure 'reasonable accommodation' (in line with Articles 2, 13 and 14 of the UN Convention on the Rights of Persons with Disabilities) to

---

[851] *Fox, Campbell and Hartley v UK*, Nos. 12244/86, 12245/86 and 12383/86, 30.8.90, para. 40; *HB v Switzerland*, No. 26899/95, 5.4.01, para. 47; *Shamayev and others v Georgia and Russia*, No. 36378/02, 12.4.05, para. 413.

[852] *Fox, Campbell and Hartley v UK*, Nos. 12244/86, 12245/86 and 12383/86, 30.8.90, para. 40.

[853] *Ibid.*

[854] No. 37555/97, 16.10.01.

[855] No. 18731/91, 28.10.94.

[856] No. 36378/02, 12.4.05.

[857] No. 26899/95, 5.4.01.

[858] No. 28973/11, 8.11.12.

address his particular condition, for example by obtaining assistance for him from a lawyer or another suitable person.

Article 5(3): right to release pending trial

Article 5(3) guarantees rights in respect of two distinct situations: the initial stage when an **6.266** individual is taken into the custody of the authorities and the period pending trial during which the suspect may be detained or released (with or without conditions).[859] The first limb of Article 5(3) requires that an accused be brought promptly before a 'judge or other officer authorised by law to exercise judicial power'. Thus decisions made by prosecutors will not comply with this provision because they lack the requisite independence and impartiality.[860] The review must be automatic—it should not require an application by the detainee.[861] The initial automatic review should encompass an assessment of the lawfulness of the arrest and detention, and whether or not there is a reasonable suspicion that the arrested person had committed an offence—but it need not *necessarily* incorporate a power to release on bail.[862] The judicial officer must have the power to release if the detention is unlawful.

Particular considerations apply to minors. The Court has emphasised that the pre-trial **6.267** detention of minors should be used only as a last resort, that it should be as short as possible and, that where detention is strictly necessary, minors should be kept apart from adults.[863]

The issue of promptness depends upon an assessment of the 'special features' of each case.[864] **6.268** The application of Article 5(3) has led to findings of violations against the UK in relation to detention of suspects in Northern Ireland. In *Brogan and others v UK*,[865] periods of detention of four days and six hours, up to six days and 16½ hours were held to violate the requirements of Article 5(3). Following that case, the UK Government entered a derogation under Article 15 of the Convention (relating to terrorism connected with the affairs of Northern Ireland). In the subsequent case of *Brannigan and McBride v UK*[866] detentions for longer periods were also found to breach the same Article, but the derogation was found to comply with Article 15 and the applicants were therefore prevented from validly claiming a violation of the Convention (the derogation has subsequently been withdrawn). There was a violation of Article 5(3) in *Kandzhov v Bulgaria*,[867] which concerned the applicant's arrest on suspicion of committing offences of insult and hooliganism during a political demonstration. He was not taken before a judge until three days and 23 hours after his arrest, a period which was found to be excessive. He was arrested on charges of a minor and non-violent offence and there were no special difficulties or exceptional circumstances which would have prevented the authorities from bringing the applicant before a judge much sooner. In *Ipek and others v Turkey*[868]

---

[859] See, e.g. *McKay v UK*, No. 543/03, 3.10.06; *Magee and others v UK*, Nos. 26289/12, 29062/12 and 29891/12, 12.5.15.

[860] See, e.g. *Niedbała v Poland*, No. 27915/95, 4.7.00; *Merit v Ukraine*, No. 66561/01, 30.3.04, paras. 62–4; *Krejčíř v Czech Republic*, Nos. 39298/04 and 8723/05, 26.3.09, para. 91; *Moulin v France*, No. 37104/06, 23.11.10.

[861] *McKay v UK*, No. 543/03, 3.10.06, para. 34.

[862] *Ibid.*, paras. 35–40. See also *Magee and others v UK*, Nos. 26289/12, 29062/12 and 29891/12, 12.5.15.

[863] *Nart v Turkey*, No. 20817/04, 6.5.08, para. 31.

[864] *Wemhoff v Germany*, Series A, No. 7, 27.7.68, para. 10; *De Jong, Baljet and Van Den Brink v Netherlands*, Nos. 8805–6/79 and 9242/81, Series A, No. 77, 22.5.84, para. 52.

[865] Nos. 11209/84, 11266/84, and 11365/85, Series A, No. 145-B, 29.11.88.

[866] Nos. 14553/89 and 14554/89, Series A, No. 258-B, 26.5.93.

[867] No. 68294/01, 6.11.08.

[868] Nos. 17019/02 and 30070/02, 3.2.09.

the Court found Article 5(3) to have been violated because of the detention of the 16-year-old applicants for three days and nine hours before being taken in front of a judge. This was less than the maximum period of four days previously applied, but account was taken of the applicants' ages, that they were denied access to a lawyer for a considerable period and that during their detention only very limited investigative steps were taken by the police.

6.269 Exceptionally, in cases where ships were intercepted on the high seas and escorted long distances to a port, the Court has found delays of 13 and 16 days before detainees on the ships were brought before a judicial officer not to be incompatible with Article 5(3).[869] However, in the similar case of *Vassis and others v France*,[870] relating to the interception of a ship off the African coast by the French navy, the Court found a violation of Article 5(3) where the crew were brought to shore after 18 days, but there was then a further 48 hours' delay before they were taken before a judge. Such a delay was not justified, given that the operation had been planned in advance, and indeed that the ship in question had been under surveillance for some weeks.

6.270 The second limb of Article 5(3) provides for an entitlement 'to trial within a reasonable time or to release pending trial'. However, the Court has found that these are not alternatives: there is a right to be released pending trial unless detention can be justified.[871] Control must be exercised by a judicial officer who is independent of both the executive and the parties to the proceedings. If the judicial officer may later intervene in criminal proceedings, his or her independence or impartiality may be open to doubt. In *HB v Switzerland*,[872] the decision to order the applicant's detention on remand was made by an investigating judge, which was found to violate Article 5(3) because the judge would have been entitled to intervene in the subsequent criminal proceedings as a representative of the prosecuting authority. Article 5(3) may be violated if the domestic law regulating pre-trial detention is insufficiently precise or foreseeable.[873]

6.271 The judge should hear the individual in person and should review the circumstances for and against detention and decide 'by reference to legal criteria, whether there are reasons to justify detention'.[874] If not, the accused should be released. If the judge lacks the power to order release then Article 5(3) will be violated. In *Caballero v UK*,[875] Article 5(3) was violated because of the effect of a statutory provision (section 25 of the Criminal Justice and Public Order Act 1994) which was automatically to deny bail to anyone charged with certain serious offences and who had a previous conviction for any of those offences. In those circumstances, the magistrates' court had no power to order Mr Caballero's release.

---

[869] *Medvedyev and others v France*, No. 3394/03, 29.3.10 (13 days) and *Rigopoulos v Spain*, No. 37388/97, dec. 12.1.99 (16 days). In *Medvedyev* the decision was reached by a majority of the Grand Chamber, by nine votes to eight.

[870] No. 62736/09, 27.6.13. See also *Ali Samatar and others v France*, Nos. 17110/10 and 17301/10, 4.12.14 and *Hassan and others v France*, Nos. 46695/10 and 54588/10, 4.12.14.

[871] *Wemhoff v Germany*, Series A, No. 7, 27.7.68, paras. 4–5.

[872] No. 26899/95, 5.4.01.

[873] See, e.g. *Krejčíř v Czech Republic*, Nos. 39298/04 and 8723/05, 26.3.09.

[874] *Schiesser v Switzerland*, Series A, No. 34, 4.12.79, para. 31; *Assenov v Bulgaria*, No. 24760/94, 28.10.98, para. 146; *Huber v Switzerland*, No. 12794/87, 23.10.90, para. 43; *HB v Switzerland*, No. 26899/95, 5.4.01, para. 55.

[875] No. 32819/96, 8.2.00. For full reasoning in that case see the European Commission Report of 30.6.98. See also *SBC v UK*, No. 39360/98, 19.6.01; *Piruzyan v Armenia*, No. 33376/07, 26.6.12.

Whilst there must continue to be reasonable suspicion of the accused's involvement in an **6.272** offence for the detention to continue, that will not be enough in itself to satisfy the Article 5(3) requirements: 'after a certain lapse of time, it no longer suffices; the court must then establish whether the other grounds cited by the judicial authorities continue to justify the deprivation of liberty'.[876] Noting the vagueness of the phrase 'after a certain lapse of time', in *Buzadji* v *Moldova*[877] the Grand Chamber stipulated that the requirement on the judicial officer to give relevant and sufficient reasons for the detention applies at the time of the first decision ordering detention on remand (in other words, 'promptly' after an arrest, mirroring the requirement under the first limb of Article 5(3)).

The grounds for detention must be both 'relevant' and 'sufficient'[878] and the Court must consider whether the national authorities showed 'special diligence' in conducting the proceedings. Relevant grounds have been held to be:

- a danger of absconding.[879] The Court has constantly reiterated that this must not be assessed solely on the basis of the severity of the possible sentence.[880] Accordingly, account must be taken, in particular, of the following: the character of the person involved, her/his morals, assets, links with the state in which they are being prosecuted and international contacts;[881]
- interference with the course of justice;[882]
- the prevention of crime;[883] and
- the preservation of public order.[884]

grounds for detention!

There must, however, be a *real application* of such grounds to the case in question: 'continued **6.273** detention can be justified in a given case only if there are specific indications of a genuine requirement of public interest which, notwithstanding the presumption of innocence, outweighs the rule of respect for individual liberty'.[885] Thus a failure to give adequate reasons, or even a court's use of 'stereotyped' reasons, is likely to violate Article 5(3).[886] In *Bouchet* v *France*[887] the Court found no violation of Article 5(3) (by four votes to three) where the defendant, who was accused of raping his former partner, was held on remand[888] for more

---

[876] *Letellier* v *France*, No. 12369/86, Series A, No. 207, 26.6.91, para. 35; see also, e.g. *Ječius* v *Lithuania*, No. 34578/97, 31.7.00; *Kudla* v *Poland*, No. 30210/96, 26.10.00, para. 111; *Idalov* v *Russia*, No. 5826/03, 22.5.12, para. 140.

[877] No. 23755/07, 5.7.16.

[878] See, e.g. *Nedim Şener* v *Turkey*, No. 38270/11, 8.7.14 and *Şık* v *Turkey*, No. 53413/11, 8.7.14 (grounds neither relevant nor sufficient to justify pre-trial detention of journalists for one year and a week—violation of Article 5(3)). The requirements are the same regardless of the distinctions between different types of detention: *Buzadji* v *Moldova*, No. 23755/07, 5.7.16, paras. 113–14.

[879] See, e.g. *Letellier* v *France*, No. 12369/86, Series A, No. 207, 26.6.91, (1992) 14 EHRR 83 and *Tomasi* v *France*, No. 12850/87, Series A, No. 241-A, 27.8.92.

[880] See, e.g. *Ilijkov* v *Bulgaria*, No. 33977/96, 26.7.01.

[881] *W* v *Switzerland*, No. 14379/88, 26.1.93, Series A, No. 254-A.

[882] See, e.g. *Clooth* v *Belgium*, No. 12718/87, Series A, No. 225, 12.12.91.

[883] See, e.g. *Muller* v *France*, No. 21802/93, 17.3.97.

[884] See, e.g. *Letellier* v *France*, No. 12369/86, Series A, No. 207, 26.6.91.

[885] *W* v *Switzerland*, No. 14379/88, 26.1.93, Series A No. 254-A, para. 30.

[886] See, e.g. *Demirel* v *Turkey*, No. 39324/98, 28.1.03; *Smirnova* v *Russia*, Nos. 46138/99 and 48183/99, 24.7.03; *Khodorkovskiy* v *Russia*, No. 5829/04, 31.5.11, para. 193.

[887] No. 33591/96, 20.3.01.

[888] A suspect on remand is entitled to have her/his case prioritised and 'conducted with special diligence': *Matznetter* v *Austria*, No. 2178/64, 10.11.69, Series A, No. 10, para. 12.

than 17 months. This was found to be justified by the seriousness of the crime, the applicant's tormented and aggressive state and the victim's vulnerability.

6.274 In *Lelievre* v *Belgium*[889] the Court found that the applicant's pre-trial detention had been justified by the continuing existence of plausible reasons for suspecting him of having committed various serious offences, including kidnapping and imprisonment, and because of the risk that he would abscond and not appear for trial. However, Article 5(3) was held to have been breached because the applicant had proposed various alternatives to his pre-trial detention (including electronic surveillance and the obligation to report to a police station several times a day) but the authorities had failed to respond and not given reasons for not applying alternative measures to detention (during a period of detention of almost eight years). There was a violation of Article 5(3) in *Khodorkovskiy* v *Russia*[890] in the absence of compelling reasons to detain the applicant: no reasons were given in two of the domestic court decisions; the courts had relied on material obtained in violation of the lawyer–client privilege; and the courts failed to give serious consideration to other possible measures of restraint.

6.275 The right to trial within a reasonable time under Article 5(3) overlaps with the similar requirement in Article 6(1). Under Article 5(3), time will run from the initial arrest until first instance conviction or acquittal and/or sentence, but not appeal proceedings (which are covered by Article 6(1)). Rather than lay down specific time limits or even rigid criteria, the Court has stated that continued pre-trial detention must be justified by relevant and sufficient reasons. In *Kalashnikov* v *Russia*,[891] the applicant's detention was said to be justified due to the strong suspicion of his involvement in serious offences and the danger of his obstructing the examination of the case. However, the domestic courts had failed to provide any factual basis for such a decision and therefore the reasons justifying detention lost their relevance and sufficiency over time. The delays in the case were caused neither by its complexity, nor by the applicant's conduct. Accordingly, Article 5(3) was violated as the detention pending trial exceeded a reasonable time (a total of four years, one month and four days, of which only one year, two months and 29 days were admissible *ratione temporis*).[892] See also below at 6.362 in relation to Article 6(1).

6.276 Article 5(3) also provides that 'release may be conditioned by guarantees to appear for trial'. Conditions that have been found to be permissible include residence requirements, an obligation to surrender travel documents and the imposition of bail or a surety. The amount of bail must be assessed primarily in relation to the person concerned, including their assets: 'to the degree of confidence that is possible that the prospects of loss of security … in the event of his non-appearance at a trial will act as a sufficient deterrent to dispel any wish on his part to abscond'.[893] The accused is required to provide sufficient information (which can be checked) in order for the amount of bail to be fixed. However, in view of the fundamental

---

[889] No. 11287/03, 8.11.07.

[890] No. 5829/04, 31.5.11.

[891] No. 47095/99, 15.7.02.

[892] See also, e.g. *Ilowiecki* v *Poland*, No. 27504/95, 4.10.01 (detention on remand of one year, nine months and 19 days violated Article 5(3)). However, detention on remand for periods of more than five years have been found, on their particular facts, not to violate Article 5(3). See, e.g. *Korchuganova* v *Russia*, No. 75039/01, 8.6.06; *Chraidi* v *Germany*, No. 65655/01, 26.10.06; *Ereren* v *Germany*, No. 67522/09, 6.11.14.

[893] *Neumeister* v *Austria*, Series A, No. 8, 27.6.68, para. 14. See also *Toshev* v *Bulgaria*, No. 56308/00, 10.8.06.

right to liberty, the authorities must take as much care in fixing the appropriate level of bail as in deciding whether the accused's continued detention is necessary.[894] In *Iwanczuk* v *Poland*,[895] Article 5(3) was violated as the proceedings relating to the setting of bail and the appropriate method of payments lasted for more than four months, during which period the applicant remained in detention, despite the fact that it had already been decided that his continued detention was not necessary. The case of *Mangouras* v *Spain*[896] concerned the setting of bail of €3 million in respect of the applicant, a Greek ship-master, after his ship sustained a leak, causing its cargo of 70,000 tonnes of oil to be spilled into the Atlantic Ocean. The Grand Chamber found, by a majority of ten votes to seven, that, exceptionally, imposing such a high figure did not breach Article 5(3). It noted that in setting bail, the domestic courts had taken account of the applicant's personal situation, the seriousness of the offence of which he was accused and his 'professional environment'. The domestic courts had considered the level of bail essential to ensure his appearance at trial, and it was noted that bail was paid by the company that insured the owner of the ship. Given the exceptional extent of the environmental damage caused by the oil-spill, it could legitimately be asked whether a level of bail set solely by reference to the applicant's assets would have been sufficient to ensure his attendance at the trial. The majority concluded that in view of the disastrous environmental and economic consequences of the spill, the domestic courts had been justified in taking into account both the seriousness of the offences and the amount of the loss imputed to the applicant.[897]

Article 5(4): right of access to court to challenge detention

According to Article 5(4), everyone who is deprived of their liberty by arrest or detention is entitled to take proceedings to challenge the 'lawfulness' of the detention (in terms both of domestic and Convention law). In some cases the judicial supervision may be incorporated in the original decision ordering detention, if taken by a body which constitutes a 'court'. **6.277**

Such proceedings should be directly available to the detainee,[898] they should be accessible[899] and should be decided by a body with the powers of a 'court' (see the relevant requirements set out above at 6.229 in relation to Article 5(1)(a)), including the power to order release if the detention is found to be unlawful. There is no right of appeal,[900] as such, against a decision ordering or extending detention, where the body in question meets these requirements. However, if that is not the case, then recourse must be available to a second body which provides all the guarantees of judicial procedure.[901] There was therefore a violation of Article **6.278**

---

[894] *Iwanczuk* v *Poland*, No. 25196/94, 15.11.01, para. 66.

[895] No. 25196/94, 15.11.01.

[896] No. 12050/04, 28.9.10.

[897] These conclusions were strongly refuted in the joint separate opinion of Judges Rozakis, Bratza, Bonello, Cabral Barreto, David Thór Björgvinsson, Nicolaou and Bianku.

[898] See, e.g. *Rakevich* v *Russia*, No. 58973/00, 28.10.03, paras. 45–6. Where a body only has discretionary powers of review, this will mean that the requisite remedy is not 'available' to the applicant. See, e.g. *D.L.* v *Bulgaria*, No. 7472/14, 19.5.16.

[899] The availability of legal aid may therefore be relevant to this question. See, e.g. *Suso Musa* v *Malta*, No. 42337/12, 23.7.13.

[900] However, where a system of appeal is provided for by domestic law, it must comply with Article 5(4) (see, e.g. *Toth* v *Austria*, Series A No. 224, 12.12.91, para. 84; *Lanz* v *Austria*, No. 24430/94, 31.1.02—on appeal the submissions of a senior public prosecutor were not disclosed to the applicant).

[901] *De Wilde, Ooms and Versyp* v *Belgium*, Series A, No. 12, 18.6.71, paras. 73–6; *Winterwerp* v *Austria*, Series A, No. 33, 24.10.79, paras. 60–1.

5(4) where a prosecutor's decision to detain with a view to bringing proceedings for psychiatric internment could only be challenged by appealing to higher prosecutors.[902]

6.279 The extent of the remedy required will depend upon the type of detention. In *Brogan and others* v *UK*,[903] for example, the Court acknowledged that the *habeas corpus* procedure satisfied the requirements of Article 5(4). However, in *Chahal* v *UK*,[904] the Court found that neither *habeas corpus*, nor judicial review,[905] nor the 'advisory panel procedure' were sufficient to challenge detention on the grounds of national security. Similarly in *Al-Nashif* v *Bulgaria*,[906] there was a violation of Article 5(4) because there was no judicial means of challenging detention prior to deportation on grounds of national security. Furthermore, the detention order did not state any reasons and Mr Al-Nashif was held practically incommunicado and was not allowed to see a lawyer. The Court has noted that there are means which can be employed to accommodate both national security concerns and yet provide individual, procedural justice (such as, in the UK, the appointment of 'special counsel').[907] However, such special procedures were assessed, and found wanting in terms of procedural fairness, in the case of *A and others* v *UK*,[908] which concerned the legality of the detention of the applicants under the Anti-Terrorism, Crime and Security Act 2001, on suspicion of being involved in international terrorism (discussed further at 6.260 above). The applicants brought proceedings challenging their detention before the Special Immigration Appeals Commission (SIAC), which was able to consider both 'open' and 'closed' material. Neither the applicants nor their legal advisers were entitled to see the closed material, but it was disclosed to special advocates, who were appointed by the Solicitor General to act on behalf of each applicant. In view of this lack of disclosure, the Grand Chamber concluded (in relation to four of the applicants) that proceedings before the SIAC were not adequate to enable them effectively to challenge the allegations made against them, relating to their alleged support for al'Qaeda or their membership of groups linked to it.

6.280 Article 5(4) was found to have been breached in *S.D.* v *Greece*[909] where the applicant was detained on his entry into Greece, having fled from Turkey where he was a member of an illegal political party and where he had spent several years in prison. He was immediately detained and held on remand for entering the country illegally. However, the domestic law did not permit a separate review of the lawfulness of the detention of aliens—the decision to detain was inseparable from the decision to deport. The Court was also critical of the ambiguity of the domestic law.

6.281 Article 5(4) necessarily implies various procedural requirements which in general will be similar to the obligations imposed by Article 6 (there must be equality of arms between the parties[910]), but they may not always be the same and they will vary according to the

---

[902] *Varbanov* v *Bulgaria*, No. 31365/96, 5.10.00.
[903] Nos. 11209/84, 11266/84, and 11365/85, Series A, No. 145-B, 29.11.88.
[904] No. 22414/93, 15.11.96.
[905] See also *HL* v *UK*, No. 45508/99, 5.10.04 (judicial review and *habeas corpus* were not sufficient for Article 5(4) purposes in respect of the detention of an 'informal patient' in a psychiatric institution).
[906] No. 50963/99, 20.6.02.
[907] *Jasper* v *UK*, No. 27052/95, 16.2.00; *Tinnelly* v *UK*, Nos. 20390/92 and 21322/92, 10.7.98.
[908] No. 3455/05, 19.2.09. See, by contrast, *Sher and others* v *UK*, No. 5201/11, 20.10.15 (thirteen days' detention without charge under anti-terrorism legislation—no violation of Article 5(4)).
[909] No. 53541/07, 11.6.09. See also *Rahimi* v *Greece*, No. 8687/08, 5.4.11.
[910] See, e.g. *Černák* v *Slovakia*, No. 36997/08, 17.12.13, para. 78.

deprivation of liberty in question.[911] The remedy must of course be available in practice, not just in theory.[912] There was a violation of Article 5(4) in *Castravet v Moldova*[913] because of a glass partition in the remand centre that hindered effective consultations between the applicant and his lawyer, and also because they reasonably believed that their conversations were not confidential. The manner in which a public hearing is held may violate Article 5(4), as was the case in *Ramishvili and Kokhreidze v Georgia*.[914] There, the applicants were held in a caged dock in chaotic conditions surrounded by masked guards, making it difficult to communicate with their lawyers, to hear the prosecutor or the judge, or to make their own submissions audible. The Court concluded that the proceedings, which were broadcast nationally, had tainted the presumption of innocence, were not sufficiently independent, and accordingly lacked the fundamental requisites of a fair hearing.

A court hearing an appeal need not address every argument, but it should take into account 'concrete facts' put forward by the detainee, which are 'capable of putting in doubt the existence of the conditions essential for the "lawfulness"'.[915] Sufficient reasons should be given for authorising detention—the use of brief, stereotypical wording will not do.[916] Where detention falls within the ambit of Article 5(1)(c), a hearing is required,[917] although it will not generally be necessary to hold the hearing in public.[918] In *Wloch v Poland*,[919] restrictions on the applicant's right to appear at the hearing and the denial of the applicant's access to the case file led to a finding of a violation of Article 5(4). There was a violation of Article 5(4) in *Allen v UK*[920] as a result of the judge's refusal to allow the applicant (who remained in custody) to attend the hearing of the prosecution's appeal against an order granting bail. It was central to the decision that the domestic law treated a prosecution appeal against bail as a rehearing of the application for bail, which entitled the judge to remand the accused in custody or to grant bail subject to conditions. In *Garcia Alva v Germany*[921] and *Lietzow v Germany*,[922] Article 5(4) was breached because of the failure to disclose witness statements, and there was a failure to allow the applicant's lawyer to inspect the investigating files in *Schöps v Germany*.[923] The Court reiterated the rationale for these obligations in *Garcia Alva*:[924]

6.282

---

[911] See, e.g. *Winterwerp v Netherlands*, Series A, No. 33, 24.10.79; *Wassink v Netherlands*, No. 12535/86, 27.9.90, Series A, No. 185-A; *Reinprecht v Austria*, No. 67175/01, 15.11.05; *Krejčíř v Czech Republic*, Nos. 39298/04 and 8723/05, 26.3.09.

[912] *RMD v Switzerland*, No. 19800/92, 26.9.97.

[913] No. 23393/05, 13.3.07. See also *Modarca v Moldova*, No. 14437/05, 10.5.07. See, in contrast, *Sarban v Moldova*, No. 3456/05, 4.10.05 and *Kröcher and Müller v Switzerland*, No. 8463/78, Comm. Rep. 16.12.82.

[914] No. 1704/06, 27.1.09 (as a result of the courtroom conditions there was also a violation of Article 3).

[915] See, e.g. *Yankov v Bulgaria*, No. 39084/97, 11.12.03, para. 185.

[916] See, e.g. *Svipsta v Latvia*, No. 66820/01, 9.3.06.

[917] See, e.g. *Trzaska v Poland*, No. 25792/94, 11.7.00; *Krejčíř v Czech Republic*, Nos. 39298/04 and 8723/05, 26.3.09.

[918] *Reinprecht v Austria*, No. 67175/01, 15.11.05.

[919] No. 27785/95, 19.10.00. See also *Samoila and Cionca v Romania*, No. 33065/03, 4.3.08.

[920] No. 18837/06, 30.3.10. See also, e.g. *Jankauskas v Lithuania*, No. 59304/00, dec. 16.12.03 (applicant's presence at hearing not required as he was legally represented); *Mamedova v Russia*, No. 7064/05, 1.6.06 (refusal of request for leave to appear at the hearing, but presence required due to applicant's first-hand knowledge of conditions of detention).

[921] No. 23541/94, 13.2.01.

[922] No. 24479/94, 13.2.01.

[923] No. 25116/94, 13.2.01. See also *Svipsta v Latvia*, No. 66820/01, 9.3.06; *Mooren v Germany*, No. 11364/03, 9.7.09.

[924] No. 23541/44, 13.2.01, para. 42.

in view of the dramatic impact of deprivation of liberty on the fundamental rights of the person concerned, proceedings conducted under Article 5(4) of the Convention should also meet, to the largest extent possible under the circumstances of an on-going investigation, the basic requirements of a fair trial ....

Nevertheless, the Court accepted that some information may be kept secret to prevent suspects tampering with evidence. The Court found a series of violations of Article 5(4) in *Khodorkovskiy v Russia*[925] caused by procedural defects in the applicant's detention hearings: he only received the 300-page case-file on the second day of a hearing; during one hearing he could only communicate with his lawyer in the presence of a prison officer; the defects could not be cured by an appeal hearing held two weeks later; at another hearing neither he nor his lawyer were present; and at a further hearing the court failed to assess the need for the applicant's continuing and future detention. Finally, a delay of one month and nine days in hearing an appeal against one of the detention orders also breached this provision. Article 5(4) also requires the impartiality of the Court, as was affirmed in *DN v Switzerland*[926] where the judge rapporteur, prior to being appointed, had expressed his opinion that the applicant should not be released from psychiatric detention. An appeal to the discretionary leniency of ministers will not amount to an effective remedy.[927]

6.283 The Article 5(4) guarantees also apply to situations where the relevant factors justifying detention may change over time. In those circumstances, there must be periodic reviews of the need for continued detention. Accordingly, the Court has held that there must be periodic reviews of the lawfulness of detention of mental health patients,[928] those sentenced to discretionary and mandatory life sentences (after expiry of the tariff period),[929] and juveniles sentenced to detention during 'Her Majesty's Pleasure'[930] with a power to order release, or with a procedure containing the necessary judicial safeguards, including, for example, the possibility of an oral hearing[931] and the right to call and question witnesses.[932] There was a violation of Article 5(4) in *Benjamin and Wilson v UK*[933] as the Mental Health Review Tribunal, which assessed the lawfulness of the applicants' continued detention in hospital, did not have the power to order release (which lay, rather, with the Home Secretary).[934] Placing the burden of proof on an applicant detained on mental health grounds to establish that continued detention does not satisfy the conditions of lawfulness will also violate Article 5(4), as was the case in *Hutchison Reid v UK*.[935] In *Magalhaes Pereira v Portugal*,[936] Article 5(4) was breached, in part, due to the authorities' reliance, in detaining the applicant

---

[925] No. 5829/04, 31.5.11.
[926] No. 27154/95, 29.3.01, para. 42.
[927] *Dougoz v Greece*, No. 40907/98, 6.3.01, para. 62.
[928] See, e.g. *X v UK* (1982) 4 EHRR 188, paras. 58–61; *Stanev v Bulgaria*, No. 36760/06, 17.1.12, para. 171; *Dörr v Germany*, No. 2894/08, dec. 22.1.13.
[929] *Thynne, Wilson and Gunnell v UK*, Nos. 11787/85, 11978/89 and 12009/86, Series A, No. 190, 25.10.90, paras. 68–80; *Stafford v UK*, No. 46295/99, 28.5.02, para. 89.
[930] *Hussain v UK*, No. 21928/93, 21.2.96, para. 54; and see *T and V v UK*, Nos. 24724/94 and 24888/94, 16.12.99.
[931] *Stafford v UK*, No. 46295/99, 28.5.02, para. 89.
[932] See, e.g. *Waite v UK*, No. 53236/99, 10.12.02.
[933] No. 28212/95, 26.9.02.
[934] See also *Clift v UK*, No. 7205/07, 13.7.10 (early release scheme subject to approval of Secretary of State—violation of Article 5 taken together with Article 14).
[935] No. 50272/99, 20.2.03.
[936] No. 44872/98, 26.2.02. See also *Ruiz Riviera v Switzerland*, No. 8300/06, 18.2.14.

in a secure psychiatric unit, on a medical report obtained one year and eight months previously, which did not therefore necessarily reflect the applicant's positon at the time of detention. A further factor was the appointment as the applicant's lawyer of a trainee barrister who took no part in the proceedings.

Article 5(4) requires that the determination by the Court must be carried out 'speedily', which will depend upon the circumstances of each case, including any delays caused by both the detainee and the authorities.[937] Delays of 15 months and two years between reviews of the detention of a person held on mental health grounds were found to violate Article 5(4) in *Herczegfalvy* v *Austria*,[938] as did a two-year delay between Parole Board reviews of the detention of discretionary life prisoners in *Oldham* v *UK*.[939] The initial review of detention should take place particularly quickly. For example, delays of 23 days in deciding on an application for release from police custody violated Article 5(4) in *Rehbock* v *Slovenia*,[940] as was the case in *Sanchez-Reisse* v *Switzerland*[941] where two-tier applications in extradition proceedings took 31 and 46 days respectively.[942] In *Van Glabeke* v *France*[943] the applicant was compulsorily admitted to psychiatric hospital for a period of 19 days. In that time no court ruled on applications made for her immediate release, in violation of Article 5(4). In *Shcherbina* v *Russia*[944] the applicant was detained with a view to his extradition to Kazakhstan. As the initial detention decision was made by a prosecutor, the Court held that a further period of 16 days before his case was reviewed by a court, violated the 'speediness' requirement of Article 5(4). What is more, the decision-making process was flawed as the original decision to detain him was taken *in camera*, without the applicant's involvement, and the prosecutor had acted *ultra vires* as he had had no powers to order the applicant's detention. **6.284**

The requirement for speedy review under Article 5(4) is much stricter than the right under Article 6(1) to a fair hearing within a reasonable time (see below at 6.362).

Article 5(5): right to compensation for unlawful detention

Article 5(5) provides for the right of a person arrested or detained unlawfully to an enforceable right to compensation. Therefore, for the Court to find a violation of Article 5(5) there must be a finding of a violation of one or more elements of Article 5.[945] A requirement that the detainee must have suffered damage in order to claim compensation does not contravene Article 5(5), but 'damage' includes both pecuniary and non-pecuniary loss. **6.285**

There will accordingly be a breach of Article 5(5) where the domestic law provides no enforceable right to compensation in respect of violations of other provisions of Article 5.[946] **6.286**

---

[937] See, e.g. *Sanchez-Reisse* v *Switzerland*, No. 27426/95, Series A, No. 107, 21.10.86; *S.T.S.* v *Netherlands*, No. 277/05, 7.6.11.

[938] No. 10533/83, Series A, No. 242-B, 24.9.92.

[939] No. 36273/97, 26.9.00.

[940] No. 29462/95, 28.11.00.

[941] No. 27426/95, Series A, No. 107, 21.10.86.

[942] See also *MB* v *Switzerland*, No. 28256/95, 30.11.00 (a delay of 34 days); *LR* v *France*, No. 33395/96, 7.6.02 (24 days between the applicant's request for release from a psychiatric institution and her release on trial).

[943] No. 38287/02, 7.3.06.

[944] No. 41970/11, 26.6.14.

[945] See, e.g. *Stanev* v *Bulgaria*, No. 36760/06, 17.1.12, para. 182.

[946] See, e.g. *Brogan and others* v *UK*, No. 11209/84 et al, 29.11.88; *Yankov* v *Bulgaria*, No. 39084/97, 11.12.03; *Stanev* v *Bulgaria*, No. 36760/06, 17.1.12; *Tymoshenko* v *Ukraine*, No. 49872/11, 30.4.13.

6.287 There was a violation of this provision in *Danev* v *Bulgaria*,[947] in which case compensation for unlawful detention was refused on the basis that the applicant had not proved any non-pecuniary damage. The Court concluded that, in effect, the domestic courts had required the applicant to prove that he had suffered non-pecuniary damage by producing evidence of outward signs of physical or psychological suffering *during* the detention. Such a formalistic approach meant that the award of compensation was unlikely in the large number of cases where unlawful detention lasted only a short time and did not result in a perceptible deterioration in the detainee's physical or psychological condition.

The lack of certainty in the domestic law may lead to a violation of Article 5(5), as was the case in *Shcherbina* v *Russia*.[948] There, a breach was found because of the lack of clarity as regards the availability of compensation for unlawful detention in the context of extradition proceedings.

Article 6: The Right to a Fair Hearing

6.288 Article 6 states:

1. In the determination of his civil rights and obligations or of any criminal charge against him, everyone is entitled to a fair and public hearing within a reasonable time by an independent and impartial tribunal established by law. Judgment shall be pronounced publicly but the press and public may be excluded from all or part of the trial in the interests of morals, public order or national security in a democratic society, where the interests of juveniles or the protection of the private life of the parties so require, or to the extent strictly necessary in the opinion of the court in special circumstances where publicity would prejudice the interests of justice.
2. Everyone charged with a criminal offence shall be presumed innocent until proved guilty according to law.
3. Everyone charged with a criminal offence has the following minimum rights:
    (a) to be informed promptly, in a language which he understands and in detail, of the nature and cause of the accusation against him;
    (b) to have adequate time and facilities for the preparation of his defence;
    (c) to defend himself in person or through legal assistance of his own choosing or, if he has not sufficient means to pay for legal assistance, to be given it free when the interests of justice so require;
    (d) to examine or have examined witnesses against him and to obtain the attendance and examination of witnesses on his behalf under the same conditions as witnesses against him;
    (e) to have the free assistance of an interpreter if he cannot understand or speak the language used in court.

6.289 The right to a fair hearing has been interpreted in the light of the preamble to the Convention, which declares the rule of law to be part of the common heritage of the contracting states, and which itself incorporates the principle of legal certainty.[949] It is the Convention right which is the most commonly breached: between 1959 and 2015, more than 41 per cent of

---

[947] No. 9411/05, 2.9.10.
[948] No. 41970/11, 26.6.14.
[949] *Sovtransavto Holding* v *Ukraine*, No. 48553/99, 25.7.02, para. 72.

the violations found by the Court concerned Article 6.[950] The general requirement set out in Article 6(1) for a fair hearing applies to both criminal and civil proceedings, but the additional rights set out in Articles 6(2) and 6(3) apply only in criminal cases. The rights set out in Article 6(3) are aspects of the general right to a fair trial and are not therefore exhaustive.

Despite the fundamental importance of Article 6, Article 15 does not preclude derogation from it. States are required to exercise diligence to ensure the *effective* enjoyment of Article 6 rights.[951] Where a decision to be enforced within a contracting state has been originally made by a non-contracting state, there must be a review to ensure that the original proceedings complied with Article 6.[952] Where the Court finds a violation of Article 6 in criminal proceedings it is increasingly its practice to recommend (and occasionally to *require*) that the domestic proceedings be reopened (see 3.19 Enforcement of judgments, above). The requirements of Article 6 do not prescribe any particular criminal justice system, nor is there a right to be tried before a jury.[953]

6.290

remedy!

The applicability of Article 6 and the criminal/civil distinction

The distinction between the Convention classification of cases as being 'civil' or 'criminal' is important, as Article 6(1) applies to both types of proceedings, but Articles 6(2) and 6(3) only apply to proceedings classified according to the Convention as criminal.

6.291

The terms 'civil rights' and 'criminal charge' are autonomous Convention concepts. Therefore, the domestic classification of proceedings may be relevant, but will not necessarily be decisive.

6.292

In assessing whether proceedings are criminal in nature, the Court will consider the classification of the offence under national law, the nature of the proceedings in question and the nature and degree of severity of the penalty (the '*Engel*' criteria).[954] For example, proceedings for the non-payment of the community charge (the 'poll tax') in the United Kingdom were classified in domestic law as being civil. However, in *Benham* v *UK*[955] the Court found such proceedings to be criminal in nature, on the basis that they were brought by a public authority under statutory powers of enforcement and that the applicant faced a maximum penalty of three months' imprisonment and had in fact been ordered to be imprisoned for 30 days. The application of the '*Engel*' criteria' may mean that offences defined at the national level as 'administrative' may be considered as 'criminal' by the European Court. That was the position in *Kasparov and others* v *Russia*,[956] as regards a breach of the domestic regulations on holding demonstrations. The Court has also characterised the role played by various financial and regulatory bodies (considered to be 'administrative' in the domestic context) as

6.293

---

[950] European Court of Human Rights, *Overview—1959–2015*, p. 6 (the vast majority of cases relating to fairness or the length of proceedings).

[951] See, e.g. *T* v *Italy*, No. 14104/88, 12.10.92, para. 29.

[952] See, e.g. *Pellegrini* v *Italy*, No. 30882/96, 20.7.01 (relating to a decision of the Vatican courts).

[953] See, e.g. *Taxquet* v *Belgium*, No. 926/05, 16.11.10, paras. 84–5; *Twomey, Cameron and Guthrie* v *UK*, Nos. 67318/09 and 22226/12, dec. 28.5.13, para. 30.

[954] *Engel and others* v *Netherlands*, 8.6.76, Series A No. 22. See also, e.g. *Öztürk* v *Germany*, No. 8544/79, Series A, No. 73, 21.2.84, para. 50; *JB* v *Switzerland*, No. 31827/96, 3.5.01, para. 44.

[955] No. 19380/92, 10.6.96.

[956] No. 21613/07, 3.10.13.

being criminal under the Convention.[957] In *Matyjek* v *Poland*[958] the Court was required to assess the nature of 'lustration proceedings' in which it was alleged that the applicant had lied about his collaboration with the communist-era secret services. Although the proceedings were not classified as being criminal under the domestic law, taking account of the criminal connotations of the offence and the nature and severity of the penalty, the Court concluded that the charges against the applicant constituted criminal charges within the meaning of Article 6. The Grand Chamber confirmed in *Jussila* v *Finland*[959] that the applicability of Article 6 (under its criminal head) to tax surcharge proceedings will depend upon the '*Engel criteria*'. In that case, although the tax surcharge was applied as part of a fiscal regime, it was imposed for deterrent and punitive purposes, and therefore Article 6 was held to be applicable (regardless of the minor nature of the penalty).

6.294   There may be a narrow distinction between offences defined in domestic law as disciplinary and those defined as criminal. Thus the key issue which arose in *Ezeh and Connors* v *UK*[960] was whether Article 6 applied to disciplinary proceedings brought against prisoners. By applying the '*Engel* criteria'[961] the Grand Chamber found that Article 6 was applicable to such proceedings:[962] the charges against the applicants (violent threats and assault) amounted to offences under the criminal law; additional days could be imposed for punitive reasons after a finding of culpability by the governor and which constituted fresh deprivations of liberty; 40 and seven additional days, respectively, were actually imposed on the applicants. Article 6(3)(c) was found to have been violated in *Ezeh and Connors* because the applicants had been denied the right to legal representation for their hearings before the prison governor. Despite being classified as disciplinary proceedings by the domestic courts in Austria, where the applicant in *T* v *Austria*[963] was fined for abuse of process in relation to his legal aid request, the Court classified the proceedings as criminal, in view of the amount of the penalty at stake and the possibility of converting it into a prison term.

6.295   In *Phillips* v *UK*,[964] the applicant complained of a violation of the presumption of innocence under Article 6(2) (see further 6.383 below) in view of the application of a statutory assumption applied in confiscation proceedings, following his conviction for drug trafficking. The Court found that such proceedings, which were analogous to sentencing proceedings, did not involve the bringing of a new 'charge' and hence Article 6(2) was not applicable. Nevertheless, Article 6(1) was applicable and the right to be presumed innocent in criminal cases was included within the general notion of a fair hearing. This would seem to suggest the need to invoke Article 6(1) with Article 6(2) or Article 6(3) if there is any doubt about the

---

[957] See, e.g. *Didier* v *France*, No. 58188/00, dec. 27.8.02; *Menarini Diagnostics S.r.l.* v *Italy*, No. 43509/08, 27.9.11; *Grande Stevens and others* v *Italy*, No. 18640/10 et al, 4.3.14.

[958] No. 38184/03, dec. 30.5.06.

[959] No. 73053/01, 23.11.06. See also *Steininger* v *Austria*, No. 21539/07, 17.4.12; *Julius Kloiber Schlachthof GmbH and others* v *Austria*, No. 21565/07 et al, 4.4.13. However, the Court has found that the civil aspect of Article 6 does not apply to taxation proceedings—see *Ferrazzini* v *Italy*, No. 44759/98, 12.7.01.

[960] Nos. 39665/98 and 40086/98, 9.10.03.

[961] *Engel and others* v *Netherlands*, 8.6.76, Series A No. 22, paras. 82–3.

[962] By 11 votes to six. But see: *Ferreira* v *Portugal*, No. 41921/98, dec. 28.9.00 (Article 6 not applicable to military disciplinary proceedings).

[963] No. 27783/95, 14.11.00.

[964] No. 41087/98, 5.7.01. In *Saccoccia* v *Austria*, No. 69917/01, dec. 5.7.07 the Court held that proceedings in the Austrian courts as regards the enforcement of a forfeiture order made by a US court did not engage the criminal limb of Article 6 (as the proceedings did not involve the determination of a new criminal charge) but the civil limb of Article 6 was applicable.

applicability of the latter, but in *Phillips* the Court considered Article 6(1) of its own motion: it had not been initially relied on by the applicant.

In criminal cases, Article 6 will usually apply as from the time when a suspect is charged, but **6.296** it may apply earlier (such as from the point of arrest and/or during a preliminary investigation) where a suspect's situation has been 'substantially affected' by any other measure.[965] It will continue to apply throughout all stages of criminal proceedings until the final conclusion of any appeal, including sentencing.[966] Exceptionally, Article 6 may also apply to proceedings relating to the transfer of a sentenced prisoner.[967] Article 6 will not be applicable to measures taken short of prosecution, such as police warnings.[968] It is also not applicable to extradition proceedings[969] or in cases of the application of the European arrest warrant.[970]

The application of Article 6 to civil proceedings

As regards civil proceedings, Article 6 is intended, in essence, to provide procedural protec- **6.297** tion of rights already recognised in domestic law. For Article 6 to apply in civil cases, there are three requirements:

(1) that there is a *civil right or obligation* in issue; and
(2) that there is a *dispute* in relation to a civil right; and
(3) that there is a *determination* of such a dispute.

To comply with the first condition there must be a 'right' in issue that can be said, at least on **6.298** arguable grounds, to be recognised under domestic law.[971] In general, a 'civil right' will amount to a private law right, rather than a public law right. The term has an autonomous meaning and so the domestic law classification may be relevant, but will not be decisive.[972] Public law proceedings may also fall within the ambit of Article 6(1) if they are decisive of a private law right (such as pecuniary rights). For example, the Court has found the following to amount to 'civil rights':

- the right to property in the context of planning proceedings;[973]
- the right to statutory sickness allowance;[974]

---

[965] See, e.g. *Eckle* v *Germany*, No. 8130/78, 15.7.82, para. 73. See also *Heaney and McGuinness* v *Ireland*, No. 34720/97, 21.12.00, para. 42; *Quinn* v *Ireland*, No. 36887/97, 21.12.00, para. 42; *Brennan* v *UK*, No. 39846/98, 16.10.01; *O'Halloran and Francis* v *UK*, Nos. 15809/02 and 25624/02, 29.6.07; *Aleksandr Zaichenko* v *Russia*, No. 39660/02, 18.2.10.

[966] See, e.g. *Eckle* v *Germany*, No. 8130/78, 15.7.82; *Findlay* v *UK*, No. 22107/93, 25.2.97 (sentencing); *T and V* v *UK*, Nos. 24724/94 and 24888/94, 16.12.99 (fixing of tariff).

[967] See, e.g. *Buijen* v *Germany*, No. 27804/05, 1.4.10. But Article 6(1) will usually *not* be applicable to such proceedings. See: *Veermae* v *Finland*, No. 38704/03, dec. 15.3.05; *Csoszánski* v *Sweden*, No. 22318/02, dec. 27.6.06; *Szabo* v *Sweden*, No. 28578/03, dec. 27.6.06.

[968] See, e.g. *R* v *UK*, No. 33506/05, dec. 4.1.07 (police warning to schoolboy re allegations of indecent assault; entry placed on sex offenders register for two and a half years and recorded on police national computer, access to which was restricted—Article 6 not applicable).

[969] See, e.g. *Peñafiel Salgado* v *Spain*, No. 65964/01, dec. 16.4.02.

[970] *Monedero Angora* v *Spain*, No. 41138/05, dec. 7.10.08.

[971] See, e.g. *Kunkova and Kunkov* v *Russia*, No. 74690/01, 12.10.06; *Ladbrokes Worldwide Betting* v *Sweden*, No. 27968/05, dec. 6.5.08; *Ahtinen* v *Finland*, No. 48907/99, 23.9.08; *De Bruin* v *Netherlands*, No. 9765/09, dec. 17.9.13. Article 6(1) *may* be applicable where a right is recognised under domestic law on a discretionary basis. See, e.g. *Fodor* v *Germany*, No. 25553/02, 11.12.06; *Regner* v *Czech Republic*, No. 35289/11, 26.11.15 (case referred to Grand Chamber 2.5.16).

[972] See, e.g. *Ferrazzini* v *Italy*, No. 44759/98, 12.7.01, para. 24.

[973] See, e.g. *Bryan* v *UK*, No. 19178/91, Series A, No. 335-A, 22.11.95.

[974] *Feldbrugge* v *Netherlands*, No. 8562/79, Series A, No. 99, 29.5.86.

- the right to a disability allowance;[975]
- a disabled carer's allowance;[976]
- a right to accommodation;[977]
- the right of people required to carry out forced labour during World War II to claim compensation;[978]
- the right to continue one's education;[979]
- the right to participate in a programme for the unemployed not to be arbitrarily revoked;[980]
- the right to practise a profession (in relation to the individual's pecuniary interests);[981]
- the right to operate a commercial venture, for example in the context of the removal of a licence;[982]
- applications for employment permits for foreign employees;[983]
- an application to register an association;[984]
- the right to enjoy a good reputation;[985]
- a civil claim for compensation against the state;[986]
- a right to obtain adequate protection of physical integrity against environmental risks (as recognised by the domestic law);[987]
- the right of civil society associations to challenge decisions relating to the environment;[988] and
- a right to fish for salmon and sea trout in particular waters.[989]

6.299 The following have been found *not* to concern 'civil rights':

- taxation proceedings[990] (including customs duties or charges);[991]

---

[975] *Salesi v Italy*, No. 13023/87, 26.2.93.

[976] *Mennitto v Italy*, No. 33804/96, 5.10.00.

[977] *Fazia Ali v UK*, No. 40378/10, 20.10.15.

[978] *Woś v Poland*, No. 22860/02, dec. 1.3.05.

[979] *Emine Araç v Turkey*, No. 9907/02, 23.9.08 (university education); *Oršuš and others v Croatia*, No. 15766/03, 16.3.10 (primary education).

[980] *Mendel v Sweden*, No. 28426/06, 7.4.09.

[981] *De Moor v Belgium*, No. 16997/90, Series A, No. 292-A, 23.7.94. See also *Kök v Turkey*, No. 1855/02, 19.10.06 (dispute over the recognition of specialist medical training in another country—Article 6(1) applicable).

[982] See, e.g. *Benthem v Netherlands*, No. 8848/80, 23.10.85.

[983] *Jurisic and Collegium Mehrerau v Austria*, No. 62539/00, 27.7.06; *Coorplan-Jenni Gmbh and Hascic v Austria*, No. 10523/02, 27.7.06.

[984] *APEH Uldozotteinek Szovetsege and others v Hungary*, No. 32367/96, 5.10.00.

[985] *Tolstoy Miloslavsky v UK*, No. 18139/91, 13.7.95, para. 58; *Kurzac v Poland*, No. 31382/96, 22.2.01, para. 20; Cases of *Cordova v Italy (No. 1)* and *(No. 2)*, Nos. 40877/98 and 45649/99, 30.1.03; *Kuśmierek v Poland*, No. 10675/02, 21.9.04.

[986] See, e.g. *Aksoy v Turkey*, No. 21987/93, 18.12.96.

[987] *Taşkın and others v Turkey*, No. 46117/99, 10.11.04. See also *Okyay and others v Turkey*, No. 36220/97, 12.7.05.

[988] See, e.g. *Collectif national d'information et d'opposition à l'usine Melox–Collectif stop Melox et Mox v France*, No. 75218/01, dec. 28.3.06; *L'Erablière A.S.B.L v Belgium*, No. 49230/07, 24.2.09.

[989] *Posti and Rahko v Finland*, No. 27824/95, 24.9.02, para. 52. See also *Alatulkkila v Finland*, No. 33538/96, 28.7.05.

[990] *Ferrazzini v Italy*, No. 44759/98, 12.7.01 (albeit by 11 votes to six). See, however, *O.B. Heller A.S. and Československá Obchodní banka A.S. v Czech Republic*, Nos. 55631/00 and 55728/00, dec. 9.11.04 (proceedings brought by customs authorities concerning the content of letters of guarantee contracted between the applicant companies and the import companies—therefore they were 'civil' within the meaning of Article 6(1)), and *Ravon v France*, No. 18497/03, 21.2.08 (a dispute concerning the lawfulness of searches carried out by the tax authorities of residential premises—the 'civil right' to respect for the applicants' home was therefore in issue).

[991] *Emesa Sugar N.V. v Netherlands*, No. 62023/00, dec. 13.1.05.

- the right to stand for election[992] or to receive an MP's pension;[993]
- the reporting of public court proceedings;[994]
- the right of access of an election observer to election-related documents;[995]
- the discretionary award of compensation following acquittal in criminal proceedings;[996]
- a prisoner's requests for temporary leave of absence;[997] and
- the right to freedom of movement within the EU.[998]

not civil rights

In *Maaouia* v *France*,[999] the Grand Chamber of the Court confirmed previous Commission **6.300** decisions to the effect that decisions regarding the entry, stay and deportation of aliens (such as proceedings for the rescission of an exclusion order) do not concern the determination of a 'civil right' (nor a criminal charge, being special preventive measures for the purpose of immigration control).[1000]

The applicability of Article 6(1) to disputes between public officials and their employers has **6.301** proved contentious. In its 1999 judgment in *Pellegrin* v *France* the Court sought to clarify previous inconsistencies in the law in this area and laid down a 'functional criterion' which stipulated that claims brought by officials whose posts involved the exercise of powers conferred by public law fell outside the scope of Article 6 (reflecting the fact that certain civil servants were bound by a special bond of trust and loyalty to their employer).[1001] However, in

---

[992] *Pierre-Bloch* v *France*, No. 24194/94, 21.10.97; *Hoon* v *UK*, No. 14832/11, dec. 13.11.14.

[993] *Papon* v *France*, No. 344/04, dec. 11.10.05.

[994] *Mackay and BBC Scotland* v *UK*, No. 10734/05, 7.12.10; *Truckenbrodt* v *Germany*, No. 49849/08, dec. 30.6.15.

[995] *Geraguyn Khorhurd Patgamavorakan Akumb* v *Armenia*, No. 11721/04, dec. 14.4.09.

[996] *Masson and van Zon* v *Netherlands*, No. 15346/89, 28.9.95.

[997] *Boulois* v *Luxembourg*, No. 37575/04, 3.4.12.

[998] *Adams and Benn* v *UK*, Nos. 28979/95 and 30343/96, dec. 13.1.97.

[999] No. 39652/98, 5.10.00.

[1000] See also, e.g. *Panjeheighalehei* v *Denmark*, No. 11230/07, dec. 13.10.09; *Dalea* v *France*, No. 964/07, dec. 2.2.10. A similar decision in respect of extradition proceedings to Uzbekistan was made by the Court in *Mamatkulov and Askarov* v *Turkey*, Nos. 46827/99 and 46951/99, 4.2.05. The applicants also complained in that case about the unfairness of criminal proceedings in Uzbekistan. The Court in *Mamatkulov* cited with approval a passage in the *Soering* judgment where it stated that 'the Court does not exclude that an issue might exceptionally be raised under Article 6 by an extradition decision in circumstances where the fugitive has suffered or risks suffering a flagrant denial of a fair trial'. In spite of the fact that the applicants' representatives had been unable to contact the applicants following their extradition from Turkey to Uzbekistan, the Court rejected their Article 6 complaint on the basis that there was not 'sufficient evidence to show that any possible irregularities in the trial were liable to constitute a flagrant denial of justice' (para. 91)—but see also the joint partly dissenting opinion of Judges Bratza, Bonello and Hedigan arguing that Article 6 had been violated. See also *Stapleton* v *Ireland*, No. 56588/07, dec. 4.5.10. In *Mamatkulov* the lack of contact between the applicants and their lawyers led the Court to find a separate violation of Article 34 (see further at 2.59–2.6, above). Issues under Article 5 might arise if there was a flagrant risk of arbitrary detention (*Othman (Abu Qatada)* v *UK*, No. 8139/09, 17.1.12, para. 233; *Tomic* v *UK*, No. 17387/03, dec. 14.10.03). The application of the European arrest warrant procedure will also not engage Article 6 (under either its civil or criminal heads): see *Monedero Angora* v *Spain*, No. 41138/05, dec. 7.10.08.

[1001] *Pellegrin* v *France*, No. 28541/95, 18.12.99. See also, e.g. *Martinez-Caro* v *Spain*, No. 42646/98 et al, dec. 7.3.00 (senior diplomatic and embassy officers); *Kajanen* v *Finland*, No. 36401/97, dec. 19.10.00 and *Pitkevich* v *Russia*, No. 47936/99, dec. 8.2.01 (judges); *Castanheira Barros* v *Portugal*, No. 36945/97, 26.10.00 and *Werner* v *Poland*, No. 26760/95, 15.11.01 (judicial liquidators); *Devlin* v *UK*, No. 29545/95, 30.10.01 (civil service administrative assistant); *Knauth* v *Germany*, No. 4111/98, dec. 22.11.01 (teacher); *Petersen* v *Germany*, No. 39793/98, dec. 22.11.01 (university lecturer); *Mickovski* v *former Yugoslav Republic of Macedonia*, No. 68329/01, dec. 10.11.05 (Deputy Solicitor General); *Martinie* v *France*, No. 58675/00, 12.4.06 (school accountant); *Kanayev* v *Russia*,

the light of anomalies that had subsequently arisen in applying this test, the Grand Chamber in its 2007 judgment in *Vilho Eskelinen* v *Finland*[1002] re-evaluated the position, holding that Article 6(1) would only be inapplicable to civil servants if: (1) the domestic law expressly excludes access to a court for the post or category of staff in question; and (2) the exclusion is justified on objective grounds in the state's interest.[1003]

6.302　The second condition (for Article 6(1) to apply to civil proceedings) is the existence of an actionable claim in domestic law in relation to the civil right in question—a dispute that is 'genuine and serious'.[1004] This requirement has created most contention in cases where there has been a procedural limitation to a substantive right. For example, in *Osman* v *UK*,[1005] the Government argued that there was no substantive right in domestic law to sue the police in negligence for failing to prevent the shooting of the second applicant and his son and therefore Article 6(1) had no application. The European Court, however, found that Article 6(1) was applicable on the basis that the applicants did have a right to sue in negligence that had been subject to a rule, applied by the domestic courts on public policy grounds, excluding the police from liability in negligence in the context of the investigation and suppression of crime (but see the later judgment of *Z* v *UK*, referred to at 6.319). Article 6(1) does not necessarily require the existence of a remedy that is *formally* recognised in the domestic law. For example, in *Gorou* v *Greece (No. 2)*[1006] the applicant civil servant made a criminal complaint against a colleague, and applied to join the proceedings as a civil party. When her colleague was acquitted by the criminal court, the applicant requested the public prosecutor at the Court of Cassation to lodge an appeal on points of law. In order to make such a request, the applicant relied not on the law itself, but on established judicial practice. The Government contested the applicability of Article 6(1), arguing that the applicant's request could not be characterised as a 'remedy'. However, taking account of the undisputed judicial practice relating to such requests, and having found that the request was considered to form an integral part of the whole of the proceedings that the applicant had joined as a civil party in seeking to obtain compensation, the majority of the Grand Chamber accepted that her request related to a 'dispute over a civil right' for the purposes of Article 6(1).[1007]

No. 43726/02, 27.7.06 (naval captain); *Stojakovic* v *Austria*, No. 30003/02, 9.11.06 (director of federal research institute).

[1002] No. 63235/00, 19.4.07 (albeit by 12 votes to five).

[1003] Applying these criteria, Article 6(1) has been found to be *inapplicable* to a decision by a military council to discharge a soldier on disciplinary grounds (*Sukut* v *Turkey*, No. 59773/00, dec. 11.9.07) but *applicable* to disciplinary proceedings brought against judges (*Olujić* v *Croatia*, No. 22330/05, 5.2.09; *Harabin* v *Slovakia*, No. 58688/11, 20.11.12; *Oleksandr Volkov* v *Ukraine*, No. 21722/11, 9.1.13; *Baka* v *Hungary*, No. 20261/12, 23.6.16), to proceedings brought by parliamentary staff (*Savino and others* v *Italy*, Nos. 17214/05, 20329/05 and 42113/04, 28.4.09); to proceedings relating to the dismissal of embassy employees (*Cudak* v *Lithuania*, No. 15869/02, 23.3.10; *Sabeh El Leil* v *France*, No. 34869/05, 29.6.11); to the dismissal of a Ministry of Internal Affairs official (*Fazliyski* v *Bulgaria*, No. 40908/05, 16.4.13); and to the dismissal of a police investigator (*Nikolova and Vandova* v *Bulgaria*, No. 20688/04, 17.12.13).

[1004] See, e.g. *Skorobogatykh* v *Russia*, No. 37966/02, dec. 8.6.06.

[1005] No. 23452/94, 28.20.98—discussed further below at 6.318. But see also *Powell and Rayner* v *UK*, No. 9310/81, Series A, No. 172, 21.2.90.

[1006] No. 12686/03, 20.3.09.

[1007] However, six judges dissented on this point, arguing that Article 6(1) was not applicable to a judicial practice which ran counter to the domestic legislation, and that the applicant's request could not be considered to be a 'remedy'.

The third condition for Article 6(1) to apply to civil proceedings is that the procedure must **6.303** lead to a *determination* of a 'civil right'.[1008] The result of the proceedings in question must be 'directly decisive' of a 'civil right'; mere tenuous connections or remote consequences will not bring Article 6 into play. In *Fayed* v *UK*,[1009] the applicants complained about the publication of a report by Government inspectors about the House of Fraser company. They argued that the inspectors' findings of dishonesty meant that the inquiry was decisive for their civil right to a good reputation. However, the Court held that the inspectors' functions were essentially investigative and were not determinative of any of the applicants' civil rights. In *Gutfreund* v *France*,[1010] the Court found Article 6(1) to be inapplicable to an application for legal aid in criminal proceedings, as it was not determinative of a civil right (or of a criminal charge).

Article 6(1) is not usually applicable to extraordinary appeal processes which seek to reo- **6.304** pen judicial proceedings, because they do not involve the determination of 'civil rights and obligations' or of 'any criminal charge'. However, this does depend on the nature, scope and specific features of the proceedings in question.[1011]

The applicability of Article 6 to interim or interlocutory court orders will depend upon an **6.305** assessment as to whether the proceedings have *determined* a 'civil right or obligation'.[1012] This principle was reaffirmed in *Micallef* v *Malta*,[1013] although the Grand Chamber found that there would be exceptional cases where it might not always be possible, in the course of interim proceedings, to comply immediately with all of the requirements of Article 6. An 11–six majority of the Court in *Micallef* found Article 6 to be applicable to injunction pro- ceedings, which were then held to have breached the requirement of impartiality because the presiding judge was related to advocates for the party opposing the applicant. The obligation to appear before, and give evidence to, a parliamentary commission of inquiry has been held not to fall within the scope of Article 6.[1014]

Proceedings determining liability for costs and in relation to enforcement will be subject to **6.306** Article 6(1).

Where a determination is made by an administrative body that does not comply with **6.307** Article 6(1), there may nevertheless be no breach of the Convention if that body is subject to a court or tribunal that does provide the Article 6(1) protections (see 6.368 below).[1015] In the UK, the availability of judicial review proceedings before the High Court may satisfy the Article 6 standards.[1016]

[1008] See, e.g. *Kervoelen* v *France*, No. 35585/97, 27.3.01.

[1009] No. 17101/90, Series A, No. 294-B, 21.9.94.

[1010] No. 45681/99, 12.6.03.

[1011] *Bochan* v *Ukraine (No. 2)*, No. 22251/08, 5.2.15, para. 50.

[1012] As was found to have been the case in *Markass Car Hire Ltd* v *Cyprus*, No. 51591/99, dec. 23.10.01. But contrast with: *X* v *UK*, No. 7990/77, dec. 11.5.81, DR 24, p. 57; *X* v *Belgium*, No. 8988/80, dec. 10.3.81, DR 24, p. 198; *Ribstein* v *France*, No. 31800/96, dec. 12.4.98; *Jaffredou* v *France*, No. 39843/98, dec. 15.12.98; *Kress* v *France*, No. 39594/98, dec. 29.2.00.

[1013] No. 17056/06, 15.10.09. See also, *Mercieca and others* v *Malta*, No. 21974/07, 14.6.11. In *Central Mediterranean Development Corporation Limited* v *Malta (No. 2)*, No. 18544/08, 22.11.11 Article 6 was also held to be applicable to proceedings for a stay of execution.

[1014] *Van Vondel* v *Netherlands*, No. 38258/03, dec. 23.3.06.

[1015] See, e.g. *Albert and Le Compte* v *Belgium*, No. 7299/75, 27.9.82; *Ozturk* v *Germany*, No. 8544/79, Series A, No. 73, 21.2.84; *Schmautzer* v *Austria*, No. 15523/89, Series A, No. 328-A, 23.10.95; *Bryan* v *UK*, No. 19178/91, Series A, No. 335-A, 22.11.95; *Holding and Barnes PLC* v *UK*, No. 2352/02, dec. 12.3.02.

[1016] But see *Kingsley* v *UK*, No. 35605/97, 7.11.00.

6.308 Legislative intervention in respect of extant civil proceedings is likely to fall foul of Article 6. Whilst the Court has found that the legislature is not necessarily precluded in civil matters from introducing new retrospective provisions that regulate rights under existing laws,[1017] where measures are introduced with a view to influencing the judicial determination of a dispute (including private law disputes between individuals), there will be a violation of the right to a fair trial under Article 6.[1018] In a number of cases, notably involving Greece, violations have been found where the legislature has intervened whilst proceedings involving the state were pending.[1019]

6.309 In *Perez* v *France*,[1020] the Grand Chamber sought to end the uncertainty arising from the Court's previous case law in confirming that Article 6 is applicable to 'civil-party proceedings': where a victim has the right to bring civil proceedings in the criminal courts, simultaneously with the prosecution (but not in respect of any independent right to have third parties prosecuted or sentenced for a criminal offence).

6.310 Specific aspects of the right to a fair trial in civil, as well as criminal, proceedings are discussed below at 6.311 to 6.416.

Access to court

6.311 Although not expressly referred to in Article 6, the European Court has found the right of access to court to be an inherent element of Article 6.[1021] Although the majority of decided cases concern *legal* impediments, the impossibility for a person to bring legal proceedings because of a lack of access to court buildings for persons with reduced mobility may also raise issues under Article 6.[1022]

[1017] See, e.g. *Zielinski and others* v *France*, Nos. 24846/94, 34165/96–34173/96, 28.10.99, para. 57; *EEG-Slachthuis Verbist* v *Belgium*, No. 60559/00, dec. 10.11.05. (legislation enacted, with retrospective effect, to re-establish a statutory basis for contributions previously payable on domestic products—no violation of the equality-of-arms principle); *Azienda Agricola Silverfunghi S.A.S. and others* v *Italy*, No. 48357/07 et al, 24.6.14 (legislative interference with property right through retroactive legislation, with the intention of decreasing public expenditure—no violation of Article 1 of Protocol No. 1).

[1018] See, e.g. *Crişan* v *Romania*, No. 42930/98, 27.5.03 (adoption, during court proceedings, of a law excluding judicial review of the decisions of an administrative commission); *Arnolin and others and 24 others* v *France*, No. 20127/03 et seq., 9.1.07; *Arras and others* v *Italy*, No. 17972/07, 14.2.12. In contrast, see *Maurice* v *France*, No. 11810/03, 6.10.05 and *Draon* v *France*, No. 1513/03, 6.10.05 (in each case, the Grand Chamber held that it was not necessary to examine separately Article 6, by 12 votes to five).

[1019] *Stran Greek Refineries and Stratis Andreadis* v *Greece*, No. 13427/87, Series A, No. 301-B, 9.12.94; *Papageorgiou* v *Greece*, No. 24628/94, 22.10.97; *Anagnostopoulous and others* v *Greece*, No. 39374/98, 7.11.00; *Agoudimos and Cefallonia Sky Shipping Co.* v *Greece*, No. 38703/97, 28.6.01; *SCM Scanner de l'Ouest Lyonnais and others* v *France*, No. 12106/03, 21.6.07; *Maggio and others* v *Italy*, No. 46286/09, 31.5.11; *M.C. and others* v *Italy*, No. 5376/11, 3.9.13; *Stefanetti and others* v *Italy*, No. 21838/10 et al, 15.4.14. See also *Kutić* v *Croatia*, No. 48778/99, 1.3.02 (discussed at 6.327 below).

[1020] No. 47287/99, 12.2.04. See also, e.g. *Torri* v *Italy*, No. 26433/95, 1.7.97; *Calvelli and Ciglio* v *Italy*, No. 32967/96, 17.1.02; *Sottani* v *Italy*, No. 26775/02, dec. 24.2.05; *Gorou* v *Greece (No. 2)*, No. 12686/03, 20.3.09; *Mihova* v *Italy*, No. 25000/07, dec. 30.3.10. In *Anagnostopoulos* v *Greece*, No. 54589/00, 3.4.03 there was a violation of the right of access to court under Article 6 where the applicant lodged a criminal complaint and sought compensation as a civil party in the criminal proceedings, which were subsequently time-barred as a result of the authorities' delay in prosecuting the case. The applicant could not then be expected to bring fresh civil proceedings.

[1021] *Golder* v *UK*, Series A, No. 18, 21.2.75. The Grand Chamber has underlined the particular need for direct access to the courts for any partially incapacitated persons wishing to have their status reviewed: *Stanev* v *Bulgaria*, No. 36760/06, 17.1.12.

[1022] *Farcaş* v *Romania*, No. 32596/04, dec. 14.9.10.

Article 6(1) may require individual access to a tribunal to challenge a decree, decision **6.312** or other measure that affects 'civil rights', even though the decision may not formally be addressed to any individual. For example, there was a violation of this principle in *Posti and Rahko v Finland*,[1023] as a result of a regulation concerning fishing rights that could not be challenged. In this decision the Court relied on EC law, notably the principle that a general measure such as a regulation can be susceptible to individual action for annulment before the EC courts.[1024] The right of access to court can be violated by the denial of access to documents, as was the case in *K.H. and others v Slovakia*,[1025] which concerned the applicants' inability to obtain copies of their medical records, resulting in violations of both Articles 6 and 8. Article 6(1) may be violated where a person who has been deprived of legal capacity has no right of direct access to a court with a view to having their legal capacity restored.[1026]

The state is left a free choice of the means to secure the right of access to court that **6.313** may be subject to limitations, provided that they do not impair the very essence of the right,[1027] provided that they are in pursuance of a legitimate aim and are proportionate,[1028] provided that they are sufficiently foreseeable,[1029] and that they comply with the equality of arms principle.[1030] Limitations considered by the Court have included, for example, the requirement to attempt to settle a civil claim before instituting proceedings,[1031] general procedural rules about the submission of appeals,[1032] time limits for the submission of documents to a court,[1033] other conditions of admissibility of an appeal,[1034] the imposition of security for costs,[1035] civil court fees,[1036] stamp

---

[1023] No. 27829/95, 24.9.02, para. 53.

[1024] Now under Article 263 TFEU (former Articles 230 and 177 of the EC Treaty); and see e.g. Case C-358/89 *Extramet Industrie SA v Council of the European Communities* [1991] ECR I-2501, 13.

[1025] No. 32881/04, 28.4.09.

[1026] *D.D. v Lithuania*, No. 13469/06, 14.2.12; *Nataliya Mikhaylenko v Ukraine*, No. 49069/11, 30.5.13; *A.N. v Lithuania*, No. 17280/08, 31.5.16.

[1027] *Winterwerp v Netherlands*, Series A, No. 33, 24.10.79. See also, e.g. *Dunayev v Russia*, No. 70142/01, 24.5.07; *Célice v France*, No. 14166/09, 8.3.12; *Josseaume v France*, No. 39243/10, 8.3.12; *R.P. and others v UK*, No. 38245/08, 9.10.12 (appointment of Official Solicitor to represent mother with learning disabilities in child care proceedings: no violation of Article 6(1)).

[1028] See, e.g. *Khalfaoui v France*, No. 34791/97, 14.12.99; *Saez Maeso v Spain*, No. 77837/01, 9.11.04; *Melnyk v Ukraine*, No. 23436/03, 28.3.06.

[1029] See, e.g. *Ligue du monde islamique and Organisation islamique mondiale du secours islamique v France*, Nos. 36497/05 and 37172/05, 15.1.09.

[1030] *Bayar and Gürbüz v Turkey*, No. 37569/06, 27.11.12.

[1031] *Momčilović v Croatia*, No. 11239/11, 26.3.15.

[1032] *MPP Golub v Ukraine*, No. 6778/05, dec. 18.10.05; *Liakopoulou v Greece*, No. 20627/04, 24.5.06 (Court of Cassation took overly formalistic approach re clarity of grounds of appeal).

[1033] *Rodriguez Valin v Spain*, No. 47792/99, 11.10.01; *Stone Court Shipping Company, S.A v Spain*, No. 55524/00, 28.10.03; *Vodárenská Akciová Společnost, AS v Czech Republic*, No. 73577/01, 24.2.04.

[1034] See, e.g. *Valchev and others v Bulgaria*, Nos. 47450/11, 26659/12 and 53966/12, dec. 1.1.14; *Arribas Antón v Spain*, No. 16563/11, 20.1.15. The refusal to hear a cassation appeal because the accused had not surrendered to custody has been found to be a disproportionate interference with the right of access: e.g. *Guérin v France*, No. 25201/94, 29.7.98 and *Omar v France*, No. 24767/94, 29.7.98. See also: *Goedhart v Belgium*, No. 34989/97, 20.3.01; *Khalfaoui v France*, No. 34791/97, 14.12.99; *Krombach v France*, No. 29731/96, 13.2.01; *Papon v France*, No. 54210/00, 25.7.02 (but contrast these decisions with *Eliazer v Netherlands*, No. 38055/97, 16.10.01). In *Chatellier v France*, No. 34658/07, 31.3.11, the striking out of the applicant's appeal because he had failed to comply with a first instance judgment (to repay a bank loan of more than €600,000) was held to be disproportionate.

[1035] See, e.g. *Tolstoy Miloslavsky v UK*, No. 18139/91, 13.7.95, para. 59 and *Aït-Mouhoub v France*, No. 22924/93, 8.10.98.

[1036] *Kreuz v Poland*, No. 28249/95, 19.6.01, para. 60 (court fee equal to the annual average salary in Poland was found to be excessive); *Mehmet and Suna Yiğit v Turkey*, No. 52658/99, 17.7.07 (requirement to pay court

duty,[1037] the imposition of fines for vexatious applications[1038] or to prevent the build-up of cases,[1039] restrictions on the right to bring proceedings by particular categories of litigants,[1040] limitation periods,[1041] and limitation giving effect to an international agreement excluding jurisdiction.[1042] However, clerical errors,[1043] or delays,[1044] by courts or public officials for which a litigant is not responsible, or ambiguities in the procedural law,[1045] or a lack of clarity as to the identity of the authority responsible for a particular situation,[1046] which have the effect of barring access to court, will violate Article 6. There was a violation of the right of access to court in *Atanasova v Bulgaria*[1047] where the applicant's claim for compensation as a civil party to criminal proceedings was unsuccessful because the criminal proceedings became time-barred as a result of the authorities' delays in dealing with the prosecution of the case. There was a violation of Article 6(1) in conjunction with Article 6(3)(c) in *Kulikowski v Poland*[1048] and *Antonicelli v Poland*,[1049] as a result of the failure of the court of appeal to advise the unrepresented applicants of the applicable time limit for lodging an appeal in criminal proceedings, as it was obliged to do under the relevant domestic law. The right to a fair hearing may be violated because of the failure to give a litigant sufficient notification of a hearing.[1050]

6.314 The applicant (a Russian national) in *Zylkov v Russia*[1051] sought to challenge a decision by the Russian Embassy in Lithuania to reject his application for child allowance under Russian law. His appeal was rejected by a district court in Moscow which suggested that the matter should be decided by the Lithuanian courts. However, the court's failure to refer to any laws giving the Lithuanian courts jurisdiction was held to breach Article 6(1) as it impaired the very essence of the applicant's right of access to court. There was also a violation of this

---

fees amounting to more than four times monthly minimum wage); *Apostol v Georgia*, No. 40765/02, 28.11.06 (requirement to pay 'preliminary expenses' which the applicant could not afford); *Stankov v Bulgaria*, No. 68490/01, 12.7.07 (claimant in civil action required to pay court fees calculated as fixed percentage of any part of his claim that was disallowed, with no upper limit and no judicial discretion).

[1037] *Weissman v Romania*, No. 63945, 24.5.06 (requirement to pay €320,000 in stamp duty disproportionate); *Iordache v Romania*, No. 6817/02, 14.10.08.

[1038] *Toyaksi and others v Turkey*, No. 43569/08 et seq., dec. 20.10.10.

[1039] *Sace Elektrik Ticaret ve Sanayi A.Ş. v Turkey*, No. 20577/05, 22.10.13 (mandatory 10 per cent fine for challenging forced sale at public auction—disproportionate).

[1040] *Winterwerp v Netherlands*, Series A, No. 33, 24.10.79.

[1041] *Stubbings v UK*, No. 22083/93, 22.10.96; *Stagno v Belgium*, No. 1062/07, 7.7.09; *Howald Moor and others v Switzerland*, Nos. 52067/10 and 41072/11, 11.3.14 (fixed 10 year limitation period for asbestos claims which ignored latency period was disproportionate—violation of Article 6(1)); *Sefer Yılmaz and Meryem Yılmaz v Turkey*, No. 611/12, 17.11.15 (limitation period starting from date of incident rather than date of knowledge—violation of Article 6(1)).

[1042] *Prince Hans-Adam II of Liechtenstein v Germany*, No. 42527/98, 12.7.01.

[1043] See, e.g. *Société Anonyme 'Sotiris and Nikos Koutras Attee' v Greece*, No. 39442/98, 16.11.00; *Platakou v Greece*, No. 38460/97, 11.1.01.

[1044] See, e.g. *Kaufmann v Italy*, No. 14021/02, 19.5.05; *Kristiansen and Tyvik AS v Norway*, No. 25498/08, 2.5.13.

[1045] *Hajiyev v Azerbaijan*, No. 5548/03, 16.11.06.

[1046] See, e.g. *Georgel and Georgeta Stoicescu v Romania*, No. 9718/03, 26.7.11.

[1047] No. 72001/01, 2.10.08.

[1048] No. 18353/03, 28.5.09. See also *Assunção Chaves v Portugal*, No. 61226/08, 31.1.12 (lack of official information for unrepresented appellant concerning avenues of appeal and the formal requirements for lodging appeal—violation of Article 6(1) (by four votes to three)).

[1049] No. 2815/05, 28.5.09.

[1050] See, e.g. *Zavodnik v Slovenia*, No. 53723/13, 21.5.15.

[1051] No. 5613/04, 21.6.11.

right in *Arlewin* v *Sweden*[1052] because of the domestic courts' refusal to exercise jurisdiction in respect of defamation proceedings concerning a television programme broadcast from the UK.

The Court has underlined that the 'accessibility, clarity and foreseeability of legal provisions and case-law' will be relevant to the right of access to court.[1053] Developments in case law will only be problematic if they lack reasonable forseeability.[1054] There was a breach of Article 6(1) in *Petko Petkov* v *Bulgaria*,[1055] because a new interpretation of the relevant domestic law on inheritance which applied retroactively in the applicant's pending case had not been sufficiently foreseeable and had the effect of blocking his claim.

The effective exercise of the right of access to court may create other obligations on the state, **6.315** such as the provision of legal aid in civil proceedings[1056] where legal representation is made compulsory for certain types of litigation or simply because of the complexity of the procedure or the particular case: whether legal aid is necessary for a fair hearing will be decided on the particular circumstances of each case, depending upon, for example, the importance of what is at stake for the applicant in the proceedings, the complexity of the law and procedure and the applicants' capacity to represent themselves effectively.[1057] In *P, C and S* v *UK*,[1058] Article 6 was violated where the applicant P had to represent herself in child care and adoption proceedings concerning her daughter. She was initially represented, but her lawyers withdrew and P was not given time to instruct alternative representatives. On the facts the Court found that legal representation was indispensable in the exceptionally complex proceedings (involving complex expert evidence) and in view, also, of what was at stake for the applicant. In *Anakomba Yula* v *Belgium*[1059] the Court found a violation of Article 6, in conjunction with Article 14, where the applicant was denied legal aid to bring proceedings to contest the paternity of her child. The basis for the refusal to grant legal aid was that she was not lawfully resident in Belgium. The Court held that given the serious nature of the family proceedings in question, there needed to be particularly compelling reasons to justify the difference in treatment between those with a residence permit and those without one.

Where the state provides legal representation through a legal aid scheme, it will need to **6.316** ensure that in practice an applicant's right of access to court is upheld. Whilst the applicant in *Bertuzzi* v *France*[1060] was granted legal aid to bring civil proceedings in negligence against a lawyer for allegedly providing bad advice, each of the three lawyers who were assigned to his case applied to withdraw because of their personal connections with the defendant lawyer. The applicant had therefore had to represent himself, which was found to violate

---

[1052] No. 22302/10, 1.3.16.
[1053] *Petko Petkov* v *Bulgaria*, No. 234/06, 19.2.13, para. 32.
[1054] See, e.g. *Legrand* v *France*, No. 23228/08, 26.5.11; *Hoare* v *UK*, No. 16261/08, dec. 12.4.11; *Petko Petkov* v *Bulgaria*, No. 234/06, 19.2.13.
[1055] No. 234/06, 19.2.13.
[1056] *Airey* v *Ireland*, Series A, No. 32, 9.10.79; *Aerts* v *Belgium*, No. 25357/94, 30.7.98; *Bakan* v *Turkey*, No. 50939/99, 12.6.07 (but contrast with *Del Sol* v *France*, No. 46800/89, 26.2.02 and *Essaadi* v *France*, No. 49384/99, 26.2.02). See also *Granos Organicos Nacionales S.A.* v *Germany*, No. 19508/07, 22.3.12 (refusal of legal aid to foreign company wanting to issue civil proceedings in German courts—no violation of Article 6(1)).
[1057] *Steel and Morris* v *UK*, No. 68416/01, 15.2.05, para. 61. See also *Blake* v *UK*, No. 68890/01, dec. 25.10.05.
[1058] No. 56547/00, 16.7.02.
[1059] No. 45413/07, 10.3.09.
[1060] No. 36378/97, 13.2.03.

the principle of equality of arms. The very failure of the domestic courts to make a formal decision in response to the applicant's request for a lawyer in the course of civil proceedings in *AB* v *Slovakia*[1061] was found to violate Article 6(1). Where a legal aid lawyer refuses to take a particular step in legal proceedings (such as lodging an appeal), Article 6(1) may be violated where the lawyer fails to give written reasons to the client[1062] or communicates with the client at such a late stage that the proceedings cannot in any event be pursued.[1063]

6.317 In *McVicar* v *UK*,[1064] the unavailability of legal aid to defend defamation proceedings did not violate Article 6. The applicant, a well-educated and experienced journalist, was not found to have been prevented from presenting his defence effectively. However, the applicants in *Steel and Morris* v *UK*[1065] were in a rather different position. They were members of a campaigning organisation who were sued for defamation by McDonald's, after distributing leaflets that were highly critical of the company's practices. The financial consequences of losing the case would have been significant for the applicants who were on low incomes. The libel proceedings were exceptionally complex: the trial at first instance lasted 313 court days; the appeal hearing lasted 23 days; there were 40,000 pages of documentary evidence and 130 oral witnesses, including experts; the case was legally complex (100 days of legal argument—38 separate written judgments); the judgments of the trial court and the Court of Appeal exceeded 1,100 pages. Consequently, the Court held that Article 6(1) had been violated, concluding that the denial of legal aid deprived the applicants of the opportunity to present their case effectively and contributed to an unacceptable inequality of arms.

6.318 In adjudicating on claims relating to the right of access to court, the European Court has in a number of cases had to discern the difference between *substantive* and *procedural* limitations in domestic case law. Where the domestic law delimits the substantive content of the 'right' itself, Article 6 will not apply, but Article 6 will apply to provisions of domestic law that bar or restrict access to a judicial remedy to determine the merits of claims relating to 'civil rights' recognised by the domestic law. The distinction between substantive and procedural limitations can be problematic, as is indicated by some of the decisions discussed below which have split the Court.[1066] The application of the principle of immunity from suit in negligence proceedings in the United Kingdom has been the subject of a number of Court judgments. In *Osman* v *UK*,[1067] the Court found a violation of Article 6 arising from the domestic courts' application of the immunity that the police enjoyed from liability in negligence in relation to the investigation and suppression of crime. Ahmet Osman had

---

[1061] No. 41784/98, 4.3.03.

[1062] *Staroszczyk* v *Poland*, No. 59519/00, 22.3.07.

[1063] *Siałkowska* v *Poland*, No. 8932/05, 22.3.07. See, by contrast, *Kulikowski* v *Poland*, No. 18353/03 and *Antonicelli* v *Poland*, No. 2815/05, 28.5.09.

[1064] No. 46311/99, 9.5.02.

[1065] No. 68416/01, 15.2.05. See also *Faulkner* v *UK*, No. 30308/96, 30.11.99 (the unavailability of civil legal aid in Guernsey was found by the former Commission to violate the applicant's right of access to court. The case was settled before the Court, inter alia, on the Government's undertaking to establish a civil legal aid system in Guernsey).

[1066] See also *Greek-Catholic Parish of Lupeni and others* v *Romania*, No. 76943/11, 29.11.16 (decision about restitution of places of worship based on 'wishes of the adherents of the communities which owned the properties'—case held to relate to a substantive provision, not a procedural obstacle—no violation of right of access to court under Article 6(1) (by 12 votes to five)).

[1067] No. 23452/94, 28.2.98.

been injured (and his father shot dead) by a former teacher who had developed an obsession with him. The shooting followed a series of incidents involving the teacher that had been reported to the police. The applicants (Ahmet Osman and his mother) brought negligence proceedings against the police for failing to take adequate measures to apprehend the teacher. The action was struck out by the Court of Appeal on the basis that public policy required immunity from suit for the police in such situations. It was considered that the imposition of liability in negligence might lead to 'detrimentally defensive' policing and that a great deal of police time, trouble and expense might be diverted away from the suppression of crime and into defending litigation and that the threat of litigation itself would be a distraction.[1068] The European Court, however, unanimously found that the application of the exclusion of liability, without consideration of competing public interest factors, operated in a disproportionate manner to restrict the applicants' right of access to court, in violation of Article 6(1). In coming to this conclusion, the Court noted that the applicants had satisfied the proximity test applied in negligence proceedings and that this test would serve as a threshold to limit the number of negligence cases against the police that would be likely to proceed to trial.

However, the decision was reviewed in *TP and KM v UK*,[1069] where the applicants alleged **6.319** a denial of access to court due to the striking out of their claims in negligence against the local authority, which related to the removal of their children into care. The Court found no violation of Article 6 as the cases had been struck out as disclosing no reasonable cause of action, and not because of any exclusionary rule or limitation period. In the judgment in *Z and others v UK*,[1070] the Court found that its reasoning in *Osman* 'was based on an understanding of the law of negligence ... which has to be reviewed in the light of the clarifications subsequently made by the domestic courts and notably the House of Lords',[1071] which had found that the law of negligence did not disclose the operation of an immunity. A similar conclusion was reached by a majority of the Grand Chamber in *Roche v UK*[1072] concerning the application of the Crown Proceedings Act, which limited the liability of the state in tort to servicemen, and prevented the applicant from bringing proceedings relating to chemical testing in the 1960s. The provision in question was held to be a provision of *substantive* law that limited the rights of servicemen in respect of damages claims against the state—it was *not* a procedural bar. Accordingly, the applicant had no 'civil right' and Article 6 was inapplicable. In the case of *Markovic and others v Italy*[1073] the applicants were relatives of victims of the NATO bombing of the RTS broadcasting centre in Belgrade in 1999 who sought to bring tortious claims in the Italian courts, but which were dismissed by the Court of Cassation. By a majority of ten votes to seven, the Grand Chamber found no violation of Article 6, taken together with Article 1, on the basis that the domestic case law excluded

---

[1068] *Osman and another v Ferguson and another* [1993] 4 All ER 344. See also, *Hill v Chief Constable of West Yorkshire* [1989] AC 53 and *Swinney and another v Chief Constable of Northumbria* [1996] 3 All ER 449.

[1069] No. 28945/95, 10.5.01.

[1070] No. 29392/95, 10.5.01.

[1071] *Ibid.*, para. 100.

[1072] No. 32555/96, 19.10.05 (eight members of the Grand Chamber dissented, arguing that the applicant had had a civil right in respect of the tort of negligence, which was subject to a *procedural* limitation).

[1073] No. 1398/03, 14.12.06 (see also the comments on this case re Article 1 at section 6.05 above). See also *Chapman v Belgium*, No. 39619/06, dec. 5.3.13 (Belgian courts' refusal to examine merits of applicant's complaints due to NATO's immunity from jurisdiction—no impairment of very essence of right to a court—inadmissible).

any possibility of the state being held liable in such circumstances. There was, therefore, no limitation on the applicants' access to a court.[1074]

6.320 Where a government intervenes to block court proceedings, this is likely to violate the right of access to court, as was the case in *Tinnelly v UK*[1075] and *Devlin v UK*,[1076] where the Government had issued certificates on national security grounds to halt proceedings for discrimination being brought against the state. There had been no independent scrutiny of the facts leading to the issuing of the certificates and their effect was conclusively to prevent a judicial determination of the applicants' complaints. Therefore, this was not justified even by security considerations. The applicant in *Baka v Hungary*[1077] complained that his six-year mandate as president of the Supreme Court had been terminated prematurely, after he had been critical about proposed legislative reforms relating to the judiciary. Finding that this decision was not open to review, either by an ordinary tribunal or any other body exercising judicial powers, the Grand Chamber also noted that the lack of judicial review was the result of legislation whose compatibility with the requirements of the rule of law was doubtful. Accordingly, the applicant was denied the right of access to court in violation of Article 6(1). The case of *Fazliyski v Bulgaria*[1078] concerned the dismissal of a Ministry of Internal Affairs intelligence officer, after officials at the Psychology Institute (which was part of the same Ministry) certified him to be mentally unfit for work. There was a violation of Article 6(1) because in reviewing the case, the judges of the supreme administrative court considered themselves to be bound by this certification and refused to scrutinise it independently, thus depriving themselves of jurisdiction.[1079] At issue in *Al-Dulimi and Montana Management Inc. v Switzerland*[1080] was the applicants' inability to challenge the imposition of sanctions by the Swiss authorities, pursuant to UN Security Council Resolution 1483 requiring the assets of former Iraqi government representatives to be frozen. The Grand Chamber found that Resolution 1483 did not contain any clear or explicit wording excluding the possibility of judicial supervision of the measures taken for its implementation. The Swiss authorities had had a duty to ensure that the listing of the applicants by the UN Sanctions Committee had not been arbitrary, but they were not given the opportunity to submit any evidence and therefore the very essence of their right of access to a court was impaired, and accordingly there was a violation of Article 6(1) (by 15 votes to two).

6.321 Granting state immunity (to a foreign state) has been interpreted as a procedural bar on the national courts' power to determine the right in question, rather than as qualifying a substantive right.[1081] The granting of state immunity in *Al-Adsani v UK*,[1082] a case concerning

---

[1074] The President of the Court, Judge Costa, described the majority's reasoning as being 'unconvincing and self-contradictory' and six judges joined Judge Zagrebelsky in his dissenting opinion which concluded that the majority decision struck 'a blow at the very foundation of the Convention'.

[1075] Nos. 20390/92 and 21322/92, 10.7.98.

[1076] No. 29545/95, 30.10.01. See also *Devenney v UK*, No. 24265/94, 19.3.02.

[1077] No. 20261/12, 23.6.16. There was also a violation of Article 10 (discussed below at 6.595).

[1078] No. 40908/05, 16.4.13.

[1079] There was also a separate violation of Article 6(1) in *Fazliyski* because of the domestic court's failure to deliver its judgments publicly.

[1080] No. 5809/08, 21.6.16. See also *Nada v Switzerland*, No. 10593/08, 12.9.12 (imposition of travel ban pursuant to UN Security Council resolution—violation of Article 8)—discussed below at 6.519.

[1081] *Al-Adsani v UK*, No. 35763/97, 21.11.01; *Fogarty v UK*, No. 37182/97, 21.11.01; *McElhinney v Ireland*, No. 31253/96, 21.11.01.

[1082] No. 35763/97, 21.11.01. See also *Jones and others v UK*, Nos. 34356/06 and 40528/06, 14.1.14 (as regards torture allegedly committed by Saudi Arabian officials—in which the Court also considered the

torture allegedly committed by the Kuwaiti authorities, was, however, found to pursue a legitimate aim, which sought to comply with international law 'to promote comity and good relations between states through the respect of another state's sovereignty'. The Court found that such measures, which reflected generally recognised rules of public international law on state immunity, could not in principle be regarded as imposing a disproportionate restriction on the right of access to court. There was no acceptance in international law of the proposition that states are not entitled to immunity regarding civil claims for alleged torture committed outside the forum state. There was accordingly no violation of Article 6(1) in *Al-Adsani* as the application by the domestic courts of legislation which upheld Kuwait's claim to immunity did not amount to an unjustified restriction on the applicants' right of access to court (by just nine votes to eight).[1083] In *Fogarty* v *UK*,[1084] there was no violation of Article 6 where the UK courts conferred immunity on the United States, in relation to proceedings for discrimination brought by an applicant for an embassy post. There were similarities to *Fogarty* in the case of *Cudak* v *Lithuania*,[1085] which concerned the application of state immunity in proceedings relating to the dismissal of a telephone operator in the Polish Embassy. However, taking account of the international law trend towards limiting state immunity in respect of employment-related disputes, and that the applicant's duties could not be claimed to have been related to the sovereign interests of the Polish Government, the Grand Chamber in *Cudak* found that the application of state immunity in her case was disproportionate and impaired the essence of her right of access to court, in violation of Article 6(1). In *Oleynikov* v *Russia*,[1086] the domestic courts' refusal to examine the applicant's debt claim against a Korean Embassy Trade Counsellor, on the basis of absolute state immunity from jurisdiction, was found to be a disproportionate restriction on his right of access to court, in breach of Article 6(1).

In *Kalogeropoulou and 256 others* v *Germany and Greece*,[1087] the applicants were the rela- **6.322** tives of victims of a massacre by Nazi occupation forces at Distomo in 1944. Their complaint about the Greek state's refusal to allow them to enforce compensation awards against Germany because of the application of sovereign immunity was declared inadmissible under Article 6(1).

---

particular position of 'state officials', and came to the same conclusions as regards the granting of immunity to the state, as it did in *Al-Adsani*). See further *Naït-Liman* v *Switzerland*, No. 51357/07, 21.6.16 (absence of universal jurisdiction of civil courts in torture cases—no violation of Article 6(1)) (case referred to Grand Chamber 28.11.16).

[1083] Seven judges in the minority argued that if it was accepted that the prohibition of torture was *jus cogens*, then states could not hide behind rules of state immunity (which were hierarchically lower rules) to avoid the consequences of the illegality of its actions. The UK courts should not therefore have accepted a plea of immunity. However, in the later case of *Jones* v *UK*, Nos. 34356/06 and 40528/06, 14.1.14, noting the judgment of the International Court of Justice in *Germany* v *Italy*, 3 February 2012, the Court found that no *jus cogens* exception to state immunity had yet been recognised.

[1084] No. 37182/97, 21.11.01. See also *Manoilescu and Dobrescu* v *Romania*, No. 60861/00, dec. 3.3.05 (foreign state diplomatic immunity barred applicants' claim for restitution of property used as Russian embassy—declared inadmissible).

[1085] No. 15869/02, 23.3.10. See also *Sabeh El Leil* v *France*, No. 34869/05, 29.6.11 (the applicant had been an accountant in the Kuwaiti embassy in Paris); *Wallishauser* v *Austria*, No. 156/04, 17.7.12 (failure of domestic courts to accept service of legal proceedings against foreign state made in accordance with rules of customary international law); *Naku* v *Lithuania and Sweden*, No. 26126/07, 8.11.16.

[1086] No. 36703/04, 14.3.13.

[1087] No. 59021/00, dec. 12.12.02. See also *Grosz* v *France*, No. 14717/06, dec. 16.6.09.

6.323 The Court has confirmed the legitimacy of states granting immunity from domestic jurisdiction to international organisations, in view, in particular, of the trend towards enhancing international co-operation, in many areas. Furthermore, measures taken which reflect generally recognised rules of public international law as regards the immunity of international organisations will not in principle be considered as a disproportionate restriction on the right of access to court.[1088] For example, the case of *Stichting Mothers of Srebrenica and others v Netherlands*[1089] concerned the refusal of the Dutch courts to hear a claim against the UN arising out of the Srebrenica massacre. It was found inadmissible on the basis that granting immunity to the UN served a legitimate purpose and was not disproportionate.

6.324 Parliamentary privilege survived a challenge under Article 6(1) in *A v UK*,[1090] where the applicant was named by her constituency MP during a parliamentary debate as being a 'neighbour from hell'. She was unable to bring civil defamation proceedings as the MP was protected by absolute parliamentary privilege. The Court found that the parliamentary immunity enjoyed by the MP pursued the legitimate aims of protecting free speech in Parliament and maintaining the separation of powers between the legislature and the judiciary. Whilst the Court found the MP's statements in question to be 'particularly regrettable', the Court held the restrictions on the applicant's right of access to Court not to be disproportionate having regard to the importance of protecting freedom of speech in Parliament, and bearing in mind that the privilege only attached to statements made during parliamentary debates.

6.325 In contrast, there was a violation of Article 6(1) arising from the application of parliamentary immunity in the case of *Cordova v Italy*.[1091] There, the applicant public prosecutor had commenced civil party proceedings for damage to his reputation as a result of statements made by two Members of Parliament. Those proceedings were terminated after resolutions were passed by the Senate and Chamber of Deputies finding that they were covered by parliamentary immunity. As the statements in question were found to have been made in the context of personal disputes, rather than arising out of the MPs' parliamentary duties, as such, and as the decisions restricting the applicant's access to court were made by political bodies, the Court found that the notion of proportionality between the aim pursued and the means employed should be interpreted narrowly. Furthermore, Article 6 had been violated as there were no alternative means for the applicant to protect his rights. Article 6(1) was also breached in *Urechean and Pavlicenco v Moldova*[1092] due to the Moldovan President's immunity from libel proceedings. Although the immunity only applied 'in the exercise of his mandate', the domestic courts had failed to assess whether, as regards the President's statements in issue, he had been acting in the course of his official duties or not. Therefore, his immunity was, in effect, perpetual and absolute. Such a blanket immunity amounted to a disproportionate restriction on the applicants' right of access to a court.

[1088] See, e.g. *Waite and Kennedy v Germany*, No. 26083/94, 18.2.99, para. 63; *Fogarty v UK*, No. 37182/97, 21.11.01, para. 36.

[1089] No. 65542/12, dec. 11.6.13. Noting that the applicants sought to challenge the use by the Security Council of its powers under Chapter VII of the United Nations Charter, the Court found that the acts or omissions of the Security Council could not be subject to domestic jurisdiction without UN agreement.

[1090] No. 35373/97, 17.12.02.

[1091] Nos. 40877/98 and 45649/99, 30.1.03. See also *de Jorio v Italy*, No. 73936/01, 3.6.04; *C.G.I.L. and Cofferati v Italy*, No. 46967/07, 24.2.09.

[1092] Nos. 27756/05 and 41219/07, 2.12.14.

In contrast to these cases, the applicant in *Kart* v *Turkey*[1093] was himself an MP who was **6.326** accused of committing criminal offences (prior to his election, whilst acting in his capacity as a lawyer), who complained that parliamentary immunity prevented him from being tried. Article 6 was held to be applicable on the basis that he was entitled to be heard by a court within a reasonable time once the judicial process had been set in motion, in order to ensure that, as an accused person, he did not have to remain too long in a state of uncertainty about the outcome of the proceedings. However, the Grand Chamber found no violation of Article 6 (by 13 votes to four—overturning a Chamber finding of a violation by four votes to three). The Court took into account that parliamentary inviolability legitimately sought to ensure the independence of Parliament by preventing any possibility of politically motivated criminal proceedings, and that states were permitted a wide margin of appreciation as to this question. It also noted that the scope of the protection was limited: to the duration of an MP's term; to criminal proceedings (not civil); and that immunity could be lifted. As to the applicant's particular circumstances, the Court found that when he stood for office, he would have been aware of the consequences of his election for the pending criminal proceedings against him. The procedure did not affect the presumption of innocence and there was no reason to believe that he would not have a fair trial when he ceased to be an MP. Accordingly, the Court concluded that the failure to lift the applicant's parliamentary immunity did not impair his right to a court to an extent that was disproportionate to the legitimate aim pursued.

The right of access to court must include a right to obtain a *determination* of a dispute, **6.327** not just a right to instigate proceedings. Therefore, this right also requires the implementation of final and binding judicial decisions which must not remain inoperative to the detriment of one of the parties.[1094] This principle was breached in *Immobiliare Saffi* v *Italy*[1095] where a final judgment was stayed for over six years as a result of the intervention of the legislature. In *Burdov* v *Russia*,[1096] there had been delays in the payment of an award of compensation (in respect of the applicant's exposure to radioactive emissions). The Court has emphasised that financial difficulties experienced by the state cannot justify failing to honour a judgment debt (although it could justify a delay, provided of course that the essence of the right under Article 6(1) is not impaired).[1097] In *Kutić* v *Croatia*,[1098] the applicant's house had been blown up in 1991 and a civil action for damages had been barred (at a stage prior to judgment) by legislation in 1996 that stayed a series of civil proceedings resulting from 'terrorist acts'. The Court found a violation of Article 6(1) as the applicants had been prevented from having their civil claims determined by the domestic

---

[1093] No. 8917/05, 3.12.09.
[1094] *Hornsby* v *Greece*, No. 18357/91, 19.3.97; *Turczanik* v *Poland*, No. 38064/97, 5.7.05; *Jeličić* v *Bosnia and Herzegovina*, No. 41183/02, 31.10.06.
[1095] No. 22774/93, 28.7.99.
[1096] No. 59498/00, 7.5.02. See also *Timofeyev* v *Russia*, No. 58263/00, 23.10.03.
[1097] See, e.g. *Prodan* v *Moldova*, No. 49806/99, 18.5.04, para. 53; *Qufaj Co. Sh.p.k.* v *Albania*, No. 54268, 18.11.04, para. 38; *Poznakhirina* v *Russia*, No. 25964/02, 24.2.05, para. 23; *Amat-G Ltd and Mebaghishvili* v *Georgia*, N0. 2507/03, 27.9.05, para. 48.
[1098] No. 48778/99, 1.3.02. See also: *Multiplex* v *Croatia*, No. 58112/00, 19.6.03; *Aćimović* v *Croatia*, No. 61237/00, 9.10.03 (however in *Aćimović* there was no additional violation of Article 6 as a result of the Liability Act of 2003 which enabled the courts to proceed with the applicant's case but imposed new conditions under which the state was liable for damage caused to the applicant's property, as it was yet to be seen how the domestic courts would interpret the new legislation).

courts for a long period. The failure to implement a judgment awarding compensation to the applicant (following the nationalisation of her plot of land and the destruction of her house) in *Jasiūnienė v Lithuania*[1099] was said to be 'aggravated' by the Government's challenge in the European Court proceedings to the very merit of the applicant's property claims and the Government's attempts to impose on the applicant particular obligations as a result of regulations that post-dated the judgment in question. In *Garcia Mateos v Spain*[1100] there was a violation of Article 6(1) taken together with Article 14 because of the failure to enforce a judgment acknowledging gender discrimination against the applicant, a working mother.

6.328 The non-enforcement (or delayed enforcement) of domestic court judgments has reached such a scale in a number of states, that the Court has issued 'pilot judgments' identifying them as systemic violations requiring the implementation of effective domestic remedies (see 3.23 above).[1101]

6.329 Both the rule of law and the principle of legal certainty are further important aspects of the requirement to be able to obtain a binding determination of a dispute. In *Brumarescu v Romania*,[1102] this principle was violated as the Procurator-General was able to overturn an entire judicial process. In *Sovtransavto Holding v Ukraine*,[1103] the 'supervisory review' procedure was held to fall foul of the principle of legal certainty. There, final court judgments were in effect reviewable indefinitely because of the discretionary power of the President of the Supreme Arbitration Tribunal, the Attorney-General and their deputies, to challenge court decisions. The Court was critical that the Ukrainian authorities, 'acting at the highest level', intervened in the proceedings on a number of occasions, which was held to be incompatible with the notion of an independent and impartial tribunal (see further 6.368 below).

6.330 The right of access to court was found to have been violated in *Khamidov v Russia*,[1104] where the applicant was prevented from bringing a civil claim concerning his eviction by the police from his land and buildings in Chechnya, because the judicial system was inoperative in Chechnya between October 1999 and January 2001 (due to the armed conflict) and yet he was required by the domestic law to issue proceedings in the region where he lived.

[1099] No. 41510/98, 6.3.03.

[1100] No. 38285/09, 19.2.13.

[1101] See, e.g. *Burdov (No. 2) v Russia*, No. 33509/04, 15.1.09; *Olaru and others v Moldova*, Nos. 476/07, 22539/05, 17911/08 and 13136/07, 28.7.09; *Yuriy Nikolayevich Ivanov v Ukraine*, No. 40450/04, 15.10.09.

[1102] No. 28342/95, 23.1.01.

[1103] No. 48553/99, 25.7.02. See also *Ryabykh v Russia*, No. 52854/99, 24.7.03. There was, however, no violation of Article 6 arising from the use of the supervisory review procedure in *Protsenko v Russia*, No. 13151/04, 31.7.08 (application brought by a third party who had not been aware of the proceedings and had therefore not been able to lodge an ordinary appeal). The reforms carried out in 2003 as regards supervisory review at the Russian Supreme Commercial Court (abolishing the discretion of the President and Deputy President to initiate supervisory review proceedings) have been found to comply with Article 6—see *OOO Link Oil SPB v Russia*, No. 42600/05, dec. 25.6.09. There, the commercial court decisions concerning the applicant company were only open to challenge once, on the defendant party's request, on the basis of restricted grounds and within a clearly defined and limited time-frame. There was also no violation of Article 6 in *Trapeznikov and others v Russia*, No. 5623/09 et al, 5.4.16 as regards the application of supervisory review in civil proceedings, following amendments made between 2008 and 2012.

[1104] No. 72118/01, 15.11.07.

Fair hearing

The right to a fair hearing in Article 6(1) applies both to criminal and civil proceedings. The **6.331** Court has constantly emphasised that its role is to consider whether the proceedings *as a whole* were fair.[1105] The Court may overlook minor infringements provided that overall the proceedings were fair and, conversely, unfairness may still arise even though the relevant formal requirements may have been complied with. The Court has reiterated that it will not be concerned with applicants' complaints about errors of fact or law committed by domestic courts, unless rights protected by the Convention have as a result been infringed. It is not a 'court of appeal' from the domestic courts.

The Court's default position is not to question the interpretation of domestic law by the **6.332** national courts, unless there is 'evident arbitrariness' or where the domestic courts have applied the law 'manifestly erroneously or so as to reach arbitrary conclusions and/or a denial of justice'.[1106] The case of *Andelković v Serbia*,[1107] concerned the applicant's claim for holiday pay which was initially upheld, but was overturned on appeal. The European Court found that the appeal court decision had no legal foundation, that it was based on 'an abstract assertion quite outside of any reasonable judicial discretion'[1108] and accordingly that such an arbitrary decision denied the applicant a fair hearing, in violation of Article 6(1). There was a similar finding in *Bochan v Ukraine (No. 2)*[1109] arising from the Ukrainian Supreme Court's gross misrepresentation of an earlier Strasbourg judgment in the applicant's case. According to the Supreme Court, the European Court had found that the domestic courts' decisions in her case had been lawful and well-founded, which was quite incorrect, and which the Grand Chamber of the European Court held to be 'grossly arbitrary' or amounting to a 'denial of justice'. In the criminal sphere, the Court is attuned to detect what may amount to political prosecutions. The case of *Navalnyy and Ofitserov v Russia*[1110] concerned the prosecution and conviction of the applicants for fraud-related offences. The first applicant was the political opposition leader, Aleksey Navalnyy, who had been conducting an anti-corruption campaign targeting, inter alios, the Russian President, the Deputy Prime Minister and the Chief of the Investigative Committee. The Court noted that the domestic courts had found the second applicant guilty of acts which were indistinguishable from regular commercial activities, and the first applicant for fostering them. This led the Court to conclude that 'the criminal law was arbitrarily and unforeseeably construed to the detriment of the applicants, leading to a manifestly unreasonable outcome of the trial'.[1111] It also took account of the fact that the courts had dismissed out of hand the applicants' allegations of political persecution, which it considered were at least arguable (noting that the opening and re-opening of the criminal prosecution coincided with the first applicant's activities, and that his conviction

---

[1105] See, e.g. *Khan v UK*, No. 35394/97, 12.5.00, paras. 34 and 38; *D.D. v Lithuania*, No. 13469/06, 14.2.12, para. 126.

[1106] See, e.g. *De Moor v Belgium*, No. 16997/90, 23.6.94; *Farbers and Harlanova v Latvia*, No 57313/00, dec. 6.9.01; *Adamsons v Latvia*, No. 3669/03, 24.6.08, para. 118; *Barać and others v Montenegro*, No. 47974/06, 13.12.11; *Andelković v Serbia*, No. 1401/08, 9.4.13, para. 24.

[1107] No. 1401/08, 9.4.13.

[1108] *Ibid.*, para. 27.

[1109] No. 22251/08, 5.2.15.

[1110] Nos. 46632/13 and 28671/14, 23.2.16. In their joint partly dissenting opinion, Judges Nicolaou, Keller and Dedov argued that the Court should also have considered on the merits the applicants' complaint under Article 18 together with Article 6 (which was declared inadmissible by a majority).

[1111] *Ibid.*, para. 115.

meant that he could not stand for election and led to restrictions on his movements and a ban on his making public statements).

6.333   As to the 'overall fairness' test, the Court has held that

> ... regard must be had to whether the rights of the defence were respected. It must be examined in particular whether the applicant was given the opportunity to challenge the authenticity of the evidence and to oppose its use. In addition, the quality of the evidence must be taken into consideration, including whether the circumstances in which it was obtained cast doubt on its reliability or accuracy.[1112]

Therefore, where it is alleged that evidence has been planted on a suspect, the Court will review whether the circumstances in which it was obtained casts doubt on its reliability or accuracy and also whether the applicant was given the opportunity to challenge its authenticity in the domestic proceedings. In several cases against Azerbaijan in which it was alleged that the police had planted drugs on suspects, the Court found violations of Article 6(1) on this basis, not least because the police had failed to conduct a search immediately after an arrest without good reason, and the domestic courts had failed to rule at all on the question of the authenticity of the evidence.[1113]

6.334   Furthermore, this principle may be breached where, for example, the domestic courts simply ignore 'pertinent and important points' made by a defendant,[1114] or rely too readily on the version of events put forward by the authorities.[1115] In *Jokšas* v *Lithuania*[1116] the applicant brought legal proceedings to challenge his dismissal from the armed forces. Applying the overall fairness test, the Court found a violation of Article 6(1) because the administrative courts failed to address the applicant's allegation of discrimination which was considered to be at the heart of his case. The Court has held that it is a requirement of fairness that the prosecuting authorities disclose to the defence all material evidence for or against the accused. The failure to do so gave rise to a defect in the trial proceedings in *Edwards* v *UK*,[1117] but there was no violation of Article 6 as the defects in the original trial were found to have been remedied by the subsequent procedure before the Court of Appeal that had examined the transcript of the trial and considered the impact of the new information on the conviction. In *CG* v *UK*,[1118] the Court commented on the 'excessive and undesirable' way in which the judge had interrupted the applicant's counsel in domestic criminal proceedings, but there was no violation of Article 6 because, as a whole, the proceedings were nevertheless not deemed to be unfair.

6.335   The right to a fair trial includes the right of legal certainty, and accordingly Article 6 may be violated where there is inconsistent adjudication of claims brought by people in similar situations and which leads to a state of uncertainty. The possibility of conflicting decisions is inherent in any judicial system, and so the Court will assess whether there are 'profound

---

[1112] See, e.g. *Sevinç and others* v *Turkey*, No. 8074/02, dec. 8.1.08; *Bykov* v *Russia*, No. 4378/02, 10.3.09; *Lisica* v *Croatia*, No. 20100/06, 25.2.10; *Erkapić* v *Croatia*, No. 51198/08, 25.4.13.

[1113] *Layijov* v *Azerbaijan*, No. 22062/07, 10.4.14; *Sakit Zahidov* v *Azerbaijan*, No. 51164/07, 12.11.15.

[1114] See, e.g. *Nechiporuk and Yonkalo* v *Ukraine*, No. 42310/04, 21.4.11; *Vyerentsov* v *Ukraine*, No. 20372/11, 11.4.13.

[1115] See, e.g. *Kasparov and others* v *Russia*, No. 21613/07, 3.10.13.

[1116] No. 25330/07, 12.11.13.

[1117] No. 13071/87, 25.11.92.

[1118] No. 43773/98, 19.12.01.

and long-standing differences' in the case-law, whether the domestic law provides a means to overcome such inconsistencies, and also whether those mechanisms have been applied and, if so, to what effect.[1119] The Court has considered claims relating to decisions made by a single court,[1120] and also claims relating to decisions made by different courts.[1121] States are required to establish mechanisms which ensure consistency in court practice and uniformity of the courts' case-law[1122] and also to organise their legal systems in such a way as to avoid the adoption of discordant judgments.[1123]

The notion of a fair hearing also incorporate the right to adversarial proceedings: 'the parties must have the opportunity not only to have made known any evidence needed for their claims to succeed, but also to have knowledge of, and comment on, all evidence adduced or observations filed, with a view to influencing the court's decision'.[1124] The Court has held that stricter scrutiny of the fairness of proceedings is required where the measures taken have a strong impact on a person's private life, such as divesting someone of their legal capacity.[1125] The right to a fair hearing may be violated because of the failure to give a litigant sufficient notification of a hearing.[1126] The conditions in a court room (such as the use of glass cabins for defendants) may violate the right to a fair hearing.[1127]

6.336 In *Avotiņš* v *Latvia*[1128] the applicant complained about the enforcement in Latvia of a judgment delivered in Cyprus in his absence. The Grand Chamber reiterated that Article 6(1) is applicable to the execution of foreign final judgments—the issue before the Court was whether the Latvian courts acted in compliance with the Convention in finding the Cypriot judgment enforceable, which they had done in accordance with the 'Brussels I Regulation' concerning the recognition and enforcement of judgments in civil and commercial matters[1129] (which the applicant alleged had been breached). Therefore, as Latvia had been acting pursuant to its obligations as a member of the European Union, the Court

---

[1119] *Nejdet Şahin and Perihan Şahin* v *Turkey*, No. 13279/05, 20.10.11, para. 53 (alleged disparities between the judgments of two hierarchically unrelated, different and independent types of court—no violation of Article 6 (by 10 votes to 7). The seven dissenting judges argued that the machinery for settling conflicts between courts was inadequate: 'If justice is not to degenerate into a lottery, the scope of litigants' rights should not depend simply on which court hears their case. The fact that litigants can receive diametrically opposite answers to the same legal question depending on which type of court examines their case can only undermine the credibility of the courts and weaken public confidence in the judicial system').

[1120] See, e.g. *Tudor Tudor* v *Romania*, No. 21911/03, 24.3.09.

[1121] See, e.g. *Ştefănică and others* v *Romania*, No. 38155/02, 2.11.10. See also *S.C. IMH Suceava S.R.L.* v *Romania*, No. 24935/04, 29.10.13 (two different decisions by different courts as to the admissibility of the same piece of evidence—insufficient reasoning—violation of Article 6(1)).

[1122] *Schwarzkopf and Taussik* v *Czech Republic*, No. 42162/02, dec. 2.12.08.

[1123] *Vrioni and others* v *Albania*, No. 2141/03, 24.3.09; *Mullai and others* v *Albania*, No. 9074/07, 23.3.10; *Brezovec* v *Croatia*, No. 13488/07, 29.3.11.

[1124] See, e.g. *K.S.* v *Finland*, No. 29346/95, 31.5.01, para. 21.

[1125] *X and Y* v *Croatia*, No. 5193/09, 3.11.11 (applicant was neither notified of the proceedings concerning her legal capacity, nor was she summoned by the court to give evidence, nor seen by the judge conducting the proceedings—violations of Articles 6 and 8).

[1126] See, e.g. *Zavodnik* v *Slovenia*, No. 53723/13, 21.5.15.

[1127] See, e.g. *Yaroslav Belousov* v *Russia*, Nos. 2653/13 and 60980/14, 4.10.16 (defendants held in over-crowded glass cabin in court room—unnecessary and disproportionate restrictions on applicant's rights to participate effectively in proceedings and to receive practical and effective legal assistance—violation of Article 6 (and Article 3)).

[1128] No. 17502/07, 23.5.16.

[1129] Council Regulation (EC) No. 44/2001 of 22 December 2000 on jurisdiction and the recognition and enforcement of judgments in civil and commercial matters.

applied the presumption of equivalent protection (the 'Bosphorus presumption')[1130]—in other words, that EU law incorporates protections equivalent to those in the European Convention. This presumption is subject to two conditions: the absence of any margin of manoeuvre on the part of the domestic authorities and the deployment of the full potential of the supervisory mechanism provided for by European Union law. On the first point, the Court found that the Regulation had been directly applicable in Latvia and the Latvian court had had no 'margin of manoeuvre'. The Court also found the second condition satisfied (and that it had not been necessary for the Latvian court to request a preliminary ruling from the CJEU). Therefore, the Bosphorus presumption was applicable. Noting in particular that the applicant could have challenged the judgment in question in the Cypriot courts, but had not done so, the Grand Chamber concluded on the facts that the protection of fundamental rights had not been manifestly deficient such that the presumption of equivalent protection was rebutted. Accordingly, there was no violation of Article 6.

6.337 The fair hearing principle was breached in *Milatová and others* v *Czech Republic*,[1131] where, during appeal proceedings before the Constitutional Court, the Court was not required to serve on the applicants copies of written observations submitted by the lower court and the defendant to the proceedings. The refusal to allow a litigant to adduce expert evidence may breach the right to a fair hearing.[1132]

6.338 The Court found a violation of Article 6 in *Perlala* v *Greece*[1133] because the Court of Cassation declared inadmissible the applicant's ground of appeal claiming a violation of Article 6, on the basis that Article 6 was not directly applicable in the case and that, for it to be taken into consideration, the applicant would have had to rely on it in conjunction with one of the grounds of appeal in the Code of Criminal Procedure. As, under the Constitution, the Convention was an integral part of the domestic legal system, the European Court found that such a decision considerably undermined the protection of individuals' rights before the highest domestic court. In *Natsvlishvili and Togonidze* v *Georgia*,[1134] the Court found no violation of Article 6(1) (or of Article 2 of Protocol No. 7) as a result of plea bargaining. This amounted to a waiver of the first applicant's right to a hearing of his case on the merits, and to appellate review, which had been agreed to on a voluntary basis, without any duress or false promises by the prosecution, and which was accompanied by adequate safeguards against possible abuse of process.

6.339 The application of the general principle of the right to a fair trial is discussed further below in relation to the following aspects: admissibility of evidence (6.340); privilege against self-incrimination and the right to silence (6.347); and equality of arms (6.353).

Admissibility of evidence

6.340 The Court has repeatedly emphasised that the question of the admissibility of evidence is primarily a matter for regulation by national law and a matter for national courts to assess.

[1130] See the discussion of the Bosphorus presumption at 4.158.
[1131] No. 61811/00, 21.6.05. See also *Krčmář and others* v *Czech Republic*, No. 35376/97, 3.3.00.
[1132] See, e.g. *Schlumpf* v *Switzerland*, No. 29002/06, 8.1.09.
[1133] No. 17721/04, 22.2.07.
[1134] No. 9043/05, 29.4.14.

The Court's task is to assess the fairness of the whole proceedings, rather than to decide whether evidence was properly admitted or not.[1135] Accordingly, Article 6 does not lay down any rules as to the admissibility of evidence as such, which is considered to be primarily a matter for domestic regulation.[1136]

The use in evidence of a confession obtained from a detainee who did not have access to a **6.341** lawyer is likely to violate Article 6. This was the case in *Salduz* v *Turkey*,[1137] in which the 17-year-old applicant was arrested on suspicion of aiding and abetting an illegal organisation. Without a lawyer being present, he gave a statement to the police admitting that he had taken part in an unlawful demonstration and written a slogan on a banner, but he subsequently retracted the statement, claiming it had been extracted under duress. The denial of access to a lawyer had been an automatic consequence of the domestic law, as the offence in issue fell within the jurisdiction of the state security courts, and therefore there had been no assessment of the need for this restriction in the particular circumstances of the case (and no consideration of the applicant's age). The statement was the main evidence used to convict the applicant and the Court concluded that neither the subsequent legal assistance he received nor the adversarial nature of the proceedings cured the defects that had occurred during police custody.

The Court has declined to decide whether, as a matter of principle, unlawfully obtained evi- **6.342** dence should be inadmissible, but will consider whether the proceedings as a whole, including the way in which evidence was obtained, were fair. This will entail an examination of the 'unlawfulness' in question and the nature of any violation of another Convention right. The applicant in *Khan* v *UK*,[1138] complained about the admission in evidence of material obtained from a police bugging device, the use of which was found by the Court to violate Article 8 because of the lack of any domestic legal regulation. Applying the overall fairness test, the Court found no violation of Article 6. It was noted that the use of the listening device had not been contrary to domestic criminal law and whilst the material was the only evidence against the applicant, it was considered to be very strong evidence. Finally, the Court noted that the applicant had had ample opportunity to challenge the authenticity and use of the recording and that the domestic courts had assessed the effect of the admission of the evidence on the fairness of the trial.[1139]

Rather different considerations will apply, however, in relation to evidence that is obtained **6.343** in violation of Article 3. Thus, the Court has sought to emphasise that:[1140]

[1135] See, e.g. *Doorson* v *Netherlands*, No. 20524/92, 26.3.96, para. 67.

[1136] See, e.g. *Schenk* v *Switzerland*, No. 10862/84, Series A, No. 140, 12.7.88 and *Teixeira de Castro* v *Portugal*, No. 25829/94, 9.6.98.

[1137] No. 36391/02, 27.11.08. See also *Panovits* v *Cyprus*, No. 4268/04, 11.12.08; *A.T.* v *Luxembourg*, No. 30460/13, 9.4.15. In contrast see *Yoldaş* v *Turkey*, No. 27503/04, 23.2.10 (free and unequivocal waiver by suspect of right to a lawyer in police custody—no violation of Article 6(1) or 6(3)(c), by four votes to three); *Bandaletov* v *Ukraine*, No. 23180/06, 31.10.13 (no legal representation at initial stage of investigation when applicant made confession during interview as witness—no violation of Article 6(3)(c)).

[1138] No. 35394/97, 12.5.00.

[1139] See also *PG and JH* v *UK*, No. 44787/98, 25.9.01. In her dissenting opinion in this case, Judge Tulkens argued that a trial could not be considered 'fair' where evidence obtained in breach of another Convention right (Article 8) had been admitted during the trial. This issue was revisited by the Grand Chamber in *Bykov* v *Russia*, No. 4378/02, 10.3.09, notably by the concurring and dissenting opinions.

[1140] See also: *Gäfgen* v *Germany*, No. 22978/05, 1.6.10, para. 173; *El Haski* v *Belgium*, No. 649/08, 25.9.12, para. 85; *Turbylev* v *Russia*, No. 4722/09, 6.10.15, para. 90.

the use in criminal proceedings of statements obtained as a result of a violation of Article 3—irrespective of the classification of the treatment as torture, inhuman or degrading treatment—renders the proceedings as a whole automatically unfair, in breach of Article 6.

The proceedings will accordingly be considered unfair, irrespective of the probative value of the confession statement and irrespective of whether its use was decisive in securing the defendant's conviction.

6.344 The Court has also found that the same principle applies to the use of *real evidence* obtained as a direct result of torture. However, the admission of real evidence obtained as a result of an act qualified as inhuman treatment in breach of Article 3, but falling short of torture, will only breach Article 6 if it has been shown that the breach of Article 3 had a bearing on the outcome of the proceedings against the defendant—in other words, that it had an impact on his or her conviction or sentence.[1141] These principles apply both where the victim of the treatment contrary to Article 3 is the actual defendant, and also where the victim is a third party.[1142] In *Jalloh* v *Germany*[1143] the Grand Chamber found that forcefully administering emetics to the applicant, using a nasogastric tube, in order to recover drugs which he had swallowed, amounted to inhuman and degrading treatment in violation of Article 3. There, a majority of the Court found that the applicant's trial was unfair under Article 6 (by 11 votes to six), having regard to the fact that the drugs regurgitated by the applicant were the decisive element in securing his conviction, and that he was a small-scale drug-dealer who received a six-month suspended prison sentence.

6.345 In *Göçmen* v *Turkey*,[1144] the Court found a violation of the right to a fair trial in circumstances where the procedural guarantees had not prevented the use of evidence obtained in violation of Article 3 (the applicant had been ill-treated in police custody), in the absence of a lawyer and in breach of the privilege against self-incrimination. Article 6 was violated in *Harutyunyan* v *Armenia*[1145] as a confession was obtained from the applicant after prolonged ill-treatment in custody by military police and it was then relied upon in criminal proceedings to convict the applicant of murder. In *El Haski* v *Belgium*[1146] the applicant was a Moroccan national who was convicted of terrorism-related offences on the basis of statements made by a witness to the Moroccan authorities, which the applicant claimed had resulted from torture. On the facts, the Court found it established that there was a 'real risk' that the statements had been obtained using treatment prohibited by Article 3. Therefore, Article 6 required the domestic courts not to admit them in evidence, unless they had first verified that they had not been obtained through torture. However, in rejecting the applicant's request for the exclusion of the statements, the Court of Appeal had simply found that he had not adduced any 'concrete evidence' that would be capable of raising reasonable doubt about that. Accordingly, there was a violation of Article 6.

6.346 However, there was no violation of Articles 6(1) or 6(3) in *Gäfgen* v *Germany*,[1147] in spite of the fact that the applicant's statement was extracted by the police using 'inhuman treatment'

[1141] *Gäfgen* v *Germany*, No. 22978/05, 1.6.10, para. 178.

[1142] *Othman (Abu Qatada)* v *UK*, No. 8139/09, 17.1.12, para. 267; *El Haski* v *Belgium*, No. 649/08, 25.9.12, para. 85.

[1143] No. 54810/00, 11.7.06. There was also a separate finding of a violation of the privilege against self-incrimination—see 6.267 below.

[1144] No. 72000/01, 17.10.06.

[1145] No. 36549/03, 28.6.07.

[1146] No. 649/08, 25.9.12.

[1147] No. 22978/05, 1.6.10.

in violation of Article 3 (they threatened him with 'intolerable pain' if he refused to disclose the whereabouts of a boy whom he had abducted). The domestic court had treated the applicant's statement as being inadmissible, but the real evidence that had become known as a consequence (such as the discovery of the boy's body, the autopsy report, tyre tracks left by the applicant's car, and the applicant's personal effects) were treated as being admissible. However, the domestic court expressly based its findings of fact exclusively on a separate confession made by the applicant at the trial, and that was corroborated by other 'untainted' evidence (obtained without breaching Article 3). The Court also excluded the possibility that the breach of Article 3 in the course of the investigation proceedings had had a bearing on the applicant's confession at the trial: prior to making his trial confession he had been informed about his right to silence and that none of the statements he had previously made could be used as evidence against him. An 11–six majority of the Grand Chamber therefore concluded that the failure to exclude the real evidence did not have a bearing on the applicant's conviction and sentence, and that as his defence rights were respected, his trial as a whole was considered to have been fair.[1148]

See also below at 6.406 as to the attendance and examination of witnesses.

Privilege against self-incrimination and the right to silence

The Court has found that the privilege against self-incrimination and the right to silence **6.347** are at the heart of the notion of a fair procedure under Article 6. These rights have usually been considered by the Court in relation to Article 6(1), rather than Article 6(2).[1149] These principles presuppose that the authorities should seek to prove their case without resorting to evidence obtained coercively or oppressively in defiance of the will of the suspect—in order to avoid miscarriages of justice.[1150] In *Aleksandr Zaichenko v Russia*,[1151] the applicant was stopped in his car on his way home from work by police officers investigating the theft of fuel from his employer. Without cautioning him, the officers questioned him and he signed a record of inspection in which he admitted having taken the fuel from his service car. The applicant was subsequently convicted of theft. The Court found a violation of Article 6(1) because the trial court based the conviction on the statement that the applicant had given to the police without being informed of his right to not incriminate himself, and the detriment that he suffered in the pre-trial proceedings was not remedied at the trial.

The privilege against self-incrimination may be invoked in order to prevent the use of **6.348** certain evidence in criminal proceedings, although it may not prevent the authorities from obtaining the information, as in *Saunders v UK*.[1152] There, the admission in evidence in criminal proceedings of statements taken by inspectors from the Department of Trade

---

[1148] In their joint partly dissenting opinion, Judges Rozakis, Tulkens, Jebens, Ziemele, Bianku and Power argued that Article 6 was breached because real evidence secured as a result of a violation of Article 3 was admitted at the applicant's trial.

[1149] But see, e.g. *Heaney and McGuinness v Ireland*, No. 34720/97, 21.12.00 and *Quinn v Ireland*, No. 36887/97, 21.12.00—violations of both Article 6(1) and 6(2).

[1150] See, e.g. *John Murray v UK*, No. 18731/91, 8.2.96, para. 45.

[1151] No. 39660/02, 18.2.10.

[1152] No. 19187/91, 17.12.96. See also *IJL, GMR and AKP v UK*, Nos. 29522/95, 30056/96 and 30574/96, 19.9.00; *Kansal v UK*, No. 21413/02, 27.4.04 (statements taken under compulsory powers by the Official Receiver in the course of bankruptcy proceedings). But see: *King v UK*, No. 13881/02, dec. 8.4.03 (taxpayers' obligation to provide information about their financial affairs—inadmissible); *Staines v UK*, No. 41552/98, dec. 16.5.00.

and Industry under statutory powers of compulsion, was found to violate the privilege against self-incrimination. In *JB* v *Switzerland*,[1153] the applicant received several disciplinary fines (during the course of administrative taxation proceedings) for failing to produce documents that provided information about his income and could have led to criminal charges for tax evasion. There was accordingly a violation of Article 6(1). The right not to incriminate oneself will still apply even if the allegedly incriminating evidence obtained by coercion is not actually used in criminal proceedings.[1154] Thus, in *Shannon* v *UK*,[1155] the fact that the applicant was required to attend an interview with financial investigators and was compelled to answer questions in connection with events in respect of which he had already been charged with offences, was found to violate his right not to incriminate himself, even though the criminal proceedings were not pursued and the evidence obtained was not therefore used. In *O'Halloran and Francis* v *UK*,[1156] the Grand Chamber found that the obligation on the applicants, as the registered owners of their cars, to provide information identifying the driver when a road-traffic offence was suspected, did not breach the essence of their right to remain silent or the privilege against self-incrimination. It reached this conclusion having assessed the nature and degree of compulsion used to obtain the evidence, the existence of safeguards in the procedure, and the use to which the material obtained was then put.

6.349 The privilege against self-incrimination is primarily concerned with respecting the right of the accused to remain silent. It does not prevent the admission in evidence of material that has an existence independent of the will of the suspect, such as breath, blood or urine samples, bodily tissue for the purpose of DNA testing, or documents obtained under a warrant.[1157] The case of *Jalloh* v *Germany* (see 6.344 above), however, was exceptional. There, a majority of the Grand Chamber found that forcefully administering emetics to the applicant in order to recover drugs that he had swallowed amounted to inhuman and degrading treatment in violation of Article 3.[1158] This evidence was then used to convict him. In such circumstances, an 11–six majority found that the privilege against self-incrimination did apply—and was breached—because the measures taken were used to obtain real evidence in defiance of the applicant's will, and in light of the extent of the force used (in comparison for example with taking blood or hair samples) in the course of a procedure that violated Article 3. Furthermore, the public interest in securing a conviction did not justify such a grave interference with the applicant's physical and mental integrity.

6.350 The state's use of informers may infringe the right to remain silent, on the basis that it will be:

> effectively undermined in a case in which, the suspect having elected to remain silent during questioning, the authorities use subterfuge to elicit, from the suspect, confessions or other statements of an incriminatory nature, which they were unable to obtain during such questioning and where the confessions or statements thereby obtained are adduced in evidence at trial.[1159]

[1153] No. 31827/96, 3.5.01.
[1154] See, e.g. *Heaney and McGuinness* v *Ireland*, No. 34720/97, 21.12.00.
[1155] No. 6563/03, 4.10.05.
[1156] Nos. 15809/02 and 25624/02, 29.6.07.
[1157] *Saunders* v *UK*, No. 19187/91, 17.12.96, para. 69.
[1158] No. 54810/00, 11.7.06 (violation of Article 3 by ten votes to seven).
[1159] *Allan* v *UK*, No. 48539/99, 5.11.02, para. 50.

There was a violation of these principles in *Allan* v *UK*[1160] in circumstances where a long-standing police informer was placed in the applicant's police cell, and later in his prison cell, with the specific purpose of obtaining evidence against him. Accordingly, the applicant's admissions were not 'spontaneous and unprompted' statements volunteered by him, but were 'induced by the persistent questioning' of the informer. Whilst there had been no direct coercion, the Court found that the applicant would have been subjected to psychological pressures that impinged on the 'voluntariness' of the disclosures. The case of *Bykov* v *Russia*[1161] concerned a covert operation carried out by the authorities during an investigation of the applicant's alleged incitement to commit murder, that included the spurious staging by the police of two deaths, which were then widely publicised. The applicant objected to the use at his trial of a recording made by a radio-transmitting device carried by a police informer. The lack of sufficient legal regulation of the device led to a finding of a violation of Article 8. As regards Article 6, the Court noted that the applicant had had the opportunity to challenge the admissibility of the evidence at first instance and on appeal. The recording was not the only evidence relied on by the domestic court in convicting the applicant—it was corroborated by other conclusive evidence. The applicant also argued that his conviction had resulted from trickery and subterfuge and that the police had overstepped the limits of permissible behaviour by secretly recording his conversation with an informer who was acting on their instructions. However, the Grand Chamber distinguished the case from *Allan* v *UK*, noting that the applicant was not detained on remand, but was at liberty and had not been under any pressure to receive the police informer and speak to him. He had been free to refuse to do so. The Court accordingly concluded that the obtaining of evidence was not 'tainted with the element of coercion or oppression' that had led it in the *Allan* case to find a breach of the applicant's right to remain silent. There was therefore no violation of Article 6.[1162]

6.351 The right to silence is not an absolute right, but the drawing of adverse inferences from silence may violate Article 6, depending on all the circumstances of the case, including the situations where inferences may be drawn, the weight attached to them by the national courts in their assessment of the evidence and the degree of compulsion involved. It will be incompatible with the right to silence to found a conviction solely or mainly on the accused's silence or on a refusal to answer questions or give evidence. However, the accused's silence may be taken into account in situations that clearly call for an explanation.[1163]

6.352 In *Condron* v *UK*,[1164] the applicants remained silent when interviewed by the police on advice from their solicitor that they were unfit to answer questions, because of the effect of drugs. The Court found that Article 6 had been violated because of the insufficient direction to the jury:

> as a matter of fairness, the jury should have been directed that if it was satisfied that the applicants' silence at the police interview could not sensibly be attributed to their having no answer or none that would stand up to cross-examination it should not draw an adverse inference.

[1160] No. 48539/99, 5.11.02.
[1161] No. 4378/02, 10.3.09. See also *Heglas* v *Czech Republic*, No. 5935/02, 1.3.07.
[1162] Note, however, the compelling partially dissenting opinion as regards Article 6 of Judge Spielmann, joined by Judges Rozakis, Tulkens, Casadevall and Mijović.
[1163] *John Murray* v *UK*, No. 18731/91, 8.2.96, paras. 44–7.
[1164] No. 35718/97, 2.5.00. See also *Beckles* v *UK*, No. 44652/98, 8.10.02.

This was particularly important given that it was impossible to know what weight was given to the applicants' silence by the jury. The European Court also noted that the Court of Appeal had no means of making that assessment and was concerned with the 'safety' of the conviction, rather than whether there had been a fair trial.

Equality of arms

6.353 The principle of 'equality of arms' is a fundamental aspect of the broader right to a fair hearing and applies in both criminal and civil cases (including appeals and ancillary proceedings, such as those relating to costs).[1165] It has been defined by the Court as requiring 'that each party must be afforded a reasonable opportunity to present his case under conditions that do not place him at a substantial disadvantage vis-à-vis his opponent'.[1166] The principle has application, for example, in relation to the duty of disclosure;[1167] thus it requires, in principle, the opportunity for parties to civil and criminal proceedings, to have knowledge of, and to be able to comment on, all evidence adduced or observations filed. Therefore, it will require disclosure, for example, of third party submissions lodged by a public prosecutor or the Attorney-General.[1168] In a series of cases (concerning domestic civil, criminal and disciplinary proceedings) the Court has found Article 6(1) to have been violated as a result of the role played by the Advocate-General, or similar officers at the Court of Cassation or Supreme Court in Austria, Belgium, France, Netherlands and Portugal.[1169] In these cases there was a failure to disclose in advance either the submissions of the officer concerned or those contained in the reporting judge's report, and an inability of the applicants to reply to them. In *Yvon* v *France*[1170] the principle of equality of arms was found to be violated where the applicant in proceedings assessing compensation for the expropriation of land had both the expropriating authority and the 'Government Commissioner' as opponents. The Court took into account the fact of the Government Commissioner's advantages in terms of access to certain information and the dominant role played by the official in the proceedings.

6.354 In *Wynen* v *Belgium*,[1171] a Chamber majority of four to three found a violation of the principle of equality of arms because rules about time limits on lodging pleadings before the Court of Cassation in civil appeal proceedings did not apply to the respondent, as they did to the appellant, which had the effect of preventing the appellant from replying to the respondent's submissions. The issue raised by the case of *Varnima Corporation International S.A.* v *Greece*[1172] was the disparity in limitation periods applicable to the

---

[1165] See, e.g. *Beer* v *Austria*, No. 30428/96, 6.2.01, para. 18.

[1166] See, e.g. *De Haes and Gijsels* v *Belgium*, No. 19983/92, 24.2.97.

[1167] See, e.g. *McMichael* v *UK*, No. 16424/90, 24.2.95, Series A, No. 308; *Feldbrugge* v *the Netherlands*, No. 8562/79, Series A, No. 99, 29.5.86 and *Matyjek* v *Poland*, No. 38184/03, 24.4.07.

[1168] See, e.g. *Bulut* v *Austria*, No. 17358/90, 22.2.96; *APEH Uldozotteinek Szovetsege and others* v *Hungary*, No. 32367/96, 5.10.00.

[1169] See, e.g. *Borgers* v *Belgium*, No. 12005/86, Series A, No. 214, 30.10.91; *Vermeulen* v *Belgium*, No. 19075/91, 20.2.96; *Lobo Machado* v *Portugal*, No. 15764/89, 20.2.96; *Van Orshoven* v *Belgium*, No. 20122/92, 25.6.97; *JJ* v *Netherlands and KDB* v *Netherlands*, Nos. 21351/93 and 21981/93, 27.3.98; *Reinhardt and Slimane-Kaid* v *France*, No. 22921/93, 31.3.98; *Fischer* v *Austria*, No. 33382/96, 17.1.02; *Meftah and others* v *France*, Nos. 32911/96, 35237/97 and 34595/97, 26.7.02 (finding of a violation by 12 votes to five).

[1170] No. 44962/98, 24.4.03. See also *Martinie* v *France*, No. 58675/00, 12.4.06 and *Tedesco* v *France*, No. 11950/02, 10.5.07 (participation of Government Commissioner and rapporteur (*Tedesco*) in deliberations of the Court of Audit). In contrast, there was no violation of the principle of equality of arms in *Batsanina* v *Russia*, No. 3932/02, 26.5.09, where civil proceedings were instigated by the public prosecutor's office.

[1171] No. 32576/96, 5.11.02.

[1172] No. 48906/06, 28.5.09.

applicant company and to the state. The applicant entered into a contract with the state for the importation of petroleum products. The state brought a claim for damages for breach of contract against the applicant, which made a counterclaim. The application of a limitation period of one year to the action brought by the company, but a 20-year period to the state's case, was found to breach the equality of arms principle (taking account of the fact that the disputes concerned a private commercial transaction, rather than a sovereign act of authority by the state).

The Court has found that the lack of neutrality of a court-appointed expert may give rise **6.355** to a breach of the principle of equality of arms.[1173] The principle may also apply to the failure to admit evidence or to hear or allow the cross-examination of witnesses. In relation to criminal proceedings, it is therefore likely to overlap with other constituent rights in Article 6(3) (see below at 6.390). There was a violation of Article 6(1) in *Matytsina v Russia*[1174] due to the inequality of arms as regards the admission of expert evidence in criminal proceedings. The court only admitted expert reports obtained by the prosecution, without any participation by the defence, and one expert witness, whose evidence was critical, was not called to appear at the trial and therefore could not be questioned by the defence. Furthermore, requests by the defence for an additional expert to be called by the court were denied, as were the defence requests to commission its own expert witnesses. The defence was permitted to call 'specialists' but they had a lesser status than 'experts' under the domestic law. Accordingly, overall, the defence had been at a 'net disadvantage vis-à-vis the prosecution'.

Right to public hearing and reasoned judgment

The right to a public hearing[1175] is expressly included in Article 6(1), as is the public pro- **6.356** nouncement of judgments. The press and public may only be excluded for the reasons set out in the Article. There is a high expectation of publicity in criminal cases, but there may be exceptions, such as to protect the safety or privacy of witnesses, or to promote the free exchange of information and opinions.[1176] In *B and P v UK*[1177] the Court found it a justifiable exception to decide to hold private hearings (on a discretionary basis) under the Children Act 1989 in order to determine the residence of each of the applicants' sons, following divorce or separation. However, in *Nikolova and Vandova v Bulgaria*,[1178] there was a violation of Article 6(1) because of the lack of a public hearing in the course of proceedings brought to challenge the dismissal of the applicant as a police investigator (for corruption-related charges). The Court noted that as the Ministry of Interior had claimed that the documents in the case-file were classified, the administrative court had then automatically excluded the public, without giving reasons. In addition, there was a separate breach of Article 6(1) because of the failure to deliver the judgments in the case publicly, or to make them available to the public for some considerable time.

[1173] See, e.g. *Bönisch v Austria*, No. 8658/79, Series A, No. 92, 6.5.85; *Brandstetter v Austria*, Nos. 11170/84, 12876/87 and 13468/87, Series A no. 211, 28.8.91; *Sara Lind Eggertsdóttir v Iceland*, No. 31930/04, 5.7.07.
[1174] No. 58428/10, 27.3.14.
[1175] See, e.g. *Scarth v UK*, No. 33745/96, 22.7.99.
[1176] See, e.g. *Doorson v Netherlands*, No. 20524/92, 26.3.96; *Z v Finland*, No. 22009/93, 25.2.97.
[1177] Nos. 36337/97 and 35974/97, 24.4.01.
[1178] No. 20688/04, 17.12.13.

6.357 Unless there are exceptional circumstances that justify dispensing with a hearing, the right to a public hearing implies a right to an oral hearing at least before one instance.[1179] The Court has held, however, that, even in the criminal sphere, the obligation to hold a hearing is not absolute—it will depend upon the circumstances of the case, notably whether a question of fact or law has been raised which could not be adequately resolved on the basis of the case file.[1180] In criminal cases there is a general right for the accused to be present at the first instance trial hearing, although this right may be waived and trial in absentia may be permissible.[1181] Whether the defendant's personal attendance is necessary at an appeal hearing will depend upon the nature of the particular proceedings, and the way in which the defendant's interests are presented and protected.[1182] The use of video links may be compatible with the Convention (provided that the rights of the defence are adequately respected).[1183] The right to a public hearing can also be waived, provided that the waiver is unequivocal and that there are no public interest reasons for the public's presence. It is not always necessary for administrative or other tribunals determining 'civil rights' to hold public hearings, provided that a public appeal court hearing is available.[1184] Furthermore, a hearing may not be necessary due to particular circumstances, for example when any questions of fact or law which arise can adequately be resolved on the basis of the parties' written observations.[1185]

A trial held in a prison will violate this provision if in practice the public and media are not informed and granted effective access.[1186]

6.358 The prosecution of children will raise particular issues as to their ability to participate effectively in criminal proceedings.[1187] Full account must be taken of their age, level of maturity and intellectual and emotional capacities and steps must be taken to promote their ability

---

[1179] See, e.g. *Lundevall v Sweden*, No. 38629/97, 12.11.02; *Salomonsson v Sweden*, No. 38978/97, 12.11.02; *Miller v Sweden*, No. 55853/00, 8.2.05 (absence of public hearing re social security benefit claims violated Article 6(1)); *Schlumpf v Switzerland*, No. 29002/06, 8.1.09; *Koottummel v Austria*, No. 49616/06, 10.12.09; *Pönkä v Estonia*, No. 64160/11, 8.11.16.

[1180] *Jussila v Finland*, No. 73043/01, 23.11.06; *Suhadolc v Slovenia*, No. 57655/08, dec. 17.5.11; *Grande Stevens and others v Italy*, No. 18640/10 et al, 4.3.14.

[1181] See, e.g. *Medenica v Switzerland*, No. 20491/92, 14.6.01 (where the defendant was found to be at fault). But it will be problematic if the defendant is not served with a court summons, as in *Colozza v Italy*, No. 9024/80, 12.2.85, or where the accused is denied the assistance of a lawyer: *Poitrimol v France*, No. 14032/88, 23.11.93. As regards civil proceedings, see also *Dilipak and Karakaya v Turkey*, Nos. 7942/05 and 24838/05, 4.3.14 (failure to take sufficient steps to identify address for service in civil proceedings and no opportunity for new trial—violation of Article 6(1)) and *Yevdokimov and others v Russia*, No. 27236/05 et al, 16.2.16 (detainees' inability to attend hearings in civil proceedings to which they were parties—violation of Article 6(1)). Article 6(1) may be breached where a defendent convicted *in absentia* is subsequently unable to obtain a fresh decision (as regards both law and fact), where it has not been unequivocally established that he has waived his right to appear and to defend himself. See, e.g. *Sanader v Croatia*, No. 66408/12, 12.2.15, para. 68.

[1182] See, e.g. *Belziuk v Poland*, No. 23103/93, 25.3.98; *Josef Prinz v Austria*, No. 23867/94, 8.2.00; *Michael Edward Cooke v Austria*, No. 23867/94, 8.2.00; *Hermi v Italy*, No. 18114/02, 18.10.06; *Bazo González v Spain*, No. 30643/04, 16.12.08; *Igual Coll v Spain*, No. 37496/04, 10.3.09; *Sibgatullin v Russia*, No. 32165/02, 23.4.09; *Sobolewski v Poland (No.2)*, No. 19847/07, 9.6.09.

[1183] *Marcello Viola v Italy*, No. 45106/04, 5.10.06.

[1184] See, e.g. *Malhous v Czech Republic*, No. 33071/96, 12.7.01.

[1185] See, e.g. *Fredin v Sweden (No. 2)*, No. 18928/91, 23.2.94, paras. 21–2; *Fischer v Austria*, No. 16922/90, 26.4.95, para. 44; *Döry v Sweden*, No. 28394/95, 12.11.02; *Rippe v Germany*, No. 5398/03, dec. 2.2.06.

[1186] *Riepan v Austria*, No. 35115/97, 14.11.00; *Hummatov v Azerbaijan*, Nos. 9852/03 and 13413/04, 29.11.07.

[1187] See, e.g. *Güveç v Turkey*, No. 70337/01, 20.1.09.

to understand and participate in the proceedings. There was a violation of Article 6(1) in *T and V v UK*,[1188] arising from the Crown Court trial of 11-year-old defendants for murder, because of the incomprehensible and intimidating formality and ritual of the court, which was accompanied by a blaze of publicity, and the defendants' inability to follow the proceedings and take decisions in their own best interests. There was similarly a violation of Article 6(1) in *SC v UK*,[1189] which concerned the prosecution in the Crown Court of an 11-year-old for attempted robbery. The Court found that in view of his age, and, in particular, because of his limited intellectual ability, the applicant had been unable to participate adequately in the proceedings.

Although Article 6 does not provide on its face for limiting the public pronouncement **6.359** of a judgment, the right has in fact been found to be satisfied by its publication in writing.[1190] Article 6 requires reasoned judgments to be made available to the general public,[1191] although there may be exceptions to the rule, such as in proceedings concerning children's residence.[1192] More controversially, in *Sutter v Switzerland*,[1193] the Court held Article 6(1) to have been satisfied where anyone who could establish an interest could consult or obtain a copy of the full text of a judgment of the Military Court of Cassation.[1194]

There is a duty under Article 6 to give reasons in both civil and criminal cases, although the **6.360** extent of the reasoning required will vary depending on the nature of the decision.[1195] This may not require a detailed answer to every argument and an appellate court may, in principle, endorse the reasons for a lower court's decision.[1196] The Court may therefore find a violation of Article 6(1) on account of a domestic court's inadequate reasoning (based on the principle that the prosecution is required to prove its case beyond reasonable doubt).[1197] The failure of the District Court to provide reasons for its refusal to admit certain evidence proposed by the applicant in civil proceedings led to a finding of a violation of Article 6(1) in *Suominen v Finland*.[1198] The problem raised by the case of *Kuznetsov and others v Russia*[1199] was one of arbitrariness. The applicants, who were Jehovah's Witnesses, complained about the unjustified termination of their meeting by the regional human rights commissioner and two police officers. Their civil action was rejected. The Court held that Article 6 had been violated—the domestic courts had failed to provide the reasons on which their decisions were based and to demonstrate that the parties had been heard in a fair and equitable manner.

[1188] Nos. 24724/94 and 24888/94, 16.12.99.

[1189] No. 60958/00, 15.6.04.

[1190] *Pretto and others v Italy*, No. 7984/77, 8.12.83.

[1191] See, e.g. *Ryakib Biryukov v Russia*, No. 14810/02, 17.1.08; *Fazliyski v Bulgaria*, No. 40908/05, 16.4.13.

[1192] *B and P v UK*, Nos. 36337/97 and 35974/97, 24.4.01.

[1193] No. 8209/78, 22.2.84.

[1194] See the concurring opinion of Sir Nicolas Bratza in *B and P v UK*, Nos. 36337/97 and 35974/97, 24.4.01.

[1195] See, e.g. *Zoon v Netherlands*, No. 29202/95, 7.12.00 (concerning an abridged judgment).

[1196] *Garcia Ruiz v Spain*, No. 30544/96, 21.1.99, para. 26. A lower court or authority is required to give reasons so as to enable the parties to make effective use of any existing right of appeal: *Hirvisaari v Finland*, No. 49684/99, 27.9.01, para. 30. See also *Hansen v Norway*, No. 15319/09, 2.10.14 (inadequate reasoning by High Court for refusing to admit applicant's appeal—violation of Article 6(1)).

[1197] See, e.g. *Ajdarić v Croatia*, No. 20883/09, 13.12.11 (including the failure adequately to address obvious discrepancies in statements of witnesses).

[1198] No. 37801/97, 1.7.03.

[1199] No. 184/02, 11.1.07.

6.361 *Taxquet* v *Belgium*[1200] concerned the applicant defendant's complaint of the lack of reasoning given in the course of criminal proceedings for murder and attempted murder, before the Assize Court sitting with a lay jury. The Grand Chamber found that, as a principle, the Convention does not require jurors to give reasons for their decisions and that Article 6 does not preclude a defendant from being tried by a lay jury even where reasons are not given for the verdict, however, for a fair trial to be satisfied, it must be possible to understand the verdict. This will require an assessment of whether there were sufficient safeguards to prevent any risk of arbitrariness, such as guidance from the judge on the legal issues arising or the evidence adduced, as well as 'precise, unequivocal questions put to the jury by the judge, forming a framework on which the verdict is based or sufficiently offsetting the fact that no reasons are given for the jury's answers'. The extent to which there are possibilities to appeal will also be relevant. On the facts of the case in *Taxquet* the Grand Chamber unanimously found a violation of Article 6(1) because neither the indictment nor the questions to the jury contained sufficient information about the applicant's involvement in the offences in question. None of the questions to the jury referred to any specific circumstances that could have enabled the applicant to understand the reasons for his conviction. Finally, it was noted that there was no right of ordinary appeal in Belgium against judgments of the Assize Court (as opposed to appeals on points of law).[1201]

Hearing within a reasonable time

6.362 The right to a hearing within a reasonable time applies to both civil and criminal proceedings. In civil cases time will generally start to run from the outset of the proceedings,[1202] and will continue until the proceedings are determined, including appeals processes.[1203] In criminal cases, time begins to run as soon as a person is 'charged', which has been defined by the Court as 'the official notification given to an individual by the competent authority of an allegation that he has committed a criminal offence'.[1204] This may occur, for example, at the time of arrest,[1205] or when preliminary proceedings are opened. If a defendant absconds, they will not usually be able to complain about the length of proceedings after that point.[1206] Where proceedings are reopened following a previous order that they be discontinued, the total length of time of the various phases of the proceedings should be taken into account for the purposes of Article 6(1).[1207]

[1200] No. 926/05, 16.11.10.

[1201] See also *Agnelet* v *France*, No. 61198/08 and *Legillon* v *France*, No. 53406/10, 10.1.13; *Matis* v *France*, No. 43699/13, dec. 6.10.15. See further *Lhermitte* v *Belgium*, No. 34238/09, 29.11.16 (complaint of lack of adequate procedural safeguards to enable accused to understand reasons for jury's guilty verdict in assize court—no violation by ten votes to seven). See, by contrast, *Judge* v *UK*, No. 35863/10, dec. 8.2.11 (re jury system in Scotland—inadmissible).

[1202] Where the domestic law requires a preliminary administrative procedure to be pursued, before an applicant can bring court proceedings, the proceedings before the administrative body are to be included: see, e.g. *Kiurkchian* v *Bulgaria*, No. 44626/98, 24.3.05, para. 51.

[1203] See, e.g. *Svetlana Orlova* v *Russia*, No. 4487/04, 30.7.09 (case pending for one year and 11 months, but, due to the application of repeated supervisory review proceedings, they were spread over almost seven years—violation of Article 6(1)).

[1204] *Deweer* v *Belgium*, Series A, No. 35, 27.2.80, para. 42.

[1205] See, e.g. *McFarlane* v *Ireland*, No. 31333/06, 10.9.10, para. 144.

[1206] *Vayiç* v *Turkey*, No. 18078/02, 20.6.06.

[1207] See, e.g. *Stoianova and Nedelcu* v *Romania*, Nos. 77517/01 and 77722/01, 4.8.05.

The Court will not lay down particular time limits: what is 'reasonable' will depend upon the particular circumstances of each case, taking into account its complexity, the extent to which the authorities,[1208] other parties or the applicant[1209] are responsible for any delays, and what is at stake for the applicant.[1210] The Court has reiterated that the existence of a possibility for an applicant to take steps to expedite proceedings, does not dispense the state from ensuring, in the first place, that the proceedings progress reasonably quickly.[1211] In *Robins* v *UK*[1212] the Court found that a period of more than four years to resolve straightforward costs proceedings, in part due to unjustifiable delays caused by the court and the Department of Social Security, violated the reasonable time requirement in Article 6(1). In *Cherakrak* v *France*,[1213] criminal proceedings that had lasted for four years and nine months were found to violate Article 6(1). *Šleževičius* v *Lithuania*[1214] concerned criminal proceedings for financial impropriety taken against a former Prime Minister of Lithuania. The proceedings were discontinued by the authorities after four years and two months, which was found to violate Article 6(1) because of the lack of diligence shown by the authorities, which failed to formulate clear charges. However, in *Wloch* v *Poland*,[1215] a six-year delay in criminal proceedings (concerning trading in children) was found not to violate Article 6(1) as the Polish authorities were not responsible for the delays, which had been caused by the fact that evidence had to be taken upon letters rogatory submitted to the Italian, French and US judicial authorities. There was no violation of Article 6(1) in *Sari* v *Turkey and Denmark*[1216] where the applicant was accused of murder in Denmark, but absconded to Turkey. The resulting criminal proceedings in Turkey lasted for more than eight years and seven months, but the delays were caused by the relative complexity of the case, to which the applicant was found to have contributed. **6.363**

In *Gheorghe* v *Romania*,[1217] the Court found that particular diligence will be required of the authorities when an applicant is suffering from a serious illness and his state of health declining rapidly. The applicant, who suffered from haemophilia A, brought civil proceedings relating to the extent of his disability, which lasted for more than two years and 11 months, which the Court held violated the reasonable time requirement. **6.364**

The inadequacies in the application of the 'Pinto law', which was introduced into the domestic law in Italy in 2001 in order to provide redress in cases concerning the length of proceedings, have resulted in further findings of violations of Article 6. This was the case in *Simaldone* v *Italy*[1218] not only because the compensation awarded by the domestic court was considered to be too low (€700 in respect of proceedings lasting more than ten years), but also because there had been an unacceptable delay (of 12 months) before payment was actually made to the applicant. The judgment in *Gaglione and others* v *Italy*[1219] concerned the delays in paying **6.365**

[1208] See, e.g. *Mitchell and Holloway* v *UK*, No. 44808/98, 17.12.02.
[1209] See, e.g. *Mangualde Pinto* v *France*, No. 43491/98, 9.4.02 (delays caused by applicant's failure to attend hearings).
[1210] See, e.g. *Matter* v *Slovakia*, No. 31534/96, 5.7.99; *Pelissier and Sassi* v *France*, No. 25444/94, 25.3.99.
[1211] See, e.g. *McFarlane* v *Ireland*, No. 31333/06, 10.9.10, para. 152.
[1212] No. 22410/93, 23.9.99.
[1213] No. 34075/96, 2.8.00.
[1214] No. 55479/00, 13.11.01.
[1215] No. 27785/95, 19.10.00.
[1216] No. 21889/93, 8.11.01.
[1217] No. 19215/04, 15.3.07.
[1218] No. 22644/03, 31.3.09.
[1219] No. 45867/07, 21.12.10.

compensation in 475 Pinto law cases, which the Court described as a 'widespread problem' given the 3,900 similar cases that were then pending before the Court.[1220]

6.366 The 'pilot judgment procedure' (or Article 46) has been applied in relation to systemic length of proceedings problems in judicial proceedings in various states, including Slovenia,[1221] in civil cases in Germany,[1222] in administrative cases in Greece,[1223] and in criminal proceedings in Bulgaria[1224] (see further at 3.30 above).

6.367 As a result of the Grand Chamber judgment in *Kudla* v *Poland*,[1225] it is possible to complain of the denial of an effective remedy in violation of Article 13 where there has been a failure to provide a trial within a reasonable time under Article 6 (see 6.694 below).

Independent and impartial tribunal established by law

6.368 Article 6(1) expressly includes the right to a hearing by an independent and impartial tribunal established by law. This must be a body capable of reaching binding decisions. The inclusion of the phrase 'established by law' means that the judicial system must not be dependent on the discretion of the executive, but rather regulated by law emanating from Parliament.[1226] The phrase applies to the legal basis for the existence of a 'tribunal', to the tribunal's compliance with the rules governing it, and to its composition.[1227] A District Court in *Posokhov* v *Russia*[1228] was found not to have been 'established by law' where the participation of two lay judges had been in contravention of the relevant domestic law. A lack of clear regulations, and safeguards, in respect of the assignment of cases to judges may also violate the right to have a hearing before a tribunal established by law.[1229]

6.369 Where a criminal penalty is imposed, the Court has underlined that there must be the possibility of review by a court which satisfies the requirements of Article 6(1). This means that (as is the case in civil proceedings) if a decision is taken by an administrative authority which does not itself satisfy the requirements of Article 6(1), it must be subject to subsequent review by a judicial body with full jurisdiction.[1230] Such a body should be capable of examining all questions of fact and law relevant to the dispute before it, and its powers should include the power to quash in all respects, on questions of fact and law, the decision of the body below.[1231]

[1220] See also: Recommendation CM/Rec(2010)3 of the Committee of Ministers to member states on effective remedies for excessive length of proceedings, 24 February 2010. See further the other Pinto Law-related cases at 4.92.

[1221] *Lukenda* v *Slovenia*, No. 23032/02, 6.10.05.

[1222] *Rumpf* v *Germany*, No. 46344/06, 2.9.10.

[1223] *Vassilios Athanasiou and others* v *Greece*, No. 50973/08, 21.12.10.

[1224] *Dimitrov and Hamanov* v *Bulgaria*, No. 48059/07 and 2708/09, 10.5.11.

[1225] No. 30210/96, 26.10.00.

[1226] See, e.g. *Fruni* v *Slovakia*, No. 8014/07, 21.6.15, para. 134.

[1227] See, e.g. *Buscarini* v *San Marino*, No. 31657/96, dec. 4.5.00; *Sokurenko and Strygun* v *Ukraine*, Nos. 29458/04 and 29465/04, 20.7.06; *Oleksandr Volkov* v *Ukraine*, No. 21722/11, 9.1.13.

[1228] No. 63486/00, 4.3.03. See also *Fedotova* v *Russia*, No. 73225/01, 13.4.06 (Town Court). In *Pandjikidzé* v *Georgia*, No. 30323/02, 27.10.09 there was not a sufficient legal basis in the domestic law for the practice of lay judges presiding with a professional judge in the Supreme Court.

[1229] *DMD GROUP, a.s.* v *Slovakia*, No. 19334/03, 5.10.10.

[1230] See, e.g. *Julius Kloiber Schlachthof GmbH and others* v *Austria*, No. 21565/07 et al, 4.4.13; *Grande Stevens and others* v *Italy*, No. 18640/10 et al, 4.3.14.

[1231] See, e.g. *Grande Stevens and others* v *Italy*, No. 18640/10 et al, 4.3.14, para. 139.

The test of independence applied by the Court (in both civil and criminal proceedings) **6.370**
includes consideration of the following: the manner of appointment of the tribunal's members, their term of office, the existence of guarantees against outside pressure, and whether
the tribunal presents an appearance of independence. In *Bryan* v *UK*,[1232] the Court found
that a planning inspector did not have the requisite appearance of independence, given that
the Home Secretary could at any time revoke the inspector's power to decide an appeal and in
circumstances where the policies of the executive could be in issue (even where the power had
not in fact been exercised). However, even where an adjudicatory body determining disputes
over civil rights does not comply with Article 6(1), there will be no violation where that body
is itself subject to the control of an Article 6-compliant judicial body with full jurisdiction.
In *Bryan*, the scope of the review of the inspector's decision provided by the High Court was
found to be sufficient. This can be contrasted with, for example, *Kingsley* v *UK*,[1233] where
judicial review was found to be insufficient as, where the applicant complained of lack of
impartiality by the Gaming Board, the High Court had no power to refer the case back for
a new decision by an independent body. In *Capital Bank AD* v *Bulgaria*,[1234] Article 6 was
violated as the relevant legislation excluded from the scope of judicial review a decision by
the Bulgarian National Bank to revoke the applicant bank's licence on the ground of insolvency. There was also a further finding of a violation of Article 6 because the bank had not
been able to participate fully in the proceedings, as it was represented by persons who were
dependent on the other party to the proceedings (special administrators appointed by the
Bulgarian National Bank).

Systemic problems concerning the disciplining and dismissal of the judiciary were identified **6.371**
in *Oleksandr Volkov* v *Ukraine*.[1235] The applicant was a supreme court judge who was dismissed
from office for breach of oath. The proceedings brought against him were found not to be
compatible with the principles of independence and impartiality under Article 6(1). There
were structural deficiencies in the body which instigated the proceedings, the High Council
of Justice, which comprised various political appointees (including the Minister of Justice
and Prosecutor General) and only a small minority of judges. Two members of the Council
both instigated the inquiry against the applicant and were then instrumental in bringing
the charges against him (and there were also appearances of personal bias as regards one of
them). The case was then heard by the Parliament (the *Verkhovna Rada*) which, according to
the Court, 'only served to contribute to the politicisation of the procedure and to aggravate
the inconsistency of the procedure with the principle of the separation of powers'.[1236] Two
members of the parliamentary committee which considered the case had also been members
of the High Council of Justice. These defects were not then remedied by the review carried
out by the Higher Administrative Court, because it did not have the power to quash the
decisions in question and it did not fully address a number of issues raised by the applicant.
Furthermore, the judges of the Higher Administrative Court were also themselves under the

---

[1232] No. 19178/91, Series A, No. 335-A, 22.11.95. See also, e.g. *Fazia Ali* v *UK*, No. 40378/10, 20.10.15.
[1233] No. 35605/97, 7.11.00.
[1234] No. 49429/99, 24.11.05.
[1235] No. 21722/11, 9.1.13. See also *Mitrinovski* v *former Yugoslav Republic of Macedonia*, No. 6899/12,
30.4.15; *Gerovska Popčevska* v *former Yugoslav Republic of Macedonia*, No. 48783/07, 7.1.16; *Jakšovski and
Trifunovski* v *former Yugoslav Republic of Macedonia*, Nos. 56381/09 and 58738/09, 7.1.16; *Kulykov and others*
v *Ukraine*, No. 5144/09, et al, 19.1.17.
[1236] *Oleksandr Volkov* v *Ukraine*, No. 21722/11, 9.1.13, para. 118.

disciplinary jurisdiction of the High Council of Justice. Additionally, separate violations of Article 6(1) were found because of breaches of the principle of legal certainty: proceedings for breach of oath were not subject to any limitation period, and during the vote taken by the plenary parliament, MPs had used the electronic voting system to cast multiple votes on behalf of MPs who were not present in the chamber. There was a further breach of Article 6(1) because the chamber of the Higher Administrative Court which heard the applicant's case had not been 'established by law' because the procedure for appointing presidents of the Court had not been regulated by any domestic law at the relevant time.

6.372 Article 6(1) requires independence not only from the parties but also from the executive,[1237] in both civil and criminal proceedings. A prosecutor will not be considered to be an 'independent and impartial tribunal' in the context of either criminal or civil proceedings.[1238] In *Henryk Urban and Ryszard Urban v Poland*,[1239] the use of an 'assessor' in the District Court was found to violate Article 6 as she could have been removed at any point by the Minister of Justice and there were insufficient guarantees to prevent arbitrariness. This could not have been rectified on appeal as the Regional Court did not have the power to quash the judgment of the District Court on the basis of the position of the assessor. In *Crişan v Romania*,[1240] the applicant had sought confirmation from a commission that he had the status of a person persecuted for political reasons during the Communist era. Article 6 was violated as the commission was found not to be independent of the executive because of its composition and the membership of its review body, and its decisions were not susceptible to challenge in the courts. The question of the objective impartiality of 'Maritime Chambers' was in issue in *Brudnicka and others v Poland*,[1241] a case concerning proceedings to determine the causes of a ferry shipwreck. There was a violation of Article 6 as the members of the Maritime Chambers were appointed and removed from office by the Minister of Justice and the Minister of Transport and Maritime Affairs, and were therefore subordinate to them. Furthermore, there was also no provision for an appeal on points of law against the decisions of the Maritime Appeals Chamber. Repeated changes in the composition of a court hearing criminal proceedings led to the finding of a violation of Article 6 in *Moiseyev v Russia*.[1242] There were 11 judicial replacements during the trial of the applicant for high treason on account of espionage, the reasons for which were only made known on two occasions. Furthermore, the domestic law allowed the court president an unfettered discretion to reassign a pending criminal case to another presiding judge. Accordingly, the Court concluded that the domestic law 'failed to provide the guarantees that would have been sufficient to exclude any objective doubt as to the absence of inappropriate pressure on judges in the performance of their judicial duties'. The involvement of ministers in any aspect of the criminal justice process is likely to cause problems under Article 6, because of the notion of the separation of powers between the executive and the judiciary.[1243] In *T and*

[1237] See, e.g. *Glod v Romania*, No. 41134/98, 16.9.03 (Administrative Commission constituted and directed by provincial governor).

[1238] See, e.g. *Zlínsat, spol. s r.o. v Bulgaria*, No. 57785/00, 15.6.06 (decision by prosecution authorities to suspend privatisation which was not susceptible to judicial review—violation of Article 6(1)).

[1239] No. 23614/08, 30.11.10.

[1240] No. 42930/98, 27.5.03.

[1241] No. 54723/00, 3.3.05.

[1242] No. 62936/00, 9.10.08.

[1243] As to the growing importance in the Court's case law of the concept of the separation of powers, see *Kleyn and others v Netherlands*, Nos. 39343/98, 39651/98, 43147/98 and 46664/99, 6.5.03, para. 193.

V v *UK*,[1244] the Court found that in setting the applicants' tariff following their convictions for murder and sentences of detention during 'Her Majesty's pleasure', the Home Secretary was exercising sentencing powers but was clearly not independent of the executive.[1245]

There are two aspects to the requirement of impartiality: the tribunal must be *subjectively* free **6.373** of personal prejudice or bias, and it must be impartial from an *objective* viewpoint. The Court has stressed that it is of fundamental importance in a democratic society that the courts inspire confidence in the public, including the parties to the proceedings.[1246] The concepts of independence and objective impartiality are therefore closely linked. In *McGonnell* v *UK*,[1247] which concerned the objective impartiality of the Bailiff of Guernsey in relation to planning proceedings, the Court found that the mere fact that the Bailiff presided over the legislature when the relevant regulation was adopted, was capable of casting doubt on his impartiality when he subsequently determined, as the sole judge of the law in the case, the applicant's planning appeal. Even in the absence of any actual bias or prejudice, the applicant was considered to have had legitimate grounds for fearing that the Bailiff may have been influenced by his prior participation in the adoption of the regulation in question. Questions of the apparent lack of impartiality may also be raised where an authority exercises both advisory and judicial functions,[1248] although the majority of the Grand Chamber found no violation of Article 6 in *Kleyn and others* v *Netherlands*,[1249] as although the Council of State had exercised an advisory role in relation to the Transport Infrastructure Planning Bill, its role in the applicant's subsequent proceedings relating to a 'Routing Decision' was found not to involve the 'same case' or the 'same decision'. There was a violation of Article 6 in *Dubus S.A.* v *France*[1250] as a result of the lack of any clear distinction between the prosecutorial, investigative and judicial functions of the Banking Commission, a body that exercised both supervisory and disciplinary functions, and in *Vernes* v *France*[1251] the applicant's complaint about the lack of impartiality of the Stock Exchange Regulatory Authority was upheld because the domestic law prevented the disclosure of the identity of its members. The requirement for impartiality was found to have been breached in *Karelin* v *Russia*[1252] because of the absence of any prosecuting party in administrative proceedings brought against the applicant for disorderly behaviour in a public place.

Disciplinary proceedings brought against judges have been found to violate the obligation **6.374** to ensure impartiality. For example, *Harabin* v *Slovakia*[1253] concerned disciplinary proceedings against the President of the Slovakian Supreme Court before the Constitutional Court. The applicant had challenged on grounds of bias, four Constitutional Court judges, two of whom had been excluded for lack of impartiality in earlier cases involving the applicant. By

---

[1244] Nos. 24724/94 and 24888/94, 16.12.99.
[1245] See also *Stafford* v *UK*, No. 46295/99, 28.5.02, para. 78; *Clift* v *UK*, No. 7205/07, 13.7.10 (early release scheme subject to approval of Secretary of State—violation of Article 5 taken together with Article 14).
[1246] See, e.g. *DN* v *Switzerland*, No. 27154/95, 29.3.01, para. 46.
[1247] No. 28488/95, 8.2.02.
[1248] *Procola* v *Luxembourg*, No. 14570/89, 28.9.95.
[1249] Nos. 39343/98, 39651/98, 43147/98 and 46664/99, 6.5.03 (no violation by 12 votes to five).
[1250] No. 5242/04, 11.6.09.
[1251] No. 30183/06, 20.1.11.
[1252] No. 926/08, 20.9.16.
[1253] No. 58688/11, 20.11.12. See also *Mitrinovski* v *former Yugoslav Republic of Macedonia*, No. 6899/12, 30.4.15 (roles played by the President of the Supreme Court in misconduct proceedings against the applicant failed both the subjective and objective impartiality tests—violation of Article 6(1)).

retaining the two judges on the basis of the need to maintain its capacity to determine the case, the Constitutional Court was considered to have failed convincingly to dissipate any doubts about the impartiality of the two judges. Furthermore, the Constitutional Court was also found to have failed to adequately assess the merits of other challenges by the parties to the impartiality of several judges.

6.375   The role of the Government Commissioner in France, sitting in on deliberations of judges in the *Conseil d'Etat*, but not voting, was found by the Grand Chamber to create appearances of a lack of independence or impartiality in *Kress* v *France*,[1254] albeit by ten votes to seven. In *Daktaras* v *Lithuania*,[1255] the applicant's doubts as to the impartiality of the Supreme Court were found to be justified in circumstances where the President of the Criminal Division of that court had lodged a petition seeking the Court of Appeal decision to be quashed and where he had also appointed the judge rapporteur and the members of the Chamber in the case. In *Rojas Morales* v *Italy*,[1256] criminal proceedings against the applicant fell foul of the objective impartiality test where two of the judges involved had previously given judgment against a co-accused that had identified the applicant as leading an organisation involved in drug trafficking. There was an objective lack of impartiality too in *Werner* v *Poland*[1257] because a motion to dismiss a judicial liquidator was presented by an insolvency judge who had also sat on the bench that had decided the motion. In *Perote Pellon* v *Spain*,[1258] the applicant (a reserve army colonel) was convicted of disclosing official secrets. Two of the trial judges in the Central Military Court had previously sat in the case and upheld the decision to charge the applicant on appeal, and they had dismissed an appeal against that decision.[1259] Therefore, the applicant's fears about the judges' impartiality were objectively justified. This principle may also circumscribe the state's reliance on part-time judges. There was a violation of Article 6 in *Wettstein* v *Switzerland*[1260] where two administrative court judges had themselves (or through their office partner) acted against the applicant in other proceedings.

[1254] No. 39594/98, 7.6.01. See also *Martinie* v *France*, No. 58675/00, 12.4.06. In *Sacilor Lormines* v *France*, No. 65411/01, 9.11.06 the Court in addition found justified the applicant mining company's concerns about the appointment of a member of the *Conseil d'Etat* to a senior position in the Ministry responsible for mines, and who had previously participated in a decision of the *Conseil d'Etat* in the course of litigation involving the applicant company and the Ministry—violation of Article 6(1) (by four votes to three).

[1255] No. 42095/98, 10.10.00. Contrast with the decision in *Gregory* v *UK*, No. 22299/93, 25.2.97.

[1256] No. 39676/98, 16.11.00. However, see also: *Schwarzenberger* v *Germany*, No. 75737/01, 10.8.06; *Poppe* v *Netherlands*, No. 32271/04, 24.3.09; *Miminoshvili* v *Russia*, No. 20197/03, 28.6.11; *Khodorkovskiy and Lebedev* v *Russia*, Nos. 11082/06 and 13772/05, 25.7.13.

[1257] No. 26760/95, 15.11.01.

[1258] No. 45238/99, 25.7.02. See also *Ekeberg and others* v *Norway*, Nos. 11106/04, 11108/04, 11116/04, 11311/04 and 13276/04, 31.7.07 (violation of Article 6 where judge had been involved in decision on the extension of defendant's detention, in assessing whether to endorse jury's decision to convict, and in sentencing).

[1259] See also, e.g. *Chesne* v *France*, No. 29808/06, 22.4.10 (justified doubts about objective impartiality of two judges of Criminal Appeals Division who had been members of investigation division of Court of Appeal); *Cardona Serrat* v *Spain*, No. 38715/06, 26.10.10 (justified doubts as to impartiality where two judges who had ordered applicant's detention pending trial subsequently sat on bench that convicted him); *Fazlı Aslaner* v *Turkey*, No. 36073/04, 4.3.14 (hearing of successive civil appeals on points of law by bench including same three judges—violation of Article 6(1)).

[1260] No. 33958/96, 21.12.00. But there was no violation of Article 6 in *Puolitaival and Pirttiaho* v *Finland*, No. 54857/00, 23.11.04 (where, by contrast, the judge's prior involvement had been remote in time, and the subject matter of the two sets of proceedings was completely different). See also *Chmelíř* v *Czech Republic*, No. 64935, 7.6.05 (violation found where the judge presiding in High Court criminal proceedings against the applicant was also, at the same time, a defendant in civil proceedings brought by the applicant for the protection of personality rights).

Links between a judge and a party to litigation may give rise to questions of impartiality, as in *Sigurðsson* v *Iceland*[1261] where the Court found a violation of Article 6(1) because of the appearance of a link between the financial arrangements made by a Supreme Court judge in support of her husband and the advantages he thereby obtained from the National Bank, with which the applicant was involved in litigation before the Supreme Court. Whilst there was no suggestion of actual bias, the applicant's complaints about the lack of objective impartiality were found to be justified. A similar conclusion was reached in *Belukha* v *Ukraine*[1262] in which the applicant complained that the president of a court, who presided alone over her first instance proceedings, had demanded and received certain assets (for the court building) from the defendant company for free. Article 6 was also violated in *Mežnarić* v *Croatia*[1263] because one of the judges who heard the applicant's constitutional court complaint had previously acted for his opponent in the same proceedings (as had the judge's daughter). In *Micallef* v *Malta*,[1264] Article 6 was found to have been breached in the course of injunction proceedings because the presiding judge was related to advocates for the party opposing the applicant. The domestic law was inadequate because it did not recognise that a sibling (or other) relationship between a judge and advocate could be a ground for challenge on the basis of impartiality. **6.376**

Judicial or ministerial comments in the press are likely to be very carefully scrutinsed by the Court. In *Lavents* v *Latvia*,[1265] the Court found a violation of the judicial impartiality requirement (and of the presumption of innocence under Article 6(2)) as a result of statements made to the media by the presiding judge of the regional court in respect of criminal proceedings that were pending against the applicant. The judge had criticised the attitude of the defence in the court proceedings, made predictions about the outcome of the trial and had even expressed surprise that the applicant was persisting in pleading not guilty. Derogatory public statements about the applicant made by the President of the National Judicial Council (and two of its members) in *Olujić* v *Croatia*,[1266] resulted in a finding by the Court that the Council lacked impartiality as regards disciplinary proceedings brought against the applicant judge. The case of *Ivanovski* v *former Yugoslav Republic of Macedonia*[1267] concerned the removal from public office of the President of the Constitutional Court, as a result of lustration proceedings. One of the main reasons why the European Court found the proceedings to be unfair, and in violation of Article 6(1), was the publication by the Prime Minister (while the case was still pending) of an open letter denouncing the applicant as a collaborator of the secret police in the former regime. **6.377**

The personal impartiality of both judges and jurors will be presumed, unless there is contrary proof. In *Sander* v *UK*,[1268] the applicant complained that he had not been heard by an **6.378**

[1261] No. 39731/98, 10.4.03. See also, e.g. *Pescador Valero* v *Spain*, No. 62435/00, 17.6.03.
[1262] No. 33949/02, 9.11.06.
[1263] No. 71615/01, 15.7.05. See also *Švarc and Kavnik* v *Slovenia*, No. 75617/01, 8.2.07.
[1264] No. 17056/06, 15.10.09.
[1265] No. 58442/00, 28.11.02.
[1266] No. 22330/05, 5.2.09.
[1267] No. 29908/11, 21.1.16.
[1268] No. 34129/96, 9.5.00, para. 34. See, by contrast, *Ekeberg and others* v *Norway*, Nos. 11106/04, 11108/04, 11116/04, 11311/04 and 13276/04, 31.7.07 (juror disqualified as had given witness statement to the police concerning the case—no violation, by four votes to three); *Szypusz* v *UK*, No. 8400/07, 21.9.10 (police officer responsible for operating video equipment permitted to remain alone with jury while it viewed video evidence—no violation, by five votes to two).

impartial tribunal because the jury had been racially prejudiced. During his trial the judge had been passed a note from a juror stating that other jurors had been making racist remarks and jokes, which was admitted by one juror. The European Court found that that did not in itself amount to evidence that the juror was actually biased against the applicant. However, the judge's redirection to the jury was held to be insufficient to dispel the reasonable impression and fear of a lack of impartiality:

> given the importance attached by all contracting states to the need to combat racism ... the judge should have reacted in a more robust manner than merely seeking vague assurances that the jurors could set aside their prejudices and try the case solely on the evidence.

There was therefore a violation of Article 6(1) (by four votes to three). Where a police officer sat on a jury which convicted the applicants in *Hanif and Khan v UK*,[1269] they were found not to have been tried by an impartial tribunal, as there was an important conflict about the police evidence in the case and the police officer on the jury was personally acquainted with the officer who gave the relevant witness evidence. There was also a breach of Article 6(1) in *Kristiansen v Norway*[1270] because one of the jurors in a rape case had been personally acquainted with the victim and had commented on her character. The Court was critical of the domestic court's failure either to discharge the juror or to issue a redirection to the jury.

6.379   Unusually, in *Kyprianou v Cyprus*,[1271] the Grand Chamber found a violation of both the subjective and objective elements of impartiality. The applicant lawyer had been interrupted during his cross-examination of a witness in a criminal trial. His reaction to being interrupted led to his conviction by the same judges for contempt of court. The matter should have been referred to the prosecuting authorities, and, if necessary, the question tried before different judges. Their lack of subjective impartiality was indicated by the fact that their decision recorded that they had been personally offended and their emphatic language conveyed a sense of indignation and shock that showed they did not have a detached approach. The Court also noted their haste in trying him summarily for a criminal offence, and the imposition of immediate imprisonment.

6.380   The requirement for independence and impartiality may cause particular difficulties in respect of military courts or tribunals.[1272] The case of *Findlay v UK*[1273] concerned the fairness of the courts-martial system in the UK. When serving in Northern Ireland the applicant, who was suffering from post-traumatic stress disorder, threatened to shoot himself and his colleagues and he was arrested and taken before a court-martial, which resulted in his

---

[1269] Nos. 52999/08 and 61779/08, 20.12.11. See, by contrast, *Peter Armstrong v UK*, No. 65282/09, 9.12.14 (police officers' participation on jury in case where police evidence was undisputed and officers were not acquainted with police officers giving evidence—no violation of Article 6(1)).

[1270] No. 1176/10, 17.12.15.

[1271] No. 73797/01, 15.12.05. The treatment of Mr Kyprianou also led to a finding in a separate case that his client's Article 6 rights had been violated—see *Panovits v Cyprus*, No. 4268/04, 11.12.08.

[1272] Although Article 6 does not, in principle, exclude the determination by military tribunals of criminal charges against military personnel (see *Cooper v UK*, No. 48843/99, 16.12.03, para. 110). But see *Miroshnik v Ukraine*, No. 75804/01, 27.11.08 (applicant's concerns about independence of military courts as regards proceedings concerning his dismissal from military service were objectively justified). See also *Ibrahim Gürkan v Turkey*, No. 10987/10, 3.7.12 (involvement of serving military officer in military criminal court—violation of Article 6(1)); *Tanışma v Turkey*, No. 32219/05, 17.11.15 (presence of serving military officers on Supreme Military Administrative Court—violation of Article 6(1))).

[1273] No. 22107/93, 27.2.97.

dismissal from the armed forces, a reduction in rank, and two years' imprisonment. At the time, a court-martial comprised a President (usually a brigadier or colonel in the army) and at least four other army officers, all of whom were appointed by the 'convening officer', a serving officer. It was also the responsibility of the convening officer to decide the charges to be brought, to procure the attendance of witnesses for both the prosecution and the defence, and his consent was usually obtained for charges to be withdrawn. In finding a violation of the right to a fair hearing under Article 6, the Court found that the applicant's concerns about the independence and impartiality of the tribunal were objectively justified. The following factors were the most significant:

(1) All the members of the court-martial who were appointed by the convening officer were subordinate in rank to him.

(2) Many of the court-martial members (including the President) were directly or ultimately under his command.

(3) The convening officer had the power to dissolve the court-martial either before or during the trial.

(4) The convening officer also acted as 'confirming officer' and the decision of the court-martial was therefore not effective until he ratified it, and he also had the power to vary the sentence imposed.

6.381 In the light of the *Findlay* case, the court-martial system was amended,[1274] but even those changes which were designed specifically to comply with the requirements of Article 6 proved to be inadequate as a result of the later judgment in *Morris v UK*.[1275] There, the Court found a violation of Article 6(1) arising from the general structure of the court-martial system. While the changes were found to have done much to meet the Court's concerns about the structure of the system, there were still systemic flaws. The Court acknowledged that the Permanent President's term of office and de facto security of tenure and the relative separation from the army command structure meant that the post was a significant guarantee of independence. However, the applicant's misgivings about the independence of the court-martial were found to be objectively justified due to the involvement of two relatively junior serving officers appointed on an ad hoc basis who had no legal training and who remained subject to army discipline and reports. The Grand Chamber subsequently held the reformed court-martial system to be in breach of Article 6 in the case of *Grieves v UK*.[1276] There, the Royal Navy court-martial system was found to have insufficient safeguards to ensure independence because of the ad hoc appointment of presidents for each court-martial, and the fact that judge advocates were serving naval officers, rather than civilians. However, in *Cooper v UK*[1277] the Grand Chamber reached a different conclusion to that of the Chamber in *Morris*, finding that there were sufficient safeguards to ensure the independence of the ordinary members of the court-martial. In Turkey, problems arose because a military judge sat (with

---

[1274] By the Armed Forces Act 1996.

[1275] No. 38784/97, 26.2.02. However, a subsequent decision of the House of Lords in *R v Spear* [2002] UKHL 31 reached a different conclusion to that of the European Court in *Morris*. In *Spear*, the House of Lords found that there *were* sufficient safeguards within the reformed court-martial system to ensure the independence of the two officers. The fact that the Reviewing Authority could only make a decision which was favourable to the defendant was important, and the House of Lords was also critical of the totality of the evidence which had been provided to the European Court in *Morris*.

[1276] No. 48843/99, 16.12.03.

[1277] No. 48843/99, 16.12.03, paras. 119–26. See also *Thompson v UK*, No. 36256/97, 15.6.04.

two civilians judges) on the state security courts that try civilians in serious cases considered to be threatening to the security of the state. In *Incal* v *Turkey*,[1278] the applicant was prosecuted for distributing a leaflet that was critical of measures taken by the local authorities in Izmir in western Turkey in respect of squatters' camps (of predominantly Kurdish people) that had been developing around the city. He was convicted of disseminating separatist propaganda and was sentenced to imprisonment and a fine. The Court found that whilst the status of military judges sitting as members of the State Security Court provided certain guarantees of independence,[1279] there were a number of fundamental concerns about their position on the court, which went further than the concerns raised by the *Findlay* case:[1280]

(1) military judges were servicemen who still belonged to the army, which took its orders from the executive;
(2) military judges remained subject to military discipline and assessment reports were compiled on them by the army for that purpose;
(3) decisions relating to the appointment of military judges were to a great extent taken by the army's administrative authorities; and
(4) their term of office was only four years and could be renewed.

[handwritten margin note: military!]

Consequently, the Court found a violation of Article 6 of the Convention,[1281] concluding that 'the applicant could legitimately fear that because one of the judges of the [court] was a military judge, it might allow itself to be unduly influenced by considerations which had nothing to do with the nature of the case'.[1282]

6.382 As a result of *Incal*, the Turkish Parliament amended the Constitution in 1999 so as to exclude all military judges from State Security Courts.[1283] The Court was subsequently inundated with similar cases concerning State Security Courts,[1284] and in a number of them it stipulated that the most appropriate form of redress would be for the applicants to be retried by an independent and impartial court.[1285]

Presumption of innocence

6.383 Article 6(2) guarantees the presumption of innocence in criminal proceedings.[1286] Accordingly, members of a court must not start with the preconceived idea that the accused

---

[1278] No. 22678/93, 9.6.98.

[1279] For example, they had the same professional training as civilian judges and they enjoyed the same Constitutional safeguards; most could not be removed or forced to retire early without their consent; they sat as individuals; according to the Constitution, they had to be independent and could not be given instructions by any public authorities about their judicial activities.

[1280] The Court also took note of the context within which the State Security Courts operated: that they were set up pursuant to the Constitution to deal with offences affecting Turkey's territorial integrity and national unity, its democratic regime and its State security, and that their main distinguishing feature was that one of their judges was always a member of the Military Legal Service.

[1281] By 12 votes to eight. There was also a unanimous finding of a violation of Article 10 of the Convention.

[1282] *Incal* v *Turkey*, No. 22678/93, 9.6.98, paras. 71–2.

[1283] Article 143 of the Constitution was amended on 18 June 1999.

[1284] In cases where military judges have been replaced by civilian judges during the course of domestic proceedings, the Court will assess whether the doubts concerning the proceedings as a whole have been sufficiently dispelled by the change in the composition of the bench. See, e.g. *İmrek* v *Turkey*, No. 57175/00, dec. 28.1.03; *Öcalan* v *Turkey*, No. 46221/99, 12.5.05; *Ceylan* v *Turkey*, No. 68953/01, dec. 30.8.05.

[1285] See, e.g. *Ükünç and Güneş* v *Turkey*, No. 42775/98, 18.12.03.

[1286] Accordingly, it will not be applicable where there has not been the determination of a criminal charge. See, e.g. *McParland* v *UK*, No. 47898/99, dec. 30.11.99; *Bingöl* v *Netherlands*, No. 18450/07, dec. 20.3.12.

has committed the offence[1287]—the burden of proof is on the prosecution and any doubt should benefit the accused.[1288]

It may be in issue, for example, where the burden of proof is transferred to the accused to establish a defence[1289] or where a presumption of law or fact is applied against the accused. Such presumptions must be confined within reasonable limits that take into account the importance of what is at stake and maintain the rights of the defence.[1290] For example, there was a violation of both Articles 6(1) and 6(2) in *Klouvi v France*[1291] where the applicant was prevented from effectively defending herself against a charge of malicious prosecution because of the application of two presumptions in the domestic law. For example, as the courts had found 'no case to answer' as regards her allegations of rape and sexual harassment, according to the criminal code this 'necessarily' meant that her accusations had been false.

6.384

In addition to issues relating to the burden of proof and presumptions of law, the Court has also stipulated that the presumption of innocence has effects which extend beyond the termination of the criminal process:

6.385

> … where there has been a criminal charge and criminal proceedings have ended in an acquittal, the person who was the subject of the criminal proceedings is innocent in the eyes of the law and must be treated in a manner consistent with that innocence. To this extent, therefore, the presumption of innocence will remain after the conclusion of criminal proceedings in order to ensure that, as regards any charge which was not proven, the innocence of the person in question is respected.[1292]

The Court has underlined that Article 6(2) does not guarantee someone charged with a criminal offence a right to compensation for lawful detention on remand, or for costs, where proceedings are subsequently discontinued or end in an acquittal, and nor does it mean that a defendant acquitted of a criminal offence has a right to compensation for a miscarriage of justice.[1293] However, Article 6(2) will be violated if, without any finding of guilt, there is a judicial decision reflecting that an accused is guilty,[1294] such as the refusal

---

The principle of the presumption of innocence is also applicable after conviction while a case is still pending on appeal. See *Konstas v Greece*, No. 53466/07, 24.5.11.

[1287] This principle was also applied in relation to an inspector during an administrative inquiry in *Poncelet v Belgium*, No. 44418/07, 30.3.10 (violation of Article 6(2) by four votes to three). See also *Dicle and Sadak v Turkey*, No. 48621/07, 16.6.15 (use of the term 'the accused/convicted person' during the course of a re-trial—indication of the criminal conviction on the applicants' criminal record after the reopening of the trial—violation of Article 6(2)).

[1288] See, e.g. *Barberà, Messegué and Jabardo v Spain*, Nos. 10588/83, 10589/83 and 10590/83, 6.12.88, Series A, No. 146, para. 77.

[1289] As in *Telfner v Austria*, No. 33501/96, 20.3.01, where the burden of proof was shifted from the prosecution to the defence by requiring the applicant to provide an explanation of his alleged involvement in a traffic accident even though it had not been possible to establish a convincing case against him.

[1290] *Salabiaku v France* No. 10589/83, Series A, No. 141-A, 7.10.88, para. 28; *Phillips v UK*, No. 41087/98, 5.7.01, paras. 40–7.

[1291] No. 30754/03, 30.6.11.

[1292] *Allen v UK*, No. 25424/09, 12.7.13, para. 103.

[1293] See, e.g. *Allen v UK*, No. 25424/09, 12.7.13, para. 82.

[1294] See, e.g. *Rushiti v Austria*, No. 28389/95, 21.3.00; *El Kaada v Germany*, No. 2130/10, 12.11.15 and, by contrast, *Tripon v Romania*, No. 27062/04, dec. 7.2.12 (dismissal of official held in pre-trial detention did not amount to a statement or act reflecting an opinion as to his guilt—inadmissible). See also the list of cases referred to in *Allen v UK*, No. 25424/09, 12.7.13, para. 98.

to pay costs to an acquitted defendant,[1295] the refusal to compensate an applicant for a period in detention,[1296] the imposition of a confiscation order,[1297] the pre-trial termination of criminal proceedings by a prosecutor on terms which presuppose the commission of the criminal act at issue,[1298] or the decision of a civil court to terminate proceedings, based to a decisive extent on prior comments made by the prosecutor as to the applicant's guilt when discontinuing criminal proceedings.[1299] The Court has also underlined that in accordance with the principle of *in dubio pro reo*, there should be no qualitative difference between an acquittal for lack of evidence and an acquittal resulting from a finding that the person's innocence was beyond doubt.[1300] The Court acknowledges a distinction between domestic court decisions describing a 'state of suspicion', and those that contain a 'finding of guilt'—only the latter is incompatible with Article 6(2).[1301] Thus in *O* v *Norway, Hammern* v *Norway* and *Y* v *Norway*,[1302] there was a violation of Article 6(2) because of the reasoning adopted by the Norwegian courts in refusing the applicants' compensation claims against the state in respect of damage sustained in criminal proceedings in which they had been acquitted. Whilst the applicants had not been 'charged with a criminal offence' in the proceedings for compensation, Article 6(2) was considered to be applicable because of the link between the conditions for obtaining compensation and the issue of criminal responsibility. The domestic courts' decisions were found to have called into doubt the correctness of the applicants' acquittals, in a manner incompatible with the presumption of innocence.[1303] There was no violation of Article 6(2) in *Allen* v *UK*[1304] where the applicant's conviction for the manslaughter of her baby was quashed by the Court of Appeal on the basis that it was 'unsafe' because new evidence might have affected the jury's decision had it been available at trial, but she was subsequently refused compensation. Having reviewed the language used by the domestic courts in reaching their decisions, the Court was satisfied that they did not

---

[1295] *Minelli* v *Switzerland*, No. 8660/79, Series A, No. 62, 25.3.83, paras. 37–41. The Court draws a distinction between a refusal to make a costs order because of reliance on suspicions as to the applicant's innocence after acquittal, and where an order is refused because it was felt that the defendant had brought suspicion on himself: *Ashendon and Jones* v *UK*, Nos, 35730/07 and 4285/08, 13.9.11.

[1296] See, e.g. *Weixelbraun* v *Austria*, No. 33730/96, 19.12.01—a compensation claim was rejected on the ground that the applicant had not been acquitted because his innocence had been proven, but that he had been given the benefit of the doubt; *Del Latte* v *Netherlands*, No. 44760/98, 9.11.04 (compensation refused on the basis that the applicants would have been convicted had they also been prosecuted for an additional charge); *Capeau* v *Belgium*, No. 42914/98, 13.1.05 (reversal of burden of proof as part of compensation proceedings); *Puig Panella* v *Spain*, No. 1483/02, 25.4.06 (compensation for prison sentence refused owing to lack of evidence amounting to total certainty of convicted person's innocence); *Tendam* v *Spain*, No. 25720/05, 13.7.10 (compensation for pre-trial detention refused because applicant acquitted for lack of proof).

[1297] See, e.g. *Geerings* v *Netherlands*, No. 30810/03, 1.3.07 (cf *Phillips* v *UK*, No. 41087/98, 5.7.01; *Van Offeren* v *Netherlands*, No. 19581/04, dec. 5.7.05; *Grayson and Barnham* v *UK*, Nos. 19955/05 and 15085/06, 23.9.08). As regards Article 7, see also *Varvara* v *Italy*, No. 17475/09, 29.10.13.

[1298] *Virabyan* v *Armenia*, No. 40094/05, 2.10.12.

[1299] *Teodor* v *Romania*, No. 46878/06, 4.6.13.

[1300] *Vassilios Stavropoulos* v *Greece*, No. 35522/04, 27.9.07, para. 39.

[1301] See, e.g. *Baars* v *Netherlands*, No. 44320/98, 28.10.03, para. 28.

[1302] Nos. 29327/95, 30287/96, 34964/97 and 56568/00, 11.2.03. But see *Ringvold* v *Norway*, No. 34964/97, 11.2.03.

[1303] See also: *Lagardère* v *France*, No. 18851/07, 12.4.12 (posthumous finding of guilt engaging liability of heirs—violations of Articles 6(1) and 6(2)). See, in contrast, e.g. *Moullet* v *France*, No. 27521/04, dec. 13.9.07 (finding by *Conseil d'Etat* of breach of disciplinary rules on the basis of the factual findings of a criminal court—inadmissible); *Silickiene* v *Lithuania*, No. 20496/02, 10.4.12 (confiscation of property of an accused's widow—no violation of Articles 6(1), 6(2) or Article 1 of Protocol No. 1).

[1304] No. 25424/09, 12.7.13.

undermine the applicant's acquittal or otherwise show a lack of respect for her right to the presumption of innocence.

Statements implying a person's guilt made in the course of related judicial proceedings, whilst criminal proceedings are pending (or after they have been discontinued[1305]), may violate Article 6(2). In *Diamantides v Greece (No. 2)*,[1306] pending criminal proceedings against the applicant for fraud and forgery were mentioned in a television programme. Consequently, the applicant lodged a defamation case. The domestic courts found that there had been no defamation and their decisions intimated that the applicant had committed the criminal offences. Article 6(2) was held to be applicable as the statements had been made in judical proceedings at the same time as, and in connection with, the criminal proceedings against the applicant. There was a violation of the presumption of innocence because the courts' statements left no doubt as to the applicant's guilt, even though he had either been acquitted of the charges, or criminal proceedings were still pending. In *Blake v UK*[1307] the test applied by the Court was whether the statements made (in the course of civil proceedings) could be said to have cast doubt on any previous criminal proceedings or to have prejudged any future criminal proceedings. In the case of *Ismoilov and others v Russia*,[1308] the Russian deputy prosecutor-general ordered the extradition of the applicants to Uzbekistan, noting that they had 'committed' acts of terrorism and other criminal offences. Article 6(2) was found to be applicable in view of the close link between the criminal proceedings in Uzbekistan and the extradition proceedings in Russia, and it was held to be violated because of the statement of the applicants' guilt without any qualification or reservation. There was a breach of Article 6(2) in *Kapetanios and others v Greece*[1309] where the applicants were acquitted in criminal proceedings on contraband charges, after which they were fined in administrative proceedings in relation to the same conduct. However, there was no violation of Article 6(2) in *Karaman v Germany*[1310] as a result of statements concerning the applicant (who was a suspect under investigation) made in a judgment convicting his co-accused who were tried separately. The Court found that the references to the applicant had been unavoidable and that the language of the judgment had made it sufficiently clear that any mention of the applicant did not entail a determination of his guilt. It also noted that the domestic law ruled out the drawing of inferences as to the guilt of individuals from criminal proceedings in which they had not participated.

6.386

Restrictions on the right to silence have been considered by the Court in relation to Article 6(1), rather than Article 6(2)[1311] (see above at 6.347).

6.387

[1305] *Vulakh and others v Russia*, No. 33468/03, 10.1.12.

[1306] No. 71563/01, 19.5.05.

[1307] No. 68890/01, dec. 25.10.05. See also *Zollmann v UK*, No. 62902/00, dec. 27.11.03 (re MP's statement made in the House of Commons).

[1308] No. 2947/06, 24.4.08.

[1309] Nos. 3453/12, 42941/12 and 9028/13, 30.4.15. There was also a breach of Article 4 of Protocol No. 7.

[1310] No. 17103/10, 27.2.14. See also *Müller v Germany*, No. 54963/08, 27.3.14 (statement in expert report that applicant was guilty of a criminal offence of which he had been acquitted—no violation of Article 6(2)). See, by contrast, *Navalnyy and Ofitserov v Russia*, Nos. 46632/13 and 28671/14, 23.2.16 (conviction of political activist and his alleged accomplice—prejudicial comments made in related criminal proceedings against third party—violation of Article 6(1)).

[1311] See, e.g. *Condron v UK*, No. 35718/97, 2.5.00, para. 72.

6.388 The presumption of innocence may also prevent prejudicial public comment concerning suspects, including statements by the police,[1312] prosecutors,[1313] judges,[1314] and politicians.[1315] It may apply to a person who has been arrested by the police, even before being charged. In *Allenet de Ribemont* v *France*[1316] senior police officers, together with a Minister, gave a press conference about the applicant, who had just been arrested, and named him as having been involved in the murder of an MP. The applicant was subsequently charged with aiding and abetting murder, but was later released and discharged. The Court held that Article 6(2) applied because at the time of the press conference a judicial investigation into the case had begun, and accordingly the applicant was considered to have been 'charged with a criminal offence'. Article 6(2) was violated because there had been a clear statement of the applicant's guilt that would have led the public to consider him guilty and which prejudged the findings of the judicial authorities. The Court acknowledged that in view of the right in Article 10 of the authorities to receive and impart information, Article 6(2) could not prevent the police from informing the public about ongoing criminal investigations, but they should do so with all the discretion and circumspection necessary if the presumption of innocence was to be respected.[1317] In *Butkevičius* v *Lithuania*,[1318] the applicant was a former Minister of Defence who objected to comments relating to his alleged guilt made by the Prosecutor-General and by the Chairman of Parliament in an interview with the national press, just a few days after his arrest for obtaining property by deception. Whilst acknowledging the importance of informing the public of the alleged offence, the Court found a violation of Article 6(2). Statements made to the press by the presiding regional court judge in *Lavents* v *Latvia*[1319] led to a finding of a violation of the presumption of innocence, where the judge implied that she was persuaded of the applicant's guilt and suggested that he should prove that he was not guilty.

6.389 There was a violation of Article 6(2) in *Samoila and Cionca* v *Romania*,[1320] not only because of prejudicial comments made by a prosecutor and a police commander about the applicant

---

[1312] See, e.g. *Samoila and Cionca* v *Romania*, No. 33065/03, 4.3.08.

[1313] *Daktaras* v *Lithuania*, No. 42095/98, 10.10.00; *Samoila and Cionca* v *Romania*, No. 33065/03, 4.3.08; *Khuzhin and others* v *Russia*, No. 13470/02, 23.10.08; *Fatullayev* v *Azerbaijan*, No. 40984/07, 22.4.10; *Muradverdiyev* v *Azerbaijan*, No. 16966/06, 9.12.10; *Ilgar Mammadov* v *Azerbaijan*, No. 15172/13, 22.5.14.

[1314] *Lavents* v *Latvia*, No. 58442/00, 28.11.02.

[1315] *Konstas* v *Greece*, No. 53466/07, 24.5.11. See also: *Arrigo and Vella* v *Malta*, No. 6569/04, dec. 10.5.05 (declared inadmissible in Strasbourg as the applicants could no longer claim to be 'victims' of a Convention violation, because the domestic courts had already acknowledged the breach of the applicants' right to presumption of innocence and provided redress); *Kouzmin* v *Russia*, No. 58939/00, 18.3.10 (violation of Article 6(2), by four votes to three, as a result of prejudicial comments made on television about the applicant by a candidate for the post of governor, who was also a retired army general, and a prominent figure in Russian society who had occupied various posts as a senior government official—but see the dissenting judgment disputing that the remarks could be considered to have been made by an agent of the state); *Gutsanovi* v *Bulgaria*, No. 34529/10, 15.10.13; *Mulosmani* v *Albania*, No. 29864/03, 8.10.13 (accusation of murder made by chairman of independent political party—inadmissible). In *Mustafa Kamal Mustafa* v *UK* (No. 31411/07, dec. 18.1.11) the complaints made by the Muslim cleric Abu Hamza that his right to be presumed innocent was infringed by the Home Secretary's decision to deprive him of his citizenship was rejected by the Court because there was held to be no direct link between that decision and the later decision of the CPS to prosecute him. See also *Rywin* v *Poland*, Nos. 6091/06, 4047/07 and 4070/07, 18.2.16 (alleged influence of parliamentary commission of inquiry and media coverage on criminal trial—no violation of Article 6(2), or of Article 6(1)).

[1316] No. 15175/89, 10.2.95, Series A, No. 308.

[1317] *Ibid.*, para. 38.

[1318] No. 48297/99, 26.3.02.

[1319] No. 58442/00, 28.11.02.

[1320] No. 33065/03, 4.3.08.

police officers who had been charged with corruption, but also because they were brought before the court in prison garments that were normally only worn by convicts.

Article 6(3): further rights in criminal cases

6.390 The following further rights under Article 6(3) are discussed below: prompt information on charge (6.393); adequate time, facilities and legal representation (6.395); attendance and examination of witnesses (6.406); and interpreters (6.415).

6.391 The rights set out in Article 6(3) are aspects of the general rights to a fair hearing—they are therefore not exhaustive. In addition, applicants who are not fully capable of representing themselves for mental health reasons may require 'special procedural safeguards'.[1321]

6.392 The Court has acknowledged that an issue may exceptionally be raised under Article 6 by an extradition decision 'in circumstances where the fugitive has suffered or risks suffering a flagrant denial of justice in the requesting country'.[1322] For an applicant to establish a 'flagrant denial of justice' this will necessitate 'a breach of the principles of fair trial guaranteed by Article 6 which is so fundamental as to amount to a nullification, or destruction of the very essence, of the right guaranteed by that Article'.[1323] Such a test prevents the admission of evidence obtained through torture:

> … the admission of torture evidence is manifestly contrary, not just to the provisions of Article 6, but to the most basic international standards of a fair trial. It would make the whole trial not only immoral and illegal, but also entirely unreliable in its outcome. It would, therefore, be a flagrant denial of justice if such evidence were admitted in a criminal trial.[1324]

In *Othman (Abu Qatada)* v *UK*[1325] the Court found that the applicant's deportation to Jordan would amount to a flagrant denial of justice, in violation of Article 6, because of the real risk that evidence obtained by torture of third persons would be admitted at the applicant's retrial, given that torture was widespread in Jordan, and the compelling evidence that the two witnesses who had made incriminating statements in his earlier trial in Jordan had been tortured. The cases of *Al Nashiri* v *Poland*,[1326] and *Husayn (Abu Zubaydah)* v *Poland*,[1327] concerned the detention of the applicants by the CIA in Poland and their 'extraordinary rendition', ultimately, to the US naval base at Guantánamo Bay. The Court found that, having been subjected to torture in the course of detention, there was also a violation of Article 6(1) of the Convention because, at the time of their transfer from Poland, there was a real risk that their trials before US military commissions would amount to a flagrant denial of justice. It was noted that the military commissions were composed exclusively of commissioned

---

[1321] *Megyeri* v *Germany*, No. 13770/88, Series A, No. 237-A, 12.5.92, paras. 11–12.

[1322] See *Soering* v *UK*, No. 14038/88, Series A, No. 161, 7.7.89, para. 113; *Drozd and Janousek* v *France and Spain*, No. 12747/87, 26.6.92, Series A No. 240, para. 110; *Einhorn* v *France*, No. 71555/01, dec. 16.10.01; *Wilcox and Hurford* v *UK*, Nos. 43759/10 and 43771/12, dec. 8.1.13, paras. 94–8. See also the joint partly dissenting opinion of Judges Bratza, Bonello and Hedigan in *Mamatkulov and Askarov* v *Turkey*, Nos. 46827/99 and 46951/99, 4.2.05 (arguing that there had been a violation of Article 6 in circumstances where the two applicants had been extradited to Uzbekistan, in breach of the Court's interim measures indication under Rule 39) (see further at 2.59–2.61 above).

[1323] *Ahorugeze* v *Sweden*, No. 37075/09, 27.10.11, para. 115. See also the factors set out in *Othman (Abu Qatada)* v *UK*, No. 8139/09, 17.1.12, paras. 258–9.

[1324] *Othman (Abu Qatada)* v *UK*, No. 8139/09, 17.1.12, para. 267.

[1325] No. 8139/09, 17.1.12.

[1326] No. 28761/11, 24.7.14.

[1327] No. 7511/13, 24.7.14.

officers of the US armed forces, that the US Supreme Court had found that they violated US and international law, and that their rules did not necessarily exclude any evidence, including evidence obtained under torture.

As to the requirement in Article 5(1)(a) that a conviction must be delivered by a competent court, see 6.229 above.

Prompt information on charge

6.393 Whereas Article 5(2) requires prompt reasons for an arrest (see above at 6.262), Article 6(3)(a) requires prompt information to be given when a suspect is charged or otherwise at the start of criminal proceedings. The Court has reiterated that 'the provision of full, detailed information to the defendant concerning the charges against him—and consequently the legal characterisation that the court might adopt in the matter—is an essential prerequisite for ensuring that the proceedings are fair'.[1328] Furthermore, the right under Article 6(3)(a) to be informed of the nature and the cause of the accusation should also be considered in the light of the defendant's right to prepare his defence under Article 6(3)(b).[1329] Thus in *Sadak and others* v *Turkey*,[1330] the authorities decided to change the nature of the charges against the applicants, without giving them adequate time to prepare their defence, in violation of both Articles 6(3)(a) and 6(3)(b).

6.394 In *Brozicek* v *Italy*,[1331] Article 6(3)(a) was satisfied by the provision of information to the applicant which was intended to inform him of the institution of proceedings against him (for resisting the police, assault and wounding), which listed the offences of which he was accused, with places and dates, and which named the victim and referred to the relevant criminal code provisions. However, Article 6(3)(a) was violated because it was not communicated in a language that the applicant could understand, even after he notified the authorities that he could not understand Italian. Extra steps may be required by the authorities to ensure that defendants with mental health problems are able sufficiently to understand the proceedings and to be informed in detail of the nature and cause of any accusation.[1332]

Adequate time, facilities and legal representation

6.395 Article 6(3)(b) and (c) provide that everyone charged with a criminal offence has the right to have adequate time and facilities for the preparation of his defence, and to defend himself in person or through the provision of legal assistance of his own choosing.[1333] The adequacy of the time given will depend upon the complexity of the particular case.[1334] For example, in the case of *Moiseyev* v *Russia*,[1335] which concerned criminal proceedings against the applicant for

---

[1328] *Pélissier and Sassi* v *France*, No. 25444/94, 25.3.99, para. 52.

[1329] *Ibid.*, para. 54.

[1330] Nos. 29900/96, 29901/96, 29902/96 and 29903/96, 17.7.01. When their cases were re-opened at the domestic level, the applicants in the *Sadak* case subsequently successfully complained to the Court about the unfairness of those proceedings (*Dicle and Sadak* v *Turkey*, No. 48621/07, 16.6.15). See also *Miraux* v *France*, No. 73529/01, 26.9.06; *Mattei* v *France*, No. 34043/02, 19.12.06; *Varela Geis* v *Spain*, No. 61005/09, 5.3.13. But by contrast see *Bäckström and Andersson* v *Sweden*, No. 67930/01, dec. 5.9.06.

[1331] No. 10964/84, Series A, No. 167, 19.12.89.

[1332] *Vaudelle* v *France*, No. 35683/97, 30.1.01, para. 61.

[1333] See, e.g. *Bonzi* v *Switzerland*, No. 7854/77, dec. 12.7.78, 12 DR 185.

[1334] For example, there was a violation of this right in *Galstyan* v *Armenia*, No. 26986/03, 15.11.07.

[1335] No. 62936/00, 9.10.08. See, by contrast, *Khodorkovskiy and Lebedev* v *Russia*, Nos. 11082/06 and 13772/05, 25.7.13 (where the Court acknowledged a series of difficulties faced by the defendants and their

high treason due to espionage, the Court found violations of the right to a fair trial because of a series of failings: the prosecuting authority had unrestricted control over visits to the applicant in detention by his lawyer and the exchange of documents; all documents exchanged between the applicant and his defence team were routinely read by the authorities; access by the applicant and his defence lawyers to the case file and their own notes was severely limited; and the applicant had not been provided with adequate conditions in which he could prepare his defence because of the inhuman conditions of confinement and transportation to which he was subjected.

The right to be represented by a lawyer of the defendant's choice is not absolute; it is subject **6.396** to limitations: the wishes of the defendant may be overriden where there are relevant and sufficient reasons in the interests of justice.[1336] Where there are no such reasons, the Court will go on to consider the 'overall fairness' test.

In accordance with this principle, it may be justified for the state to appoint representa- **6.397** tion or to lay down specific rules for access to particular courts, such as supreme courts, including, for example, the use of specialist lawyers.[1337] An absolute bar on defendants being tried in absentia from having legal representation will violate this provision.[1338] A refusal to allow a lawyer to defend himself in criminal proceedings may fall within the state's margin of appreciation.[1339] There was a violation of Articles 6(1) and 6(3)(c) in *Dvorski* v *Croatia*,[1340] where the applicant (a suspect in police custody) was denied access to a lawyer who had been appointed to represent him by his parents. The lawyer went to the police station to see the applicant but was turned away by the police who did not inform the applicant. In view of those circumstances, his 'choice' of another lawyer to represent him was not considered to be an informed choice. The Court rejected the Government's suggestion that the lawyer had not had a proper power of attorney and accordingly found that the reasons for refusing the applicant access to his lawyer were not relevant or sufficient. Furthermore, the overall fairness of the proceedings was undermined because during police questioning, the applicant confessed to the crimes with which he was charged and his confession was later admitted in evidence at his trial. The Court also found that the courts did not properly address this issue, and failed to take adequate remedial measures to ensure fairness.

In *Vyerentsov* v *Ukraine*[1341] the denial of the applicant's right under the domestic law to be **6.398** represented by a lawyer of his choosing, purely on the basis that he was himself a 'human rights defender' was found to violate Article 6(1) together with Article 6(3)(c).

---

lawyers in the domestic criminal proceedings, but concluded that there was no violation of Articles 6(1) and 6(3)(b)).

[1336] *Croissant* v *Germany*, No. 13611/88, Series A, No. 237-B, 25.9.92, para. 29; *Dvorski* v *Croatia*, No. 25703/11, 20.10.15, para. 79.

[1337] *Meftah and others* v *France*, Nos. 32911/96, 35237/97 and 34595/96, 26.7.02, para. 45—the Court held there was no violation of Article 6 where the applicants were not given the opportunity to plead their cases orally before the Court of Cassation, either in person or through members of the ordinary bar. See also *Fontaine and Bertin* v *France*, Nos. 38410/97 and 40373/98, 8.7.03.

[1338] *Poitrimol* v *France*, No. 14032/88, 23.11.93; *Krombach* v *France*, No. 29731/96, 13.2.01. See also *Haziri* v *France*, No. 59480/00, 29.3.05 (applicant forcibly removed to Algeria).

[1339] *Correia de Matos* v *Portugal*, No. 48188/99, dec. 15.11.01.

[1340] No. 25703/11, 20.10.15.

[1341] No. 20372/11, 11.4.13.

6.399 In the context of Article 8, the importance of the right of communication with a lawyer has been emphasised in a series of cases concerning prisoners, such as *Campbell* v *UK*[1342] in which the Court stressed that procedures concerning communication with lawyers should 'favour full and uninhibited discussion'. In *S* v *Switzerland*[1343] the applicant was arrested, with 27 others, and detained on suspicion of his involvement in cases of arson and attacks using explosives. Correspondence with his lawyer was intercepted and visits from his lawyer were supervised by police officials. In finding a violation of Article 6(3)(c), the Court rejected the Government's arguments that the possibility of collusion between defence counsel could justify such interferences. The Court emphasised that 'an accused's right to communicate with his advocate out of the hearing of a third person is one of the basic requirements of a fair trial in a democratic society'.[1344] In *Brennan* v *UK*,[1345] a police officer's presence at one interview (the first meeting of the accused with his solicitor) violated Article 6(3) in conjunction with Article 6(1). Surveillance by an investigating judge of contacts between a detainee and a lawyer, as in *Lanz* v *Austria*[1346] is a 'serious interference with an accused's defence rights and very weighty reasons should be given for its justification'. Article 6 was violated in *Lanz*: a risk of collusion was found to be insufficient. In *Zagaria* v *Italy*,[1347] while the applicant was following his court proceedings from a video-conferencing room in his detention centre, a superviser in the room eavesdropped on his conversation with his lawyer, resulting in the finding of a violation of Article 6(3)(c) taken together with Article 6(1). In *Khodorkovskiy and Lebedev* v *Russia*,[1348] there was a breach of Article 6(3)(c) where investigators searched the applicants' lawyer's office and seized his working files. This was found to amount to an infringement of the secrecy of the lawyer–client relationship, for which there was no justification and which had been carried out without adequate procedural safeguards (there had been no court warrant). The provision was also breached, for several other reasons: correspondence and notes passed between the applicants and their lawyers at the pre-trial stage was routinely monitored by the prison authorities; during their trial their legal correspondence was monitored by the judge; and the presence of escort officers in the courtroom meant that they did not have the opportunity to have private oral communications with their lawyers.

6.400 The Court has emphasised that Article 6 will normally require an accused to be given access to a lawyer at the initial stages of a criminal investigation and/or police interrogation,[1349] but that this right may be restricted if there are compelling reasons for doing so.[1350] *Ibrahim*

[1342] No. 13590/88, Series A, No. 233-A, 25.3.92.

[1343] Nos. 12629/87 and 13965/88, Series A, No. 220, 28.11.91.

[1344] Nos. 12629/87 and 13965/88, Series A, No. 220, 28.11.91, para. 48. See also *Öcalan* v *Turkey*, No. 46221/99, 12.5.05 (Article 6(3)(c) violated where the applicant was always required to consult with his lawyers within the hearing of the security forces).

[1345] No. 39846/98, 16.10.01, para. 63.

[1346] No. 24430/94, 31.1.02.

[1347] No. 58295/00, 27.11.07.

[1348] Nos. 11082/06 and 13772/05, 25.7.13.

[1349] Judges Zagrebelsky, Casadevall, Türmen and Bratza argued in their concurring opinions in the Grand Chamber judgment in *Salduz* v *Turkey*, No. 36391/02, 27.11.08 that Article 6 requires that suspects should be granted access to legal advice from the moment they are taken into police custody or pre-trial detention. See also *Dayanan* v *Turkey*, No. 7377/03, 13.10.09; *Stojkovic* v *France and Belgium*, No. 25303/08, 27.10.11; *Aras* v *Turkey (No. 2)*, No. 15065/07, 18.11.14; *Borg* v *Malta*, No. 37537/13, 12.1.16.

[1350] *Brennan* v *UK*, No. 39846/98, 16.10.01, para. 45; *Salduz* v *Turkey*, No. 36391/02, 27.11.08, para. 55; *Pishchalnikov* v *Russia*, No. 7025/04, 24.9.09, para. 70.

and others v *UK*[1351] concerned delays in the applicants' access to a lawyer during police questioning. Three of the applicants were arrested on suspicion of attempting to explode bombs on the London transport system, and were denied access to a lawyer for periods of between four and eight hours. The Grand Chamber reiterated that, as a rule, access to a lawyer should be provided from the first police interview of a suspect, unless: firstly, it could be shown that there were 'compelling reasons' to restrict that right; and, secondly, the Court was also required to evaluate the prejudice caused to the rights of the defence by the restriction, which meant assessing whether the proceedings as a whole were fair.[1352] In considering whether there were 'compelling reasons' (which had to be done on a case-by-case basis) it was relevant to consider whether the decision to restrict legal advice had a basis in domestic law and whether the scope and content of any restrictions on legal advice were sufficiently circumscribed by law so as to guide operational decision-making. For three of the applicants, there was no violation of Article 6(1) or 6(3)(c) (by 15 votes to two). The Court concluded that there had been an urgent need to avert serious adverse consequences for the life and physical integrity of the public, and hence there were compelling reasons for the temporary restrictions on their right to legal advice. In spite of those delays, and the admission at trial of statements made in the absence of legal advice, the Court concluded that the proceedings as a whole were fair. The fourth applicant was initially interviewed as a witness by police and his interview was suspended when he started to incriminate himself (having sheltered one of the other applicants). However, at that stage he was not cautioned and nor was he informed of his right to remain silent—decisions which had no basis in domestic law. Therefore, there were no compelling reasons for the restriction of the fourth applicant's right to legal advice. Accordingly, the burden of proof shifted to the Government to demonstrate convincingly why the overall fairness of the trial was not irretrievably prejudiced by the restriction on access to legal advice. On the facts of the case, this test was not met and therefore there was a violation of Articles 6(1) and 6(3)(c) (by 11 votes to six).

Particular emphasis has been placed on the fundamental importance of providing access to **6.401** a lawyer where the person in custody is a minor.[1353] There was a violation of Articles 6(1), 6(3)(c) and 6(3)(d) in *Blokhin* v *Russia*,[1354] in relation to proceedings which led to the temporary detention of a twelve-year-old suffering from ADHD. Not only was he denied legal assistance during police questioning, but he was also prevented from cross-examining the witnesses whose evidence against him had been decisive. The Grand Chamber further noted that as the applicant had been under the age of criminal responsibility he had not therefore been provided with the usual procedural guarantees provided for by the Code of Criminal Procedure.

Where there are multiple complaints about restrictions on an applicant's capability to prepare for trial, the Court will consider the cumulative effect of those restrictions on the overall fairness of the proceedings. In *Öcalan* v *Turkey*,[1355] the Court found a violation of Article

---

[1351] No. 50541/08 et al, 13.9.16.
[1352] See the non-exhaustive list of ten factors relevant to the overall fairness assessment, at para. 274 of *Ibrahim* (*Ibid.*).
[1353] *Salduz* v *Turkey*, No. 36391/02, 27.11.08, para. 60. See also *Panovits* v *Cyprus*, No. 4268/04, 11.12.08; *Adamkiewicz* v *Poland*, No. 54729/00, 2.3.10; *Blokhin* v *Russia*, No. 47152/06, 23.3.16.
[1354] No. 47152/06, 23.3.16 (by a majority of 11 to 6).
[1355] No. 46221/99, 12.5.05.

6 for a variety of reasons: the applicant was not assisted by his lawyers when questioned in police custody; he was unable to communicate with his lawyers out of hearing of officials; neither he nor his lawyers were allowed direct access to the case file until a very late stage in the proceedings; restrictions were imposed on the number and length of his lawyers' visits; and, finally, the applicant was not tried by an independent and impartial tribunal.

6.402 It has been acknowledged that the right of access to legal advice is of particular importance in the context of restrictions on a suspect's right to silence. In *John Murray* v *UK*[1356] the Court found a violation of Article 6(1) in conjunction with Article 6(3)(c) where the applicant had been denied access to a lawyer for the first 48 hours of his detention. Under the Criminal Evidence (Northern Ireland) Order 1988, the drawing of adverse inferences was permitted from the refusal to answer questions in interview and in such circumstances the Court held that the denial of access to a lawyer violated Article 6. However, in *Brennan* v *UK*,[1357] the deferral of access to a solicitor for 24 hours was found to be justified on reasonable grounds because of risks that others allegedly involved in the offence might have been alerted. It was significant that no incriminating statements were made in the 24-hour period and no inferences were drawn as a result of any statements or omissions made in that period.

6.403 Free legal assistance will only be required where the defendant has insufficient means to pay and where it is required in the interests of justice,[1358] which will depend upon both the severity of the penalty and the complexity of the case in question.[1359] Thus, the Court will assess whether a defendant can present a case adequately without a lawyer, and whether they have sufficient understanding of the language used in court and the judicial system.

6.404 Where deprivation of liberty is at stake, the interests of justice in principle require legal representation. Applying these criteria, the Court found a violation of Articles 6(1) and 6(3)(c) in *Benham* v *UK*[1360] where legal aid was not available for magistrates' court proceedings for non-payment of the community charge. Having found that Article 6 was applicable to disciplinary proceedings brought against prisoners, the Grand Chamber in *Ezeh and Connors* v *UK*[1361] found that Article 6(3)(c) had been violated because the applicants had been denied the right to legal representation for their hearings before the prison governor. The interests of justice require a fair procedure, which imposes an obligation on the state to offer defendants a realistic chance to defend themselves throughout the entire trial, including in cassation or appeal courts.[1362] In *RD* v *Poland*,[1363] the domestic law did not give the convicted appellant the choice between appointing a lawyer or preparing his appeal himself. It was compulsory to have an advocate, but the appellant was refused free legal assistance and was only informed eight days before the expiry of the time limit for submitting his cassation appeal.

[1356] No. 18731/91, 28.10.94. See also, *Magee* v *UK*, No. 28135/95, 6.6.00 and *Averill* v *UK*, No. 36408/97, 6.6.00. In contrast, see *Latimer* v *UK*, No. 12141/04, dec. 31.5.05.

[1357] No. 39846/98, 16.10.01, paras. 45–8.

[1358] *Pham Hoang* v *France*, No. 13191/87, 25.9.92, para. 39.

[1359] See, e.g. *Barsom and Varli* v *Sweden*, Nos. 40766/06 and 40831/06, dec. 4.1.08; *Volkov and Adamskiy* v *Russia*, Nos. 7614/09 and 30863/10, 26.3.15; *Mikhaylova* v *Russia*, No. 46998/08, 19.11.15.

[1360] No. 19380/92, 10.6.96.

[1361] Nos. 39665/98 and 40086/98, 9.10.03 (see also 6.294 above).

[1362] *Vacher* v *France*, No. 20368/92, 17.12.96, para. 30.

[1363] Nos. 29692/96 and 34612/97, 18.12.01.

The inability of appellants in criminal appeal proceedings in Greece to obtain legal aid has been found to violate Articles 6(1) and 6(3)(c).[1364]

Where a defendant is assigned a lawyer under a state legal aid scheme, it has often been said by the Court that the state cannot be held responsible for every shortcoming on the part of a lawyer appointed for legal-aid purposes: the authorities will be required under Article 6(3)(c) to intervene only if a failure by a legal aid lawyer to provide effective representation is 'manifest or sufficiently brought to their attention in some other way'. There was a violation of this obligation in *Czekalla v Portugal*[1365] where a procedural error by the defendant's state-assigned lawyer meant that he was denied access to appeal to the Supreme Court. According to the European Court, this situation 'therefore imposed on the relevant court the positive obligation to ensure practical and effective respect for the applicant's right to due process', such as intervening to correct the error. In *Sakhnovskiy v Russia*[1366] there was a violation of Article 6(1) and Article 6(3)(c) in circumstances where the applicant, appealing against his conviction for murder, was only given 15 minutes to consult with his newly appointed legal aid counsel prior to an appeal hearing. This was clearly insufficient given the seriousness and complexity of the case. Furthermore, he was only able to do so by video link from his detention centre in Novosibirsk, while his lawyer was in Moscow. **6.405**

Attendance and examination of witnesses

Article 6(3)(d) provides defendants with the right both to examine prosecution witnesses and to call witnesses and have them examined under similar conditions: 'all the evidence must normally be produced in the presence of the accused at a public hearing with a view to adversarial argument'.[1367] Although the Article refers to 'witnesses', the principle has also been held to apply to victims, expert witnesses and others who testify before a court, as well as to documentary evidence.[1368] The Convention does not completely prohibit relying on evidence that has not been examined in adversarial proceedings, but in such circumstances the Court has held that the evidence should be treated 'with extreme care'.[1369] **6.406**

As regards the non-attendance of a witness, the Grand Chamber in *Al-Khawaja and Tahery v UK*[1370] held that there are two tests; first, there must be a good reason for it,[1371] and, secondly, when a conviction is based solely or to a decisive degree on depositions that have been made **6.407**

[1364] *Twalib v Greece*, No. 24294/94, 9.6.98; *Biba v Greece*, No. 33170/96, 26.9.00. In *Biba*, the applicant was an Albanian national convicted of murder and sentenced to life imprisonment and yet legal aid was not available for cassation proceedings.

[1365] No. 38830/97, 10.10.02. See also *Sannino v Italy*, No. 30961/03, 27.4.06; *Bogumil v Portugal*, No. 35228/03, 7.10.08; *Vamvakas v Greece*, No. 2870/11, 9.4.15. But contrast, e.g. with *Rutkowski v Poland*, No. 45995/99, dec. 19.10.00.

[1366] No. 21272/03, 2.11.10.

[1367] See, e.g. *Lüdi v Switzerland*, No. 12433/86, Series A, No. 238, 15.6.92, para. 47.

[1368] See, e.g. *Mirilashvili v Russia*, No. 6293/04, 11.12.08, para. 158–9; *Khodorkovskiy and Lebedev v Russia*, Nos. 11082/06 and 13772/05, 25.7.13, para. 711 (as to expert witnesses).

[1369] *S.N. v Sweden*, No. 34209/96, 2.7.02, para. 53.

[1370] Nos. 26766/05 and 22228/06, 15.12.11. This is a leading authority on hearsay evidence (tempering the position of the chamber judgment in the case—20.1.09), and earlier case-law should be reviewed in the light of the principles which it sets out. See also *Donohoe v Ireland*, No. 19165/08, 12.12.13 (admission in evidence of police testimony based on undisclosed sources against person accused of IRA membership—no violation of Article 6(1)); *Paić v Croatia*, No. 47082/12, 29.3.16 (conviction on basis of statement of overseas witness who could not be cross-examined—violation of Article 6(3)(d)).

[1371] See, e.g. *Rudnichenko v Ukraine*, No. 2775/07, 11.7.13.

by a person whom the accused has had no opportunity to examine (during the investigation or at the trial), the rights of the defence may be restricted to an extent that is incompatible with Article 6. However, the Court also clarified that where a hearsay statement is the sole or decisive evidence, its admission will not automatically violate Article 6. Nevertheless, in that situation, the Court must exercise 'the most searching scrutiny'—to ascertain whether there are sufficient counterbalancing factors in place, including measures that permit a fair and proper assessment of the reliability of the evidence to be carried out.[1372] Applying the *Al-Khawaja* tests, the Court found no violation arising from convictions based on statements by absent witnesses in *Horncastle and others* v *UK*.[1373] As regards the first and second applicants, the victim's death had made it necessary to admit his witness statement as hearsay evidence. The victim in the other case had refused to give evidence because of her fear for her family's safety—the Court was satisfied that the trial judge had undertaken appropriate enquiries concerning the level of her fear to demonstrate the need to admit her written statement. The Court further found that the statements were not considered to be 'decisive', and in any event, as regards the first and second applicants, the Court took account of the safeguards provided by the legislative framework regulating the circumstances in which hearsay evidence could be admitted and the possibility for the applicants to challenge its admission. In 2015, the Grand Chamber further refined the *Al-Khawaja* test in the case of *Schatschaschwili* v *Germany*,[1374] stipulating that the absence of a good reason for the non-attendance of a witness is not *of itself* conclusive of the unfairness of a trial (although it is a very important factor in assessing its overall fairness). The Court also clarified that even in the absence of a finding that the hearsay evidence in question was the 'sole or decisive' evidence in convicting the accused, it should still assess whether there were sufficient counter-balancing factors in place (given that the Court is ascertaining the overall fairness of the proceedings). Finally, the Court found that the three steps in the *Al-Khawaja* test would usually be considered in the same order as in that case, but that it may be necessary in some cases to consider them in a different order. The difficulty of making an assessment of fairness using the *Al-Khawaja* criteria is perhaps illustrated by the decision on the merits in *Schatschaschwili*—a finding of a violation of Article 6(1) by nine votes to eight. There, the majority of the Court found that there had been good reason (from the domestic court's perspective) for the non-attendance of two key witnesses to the robbery in question because, in effect, they could not be reached in Latvia, or compelled to attend the trial in Germany. It also held that as they were the only eye-witnesses to the robbery, their evidence was to be considered 'decisive'. Finally, as regards the compensatory procedural measures available to the applicant, the Grand Chamber found that the prosecution authorities had not given the applicant an opportunity to have the two witnesses questioned at the investigation stage by a lawyer appointed to represent him, and therefore the trial as a whole was considered unfair, in violation of Articles 6(1) and 6(3)(d).[1375]

[1372] *Al-Khawaja and Tahery* v *UK*, Nos. 26766/05 and 22228/06, 15.12.11, para. 147.

[1373] No. 4184/10, 16.12.14. See, by contrast, *Balta and Demir* v *Turkey*, No. 48628/12, 23.6.15 (conviction based on statements of anonymous witness whom the defendant had been unable to question—violation of Article 6(1)).

[1374] No. 9154/10, 15.12.15. Note, however, that the majority's refinements to the *Al-Khawaja* tests were disputed in the joint concurring opinion of Judges Spielmann, Karakaş Sajó and Keller. See also *Constantinides* v *Greece*, No. 76438/12, 6.10.16.

[1375] Six dissenters (Judges Hirvelä, Popović, Pardalos, Nussberger, Mahoney and Kūris) argued that, on the contrary, there were sufficient procedural protections available to the defendant.

In *Craxi* v *Italy*,[1376] the applicant, the former Italian Prime Minister Benedetto Craxi, had **6.408** been convicted solely on the basis of statements made before his trial by other defendants who had chosen not to give evidence in court, and by a person who had subsequently died. The Court found a violation of Article 6(3)(d) together with Article 6(1) as the applicant and his lawyers had not had the opportunity of cross-examining those witnesses and had consequently not been able to challenge the statements that had formed the legal basis for the applicant's conviction. There was a violation of these provisions in *Orhan Çaçan* v *Turkey*,[1377] where the applicant's conviction was based to a decisive extent on the statements of a key witness who did not appear at the hearing and who had subsequently retracted his evidence. However, there was no violation of Article 6 in *Mika* v *Sweden*[1378] where the applicant was convicted of raping a woman who committed suicide a few days later. Her statement to the police was used as evidence to convict him. The authorities could not be blamed for the applicant not having had the opportunity to question her. Furthermore, her statement was not the sole evidence used in the proceedings against him, but had been corroborated by additional oral and written evidence. There was a violation of Article 6(3)(d) in *Khodorkovskiy and Lebedev* v *Russia*,[1379] because the applicant's request to have two expert witnesses attend their trial in order to be cross-examined was denied by the district court simply on the basis that the court already had their written opinions—the Court concluded that there had been no good reasons for them not to attend the trial. There was also a breach because the defence had been prevented from adducing expert audit evidence on grounds of admissibility under the domestic law, which the Court held violated the principle of equality of arms. In *Al-Khawaja and Tahery* v *UK*[1380] the Court reached differing conclusions as to the position of the two applicants. For Mr Al-Khawaja, it had been necessary to admit the statement of a witness who had died, whose evidence was found to be 'decisive'. However, there were sufficient counter-balancing factors to conclude that its admission did not breach the Convention, notably the strong corroborative evidence in the case and the judge's direction to the jury indicating that the statement should carry less weight. In Mr Tahery's case the witness did not attend the trial because she was afraid to do so. The Court found it had been justified to admit her statement (which was also 'decisive'), but as there had not been any strong corroborative evidence in the case, the jury had been unable to conduct a fair and proper assessment of the reliability of the witness's evidence. There was therefore a violation of Article 6(1) taken together with Article 6(3)(d).

The non-appearance of witnesses living abroad may give rise to a violation of the Convention, **6.409** depending on the measures taken by the authorities to try to summon them to give evidence in person, and other factors such as the extent of corroboration and the question of the overall fairness of the proceedings.[1381] There was a violation of Article 6(1) in *Mirilashvili* v *Russia*,[1382] where a military court placed substantial reliance on statements given by three

---

[1376] No. 34896/97, 5.12.02.
[1377] No. 26437/04, 23.3.10.
[1378] No. 31243/06, dec. 27.1.09. There was a similar outcome in *Gani* v *Spain*, No. 61800/08, 19.2.13, as a result of the admission in evidence of a statement by the sole prosecution witness in a rape case who could not be cross-examined because of her post-traumatic stress disorder.
[1379] Nos. 11082/06 and 13772/05, 25.7.13.
[1380] Nos. 26766/05 and 22228/06, 15.12.11.
[1381] See, e.g. *Klimentyev* v *Russia*, No. 46503/99, 16.11.06 (no violation of Article 6(3)(d)).
[1382] No. 6293/04, 11.12.08.

witnesses in Georgia who did not appear before the court. It was accepted that the court had requested the Georgian authorities to secure their attendance at the trial, but without success. However, the court then refused to admit statements taken from the witnesses in Georgia by the applicant's lawyers in which they retracted their previous testimonies, which was not considered to be justified and led to a finding that the proceedings as a whole were not fair.

6.410 The use of anonymous witnesses (for example where there is a threat of witness intimidation) may violate the Convention because the defence is unable to test the witness's reliability or question their credibility.[1383] Convictions should not therefore be founded either solely or to a decisive extent on statements of anonymous witnesses.[1384] Furthermore, the Court has stated that, when assessing whether the procedures followed in questioning anonymous witnesses were sufficient to counter-balance the difficulties caused to the defendants, due weight should be given to the extent to which their evidence was decisive in convicting the defendant.[1385] It may be necessary to refer to depositions taken at the investigation stage (where, for example, a witness refuses to repeat his allegations in public), but in that case the defendant should have been given the opportunity to challenge those statements, either when they were made, or subsequently.[1386] This also applies to statements made by a co-accused: in *Luca* v *Italy*,[1387] there was a violation of Article 6(3)(d) because the applicant was convicted on the basis of statements made to the public prosecutor in connected proceedings, by his co-accused, and the applicant was not given the opportunity to examine them.

6.411 The Convention system recognises that there may be competing interests between the defence and prosecution witnesses, especially where life, liberty or the security of the person are at stake, as well as rights under Article 8.[1388] Only such measures restricting the rights of the defence that are strictly necessary are permissible under Article 6(1).[1389] The Court has recognised the need to take steps to protect the interests of juvenile witnesses, in particular in proceedings involving sexual offences. Article 6(3)(d) was violated in *PS* v *Germany*[1390] where the defendant was accused of sexually abusing an eight-year-old girl and the domestic courts based their finding of guilt to a decisive extent on the girl's statements. However, at no stage was she questioned by a judge and the applicant had no opportunity to test her reliability. That finding can be contrasted with the decision in *SN* v *Sweden*[1391] in which the Court found no violation in comparable circumstances. There, the defendant was accused of the sexual abuse of a young boy, whose interviews were recorded by video and audio tape and were played during the proceedings. This was found to be sufficient to enable the defendant

---

[1383] See, e.g. *Kostovski* v *Netherlands*, No. 11454/85, Series A, No. 166, 20.11.89; *Visser* v *Netherlands*, No. 26668/95, 14.2.02; *Birutis and others* v *Lithuania*, Nos. 47698/99 and 48115/99, 28.3.02; and *Doorson* v *Netherlands*, No. 20524/92, 26.3.96 (where, exceptionally, the maintenance of witnesses' anonymity did not violate Article 6).

[1384] *Van Mechelen* v *Netherlands*, Nos. 21363/93, 21427/93 and 22056/93, 23.4.97, para. 55; *Krasniki* v *Czech Republic*, No. 51277/99, 28.2.06; *Sapunarescu* v *Germany*, No. 22007/03, dec. 11.9.06.

[1385] *Kok* v *Netherlands*, No. 43149/98, dec. 4.7.00; *Visser* v *Netherlands*, No. 26668/95, 14.2.02.

[1386] See, e.g. *Unterpertinger* v *Austria*, No. 9120/80, Series A, No. 238, 24.11.86, paras. 31–3.

[1387] No. 33354/96, 27.2.01, para. 41.

[1388] *Doorson* v *Netherlands*, No. 20524/92, 26.3.96, para. 70.

[1389] See, e.g. *Van Mechelen and others* v *Netherlands*, No. 21363/93, 21427/93 and 22056/93, 23.4.97.

[1390] No. 33900/96, 20.12.01, para. 28.

[1391] No. 34209/96, 2.7.02 (no violation, by five votes to two, with Judges Türmen and Maruste dissenting). See also *Accardi and others* v *Italy*, No. 30598/02, dec. 20.1.05.

to challenge the boy's statements. The Court reiterated that in criminal proceedings concerning sexual offences, Article 6(3)(d) cannot require in all cases that questions be put by the defendant or the defendant's lawyer, by way of cross-examination, or otherwise. Indeed, in assessing whether the accused has had a fair trial, account should be taken of the right to respect for the private life of the perceived victim.[1392]

In *Papageorgiou* v *Greece*,[1393] criminal proceedings for fraud were found to have violated **6.412** Articles 6(1) and 6(3)(d) as the court failed, despite the applicant's repeated requests, to produce the originals of the cheques in question, which was considered to be vital to the applicant's case and which might have enabled him successfully to establish that the allegation was unfounded.

The use of evidence obtained as a result of police incitement (for example, by undercover **6.413** agents) will not, however, be justified by the public interest. Thus in *Teixeira de Castro* v *Portugal*[1394] the Court found that the activities of two police officers (in an investigation of drug dealing) had gone beyond that of undercover agents, in that they had not 'confined themselves to investigating the applicant's criminal activity in an essentially passive manner', but had 'exercised an influence such as to incite the commission of the offence'.[1395] Thus the first consideration for the Court will be whether the offence would have been committed without the intervention of the authorities. This will involve assessing the reasons for the operation in question and examining the conduct of the authorities in carrying it out. Secondly, the Court will examine the way the domestic courts dealt with the applicant's plea of incitement. This will mean verifying whether an arguable complaint of incitement amounts to a substantive defence under domestic law, or could lead to the exclusion of evidence, or similar consequences.[1396] Applying this second test in *Lagutin and others* v *Russia*[1397] the Court found a violation of Article 6(1) because of the domestic courts' failure to deal adequately with the applicant defendants' allegations of entrapment. In particular, they took no steps to verify the content of the police operational files allegedly implicating them in drug trafficking.

Where evidence is withheld on public interest grounds, it should be the trial judge, rather **6.414** than the prosecution, who attempts to assess the importance of concealed information to the defence and weigh this against the public interest in keeping the information secret. For this reason there was a violation of Article 6(1) in *Rowe and Davis* v *UK*.[1398] There,

---

[1392] See *Y.* v *Slovenia*, No. 41107/10, 28.5.15 (failure to protect girl's personal integrity in criminal proceedings concerning sexual abuse—violation of Article 8 (discussed further at 6.486 below).

[1393] No. 59506/00, 9.5.03.

[1394] No. 25829/94, 9.6.98.

[1395] See also *Vanyan* v *Russia*, No. 53203/99, 15.12.05; *Khudobin* v *Russia*, No. 59696/00, 26.10.06; *Ramanauskas* v *Lithuania*, No. 74420/01, 5.2.08. In contrast, see *Calabro* v *Italy*, No. 59895/00, dec. 21.3.02; *Sequeira* v *Portugal*, No. 73557/01, dec. 6.5.03; *Miliniene* v *Lithuania*, No. 74355/01, 24.6.08; *Veselov and others* v *Russia*, Nos. 23200/10, 24009/07 and 556/10, 2.10.12. See further *Shannon* v *UK*, No. 67537/01, dec. 6.4.04 (entrapment by a private individual—a journalist).

[1396] See also *Bannikova* v *Russia*, No. 18757/06, 4.11.10 which includes an extensive review of the Court's case law on entrapment at paras. 33–65.

[1397] No. 6228/09 et al, 24.4.14. See, by contrast, *Kuzmickaja* v *Lithuania*, No. 27968/03, dec. 10.6.08; *Volkov and Adamskiy* v *Russia*, Nos. 7614/09 and 30863/10, 26.3.15.

[1398] No. 28901/95, 16.2.00. See also *Altan* v *UK*, No. 36533/97, 19.6.01; *Dowsett* v *UK*, No. 39482/98, 24.6.03 (note the concurring opinion of Judge Bratza, joined by Judge Costa, arguing that the failure of the defence to apply to the Court of Appeal to review the material in question did not distinguish the case from

the Court held that the defect in the trial proceedings was not remedied by the Court of Appeal, which was dependent for its understanding of the possible relevance of the undisclosed material on transcripts of the Crown Court hearings and on the account of the issues given by prosecuting counsel. The Court also noted that the first instance judge would have been in a position to monitor the need for disclosure throughout the trial, whereas the Court of Appeal was obliged to carry out its appraisal ex post facto. Where allegations of entrapment had arisen in *Edwards and Lewis* v *UK*,[1399] the European Court was not in a position to ascertain whether there had in fact been entrapment as the relevant information had not been disclosed by the prosecuting authorities (on public interest grounds, following an ex parte application). Accordingly, its role was to examine the way in which the plea of entrapment had been considered. The Court found that the applicants had been denied access to the evidence, making it impossible for the defence to argue the case of entrapment in full before the trial judge, in violation of the requirements to provide adversarial proceedings and equality of arms under Article 6(1). In *Mirilashvili* v *Russia*,[1400] the Court was critical of the domestic court's decision-making process in refusing to disclose to the defence materials related to the telephone tapping of the applicant in the course of criminal proceedings, because in doing so it failed to weigh up the public interest against the rights of the accused.

Interpreters

6.415   Article 6(3)(e) provides an unqualified right to free interpretation for those who cannot understand or speak the language used in court. This right extends prior to trial to the translation or interpretation of all documents and statements in the proceedings that it is necessary for a defendant to understand in order to have a fair trial.[1401] Therefore, the Court has held that the assistance of an interpreter should be provided during the investigating stage, unless there are compelling reasons in a particular case to restrict this right.[1402] Accordingly, there was a violation of this provision in *Baytar* v *Turkey*[1403] where the applicant was not provided with an interpreter when being questioned in police custody, and the statements she made were subsequently relied on by the court in finding her guilty.

6.416   There was a violation of this provision in *Cuscani* v *UK*[1404] where the defendant, an Italian national, was not provided with an interpreter during his hearing on sentencing, after the defendant's counsel suggested that they could 'make do and mend' by using the applicant's brother as interpreter. Taking into account the fact that the trial judge had been made aware of the defendant's poor command of English, and that he had pleaded guilty to serious

---

Rowe and Davis). But see *Jasper* v *UK*, No. 27052/95, 16.2.00; *Fitt* v *UK*, No. 29777/96, 16.2.00; *PG and JH* v *UK*, No. 44787/98, 25.9.01; *Botmeh and Alami* v *UK*, No. 15187/03, 7.6.07.

[1399] Nos. 39647/98 and 40461/98, 22.7.03. This decision was referred to the Grand Chamber under Article 43, at the Government's request. However, the Government subsequently decided not to pursue the matter before the Grand Chamber, which merely endorsed the Chamber's decision (Grand Chamber judgment of 27.10.04).

[1400] No. 6293/04, 11.12.08.

[1401] *Luedicke, Belkacem and Koç* v *Germany*, Series A, No. 29, 28.11.78, para. 48 and *Kamasinski* v *Austria*, No. 9783/82, Series A, No. 168, 19.12.89, para. 74. The provision does not necessitate a written translation of *any* documentary evidence or official paper in a criminal case file: *Husain* v *Italy*, No. 18913/03, dec. 24.2.05.

[1402] See, e.g. *Diallo* v *Sweden*, No. 13205/07, dec. 5.1.10.

[1403] No. 45440/04, 14.10.14.

[1404] No. 32771/96, 24.9.02. See also *Baytar* v *Turkey*, No. 45440/04, 14.10.14, para. 57.

charges of fraud, the Court held that the position should have been verified by the judge, who was required to treat the defendant's interests with 'scrupulous care', and was therefore required to satisfy himself that the absence of an interpreter would not prejudice the defendant's full involvement in the proceedings. In *Isyar v Bulgaria*[1405] there was a violation of Article 6(3)(e) as the applicant was required to pay all the interpreting costs incurred in the criminal proceedings against him.

Article 7: No Punishment Without Law

Article 7 states: **6.417**

1. No one shall be held guilty of any criminal offence on account of any act or omission which did not constitute a criminal offence under national or international law at the time when it was committed. Nor shall a heavier penalty be imposed than the one that was applicable at the time the criminal offence was committed.
2. This article shall not prejudice the trial and punishment of any person for any act or omission which, at the time when it was committed, was criminal according to the general principles of law recognised by civilised nations.

The first sentence of Article 7(1) embodies two key principles. Firstly, Article 7 prevents **6.418** the retrospective application of the criminal law. Thus in *Veeber v Estonia (No. 2)*[1406] there was a violation of this principle where the applicant company director was convicted of tax offences committed in 1993 and 1994, under an amendment to the criminal law that had only entered into force in 1995, and where the conduct in question had not previously amounted to a criminal offence.

Secondly, Article 7 also requires sufficient accessibility and precision of the criminal law. In **6.419** *Kokkinakis v Greece*[1407] the Court stated that Article 7:

embodies, more generally, the principle that only the law can define a crime and prescribe a penalty ... and the principle that the criminal law must not be extensively construed to an accused's detriment, for instance by analogy; it follows from this that an offence must be clearly defined in law. This condition is satisfied where the individual can know from the wording of the relevant provision and, if need be, with the assistance of the courts' interpretation of it, what acts and omissions will make him liable.

There was a violation of this principle in *Kafkaris v Cyprus*[1408] as the domestic law in Cyprus **6.420** was found not to be formulated with sufficient precision as to enable the applicant to discern,

---

[1405] No. 391/03, 20.11.08.
[1406] No. 45771/99, 21.1.03. See also *Puhk v Estonia*, No. 55103/00, 10.2.04.
[1407] No. 14307/88, Series A, No. 260-A, 25.5.93.
[1408] No. 21906/04, 12.2.08. See also, e.g. *Sud Fondi srl and others v Italy*, No. 75909/01, 20.1.09 (imposition of penalty of confiscation of properties insufficiently prescribed by law) and the comparable case of *Varvara v Italy*, No. 17475/09, 29.10.13; *Vyerentsov v Ukraine*, No. 20372/11, 11.4.13 (absence of clear and foreseeable legislation laying down the rules for the holding of peaceful demonstrations); *Plechkov v Romania*, No. 1660/03, 16.9.14 (conviction for illegal fishing based on unforeseeable application of legislation— violation of Article 7). The situation in *Kafkaris* was contrasted by the Grand Chamber with the position of the applicants in *A and others v UK*, No. 3455/05, 19.2.09, who were detained under the Anti-Terrorism, Crime and Security Act 2001. Whilst they had been left in a state of uncertainty, the Court found that it could not be said that the applicants in *A and others* were without any prospect or hope of release. See also *Dallas v UK*, No. 38395/12, 11.2.16 (juror's committal for contempt of court for disobeying judge's instructions not to conduct internet research—law of contempt considered to be accessible and foreseeable—no violation of Article 7).

even with appropriate advice, the scope of the penalty of life imprisonment that was imposed on him following his conviction for murder, or the manner of its execution. It was simply not clear what the penalty of life imprisonment entailed at the particular time. In *Camilleri* v *Malta*[1409] the prosecutor had a discretion as to which court (criminal court or magistrates' court) would hear the criminal proceedings against the applicant, which meant that there were two possible ranges of sentences. The domestic law did not contain any criteria as to how the prosecutor's discretion would be exercised, and therefore it did not satisfy the foreseeability principle as required by Article 7.

6.421 Article 7 must be construed in line with its object and purpose, so as 'to provide effective safeguards against arbitrary prosecution, conviction and punishment'.[1410] No derogation from Article 7 is ever possible.

6.422 Article 7 applies only in circumstances where there is a finding of guilt in criminal proceedings and/or the imposition of a criminal penalty.[1411] However, the fact that proceedings may be defined by the domestic authorities as 'civil' rather than criminal will not be decisive: the Court has found 'criminal proceedings' to be an autonomous concept.

6.423 The Court has stated that Article 7(1) permits an element of judicial interpretation, where there is a need for the elucidation of doubtful points,[1412] and for adaptation to changing circumstances—such as the succession of one state over another. The cases brought following the reunification of Germany illustrate this latter point. In *Streletz, Kessler and Krenz* v *Germany*,[1413] the applicants were former senior leaders of the German Democratic Republic (GDR), which operated a border-policing policy (including anti-personnel mines and automatic firing systems) that flagrantly infringed human rights standards. The Court found that they had 'created the appearance of legality' emanating from the GDR's legal system, but as they had implemented or continued a practice that disregarded the very principles of that system, they could not plead the protection of Article 7(1) of the Convention. Similarly, an application under Article 7 brought by a former prosecutor of political trials during the communist era in Czechoslovakia was rejected by the Court in *Polednová* v *Czech Republic*.[1414] The application of the criminal law, leading to her conviction for murder, was not considered arbitrary, indeed: 'the practice of eliminating opponents to a political regime through the death penalty, imposed at the end of trials which flagrantly infringed the right to a fair trial and, in particular, the right to life, cannot be described as "law" within the meaning of Article 7 of the Convention'.

6.424 There was a violation of Article 7(1) in *Dragotoniu and Militaru-Pidhorni* v *Romania*[1415] where employees of a private bank were convicted of accepting bribes under a provision of the Criminal Code that, at the material time, was only applicable to public servants or

---

[1409] No. 42931/10, 22.1.13.
[1410] *SW and CR* v *UK*, No. 20166/92, Series A, No. 355-B, 22.11.95.
[1411] See, e.g. *Berland* v *France*, No. 42875/10, 3.9.15 (compulsory hospitalisation and other measures imposed following declaration of exemption from criminal responsibility, not amounting to a 'penalty'—Article 7 not applicable).
[1412] See, e.g. *Ashlarba* v *Georgia*, No. 45554/08, 15.7.14 (applicant's conviction for being a member of the 'thieves' underworld' was sufficiently foreseeable—no violation of Article 7).
[1413] Nos. 34044/96, 35532/97 and 44801/98, 22.3.02. See also *K-HW* v *Germany*, No. 37201/97, 22.3.01.
[1414] No. 2615/10, dec. 21.6.11.
[1415] Nos. 77193/01 and 77196/01, 24.5.07.

people working for a state-owned company. There was no violation of Article 7(1) in *Jorgic v Germany*[1416] where the Court found that the national courts' interpretation of the crime of genocide under domestic law, so as to cover the applicant's acts committed in the course of ethnic cleansing in Bosnia and Herzegovina, was consistent with the essence of the offence and could reasonably have been foreseen by the applicant. The applicants in *Khodorkovskiy and Lebedev v Russia*[1417] sought to raise Article 7 in order to challenge the unforeseeability of the domestic law on 'tax evasion'. The Court concluded that although their case had involved a 'novel interpretation' of the concept of tax evasion, it had been based on a reasonable interpretation of the criminal code, which was consistent with the essence of the offence. The Court reiterated that Article 7 'is not incompatible with judicial law-making and does not outlaw the gradual clarification of the rules of criminal liability through judicial interpretation from case to case, provided that the resultant development is consistent with the essence of the offence and could reasonably be foreseen'.[1418]

The prohibition of the retrospective application of the criminal law includes developments **6.425** through the common law where the definition of a criminal offence is extended to include conduct that had not previously been considered to be a crime. There will be no breach of Article 7, however, where common law developments are consistent with the essence of the offence in question and where they could have been reasonably foreseen. For example, the applicants in *SW and CR v UK*[1419] argued that the House of Lords' removal of the marital rape exemption violated Article 7. However, the Court held that the change in the law had been gradually evolved through judicial interpretation and was reasonably foreseeable and accordingly Article 7 had not been violated.

The Court has also confirmed that it is legitimate under Article 7 for a state to bring criminal **6.426** proceedings against persons who have committed crimes under a former regime, and that the courts of such a state, having taken the place of those that existed previously, cannot be criticised for applying and interpreting the legal provisions in force at the material time.[1420] The applicant in *Glässner v Germany*,[1421] in his capacity as public prosecutor in the former GDR, had intentionally called for a manifestly disproportionate sentence during the trial of a famous East German dissident in the 1970s, concerning his authorship of a book advocating reform of the socialist regime. The case was declared inadmissible as at the time when it was committed the applicant's act constituted an offence (perversion of the course of justice) that was defined with sufficient accessibility and foreseeability in the domestic law of the GDR.

The applicant in *Achour v France*[1422] was convicted of a second drug-trafficking offence, and **6.427** his sentence was increased as a result of an amended law on recidivism that had been introduced after he had been convicted of the first drug-trafficking offence and served his sentence. He argued that the harsher provisions of the new law on recidivism had been applied

---

[1416] No. 74613/01, 12.7.07. See also, e.g. *Moiseyev v Russia*, No. 62936/00, 9.10.08 (domestic court's interpretation of crime of espionage considered reasonably foreseeable).
[1417] Nos. 11082/06 and 13772/05, 25.7.13.
[1418] *Ibid.*, para. 821.
[1419] No. 20166/92, Series A, No. 355-B, 22.11.95.
[1420] *Glässner v Germany*, No. 46362/99, dec. 28.6.01.
[1421] *Ibid.*
[1422] No. 67335/01, 29.3.06.

retrospectively, in violation of Article 7. The Grand Chamber rejected his claim, finding that the sentence imposed on the applicant, who was found guilty and held to be a recidivist in those proceedings, was applicable at the time when the second offence was committed, in accordance with a law that was sufficiently accessible and foreseeable as to its effect.

6.428 The second sentence of Article 7(1) prevents the imposition of a heavier penalty than that which could have been imposed when the offence was committed. For example, there was a violation of this principle in *Gabarri Moreno* v *Spain*[1423] because of the failure of the domestic courts to reduce the applicant's sentence in accordance with the relevant law on mitigating circumstances. There was also a breach of Article 7 in *Maktouf and Damjanović* v *Bosnia and Herzegovina*,[1424] where the applicants were convicted of war crimes against civilians committed in the early 1990s and they were sentenced (to five years' and eleven years' imprisonment, respectively) under the 2003 Criminal Code, rather than under the 1976 Criminal Code which was applicable at the time of the commission of the offences, and which provided for more lenient minimum sentences.

6.429 The Court draws a distinction between a measure that constitutes in substance a 'penalty' (to which Article 7 applies) and one which concerns the 'execution' or 'enforcement' of a penalty (to which Article 7 does not apply).[1425] Thus, a measure concerning the remission of a sentence, or a change in a regime for early release, or a transfer under the Additional Protocol to the Convention on the Transfer of Sentenced Prisoners, do not amount to a 'penalty' within the meaning of Article 7.[1426]

6.430 However, this distinction is not always very evident. In *Del Río Prada* v *Spain*[1427] the date of the applicant's release from prison was delayed (from July 2008 to June 2017) when the case law relating to the remission of sentences was amended while she was in prison. This change was held to amount to a redefinition of the scope of the 'penalty' imposed and therefore Article 7 was applicable. It resulted from a departure by the Supreme Court from previous case law, which had not been reasonably foreseeable (unlike the position in *SW and CR* v *UK*, discussed above at 6.425), and accordingly, the Grand Chamber found a violation of Article 7. The Court also found that the applicant's detention since July 2008 had not been lawful, in breach of Article 5(1), and it ordered the state to ensure her release at the earliest possible date.

6.431 Like 'criminal offence', the term 'penalty' has an autonomous meaning;[1428] so the classification of a particular provision under domestic law will not be decisive. In *Welch* v *UK*[1429] the Court applied the following factors in determining whether a confiscation order imposed under the Drug Trafficking Offences Act 1986 amounted to a penalty: whether the measure was imposed following conviction for a criminal offence; the nature and purpose of the measure in question; its characterisation under national law; the procedures involved in the making and implementation of the measure; and its severity. In *Welch*, the Court found

---

[1423] No. 68066/01, 22.7.03.
[1424] Nos. 2312/08 and 34179/08, 18.7.13.
[1425] See, e.g. *Kafkaris* v *Cyprus*, No. 21906/04, 12.2.08, para. 142; *Grava* v *Italy*, No. 43522/98, 10.7.03.
[1426] *Müller* v *Czech Republic*, No. 48058/09, dec. 6.9.11.
[1427] No. 42750/09, 21.10.13.
[1428] *Welch* v *UK*, No. 17440/90, Series A, No. 307-A, 9.2.95; See also, e.g. *Valico* v *Italy*, No. 70074/01, dec. 21.3.06; *SUD FONDI srl and others* v *Italy*, No. 75909/01, dec. 30.8.07.
[1429] *Welch* v *UK*, No. 17440/90, Series A, No. 307-A, 9.2.95.

the following to be indicative of a regime of punishment under the 1986 Act: the statutory assumptions that all property passing through the offender's hands over a six-year period was the fruit of drug trafficking unless he could prove otherwise; the fact that the confiscation order was directed to the proceeds involved in drug dealing and was not limited to actual enrichment or profit; the discretion of the judge in fixing the amount of the order to take into consideration the degree of culpability of the accused; and the possibility of imprisonment in default of payment by the offender. The Court concluded that 'looking behind appearances at the realities of the situation, whatever the characterisation of the measure of confiscation, the fact remains that the applicant faced more far-reaching detriment as a result of the order than that to which he was exposed at the time of the commission of the offences for which he was convicted'.[1430] In *M v Germany*[1431] the Court was required to consider whether 'preventive detention' under the German Criminal Code amounted to a 'penalty' for the purposes of Article 7(1). Under the domestic law, such a measure was consided to be one of correction and prevention, rather than a penalty. However, the Court found that it was a 'penalty', given that: it was ordered by the criminal sentencing court; it entailed a deprivation of liberty; persons subject to it were detained in ordinary prisons; and it was a severe measure as there was no longer any maximum duration. The Court went on to find a violation of Article 7(1), as at the time the applicant was sentenced, preventive detention could only be imposed for a maximum of 10 years, but a subsequent amendment to the law had abolished the time limit, thus allowing detention for an unlimited duration.

In *Ecer and Zeyrek v Turkey*,[1432] the applicants complained that following their conviction, **6.432** a heavier penalty was imposed on them than had been available at the time the offences were committed. The Court found a violation of Article 7 as they were sentenced under a 1991 Act in relation to offences committed in 1988 and 1989, of assisting the Kurdish Workers' Party (PKK). The Court rejected the Government's argument that the applicants were charged with continuing offences, as this had been reflected neither in the indictment nor the judgment. In *EK v Turkey*,[1433] there was a violation of Article 7 where the applicant was convicted for publishing a book that was found by the domestic courts to undermine the territorial integrity and the unity of the nation: the application of a prison sentence to a book publisher, as opposed to publishers of newspapers or magazines, was found not to be in accordance with the relevant domestic law. Cases challenging the requirement to be placed on a sex offenders register have been declared inadmissible by the Commission and Court.[1434] The applicants claimed a violation of Article 7 on the basis that the requirement to register with the police amounted to a heavier penalty than that which could have been imposed at the time the offences were committed. However, the registration scheme was found not to amount to a 'penalty' within the meaning of Article 7. Similarly, the taking of a mouth swab, so that a DNA profile could be retained following a conviction, has not been found to constitute a 'penalty'.[1435]

[1430] *Ibid.*, para. 34.

[1431] No. 19359/04, 17.12.09 (there was also a violation of Article 5(1)). See also *Jendrowiak v Germany*, No. 30060/04, 14.4.11; *Glien v Germany*, No. 7345/12, 28.11.13.

[1432] Nos. 29295/95 and 29363/95, 27.2.01.

[1433] No. 28496/95, 7.2.02.

[1434] *Ibbotson v UK*, No. 40146/98, dec. 21.10.98; *Adamson v UK*, No. 42293/98, dec. 26.1.99; *Gardel v France*, No. 16428/05, 17.12.09.

[1435] *Van der Velden v Netherlands*, No. 29514/05, dec. 7.12.06.

6.433   Several aspects of Article 7 were raised by the applicant in the case of *Rohlena* v *Czech Republic*,[1436] heard by the Grand Chamber. The applicant was charged with repeatedly physically and mentally abusing his wife while drunk (between 2000 and 2006), and was convicted of the continuing offence of abusing a person living under the same roof (as defined in the Criminal Code since 1 June 2004). There were two issues under Article 7 to consider. First, whether, at the time they were committed, the applicant's acts, including those carried out before 1 June 2004, constituted an offence defined with sufficient foreseeability by the domestic law. The Court answered that question in the affirmative: since the applicant's conduct before 1 June 2004 amounted to punishable criminal offences under various provisions of the Criminal Code, the Court accepted that this did not constitute retroactive application of more detrimental criminal law. Secondly, the Court had to assess whether the application of the law to include acts committed before 1 June 2004 meant that the applicant had been subjected to a heavier penalty. This question was answered in the negative: all the constituent elements of the 'continuous offence' were made out also with regard to the acts committed by the applicant prior to 1 June 2004, and there was nothing to indicate that the domestic courts' approach had the adverse effect of increasing the severity of the applicant's punishment (in fact, if his acts prior to that date had been assessed separately, he may have received a harsher sentence). Accordingly, there was no violation of Article 7. The Grand Chamber concluded by commenting more broadly on the approach of the Czech courts: 'by reinforcing the national legal protection against domestic violence … it also conforms to the fundamental objectives of the Convention, the very essence of which is respect for human dignity and freedom'.[1437]

6.434   In *Scoppola* v *Italy (No. 2)*[1438] a majority of the Grand Chamber overturned previous European Commission case law,[1439] in finding that Article 7 also incorporates the principle of retroactivity of the more *lenient* criminal law.[1440] This accordingly means that that where there are differences between the criminal law in force at the time of the commission of an offence and subsequent criminal laws introduced before the final judgment, the courts are required to apply the law whose provisions are most favourable to the defendant. The applicant had been convicted, inter alia, of murdering his wife and was sentenced to life imprisonment in 2002, after he had elected to be tried according to a summary procedure. However, as a more lenient sentence had been introduced into the domestic law after the commission of the offence (namely 30 years' imprisonment), the Court found that Article 7 had been violated (by 11 votes to six).[1441]

[1436] No. 59552/08, 27.1.15.

[1437] *Ibid.*, para. 71.

[1438] No. 10249/03, 17.9.09.

[1439] *X* v *Germany*, No. 7900/77, dec. 6.3.78, (DR) 13, pp. 70-72. See also *Ian Le Petit* v *UK*, No. 35574/97, dec. 5.12.00 and *Zaprianov* v *Bulgaria*, No. 41171/98, dec. 6.3.03.

[1440] See also *Gouarré Patte* v *Andorra*, No. 33427/10, 12.1.16; *Ruban* v *Ukraine*, No. 8927/11, 12.7.16. However, the Court has further clarified that limitation periods are considered to be procedural laws which do not define substantive offences or their corresponding penalties, but rather lay down a prior condition, and accordingly would not be subject to this aspect of Article 7. See *Coëme and others* v *Belgium*, Nos. 32492/96 et al, 22.6.00; *Scoppola* v *Italy (No. 2)*, No. 10249/03, 17.9.09.

[1441] There was also a violation of Article 6 on the basis that as he had elected for summary proceedings, the applicant had had a legitimate expectation that, according to the domestic law, the maximum sentence applicable was 30 years' imprisonment, which was, however, frustrated by a later legislative decree.

According to Article 7(1), retrospectivity in the application of the criminal law will not, how- **6.435**
ever, violate the Convention if the act in question had been a crime under international law
at the time of its commission.[1442] There was a violation of Article 7 in *Korbely* v *Hungary*[1443] as
a result of the conviction of the applicant in 2001, for committing a crime against humanity
through multiple homicide (under Article 3 of the 1949 Geneva Convention) whilst serving as a military officer during the 1956 revolution. As the conviction was based exclusively
on international law, the Court was required to consider whether it had been foreseeable
that the applicant's acts constituted a crime against humanity under international law. On
the facts of the case, the Court found that it was open to question whether the constituent
elements of a crime against humanity had been committed and accordingly a majority of
the Court found a violation of Article 7 (by 11 votes to six).[1444] By contrast, there was no
violation of Article 7 in *Kononov* v *Latvia*[1445] arising from the conviction of the applicant
in 2004 for war crimes committed in 1944. He had been found to have led a Soviet com-
mando unit of Red Partizans in a punitive expedition against a village, during which several
villagers had been killed. The Grand Chamber held that there had been a sufficiently clear
legal basis in international law in 1944 (under the Hague Regulations 1907 and the Lieber
Code 1863) for the applicant to have been convicted and punished for war crimes (the
ill-treatment, wounding and killing of villagers, the treacherous wounding and killing of
villagers, the burning to death of a pregnant woman and attacks on undefended localities).
Moreover, the charges were not statute-barred either by domestic law or international law.
The Court also rejected the applicant's argument that he could not have foreseen that the
acts constituted war crimes, or have anticipated that he would be subsequently prosecuted,
concluding that the international laws and customs of war in 1944 were sufficient to found
individual criminal responsibility.[1446]

Article 7(2) also permits retrospectivity in relation to conduct that 'was criminal accord- **6.436**
ing to the general principles of law recognised by civilised nations'. In *Kolk and Kislyiy*
v *Estonia*[1447] the applicants had been convicted of crimes against humanity, as a result
of their involvement in the deportation of civilians from Estonia to remote parts of the
Soviet Union in 1949. Their complaint of a violation of Article 7, on the basis that at
the time there was no such offence in the domestic law, was declared inadmissible by
the Court. The Court agreed with the conclusion of the Estonian courts that even if the
acts committed by the applicants had been lawful under the Soviet law at the time, they

---

[1442] *Streletz, Kessler and Krenz* v *Germany*, Nos. 34044/96, 35532/97 and 44801/98, 22.3.02; *K-HW* v
Germany, No. 37201/97, 22.3.01.

[1443] No. 9174/02, 19.9.08.

[1444] See also *Vasiliauskas* v *Lithuania*, No. 35343/05, 20.10.15 (conviction in 2004 for alleged genocide of
Lithuanian partisans in 1953, as members of a political group—conviction not consistent with essence of offence
of genocide as defined in international law at the material time and had not been reasonably foreseeable—
violation of Article 7 (by nine votes to eight)) and *Žaja* v *Croatia*, No. 37462/09, 4.10.16 (inconsistent interpretation by domestic courts of ambiguous provision of domestic law—violation of Article 7). See, by contrast,
Ould Dah v *France*, No. 13113/03, dec. 17.3.09 (universal jurisdiction of contracting state to prosecute torture
and barbaric acts despite amnesty law in state where such acts had been committed—inadmissible).

[1445] No. 36376/04, 17.5.10. In *Larionovs and Tess* v *Latvia*, Nos. 45520/04 and 19363/05, dec. 25.11.14
the Court declared inadmissible the applicants' complaints concerning the retroactivity of the criminal provisions on genocide, for failing to first lodge a complaint with the Constitutional Court.

[1446] See also *Van Anraat* v *Netherlands*, No. 65389/09, dec. 6.7.10 (conviction under War Crimes Act for
selling to Iraqi authorities chemical substances used to manufacture poisonous gas—inadmissible).

[1447] Nos. 23052/04 and 24018/04, dec. 17.1.06.

nevertheless constituted crimes against humanity under international law at the time of their commission.

Overview of Articles 8 to 11

6.437 Articles 8 to 11 set out the extent of the rights to respect for private and family life, home and correspondence, to freedom of thought, conscience and religion, to freedom of expression, and to freedom of assembly and association. In each case the right is not absolute; the Convention expressly permits interferences with the rights on certain conditions. The burden is primarily on the respondent to justify an interference with these rights.

6.438 Articles 8 to 11 have a similar structure in that the first paragraph describes in general terms the extent of the right and the second paragraph describes the circumstances in which interferences with the rights are permissible. In each case, any interference must be 'in accordance with the law' or 'prescribed by law', and must be 'necessary in a democratic society' for one of the legitimate aims set out in the second paragraph. Because of their similar structures, each of these Articles can be considered by asking five questions in turn:

1. In accordance w/ law
2. necessary to a democratic society

1. Can the applicant claim that the right under the first paragraph of the relevant Article is engaged?

6.439 The first question to consider is therefore whether the matter complained about falls within the scope of the relevant substantive right. For example, in *Halford* v *UK*[1448] the Government argued that telephone calls made by the applicant, the former Assistant Chief Constable of Merseyside, from her workplace, fell outside the scope of Article 8 because she could have had no reasonable expectation of privacy in relation to them. However, the Court rejected the Government's submissions, finding that telephone calls from business premises were covered by the notions of 'private life' and 'correspondence' under Article 8(1).

6.440 In *Botta* v *Italy*,[1449] however, the applicant's complaints in relation to his right as a disabled person to gain access to the beach and the sea on his holidays were not found to fall within the scope of 'private life' under Article 8. Nevertheless, the Court has found that Article 8 will be applicable

> in exceptional cases where … lack of access to public buildings and buildings open to the public affects [an applicant's] life in such a way as to interfere with her right to personal development and her right to establish and develop relationships with other human beings and the outside world.[1450]

2. If so, has there been an interference with the applicant's right?

6.441 Whether there has been an 'interference' with a substantive right is rarely disputed. For example, in *Bowman* v *UK*[1451] the applicant (the director of the Society for the Protection of the Unborn Child) had been prosecuted and acquitted under the Representation of the People

---

[1448] No. 20605/92, 25.6.97.
[1449] No. 21439/93, 24.2.98.
[1450] *Zehnalova and Zehnal* v *Czech Republic*, No. 38621/97, dec. 14.5.02; *Sentges* v *Netherlands*, No. 27677/02, dec. 8.7.03; *Pentiacova and others* v *Moldova*, No. 14462/03, dec. 4.1.05.
[1451] No. 24839/94, 4.12.95.

Act 1983 for spending more than £5 on publications prior to an election in order to publicise the candidates' views on abortion. The Government argued that there had been no restriction of the applicant's right to freedom of expression. The Court acknowledged that the Act did not directly restrain freedom of expression, but limited election expenditure, and that it did not restrict expenditure on the transmission of information or opinions generally, but only expenditure incurred during an election period with a view to promoting the election of a candidate. Nevertheless, the Court found that the applicant's freedom of expression had been restricted. In *Steur* v *Netherlands*[1452] the Court rejected the respondent Government's argument that there had been no interference with the applicant lawyer's rights under Article 10 on the basis that although no sanction had been imposed on the applicant, he had been subject to a finding that he had breached professional standards.

3. Was the interference with the right 'in accordance with the law' or 'prescribed by law'?

The legal basis for any interference must be both adequately accessible and must be formu- **6.442** lated with sufficient precision to enable a person to regulate their conduct: a person 'must be able—if need be with appropriate advice—to foresee, to a degree that is reasonable in the circumstances, the consequences which a given action may entail'.[1453] It is therefore a very important principle that this condition not only requires a specific legal rule or regime authorising the interference, but also relates to the *quality* of the particular domestic legal provision.[1454] This means that, for example, where the domestic law confers a discretion, it should also indicate the scope of that discretion.[1455] The degree of 'certainty' required in the law will differ depending upon the nature of the right being exercised and the nature of the interference. The Court has also reiterated that it will depend 'to a considerable degree on the content of the instrument in question, the field it is designed to cover and the number and status of those to whom it is addressed'.[1456] It is important to note that in common law jurisdictions the 'prescribed by law' test does not prevent the gradual clarification of the law through judicial law-making.[1457]

There are a number of examples below at 6.447 to 6.552 of interferences carried out both in the absence of any legal regulation and where the relevant law was insufficiently precise. Perhaps the strictest application of this test has been in relation to state surveillance (see below at 6.462–6.477).

4. Did the interference pursue one or more of the legitimate aims set out in the second paragraph?

The aims listed in the second paragraphs of Articles 8 to 11 are very broadly drawn. **6.443** Respondent states will often raise more than one such aim. The state must produce some evidence that the particular aim was being pursued by the measure in question, but in

---

[1452] No. 39657/98, 28.10.03.
[1453] *Sunday Times* v *UK* (*No. 1*), Series A, No. 30, 26.4.79, para. 49.
[1454] See, e.g. *Oleksandr Volkov* v *Ukraine*, No. 21722/11, 9.1.13.
[1455] *Silver* v *UK*, Nos. 5947/72, 6205/73, 7052/75, 7061/75, 7107/75, 7113/75 and 7136/75, Series A, No. 61, 25.3.83, paras. 88–9 (restriction on prisoners' correspondence on the basis of unpublished prison orders).
[1456] See, e.g. *Maestri* v *Italy*, No. 39748/98, 17.2.04, para. 30.
[1457] See, e.g. *S.W. and C.R.* v *UK*, No. 20166/92, 22.11.95, para. 36; *Blake* v *UK*, No. 68890/01, dec. 25.10.05, para. 141.

many cases this is not disputed and the Court, in practice, rarely finds that an interference did not comply with at least one of the aims stipulated in the second paragraph. However, in *İzmir Savaş Karşıtları Derneği v Turkey*,[1458] the Court found that a legal requirement for the applicant anti-war association to obtain the prior permission of the Ministry of the Interior in order to participate in meetings abroad could not be regarded as pursuing any of the legitimate aims set out in Article 11(2). In *Toma v Romania*,[1459] the decision of the police to allow journalists to film and photograph the applicant in police custody could not be justified by any of the legitimate aims provided for in Article 8(2). The case of *Perinçek v Switzerland*[1460] related to the criminal prosecution of the applicant, a Turkish national, for denying the Armenian genocide. The Court rejected the Government's argument that the restriction on the applicant's Article 10 rights pursued the 'prevention of disorder', as the Government had not shown that the applicant's statements were capable of leading, or actually led, to disorder, and that in acting to penalise them, the Swiss authorities had had that in mind. Nevertheless, the Court accepted that it had the legitimate aim of protecting the 'rights of others'.

The second paragraphs of Articles 8 to 11 differ slightly. For example, Article 8(2) includes the 'economic well-being of the country'[1461] and Article 9 has no national security limitation.

5. Was the interference 'necessary in a democratic society'?

6.444   The condition that any interference must be 'necessary in a democratic society', requires the existence of a 'pressing social need' and that the interference is proportionate to the legitimate aim pursued.[1462] 'Necessity' is more than 'useful', 'reasonable', or 'desirable'.

In assessing the proportionality of a particular measure, the Court will consider whether there is an alternative means of protecting the relevant public interest without an interference or by means which are less intrusive. The Court will assess whether the reasons for the interference are 'relevant' and 'sufficient' to justify it. It is a further requirement that the decision-making process leading to the measure of interference should be fair. The existence of effective controls on measures taken by the authorities is also a relevant factor in assessing proportionality.

6.445   In considering proportionality, the Strasbourg organs have developed the concept of the 'margin of appreciation' (see also above at 5.11): that national authorities are in principle in a better position to give an opinion on the necessity of a restriction, and that it is for the national authorities to make the initial assessment of the reality of the pressing social need. This doctrine reflects the European Court's status as a supervisory mechanism. The extent of the margin of appreciation will vary depending on the issue in question. For example, the state has a wider discretion in relation to the protection of morals, but it is narrower in relation to maintaining the authority and impartiality of the judiciary. The latter is considered to be a more objective notion in respect of which there is a lot of common ground among the law and practice of the contracting states.

[1458] No. 46257/99, 2.3.06.
[1459] No. 42716/02, 24.2.09.
[1460] No. 27510/08, 15.10.15.
[1461] See, e.g. *Hatton and others* v *UK*, No. 36022/97, 8.7.03, para. 121.
[1462] See, e.g. *Olsson* v *Sweden (No. 1)*, No. 10465/83, Series A, No. 130, 24.3.88, para. 67.

The scope of the margin of appreciation will vary from case to case. The extent of the discretion allowed to states will depend upon a number of factors: **6.446**

[handwritten: ❋ extent of discretion / margin of error]

- the importance of the protected right;
- whether there is a 'European standard' on the issue in question—if there is, it is more difficult for the state to justify an interference with a right, contrary to that standard;
- the weight of the (other, public) interest being protected;
- the extent or significance of the interference—what were the effects in the particular circumstances of the case?

Applying these principles, the Court has found, for example, that employers' mandatory drug and/or alcohol testing of employees on board a ferry[1463] and at a nuclear power station,[1464] is not a disproportionate interference with the employees' rights under Article 8.

These concepts will be examined and illustrated further below in connection with Articles 8 to 11.

Article 8: The Right to Respect for Private and Family Life, Home and Correspondence

Article 8 states: **6.447**

1. Everyone has the right to respect for his private and family life, his home and his correspondence.
2. There shall be no interference by a public authority with the exercise of this right except such as is in accordance with the law and is necessary in a democratic society in the interests of national security, public safety or the economic well-being of the country, for the prevention of disorder or crime, for the protection of health or morals, or for the protection of the rights and freedoms of others.

Article 8(1) has four elements: private life; family life; home and correspondence. The state's **6.448** primary obligation under Article 8 is negative, that is, not to interfere with those rights. However, in certain circumstances the Article imposes positive obligations—a duty to take appropriate steps to ensure protection of the rights in question (see, e.g., *Chapman* v *UK*,[1465] and related cases on the positive obligation to 'facilitate the gypsy way of life'). It is well established that positive obligations are inherent in the concept of the right to 'respect' for private life under Article 8.[1466] Such obligations may arise directly in relation to a public body, but the obligations under Article 8 may also arise where there is, or ought to be, a duty on a public authority to prevent an individual (or other private entity) from violating the rights of another individual.[1467] In any particular case, in order to determine whether or not a positive obligation exists, the Court will assess the fair balance between the general interests of the community and the interests of the individual. For example, there was a violation of Article 8 in *K.U.* v *Finland*[1468] because the relevant domestic legislation prevented the

[handwritten: ❋ positive obligations]

[1463] *Madsen* v *Denmark*, No. 58341/00, dec. 7.11.02.
[1464] *Wretlund* v *Sweden*, No. 46210/99, dec. 9.3.04.
[1465] No. 24882/94, 18.1.01.
[1466] See, e.g. *Sheffield and Horsham* v *UK*, Nos. 22985/93 and 23390/94, 30.7.98, para. 52.
[1467] See, e.g. *MC* v *Bulgaria*, No. 39272/98, 4.12.03, referred to at 6.123 above.
[1468] No. 2872/02, 2.12.08.

authorities from compelling an internet service provider to disclose the identity of a person wanted for placing an indecent advertisement about a minor on an internet dating site. *Schüth* v *Germany*[1469] concerned the dismissal of the applicant by the Catholic Church from his position as a choirmaster and organist, on the grounds that he had had an extra-marital relationship. The respondent Government was found not to have complied with its positive obligations under Article 8, as the German labour courts had failed to weigh the applicant's rights against those of the Church, as employer, in a manner that was compatible with the Convention. The Court was critical, for example, that the domestic courts had given inadequate consideration of the applicant's de facto family life. It was also noted that it would be very difficult for an employee in the applicant's position to find a new job outside the Church.

6.449 Aside from the question of positive obligations, governments have on occasion sought to argue that there has been no interference with Article 8(1) rights *by a public authority* on the basis that the interference in question has been carried out by a private individual rather than the authorities. Such arguments are likely to be rejected by the Court if there was in fact state involvement, as was the case in *MM* v *Netherlands*[1470] where it was clear that the recording of the applicant's telephone conversation by a Mrs S was carried out at the suggestion, and instigation, of the police.

Private life

6.450 The concept of private life has not been conclusively defined, but it has been invoked in a very wide range of contexts. The Court has held that the notion of privacy is not limited to the 'inner circle' of an individual's private life, but includes the right to establish and develop relationships with other human beings. On that basis, the concept of private life includes 'the totality of social ties between settled migrants and the community in which they are living'.[1471] Private life includes respect for human dignity,[1472] as well as physical, psychological, and moral integrity[1473]—incorporating 'multiple aspects' of a person's physical and social identity.[1474] This includes mental health,[1475] a right to personal development (which includes the right to protect one's image),[1476] an individual's ethnic identity,[1477] the right to determine personal identity (including, for example, the circumstances of a child's birth[1478] and a person's sexual identity), sexual orientation and the right to establish and develop

---

[1469] No. 1620/03, 23.9.10. See, by contrast, *Obst* v *Germany*, No. 425/03, 23.9.10 (dismissal of church employee for adultery—no violation of Article 8); *Fernández Martínez* v *Spain*, No. 56030/07, 12.6.14 (refusal to renew Catholic teacher's contract after he publicly revealed his position as a married priest—no violation of Article 8 (by nine votes to eight)); *Travaš* v *Croatia*, No. 75581/13, 4.10.16 (dismissal of religious education teacher following withdrawal of canonical mandate—no violation of Article 8).

[1470] No. 39339/98, 8.4.03. See also *A* v *France*, No. 14838/89, 23.11.93, Series A No. 277-B.

[1471] See, e.g. *Osman* v *Denmark*, No. 38058/09, 14.6.11, para. 55.

[1472] See, e.g. *Lindström and Mässeli* v *Finland*, No. 24630/10, 14.1.14, para. 58.

[1473] See *X and Y* v *Netherlands*, No. 8978/80, Series A, No. 91, 26.3.85, para. 22 (sexual assault on 16-year-old girl with mental health problems); *Sandra Janković* v *Croatia*, No. 38478/05, 5.3.09, paras. 31 and 45.

[1474] See, e.g. *Dadouch* v *Malta*, No. 38816/07, 20.7.10, para. 47.

[1475] *Bensaid* v *UK*, No. 44599/98, 6.2.01, para. 47.

[1476] *Reklos and Davourlis* v *Greece*, No. 1234/05, 15.1.09.

[1477] *S and Marper* v *UK*, Nos. 30562/04 and 30566/04, 4.12.08, para. 66; *Ciubotaru* v *Romania*, No. 27138/04, 27.4.10, paras. 49 and 53 (inability to change registration of ethnic origin in official records—violation of Article 8).

[1478] *Odièvre* v *France*, No. 42326/98, 13.2.03, para. 29.

relations with others[1479] (including the state's recognition of marital status,[1480] and relations in the professional[1481] and commercial spheres).[1482] The Court has found that legislation regulating the interruption of pregnancy concerns the sphere of private life, since whenever a woman is pregnant her private life becomes closely connected with the developing foetus.[1483] A person's name is considered to fall within the scope of 'private and family life'.[1484] Article 8 also applies to the protection of reputation, provided that the issue in question relates to the sphere of private or family life.[1485]

However, Article 8 does not extend to the loss of reputation which is the foreseeable consequence of one's own actions, such as in committing a criminal offence.[1486] An absolute ban on prisoners growing beards has been found to engage (and indeed violate) the right to a private life under Article 8.[1487]   **6.451**

The authorities' failure to provide appropriate access for disabled people to public services and facilities may impinge on personal autonomy, and accordingly may be subject to Article 8.[1488] In *Pretty* v *UK*,[1489] the Court did not exclude that preventing an applicant from   **6.452**

[1479] *Bensaid* v *UK*, No. 44599/98, 6.2.01, para. 47.

[1480] *Dadouch* v *Malta*, No. 38816/07, 20.7.10, para. 48.

[1481] See, e.g. *Bigaeva* v *Greece*, No. 26713/05, 28.5.09; *Oleksandr Volkov* v *Ukraine*, No. 21722/11, 9.1.13; *Fernández Martínez* v *Spain*, No. 56030/07, 12.6.14; *Emel Boyraz* v *Turkey*, No. 61960/08, 2.12.14; *Sodan* v *Turkey*, No. 18650/05, 2.2.16.

[1482] See, e.g. *Albanese* v *Italy*, No. 77924/01, 23.3.06, para. 53 (declaration of personal bankruptcy automatically entailed various consequences, including the handing over of all correspondence to the trustee in bankruptcy, and a prohibition on leaving place of residence without authorisation from the insolvency judge—violation of right to respect for private life under Article 8).

[1483] *Tysiąc* v *Poland*, No. 5410/03, 20.3.07, para. 106; *A, B & C* v *Ireland*, No. 25579/05, 16.12.10, para. 213. See also *Ternovszky* v *Hungary*, No. 67545/09, 14.12.10 (uncertainty of domestic law prevented mother from giving birth at home—violation of Article 8).

[1484] See, e.g. *Burghartz* v *Switzerland*, No. 16213/90, 22.2.94, para. 24; *Ünal Tekeli* v *Turkey* No. 29865/96, 16.11.04, para. 42; *Daróczy* v *Hungary*, No. 44375/05, 1.7.08; *Güzel Erdagöz* v *Turkey*, No. 37483/02, 21.10.08; *Garnaga* v *Ukraine*, No. 20390/07, 16.5.13; *Henry Kismoun* v *France*, No. 32265/10, 5.12.13; *Gözüm* v *Turkey*, No. 4789/10, 20.1.15. By contrast, see: *Mentzen alias Mencena* v *Latvia*, No. 71074/01, dec. 7.12.04 (complaint about rules regulating the spelling of surnames in passports in the national language—declared inadmissible); *Kemal Taşkın and others* v *Turkey*, No. 30206/04, 23.2.10 (requirement for names in official documents to be spelt with letters from official Turkish alphabet—no violation). A refusal to register a particular name may be considered reasonable under Article 8 on the basis of the aim of protecting a child from the possible prejudice caused by a name which might be considered inappropriate by others (see, e.g. *Guillot* v *France*, No. 22500/93, 24.10.96; *Salonen* v *Finland*, No. 27868/95, dec. 2.7.97; *Johansson* v *Finland*, No. 10163/, 6.9.07).

[1485] *Chauvy and others* v *France*, No. 64915/01, 29.6.04; *Sanchez Cardenas* v *Norway*, No. 12148/03, 4.10.07; *Pfeifer* v *Austria*, No. 12556/03, 15.11.07; *Gunnarsson* v *Iceland*, No. 4591/04, dec. 20.10.05 (inadmissible); *Petrina* v *Romania*, No. 78060/01, 14.10.08; *Taliadorou and Stylianou* v *Cyprus*, Nos. 39627/05 and 39631/05, 16.10.08; *Kyriakides* v *Cyprus*, No. 39627/05 and 39631/05, 16.10.08. See also: *A* v *Norway*, No. 28070/06, 9.4.09 (publication in newspaper articles of information in which applicant could be perceived as prime suspect in murder case—violation of Article 8); *Karakó* v *Hungary*, No. 39311/05, 28.4.09 (dismissal of criminal libel proceedings against political opponent—where the Court notes the difference between the notions of personal intergrity and reputation under Article 8); *Putistin* v *Ukraine*, No. 16882/03, 21.11.13 (claimed failure to secure right to reputation of applicant whose father was allegedly defamed—no violation of Article 8); *Dzhugashvili* v *Russia*, No. 41123/10, dec. 9.12.14 (dismissal of claim for defamation of Stalin brought by grandson—inadmissible).

[1486] *Gillberg* v *Sweden*, No. 41723/06, 3.4.12.

[1487] *Biržietis* v *Lithuania*, No. 49304/09, 14.6.16.

[1488] *Mółka* v *Poland*, No. 56550/00, dec. 11.4.06.

[1489] No. 2346/02, 29.4.02, para. 67. See also *Haas* v *Switzerland*, No. 31322/07, 20.1.11 (applicant's inability to obtain a lethal substance without a medical prescription, to permit a dignified suicide—no violation of Article 8); *Koch* v *Germany*, No. 497/09, 19.7.12 (refusal of domestic courts to hear merits of application re

exercising her choice to avoid an undignified and distressing end to her life might constitute an interference with the right to respect for private life (although on the facts of the case it was found to be proportionate). The Court has also found that restrictions on taking up public or private sector employment may also affect 'private life'.[1490] In *Hadri-Vionnet* v *Switzerland*[1491] the Court found that Article 8 was applicable to the question whether the applicant had been entitled to attend her stillborn baby's burial, and to have the body transported in a suitable vehicle. The issue of access to relatives' graves has also been found to fall within the notion of private and family life.[1492]

6.453 The Court has recognised 'a zone of interaction of a person with others, even in a public context' which may fall within the scope of private life.[1493] As to notions of private life within the public sphere, the Court said this in *PG and JH* v *UK*:[1494]

> There are a number of elements relevant to a consideration of whether a person's private life is concerned by measures effected outside a person's home or private premises. Since there are occasions when people knowingly or intentionally involve themselves in activities which are or may be recorded or reported in a public manner, a person's reasonable expectations as to privacy may be a significant, although not necessarily conclusive, factor. A person who walks down the street will, inevitably, be visible to any member of the public who is also present. Monitoring by technological means of the same public scene (for example, a security guard viewing through closed-circuit television) is of a similar character. Private-life considerations may arise, however, once any systematic or permanent record comes into existence of such material from the public domain.

6.454 Applying such principles in *Peck* v *UK*,[1495] the Court found there had been a serious interference with the right to respect for the applicant's private life where local authority closed-circuit television (CCTV) footage of the applicant was disclosed to the media, which subsequently

---

legality of refusal to authorise applicant's wife to obtain lethal dose of drug, to enable her to commit suicide—violation of Article 8); *Gross* v *Switzerland*, No. 67810/10, 14.5.13 (a chamber judgment found a violation of Article 8 by four votes to three as a result of the absence of clear guidelines regulating the prescription of a drug to enable an individual who was not suffering from a terminal illness to commit suicide. The case was referred to the Grand Chamber which found the application inadmissible (by nine votes to eight) as an abuse of application (*Gross* v *Switzerland*, No. 67810/10, 30.9.14)).

[1490] *Sidabras and Džiautas* v *Lithuania*, Nos. 55480/00 and 59330/00, 27.7.04, para. 47. See also: *Karov* v *Bulgaria*, No. 45964/99, 16.11.06 (suspension of police officer subject to criminal proceedings—no violation of Article 8); *D.M.T. and D.K.I.* v *Bulgaria*, No. 29476/06, 24.7.12 (prolonged suspension from civil service position, plus general ban on taking up employment in public or private sector—violation of Article 8); *Ivanovski* v *former Yugoslav Republic of Macedonia*, No. 29908/11, 21.1.16 (removal from public office of President of Constitutional Court, as a result of lustration proceedings—violation of Articles 6 and 8).

[1491] No. 55525/00, 14.2.08.

[1492] *Sargsyan* v *Azerbaijan*, No. 40167/06, 16.6.15.

[1493] *PG and JH* v *UK*, No. 44787/98, 25.9.01, para. 56; *Von Hannover* v *Germany*, No. 59320/00, 24.6.04, para. 50. See also: *Perry* v *UK*, No. 63737/00, 17.7.03 (covert video film, taken in a custody suite of a police station to be used for identification purposes, was found to engage Article 8(1)); *Van der Graaf* v *Netherlands*, No. 8704/03, dec. 1.6.04 (suspect placed under permanent camera surveillance whilst in custody on remand found to engage Article 8 but to be justified); and *Uzun* v *Germany*, No. 35623/05, 2.9.10 (surveillance of terrorist suspect using global-positioning system (GPS)—Article 8 applicable, but no violation). In the admissibility decision in *Steel and Morris* v *UK*, No. 68416/01, dec. 22.10.02, the Court stated that the concept of private life was 'inapplicable to places which are freely accessible to the public and which are used for activities which do not relate to the private sphere'.

[1494] No. 44787/98, 25.9.01, para. 57.

[1495] No. 44647/98, 28.1.03. See also *Bremner* v *Turkey*, No. 37428/06, 13.10.15 (television broadcast showing non-blurred image of individual obtained using hidden camera—violation of Article 8).

broadcast identifiable images of him. The CCTV film had been taken of the applicant in a public street in the immediate aftermath of his suicide attempt. The Court confirmed that merely monitoring a person in a public place will not engage Article 8, but rather it is the recording of the data or the creation of systematic or permanent records that may do so. The factors found to be relevant in *Peck* were as follows: the applicant had been in a public street, but not for the purposes of participating in a public event; he was not a public figure; it was late at night and he was in some distress; he was not charged with any offence; footage of the immediate aftermath of his suicide attempt was recorded and disclosed by the council directly to the public and the media, for broadcast and publication purposes; the applicant's identity was not adequately, or in some cases not at all, masked in the photographs and footage; and he was recognised by members of his family and by his friends, neighbours and colleagues. Therefore, the Court concluded that 'as a result, the relevant moment was viewed to an extent which far exceeded any exposure to a passer-by or to security observation ... and to a degree surpassing that which the applicant could possibly have foreseen'.[1496] In *Von Hannover v Germany*,[1497] the Court found that there was 'no doubt' that the publication by various German magazines of photos of the applicant, the daughter of Prince Rainier III of Monaco, in her daily life (either on her own or with other people), fell within the scope of her private life under Article 8. Indeed, the Court laid emphasis on the intrusiveness of tabloid newspapers: 'photos appearing in the tabloid press are often taken in a climate of continual harassment which induces in the person concerned a very strong sense of intrusion into their private life or even of persecution'.[1498] The Court in *Von Hannover* expressly acknowedged that the protection of private life has to be balanced against the right to freedom of expression under Article 10.[1499] However, in finding a violation of Article 8, the Court found that a 'fundamental distinction' had to be made between reporting information that was capable of contributing to a debate in a democratic society, and reporting details of the private life of an individual who does not exercise official functions: to 'satisfy the curiosity of a particular readership regarding the details of the applicant's private life, cannot be deemed to contribute to any debate of general interest to society'.[1500] In *Mosley v UK*,[1501] the Court found that the positive obligations inherent in Article 8 did *not* require there to be a legal duty on the media to provide prior notification to the subjects of media reports, having regard to Article 10 and the chilling effect which might be caused by such a requirement. There was a violation of Article 8 in *Alkaya v Turkey*[1502] due to the disclosure by a national newspaper of the

---

[1496] *Peck v UK*, No. 44647/98, 28.1.03, para. 62.

[1497] No. 59320/00, 24.6.04, para. 53. See also *Sciacca v Italy*, No. 50774/99, 11.1.05 (release by police to press of photo of suspect under house arrest).

[1498] *Von Hannover v Germany*, No. 59320/00, 24.6.04, para. 59.

[1499] See also on that point *Karakó v Hungary*, No. 39311/05, 28.4.09 (dismissal of criminal libel proceedings against political opponent). See further *Kahn v Germany*, No. 16313/10, 17.3.16 (no award of damages against publisher for breaching injunction not to publish photographs of children of former international footballer—no violation of Article 8). In *MGN Limited v UK*, No. 39401/04, 18.1.11, the Court found no violation of the applicant newspaper's rights under Article 10 as a result of successful proceedings for breach of confidence taken against it by the model Naomi Campbell resulting from its coverage of her treatment for drug addiction.

[1500] *Von Hannover v Germany*, No. 59320/00, 24.6.04, para. 65. See, by contrast, the subsequent Grand Chamber judgment in *Von Hannover v Germany (No. 2)*, Nos. 40660/08 and 60641/08, 7.2.12 (not unreasonable for domestic courts to find that press reporting on the poor health of Prince Rainier of Monaco contributed to a debate of general interest—no violation of Article 8).

[1501] No. 48009/08, 10.5.11.

[1502] No. 42811/06, 9.10.12.

private address of the applicant (who was a well-known actress) in a report about a burglary at her house. There was no public interest in giving details of her home address (as opposed to reporting the burglary) and the domestic courts had failed to weigh up adequately the competing interests at stake.

In *Friends and others* v *UK*[1503] the Court declared inadmissible a complaint about the hunting ban in the United Kingdom, on the basis that hunting was essentially a public activity and therefore there was no interference with the applicants' Article 8 rights.

Family life

6.455 Whether an applicant can invoke the right to respect for family life will depend on the particular circumstances of each case. The Court in *Marckx* v *Belgium*[1504] stated that this means that the domestic legal system must allow people 'to lead a normal family life' and for family ties to develop normally. Clearly, where there are biological ties, there is a strong presumption that family life exists[1505] and only in exceptional circumstances will such relationships not be protected by the concept of family life. Family life not only protects families based on marriage, but also other de facto relationships, demonstrated by living together or other factors.[1506] Depending upon the circumstances, family life may include unmarried adults,[1507] relations with illegitimate children, and adoptive and foster families.[1508] Links between grandparents and grandchildren, aunts and uncles and other relatives may fall within the notion of family life, provided that there are found to be sufficiently close links. The notion of family life may also encompass issues concerning succession and inheritance.[1509] It is an important principle that the Convention is to be interpreted as a 'living instrument', which in this context means that the notion of family life will continue to evolve. In *Schalk and Kopf* v *Austria*,[1510] the Court found that a same-sex relationship falls within the concept of family life.[1511] In *X, Y and Z* v *UK*,[1512] the Court held that family life included the relationship between a woman, her transsexual partner and a child born to the woman by artificial insemination from an anonymous donor.

[1503] Nos. 16072/06 and 27809/08, dec. 24.11.09.

[1504] Series A, No. 31, 13.6.79.

[1505] See, e.g. *Kroon* v *Netherlands*, No. 18535/91, Series A, No. 297-C, 27.10.94, para. 30. See also *Paradiso and Campanelli* v *Italy*, No. 25358/12, 24.1.17. This case concerned the removal of a child born abroad as a result of an illegal surrogacy arrangement. As there was no biological link between the applicants and the child, there was found to be no de facto family life, but the right to respect for private life was engaged.

[1506] See, e.g. *Wagner and J.M.W.L.* v *Luxembourg*, No. 76240/01, 28.6.07, para. 117; *Şerife Yiğit* v *Turkey*, No. 3976/05, 2.11.10, para. 94.

[1507] There have been conflicting decisions of the Court as to whether 'family life' is considered to exist as between adult offspring and their parents. For example, family life was found to exist in *Bouchelkia* v *France*, No. 23078/93, 29.1.97 and *Boujlifa* v *France*, No. 25404/94, 21.10.97, but not in *Onur* v *UK*, No. 27319/07, 17.2.09 or *A. W. Khan* v *UK*, No. 47486/06, 21.1.10.

[1508] See, e.g. *Kopf and Liberda* v *Austria*, No. 1598/06, 17.1.12 (foster parents); *Nazarenko* v *Russia*, No. 39438/13, 16.7.15 (applicant who had raised child, but was not her biological father).

[1509] See, e.g. *Marckx* v *Belgium*, Series A, No. 31, 13.6.79; *Pla Puncernau and Puncernau Pedro* v *Andorra*, No. 69498/01, 13.7.04; and *Velcea and Mazăre* v *Romania*, No. 64301/01, 1.12.09.

[1510] No. 30141/04, 24.6.10.

[1511] This point had been left open by the Court in *Karner* v *Austria*, No. 40016/98, 24.7.03, in a case concerning the inheritance of a flat by a partner in a same-sex relationship.

[1512] No. 21830/93, 22.4.97. But see *J.R.M.* v *Netherlands*, No. 16944/90, dec. 8.3.93 (sperm donor—inadmissible).

Home

Article 8 upholds the right to respect for one's home. It does not establish a right to be **6.456** provided with a home, as such,[1513] but exceptionally may require the provision of shelter to particularly vulnerable people.[1514] The notion of 'home' includes permanent and temporary places of residence,[1515] offices and business premises,[1516] and places of residence that are not legally established.[1517] It also includes the right to enjoy the home. There will often be an element of overlap with other aspects of Article 8(1) and with property rights under Article 1 of Protocol No. 1 (see below at 6.759).

The Court has reiterated that whether a property can be classified as a 'home' is a question **6.457** of fact and does not depend on the lawfulness of the occupation under domestic law.[1518] In *Prokopovich* v *Russia*[1519] the applicant complained of having been evicted from her flat following the death of her partner. Article 8 was found to be applicable as, although she had not been formally registered there, it was established on the facts that it had been her actual place of residence. Her eviction, without a court order, breached the domestic law, and therefore was not 'in accordance with the law' as required by Article 8. In *Novoseletskiy* v *Ukraine*[1520] the state was found to have breached its positive obligation to restore and protect the applicant's effective enjoyment of the right to respect for his home and his private and family life. The applicant's right to occupy a state-owned flat had been revoked by his employer, a teacher training institute, as a result of which he and his wife had to live with another household for several years. The state's responsibility was engaged both because the institute was found to be a governmental organisation exercising public duties, and in view of the failure of the domestic courts to take sufficient steps to restore the applicant's rights within a reasonable time. In the case of *Yordanova* v *Bulgaria*,[1521] the Court found that the proposed eviction of members of a Roma community (comprising several hundred people) engaged the right to respect for their private life, their family life and their home. They lived in a settlement on municipal land in Sofia. Constructed without authorisation, the homes had neither sewerage nor plumbing. The Court found that:

[1513] See, e.g. *Chapman* v *UK*, No. 27238/95, 18.1.01, para. 99. But see *Marzari* v *Italy*, No. 36448/97, dec. 4.5.99—a refusal of the authorities to provide assistance with a housing problem to the severely ill might raise an issue under Article 8.

[1514] *Yordanova* v *Bulgaria*, No. 2544/06, 24.4.12, para. 130.

[1515] See, e.g. *Collins* v *UK*, No. 11909/02, dec. 15.10.02 (long stay residence within a hospital complex); *Demades* v *Turkey*, No. 16219/90, 31.7.03 (second homes). There must, however, have been a sufficiently concrete tie with the 'home' in question: *Demopoulos and others* v *Turkey*, No. 46113/99 et al, dec. 1.3.10.

[1516] See, e.g. *Société Colas Est and others* v *France*, No. 37971/97, 16.4.02, paras. 40–1; *Buck* v *Germany*, No. 41604/98, 28.4.05, para. 31 (where the Court noted that the the word '*domicile*' in the French version of the Convention has a broader connotation than the word 'home'). But the concept of 'home' does not include farm buildings where livestock are kept: see *Leveau and Fillon* v *France*, Nos. 63512/00 and 63513/00, dec. 6.9.05; or industrial buildings: see *Khamidov* v *Russia*, No. 72118/01, 15.11.07; or a laundry room: see *Chelu* v *Romania*, No. 40274/04, 12.1.10.

[1517] *Gillow* v *UK*, No. 9063/80, 24.11.86, para. 46; *Buckley* v *UK*, No. 20348/92, 25.9.96, paras. 53–4; *Kalanyos and others* v *Romania*, No. 57884/00, dec. 19.5.05.

[1518] See, e.g. *McCann* v *UK*, No. 19009/04, 13.5.08, para. 46; *Yordanova* v *Bulgaria*, No. 2544/06, 24.4.12, para. 103; *Winterstein and others* v *France*, No. 27013/07, 17.10.13, para. 141.

[1519] No. 58255/00, 18.11.04.

[1520] No. 47148/99, 22.2.05.

[1521] No. 2544/06, 24.4.12.

... the disadvantaged position of the social group to which the applicants belong could and should have been taken into consideration, for example, in assisting them to obtain officially the status of persons in need of housing which would make them eligible for the available social dwellings on the same footing as others.[1522]

It concluded that, if enforced, the eviction order would breach Article 8 as it was based on legislation which did not require the examination of proportionality and was issued and reviewed under a flawed decision-making procedure.

6.458   The Court has held that Article 8 applies to severe environmental pollution that may affect individuals' well-being and prevent them from enjoying their homes in such a way as to affect their private and family life adversely (even if their health is not seriously endangered).[1523] In *Moreno Gómez* v *Spain*,[1524] the Court explained the applicability of Article 8 in the environmental context in this way:

> A home will usually be the place, the physically defined area, where private and family life develops. The individual has a right to respect for his home, meaning not just the right to the actual physical area, but also to the quiet enjoyment of that area. Breaches of the right to respect of the home are not confined to concrete or physical breaches, such as unauthorised entry into a person's home, but also include those that are not concrete or physical, such as noise, emissions, smells or other forms of interference. A serious breach may result in the breach of a person's right to respect for his home if it prevents him from enjoying the amenities of his home ...

6.459   In a number of cases involving Turkey, the security forces have been found to have destroyed the applicants' homes and forced them and their families to leave, amounting to a grave and unjustified violation of Article 8 (and of Article 1 of Protocol No. 1).[1525] Similar decisions have been made in cases concerning aerial attacks on homes in the course of the conflict in Chechnya.[1526] In *Cyprus* v *Turkey*,[1527] the denial of displaced persons of the right to return to their homes was found to amount to a continuing violation of Article 8, which had no basis in law. The Romanian authorities were found to have failed to have taken adequate steps to uphold the rights of the applicants in *Moldovan and others* v *Romania*.[1528] The applicants were Roma agricultural workers whose homes had been burnt by a mob, with the acquiescence of the police. The public prosecutor failed to institute criminal proceedings, the courts had failed to award damages in respect of the loss of their homes or property and the Court concluded that the general attitude of the authorities (including the prosecutors, criminal and civil courts, Government and local authorities) had the effect of perpetuating the applicants' feelings of insecurity and amounted to a hindrance of their right to respect for their private and family life and their homes, and thus a serious and continuing violation of Article 8.[1529]

[1522] *Yordanova* v *Bulgaria*, No. 2544/06, 24.4.12, para. 132.

[1523] See, e.g. *Taşkin and others* v *Turkey*, No. 46117/99, 10.11.04, para. 113; see also the section on 'Environmental issues' at 6.527 below.

[1524] No. 4143/02, 16.11.04, para. 53.

[1525] See, e.g. *Bilgin* v *Turkey*, No. 23819/94, 16.11.00; *Dulaş* v *Turkey*, No. 25801/94, 30.1.01; *Orhan* v *Turkey*, No. 25656/94, 18.6.02; *Yöyler* v *Turkey*, No. 26973/95, 24.7.03; *Ayder and others* v *Turkey*, No. 23656/94, 8.1.04; *Ahmet Özkan and others* v *Turkey*, No. 21689/93, 6.4.04.

[1526] See, e.g. *Esmukhambetov and others* v *Russia*, No. 23445/03, 29.3.11; *Kerimova and others* v *Russia*, No. 17170/04 et al, 3.5.11.

[1527] No. 25781/94, 10.5.01.

[1528] Nos. 41138/98 and 64320/01, 12.7.05 (judgment No. 2).

[1529] Article 3 was also violated—see 6.182 above, as was Article 14, taken together with both Articles 8 and 6.

Correspondence

Article 8 will be engaged where there is interference with a wide range of communications, **6.460** including by post, telephone, fax, email and personal internet usage.[1530] These forms of communication may be protected by the other elements of Article 8(1), such as private and family life, as well as the right to respect for correspondence.

The various constituent elements of Article 8(1) and the justification for interferences with **6.461** the rights are examined and illustrated below under the following headings:

- Communications, surveillance and searches: policing and prisons (6.462);
- Police retention, use and disclosure of personal information (6.478);
- Protecting physical, psychological and personal integrity through the law (6.482);
- Family relations (6.487);
- Immigration, asylum and travel restrictions (6.509);
- Sexual identity and relations (6.520);
- Rights of minorities and housing (6.525);
- Environmental issues (6.527);
- Access to personal records (6.535);
- Confidentiality of personal data (6.540);
- Employment (6.544); and
- Medical treatment (6.546).

Communications, surveillance and searches: policing and prisons

Cases of secret surveillance, for example by telephone tapping and by filming, have often **6.462** focused on the adequacy of the legal regime regulating such surveillance. There will clearly be a violation of Article 8 where the authorities carry out surveillance in contravention of the domestic law, as was the case in *Perry v UK*,[1531] where the applicant suspect was covertly filmed in a police station custody suite, in breach of the statutory code of practice. There was also a breach of the domestic law in *Craxi (No. 2) v Italy*,[1532] as a result of the failure of the Public Prosecutor to lodge transcripts of private telephone conversations in the court registry, prior to their use in criminal proceedings.

More often, however, it is the *quality* of the domestic law, or even the absence of legal regu- **6.463** lation, that leads to violations of Article 8 of the Convention. As a suspected receiver of stolen goods, the telephone conversations of the applicant in the case of *Malone v UK*[1533] were intercepted by the police under a warrant issued by the Home Secretary.[1534] After his acquittal, he challenged the legality of such interceptions in the domestic courts and under the Convention. In its judgment in the *Malone* case, the Court acknowledged that where the state exercises its powers in secret, there are obvious risks of arbitrariness. However, the Court agreed with the UK Government that the requirements of the Convention (particu- larly in relation to foreseeability) cannot be the same in the context of police investigations

---

[1530] See, e.g. *Copland v UK*, No. 62617/00, 3.4.07, para. 41.
[1531] No. 63737/00, 17.7.03.
[1532] No. 25337/94, 17.7.03.
[1533] No. 8691/79, 2.8.84, Series A, No. 82.
[1534] The UK Government's usual practice, as was the case in *Malone*, is not to disclose the extent to which an applicant has been the subject of surveillance, if at all. They did accept, however, that Malone was a member of a class of persons who were liable to be the subject of interception: para. 64.

as they are where the aim of the law is to restrict the conduct of individuals. Nevertheless, the Court emphasised that there has to be an adequate indication of the circumstances in which the police or other authorities can rely on 'this secret and potentially dangerous interference with the right to respect for private life and correspondence' in order to protect against arbitrary interference. The Court held that Article 8 had been violated in *Malone* because of the obscurity and uncertainty of the relevant domestic law which applied at that time. As a result of this judgment, the UK Government introduced the Interception of Communications Act 1985 to regulate the interception of communications by mail and by telephone (including mobile phones). In a subsequent admissibility decision concerning allegations of the interception of telexes sent by trade unions in Eastern Europe to the General Secretary of the Scottish TUC, the European Commission found that this system provided the requisite degree of certainty.[1535]

6.464 In the case of *Halford* v *UK*[1536] the Court found a violation of Article 8 arising from the interception of the applicant's telephone calls by her employer, Merseyside Police, within the internal telephone system at the Merseyside Police Headquarters. In those circumstances, as the Interception of Communications Act 1985 only applied to a 'public telecommunications system', it did not regulate interception of internal systems, and on that basis the Court found that the interference was not 'in accordance with the law'.[1537] Similarly, the absence of law regulating the surveillance by an employer of an employee's telephone, email and use of the internet was found to violate Article 8 in *Copland* v *UK*.[1538]

6.465 The absence of legal regulation has also been decisive in relation to the use of police surveillance devices. In the case of *Khan* v *UK*,[1539] the Court unanimously found a violation of both Articles 8 and 13 arising from the use of a listening device by the police, which was subject only to non-statutory Home Office guidelines, the disclosure of which to the applicant was refused on the basis of public interest immunity. There was no domestic law whatsoever regulating the use of covert listening devices at the relevant time and accordingly the Court found that the interference was not 'in accordance with the law'. In *Heglas* v *Czech Republic*,[1540] the insufficiently clear legal basis for the use of body-mounted listening devices was found to breach Article 8, and there was a violation for similar reasons in *Bykov* v *Russia*[1541] (as regards the use of a radio-transmitting device) and *Van Vondel* v *Netherlands*[1542] (in relation to assistance given by the police to an individual in order to record his telephone conversations with the applicant). In *PG and JH* v *UK*,[1543] the obtaining by the police of

---

[1535] *Campbell Christie* v *UK*, No. 21482, Series A, No. 78, dec. 27.6.94, DR 119. The European Commission's admissibility decisions in *Esbester* v *UK*, No. 18601/91, dec. 2.4.93 and *Hewitt and Harman* v *UK*, No. 20317/92, dec. 1.9.93, came to similar conclusions in relation to the analogous system for the Security Service established by the Security Service Act 1989.

[1536] No. 20605/92, 25.6.97.

[1537] *Ibid.*, para. 51.

[1538] No. 62617/00, 3.4.07. See, by contrast, *Bărbulescu* v *Romania*, No. 61496/08, 12.1.16 (monitoring of an employee's use of internet at work and use of data collected to justify his dismissal—no violation of Article 8) (case referred to Grand Chamber 6.6.16).

[1539] No. 35394/97, 12.5.00. See also *Govell* v *UK*, No. 27237/95, Comm. Rep. 26.2.97; *Taylor-Sabori* v *UK*, No. 47114/99, 22.10.02 (interception of pagers unregulated by statute).

[1540] No. 5935/02, 1.3.07.

[1541] No. 4378/02, 10.3.09.

[1542] No. 38258/03, 25.10.07.

[1543] No. 44787/98, 25.9.01.

information relating to numbers called on a telephone in the applicant's flat (the process of 'metering') was found to amount to an interference with the applicants' private lives or correspondence, but there was no violation of Article 8 as the process was sufficiently prescribed by domestic law and was used in a proportionate manner. However, the recording of the applicants' voice samples in the police station and in police cells violated Article 8 as such surveillance was not regulated by domestic law (prior to the Regulation of Investigatory Powers Act 2000 coming into force).

The *quality* of the law regulating telephone tapping in France (which was permitted under **6.466** warrant issued by an investigating judge) led to findings of violations of Article 8 by the Court in *Kruslin* v *France*[1544] and *Huvig* v *France*.[1545] Whilst interception was regulated by the French Criminal Code, the Court found there were insufficient controls in a number of ways. For example, there was no definition of the categories of people liable to be subject to interception or the nature of offences which might give rise to an order for interception. There was also no obligation to limit the duration of the warrant, and there was no procedure for the destruction of the tapes, particularly following discharge or acquittal.[1546] In *Rotaru* v *Romania*,[1547] the Court found insufficient legal controls on the collection and storage of information by the Romanian secret services, in violation of Article 8. In the context of secret surveillance, the Court has stressed that 'the values of a democratic society must be followed as faithfully as possible in the supervisory procedures if the bounds of necessity, within the meaning of Article 8(2), are not to be exceeded'.[1548] In *Dragojević* v *Croatia*[1549] the Court found a violation of Article 8 because of inadequacies in the domestic courts' application of the legislation regulating surveillance. As he was suspected of being involved in drug-trafficking, the applicant's telephone was monitored, under authorisations issued by an investigating judge. However, the judicial orders were found to be inadequately reasoned, as they contained no details about the particular case. The Court did not accept that such decisions could be retrospectively justified by the domestic courts, especially as the relevant statute required prior judicial scrutiny and detailed reasons to be given in the authorisation itself.

The Bulgarian legislation permitting secret surveillance was found to fall short of the Article **6.467** 8 requirements in the *Case of the Association for European Integration and Human Rights and Ekimdzhiev* v *Bulgaria*,[1550] as was found to be the case with the equivalent Moldovan legislation in *Iordachi* v *Moldova*[1551] and as regards the domestic law in Hungary in *Szabó and Vissy* v

---

[1544] No. 11801/85, Series A, No. 176-B, 24.4.90.

[1545] No. 11105/84, Series A, No. 176-B, 24.4.90. See also *Prado Bugallo* v *Spain*, No. 58496/00, 18.2.03.

[1546] *Kruslin* v *France*, No. 11801/85, 24.4.90, Series A, No. 176-B, paras. 34–5; *Huvig* v *France*, No. 11105/84, Series A, No. 176-B, 24.4.90, paras. 33–4. For a similar decision concerning the use of listening devices, see *Vetter* v *France*, No. 59842/00, 31.5.05. See also *Lambert* v *France*, No. 23618/94, 24.8.98—unanimous violation of Article 8 where the domestic courts refused the applicant's complaint of the interception of his telephone calls on the ground that it was a third party's line which had been tapped. In *Nasir Choudhary* v *UK*, No. 40084/98, dec. 4.5.99, the Court found that the Interception of Communications Act 1985, s. 1 was sufficiently clear for the purposes of Article 8(2) in permitting interception of telephone calls where there were reasonable grounds for believing that one of the parties to the call had consented to the interception.

[1547] No. 36437/97, 4.5.00. See also *Dumitru Popescu* v *Romania*, No. 71525/01, 26.4.07; *Association '21 December 1989' and others* v *Romania*, No. 33810/07, 24.5.11.

[1548] *Klass and others* v *Germany*, Series A, No. 28, 6.9.78, para. 55.

[1549] No. 68955/11, 15.1.15.

[1550] No. 62540/00, 28.6.07.

[1551] No. 25198/02, 10.2.09.

Hungary.[1552] In *Liberty and others* v *UK*,[1553] three civil liberties organisations complained that their communications had been intercepted by an agency of the Ministry of Defence, under wide powers granted by the Interception of Communications Act 1985. The Court found a violation of Article 8 on the basis that the domestic law gave the authorities a very wide discretion to intercept telephone calls, emails and other communications, without there being adequate safeguards against abuse of power. There were also no publicly available criteria as regards the procedure to be followed for selecting for examination, sharing, storing and destroying intercepted material. In *Klass and others* v *Germany*,[1554] concerning the system of secret surveillance in Germany, the Court stated that 'in a field where abuse is potentially so easy in individual cases and could have such harmful consequences for democratic society as a whole, it is in principle desirable to entrust supervisory control to a judge'. The Court has more recently reiterated that there must be clear, detailed rules on interception of telephone conversations, but it has also said as regards secret measures of surveillance, such as the interception of communications, that the need for 'foreseeability' of the law does *not* require that individuals should be able to foresee when the authorities are likely to intercept their communications so that they can adapt their conduct accordingly.[1555] The case of *Roman Zakharov* v *Russia*[1556] concerned the manifold inadequacies of the legal framework governing secret surveillance of mobile telephone communications by the security services (FSB) in Russia. The Grand Chamber noted that service providers were required to install equipment giving the authorities direct access to all users' mobile telephone communications, which it found meant that the system was particularly prone to abuse. The Court identified a plethora of problematic issues, including the following: that secret interception of communications was allowed in respect of a very wide range of offences; interception could be ordered in respect of witnesses as well as suspects; the authorities had an almost unlimited discretion to carry out interception in relation to activities endangering Russia's national, military, economic or ecological security; there were insufficient guarantees about the discontinuation of surveillance; there was no requirement to destroy immediately any data that were not relevant to the purpose for which they were obtained; judicial scrutiny of the authorisation of interceptions was too limited in scope and the law did not set out requirements as to the content of interception requests or authorisations; the urgent authorisation procedure did not provide sufficient safeguards to ensure that it was used sparingly and only in duly justified cases; the arrangements for supervision (including by prosecutors) were inadequate; and there were insufficient provisions as to notification of surveillance[1557] and in relation to the availability of remedies.

6.468 *Kopp* v *Switzerland*[1558] concerned the interception of a law firm's telephone calls, and therefore brought into play the question of legal professional privilege. There, the Court[1559] found it

---

[1552] No. 37138/14, 12.1.16.

[1553] No. 58243/00, 1.7.08. See also *10 human rights organisations* v *UK*, No. 24960/15 et al, communicated 24.11.15 (a complaint about the alleged mass surveillance of human rights organisations).

[1554] Series A, No. 28, 6.9.78.

[1555] *Weber and Saravia* v *Germany*, No. 54934/00, dec. 29.6.06, para. 93 (concerning the Restrictions on the Secrecy of Mail, Post and Telecommunications Act 1968). See also *Kennedy* v *UK*, No. 26839/05, 18.5.10 (adequacy of safeguards contained in Regulation of Investigatory Powers Act 2000 as regards interception of communications—no violation of Articles 8 or 6(1)).

[1556] No. 47143/06, 4.12.15.

[1557] As to notification requirements, see also *Cevat Özel* v *Turkey*, No. 19602/06, 7.6.16.

[1558] No. 23224/94, 25.3.98.

[1559] *Ibid.*, para. 74.

astonishing that this task should be assigned to an official of the Post Office's legal department, who is a member of the executive, without supervision by an independent judge, especially in this sensitive area of the confidential relations between a lawyer and his clients, which directly concern the rights of the defendant.

At issue in *R.E.* v *UK*[1560] was the covert surveillance of a detainee's consultations with his lawyer, and with the person appointed to assist him, as a vulnerable person, following his arrest in connection with the murder of a police officer. Article 8 was found to have been breached during the legal consultations because there were insufficient safeguards in the domestic statute (the Regulation of Investigatory Powers Act 2000) as regards the examination, use and storage of the material, the precautions to be taken when communicating the material to other parties, and the circumstances in which recordings would be erased or the material destroyed. However, there was no breach of Article 8 in relation to the surveillance of consultations between the detainee and the appropriate adult which were not subject to legal privilege and therefore did not attract the 'strengthened protection' given to legal consultations. The clarity of the law was found wanting in *Vukota-Bojić* v *Switzerland*[1561] which concerned surveillance of the activities of a social-insurance claimant by private investigators commissioned by an insurance company. The domestic law was not sufficiently clear in setting out the scope and manner of exercise of the discretion conferred on insurance companies to conduct secret surveillance, and it did not incorporate sufficient safeguards against abuse. There was no violation of Article 8 in *Uzun* v *Germany*,[1562] which concerned the surveillance of a terrorist suspect's movements in public using a global-positioning system (GPS) device. In the course of its consideration of the compliance of the domestic law with the principles of foreseeability and the rule of law, the Court noted that as the use of GPS caused less of an interference with a person's private life than surveillance of telecommunications, the stricter standards applied in such cases were not directly applicable.

The searching of premises by the authorities has been examined both in respect of the legality of the measures used and their proportionality. In *Funke* v *France*,[1563] which concerned the search of the applicant's home by French customs authorities and the seizure of financial papers, the Court considered that three of the four component rights protected by Article 8(1) were in issue, namely the right to respect for private life, home and correspondence. The measures taken were found to be disproportionate to the legitimate aim being pursued by the authorities. The prime reason was the absence of the need for a judicial warrant. The other relevant restrictions and conditions under French law were considered to be 'too lax and full of loopholes', leaving the customs authorities very wide powers, including the exclusive competence to assess the expediency, number, length and scale of inspections.[1564] The domestic law relating to search and seizure of correspondence also fell foul of the 'prescribed by law' test in *Lavents* v *Latvia*[1565] primarily because it did not specify the period of validity of the measure or the reasons that might warrant it. Where the authorities may order and carry out

6.469

[1560] No. 62498/11, 27.10.15.

[1561] No. 61838/10, 18.10.16.

[1562] No. 35623/05, 2.9.10.

[1563] No. 10828/84, Series A, No. 256-A, 25.2.93. See also *Cremieux* v *France*, No. 11471/85, 25.2.93 and *Miailhe* v *France*, No. 12661/87, 25.2.93.

[1564] No. 10828/84, Series A, No. 256-A, 25.2.93, para. 57.

[1565] No. 58442/00, 28.11.02. See also *Estrikh* v *Latvia*, No. 73819/01, 18.1.07 (prisoners' rights to long-term visits prescribed by a law that had not been made public—violation of Article 8).

searches without a judicial warrant, there must be 'very strict limits' on such powers in order to prevent violations of Article 8.[1566]

6.470 In *Chappell* v *UK*[1567] the applicant was a videotape dealer who operated from premises that combined his office with his home. The case concerned the execution of a search warrant by the police looking for obscene videos at the same prearranged time as a search order was executed by the plaintiff in proceedings for breach of copyright. The Court noted the High Court judge's concerns that simultaneous searches (by 16 or 17 people) made the execution of the order 'more oppressive than it should have been'[1568] but the interference with the applicant's Article 8 rights was found to be proportionate to the legitimate aim of protecting the plaintiff's copyright. The searches of the applicant journalists' homes, offices and cars in *Ernst and others* v *Belgium*[1569] was found to be disproportionate because of the wording of the search warrants, which permitted the search for and seizure of 'any document or object that might assist the investigation', without limitation. The warrants also gave no information about the investigation, the premises to be searched or the objects to be seized, and the applicants were not informed of the reasons for the searches.

6.471 The case of *Niemetz* v *Germany*[1570] confirmed that the search of office premises would fall to be considered under Article 8. There, the applicant lawyer's office was searched by the police who examined four filing cabinets containing information relating to clients. The search would therefore have included 'correspondence' and the Court noted that Article 8(1) did not include any qualification of the word 'correspondence', as it did for the word 'life'.[1571] It did not matter that the correspondence was of a professional nature. The search was found to impinge on professional secrecy to an extent that was disproportionate, primarily because the warrant had been drawn in very wide terms, permitting the search and seizure of 'documents', without limitation.[1572] The failure to comply with procedural safeguards when police searched a lawyer's computer files led to a finding that the search and seizure was disproportiante in violation of Article 8 in *Wieser and Bicos Beteiligungen GmbH* v *Austria*.[1573] In *Buck* v *Germany*,[1574] a police search of the applicant's residential and business premises was found (by four votes to three) to be a disproportionate interference with his Article 8 rights because it related to criminal proceedings against his son (and not

---

[1566] See also, *Camenzind* v *Switzerland*, No. 21353/93, 16.12.97; *Van Rossem* v *Belgium*, No. 41872/98, 9.12.04.

[1567] No. 10461/83, Series A, No. 142, 30.3.89.

[1568] *Ibid.*, para. 65.

[1569] No. 33400/96, 15.7.03. There was also a violation of Article 10.

[1570] No. 13710/88 16.12.92. See also: *Société Colas Est and others* v *France*, No. 37971/97, 16.4.02; *Roemen and Schmit* v *Luxembourg*, No. 51772/99, 25.2.03.

[1571] *Ibid.*, para. 32.

[1572] *Ibid.*, para. 37. See also, e.g. *Elçi and others* v *Turkey*, Nos. 23145/93 and 25091/94, 13.11.03 (searches of lawyers' offices and privileged professional materials taken without authorisation); *Smirnov* v *Russia*, No. 71362/01, 7.6.07 (search of lawyer's home without safeguards against interference with professional secrecy); *André and others* v *France*, No. 18603/03, 24.7.08 (search of law office and seizures by tax inspectors seeking evidence against a corporate client).

[1573] No. 74336/01, 16.10.07. See also: *Robathin* v *Austria*, No. 30457/06, 3.7.12 (authorisation of search and seizure of all electronic data in law office without sufficient reason—violation of Article 8); *Vinci Construction and GTM Génie Civil et Services* v *France*, Nos. 63629/10 and 60567/10, 2.4.15 (search and seizure of companies' electronic data including e-mails subject to lawyer–client privilege—violation of Article 8); *Bernh Larsen Holding AS and others* v *Norway*, No. 24117/08, 14.3.13 (requirement for applicant company to provide to tax authorities data on server which it shared with other companies—no violation of Article 8).

[1574] No. 41604/98, 28.4.05.

the applicant) that concerned a relatively minor road traffic offence (speeding). In *Saint-Paul Luxembourg S.A.* v *Luxembourg*[1575] a police search and seizure operation at a newspaper premises, conducted in order to establish the identity of the author of an article, was found to be disproportionate, because other less intrusive means could have been carried out to achieve the same ends.

The use by the police of powers to stop and search people in public will engage Article 8 rights. This was confirmed in the case of *Gillan and Quinton* v *UK*,[1576] which concerned the searching of the applicants in the vicinity of an arms fair, where a demonstration had been planned. The Court held that the use of coercive powers, under the Terrorism Act 2000, to require individuals to submit to detailed searches of their person, clothing and personal belongings amounted to a clear interference with the right to respect for private life. The Court went on to find that the legislation was not sufficiently circumscribed or subject to adequate legal safeguards against abuse. The 2000 Act allowed the police to stop and search a pedestrian in a specified area if it was considered 'expedient' for the prevention of acts of terrorism. The use of the power need not be considered 'necessary' and there was no requirement to assess its proportionality. The authorisation was limited to a 28-day period, but was renewable, and could cover a large geographical area. A search had to be carried out for the purpose of looking for articles that could be used in connection with terrorism, but the officer conducting the search need not have 'reasonable suspicion', nor was there even a requirement for the officer subjectively to suspect anything about the person stopped and searched. Neither powers of confirmation or review conferred on the Secretary of State and the Independent Reviewer, nor the possibility of judicial review, were considered adequate to limit the potential for the abuse of power. Therefore, the Court concluded that there was a violation of Article 8. **6.472**

In *McLeod* v *UK*,[1577] the Court found that the entry of the police into the applicant's house in order to prevent a breach of the peace amounted to an interference with her rights under Article 8(1). The police entered the house ostensibly to prevent any disputes that might have arisen when the applicant's former husband sought to remove various items of property from the house. The power to enter premises to prevent a breach of the peace was considered to be sufficiently accessible and foreseeable in domestic law. The interference was found to be aimed at preventing disorder or crime, but the means employed by the police were held to be disproportionate to that aim. The police had failed to verify whether the ex-husband was entitled to enter the applicant's home (he had not been so entitled) and once the police had been informed that the applicant was not present, they should not have entered the house, as it should have been clear that there was little or no risk of disorder or crime. There was accordingly a breach of Article 8. A similar finding was made in *Keegan* v *UK*[1578] in which the police had obtained a warrant to search a house for the proceeds of a robbery. However, the applicants had been living at the house for six months and had no connection with the suspect, and the police were found not to have made the requisite enquiries prior to making an early morning raid. **6.473**

[1575] No. 26419/10, 18.4.13.
[1576] No. 4158/05, 12.1.10. See also *Colon* v *Netherlands*, No. 49458/06, dec. 15.5.12.
[1577] No. 24755/94, 23.9.98.
[1578] No. 28867/03, 18.7.06.

6.474 The interception of detainees' letters (to family members, lawyers, medical specialists, Strasbourg institutions and other international organisations) has been the subject of a number of Convention cases.[1579] Italian legislation authorising interception was found to violate Article 8 because it lacked sufficient detail: it neither prescribed the period of time in which monitoring could take place, nor the reasons that would lead to such measures being taken.[1580] There was a breach of Article 8 in *Mehmet Nuri Özen and others* v *Turkey*[1581] where prisoners' letters were not sent on to addressees because they were written in Kurdish, rather than Turkish, and therefore the authorities argued that they could not know if the letters contained 'offensive' material. Such an interference with the applicants' Article 8 rights was not considered to be 'in accordance with the law' as the domestic law only permitted restrictions on the basis of the contents of the letters, not their language. In *Cotlet* v *Romania*,[1582] Article 8 was violated because of interferences with the applicant prisoner's correspondence with the European Commission and Court of Human Rights: the post was delayed; his letters were opened; and he was not provided with adequate writing materials. Whilst some measure of control of prisoners' correspondence is accepted, the fact that the opportunity to write and receive letters may be the only contact with the outside world is an important factor to be taken into account. In *Silver* v *UK*,[1583] the legal regime for the interception of prison mail (statute, rules and standing orders) to MPs, solicitors and others was in various respects found to be insufficiently foreseeable or to impose unjustifiable restrictions in violation of Article 8.[1584] In *Campbell* v *UK*,[1585] the Court emphasised the particular importance of correspondence with a lawyer, which in principle is privileged. Therefore, such correspondence should only be opened where there are reasonable grounds to believe it contains an illicit enclosure. Privileged letters should, even then, not be read, other than in exceptional circumstances. But Article 8 does not guarantee a right for prisoners to make telephone calls (particularly where facilities for contact by way of correspondence are available and adequate),[1586] or to receive emails.[1587]

6.475 The importance of legally privileged correspondence was reiterated in *Foxley* v *UK*,[1588] where the applicant's post, including correspondence with his legal advisers, was redirected under a court order to his trustee in bankruptcy (who was also the court-appointed receiver), who

---

[1579] See, e.g. *Puzinas* v *Lithuania*, No. 44800/98, 14.3.02; *Petrov* v *Bulgaria*, No. 15197/02, 22.5.08; *Moiseyev* v *Russia*, No. 62936/00, 9.10.08; *Gagiu* v *Romania*, No. 63258/00, 24.2.09; *Szuluk* v *UK*, No. 36936/05, 2.6.09; *Yefimenko* v *Russia*, No. 152/04, 12.2.13; *D.L.* v *Bulgaria*, No. 7472/14, 19.5.16 (blanket monitoring of correspondence and telephone conversations of residents of closed educational institution for juveniles—violation of Article 8).

[1580] *Calogero Diana* v *Italy*, No. 15211/89, 15.11.96; *Domenichini* v *Italy*, No. 15943/90, 15.11.96; *Messina (No. 2)* v *Italy*, No. 25498/94, 28.9.00.

[1581] No. 15672/08, 11.1.11. See also: *Nusret Kaya and others* v *Turkey*, No. 43750/06 et al, 22.4.14 (restrictions on prisoners using Kurdish in telephone calls—violation of Article 8); *Mesut Yurtsever and others* v *Turkey*, No. 14946/08 et al, 20.1.15 (ban on Kurdish language newspaper in Turkish prisons—violation of Article 10).

[1582] No. 38565/97, 3.6.03 (there was also a violation of Article 34).

[1583] Nos. 5947/72, 6205/73, 7052/75, 7061/75, 7107/75, 7113/75 and 7136/75, Series A, No. 61, 25.3.83.

[1584] See also *Radaj and others* v *Poland*, Nos. 29537/95 and 35453/97, 28.11.02; *Nilsen* v *UK*, No. 36882/05, dec. 9.3.10 (measures taken by Prison Service to prevent publication of autobiography by serial killer—inadmissible).

[1585] No. 13590/88, Series A, No. 233-A, 25.3.92. See also *Ekinci and Akalın* v *Turkey*, No. 77097/01, 30.1.07.

[1586] *A.B.* v *Netherlands*, No. 37328/97, 29.1.02, para. 92.

[1587] *Helander* v *Finland*, No. 10410/10, dec. 10.9.13.

[1588] No. 33274/96, 20.6.00.

opened the letters, read them, photocopied them and placed them on file. Such interference was found to be disproportionate in violation of Article 8.[1589]

6.476 Article 8 will also protect the right of detainees to contact their family. In *Poltoratskiy* v *Ukraine*,[1590] the restrictions on the applicant prisoner's contact with his family (and lawyer) were the result of a Ministry of Justice internal 'Instruction', which was an unpublished document that was not accessible to the public. Accordingly, the limitations placed on the applicant's Article 8 rights were not 'in accordance with the law'. There was a similar outcome in *Kurkowski* v *Poland*[1591] as the authorities had an absolute discretion as to the restrictions which could be placed on family visits with the applicant, who was in pre-trial detention. Article 8 was also breached because during several visits the applicant was physically separated from his family by a Perspex partition, for which there was no justification. Article 8 may be violated where detainee are held in a location far away from their families. This was the case in *Khodorkovskiy and Lebedev* v *Russia*,[1592] where the applicants, having been convicted of tax evasion offences, were sent to serve their prison sentences in remote penal colonies thousands of miles away from their families.

6.477 In *McVeigh, O'Neill and Evans* v *UK*,[1593] the applicants complained of violations of their rights under Article 8 to respect for their family life on the basis that they were prevented from communicating with their wives during their detention by the police under the Prevention of Terrorism (Supplemental Temporary Provisions) Order 1976. The European Commission found a violation of Article 8 in that case as there had been no risk that accomplices might have been alerted, or might have escaped, destroyed or removed evidence, or committed offences.[1594] The Commission acknowledged that 'at the time when a person is arrested his ability to communicate rapidly with his family may be of great importance. The unexplained disappearance of a family member even for a short period of time may provoke great anxiety.'[1595] Similarly, there was a violation of Article 8 in *Ferla* v *Poland*[1596] as a result of restrictions on contacts between the applicant remand prisoner and his wife, on the basis that she might be called as a prosecution witness: allowing just one visit in 11 months was found to be disproportionate. The applicant's wife had told the authorities that she had no information to offer, and they had failed to consider other means of preventing any possible collusion (such as supervision by a prison officer). Other forms of restrictions placed on prisoners may impinge upon their Article 8 rights, in view of the need to respect human dignity. For example, in *Lindström and Mässeli* v *Finland*[1597] the Court found a violation of Article 8 as a result of the requirement for prisoners in isolation to wear 'closed overalls' sealed with plastic strips—a practice that was found to have an insufficient legal basis.

[1589] See also *Luordo* v *Italy*, No. 32190/96 and *Bottaro* v *Italy*, No. 56298/00, 17.7.03 (bankrupt applicants' correspondence intercepted for excessive periods).

[1590] No. 38812/97, 29.4.03, para. 148. See further at 6.147 and 6.565. See also, e.g. *Sarı and Çolak* v *Turkey*, Nos. 42596/98 and 42603/98, 4.4.06 (detention in police custody); *Kučera* v *Slovakia*, No. 48666/99, 17.7.07; *Moiseyev* v *Russia*, No. 62936/00, 9.10.08.

[1591] No. 36228/06, 9.4.13.

[1592] Nos. 11082/06 and 13772/05, 25.7.13. See also *Polyakova and others* v *Russia*, No. 35090/09, 7.3.17.

[1593] Nos. 8022/77, 8025/77 and 8027/77, 18.3.81.

[1594] *Ibid.*, paras. 237–40.

[1595] *Ibid.*, para. 237.

[1596] No. 55470/00, 20.5.08.

[1597] No. 24630/10, 14.1.14. There was, however, no violation of Article 3.

Police retention, use and disclosure of personal information[1598]

6.478 The collection and retention in police records of information about suspects (including fingerprints, cellular samples and DNA profiles)[1599] gives rise to a number of questions, such as the necessity of retaining the information and the circumstances in which the information should be disclosed to the suspect or to third parties. The right to respect for private and family life in Article 8 will provide a degree of protection for those about whom information is held on police files. An interference with a suspect's Article 8(1) rights may be justified by the police on the basis, for example, that the retention of the information is necessary for the prevention of disorder or crime or is in the interests of public safety, provided also, that the measure in question is both in accordance with the law and proportionate to the aim being pursued. Whether Article 8(1) is engaged in such circumstances is not usually in issue. For example, it was undisputed in *Murray* v *UK*[1600] that various measures carried out by the army, including the recording of personal details about the first applicant and her family, and their taking her photograph without her knowledge or consent, interfered with the applicants' rights under Article 8(1).

6.479 In *Leander* v *Sweden*[1601] it was not disputed that information contained in a secret police register related to the applicant's private life. The Court found that both the storing and the release of such information, coupled with a refusal to allow the applicant the opportunity to refute it, amounted to an interference with his right to respect for private life under Article 8(1). *Leander* concerned the retention of information relating to employment in national security sensitive positions. Swedish law conferred a wide discretion as to the collection of information on a secret police register, but it was limited in that information could not be recorded merely because by belonging to an organisation, or by other means, a person had expressed a political opinion. The discretion was further limited by Governmental instructions (only one of which was public and therefore sufficiently accessible to be taken into account by the Court) and by the requirements that the information had to be necessary for the secret police service and intended to serve the purpose of preventing or detecting 'offences against national security, etc'. There were also explicit and detailed provisions as to what information could be disclosed, the authorities to which, and circumstances in which, information could be communicated, as well as the procedure to be followed when taking decisions to release information. Such requirements were considered by the Court to provide an adequate indication as to the scope and manner of exercise of the discretion conferred on the police.[1602] The inaccessibility of the relevant domestic law led to a finding of a violation of Article 8 in *Shimovolos* v *Russia*.[1603] There, the applicant human rights activist had been listed in a police 'surveillance database', the legal basis for which was an unpublished ministerial order. Therefore, the grounds for registering a person's name, the authorities competent to make such an order, its duration, the nature of the data collected, the procedures for storing and using the data and the controls to prevent abuse were not open to public scrutiny.

[1598] The issues of access to personal records and the confidentiality of personal data are considered below at 6.535 and 6.540.

[1599] *Van der Velden* v *Netherlands,* No. 29514/05, dec. 7.12.06; *S. and Marper* v *UK*, Nos. 30562/04 and 30566/04, 4.12.08.

[1600] No. 18731/91, 28.10.94.

[1601] No. 9248/81, Series A, No. 116, 26.3.87.

[1602] *Ibid.*, paras. 54–6.

[1603] No. 30194/09, 21.6.11.

In *S and Marper* v *UK*,[1604] the applicants challenged the effect of legislation which enabled fingerprints and DNA samples taken from a person suspected of a criminal offence to be retained without a time limit, even if the criminal proceedings resulted in an acquittal or discharge. While the Court acknowledged that a national DNA database had contributed to the detection and prevention of crime, it was critical of the blanket and indiscriminate nature of the power of retention of samples, which existed irrespective of the nature or gravity of the suspected offence or the age of the individual concerned. There were only limited possibilities for someone acquitted to have the data removed from the database, and there was no provision for independent review of the justification for the retention according to defined criteria. The Court expressed its concern about the risks of stigmatisation of those who were entitled to be presumed innocent (especially minors). There had accordingly been a disproportionate interference with the applicants' rights, in violation of Article 8. The applicant in *M.M.* v *UK*[1605] complained about the retention of her police caution for life, and her obligation to disclose it to a prospective employer some years afterwards. The Court found a violation of Article 8 because of the absence in Northern Ireland of a clear legislative framework for the collection and storage of data, and the lack of clarity as to the scope, extent and restrictions of the common law powers of the police to retain and disclose caution data. However, there was no violation of Article 8 in *Gardel* v *France*,[1606] as a result of the applicant's registration on a national sex offenders register for a 30-year period, following his conviction for rape of 15-year-olds and his sentencing to life imprisonment. The interference with the applicant's rights was considered not to be disproportionate, taking into account the state's duty to protect children and other vulnerable people, the procedural provisions available to the applicant and the breadth of the state's margin of appreciation.

There was a violation of Article 8 in *Cemalettin Canlı* v *Turkey*[1607] as a result of the disclosure **6.480** by the police of information about the applicant to a court, which stated, inaccurately, that he was a member of an illegal organisation (in breach of the relevant police regulations). *Mikolajova* v *Slovakia*[1608] concerned the disclosure by the police to a health insurance company of information suggesting that the applicant had been guilty of a violent criminal offence, even though she had not even been charged—the Court found a violation of Article 8, noting also the lack of any available domestic recourse for her. In *Turek* v *Slovakia*[1609] the applicant complained that the state security agency retained a file identifying him as a former collaborator, and objected to the issuing of a negative security clearance on him. There was a breach of Article 8 because of the lack of any effective procedure by which the applicant could seek to protect the right to respect for his private life. The domestic courts required the applicant to prove that the interference was contrary to the applicable rules, but the rules

---

[1604] Nos. 30562/04 and 30566/04, 4.12.08. See also *M.K.* v *France*, No. 19522/09, 18.4.13 (lack of safeguards for collection, preservation and deletion of fingerprint records of persons suspected but not convicted of criminal offences—violation of Article 8) and *Khelili* v *Switzerland*, No. 16188/07, 18.10.11 (police records describing applicant's occupation as 'prostitute', despite lack of conviction for prostitution-related offences—violation of Article 8). See, by contrast, *Peruzzo and Martens* v *Germany*, Nos. 7841/08 and 57900/12, dec. 4.6.13 (taking and retention of DNA profiles found to be proportionate—inadmissible).

[1605] No. 24029/07, 13.11.12.

[1606] No. 16428/05, 17.12.09. See also: *Bouchacourt* v *France*, No. 5335/06, 17.12.09; *M.B.* v *France*, No. 22115/06, 17.12.09; and *Hautin* v *France*, No. 6930/06, dec. 24.11.09.

[1607] No. 22427/04, 18.11.08.

[1608] No. 4479/03, 18.1.11.

[1609] No. 57986/00, 14.2.06.

were secret and the applicant did not have full access to them. The collection and retention of information by MI5 (the UK security service) concerning the private lives of Patricia Hewitt and Harriet Harman[1610] was found by the European Commission of Human Rights to violate Article 8 because such interference was based on a non-binding and unpublished Government directive and was not therefore 'in accordance with the law'.[1611] In *Amann v Switzerland*,[1612] the retention of information on the applicant by the police in a national security card index, identifying him as a contact with the Russian embassy, was found to violate Article 8, as the relevant domestic law was insufficiently foreseeable.

6.481 In *Friedl v Austria*[1613] the applicant took part in a demonstration in Vienna about homelessness. He was photographed and filmed by the police who also checked his identity and took down personal details. The information was stored in administrative files that were to be destroyed in 2001, but it was not retained on computer files. The Commission found that the taking and retention of the photographs did not interfere with the applicant's rights under Article 8(1), as there had been no intrusion into the 'inner circle' of his private life; they concerned a public incident in which the applicant had voluntarily taken part and they were taken solely for the purpose of recording and investigating the incident in question. The retention of personal information was considered to be an interference with the Article 8(1) rights, but was found to be necessary in a democratic society for the prevention of disorder or crime. The Court judgment in *Sciacca v Italy*[1614] confirmed that, following *Van Hannover* (see 6.454 above), the *publication* of a photograph falls within the scope of private life under Article 8. There, the publication at a press conference by the revenue police of a photograph of a suspect under house arrest was found to violate Article 8 as it was subject only to practice, and was therefore not 'in accordance with the law'. There was a similar conclusion in *Giorgi Nikolaishvili v Georgia*[1615] where 'wanted' posters of the applicant were displayed by the police. The applicant was not himself a suspect, but was being sought as a witness in a murder case. There was no domestic legal basis for the publication of his photograph and therefore the interference with his Article 8 rights was not 'in accordance with the law'. In *Toma v Romania*,[1616] the decision of the police to allow journalists to film and photograph the applicant in police custody could not be justified by any of the legitimate aims provided for in Article 8(2), and there was accordingly a violation of Article 8.

Protecting physical, psychological and personal integrity through the law

6.482 There are positive obligations on the state under Article 8 to take reasonable and appropriate measures to secure and protect individuals' rights to respect for their private life, including the right to physical and psychological integrity.[1617] Children, people with disabilities and other vulnerable people are, in particular, entitled to effective protection.[1618] These

---

[1610] Former staff members of the human rights organisation, Liberty, who subsequently became MPs and government ministers.

[1611] No. 20317/92, 1.9.93.

[1612] No. 27798/95, 26.2.00.

[1613] No. 15225/89, Series A, No. 305-B, 31.1.95.

[1614] No. 50774/99, 11.1.05. See also *Khuzhin and others v Russia*, No. 13470/02, 23.10.08.

[1615] No. 37048/04, 13.1.09.

[1616] No. 42716/02, 24.2.09.

[1617] See, e.g. *Storck v Germany*, No. 61603/00, 16.6.05, para. 149; *Tysiąc v Poland*, No. 5410/03, 20.3.07, paras. 110–13.

[1618] *C.A.S. and C.S. v Romania*, No. 26692/05, 20.3.12, para. 71; *B v Romania* (No. 2), No. 1285/03, 19.2.13, para. 86.

obligations may be breached if there are inadequacies in the process leading to psychiatric detention.[1619]

Article 8 therefore imposes a broad obligation on states to adopt adequate positive measures by means of criminal law protection to protect individuals against acts of violence by other individuals (and indeed from other threats).[1620] This will include an obligation to carry out an adequate investigation into incidents of alleged racial abuse.[1621] There may be a degree of overlap with the obligations contained in Article 3. For example in *MC* v *Bulgaria*[1622] (discussed above at 6.123) the Court held that states have a positive obligation inherent in Articles 3 and 8 'to enact criminal-law provisions effectively punishing rape and to apply them in practice through effective investigation and prosecution'. The Grand Chamber found a violation of Article 8 in *Söderman* v *Sweden*[1623] in which a 14-year-old girl was covertly filmed by her stepfather while changing in the bathroom. He was acquitted of an offence of sexual molestation on the basis that his conduct was not covered by such an offence. Noting that there were no other criminal or civil law remedies available to the applicant, the Court found that there was an inadequate legal framework to protect her physical integrity. **6.483**

Sandra Janković v *Croatia*[1624] was a case in which the extent of the positive obligations under Article 8 was in issue. The applicant was physically assaulted by three individuals when she attempted to re-enter her flat, in relation to which she had obtained a court order entitling her to do so. The Court emphasised that in order for the state to meet its positive obligations the Convention does not require state-assisted prosecution in all cases—the ability for a victim to act as a private prosecutor or as the injured party in the role of a subsidiary prosecutor, as was possible in the Croatian system, may be sufficient. The applicant lodged a detailed complaint with the State Attorney's Office, describing the acts of violence and providing the names and addresses of the attackers. However, her complaint was ruled inadmissible as being incomplete, but without reasons being given. Accordingly, as the authorities neither prosecuted the alleged perpetrators of the attack, nor allowed the applicant to bring a private prosecution, the criminal law mechanisms were found to be defective, in violation of the positive obligations under Article 8. **6.484**

Cases of domestic violence are increasingly coming before the Strasbourg Court, in many of which the Court has found the national authorities to have taken insufficient steps to protect the victims.[1625] In *A* v *Croatia*[1626] the domestic courts had instigated several sets of proceedings in an attempt to prevent the applicant from being attacked by her husband. However, many of the stipulated measures, such as periods of detention, fines, psycho-social treatment **6.485**

[1619] See, e.g. *B* v *Romania (No. 2)*, No. 1285/03, 19.2.13.
[1620] See, e.g. *Georgel and Georgeta Stoicescu* v *Romania*, No. 9718/03, 26.7.11 (attack by stray dogs—violation of Article 8). By contrast, see *Berü* v *Turkey*, No. 47304/07, 11.1.11.
[1621] *R.B.* v *Hungary*, No. 64602/12, 12.4.16. Article 8 may also be engaged in relation to the adequacy of the state's response to demonstrations. In *Király and Dömötör* v *Hungary*, No. 10851/13, 17.1.17, there was a violation of Article 8 due to the authorities' inadequate response to an anti-Roma demonstration, because of a series of shortcomings in the investigation.
[1622] No. 39272/98, 4.12.03.
[1623] No. 5786/08, 12.11.13.
[1624] No. 38478/05, 5.3.09.
[1625] See also *Kalucza* v *Hungary*, No. 57693/10, 24.4.12 and the domestic violence cases discussed in relation to Article 2 at 6.71–6.72 above, and Article 3 at 6.124 above.
[1626] No. 55164/08, 14.10.10.

and imprisonment, had simply not been enforced, and there were delays in imposing others, such as the provision of psychiatric treatment. As a result of the failure to implement these measures, the Court held that the respondent government had breached its positive obligations under Article 8 to ensure the right to respect for the applicant's private life. The state's positive obligations under Article 8 were also found to have been violated in *Hajduová v Slovakia*,[1627] because of the authorities' failure to protect the applicant from her husband who was found to be suffering from a serious personality disorder. In particular, it was noted that the domestic court had not complied with its statutory obligation to order his detention for psychiatric treatment following his conviction for violent behaviour towards the applicant. In *Bevacqua and S. v Bulgaria*,[1628] the Court was critical in particular of the domestic court's failure to act swiftly to adopt interim custody measures to protect the first applicant's son and that insufficient sanctions were imposed to control the applicant's husband's conduct. In that case the Court held that cases of domestic violence would not necessarily require prosecution by the state in every case, as opposed to proceedings being brought by the victim.[1629] The case of *Eremia v Moldova*[1630] concerned the failure of the authorities to take adequate measures to protect the applicant and her teenage daughters from domestic violence perpetrated by the applicant's husband, a police officer, who frequently beat his wife in the presence of their daughters. Accordingly, the Article 8 rights of the daughters were breached because of the authorities' failure to protect their psychological well-being.[1631]

6.486 The case of *Y. v Slovenia*[1632] concerned criminal proceedings brought against a man accused of sexually assaulting the applicant (when aged 14). There was a violation of Article 8 because of the failure to protect the applicant's personal integrity during the trial, notably because of the manner of her cross-examination, which took place over a period of seven months. Some of the questioning was conducted by the defendant himself, and was found to intend to denigrate the applicant's character. The Court was also critical of the way in which she was questioned by an expert in gynaecology, and the way in which her application to have the defendant's counsel disqualified was dealt with.

Family relations

6.487 The right to respect for family life protects and upholds contact and relations between family members (see above at 6.455 as to the definition of family). This right is essentially concerned with preventing arbitrary interference in people's lives by public authorities, but in certain circumstances includes positive obligations on the state that may require steps to be taken to ensure respect for family life as between individuals and/or private bodies.[1633] For example, the case of *Zorica Jovanović v Serbia*,[1634] concerned a spate of 'missing baby'

[1627] No. 2660/03, 30.11.10. See also *E.S. and others v Slovakia*, No. 8227/04, 15.9.09 (state failed to provide adequate protection for wife and children against violent and abusive husband/father—violations of Articles 3 and 8).

[1628] No. 71127/01, 12.6.08.

[1629] *Bevacqua and S. v Bulgaria*, No. 71127/01, 12.6.08, para. 82.

[1630] No.3564/11, 28.5.13.

[1631] There were also violations of Article 3 and Article 14 taken together with Article 3.

[1632] No. 41107/10, 28.5.15 (see also 6.411 above).

[1633] See, e.g. *Airey v Ireland*, Series A, No. 32, 9.10.79, para. 32; *Glaser v UK*, No. 32346/96, 19.9.00, para. 63.

[1634] No. 21794/08, 26.3.13.

cases, in Serbian hospitals in the 1970s to the 1990s. The applicant had been told that her baby had died, but his body had never been released to her and the cause of death was never determined. The Court held that Article 8 had been violated because of the authorities' failure to comply with their positive obligations to provide credible information about the fate of the applicant's son.

The Court has constantly reiterated[1635] that:

6.488

> where the existence of a family tie with a child has been established, the state must act in a manner calculated to enable that tie to be developed and legal safeguards must be created that render possible, as from the moment of birth, the child's integration into his or her family.

There have been many cases relating to Article 8 concerning contact with children, such as residence and access cases and those relating to the placing of children into care. The Court's role is to review the decisions made by the domestic authorities as against the standards of the Convention, and not to replace those authorities. It has often been emphasised that in domestic judicial decisions where the rights under Article 8 of parents and of a child are at stake, the child's rights must be the paramount consideration. Furthermore, if any balancing of interests is necessary, the interests of the child must prevail.[1636]

The Court has underlined that the taking into care of a child should normally be a temporary measure and that any measures taken should be consistent with the ultimate aim of reuniting the natural parent and child.[1637] The Convention upholds the right of a non-resident parent to have access or contact with the child, subject to the child's best interests. Many cases therefore depend upon the proportionality of the restriction on residence or contact. The automatic denial of parental rights through the application of the law, without judicial review of such a decision, or of the interests of the child, is highly likely to violate Article 8.[1638]

6.489

The Court has stressed that 'it is an interference of a very serious order to split up a family',[1639] Such a measure could very rarely be justified, for example, simply by material difficulties (such as inadequate housing).[1640] In *Johansen v Norway*[1641] the Court emphasised that consideration of what was in the best interests of the child was of 'crucial importance', and that the national authorities have a wide margin of appreciation in assessing the necessity of taking a child into care. However, the Court will exercise a stricter scrutiny in relation to restrictions on parental rights and access on the basis that such restrictions could effectively curtail family relations between parent and child.[1642] The Court found the taking of the child into care to be proportionate in *Johansen*, but the deprivation of the mother's access and parental rights in respect of her daughter was held to be unjustified and beyond the state's margin of appreciation. There was a violation of Article 8 in *Ageyevy v Russia*[1643] as a result of the revocation

6.490

[1635] See, e.g. *Keegan v Ireland*, No. 16969/90, Series A, No. 290, 26.5.94, para. 50; *Kroon v Netherlands*, No. 27.10.94, 27.10.94, Series A, No. 297-C, para. 32; *Yousef v Netherlands*, No. 33711/96, 5.11.02, para. 52.

[1636] See, e.g. *Elsholz v Germany*, No. 25735/94, 31.7.00, para. 52; *TP and KM v UK*, No. 28945/95, 10.5.01, para. 72.

[1637] See, e.g. *Olsson v Sweden (No. 1)*, No. 10465/83, Series A, No. 130, 24.3.88, para. 81.

[1638] See, e.g. *Iordache v Romania*, No. 6817/02, 14.10.08; *M.D. and others v Malta*, No. 64791/10, 17.7.12.

[1639] *Olsson v Sweden (No. 1)*, No. 10465/83, Series A, No. 130, 24.3.88, para. 72.

[1640] *Wallová and Walla v Czech Republic*, No. 23848/04, 26.10.06. See also *Saviny v Ukraine*, No. 39948/06, 18.12.08.

[1641] No. 17383/90, 7.8.96.

[1642] See also, e.g. *Clemeno v Italy*, No. 19537/03, 21.10.08.

[1643] No. 7075/10, 18.4.13.

of the applicant parents' adoption of two children, following an incident at home in which one of the children had been found with burns and other injuries. The court orders in question were irreversible and had the effect of totally depriving the applicants of their family life with the children. The European Court was critical of the domestic courts' superficial examination of the case and found their analysis to be 'seriously deficient' and their conclusions to be 'unconvincing and too far-reaching'. There were separate violations of Article 8 due to: (i) the denial of the applicants' access to the children for more than 14 months; (ii) the conduct of hospital officials (who took and disseminated photographs of the applicant's son and disclosed confidential information to the media—for which there was no basis in domestic law); (iii) the authorities' failure effectively to investigate the applicants' complaint about the unauthorised disclosure of their son's adoption status to the media; and (iv) the domestic courts' failure to protect the mother's reputation in defamation proceedings which she brought in respect of media reports describing the alleged ill-treatment of her son. In *K and T v Finland*,[1644] the applicants' children had been taken into care following the mother's long history of mental illness. Her younger child was taken away directly from the hospital delivery room, without her even being able to feed the child. The Grand Chamber of the Court found that different considerations apply to normal care orders and emergency care orders, as in the latter situation it may not be possible to include all those with an interest in the decision-making process. The Court found that there must be 'extraordinarily compelling reasons' to justify a baby being taken from the mother against her will immediately after the birth, where neither she nor her partner had been involved in the process.[1645] There was a violation of Article 8 in *K and T* because of the failure to take adequate steps to facilitate family reunification.

6.491   There were two distinct violations of Article 8 in *PC and S v UK*:[1646] firstly, due to the removal by the local authority of a baby from her mother at birth, in light of evidence that the mother may have had a propensity to harm her children. It was not the decision to obtain an emergency protection order, but the manner of its implementation which violated Article 8. The Court was critical of the draconian step of removing the child from her mother shortly after birth—this was not shown to have been necessary, as, for example, the baby could have been left in the mother's care in hospital under supervision. The second violation of Article 8 in *P, C and S* resulted from the making of a care order and a freeing for adoption order. Article 8 was found to have been violated because of the lack of legal representation for such proceedings, and the lack of any real lapse of time between the two sets of proceedings, which had the effect of depriving the applicants of being adequately involved in the decision-making process.[1647] In *Scozzari and Giunta v Italy*,[1648] however, there was no violation of Article 8 as a result of the suspension of the mother's parental rights and the temporary removal of her child. There, the mother was found to be suffering from a personality disorder and that she was therefore incapable of managing her family and children. Nevertheless, Article 8 was violated in *Scozzari and Giunta* because of the restrictions on contact and as a result of the placing of the child in *Il Forteto*, a community, two of whose leaders had been convicted of

---

[1644] No. 25702/94, 12.7.01.
[1645] *Ibid.*, para. 168. See also *Haase v Germany*, No. 11057/02, 8.4.04; *Hanzelkovi v Czech Republic*, No. 43643/10, 11.12.14.
[1646] No. 56547/00, 16.7.02.
[1647] This also led to a separate finding of a violation of Article 6.
[1648] Nos. 39221/98 and 41963/98, 13.7.00.

ill-treatment and of abusing handicapped people in the community. The taking of the appli-cant's child into care was found to be justified in *Gnahoré v France*,[1649] after the child had been admitted into hospital with various bodily wounds, bruises, scratches and scars (and despite the fact that proceedings for assault against the applicant had been discharged). An erroneous diagnosis by health professionals, leading to a child being taken into care will not necessarily result in a breach of the Convention:[1650]

> … mistaken judgments or assessments by professionals do not *per se* render child-care meas-ures incompatible with the requirements of Article 8. The authorities, medical and social, have duties to protect children and cannot be held liable every time genuine and reasonably-held concerns about the safety of children *vis-à-vis* members of their families are proved, retrospec-tively, to have been misguided.

In *A.D. and O.D. v UK*[1651] a young child was placed on the 'at risk' register, and an interim **6.492** care order was made, after fractures of the child's ribs were detected. The family were required to relocate to a family resource centre about 150 miles from their home, in order that a risk assessment could be carried out, and the child was then placed with foster par-ents for four months. The care order was later discharged after it was established that the child suffered from brittle bone disease. While the Court found that the initial protective measures had been justified, it found a violation of Article 8 because of subsequent fail-ings by the local authority that were considered to be disproportionate: the wrong type of assessment was carried out; the family were required to relocate for a period of 12 weeks; the child was removed from his parents when the risk assessment was carried out (when less intrusive means may have been available) and in view of the delay in returning the child to his parents' care once the assessment was completed. There was a violation of Article 8 in *B.B. and F.B. v Germany*[1652] because of the withdrawal of parental authority solely on the basis of uncorroborated allegations against a father, of repeated physical abuse, made by two minor children. Both an interim and then a full care order were made and the children were placed in a children's home. There was no parental contact for a year and at the first meeting with the parents, the daughter admitted that she had lied about the abuse. The Court found that the children's immediate removal had been justified, but it was critical of the failure by the domestic courts to investigate the facts, given that there had been no objective evidence of the alleged abuse. In *M.A.K. and R.K. v UK*,[1653] a nine-year-old girl was admitted to hospital with injuries to her legs. The hospital initially suspected that she may have been a victim of sexual abuse, and restrictions were placed on the father's right to see his daughter. She was later diagnosed with a rare skin disease and was discharged from hospital. The Court accepted that there were sufficient reasons to suspect abuse at the time of the girl's admission, but found that the father and daughter's right to respect for their family life had been breached because of a delay of four days before a dermatologist was con-sulted about the girl's condition. There was also a separate finding of a violation of Article 8 because of the hospital's decision to take a blood test and photograph the girl against her parents' express instructions.

[1649] No. 40031/98, 19.9.00. See also *Covezzi and Morselli v Italy*, No. 52763/99, 9.5.03 (care order follow-ing allegations of sexual abuse).
[1650] *R.K. and A.K. v UK*, No. 38000/05, 30.9.08, para. 36.
[1651] No. 28680/06, 16.3.10.
[1652] Nos. 18734/09 and 9424/11, 14.3.13.
[1653] Nos. 45901/05 and 40146/06, 23.3.10.

6.493 Article 8 may also be violated where the authorities fail to take reasonable steps with a view to reuniting a family after children have been taken into care. There was a violation for such reasons in *K.A. v Finland*[1654] because of the absence of a 'serious and sustained effort on the part of the social welfare authority directed towards facilitating a possible family reunification'.

6.494 Article 8 was found to have been violated in *Kutzner v Germany*[1655] as a result of the withdrawal of the parents' responsibility for their two daughters, and their placement with foster parents. This was done primarily because the applicants were not considered to have the requisite intellectual capacity to bring up their children, but was also to a certain extent due to the children's emotional under-development. There were, however, no allegations of neglect or ill-treatment against the applicants and accordingly such reasons were found to be insufficient to justify the severing of the relationships. There were multiple reasons for the finding of several violations of Article 8 in the case of *Soares de Melo v Portugal*[1656] which concerned court orders to the effect that the applicant mother's seven youngest children (of ten) should be taken into care, with a view to adoption, and that she should be deprived of parental responsibility in respect of those children and denied all contact with them. The Court found that although the applicant's situation (as a single mother of ten who was reliant on food banks) was one of 'manifest material deprivation',[1657] the domestic authorities had not made any attempt to compensate for this by providing additional financial support to meet the family's basic needs: as vulnerable individuals, they should have had increased protection. There had been no suggestion of any mistreatment or abuse—the emotional ties between the applicant and her children had been found to be strong. Furthermore, she had been required to undergo sterilisation, which could never be a condition for retaining parental rights. In addition, the applicant's views had not been properly considered in the course of the domestic proceedings, and she had not been legally represented.

6.495 Article 8 has been found implicitly to incorporate certain procedural rights, which were found to have been violated in relation to the placing of the applicants' son into care in the case of *McMichael v UK*[1658] because of the failure to disclose certain documents during the domestic legal proceedings:

> what … has to be determined is whether, having regard to the particular circumstances of the case and notably the serious nature of the decisions to be taken, the parents have been involved in the decision-making process, seen as a whole, to a degree sufficient to provide them with the requisite protection of their interests.

The Court has also stipulated that the decision-making process must ensure that the views of the natural parents are known to, and considered by, the local authority, and that they have access to appropriate remedies. There was accordingly a violation of Article 8 in *A.K. and L. v Croatia*,[1659] because of the failure to provide legal representation to the applicant (who had a mental disability) in proceedings which led to her loss of parental rights. As a result she was considered to have been insufficiently involved in the decision-making process.

[1654] No. 27751/95, 14.1.03.
[1655] No. 46544/99, 26.2.02. See also *S.H. v Italy*, No. 52557/14, 13.10.15.
[1656] No. 72850/14, 16.2.16.
[1657] 'dénuement matériel manifeste' (*Ibid.*, para. 106).
[1658] No. 16424/90, Series A, No. 308, 24.2.95.
[1659] No. 37956/11, 8.1.13. See also *B v Romania (No. 2)*, No. 1285/03, 19.2.13.

The Court further stipulated in *T.P. and K.M.* v *UK*,[1660] that 'it is essential that a parent be **6.496** placed in a position where he or she may obtain access to information which is relied on by the authorities in taking measures of protective care'. A parent may therefore claim an interest in being informed of the nature and extent of the allegations of abuse made by their child. Article 8 was breached in *T.P. and K.M.* v *UK* because of the failure to disclose a video recording of an interview with the child by a medical professional, or to submit the question to the High Court for determination. Disclosure was required even where no request for disclosure had been made. The failure of the domestic courts to inform a parent of additional evidence obtained during appeal proceedings may also violate the obligation to provide for sufficient parental involvement in the decision-making process.[1661] However, the Court has also emphasised that where action has to be taken by the authorities to protect a child in an emergency, it might not always be possible, because of the urgency of the situation, to involve those who have custody of the child in the decision-making process. Indeed, it might not be desirable to do so if those with custody of the child are considered to be the source of an immediate threat to the child.[1662]

In relation to parent–child contact or access rights, the Court has held that what is decisive **6.497** is whether the national authorities have taken all necessary steps to facilitate reunion as can reasonably be demanded in the special circumstances of each case.[1663] If rights of contact are granted, they should be effective in practice.[1664] The authorities may be required to take 'realistic coercive measures' in respect of a parent who is unwilling to permit access, as required by the domestic courts.[1665] The speed of proceedings involving children will also be an important factor in view of the risk that any procedural delay may effectively determine the issue in question.[1666] However, the margin of appreciation permitted to states in respect of parental access is stricter than that in relation to custody.[1667] The Court has stated in relation to questions of access[1668] that:

> Article 8 requires that the domestic authorities should strike a fair balance between the interests of the child and those of the parents and that, in the balancing process, particular importance should be attached to the best interests of the child, which, depending on their nature and seriousness, may override those of the parents.

In *Hokkanen* v *Finland*[1669] the applicant's daughter was cared for by her maternal grandpar- **6.498** ents after the death of the applicant's wife. The grandparents refused to comply with court orders granting the applicant custody and access that were not enforced by the authorities. The Court found a violation of the applicant's right to respect for his family life arising from the denial of access up to the point when the child had become sufficiently mature enough for her opinion, which was to oppose the applicant's access, to be taken into account.

[1660] No. 28945/95, 10.5.01.
[1661] *Buchberger* v *Austria*, No. 32899/96, 20.12.01.
[1662] See, e.g. *Venema* v *Netherlands*, No. 35731/97, 17.12.02. But in contrast see *Covezzi and Morselli* v *Italy*, No. 52763/99, 9.5.03.
[1663] *Olsson* v *Sweden (No. 2)*, No. 13441/87, 27.11.92, para. 90.
[1664] See, e.g. *Gluhaković* v *Croatia*, No. 21188/09, 12.4.11.
[1665] See, e.g. *Hansen* v *Turkey*, No. 36141/97, 23.9.03, para. 105.
[1666] *H* v *UK*, No. 9580/81, 8.7.87, paras. 89–90.
[1667] See, e.g. *Sahin* v *Germany*, No. 30943/96, 8.7.03, para. 65.
[1668] *Ibid.*, para. 66.
[1669] No. 19823/92, Series A, No. 299-A, 23.9.94.

The applicant in *Amanalachioai v Romania*[1670] similarly complained about the refusal of his daughter's maternal grandparents to return his daughter, after the school holidays. In refusing to order the daughter's return to the applicant, the domestic courts had based their decisions on the material conditions provided by the applicant and on his conduct, on the potential difficulty for her to integrate into her new family and on her deep attachment to her grandparents. However, the Court found that the reasons given did not amount to the 'very exceptional' circumstances that might justify the severance of family ties. The Court was also critical of the inactive attitude of the authorities, and the delays, in response to the applicant's attempts to oblige the grandparents through legal proceedings to return the child. This had the effect of favouring her integration into her new environment and had consolidated a de facto situation that contravened the applicant's right under Article 8. In *Glaser v UK*[1671] the applicant complained of both the English and Scottish courts' failure to enforce contact orders with his children, in the face of their mother's refusal to comply. The Court found no violation of Article 8, in part because of the existence of an 'accessible and coherent' system (in England and Scotland) for the enforcement of contact orders. The Court reiterated that such a process would involve a balancing of competing interests, particularly where children were at risk if coercive measures were taken to enforce contact. In reviewing the various stages of the domestic proceedings, the Court found that at no stage could the authorities have taken more coercive steps.[1672] In contrast, Article 8 was violated in *Zawadka v Poland*[1673] as the domestic courts were deemed to have failed to take sufficient steps to enable the applicant father to enforce his rights of contact with his son, when faced with the mother's unwillingness to comply with a settlement that had earlier been agreed by the parents. He had in the end lost permanent contact with the child, even though his parenting skills had never been in question. In *Eberhard and M. v Slovenia*[1674] the failure of the authorities to enforce an access order in favour of the applicant father, and the fact that the resulting court proceedings lasted for more than four and a half years, led to the finding of a violation of Article 8.

6.499   There was no violation of Article 8 in *Sahin v Germany*[1675] arising from the denial of access rights to the applicant father, because of the serious tensions between the parents that would have affected their daughter. Whilst the Chamber in that case had found the decision-making process to be flawed because of the failure of the domestic courts to hear the applicant's five-year-old daughter, the Grand Chamber[1676] found it reasonable for the courts to have relied instead on the findings of an expert psychologist. By contrast in *Sommerfeld v Germany*[1677] the Grand Chamber found it justifiable for the domestic courts not to have obtained an additional psychological report in circumstances where the applicant's 13-year-old daughter had clearly expressed her wish not to see her father. Inadequacies in the decision-making procedure were held to violate Article 8 in *C v Finland*[1678] in which an order granting custody to

---

[1670] No. 4023/04, 26.5.09.

[1671] No. 32343/96, 19.9.00. As to the enforcement of rights of contact in the UK, see, by contrast, *M.A. v UK*, No. 35242/04, dec. 26.4.05.

[1672] *Ibid.*, para. 86.

[1673] No. 48542/99, 23.6.05 (a finding by four votes to three).

[1674] Nos. 8673/05 and 9733/05, 1.12.09.

[1675] No. 30943/96, 8.7.03. There was, however, a violation of Article 14 taken together with Article 8—see 6.741 below.

[1676] Albeit by 12 votes to five.

[1677] No. 31871/96, 8.7.03.

[1678] No. 18249/02, 9.5.06.

the applicant over his two 12-year-old children had been overturned by the Supreme Court (in favour of their mother's partner). That court was found to have placed exclusive weight on the children's views, without considering any other factors, in particular the applicant's rights as a father, thus giving the children 'an unconditional veto', and reversing previous decisions in the applicant's favour. It was also criticised for not holding an oral hearing and for not taking further steps, such as hearing expert evidence, in order to reach a decision. The failure of a court to hear and consider the views of a child at all during custody proceedings is likely to breach Article 8.[1679]

The failure of the authorities to take adequate steps to ensure the enforcement of final return orders in international child abduction cases (notably under the Hague Convention), or delays in doing so, may also violate Article 8.[1680] In *Bajrami v Albania*,[1681] the Court found a violation of Article 8 because of the authorities' failure to implement a court decision awarding the applicant custody of his daughter (whom his wife had taken to Greece). The Court was critical that there was no specific remedy in relation to cases of abduction of children—Albania was not party to the Hague Convention and had not implemented the UN Convention on the Rights of the Child. However, in *Neulinger and Shuruk v Switzerland*[1682] the Grand Chamber found that a Swiss court order requiring the return of the first applicant's child to Israel would violate Article 8 if it were implemented (even though the child's original removal from Israel by his mother was considered to be wrongful). The Court reiterated that a child's return should not be ordered 'automatically or mechanically' when the Hague Convention is applicable, as the child's best interests will depend on a variety of circumstances. It noted that the child had arrived in Switzerland in 2005 at the age of two and had lived there continuously ever since. He had attended nursery and then school, spoke French and had Swiss nationality. Medical reports indicated that, if he were uprooted, it would have serious consequences for him. Therefore, it concluded that it would not be in his best interests to return to Israel.

6.500

Issues relating to adoption may raise questions under Article 8, although there is no right in the Convention to adopt, as such.[1683] In *Keegan v Ireland*[1684] there was a violation of the right

6.501

[1679] See *M. and M. v Croatia*, No. 10161/13, 3.9.15; *N. Ts. and others v Georgia*, No. 71776/12, 2.2.16.

[1680] See: *Ignaccolo-Zenide v Romania*, No. 31679/96, 25.1.00; *Sylvester v Austria*, Nos. 36812/97 and 40104/98, 24.4.03; *Iglesias Gil and AUI v Spain* No. 56673/00, 29.4.03; *Maire v Portugal*, No. 48206/99, 26.6.03; *Karadžić v Croatia*, No. 35030/04, 15.12.05; *Bianchi v Switzerland*, No. 7548/04, 22.6.06; *Carlson v Switzerland*, No. 49492/06, 6.11.08; *Macready v Czech Republic*, Nos. 4824/06 and 15512/08, 22.4.10; *Shaw v Hungary*, No. 6457/09, 26.7.11; *Raw and others v France*, No. 10131/11, 7.3.13; *Hromadka and Hromadkova v Russia*, No. 22909/10, 11.12.14; *M.A. v Austria*, No. 4097/13, 15.1.15. In cases such as *Shaw, Raw and others* and *M.A.* the Court also took account of the strictures contained in the Brussels IIa Regulation (Council Regulation (EC) No. 2201/2003 of 27 November 2003). See, in contrast to these cases, *Maumousseau and Washington v France*, No. 39388/05, 6.12.07 (objection to return of child to father in US under Hague Convention—no violation of Article 8); *Serghides v Poland*, No. 31515/04, 2.11.10 (revocation of order for return of applicant's daughter following her abduction by mother, due to unsatisfactory conduct by both parents—no violation of Article 8).

[1681] No. 35853/04, 12.12.06.

[1682] No. 41615/07, 6.7.10. See also *Šneersone and Kampanella v Italy*, No. 14737/09, 12.7.11; *Karrer v Romania*, No. 16965/10, 21.2.12; *B. v Belgium*, No. 4320/11, 10.7.12; *X v Latvia*, No. 27853/09, 26.11.13 (inadequate decision-making process as regards decision to return a child pursuant to Hague Convention—violation of Article 8 (by nine votes to eight)); *López-Guió v Slovakia*, No. 10280/12, 3.6.14 (lack of participation of parent in proceedings concerning return of child under Hague Convention—violation of Article 8); *R.S. v Poland*, No. 63777/09, 21.7.15 (failure to consider father's parental rights in child abduction case—violation of Article 8 (by four votes to three)).

[1683] *Fretté v France*, No. 36515/97, 26.2.02, para. 32.

[1684] No. 27229/95, 6.9.99.

to family life where the domestic law permitted the mother of a child to place the child for adoption shortly after her birth without the knowledge or consent of the father:[1685]

> such a state of affairs not only jeopardised the proper development of the applicant's ties with the child but also set in motion a process which was likely to prove to be irreversible, thereby putting the applicant at a significant disadvantage in his contest with the prospective adopters for the custody of the child.

6.502 However, in *Söderbäck v Sweden*,[1686] there was no violation of Article 8 following the adoption of the applicant's child, even where its effect was totally to deprive the applicant of a family life with his daughter, because of the infrequency of the contact between him and his daughter and because she had been living with her adoptive father since she was eight months old. The first applicant in *Wagner and J.M.W.L. v Luxembourg*,[1687] complained about the authorities' refusal to declare a Peruvian judgment enforceable according to which the applicant had legally adopted a three-year-old girl in Peru who had been abandoned (the second applicant). This was a result of the absence of a provision in Luxembourg law enabling a single person to be granted full adoption of a child. The Court found that the child's best interests had to take precedence—the domestic courts could not reasonably disregard the legal status which had been created on a valid basis in Peru and which corresponded to family life within the meaning of Article 8. In *Emonet and others v Switzerland*[1688] the applicants complained that the effect of the adoption of an adult (who was seriously disabled) by her mother's partner was, in law, to terminate the mother–daughter relationship. Finding that the blindly automatic application of legal provisions to the applicants' situation failed to take account of the biological and social realities, the Court held there had been a violation of Article 8. Procedural failings led to the finding of a violation of Article 8 in *X v Croatia*.[1689] The applicant suffered from paranoid schizophrenia. As a result of a decision divesting her of the capacity to act, she was completely excluded from the proceedings for the adoption of her daughter (even though her parental rights were still intact). In *I.S. v Germany*[1690] the Court found no violation of Article 8 in a case brought by the biological mother of children who had given them up for adoption, as a result of the authorities' subsequent refusal to allow her to have contact with them or information about them. The Court noted that her decision had been taken in the full knowledge of the legal and factual consequences. The annulment of an adoption order led to a finding of a violation of Article 8 in *Zaieţ v Romania*.[1691] The annulment was made at the request of the applicant's sister, 31 years after the adoption order had been made, and after the death of their mother, and resulted in the applicant's loss of inheritance rights. The Court doubted whether the order was in accordance with the law, or pursued a legitimate aim, but in any event found it not to have been justified.

6.503 In *Marckx v Belgium*[1692] the illegitimacy laws in Belgium, which included restrictions on giving or bequeathing property, were found to violate the right to respect for family life under

---

[1685] *Keegan v Ireland*, No. 16969/90, Series A, No. 290, 26.5.94, para. 55.

[1686] No. 24484/97, 28.10.98.

[1687] No. 76240/01, 28.6.07. See also *Chbihi Loudoudi and others v Belgium*, No. 52265/10, 16.12.14 (refusal to grant adoption of child placed in *kafala* care to applicants by her biological parents—no violation of Article 8).

[1688] No. 39051/03, 13.12.07.

[1689] No. 12233/04, 17.7.08.

[1690] No. 31021/08, 5.6.14.

[1691] No. 44958/05, 24.3.15.

[1692] No. 6833/74, Series A, No. 31, 13.6.79.

Article 8.[1693] In *Kroon v Netherlands*[1694] the applicant father's paternity of his child could not be recognised unless the mother's husband denied paternity. This was found to violate Article 8: 'respect for family life requires that biological and social reality prevail over a legal presumption which, as in the present case, flies in the face of both established fact and the wishes of those concerned without actually benefiting anyone'.[1695] This principle was also applied in *Znamenskaya v Russia*[1696] where the failure of the authorities to recognise the paternity of the biological father of a stillborn child was found to violate Article 8. The name of the applicant's former husband had been entered on the child's birth certificate, because of a legal presumption that the husband was the father of a child born within 300 days of the dissolution of a marriage, and the applicant was unable to have the name changed, even though the issue of paternity was not contested. Article 8 was violated in *Różański v Poland*[1697] because of the lack of any directly accessible procedure by which the applicant could have his paternity established. By contrast, in *Shofman v Russia*[1698] the applicant's complaint was that he had no means of challenging a presumption of paternity (that he was the father of his wife's son), in circumstances where he had only been made aware that he was not the father after the expiry of the relevant limitation period (one year after the child's birth), and even though DNA tests established in court proceedings that he was not the father. This situation was held not to strike a fair balance, and to have breached Article 8. The applicant in *Krušković v Croatia*[1699] had been divested of his legal capacity, and, as a consequence, there was no possibility for him to institute legal proceedings in order to establish his paternity. In circumstances where it was not disputed between the applicant and the mother of the child in question that he was the father, the Court found the state had failed to meet its positive obligations under Article 8.

The right to *become* a parent (or not to do so) was in issue in *Evans v UK*.[1700] The applicant **6.504** complained that, following *in vitro* fertilisation (IVF) treatment, the domestic law permitted her former partner to withdraw his consent to the storage and use by her of embryos created jointly by them (after her ovaries had been removed because of her medical condition). The Grand Chamber found that the issue engaged the applicant's right to respect for her private life,[1701] noting that the case involved a conflict between the rights of two individuals, which were entirely irreconcilable. It examined the positive obligations that arose, in order to decide whether the law was applied in a way that struck a fair balance between the competing

---

[1693] See also *Camp and Bourimi v Netherlands*, No. 28369/95, 3.10.00. But contrast with the decision in *Haas v Netherlands*, No. 36983/97, 13.1.04 (Article 8 inapplicable as the very limited contact between an illegitimate, unrecognised son with his alleged father could not be construed as 'family life').

[1694] No. 18535/91, Series A, No. 297-C, 27.10.94.

[1695] *Ibid.*, para. 40. But contrast this decision with *Yousef v Netherlands*, No. 33711/96, 5.11.02 (no violation of Article 8 where the applicant was found to have the intention of disrupting his daughter's family situation). See also *Nylund v Finland*, No. 27110/95, dec. 29.6.99 (paternity proceedings not arbitrary).

[1696] No. 77785/01, 2.6.05. However, Judges Rozakis, Botoucharova and Hajiyev dissented, disputing that the private life of the *mother* included a right to ask for recognition of the paternity of the stillborn child, as part of the state's positive obligations under Article 8.

[1697] No. 55339/00, 18.5.06. See also *L.D. and P.K. v Bulgaria*, Nos. 7949/11 and 45522/13, 8.12.16.

[1698] No. 74826/01, 24.11.05. See also *Mizzi v Malta*, No. 26111/02, 12.1.06; *Paulík v Slovakia*, No. 10699/05, 10.10.06; *Tavlı v Turkey*, No. 11449/02, 9.11.06; *Phinikaridou v Cyprus*, No. 23890/02, 20.12.07.

[1699] No. 46185/08, 21.6.11.

[1700] No. 6339/05, 10.4.07. See also *Knecht v Romania*, No. 10048/10, 2.10.12 (local authorities' confiscation of embryos from clinic pursuant to investigation, and delay in returning them—no violation of Article 8).

[1701] In *Parrillo v Italy*, No. 46470/11, 27.8.15, the Grand Chamber found that the applicant's 'private life' was engaged as regards the fate of embryos created following IVF treatment, but that Article 8 was not violated by the refusal to allow them to be donated for scientific research.

public and private interests involved. The Court concluded that there was no violation of Article 8 on the basis that there was no European consensus in relation to this aspect of IVF treatment, that the domestic rules were clear and had been brought to the attention of the applicant, and that the rules struck a fair balance. The Grand Chamber also found no violation of Article 8 in *S.H. and others v Austria*[1702] as a result of the domestic law prohibition on the use of ova and sperm from donors for *in vitro* fertilisation. The Court took account of the fact that the case raised sensitive moral and ethical questions, that there was no common ground across Europe on the issue, that the Austrian legislature had adopted a careful and cautious approach 'in seeking to reconcile social realities with its approach of principle in this field', and it allowed the state a wide margin of appreciation. As it was an evolving and dynamic area, however, it was one to be kept under review by Council of Europe states. The applicant couple in *Costa and Pavan v Italy*[1703] were healthy carriers of cystic fibrosis who wanted to have a second child who would not be affected by the disease, but medically-assisted procreation techniques were only available to certain groups in Italy (which did not include them) and embryo screening was banned altogether. The only option for the applicants was therefore to initiate a pregnancy by natural means and to terminate it if prenatal testing showed the foetus to be infected. As a result of the inconsistency in the domestic law, the Court found the interference with the applicants' Article 8 rights to be disproportionate. There was also a violation of Article 8 in *Labassee v France*[1704] and *Mennesson v France*[1705] because of the French authorities' refusal to recognise parent–child relationships born as a result of surrogacy treatment[1706] in the United States. The applicants were denied the right to record entries in the register of births, marriages and deaths as the surrogacy agreement was null and void on public-policy grounds under the French Civil Code. As there was no European consensus on the lawfulness of surrogacy arrangements, the authorities enjoyed a wide margin of appreciation as regards surrogacy-related decisions, although there was a narrow margin of appreciation in respect of matters of parentage. The practical obstacles the applicants faced were not such as to mean there was a breach of the right to respect for their *family life*, but there was a violation of Article 8 because of the impact on the applicant children's right to respect for their *private life*, taking account of their best interests. The children faced uncertainty as to their ability to obtain French nationality and the lack of legal recognition of their situation in France had implications for their inheritance rights. Further, the authorities' decision also had the effect of not recognising the tie between the children and their biological fathers.

6.505 The right to family life has particular importance for prisoners and the Court has stressed that 'even if a detainee by the very nature of his situation must be subjected to various limitations of his rights and freedoms, every such limitation must be nevertheless justifiable as necessary in a democratic society'.[1707] The Court has also affirmed that whilst imprisonment

---

[1702] No. 57813/00, 3.11.11 (the chamber judgment (1.4.10) had found a breach of Article 14 taken together with Article 8).

[1703] No. 54270/10, 28.8.12.

[1704] No. 65941/11, 26.6.14.

[1705] No. 65192/11, 26.6.14.

[1706] On the issue of surrogacy, see also *Paradiso and Campanelli v Italy*, No. 25358/12, 24.1.17 (removal of a child born abroad as a result of illegal surrogacy arrangement—no biological link between applicants and child—no de facto family life—right to respect for private life engaged—fair balance struck by Italian courts—no violation of Article 8).

[1707] *Ploski v Poland*, No. 26761/95, 12.11.02, para. 35.

necessarily entails limitations on private and family life, Article 8 requires prison authorities to assist prisoners in maintaining contact with their close family,[1708] which may require prisoners to be transferred closer to home.[1709] Limitations on family visits will engage Article 8, although there was no violation in *Messina v Italy (No. 2)* where a convicted Mafia member was subject to a special prison regime, with, on average, fewer than two visits per month permitted. However, an absolute ban on visits to the applicant in prison by his wife and young daughter was held to be a disproportionate interference with Article 8 in *Lavents v Latvia*,[1710] as was the very restrictive visiting regime for life sentence prisoners in *Khoroshenko v Russia*.[1711] The refusal to allow a prison inmate to visit a dying relative[1712] or attend a close relative's funeral may violate Article 8.[1713] The separation of a mother and her baby in prison will also engage Article 8 rights.[1714]

In *Dickson v UK*[1715] the Grand Chamber found that a refusal to allow a convicted prisoner **6.506** access to artifical insemination facilities violated Article 8 (by 12 votes to five). The applicants were a married couple who had met while serving prison sentences. The second applicant had served her sentence, but her husband had not. Artificial insemination had remained their only realistic hope of having a child together in view of the second applicant's age and the first applicant's release date. The Court rejected the Government's arguments that losing the opportunity to have children was an inevitable consequence of imprisonment. The Government also argued that public confidence in the prison system would be undermined if artificial insemination were allowed, but the Court reiterated that the automatic forfeiture of rights by prisoners could not be based on what might offend public opinion. Finally, the Government argued that the absence of a parent for a long period would have a negative impact on any child conceived, but the Court found that this could not prevent parents from attempting to conceive a child in the situation of the particular case, noting that the second applicant was at liberty and would have taken care of the child until her husband was released. In practice, rights of artificial insemination were only granted so exceptionally that the Court found that there was not the requisite assessment of proportionality in individual cases.

At issue in the case of *Van der Heijden v Netherlands*[1716] was the refusal to grant a long-term **6.507** cohabitee the right not to testify in criminal proceedings against her partner. The obligation to give evidence amounted to an interference with the right to respect for her private life. However, there was no violation of Article 8 as the requirement was lawful and was held to be proportionate to the legitimate aim of securing evidence for the purpose of detecting and prosecuting crime. The Grand Chamber found (by ten votes to seven) that the legislature

---

[1708] *Messina v Italy (No. 2)*, No. 25498/94, 28.9.00, para. 61.
[1709] *Khodorkovskiy and Lebedev v Russia*, Nos. 11082/06 and 13772/05, 25.7.13; *Vintman v Ukraine*, No. 28403/05, 23.10.14.
[1710] No. 58442/00, 28.11.00. See also *Nowicka v Poland*, No. 30218/96, 3.12.02 (violation of Article 8 where visiting restricted to one visit per month).
[1711] No. 41418/04, 30.6.15.
[1712] *Lind v Russia*, No. 25664/05, 6.12.07.
[1713] *Ploski v Poland*, No. 26761/95, 12.11.02 (in contrast to the earlier decisions in *Marincola and Sestito v Italy*, No. 42662/98, 25.11.99, and *Georgiou v Greece*, No. 45138/98, 13.1.00).
[1714] *Togher v UK*, No. 28555/95, 16.4.98. But see *Kleuver v Norway*, No. 45837/99, dec. 30.4.02.
[1715] No. 44362/04, 4.12.07.
[1716] No. 42857/05, 3.4.12.

was entitled to limit the availability of the privilege not to testify to spouses and those in registered partnerships (rather than other de facto relationships).[1717]

6.508 The case of *Maskhadova and others* v *Russia*[1718] concerned the aftermath of the death of the Chechen separatist leader Aslan Maskhadov whose body was discovered following a security services operation. His family complained under Article 8 about the authorities' refusal to return the body for burial. The Court noted that the authorities' decision had prevented the family from organising and taking part in Maskhadov's burial. They also did not know where he was buried, and therefore could not visit the grave-site. As a result, the Court found that this constituted an interference with their private and family life under Article 8. It was satisfied that the authorities' stance had a sufficient legal basis in the domestic law, and that it pursued a legitimate aim, namely the protection of the rights and freedoms of others (including minimising the informational and psychological impact of terrorist acts on the population and the protection of the feelings of relatives of the victims of terrorist acts). Nevertheless, the refusal to return the body was held to be disproportionate and in violation of Article 8.[1719] Given Maskhadov's role in the insurgency movement, the Court was prepared to accept that measures limiting the family's rights in respect of his funeral arrangements could be justified, and that the authorities were entitled to be concerned to prevent possible disturbances (or unlawful activity) by those who supported or opposed the causes espoused by Maskhadov, during or after any burial ceremonies. However, the total ban on the disclosure to the family of the location of the grave was considered disproportionate as it prevented them from paying their last respects.

Immigration, asylum and travel restrictions

6.509 Article 8 does not provide a right of entry or residence or a right to remain in a Convention state. The Court acknowledges that it is for states to maintain public order, 'in particular by exercising their right, as a matter of well-established international law and subject to their treaty obligations, to control the entry, residence and expulsion of aliens'.[1720] Article 8 may, nevertheless, be engaged, depending upon the extent of the effects upon family life, by a decision to deport, exclude or expel.

6.510 Article 8 protects only established families—it does not guarantee a right of entry to create a new family.[1721] There are a number of factors that the Court will weigh up in deciding whether a family is established in the Convention state. These factors include the length of time members of the family have lived in the country in question and the length of any periods of separation of family members. The Court will consider how easy it would be for the family to settle in the country of origin of the non-national family member, which includes consideration of how 'adaptable' any children would be to living in the other country. The

---

[1717] The dissenting judges pointed, amongst other things, to the fact that the majority of Council of Europe states would have exempted the applicant from testifying.

[1718] No. 18071/05, 6.6.13. See also *Sabanchiyeva and others* v *Russia*, No. 38450/05, 6.6.13.

[1719] Judges Hajiyev and Dedov dissented on the finding of a violation of Article 8, arguing that 'the terrorists waived their social obligation to maintain peace and left their homes to wage war—and not merely war, but a war against civilians—and that terrorists usually sacrifice their own bodies in their attacks …'.

[1720] See, e.g. *Beldjoudi* v *France*, No. 12083/86, Series A, No. 234-A, 26.3.92, para. 74. In cases where an individual may be expelled to a country where they risk ill-treatment in any form, Articles 2 or 3 may be engaged (see above at 6.65 and 6.164).

[1721] *Abdulaziz, Cabales and Balkandali* v *UK*, Nos. 9473/81 and 9474/81, Series A, No. 94, 28.5.85.

Court may also take into account difficulties connected with language, health, employment and other social, cultural and religious issues. If the Court is satisfied that the right to family life is engaged, then it will apply the usual tests to any interference: is it 'in accordance with the law', does it pursue a legitimate aim and does it pass the test of proportionality?

Decisions in the immigration field that are considered to be arbitrary are unlikely to be compatible with Article 8. For example, in *Al-Nashif* v *Bulgaria*,[1722] there was a violation of Article 8 because the order for the deportation on national security grounds of the applicant (who was of Palestinian origin, but stateless) was made pursuant to a legal regime that did not provide the necessary safeguards against arbitrariness. Under Bulgarian domestic law, the Minister of the Interior could issue deportation orders without giving reasons, without the need for any adversarial procedure and without any possibility of appeal. The expulsion of the applicant while his appeal was still pending was found not to be 'in accordance with the law', in violation of Article 8 in *Estrikh* v *Latvia*.[1723] In *Liu and Liu* v *Russia*[1724] the domestic legal provisions themselves failed the 'quality of law' test. There, the decision to deport the first applicant, a Chinese national, was based on both the Foreign Nationals Act (a residence permit could be refused if the foreign national posed a threat to the security of the state or its citizens) and the Entry Procedure Act (a foreign national's presence on Russian territory could be declared undesirable). The decision to reject the applicant's request for a residence permit was made by the local police, who gave no reasons, and it was not in practice susceptible to effective scrutiny by a court as no reasons were provided to the court to explain why the first applicant was considered to pose a risk to national security. His subsequent deportation was ordered by the Federal Migration Service at the instigation of the police, without hearing the applicant (and it was not clear whether there was a right of appeal to a court). The Court concluded that the legal regime failed to provide an adequate degree of protection against arbitrary interference, in violation of Article 8. **6.511**

In *Moustaquim* v *Belgium*,[1725] the applicant's deportation following his conviction for various offences was found to be a disproportionate interference with his right to respect for family life under Article 8.[1726] It was important that the applicant, a Moroccan national, had been only two years old when he arrived in Belgium and he had lived there for about 20 years, and that at the time of the deportation order, all his close relatives had been living in Belgium for a long period. It was also relevant that the applicant had returned just twice to Morocco, for holidays, and that he had received all his schooling in French. Similarly, in *Beldjoudi* v *France*,[1727] the proposed deportation of a convicted criminal, an Algerian citizen, was held to be a disproportionate interference with family life. Mr Beldjoudi was born in France of French parents, but had lost his French nationality because of his parents' failure to make a declaration on his behalf. He had spent his whole life (40 years) in France, had married a French woman, had been educated in French, appeared not to know Arabic and had no links **6.512**

[1722] No. 50963/99, 20.6.02. See also *Musa and others* v *Bulgaria*, No. 61259/00, 11.1.07; *C.G. and others* v *Bulgaria*, No. 1365/07, 24.4.08. By contrast, see *I.R. and G.T.* v *UK*, Nos. 14876/12 and 63339/12, dec. 28.1.14 (exclusion on grounds of national security—Special Immigration Appeals Tribunal offered sufficient procedural safeguards—inadmissible).

[1723] No. 73819/01, 18.1.07.

[1724] No. 42086/05, 6.12.07.

[1725] No. 12313/86, Series A, No. 193, 18.2.91.

[1726] See also *Ezzouhdi* v *France*, No. 41760/99, 13.2.01.

[1727] No. 12083/86, Series A, No. 234-A, 26.3.92.

with Algeria. However, in *Boughanemi v France*[1728] the Court found no violation of Article 8 in similar circumstances. The decisive difference from *Moustaquim* and *Beldjoudi* was the seriousness of the offences of which Mr Boughanemi had been convicted, and, apparently, that he kept his Tunisian nationality and 'never manifested a wish to become French'. The Court's approach to such cases has been rightly criticised as being arbitrary.[1729] However, in 2001 in the case of *Boultif v Switzerland*,[1730] the Court set out guiding principles to assess the proportionality of expulsion where the main obstacle is the difficulty for spouses to stay together and in particular for a spouse and/or the children to live in the other's country of origin.

6.513   The relevant factors are as follows:[1731]

- the nature and seriousness of the offence committed by the applicant;
- the length of the applicant's stay in the country from which they are going to be expelled;
- the time elapsed since the offence was committed and the applicant's conduct in that period;
- the nationalities of the persons concerned;
- the applicant's family situation (such as the length of any marriage);
- other factors revealing whether the couple led a real and genuine family life;
- whether the spouse knew about the offence when they entered into the family relationship;
- whether there are children in the marriage and, if so, their ages;
- the seriousness of the difficulties that the spouse is likely to encounter in the country of origin;
- the best interests and well-being of the children, in particular the seriousness of the difficulties which any children of the applicant are likely to encounter in the country to which the applicant is to be expelled; and
- the solidity of social, cultural and family ties with the host country and with the country of destination.

6.514   Considering the position of the Algerian applicant and his Swiss wife in *Boultif*, the Court found Article 8 to have been violated, because it was practically impossible for him and his family to live outside Switzerland and the applicant had only represented a comparatively limited danger to public order[1732] (albeit a ruthless and brutal robbery). In *Amrollahi v Denmark*[1733] the decision to deport the Iranian applicant (whose wife was Danish), following his conviction for drug trafficking, was found to violate Article 8, as, on the facts, it

---

[1728] No.22070/93, 24.04.96. See also *Benhabba v France*, No. 53441/99, 10.7.03 (no violation of Article 8 arising from 10-year exclusion order, having regard, inter alia, to persistent drug offences).

[1729] See, e.g. the dissenting judgment of Martens J in *Boughanemi v France*, No. 22070/93, 24.4.96.

[1730] No. 54273/00, 2.8.01.

[1731] As set out in *Boultif v Switzerland*, No. 54273/00, 2.8.01 and supplemented by the Grand Chamber in *Üner v Netherlands*, No. 46410/99, 18.10.06. See, also, e.g., *A.A. v UK*, No. 8000/08, 20.9.11; *Kolonja v Greece*, No. 49441/12, 19.5.16. Given the 'economic well-being of the country' factor in Article 8(2), the state authorities may be able to take account of an applicant's indebtedness or their dependency on welfare benefits, but these factors were outweighed by other factors in *Hasanbasic v Switzerland*, No. 52166/09, 11.6.13 (relating to the refusal to renew a residence visa), including the considerable period of time already spent in the country.

[1732] *Ibid.*, para. 55. See also, e.g. *Yildiz v Austria*, No. 37295/97, 31.10.02; *Omojudi v UK*, No. 1820/08, 24.11.09.

[1733] No. 56811/00, 11.7.02. See also, e.g. *Mokrani v France*, No. 52206/99, 15.7.03 (violation of Article 8 arising from deportation order following conviction for heroin trafficking, having regard in particular to the applicant's close personal ties with France).

would have been impossible for them to continue their family life outside Denmark. There was a violation of Article 8 in *Yilmaz v Germany*[1734] in particular because of the indefinite term of the applicant's expulsion from Germany where he lived with his partner, a German national, and young son. In *Maslov v Austria*[1735] the Grand Chamber found a violation of Article 8 as a result of the imposition of a ten-year exclusion order on the Bulgarian applicant when aged 16. This was found to be disproportionate having regard to the primarily non-violent nature of the offences that he had committed as a minor, the ten years he had lived in Austria, the time that had elapsed since the commission of his offences and his family, social and linguistic ties with Austria. *Udeh v Switzerland*[1736] concerned the proposed deportation of the applicant, a Nigerian national, following his convictions for possessing cocaine and drug-trafficking. The Court found that his expulsion would violate Article 8, taking account of the fact that he had two children in Switzerland, with whom there was a genuine family relationship, that he had lived in Switzerland for seven and a half years, that the applicant had committed only one serious offence and that his subsequent conduct has been irreproachable. However, the Grand Chamber found no violation of Article 8 in *Üner v Netherlands*,[1737] in respect of the Turkish applicant's deportation and ten-year exclusion, which followed his conviction for manslaughter and assault. A fair balance was found to have been struck, having regard to the seriousness of the offence, the limited nature of the exclusion, the short time during which he had lived with his partner and older son in the Netherlands, the adaptable age of his young children and the fact that, as Dutch nationals, they would be able to go to Turkey, and then return to the Netherlands.

A deportation of an applicant where there is no criminality will be more difficult to justify **6.515** under Article 8.[1738] The applicant in *Nunez v Norway*[1739] was the subject of a deportation order and two-year expulsion, after committing a series of breaches of immigration laws. The Court found that the public interest weighed heavily in favour of her deportation, for various reasons including her disregard for a re-entry ban and her provision of false information. Nevertheless, the Court still found that Article 8 would be violated if she were deported because of the authorities' failure to consider the best interests of her two young children, who would have been separated from their mother had she been deported.

The Dutch authorities were held to have breached Article 8 by refusing to grant a residence permit to the applicant's daughter in *Sen v Netherlands*.[1740] Whilst the daughter had strong links with the linguistic and cultural environment of Turkey, the major obstacle to the

---

[1734] No. 52853/99, 17.4.03.

[1735] No. 1638/03, 23.6.08. See, by contrast, *Mutlag v Germany*, No. 40601/05, 25.3.10 (no violation of Article 8, having regard in particular to the applicant's serious and repeated violent offences); *Samsonnikov v Estonia*, No. 52178/10, 3.7.12 (no violation of Article 8 re expulsion of long-term resident following series of criminal convictions).

[1736] No. 12020/09, 16.4.13.

[1737] No. 46410/99, 18.10.06.

[1738] See, e.g. *Berrehab v Netherlands*, No. 10730/84, Series A, No. 138, 21.6.88.

[1739] No. 55597/09, 28.6.11. See also *Jeunesse v Netherlands*, No. 12738/10, 3.10.14 (refusal to grant residence permit on ground of family life despite existence of exceptional circumstances—violation of Article 8).

[1740] No. 31465/96, 21.12.01. See also *Rodrigues da Silva and Hoogkamer v Netherlands*, No. 50435/99, 31.1.06 (refusal to allow Brazilian mother to remain in the Netherlands—violation of Article 8); *Osman v Denmark*, No. 38058/09, 14.6.11 (refusal to re-issue residence permit to minor who had been sent abroad by her parents against her will—violation of Article 8).

family returning to Turkey was the length of time they had lived in the Netherlands, and two other children only knew the Netherlands, where they had been born and attended school. The application of a residence prohibition to a 16-year-old Bosnian national in *Jakupovic* v *Austria*[1741] was found to be disproportionate (albeit by four votes to three), the Court emphasising that:

> very weighty reasons have to be put forward to justify the expulsion of a young person ..., alone, to a country which has recently experienced a period of armed conflict with all its adverse effects on living conditions and with no evidence of close relatives living there.

6.516 In *Radovanovic* v *Austria*,[1742] however, the main basis for finding a violation of Article 8 was the imposition of a residence prohibition on the applicant that was unlimited. In *Mubilanzila Mayeka and Kaniki Mitunga* v *Belgium*[1743] the Belgian authorities were found to have failed to facilitate a family's reunification, in violation of Article 8, by holding an unaccompanied five-year-old child (who was an illegal alien) in an adult immigration centre for two months and then deporting her to the Democratic Republic of Congo, even though the authorities were aware that the child's mother was in Canada. Given her young age, the child could not be held responsible for any deception of the authorities by the family. Article 8 was violated in *Cyprus* v *Turkey*[1744] as a consequence of the restrictions imposed by the authorities of the 'Turkish Republic of Northern Cyprus' in refusing permission for Greek Cypriots who had left northern Cyprus to return, which was found to have no legal basis, and which resulted in the enforced separation of families and the denial of the possibility of their leading a normal family life.[1745]

6.517 The Court has also held that, in view of the importance of protecting the best interests of the child, and the principle that minors should only be detained as a last resort, the very fact of detaining a family with children in an administrative detention centre pending their expulsion may violate Article 8.[1746]

6.518 The case of *Slivenko* v *Latvia*[1747] concerned the applicant family's removal from Latvia as a result of a treaty concluded with Russia relating to the withdrawal of Russian troops, and their families, from Latvia. The first applicant's husband had already retired from the army and she and her daughter had lived for many years in Latvia. Whilst not originally from Latvia, they had developed personal, social and economic ties in Latvia. The Court held that although such an agreement by way of a treaty was not in itself in violation of Article 8, the rights of the applicants had been violated because of the authorities' failure to consider their particular circumstances.[1748] The case of *Kurić and others* v *Slovenia*[1749] concerned

---

[1741] No. 36757/97, 6.2.03.
[1742] No. 42703/98, 22.4.04.
[1743] No. 13178/03, 12.10.06 (Article 8 was also violated as a result of both the detention and the deportation).
[1744] No. 25781/94, 10.5.01.
[1745] *Ibid.*, paras. 292–3.
[1746] *Popov* v *France*, Nos. 39472/07 and 39474/07, 19.1.12.
[1747] No. 48321/99, 9.10.03.
[1748] An approach disputed by six dissenters (Judges Wildhaber, Ress, Bratza, Cabral Barreto, Greve and Maruste) in the light of 'the particular context of the withdrawal of the Russian armed forces from the territory of Latvia after almost 50 years of Soviet presence there'. See, in contrast, *Slivenko, Kolosovskiy* v *Latvia*, No. 50183/99, dec. 29.1.04. See further *Petropavlovskis* v *Latvia*, No. 44230/06, 13.1.15 (refusal to grant citizenship to leader of protest movement against Government's language policy—Articles 10 and 11 not applicable).
[1749] No. 26828/06, 26.6.12. See also *Anastasov and others* v *Slovenia*, No. 65020/13, dec. 18.10.16.

the position of the 'erased'—former citizens of Yugoslavia who complained they had been arbitrarily deprived of the possibility of acquiring Slovenian citizenship, and whose names were taken off the register of permanent residents, and who became de facto stateless after Slovenian independence. The Court found there were serious doubts as to the foreseeability that the domestic legal provisions in question would lead to such an extreme measure as their 'erasure', which was also carried out automatically and without prior notification, and the applicants were not given the opportunity to challenge it before the domestic courts. Furthermore, the Constitutional Court had declared the provision of the Aliens Act in question to be unconstitutional, but it had taken more than seven years to comply with that decision and amend the legislation. Therefore, the interference was 'not in accordance with the law'. The Court also found that the authorities should have regularised the residence status of former Yugoslav citizens, and that the prolonged impossibility for the applicants to obtain valid residence permits was disproportionate.[1750]

The case of *Nada v Switzerland*[1751] concerned a travel ban imposed on the applicant — **6.519** resulting from legislation (the Swiss Federal Taliban Ordinance) implementing UN Security Council resolutions—on the basis that he was suspected of being associated with the Taliban and al-Qaeda. The applicant, an Egyptian national, had been living in Campione d'Italia, a tiny Italian enclave surrounded by a Swiss Canton, and the effect of the ban was to prevent him from entering or transiting through Switzerland. The Grand Chamber held the ban to be lawful and to pursue a legitimate aim but it was found to be disproportionate and in violation of Article 8. Contrary to the arguments of the Government, the Court found that the Swiss authorities did have a degree of latitude as to how to implement the UN Security Council resolutions. It was noted that the Swiss and Italian authorities had themselves concluded that the suspicions about the applicant's participation in activities related to international terrorism were clearly unfounded, but there had been a considerable delay before the Swiss authorities informed the UN Sanctions Committee about their conclusions. The Swiss authorities had failed to take sufficient account of the realities of the applicant's situation, confined to Campione d'Italia (and unable to travel to any other part of Italy), or of the considerable duration of the measures imposed or his nationality, age and health. There should therefore have been at least some alleviation of the sanctions regime, in order to avoid interference with his private and family life.

Sexual identity and relations

The Court has acknowledged that sexual relations are 'a most intimate aspect' of a person's **6.520** private life. Where there are restrictions on an intimate aspect of an individual's private life, there must be 'particularly serious reasons' to satisfy Article 8(2). In *Dudgeon v UK*,[1752] the Court found that the criminalisation in Northern Ireland of consensual homosexual activity between men over the age of 21 violated the right to respect for private life under Article 8. Despite the lack of enforcement of the legislation, its very existence was considered to have affected the applicant's private life and there was held to be no pressing social need for

---

[1750] In addition to finding a violation of Article 8, the Grand Chamber also found violations of Article 13 and Article 14 in conjunction with Article 8.
[1751] No. 10593/08, 12.9.12. See also the discussion at 6.320 of *Al-Dulimi and Montana Management Inc. v Switzerland*, No. 5809/08, 21.6.16 (lack of access to court in relation to imposition of sanctions under UN resolution—violation of Article 6(1)).
[1752] No. 7525/76, Series A, No. 45, 23.9.81.

the legislation. There have been equivalent decisions in the case of *Norris* v *Ireland*,[1753] and in *Modinos* v *Cyprus*.[1754]

6.521 *Sutherland* v *UK*[1755] concerned the discrimination in having a homosexual age of consent at 18 rather than 16. By a majority of 14 to four the Commission decided that the law violated the applicant's right to respect for his private life, and that the provision was discriminatory. The Commission rejected the arguments that men between 16 and 20 were in special need of protection against being 'recruited' into homosexuality by predatory older men. The Commission also did not accept that 'society's claimed entitlement to indicate disapproval of homosexual conduct and its preference for a heterosexual lifestyle' could provide an objective or reasonable justification for the inequality of treatment under the criminal law. In overturning the Commission's previous case law on the age of consent issue going back more than 20 years,[1756] the case represents a good example of the Convention being interpreted as a living instrument.

6.522 The applicant members of the armed forces in *Smith and Grady* v *UK* and *Lustig-Prean and Beckett* v *UK*,[1757] complained about investigations into their homosexuality and about their automatic discharge from service solely on the ground of their sexual orientation. Neither was found by the Court to be justified under Article 8(2). The investigation process was found to be exceptionally intrusive and offensive, as it included detailed questions about particular sexual practices and preferences. The effect of discharge had a profound effect on the applicants' careers and prospects. The absolute and general character of the armed forces' policy was also decisive: immediate discharge followed, irrespective of an individual's conduct or service record. The Government was found to have failed to substantiate the allegation that the policy was required in order to maintain operational effectiveness. As to the reported negative attitudes amongst armed forces personnel towards homosexuals, the Court held[1758] that:

> to the extent that they represent a predisposed bias on the part of a heterosexual majority against a homosexual minority, these negative attitudes cannot, of themselves ... amount to sufficient justification for the interferences with the applicants' rights ... any more than similar negative attitudes towards those of a different race, origin or colour.

6.523 Like the issue of the age of consent, the Strasbourg cases concerning transsexual and transgendered people illustrate the notion that the European Convention is a 'living instrument', in other words that the rights contained in the Convention are not static, but can evolve and develop with changes in society. There have been a number of cases aimed at achieving legal recognition of gender reassignment, by challenging the refusal to alter birth registers and arguing that this refusal fails to respect the right to a private life. In 1986 the case of *Rees* v *UK*[1759] was rejected by a 12 to three majority of the Court, although the Court specifically

---

[1753] No. 10581/83, Series A, No. 142, 26.10.88.

[1754] No. 15070/89, 22.4.93.

[1755] No. 25186/94, Comm. Rep. 1.7.97. See also the judgment of 27.3.01 (striking out).

[1756] *X* v *UK*, No. 7215/75, 12.10.78, DR 19 66; *WZ* v *Austria*, No. 17279/90, 13.5.92; *HF* v *Austria*, No. 22646/93, 26.6.95.

[1757] Nos. 33985/96 and 33986/96, 27.9.99 and Nos. 31417/96 and 32377/96, 27.9.99. See also: *Perkins and R* v *UK*, Nos. 43208/98 and 44875/98, 22.10.02; *Beck, Copp and Bazeley* v *UK*, Nos. 48535/99, 48536/99 and 48537/99, 22.10.02.

[1758] *Smith and Grady* v *UK*, Nos. 33985/96 and 33986/96, 27.9.99, para. 97.

[1759] No. 9532/81, 17.10.86.

acknowledged the seriousness of the problems and the distress caused. But by 1990, in the case of *Cossey* v *UK*,[1760] the majority against the applicant was down to ten to eight. Whereas in 1986 the Court found that only five European countries recognised gender reassignment through allowing changes to the birth register, by 1990 that number had risen to 14. In *Sheffield and Horsham* v *UK*,[1761] the Court found against the applicants by an 11 to nine majority on the basis that the UK Government could rely on its margin of appreciation in refusing to recognise in law the sexual identity of a post-operative transsexual. However, in *Goodwin* v *UK*, and *I* v *UK*,[1762] the Grand Chamber of the Court in 2002 re-evaluated the position and finally accepted that the failure to recognise legally the new identity of transsexuals violates Article 8. The applicant in *Goodwin* had been registered at birth as being male and had undergone gender reassignment surgery on the National Health Service (NHS). She therefore lived in society as a female, but remained male for legal purposes. The Court acknowledged that the failure to recognise her personal identity caused her stress and alienation. Although the NHS carried out the surgery, she had been permitted, illogically, no legal recognition of her status. Whilst the state of medical knowledge did not provide determining arguments concerning the legal recognition of transsexuals, the Court took into account the clear international trend in favour of such recognition. A violation of Article 8 arose in *L* v *Lithuania*[1763] because of the absence of law regulating full gender-reassignment surgery. In *Van Kück* v *Germany*,[1764] there was a violation of Article 8 because of the domestic courts' refusal to order an insurance company to reimburse the costs of the applicant transsexual's gender reassignment treatment, having questioned the necessity of such treatment. The Court found that in view of the impact of the decision on the applicant's right to respect for her sexual self-determination, it was disproportionate to require her to prove the necessity of the treatment. However, the Grand Chamber found no violation of Article 8 in *Hämäläinen* v *Finland*[1765] as a result of the refusal to give the applicant a female identity number following her sex change, unless her existing marriage was transformed into a civil partnership. The applicant and her spouse wanted to remain married, but under the domestic law, marriage was only permitted between persons of the opposite sex. The Court noted that Article 8 had not been interpreted to require states to allow same-sex couples to marry, and there was no European consensus on allowing same-sex marriage. Taking account of the various options open to the applicant (remain married, enter into a registered partnership or divorce), the Court held that the Finnish system was not disproportionate.

In the 2015 judgment in *Oliari and others* v *Italy*[1766] the Court held that the failure to give **6.524** legal recognition to same-sex partnerships violated Article 8. The Court found that there were insufficient legal protections for same-sex couples in Italy, as the registration of same-sex unions did not confer any rights as such, and 'cohabitation agreements' had only a limited scope. Furthermore, in its judgments, the Italian Constitutional Court had repeatedly

---

[1760] No. 10843/84, Series A, No. 184, 27.9.90.

[1761] Nos. 22985/93 and 23390/94, 30.7.98.

[1762] No. 28957/95, 11.7.02; No. 25680/94, 11.7.02. See also *Grant* v *UK*, No. 32570/03, 23.5.06.

[1763] No. 27527/03, 11.9.07. See also *Y.Y.* v *Turkey*, No. 14793/08, 10.3.15 (inability to procreate as a prerequisite to having gender reassignment surgery—violation of Article 8).

[1764] No. 35968/97, 12.6.03. See also *Schlumpf* v *Switzerland*, No. 29002/06, 8.1.09 (unnecessarily long proceedings relating to the reimbursement of medical costs for a sex change operation).

[1765] No. 37359/09, 16.7.14.

[1766] Nos. 18766/11 and 36030/11, 21.7.15.

called for the recognition of same-sex unions (which required Parliamentary legislation). The Court also took account of the fact that 24 of the 47 Council of Europe states had legislated in order to provide legal recognition of same-sex couples.

Rights of minorities and housing

6.525 In a series of cases concerning planning and enforcement measures taken against gypsies or travellers living in caravans, the Court has accepted that three separate aspects of Article 8 were in issue: the right to respect for their private life, family life and home. This was because the measures in question affected the positioning of the applicants' caravans, but also affected their ability to maintain their identity as gypsies or travellers, and to lead their private and family life in accordance with their tradition. The Court has accordingly affirmed a positive obligation on states under Article 8 'to facilitate the gypsy way of life',[1767] and it has found that the occupation of a caravan is integral to travellers' identity.[1768] Nevertheless, on the facts of *Chapman v UK*, the Grand Chamber of the Court was split by ten votes to seven in finding no violation of Article 8 (following *Buckley v UK*[1769] in which the Court had found no violation by six votes to three). The Court was not prepared to accept that there was an obligation on the authorities to make available to the gypsy community an adequate number of suitably equipped sites.[1770] However, the Court found Article 8 to have been violated in *Connors v UK*[1771] as a result of the applicant's family's summary eviction, on grounds of causing a nuisance, from a local authority caravan site where he and his family had lived for more than 13 years. There, the serious interference with the applicant's Article 8 rights necessitated 'particularly weighty reasons' and a narrow margin of appreciation and the Court held that summary eviction, in the absence of any form of security of tenure, could not be justified by a 'pressing social need' under Article 8. There was a similar finding in *McCann v UK*,[1772] because of the use of summary proceedings to dispossess the applicant of his home: he and his wife were joint secure tenants and the local authority obtained a signed 'notice to quit' from the applicant's wife, who was unaware of the effects of the notice. The Court held that Article 8 had been violated because of the lack of procedural safeguards, given that there was no means of having the proportionality of the measure assessed by an independent tribunal (which would have been the case had the local authority used the statutory scheme).[1773] In cases concerning the eviction of numbers of people from Roma or traveller communities, the Court has found the measures taken by the authorities to be disproportionate and in breach of Article 8. In *Winterstein and others v France*,[1774] the eviction of traveller families from private land on which they had been living for many years was held to violate Article 8, as the domestic courts had failed to assess the proportionality of such a measure and the authorities failed to take account of the consequences of the removal for the applicants or their position as members of a vulnerable minority.

[1767] *Chapman v UK*, No. 27238/95, 18.1.01, para. 96. See also *Muñoz Díaz v Spain*, No. 49151/07, 8.12.09, paras. 60–1.

[1768] *Winterstein and others v France*, No. 27013/07, 17.10.13, para. 142.

[1769] No. 20348/92, 25.6.96.

[1770] *Ibid.*, para. 98.

[1771] No. 66746/01, 27.5.04.

[1772] No. 19009/04, 13.5.08.

[1773] See also *Ćosić v Croatia*, No. 28261/06, 15.1.09.

[1774] No. 27013/07, 17.10.13. See also *Yordanova v Bulgaria*, No. 2544/06, 24.4.12; *Bagdonavicius and others v Russia*, No. 19841/06, 11.10.16.

The Court has held that people who lack legal capacity are particularly vulnerable and that **6.526** therefore states may have a positive obligation under Article 8 to provide them with specific protection under the law. In *Zehentner* v *Austria*[1775] the Court found a violation of Article 8 because of the sale of the applicant's apartment and her eviction in summary proceedings. The applicant had lacked legal capacity (as she suffered from paranoid psychosis) and had not been able to participate effectively in the proceedings.

Environmental issues

The Court has stated that whilst 'there is no explicit right in the Convention to a clean and **6.527** quiet environment, ... where an individual is directly and seriously affected by noise or other pollution, an issue may arise under Article 8'.[1776] Environmental complaints must establish both that there has been an interference with the applicant's private sphere, and that it was of a sufficient level of severity.[1777] The assessment of the minimum level will depend on all the circumstances of the case, including the intensity and duration of the nuisance and its physical or mental effects.[1778] Accordingly, an individual's well-being and the enjoyment of their home may be affected by severe environmental pollution, such that the right to private and family life may be adversely affected, even without there being any serious danger to health. Where there is no direct evidence of damage to applicants' health, the Court will assess whether the potential risks to the environment establish a close link with the applicants' private life and home sufficient to affect their 'quality of life'.[1779] The state may be held liable under Article 8 not only where a public body causes the pollution, but also where the state's responsibility arises because of the failure to regulate private industry.[1780]

In *Lopez Ostra* v *Spain*,[1781] the Court found a violation of Article 8 arising from the failure of **6.528** the municipal authorities to prevent pollution from a waste treatment plant:[1782] the authorities had failed to strike a fair balance between the interest of the town's economic well-being and the applicant's effective right to respect for her home and her private and family life. The applicant prisoner in *Brânduşe* v *Romania*[1783] invoked Article 8 in complaining about offensive fumes and smells coming from a site formerly used as a refuse tip, situated about 20 metres from the prison, run by the city council. Environmental impact assessments established that although his health had not deteriorated, his quality of life and well-being had been detrimentally affected, thus engaging Article 8. The authorities had failed to follow proper procedures to ensure the tip had the appropriate authorisation for its operation or for its closure, and there was a high level of pollution which exceeded acceptable

---

[1775] No. 20082/02, 16.7.09.

[1776] *Hatton and others* v *UK*, No. 36022/97, 8.7.03, para. 96.

[1777] *Fadeyeva* v *Russia*, No. 55723/00, 9.6.05. See, by contrast, *Furlepa* v *Poland*, No. 62101/00, dec. 18.3.08 and *Greenpeace E. V. and others* v *Germany*, No. 18215/06, dec. 12.5.09.

[1778] See, e.g. *Dzemyuk* v *Ukraine*, No. 42488/02, 4.9.14, para. 78.

[1779] *Dzemyuk* v *Ukraine*, No. 42488/02, 4.9.14, para. 82. See also, e.g. *Hardy and Maile* v *UK*, No. 31965/07, 14.2.12.

[1780] See, e.g. *Hatton and others* v *UK*, No. 36022/97, 8.7.03, para. 98. See also, e.g. *Fadeyeva* v *Russia*, No. 55723/00, dec. 16.10.03; *Tatar* v *Romania*, No. 67021/01, 27.1.09.

[1781] No. 16798/90, Series A, No. 303-C, 9.12.94.

[1782] As regards water pollution, see also *Dubetska and others* v *Ukraine*, No. 30499/03, 10.2.11; *Dzemyuk* v *Ukraine*, No. 42488/02, 4.9.14.

[1783] No. 6586/03, 7.4.09.

standards. There was therefore a violation of Article 8. A similar decision was reached in *Di Sarno and others* v *Italy*[1784] because of a prolonged failure by municipal authorities to ensure the collection, treatment and disposal of rubbish. In *Dzemyuk* v *Ukraine*[1785] the Court held that the placing of a cemetery close to the applicant's home, and the resulting pollution, was illegal under domestic regulations in a number of ways, and accordingly was not 'in accordance with the law', within the meaning of Article 8.

6.529 Where it is not the state that is the polluter, the Court will examine the extent of the positive obligations on the authorities to prevent environmental damage, for example by regulating private industry. In such cases, the interests of the individuals concerned have to be weighed against any wider public interest issues, and considered in the light of the state's margin of appreciation. However, in making such an assessment, the Court has stated that it will not assert any 'special status' for environmental human rights.[1786] The applicant in *Fadeyeva* v *Russia*[1787] complained about pollution emanating from a privately owned steel plant. She argued that the domestic law required her resettlement from within the 'sanitary security zone' around the steel plant, and that a failure to rehouse her accordingly violated the state's positive obligations under Article 8. The available evidence in *Fadeyeva* was such that the Court accepted that the actual detriment to the applicant's health and well-being reached a level sufficient to bring it within the scope of Article 8. The applicant lived in a zone where housing was prohibited by the domestic law, and where the levels of pollution exceeded domestic environmental standards, but the authorities did not provide her with any assistance to move away from the area. Furthermore, the Government failed to establish that adequate measures had been taken to regulate the levels of pollution from the steel plant. As a result, Article 8 was held to have been violated. The applicant in *Giacomelli* v *Italy*[1788] complained of pollution from a privately-owned toxic waste treatment plant 30 metres from her home. Article 8 was violated because the authorities failed for more than 14 years to require that an environmental impact assessment be carried out (in accordance with the domestic law) and did not implement court decisions necessitating the suspension of the plant's operations. Article 8 was found to have been violated in *Tatar* v *Romania*[1789] as a result of the environmental hazards caused by a company mining gold and silver. The authorities were criticised for having failed to carry out adequate prior assessments of the environmental risks, for not making sufficient information publicly available and for not having put a stop to the industrial activity after a serious incident in which rivers were polluted with sodium cyanide and other pollutants. It was also the inadequacy of the availability of essential information which led to a finding of a violation of Article 8 in *Vilnes and others* v *Norway*.[1790] The case concerned the risks to which North Sea divers had been exposed from the 1960s to the 1990s. The Court found the authorities had failed to ensure that the applicant divers had received essential information relating to the impact of decompression, which would have enabled them to assess the risks to their health and safety.

[1784] No. 30765/08, 10.1.12.
[1785] No. 42488/02, 4.9.14.
[1786] *Hatton and others* v *UK*, No. 36022/97, 8.7.03, para. 122. See also: *Ashworth and others* v *UK*, No. 39561/98, dec. 20.1.04 (aircraft noise).
[1787] No. 55723/00, 9.6.05.
[1788] No. 59909/00, 2.11.06.
[1789] No. 67021/01, 27.1.09.
[1790] Nos. 5286/09 and 22703/10, 5.12.13.

The case of *Moreno Gómez* v *Spain*,[1791] concerned noise from night-clubs and bars in the **6.530** centre of Valencia. It had been established that the noise at night had exceeded permitted levels for several years, but the City Council had failed to enforce effectively relevant bye-laws dealing with noise and vibration. As a result there was a serious infringement of the applicant's right to respect for her home, in violation of Article 8. In *Deés* v *Hungary*,[1792] it was traffic noise that led to a finding of a violation of Article 8.[1793]

In the Chamber judgment in *Hatton* v *UK*, concerning the effect on local residents of night- **6.531** time aircraft noise at Heathrow Airport, the Court stated[1794] that:

> in the particularly sensitive field of environmental protection, mere reference to the economic well-being of the country was not sufficient to outweigh the rights of others … States are required to minimise, as far as possible, the interference with Article 8 rights, by trying to find alternative solutions and by generally seeking to achieve their aims in the least onerous way as regards human rights. In order to do that, a proper and complete investigation and study, with the aim of finding the best possible solution which would, in reality, strike the right balance, should precede the relevant project.

Applying this test, the Chamber in *Hatton* held (by five votes to two) that there had been a violation of Article 8.[1795] However, the 'minimal interference' test was challenged by the Government before the Grand Chamber which found no violation of Article 8 (by 12 votes to five). Rather than relying on a 'minimal interference' test, on the basis that the Court's supervisory function is of a 'subsidiary nature' the Grand Chamber stated that it was limited to assessing whether or not the measure in question had struck a 'fair balance'. An important factor was that unlike both *Lopez Ostra* and *Guerra* (see below at 6.536) there had been no failure to comply with domestic regulations in *Hatton*. In finding that a fair balance had been struck, the Court noted the following: that there was a scheme in place restricting night flights, in order to keep noise disturbance to an acceptable level, which was kept under review; that it was reasonable to assume that night flights contributed to a certain extent to the general economy; that a series of noise mitigation or abatement measures had been put in place at Heathrow; that house prices in the area had not been adversely affected by night noise; and that the applicants could leave the area without financial loss.[1796]

Where there is a challenge to a state decision affecting environmental issues, the Court has **6.532** said that in addition to assessing the substantive merits of the Government's decision, to ensure its compatibility with Article 8, it may also scrutinise the decision-making process to ensure that due weight has been accorded to the interests of the individual. This may

---

[1791] No. 4143/02, 16.11.04.

[1792] No. 2345/06, 9.11.10.

[1793] See also *Mileva and others* v *Hungary*, Nos. 43449/02 and 21475/04, 25.11.10 (noise from computer club open 24 hours a day—violation of Article 8). See, by contrast, *Ruano Morcuende* v *Spain*, No. 75287/01, dec. 6.9.05 (noise from an electric transformer); *Fägerskiöld* v *Sweden*, No. 37664/04, dec. 26.2.08 (noise from a wind turbine); *Borysiewicz* v *Poland*, No. 71146/01, 1.7.08 (lack of evidence to establish level of noise from tailoring shop); *Leon and Agnieszka Kania* v *Poland*, No. 12605/03, 21.7.09 (noise from lorry maintenance and metal cutting and grinding workshop); *Galev and others* v *Bulgaria*, No. 18324/04, dec. 29.9.09 (opening of dental surgery in residential block).

[1794] *Hatton and others* v *UK*, No. 36022/97, 8.7.03, (para. 86 of Grand Chamber judgment, referring to para. 97 of the chamber judgment of 2.10.01).

[1795] No. 36022/97, 2.10.01.

[1796] The dissenting judges (Judges Costa, Ress, Türmen, Zupančič and Steiner) argued that the majority's decision represented a 'step backwards' in terms of environmental human rights protection and that it gave 'precedence to economic considerations over basic health conditions in qualifying the applicants' "sensitivity to noise" as that of a small minority of people'.

include an inquiry into the type of policy or decision involved, the extent to which the views of individuals (including the applicants) were taken into account throughout the procedure, and the procedural safeguards available.[1797] The Court has stated[1798] that:

> a governmental decision-making process concerning complex issues of environmental and economic policy … must necessarily involve appropriate investigations and studies in order to allow them to strike a fair balance between the various conflicting interests at stake,

but this will not necessarily require 'comprehensive and measurable data' to be available in relation to 'each and every aspect of the matter to be decided'. In *Taşkın and others* v *Turkey*,[1799] the applicants complained about the grant of operating permits issued to a gold mine near to where they lived. Article 8 was found to have been violated because the mine was not ordered to be closed until ten months after a judgment of the administrative court had been issued annulling the decision by the Ministry of the Environment to grant the permit (on environmental grounds). Furthermore, the Council of Ministers had subsequently authorised the continuation of the mine (in an unpublished decision). Thus, the applicants were found to have been deprived of their procedural guarantees. In *Hatton* v *UK*, the decision-making process did not conflict with Article 8 because there had been sufficient investigations and studies into the problem of sleep disturbance, and there had been constant monitoring of night-time noise. Furthermore, the Government had publicised its consultation paper on the question, in respect of which the applicants could have made representations.

6.533 The case law of the Court records various types of effective measures that have been taken in order to prevent or minimise environmental pollution, such as:

(1) imposing operating conditions—as was the case with the steel plant in *Asselbourg and others* v *Luxembourg*;[1800]

(2) carrying out inspections and studies into levels of pollution—as in *Gronus* v *Poland*;[1801]

(3) the provision of public access to information—highlighted in *Guerra* v *Italy*,[1802] in which there was a violation of Article 8 because the applicants were not given essential information that would have enabled them to assess the risks they and their families might run if they continued to live near a chemical factory;

(4) an obligation to consult local people—as in *Ashworth* v *UK*;[1803]

(5) applying sanctions—part of the operation of a waste treatment plant was ordered to be stopped in *Lopez Ostra* v *Spain*[1804] and residents were rehoused for a period of months; and

(6) providing effective civil or criminal remedies—there were such effective remedies available to the applicants in *Asselbourg* and in *Astrid Moe* v *Norway*.[1805]

6.534 In the context of planning decisions, the Court has acknowledged that where a house is erected without the requisite permission, there is a conflict between the owner's Article 8

[1797] See, e.g. *Hatton and others* v *UK*, No. 36022/97, 8.7.03, paras. 99 and 104. See also, e.g. *Hardy and Maile* v *UK*, No. 31965/07, 14.2.12.

[1798] *Hatton and others* v *UK*, No. 36022/97, 8.7.03, para. 128.

[1799] No. 46117/99, 10.11.04. See also *Lemke* v *Turkey*, No. 17381/02, 5.6.07.

[1800] No. 29121/95, dec. 29.6.99.

[1801] No. 39695/96, dec. 2.12.99.

[1802] No. 14967/89, 19.2.98.

[1803] No. 39561/98, dec. 20.1.04.

[1804] No. 16798/90, Series A, No. 303-C, 9.12.94.

[1805] No. 30966/96, dec. 14.12.99.

rights and the community's right to environmental protection. Whether or not the home was established lawfully will be an important factor in deciding whether it would be legitimate to require that person to move. The availability of alternative suitable accommodation will also be important.[1806]

See also the commentary on access to personal records at 6.535 below.

Access to personal records

The question of access to personal records will engage Article 8. The applicant in *Gaskin* v **6.535** *UK*[1807] sought documents from his local authority relating to the period of time when he was in care. Whilst acknowledging the applicant's interest in obtaining information about his childhood and early development, the Court also emphasised that the confidentiality of public records is of importance for receiving objective and reliable information, and that such confidentiality can also be necessary for the protection of third persons.[1808] In such circumstances, in order to comply with the principle of proportionality, it should have been an independent authority that decided whether access should be granted. In similar circumstances in *MG* v *UK*,[1809] the Court noted that the Government's disclosure of copy records during the European Convention proceedings demonstrated the need for an independent appraisal, as significant portions of the records were blanked out and various documents were retained in order to protect the confidentiality of third parties. The Court reiterated in *K.H. and others* v *Slovakia*[1810] that the positive obligations established by Article 8 may require that the authorities make available to data subjects copies of their data files. Article 8 was violated in that case because the applicants (Roma women who believed they may have been sterilised without their knowledge or consent)[1811] were prevented from obtaining copies of their medical records. The denial of access to personal records may also violate the right of access to court under Article 6, as was the case in *K.H. and others*.

The failure to provide environmental information may also violate Article 8. The 40 appli- **6.536** cants in *Guerra and others* v *Italy*[1812] lived within one kilometre of a chemical factory, which had been classified as high risk. Article 8 was engaged by the direct effect of the factory's toxic emissions on the applicants' rights to respect for their private and family life, and the failure to provide them with information that would have enabled them to assess the risks that they faced from the factory was found to violate Article 8.[1813] The applicants in *McGinley and Egan* v *UK*[1814] had taken part, as servicemen, in the UK's nuclear testing programme in the 1950s and 1960s. The Court stated that:

> where a government engages in hazardous activities … which might have hidden adverse consequences on the health of those involved in such activities, respect for private and family life

---

[1806] See *Chapman* v *UK*, No. 27238/95, 18.1.01, paras. 102–4.

[1807] No. 10454/83, Series A, No. 160, 7.7.89. But contrast with *Martin* v *UK*, No. 27533/95, dec. 28.2.96.

[1808] *Ibid.*, para. 49.

[1809] No. 39393/98, 24.9.02.

[1810] No. 32881/04, 28.4.09.

[1811] See also *V.C.* v *Slovakia*, No. 18968/07, dec. 16.6.09.

[1812] No. 14967/89, 19.2.98.

[1813] Re applicability to Article 2, see *Öneryildiz* v *Turkey*, No. 48939/99, 18.6.02, para. 84 (Chamber) and 30.11.04, para. 90 (Grand Chamber).

[1814] Nos. 21825/93 and 23414/94, 9.6.98. In addition to Article 8, Article 6 was also in issue as a result of the effect of the non-disclosure of documents on the applicants' right of access to the Pensions Appeal Tribunal. See also *Roche* v *UK*, No. 32555/96, 19.10.05. As to Article 6(1), see also *Okyay* v *Turkey*, No. 36220/97, 12.7.05 (complaint concerning the emission of toxic fumes by three coal-power stations).

under Article 8 requires that an effective and accessible procedure be established which enables persons to seek all relevant and appropriate information.

The Grand Chamber drew a similar conclusion in *Roche v UK*,[1815] which concerned records relating to chemical tests carried out on armed forces personnel in the 1960s. Unlike *McGinley and Egan*,[1816] Article 8 was violated in *Roche* because of the failure to provide an effective and accessible procedure enabling the applicant to have access to all the information that would enable him to assess any risk to which he had been exposed during his participation in the tests.

6.537 The right to respect for private life is also engaged where a child born outside marriage brings proceedings to establish the identity of a natural parent. In *Mikulic v Croatia*[1817] this was found to be the only means for the child to establish the identity of her biological father, as there was no provision under domestic law to compel a person to undergo DNA testing and there was no alternative means of establishing paternity (although the Court also acknowledged the need to protect third parties from compulsion to medical testing, including DNA). The applicant in *Odièvre v France*[1818] was an adopted child who sought to trace her natural mother, who had abandoned her at birth and who had requested that information about the birth should remain confidential. The Grand Chamber in *Odièvre* acknowledged the difficulty in reconciling the competing interests of two adult parties. There were also third party interests to consider, and the 'general interest' in that the relevant French legislation sought to protect a mother's and child's health during pregnancy, and to avoid abortions. The Grand Chamber was split by ten votes to seven, in finding no violation of Article 8, taking into account the state's 'margin of appreciation', that changes in the domestic legislation had improved the prospects of a mother in a similar situation waiving confidentiality, and the fact that the applicant had been given access to certain 'non-identifying' information about her natural mother. The seven dissenting judges[1819] argued that the domestic law failed to allow a balancing of the respective rights of mother and child, as the mother effectively had a veto over the child's right to information: 'the mother thus has a discretionary right to bring a suffering child into the world and to condemn it to lifelong ignorance'.

6.538 In *Smirnova v Russia*,[1820] the applicant complained about the domestic court's withholding of her identity papers (or 'internal passport') following her release from custody on remand. This was found to amount to an interference with the applicant's right to respect for her private life under Article 8 because 'in their everyday life Russian citizens have to

---

[1815] No. 32555/96, 19.10.05.

[1816] There, the proceedings before the Pensions Appeal Tribunal were considered to have met the Article 8 obligation.

[1817] No. 53176/99, 7.2.02, para. 55. See also *Jäggi v Switzerland*, No. 58757/00, 13.7.06 (refusal to permit DNA test on deceased person); *A.M.M. v Romania*, No. 2151/10, 14.2.12 (inadequate procedure to establish paternity of minor with disabilities—violation of Article 8); *Menéndez García v Spain*, No. 21046/07, dec. 5.5.09 (insufficient locus standi to establish applicant's father's paternity—inadmissible); *Canonne v France*, No. 22037/13, dec. 2.6.15 (finding of paternity based on alleged father's refusal to submit to DNA tests—inadmissible).

[1818] No. 42326/98, 13.2.03. See, by contrast, *Godelli v Italy*, No. 33783/09, 25.9.12, in which the Court found a violation of Article 8, because of the failure of the domestic law in Italy to reflect a balance of the competing rights as between a child and her birth mother.

[1819] Judges Wildhaber, Bratza, Bonello, Loucaides, Cabral Barreto, Tulkens and Pellonpää.

[1820] Nos. 46138/99 and 48183/99, 24.7.03.

prove their identity unusually often', including in order to obtain employment, receive medical care, exchange currency and buy train tickets. There was a violation of Article 8 because the Government failed to show that the measure taken had had any basis in domestic law. In *İletmiş* v *Turkey*,[1821] the confiscation of the applicant's passport for a period of 15 years, while he lived in Germany, was found to be a disproportionate interference with his Article 8 rights.

The applicant in *Brinks* v *Netherlands*[1822] sought information held on him by the **6.539** Netherlands National Security Service, in relation to his time working in the GDR in the 1980s as an academic and journalist. The Security Service's decision to limit his access to information that it held on him to outdated information that did not contain any personal data relating to third parties, and did not give any insight into its sources, working methods and current level of knowledge, was found to be adequately subject to the law and was not disproportionate. In *Haralambie* v *Romania*[1823] the procedure established to enable individuals to obtain access to personal files held by the security forces within a reasonable time was found to be ineffective in practice (given a six-year delay), in violation of Article 8.

Confidentiality of personal data

The Court has not to date found that Article 8 creates a general right of access to personal **6.540** data, but it has acknowledged the fundamental importance of the protection of personal data under Article 8.

In *Peck* v *UK*,[1824] the Court found a violation of Article 8 where local authority CCTV foot- **6.541** age of the applicant was disclosed to the media, which subsequently broadcast identifiable images of him. The CCTV film had been taken of the applicant in a public street in the immediate aftermath of his suicide attempt. This was found to be disproportionate because of the failure of the local authority to maintain adequate safeguards to prevent the disclosure of his identity. It could either have obtained his consent or masked the images in question (or ensured that the media did so) (see also the discussion of this case at 6.454, above). Article 8 was found to have been violated in *Reklos and Davourlis* v *Greece*,[1825] where a medical clinic permitted a photographer to take photographs of a new-born baby, without the consent of the parents. In *Craxi* (*No. 2*) v *Italy*,[1826] confidential telephone conversations made by the former Italian Prime Minister, Benedetto Craxi, were published by the press. The recordings had been made in the course of criminal proceedings and transcripts had been deposited by the Public Prosecutor in its registry. As the published conversations had no little or relevance to the criminal proceedings, there was a violation of Article 8, which was found to be imputable to the state because of the failure to ensure that they did not pass into the public domain. In *Sõro* v *Estonia*[1827] the authorities' publication of information (under the Disclosure Act)

[1821] No. 29871/96, 6.12.05. See also *Kotiy* v *Ukraine*, No. 28718/09, 5.3.15. By contrast, see *M* v *Switzerland*, No. 41199/06, 26.4.11.
[1822] No. 9940/04, dec. 5.4.05.
[1823] No. 21737/03, 27.10.09.
[1824] No. 44647/98, 28.1.03.
[1825] No. 1234/05, 15.1.09.
[1826] No. 25337/94, 17.7.03. See also *Apostu* v *Romania*, No. 22765/12, 3.2.15.
[1827] No. 22588/08, 3.9.15. See also *Ivanovski* v *former Yugoslav Republic of Macedonia*, No. 29908/11, 21.1.16.

about the applicant's former employment as a driver for the KGB was held to breach Article 8 (by four votes to three). The majority of the Court found the effect of the relevant legislation to be disproportionate because there was no assessment of the specific tasks carried out by former employees of the security services, so as to be able to differentiate the danger they might pose several years after their security service careers had ended.

6.542 The Court has also recognised the particular importance of health records:[1828]

> Respecting the confidentiality of health data is a vital principle in the legal systems of all the Contracting Parties to the Convention. It is crucial not only to respect the sense of privacy of a patient but also to preserve his or her confidence in the medical profession and in the health services in general.

> Without such protection, those in need of medical assistance may be deterred from revealing such information of a personal and intimate nature as may be necessary in order to receive appropriate treatment and, even, from seeking such assistance, thereby endangering their own health and, in the case of transmissible diseases, that of the community.

6.543 There must therefore be adequate safeguards in domestic law to prevent the communication or disclosure of personal health data in contravention of Article 8.[1829] Disclosure may be particularly damaging in certain circumstances, such as where it relates to HIV infection.[1830] In *I v Finland*,[1831] the Court found that the state had failed in its positive obligation to ensure respect for the applicant's private life as a result of the lack of confidentiality of medical records. The applicant was a nurse who was HIV-positive. She was being treated at the same hospital where she worked and began to suspect that her colleagues were aware of her illness. Article 8 was found to be violated because hospital staff had had free access to patient registers (the system was amended so that only a treating clinic's personnel had access to patient information). The case of *Biriuk v Lithuania*[1832] related to what the Court described as an 'outrageous abuse of press freedom'. The country's most popular national newspaper published a front page article in which it disclosed the applicant's HIV-positive status. The applicant complained that although her privacy case in the domestic courts had been successful, she had only been awarded derisory damages (equivalent to about €2,900). The Court found a violation of Article 8 on the basis that the state had failed to secure the applicant's right to respect for her private life, because the domestic law placed severe limitations on judicial discretion in awarding damages in such circumstances. In *Panteleyenko v Ukraine*,[1833] in the course of defamation proceedings, a domestic court obtained from a psychiatric hospital confidential information concerning the applicant's mental state and medical treatment. This information was then disclosed by the judge to the parties and others present in the courtroom at a public hearing. This was found to breach the domestic law, and hence the interference was not 'in accordance with the law' in violation of Article 8. In

---

[1828] *Z v Finland*, No. 22009/93, 25.2.97, para. 95. See also *Avilkina and others v Russia*, No. 1585/09, 6.6.13 (disclosure of confidential medical information relating to refusal by Jehovah's Witnesses to undergo blood transfusion—violation of Article 8).

[1829] See also *L.L. v France*, No. 7508/02, 10.10.06; *L.H. v Latvia*, No. 52019/07, 29.4.14.

[1830] See, e.g. *Biriuk v Lithuania*, No. 23373/03, 25.11.08; *C.C. v Spain*, No. 1425/06, 6.10.09 (disclosure of applicant's HIV status in court judgment).

[1831] No. 20511/03, 17.7.08. See, by contrast, *Y v Turkey*, No. 648/10, dec. 17.2.15.

[1832] No. 23373/03, 25.11.08. See also *Armonienė v Lithuania*, No. 36919/02, 25.11.08, and *A v Norway*, No. 28070/06, 9.4.09 (publication in newspaper articles of information in which applicant could be perceived as prime suspect in murder case—violation of Article 8).

[1833] No. 11901/02, 29.6.06.

P. and S. v Poland[1834] the disclosure of information by a hospital about a case of a pregnant girl who was seeking an abortion after being raped was found neither to have a legitimate aim, nor to be lawful, in violation of Article 8.

In relation to police information, see above at 6.478.

Employment

Dismissal from employment may raise issues under Article 8. For example, in *Oleksandr*   **6.544**
Volkov v *Ukraine*,[1835] which concerned the applicant's dismissal as a supreme court judge, the Court held that his dismissal

> … affected a wide range of his relationships with other persons, including relationships of a professional nature. Likewise, it had an impact on his 'inner circle' as the loss of his job must have had tangible consequences for the material well-being of the applicant and his family. Moreover, the reason for the applicant's dismissal, namely breach of the judicial oath, suggests that his professional reputation was affected.[1836]

Article 8 was violated because the domestic law relating to proceedings against judges for breach of oath was not sufficiently foreseeable, as there were no guidelines or practice establishing a consistent interpretation of the offence of breach of oath and there was also a lack of appropriate legal safeguards.

In *Fernández Martínez* v *Spain*[1837] a nine–eight majority of the Grand Chamber found no   **6.545**
violation of Article 8 because of the refusal to renew a Catholic teacher's contract after he publicly revealed his position as a married priest. The majority found no disproportionality taking into account a range of factors, including the state's duty to protect the autonomy of the Church, the duty of those working for religious organisations to show loyalty to their employers and the extent to which the applicant's dismissal was reviewed by the domestic courts. The Court found that by entering into successive employment contracts, the applicant knowingly and voluntarily accepted a heightened duty of loyalty towards the Catholic Church.

Medical treatment

The Court has reiterated that 'a person's body concerns the most intimate aspect of one's pri-   **6.546**
vate life'.[1838] Accordingly, any form of compulsory medical intervention, however minor, will amount to an *interference* with this right.[1839] There was a violation of Article 8 in *YF* v *Turkey*,[1840] where the applicant's wife, whilst in police custody, was forced by the police to

---

[1834] No. 57375/08, 30.10.12. See also 6.189 (re Article 3).

[1835] No. 21722/11, 9.1.13.

[1836] *Ibid.*, para. 166. There were also several violations of Article 6(1) (see 6.371 above).

[1837] No. 56030/07, 12.6.14. The eight dissenting judges (Judges Spielmann, Sajó, Karakaş, Lemmens, Jäderblom, Vehabović, Dedov and Saiz Arnaiz) had 'points of disagreement on almost every aspect of the case: the establishment of the facts; the characterisation of the facts in the light of Article 8; and the application of Article 8 to the facts of the case'.

[1838] *YF* v *Turkey*, No. 24209/94, 22.7.03, para. 33.

[1839] *X* v *Austria*, no. 8278/78, dec. 13.12.79; DR 18, p. 155; *Acmanne and others* v *Belgium*, No. 10435/83, dec. 10.12.84; DR 40, p. 254; *YF* v *Turkey*, No. 24209/94, 22.7.03, para. 33; *Glass* v *UK*, No. 61827/00, 9.3.04, para. 70.

[1840] No. 24209/94, 22.7.03. See also *Juhnke* v *Turkey*, No. 52515/99, 13.5.08; *Yazgül Yılmaz* v *Turkey*, No. 36369/06, 1.2.11 (gynaecological examination of a 16-year-old girl detained by the police).

~~undergo a gynaecological examination.~~ The Court rejected the Government's arguments that she had consented, finding that she had been in no position to resist submitting to an examination, which had not been justified by a medical necessity, nor was it otherwise prescribed by the domestic law. In *Glass v UK*,[1841] the first applicant was a severely mentally and physically disabled child. Against the clearly expressed instructions of his mother, the second applicant, diamorphine was administered to him in hospital to relieve his distress during respiratory failure. The Government argued that this had been carried out as a matter of urgency in order to relieve his distress and that it would not have been practicable to seek the approval of the courts. However, this practice was found to violate Article 8 as the Court remained unpersuaded that an emergency High Court application could not have been made at an earlier stage. The Court declined to deal with a complaint that a 'do not resuscitate' notice had been included in the child's notes without the knowledge or consent of his mother. In *X v Finland*[1842] the Court underlined that the forced administration of medication amounts to a serious interference with a person's physical integrity, and must therefore be based on a law that guarantees proper safeguards against arbitrariness. There was a violation of Article 8 in that case because under Finnish law, the decision to detain the applicant for involuntary treatment in a mental hospital included an automatic authorisation for the forcible administration of medication if the applicant refused the treatment. Furthermore, there was no remedy available by which the applicant could require a court to rule on the lawfulness or proportionality of the administration of medication, or to have it discontinued.

6.547   It was the lack of precision of the domestic law relating to the removal of organs for transplantation which led to the finding of a violation of Article 8 in *Petrova v Latvia*.[1843] There, the applicant's son died in hospital in Riga as a result of serious injuries sustained in a car accident. She found out later that her son's kidneys and spleen had been removed immediately after his death without her knowledge or consent. Although the domestic law allowed the closest relatives to express their wishes as to organ transplantation, she had not in practice been able to do so, as she had not been consulted, and the domestic law was unclear about the extent of the duty on the authorities to inform the nearest relatives or obtain their consent.

6.548   There was a violation of Article 8 in *Shtukaturov v Russia*,[1844] as a result of proceedings that led to an order depriving the applicant, a patient suffering from mental illness, of his legal capacity. As a consequence he became dependent upon his guardian in most areas of his life. The legal proceedings themselves were flawed as the applicant did not take part in them and he was not called to appear before the judge. The Court emphasised that in order to justify full incapacitation the mental disorder must be 'of a kind or degree' that warranted such a measure, and the applicant's incapacity had not been analysed in sufficient detail.

6.549   The positive obligations imposed on the state by Article 8 will require, for example, the existence of an effective judicial mechanism sufficient to enable investigations to be carried

---

[1841]   No. 61827/00, 9.3.04.
[1842]   No. 34806/04, 3.7.12.
[1843]   No. 4605/05, 24.6.14. See also *Elberte v Latvia*, No. 61243/08, 13.1.15.
[1844]   No. 44009/05, 27.3.08. See also *X and Y v Croatia*, No. 5193/09, 3.11.11; *R.P. and others v UK*, No. 38245/08, 9.10.12 (appointment of Official Solicitor to represent mother with learning disabilities in child care proceedings—no violation of Article 6(1)).

out in cases of alleged medical negligence that may have violated a person's physical integrity pursuant to Article 8.[1845]

The Court grants states a wide margin of appreciation as regards healthcare policy, and in **6.550** respect of the availability of particular treatment. For example in *Hristozov and others* v *Bulgaria*[1846] the Court found no violation of Article 8 (albeit by four votes to three) arising from the denial of an unauthorised experimental drug to patients suffering from cancer: a fair balance was found to have been struck between the competing interests of the individuals and of the community as a whole.

In *Tysiąc* v *Poland*,[1847] the applicant, who suffered from severe myopia, was denied a thera- **6.551** peutic abortion, even though she was advised that if she carried her pregnancy to full term there would be a serious risk to her eyesight. During her pregnancy, and after the birth of her child, the applicant's eyesight substantially deteriorated and she was declared significantly disabled. As a result of the uncertain position in the domestic law, the Court concluded that the law did not incorporate effective mechanisms capable of determining whether the conditions for obtaining a lawful abortion had been met in the applicant's case. This created a situation of prolonged uncertainty that caused her severe distress and anguish, in violation of Article 8.

At issue in the case of *A, B & C* v *Ireland*[1848] was the prohibition of abortion in Ireland. Each **6.552** of the applicants had travelled to the United Kingdom to have an abortion, after becoming pregnant unintentionally. A majority of the Grand Chamber (11 votes to six) found that there was no violation of the right to respect for the private life of two of the applicants who were found to have had an abortion for reasons of health and well-being, but for whom there had been no risk to their lives. Taking into account the wide margin of appreciation afforded to the state on such questions, and the 'profound moral views of the Irish people as to the nature of life', the Court held that a fair balance had been struck in their cases. However, Article 8 was unanimously found to have been violated in the case of the third applicant. The question that arose in her case was the extent to which the state met its positive obligation to provide an effective and accessible procedure allowing her to establish her entitlement to a lawful abortion in Ireland. The third applicant had a rare form of cancer, and when she discovered she was pregnant she feared for her life as she believed that her pregnancy increased the risk of her cancer returning and that she would not obtain treatment for cancer in Ireland while pregnant. The Court noted that the Irish Constitution (as interpreted by the Supreme Court) provides that an abortion is available in Ireland if it is established as a matter of probability that there is a real and substantial risk to the life, as distinct from the health, of the mother, including a risk of self harm, which can only be avoided by a termination of the pregnancy. However, it found that there was substantial uncertainty as to how these principles would be interpreted. Therefore both she and any doctor ran a serious risk

---

[1845] See, e.g. *Codarcea* v *Romania*, No. 31675/04, 2.6.09.

[1846] Nos. 47039/11 and 358/12, 13.11.12.

[1847] No. 5410/03, 20.3.07. See also *R.R.* v *Poland*, No. 27617/04, 26.5.11 (denial of access to prenatal genetic tests, which also prevented an abortion on grounds of foetal abnormality—violation of Articles 3 and 8 (discussed at 6.189)); *P. and S.* v *Poland*, No. 57375/08, 30.10.12 (breach of positive obligation to secure effective respect for private life through access to a lawful abortion—disclosure of information by hospital about pregnant minor seeking abortion after being raped—violations of Article 8).

[1848] No. 25579/05, 16.12.10.

of criminal prosecution were a decision made that she was entitled to an abortion, but which later was found to contravene the Constitution. Nor would judicial proceedings constitute an effective or accessible procedure to enable someone in the third applicant's position to establish her right to a lawful abortion.

Article 9: Freedom of Thought, Conscience and Religion

6.553   Article 9 states:

1.   Everyone has the right to freedom of thought, conscience and religion; this right includes freedom to change his religion or belief and freedom, either alone or in community with others and in public or private, to manifest his religion or belief, in worship, teaching, practice and observance.
2.   Freedom to manifest one's religion or beliefs shall be subject only to such limitations as are prescribed by law and are necessary in a democratic society in the interests of public safety, for the protection of public order, health or morals, or for the protection of the rights and freedoms of others.

6.554   Freedom of thought, conscience and religion is said to be one of the foundations of a 'democratic society': 'It is, in its religious dimension, one of the most vital elements that go to make up the identity of believers and of their conception of life, but it is also a precious asset for atheists, agnostics, sceptics and the unconcerned.'[1849] The right to freedom of thought, conscience and religion in Article 9 is closely connected to both the right to freedom of expression in Article 10 and the rights to peaceful assembly and of association in Article 11.[1850] In cases where the applicant's freedom of thought, conscience and religion is in issue, both Articles 10 and 11 should also be carefully considered.

6.555   Article 9(1) expressly clarifies the extent of the right to freedom of religion as including two aspects: the right to *change* one's religion or belief and to *manifest* one's religion or belief. To be able to rely on the right to manifest one's religion, an applicant must establish that he or she is in fact an adherent of the religion in question and that the manifestation in question is an essential part of that religion. Article 9(1) specifically refers to 'worship,[1851] teaching, practice and observance' as being forms of manifestation of one's religion or belief, which includes bearing witness in words and deeds and the right to try to convince others.

6.556   The Court has emphasised that Article 9 includes the right to manifest one's religion in community with others, in public and within the circle of those whose faith one shares: 'bearing witness in words and deeds is bound up with the existence of religious convictions'. It therefore protects the freedom to hold, or not to hold, religious beliefs, and to practise, or not to practise, a religion.[1852] The scope of Article 9 has generally been interpreted widely in terms of the nature of the belief (which includes non-religious beliefs, such as secularism,[1853]

[1849]   *Kokkinakis* v *Greece*, No. 14307/88, Series A, No. 260-A, 25.5.93, para. 31.

[1850]   See, e.g. *Metropolitan Church of Bessarabia* v *Moldova*, No. 45701/99, 13.12.01; *Moscow Branch of the Salvation Army* v *Russia*, No. 72881/01, 5.10.06; *Kuznetsov and others* v *Russia*, No. 184/02, 11.1.07.

[1851]   The notion of 'worship' includes ritual and ceremonial acts giving direct expression to belief, including ceremonies following deaths: *Güler and Uğur* v *Turkey*, No. 31706/10 and 33088/10, 2.12.14, para. 41.

[1852]   See, e.g. *Kokkinakis* v *Greece*, No. 14307/88, Series A, No. 260-A, 25.5.93, (1994) 1, para. 31; *Buscarino* v *San Marino*, No. 24645/94, 18.2.99, para. 34.

[1853]   *Lautsi and others* v *Italy*, No. 30814/06, 18.3.11, para. 58.

pacifism and anti-militarism[1854]), but much more restrictively in relation to the manifestation or practices which are claimed to be motivated by one's religion or belief. The act in question must be 'intimately linked' to the religion or belief. Article 9 therefore does not protect every act which an individual considers to be required by their belief.[1855] The Court has found, for example, that observing dietary rules may be considered a direct expression of beliefs in practice–and in *Jakóbski v Poland*[1856] the Court found a violation of Article 9 because of the prison authorities' refusal to provide the applicant with a meat-free diet in prison, contrary to the dietary rules of his Buddhist faith. In general, however, Article 9 will not be violated by the application of general laws to individuals who object on the basis that the law offends against their religion or belief.[1857] The Court has also stipulated that in democratic societies, where several religions coexist, it may be necessary to place restrictions on freedom to manifest one's religion or belief in order to reconcile the interests of the various groups and ensure that everyone's beliefs are respected.[1858] Where restrictions to Article 9 rights are the result of the actions of a private entity, the Court will assess the extent of the positive obligation on the state to secure the rights under Article 9.[1859]

The Court has stressed the need for the state to ensure the preservation of religious pluralism, which requires that religious communities should be able to exist autonomously. As well as restraining state interference with religious organisations, this also obliges the authorities to ensure that different organisations or denominations (which might be considered to be 'in competition') tolerate each other.[1860] Furthermore, the right to freedom of religion excludes the assessment by the state of the legitimacy of religious beliefs, or the ways in which such beliefs are expressed.[1861] States will not be precluded from requiring the registration of religious denominations in a manner that is compatible with Articles 9 and 11 of the Convention, but that does not mean that members of an unregistered religious denomination can then be sanctioned for praying or manifesting their religious beliefs in other ways.[1862] Where religious organisations are subject to a system of prior authorisation, it will not be compatible with Article 9 for a recognised ecclesiastical authority to be involved in the procedure for granting authority.[1863] In *Hasan and Chaush v Bulgaria*,[1864] the Grand Chamber of the Court confirmed the applicability of Article 9 to the organisation of religious communities:[1865]

6.557

> Where the organisation of the religious community is at issue, Article 9 of the Convention must be interpreted in the light of Article 11, which safeguards associative life against unjustified

---

[1854] *Savda v Turkey*, No. 42730/05, 12.6.12.

[1855] See, e.g. *Arrowsmith v UK*, (1978) 19 DR 5; *Hasan and Chaush v Bulgaria*, No. 30985/96, 26.10.00; *Pichon and Sajous v France*, No. 49853/99, dec. 2.10.01 (pharmacists' application concerning refusal to sell contraceptives declared inadmissible); *Mann Singh v France*, No. 24479/07, dec. 13.11.08 (obligation to remove turban for driving licence photograph—inadmissible); *Francesco Sessa v Italy*, No. 28790/08, 3.4.12 (refusal to adjourn a hearing scheduled on a Jewish holiday—no violation of Article 9 (by four votes to three)); *Austrianu v Romania*, No. 16117/02, 12.2.13 (confiscation of prisoner's cassette recorder used to listen to religious tapes—inadmissible).

[1856] No. 18429/06, 7.12.10.

[1857] See, e.g. *Skugar and others v Russia*, No. 40010/04, dec. 3.12.09.

[1858] See, e.g. *Leyla Şahin v Turkey*, No. 44774/98, 10.11.05, para. 106.

[1859] See, e.g. *Eweida v UK*, No. 48420/10, 15.1.13, para. 84.

[1860] *Serif v Greece*, No. 38178/97, 14.12.99, para. 53.

[1861] *Ibid.*, para. 52.

[1862] *Masaev v Moldova*, No. 6303/05, 12.5.09, para. 26.

[1863] *Pentidis and others v Greece*, No. 23238/94, Comm. Rep. 9.6.97, para. 46.

[1864] No. 30985/96, 26.10.00. See also *Supreme Holy Council of the Muslim Community v Bulgaria*, No. 39023/97, 16.12.04.

[1865] *Ibid.*, para. 62.

State interference. Seen in this perspective, the believers' right to freedom of religion encompasses the expectation that the community will be allowed to function peacefully, free from arbitrary State intervention. Indeed, the autonomous existence of religious communities is indispensable for pluralism in a democratic society and is thus an issue at the very heart of the protection which Article 9 affords. It directly concerns not only the organisation of the community as such but also the effective enjoyment of the right to freedom of religion by all its active members. Were the organisational life of the community not protected by Article 9 of the Convention, all other aspects of the individual's freedom of religion would become vulnerable.

6.558 In *İzzettin Doğan and others* v *Turkey*[1866] the Grand Chamber found a violation of Article 9 (by 12 votes to five) because of the authorities' refusal to provide public religious services to adherents to the Alevi faith. This was found to infringe the Alevi community's right to an autonomous existence. Furthermore, the domestic law laid down a number of significant prohibitions, including the banning of certain practices and the imposition of imprisonment or fines for contraventions. Followers of the Alevi faith also faced other legal, organisational and financial problems with regard to building places of worship, receiving donations or subsidies and having access to the courts. The Government had failed to set out relevant and sufficient reasons to justify refusing the recognition to the Alevi community. There was a violation of Article 9 in *Hasan and Chaush* v *Bulgaria* arising from Government proclamations ordering changes in the leadership and statute of the Muslim community in Bulgaria, without reasons being given. The Government's interference failed the 'prescribed by law' test, as its decisions were based on legal provisions that gave the executive an unfettered discretion and that were not adequately clear or foreseeable.[1867] The authorities' interference with the applicant's Article 9 rights in *Perry* v *Latvia*[1868] also breached the prescribed by law test. The applicant was an American evangelical pastor who had founded a religious community in Latvia in 1997 and had been granted temporary residence permits. However, in 2000 he was issued with a residence permit that forbade him to carry out religious activities, on the basis of 'negative operational information' about him. The Court found that the domestic law could not be used to issue him with a residence permit subject to conditions restricting his rights to engage in religious activity. The applicants in the case of *Association Les Témoins de Jéhovah* v *France*[1869] successfully claimed that, because of the lack of clarity in the application of the relevant law, a tax on donations to religious associations had been 'unforeseeable' and accordingly was not prescribed by law under Article 9. In *Kuznetsov and others* v *Russia*,[1870] the applicants, who were Jehovah's Witnesses, complained about the unjustified termination of their meeting by the regional

---

[1866] No. 62649/10, 26.4.16. There was also a violation of Article 14 taken together with Article 9.

[1867] See also *Holy Synod of the Bulgarian Orthodox Church (Metropolitan Inokentiy) and others* v *Bulgaria*, Nos. 41203 and 35677/04, 22.1.09 (Governmental interference with the Orthodox Church—violation of Article 9); *Mirolubovs* v *Latvia*, No. 798/05, 15.9.09 (state intervention in dispute between members of Orthodox communities—violation of Article 9).

[1868] No. 30273/03, 8.11.07.

[1869] No. 8916/05, 30.6.11. In the subsequent just satisfaction judgment (5.7.12), the Court awarded the applicant association pecuniary damages of €4,590,295 (the amount which had already been paid) and, invoking Article 46, stipulated that the tax measure in question (which was still in force) should be discontinued.

[1870] No. 184/02, 11.1.07. See also *Krupko and others* v *Russia*, No. 26587/07, 26.6.14 (disruption of Jehovah's Witnesses meeting by armed riot police—violation of Article 9); *Association for Solidarity with Jehovah's Witnesses and others* v *Turkey*, Nos. 36915/10 and 8606/13, 24.5.16 (planning restrictions preventing religious community from having a place of worship—violation of Article 9).

human rights commissioner and two police officers. This was found by the Court to breach Article 9 as it had no legal basis.

Article 9 was violated in *Nolan and K. v Russia*,[1871] because of the banning from Russia of **6.559** the applicant, an active member of the Unification Church, on the basis that he was said to pose a threat to national security. However, the Court concluded that the ban was designed to repress the exercise of his right to freedom of religion and stifle the spreading of the teaching of the Unification Church, and that there was no plausible legal or factual justification for it. There was a violation of Article 9 in the case of *97 members of the Gldani Congregation of Jehovah's Witnesses and 4 others v Georgia*,[1872] which concerned an organised, sustained attack on the applicant Jehovah's Witnesses during a congregation meeting by members of a group of Orthodox extremists. Their religious literature was confiscated and burnt, and one applicant had his head shaved to the sound of prayers, as a religious punishment. The applicants' complaints to the authorities were then met with 'total indifference'. The Court found that this 'opened the doors to a generalisation of religious violence throughout Georgia' by the same group. Similarly, the case of *Karaahmed v Bulgaria*[1873] concerned the disruption of Muslim prayers at a mosque in Sofia caused by demonstrators from a right-wing political party. Not only was the police response held to be inadequate, but also the ensuing investigation was ineffective, meaning that the authorities had failed to comply with their positive obligations under Article 9. The applicant's conviction for usurping the functions of a minister of a 'known religion' was found to be a disproportionate interference with his rights under Article 9 in *Agga v Greece (No. 2)*,[1874] following a dispute as to who should succeed as the Muslim Mufti of Xanthi—the Court remained unpersuaded by the need for such a measure even in the light of the Government's arguments that it had been necessary to prevent religious tensions in the region.

The extent of state control over religious organisations was also in issue in *Metropolitan* **6.560** *Church of Bessarabia v Moldova*,[1875] because of the state's refusal to recognise the applicant church. The domestic law provided that only religions recognised by the state could be practised, and so priests from the applicant church, which had not been recognised, could not conduct services, its members were not permitted to meet, and the church was not entitled to judicial protection of its assets. The dissolution of the applicant community by the domestic courts, and the ban on its activities, was found to violate Article 9 (read in the light of Article 11) in *Jehovah's Witnesses of Moscow v Russia*.[1876] These measures were found to have the effect of stripping it of legal personality, and preventing it from owning or renting property, maintaining bank accounts, hiring employees, or ensuring the judicial protection of the community, its members and its assets. The domestic courts had found that the

---

[1871] No. 2512/04, 12.2.09. See also *Cox v Turkey*, No. 2933/03, 20.5.10 (American academic prevented from re-entering Turkey because of her statements about Kurds and Armenian massacre—violation of Article 10).

[1872] No. 71156/01, 3.5.07. See also *Begheluri v Georgia*, No. 28490/02, 7.10.14.

[1873] No. 30587/13, 24.2.15.

[1874] Nos. 50776/99 and 52912/99, 17.10.02.

[1875] No. 45701/99, 13.12.01. See also *Svyato-Mykhaylivska Parafiya v Ukraine*, No. 77703/01, 14.6.07 (violation of Article 9 as a result of the authorities' refusal to register amendments to statute of Orthodox parish); *Magyar Kereszteny Mennonita Egyhaz and others v Hungary*, No. 70945/11 et al, 8.4.14 (requirement for churches to re-register in order to regain benefits from state—violation of Article 11 read in the light of Article 9).

[1876] No. 302/02, 10.6.10. See also *Biblical Centre of the Chuvash Republic v Russia*, No. 33203/08, 12.6.14 (dissolution of religious community—violation of Article 9 interpreted in the light of Article 11).

applicant community forced families to break up, that it infringed the rights and freedoms of its members or third parties, that it incited its followers to commit suicide or refuse medical care, that it impinged on the rights of non-Witness parents or their children, and that it encouraged members to refuse to fulfil legal duties. Having carried out an extensive review of these allegations, the European Court, however, held that the domestic courts had failed to adduce relevant and sufficient reasons to justify such findings. There was also a separate violation of Article 11 (read in the light of Article 9) because of the refusal to re-register the association. In *Religionsgemeinschaft der Zeugen Jehovas and others v Austria*[1877] Article 9 was breached because the applicant religious organisation had to wait 20 years for it to be granted legal personality.

6.561 The freedom to manifest one's religion or belief also includes a negative aspect—the right of individuals *not* to act in such a way that it could be inferred that they have, or do not have, particular beliefs. In *Buscarini and others v San Marino*,[1878] the applicant MPs were required to swear an oath on the Gospels, or they would forfeit their parliamentary seats. This was found to violate Article 9 as the MPs were obliged to swear allegiance to a particular religion. There was a violation of Article 9 in *Sinan Işık v Turkey*,[1879] because of the authorities' refusal to change the statement of religion on the applicant's identity card from 'Islam' to 'Alevi'. Whilst being sworn in as a lawyer, the applicant in *Alexandridis v Greece*[1880] was in practice forced to disclose that he was not a member of the Orthodox Church and did not wish to take a religious oath, which was held to violate Article 9. In *Kokkinakis v Greece*[1881] the applicant, a Jehovah's Witness, complained of his conviction for proselytism, which was found by the Court to be a disproportionate interference in violation of Article 9 given that the domestic courts had failed to set out in what way the applicant had used improper means. The Court made a distinction between bearing Christian witness through true evangelism and improper proselytism, through offering material or social advantages to gain new members, exerting improper pressure or even the use of violence or brainwashing. However, in *Otto-Preminger-Institut v Austria*[1882] the Court stated that those who manifest their religion cannot reasonably expect to be exempt from all criticism: 'they must tolerate and accept the denial by others of their religious beliefs and even the propagation by others of doctrines hostile to their faith'. Measures taken by the authorities to restrict the publication or broadcast of provocative portrayals of objects of religious veneration may be justified to protect the respect for the religious feelings of believers.[1883]

[1877] No. 40825/98, 31.7.08 (there was also a violation of Article 14 taken together with Article 9 because it was unjustifiably granted the status of a 'religious community' rather than a 'religious society' which conferred various privileges). See also *Kimlya and others v Russia*, No. 76836/01 and 32782/03, 1.10.09 (legal requirement of 15 years' prior existence in order to register religious group—violation of Article 9); *Savez crkava 'Riječ života' and others v Croatia*, No. 7798/08, 9.12.10 (refusal to conclude legal status of Reformist churches—violation of Article 14 in conjunction with Article 9).

[1878] No. 24645/94, 18.2.99.

[1879] No. 21924/05, 2.2.10.

[1880] No. 19516/06, 21.2.08. See also *Dimitras and others v Greece*, No. 42837/06 et al, 3.6.10 (obligation to disclose religious convictions to avoid having to take religious oath in criminal proceedings—violation of Article 9); *Wasmuth v Germany*, No. 12884/03, 17.2.11 (obligation to indicate on wage-tax card membership of church or religious society entitled to levy church tax—no violation of Article 9).

[1881] No. 14307/88, Series A, No. 260-A, 25.5.93.

[1882] No. 13470/87, Series A, No. 295-A, 20.9.94.

[1883] *Wingrove v UK*, No. 17419/90, 25.11.96, paras. 46–51.

Some of the older case-law of the Court and Commission suggests that if complainants can **6.562** circumvent restrictions on their right to freedom of religion then there will be no *interference* with Article 9(1). However, in *Eweida v UK*,[1884] the Court clarified that where there are restrictions on freedom of religion in the workplace, rather than considering whether an employee could move jobs (and thus avoid the restriction), this is a factor to be considered in weighing up the proportionality of the measure in question, under Article 9(2). The first applicant in *Eweida* was a Coptic Christian who complained that the uniform code applied by her employer, British Airways, prevented her from wearing a cross at work. The Court found a violation of Article 9 as her right to manifest her religion had not had sufficient protection, given that too much weight had been placed on the employer's desire to maintain a certain corporate image, and that there had been no particular encroachment on the interests of others. However, there was no violation of Article 9 as regards a similar complaint brought by the second applicant, a nurse, because the restrictions on the wearing of jewellery (including religious symbols) within the National Health Service had been imposed for health and safety reasons. There was also no breach of Article 9 as regards the other two applicants in *Eweida*. The third applicant was a Christian registrar who lost her job because she refused to officiate over civil partnerships due to her belief that same-sex unions were contrary to God's will. This was found to be proportionate because the local authority's policy sought to protect the Convention rights of others. The fourth applicant was also dismissed (from the private company, Relate) when he refused to provide psycho-sexual counselling to same-sex couples, due to his Christian beliefs. However, there was again no violation because the employer's policy had been aimed at providing a service without discrimination. The applicant in *Ebrahimian v France*[1885] was employed as a social worker in the psychiatric department of a hospital, but was told that her contract would not be reviewed because of her refusal to remove her veil, and because of complaints which had been made against her by some patients. The Court noted that French public servants had a right to respect for their freedom of conscience, but they were also forbidden from manifesting their religious beliefs in discharging their duties. It found that the authorities had attempted to persuade her to refrain from displaying her religious convictions and that the decision was made on the basis of protecting other people's right to respect for freedom of religion. The authorities had been justified in finding that there was no possibility of reconciling the applicant's religious convictions with the obligation to refrain from manifesting them, and accordingly there was no violation of Article 9.

The dismissal of a non-academic school employee was found to violate Article 9 in *Ivanova v* **6.563** *Bulgaria*.[1886] The applicant was a follower of an evangelical Christian group (whose registration as a non-profit organisation had been turned down by the Council of Ministers). The Court found that, contrary to the Government's position, her employment had been terminated on account of her religious beliefs, and that there was no evidence that she had been involved in proselytism at the school. The applicant had been asked to resign or renounce her faith (which she refused to do)—described by the Court as a flagrant violation of her Article 9 rights.

[1884] No. 48420/10, 15.1.13.
[1885] No. 64846/11, 26.11.15.
[1886] No. 52435/99, 12.4.07. See also *Sodan v Turkey*, No. 18650/05, 2.2.16 (transfer of official to less important post on account of religious convictions—violation of Article 8).

6.564   The Turkish authorities were found to have breached Article 9 in *Cyprus* v *Turkey*[1887] because of restrictions placed on the freedom of movement of the Greek Cypriot population in northern Cyprus, which 'considerably curtailed their ability to observe their religious beliefs', in particular by restricting their access to places of worship outside their villages.

6.565   In *Poltoratskiy* v *Ukraine*,[1888] the Court found a violation of Article 9 because the applicant prisoner, who was on 'death row', was not permitted to be visited by a priest. The fact that this restriction was the subject of an internal and unpublished Ministry of Justice 'Instruction' meant that it had not been carried out 'in accordance with the law'.

6.566   In *Leyla Şahin* v *Turkey*,[1889] the Grand Chamber found that a ban on university students wearing Muslim headscarves was a proportionate interference with the applicant's rights under Article 9. The measure was justified under Turkish law in order to respect the principles of secularism and gender equality, and the Court found that upholding secularism was considered necessary to protect the democratic system in Turkey. The ban met a 'pressing social need' to protect the rights and freedoms of others (those who chose not to wear the headscarf) and to maintain public order, in view of the political significance of the headscarf in Turkey and the presence of extremist political movements. It was accepted that practising Muslim students in Turkish universities were otherwise free to manifest their religion in accordance with habitual forms of Muslim observance. Furthermore the adoption of the regulations in question had followed several years of debate in Turkish society, and there was settled domestic case law on the issue.[1890] The obligation to remove a turban in order to pass through airport screening has been justified as being in the interests of public safety.[1891] In *Ahmet Arslan and others* v *Turkey*,[1892] the Court found a violation of Article 9 as a result of the criminal convictions of the members of a religious group for wearing particular religious attire in public (a turban, 'salvar', tunic and stick). However, the Grand Chamber found (by 15 votes to two) no violation of Articles 8 or 9 in *S.A.S.* v *France*[1893] in relation to a Muslim woman who wished to wear a full-face veil and who accordingly faced prosecution under a 2010 law prohibiting anyone concealing their face in public places. The Court distinguished the case from *Ahmet Arslan* on the basis that the full-face Islamic veil entirely concealed the face (except possibly for the eyes). The ban was not considered necessary for public safety as there was no general threat to public safety, however, it was held to be proportionate to the

---

[1887] No. 25781/94, 10.5.01.

[1888] No. 38812/97, 29.4.03, para. 148. See further at 6.147 and 6.476. See also *Mozer* v *Moldova and Russia*, No. 11138/10, 23.2.16.

[1889] No. 44774/98, 10.11.05. See also: *Karaduman* v *Turkey*, No. 16278/90, dec. 3.5.93, DR 74, p. 93; *Dahlab* v *Switzerland*, No. 42393/98, dec. 15.2.01 (schoolteacher); *Kurtulmuş* v *Turkey*, No. 65500/01, dec. 24.1.06 (university lecturer); *Köse and 93 others* v *Turkey*, No. 26625/02, dec. 24.1.06 (school children); *Dogru* v *France*, No. 27058/05, 4.12.08 and *Kervanci* v *France*, No. 31645/04, 4.12.08 (school pupils expelled for refusing to remove headscarves during P.E. and sports classes); *Aktas* v *France*, No. 43563/08, *Bayrak* v *France*, No. 14308/08, *Gamaleddyn* v *France*, No. 18527/08, *Ghazal* v *France*, No. 29134/08, *J. Singh* v *France*, No. 25463/08, *R. Singh* v *France*, No. 27561/08, decs. 30.6.09 (expulsion of school pupils wearing either headscarves or the Sikh keski—inadmissible). In *Osmanoğlu and Kocabaş* v *Switzerland*, No. 29086/12, 10.1.17, there was no violation of Article 9 where parents were fined for refusing, on religious grounds, to allow their daughters to attend compulsory mixed swimming lessons at their primary school.

[1890] See, however, the persuasive dissenting opinion of Judge Tulkens.

[1891] *Phull* v *France*, No. 35753/03, dec. 11.1.05. See also *El Morsli* v *France*, No. 15585/06, dec. 4.3.08 (obligation on Muslim woman to remove headscarf at consulate security checkpoint).

[1892] No. 41135/98, 23.2.10.

[1893] No. 43835/11, 1.7.14.

aim of preserving conditions for 'living together' as an element of the protection of the rights and freedoms of others. While the scope of the ban was broad (applying to all public spaces) it only applied to clothing which concealed the face. Although a criminal sanction was applicable, a breach of the ban would only lead to a low fine. Furthermore, the authorities enjoyed a wide margin of appreciation in respect of a societal choice of this nature, and there was no European consensus against imposing such a ban.

6.567 Article 9 cannot be relied on by corporate bodies, but churches can do so, on behalf of their members and as separate entities themselves.[1894] Associations cannot invoke the right to freedom of conscience.[1895]

6.568 It was only in 2011, in its judgment in *Bayatyan v Armenia*,[1896] that the Grand Chamber found that Article 9 permitted conscientious objectors to resist military service (before that such arguments had been resisted because of the express reference in Article 4(3)(b) to compulsory military service).[1897] *Bayatyan* concerned the conviction for draft evasion (and sentence to two and a half years' imprisonment) of the applicant, a Jehovah's Witness, who had informed the authorities of his refusal to perform military service, but that he would have been willing to carry out alternative civilian service. Overturning the previous Strasbourg case-law, the Court held that 'opposition to military service, where it is motivated by a serious and insurmountable conflict between the obligation to serve in the army and a person's conscience or his deeply and genuinely held religious or other beliefs, constitutes a conviction or belief of sufficient cogency, seriousness, cohesion and importance to attract the guarantees of Article 9'.[1898] Noting that an alternative option of civilian service was not available in Armenia, the Court held that the applicant's conviction was not 'necessary in a democratic society' within the meaning of Article 9.

6.569 In *Z and T v UK*[1899] the Court rejected a complaint from Pakistani Christians, whose asylum claims had been dismissed, that their return to Pakistan would violate Article 9 (without claiming that their rights under Articles 2 or 3 were at risk). The Court noted that:

> ... protection is offered to those who have a substantiated claim that they will either suffer persecution for, *inter alia*, religious reasons or will be at real risk of death or serious ill-treatment, and possibly flagrant denial of a fair trial or arbitrary detention, because of their religious affiliation (as for any other reason). Where however an individual claims that on return to his own country he would be impeded in his religious worship in a manner which falls short of those proscribed levels, the Court considers that very limited assistance, if any, can be derived from Article 9 by itself. Otherwise it would be imposing an obligation on Contracting States effectively to act as indirect guarantors of freedom of worship for the rest of [the] world.

[1894] *Chappell v UK* (1987) 53 DR 214; *Metropolitan Church of Bessarabia v Moldova*, No. 45701/99, 13.12.01, para. 101.

[1895] *Vereniging Rechtswinkels Utrecht v Netherlands* (1986) 46 DR 200. As to the application of Article 9 to members of the armed forces, see, e.g. *Pektas v Turkey*, No. 39682/98, 3.10.02.

[1896] No. 23459/03, 7.7.11. See also: *Erçep v Turkey*, No. 43965/04, 22.11.11; *Feti Demirtaş v Turkey*, No. 5260/07, 17.1.12; *Savda v Turkey*, No. 42730/05, 12.6.12. See further *Papavasilakis v Greece*, No. 66899/14, 15.9.16 (absence of procedural safeguards as regards request for alternative civil service—violation of Article 9).

[1897] See: the dissenting and concurring opinions in *Thlimmenos v Greece*, No. 34369/97, Comm. Rep. 4.12.98; the earlier chamber judgment in *Bayatyan* (27.10.09) and the dissenting opinion of Judge Power. In *Taştan v Turkey*, No. 63748/00, 4.3.08 the Court held that requiring a 71-year-old man to perform military service amounted to degrading treatment, in violation of Article 3.

[1898] *Bayatyan v Armenia*, No. 23459/03, 7.7.11, para. 110.

[1899] No. 27034/05, dec. 28.2.06.

6.570 It is important to note that the limitations set out in Article 9(2) only apply to the right to *manifest* one's religion or beliefs. Article 9(2) does not apply to the right to hold a particular belief or to the rights to freedom of thought or conscience, which are therefore unqualified.

6.571 Where it is accepted that Article 9(1) rights are engaged, the Court has frequently found the restrictions applied to be proportionate. For example, in *Leela Förderkreis E.V. and others v Germany*,[1900] the applicant religious associations complained about the authorities' information campaign against such groups that had been labelled as 'sects' or 'psycho sects'. However, the Court found no violation of Article 9 as the campaign had legitimately been aimed at warning people about the emergence of new religions, which had been viewed by some as disturbing. This was considered to fall within the state's margin of appreciation and the applicant associations' freedom to manifest their religion or beliefs had not been prohibited. In *Pendragon v UK*,[1901] a ban on assemblies at Stonehenge under the Public Order Act 1986 (which applied for four days over a four-mile radius) was found to have interfered with the rights of the applicant (who had intended to hold a Druidic service at the summer solstice) under Article 11(1), and brought Article 9(1) into consideration. However, in view of the violence at Stonehenge in previous years, the restriction was not found to be disproportionate.

Article 10: Freedom of Expression

6.572 Article 10 states:

1. Everyone has the right to freedom of expression. This right shall include freedom to hold opinions and to receive and impart information and ideas without interference by public authority and regardless of frontiers. This article shall not prevent states from requiring the licensing of broadcasting, television or cinema enterprises.
2. The exercise of these freedoms, since it carries with it duties and responsibilities, may be subject to such formalities, conditions, restrictions or penalties as are prescribed by law and are necessary in a democratic society, in the interests of national security, territorial integrity or public safety, for the prevention of disorder or crime, for the protection of health or morals, for the protection of the reputation or rights of others, for preventing the disclosure of information received in confidence, or for maintaining the authority and impartiality of the judiciary.

6.573 The Court has consistently underlined the importance of the right to freedom of speech as one of the essential foundations of a democratic society, acknowledging in particular the function which the media plays (a vital role in providing information and as 'public watchdog')[1902] and its duty to impart information and ideas of public interest, without overstepping certain bounds. This duty is said to be mirrored by the public's right to receive such

---

[1900] No. 58911/00, 6.11.08.

[1901] No. 31416/96, dec. 19.10.98. See also *Christians Against Racism and Fascism* v *UK*, No. 8440/78, dec. 16.7.80: police ban on processions in London not found to be disproportionate.

[1902] See, e.g. *Jersild* v *Denmark*, No. 15890/8, Series A, No. 298, 23.9.94, para. 31; *Cumpănă and Mazăre* v *Romania*, No. 33748, 17.12.04, para. 93; *Dammann* v *Switzerland*, No. 77551/01, 25.4.06, para. 57; *Kobenter and Standard Verlags Gmbh* v *Austria*, No. 60899/00, 2.11.06, para. 31; *July and Sarl Libération* v *France*, No. 20893/03, 14.2.08, para. 76; *Fatullayev* v *Azerbaijan*, No. 40984/07, 22.4.10, para. 88.

information. Freedom of expression is also considered to be one of the basic conditions required for each individual's self-fulfilment.

Article 10 is related to, and frequently invoked with, Article 9 (freedom of thought, con- **6.574** science and religion) and Article 11 (right to peaceful assembly and association). As with Articles 8, 9 and 11, the substantive right is set out in Article 10(1) and the permitted restrictions are set out in Article 10(2) (see also above at 6.437). These restrictions must be narrowly interpreted and the need for the restriction must be convincingly established.[1903] The right to freedom of expression is therefore subject to duties and responsibilities, the extent of which will vary according to the context.

Some situations will require an assessment of the fair balancing as between competing **6.575** rights, notably freedom of expression and privacy. In *Axel Springer AG v Germany*,[1904] the Grand Chamber reviewed the factors which are relevant to the 'balancing exercise' between the rights under Articles 8 and 10: (i) the contribution to a debate of general interest; (ii) how well known the person concerned is and the nature of the subject of the report; (iii) the prior conduct of the person concerned; (iv) the method of obtaining the information and its veracity; (v) the content, form and consequences of the publication; and (vi) the severity of the sanction imposed. Applying those principles in the case, the Court found that the application of injunctions to prevent a national daily newspaper from publishing information about the arrest and conviction of a famous actor was disproportionate and in violation of Article 10 (by 12 votes to five). Applying the same principles in *Couderc and Hachette Filipacchi Associés v France*[1905] the Grand Chamber unanimously found a violation of Article 10 as a result of a court finding of liability against the publishers of an article and photographs about the existence of the Prince of Monaco's 'secret child' who had been born out of wedlock. Contrary to the position of the domestic courts, the Court found that the publications went beyond the private sphere and that there was a genuine public interest in the existence of the Prince's child who had been unknown, and the possible consequences on the succession to the throne in a hereditary monarchy. In *Hachette Filipacchi Associés v France*[1906] the applicant company owned the magazine *Paris-Match*, which published an article with a photograph of the body of the Prefect of Corsica moments after he had been murdered. The Prefect's relatives sought an injunction and consequently the company was required to publish in its magazine a statement to inform readers that the photograph had been published without the consent of the family, who considered its publication an intrusion into the intimacy of their private life. The Court held there was no violation of Article 10 (by five votes to two), finding that the domestic courts had given reasons for the interference that were both 'relevant and sufficient', and concluding that it was proportionate to the legitimate aim pursued and 'necessary in a democratic society'.

[1903] See, e.g. *Ahmed and others v UK*, No. 22954/93, 12.9.95, para. 55.

[1904] No. 39954/08, 7.2.12. See also *Axel Springer AG v Germany (No. 2)*, No. 48311/10, 10.7.14 and *Aksu v Turkey*, Nos. 4149/04 and 41029/04, 15.3.12. There was a violation of Article 10 in *Haldimann and others v Switzerland*, No. 21830/09, 24.2.15 where the applicant journalists were convicted for secretly filming and broadcasting (for public interest purposes) an interview with an insurance broker, whose face had been pixelated and his voice altered.

[1905] No. 40454/07, 10.11.15.

[1906] No. 71111/01, 14.6.07.

6.576 The Court has held that there is a duty not to be gratuitously offensive in relation to objects of religious veneration.[1907] However, in situations where there is a clash of rights under Articles 9 and 10, the Court has emphasised that:[1908]

> Those who choose to exercise the freedom to manifest their religion, irrespective of whether they do so as members of a religious majority or a minority, cannot reasonably expect to be exempt from all criticism. They must tolerate and accept the denial by others of their religious beliefs and even the propagation by others of doctrines hostile to their faith.

6.577 In *I.A.* v *Turkey*,[1909] the applicant was convicted of blasphemy, following the publication by his publishing house of a book discussing philoshophical and theological issues. The European Court found, by four votes to three, that this did not violate Article 10, as the book was considered to include abusive or offensive attacks on matters deemed sacred by Muslims. The dissenting judges acknowledged that there were insulting statements in the book that could be deeply offensive to Muslims, but argued that that did not justify the prosecuting authorities instituting criminal proceedings: 'a democratic society is not a theocratic society'.[1910] By contrast, Article 10 was found to have been violated in *Giniewski* v *Poland*[1911] as a result of the applicant's prosecution and conviction for defaming the Christian community as a result of the applicant's newspaper article criticising the Pope. The article was found not to be gratuitously offensive or insulting, and had not incited disrespect or hatred.

6.578 In principle, Article 10 will protect the right to express oneself in a way that may be seen as offensive, shocking or disturbing, reflecting the need in a democratic society for pluralism, tolerance and broadmindedness.[1912] However, measures taken by the authorities to restrict or prevent the publication of statements inciting racial hatred or which amount to hate speech more generally, or calls to violence, are likely to be considered compliant with Article 10,[1913] and certain forms of expression, such as offensive racist statements, may not be protected by Article 10 at all.[1914]

6.579 Where a form of expression is protected by Article 10(1), this will be subject to the permissible restrictions in Article 10(2), provided that they are lawful ('prescribed by law') and proportionate ('necessary in a democratic society'). For example, in *RTBF* v *Belgium*,[1915] the Court held that the domestic law relating to court injunctions preventing the broadcasting of a television programme was not sufficiently clear or foreseeable, because it had not been applied in a consistent way by the Belgian courts. In common law jurisdictions the 'prescribed by law' test does not prevent the gradual clarification of the law through judicial law-making.[1916] The majority of cases, however, turn on whether or not an interference with

---

[1907] See, e.g. *Wingrove* v *UK*, No. 17419/90, 25.11.96, para. 52.
[1908] See, e.g. *Otto-Preminger-Institut* v *Austria*, No. 13470/87, 20.9.94, para. 47.
[1909] No. 42571/98, 13.9.05.
[1910] Joint dissenting opinion of Judges Costa, Cabral Barreto and Jungwiert.
[1911] No. 64016/00, 31.1.06. See also *Klein* v *Slovakia*, No. 72208/01, 31.10.06.
[1912] See, e.g. *Handyside* v *UK*, Series A, No. 24, 7.12.76, para. 49; *Fatullayev* v *Azerbaijan*, No. 40984/07, 22.4.10, para. 86; *PETA Deutschland* v *Germany*, No. 43481/09, 8.11.12, para. 46.
[1913] See, e.g. *Balsytė-Lideikienė* v *Lithuania*, No. 72596/01, 4.11.08; *Féret* v *Belgium*, No. 15615/07, 16.7.09 (conviction of president of extreme right wing party for publishing leaflets inciting racial hatred—no violation of Article 10, by four votes to three). See also the digest of cases concerning hate speech and calls to violence in *Perinçek* v *Switzerland*, No. 27510/08, 15.10.15, paras. 204–8.
[1914] See, e.g. *Jersild* v *Denmark*, No. 15890/8, Series A, No. 298, 23.9.94 1, para. 35.
[1915] No. 50084/06, 29.3.11.
[1916] See, e.g. *Blake* v *UK*, No. 68890/01, dec. 25.10.05, para. 141.

the right was proportionate or not (which in some cases will be decided by the narrowest of margins). In assessing the proportionality of restrictions on the right to freedom of expression, the Court allows the authorities a discretion, or 'margin of appreciation' (see also above at 6.444) which varies according to the subject matter. For example, a wider margin of appreciation is allowed in respect of issues of morality and commercial speech, but a narrower margin of appreciation is applied in relation to political speech.[1917] The factors to be taken into account when assessing the proportionality of an interference will include the nature and severity of the penalties imposed.[1918]

The Court acknowledges the difference between statements of fact[1919] and value judgements **6.580** (as is reflected in the defamation laws of a number of Council of Europe states) and the impossibility of proving the latter.[1920] There must, however, be a sufficient factual basis for any such value judgement.[1921]

There may also be positive obligations under Article 10, for example where the authorities **6.581** fail to take steps to investigate and provide protection against unlawful acts of violence.[1922] In *Palomo Sánchez and others* v *Spain*,[1923] the Grand Chamber found that trade union members should be able to express to their employer the demands by which they seek to improve the situation of workers in their company. The applicants complained they had been dismissed by their employer (a private company) because of their trade union activities, but on the pretext of allegedly offensive content in their union newsletter aimed at two other employees. The Court held that a state's responsibility could be engaged in such circumstances if it failed to meet its positive obligation to uphold the applicants' Article 10 rights. However, on the facts, the dismissal of their cases by the judicial authorities was not deemed to violate Article 10 (by a majority of 12 votes to five), as the article and cartoon in question was considered to have crossed the boundary between criticism and offensive insult. As well as protecting

---

[1917] See, e.g. *Vgt Verein Gegen Tierfabriken* v *Switzerland*, No. 24699/94, 28.6.01, paras. 69–71.

[1918] See, e.g. *Ceylan* v *Turkey*, No. 23556/94, 8.7.99, para. 37; *Salov* v *Ukraine*, No. 65518/01, 6.9.05, para. 115; *Dabrowski* v *Poland*, No. 18235/05, 19.12.06, para. 36; *Kwiecień* v *Poland*, No. 51744/99, 9.1.07, para. 56; *Yılmaz and Kılıç* v *Turkey*, No. 68514/01, 17.7.98, para. 67; *Balsytė-Lideikienė* v *Lithuania*, No. 72596/01, 4.11.08, para. 83; *Tešić* v *Serbia*, Nos. 4678/07 and 50591/12, 11.2.14 (award of damages in defamation proceedings led, inter alia, to enforcement order amounting to two-thirds of the applicant's pension—violation of Article 10); *Murat Vural* v *Turkey*, No. 9540/07, 21.10.14 (13 year sentence for pouring paint over statues of Kemal Atatürk—violation of Article 10); *Erdoğan Gökçe* v *Turkey*, No. 31736/04, 14.10.14 (imposition of prison sentence on candidate in municipal elections for disseminating press release before statutory electioneering period—violation of Article 10).

[1919] As in *Pedersen and Baadsgaard* v *Denmark*, No. 49017/99, 17.12.04. In *Salov* v *Ukraine*, No. 65518/01, 6.9.05 (para. 112), the Court characterised the statement in question as a 'false statement of fact'. In *Brosa* v *Germany*, No. 5709/09, 17.4.14 the Court did not agree with the domestic courts' assessment that a statement to the effect that an association was a dangerous neo-Nazi organisation was a mere allegation of fact, but also included a clear element of value judgement which was not fully susceptible to proof.

[1920] See, e.g. *Jerusalem* v *Austria*, No. 26958/95, 27.2.01, para. 42; *Feldek* v *Slovakia*, No. 29032/95, 12.7.01, paras. 76 and 85; *Karman* v *Russia*, No. 29372/02, 14.12.06, para. 41; *Gorelishvili* v *Georgia*, No. 12979/04, 5.6.07 (the domestic law made no distinction between value judgements and statements of fact); *Stojanović* v *Croatia*, No. 23160/09, 19.9.13; *Morice* v *France*, No. 29369/10, 23.4.15, paras.155–6; *Kharlamov* v *Russia*, No. 27447/07, 8.10.15.

[1921] See, e.g. *De Haes and Gijsels* v *Belgium*, No. 19983/92, 24.2.97, para. 47; *Scharsach and News Verlagsgesellschaft* v *Austria*, No. 39394/98, 13.11.03, para. 39; *Cumpănă and Mazăre* v *Romania*, No. 33748, 17.12.04, paras. 98–102. The Court's judgment in *Ukrainian Media Group* v *Ukraine*, No. 72713/01, 29.3.05 highlighted the fact that the domestic law did not distinguish between statements of fact and value judgements.

[1922] See *Özgür Gündem* v *Turkey*, No. 23144/93, 16.3.00; *Dink* v *Turkey*, No. 2668/07, 14.9.10.

[1923] No. 28955/06, 12.9.11.

the substance of the information or ideas expressed, Article 10 also protects the manner in which they are conveyed.

6.582 The application of Article 10 is discussed further below under the following headings: political expression (6.583); public officials and lawyers; whistleblowing (6.591); public protest (6.597); the media (6.602); artistic expression (6.620); expression in the commercial context (6.625); maintaining the authority and impartiality of the judiciary (6.628) and the right to receive information (6.631).

Political expression

6.583 Freedom of expression has particular importance for elected political representatives and so interferences with the freedom of speech of politicians will be closely scrutinised. In *Castells* v *Spain*,[1924] for example, the conviction of a Basque opposition senator for writing an article critical of the Government was found to violate Article 10.[1925] Given the importance of free speech within a democracy, very strong reasons will be required to justify restrictions on political speech[1926] or interferences with statements made within parliaments or other elected bodies such as municipal councils.[1927] In *Karácsony and others* v *Hungary*[1928] the applicant opposition MPs had brought a placard and banners into the parliamentary chamber during a debate (and one had used a megaphone). As a result, they were fined, on a motion introduced by the speaker. Such disciplinary sanctions in themselves were found to be justified, but Article 10 was breached because of the absence of any procedural safeguards allowing the applicant MPs to be heard. The Court has underlined that the application of a prison sentence for an offence in the area of political speech will only be compatible with Article 10 in exceptional circumstances.[1929]

6.584 Freedom of political debate is considered by the Court to be at the very core of the concept of a democratic society and the freedom of the press provides the public with one of the best means of discovering and forming an opinion of the ideas and attitudes of political leaders.[1930] The Court has also affirmed the 'watchdog' role of non-governmental organisations (including small and informal campaigning groups),[1931] in commenting on matters of public interest, as being essential in a democracy.[1932] Accordingly, whilst politicians are entitled to protect their reputations, the limits of acceptable criticism are wider in relation to a politician than a private individual.[1933] A politician:

[1924] No. 11798/85, Series A, No. 236, 23.4.92.

[1925] See also *Ibrahim Aksoy* v *Turkey*, Nos. 28635/95, 30171/96 and 34535/97, 10.10.00; *Jerusalem* v *Austria*, No. 26958/95, 27.2.01; *Mamère* v *France*, No. 12697/03, 7.11.06; *Lombardo and others* v *Malta*, No. 7333/06, 24.4.07; *Otegi Mondragon* v *Spain*, No. 2034/07, 15.3.11.

[1926] See, e.g. *Malisiewicz-Gąsior* v *Poland*, No. 43797/98, 6.4.06; *Karman* v *Russia*, No. 29372/02, 14.12.06.

[1927] *Jerusalem* v *Austria*, No. 26958/95, 27.2.01, para. 40.

[1928] Nos. 42461/13 and 44357/13, 17.5.16.

[1929] See, e.g. *Bingöl* v *Turkey*, No. 36141/04, 22.6.10, para. 41; *Otegi Mondragon* v *Spain*, No. 2034/07, 15.3.11, para. 59.

[1930] See, e.g. *Oberschlick* v *Austria*, No. 11662/85, Series A, No. 204, 23.5.91, para. 58.

[1931] *Steel and Morris* v *UK*, No. 68416/01, 15.2.05, para. 89.

[1932] *Vides Aizsardzības Klubs* v *Latvia*, No. 57829/00, 27.5.04.

[1933] See, e.g. *Lingens* v *Austria*, No. 9815/82, Series A, No. 103, 8.7.86; *Feldek* v *Slovakia*, No. 29032/95, 12.7.01; *Lepojić* v *Serbia*, No. 13909/05, 6.11.07; *Vellutini and Michel* v *France*, No. 32820/09, 6.10.11. The extent of the 'public figure status' of the persons concerned will be an important factor in deciding whether comment is in the public interest or not: see, e.g. *Tammer* v *Estonia*, No. 41205/98, 6.2.01, para. 67. Whether the person is actually known to the public is of lesser importance; what counts is whether the person has entered

inevitably and knowingly lays himself open to close scrutiny of his every word and deed by both journalists and the public at large, and he must display a greater degree of tolerance, especially when he himself makes public statements that are susceptible of criticism.[1934]

Furthermore, journalists are permitted 'a degree of exaggeration, or even provocation'.[1935] Unnecessarily offensive language will not, however, be protected.[1936] In *Ukrainian Media Group v Ukraine*, the applicant company had published articles in its daily newspaper that were critical of two politicians, both of whom were presidential candidates. The politicians brought civil proceedings that resulted in the applicant being ordered to pay them compensation and publish an apology. The Court found the interference with the right to freedom of expression to be unjustified, noting[1937] that:

> … the publications contained criticism of the two politicians in strong, polemical, sarcastic language. No doubt the plaintiffs were offended thereby, and may have even been shocked. However, in choosing their profession, they laid themselves open to robust criticism and scrutiny; such is the burden which must be accepted by politicians in a democratic society.

Disproportionate awards of damages or legal costs in defamation proceedings may lead to a finding of a violation of Article 10,[1938] depending on whether or not there are adequate and effective safeguards to ensure there is a reasonable degree of proportionality as between the award and the injury to reputation.[1939]

The applicant journalist in *Oberschlick v Austria*[1940] was convicted of defamation for publishing a criminal information laid against the Secretary-General of the Austrian Liberal Party who had advocated discrimination against immigrant families in relation to family allowances. The Court found that the applicant had contributed to a public debate on an important political question and that a politician who expressed himself in such a way could expect a strong reaction from journalists and the public. The applicant was held not to have exceeded the limits of freedom of expression and there was therefore a violation of Article 10. In *Unabhängige Initiative Informationsvielfalt v Austria*,[1941] the applicant was injuncted from repeating statements that Jorg Haider, the leader of the Austrian Freedom Party, had incited people to 'racist agitation'. This, however, was considered to be fair comment on a matter of public opinion, and a value judgement.[1942] The case of *Perinçek v*

6.585

'the public arena': *Krone Verlag GmbH v Austria*, No. 34315/96, 26.2.02, para. 37. See also *Hrico v Slovakia*, No. 49418/99, 20.7.04; *Lombardo and others v Malta*, No. 7333/06, 24.4.07.

[1934] *Ibid*. See also, e.g. *Lopes Gomes Da Silva v Portugal*, No. 37698/97, 28.9.00, paras. 32–7; *Lindon, Otchakovsky-Laurens and July v France*, Nos. 21279/02 and 36448/02, 22.10.07, para. 56 (concerning a novel relating to Jean-Marie Le Pen and the *Front National*); *Brosa v Germany*, No. 5709/09, 17.4.14, para. 41; *Mladina d.d. Ljubljana v Slovenia*, No. 20981/10, 17.4.14, para. 40.

[1935] *Prager and Oberschlick v Austria*, No. 15974/90, 26.4.95, para. 38; *Lopes Gomes Da Silva v Portugal*, No. 37698/97, 28.9.00, para. 34.

[1936] *Tammer v Estonia*, No. 41205/98, 6.2.01, para. 67. However, 'even offensive language, which may fall outside the protection of freedom of expression if its sole intent is to insult, may be protected by Article 10 when serving merely stylistic purposes' (see, e.g. *Mladina d.d. Ljubljana v Slovenia*, No. 20981/10, 17.4.14, para. 45).

[1937] No. 72713/01, 29.3.05, para. 67. It was also significant that the domestic law failed to distinguish between statements of fact and value judgements.

[1938] See, e.g. *Tolstoy Miloslavsky v UK*, No. 18139/91, 13.7.95; *M.G.N. Limited v UK*, No. 39401/04, 18.1.11.

[1939] *Independent News and Media and Independent Newspapers Ireland Limited v Ireland*, No. 55120/00, 16.6.05, para. 113.

[1940] No. 11662/85, Series A, No. 204, 23.5.91.

[1941] No. 28525/95, 26.2.02.

[1942] See also *Scharsach and News Verlagsgesellschaft v Austria*, No. 39394/98, 13.11.03.

Switzerland[1943] concerned the criminal prosecution of the applicant, the chairman of the Turkish Workers' Party, for denying the Armenian genocide. His statements concerned a matter of public interest, and were entitled to heightened protection under Article 10. Whilst virulent and expressed intransigently, they did not amount to a call for hatred, violence or intolerance towards the Armenians. There had been no particular 'heightened tensions' in Switzerland, and the statements did not affect the dignity of the Armenian community to the point of requiring a criminal law response. Furthermore, there was no obligation in international law for Switzerland to criminalise such statements, the Swiss courts had not adequately sought to assess the proper balance between the applicant's right to freedom of expression and the Armenians' right to the protection of their dignity, and the interference took the serious form of a criminal conviction. Accordingly, the applicant's conviction was found to be disproportionate and in violation of Article 10 (by ten votes to seven).

6.586 The limits of permissible criticism are wider still in relation to the government, which must be subject to the close scrutiny of the press and public. Whilst it may be appropriate for the authorities to invoke criminal sanctions in certain circumstances to achieve the Article 10(2) legitimate aims, the Court has stressed that the government should exercise restraint in resorting to criminal proceedings, in view of its dominant position, and particularly where there are other means of replying to attacks from opponents or in the media.[1944] A series of cases against Turkey, relating to criminal prosecutions resulting from statements concerning the conflict in the south-east of the country, has involved an assessment by the Court of the limits of permissible criticism. The Court has emphasised that one of the principal characteristics of democracy is the possibility it offers of resolving a country's problems through dialogue and without recourse to violence, even when it is 'irksome'. It is also said to be of the essence of democracy to permit various political programmes to be put forward and debated, even those calling into question the way in which the state is organised, provided that they do not damage democracy itself.[1945] In *Sürek* v *Turkey (No. 1)*,[1946] the Court found no violation of Article 10 (by 11 votes to six) resulting from prosecutions relating to articles condemning military activity in south-east Turkey. One article was found to have named individuals and thereby exposed them to risk of physical violence and was considered to amount to hate speech and the glorification of violence.

6.587 Similarly, there was no violation of Article 10 in *Falakaoğlu and Saygılı* v *Turkey*,[1947] which concerned the applicants' convictions for publishing in a newspaper a declaration made by a group of detainees held on charges of belonging to an armed terrorist group, without any additional editorial analysis. The declaration appealed to public opinion to mobilise 'support' for an action to 'demolish' F-type prisons—an action that had already caused violent clashes between detainees and the security forces, leading to the loss of lives. In *Colombani and others* v *France*,[1948] the conviction of the editor-in-chief of *Le Monde*, and a *Le Monde*

[1943] No. 27510/08, 15.10.15.

[1944] See, e.g. *Castells* v *Spain*, No. 11798/85, Series A, No. 236, 23.4.92, para. 46.

[1945] See, e.g. *Ibrahim Aksoy* v *Turkey*, Nos. 28635/95, 30171/96 and 34535/97, 10.10.00.

[1946] No. 26682/95, 8.7.99. See, by contrast, *Yalçınkaya and others* v *Turkey*, No.25764/09 et al, 1.10.13 (conviction for offering mark of respect to leader of PKK, without any propaganda or incitement to acts of violence—violation of Article 10).

[1947] Nos. 22147/02 and 24972/03, 23.1.07.

[1948] No. 51279/99, 25.6.02.

journalist, for insulting a head of state, was found to be disproportionate and in violation of Article 10. Their article concerned the extent of drug production in Morocco, relying on an authoritative official report. It was reasonable for the journalists to have relied on the report without having verified its accuracy. It was also problematic that the domestic law prevented justification from being pleaded (in order to prove the truth of the allegations). The applicant political activist in *Eon* v *France*[1949] was convicted of insulting President Sarkozy, for waving a placard which read 'Casse toi pov'con' ('Get lost, you sad prick')—a phrase which the President had himself used. Taking account of the applicant's use of 'irreverent satire', that the phrase had been used by the President himself which had attracted a lot of media attention, the Court found the authorities' recourse to criminal sanctions was disproportionate and in violation of Article 10. Whilst an interim injunction was found to be justifiable in *Plon (société)* v *France*[1950] in order to prevent publication of a book and thereby protect the medical confidentiality of a recently deceased head of state, a continuing ban some nine months after the death was not 'necessary in a democratic society', not least because 40,000 copies of the book had already been sold and it had been published on the internet. The Court has reiterated that the Convention is likely to be breached where the domestic law provides greater levels of protection to heads of state (for example, through a special law on insults) than other individuals or institutions (such as the government or parliament).[1951]

6.588 There was a violation of Article 10 in *Gaweda* v *Poland*[1952] as a result of the refusal of the authorities to register the applicant's political journals, which accordingly prevented their publication. Registration was refused because the titles of the journals[1953] were said to be 'in conflict with reality'. The Court held that the interpretation of the domestic law by the Polish courts had introduced new criteria that could not have been foreseen from the text, thus failing the 'prescribed by law' requirement.

6.589 Article 10 protects the use of symbols, and other forms of expression, in addition to freedom of speech. For example, in *Vajnai* v *Hungary*[1954] the Court found a violation of Article 10 because of the applicant politician's conviction for wearing a red star at a political demonstration. It was a criminal offence to display symbols that were considered to be 'totalitarian.' The constitutionality of that provision had been upheld by the Constitutional Court, which found that the use of such symbols would offend those committed to democracy, in particular those who had been persecuted by Nazism and Communism. The ban was found to be indiscriminate, in that merely wearing the red star could lead to a criminal sanction, and it had been worn by the applicant, the vice-president of a left wing workers' party, at a lawfully organised, peaceful demonstration.[1955]

[1949] No. 26118/10, 14.3.13.

[1950] No. 58148/00, 18.5.04.

[1951] *Colombani and others* v *France*, No. 51279/99, 25.6.02; *Otegi Mondragon* v *Spain*, No. 2034/07, 15.3.11.

[1952] No. 26229/95, 14.3.02.

[1953] 'Germany—A Thousand Year Old Enemy of Poland' and 'The Social and Political Monthly—A European Moral Tribunal'.

[1954] No. 33629/05, 8.7.08. See also *Fáber* v *Hungary*, No. 40721/08, 24.7.12 (fine for displaying flag with controversial historical connotations in protest against anti-racist demonstration—violation of Article 10).

[1955] By contrast, in *Donaldson* v *UK*, No. 56975/09, dec. 25.1.11, a ban on prisoners in Northern Ireland wearing emblems (which prevented the applicant from wearing an Easter lily in commemoration of Irish republicans who died during the 1916 Easter Rising) was found to be proportionate.

6.590   Free political debate is closely related to, and one of the conditions needed to ensure, the right to free elections. Therefore the free circulation of opinions and information is particularly important prior to an election.[1956] Article 10 was violated in *Bowman v UK*[1957] arising from the rules relating to election expenditure that prevented the applicant from informing the electorate about candidates' views on abortion. Restrictions on political advertising also attract a relatively narrow margin of appreciation (although the Court is wary of the possibility of powerful financial groups obtaining competitive advantage in commercial advertising). A ban in Switzerland on political advertising on television and radio, but not other media, was found to be disproportionate.[1958] However, in the subsequent case of *Animal Defenders International v UK*,[1959] the Grand Chamber was split nine–eight in finding no violation of Article 10 in a comparable case from the UK. The applicant NGO was prevented from broadcasting a campaign relating to the abuse of primates, because of the general statutory ban on political advertising. Therefore, as the restriction was imposed as a result of a 'general measure', the Court underlined that the quality of both the parliamentary and the judicial review of the necessity of the measure were important factors to consider (in assessing whether the legislature acted within its 'margin of appreciation'). The Court found that there had been 'exacting and pertinent reviews',[1960] by both parliamentary and judicial bodies, and that the prohibition was specifically circumscribed in various ways. The lack of European consensus on the issue of political advertising also meant that the state was allowed a wider margin of appreciation, and the Court also took account of the fact that other forms of media were open to the NGO applicant. States are allowed a wide margin of appreciation as to linguistic policies during elections, but the imposition of a blanket ban on the use of any language other than Turkish was found to breach Article 10 in *Şükran Aydın and others v Turkey*.[1961] The applicants were politicians who had been prosecuted for speaking Kurdish during an election campaign, to audiences some of whom would not have been able to understand Turkish.

Public officials and lawyers; whistleblowing

6.591   Where the freedom of expression of public servants is in issue, the court will carefully consider the extent of their 'duties and responsibilities' that assume a 'special significance'.[1962] The Court will attempt to strike a fair balance between the rights of the individual and the interests of the state in ensuring the functioning of the civil service.[1963] Civil servants, including

---

[1956]   See, e.g. *Bowman v UK*, No. 24839/94, 4.12.95, para. 42.

[1957]   No. 24839/94, 4.12.95.

[1958]   *Vgt Verein Gegen Tierfabriken v Switzerland*, No. 24699/94, 28.6.01and *Verein Gegen Tierfabriken Schweiz (VgT) v Switzerland (No. 2)*, No. 32772/02, 30.6.09. See also *TV Vest As & Rogaland Pensjonistparti v Norway*, No. 21132/05, 11.12.08—breach of Article 10 because of the imposition of a fine on a television station for having broadcast a political party's advertisement, in breach of the statutory prohibition of any televised political advertising.

[1959]   No. 48876/08, 22.4.13.

[1960]   *Ibid.*, para. 116.

[1961]   No. 49197/06, 22.1.13. See also *Semir Güzel v Turkey*, No. 29483/09, 13.9.16 (prosecution of politician for failing to prevent political meeting being held in Kurdish—violation of Article 10).

[1962]   See, e.g. *Ahmed and others v UK*, No. 22954/93, 12.9.95, para. 61 (local government officers); *Glasenapp v Germany*, No. 9228/80, Series A, No. 104, 28.8.86 and *Kosiek v Germany*, No. 9704/82, Series A, No. 105, 28.8.86 (teachers); *De Diego Nafría v Spain*, No. 46833/99, 14.3.02 (employees of national bank).

[1963]   *Vogt v Germany*, No. 17851/91, Series A, No. 323, 26.9.95, para. 53. See also *Otto v Germany*, No. 27574/02, dec. 24.11.05; *Kern v Germany*, No. 26870/04, dec. 29.5.07; *Karapetyan and others v Armenia*, No. 59001/08, 17.11.16.

judges, public prosecutors[1964] and the police,[1965] should enjoy public confidence and it may therefore be necessary to protect them from 'offensive and abusive verbal attacks'.[1966] The Court has also held that any interference with the freedom of expression of a member of the legal service, such as a prosecutor, will require close scrutiny, because of the chilling effect that such measures could have on the wider profession.[1967]

However, the Court has also acknowledged that civil servants acting in an official capacity **6.592** are subject to wider limits of acceptable criticism than ordinary citizens,[1968] and the Court has reiterated that, even in the face of insults, 'civil servants have a duty to exercise their powers by reference to professional considerations only, without being unduly influenced by personal feelings'.[1969] Inevitably, in view of the conflict involved between the right to impart information and the protection of the reputation or rights of others, some cases can be very difficult to call. For example, in *Pedersen and Baadsgaard v Denmark*, by a majority of nine to eight, the Grand Chamber found no violation of Article 10 arising from the applicant television journalists' convictions for defamation, following their criticisms of the police's handling of a murder investigation.[1970]

The Court has held that 'whistleblowing' both in the private sector,[1971] and by a public offi- **6.593** cial, may be protected by Article 10:[1972]

> ... the signalling by a civil servant or an employee in the public sector of illegal conduct or wrongdoing in the workplace should, in certain circumstances, enjoy protection. This may be called for where the employee or civil servant concerned is the only person, or part of a small category of persons, aware of what is happening at work and is thus best placed to act in the public interest by alerting the employer or the public at large.

In *Guja v Moldova*,[1973] the Court noted that civil servants often have access to information **6.594** that governments may legitimately want to keep confidential, and accordingly they owe a duty of discretion to their employers. Therefore, disclosure should first be made to a superior,

---

[1964] See, e.g. *Rizos and Daskas v Greece*, No. 65545/01, 27.5.04.

[1965] See, e.g. *Pedersen and Baadsgaard v Denmark*, No. 49017/99, 17.12.04; *Stângu and Scutelnicu v Romania*, No. 53899/00, 31.1.06; *Coutant v France*, No. 17155/03, dec. 24.1.08.

[1966] *Janowski v Poland*, No. 25716/94, 21.1.99, para. 33.

[1967] See, e.g. *Kayasu v Turkey*, Nos. 64119/00 and 76292/01, 13.11.08.

[1968] See, e.g. *Mamère v France*, No. 12697/03, 7.11.06.

[1969] *Yankov v Bulgaria*, No. 39084/97, 11.12.03, para. 142.

[1970] No. 49017/99, 17.12.04. The majority emphasised the following factors: that the accusation against a named police officer (of deliberately suppressing vital evidence) was an allegation of fact susceptible of proof; it was very serious and would have resulted in prosecution had it been true (punishable with up to nine years' imprisonment); the applicants did not seek to provide any justification for their allegation; the applicants were themselves the authors of the allegations—they were not convicted for reproducing or reporting the statements of others; the allegation was made at peak viewing time on national television; the audiovisual media often have a much more immediate and powerful effect than the print media; the applicants placed undue reliance upon the statement of one witness and the majority were critical of the applicants' assessment of the evidence generally; there was no reason to doubt the Supreme Court's finding that the applicants lacked a sufficient factual basis for the allegation; and the penalties imposed on the applicants (orders for the payment of fines and compensation) were not excessive. By contrast, in arguing in favour of a violation the eight dissenting judges emphasised the importance of the work of senior police officers being subject to close and rigorous scrutiny by the press.

[1971] *Heinisch v Germany*, No. 28274/08, 21.7.11.

[1972] *Guja v Moldova*, No. 14277/04, 12.2.08, para. 72.

[1973] No. 14277/04, 12.2.08. See also *Marchenko v Ukraine*, No. 4063/04, 19.2.09 (schoolteacher who made allegations against school director).

or other competent authority, and, where that is impracticable, it should only be made public as a last resort. The assessment of proportionality of such a disclosure will depend upon the public interest in the information and its authenticity, the damage to the public authority caused by disclosure, the motive of the 'whistleblower' and the nature of any penalty imposed. The Grand Chamber in *Guja* unanimously found a violation of Article 10 as a result of the dismissal of the head of press at the prosecutor-general's office for disclosing to the national press two letters from MPs to the prosecutor-general relating to investigations into police malpractice. There was no domestic provision for the reporting of irregularities by someone in the applicant's position. The disclosure was found to raise important questions about the separation of powers, improper conduct by a high-ranking politician and the Government's attitude towards police brutality. The Court also concluded that the public interest in having information revealed about wrongdoing within the prosecutor's office was so important that it outweighed the interest in maintaining public confidence in that office. The applicant had acted in good faith and, by being dismissed, had had the heaviest sanction imposed on him. The case of *Bucur and Toma* v *Romania*[1974] concerned the criminal prosecution of an employee of the Romanian Intelligence Service after he publicised information concerning irregular telephone tapping practices. Such a measure was found to be disproportionate and in violation of Article 10 due to the following factors: there was no other official means for the applicant to impart the information; there was a high public interest in it; the applicant had had reasonable grounds to believe that the information he divulged was true; the importance of the information prevailed over any countervailing interest in maintaining public confidence in the intelligence service; and the absence of any reason to question the applicant's *bona fides*. There was a violation of Article 10 in *Heinisch* v *Germany*[1975] as a result of the dismissal without notice of a geriatric nurse after she had lodged a criminal complaint alleging shortcomings in the care provided by the nursing home where she worked (as a result of staff shortages). The following factors were held to be relevant: that there was a public interest in the disclosure (outweighing the interests of the state-owned company which ran the home); her previous complaints to her employer had not led to improvements; the allegations were authentic and made in good faith; and she was subjected to the most severe sanction (dismissal).

6.595 The case of *Kudeshkina* v *Russia*[1976] concerned the applicant judge's removal from office, after she made statements in the media criticising the Russian judiciary. Her criticisms were based in part on her removal from a criminal case against a police investigator by the President of the Moscow City Court, allegedly as a result of external pressure. The Court found that there was a factual basis to such complaints as 'confidential reports by relevant agencies' were acknowledged by the authorities to have influenced the decision to remove her from the case. The Court reiterated that the duty of loyalty and discretion owed by civil servants (especially the judiciary) required that the dissemination even of accurate information must be carried out with 'moderation and propriety'. The applicant's statements were not found to amount to a gratuitous personal attack but were considered by the Court to be fair comment on a matter of great public importance. The Court also took account

---

[1974] No. 40238/02, 8.1.13.
[1975] No. 28274/08, 21.7.11. See, by contrast, *Langner* v *Germany*, No. 14464/11, 17.9.15 (applicant's criticism of deputy mayor found to be motivated by personal misgivings—it was therefore not a 'whistle-blowing' case—no violation of Article 10).
[1976] No. 29492/05, 26.2.09.

of the fact that the disciplinary proceedings against the applicant were conducted by the Moscow City Court, in spite of her justifiable fears of its lack of impartiality, and that the penalty imposed on her was severe—removal from judicial office, and of any possibility of exercising the profession of judge. As a result, the Court held, by a majority of four votes to three, that there had been a violation of Article 10. The applicant in *Baka* v *Hungary*[1977] complained that his mandate as President of the Supreme Court had been terminated prematurely, after he had spoken out against proposed legislative reforms relating to the judiciary. The Grand Chamber found that the decision neither had a legitimate aim and nor was it proportionate, in breach of Article 10. Noting that the applicant's duties included expressing his views on the legislative reforms which were likely to have an impact on the judiciary and its independence, the Court also took account of the fact that he had been removed from office three and a half years before the end of his term, and that there were insufficient safeguards to prevent abuse.

The Court has reiterated that lawyers are entitled to comment in public on the administra- **6.596** tion of justice, provided that their criticism does not overstep certain bounds, although different considerations apply to comments made in the courtroom, and those made outside.[1978] The particular position of lawyers was highlighted by the case of *Nikula* v *Finland*[1979] in which the applicant was convicted of defamation for criticising (in her capacity as defence counsel) the public prosecutor's decision to press charges against a witness, and thereby preventing her client from being able to examine him. In finding a violation of Article 10, the Court stated that it would be 'only in exceptional cases that restriction—even by way of a lenient criminal sanction—of defence counsel's freedom of expression can be accepted as necessary in a democractic society'. It also said that 'while lawyers too are certainly entitled to comment in public on the administration of justice, their criticism must not overstep certain bounds'. In such cases, the Court will seek to strike a balance between the public's right to receive information about questions arising from judicial decisions, the requirements of the proper administration of justice and the dignity of the legal profession. In *Nikula*, the Court found that although some of the terms used by the lawyer were inappropriate, her criticisms were strictly limited to the performance of the public prosecutor in the case, they were made in the court room (as opposed to being made directly to the media) and they did not involve personal insult. The Court also commented that an interference with a defence lawyer's freedom of expression in the course of a trial could raise an issue in respect of the defendant's Article 6 rights. There was also a violation of Article 10 in *Bono* v *France*[1980] where a disciplinary penalty was imposed on the applicant, in his capacity as defence counsel, for accusing an investigating judge of complicity in torture. The applicant represented a terrorism suspect arrested in Syria. Various case documents were obtained, after the judge travelled to Syria, which included records of interview, which the applicant

---

[1977] No. 20261/12, 23.6.16. There was also a violation of the applicant's right of access to court under Article 6(1).

[1978] *Morice* v *France*, No. 29369/10, 23.4.15, paras.132–9, 148.

[1979] No. 31611/96, 21.3.02. See also *Steur* v *Netherlands*, No. 39657/98, 8.10.03; *Kyprianou* v *Cyprus*, No. 73797/01, 15.12.05; *Foglia* v *Switzerland*, No. 35865/04, 13.12.07; *Reznik* v *Russia*, No. 4977/05, 4.4.13. See by contrast *Schmidt* v *Austria*, No. 513/05, 17.7.08 (lawyer subject to written reprimand—no violation); *Furuholmen* v *Norway*, No. 53349/08, dec. 18.3.10 (defence counsel fined for disclosing inadmissible trial evidence to press—inadmissible); *Peruzzi* v *Italy*, No. 39294/09, 30.6.15 (lawyer's defamation conviction for criticism of judge outside courtroom—no violation of Article 10).

[1980] No. 29024/11, 15.12.15.

claimed were obtained under torture by the Syrian security services. His application to have this evidence excluded was granted, but his client was found guilty. He was subsequently issued with a reprimand and disqualified from professional bodies for five years, because of his allegations against the judge. The Court found that the disciplinary sanction did not strike a fair balance in the context of the proper administration of justice, noting in particular that the remarks had been made in written submissions (and had therefore not left the courtroom) with the aim of excluding the statements in question made under torture, which had been accepted by the national courts. However, in *Lesnik v Lithuania*,[1981] there was no violation of Article 10 as a result of the applicant businessman's conviction for making allegations about a public prosecutor of unlawful and abusive conduct. Such allegations were found to be statements of fact (rather than value judgements) that were not justified by the available evidence. Judges Bratza and Maruste dissented on the basis that the applicant's criticisms were not made publicly, but in two letters to the prosecutor himself and the General Prosecutor. There was a violation of Article 10 in *Mor v France*[1982] where the applicant lawyer received a criminal conviction for commenting to the press about a confidential expert report (prepared in the course of a criminal investigation) which had already become publicly available.

Public protest

6.597 Linked to political speech is expression in the form of public protest or demonstration that will also engage Article 10. For example, in the case of *Karademirci and others v Turkey*,[1983] the applicants were members of a health workers' union who held a press conference outside a school and read out a statement protesting about the ill-treatment of pupils. As a consequence they were prosecuted and convicted under legislation that imposed conditions and prior formalities on 'publishing or distributing leaflets, written statements and similar publications'. The Court found Article 10 to have been violated as the authorities had extended the scope of the criminal law to the applicants in a way that could not have been foreseen. The Court acknowledged that the exercise of freedom of expression may be made subject to compliance with particular formalities, but emphasised that where a failure to comply with a formal procedure amounts to a criminal offence, the law must clearly define the circumstances in which it will apply. In *Kandzhov v Bulgaria*,[1984] the applicant's arrest for committing offences of insult and hooliganism during a political demonstration breached Article 10 both because it was not 'prescribed by law' and it was disproportionate. According to the domestic law, charges of 'insult' could not justify being detained. He had been accused of hooliganism on the basis that he had gathered signatures calling for the resignation of the Minister of Justice and displayed posters describing him as a 'top idiot', however, the Supreme Court found that such actions did not amount to the constituent elements of the offence of hooliganism. As to the question of proportionality, the Court noted that the applicant's actions had been entirely peaceful, did not obstruct any passers-by and were not likely to provoke others to violence. It was also relevant that he was detained in custody for nearly four days before being taken before a judge (who ordered his release).

[1981] No. 35640/97, 11.3.03. See also *Perna v Italy*, No. 48898/99, 6.5.03; *Belpietro v Italy*, No. 43612/10, 24.9.13.
[1982] No. 28198/09, 15.12.11.
[1983] Nos. 37096/97 and 37101/96, 25.1.05.
[1984] No. 68294/01, 6.11.08.

The applicants in *Steel and Morris* v *UK*,[1985] were members of a small campaigning organisa- **6.598**
tion, 'London Greenpeace', who were sued for defamation by McDonald's, after distributing leaflets that were highly critical of the company's practices. The Court found Article
10 to have been violated because of the lack of procedural fairness (the denial of legal aid
had resulted in a violation of Article 6—see 6.317 above) and the disproportionate award
of damages, which were substantial in comparison to the applicants' incomes. By contrast,
there was no violation of Article 10 in *PETA Deutschland* v *Germany*[1986] in which an injunction was obtained by the Central Jewish Council in Germany against the applicant animal
rights association's poster campaign entitled 'The Holocaust on your Plate', which featured
photos of concentration camp inmates alongside pictures of animals kept in mass stocks. It
was acknowledged that the campaign was in the public interest, however, the ban was found
to be a proportionate measure. The case had been carefully examined by the domestic courts
which had found that the campaign had confronted the plaintiffs with their suffering and
persecution in the interest of animal protection and that this 'instrumentalisation' of their
suffering had violated their personality rights in their capacity as Jews living in Germany
and as survivors of the Holocaust. The Court also noted that a reference to the Holocaust
had to be seen in the specific context of the German past, and it accepted the Government's
position that they considered themselves under a special obligation towards Jews living
in Germany.

The case of *Steel and others* v *UK*[1987] concerned various forms of peaceful protest against a **6.599**
grouse shoot, a motorway extension and outside a fighter helicopter conference. Rejecting
the Government's argument that Article 10 was not applicable because the protests were
not peaceful, the Court found that although the applicants had physically impeded the
activities of which they disapproved, they nonetheless constituted expressions of opinion
within the meaning of Article 10. Three of the applicants had been protesting against the
sale of fighter helicopters by handing out leaflets and holding up a banner that said: 'Work
for peace and not war'. They were arrested on the basis that their conduct was likely to cause
a breach of the peace and they were held for about seven hours. Subsequent proceedings
against them were withdrawn by the magistrates when no evidence was produced. The
Court found a violation of their right to freedom of expression as there were no reasonable grounds for the police to believe that the applicants' peaceful protest would cause a
breach of the peace. Accordingly, their arrest and detention had not been 'necessary in
a democratic society'. It was held to be disproportionate to fine the applicants in *Tatár
and Fáber* v *Hungary*,[1988] for their symbolic protest which involved hanging items of dirty
laundry on a fence outside the parliament building in Budapest. Given that the protest
had only involved the two applicants, for a few minutes, it had not been justified for the
authorities to classify it as an 'assembly' which under the relevant domestic law required
prior notification (which the applicants had not provided). Article 10 was breached in
Shvydka v *Ukraine*,[1989] where the applicant, an opposition politician, was sentenced to ten
days' detention for publicly detaching part of a ribbon from a wreath laid by the Ukrainian
President at a commemorative ceremony. There was a disproportionate interference with

---

[1985] No. 68416/01, 15.2.05.
[1986] No. 43481/09, 8.11.12.
[1987] No. 24838/94, 23.9.98.
[1988] Nos. 26005/08 and 26160/08, 12.6.12.
[1989] No. 17888/12, 30.10.14.

the applicants' Article 10 rights in *Women on Waves and others* v *Portugal*.[1990] The association *Women on Waves*, which campaigned for reproductive rights, chartered a ship and set sail for Portugal where they planned to campaign for the decriminalisation of abortion. However, the ship was banned by a Portuguese ministerial order and blocked by a warship. There was, however, no evidence that the applicants would have breached Portuguese law on abortion, and the authorities could have taken other less drastic measures with the aim of preventing disorder or protecting health.

6.600   The Court will give particular scrutiny to cases where imprisonment is imposed by the authorities for non-violent conduct. Thus in *Taranenko* v *Russia*[1991] the Court found the authorities' response disproportionate where the applicant was arrested during a demonstration in the building of the President's Administration, charged with mass disorder, remanded in custody for a year and given a three year suspended prison sentence.

6.601   The case of *Appleby and others* v *UK*[1992] concerned a ban on environmental protestors leafletting members of the public in a privately owned area of a town centre that was open to the public, raising questions about the extent of the positive obligations on the state. The Court noted the trend in US case law to accommodate freedom of expression in privately owned property that was open to the public, and stated that it would not exclude that a positive obligation could arise for the state to protect the enjoyment of Convention rights by regulating property rights, citing the example of 'the corporate town, where the entire municipality was controlled by a private body'.[1993] However, as the applicants were prevented from leafletting in a particular limited area of the town, and, as there were other means available to them to express their views to the public, the Government was not considered to have failed in its positive obligations to protect the applicants' freedom of expression. It is suggested that this was a decision that fails to take sufficient account of the restrictions placed on fundamental rights caused by the ever-increasing privatisation of public space. Indeed, in his partly dissenting opinion, Judge Maruste argued that 'the property rights of the owners of the shopping mall were unnecessarily given priority over the applicants' freedom of expression and assembly'. The circumstances of the case of *Mouvement raëlien suisse* v *Switzerland*,[1994] concerning a ban on the applicant association's poster campaign, were distinguished by the Grand Chamber from the *Appleby* case on the basis that it did not relate to a general ban, but a ban on the use of regulated and supervised facilities in public space. The aim of the association was to establish good relations with extraterrestrials and the Court found that the proselytising function of its posters meant that its form of expression was closer to commercial than political speech, and accordingly the state had a wider margin of appreciation. By a majority of nine votes to eight, the Grand Chamber found the restrictions to be justified, concurring with the conclusions drawn by the domestic courts that the ban was proportionate because the posters displayed the association's website which promoted human cloning and 'geniocracy', and in the light of accusations against certain of the association's members of sexual abuse of minors. However, seven of the dissenting judges were concerned that the

---

[1990] No. 31276/05, 3.2.09.
[1991] No. 19554/05, 15.5.14. See also, e.g. *Yılmaz and Kılıç* v *Turkey*, No. 68514/01, 17.7.08; *Barraco* v *France*, No. 31684/05, 5.3.09.
[1992] No. 44306/98, 6.5.03. See also *Anderson and others* v *UK*, No. 33689/96, dec. 27.10.97.
[1993] See *Marsh* v *Alabama* 326 US 501, 66 S Ct 276, 90 L Ed 265 (1946).
[1994] No. 16354/06, 13.7.12.

majority Court had justified the ban 'indirectly', on the basis of the contents of the association's website.[1995]

The media

The importance of freedom of speech of the media is referred to in the introductory section above (see 6.573). The Court has acknowledged the importance of the internet in the exercise of freedom of expression.[1996] Prior restraint of the media will require particular justification,[1997] and measures such as interim injunctions will be carefully scrutinised by the Court as they necessitate suitable procedural safeguards to prevent arbitrary encroachments upon freedom of expression.[1998] Orders requiring the disclosure of journalists' sources (or material containing information capable of identifying journalistic sources)[1999] must be justified by an overriding requirement in the public interest.[2000] The Court has emphasised[2001] that disclosure orders: **6.602**

> … have a detrimental impact not only on the source in question, whose identity may be revealed, but also on the newspaper against which the order is directed, whose reputation may be negatively affected in the eyes of future potential sources by the disclosure, and on the members of the public, who have an interest in receiving information imparted through anonymous sources and who are also potential sources themselves.

In *Sanoma Uitgevers B.V. v Netherlands*,[2002] the Grand Chamber assessed the police seizure of a CD-ROM containing photographs of illegal street racing taken by journalists for a car magazine, owned by the applicant company. The basis for the seizure was the Code of Criminal Procedure; however, the quality of the domestic law was not considered sufficient to pass the 'prescribed by law' test. The Court emphasised that orders requiring journalists to disclose their sources must be subject to the guarantee of review by a judge or other independent and impartial decision-making body. That was not the case in the Netherlands, **6.603**

[1995] See the joint dissenting opinion of Judges Tulkens, Sajó, Lazarova Trajkovska, Bianku, Power-Forde, Vučinić and Yudkivska. There were also separate dissenting opinions from Judges Sajó, Lazarova Trajkovska and Vučinić, and from Judge Pinto de Albuquerque.

[1996] *Fatullayev v Azerbaijan*, No. 40984/07, 22.4.10, para. 95; *Ahmet Yıldırım v Turkey*, No. 3111/10, 18.12.12, para. 48, and para. 54: '… the Internet has now become one of the principal means by which individuals exercise their right to freedom of expression and information, providing as it does essential tools for participation in activities and discussions concerning political issues and issues of general interest'. See also *Akdeniz v Turkey*, No. 20877/10, dec. 11.3.14 (application by internet user concerning measures blocking access to internet music providers—inadmissible); *Kalda v Estonia*, No. 17429/10, 19.1.16 (restrictions on prisoner's access to internet sites—violation of Article 10); *Jankovskis v Lithuania*, No. 21575/08, 17.1.17 (restriction on prisoner's access to internet site providing educational information—violation of Article 10).

[1997] See, e.g. *Observer and Guardian v UK*, No. 13585/88, 26.11.91; *Ekin Association v France*, No. 39288/98, 17.7.01, paras. 56–7; *Mosley v UK*, No. 48009/08, 10.5.11, para. 117; *Ahmet Yıldırım v Turkey*, No. 3111/10. 18.12.12, para. 64.

[1998] See, e.g. *Cumhuriyet Vakfı and others v Turkey*, No. 28255/07, 8.10.13, para. 61.

[1999] See, e.g. *Sanoma Uitgevers B.V. v Netherlands*, No. 38224/03, 14.9.10.

[2000] *Goodwin v UK*, No. 17488/90, 27.3.96, para. 39; *Voskuil v Netherlands*, No. 64752/01, 22.11.07, para. 65; *Tillack v Belgium*, No. 20477/05, 27.11.07, para. 53; *Financial Times Ltd and others v UK*, No. 821/03, 15.12.09, para. 59. See also *Roemen and Schmit v Luxembourg*, No. 51772/99, 25.2.03 (where the Court stated that a search undertaken with a view to finding out a journalist's source was even more intrusive than an order for the disclosure of a source's identity); *Saint-Paul Luxembourg S.A. v Luxembourg*, No. 26419/10, 18.4.13; *Nagla v Latvia*, No. 73469/10, 16.7.13.

[2001] *Financial Times Ltd and others v UK*, No. 821/03, 15.12.09, para. 63.

[2002] No. 38224/03, 14.9.10. See also *Görmüş and others v Turkey*, No. 49085/07, 19.1.16 (search and seizure operation to identify journalistic source of military documents classified as confidential—violation of Article 10).

where the decision was made by the public prosecutor. The Grand Chamber reiterated the following requirements for such a review:

(1) there must be a weighing of the potential risks and respective interests prior to any disclosure and with reference to the material that it is sought to have disclosed so that the arguments of the authorities seeking the disclosure can be properly assessed;

(2) the review should be governed by clear criteria, including whether a less intrusive measure may be sufficient;

(3) it should be possible for the judge or other authority to refuse to make a disclosure order or to make a limited or qualified order so as to protect sources from being revealed, whether or not they are specifically named in the withheld material, on the grounds that the communication of such material creates a serious risk of compromising the identity of journalists' sources;

(4) in urgent situations, there should be a procedure to identify and isolate, prior to the exploitation of the material by the authorities, information that could lead to the identification of sources from information that carries no such risk.[2003]

6.604 At issue in *Telegraaf Media Nederland Landelijke Media B.V. and others* v *Netherlands*[2004] was the use of surveillance powers by the Netherlands secret services to circumvent the protection of journalistic sources, after the applicant company published newspaper articles alleging that information on pending investigations by the secret services into drugs and arms dealings had fallen into criminal hands. Those powers had been exercised without prior review by an independent body with the capability of preventing or terminating them. Accordingly, the Court found that the domestic law did not provide adequate safeguards, in breach of both Articles 8 and 10. Furthermore, the order imposed on the company to surrender the documents in question was also held to violate Article 10. The Court found that there was no overriding requirement in the public interest to justify the disclosure of the applicant's journalistic source—not even by the need to identify the secret services official who had leaked the documents.

6.605 The Court has acknowledged the importance of the role played by investigative journalism, and that journalists will be inhibited if they run the risk of imprisonment. The case of *Cumpănă and Mazăre* v *Romania*[2005] concerned the applicant journalists' convictions for insult and defamation of a city council official. The Court found that the authorities had been justified in bringing proceedings to protect the official's reputation and dignity; nevertheless, Article 10 was violated in view of the severity of the sanctions imposed: imprisonment and a ban from working as journalists for a year.

6.606 The Court has also frequently reiterated that the exercise of media freedom (including in relation to matters of serious public concern) involves 'duties and responsibilities', in particular where it may affect the reputation of private individuals.[2006] The Court has

---

[2003] *Sanoma Uitgevers B.V.* v *Netherlands*, No. 38224/03, 14.9.10, para. 92.

[2004] No. 39315/06, 22.11.12.

[2005] No. 33748, 17.12.04.

[2006] See, e.g. *Bladet Tromsø and Stensaas* v *Norway*, No. 21980/93, 20.5.99, para. 65; *Selistö* v *Finland*, No. 56767/00, 16.11.04, para. 54; *Flux* v *Moldova (No. 6)*, No. 22824/04, 29.7.08, para. 26. See also *A* v *Norway*, No. 28070/06, 9.4.09 (publication in newspaper articles of information in which applicant could be perceived as prime suspect in murder case—violation of Article 8); *Björk Eiðsdóttir* v *Iceland*, No. 46443/09, 10.7.12 (award of damages against journalist for publishing interview with strip dancer accusing her former employer of criminal conduct—violation of Article 10).

emphasised that the 'safeguard afforded by Article 10 to journalists in relation to reporting on issues of general interest is subject to the proviso that they are acting in good faith in order to provide accurate and reliable information in accordance with the ethics of journalism'.[2007] For example, the case of *Standard Verlagsgesellschaft mbH (No. 2) v Austria*[2008] related to an injunction restraining a newspaper from printing defamatory material purportedly based on an expert opinion. However, the Court found that the article in question had in fact wrongly cited the expert opinion, as the newspaper had relied on a press release from a political party that had summarised the opinion incorrectly. Accordingly, the Court held there was no violation of Article 10 (by four votes to three). There was also no violation of Article 10 in *Rumyana Ivanova v Bulgaria*[2009] which concerned the applicant journalist's conviction for defamation of a politician having made unsubstantiated allegations of fact. The case of *Leroy v France*[2010] concerned convictions for condoning terrorism as a result of the publication in a newspaper of a cartoonist's sketch of the attack on the Twin Towers of the World Trade Center in September 2001, together with a parody of an advertising slogan: 'We have all dreamt of it. Hamas did it.' The Court found no violation of Article 10 on the basis that the cartoonists's intention had not merely been to criticise American imperialism, but also to support and glorify its violent destruction. The Court concluded that the applicant had expressed his moral support for, and solidarity with, the perpetrators of the attacks, demonstrated approval of the violence, and undermined the dignity of the victims.

6.607 The applicant newspaper editor in *Wizerkaniuk v Poland*[2011] was convicted for failing to obtain prior authorisation from an MP to publish the verbatim record of an interview which had been conducted with him. In finding a violation of Article 10, the Court noted that the conviction was upheld purely on the basis of the failure to obtain the interviewee's consent, and was regardless of the substance of the article published. It was not disputed that the article contained no distortions or inaccuracies. The Court found that the domestic law gave 'interviewees *carte blanche* to prevent a journalist from publishing any interview they regard as embarrassing or unflattering, regardless of how truthful or accurate it is'.[2012]

6.608 The Court has underlined the valuable role of media internet archives in preserving and making available news and information, and as constituting an important source for education and historical research. However, states will be afforded a wider margin of appreciation in relation to such news archives:[2013]

[2007] See, e.g. *Standard Verlagsgesellschaft mbH (No. 2) v Austria*, No. 37464/02, 22.2.07, para. 38.

[2008] No. 37464/02, 22.2.07.

[2009] No. 36207/03, 14.2.08.

[2010] No. 36109/03, 2.10.08 (the case was declared admissible, but the Court found no violation of Article 10).

[2011] No. 18990/05, 5.7.11.

[2012] *Ibid.*, para. 81.

[2013] *Times Newspapers Ltd (Nos. 1 and 2) v UK*, Nos. 3002/03 and 23676/03, 10.3.09, para. 45. The Court held in that case that there was no violation of Article 10 as a result of the application of a common law rule that a new cause of action accrues every time defamatory material on the internet is accessed. The Court concluded that the requirement to publish an appropriate qualification to an article contained in an internet archive, where a libel action has been initiated in respect of the same article published in the written press, did not amount to a disproportionate interference with the right to freedom of expression. See also *Węgrzynowski and Smolczewski v Poland*, No. 33846/07, 16.7.13 (court's refusal to order newspaper to remove article damaging applicant's reputation from its internet archive—no violation of Article 8).

> … the duty of the press to act in accordance with the principles of responsible journalism by ensuring the accuracy of historical, rather than perishable, information published is likely to be more stringent in the absence of any urgency in publishing the material.

6.609 In assessing the duties and responsibilities of journalists, the Court recognises that the audio-visual media often have a much more immediate and powerful effect than the print media.[2014] This was a relevant factor in the Court's finding of no violation of Article 10 in *Murphy* v *Ireland*.[2015] There, the ban on the broadcasting of an advertisement submitted by the applicant, a pastor of the Irish Faith Centre, was found to be justifiable in view of the sensitivity concerning religious advertisements in Ireland and the state's wide margin of appreciation in that area.[2016]

6.610 The Court has held that there will have to be particularly strong reasons for punishing journalists for assisting in disseminating the statements of others.[2017] In *Jersild* v *Denmark*,[2018] the applicant was prosecuted and convicted after making a television documentary about self-proclaimed racist youths. The Court found that the applicant had not intended to propagate racist ideas, but to raise an issue of important public concern: news reporting based on interviews was said to be one of the most important means of fulfilling the public watchdog role of the press. Despite the low level of the fine, the fact that the applicant was convicted was disproportionate and was found to have violated Article 10 (by 12 votes to seven) (see also the effect of Article 17 above at 5.32).

6.611 The case of *Editorial Board of Pravoye Delo and Shtekel* v *Ukraine*[2019] concerned defamation proceedings brought against a newspaper as a result of its publication of a letter which had been taken verbatim from a news website. The Court found a violation of Article 10, because, unlike the position as regards the publication of items taken fron the press, there were no safeguards in the domestic law to protect journalists who had published material taken from internet sources. Furthermore, the decision of the domestic court, in the course of defamation proceedings, to order the applicants to publish an apology was found not to be 'prescribed by law' and therefore in violation of Article 10, as the domestic law did not provide for such a measure to be taken. The failure of the domestic court to give adequate reasons for the closure of a newspaper led to a finding of a violation of Article 10 in *Kommersant Moldovy* v *Moldova*.[2020] Following the publication of a series of articles that were highly critical of the Moldovan authorities over its policy towards the break away Moldavian Republic of Transdniestria, the court cited national security reasons as the basis for the closure. However, the European Court was critical of the failure to identify specific passages that were problematic or to explain how they endangered national security.

[2014] See, e.g. *Jersild* v *Denmark*, No. 15890/8, Series A, No. 298, 23.9.94, para. 31.
[2015] No. 44179/98, 10.7.03.
[2016] For a critical analysis of this decision (comparing it with the Court's decision in *Vgt Verein Gegen Tierfabriken* v *Switzerland*, No. 24699/94, 28.6.01) see: A. Geddis, 'You Can't Say "God" on the Radio: Freedom of Expression, Religious Advertising and the Broadcast Media after Murphy v Ireland' [2004] EHRLR 181.
[2017] See, e.g. *Thoma* v *Luxembourg*, No. 38432/97, 29.3.01; *Björk Eiðsdóttir* v *Iceland*, No. 46443/09, 10.7.12.
[2018] No. 15890/8, Series A, No. 298, 23.9.94. See, by contrast, *Pedersen and Baadsgaard* v *Denmark*, No. 49017/99, 17.12.04.
[2019] No. 33014/05, 5.5.11.
[2020] No. 41827/02, 9.1.07.

In *Fatullayev* v *Azerbaijan*,[2021] the Court underlined that seeking historical truth is an integral **6.612** part of freedom of expression. There, the applicant newspaper editor was the subject of both criminal and civil proceedings as a result of his articles (in print and postings on the internet) relating to a massacre committed during the conflict over Nagorno-Karabakh. The Court emphasised that it is essential in a democratic society that a debate on the causes of acts that may amount to war crimes or crimes against humanity should be able to take place freely. Although the applicant had been critical of elements of the Azerbaijani military, he had not directly accused them of committing war crimes. The Court also did not consider justified the domestic court's finding that the applicant had defamed civilian refugees of the massacre or former soldiers (who had brought proceedings against him). Taking account of the role of the press as a 'public watchdog', whilst finding that the applicant had made exaggerated or provocative assertions, the Court found that he had not crossed the limits of journalistic freedom in performing his duty to impart information on matters of general interest. The sentence of two and a half years' imprisonment was considered to be 'very severe'. There was a second violation of Article 10 because of the applicant's separate conviction on charges of threat of terrorism and incitement to ethnic hostility, and his sentence of eight years' imprisonment, resulting from an article critical of the Government concerning international politics relating to US–Iranian relations. The Court found that the domestic courts had failed to provide any relevant reasons for the conviction. Invoking Article 46, the Court went on to order the state to secure the applicant's immediate release. The importance of the search for historical truth was also an integral part of the Court's reasoning in *Dink* v *Turkey*,[2022] where the Court found a violation of Article 10 as a result of journalist Hrant Dink's conviction for denigrating Turkish identity, after writing articles about Turkish–Armenian relations, including the Armenian genocide. The authorities had furthermore failed to protect him against known threats made by ultra-nationalist extremists, which led to a finding of a violation of the positive obligations under Article 10 (as well as violations of Article 2).

Various cases concerning freedom of expression via the internet have been considered by **6.613** the Court. The applicant in *Ahmet Yıldırım* v *Turkey*[2023] complained that he was unable to access his website (set up on the Google Sites website) on which he published his own academic articles. Access had been prevented because of a court order issued in the course of criminal proceedings concerning an unrelated website, which ordered the blocking of all access to Google Sites. Such a restriction was found not to be 'prescribed by law' under Article 10 because it was not sufficiently foreseeable. The Court noted that neither the applicant's website, nor Google Sites had been the subject of legal proceedings, and the relevant law did not provide for the wholesale blocking of access to an entire internet domain: 'the judicial review of such a measure ... is inconceivable without a framework establishing precise and specific rules regarding the application of preventive restrictions on freedom of

---

[2021] No. 40984/07, 22.4.10.

[2022] No. 2668/07, 14.9.10. See also *Altuğ Taner Akçam* v *Turkey*, No 27520/07, 25.10.11. There, the opening of a criminal investigation against the applicant (which was not, however, pursued) together with a linked public campaign, meant that there was a considerable risk of prosecution, and accordingly Article 10 was engaged. The criminal offence of 'denigrating Turkishness' was not 'prescribed by law' and therefore breached Article 10. The Court also referred to the importance of historical truth in *Ungváry and Irodalom Kft.* v *Hungary*, No. 64520/10, 3.12.13 (damages awarded against historian and publisher for alleging that public official had collaborated with state security services during Communist era—violation of Article 10).

[2023] No. 3111/10, 18.12.12.

expression'.[2024] Furthermore, the domestic court which issued the order had failed to weigh up the competing interests at stake. The case of *Cengiz and others* v *Turkey*[2025] concerned the wholesale blocking of the YouTube website by an Ankara court, on the basis that selected pages of the site had infringed the prohibition on insulting the memory of Kemal Atatürk. This was found to breach the Article 10 rights of the applicants (a group of users of the YouTube website) as there was no statutory basis for such a broad blocking order. The case of *Delfi AS* v *Estonia*[2026] was the first in which the Court had to consider the liability of an internet provider in respect of comments posted on its news portal by the public. The company which owned the portal was subject to defamation proceedings in respect of comments amounting to threats and offensive statements relating to the owner of a ferry company, which was the subject of an article on the site. The Grand Chamber found no violation of Article 10 (by 15 votes to two), noting that the comments constituted hate speech and direct incitements to violence and taking account of the professional and commercial nature of the news portal, and to the fact that the applicant company had an economic interest in the posting of comments. It also found that the filtering mechanism for dealing with inappropriate postings had been inadequate, as the unlawful comments had remained online for six weeks. Furthermore, the fine imposed (of €320) was not disproportionate. By contrast, the Court unanimously found a violation of Article 10 in *Magyar Tartalomszolgáltatók Egyesülete and Index. hu Zrt* v *Hungary*[2027] in which the applicants, providers and owners of news portals, were the subject of civil proceedings as a result of derogatory third party comments posted about a real estate website. Although the comments were deemed to be offensive and vulgar, unlike in *Delfi*, they were not unlawful, and they did not amount to hate speech or incitement to violence. The Court was critical that the domestic courts had found the applicants liable for the defamatory statements without considering issues of proportionality and assessing the respective liabilities of the authors of the comments and of the applicants. It was also noted that the applicants had immediately removed the comments when they were informed of the initiation of civil proceedings, and that they had various measures in place to prevent or remove defamatory comments on their portals (including a disclaimer, a team of moderators, and a 'notice-and-take-down' system).

6.614 Publication of information and comment about court proceedings is acknowledged to be an important media function.[2028] However, there may be competing interests. The Court has stated[2029] that:

> the public interest in receiving information only covers facts which are connected with the criminal charges brought against the accused. This must be borne in mind by journalists when reporting on pending criminal proceedings, and the press should abstain from publishing information which is likely to prejudice, whether intentionally or not, the right to respect for the private life and correspondence of the accused persons.

A general and absolute prohibition on reporting criminal proceedings instituted on a complaint accompanied by a civil party action was found to be a disproportionate interference

---

[2024] *Ibid.*, para. 64.
[2025] Nos. 48226/10 and 14027/11, 1.12.15.
[2026] No. 64569/09, 16.6.15.
[2027] No. 22947/13, 2.2.16.
[2028] See, e.g. *Worm* v *Austria*, No. 22714/93, 29.8.97; *Dupuis and others* v *France*, No. 1914/02, 7.6.07; *Obukhova* v *Russia*, No. 34736/03, 8.1.09; *Axel Springer AG* v *Germany*, No. 39954/08, 7.2.12.
[2029] *Craxi (No. 2)* v *Italy*, No. 25337/94, 17.7.03, para. 65.

with Article 10 in *Du Roy and Malaurie* v *France*.[2030] In *Worm* v *Austria*,[2031] however, an article commenting on trial proceedings was considered to go beyond the bounds required by the proper administration of justice, as it stated, inter alia, that the defendant was guilty of tax evasion. There was therefore no violation of Article 10, as the article was considered to be capable of influencing the outcome of the proceedings. There was no violation of Article 10 in *Leempoel & S.A. ED. Ciné Revue* v *Belgium*[2032] where a weekly magazine had been withdrawn from sale and its further distribution prohibited because it had disclosed documents classified as secret in the context of a parliamentary inquiry into the handling by the police and judiciary of an abduction case. This was found to be justified because of the interference with one of the judge's defence rights and her right to respect for privacy, as well as the confidentiality of the parliamentary proceedings. In *P4 Radio Hele Norge* v *Norway*,[2033] a complaint concerning the denial of an application to broadcast a murder trial live on radio was declared inadmissible by the Court, as being a measure that lay within the state's margin of appreciation, having regard to the different positions taken by Council of Europe states as to the live broadcasting of legal proceedings. The case of *Egeland and Hanseid* v *Norway*[2034] concerned the convictions of two national newspaper editors pursuant to a law prohibiting the taking of photographs of a convicted person, without their consent, on their way to or from a court hearing. The photographs depicted a woman in a distraught state just after she had been convicted of triple murder and sentenced to 21 years' imprisonment. The Court concluded that the measures taken were justified in order both to protect the woman's privacy and to safeguard due process, and accordingly there was no violation of Article 10. In *Schweizerische Radio- und Fernsehgesellschaft SRG* v *Switzerland*,[2035] the absolute refusal by the prison authorities to allow the applicant broadcasting company to interview a prisoner within the prison was held to be disproportionate and in violation of Article 10: they failed to explain how, in practice, order and security in the prison would have been threatened.

The case of *Stoll* v *Switzerland*[2036] concerned the conviction of the applicant journal- **6.615** ist for publishing extracts from a confidential diplomatic document relating to the Swiss Government's strategy as regards the payment of compensation due to Holocaust victims for unclaimed assets deposited in Swiss bank accounts. The Grand Chamber held that the phrase 'preventing the disclosure of information received in confidence' in Article 10(2) applied to confidential information disclosed both by a person subject to a duty of confidence, and by a third party such as a journalist. The Court emphasised that 'press freedom assumes even greater importance in circumstances in which state activities and decisions escape democratic or judicial scrutiny on account of their confidential or secret nature'.[2037] However, on the facts of the case the Court found no violation of Article 10 by 12 votes to five. The Court acknowledged that it was vital to diplomatic services and the smooth functioning of international relations for diplomats to be able to exchange confidential or secret information. The applicant's articles had been liable to cause considerable damage

---

[2030] No. 34000/96, 3.10.00.
[2031] No. 22714/93, 29.8.97.
[2032] No. 64772/01, 9.11.06.
[2033] No. 76682/01, dec. 6.5.03.
[2034] No. 34438/04, 16.4.09.
[2035] No. 34124/06, 21.6.12.
[2036] No. 69698/01, 10.12.07. See also *Bojolyan* v *Armenia*, No. 23693/03, dec. 3.11.09.
[2037] *Ibid.*, para. 110.

to the interests of the Swiss authorities. The majority of the Court was critical of the applicant's articles as being capricious, insinuating, imprecise and liable to mislead the reader, which detracted from the importance of their contribution to the public debate protected by Article 10. Finally, the applicant's fine (800 Swiss francs) had not been disproportionate. The case of *Bédat* v *Switzerland*[2038] concerned the applicant journalist's prosecution and fine for having published information covered by the secrecy of criminal investigations, using as its source court papers in a criminal case brought against a motorist for ramming his car into a group of pedestrians. In order to weigh up the competing interests involved in such a case, the Court will consider six criteria: how the journalist came into possession of the information; the content of the article; its contribution to the public interest; its influence on the criminal proceedings; any infringement of the accused's private life; and the proportionality of the penalty imposed. In finding no violation of Article 10 (by 15 votes to two), the Grand Chamber noted the sensationalist tone of the article and that the applicant would have been aware of the confidentiality of the information he was publishing. Furthermore, the article made little or no contribution to the public interest and its negative slant on the defendant risked influencing the course of the criminal proceedings. Finally, the fine imposed had not been a disproportionate penalty.

6.616 The execution of search warrants in respect of the homes or offices of journalists should comply with the requirements as to lawfulness and proportionality under Article 10 (in addition to Article 8).[2039]

6.617 The Court has underlined that physical ill-treatment by state agents of journalists while they are performing their professional duties seriously hampers their exercise of the right to receive and impart information (regardless of any intention to interfere with journalistic activity). There was a violation of Article 10 in *Najafli* v *Azerbaijan*[2040] where the applicant journalist was beaten up by the police dispersing a demonstration on which he was reporting. In contrast, there was no violation of Article 10 (by 13 votes to four) in *Pentikäinen* v *Finland*.[2041] There, the applicant, a journalist and photographer, was detained at a demonstration which turned violent, held for over 17 hours, charged and found guilty of having disobeyed the police. On the facts, the Court found that the preventive measures taken by the police had been justified to protect public safety and prevent disorder—the applicant had been aware of the police order to disperse, but chose not to comply. The applicant had not been prevented from reporting on the event, and his equipment was not confiscated when he was detained. The Court also noted that the applicant had not been identifiable as a journalist from his appearance. He had not been convicted for his journalistic activities as such, but for disobeying police orders, and the domestic court's reasoning was considered relevant and sufficient. Moreover, no penalty had been imposed.

6.618 Article 10(1) expressly permits the licensing of broadcasting, television and cinema. The refusal to grant a broadcasting licence will amount to an interference with a company's freedom to impart information and ideas.[2042] The denial of licences or the extent of

---

[2038] No. 56925/08, 29.3.16.

[2039] See, e.g. *Ernst and others* v *Belgium*, No. 33400/96, 15.7.03.

[2040] No. 2594/07, 2.10.12.

[2041] No. 11882/10, 20.10.15.

[2042] See, e.g. *Meltex Ltd and Mesrop Movsesyan* v *Armenia*, No. 32283/04, 17.6.08, para. 74.

conditions placed on licences will be subject to the requirements of Article 10(2).[2043] The Court has emphasised that the grant of a licence may be made conditional on various grounds, such as the nature and objectives of a proposed station, its potential audience, the rights and needs of a specific audience and the obligations deriving from international standards.[2044] The monopoly broadcasting system in Austria was found not to be inconsistent, as such, with the third sentence of Article 10, because it was considered to be capable of contributing to the quality and balance of programmes.[2045] However, a complete monopoly of terrestrial television was found to be a disproportionate interference with Article 10.[2046] The Court has accepted the legitimacy of a monopoly of terrestrial television where private broadcasters have been granted broadcasting rights over cable television.[2047] There was a violation of Article 10 in *Meltex Ltd and Mesrop Movsesyan v Armenia*[2048] because the licensing authority failed to provide any reasons for its repeated refusals to grant the applicant company a broadcasting licence. The problem identified by the Grand Chamber in *Centro Europa 7 S.r.l. and Di Stefano v Italy*[2049] was the lack of clarity and precision in the domestic legal framework regulating the allocation of broadcasting frequencies. As a consequence, the applicant company had been awarded a licence but had not in practice been able to take it up because of the failure over ten years to be allocated a frequency.

The Court has also found that where a state establishes a public broadcasting system, **6.619** Article 10 requires that domestic law and practice must guarantee that the system provides a pluralistic service. This important principle was violated in *Manole and others v Moldova*,[2050] because of a deficient legislative framework regulating broadcasting in Moldova. The law did not prevent Governmental interference with Teleradio-Moldova (TRM), which had a virtual monopoly of audio-visual broadcasting, by controlling the appointment of its senior management. The applicants made complaints (which were upheld) that as journalists at TRM they had been pressurised by its management to avoid topics embarrassing to the Government, and to give disproportionate coverage to members of the ruling party.

Artistic expression

The right to freedom of artistic expression is protected by Article 10: **6.620**

> Those who create, perform, distribute or exhibit works of art contribute to the exchange of ideas and opinions which is essential for a democratic society.[2051]

[2043] See, e.g. *Autronic AG v Switzerland*, No. 12726/87, Series A, No. 178, 22.5.90; *Glas Nadezhda EOOD and Elenkov v Bulgaria*, No. 14134/02, 11.10.07.

[2044] See, e.g. *United Christian Broadcasters Ltd v UK*, No. 44802/98, dec. 7.11.00.

[2045] *Informationsverein Lentia v Austria*, Nos. 13914/88, 15041/89, 15717/89, 15779/89 and 17207/90, Series A, No. 276, 24.11.93, para. 33; *Radio ABC v Austria*, No. 19736/92, 20.10.97, para. 28.

[2046] *Informationsverein Lentia v Austria*, Nos. 13914/88, 15041/89, 15717/89, 15779/89 and 17207/90, Series A, No. 276, 24.11.93.

[2047] *Tele 1 Privatfernsehgesellschaft MBH v Austria*, No. 32240/96, 21.9.00.

[2048] No. 32283/04, 17.6.08.

[2049] No. 38433/09, 7.6.12.

[2050] No. 13936/02, 17.9.09. See also *Saliyev v Russia*, No. 35016/03, 21.10.10 (withdrawal of copies of municipal newspaper containing applicant's article—violation of Article 10).

[2051] *Müller and others v Switzerland*, No. 10737/84, Series A, No. 133, 24.5.88, para. 33; *Lindon, Otchakovsky-Laurens and July v France*, Nos. 21279/02 and 36448/02, 22.10.07, para. 47 (a case relating to a novel).

6.621 This was confirmed in *Müller and others* v *Switzerland*,[2052] where the Court found Article 10 to be applicable to the confiscation of paintings under obscene publications laws[2053] and convictions for exhibiting the paintings. There was an interference with this right in *Wingrove* v *UK*,[2054] arising from the refusal of the British Board of Film Classification to certify the applicant's video film *Visions of Ecstacy* (on the grounds it was blasphemous) and from the criminal sanctions applicable to the distribution of a video without a certificate. However, the Court found no violation of Article 10. The video portrayed a female character astride the crucified Christ engaged in an overtly sexual act. Taking account of the high threshold of profanation required by the offence of blasphemy in the domestic law, and the state's margin of appreciation, the Court considered that the steps taken were both relevant and sufficient, in accordance with Article 10(2). There was a violation of Article 10 in *Akdaş* v *Turkey*[2055] as a result of the seizure of the Turkish translation of the erotic novel *Les Onze Mille Verges* by Guillaume Apollinaire, and the applicant publisher's conviction and fine. These were found to be disproportionate measures in relation to a book published in 1907, which had been published in various languages in many countries and which formed part of the European literary heritage.

6.622 As in the examples cited above, many of the cases relating to artistic expression have concerned criminal proceedings instituted in order to protect public morals or prevent disorder. Rather different was the case of *Ehrmann and SCH VHI* v *France*[2056] in which the applicant artists complained that they had been found to be in breach of planning laws, for displaying their artistic works on the exterior of their property, which was situated near to two historic buildings. However, the Court found the measures taken to be proportionate, as being intended to respect both the 'common good' and the 'collective intent as expressed in planning choices'.

6.623 In *Ululsoy and others* v *Turkey*[2057] the decision of the Regional Governor's Office to refuse to authorise a Kurdish-language production of a play was held to violate Article 10. The domestic law failed to indicate with sufficient clarity the extent of the authorities' discretion on such matters, or the manner in which the discretion was to be exercised; it also failed to provide adequate safeguards against abuses and there was no evidence of any threat to public order.

6.624 The Court has found that the *form* or *medium* of artistic expression (such as poetry[2058] or novels[2059]) may be relevant in construing their meaning, not least because they may have fewer readers than, for example, newspaper reports, or because they employ satire or caricature.[2060] The majority of the Grand Chamber found no violation of Article 10 in *Lindon, Otchakovsky-Laurens and July* v *France*,[2061] resulting from the applicants' convictions for

---

[2052] *Ibid.*

[2053] See also *Perrin* v *UK*, No. 5446/03, dec. 18.10.05 (obscene images on the internet—declared inadmissible).

[2054] No. 17419/90, 25.11.96. See also *Otto-Preminger-Institut* v *Austria*, No. 13470/87, 20.9.94.

[2055] No. 41056/04, 16.2.10.

[2056] No. 2777/10, dec. 7.6.11.

[2057] No. 34797/03, 3.5.07.

[2058] *Karataş* v *Turkey*, No. 23168/94, 8.7.99.

[2059] *Alınak* v *Turkey*, No. 40287/98, 29.3.05. See also *Jelševar and others* v *Slovenia*, No. 47318/07, dec. 11.3.14.

[2060] *Vereinigung Bildender Künstler* v *Austria*, No. 68354/01, 25.1.07.

[2061] Nos. 21279/02 and 36448/02, 22.10.07.

defamation as a consequence of publishing a novel about the extremist politician Jean-Marie Le Pen and the *Front National* party. However, in a powerful dissenting judgment a minority of the Court[2062] argued that insufficient account had been taken of the fact that the form of expression in issue was a novel, and that artistic works should be given a higher level of protection. They were critical of the majority, inter alia, on the basis that:

> … the question whether words or expressions attributed to fictional characters are to be regarded as defamatory is made to depend on whether the author is to be seen as having sufficiently distanced himself in the novel from the words spoken. This seems to us to be a very fragile foundation on which to conclude that an author is guilty of defamation.

They also suggested that as regards Le Pen:

> … it may reasonably be argued that he should accept an even higher degree of tolerance precisely because he is a politician who is known for the virulence of his discourse and for his extremist views.

Expression in the commercial context

Article 10 also protects commercial freedom of expression[2063]—the right is guaranteed to 'everyone,' including profit-making corporate bodies. The state's margin of appreciation in regulating this area is likely to be wider: the Court has found the margin of appreciation to be essential in commercial matters, such as unfair competition and advertising.[2064] **6.625**

Restrictions on advertising can be justified on the basis of preventing unfair competition and untruthful or misleading messages, and restrictions may also be permissible in order to ensure respect for the rights of others or 'owing to the special circumstances of particular business activities and professions', such as lawyers and medical practitioners.[2065] In *Stambuk v Germany*,[2066] the applicant ophthalmologist was the subject of disciplinary proceedings resulting in a fine, because he took part in an interview with a journalist to discuss laser operation techniques. The resulting article was considered by the disciplinary court to amount to advertising prohibited by rules relating to medical practitioners. According to the European Court, however, this was an overly strict application of the rules and, in the light of the public interest in new laser techniques, it was considered to be a disproportionate interference with his rights under Article 10. **6.626**

The cases of *Hachette Filipacchi Presse Automobile and Dupuy v France*[2067] and *Société de Conception de Presse et d'Edition and Ponson v France*[2068] concerned the conviction of the publishers of two magazines for illegal advertising of tobacco, after having published photographs of famous racing drivers sporting logos for cigarette brands. The Court noted that restrictions on tobacco-related advertising were founded on public health considerations that could prevail over economic matters and also over fundamental rights such as freedom **6.627**

[2062] Judges Rozakis, Bratza, Tulkens and Šikuta.

[2063] See, e.g. *Markt Intern Verlag GmbH and Klaus Beermann v Germany*, No. 10572/83, 20.11.89, para. 2.6.

[2064] *Casado Coca v Spain*, No. 15450/89, 24.2.94, Series A No. 285-A, para. 50 and *Jacubowski v Germany*, No. 15088/89, 23.6.94, para. 26.

[2065] See, e.g. *Casado Coca v Spain*, No. 15450/89, 24.2.94, Series A no. 285-A; *Stambuk v Germany*, No. 37928/97, 17.10.02; *Krone Verlag GmbH and Co KG v Austria*, No. 39069/97, 11.12.03.

[2066] No. 37928/97, 17.10.02.

[2067] No. 13353/05, 5.3.09.

[2068] No. 26935/05, 5.3.09.

of expression, and there was a European consensus on the need for strict regulation of such advertising. The Court found that the cigarette logos could easily have been blurred, and also that the fines imposed were not excessive. Accordingly, the measures taken were not considered to be disproportionate and there was no violation of Article 10.

Maintaining the authority and impartiality of the judiciary

6.628 One of the legitimate aims in Article 10(2) (which is not to be found in Articles 8, 9 or 11) is the maintenance of the authority and impartiality of the judiciary.[2069]

6.629 This term has to be interpreted in a way that reflects the fundamental principle of the rule of law.[2070] It encompasses both the machinery of justice or the judicial branch of government, as well as judges in their official capacity. The rationale for this restriction is that the public should have respect for and confidence in the courts' ability to fulfil their function of clarifying legal rights and deciding on legal disputes.[2071] In *Skalka* v *Poland*,[2072] the Court recognised the legitimate aim in the applicant's conviction for insulting the judiciary. However, the fact that he did so in an internal exchange of letters with the President of the Regional Court that were not publicised meant that the conviction and sentence to eight months' imprisonment were disproportionate and in violation of Article 10. The applicant lawyer in *Amihalachioaie* v *Moldova*[2073] had been critical in the press of the Moldovan Constitutional Court following its decision to declare unconstitutional statutory provisions requiring lawyers to be members of the Union of Lawyers of Moldova (of which the applicant was president). His fine was found to be a disproportionate violation of the applicant's rights under Article 10 given the controversy created by the decision and his moderate criticisms of the judges.

6.630 In *Seckerson and Times Newspapers Limited* v *UK*,[2074] the applicant jury foreman and the Times newspaper had been found guilty of contempt of court, and fined, for breaching the secrecy of jury deliberations, following the publication of an article in which the foreman expressed his concerns about the trial in which he had been involved. In finding the application inadmissible, the Court emphasised that rules imposing requirements of confidentiality of judicial deliberations are important in maintaining the authority and impartiality of the judiciary, and that even the absolute secrecy of jury deliberations was not unreasonable.

The right to receive information

6.631 Whilst Article 10 expressly refers to the right to receive information, this has been narrowly interpreted as prohibiting the authorities from restricting a person from receiving information that others wish to impart. It has not been held to impose a positive obligation on the state to collect and disseminate information of its own motion. For example, in *Guerra and*

[2069] See, e.g. *Prager and Oberschlick* v *Austria*, No. 15974/90, 26.4.95 and *De Haes and Gijsels* v *Belgium*, No. 19983/92, 24.2.97.

[2070] See, e.g. *Sunday Times* v *UK (No. 1)*, Series A, No. 30, 26.4.79, para. 55.

[2071] See, e.g. *Morice* v *France*, No. 29369/10, 23.4.15, paras. 128–30.

[2072] No. 43425/98, 27.5.03. See also *Saday* v *Turkey*, No. 32458/96, 30.3.06 (sentence of two months' solitary confinement for contempt of court was disproportionate); *Ümit Bilgiç* v *Turkey*, No. 22398/05, 3.9.13 (applicant's conviction for contempt of court and placement in psychiatric detention found to be disproportionate); *Mustafa Erdoğan and others* v *Turkey*, Nos. 346/04 and 39779/04, 27.5.14 (damages awarded for defamation following publication of article criticising Constitutional Court decision ordering dissolution of political party—violation of Article 10).

[2073] No. 60115/00, 20.4.04.

[2074] Nos. 32844/10 and 33510/10, dec. 24.1.12.

others v *Italy*[2075] Article 10 was found not to be applicable where the applicants complained that the authorities had failed to ensure that the public were informed about the risks created by the operation of a chemical factory.

However, in recent years the Court has evolved a broader interpretation of the right to receive information. In *Társaság a Szabadságjogokért* v *Hungary*,[2076] the Court compared the role of non-governmental organisations with that of the press, in promoting access to information. There, the Hungarian Civil Liberties Union successfully invoked Article 10 in relation to the refusal by the Constitutional Court to provide it with access to a pending complaint (which had been submitted by an MP and which concerned the constitutionality of criminal legislation relating to drug offences). Noting that the NGO was involved in the legitimate gathering of information on a matter of public importance, the Court held that the state had an obligation not to impede the flow of information sought by the NGO, and that the Court's refusal of access amounted to a disproportionate interference with its Article 10 rights. The right to receive information was also breached in *Österreichische Vereinigung zur Erhaltung, Stärkung und Schaffung eines wirtschaftlich gesunden land- und forstwirtschaftlichen Grundbesitzes* v *Austria*[2077] where a regional authority concerned with approving agricultural and forestry land transactions refused to provide information to an NGO involved in research. Although the NGO's request concerned numerous decisions over a lengthy period, the Court found that much of the difficulty anticipated in complying with the request was caused by the authority's stance in not publishing any of its decisions. An outright refusal was accordingly held to be disproportionate. There was a violation of Article 10 in *Kenedi* v *Hungary*[2078] as a result of the authorities' refusal to comply with court orders obtained by the applicant historian, entitling him to gain access to documents relating to the state security service. In *Youth Initiative for Human Rights* v *Serbia*,[2079] the applicant NGO sought information from the Serbian intelligence agency as to how many people it had subjected to electronic surveillance. Its refusal to provide this information was found by the Information Commissioner to be unlawful, and ordered its disclosure. Accordingly the Court found the refusal not to be 'in accordance with the law', in violation of Article 10 (and it ordered the state to ensure that the agency disclose the information sought). The extent of the right of access to information was reviewed by the Grand Chamber in *Magyar Helsinki Bizottság* v *Hungary*.[2080] There, the Court clarified that Article 10 does not confer a right of access to information held by a public authority, nor oblige the Government to impart such information to the individual. However, such a right may arise where disclosure of information has been ordered by a judge, and also where access to the information is instrumental for the applicants' exercise of their right to freedom of expression, and where its denial constitutes an interference with that right.[2081] The criteria relevant to such an assessment include: the purpose of the information request; the nature of the information sought; the role of the applicant; and whether

6.632

[2075] No. 14967/89, 19.2.98. See also, *Leander* v *Sweden*, No. 9248/81, Series A, No. 116, 26.3.87, para. 74.
[2076] No. 37375/05, 14.4.09. See also *Sdružení Jihočeské Matky* v *Czech Republic*, No. 19101/03, dec. 10.7.06.
[2077] No. 39534/07, 28.11.13.
[2078] No. 31475/05, 26.5.09. See also *Roşiianu* v *Romania*, No. 27329/06, 24.6.14; *Guseva* v *Bulgaria*, No. 6987/07, 17.2.15.
[2079] No. 48135/06, 25.6.13.
[2080] No. 18030/11, 8.11.16.
[2081] *Ibid.*, para. 156.

the information is 'ready and available'.[2082] There was a violation of Article 10 in that case because the denial of access to information held by police departments about the identity of public defenders, in response to a request by the Hungarian Helsinki Committee in order to carry out a survey on the functioning of the public defenders' scheme, was held to be disproportionate.

6.633 In *Cyprus* v *Turkey*,[2083] the widespread practice of the authorities of the 'Turkish Republic of Northern Cyprus' was to censor primary school books that were being used by Greek Cypriots. This was found by the Court to be unjustified and a denial of the right to freedom of information. The prohibition on the distribution of the *Ülkede Gündem* newspaper within a region of Turkey proclaimed as a state of emergency violated this principle in *Çetin and others* v *Turkey*,[2084] as a result of the authorities' failure to provide detailed reasons for the ban and the absence of any powers of judicial review of the decision. There was a violation of Article 10 in *Mesut Yurtsever and others* v *Turkey*,[2085] because the applicant prisoners were denied access to Kurdish language newspapers. The authorities had stated that they could not assess the content of the newspapers (as was required by statute), as they could not understand the language in which they were written. There was also no power to restrict the receipt of publications on the basis of their language. The authorities' decisions had accordingly not been based on any grounds provided for by law.

6.634 The applicants' Article 10 rights were violated in *Khurshid Mustafa and Tarzibachi* v *Sweden*,[2086] where a private landlord terminated their tenancy agreement, and evicted them, because they had used a satellite dish to receive television programmes in Arabic and Farsi, in breach of an obligation not to install outside antennae. The Court acknowledged that it was particularly important for the applicants, a family of Iraqi origin, to receive broadcasts from their native region, for political and social news and entertainment. The domestic courts were found to have failed to take sufficient account of Article 10 in weighing up the competing interests.

Article 11: Freedom of Peaceful Assembly and Association

6.635 Article 11 states:

1. Everyone has the right to freedom of peaceful assembly and to freedom of association with others, including the right to form and to join trade unions for the protection of his interests.
2. No restrictions shall be placed on the exercise of these rights other than such as are prescribed by law and are necessary in a democratic society in the interests of national security or public safety, for the prevention of disorder or crime, for the protection of health or morals or for the protection of the rights and freedoms of others. This article shall not prevent the imposition of lawful restrictions on the exercise of these rights by members of the armed forces, of the police or of the administration of the state.

[2082] *Ibid.*, paras. 157–70.
[2083] No. 25781/94, 10.5.01, paras. 248–54.
[2084] Nos. 40153/98 and 40160/98, 13.2.03.
[2085] No. 14946/08 et al, 20.1.15. See also *Mehmet Nuri Özen and others* v *Turkey*, No. 15672/08, 11.1.11 (ban on distribution of prisoners' letters in Kurdish—violation of Article 8).
[2086] No. 23883/06, 16.12.08.

The rights to freedom of peaceful assembly and association are linked to the right to freedom **6.636** of expression in Article 10 and the right to freedom of thought, conscience and religion in Article 9. The Court has stressed that Articles 9 and 10 would be of very limited scope if there was not also a guarantee of being able to share beliefs and ideas in community with others, particularly through associations of individuals with the same beliefs, ideas or interests.[2087] Equally, one of the objectives of the right to freedom of peaceful assembly and association is the freedom to hold opinions and to receive and impart information and ideas.[2088] Where Articles 9, 10 and/or 11 are invoked together, the Court may decide to deal with one of those rights as the *lex specialis*, in which case in doing so it may take into account the other rights. For example, in *Hasan and Chaush v Bulgaria*,[2089] the Grand Chamber of the Court underlined the application of Article 9, interpreted in the light of Article 11, to religious communities (see 6.557 above). The Court may also find violations of more than one of Articles 9 to 11, depending on the particular circumstances of the case.

Freedom of peaceful assembly

The right to freedom of peaceful assembly is considered to be one of the foundations of a **6.637** democratic society and it is therefore not to be restrictively interpreted. The assembly must be peaceful: Article 11 does not protect those who have violent intentions which result in public disorder, or those who incite violence or otherwise reject the foundations of a democratic society.[2090] Article 11 will, however, apply to an assembly where there is a real risk of a violent counter-demonstration, where the violence would be outside the control of the organisers.[2091] The right has been applied to private meetings and meetings in the streets and other public places, marches, processions and 'sit-ins'. Article 11 will still be applicable even where the effect of a demonstration is to block roads and disrupt traffic.[2092] States have a wide discretion as to the reasonable and appropriate measures to be taken to enable lawful demonstrations to proceed peacefully. Meetings in public may therefore legitimately require prior authorisation.[2093] However, the fact that a demonstration is considered to be unlawful (for example because of a failure to give prior notification) does not justify an infringement of freedom of assembly.[2094] The Court expects public authorities to 'show a certain degree of tolerance towards peaceful gatherings if the freedom of assembly guaranteed by Article 11 of the Convention is not to be deprived of all substance'.[2095] There are positive obligations

---

[2087] See, e.g. *Chassagnou and others v France*, Nos. 25088/94, 28331/95 and 28443/95, 29.4.99, para. 100.

[2088] See, e.g. *Ahmed and others v UK*, No. 22954/93, 12.9.95, para. 70.

[2089] No. 30985/96, 26.10.00.

[2090] See, e.g. *G v Germany*, No. 13079/87, dec. 6.3.89; *Stankov and the United Macedonian Organisation Ilinden v Bulgaria*, Nos. 29221/95 and 29225/95, 2.10.01, para. 77; *Kudrevičius and others v Lithuania*, No. 37553/05, 15.10.15, paras. 92–4. See also *Osmani and others v former Yugoslav Republic of Macedonia*, No. 50841/99, 11.10.01. However, the Court has emphasised that '... an individual does not cease to enjoy the right to peaceful assembly as a result of sporadic violence or other punishable acts committed by others in the course of the demonstration if the individual in question remains peaceful in his or her own intentions or behaviour' (see, e.g. *Primov and others v Russia*, No. 17391/06, 12.6.14, para. 155).

[2091] *Christians Against Racism and Fascism v UK*, No. 8440/78, dec. 16.7.80, para. 4.

[2092] *Kudrevičius and others v Lithuania*, No. 37553/05, 15.10.15.

[2093] *Rassemblement Jurassien and Unité Jurassien v Switzerland*, No. 8191/78, dec. 10.10.79; *Ziliberberg v Moldova*, No. 61821/00, dec. 4.5.04; *Skiba v Poland*, No. 10659/03, dec. 7.7.09; *Rai and Evans v UK*, Nos. 26258/07 and 26255/07, dec. 17.11.09.

[2094] See, e.g. *Oya Ataman v Turkey*, No. 74552/01, 5.12.06.

[2095] *Oya Ataman v Turkey*, No. 74552/01, 5.12.06, para. 42; *Bukta and others v Hungary*, No. 25691/04, 17.7.07, para. 37; *Patyi and others v Hungary*, No. 5529/05, 7.10.08, para. 43; *Sergey Kuznetsov v Russia*, No. 10877/04, 23.10.08, para. 44; *Primov and others v Russia*, No. 17391/06, 12.6.14, paras. 118 and 145; *Yılmaz*

inherent in Article 11, such as the duty of the police to communicate with the leaders of a march or demonstration, in order to ensure that the assembly is peaceful and to prevent disorder.[2096] An interference with the right of peaceful assembly may be found to be disproportionate even if the restriction in question (such as the imposition of a small fine) is relatively limited.[2097] Article 11 protects the communication of opinions by word, gesture and silent demonstrations.[2098] Those who organise[2099] (both individuals and corporate bodies) and participate in a peaceful assembly can invoke Article 11. Interference with the right of freedom of assembly as the exercise of political expression will receive particular scrutiny by the Court: 'public events related to political life in the country or at the local level must enjoy strong protection under [Article 11], and rare are the situations where a gathering may be legitimately banned in relation to the substance of the message which its participants wish to convey'.[2100] The Court will be especially wary of the chilling effect of measures taken by the authorities which deter opposition supporters and the public at large from attending demonstrations or participating in open political debate.[2101] In a stark judgment in *Huseynli and others v Azerbaijan*[2102] the Court concluded that administrative proceedings brought against the applicants (leading opposition activists and politicians), were aimed at deterring them from taking part in demonstrations, and at punishing them for having done so, in violation of Article 11. This finding was underpinned by evidence that pre-emptive or retaliatory arrests (and convictions) were widely used by the Azerbaijani authorities to supress support for the opposition. Other measures used included police warnings not to attend demonstrations, and the targeting of human rights organisations by closing them down or demolishing the buildings where they were located. The applicants themselves had been arrested and convicted on the same day—two days before a scheduled demonstration—and sentenced to seven days' administrative detention, in similar circumstances and on what the Court found to be 'dubious grounds'.

6.638 Any interference with the right to freedom of peaceful assembly must be adequately 'prescribed by law'. This was not the case in *Djavit An v Turkey*,[2103] where the Turkish Cypriot applicant complained that the authorities repeatedly refused him permission to cross the 'green line' from northern Cyprus to the south in order to participate in bi-communal talks about the island's future. Article 11 was violated simply because of the absence of any law regulating the issuing of permits in such circumstances. There was a violation of Article 11 in *Bączkowski and others v Poland*[2104] because the decision to ban a minority rights march and demonstrations in Warsaw was found by the domestic courts to have been unlawful. The

---

Yıldız and others v Turkey, No. 4524/06, 14.10.14, para. 45; *Navalnyy and Yashin v Russia*, No. 76204/11, 4.12.14, para. 63.

[2096] See, e.g. *Frumkin v Russia*, No. 74568/12, 5.1.16.

[2097] See, e.g. *Sergey Kuznetsov v Russia*, No. 10877/04, 23.10.08 (fine equivalent to €35 for having breached the procedure for organising and holding a public assembly).

[2098] See, e.g. *Ezelin v France*, No. 11800/85, Series A, No. 202, 26.4.91, para. 52.

[2099] See, e.g. *Gün and others v Turkey*, No. 8029/07, 18.6.13.

[2100] *Primov and others v Russia*, No. 17391/06, 12.6.14, para. 135.

[2101] See, e.g. *Nemtsov v Russia*, No. 1774/11, 31.7.14, para. 78; *Frumkin v Russia*, No. 74568/12, 5.1.16, para. 141.

[2102] Nos. 67360/11, 67964/11 and 69379/11, 11.2.16.

[2103] No. 20652/92, 20.2.03. See also *Adalı v Turkey*, No. 38187/97, 31.3.05.

[2104] No. 1543/06, 3.5.07. See also *Patyi v Hungary*, No. 35127/08, 17.1.12 (refusal by police to allow demonstration in 'security operational zone' near Parliament—violation of Article 11 due to retroactive removal of legal basis of ban).

applicant in *Mkrtchyan* v *Armenia*[2105] organised an authorised demonstration in Yerevan, as a result of which he was later arrested, found to have committed an administrative offence and fined. However, the Court held that the Government could not identify any legal act that prescribed the rules for holding rallies and street processions that the applicant was found to have breached. Therefore, Article 11 was violated because the domestic law was not formulated with sufficient precision to enable the applicant reasonably to foresee the consequences of his actions. The applicant in *Vyerentsov* v *Ukraine*[2106] was subject to three days' administrative detention for breaching the procedure for holding demonstrations. The interference with the applicant's Article 11 rights was found not to be prescribed by law, because the only applicable law was a 1988 decree (which was insufficiently precise) and in the ensuing period the Ukrainian parliament had failed to enact a legislative framework to regulate the holding of peaceful demonstrations (as envisaged in the Ukrainian Constitution). The evidence of political demonstrations effectively having been banned in Baku led the Court in *Gafgaz Mammadov* v *Azerbaijan*[2107] to express its serious concerns about the foreseeability and precision of the Azerbaijani legislation governing public assemblies, and about the possibility of public assemblies being abusively banned or dispersed.

Turning to the question of proportionality, public demonstrations will often involve a certain level of disruption—notably to traffic—which will accordingly require an assessment of the balance between competing interests. This was the case in *Kudrevičius and others* v *Lithuania*[2108] which concerned the applicant farmers' conviction for blocking traffic on major roads for two days, as a result of their demonstrations aimed at highlighting the difficulties faced by the agricultural sector. The demonstrations had received prior authorisation; however, the organisers decided to move out of the designated areas and drove their tractors onto major highways. This was a clear violation of the stipulated conditions, and the authorities were not given prior notification. Thus, the organisers' deliberate intent to create roadblocks was what distinguished the case from others in which there was incidental disruption to ordinary life caused by demonstrations: the restrictions imposed as a result of the almost complete obstruction of three major highways were considered justifiable. It was also noted that the police had not sought to disperse the gatherings at the time, and the applicants had only been subjected to a suspended sentence. As a result, the Grand Chamber found no violation of Article 11.

6.639

General or blanket bans on demonstrations will require far more justification than bans on particular assemblies. Thus in *Alekseyev* v *Russia*,[2109] the repeated banning of Gay Pride marches in Moscow was found to violate Article 11 as being a disproportionate restriction on the applicant activist's right to freedom of peaceful assembly. The Government in *Alekseyev* referred to the risk of public disorder, as evidenced by petitions submitted against the rally, but the Court noted that the authorities had not carried out assessments of the risks posed

6.640

[2105] No. 6562/03, 11.1.07.

[2106] No. 20372/11, 11.4.13.

[2107] No. 60259/11, 15.10.15. The applicant's conviction and sentence to five days' detention for failing to obey police orders to stop participating in an unauthorised demonstration was found to be disproportionate and in violation of Article 11.

[2108] No. 37553/05, 15.10.15. See also, e.g. *Lucas* v *UK*, No. 39013/02, dec. 18.3.03; *Bukta and others* v *Hungary*, No. 25691/04, 17.7.07; *Barraco* v *France*, No. 31684/05, 5.3.09.

[2109] Nos. 4916/07, 25924/08 and 14599/09, 21.10.10. See also *Genderdoc-M* v *Moldova*, No. 9106/06, 12.6.12.

by counter-demonstrations or of public disorder. Had there been a counter-demonstration, the authorities would have been required to take sufficient measures to ensure that both events proceeded peacefully and lawfully. The Court also noted that the mayor of Moscow had frequently expressed his opposition to such marches. In *Rai, Allmond and 'Negotiate Now' v UK*,[2110] however, the Commission found that banning the applicants from holding a rally in Trafalgar Square in London was not disproportionate as they were prevented from demonstrating in only one high profile location in central London.[2111]

6.641 A general ban will only be justifiable if there is a real danger of disorder that cannot be prevented by other less stringent measures. An important factor to be taken into account is the effect on assemblies that do not pose a risk of disorder but that are nevertheless caught by the ban. In *Christians Against Racism and Facism v UK*,[2112] the Commission found a blanket ban on demonstrations in London for two months, which was aimed at preventing a National Front march but which also prohibited the applicant's demonstration, to be 'necessary in a democratic society' because of the tense atmosphere at that time created by a series of National Front demonstrations. Where there is a foreseeable danger to public safety that the authorities must deal with at short notice, the state is likely to be given a wide margin of appreciation in placing restrictions on the right to assembly.[2113]

6.642 There was a disproportionate interference with the applicants' Article 11 rights in *Schwabe and M.G. v Germany*[2114] when they were arrested for preventive purposes on their way to a demonstration against a G8 summit, and their detention continued for the whole duration of the summit (almost six days). In taking part in the demonstration the applicants had intended to participate in a debate on matters of public interest—the effects of globalisation. There had been nothing to indicate that either the applicants or the organisers of the demonstrations had violent intentions. The Court also took account of the fact that other less intrusive measures could have been used (such as seizing the applicants' banners). In *Gün and others v Turkey*,[2115] the Court found the criminal conviction of the organisers of a demonstration to be disproportionate—they had been sentenced to 18 months' imprisonment in respect of a demonstration in Cizre marking the anniversary of the arrest of Abdullah Öcalan, the head of the PKK, which had ended with clashes between the police and about ten demonstrators. The demonstration had been tacitly tolerated by the police, and the applicants' intentions had been peaceful. The Court found the sentences to be excessive, and also found that the damage caused by a group of unidentified individuals after the demonstration could not have justified the suspension of all events and demonstrations for one week.

6.643 In *Cisse v France*,[2116] the police evacuation of a church that had been occupied for two months by 200 illegal immigrants (some of whom were on hunger strike) was found by the Court not to be a disproportionate interference with their Article 11 rights. The Court was critical of the sudden and indiscriminate manner in which the police had intervened, but there was no

---

[2110] No. 25522/94, dec. 6.4.95.

[2111] See also, *Gypsy Council v UK*, No. 66336/01, dec. 14.5.02 (ban on annual Romany horse fair in village).

[2112] No. 8440/78, dec. 16.7.80.

[2113] *Rassemblement Jurassien and Unité Jurassien v Switzerland*, No. 8191/78, 10.10.79, para. 9.

[2114] Nos. 8080/08 and 8577/08, 1.12.11. There was also a violation of Article 5(1)—see 6.240.

[2115] No. 8029/07, 18.6.13.

[2116] No. 51346/99, 9.4.02.

violation of Article 11 because the long period of occupation of the church had meant that they were able to make their symbolic protest, and intervention was also justified because of health concerns. There was no violation of Article 11 in *Osmani and others v former Yugoslav Republic of Macedonia*,[2117] as a result of the prosecution of a local mayor following a public meeting at which he made an inflammatory pro-Albanian speech that was found to have encouraged the use of violence. Such measures were not disproportionate, given also that the applicant's actions were a causal factor in public riots which ensued. There was found to be no violation of Article 11 in *Çiloğlu and others v Turkey*,[2118] where the police stopped a sit-in on a public highway, of which no prior notice had been given.

The Court has emphasised[2119] that: 'It would be incompatible with the underlying values of the Convention if the exercise of Convention rights by a minority group were made conditional on its being accepted by the majority.' Thus, in *Barankevich v Russia*[2120] the authorities' refusal to allow an evangelical church to hold an act of worship in a park could not be justified by the fact that the religion in question was practised by a minority of the local residents. Children are owed particular protection, thus the arrest, detention or imprisonment of a child should only be used as a measure of last resort and for the shortest period of time.[2121] **6.644**

Article 11 will be breached where the authorities act in an arbitary way in restricting the right of peaceful assembly. For example, in *Makhmudov v Russia*[2122] the local authorities withdrew permission for a demonstration against Moscow town-planning policies, ostensibly on the basis that it was expecting 'an outbreak of terrorist activities'. However, the Court found a violation of Article 11 as the Government failed to produce any evidence to substantiate such a threat. The severity of the penalty imposed will be relevant to the Court's assessment of proportionality. For example, there was a violation of Article 11 in *Galstyan v Armenia*,[2123] where the applicant demonstrator was arrested and sentenced to three days' administrative detention for obstructing street traffic and 'making a loud noise'. The traffic had in fact already been suspended by the authorities, in anticipation of a lawful demonstration (protesting against the Government), and there was no suggestion that the applicant's conduct involved any obscenity or incitement to violence. The Court accordingly concluded that the applicant had been sanctioned for merely being present and proactive at the demonstration. **6.645**

In the context of the disruption of a demonstration by counter-demonstrators, the Court has confirmed that the right to freedom of assembly may entail positive obligations on the state to provide protection of peaceful protestors. In *Plattform 'Ärzte für das Leben' v Austria*[2124] the applicants complained about the lack of police protection to prevent the disruption of their anti-abortion demonstrations by pro-abortionist groups. The Court stated as follows:[2125] **6.646**

> A demonstration may annoy or give offence to persons opposed to the ideas or claims that it is seeking to promote. The participants must, however, be able to hold the demonstration without

---

[2117] No. 50841/99, dec. 11.10.01.
[2118] No. 73333/01, 6.3.07.
[2119] See, e.g. *Barankevich v Russia*, No. 10519/03, 26.7.07, para. 31.
[2120] No. 10519/03, 26.7.07.
[2121] *Gülcü v Turkey*, No. 17526/10, 19.1.16, para. 115.
[2122] No. 35082/04, 26.7.07.
[2123] No. 26986/03, 15.11.07.
[2124] No. 10126/82, Series A, No. 139, 21.6.88. See also, e.g. *97 members of the Congregation of Jehovah's Witnesses in Gldani and others v Georgia*, No. 71156/01, 3.5.07.
[2125] *Ibid.*, para. 32.

having to fear that they will be subjected to physical violence by their opponents; such a fear would be liable to deter associations or other groups supporting common ideas or interests from openly expressing their opinions on highly controversial issues affecting the community. In a democracy the right to counterdemonstrate cannot extend to inhibiting the exercise of the right to demonstrate.

6.647 Article 11 was violated in *Öllinger v Austria*,[2126] as a result of the authorities' unconditional prohibition of the applicant MP's proposed assembly in a cemetery on All Saints' Day to commemorate Salzburg Jews murdered by the SS during World War II. It would have coincided with a gathering of an association of former SS members. Given the expected size of the gathering (only a small number of participants were expected) and its peaceful nature, the ban could not be justified in order to protect either the rights of the association or regular cemetery-goers. In *Identoba and others v Georgia*[2127] the Court found a violation of Article 11 in conjunction with Article 14 because of the authorities' failure to ensure that a demonstration organised by LGBT activists could take place, by sufficiently containing homophobic and violent counter-demonstrators.

Freedom of association

6.648 The Court has consistently stated[2128] that:

> The right to form an association is an inherent part of the right set forth in Article 11 of the Convention. The ability to form a legal entity in order to act collectively in a field of mutual interest is one of the most important aspects of the right to freedom of association, without which that right would be deprived of any meaning.

6.649 The right to freedom of association applies to private law bodies, but not public law bodies that are not considered to be 'associations' within the meaning of Article 11.[2129] In *Le Compte, Van Leuven and De Meyere v Belgium*[2130] the applicant doctors complained about being required to join the *Ordre des Médecins* and being subjected to its disciplinary system. The Court held that the *Ordre* was not an 'association', taking into account its public law status and its functions of controlling the practice of medicine and maintaining the register of practitioners, as well as its administrative, rule-making and disciplinary powers.[2131] As there were also no restrictions on practitioners setting up or joining their own professional associations, there was no interference with the applicant's Article 11 rights. The term 'association' is, however, an autonomous concept—the classification of an organisation in the national law will be a factor, but will not be decisive in establishing whether the right to freedom of association is applicable. For example, hunters' associations in France were found to be 'associations' within the meaning of Article 11, despite the Government's arguments that they were public law, para-administrative institutions outside its scope.[2132] The Court has underlined that the

---

[2126] No. 76900/01, 29.6.06.

[2127] No. 73235/12, 12.5.15 (there was also a violation of Article 3 taken together with Article 14—see the discussion of this case at 6.119).

[2128] See, e.g. *Sidiropoulos and others v Greece*, No. 26695/95, 10.7.98, para. 40; *The Moscow Branch of the Salvation Army v Russia*, No. 72881/01, 5.10.06, para. 59; *Ramazanova and others v Azerbaijan*, No. 44363/02, 1.2.07, para. 54; *Zhechev v Bulgaria*, No. 57045/00, 21.6.07, para. 34.

[2129] See, e.g. *Mytilinaios and Kostakis v Greece*, No. 29389/11, 3.12.15.

[2130] Nos. 6878/75 and 7238/75, Series A, No. 43, 23.6.81.

[2131] See also *OVR v Russia*, No. 44319/98, dec. 3.4.01 (an association of notaries).

[2132] *Chassagnou and others v France*, Nos. 25088/94, 28331/95 and 28443/95, 29.4.99, para. 100.

outright dissolution of an association is a harsh measure which can only be taken in the most serious cases.[2133]

Political parties

Political parties are protected by the right to freedom of association under Article 11,[2134] not least because they are 'essential to the proper functioning of democracy'.[2135] Because of this, the exceptions in Article 11(2) are to be strictly construed in relation to political parties: convincing and compelling reasons will be needed to justify restrictions and the state will be allowed only a limited margin of appreciation. The right to freedom of association in Article 11 encompasses the functioning of political parties, although the justifiability of restrictive measures taken against such parties by the state may depend upon the aims and means employed by the organisation. Restrictions imposed on political parties must be legally foreseeable.[2136] A political party may campaign for changes in the law, provided that it uses legal and democratic means and that the changes proposed are compatible with democratic principles.[2137] The Court has accepted that an organisation's programme may conceal objectives and intentions that are different from its stated aims, and therefore that it may be necessary to compare its programme with the organisation's actions and the positions it defends.[2138] **6.650**

An essential factor is whether there has been a call for the use of violence, uprising or any other activity which amounts to a 'rejection of democratic principles'.[2139] Furthermore, preventive intervention may be justified, as the state 'cannot be required to wait until a political party has seized power and begun to take concrete steps to implement a policy incompatible with the standards of the Convention and democracy',[2140] not least because of the positive obligations on the state under Article 1 of the Convention to ensure that the Convention standards are upheld for everyone within its jurisdiction. A ban on political parties receiving funds from foreign political parties is not in itself incompatible with Article 11.[2141] **6.651**

A temporary ban on the Christian Democratic People's Party in Moldova was imposed because of gatherings it had organised in order to protest against government plans to make the study of Russian compulsory for schoolchildren. However, as the party's gatherings were entirely peaceful, without any acts that undermined the principles of pluralism and democracy, the ban was found to be disproportionate to the aim pursued, did not meet a 'pressing social need', and accordingly violated Article 11.[2142] **6.652**

[2133] *Association Rhino and others* v *Switzerland*, No. 48848/07, 11.10.11, para. 62 (dissolution of squatters' association—violation of Article 11).

[2134] See, e.g. *Presidential Party of Mordovia* v *Russia*, No. 65659/01, 5.10.04, para. 28.

[2135] *United Communist Party of Turkey and others* v *Turkey*, No. 19392/92, 30.1.98, para. 25. See also, *Socialist Party and others* v *Turkey*, No. 21237/93, 25.5.98 and *Freedom and Democracy Party (Özdep)* v *Turkey*, No. 23885/94, 8.12.99.

[2136] See, e.g. *Cumhuriyet Halk Partisi* v *Turkey*, No. 19920/13, 26.4.16 (confiscation of political party's assets not legally foreseeable—violation of Article 11).

[2137] *Socialist Party and others* v *Turkey*, No. 21237/93, 25.5.98, paras. 46–7.

[2138] *United Communist Party* v *Turkey*, No. 19392/92, 30.1.98, para. 58.

[2139] *Freedom and Democracy Party (Özdep)* v *Turkey*, No. 23885/94, 8.12.99, para. 40. See also the discussion of Article 17 at 5.33 above, including cases such as *Hizb Ut-Tahrir and others* v *Germany*, No. 31098/08, dec. 12.6.12.

[2140] *Refah Partisi (the Welfare Party) and others* v *Turkey*, Nos. 41340/98, 41342/98, 41343/98 and 41344/98, 13.2.03, para. 102.

[2141] *Parti Nationaliste Basque–Organisation Régionale d'Iparralde* v *France*, No. 71251/01, 7.6.07, para. 47.

[2142] *Christian Democratic People's Party* v *Moldova*, No. 28793/02, 14.2.06.

6.653 The dissolution of a political party is a drastic step which will rarely be justifiable. In a series of cases against Turkey, the Court has found the dissolution of various political parties by the Turkish Constitutional Court to be a disproportionate interference with the organisations' Article 11 rights.[2143] In the case of *United Communist Party of Turkey and others* v *Turkey*,[2144] the Court stressed that:

> there can be no justification for hindering a political group solely because it seeks to debate in public the situation of part of the state's population and to take part in the nation's political life in order to find, according to democratic rules, solutions capable of satisfying everyone concerned.

However, there was no violation of Article 11 in *Refah Partisi (the Welfare Party) and others* v *Turkey*,[2145] where the Court stated that in assessing whether the dissolution of a political party on account of a risk of democratic principles being undermined met a 'pressing social need' would depend upon consideration of the following:[2146]

(1) whether there was plausible evidence that the risk to democracy, supposing it had been proved to exist, was sufficiently imminent;
(2) whether the acts and speeches of the leaders and members of the political party concerned were imputable to the party as a whole; and
(3) whether the acts and speeches imputable to the political party formed a whole that gave a clear picture of a model of society conceived and advocated by the party that was incompatible with the concept of a 'democratic society'.

6.654 Whilst the Chamber of the Court had been divided by four votes to three in finding no violation of Article 11 in the *Refah Partisi* case, the Grand Chamber unanimously found no violation. The Constitutional Court's dissolution of the party was found to be proportionate in view of the following factors: at the time of its dissolution, the party had the real potential to seize political power; the acts and speeches of the party's leaders and members were justifiably imputable to the party as a whole; the party's aim of introducing a plurality of legal systems was incompatible with the Convention because it would involve discrimination on the basis of religion; the aim of introducing sharia was also incompatible with the Convention because it had no place for principles such as political pluralism; and there had been ambiguity over statements made concerning the use of violence to attain, and keep, power. This decision could be questioned, not least because, prior to its dissolution, the Refah Party had in fact come to power by forming a coalition government with another party, and therefore

---

[2143] *United Communist Party of Turkey and others* v *Turkey*, No. 19392/92, 30.1.98; *Socialist Party and others* v *Turkey*, No. 21237/93, 25.5.98: *Freedom and Democracy Party (Özdep)* v *Turkey*, No. 23885/94, 8.12.99; *Yazar and others* v *Turkey*, No. 22723–5/93, 9.4.02; *Dicle on behalf of the DEP (Democratic Party)* v *Turkey*, No. 25141/94, 10.12.02; *Socialist Party of Turkey (STP) and others* v *Turkey*, No. 26482/95, 12.11.03; *Democracy and Change Party and others* v *Turkey*, Nos. 39210/98 and 39974/98, 26.4.05; *Emek Partisi and Şenol* v *Turkey*, No. 39434/98, 31.5.05; *Demokratik Kitle Partisi and Elçi* v *Turkey*, No. 51290/99, 3.5.07; *HADEP and Demir* v *Turkey*, No. 28003/03, 14.12.10 (describing the actions of the security forces in south-east Turkey as a 'dirty war' does not incite people to hatred, revenge, recrimination or armed resistance); *Party for a Democratic Society (DTP) and others* v *Turkey*, No. 3840/10 et al, 12.1.16.

[2144] No. 19392/92, 30.1.98, para. 57.

[2145] Nos. 41340/98, 41342/98, 41343/98 and 41344/98, 13.2.03. See also *Kalifatstaat* v *Germany*, No. 13828/04, dec. 11.12.06 and *Vona* v *Hungary*, No. 35943/10, 9.7.13 (in which the Court distinguished 'social movements' from political parties—see also the discussion at 6.662).

[2146] *Refah Partisi (the Welfare Party) and others* v *Turkey*, Nos. 41340/98, 41342/98, 41343/98 and 41344/98, 13.2.03, para. 104.

even greater justification was required for its dissolution, when compared with parties that had not received such a mandate. In *Herri Batasuna and Batasuna v Spain*[2147] the Court unanimously found no violation of Article 11 resulting from the dissolution of the applicant political parties that were linked to the Basque separatist organisation, ETA. The Court saw no reason to fault the reasoning of the Supreme Court as regards the nature and extent of such links, which were found to include implicit support for a terrorist strategy and which came close to explicit support for the use of violence, thus posing a considerable threat to democracy.

In *Partidul Comunistilor (Nepeceristi) and Ungureanu v Romania*,[2148] it was held to be a **6.655** disproportionate interference under Article 11 to refuse to register the PCN communist party[2149] before its activities had been started (even allowing for Romania's experience of totalitarian communisim prior to 1989). There was nothing in the party's publications that could reasonably be construed as a call for the use of violence for political ends or as a policy in breach of the rules of democracy. The refusal by the Czech Ministry of Interior to register the Liberal Party, because its goals were said to be unconsitutional, was found to violate Article 11 in *Linkov v Czech Republic*.[2150] The Court found that there was no evidence that the party had not sought to pursue its aims by lawful and democratic means. Following the change of regime in 1989, the Czech legislature had passed laws declaring that the communist regime had breached human rights, and the Court found that the party's aim of 'breaking the legal continuity with totalitarian regimes' could be lawfully achieved through campaigning to end the impunity for offences committed during the communist era. The Court will carefully scrutinise restrictions imposed by the authorities on political parties to ascertain whether there is undue interference with their internal functioning. In *Republican Party of Russia v Russia*,[2151] the Court found that the refusal by the Ministry of Justice to register changes to the applicant party's address and list of delegates violated Article 11, because it was neither lawful, nor 'necessary in a democratic society'. The party's subsequent dissolution, on the basis of its insufficient membership and regional representation, was also found to be disproportionate and in breach of Article 11.

Minority rights, religious and other associations

In addition to political parties, the Court has recognised the importance to a functioning **6.656** democracy of other forms of associations, including 'those protecting cultural or spiritual heritage, pursuing various socio-economic aims, proclaiming or teaching religion, seeking an ethnic identity or asserting a minority consciousness'.[2152] The Court has stated that the inhabitants of a region in a country are entitled to form associations in order to promote the region's special characteristics—asserting a minority consciousness cannot in itself justify an interference with rights under Article 11.[2153]

[2147] Nos. 25803/04 and 25817/04, 30.6.09. See also *Etxeberria, Barrena Arza, Nafarroako Autodeterminazio Bilgunea and Aiarako and others v Spain*, Nos. 35579/03, 35613/03, 35626/03 and 35634/03, 30.6.09 (no violation of Article 3 of Protocol No. 1).

[2148] No. 46626/99, 3.2.05.

[2149] A party of communists who had not been members of the Romanian Communist Party—*Ibid.*, para. 1.

[2150] No. 10504/03, 7.12.06.

[2151] No. 12976/07, 12.4.11.

[2152] *Gorzelik and others v Poland*, No. 44158/98, 17.2.04, para. 92. See also, e.g. *Tebieti Mühafize Cemiyyeti and Israfilov v Azerbaijan*, No. 37083/03, 8.10.09 (dissolution of environmental NGO).

[2153] *Sidiropoulos and others v Greece*, No. 26695/95, 10.7.98, para. 44. See also the 'follow up' case of *House of Macedonian Civilisation and others v Greece*, No. 1295/10, 9.7.15.

6.657 In *Stankov and the United Macedonian Organisation Ilinden* v *Bulgaria*,[2154] the Court found that measures taken to prevent the applicant minority rights association's demonstrations could not be justified. In particular, there was no foreseeable risk of violent action or incitement to violence, or any other form of rejection of democratic principles. The Court in *Stankov* reiterated the importance of the need for free political speech in a democracy:[2155]

> ... the fact that a group of persons calls for autonomy or even requests secession of part of the country's territory—thus demanding fundamental constitutional and territorial changes—cannot automatically justify a prohibition of its assemblies. Demanding territorial changes in speeches and demonstrations does not automatically amount to a threat to the country's territorial integrity and national security. Freedom of assembly and the right to express one's views through it are among the paramount values of a democratic society. The essence of democracy is its capacity to resolve problems through open debate. Sweeping measures of a preventive nature to suppress freedom of assembly and expression other than in cases of incitement to violence or rejection of democratic principles—however shocking and unacceptable certain views or words used may appear to the authorities, and however illegitimate the demands made may be—do a disservice to democracy and often even endanger it.
>
> In a democratic society based on the rule of law, political ideas which challenge the existing order and whose realisation is advocated by peaceful means must be afforded a proper opportunity of expression through the exercise of the right of assembly as well as by other lawful means.

6.658 In *İzmir Savaş Karşıtları Derneği* v *Turkey*,[2156] the Court found that a legal requirement for the applicant anti-war association to obtain the prior permission of the Ministry of the Interior in order to participate in meetings abroad could not be regarded as pursuing any of the legitimate aims set out in Article 11(2) (rejecting the Government's arguments that its legitimate aim was the protection of national security or public safety).

6.659 Article 11 was violated in *Ouranio Toxo and others* v *Greece*[2157] because of both acts and omissions by the authorities vis-à-vis the applicant political party, whose aims included support for the Macedonian minority in Greece. Not only had the police removed a sign stating the name of the party in Macedonian, but also the local authorities incited public protests against the party and the police then failed to take adequate steps to prevent attacks on the party's headquarters.

6.660 At issue in *Association of Citizens Radko & Paunkovski* v *former Yugoslav Republic of Macedonia*,[2158] was the decision of the Constitutional Court to dissolve the applicant association on the basis that its activities were in reality directed towards the violent destruction of the constitutional order, the incitement of national or religious hatred or intolerance, and the denunciation of the free expression of the national affiliation of the Macedonian people. This was found by the European Court to be disproportionate as it had not been established that the association would use illegal or anti-democratic means to pursue its aims. The Court accepted that its ideology was likely to arouse hostility among the population, but in the absence of any evidence of a real threat to society or the state, that was not enough to justify the dissolution of the association:[2159]

[2154] Nos. 29221/95 and 29225/95, 2.10.01.
[2155] *Ibid.*, para. 97.
[2156] No. 46257/99, 2.3.06.
[2157] No. 74989/01, 20.10.05.
[2158] No. 74651/01, 15.1.09.
[2159] *Ibid.*, para. 76.

… sweeping measures of a preventive nature to suppress freedom of assembly and expression other than in cases of incitement to violence or rejection of democratic principles—however shocking and unacceptable certain views or words used may appear to the authorities, and however illegitimate the demands made may be—do a disservice to democracy and often even endanger it.

Problems with registering associations (including delays)[2160] may also raise issues under Article 11.[2161] The refusal to re-register the applicant religious organisation, resulting in its loss of legal status, was found to breach Article 11 taken together with Article 9 in *Moscow Branch of the Salvation Army* v *Russia*.[2162] A new law required all religious associations to re-submit their articles of association for registration. The authorities sought to justify the refusal on various grounds, including its 'foreign origin', and that it was said to be a 'paramilitary organisation'. The European Court found that the domestic courts' decisions were arbitrary and that the authorities had acted in bad faith. Article 11 was violated in *Zhechev* v *Bulgaria*,[2163] as a result of the refusal to register an association whose aims included repealing the Bulgarian Constitution, restoring the monarchy and 'opening' the border between the former Yugoslav Republic of Macedonia and Bulgaria. Such aims were found not to be incompatible with the principle of democracy and did not jeopardise the country's integrity or national security.[2164]

6.661

However, in *Gorzelik and others* v *Poland*,[2165] there was no violation of Article 11 as a result of the state's refusal to register an association, the 'Union of People of Silesian Nationality,' on grounds that it sought thereby to obtain particular election privileges (notably, an exemption from the 5 per cent threshold of the vote normally required to obtain seats in Parliament). The Grand Chamber held that the authorities' refusal to permit the association to use the description 'organisation of a national minority' in its memorandum of association was not disproportionate: it was not a 'comprehensive, unconditional' refusal, 'directed against the cultural and practical objectives that the association wished to pursue', but was designed to counter a specific problem relating to electoral law. *Vona* v *Hungary*[2166] concerned the dissolution of the Hungarian Guard Association which had been involved in anti-Roma rallies and paramilitary parading. Noting the differences between political parties and other 'social movements', the Court underscored that state authorities are entitled to take preventive measures to protect democracy as regards social movements 'if a sufficiently imminent prejudice to the rights of others threatens to undermine the fundamental values on the basis of which a democratic society exists and functions' (including a society free from racial segregation), and that restrictions placed on political parties necessitate greater scrutiny than social movements. Although it acknowledged the 'drastic' nature of the decision to dissolve the applicant organisation, the Court found no violation of Article 11, on the basis that the

6.662

[2160] See, e.g. *Ramazanova and others* v *Azerbaijan*, No. 44363/02, 1.2.07.

[2161] See, e.g. *Bozgan* v *Romania*, No. 25097/02, 11.10.07; *Magyar Keresztény Mennonita Egyház and others* v *Hungary*, No. 70945/11 et al, 8.4.14 (requirement for churches to re-register in order to regain benefits from state—violation of Article 11 read in the light of Article 9).

[2162] No. 72881/01, 5.10.06. See also the similar decision in *Church of Scientology Moscow* v *Russia*, No. 18147/02, 5.4.07.

[2163] No. 57045/00, 21.6.07.

[2164] See also *Bekir-Ousta and others* v *Greece*, No. 35151/05, 11.10.07 (refusal to register association established by Muslim minority in Western Thrace on the basis of mere suspicions about the founders' intentions).

[2165] No. 44158/98, 17.2.04.

[2166] No. 35943/10, 9.7.13.

domestic courts' decision had not been unreasonable or arbitrary. It agreed that the activities of, and the ideas expressed by, the association relied on a race-based comparison between the Roma minority and the ethnic Hungarian majority and it took particular account of the intimidating nature of their paramilitary rallies.

Trade unions

6.663 Expressly included within the right to freedom of association under Article 11 is the right to form and to join trade unions. For example, the inability of civil servants in Turkey to form trade unions has been found to violate Article 11,[2167] and in *Metin Turan v Turkey*[2168] the Court found a violation of Article 11 as a result of the compulsory transfer of a civil servant due to his legitimate trade union activities. There was a breach of Article 11 (and of Article 10) in *Eğitim ve Bilim Emekçileri Sendikası v Turkey*[2169] where the governor of Ankara applied to have the applicant trade union dissolved (and its statute amended) for supporting the right to education in a mother tongue other than the national language, which was held to be unjustified and disproportionate. However, there was no violation of Article 11 in *Sindicatul 'Păstorul cel Bun' v Romania*,[2170] as a result of the refusal of the county court to register a trade union of clergy and lay employees of the Romanian Orthodox Church, on the basis that its formation would have been in breach of the Church's statute. The Court found that the decision had a legal basis in the Church's statute and that, in refusing to register the trade union, the authorities had declined to become involved in the organisation and operation of the Church, which was in compliance with its duty of neutrality under Article 9 of the Convention. It noted that there was no absolute ban on the applicants founding a trade union—they could do so in accordance with the statute of the Church.

6.664 Article 11 has not been expansively interpreted in relation to trade unions, although the Court has recently recognised that, in view of its 'living instrument' principle, the essential elements of the right of association are subject to evolution, depending on developments in labour relations.[2171] The Court has held that Article 11 does not guarantee any particular treatment of trade unions, such as the right to be consulted by the state or the right to strike.[2172] However, Article 11 does require that trade unions should be heard[2173] and that they should be able to take action to protect the occupational interests of their members,[2174] an important aspect of

---

[2167] *Tüm Haber Sen and Çınar v Turkey*, No. 28602/95, 21.1.06; *Demir and Baykara v Turkey*, No. 34503/97, 12.11.08.

[2168] No. 20868/02, 14.11.06. See also *Şişman and others v Turkey*, No. 1305/05, 27.9.11 (imposition of disciplinary sanctions which infringed trade union freedoms—violation of Article 11); *Vellutini and Michel v France*, No. 32820/09, 6.10.11 (conviction of trade union leaders for strident criticism of their employer (a mayor)—violation of Article 10).

[2169] No. 20641/05, 25.9.12.

[2170] No. 2330/09, 9.7.13 (by eleven votes to six). See also *Manole and 'Romanian farmers direct' v Romania*, No. 46551/06, 16.6.15 (refusal to register farmers' trade union—no violation of Article 11).

[2171] *Demir and Baykara v Turkey*, No. 34503/97, 12.11.08, para. 146.

[2172] *Schmidt and Dahlström v Sweden*, No. 5589/72, Series A, No. 21, 6.2.76, para. 36. See also *Federation of Offshore Workers' Trade Unions and others v Norway*, No. 38190/97, dec. 27.6.02 (Government prohibition on strike); *Sanchez Navajas v Spain*, No. 57442/00, dec. 21.6.01 (refusal to pay trade union representative for time spent studying new legislation on trade union elections—inadmissible); *Swedish Transport Workers' Union v Sweden*, No. 53507/99, dec. 30.11.04 (no right for a trade union to maintain a collective agreement on a particular matter for an indefinite period—inadmissible).

[2173] *Swedish Engine Drivers' Union v Sweden*, No. 5614/72, Series A, No. 20, 6.2.76, para. 40.

[2174] *National Union of Belgian Police v Belgium*, No. 4464/70, Series A, No. 9, 27.10.75, para. 39. See also *UNISON v UK*, No. 53574/99, dec. 10.1.02.

which is the right to strike (which may be limited by regulation in particular circumstances). Article 11 was violated in *Enerji Yapı-Yol Sen* v *Turkey*[2175] as a result of disproportionate restrictions placed on the members of the applicant union in relation to their right to strike. The applicant was a union of public servants, some of whose members were subject to disciplinary proceedings for taking part in strike action, contrary to a governmental circular that deprived all public servants of the right to strike during a national day of action. The Court has confirmed that secondary industrial action (including secondary strike action) is covered by Article 11; however, there was no violation of Article 11 in *National Union of Rail, Maritime and Transport Workers* v *UK*[2176] as a result of the statutory ban in the UK on secondary strike action. There, the Court took account of the broad margin of appreciation available to the state, and had regard to the fact that the applicant union's members were able to exercise their right to freedom of association through its negotiations with the employer and its members exercising their right to strike at their place of work.

The issue of collective bargaining has been the subject of close scrutiny by the Court. In **6.665** *Wilson, the National Union of Journalists and others* v *UK*,[2177] the Court found a violation of Article 11 because the domestic law allowed an employer to de-recognise trade unions for collective bargaining purposes and it also permitted offers to be made of more favourable conditions of employment to employees who agreed not to be represented by the unions. The Court held that the absence in the domestic law of an obligation on employers to enter into collective bargaining did not in itself violate Article 11. Nevertheless, as it was possible for an employer effectively to undermine or frustrate a trade union's ability to seek the protection of its members' interests, and by permitting employers to use financial incentives to induce employees to surrender important union rights, there was a failure to comply with the positive obligations inherent in Article 11. The Grand Chamber went further in its judgment in *Demir and Baykara* v *Turkey*,[2178] by finding that, in view of developments in labour law, the right to collective bargaining with an employer had become one of the essential elements of the right to form and join trade unions. In that case, the annulment of an agreement *ex tunc* between a civil servants' trade union and a municipal authority (after it had been applied for two years) was held to be unjustifiable and in violation of Article 11.

In *Danilenkov and others* v *Russia*[2179] the Court affirmed that Article 11, taken together with **6.666** Article 14, includes a right not to be discriminated against for choosing to avail oneself of the right to be protected by a trade union—thus the state is obliged to implement measures to prevent discrimination on the ground of trade union membership. A private seaport company took various steps to discourage membership of the dockers' union, including decreasing earnings, disciplinary sanctions and dismissals. The domestic law included a blanket prohibition on all discrimination on the ground of trade union membership. In practice, however, it proved ineffective as regards the applicant union members as there was no civil remedy, and criminal proceedings required proof beyond reasonable doubt of direct intent

---

[2175] No. 68959/01, 21.4.09. See also *Hrvatski liječnički sindikat* v *Croatia*, No. 36701/09, 27.11.14 (trade union prevented from taking strike action for three years and eight months—violation of Article 11).

[2176] No. 31045/10, 8.4.14.

[2177] Nos. 30668/96, 30671/96 and 30678/96, 2.7.02. See also *Unite the Union* v *UK*, No. 65397/13, dec. 3.5.16 (inability of trade union to engage in collective bargaining owing to abolition of Agricultural Wages Board—inadmissible).

[2178] No. 34503/97, 12.11.08.

[2179] No. 67336/01, 30.7.09.

by the company to discriminate on grounds of trade union membership. Consequently, criminal proceedings were not initiated. Accordingly, the Court held that the state had not met its positive obligations to adopt effective and clear judicial protection against such discrimination, in violation of Article 14 in conjunction with Article 11.

6.667 Article 11 includes a negative right of association and therefore prevents compulsory membership of associations, which may include professional associations and trade unions.[2180] *Young, James and Webster* v *UK*[2181] concerned the applicants' dismissal for failing to join one of three unions that had concluded a 'closed shop' agreement with their employer, British Rail, so that membership was a condition of employment. The Court found that the threat of dismissal and the exertion of pressure on the applicants to join an association contrary to their convictions went to the very heart of the protections provided by Article 11, which was found to be violated by such disproportionate measures. A similar decision was made by a majority of the Grand Chamber in *Sørensen and Rasmussen* v *Denmark*,[2182] concerning pre-entry closed shop agreements within the private sector in Denmark, the Court noting that there was little support within Council of Europe states for the maintenance of closed shop agreements. There was a violation of Article 11 in *Vörður Ólafsson* v *Iceland*,[2183] as a result of the statutory obligation on the applicant, a master builder, to pay an 'industry charge' to a private industrial federation, of which he was not a member. Imposing such a levy was not found to be justifiable because the national law only defined the federation's role and duties in an open-ended manner, and also because there was a lack of transparency and accountability as to how the revenue from the charge was used.

6.668 Equally, the Court has found that a trade union has the right to choose its own members:[2184]

> Article 11 cannot be interpreted as imposing an obligation on associations or organisations to admit whosoever wishes to join. Where associations are formed by people, who, espousing particular values or ideals, intend to pursue common goals, it would run counter to the very effectiveness of the freedom at stake if they had no control over their membership.

6.669 In the case of *Associated Society of Locomotive Engineers & Firemen (ASLEF)* v *UK*,[2185] the applicant union complained that it had been prevented from expelling one of its members who was also a member of the far right British National Party. In domestic proceedings, the employment appeal tribunal had held that a union could expel a member on the ground of his conduct, but not of his membership of a political party. The Court unanimously found that Article 11 had been violated, taking into account the union's right to choose its members, that the individual member's political values clashed fundamentally with those of the union, that the union had not acted in an abusive or unreasonable way and that the expulsion of the individual would not cause him any particular hardship.

The Court has held that Article 11 binds the 'state as employer', whether relations with employees are governed by public or private law.[2186]

[2180] See, e.g. *Sigurjónsson* v *Iceland*, No. 16130/90, Series A, No. 264, 30.6.93.
[2181] Nos. 7601/76 and 7807/77, Series A, No. 44, 26.6.81.
[2182] Nos. 52562/99 and 52620/99, 11.1.06.
[2183] No. 20161/06, 27.4.10.
[2184] *Associated Society of Locomotive Engineers & Firemen (ASLEF)* v *UK*, No. 11002/05, 27.2.07, para. 39.
[2185] No. 11002/05, 27.2.07.
[2186] See, e.g. *Schmidt and Dahlström* v *Sweden*, No. 5589/72, Series A, No. 21, 6.2.76, para. 33.

Employees

The Court has recognised that Article 11 imposes positive obligations on the authorities to **6.670** provide protection against dismissal by private employers, where, for example, the dismissal is motivated by the fact that an employee belongs to a particular political party. The case of *Redfearn v UK*[2187] concerned the dismissal of the applicant, a bus driver employed by a private company to transport people with disabilities, the majority of whom were Asian in origin. However, he was dismissed when he was elected to the position of local council-lor with the British National Party, whose membership only extended to white nationals. As the applicant did not satisfy the one-year qualifying period for unfair dismissal claims, he had no domestic remedy. Therefore, Article 11 had been violated (by four votes to three) because of the failure to provide the applicant with an opportunity to challenge his dismissal.

Public officials

Article 11(2) expressly includes the right of the state to place 'lawful restrictions' on the **6.671** exercise of the Article 11(1) rights by members of the armed forces, the police and members of the 'administration of the state'. This latter term is to be narrowly interpreted—in *Vogt v Germany*[2188] the Court left open the question as to whether the term included teachers. In *Vogt* the applicant teacher's dismissal for refusing to disassociate herself from the German Communist Party was an interference with her rights under Article 11 that was held to be disproportionate. The term 'lawful restrictions' has the same meaning as the terms 'in accordance with the law' and 'prescribed by law', in requiring not only conformity with domestic law but also a certain quality of the law and sufficient foreseeability[2189] (see also above at 6.345).

An outright ban in the French Defence Code on military personnel forming or joining **6.672** any trade union body was held to be disproportionate and in violation of Article 11 in *Matelly v France*[2190] and *Adefdromil v France*.[2191] By a majority of four to three, the Court found a violation of Article 11 in *NF v Italy*,[2192] as a result of disciplinary proceedings being taken against a magistrate for having been a member of a masonic lodge. The domestic law was found to be insufficiently clear to make it foreseeable that a person (even one as well informed of the law as the applicant) in such a situation would face disciplinary sanc-tions. A similar decision was made by the Grand Chamber (divided by 11 votes to six), in *Maestri v Italy*.[2193] The requirement for candidates for public office to declare that they

---

[2187] No. 47335/06, 6.11.12.
[2188] No. 17851/91, Series A, No. 323, 26.9.95. As regards a dismissal of a school employee on religious grounds, see *Ivanova v Bulgaria*, No. 52435/99, 12.4.07 (violation of Article 9).
[2189] *Rekvényi v Hungary*, No. 25390/94, 20.5.99, para. 59.
[2190] No. 10609/10, 2.10.14.
[2191] No. 32191/09, 2.10.14.
[2192] No. 37119/97, 2.8.01.
[2193] No. 39748/98, 17.2.04. Five of the dissenting judges (Judges Bonello, Jungwiert, Stráznická, Bîrsan and Del Tufo) argued, inter alia, as follows: that the applicant judge knew, or ought reasonably to have been aware of, the consequences of joining a masonic lodge; that he had not raised the lack of foreseeability of the law in the domestic courts; and that the Italian courts were the best-placed to interpret the domestic law provi-sions: 'the judgment of the majority has totally pushed aside the principle of subsidiarity (and also those of the "fourth-instance" doctrine and the margin of appreciation), so fundamental to the proper application of the Convention'.

were not members of the freemasons has been found to be a disproportionate interference with Article 11 rights.[2194] However, in *Junta Rectora Del Ertzainen Nazional Elkartasuna (ER.N.E.) v Spain*[2195] the Court found no violation of Article 11 as a result of the refusal to allow a police officers' trade union to take strike action. A more restrictive legislative regime as regards law enforcement officers, compared with other public servants, was considered to be proportionate, given their function of ensuring national security, public safety and the prevention of disorder.

Article 12: Right to Marry

6.673   Article 12 states:

> Men and women of marriageable age have the right to marry and to found a family, according to the national laws governing the exercise of this right.

6.674   The Court has stressed that a good deal of leeway will be given to the state in interpreting this provision:[2196]

> Article 12 expressly provides for regulation of marriage by national law and given the sensitive moral choices concerned and the importance to be attached to the protection of children and the fostering of secure family environments, this Court must not rush to substitute its own judgment in place of the authorities who are best placed to assess and respond to the needs of society.

6.675   Article 12 has accordingly been narrowly interpreted. It should always be considered in conjunction with the right to respect for private and family life under Article 8. The Court has interpreted Article 12 as upholding 'traditional marriage between persons of opposite biological sex' and has found that Article 12 is mainly concerned to protect marriage as the basis of the family.[2197] In *Schalk and Kopf v Austria*,[2198] the Court noted that the reference to 'men and women' had not been included in Article 9 of the EU Charter of Fundamental Rights,[2199] leaving the decision to states whether or not to allow same-sex marriage. In the light of that, the Court concluded that it was no longer the case that the right to marry enshrined in Article 12 must in all circumstances be limited to marriage between two persons of the opposite sex. However, the Court held that Article 12 does not impose an obligation on states to grant a same-sex couple the right to marry.

6.676   In a series of cases concerning transsexuals, Article 12 was formerly interpreted as not allowing a person who has undergone gender reassignment surgery to marry someone of the opposite sex to that as which the person now lives.[2200] However, in *Goodwin v UK*[2201] and

---

[2194] *Grande Oriente d'Italia de Palazzo Giustiniani v Italy*, No. 35972/97, 2.8.01; *Grande Oriente d'Italia de Palazzo Giustiniani v Italy (No. 2)*, No. 26740/02, 31.5.07; cf *Siveri and Chiellini v Italy*, No. 13148/04, dec. 3.6.08.

[2195] No. 45892/09, 21.4.15.

[2196] *B and L v UK*, No. 36536/02, 13.9.05, para. 36.

[2197] *Rees v UK*, No. 9532/81, Series A, No. 106, 17.10.86, and, e.g. *Sheffield and Horsham v UK*, Nos. 22985/93 and 23390/94, 30.7.98, para. 66.

[2198] No. 30141/04, 24.6.10.

[2199] Article 9 of the Charter provides that: 'The right to marry and to found a family shall be guaranteed in accordance with the national laws governing the exercise of these rights.'

[2200] See, e.g. *Cossey v UK*, No. 10843/84, Series A, No. 184, 27.9.90; *Sheffield and Horsham v UK*, Nos. 22985/93 and 23390/94, 30.7.98.

[2201] No. 28957/95, 11.7.02.

I v *UK*,[2202] the Grand Chamber of the Court found that, in preventing transsexuals from marrying a person of the sex opposite to their reassigned gender under any circumstances, the very essence of the right to marry had been infringed. The Court reasoned as follows:[2203]

> Article 12 secures the fundamental right of a man and woman to marry and to found a family. The second aspect is not however a condition of the first and the inability of any couple to conceive or parent a child cannot be regarded as *per se* removing their right to enjoy the first limb of this provision.

Whilst the Court acknowledged that the first sentence of Article 12 expressly refers to the right of a man and woman to marry, it was 'not persuaded that at the date of this case it can still be assumed that these terms must refer to a determination of gender by purely biological criteria'.[2204]

Article 12 also stipulates that the exercise of the right is subject to the national laws of the states parties; however, any limitations on the right must not restrict or reduce the right to an extent which would impair the very essence of the right. Therefore restrictions on the right to marry, such as procedural requirements or limitations as to capacity or age, will be subject to a test of proportionality. **6.677**

The Court has held that it may be justified for states to prevent 'marriages of convenience', the aim of which are to gain an advantage in the context of immigration rules.[2205] However, at issue in *O'Donoghue and others* v *UK*[2206] were the conditions placed on marriage for third-country nationals by way of a certificate of approval scheme. The Court found that imposing conditions in order to ascertain whether a marriage was one of convenience would not necessarily breach the Convention. However, the certificate of approval scheme fell foul of Article 12 for three reasons. Firstly, the grant of a certificate was not based solely on the genuineness of the proposed marriage (but rather on immigration status). Secondly, the scheme imposed a blanket prohibition on the right to marry on all persons in specified categories, for which there was no justification. Thirdly, the imposition of a fixed fee of £295 was high enough to impair the very right to marry. As the scheme did not apply to marriages conducted within the Church of England, the scheme was also held to be discriminatory on the grounds of religion, in violation of Article 14 taken together with both Article 12 and Article 9. **6.678**

Other limitations on the right to marry in national laws may be in the public interest, in respect of, for example, consent, prohibited degrees of affinity or the prevention of bigamy. In *B and L* v *UK*, Article 12 was found to have been violated as a result of the prohibition in the domestic law on the marriage of a parent-in-law to a child-in-law (unless both their spouses are dead).[2207] This prevented the applicants (father-in-law and daughter-in-law) from marrying, after they moved in together following the end of their respective marriages. Whilst the legislation had legitimate aims, it did not prevent such relationships from occurring (there **6.679**

[2202] No. 25680/94, 11.7.02.
[2203] No. 28957/95, 11.7.02, para. 98.
[2204] *Ibid.*, para. 100. In *R. and F.* v *UK* (No. 35748/05, dec. 28.11.06) and *Parry* v *UK* (No. 42971/05, dec. 28.11.06) the Court declared inadmissible complaints brought by two husbands who had undergone gender reassignment surgery following their marriage but were barred by law from obtaining full gender recognition as they wished to remain married.
[2205] See, e.g. *Frasik* v *Poland*, No. 22933/02, 5.1.10, para. 89.
[2206] No. 34848/07, 14.12.10.
[2207] *B and L* v *UK*, No. 36536/02, 13.9.05.

were no criminal provisions to prevent extra-marital relationships between a parent-in-law and a child-in-law), and it could be waived in individual cases through an Act of Parliament.

6.680 The Court has emphasised that prisoners have the right to marry: 'personal liberty is not a necessary pre-condition for the exercise of the right to marry'.[2208] The applicant in *Frasik v Poland*,[2209] complained about a district court's refusal to permit him to marry whilst held on remand. He wanted to marry a woman who had complained that he had raped and battered her—they had since become reconciled. The judge wanted to prevent the victim, through marrying the applicant, from exercising her right not to testify against him. She also considered that the remand centre was not an appropriate place to marry and doubted the sincerity of the couple's intentions. Both the Supreme Court and the European Court found this interference with the applicant's Article 12 rights to be disproportionate and arbitrary. There was a similar outcome in *Jaremowicz v Poland*[2210] where the authorities arbitrarily invoked various subjective reasons for refusing to allow the applicant, a prisoner, to marry another prisoner, because their relationship was deemed to be 'very superficial' and because it had been 'developed illegally'.

6.681 Article 12 upholds the right to remarry,[2211] but does not establish a right of divorce.[2212] Overly long divorce proceedings have been held to violate Article 12, as being an unreasonable restriction on the right to marry.[2213] In *Selim v Cyprus*,[2214] the Court declared admissible in respect of Articles 8 and 12 a complaint concerning the impossibility, due to the domestic law, for a Muslim Turkish Cypriot living in Cyprus to contract a civil marriage. The case was later settled[2215] on the basis, inter alia, that the Marriage Law was extended to members of the Turkish community, and a new bill had been laid before Parliament that would apply to all Cypriots without distinction of origin.

Article 13: Right to an Effective Remedy

6.682 Article 13 states:

> Everyone whose rights and freedoms as set forth in this Convention are violated shall have an effective remedy before a national authority notwithstanding that the violation has been committed by persons acting in an official capacity.

6.683 The Court has held that Article 13 must be interpreted as guaranteeing an effective remedy before a national authority for everyone who claims that their rights and freedoms under the Convention have been violated.[2216] The Article expressly states that such

---

[2208] *Frasik v Poland*, No. 22933/02, 5.1.10, para. 91. See also *Hamer v UK*, No. 7114/75, dec. 13.10.77; *Chernetskiy v Ukraine*, No. 44316/07, 8.12.16.

[2209] No. 22933/02, 5.1.10.

[2210] No. 24023/03, 5.1.10.

[2211] See, e.g. *F v Switzerland*, No. 11329/85, Series A, No. 128, 18.12.87.

[2212] *Johnston and others v Ireland*, No. 9697/82, Series A, No. 112, 18.12.86, paras. 51–4. See also *Babiarz v Poland*, No. 1955/10, 10.1.17 (dismissal of divorce petition of spouse who wished to marry new partner—no violation of Article 12).

[2213] *V.K. v Croatia*, No. 38380/08, 27.11.12.

[2214] No. 47293/99, dec. 18.9.01.

[2215] *Selim v Cyprus*, No. 47293/99, 16.7.02.

[2216] *Klass and others v Germany*, Series A, No. 28, 6.9.78, para. 64.

remedies must be available even as against those acting in their official capacity. Article 13 has been said to give 'direct expression to the states' obligation to protect human rights first and foremost within their own legal system'.[2217] Its object is to allow individuals the potential relief at the national level before having to invoke the international machinery of the European Convention on Human Rights.[2218] The effect of Article 13 is therefore to require the provision of a domestic remedy allowing the competent national authority both to deal with the substance of the relevant Convention complaint and to grant appropriate relief.

The remedy required by Article 13 need not be provided by a court (see further below). It must be 'effective' in practice as well as in law, in particular in the sense that its exercise must not be unjustifiably hindered by the acts or omissions of the authorities of the respondent state.[2219] For example, *Al-Saadoon and Mufdhi v UK*[2220] concerned the applicants' detention by the British armed forces in southern Iraq in 2003, and their subsequent transfer to the Iraqi authorities. The applicants successfully argued that, as there had been a breach of the Court's Rule 39 interim measures indication, there was a violation of Article 34, and also that Article 13 was breached because, at the time of their transfer, the House of Lords had not had the opportunity to consider their appeal. **6.684**

Whilst Article 13 does not require a domestic remedy in relation to *any* grievance under the Convention, it can be properly invoked in relation to any *arguable claim* of a violation of another Convention right.[2221] It is important to note that in spite of the literal wording of the Article, no other Convention right need be violated in order to establish a breach of Article 13.[2222] The Court has not defined the notion of arguability, which it has said must be determined in the light of the particular facts and the nature of the legal issues raised in each case.[2223] While Article 13 guarantees the availability of a suitable forum to obtain a remedy, it cannot of course require that the applicant's claim is in fact successful. Article 13 does not guarantee a remedy to challenge domestic legislation. For example, on that basis, the Commission rejected a claim of a violation of Article 13 in *CC v UK*,[2224] which concerned the automatic denial of bail under the Criminal Justice and Public Order Act 1994. **6.685**

The 'remedy' need not be provided by a court, but the body in question providing the remedy must be capable of affording effective redress and must be sufficiently independent of the body being challenged. Remedies that are discretionary, or unenforceable, will not generally comply with Article 13. For example, in the United Kingdom, the Prison Board of Visitors and the Parliamentary Ombudsman were found to lack sufficient powers in relation to a **6.686**

[2217] *Kudla v Poland*, No. 30210/96, 26.10.00, para. 152.

[2218] *Collected Editions of the 'Travaux Préparatoires' of the European Convention on Human Rights*, Vol. II, pp. 485, 490 and Vol. III, p. 651; *Kudla v Poland*, No. 30210/96, 26.10.00, para. 152. See also Recommendation Rec(2004)6 of the Committee of Ministers to Member States on the improvement of domestic remedies, 12.5.04.

[2219] *Aksoy v Turkey*, No. 21987/93, 18.12.96, para. 95. See also *Hasan and Chaush v Bulgaria*, No. 30985/96, 26.10.00, para. 101.

[2220] No. 61498/08, 2.3.10.

[2221] See, e.g. *Silver v UK*, Nos. 5947/72, 6205/73, 7052/75, 7061/75, 7107/75, 7113/75 and 7136/75, Series A, No. 61, 25.3.83.

[2222] *Klass and others v Germany*, Series A, No. 28, 6.9.78, para. 64.

[2223] *Boyle and Rice v UK*, Nos. 9659/82 and 9658/82, Series A, No. 131, 27.4.88, para. 55.

[2224] No. 32819/96, Comm. Rep. 30.6.98.

complaint concerning the interception of prisoners' mail.[2225] The absence of a *right* of appeal (as opposed to an informal practice) to challenge a court order prohibiting reporting on a criminal trial in Scotland led to a finding of a violation of Article 13 in conjunction with Article 10 in *Mackay and BBC Scotland* v *UK*.[2226] The Court in *Khan* v *UK*[2227] found that the police complaints system did not provide an effective remedy, within the meaning of Article 13, because of the system's lack of independence. In reaching its decision, the Court took into account the fact that it was standard practice for a chief constable to appoint a member of his or her own force to carry out the investigation, and noted the role of the Home Secretary in appointing, remunerating and dismissing members of the Police Complaints Authority.

6.687 In exceptional situations, the aggregate of remedies provided by domestic law may satisfy Article 13, as was found to be the case in *Leander* v *Sweden*[2228] in the context of secret security vetting.

6.688 The scope of Article 13 will vary depending upon the nature of the Convention complaint. For example, where there has been a fatal incident (or a disappearance), and also in the context of allegations of torture or where a person's home has been destroyed by state agents, the Court has held that the notion of an 'effective remedy' under Article 13 requires 'a thorough and effective investigation capable of leading to the identification and punishment of those responsible and including effective access for the complainant to the investigatory procedure'.[2229] The Court has found a series of violations of Article 13 because of the ineffectiveness of the criminal law system in respect of actions of the security forces in south-east Turkey in the 1990s[2230] (see also the sections on Articles 2 and 3 above).

6.689 Cases concerning fatalities (Article 2) may raise particular issues under Article 13. In *Keenan* v *UK*,[2231] which concerned the suicide of the applicant's son in prison, there was a violation of Article 13 because the inquest could not provide a remedy by determining the liability of the authorities for any alleged ill-treatment or by providing compensation. The Court found that 'no effective remedy was available … which could have established where responsibility lay for the death of Mark Keenan'[2232] and also that 'in the case of a breach of Articles 2 and 3 of the Convention … compensation for the non-pecuniary damage flowing from the breach should in principle be available as part of the range of possible remedies'.[2233] In his

---

[2225] *Silver* v *UK*, Nos. 5947/72, 6205/73, 7052/75, 7061/75, 7107/75, 7113/75 and 7136/75, Series A, No. 61, 25.3.83.

[2226] No. 10734/05, 7.12.10.

[2227] No. 35394/97, 12.5.00. See also: *Govell* v *UK*, No. 27237/95, Comm. Rep. 14.1.98; *PG and JH* v *UK*, No. 44787/98, 25.9.01, para. 88.

[2228] No. 9248/81, Series A, No. 116, 26.3.87.

[2229] See, e.g. *Aksoy* v *Turkey*, No. 21987/93, 18.12.96, para. 98. See also *Aydin* v *Turkey*, No. 23178/94, 28.6.97, para. 103; *Kaya* v *Turkey*, No. 22729/93, 19.2.98, para. 107; *Kurt* v *Turkey*, No. 24276/94, 25.5.98, para. 104; *Tekin* v *Turkey*, No. 22496/93, 9.6.98, para. 66; *Yaşa* v *Turkey*, No. 22495/93, 2.9.98, para. 114; *Akkoç* v *Turkey*, Nos. 22947/93 and 22948/93, 10.10.00, para. 103; *Taş* v *Turkey*, No. 24396/94, 14.11.00, para. 91; *Bilgin* v *Turkey*, No. 23819/94, 16.11.00, para. 114.

[2230] See, e.g. *Akkoç* v *Turkey*, Nos. 22947/93 and 22948/93, 10.10.00; *Mahmut Kaya* v *Turkey*, No. 22535/93, 28.3.00, paras. 94–8; *Og̈ur* v *Turkey*, No. 21594/93, 20.5.99, para. 91; *Bilgin* v *Turkey*, No. 23819/94, 16.11.00, para. 119; *Gül* v *Turkey*, No. 22676/93, 19.12.00, para. 102.

[2231] No. 27229/95, 3.4.01.

[2232] *Ibid.*, para. 132.

[2233] *Ibid.*, para. 130. See also *McGlinchey and others* v *UK*, No. 50390/99, 29.4.03; *Bubbins* v *UK*, No. 50196/99, 17.3.05.

concurring opinion in *Keenan*, Sir Stephen Sedley suggested that an effective remedy would be provided by an inquest with procedures which assured the rights and interests of persons such as the applicant, and which had the power to determine where the responsibility lay. There was a similar outcome in *Reynolds v UK*,[2234] which concerned the death of the applicant's son who had been diagnosed with schizophrenia and had committed suicide while in voluntary psychiatric care. The Court found a violation of Article 13 together with Article 2 as it had not in practice been possible for the applicant to bring civil proceedings in order to establish liability, or to claim compensation in respect of the non-pecuniary damage which she had suffered. As regards ongoing conditions of detention, the Court has found that preventive and compensatory remedies have to be complementary to be deemed effective, as the possible receipt of compensation cannot of itself 'legitimise' treatment in breach of Article 3.[2235] There was a violation of Article 13 taken together with Article 3 in *Bamouhammad v Belgium*[2236] because there was no preventive mechanism to provide an effective response to the applicant prisoner's complaints of repeated transfers and as to the effects of the special prison regime on his health.

In relation to systems of secret surveillance by the state, the Court has recognised that an **6.690** 'effective remedy' under Article 13 must mean a remedy 'that is as effective as can be having regard to the restricted scope for recourse inherent in any system of secret surveillance'.[2237] In *Chahal v UK*,[2238] however, given the importance of Article 3 and the potential irreversible harm to the applicant (a Sikh nationalist under threat of deportation to India), the Court emphasised that the notion of an effective remedy under Article 13 required independent scrutiny of the claim that there existed substantial grounds for fearing a real risk of treatment contrary to Article 3. Article 13 was found to have been violated in *Chahal* as neither the 'advisory panel' nor the domestic courts could review the decision to deport him with reference solely to the question of risk, quite apart from any national security considerations. The advisory panel was also found not to provide sufficient procedural safeguards for Article 13 purposes, as the applicant had not been entitled to legal representation, he was given only an outline of the grounds for the decision and the panel could not make a binding decision and its advice to the minister was not disclosed. There was also a violation of Article 13 in *Al-Nashif v Bulgaria*,[2239] as there was no remedy available to the applicant who was the subject of a deportation order on grounds of national security. There, the Court stated[2240] that:

> Even where an allegation of a threat to national security is made, the guarantee of an effective remedy requires as a minimum that the competent independent appeals authority must be informed of the reasons grounding the deportation decision, even if such reasons are not publicly available. The authority must be competent to reject the executive's assertion that there is a threat to national security where it finds it arbitrary or unreasonable. There must be some form of adversarial proceedings, if need be through a special representation after a security

---

[2234] No. 2694/08, 13.3.12.

[2235] See, e.g. *Ananyev and other v Russia*, Nos. 42525/07 and 60800/08, 10.1.12; *Harakchiev and Tolumov v Bulgaria*, Nos. 15018/11 and 61199/12, 8.7.14.

[2236] No. 47687/13, 17.11.15.

[2237] See, e.g. *Klass and others v Germany*, Series A, No. 28, 6.9.78, para. 69.

[2238] No. 22414/93, 15.11.96.

[2239] No. 50963/99, 20.6.02. By contrast, see *I.R. and G.T. v UK*, Nos. 14876/12 and 63339/12, dec. 28.1.14 (exclusion on grounds of national security—Special Immigration Appeals Tribunal offered sufficient procedural safeguards—inadmissible).

[2240] *Al-Nashif v Bulgaria*, No. 50963/99, 20.6.02, para. 137.

clearance. Furthermore, the question whether the impugned measure would interfere with the individual's right to respect for family life and, if so, whether a fair balance is struck between the public interest involved and the individual's rights must be examined.

6.691 Judicial review of expulsion orders made on national security grounds was subsequently introduced in Bulgaria in 2003, but in *C.G. and others v Bulgaria*[2241] such proceedings were found not to comply with Article 13 because the domestic courts failed to carry out adequate scrutiny as to whether the decision to expel had been made on genuine national security grounds and whether there was a sufficient factual basis for the assessment that the applicant presented such a security risk. The applicant was also not given a sufficient opportunity to refute the authorities' assessment and no consideration was given by the courts to the question whether the interference with the applicants' family life was proportionate.

6.692 In *Conka v Belgium*,[2242] the applicant Slovakian asylum-seekers were served on a Friday with an order to leave Belgium, and they were deported the following Tuesday. The Government argued that a remedy was available to the applicants who could have applied to the *Conseil d'Etat* for a stay of execution under an extremely urgent procedure. However, the Court, by a majority of four votes to three, found that Article 13 (in conjunction with Article 4 of Protocol No. 4) had been violated because the deportation order was not suspensive and the authorities were not bound to await any decision of the *Conseil d'Etat*. Furthermore, whilst a practice had developed to deal with urgent cases, the Court found that there was no guarantee that it would be complied with in every case. In its subsequent judgment in *Gebremedhin [Gaberamadhien] v France*,[2243] the Court found that where a state decides to remove an alien to a country where there are substantial grounds for believing that they face a risk of torture or ill-treatment, Article 13 requires that the person should have access to a remedy with automatic suspensive effect. There was a violation of Article 13 (taken together with Article 3) in *Gebremedhin* because the applicant Eritrean, who applied for asylum on arrival at Charles de Gaulle airport in Paris, did not have access (from the airport waiting area) to a remedy with automatic suspensive effect to challenge an order refusing him entry to French territory and requiring his removal. Article 13 was found to have been violated (in conjunction with Article 8) in *De Souza Ribeiro v France*[2244] as a result of the absence of an effective and accessible remedy in relation to the applicant's removal from French Guiana to Brazil. He was expelled within less than 36 hours of his arrest, which did not enable his petition to the administrative court to be properly assessed. The applicants in *Singh and others v Belgium*[2245] applied for asylum because of their fears of being returned to Afghanistan, as members of the minority Sikh community there. However, the Belgian authorities failed to take sufficient steps to assess the risks they faced, or to authenticate their identity documents, which should not have been dismissed without close and rigorous scrutiny. As a result, there was a violation of Article 13 together with Article 3. In *Rahimi v Greece*[2246] the failure to

---

[2241] No. 1365/07, 24.4.08.
[2242] No. 51564/99, 5.2.02. See also *Hirst Jamaa and others v Italy*, No. 27765/09, 23.2.12.
[2243] No. 25389/05, 26.4.07. See also *Abdolkhani and Karimnia v Turkey*, No. 30471/08, 22.9.09; *Auad v Bulgaria*, No. 46390/10, 11.10.11; *I.M. v France*, No. 9152/09, 2.2.12; *M.A. v Cyprus*, No. 41872/10, 23.7.13; *A.C. and others v Spain*, No. 6528/11, 22.4.14; *A.M. v Netherlands*, No. 29094/09, 5.7.16.
[2244] No. 22689/07, 13.12.12. See also *Mohammed v Austria*, No. 2283/12, 6.6.13.
[2245] No. 33210/11, 2.10.12.
[2246] No. 8687/08, 5.4.11.

provide adequate procedural information to an unaccompanied minor asylum-seeker, in a language he understood, was held to breach Article 13. Article 13 was found to have been breached in *M.S.S. v Belgium and Greece*,[2247] because of 'major structural deficiencies' in the Greek asylum procedure.

Where a Court refuses to consider the substantive issues in question, on the basis that the decision-making body had full discretion, it cannot provide an effective remedy in full compliance with Article 13.[2248]   **6.693**

Prior to the Grand Chamber judgment in *Kudla v Poland*,[2249] the Court would not rule on a complaint under Article 13 in respect of a breach of the reasonable time requirement under Article 6(1). This position was reviewed in *Kudla* in the light of the excessive number of length of proceedings cases coming before the Court, and as a result it is now possible to make such a separate complaint.[2250] Thus, a remedy in relation to unduly long legal proceedings will be effective for the purposes of Article 13 either if it can lead to the expedition of the proceedings, or if it provides adequate redress for delays that have already occurred.[2251] This will ordinarily include the award of non-pecuniary damages.[2252] However, the position is different where excessively long legal proceedings impact on rights to family life (such as contact rights) in which case the available remedy must be both preventive and compensatory.[2253]   **6.694**

In *McFarlane v Ireland*,[2254] a majority of the Grand Chamber found a violation of Article 13 because of the absence of an effective remedy to claim damages for delays in criminal proceedings. The Court rejected the Government's arguments that an action for damages for a breach of the constitutional right to reasonable expedition would amount to an effective remedy. Although such a domestic right had existed in theory for 25 years, the Court noted that it had never in fact been invoked and found there were significant uncertainties as to its availability in practice. There were also doubts that the remedy would be effective in the particular situation where a delay was caused by the failure of an individual judge to deliver judgment within a reasonable time. Finally, the Court also had concerns about the likely length of such a remedy itself, as well as the availability of legal aid.[2255]   **6.695**

[2247] No. 30696/09, 21.1.11. See also: *O'Rourke v UK*, No. 39022/97, dec. 26.6.01; *Larioshina v Russia*, No. 56869/00, dec. 23.4.02; *Budina v Russia*, No. 45603/05, dec. 18.6.09.

[2248] *Hasan and Chaush v Bulgaria*, No. 30985/96, 26.10.00, para. 100.

[2249] No. 30210/96, 26.10.00.

[2250] See, e.g. *Nouhaud v France*, No. 33424/96, 9.7.02; *Konti-Arvaniti v Greece*, No. 53401/99, 10.4.03; *Doran v Ireland*, No. 50389/99, 31.7.03; *Kangasluoma v Finland*, No. 48339/99, 20.1.04; *Sürmeli v Germany*, No. 75529/01, 8.6.06; *Panju v Belgium*, No. 18393/09, 28.10.14.

[2251] *Sürmeli v Germany*, No. 75529/01, 8.6.06, para. 99. In *Vidas v Croatia*, No. 40383/04, 3.7.08 the Court found a violation of Article 13 where the applicant's complaint to the Constitutional Court about the length of civil proceedings itself took more than three years to resolve. See also *Kaić and others v Croatia*, No. 22014/04, 17.7.08 (both insufficient compensation and delay led to a finding of a violation of Article 13). A disciplinary complaint against judges will not amount to an effective remedy in relation to the length of proceedings—see *Abramiuc v Romania*, No. 37411/02, 24.2.09.

[2252] See, e.g. *Martins Castro and Alves Correia de Castro v Portugal*, No. 33729/06, 10.6.08 and *Valada Matos das Neves v Portugal*, No. 73798/13, 29.10.15.

[2253] See, e.g. *Kuppinger v Germany*, No. 62198/11, 15.1.15, para. 137.

[2254] No. 31333/06, 10.9.10.

[2255] But in their joint dissenting opinions, Judges Gyulumyan, Ziemele, Bianku and Power, and, separately, Lopez-Guerra, argued that the case should have been declared inadmissible because the applicants had failed to test the efficacy of an action for damages for a breach of the constitutional right to reasonable expedition.

6.696 The right of the applicant church to an effective remedy under Article 13 was found to have been violated in *Metropolitan Church of Bessarabia v Moldova*.[2256] The applicant Church brought proceedings in the Supreme Court to challenge the Government's refusal to recognise it. The Supreme Court held that the Government's refusal to reply to the applicant was not unlawful, or in breach of Article 9, and the Supreme Court failed to reply to the main complaint, which was that the applicant wished to practise a religion within a church which was distinct from the Metropolitan Church of Moldova, as only those denominations that were recognised by the state enjoyed legal protection.

6.697 In relation to the right to freedom of assembly, the Court has emphasised that the timing of marches and demonstrations may be significant, and accordingly that the domestic law should specify reasonable time limits within which the authorities should act in respect of requests for permission to hold public assemblies. There was a violation of Article 13 taken together with Article 11 in *Bączkowski and others v Poland*,[2257] which concerned the repeated banning of marches in Warsaw aimed at highlighting discrimination against minorities. The applicants sought to challenge the ban on their march and rallies, but they were not given a decision prior to the planned events.

6.698 In *Petkov and others v Bulgaria*,[2258] the applicants were prevented from standing for parliamentary elections because the electoral authorities failed to comply with domestic court judgments ordering their reinstatement onto the electoral lists, in violation of Article 3 of Protocol No. 1. In those circumstances the Court held that an award of compensation would not in itself be sufficient to comply with Article 13. What was required was a procedure by which the applicants could seek vindication of their right to stand for Parliament before a body capable of examining the effect which the alleged breach of their rights had on the outcome of the elections (including the power to annul the election result, wholly or in part, if necessary). It was not established that such a remedy existed, even by way of an application to the Constitutional Court and, accordingly, Article 13 was found to have been violated.

6.699 Prior to the implementation of the Human Rights Act 1998 in the UK, the European Court found that in certain circumstances judicial review would amount to an effective remedy, but in other situations it would not. The Court has contrasted the 'most anxious scrutiny' applied by the domestic courts to the individual facts in extradition or asylum cases such as *Soering v UK*[2259] or *Vilvarajah v UK*[2260] (where the test applied by the domestic courts was found to coincide with the Court's own approach under Article 3)[2261] with cases where the High Court's jurisdiction was limited and where therefore there could be no application of the test of proportionality. In *Smith and Grady v UK*,[2262] which concerned the ban on homosexuals in the armed forces, the Court found that despite the availability of judicial review proceedings, there had been a violation of Article 13 because the threshold at which the domestic courts could find the policy in question to be irrational[2263]

[2256] No. 45701/99, 13.12.01.
[2257] No. 1543/06, 3.5.07. See also *Alekseyev v Russia*, Nos. 4916/07, 25924/08 and 14599/09, 21.10.10; *Genderdoc-M v Moldova*, No. 9106/06, 12.6.12.
[2258] Nos. 77568/01, 178/02 and 505/02, 11.6.09.
[2259] No. 14038/88, Series A, No. 161, 7.7.89.
[2260] Nos. 13163/87, 13164/87, 13165/87, 13447/87 and 13448/87, Series A, No. 215, 30.10.91.
[2261] See also: *Bensaid v UK*, No. 44599/98, 6.2.01, para. 56; *Hilal v UK*, No. 45276/99, 6.3.01, para. 78.
[2262] Nos. 33985/96 and 33986/96, 27.12.99.
[2263] *Ibid.*, para. 138. See also *Hatton and others v UK*, No. 36022/97, 8.7.03, paras. 141–2.

was placed so high that it effectively excluded any consideration by the domestic courts of the question of whether the interference with the applicants' rights answered a pressing social need or was proportionate to the … aims pursued, principles which lie at the heart of the Court's analysis of complaints under Article 8 of the Convention.

A similar finding of a violation of Article 13 was made in *Peck* v *UK*,[2264] where the Court also held that complaints to various media commissions, concerning the publication or broadcast of CCTV footage of the applicant, could not have provided him with an effective remedy because the commissions lacked the power to award damages.

Article 14: Prohibition of Discrimination

Article 14 states: **6.700**

> The enjoyment of the rights and freedoms set forth in this Convention shall be secured without discrimination on any ground such as sex, race, colour, language, religion, political or other opinion, national or social origin, association with a national minority, property, birth or other status.

Article 14 prohibits discrimination in relation to the other Convention rights only. It is **6.701** therefore not a freestanding right and must be invoked in conjunction with another substantive Convention right (including the rights contained in the Protocols). The 'parasitic' nature of the right is one of the reasons why the Article 14 case law has been limited. However, Protocol No. 12 to the Convention seeks to plug this gap by establishing a freestanding, non-discrimination provision. Protocol No. 12 (see 6.909 below) was adopted on 4 November 2000 and came into force on 1 April 2005.

The Strasbourg institutions can be criticised for failing to develop Article 14 notwithstand- **6.702** ing its limited remit (although more recent seminal cases such as *Opuz* v *Turkey*[2265] and *D.H and others* v *Czech Republic*[2266]—discussed below—have demonstrated a more progressive approach). For example, in the cases concerning the ban on homosexuals in the armed forces, *Smith and Grady* v *UK*[2267] and *Lustig-Prean and Beckett* v *UK*[2268] the Court found violations of the right to respect for private life (and of Article 13 in *Smith and Grady*), but it declined to consider Article 14, finding that it did not give rise to a separate issue. This case, concerning as it did an overtly discriminatory policy, illustrates the weakness of the application of Article 14. It has been the stated practice of the Court not to examine a complaint under Article 14 where a separate breach of the substantive Article has been found, unless a clear inequality of treatment is a fundamental aspect of the case.[2269] In many cases against Turkey brought since the mid-1990s, concerning a wide range of violations of the rights of the Kurdish community in Turkey, the Court declined to find violations of Article 14. That was the position too in the earlier Roma cases brought against Bulgaria, such as *Assenov*,[2270] *Velikova*[2271] and *Anguelova*.[2272] *Anguelova* concerned the death in police custody of a 17-year-old Roma man,

---

[2264] No. 44647/98, 28.1.03.
[2265] No. 33401/02, 9.6.09.
[2266] No. 57325/00, 13.11.07, para. 188.
[2267] Nos. 33985/96 and 33986/96, 27.9.99.
[2268] Nos. 31417/96 and 32377/96, 27.9.99.
[2269] See, e.g. *Dudgeon* v *UK*, No. 7526/76, Series A. No. 59, 24.2.83, para. 67.
[2270] No. 24760/94, 28.10.98.
[2271] No. 41488/98, 18.5.00.
[2272] No. 38361/97, 13.6.02.

as a result of a skull fracture. In his forceful dissenting opinion, Judge Bonello argued that the Court's treatment of minorities was inadequate:

> Frequently and regularly the Court acknowledges that members of vulnerable minorities are deprived of life or subjected to appalling treatment in violation of Article 3; but not once has the Court found that this happens to be linked to their ethnicity. Kurds, coloureds, Islamics, Roma and others are again and again killed, tortured or maimed, but the Court is not persuaded that their race, colour, nationality or place of origin has anything to do with it. Misfortunes punctually visit disadvantaged minority groups, but only as the result of well-placed coincidence.

6.703   However, in *Nachova and others v Bulgaria* the Court found a violation of Article 14, taken together with Article 2, following the use of lethal force by the military police to stop two young Roma men who had absconded from the army (and in the light of previous similar incidents in the cases of *Velikova* and *Anguelova*). The authorities were found to have failed to investigate allegations of racist verbal abuse by the officers involved. The Court laid down a clear marker as to the requirements of Article 14 relating to the investigation of racist violence:[2273]

> … when investigating violent incidents and, in particular, deaths at the hands of State agents, State authorities have the additional duty to take all reasonable steps to unmask any racist motive and to establish whether or not ethnic hatred or prejudice may have played a role in the events. Failing to do so and treating racially induced violence and brutality on an equal footing with cases that have no racist overtones would be to turn a blind eye to the specific nature of acts that are particularly destructive of fundamental rights. A failure to make a distinction in the way in which situations that are essentially different are handled may constitute unjustified treatment irreconcilable with Article 14 of the Convention.

6.704   The Court also held that any evidence of racist verbal abuse by law enforcement agents in an operation involving the use of force against persons from any minority is highly pertinent as to whether or not unlawful, hatred-induced violence has taken place; any such evidence must therefore be verified. If it is confirmed, there must then be a thorough examination to uncover any possible racist motives.

6.705   Finally in *Nachova*, the Chamber in its 2004 judgment had found that the failure of the authorities to carry out an effective investigation into the apparently racist motive for the killing shifted the burden of proof to the Government in relation to the alleged violation of Article 14 taken together with the substantive aspect of Article 2. However, the Grand Chamber declined to follow that approach, as it would have required the Government to prove the absence of racial prejudice on the part of the officer, and found no violation of Article 14 taken together with the substantive obligation under Article 2 (by 11 votes to six). Nevertheless, the Grand Chamber held that it could not exclude the possibility 'that in certain cases of alleged discrimination it may require the respondent government to disprove an arguable allegation of discrimination and—if they fail to do so—find a violation of Article 14 of the Convention on that basis'.[2274]

[2273] *Nachova and others v Bulgaria*, Nos. 43577/98 and 43579/98, 26.2.04, para. 158 (and endorsed by the Grand Chamber in its judgment of 6.7.05, para. 160). See also *Angelova and Iliev v Bulgaria*, No. 55523/00, 26.7.07.

[2274] *Nachova and others v Bulgaria*, Nos. 43577/98 and 43579/98, 6.7.05, para. 157. See also the concurring opinion of Judge Bratza.

Equivalent principles also apply to the investigation of religiously motivated violence.[2275]

Applicability of Article 14

Article 14 can be relied upon provided that the complaint falls within the *ambit* of one or **6.706** more of the other Convention rights,[2276] but it is not necessary to establish that there has been a violation of another Convention right. In *Botta* v *Italy*,[2277] for example, the applicant's complaint about discrimination in relation to access to bathing facilities on holiday for disabled people was not considered to fall within the ambit of Article 8 and therefore Article 14 had no application. However, in *Van der Mussele* v *Belgium*,[2278] the complaint of a pupil advocate about having to perform pro bono work was found not to breach Article 4 but, as the case fell within the ambit of Article 4, Article 14 was applicable.[2279]

Article 14 also applies not only to aspects of a Convention right that the state is obliged to **6.707** protect, but also those aspects that a state chooses to guarantee, without being required to do so. In *Petrovic* v *Austria*[2280] the applicant father's complaint that the parental leave allowance was only available to mothers fell within the scope of Article 8 (despite the fact that there was no positive obligation to provide such financial assistance) because by granting such an allowance, the aim of the state was to promote family life. *Frette* v *France*[2281] concerned the rejection of the applicant homosexual's request for authority to adopt a child. Article 14 was held to be applicable, as whilst the Convention does not guarantee a right to adopt as such, French domestic law allowed all single people to apply for adoption, a right that fell within the ambit of Article 8.

Grounds of discrimination

Article 14 expressly prohibits discrimination on *any* ground: examples include sex, race, **6.708** colour, language, religion, political or other opinion, national or social origin, association with a national minority, property, or birth. However, it also prohibits discrimination on grounds of 'other status', indicating that the list is open-ended. For example, other prohibited grounds have been found to include marital status,[2282] sexual orientation,[2283] illegitimacy,[2284] disability,[2285] health status,[2286] professional status,[2287] immigration status,[2288]

[2275] *Milanović* v *Serbia*, No. 44616/07, 14.12.10.

[2276] See, e.g. *Gaygusuz* v *Austria*, No. 17371/90, 16.9.96, para. 36.

[2277] *Botta* v *Italy*, No. 21439/93, 24.2.98.

[2278] No. 8919/80, Series A, No. 70, 23.11.83.

[2279] See also *Zarb Adami* v *Malta*, No. 17209/02, 20.6.06 (violation of Article 14 taken in conjunction with Article 4(3)(d), as many more men were required in practice to do jury service). But see the concerns expressed by Judges Bratza and Garlicki in their concurring opinions as to how the case could be said to fall within the ambit of Article 4 given that jury service was a 'normal civic obligation' and was therefore excluded from the definition of 'forced or compulsory labour' under Article 4(3).

[2280] No. 20458/92, 27.3.98.

[2281] No. 36515/97, 26.2.02.

[2282] See, e.g. *Wessels-Bergevoet* v *Netherlands*, No. 34462/97, 4.6.02; *Şerife Yiğit* v *Turkey*, No. 3976/05, 2.11.10 (distinction between a civil and religious marriage).

[2283] See. e.g. *Sutherland* v *UK*, No. 25186/94, Comm. Rep. 1.7.97; *Salgueiro da Silva Mouta* v *Portugal*, No. 33290/96, 21.12.99; *Fretté* v *France*, No. 36515/97, 26.2.02; *L and V* v *Austria*, Nos. 39392/98 and 3989/98, 9.1.03.

[2284] See, e.g. *Inze* v *Austria*, No. 8695/79, Series A, No. 126, 28.10.87.

[2285] *Mandy Malone* v *UK*, No. 25290/94, dec. 28.2.96; *Glor* v *Switzerland*, No. 13444/04, 30.4.09.

[2286] *Kiyutin* v *Russia*, No. 2700/10, 10.3.11.

[2287] *Van der Mussele* v *Belgium*, No. 8919/80, Series A, No. 70, 23.11.83.

[2288] *Bah* v *UK*, No. 56328/07, 27.9.11; *Hode and Abdi* v *UK*, No. 22341/09, 6.11.12.

trade union membership,[2289] military status,[2290] and place of residence.[2291] Article 14 does *not* therefore solely proscribe different treatment based on characteristics that are 'personal', in the sense that they are innate or inherent: see, for example, the cases based on property ownership[2292] or military position.

6.709　In *Clift* v *UK*,[2293] the Court held that the applicant, who was a convicted prisoner, could legitimately complain of discrimination under Article 14 in circumstances where an early release scheme applied differently to prisoners depending on the length of their sentences. In *G.N.* v *Italy*[2294] the Court found a violation of Article 14 taken together with Article 2 where the applicants were excluded from compensation arrangements in respect of those who contracted HIV during blood transfusions, simply on the basis that their relatives had been suffering from thalassaemia as opposed to haemophilia (as stipulated by the relevant legislation).

The test of discrimination

6.710　A person is considered to have suffered discrimination if:

(1) they have been treated differently from people in a similar situation (on a prohibited ground); and

(2) there is no reasonable and objective justification for the difference in treatment.[2295]

6.711　The applicant must therefore establish that there has been less favourable treatment and that its basis was a prohibited ground of discrimination. However, there will be no violation of Article 14 if the difference in treatment related to people who were *not* in 'analogous situations'—the comparator groups therefore need not be identical, but do need to be in a 'relevantly similar situation'. In *Van der Mussele* v *Belgium*,[2296] the applicant lawyer complained about discrimination between advocates and other professions in relation to the obligation to work without payment. However, the Court held that, in view of the fundamental differences between the professions (as to legal status, conditions for entry into the profession, the nature of the functions involved, and the manner of exercise of those functions) there was no similarity between the disparate situations in question.

6.712　If an applicant establishes that there has been differential treatment in an analogous situation, then the state must prove that the difference in treatment had a 'reasonable and objective justification'. The test that the Court applies is twofold: that the difference in treatment pursued a legitimate aim; and that it was proportionate to that aim.

6.713　The test of proportionality (which is discussed further above at 5.10) requires an assessment of whether there is a reasonable relationship of proportionality between the means employed and the aim sought to be achieved. Any difference in treatment must strike a fair balance

---

[2289] See *Danilenkov* v *Russia*, No. 67336/01, 30.7.09.
[2290] *Engel and others* v *Netherlands*, Series A, No. 22, 8.6.76.
[2291] *Carson and others* v *UK*, No. 42184/05, 16.3.10, para. 71.
[2292] See, e.g. *Pine Valley Developments Ltd* v *Ireland*, No. 12742/87, Series A, No. 222, 29.11.91.
[2293] No. 7205/07, 13.7.10.
[2294] No. 43134/05, 1.12.09.
[2295] See, e.g. *Belgian Linguistic Case*, Series A, No. 6, 23.7.68.
[2296] No. 8919/80, Series A, No. 70, 23.11.83.

between the protection of the interests of the community and respect for the rights and freedoms safeguarded by the Convention.

In assessing the proportionality of a measure, the state is generally allowed a certain 'margin of appreciation', or discretion. However, the Court has found that discrimination on particular grounds, such as sex,[2297] sexual orientation,[2298] nationality,[2299] marital status,[2300] and illegitimacy[2301] will have to be justified by 'very strong or weighty' or 'particularly serious' reasons. The Commission affirmed that 'a special importance should be attached to discrimination based on race',[2302] and the Grand Chamber has described racial discrimination as a 'particularly egregious' kind of discrimination.[2303] Furthermore, vulnerable segments of society who have previously been the victims of discrimination, such as disabled people, will be further protected:[2304]

> ... if a restriction on fundamental rights applies to a particularly vulnerable group in society, who have suffered considerable discrimination in the past, such as the mentally disabled, then the State's margin of appreciation is substantially narrower and it must have very weighty reasons for the restrictions in question ...

The Court has also found that people living with HIV are a vulnerable group who have been the victims of prejudice and stigmatisation and therefore states will be permitted only a narrow margin of appreciation in providing differential treatment to them on the basis of their HIV status.[2305]

6.714

One of the relevant factors in considering the reasons for a difference in treatment is whether or not there is a common standard amongst Council of Europe states. In *Petrovic v Austria*[2306] the Court noted that there was no such common standard in respect of parental leave allowances for fathers (at the end of the 1980s most Council of Europe states did not provide for such payments) and accordingly the decision to refuse the applicant a parental leave allowance fell within the state's margin of appreciation. However, by the time of the judgment in *Konstantin Markin v Russia*[2307] in 2012, the Court noted that in a majority of European states legislation provided that parental leave applied to both mothers and fathers. Therefore, the Government could not rely on the absence of a common standard among the contracting states to justify the difference in treatment between men and women (in this case, military personnel) as regards parental leave. The automatic exclusion of all servicemen, irrespective of their position in the army, the availability of a replacement or their individual situation,

6.715

2297 See, e.g. *Abdulaziz, Cabales and Balkandali v UK*, Nos. 9473/81 and 9474/81, Series A, No. 94, 28.5.85, para. 78; *Smith and Grady v UK*, Nos. 33985/96 and 33986/96, 27.9.99, para. 90; *Lustig-Prean and Beckett v UK*, Nos. 31417/96 and 32377/96, 27.9.99, para. 82.

2298 See, e.g. *L and V v Austria*, Nos. 39392/98 and 3989/98, 9.1.03.

2299 *Gaygusuz v Austria*, No. 17371/90, 16.9.96, para. 42; *Koua Poirrez v France*, No. 40892/98, 30.9.03, para. 46.

2300 See, e.g. *Wessels-Bergevoet v Netherlands*, No. 34462/97, 4.6.02, para. 49.

2301 See, e.g. *Inze v Austria*, No. 8695/79, Series A, No. 126, 28.10.87.

2302 *East African Asians v UK*, Nos. 4403/70–4419/70, 4422/70, 4434/70, 4443/70, 4476/70–4478/70, 4486/70, 4501/70 and 4526/70–4530/70, 14.12.73, para. 207.

2303 *Nachova and others v Bulgaria*, Nos. 43577/98 and 43579/98, 6.7.05, para. 145.

2304 *Alajos Kiss v Hungary*, No. 38832/06, 20.5.10, para. 42.

2305 *Kiyutin v Russia*, No. 2700/10, 10.3.11, para. 64.

2306 No. 20458/92, 27.3.98.

2307 No. 30078/06, 22.3.12 (in effect, confirming the earlier chamber judgment in the case: 7.10.10). See also *Hulea v Romania*, No. 33411/05, 2.10.12.

was found to fall outside any acceptable margin of appreciation, and to violate Article 14 taken together with Article 8.

6.716   The foreseeability of any changes to domestic laws which have discriminatory effects will be relevant to the proportionality test. For example, there was a violation of Article 14 taken together with Article 2 of Protocol No. 1 in *Altınay v Turkey*[2308] where there was an unexpected legal change as regards university access. The applicant was prevented from going to university after changes were introduced which discriminated against him as a pupil at a vocational school, as opposed to an ordinary high school, and there were no 'corrective measures' applicable to his case.

6.717   The Court has also recognised the principle of indirect discrimination:[2309]

> ... a general policy or measure which is apparently neutral but has disproportionately prejudicial effects on persons or groups of persons who .... are [for example] identifiable only on the basis of an ethnic criterion, may be considered discriminatory notwithstanding that it is not specifically aimed at that group ... unless that measure is objectively justified by a legitimate aim and the means of achieving that aim are appropriate, necessary and proportionate.

There was a violation of Article 14 together with Article 8 in *Di Trizio v Switzerland*[2310] because in practice the method of calculation of invalidity benefits was discriminatory against women. Noting that in one year 97 per cent of all the cases in which the particular method of calculation had been applied concerned women, the Court found that such figures gave rise to a presumption of indirect discrimination.

6.718   Referral to statistics in order to establish discriminatory treatment may be important in practice. Thus the Court has found[2311] that:

> ... where an applicant is able to show, on the basis of undisputed official statistics, the existence of a prima facie indication that a specific rule—although formulated in a neutral manner—in fact affects a clearly higher percentage of women than men, it is for the respondent government to show that this is the result of objective factors unrelated to any discrimination on grounds of sex.

6.719   In *D.H. and Others v Czech Republic*,[2312] the Grand Chamber established that:

> when it comes to assessing the impact of a measure or practice on an individual or group, statistics which appear on critical examination to be reliable and significant will be sufficient to constitute the prima facie evidence the applicant is required to produce.

6.720   In the ground-breaking judgment in *Opuz v Turkey*,[2313] the Court found a violation of Article 14 taken together with Articles 2 and 3 because of the authorities' failure to respond adequately to domestic violence. The case concerned an escalating series of violent attacks on

---

[2308]   No. 37222/04, 9.7.13.
[2309]   See *Hugh Jordan v UK*, No. 24746/94, 4.5.01, para. 154; *Hoogendijk v Netherlands*, No. 58461/00, dec. 6.1.05; *Oršuš and others v Croatia*, No. 15766/03, 16.3.10, para. 150.
[2310]   No. 7186/09, 2.2.16.
[2311]   *Hoogendijk v Netherlands*, No. 58641/00, dec. 6.1.05; *D.H. and others v Czech Republic*, No. 57325/00, 13.11.07, para. 180.
[2312]   No. 57325/00, 13.11.07, para. 188.
[2313]   No. 33401/02, 9.6.09. See also *Eremia v Moldova*, No.3564/11, 28.5.13 (failure of authorities to take adequate measures to protect wife and teenage daughters from domestic violence—violations of Articles 3, 8 and Article 14 together with Article 3).

the applicant and her mother by the applicant's husband, culminating in his fatally shooting the applicant's mother. The Court took account of statistics submitted by the Diyarbakır Bar Association and Amnesty International in finding that the highest number of reported victims of domestic violence was in Diyarbakır, where the applicant lived, and that the victims were all women, primarily of Kurdish origin, and illiterate or with a low level of education. The evidence also led the Court to discern a 'general and discriminatory judicial passivity' as regards domestic violence. Accordingly, the violence suffered by the two women was to be regarded as gender-based violence, which was a form of discrimination against women.[2314] In *Hugh Jordan* v *UK*[2315] the applicant alleged that there was a violation of Article 14 because of the targeting by the security forces of the Catholic or nationalist community in Northern Ireland. Whilst the Court accepted that statistics appeared to show that the majority of people shot by the security forces were from that community, there was considered to be insufficient evidence to establish a violation of Article 14.

Gender

There was no reasonable and objective basis for the difference in treatment between men **6.721** and women in the payment of contributions to a child benefit scheme in *Van Raalte* v *Netherlands*.[2316] The domestic law exempted unmarried childless women over 45, but not men. The Court noted that 'just as women over forty-five may give birth to children, there are on the other hand men of forty-five or younger who may be unable to procreate',[2317] and that women over 45 might also become eligible for child benefit by, for example, marrying a man who had children from a previous marriage. There was also no objective and reasonable justification for the difference in treatment between married women and married men in relation to entitlement to old age pension benefits in *Wessels-Bergervoet* v *Netherlands*.[2318] There, entitlement was reduced, as for a period of 19 years the applicant was excluded from insurance because she was married to a man who was not insured (due to his employment abroad). However, a married man in the same position would not have been similarly excluded, hence the Court found a violation of Article 14 in conjunction with Article 1 of Protocol No. 1. Similarly, in *Willis* v *UK*,[2319] the difference in treatment between men and women as regards entitlement to social security payments on the death of a spouse was not found to be justified. In *Vrountou* v *Cyprus*[2320] the Court found a violation of Article 14 taken together with Article 1 of Protocol No. 1 because the applicant was denied a refugee card (which established entitlement to housing assistance) on the basis that she was the child of a displaced woman rather than a displaced man (under a scheme introduced in 1974 following the Turkish occupation of parts of Cyprus). Noting in particular that the

---

[2314] The decision in *Opuz* can be contrasted with the case of *A* v *Croatia*, No. 55164/08, 14.10.10 in which the Court found insufficient evidence to establish that measures taken in Croatia in response to domestic violence were discriminatory.

[2315] No. 24746/94, 4.5.01. See also: *Kelly and others* v *UK*, No. 30054/96, 4.5.01; *McKerr* v *UK*, No. 28883/95, 4.5.01; *Shanaghan* v *UK*, No. 37715/97, 4.5.01.

[2316] No. 20060/92, 21.2.97. See also, e.g. *Di Trizio* v *Switzerland*, No. 7186/09, 2.2.16 (method of calculation of invalidity benefits discriminatory against women—violation of Article 14 together with Article 8); *Weller* v *Hungary*, No. 44399/05, 31.3.09 (refusal to pay maternity benefit on account of parental status and nationality—violation of Article 14 together with Article 8).

[2317] *Ibid.*, para. 43.

[2318] No. 34462/97, 4.6.02.

[2319] No. 36042/97, 11.6.02.

[2320] No. 33631/06, 13.10.15.

scheme had persisted for more than forty years, the Court found there was no objective and reasonable justification for the difference in treatment, which had been based on traditional family roles.

6.722   The case of *Stec and others* v *UK*[2321] concerned differences in the entitlement for men and women to industrial injuries social security benefits. The applicants (two men and two women) complained of receiving reduced benefits because of the difference in pensionable ages in the United Kingdom (65 for men and 60 for women). The Grand Chamber held there was no violation of Article 14 taken together with Article 1 of Protocol No. 1. It found that the difference in pensionable age had originally been intended to correct the disadvantaged economic position of women, and continued to be reasonably and objectively justified on that basis. Furthermore, linking eligibility for the benefit to the pension system was reasonably and objectively justified, given that its aim was to compensate for reduced earning capacity during a person's working life.

6.723   The case of *Emel Boyraz* v *Turkey*[2322] concerned the dismissal of the applicant as a security guard, on the basis of her gender. The Court found that the reasons given—that security officers had to work on night shifts and in rural areas and might be required to use firearms and physical force—could not in itself justify the difference in treatment between men and women, and accordingly there was a breach of Article 14 in conjunction with Article 8. In *Ünal Tekeli* v *Turkey*,[2323] there was a violation of Article 14 taken together with Article 8, because of the impossibility for the applicant, a married woman, to use her maiden name in official documents, whereas married men could keep the surname they had before they were married. This gender-based difference in treatment could not be justified by the Government's stated objective of 'reflecting family unity'.

6.724   Placing an unjustifiably greater burden on men than women to carry out 'civic obligations', such as jury service and work for the fire service, has been found to violate Article 14 taken together with Article 4(3)(d).[2324] In *Khamtokhu and Aksenchik* v *Russia*[2325] a ten–seven majority of the Grand Chamber found no violation of Article 14 taken together with Article 5 where, under Russian law, a sentence of life imprisonment could be imposed on men, but not women, on the basis that there was held to be a public interest in exempting female offenders.

Ethnicity or race

6.725   Since the mid-2000s there has been a considerable body of cases before the European Court establishing that across the continent there is unjustifiable discrimination against people of Roma origin. In the leading case of *D.H. and others* v *Czech Republic*,[2326] the Grand Chamber

---

[2321] Nos. 65731/01 and 65900/01, 12.4.06. See also *Andrle* v *Czech Republic*, No. 6268/08, 17.2.11.
[2322] No. 61960/08, 2.12.14.
[2323] No. 29865/96, 16.11.04. See also *Losonci Rose and Rose* v *Switzerland*, No. 664/06, 9.11.10 (discrimination in relation to choice of surname of binational couple—violation of Article 14 together with Article 8); *Cusan and Fazzo* v *Italy*, No. 77/07, 7.1.14 (inability for married couple to give their legitimate child the wife's surname—violation of Article 14 together with Article 8).
[2324] *Zarb Adami* v *Malta*, No. 17209/02, 20.6.06; *Schmidt* v *Germany*, No. 13580/88, Series A, No. 291-B, 18.7.94.
[2325] No. 60367/08, 27.1.17 (the exemption of juveniles and offenders over 65 was also considered to be justifiable).
[2326] No. 57325/00, 13.11.07, para. 188.

found that the applicants had submitted evidence that established that a disproportionately high number of Roma children were placed in special schools in the Ostrava region in the Czech Republic. The evidence was considered to be sufficiently reliable and significant to give rise to a strong presumption of indirect discrimination, and accordingly the burden of proof then lay on the Government to show that the difference was the result of objective factors unrelated to ethnic origin. The Court found that there was a danger that psychological testing of the children was biased, as the tests failed to take account of the particular characteristics of the Roma children. The parents could not be considered to have given informed consent to the placement of their children in special schools. The Court concluded that the applicants had been placed in schools for children with mental disabilities where a more basic curriculum was followed than in ordinary schools, and that they therefore received an education that compounded their difficulties and compromised their subsequent personal development. The difference in treatment was not objectively and reasonably justified and there was a violation of Article 14 in conjunction with Article 2 of Protocol No. 1 (by 13 votes to four). There was a similar finding in *Sampanis and others v Greece*,[2327] because the Roma applicants' children were unjustifiably denied access to a primary school and were assigned to 'special classes' in a separate annex.

6.726 The case of *Oršuš and others v Croatia*[2328] also concerned the placement of children in Roma-only classes. The Grand Chamber found that the available statistics did *not* establish that there was a general policy automatically to place Roma pupils in separate classes in the particular schools in question. Nevertheless, there was a difference in treatment, because the placement of children in special schools on the basis that they had an insufficient command of the Croatian language was only applied to Roma children. After a careful analysis, a nine–eight majority of the Court concluded that this difference in treatment did not have a reasonable and objective justification, as there were not adequate safeguards to ensure that the authorities had sufficient regard to their special needs as members of a disadvantaged group. There was no clear legal basis for the separate schooling and the tests that the pupils took were not specifically designed to test language capability. The Court was not satisfied that the authorities had taken positive measures to deal with the high drop-out rates of Roma pupils. It also noted that the nature of the adapted curriculum was unclear and was critical of the lack of transparency and clear criteria as regards transfer to mixed classes, which had meant that the applicants remained in Roma-only classes for long periods of time—for some, throughout their entire primary schooling. Accordingly, there was a violation of Article 14 taken together with Article 2 of Protocol No. 1.

6.727 There was a finding of a violation of Article 14 (taken together with Articles 6 and 8) in *Moldovan and others v Romania*,[2329] a case in which the homes of Roma agricultural workers had been burnt by a mob, with the acquiescence of the police. The Court found that their failure to secure redress through the courts was a result of their ethnicity, as evidenced by the authorities' repeated discriminatory remarks made against the applicants. There was a finding of a violation of Article 14 taken together with Article 3 in *Bekos and Koutropoulos*

[2327] No. 32526/05, 5.6.08. See also *Sampani and others v Greece*, No. 59608/09, 11.12.12.
[2328] No. 15766/03, 16.3.10.
[2329] Nos. 41138/98 and 64320/01, 12.7.05 (judgment No. 2). See also *Paraskeva Todorova v Bulgaria*, No. 37193/07, 25.3.10 (refusal to suspend sentence as a result of applicant's ethnic origin—violation of Article 14 together with Article 6).

v *Greece*,[2330] a case concerning assaults on two Roma men during their arrest by the police. Despite plausible information that the alleged assaults had been racially motivated (it was claimed that they were racially verbally abused), the authorities failed to examine this question.[2331] A similar finding was made in *Šečić v Croatia*[2332] as a result of the police's failure to investigate a serious assault on a Roma man, believed to have been carried out by members of a skinhead group, and in *Cakir v Belgium*,[2333] as regards the failure to investigate a racist motivation to police brutality used when arresting the applicant.

6.728 There was a finding of a violation of Article 14 together with Article 3 in *B.S. v Spain*,[2334] as a result of the authorities' failure to investigate the alleged racist aspects of ill-treatment inflicted by the police on a Nigerian woman who was working as a prostitute. The applicant had complained that the police had made racist remarks to her, such as 'get out of here you black whore', but they had not been examined by the courts.

6.729 At issue in *Biao v Denmark*[2335] were the more favourable conditions for family reunion applying to people who had held Danish citizenship for at least 28 years. The applicants were a married couple—a naturalised Danish citizen of Togolese origin and a Ghanaian national—who were made subject to the rule that a couple applying for family reunification must not have stronger ties with another country (which did not apply to those who had been citizens for 28 years). The Grand Chamber found that the rule in question had the indirect effect of favouring Danish nationals of Danish ethnic origin, and having a disproportionately prejudicial effect on people of foreign ethnic origin. As the Government failed to show that there were compelling or very weighty reasons unrelated to ethnic origin to justify the indirect discriminatory effect of the rule, the Grand Chamber found a violation of Article 14 together with Article 8 (by a majority of 12 votes to five).

6.730 The Grand Chamber found a violation of Article 14 taken together with Article 3 of Protocol No. 1 in *Sejdić and Finci v Bosnia and Herzegovina*,[2336] which concerned the applicants' eligibility to stand for the House of Peoples (the second chamber of the state Parliament). According to the Constitution, in order to be eligible to stand for election, a candidate was required to declare affiliation with a 'constituent people' (Bosniacs, Croats and Serbs).[2337] However, the applicants described themselves as being of Roma and Jewish origin, respectively, and accordingly objected to declaring such affiliation. They were therefore excluded from standing on a basis that lacked any objective and reasonable justification. The Court took note of the Opinion of the Venice Commission that there were mechanisms of power-sharing that did not automatically lead to the total exclusion of representatives of particular communities. For the same reasons, there was also a violation of Article 1 of Protocol No. 12 as regards the applicants' inability to stand for elections to the Presidency of Bosnia and

---

[2330] No. 15250/02, 13.12.05. See also *Cobzaru v Romania*, No. 48249/99, 26.7.07; *Stoica v Romania*, No. 42722/02, 4.3.08.

[2331] But see *Ognyanova and Choban v Bulgaria*, No. 46317/99, 23.2.06 (death of Roma man in police custody—no violation of Article 14 where there was no evidence of racial prejudice).

[2332] No. 40116/02, 31.5.07.

[2333] No. 44256/06, 10.3.09.

[2334] No. 47159/08, 24.7.12.

[2335] No. 38590/10, 24.5.16.

[2336] Nos. 27996/06 and 34836/06, 22.12.09.

[2337] These provisions had been incorporated into the Constitution in order to end a brutal conflict marked by genocide and 'ethnic cleansing', and achieve peace.

Herzegovina. There was a violation of Article 14 together with Article 3 of Protocol No. 1 in *Danis and the Association of Ethnic Turks v Romania*[2338] as regards eligibility requirements to take part in parliamentary elections. The applicant association represented the Turkish minority in Romania and were required by new legislation to establish their representative nature, whereas another association representing the Turkish minority which was already represented in parliament did not need to do so. This difference in treatment had been disproportionate because the electoral legislation had been changed seven months before the elections and had introduced a new eligibility criterion (that of being granted charitable status) which it had been impossible for the applicant association to satisfy.

In *Timishev v Russia*[2339] the decision of the traffic police to refuse to allow the applicant **6.731** Chechen to cross from Ingushetia into Kabardino-Balkaria was found to be in violation of Article 14 taken together with Article 2 of Protocol No. 4 (the right to freedom of movement). The refusal was made following an order by a Ministry of Interior official not to admit 'Chechens'. Accordingly, the Court found the applicant had been the victim of racial discrimination.

Religion

The case of *Hoffmann v Austria*[2340] concerned a dispute over custody of the applicant's chil- **6.732** dren. In awarding custody to the applicant's ex-husband, the domestic courts had assessed the effects that the applicant's membership of the Jehovah's Witness community would have on the children, which included the effects on their social life of being associated with a religious minority and the hazards attached to the rejection of blood transfusions. The European Court found that there had been a difference in treatment on religious grounds that had a legitimate aim (the protection of the health and rights of the children), but that was disproportionate: a distinction based essentially on a difference in religion alone was not acceptable. However, this decision was reached by a majority of just five to four, with the dissenting judges arguing that the domestic courts had reached their decision not on religious grounds, but because of the consequences for the children of the applicant's membership of the Jehovah's Witnesses, which they considered to be legitimate grounds. There was a violation of Article 14 taken together with both Articles 3 and 9 in the case of *97 members of the Gldani Congregation of Jehovah's Witnesses and 4 others v Georgia*,[2341] which concerned an organised, sustained attack on the applicant Jehovah's Witnesses by members of a group of Orthodox extremists. The authorities' failure to intervene and their subsequent indifference to the attack was found by the Court to be 'to a large extent the corollary of the applicants' religious convictions'. In *Religionsgemeinschaft der Zeugen Jehovas and others v Austria*[2342] there was a breach of Article 9 taken together with Article 14 because of the imposition of a 10-year waiting period before the applicant religious association was granted legal personality—a period

---

[2338] No. 16632/09, 21.4.15.

[2339] Nos. 55762/00 and 55974/00, 13.12.05.

[2340] Series A, 255-C, 23.6.93. See also *Palau-Martinez v France*, No. 57967/00, 16.12.03; *Vojnity v Hungary*, No. 29617/07, 12.2.13 (denial of father's right of access to his son—violation of Article 14 together with Article 8).

[2341] No. 71156/01, 3.5.07.

[2342] No. 40825/98, 31.7.08 (there was also a violation of Article 14 taken together with Article 9 because it was unjustifiably granted the status of a 'religious community' rather than a 'religious society' that conferred various privileges). See also *Savez crkava 'Riječ života' and others v Croatia*, No. 7798/08, 9.12.10 (refusal to conclude legal status of Reformist churches—violation of Article 14 in conjunction with Article 9).

that was not necessarily applied to other organisations. This was held to be unjustifiable as regards the Jehovah's Witnesses, which had a long-standing existence internationally and which was established in Austria. There was a violation of Article 14 together with Article 9 in *Cumhuriyetçi Eğitim Ve Kültür Merkezi Vakfı v Turkey*[2343] because of the authorities' refusal to grant to the applicant Alevi association an exemption from electricity bills available to places of worship. The decision had been taken on the basis that Alevism was not a religion and could not therefore have its own places of worship. However, the Court found that such an assessment could not be used to justify the exclusion of the Alevi premises, as they, like other recognised places of worship, were premises intended for the practice of religious rituals. There was accordingly no justification for the difference in treatment. In the subsequent case of *İzzettin Doğan and others v Turkey*[2344] the Grand Chamber found a violation of Article 14 together with Article 9 because of the authorities' refusal to provide public religious services to adherents to the Alevi faith. The Court found a 'glaring imbalance' between the status conferred on the majority understanding of Islam in the form of a religious public service, and the almost blanket exclusion of the Alevi community from such a service, which could not be justified by the Government.

6.733 The case of *Manzanas Martin v Spain*[2345] concerned the difference in pension eligibility of the applicant, an evangelical priest, as compared with Catholic priests. The Court found a violation of Article 14 taken together with Article 1 of Protocol No. 1 as there was no justification for the fact that Catholic priests had been integrated into the social security regime 22 years earlier than their counterparts in the Evangelical Church.

6.734 The case of *O'Donoghue and others v UK*[2346] concerned conditions placed on marriage for third-country nationals by way of a certificate of approval scheme.[2347] As well as violating Article 12, because the scheme impaired the very essence of the right to marry, the Court also found a violation of Article 14 taken together with both Article 12 and Article 9, because the scheme did *not* apply to marriages conducted within the Church of England.

Nationality

6.735 The Court acknowledges that the pressures on state funds may justify certain differential treatment:

> a State may have legitimate reasons for curtailing the use of resource-hungry public services—such as welfare programmes, public benefits and health care—by short-term and illegal immigrants, who, as a rule, do not contribute to their funding.[2348]

Further, the Court has also recognised that it may sometimes be justifiable to differentiate between different categories of aliens residing in its territory (such as, for example, affording preferential treatment to EU nationals).[2349]

[2343] No. 32093/10, 2.12.14. See, by contrast, *The Church of Jesus Christ of Latter-Day Saints v UK*, No. 7552/09, 4.3.14 (denial of exemption from business rates for places of worship—no violation of Article 14 together with Article 9).

[2344] No. 62649/10, 26.4.16. The Court also found a violation of Article 9 (by 12 votes to five).

[2345] No. 17966/10, 3.4.12.

[2346] No. 34848/07, 14.12.10.

[2347] Under s. 19 of the Asylum and Immigration (Treatment of Claimants etc.) Act 2004.

[2348] *Ponomaryovi v Bulgaria*, No. 5335/05, 21.6.11, para. 54. See also 6.799 below.

[2349] *Ibid.*

The case of *Kurić and others* v *Slovenia*[2350] concerned the position of the 'erased'—former **6.736** citizens of Yugoslavia who complained they had been arbitrarily deprived of the possibility of acquiring Slovenian citizenship, and whose names were taken off the register of permanent residents, and who became de facto stateless after Slovenian independence. The Grand Chamber found that there was differential treatment which was based on the national origin of the persons concerned: former Yugoslav citizens were treated differently from other foreigners. This did not pursue a legitimate aim and lacked any objective and reasonable justification, in violation of Article 14 taken together with Article 8. The case of *A.H. and others* v *Russia*[2351] concerned the ban on adoption of Russian children by US nationals. The adoption proceedings initiated by the applicants were abruptly ended because of their automatic ineligibility resulting from the law introduced in 2013, and no consideration was given to the interests of the children. As there were no compelling reasons to justify the blanket ban, this was held to breach Article 14 taken together with Article 8. There was a violation of Article 14 taken together with Article 1 of Protocol No. 1 in *Koua Poirrez* v *France*.[2352] There, the applicant, an Ivory Coast national, was unjustifiably refused a disability allowance solely on the basis that he was not a French national or that he was not a national of a state with which the French Government had concluded a reciprocal agreement in respect of the allowance.[2353] There was also a violation of Article 14 taken together with Article 1 of Protocol No. 1 in *Andrejeva* v *Latvia*.[2354] The applicant had entered Latvia in the 1950s and had been resident there ever since. She had worked in the same chemical plant before and after Latvia achieved independence from the Soviet Union. In calculating her retirement pension, the authorities refused to take account of her work 'outside Latvia'. For the applicant this meant not taking account of her time working in the plant prior to independence. The sole reason for this was that she did not have Latvian citizenship, whereas a Latvian citizen would have been granted the portion of the pension that was denied to the applicant. This difference in treatment on grounds of nationality was held not to be justifiable.

In *Luczak* v *Poland*,[2355] the applicant, a French national living and working as a farmer in **6.737** Poland, complained that the domestic law permitted only Polish nationals to be admitted to the farmers' social security scheme, and that as a result he had no social security cover in the event of sickness, occupational injury or invalidity. The Court found this to be unjustifiable and in violation of Article 14 taken together with Article 1 of Protocol No. 1. There was no violation of the Convention in *Bigaeva* v *Greece*,[2356] arising from the application of

---

[2350] No. 26828/06, 26.6.12. See also *Anastasov and others* v *Slovenia*, No. 65020/13, dec. 18.10.16.

[2351] No. 6033/13 et al, 17.1.17.

[2352] No. 40892/98, 30.9.03. See also *Anakomba Yula* v *Belgium*, No. 45413/07, 10.3.09 (violation of Article 6, in conjunction with Article 14, where the applicant was denied legal aid to bring proceedings to contest the paternity of her child on the basis that she was not lawfully resident in Belgium); *Rangelov* v *Germany*, No. 5123/07, 22.3.12 (violation of Article 14 together with Article 5 due to refusal to provide to applicant prisoner social therapy or to relax his conditions of preventive detention on grounds of his foreign nationality).

[2353] See also *Fawsie* v *Greece*, No. 40080/07, 28.10.10; *Saidoun* v *Greece*, No. 40083/07, 28.10.10 and *Dhahbi* v *Italy*, No. 17120/09, 8.4.14 (refusal to grant welfare benefits to foreign nationals—violation of Article 14 together with Article 8).

[2354] No. 55707/00, 18.2.09. See, by contrast, *Si Amer* v *France*, No. 29137/06, 29.10.09 (residence requirement for entitlement to supplementary pension for employee who worked for French company in Algeria prior to independence—no violation of Article 1 of Protocol No. 1 taken together with Article 14).

[2355] No. 77782/01, 27.11.07.

[2356] No. 26713/05, 28.5.09. See, by contrast, *Zeïbek* v *Greece*, No. 46368/06, 9.7.09 (effect on pension entitlement of loss of Greek nationality—violation of Article 1 of Protocol No. 1 taken together with Article 14).

a nationality requirement as regards entry to the legal profession. As the practice of law was considered to be a service in the public interest, the application of nationality requirements fell within the authorities' margin of appreciation.

Military status

6.738 The suspension of a former military judge's pension, following the abolition of military courts, was found to violate Article 14 together with Article 1 of Protocol No. 1 in *Buchen v Czech Republic*.[2357] Some categories of former members of the armed forces continued to receive their pension (including former military judges and prosecutors who became civilian judges) and the Court found that the difference in treatment could not be justified. However, in *Janković v Croatia*,[2358] the reduction of pensions held by former servicemen of the Yugoslav People's Army was found to be justified in order to integrate them into the general Croatian pension system and therefore did not violate Article 1 of Protocol No. 1 taken together with Article 14 (even though the pensions of former Croatian officers were higher).

Property-related cases

6.739 The Court has confirmed that the imposition on landowners, who are opposed to hunting on ethical grounds, of the obligation to tolerate hunting on their property is likely to be considered disproportionate. In *Chassagnou and others v France*[2359] the Court found no objective and reasonable justification in allowing large-scale landowners, but not small-scale landowners, the right to opt out of membership of hunting associations.

6.740 The case of *Šekerović and Pašalić v Bosnia and Herzegovina*[2360] concerned structural defects in the pension system affecting people who had become IDPs as a result of the conflict in the former Yugoslavia in the mid-1990s. There was a violation of Article 14 taken together with Article 1 of Protocol No. 1 because there was no objective and reasonable justification for the difference in treatment between pensioners who had moved between the various entities of the former state, and those who had stayed in what was present-day Bosnia and Herzegovina.

Illegitimacy

6.741 Discrimination on the basis of illegitimacy, as regards inheritance rights,[2361] and in relation to the acquisition of citizenship,[2362] have been found to be unjustifiable and accordingly a violation of Article 14 in conjunction with Article 8. In *Sahin v Germany*[2363] the Grand

---

[2357] No. 36541/97, 26.11.02.

[2358] No. 43440/98, dec. 12.10.00.

[2359] Nos. 25088/94, 28331/95 and 28443/95, 29.4.99. Similar decisions have been made in *Schneider v Luxembourg*, No. 2113/04, 10.7.07 and *Herrmann v Germany*, No. 9300/07, 26.6.12. See, by contrast, *Chabauty v France*, No. 57412/08, 4.10.12 (landowner had no ethical objections to hunting—no violation of Article 14 together with Article 1 of Protocol No. 1).

[2360] Nos. 5920/04 and 67396/09, 8.3.11. See also *Karanović v Bosnia and Herzegovina*, No. 39462/03, 20.11.07.

[2361] *Marckx v Belgium*, Series A, No. 31, 13.6.79; *Camp and Bourimi v Netherlands*, No. 28369/95, 3.10.00; *Pla Puncernau and Puncernau Pedro v Andorra*, No. 69498/01, 13.7.04; *Merger and Cros v France*, No. 68864/01, 22.12.04; *Brauer v Germany*, No. 3545/04, 28.5.09. But see also *Alboize-Barthes and Alboize-Montzume v France*, No. 44421/04, dec. 21.10.08 (inadmissible). There may also be a violation of Article 14 in conjunction with Article 1 of Protocol No. 1—see *Inze v Austria*, No. 8695/79, 28.10.87, Series A, No. 126; *Mazurek v France*, No. 34406/97, 1.2.00; *Fabris v France*, No. 16574/08, 7.2.13.

[2362] *Genovese v Malta*, No. 53124/09, 11.10.11.

[2363] No. 30943/96, 8.7.03. Contrast with the decision in *Elsholz v Germany*, No. 25735/94, 31.7.00. See also *Zaunegger v Germany*, No. 22028/04, 3.12.09 (inability of father of child born out of wedlock to obtain joint custody without mother's consent—violation of Article 14 taken together with Article 8); *Anayo v*

Chamber found a violation of Article 14 taken together with Article 8 because of the unjustified difference in treatment in relation to the access rights of fathers of children born out of wedlock as compared with fathers of children born in wedlock: for the latter there was a right of access, whereas for the former access depended on the views of the mother, who could only be overriden by the courts if it were in the interests of the child. There was a similar decision in *Sommerfeld v Germany*,[2364] although seven dissenting judges[2365] argued that in reaching its conclusions the majority had wrongly relied on the provisions of the legislation in the abstract, without adequately assessing how the law was *applied* to the applicant.

Sexual orientation

As noted above, unjustifiable discrimination on grounds of sexual orientation will fall foul of Article 14.[2366] Such arguments have arisen in cases concerning differential treatment between heterosexual and homosexual sexual activity in domestic criminal law, as was the case in *L and V v Austria*,[2367] where the Court found there was no objective and reasonable justification why, according to Austrian law, young men between 14 and 18 years of age needed protection against any sexual relationship with adult men, while young women in the same age bracket did not need such protection against relations with either adult men or women. Subsequently, in *E.B. and others v Austria*[2368] the Court found a violation of Article 14 taken together with Article 8 because of the refusal to amend the applicants' criminal records (imposed under the same law as considered in *L and V v Austria*) despite a Constitutional Court ruling to the effect that the provision in question was unconstitutional. Given the reasons for amending the legislation, the Court concluded that there was no justification for maintaining their convictions on the criminal record. **6.742**

The case of *Bączkowski and others v Poland*[2369] concerned the authorities' decision to ban a minority rights march and rallies in Warsaw. The decisions were justified on 'technical' grounds, and hence the Court expressed itself unwilling to speculate on the existence of motives, other than those expressly stated in the decisions. However, it went on to find that it could not overlook an interview with the Mayor of Warsaw in which he had made known his views about the exercise of freedom of assembly and 'propaganda about homosexuality', and during which he stated that he would refuse permission to hold the assemblies. Therefore, as his position may have influenced the decision-making process, the Court found a violation of Article 14 in conjunction with Article 11. In *Identoba and others v Georgia*[2370] the Court found a violation of Articles 3 and 11, both taken in conjunction with Article 14, because of the authorities' failure to protect demonstrators from homophobic violence. **6.743**

The principle of the Convention as a 'living instrument' has undoubtedly influenced the development of cases concerning sexual orientation, as was expressly the case in *L and V v* **6.744**

Germany, No. 20578/07, 21.12.10; *Schneider v Germany*, No. 17080/07, 15.9.11 (denial of access to biological father without considering best interests of child—violation of Article 8).

[2364] No. 31871/96, 8.7.03.

[2365] Judges Wildhaber, Palm, Lorenzen, Jungwiert, Greve, Levits and Mularoni.

[2366] See, e.g. *Bączkowski and others v Poland*, No. 1543/06, 3.5.07 (see 6.743 below).

[2367] Nos. 39392/98 and 3989/98, 9.1.03.

[2368] No. 31913/07 et al, 7.11.13.

[2369] No. 1543/06, 3.5.07. See *Alekseyev v Russia*, Nos. 4916/07, 25924/08 and 14599/09, 21.10.10; see also *Genderdoc-M v Moldova*, No. 9106/06, 12.6.12.

[2370] No. 73235/12, 12.5.15 (see the discussion of this case at 6.119).

Austria. Where the domestic authorities rejected the applicant's request for authorisation to adopt a child, explicitly due to his 'lifestyle', and, as found by the Court, implicitly on grounds of his homosexual orientation, the Court in *Fretté* v *France*[2371] found no violation of Article 14. Three of the four judges in the majority (Judges Costa, Jungwiert and Traja) found Article 14 to be inapplicable on the basis that the right to adopt did not fall within the ambit of Article 8. Judge Kuris found that there was an objective and reasonable justification for the difference in treatment, having regard to the state's broad margin of appreciation in this area, and that the scientific community was divided over the possible consequences of children being brought up by homosexual parents. The three judges in the minority (Judges Bratza, Fuhrmann and Tulkens) argued emphatically, however, that the reliance on the lack of common ground in Council of Europe states on uniform principles relating to adoption by homosexuals 'paves the way for States to be given total discretion' and was 'irrelevant, at variance with the Court's case law relating to Article 14 of the Convention, and when couched in such general terms, [was] liable to take the protection of fundamental rights backwards'. Subsequently, in *E.B.* v *France*,[2372] a ten to seven majority of the Grand Chamber found a violation of the Convention as a result of the authorities' refusal to grant approval of authorisation to adopt to the applicant, a lesbian living with another woman. The Court found that one of the main reasons for the refusal was the lack of a 'paternal referent' in the applicant's household, a factor which the Court considered could have served as a pretext for rejecting the application on grounds of the applicant's homosexuality. The Court concluded that her sexual orientation had been a decisive factor in the decision to refuse her authorisation to adopt, which was unacceptable under the Convention. Another ten–seven majority of the Grand Chamber found a violation of Article 14 together with Article 8 in *X and others* v *Austria*[2373] because the domestic law did not allow second-parent adoption in same-sex couples. The applicants were two women living in a stable homosexual relationship, one of whom had a minor son and the other wanted to adopt him, but the effect of doing so under the domestic law would be to sever his ties with his mother. The couple were found to be in a relevantly similar situation to an unmarried different-sex couple (in which one partner wished to adopt the other's child—which would be permitted) and that the difference in treatment was due to their sexual orientation. The Government could not provide 'weighty and convincing reasons' to show that this distinction was necessary for the protection of the family 'in the traditional sense' or for the protection of the interests of the child.[2374]

6.745 In *Karner* v *Austria*,[2375] the Court found a violation of Article 14 taken together with Article 8 as a result of the application of legislation that prevented a surviving partner of a

---

[2371] No. 36515/97, 26.2.02.

[2372] No. 43546/02, 22.1.08. See also *Gas and Dubois* v *France*, No. 25951/07, 15.3.12 (refusal of simple adoption order for homosexual partner of biological mother—no violation of Article 14 together with Article 8).

[2373] No. 19010/07, 19.2.13.

[2374] However, there was no violation of the Convention where the applicants' situation was compared with that of a married couple, one of whom wanted to adopt the other spouse's child. See also *Boeckel and Gessner-Boeckel* v *Germany*, No. 8017/11, dec. 7.5.13 (refusal to include woman registered as mother's civil partner on child's birth certificate—applicants were not in a relevantly similar situation as a married husband and wife in respect of entries in birth certificate—inadmissible).

[2375] No. 40016/98, 24.7.03. See also *Kozak* v *Poland*, No. 13102/02, 2.3.10. Contrast these cases with *Korelc* v *Slovenia*, No. 28456/03, 12.5.09 (refusal to allow cohabiting carer to inherit tenancy—inadmissible).

couple of the same sex from inheriting the deceased partner's tenancy. The Government's suggestion that such measures were needed for 'the protection of the traditional family unit' was not found to be sufficient to demonstrate that it was necessary to exclude people living in a homosexual relationship from the application of the law. The case of *J.M.* v *UK*[2376] concerned a difference in treatment on grounds of sexual orientation in relation to child-support regulations. The applicant was divorced from her former husband and was in a long-term relationship with another woman. Her two children lived mainly with their father and the applicant was required by the child support regulations, as the non-resident parent, to contribute to the cost of the children's upbringing. The regulations provided for a reduced amount to be paid where the absent parent had entered into a new relationship (married or unmarried), but they took no account of same-sex relationships. The Court concluded that there was no justification for this difference in treatment, and accordingly that there was a violation of Article 14 taken together with Article 1 of Protocol No. 1.

In *Schalk and Kopf* v *Austria*,[2377] the Court for the first time recognised that same-sex relationships fall within the meaning of 'family life' under Article 8. By four votes to three, the Court rejected the applicants' claim that the failure to give legal recognition to their relationship (before the Registered Partnership Act came into force in 2010) violated Article 14 taken together with Article 8.[2378] However, in *Vallianatos and others* v *Greece*,[2379] the Grand Chamber found a violation of Article 14 taken together with Article 8 because a 2008 law providing legal recognition to civil unions only applied to different-sex couples, and not to same-sex couples. Noting that nine member states provided for same-sex marriage, and that another seventeen provided a form of civil partnership for same-sex couples, the Court found that the Government had failed to provide 'convincing and weighty reasons' for the exclusion of same-sex couples. **6.746**

There was a violation of Article 14 together with Article 3 in *X* v *Turkey*[2380] as a result of the applicant prisoner's total isolation from prison life, which had been ostensibly imposed to protect him from harm from other inmates, but which the Court found had been unjustifiably imposed on him because of his sexual orientation. **6.747**

Marital status

There was a violation of Article 8 taken together with Article 14 in *Petrov* v *Bulgaria*[2381] because the applicant, an unmarried prisoner, was banned from making telephone calls to his partner, unlike married prisoners, for which there was found to be no justification. **6.748**

[2376] No. 37060/06, 28.9.10.

[2377] No. 30141/04, 24.6.10. See also *X and others* v *Austria*, No. 19010/07, 19.2.13, and see the discussion of *Oliari and others* v *Italy*, Nos. 18766/11 and 36030/11, 21.7.15 (at 6.524 above)—violation of Article 8 due to the failure to provide legal recognition of same-sex partnerships.

[2378] In their joint dissenting opinion, Judges Rozakis, Spielmann and Jebens argued cogently that no justification for the difference in treatment (compared with different-sex couples) had been put forward.

[2379] Nos. 29381/09 and 32684/09, 7.11.13. See also *Pajić* v *Croatia*, No. 68453/13, 23.2.16 (discrimination between unmarried same-sex couples and unmarried different-sex couples in obtaining family reunification—violation of Article 14 in conjunction with Article 8); *Taddeucci and McCall* v *Italy*, No. 51362/09, 30.6.16 (refusal to grant residence permit for family reason to same-sex foreign partner—violation of Article 14 in conjunction with Article 8).

[2380] No. 24626/09, 9.10.12.

[2381] No. 15197/02, 22.5.08.

6.749 In *Burden and Burden* v *UK*[2382] the applicants, two unmarried sisters who lived together, complained that when either of them died the other would be subject to inheritance tax on their property (at 40 per cent), but that married couples (or couples in civil partnerships) were not liable to pay the tax. The Grand Chamber found that the relationship between siblings was qualitatively different to that between married couples and homosexual civil partners. The legal consequences that couples in both marriages and civil partnerships decided to incur distinguished those relationships from other forms of cohabitation. There was accordingly no discrimination.

6.750 At issue in *Muñoz Díaz* v *Spain*,[2383] was the Roma applicant's right to a survivor's pension following the death of her husband. She had married in 1971 in a ceremony solemnized according to the rites of the Roma community. However, she was denied a survivor's pension because their marriage had not been entered in the Civil Register. The Court noted that at the time of their marriage, it had not been possible to be married in Spain otherwise than in accordance with the rites of the Catholic Church, except by making a declaration of apostasy, and the applicant had believed in good faith that her marriage was fully valid. The Court concluded that the Spanish authorities had recognised the marriage for various other purposes, creating a legitimate expectation, and therefore it was disproportionate to discount it as regards the right to a survivor's pension. Accordingly, there was a violation of Article 14 taken together with Article 1 of Protocol No. 1. However, no such legitimate expectation arose in *Şerife Yiğit* v *Turkey*,[2384] where the applicant had married in a religious ceremony, but had not contracted a civil marriage. The domesic law was clear that she needed to do so in order to receive social security benefits and pension rights, and therefore the authorities' refusal to grant her such rights was found to be objectively justified.

6.751 The applicants in *Wagner and J.M.W.L.* v *Luxembourg*,[2385] complained about the authorities' refusal to declare a Peruvian judgment enforceable according to which the first applicant had legally adopted a three-year-old girl in Peru who had been abandoned (the second applicant). This was a result of the absence of a provision in Luxembourg law enabling a single person to be granted full adoption of a child. The second applicant was found to have been subjected to a difference in treatment compared with children whose full adoption granted abroad was recognised in Luxembourg. This was held to be unjustified and accordingly to violate Article 14 in conjunction with Article 8.

Other status

6.752 There was a violation of Article 14 taken together with Article 8 in *Glor* v *Switzerland*,[2386] as a result of the obligation on the applicant to pay a military service exemption tax, even though he had been declared unfit for service on medical grounds (on account of his diabetes). The applicant challenged the fact that two groups of people were not obliged to pay the tax: those who suffered from a 'serious disability' and those who performed the alternative civilian service (for which only conscientious objectors were eligible). The Court noted that the requirement to pay the tax for individuals who could not fulfil the obligation to carry

---

[2382] No. 13378/05, 29.4.08. See also *Korelc* v *Slovenia*, No. 28456/03, 12.5.09 (refusal to allow cohabiting carer to inherit tenancy—inadmissible).
[2383] No. 49151/07, 8.12.09.
[2384] No. 3976/05, 2.11.10.
[2385] No. 76240/01, 28.6.07.
[2386] No. 13444/04, 30.4.09.

out military or civil protection service for medical reasons was not replicated elsewhere in Europe, and that requiring the applicant to pay the tax, without allowing the possibility of performing military (or civil protection) service, was potentially in contradiction with the need to fight discrimination in respect of disabled persons and to promote their full participation in society. The level of the tax was not insignificant in comparison with the applicant's taxable income, and the Court was critical of the way the authorities had handled the case, for example by failing to give adequate consideration to the applicant's particular circumstances. It concluded that there was no objective justification for the distinction made by the authorities, particularly between those who were declared unfit for service and not liable to pay the tax, and those who were unfit for service but who were still obliged to pay it. Discrimination on the basis of disability also arose in *Çam v Turkey*[2387] where a music academy refused to enrol the applicant, who was blind, despite her having passed the requisite competitive entrance examination (in respect of the Turkish lute). A medical report stating that the applicant would be able to take lessons there was changed by the academy director to say the opposite. The Court found there was no doubt that her blindness was the sole reason for her exclusion. It also noted that the authorities had made no effort to identify the applicant's needs and failed to explain how her blindness would impede her access to musical education, and no attempts were made to consider new amenities to meet her specific educational needs. Therefore, there was a violation of Article 14 together with Article 2 of Protocol No. 1. The applicant in *Guberina v Croatia*[2388] was refused tax relief on the purchase of a house which he bought in order to care for his severely disabled child in more suitable accommodation. The Court found that the term 'other status' in Article 14 could encompass the disability of the applicant's child (as opposed to the applicant himself). In excluding the applicant from the tax exemption, the authorities had failed to take account of the specific needs of the applicant's family related to the child's disability, for which there was no objective and reasonable justification. Therefore, there was a violation of Article 14 in conjunction with Article 1 of Protocol No. 1.

6.753 The Court has recognised the widespread stigma and exclusion suffered by people living with HIV/AIDs.[2389] In *Kiyutin v Russia*[2390] the applicant, an Uzbek national, complained of discrimination as regards the rejection of his application for a residence permit on the basis of his HIV-positive status. The Court found there was no reasonable and objective justification for the applicant's treatment, in violation of Article 14 in conjunction with Article 8. There was a similar finding in *I.B. v Greece*[2391] where the applicant was dismissed from his job because of his HIV-positive status, in response to pressure from other employees. The Court found that the domestic courts had failed to weigh up the respective rights of employer and employee in a Convention-compliant way. A ban on individuals seeking employment in particular private sector spheres (because they formerly worked for the KGB) has been found to be disproportionate, in violation of Article 14, taken together with Article 8.[2392]

[2387] No. 51500/08, 23.2.16.
[2388] No. 23682/13, 22.3.16.
[2389] *Kiyutin v Russia*, No. 2700/10, 10.3.11, para. 64.
[2390] No. 2700/10, 10.3.11. See also *Novruk and others v Russia*, No. 31039/11 et al, 15.3.16.
[2391] No. 552/10, 3.10.13.
[2392] *Sidabras and Džiautas v Lithuania*, Nos. 55480/00 and 59330/00, 27.7.04. See also *Rainys and Gasparavičius v Lithuania*, Nos. 70665/01 and 74345/01, 7.4.05. The applicants in these cases subsequently brought a further case about their non-reinstatement, which was partially successful: *Sidabras and others v Lithuania*, Nos. 50421/08 and 56213/08, 23.6.15.

6.754 In *Carson and others* v *UK*,[2393] the applicants complained that, as pensioners living abroad, they were not entitled to the index-linking of their pensions, unlike pensioners still resident within the United Kingdom. By a majority of 11 to six, the Grand Chamber found no discrimination, on the basis that the applicants were not in a relevantly similar situation to pensioners living in the United Kingdom. Although the Court acknowledged that the applicants had worked in the United Kingdom and paid compulsory National Insurance contributions, it noted that such contributions were not exclusively linked to retirement pensions, but formed part of the revenue that paid for a range of social security benefits. Therefore, this was not deemed to be a sufficient basis for treating on a similar basis the position of pensioners who received index-linked pensions and those who did not. It was also relevant that the social security benefits system (including state pensions) was intended to ensure certain minimum standards of living for residents of the United Kingdom. In *Topčić-Rosenberg* v *Croatia*[2394] there was a violation of Article 14 with Article 8 because the applicant was not entitled to paid maternity leave due to her status as an adoptive mother (compared to biological mothers), which the Court concluded could not be reasonably justified.

6.755 The applicant in *Stummer* v *Austria*[2395] complained that as a working prisoner, he was not affiliated to the old age pension system. The Grand Chamber found that he was in a relevantly similar situation to ordinary employees; however, a ten–seven majority found that, taken in the wider context of the overall system of prison work, and prisoners' social cover (in respect of which the state was afforded a wide margin of appreciation), and noting that the applicant was provided with some social benefits after he left prison, the Court found that the difference in treatment was reasonable.

6.756 In *Clift* v *UK*,[2396] the applicant had been sentenced to 18 years' imprisonment for, inter alia, attempted murder. Under the legislation in force at the time, prisoners serving fixed-term sentences of 15 years or more required the approval of the Secretary of State for early release (in addition to the Parole Board's recommendation), whereas no such approval was needed for prisoners serving fixed-term sentences of less than 15 years, or life sentences. The Court held that there was no objective justification for such difference in treatment, as the Government had not established that the Minister's approval would address concerns about any perceived higher risk posed by certain prisoners upon release. There was accordingly a violation of Article 5 taken together with Article 14.[2397] The applicant in

---

[2393] No. 42184/05, 16.3.10. See also: *Pichkur* v *Ukraine*, No. 10441/06, 7.11.13 (termination of payment of retirement pension on basis that beneficiary was permanently resident abroad—violation of Article 14 together with Article 1 of Protocol No. 1); *Fábián* v *Hungary*, No. 78117/13, 15.12.15 (difference in treatment between publicly and privately employed retirees and between categories of civil servants as regards payment of old-age pension—violation of Article 14 taken together with Article 1 of Protocol No. 1) (case referred to Grand Chamber 2.5.16); *Ramaer and Van Willigen* v *Netherlands*, No. 34880/12, dec. 23.10.12 (legislative change depriving non-resident pensioners of benefits under health care insurance contracts—inadmissible).

[2394] No. 19391/11, 14.11.13.

[2395] No. 37452/02, 7.7.11. See also *S.S. and others* v *UK*, Nos. 40356/10 and 54466/10, dec. 21.4.15 (complaint of discrimination in entitlement to social security benefits of prisoners in psychiatric care compared to other persons detained for psychiatric treatment—inadmissible).

[2396] No. 7205/07, 13.7.10.

[2397] There was also a violation of Article 14 taken together with Article 5 in *Rangelov* v *Germany*, No. 5123/07, 22.3.12 (refusal of social therapy or relaxation of conditions of preventive detention—difference in treatment was due to applicant's foreign nationality and could not be objectively justified).

Laduna v *Slovakia*[2398] complained about the difference in treatment he received as a remand prisoner (in relation to visiting rights and access to television) compared with convicted prisoners. The Court found a violation of Article 14 together with Article 8, as there was no objective and reasonable justification for imposing greater restrictions on remand prisoners (who are to be presumed innocent). There was a violation of Article 14 taken together with Article 3 in *Gülay Çetin* v *Turkey*,[2399] as a result of the ineligibility of pre-trial detainees to various forms of release, where they were suffering from a terminal illness (in contrast to the position of convicted prisoners).

The failure to treat differently

The Court has also held that the right not to be discriminated against is violated when, without an objective and reasonable justification, there is a failure to treat differently, persons whose situations are significantly different. There was a violation of Article 14, in conjunction with Article 9, in *Thlimmenos* v *Greece*,[2400] on that basis. There, the applicant, a Jehovah's Witness, had been refused an appointment to a post of chartered accountant, as a result of a prior criminal conviction for disobeying an order to wear military uniform, because of his religious beliefs. He complained of the fact that no distinction was made between persons convicted of offences committed exclusively because of their religious beliefs and persons convicted of other offences. The applicant's exclusion from the profession was held to be disproportionate and did not pursue a legitimate aim. The Court also applied the principle of the failure to treat differently in *E.B. and others* v *Austria*.[2401] There, the Court found a violation of Article 14 taken together with Article 8 because of the refusal to amend the applicants' criminal records (for having homosexual relations with consenting males aged between 14 and 18) despite a Constitutional Court ruling to the effect that the provision in question was unconstitutional, and a European Court judgment finding a violation of Article 14 together with Article 8 (see *L and V* v *Austria*, discussed at 6.742 above). The Court was required to assess the proportionality of the failure to treat the applicants differently from other persons also convicted of a criminal offence, but where the offence in question had not been quashed by the Constitutional Court or otherwise abolished. Given the reasons for amending the legislation, the Court concluded that there was no justification for maintaining the applicants' convictions on the criminal record.

Positive discrimination

Positive discrimination is not automatically prohibited by Article 14; it will depend upon the justification for the difference in treatment in each case.[2402]   **6.758**

Article 1 of Protocol No. 1: Right of Property

Article 1 of Protocol No. 1 states: **6.759**

> Every natural or legal person is entitled to the peaceful enjoyment of his possessions. No one shall be deprived of his possessions except in the public interest and subject to the conditions provided for by law and by the general principles of international law.

[2398] No. 31827/02, 13.12.11. See also *Varnas* v *Lithuania*, No. 42615/06, 9.7.13 (difference in treatment of remand prisoners compared to convicted prisoners as regards conjugal visits—violation of Article 14 together with Article 8).

[2399] No. 44084/10, 5.3.13.

[2400] No. 34369/97, 6.4.00.

[2401] No. 31913/07 et al, 7.11.13. See also *Guberina* v *Croatia*, No. 23682/13, 22.3.16 (discussed at 6.752 above).

[2402] See, e.g. *Lindsay* v *UK*, No. 11089/84, dec. 11.11.86, (1986) 49 DR 181.

The preceding provisions shall not, however, in any way impair the right of a state to enforce such laws as it deems necessary to control the use of property in accordance with the general interest or to secure the payment of taxes or other contributions or penalties.

6.760 Article 1 of Protocol No. 1 provides qualified protections to the right of property. The Article expressly allows public authorities a wide discretion to interfere with the right: it permits the deprivation of a person's possessions where it is 'in the public interest', and the second paragraph allows the state to impose 'such laws as it deems necessary' in relation to taxation[2403] and other contributions or penalties. The positive obligations inherent in Article 1 of Protocol No. 1 may require certain measures by the state to protect the right of property even in cases involving litigation between individuals or companies. This means in particular that 'states are under an obligation to afford judicial procedures that offer the necessary procedural guarantees and therefore enable the domestic courts and tribunals to adjudicate effectively and fairly any disputes between private persons'.[2404]

6.761 Where there has been a violation of Article 1 of Protocol No. 1, the Court may, in certain circumstances, order restitution of the property in question, under Article 41. This is discussed further at 8.29 below.

Possessions

6.762 A 'possession' has been broadly interpreted to include: land and moveable goods, planning permission,[2405] property subject to unenforced expropriation orders and prohibition on construction,[2406] the economic interests arising from a licence to sell alcohol,[2407] accountancy and law practices and their goodwill,[2408] a permit for gravel extraction,[2409] hunting rights over land,[2410] shares,[2411] intellectual property rights (including patents and the application for a registration of a trademark),[2412] the registration of internet domain names,[2413] an enforceable debt,[2414] the right to a pension,[2415] the right to emergency

---

[2403] See, e.g. *Spampinato* v *Italy*, No. 23123/04, dec. 29.3.07.

[2404] *Sovtransavto Holding* v *Ukraine*, No. 48553/99, 25.9.02, para. 96. As to positive obligations under Article 1 of Protocol No. 1, see also *Öneryildiz* v *Turkey*, No. 48939/99, 30.11.04, para. 134.

[2405] *Pine Valley Developments Ltd* v *Ireland*, No. 12742/87, Series A, No. 222, 29.11.91.

[2406] *Sporrong and Lönnroth* v *Sweden*, Nos. 7151/75 and 7152/75, Series A, No. 52, 23.9.82.

[2407] *Tre Traktörer Aktiebolag* v *Sweden*, No. 10873/84, Series A, No. 159, 7.7.89.

[2408] *Van Marle and others* v *Netherlands*, Nos. 8543/79, 8674/79, 8675/79 and 8685/79, 26.6.86 (accountancy practice); *Döring* v *Germany*, No. 37595/99, dec. 9.11.99 (law practice); *Buzescu* v *Romania*, No. 61302/00, 24.5.05 (law practice).

[2409] *Fredin* v *Sweden*, No. 12033/86, Series A, No. 192, 18.2.91.

[2410] *Chassagnou and others* v *France*, Nos. 25088/94, 28331/95 and 28443/95, 29.4.99.

[2411] *Bramelid and Malmstrom* v *Sweden* (1982) 29 DR 64; *Sovtransavto Holding* v *Ukraine*, No. 48553/99, 25.9.02, para. 91.

[2412] *Anheuser-Busch Inc.* v *Portugal*, No. 73049/01, 11.1.07. See also *Smith Kline and French Laboratories* v *Netherlands* (1990) 66 DR 70.

[2413] *Paeffgen GMBH* v *Germany*, Nos. 25379/04, 21688/05, 21722/05 and 21770/05, dec. 18.9.07.

[2414] *Stran Greek Refineries and others* v *Greece*, No. 13427/87, Series A, No. 301-B, 9.12.94; *Burdov* v *Russia*, No. 59498/00, 7.5.02.

[2415] See, e.g. *Wessels-Bergervoet* v *Netherlands*, No. 34462/97, 4.6.02, para. 43; *Azinas* v *Cyprus*, No. 56679/00, 20.6.02 (but see the separate opinions of (1) Judges Wildhaber, Rozakis and Mularoni, (2) Judge Hadjihambis, (3) Judges Costa and Garlicki and (4) Judge Ress, in the Grand Chamber judgment in *Azinas* of 28.4.04); *Banfield* v *UK*, No. 6223/04, dec. 18.10.05; *Klein* v *Austria*, No. 57028/00, 3.3.11; *Torri and others* v *Italy*, Nos. 11838/07 and 12302/07, dec. 24.1.12.

assistance,[2416] the right to a widow's social security benefit,[2417] the right to fish in state-owned waters (under a lease),[2418] rights of grazing and pasture over common land,[2419] an entitlement to claim compensatory property,[2420] and legal claims for compensation and for the restitution of assets.[2421] However, a human embryo is not considered as a 'possession'.[2422]

This Article provides rights in respect of existing possessions or assets, which will also **6.763** include *claims* by virtue of which an applicant has at least a 'legitimate expectation' of acquiring effective enjoyment of a property right.[2423] Thus in *Jasiūnienė v Lithuania*[2424] a judgment awarding the applicant compensation in land or money, but which was not implemented, was held to amount to an enforceable claim and therefore a 'possession' within the meaning of Article 1 of Protocol No. 1. There is, however, no right under Article 1 of Protocol No. 1 to acquire property, and future income will only be considered as a 'possession' if it has already been earned or where an enforceable claim to it exists.[2425] Furthermore, 'the hope of recognition of the survival of an old property right which it has long been impossible to exercise effectively' does not amount to a 'possession'.[2426]

[2416] *Gaygusuz v Austria*, No. 17371/90, 16.9.96. The benefit in question in *Gaygusuz* was contributory, but Article 1 of Protocol No. 1 may also apply to non-contributory social benefits: see *Koua Poirrez v France*, No. 40892/98, 30.9.03, para. 37.

[2417] *Willis v UK*, No. 36042/97, 11.6.02 (where the Court also said that it was not necessary to address the question whether a social security benefit must be contributory in order for it to be a 'possession').

[2418] *Posti and Rahko v Finland*, No. 27824/95, 24.9.02, para. 76.

[2419] *Doğan and others v Turkey*, Nos. 8803–8811/02, 8813/02 and 8815–8819/02, 29.6.04.

[2420] *Broniowski v Poland*, No. 31443/96, 22.6.04.

[2421] *Pressos Compania Naviera SA and others v Belgium*, No. 17849/91, Series A, No. 332, 20.11.95, para. 31 and *National and Provincial Building Society and others v UK*, Nos. 21319/93, 21449/93 and 21675/93, 23.10.97, para. 74.

[2422] *Parrillo v Italy*, No. 46470/11, 27.8.15, para. 215.

[2423] See also, e.g. *Maurice v France*, No. 11810/03, 6.10.03; *Plechanow v Poland*, No. 22279/04, 7.7.09; *Atanasiu and others v Romania*, Nos. 30767/05 and 33800/06, 12.10.10; *Althoff and others v Germany*, No. 5631/05, 8.12.11; *N.K.M. v Hungary*, No. 66529/11, 14.5.13; *Valle Pierimpiè Società Agricola S.p.a. v Italy*, No. 46154/11, 23.9.14. In *Nerva and others v UK*, No. 42295/98, 24.9.02, the Court held that restaurant waiters had no legitimate expectation that tips paid by customers should not be treated as counting towards their remuneration, and therefore there was no 'possession' within the meaning of Article 1 of Protocol No. 1. The applicants in *Polacek and Polackova v Czech Republic*, No. 38645/97, dec. 10.7.02 were found to be 'mere claimants' for the restitution of land, without a legitimate expectation, according to the nationality conditions laid down by the domestic law. See also *Brezny and Brezny v Slovak Republic*, No. 23131/93, 4.3.96; *Malhous v Czech Republic*, No. 33071/96, dec. 13.12.00; *Kopecký v Slovakia*, No. 44912/98, 28.9.04; *Melchior v Germany*, No. 66783/01, dec. 2.2.06; *Centro Europa 7 S.r.l. and Di Stefano v Italy*, No. 38433/09, 7.6.12. In *Von Maltzan and others v Germany*, Nos. 71916/01, 71917/01 and 10260/02, dec. 2.3.05, the Grand Chamber found that the applicants could not claim a 'legitimate expectation' of realising a current and enforceable claim, by obtaining the restitution of their property or compensation, or indemnification, in respect of property expropriated during, and after, the Soviet occupation from 1945. The applicants in *Flores Cardoso v Portugal*, No. 2489/09, 29.5.12 had no 'legitimate expectation' that sums of money deposited in the Portuguese consulate in Mozambique following the outbreak of civil war, would be repaid taking account of inflation and currency depreciation. A nine–eight majority of the Grand Chamber in *Béláné Nagy v Hungary*, No. 5308/13, 13.12.16 found that the applicant had a legitimate expectation to a disability pension, after she had subsequently become ineligible because of legislative changes to the pension scheme. This was held to be disproportionate because the applicant was completely deprived of any entitlement to benefits.

[2424] No. 41510/98, 6.3.03.

[2425] See, e.g. *Ambruosi v Italy*, No. 31227/96, 19.10.00, para. 20; *Wendenburg and others v Germany*, No. 71630/01, dec. 6.2.03.

[2426] See, e.g. *Prince Hans-Adam II of Liechtenstein v Germany*, No. 42527/98, 12.7.01, para. 83; *Slivenko v Latvia*, No. 48321/99, 23.1.02, para. 12.

In *Kopecky* v *Slovakia*,[2427] the applicant brought proceedings in the 1990s for restitution of valuable coins which had been confiscated from his father in the 1950s. A majority of four judges to three found that he had a 'legitimate expectation' in respect of his claim to the coins, because he had at least an arguable claim that met the requirements of the relevant domestic legislation. However, the Grand Chamber found that no such expectation arose as the domestic law requirements were not in fact fulfilled. An option to renew a lease was found in *Stretch* v *UK*[2428] to amount to a 'possession' even in circumstances where the local authority that had originally purportedly granted the lease was later found by the domestic courts to have acted *ultra vires*: the applicant was considered to have had at least a legitimate expectation of being able to renew the lease. Whether a tenancy of residential property (as opposed to a commercial lease) will amount to a 'possession' will depend upon factors such as the extent of the formality of the arrangement (for example whether there is a formal lease) and the length of occupation of the property.[2429] In *Teteriny* v *Russia*,[2430] the Court found that a 'social tenancy agreement' granted by a town council to the applicant judge (permitting him to possess and make use of his flat, and, on certain conditions, to privatise it) constituted a 'possession' as it established a legitimate expection to acquire a pecuniary asset.

6.764 It is important to emphasise that a 'possession' is an autonomous Convention concept and so the domestic classification will not necessarily be decisive. Therefore, neither the lack of recognition in domestic law of a private interest such as a 'right,' nor the fact that domestic laws do not regard such an interest as a 'right of property' will necessarily prevent the interest in question, in some circumstances, from being a 'possession'.[2431] The applicant's house in *Öneryildiz* v *Turkey*,[2432] which had been built without the authorities' permission in a shanty town on the foot of a rubbish tip, was destroyed by a methane gas explosion. The Court was required to decide whether there was a 'possession' to which Article 1 of Protocol No. 1 would apply. Whilst the applicant had occupied land owned by the state for five years, he did not have a sufficiently established claim to transfer of the title to the land and so the land itself did not amount to a 'possession'. His house had been built in breach of planning regulations, nevertheless, he was acknowledged to be the de facto owner of the dwelling and movable goods. Accordingly, the Court found he had a substantial proprietary interest which was tolerated by the authorities, which was held to amount to a 'possession'.[2433] In *Depalle* v *France*[2434] the applicant had acquired a

---

[2427] No. 44912/98, 7.1.03 (Chamber) and 28.9.04 (Grand Chamber).

[2428] No. 44277/98, 24.6.03.

[2429] See, e.g. *Pentidis and others* v *Greece*, No. 23238/94, Comm. Rep. 27.2.96; *Panikian* v *Bulgaria*, No. 29583/96, dec. 10.7.97; *JLS* v *Spain*, No. 41917/98, dec. 27.4.99; *Blečić* v *Croatia*, No. 59532/00, 29.7.04 (Chamber) (whether a 'specially protected tenancy' amounted to a 'possession' was left open by the Court—the case was referred to the Grand Chamber (8.3.06) which declared the case inadmissible *ratione temporis*).

[2430] No. 11931/03, 30.6.05.

[2431] *Öneryildiz* v *Turkey*, No. 48939/99, 30.11.04. The 'right of use' of property as was common in the former Soviet Union, has also been recognised as constituting a 'possession'—see *Chiragov and others* v *Armenia*, No. 13216/05, 16.6.15, para. 149; *Sargsyan* v *Azerbaijan*, No. 40167/06, 16.6.15, para. 203.

[2432] No. 48939/99, 30.11.04. See also *Doğan and others* v *Turkey*, Nos. 8803–8811/02, 8813/02 and 8815–8819/02, 29.6.04.

[2433] See also, *Saghinadze and others* v *Georgia*, No. 18768/05, 27.5.10 (right of IDP from Abkhazia to use cottage belonging to Ministry of Interior for ten years—found to constitute a 'possession').

[2434] No. 34044/02, 29.3.10. See also *Brosset-Triboulet and others* v *France*, No. 34078/02, 29.3.10.

house on 'maritime public land' to which he had been granted successive rights of occupation. As it was on maritime public property, the domestic courts did not recognise that he had a 'property right'. Nevertheless, the Court found that the time that had elapsed (50 years) had the effect of vesting in the applicant a proprietary interest in the house that was sufficiently established to amount to a 'possession' for the purposes of Article 1 of Protocol No. 1.

The three principles

The Article covers three principles: **6.765**

(1) the entitlement to peaceful enjoyment of possessions;
(2) the prohibition of deprivation of possessions, subject to specified conditions; and
(3) the right of the state to control the use of property, subject to specified conditions.[2435]

These principles are inter-related: the second and third rules are to be construed in the light of the general principle contained in the first.

The notion of 'deprivation' covers both de facto deprivation as well as formal depriva-   **6.766**
tion. It is frequently in dispute as to whether there had been a 'deprivation of possessions' (second rule) or a 'control of use of property' (third rule), as the former will require greater justification than the latter. For example, in *Fredin v Sweden*[2436] the Court rejected the applicants' arguments that the revocation of their permit for gravel extraction was so serious as to amount to a de facto deprivation of possessions, finding instead that it amounted to a 'control of use of property'. Similarly, in *Air Canada v UK*[2437] the seizure of an aircraft by customs officials following the discovery of cannibis resin, and the requirement to pay £50,000 in order to have it returned, was also found to be a 'control of use of property'. This was because the seizure was temporary and did not involve a transfer of ownership, and it had been carried out as part of a scheme intended to prevent carriers from bringing prohibited drugs into the country. In *AGOSI v UK*[2438] the applicant company complained about the forfeiture of krugerrands that had been seized by Customs and Excise officers from third parties while attempting to smuggle them into the United Kingdom. The Court found that whilst the forfeiture did involve a deprivation of property, it had been a measure taken as part of the prohibition of the importation of gold coins into the United Kingdom and therefore the second paragraph of Article 1 applied. In *Pine Valley Developments Ltd v Ireland*[2439] the annulment of outline planning permission for the applicant's land was found to be a measure of control of the use of property. In *Anheuser-Busch Inc. v Portugal*,[2440] the Grand Chamber found that Article 1 of Protocol No. 1 was applicable to a dispute over a trademark registration of the brand name 'Budweiser', but that the Supreme Court's judgment setting aside the applicant company's trademark registration, in favour of a rival company, did not constitute an interference with the applicant's rights. There was nothing to suggest that the decision had been arbitary or unreasonable.

[2435] *Sporrong and Lönnroth v Sweden*, Nos. 7151/75 and 7152/75, Series A, No. 52, 23.9.82, para. 61.
[2436] No. 12033/86, Series A, No. 192, 18.2.91.
[2437] No. 18465/91, Series A, No. 316, 5.5.95. See also *Bosphorus Hava Yollari Turizm Ve Ticaret AS v Ireland*, No. 45036/98, 30.6.05.
[2438] No. 9118/80, Series A, No. 108, 24.10.86.
[2439] No. 12742/87, Series A, No. 222, 29.11.91.
[2440] No. 73049/01, 11.1.07.

6.767 The applicant in *Kotov* v *Russia*[2441] held a savings account in a private bank which went into liquidation. Under the domestic law he should have been treated as a priority creditor, but the liquidator gave priority to various categories of people who were not referred to in the legislation—'disabled persons, war veterans, the needy and persons who had participated actively in the winding-up operation'. Consequently, he only received a small proportion of the sums owed to him. The Court had to assess the question of the state's responsibility arising from the actions of the liquidator. The Court found that liquidators could not be considered as representatives of the state, as they were private professionals, accountable only to the creditors' body or individual creditors, and not to any regulatory body. They did not receive any public funding and their powers were limited to operational control and management of the insolvent company's property, without any formal delegation of powers by government. Nor did they have coercive or regulatory powers in respect of third parties. Therefore, the state could not be held responsible for the liquidator's wrongful acts. Furthermore, the legal framework which had been established satisfied the positive obligations on the state to enable someone in the applicant's position to assert their property rights. Indeed, the applicant could have brought an action in damages against the liquidator, but had not done so. Accordingly, there was no violation of Article 1 of Protocol No. 1 (by 12 votes to five).

6.768 The refusal of the authorities to comply with an order for the demolition of the applicant's neighbours' cowshed in *Paudicio* v *Italy*[2442] was found to engage the applicant's rights under the first sentence of Article 1 as it was so close to his home (but it amounted to neither a 'deprivation' nor a 'control of use' of his property).

Proportionality of interference

6.769 In assessing interferences with property under Article 1 of Protocol No. 1, the Court will attempt to strike a fair balance between the right of the individual and the general interest of the community, which will require consideration of whether the applicant has had to bear a 'disproportionate burden'.[2443] There must be a reasonable relationship of proportionality between the means employed and the aim pursued. The authorities are allowed a wide margin of appreciation both in respect of the means of enforcement and the justification of the measure taken in the general interest. The second paragraph of Article 1 is to be construed in the light of the principles set out in the first sentence.

6.770 The Court has stated that the notion of what is in the public interest is:[2444]

> necessarily extensive. In particular, the decision to enact laws expropriating property will commonly involve consideration of political, economic and social issues on which opinion in a democratic society may reasonably differ widely. The Court, finding it natural that the margin of appreciation available to the legislature in implementing social and economic policies should be a wide one, will respect the legislature's judgment as to what is 'in the public interest' unless that judgment be manifestly without reasonable foundation.

[2441] No. 54522/00, 3.4.12 (overturning the earlier chamber judgment in the case: 14.1.10).
[2442] No. 77606/01, 24.5.07.
[2443] *Chassagnou and others* v *France*, Nos. 25088/94, 28331/95 and 28443/95, 29.4.99, para. 85.
[2444] *Pressos Compania Naviera SA and others* v *Belgium*, No. 17849/91, Series A, No. 332, 20.11.95, para. 37. See also, e.g. *Koufaki and Adedy* v *Greece*, Nos. 57665/12 and 57657/12, dec. 7.5.13 (government austerity measures resulting in the reduction in remuneration, benefits, bonuses and retirement pensions of public servants—inadmissible).

This will be the case, for example, in relation to long-standing and complex areas of law **6.771**
regulating private law matters between individuals. This principle was applied in *J.A. Pye
(Oxford) Ltd and J.A. Pye (Oxford) Land Ltd v UK*,[2445] in which the Grand Chamber of the
Court found no violation of Article 1 of Protocol No. 1 (by ten votes to seven) as a result
of the application of the law of adverse possession, which had been in force for many years,
according to which the applicant companies had lost their beneficial ownership of agricultural land after 12 years' adverse possession by a farmer who used the land for grazing.

The Court has also found that similar principles apply[2446] **6.772**

> to such fundamental changes of a country's system as the transition from a totalitarian regime
> to a democratic form of government and the reform of the State's political, legal and economic
> structure, phenomena which inevitably involve the enactment of large-scale economic and
> social legislation.

The Court has recognised that, in the context of such a transition, where a state enacts legislation designed to enable those who had lost property unjustifiably expropriated by the
state to claim it back from the state, or indeed private individuals, such measures reflect an
underlying public interest 'to restore justice and respect for the rule of law'.[2447] Moreover,
in a number of cases the Court has not found to be disproportionate the reduction of pension rights previously enjoyed by members of the communist elite, political police or armed
forces in post-communist states.[2448] In view of the strong public interest considerations, the
introduction of a law that extinguished pre-existing civil claims in respect of forced labour
under the Nazi regime and that instead provided for a general compensation scheme was
found in *Poznanski and others v Germany*[2449] not to be a disproportionate interference with
the applicants' property rights.

In *Zubko and others v Ukraine*,[2450] the Court emphasised the importance of ensuring that **6.773**
judgments relating to the salary arrears of judges should be enforced, and sufficient funds
allocated, without delay, given their 'sensitive status as independent judicial officers'.

It has frequently been reiterated by the Court that in relation to regional planning and envi- **6.774**
ronmental conservation policies, where the general interest of the community is pre-eminent,
the state will be allowed a margin of appreciation that is greater than when exclusively civil
rights are at stake. Thus, for example, in *Depalle v France*[2451] there was no violation of Article
1 of Protocol No. 1 where the applicant lost his right of occupancy of a house acquired
50 years previously on 'maritime public land' under legislation introduced to protect coastal
areas (without being compensated). The applicant had always known that his right was 'pre-
carious and revocable'. However, the applicants were faced with a disproportionate burden

---

[2445] No. 44302/02, 30.8.07.
[2446] *Broniowski v Poland*, No. 31443/96, 22.6.04, para. 149.
[2447] See *Velikovi and others v Bulgaria*, Nos. 43278/98, 45437/99, 48014/99, 48380/99, 51362/99, 53367/
99, 60036/00, 73465/01 and 194/02, 15.3.07, para. 172. See also *Pincová and Pinc v Czech Republic*, No.
36548/97, 5.11.02.
[2448] See, e.g. *Domalewski v Poland*, No. 34610/97, dec.15.6.99; *Janković v Croatia*, No. 43440/98, dec.
12.10.00; *Schwengel v Germany*, No. 52442/99, dec. 2.3.00; *Lessing and Reichelt v Germany*, Nos. 49646/10
and 3365/11, dec. 16.10.12; *Cichopek and others v Poland*, No. 15189/10 et al, dec. 14.5.13.
[2449] No. 25101/05, dec. 3.7.07.
[2450] Nos. 3955/04, 5622/04, 8538/04 and 11418/04, 26.4.06.
[2451] No. 34044/02, 29.3.10. See also *Brosset-Triboulet and others v France*, No. 34078/02, 29.3.10.

in *Potomska and Potomski v Poland*[2452] as they bought a plot of farmland in order to develop it, but it was subsequently listed as a historic monument (being the former site of a Jewish cemetery). As a result, they were required to preserve the land as a historical monument and protect it from damage, and they were prohibited from carrying out any work on any of their land (over more than 20 years). They also had no enforceable right to compel the state to expropriate the land and receive compensation.

6.775   The Court has held that it is an important legitimate interest for a state to act in compliance with its legal obligations flowing from membership of the European Community. This principle was applied in *Bosphorus Hava Yollari Turizm Ve Ticaret AS v Ireland*,[2453] which concerned the impounding of the applicant's leased aircraft in Ireland, as a result of a directly effective EC Regulation implementing UN sanctions in respect of the then Federal Republic of Yugoslavia. The Court also found in *Bosphorus* that the protection of fundamental rights by Community law was 'equivalent' to that of the Convention system, and therefore a presumption arose that Ireland did not breach the Convention when it implemented legal obligations resulting from its membership of the EC.[2454] Such a presumption could be rebutted if it was considered that the protection of Convention rights was 'manifestly deficient'. On the facts of the case, that presumption had not been rebutted and accordingly there was no violation of Article 1 of Protocol No. 1.

6.776   A fair balance is unlikely to be met if there have been excessive delays by the authorities, for example in providing a remedy, or paying compensation[2455] or if otherwise the duration of the interference with an applicant's rights is excessive.[2456] However, the Court may be less sympathetic to an applicant who acquires property with prior knowledge of potential restrictions (such as planning controls) or who does so knowing that commercial or business factors may affect the value of the property.[2457]

6.777   According to the Papandreou Government, the rationale for the introduction of a new law in 1994 that took effect to expropriate the property of the former King of Greece, was the major public interest in preserving the constitutional status of the country as a republic. This reasoning was accepted by the Court, given the wide margin of appreciation in this area.[2458] In *Trajkovski v former Yugoslav Republic of Macedonia*[2459] the applicant complained about restrictions on foreign currency withdrawals imposed following the dissolution of the Federal Republic of Yugoslavia. Taking into account the difficult circumstances of the dissolution and the potential effect of large numbers of uncontrolled withdrawals on the liquidity of bank and state funds, the restrictions were considered to have struck a fair

---

[2452]   No. 33949/05, 29.3.11.

[2453]   No. 45036/98, 30.6.05.

[2454]   See also *Povse* v *Austria*, No. 3890/11, dec. 18.6.13. See, by contrast, *Michaud* v *France*, No. 12323/11, 6.12.12 (presumption of equivalent protection not applicable, as (a) the case concerned the implementation of a Directive (not a Regulation) and (b) the *Conseil d'Etat* did not refer the case to the Court of Justice for a preliminary ruling). See also *Avotiņš* v *Latvia*, No.17502/07, 23.5.16 (presumption of equivalent protection applicable as regards enforcement of Cypriot judgment—no violation of Article 6).

[2455]   See, e.g. *Almeida Garrett* v *Portugal*, Nos. 29813/96 and 30229/96, 11.1.00.

[2456]   See, e.g. *Smirnov* v *Russia*, No. 71362/01, 7.6.07 (authorities' retention for more than six years of lawyer's computer, following search of home); *Hüseyin Kaplan* v *Turkey*, No. 4508/09, 1.10.13 (restrictions on use of land assigned to public authority 20 years before its expropriation—violation of Article 1 of Protocol No. 1).

[2457]   See, e.g. *Pine Valley Developments Ltd v Ireland*, No. 12742/87, Series A, No. 222, 29.11.91.

[2458]   *Former King of Greece v Greece*, No. 25701/94, 23.11.00.

[2459]   No. 53320/99, dec. 7.3.02.

balance. By contrast, in *Suljagić v Bosnia and Herzegovina*[2460] the Court found a systemic violation of Article 1 of Protocol No. 1 to the Convention as a result of the government's failure adequately to implement domestic legislation providing for the reimbursement of applicants for foreign currency savings deposited in national banks in the former Yugoslavia before 1991.

States are granted a wide margin of appreciation in the area of taxation (being an aspect of social and economic legislation). However, in *N.K.M. v Hungary*[2461] the Court found that the imposition of an overall tax burden of 52 per cent of a civil servant's severance pay was disproportionate and in breach of Article 1 of Protocol No. 1. This rate was about three times the general personal income tax rate. **6.778**

The decision to reduce a former police officer's pension by 65 per cent, following his criminal conviction, was not found to be disproportionate in *Banfield v UK*.[2462] The Court took account of the particularly serious nature of the applicant's offences (including rape and burglary), the exceptional damage that such behaviour could cause to the reputation of the police, and the fact that he had had the benefit of extensive procedural guarantees. However, there was a violation of Article 1 of Protocol No. 1 in *Apostolakis v Greece*[2463] because the applicant was automatically deprived of his retirement pension, and his social security rights, following his conviction for falsifying paybooks (whilst serving as pensions director of an insurance fund). The effect was totally to deprive him of any personal means of subsistence, which was found to amount to a disproportionate burden. The authorities are likely to be granted a wide margin of appreciation as regards the proportionality of confiscation proceedings brought as a consequence of a criminal conviction. For example, there was no violation of Article 1 of Protocol No. 1 in *Gogitidze and others v Georgia*[2464] as a result of proceedings resulting in the forfeiture of property wrongfully acquired by a former government minister, as part of anticorruption measures.

The decision to revoke the applicant's early retirement pension in *Moskal v Poland*[2465] was found to be disproportionate and in violation of Article 1 of Protocol No. 1. This decision was made ten months after the pension had first been awarded, because it was subsequently found that the Social Security Board had made a mistake in finding her to be eligible for it. Although the Court acknowledged that public authorities should not be prevented from correcting their mistakes, it was critical of the length of time that had elapsed before the case had been reviewed. The applicant had resigned from her job in expectation of receipt of the pension, which had been her sole source of income. Therefore, the burden placed on her was found to be excessive. **6.779**

[2460] No. 27912/02, 3.11.09. See also *Ališić and others v Bosnia and Herzegovina, Croatia, Serbia, Slovenia and former Yugoslav Republic of Macedonia*, No. 60642/08, 16.7.14. In contrast, see *Likvidējamā p/s Selga and others v Latvia*, Nos. 17126/02 and 24991/02, dec. 1.10.13 (inability to recover frozen foreign-currency savings after dissolution of USSR—inadmissible).

[2461] No. 66529/11, 14.5.13.

[2462] No. 6223/04, dec. 18.10.05.

[2463] No. 39574/07, 22.10.09. See also *Klein v Austria*, No. 57028/00, 3.3.11; *Stefanetti and others v Italy*, No. 21838/10 et al, 15.4.14 (loss of two-thirds of pension due to effect of legislation introduced while litigation pending against state—violation of Article 1 of Protocol No. 1).

[2464] No. 36862/05, 12.5.15.

[2465] No. 10373/05, 15.9.09 (violation of Article 1 of Protocol No. 1 by four votes to three).

6.780 In the 'pilot judgment' of *Broniowski v Poland*,[2466] there was a violation of Article 1 of Protocol No. 1 as a result of the failure of the Polish authorities to compensate the applicant for land that his family had had to abandon after World War II. The Court accepted that 'stringent limitations' on compensation could be justified by 'radical reform of the country's political and economic system, as well as the state of the country's finances'. Nevertheless, the Government was found to have failed to provide a satisfactory explanation for continuously failing, over many years, to implement the applicant's legal entitlement to compensation. The Court has also accepted as being in the public interest legislation introduced in Italy in the face of a chronic housing shortage, which was intended to stagger the eviction of tenants, in order to reduce social tension.[2467] However, the failure of the system to ensure that landlords in urgent cases could repossess their properties, even after many years, has led to a series of judgments in which the Court has found that a fair balance was not attained: the system operated inflexibly and did not set a time limit when the landlord would regain possession; the domestic courts had no jurisdiction to rule on the question of delay; and there was no right to compensation for delay.[2468] Another systemic violation of property rights in Poland was identified in the pilot judgment *Hutten-Czapska v Poland*,[2469] relating to legislative restrictions on the rights of landlords to charge rent for their properties and to recover property maintenance costs. There, the Court recognised the difficulties created by the shortage of affordable housing in Poland, and the authorities' need to reconcile the competing interests of landlord and tenant, but concluded that the rent-control legislation placed too great a financial burden on landlords.

6.781 The case of *Klaus and Iouri Kiladze v Georgia*[2470] highlighted a 'legislative gap' that prevented victims of political repression in the Soviet era from obtaining compensation. Under a law enacted in 1997 the applicants were entitled to compensation, but the domestic courts rejected their claims because the laws to which the relevant sections of the 1997 law referred had not yet been enacted. The Government had failed to take any steps in order to introduce such laws (such as establishing the number of eligible victims) and no explanation for the omission had been provided. The Court held that having made the moral and financial decision to enact legislation to support Georgian citizens persecuted by the Soviet regime, the state had a duty to act so that the applicants were not left in a state of uncertainty for an indefinite period. The applicants had therefore been subject to a disproportionate and excessive burden in violation of Article 1 of Protocol No. 1. As up to 16,000 people were affected, the Court invoked Article 46 in also holding that the authorities were required to act swiftly to adopt legislative, administrative and budgetary measures in order to plug the gap.

6.782 There was a violation of Article 1 of Protocol No. 1 in *Burdov v Russia*[2471] because of the impossibility for the applicant to obtain execution of judgments made in his favour awarding him compensation. No reasons for this state of affairs were provided by the Government and the

---

[2466] No. 31443/96, 22.6.04.

[2467] *Spadea and Scalabrino v Italy*, Series A, No. 315-B, 28.9.95, paras. 31–2.

[2468] See, e.g. *Immobiliare Saffi v Italy*, No. 22774/93, 28.7.99.

[2469] No. 35014/97, 19.6.06. See also *Bittó and others v Slovakia*, No. 30255/09, 28.1.14; *Statileo v Croatia*, No. 12027/10, 10.7.14; *Berger-Krall and others v Slovenia*, No. 14717/04, 12.6.14 (housing reforms leading to higher rents and reduced security of tenure for tenants following move to market economy—no violation of Article 1 of Protocol No. 1).

[2470] No. 7975/06, 2.2.10. See also *Burdiashvili v Georgia*, No. 26290/12, 4.4.17.

[2471] No. 59498/00, 7.5.02.

Court reiterated that a lack of funds could not justify such a violation of the Convention.[2472] In *Sovtransavto Holding* v *Ukraine*,[2473] the applicant Russian company complained about the reduction of its shareholding in a Ukrainian public company. The fair balance between the public interest and the applicant company's rights was found to have been upset by the way in which civil proceedings were conducted, including the refusal of the tribunals of fact to comply with the directions of a higher court, the considerable difference of approach to the proceedings and the interpretation of the domestic law by the various levels of jurisdiction, and, perhaps most tellingly, interventions by the executive. These and other factors had meant that the proceedings had been repeatedly reopened and that there had been permanent uncertainty about the lawfulness of the original decision. In *Luordo* v *Italy*[2474] and *Bottaro* v *Italy*,[2475] a fair balance was not achieved as between the applicants (who had been declared bankrupt), and their creditors, because the applicants were prevented from administering or disposing of their assets for periods of more than 14 and 12 years, respectively.

6.783 The adoption of legislation that abolished, with retrospective effect, the applicants' existing claims in negligence were found to be disproportionate in *Maurice* v *France*.[2476] This prevented the applicants from arguing a particular head of damage in their legal case against a hospital concerning disabilities that had not been detected before their child's birth. The applicants had been able to claim only limited compensation and had been left in considerable uncertainty, and there was therefore a violation of Article 1 of Protocol No. 1.

6.784 In *Air Canada* the measures taken (the seizure of an aircraft following the discovery of cannabis) were found to conform to the general interest in combating international drug trafficking.[2477] By contrast, in *Ismayilov* v *Russia*[2478] the forfeiture of money (which the applicant possessed lawfully) merely for failing to report it to customs authorities on his entry into Russia, was considered to be a confiscation measure that was disproportionate and in violation of Article 1 of Protocol No. 1. The judgment was distinguished from cases in which goods had been confiscated whose importation was prohibited and also cases concerning the confiscation of assets which amounted to the proceeds of crime. In *Hentrich* v *France*,[2479] the legitimate objective in the public interest for the exercise by the Commissioner of Revenue of a right of pre-emption over land was the prevention of tax evasion. In *James* v *UK*[2480] the applicants were trustees of a substantial estate under the Duke of Westminster's will. They complained of the deprivation of part of their land following the exercise by tenants of rights of acquisition under the Leasehold Reform Act 1967. The Court rejected the applicants'

[2472] See also, e.g. *De Luca* v *Italy*, No. 43870/04, 24.9.13 (applicant's inability to recover judgment debt from local authority in receivership—violation of Article 1 of Protocol No. 1).

[2473] No. 48553/99, 25.9.02.

[2474] No. 32190/96, 17.7.03.

[2475] No. 56298/00, 17.7.03.

[2476] No. 11810/03, 6.10.05. See also *Draon* v *France*, No. 1513/03, 6.10.05; *Aubert and others and 8 others* v *France*, Nos. 31501/03 et seq., 9.1.07; *Joubert* v *France*, No. 30345/05, 23.7.09; *M.C. and others* v *Italy*, No. 5376/11, 3.9.13. In contrast: in *EEG-Slachthuis Verbist* v *Belgium*, No. 60559/00, dec. 10.11.05 there were sufficient public interest grounds to justify legislation enacted, with retrospective effect, to re-establish a statutory basis for contributions previously payable on domestic products; in *Sud Parisienne de Construction* v *France*, No. 33704/04, 11.2.10 a legislative amendment with retrospective effect to the rate of default interest applicable to public procurement contracts was justified on public interest grounds to rectify an anomaly.

[2477] *Air Canada* v *UK*, No. 18465/91, Series A, No. 316, 5.5.95.

[2478] No. 30352/03, 6.11.08. See also *Grifhorst* v *France*, No. 28336/02, 26.2.09.

[2479] No. 13616/88, Series A, No. 296-A, 22.9.94.

[2480] Nos. 8793/79, Series A, No. 98, 21.2.86.

arguments that the transfer of property from one individual to another could not be in the public interest, as 'the taking of property in pursuance of a policy calculated to enhance social justice within the community' would satisfy the public interest requirement.[2481] Moreover, the fairness of the system governing property rights as between individuals was also a matter of public concern.

Compensation

6.785 The level of compensation paid where there has been a deprivation (or control of use[2482]) of property will be a material factor in assessing proportionality. The taking of property will normally require compensation with an amount reasonably related to the value of the property, but public interest considerations (including measures designed to achieve greater social justice)[2483] may permit reimbursement of less than the full market value.[2484] A total lack of compensation can only be justified in exceptional circumstances.[2485] A failure to take account of relevant factors when calculating the level of compensation may result in a finding of a violation of Article 1.[2486] In relation to buildings of historical or cultural value, compensation should include a sum reasonably reflecting the cultural characteristics of the expropriated property.[2487]

6.786 In *Holy Monasteries* v *Greece*[2488] the transfer of land from the applicant monasteries to the Greek state without compensation was therefore found to be a deprivation of property in violation of Article 1.[2489] In *Former King of Greece* v *Greece*,[2490] the failure to pay compensation for the expropriation of the applicant's estates was not in itself found to be wrongful, but Article 1 of Protocol No. 1 was violated because the Government failed to provide any convincing explanation as to why compensation was not paid. The Court found a violation of Article 1 of Protocol No. 1 in *Vistiņš and Perepjolkins* v *Latvia*[2491] because of the 'extreme disproportion' between the official cadastral value of land situated in the port of Riga and the levels of compensation received by the applicants (the first applicant received less than one thousandth of the cadastral value of his land). A 12–five majority of the Grand Chamber accepted that it was in the public interest for the state to expropriate the land, but, even allowing for the particular context of denationalisation following Latvia's restoration of independence, found that a fair balance had not been struck. However, in *Jahn and others*

[2481] See also, *Jahn and others* v *Germany*, Nos. 46720/99, 72203/01 and 72552/01, 30.6.05, paras. 109–10.

[2482] See, e.g. *Aschan and others* v *Finland*, No. 37858/97, dec. 15.2.01 (loss of income from the sale of fishing permits).

[2483] *James* v *UK*, Nos. 8793/79 Series A, No. 98, 21.2.86, para. 54.

[2484] See, e.g. *Holy Monasteries* v *Greece*, Nos. 13092/87 and 13984/88, Series A, No. 301-A, 9.12.94, para. 71.

[2485] See, e.g. *Jahn and others* v *Germany*, Nos. 46720/99, 72203/01 and 72552/01, 30.6.05, paras. 94 and 111; *N.A.* v *Turkey*, No. 37451/97, 11.10.05, para. 41. See also *Kalinova* v *Bulgaria*, No. 45116/98, 8.11.07; *Köktepe* v *Turkey*, No. 35785/03, 22.7.08; *Turgut and others* v *Turkey*, No. 1411/03, 8.7.08; *Maksymenko and Gerasymenko* v *Ukraine*, No. 49317/07, 16.5.13; *Valle Pierimpiè Società Agricola S.p.a.* v *Italy*, No. 46154/11, 23.9.14. But see *Depalle* v *France*, No. 34044/02, 29.3.10, para. 91.

[2486] See, e.g. *Bistrović* v *Croatia*, No. 25774/05, 31.5.07.

[2487] *Kozacıoğlu* v *Turkey*, No. 2334/03, 19.2.09. See also *Helly and others* v *France*, No. 28216/09, dec. 11.10.11.

[2488] Nos. 13092/87 and 13984/88, Series A, No. 301-A, 9.12.94.

[2489] See also, e.g. *Pialopoulos and others* v *Greece*, No. 37095/97, 15.2.01.

[2490] No. 25701/94, 23.11.00.

[2491] No. 71243/01, 25.10.12.

v *Germany*,[2492] the failure to pay any compensation to the applicants for the state's expropriation of their land (acquired in the 1970s and 1980s during the regime of the German Democratic Republic) was found to be justified in the unique context of German reunification, given the uncertainty of the applicants' legal position and the social justice grounds cited by the authorities (the applicants were considered to have benefited from a 'windfall'). The failure to pay compensation following the annulment of outline planning permission for the applicant's land in *Pine Valley Developments Ltd* v *Ireland*[2493] was not found to be disproportionate, having regard to the commercial venture undertaken by the applicants and the consequential element of risk. In *Budayeva and others* v *Russia*,[2494] which concerned, inter alia, the destruction of properties caused by mudslides, the Court found that the provision of compensation at the full market rate was not required, and that in assessing the adequacy of the compensation it was necessary to take account of the complexity of the situation and the number of property owners affected, as well as the economic, social and humanitarian issues inherent in the provision of disaster relief. The applicants were provided with free substitute housing and a lump-sum emergency allowance, which was found to comply with Article 1 of Protocol No. 1. In *Perdigão* v *Portugal*,[2495] the applicants received compensation of about €197,000 as a result of the expropriation of a piece of land and a quarry, but the court fees they were required to pay (which were indexed to the sum in dispute) exceeded that figure and they accordingly received nothing. This was not considered to have achieved a 'fair balance' and the Grand Chamber found a violation of Article 1 of Protocol No. 1.

6.787 Delays in paying compensation may lead to the value of the sum in question being reduced by substantial inflation.[2496] Following the destruction of the applicant's house due to a methane gas explosion in *Öneryildiz* v *Turkey*,[2497] the applicant's award of compensation had still not been paid, even though a final judgment had been delivered. Accordingly, the Court found a violation of Article 1 of Protocol No. 1. There was a violation of Article 1 of Protocol No. 1 in *Lallement* v *France*,[2498] which concerned the expropriation of 30 per cent of the applicant's dairy farm. This step made it financially unviable to continue to farm the remaining land and the available compensation had not covered this loss of the applicant's income, which was not therefore considered to bear a reasonable relation to the value of the expropriated property.

6.788 In *Motais de Narbonne* v *France*,[2499] land was expropriated by the local authority for the purposes of building social housing. However, there had in fact been no building works for the

---

[2492] Nos. 46720/99, 72203/01 and 72552/01, 30.6.05 (the Grand Chamber found no violation of Article 1 of Protocol No. 1 by 11 votes to six, following the chamber's earlier unanimous judgment finding a violation—22.1.04). See also *Althoff and others* v *Germany*, No. 5631/05, 8.12.11 (retrospective amendment of statutory time-limit applying to claims for restitution of land in the former GDR—violation of Article 1 of Protocol No. 1); *Göbel* v *Germany*, No. 35023/04, 8.12.11 (loss of shares in land without full compensation in context of German reunification—no violation of Article 1 of Protocol No. 1).

[2493] No. 12742/87, Series A, No. 222, 29.11.91.

[2494] Nos. 15339/02, 21166/02, 20058/02, 11673/02 and 15343/02, 20.3.08. See, by contrast, *Hadzhiyska* v *Bulgaria*, No. 20701/09, dec. 15.5.12 (damage to property caused by flooding after heavy rainfall—applicant did not allege that the authorities could have foreseen or prevented the consequences of the rain—inadmissible).

[2495] No. 24768/06, 16.11.10.

[2496] See, e.g. *Baltekin* v *Turkey*, No. 19266/92, 30.1.01.

[2497] No. 48939/99, 30.11.04.

[2498] No. 46044/99, 11.4.02.

[2499] No. 48161/99, 2.7.02.

19 years since the order was made. The Court accordingly found that even where, as in this case, compensation reflecting the market value had been paid, an excessive burden had been placed on the applicant who had been denied the capital gain generated by the property. The Court warned that states should avoid keeping land in reserve for development, which had in this case amounted to a form of speculation in real estate, to the detriment of the applicant.

6.789   The Court has also held that the right to peaceful enjoyment of possessions includes an 'expectation of a reasonable consistency between inter-related, albeit separate, decisions concerning the same property'.[2500] Thus in *Jokela* v *Finland*,[2501] there was a violation of this right where the market value of the applicant's husband's land fixed for the levying of inheritance tax was assessed to be four times higher than the market value of the same land assessed for the purposes of its expropriation.

Legal regulation

6.790   An interference with property must of course be regulated by law. Thus there was a clear violation of Article 1 of Protocol No. 1 in *Frizen* v *Russia*[2502] where the Government could cite no legal provision at all to justify the forfeiture of the applicant's car, following her husband's conviction for fraud. The requirement of legal regulation also means that there must be sufficient accessibility, precision and foreseeability in domestic law and practice.[2503] Furthermore, where legislation allows the authorities a discretion, the law must also indicate the scope of the discretion with sufficient precision (having regard to the subject matter of the legislation in question). In *Hentrich* v *France*,[2504] this requirement was violated by the Commissioner of Revenue exercising a right of pre-emption following the applicants' purchase of land in a manner which was arbitrary, selective and 'scarcely foreseeable'. In *Iatridis* v *Greece*,[2505] the state ordered the applicant's eviction from a cinema in respect of which he held a licence to operate. The High Court quashed the order, but the Government refused to reinstate him. Thus the European Court held the state's actions to be manifestly in breach of the domestic law, in violation of Article 1 of Protocol No. 1.[2506]

6.791   In *Capital Bank AD* v *Bulgaria*,[2507] the decision to revoke the applicant bank's licence was found not to be subject to sufficient guarantees against arbitrariness and was therefore not lawful within the meaning of Article 1 of Protocol No. 1. The decision was made by the Bulgarian National Bank without being obliged to inform the applicant bank of the

---

[2500] *Jokela* v *Finland*, No. 28856/95, 21.5.02, para. 61.

[2501] No. 28856/95, 21.5.02.

[2502] No. 58254/00, 24.3.05. See also *Khamidov* v *Russia*, No. 72118/01, 15.11.07—the police's prolonged occupation of the applicant's land and buildings in Chechnya in the aftermath of a counter-terrorist operation was not specifically authorised by any domestic law, order or court decision.

[2503] See, e.g. *Carbonara and Ventura* v *Italy*, No. 24638/94, 30.5.00; *Baklanov* v *Russia*, No. 68443/01, 9.6.05; *Zlínsat, spol. s r.o.* v *Bulgaria*, No. 57785/00, 15.6.06; *Sud Fondi srl and others* v *Italy*, No. 75909/01, 20.1.09; *Saghinadze and others* v *Georgia*, No. 18768/05, 27.5.10; *Hoare* v *UK*, No. 16261/08, dec. 12.4.11. In *Vistiņš and Perepjolkins* v *Latvia*, No. 71243/01, 25.10.12, the Court found that the Latvian system of land expropriation which entitles the parliament, rather than the executive, to take expropriation decisions, did not, as such, raise any issue of 'lawfulness' under Article 1 of Protocol No. 1. The Court did, however, express its doubts about the lawfulness of parliament's decision to derogate from the usual procedures laid down in the expropriation law (in any event finding the expropriation to be disproportionate).

[2504] No. 13616/88, Series A, No. 296-A, 22.9.94.

[2505] No. 31107/96, 25.3.99.

[2506] See also, e.g. *Paudicio* v *Italy*, No. 77606/01, 24.5.07.

[2507] No. 49429/99, 24.11.05.

commencement of the procedure, nor did it have to take into account the applicant's representations or objections. A similar conclusion was reached in *Družstevní záložna Pria and others* v *Czech Republic*[2508] in which the Court found a violation of Article 1 of Protocol No. 1 as a result of the denial of access of a credit union in receivership to its business documents and accounts, thus preventing it in effect from challenging the decision to put it into receivership. The grant of access to the documents was in the sole discretion of the receiver. The interference with the applicants' property rights in *Apostolidi and others* v *Turkey*[2509] was found to be insufficiently foreseeable. The Greek applicants inherited their aunt's flat in Turkey, but the Turkish courts found that they could only acquire it by inheritance if Turkish nationals had the same entitlement in Greece, and that this condition of reciprocity was not satisfied. However, contrary to the findings of the Turkish courts, the European Court found that it had not been established that there was any restriction in Greece preventing Turkish nationals from acquiring property by inheritance.

6.792 The case of *OAO Neftyanaya Kompaniya Yukos* v *Russia*[2510] concerned criminal proceedings for tax evasion brought against the applicant oil company, resulting in a commercial court order that it should pay vast sums by way of taxes, interest and penalties, and subsequently in its insolvency and liquidation. The Court found that there had been a violation of the lawfulness requirement under Article 1 of Protocol No. 1 as a consequence of a Constitutional Court decision which had prevented the company from benefiting from a statutory three-year time-bar which was normally applicable to prosecutions for tax evasion. The Court found that this decision amounted to a reversal of, and departure from, the well-established practice directions of the Supreme Commercial Court. A requirement to pay double fines was also not considered to be in accordance with the law. Furthermore, the measures of enforcement proceedings imposed on the company— the seizure of its assets, the imposition of a 7 per cent enforcement fee (an additional €1.16 million) and the forced sale of the company's main production unit—were also held to be disproportionate to the legitimate aim pursued. The authorities failed to take account of all the factors that were relevant to the enforcement proceedings, and also erred in not considering possible alternative measures, especially those that could have mitigated the damage to the company.

Procedural requirements

6.793 The second paragraph of Article 1 has been held implicitly to include procedural requirements. Thus applicants should be given a reasonable opportunity to put their case to the responsible authorities for the purpose of effectively challenging the measures interfering with their rights. This will require a 'comprehensive view' to be taken of the procedure in question.[2511] Thus, domestic courts will be required to carry out an assessment of the proportionality of an interference with property rights. For example in *Džinić* v *Croatia*[2512] there was a violation of Article 1 of Protocol No. 1 because although the seizure of the applicant's property in the context of criminal proceedings had in principle been legitimate and

---

[2508] No. 2034/01, 31.7.08.
[2509] No. 45628/99, 27.3.07.
[2510] No. 14902/04, 20.9.11. There were also violations of Articles 6(1) and 6(3)(b) during the course of the tax assessment proceedings.
[2511] See, e.g. *Jokela* v *Finland*, No. 28856/95, 21.5.02, para. 45.
[2512] No. 38359/13, 17.5.16.

justified, there had been no assessment by the domestic courts as to whether the value of the seized property corresponded to the possible confiscation claim.

6.794 There was a violation of Article 1 of Protocol No. 1 for procedural reasons in *Bruncrona* v *Finland*.[2513] There, the applicants' leasehold rights over a group of islands were purportedly terminated by a letter from the National Park and Forestry Services requesting that the property be vacated. The Court held that this was not an acceptable means of terminating a right that had been enjoyed for almost 300 years. In the *AGOSI* case,[2514] the Court considered two procedural issues: whether reasonable account had been taken of the relationship between the conduct of the company and the unlawful smuggling of gold coins, and whether the company had an adequate opportunity to put its case to the authorities. In that case, the scope of judicial review (in challenging the discretion of the Commissioners of Customs and Excise) was held to satisfy the requirements of the second paragraph of Article 1.

Destruction of home and displacement from homes

6.795 In a series of cases against Turkey in the mid-1990s, the security forces were found responsible for destroying the homes and possessions of the applicants, resulting in findings of grave and unjustified violations of Article 1 of Protocol No. 1 (and of Article 8).[2515] Similar decisions have been made in cases concerning aerial attacks on homes in the course of the conflict in Chechnya.[2516] In *Doğan and others* v *Turkey*,[2517] the Court found that Article 1 of Protocol No. 1 had been violated as a result of the inability of the applicants to return to their village over a period of more than 10 years, following their expulsion in 1994 as a result of clashes between the PKK and the security forces. The applicants had been living elsewhere in extreme poverty and had received no compensation or alternative housing or employment.

6.796 The Court held[2518] that the authorities had the

> primary duty and responsibility to establish conditions, as well as provide the means, which allow the applicants to return voluntarily, in safety and with dignity, to their homes or places of habitual residence, or to resettle voluntarily in another part of the country.

In the inter-state case of *Cyprus* v *Turkey*,[2519] there was found to be a continuing violation of Article 1 of Protocol No. 1 due to the denial to Greek Cypriot property owners of their access to, and control, use and enjoyment of, their property, and the absence of any compensation.

6.797 In two cases concerning applicants who were displaced from their homes during the Nagorno-Karabakh conflict between Armenia and Azerbaijan in the early 1990s, and who had subsequently been unable to return, the Court found continuing violations of Article 1 of Protocol No. 1, as well as Article 8.[2520]

[2513] No. 41673/98, 16.11.04.

[2514] No. 9118/80, Series A, No. 108, 24.10.86.

[2515] *Akdivar* v *Turkey*, No. 21893/93, 16.9.96; *Mentes and others* v *Turkey*, No. 23186/94, 28.11.97, *Selçuk and Asker* v *Turkey*, Nos. 23184/94 and 23185/94, 24.4.98; *Bilgin* v *Turkey*, No. 23819/94, 16.11.00; *Dulaş* v *Turkey*, No. 25801/94, 30.1.01; *Orhan* v *Turkey*, No. 25656/94, 18.6.02; *Yöyler* v *Turkey*, No. 26973/95, 24.7.03; *Ayder and others* v *Turkey*, No. 23656/94, 8.1.04; *Ipek* v *Turkey*, No. 25760/94, 17.2.04.

[2516] See, e.g. *Esmukhambetov and others* v *Russia*, No. 23445/03, 29.3.11; *Kerimova and others* v *Russia*, No. 17170/04 et al, 3.5.11.

[2517] Nos. 8803–8811/02, 8813/02 and 8815–8819/02, 29.6.04.

[2518] *Ibid.*, para. 154.

[2519] No. 25781/94, 10.5.01.

[2520] *Chiragov and others* v *Armenia*, No. 13216/05, 16.6.15; *Sargsyan* v *Azerbaijan*, No. 40167/06, 16.6.15.

The expropriation and destruction of city centre homes, for development purposes, has been **6.798** found to violate Article 1 of Protocol No. 1. For example, in *Akhverdiyev v Azerbaijan*[2521] the Court found that the expropriation of the applicant's house in Baku, as a result of the assignment of land to a private developer, had not been lawful.

Article 2 of Protocol No. 1: Right to Education

Article 2 of Protocol No. 1 states: **6.799**

> No person shall be denied the right to education. In the exercise of any functions which it assumes in relation to education and to teaching, the state shall respect the right of parents to ensure such education and teaching is in conformity with their own religious and philosophical convictions.

The overriding aim of this Article is to ensure a right of access, in principle, to 'the means of instruction existing at a given time'. It has been held to guarantee a right of access to existing educational institutions and the right to obtain official recognition of studies completed. The provision applies to all levels of education, including higher education,[2522] and allows for no exceptions,[2523] and does not distinguish between state and private education.[2524] It should be interpreted in the light of Articles 8, 9 and 10 of the Convention.[2525] Article 14 may be relevant where there is a discriminatory aspect to the provision of education. For example, in *Ponomaryovi v Bulgaria*[2526] there was a violation of Article 14 taken together with Article 2 of Protocol 1 as a result of the requirement imposed on aliens who did not have residence status (but not Bulgarian nationals) to pay fees to attend secondary school. There, the Court found that states have a wider margin of appreciation as regards higher education, but that it was much narrower in respect of primary education (with secondary education falling between the two).

Article 2 does not necessarily ensure a right of access to a particular educational institu- **6.800** tion.[2527] Article 2 does not require states to establish, either at their own expense, or to subsidise, education of a particular type or at a particular level. The Article also does not lay down requirements for the content and purpose of the education or teaching: the setting and planning of the curriculum falls in principle within the state's competence. There is no denial of the right to education where individuals are prevented from continuing their education because they have been lawfully convicted and detained in prison, and nor is there any obligation on the prison authorities to set up particular educational courses.[2528] However, there was a violation of Article 2 of Protocol No. 1 in *Velyo Velev v Bulgaria*[2529] where the applicant remand prisoner (who had not yet completed his secondary education)

[2521] No. 76254/11, 29.1.15.
[2522] *Leyla Şahin v Turkey*, No. 44774/98, 10.11.05, paras. 134–42; *Mürsel Eren v Turkey*, No. 60856/00, 7.2.06.
[2523] *Timishev v Russia*, Nos. 55762/00 and 55974/00, 13.12.05, para. 64.
[2524] For an overview of the application of Article 2 of Protocol No. 1 see, in particular, the Grand Chamber judgment in *Folgerø and others v Norway*, No. 15472/02, 29.6.07, para. 84.
[2525] *Ibid.*
[2526] No. 5335/05, 21.6.11.
[2527] *Simpson v UK*, No. 14688/89, 24.2.98.
[2528] *Epistatu v Romania*, No. 29343/10, 24.9.13.
[2529] No. 6032/07, 27.5.14.

was denied access to a pre-existing prison school. The Court found that the decision was neither sufficiently foreseeable, nor did it pursue a legitimate aim and nor was it shown to be proportionate.

6.801 The right to education is not absolute; it may be subject to limitations and to regulation that will vary in time and place according to the needs and resources of the community and of individuals. Any restrictions must be foreseeable, pursue legitimate aims and be proportionate. In *Tarantino and others v Italy*[2530] the Court found no violation of Article 2 of Protocol No. 1 as a result of legislation imposing limits on the number of candidates able to enter university to study medicine and dentistry. Such limits had been introduced in order to reflect the capacity and resource potential of universities, and society's need for a particular profession, which the Court held to be proportionate grounds. The case of *Memlika v Greece*[2531] concerned the exclusion of children from their primary school for more than three months after they were wrongly diagnosed with leprosy. The initial exclusion had been legitimate in preventing a risk of contamination, but the subsequent delay in setting up a panel responsible for deciding on the children's return to school had been disproportionate, in violation of Article 2 of Protocol No. 1.

Disciplinary measures such as suspension or expulsion are permissible.[2532] As regards exclusions from school, the Court will assess whether a 'fair balance' was struck by the authorities, taking account of factors such as the procedural safeguards available to challenge the exclusion, the duration of the exclusion, the extent of the co-operation shown by the pupil with respect to attempts at re-integration, the steps taken by the authorities to minimise the effects of exclusion, and the adequacy of alternative education provided by the school during the period of exclusion.[2533]

6.802 There is no requirement that education should be available in any particular language, other than the national language (or one of the national languages).[2534] However, in *Cyprus v Turkey*,[2535] where the authorities of the 'Turkish Republic of Northern Cyprus' had assumed responsibility for Greek-language primary schooling, the Court found that the Turkish authorities should have made continued provision for Greek-language schooling at secondary level. The applicants in *İrfan Temel and others v Turkey*[2536] were university students who were temporarily suspended for having petitioned university authorities to provide optional Kurdish language courses. This was considered to be neither reasonable nor proportionate, in violation of Article 2 of Protocol No. 1. A ban on university students wearing Islamic headscarves was found not to violate the first sentence of Article 2 of Protocol No. 1 in *Leyla Şahin v Turkey*.[2537] In *Mürsel Eren v Turkey*,[2538] the annulment of the applicant's university entrance exam results, without any legal or rational basis, was held to violate his right to education.

[2530] Nos. 25851/09, 29284/09 and 64090/09, 2.4.13.
[2531] No. 37991/12, 6.10.15.
[2532] *Ali v UK*, No. 40385/06, 11.1.11.
[2533] *Ibid.*, para. 58.
[2534] *Belgian Linguistic Case (No. 2)*, Series A, No. 6, dec. 23.7.68, paras. 3 and 6.
[2535] No. 25781/94, 10.5.01.
[2536] No. 36458/02, 3.3.09.
[2537] No. 44774/98, 10.11.05. There was also no violation of Article 9: see the discussion at 6.566 above. See also *Köse and 93 others v Turkey*, No. 26625/02, dec. 24.1.06 (secondary school students).
[2538] No. 60856/00, 7.2.06.

Education in conformity with parents' religious and philosophical convictions

The aim of the second sentence of Article 2 is to safeguard the possibility of pluralism in edu- **6.803**
cation.[2539] Article 2 does not allow for a distinction to be drawn between religious instruction and other subjects—the state is required to respect parents' convictions throughout the
entire state education programme.[2540]

The term 'philosophical convictions' has been defined as meaning 'such convictions as are **6.804**
worthy of respect in a "democratic society" and are not incompatible with human dignity'.
In addition, such convictions must not conflict with the fundamental right of the child to
education: the whole of Article 2 being dominated by its first sentence.[2541] For example,
opposition to corporal punishment satisfies these criteria. The second sentence requires that
information or knowledge included in the curriculum should be conveyed in an 'objective,
critical and pluralistic manner', and without indoctrination.

In *Campbell and Cosans* v *UK*[2542] the applicants complained about the system of corporal **6.805**
punishment in state schools. The Court rejected the Government's arguments that the disciplinary system did not fall within the 'functions' relating to education or teaching, and
confirmed that any function ancillary to education and teaching would be subject to Article
2 of Protocol No. 1. It was also held that the obligation to respect parents' philosophical and
religious convictions not only applies to the content of education, but also to other functions
including the organisation and financing of education and the disciplinary system. The existence of corporal punishment was found to violate the applicants' rights under the second
sentence of the Article, and the suspension of Jeffrey Cosans from school for nearly a year was
unreasonable and accordingly violated the first sentence.

The applicants in *Kjeldsen, Busk, Madsen and Pedersen* v *Denmark*,[2543] as Christian parents, **6.806**
objected to compulsory sex education in schools. The Court found no violation of Article 2
on the basis that the relevant legislation did not advocate a specific kind of sexual behaviour
or incite pupils to indulge in practices that might be dangerous for their stability, health or
future. Therefore, it was not considered to offend the applicants' convictions to the extent
forbidden by the second sentence of the Article. However, in *Folgerø and others* v *Norway*[2544]
the Grand Chamber of the Court found (by nine votes to eight) that Article 2 of Protocol
No. 1 had been violated because of the authorities' refusal to grant full exemption to the
humanist applicants' children from instruction in Christianity, religion and philosophy in
state primary schools. The Court found that 'preponderant weight' was given to Christianity,
notably through reliance on the 'Christian object clause' in the legislation, according to which
the object of primary and lower secondary education was to help give pupils a Christian and
moral upbringing. In practice, the system of partial exemption could be unduly onerous on

---

[2539] *Kjeldsen, Busk, Madsen and Pedersen* v *Denmark*, Nos. 5095/71, 5920/72 and 5926/72, Series A, No.
23, 7.12.76, para. 50.
[2540] See, e.g. *Folgerø and others* v *Norway*, No. 15472/02, 29.6.07, para. 84.
[2541] *Campbell and Cosans* v *UK*, Nos. 7511/76 and 7743/76, Series A, No. 48, 25.2.82, para. 36.
[2542] Nos. 7511/76 and 7743/76, Series A, No. 48, 25.2.82.
[2543] Nos. 5095/71, 5920/72 and 5926/72, Series A, No. 23, 7.12.76. See also *Knock and others* v *Germany*,
No. 35504/03, dec. 11.9.06 and *Appel-Irrgang* v *Germany*, No. 45216/07, dec. 6.10.09 (Protestant parents
objecting to compulsory secular ethics classes in state schools—inadmissible); *Dojan and others* v *Germany*,
No. 319/08, dec. 13.9.11 (members of the Christian Evangelical Baptist Church whose children were refused
exemption from sex education classes—inadmissible).
[2544] No. 15472/02, 29.6.07.

parents and parents might also be deterred from applying for exemption by a risk of exposure of their private lives and potential conflict. Having analysed the relevant legal framework, and its application in practice, the Court concluded that the authorities had not taken sufficient care to ensure that information and knowledge included in the curriculum should be conveyed in an objective, critical and pluralistic manner for the purposes of Article 2 of Protocol No. 1.

6.807 The applicants in *Catan and others v Moldova and Russia*[2545] were Moldovans who lived in Transdniestria and who were pupils at three Moldovan-language schools, and their parents. They complained about the closure of their schools and their harassment by the separatist Transdniestrian authorities. The Court found that the use of the Latin alphabet was an offence in the 'MRT', that the schools had had to move to new buildings significant distances away, and that the number of pupils attending the schools had significantly decreased. Accordingly, such measures, and the applicants' harassment, amounted to interferences with their right of access to educational institutions and to be educated in their national language, as well as amounting to an interference with the parents' rights to ensure their children's education and teaching in accordance with their philosophical convictions. The Court held that there was no legitimate aim for such measures, and indeed that they were intended to enforce the Russification of the language and culture of the Moldovan community living in Transdniestria. The Moldovan Government had made considerable efforts to support the applicants (notably paying for the schools' costs), and were therefore considered to have met their positive obligations. However, due to its continued support for the 'MRT', Russia was held to be responsible for the violation of Article 2 of Protocol No. 1.

6.808 The Grand Chamber of the Court found no violation of Article 2 of Protocol No. 1 in *Lautsi and others v Italy*,[2546] as a result of the display of crucifixes in classrooms in state schools. The applicant complained that this was contrary to the principle of secularism, in accordance with which she wished to bring up her children. In initially finding a violation of the Convention, the Chamber[2547] took particular account of:

> the nature of the religious symbol and its impact on young pupils, especially the applicant's children, because in countries where the great majority of the population owe allegiance to one particular religion the manifestation of the observances and symbols of that religion, without restriction as to place and manner, may constitute pressure on students who do not practise that religion or those who adhere to another religion.

The Chamber concluded that the compulsory display by a public authority of a symbol of a particular faith, especially in classrooms, restricted the right of parents to educate their children in conformity with their convictions and the right of schoolchildren to believe or not believe. However, the Grand Chamber emphasised that there was no evidence that the display of the crucifix (an 'essentially passive symbol') in classrooms had any effect on pupils. The crucifix was not associated with compulsory teaching about Christianity, and Italian schools were equally open to other religions (allowing apparel and symbols of other faiths). Noting that there was no European consensus on this question, the Court concluded that it was a matter that fell within states' margin of appreciation.

[2545] Nos. 43370/04, 8252/05 and 18454/06, 19.10.12.
[2546] No. 30814/06, 18.3.11.
[2547] No. 30814/06, 3.11.09, para. 50.

In the case of *Hasan and Eylem Zengin* v *Turkey*,[2548] the applicants, who were adherents of **6.809** Alevism, complained about the refusal to exempt state primary and secondary school pupils from mandatory lessons on religion and morals. Article 2 of Protocol No. 1 was violated as the teaching of religion was found not to be sufficiently objective or to reflect the religious diversity in Turkey. There was little or no teaching on the Alevi faith. Furthermore, only Jewish or Christian children could be exempted from religious education (where a prior declaration of adherence to either of those religions had been made).

Discrimination

In *D.H. and others* v *Czech Republic*,[2549] the Grand Chamber found a violation of Article 14 taken **6.810** together with Article 2 of Protocol No. 1, as a result of the disproportionately high number of Roma children placed in special schools in the Ostrava region in the Czech Republic (on this case, and *Sampanis and others* v *Greece*,[2550] see 6.725 above). There was a violation of Article 14 taken together with Article 2 of Protocol No. 1 in *Altınay* v *Turkey*[2551] due to an unforeseeable legal change as regards university access which was held to be disproportionate (see 6.716 above).

Special educational needs

The authorities are given a wide discretion in utilising resources to provide for the education **6.811** of children with special educational needs.[2552] For example, in *SP* v *UK*,[2553] the applicant complained about the provision of education to her son who was dyslexic. The application was declared inadmissible as there had been no question of his being excluded from the educational facilities provided by the state.

UK reservation

At the time of signing the first Protocol, the UK Government entered into a reservation in respect **6.812** of this provision, which is incorporated into the Human Rights Act 1998 (Schedule 3):[2554]

> ... in view of certain provisions of the Education Acts in force in the United Kingdom, the principle affirmed in the second sentence of Article 2 is accepted by the United Kingdom only so far as it is compatible with the provision of efficient instruction and training, and the avoidance of unreasonable public expenditure.

Article 3 of Protocol No. 1: Right to Free Elections

Article 3 of Protocol No. 1 states: **6.813**

> The High Contracting Parties undertake to hold free elections at reasonable intervals by secret ballot, under conditions which will ensure the free expression of the opinion of the people in the choice of the legislature.

[2548] No. 1448/04, 9.10.07. See also *Mansur Yalçın and others* v *Turkey*, No. 21163/11, 16.9.14 (finding a similar violation, even in the light of changes to the curriculum introduced following the judgment in *Hasan and Eylem Zengin*). See further *Sinan Işık* v *Turkey*, No. 21924/05, 2.2.10 (refusal to change indication of religion on identity card from 'Islam' to 'Alevi'—violation of Article 9).

[2549] No. 57325/00, 13.11.07, para. 188.

[2550] No. 32526/05, 5.6.08.

[2551] No. 37222/04, 9.7.13.

[2552] See, e.g. *Molly McIntyre* v *UK*, No. 29046/95, dec. 21.10.98.

[2553] No. 28915/95, 17.1.97.

[2554] See further 7.23 below.

6.814 The Court has described this Article as being 'of prime importance in the Convention system' as it enshrines a characteristic principle of democracy.[2555] Unlike the majority of other Convention rights, it is primarily concerned with a positive obligation—to hold democratic elections. There is a strong link with Article 10: 'free elections and freedom of expression, particularly freedom of political debate, together form the bedrock of any democratic system'.[2556] In its judgment in the case of *Ždanoka v Latvia*,[2557] the Grand Chamber set out the relevant principles in applying this provision. As it is phrased in 'collective and general terms', the standards applied in establishing compliance with Article 3 of Protocol No. 1 are less stringent than those applied under Articles 8 to 11 of the Convention. Article 3 of Protocol No. 1 also incorporates certain procedural positive obligations, such as requiring a domestic system for the effective examination of individual complaints and appeals concerning electoral rights.[2558]

6.815 Limitations are to be implied (which may go beyond the list of 'legitimate aims' set out in Articles 8 to 11). In considering compliance with Article 3 of Protocol No. 1, the Court will mainly consider whether there has been arbitrariness or a lack of proportionality, and whether the restriction has interfered with the free expression of the opinion of the people. Furthermore, states are granted a wide 'margin of appreciation' and the assessment of any electoral legislation should be made 'in the light of the political evolution of the country concerned'. The Court will seek to assess the nature, type, duration and consequences of any statutory restrictions that are alleged to violate an individual's rights.

6.816 Article 3 of Protocol No. 1 applies only to the election of a 'legislature.' In addition to national parliaments, the Court has held that, depending on the constitutional structure of the state in question, the Article may apply to other bodies. In *Mathieu-Mohin and Clerfayt v Belgium*[2559] the Court found that a regional council had sufficient competence and powers to make it a constituent part of the Belgian 'legislature' and the Parliaments of the Spanish Autonomous Communities have also been found to be part of the 'legislature' within the meaning of Article 3 of Protocol No. 1.[2560] It will not, however, apply to presidential elections.[2561]

[2555] *Mathieu-Mohin and Clerfayt v Belgium*, No. 9267/81, Series A, No. 113, 2.3.87, para. 47.

[2556] *Bowman v UK*, No. 24839/94, 4.12.95, para. 42.

[2557] No. 58278/00, 16.3.06, para. 115.

[2558] *Namat Aliyev v Azerbaijan*, No. 18705/06, 8.4.10.

[2559] No. 9267/81, Series A, No. 113, 2.3.87.

[2560] *Federacion Nationalista Canaria v Spain*, No. 56618/00, dec. 7.6.01. See also *Py v France*, No. 66289/01, 11.1.05 (Article 3 of Protocol No. 1 applicable to elections to the Congress in New Caledonia). But see *Booth-Clibborn v UK* (1985) 43 DR 236 (metropolitan county councils were not considered to be 'legislatures' because their powers were delegated by Parliament); *Cherepkov v Russia*, No. 51501/99, dec. 25.1.00 (a municipal council and mayor do not exercise legislative power); *Malarde v France*, No. 46813/99, dec. 5.9.00 (Article 3 of Protocol No. 1 not applicable to Regional Councils in France); *Salleras Llinares v Spain*, No. 52226/99, dec. 12.10.00 (Article 3 of Protocol No. 1 not applicable to municipal authorities in Spain); *Santoro v Italy*, No. 36681/97, dec. 16.1.03 (Article 3 of Protocol No. 1 not applicable to provincial authorities in Italy); *Zdanoka v Latvia*, No. 58278/00, dec. 6.3.03 (Latvian local councils not part of the 'legislature'); *Mółka v Poland*, No. 56550/00, dec. 11.4.06 (Article 3 of Protocol No. 1 not applicable to municipal councils, district councils or regional assemblies).

[2561] *Guliyev v Azerbaijan*, No. 35584/02, dec. 27.5.04; *Boškoski v former Yugoslav Republic of Macedonia*, No. 11676/04, dec. 2.9.04; *Paksas v Lithuania*, No. 34932/04, 6.1.11, para. 72.

In *Matthews* v *UK*[2562] the applicant complained about the exclusion of Gibraltar from the **6.817** franchise for the European parliamentary elections. The Court rejected the Government's arguments that, as a supranational body, the European Parliament fell outside the ambit of Article 3 of Protocol No. 1. The Court in *Matthews* considered the actual powers of the European Parliament in the context of the EC legislative process, notably since the Maastricht Treaty, and concluded that it was sufficiently involved in the general democratic supervision of the EC to constitute part of the 'legislature' of Gibraltar. As the applicant had been completely denied the opportunity to express her opinion in choosing members of the European Parliament, Article 3 of Protocol No. 1 was violated.

Article 3 of Protocol No. 1 includes both the right to vote and the right to stand for election **6.818** to the legislature (including the right to sit as an MP once elected).[2563] Indeed, the annulment of election results (if found to be unlawful or arbitrary) could violate the rights of both voters and election candidates.[2564] The Court has noted[2565] that:

> There are numerous ways of organising and running electoral systems and a wealth of differences, *inter alia*, in historical development, cultural diversity and political thought within Europe which it is for each Contracting State to mould into their own democratic vision.

Accordingly, the state has a wide margin of appreciation in setting conditions on those rights **6.819** (such as minimum age requirements) but any conditions must pursue a legitimate aim and be proportionate and must not impair the very essence of the rights.[2566] Minimum thresholds for representation in Parliament will not violate Article 3 of Protocol No. 1 provided that the electoral law is not arbitrary, disproportionate or capable of undermining 'the free expression of the opinion of the people in the choice of the legislature'.[2567] This principle was confirmed by the Grand Chamber in *Yumak and Sadak* v *Turkey*[2568] in which the applicants sought to challenge the imposition of a 10 per cent national threshold (the highest in Europe) in order for a political party to be represented in Parliament. Although it acknowledged that a 10 per cent threshold was excessive, the majority of the Court found no violation of Article 3 of Protocol No. 1 (by 13 votes to four), having regard to the political climate of crisis in Turkey at the time of the elections and the attendant safeguards (such as the role played by the Constitutional Court).

[2562] No. 24883/94, 18.2.99.

[2563] *Ganchev* v *Bulgaria*, No. 28858/95, Comm. Rep. 25.11.96, para. 130; *Gaulieder* v *Slovak Republic*, No. 36909/97, Comm. Rep. 10.9.99, para. 41; *Sadak and others* v *Turkey*, Nos. 25144/94, 26149/95, 26154/95, 27100/95 and 27101/95, 11.6.02, para. 33. See also *Russian Conservative Party of Entrepreneurs and Zhukov and Vasilyev* v *Russia*, Nos. 55066/00 and 55638/00, dec. 18.3.04.

[2564] See, e.g. *Riza and others* v *Bulgaria*, Nos. 48555/10 and 48377/10, 13.10.15 (annulment of election results in several polling stations in Turkey—flawed review by Constitutional Court and no possibility of holding new elections—violations of Article 3 of Protocol No. 1).

[2565] *Hirst* v *UK (No. 2)*, No. 74025/01, 6.10.05.

[2566] See, e.g. *Benkaddour* v *France*, No. 51685/99, dec. 18.11.03.

[2567] *Federacion Nationalista Canaria* v *Spain*, No. 56618/00, dec. 7.6.01; *Partija 'JAUNIE DEMOKRĀTI'* v *Latvia*, No. 10547/07 and *Partija 'MŪSU ZEME'* v *Latvia*, No. 34049/07, decs. 29.11.07. See also *Partei Die Friesen* v *Germany*, No. 65480/10, 28.1.16 (application of 5 per cent threshold in parliamentary elections in Lower Saxony—no violation of Article 3 of Protocol No. 1 taken together with Article 14); *Strack and Richter* v *Germany*, Nos. 28811/12 and 50303/12, dec. 5.7.16 (refusal to terminate mandate of European Parliament members elected as a result of 5 per cent eligibility threshold declared unconstitutional—inadmissible).

[2568] No. 10226/03, 8.7.08. See also *Özgürlük ve Dayanışma Partisi (ÖDP)* v *Turkey*, No. 7819/03, 10.5.12 (refusal of financial aid to political party as it had not received the statutory minimum number of votes (7 per cent) to be eligible for aid—no violation of Article 14 taken together with Article 3 of Protocol No. 1).

The right to vote

6.820 Restrictions on being placed on the electoral role may interfere with rights under Article 3 of Protocol No. 1. In *Matthews v UK*,[2569] the Court distinguished the position of the applicant resident of Gibraltar, who had no voting rights in relation to the European Parliament, with that of people who live outside the jurisdiction on the basis that 'such individuals have weakened the link between themselves and the jurisdiction'. Accordingly, the Court has stated that residence requirements in relation to the right to vote are not unreasonable per se.[2570] Thus the imposition of a ten-year residence requirement in order to be able to participate in elections to the Congress in New Caledonia was considered to be justifiable in *Py v France*,[2571] having regard to the 'local requirements' under Article 56(3) of the Convention: it had had a turbulent history and was at the time in a process of transition, leading to full sovereignty. The applicants in *Sevinger and Eman v Netherlands*[2572] complained that as Netherlands nationals resident in Aruba, they were not eligible to vote in the elections for the Lower House of the Netherlands Parliament. However, this was not considered to be unreasonable or arbitrary as they could vote in the elections for members of the Parliament of Aruba, which was entitled to send special delegates to the Netherlands Parliament. In *Sitaropoulos and Giakoumopoulos v Greece*,[2573] the applicants were expatriates living in France who complained that they could not exercise the right to vote in Greek parliamentary elections, even though the Greek Constitution had authorised the legislature to provide for such rights. The Grand Chamber of the Court found that there was no obligation, in international law generally, on states to enable citizens living abroad to exercise the right to vote, and it noted that there were widely differing approaches as to the arrangements for exercising such a right in states which did allow voting from abroad. Accordingly it unanimously found no violation of Article 3 of Protocol No. 1.

6.821 In *Labita v Italy*,[2574] the applicant, who was suspected of belonging to the Mafia, was automatically struck off the electoral register even after his acquittal.[2575] This was found by the Court to be disproportionate and in violation of Article 3 of Protocol No. 1. The automatic suspension of the applicant's electoral rights during bankruptcy proceedings, which lasted several years, was found in *Albanese v Italy*[2576] not to pursue any legitimate aim—they were civil proceedings that did not imply any deceit or fraud by the bankrupt. In *Aziz v Cyprus*,[2577] the applicant was denied the right to be placed on the Greek Cypriot electoral role by the Constitution because he was a Turkish Cypriot, which was found to violate both Article 3 of Protocol No. 1 and Article 14 of the Convention.

[2569] No. 24883/94, 18.2.99.
[2570] See, e.g. *Melnychenko v Ukraine*, No. 17707/02, 19.10.04, para. 56; *Doyle v UK*, No. 30158, dec. 6.2.07; *Sevinger and Eman v Netherlands*, Nos. 17173/07 and 17180/07, dec. 6.9.07; *Shindler v UK*, No. 19840/09, 7.5.13.
[2571] No. 66289/01, 11.1.05.
[2572] Nos. 17173/07 and 17180/07, dec. 6.9.07.
[2573] No. 42202/07, 15.3.12 (overturning an earlier chamber Judgment: 8.7.10). See also *Oran v Turkey*, Nos. 28881/07 and 37920/07, 15.4.14.
[2574] No. 26772/95, 6.4.00.
[2575] See also *Santoro v Italy*, No. 36681/97, 1.7.04.
[2576] No. 77924/01, 23.3.06.
[2577] No. 69949/01, 22.6.04.

Restrictions on the voting rights of prisoners may violate the Convention. The Commission found that the deprivation of the right to vote following a conviction by a court for uncitizenlike conduct did not affect the expression of the opinion of the people and was not arbitrary. This view was based on 'the notion of dishonour that certain convictions carry with them for a specific period, which may be taken into consideration by legislation in respect of the exercise of political rights'.[2578] However, a statutory ban on all convicted prisoners voting in parliamentary elections was found by a majority of the Grand Chamber (by 12 votes to five) to violate Article 3 of Protocol No. 1 in *Hirst* v *UK (No. 2)*.[2579] The Representation of the People Act 1983 was held to be a 'blunt instrument' which imposed a blanket restriction on all convicted prisoners in prison. The Court found this absolute ban to be indiscriminate and disproportionate, as it applied irrespective of the length of the sentence or of the nature or gravity of the offence, or the prisoner's individual circumstances. Whilst accepting that states had a wide margin of appreciation, the Court also observed that the UK legislature had never sought to weigh the competing interests or to assess the proportionality of the ban as it affected convicted prisoners. As successive UK governments failed to amend the domestic law in response to *Hirst* and, in the light of 2,500 similar pending cases, the Court issued a 'pilot judgment' (see 3.30) in 2010 in the case of *Greens and M. T.* v *UK*.[2580] Finding a violation of the Convention on the same basis as *Hirst*, the Court also stipulated that the Government was required to bring forward proposals to amend the legislation within six months of the judgment becoming final. **6.822**

The provision of disenfranchisement challenged in *Frodl* v *Austria*[2581] did not apply to all prisoners—just to those sentenced to more than a year's imprisonment for offences committed with intent. Nevertheless, there was a violation of Article 3 of Protocol No. 1 because of a failure to comply with the requirements laid down in *Hirst*, namely that the decision to disenfranchise should be taken by a judge taking account of all the relevant circumstances, and that there should be a link between the offence and issues relating to elections and democratic institutions. However, in *Scoppola* v *Italy (No. 3)*,[2582] the Grand Chamber subsequently clarified its view that removal of the right to vote without a judicial decision in the particular case, does not, as such, violate Article 3 of Protocol No. 1.

Applying the *Hirst* principles in *Alajos Kiss* v *Hungary*[2583] the Court found a violation of Article 3 of Protocol No. 1 because the applicant, who was suffering from manic depression, was deprived of the right to vote as a result of a partial guardianship order. This resulted from an automatic, blanket ban on those under partial guardianship that was held to be indiscriminate, in the absence of an individualised judicial evaluation. In *Moore* v *UK*,[2584] the applicant invoked Article 3 of Protocol No. 1, together with Article 14, in challenging a rule preventing mental health patients from using a hospital as their residential address for **6.823**

[2578] See, e.g. *Patrick Holland* v *Ireland*, No. 24827/94, dec. 14.4.98. See also *Iwanczuk* v *Poland*, No. 25196/94, 15.11.01 (a case concerning voting in prison, but where this right was not raised).

[2579] No. 74025/01, 6.10.05.

[2580] Nos. 60041/08 and 60054/08, 23.11.10. See also *Anchugov and Gladkov* v *Russia*, Nos. 11157/04 and 15162/05, 4.7.13; *Söyler* v *Turkey*, No. 29411/07, 17.9.13; *Murat Vural* v *Turkey*, No. 9540/07, 21.10.14; *Kulinski and Sabev* v *Bulgaria*, No. 63849/09, 21.1.16.

[2581] No. 20201/04, 8.4.10.

[2582] No. 126/05, 22.5.12.

[2583] No. 38832/06, 20.5.10.

[2584] No. 37841/97, 30.5.00.

the purposes of registering on the electoral roll. The case was struck off the Court's list of cases after the UK Government agreed to amend the Representation of the People Act 1983 to allow mental health patients to use the hospital as their address.

6.824 The Article does not require a particular electoral system, such as proportional representation, as states have a wide margin of appreciation in relation to appointments to the legislature. The Court has stated[2585] that:

> any electoral system must be assessed in the light of the political evolution of the country concerned; features that would be unacceptable in the context of one system may accordingly be justified in the context of another, at least so long as the chosen system provides for conditions which will ensure the free expression of the opinion of the people in the choice of the legislature.

The right to stand for election

6.825 Restrictions on the right to stand for election to the legislature are increasingly being raised before the European Court. The Court has reiterated that domestic authorities are obliged to avoid arbitrary decisions and abuse of power in the context of elections, notably as regards the registration of candidates,[2586] and that legislation regulating the right to stand for election must be sufficiently precise and foreseeable,[2587] and balance the legitimate interests of society as a whole with the right of prospective parties to be represented in parliamentary elections.[2588] The applicant MPs in *Sadak and others v Turkey*[2589] complained of the automatic forfeiture of their parliamentary seats following the dissolution of their party, the Democracy Party, by the Turkish Constitutional Court. As the dissolution had been ordered as a result of speeches made by a former chairman of the party, and because of a written declaration made by the party's central committee, the forfeiture of the applicants' parliamentary seats was found to be disproportionate because it happened regardless of their personal political activities.[2590] Unreasonable language requirements were found to have violated the applicant's right to stand for election in *Podkolzina v Latvia*.[2591] There, the applicant's name was removed from a list of candidates standing at a general election because of her insufficient knowledge of Latvian. The Court reiterated that states have a broad latitude to establish constitutional rules on the status of MPs, including eligibility criteria, which may vary according to 'historical and political factors specific to each state'. The Court also stated that electoral legislation must be assessed in the light of the political evolution of the country,

---

[2585] *Mathieu-Mohin and Clerfayt v Belgium*, No. 9267/81, Series A, No. 113, 2.3.87, para. 54.

[2586] See, e.g. *Petkov and others v Bulgaria*, Nos. 77568/01, 178/02 and 505/02, 11.6.09; *Tahirov v Azerbaijan*, No. 31953/11, 11.6.15; *Annagi Hajibeyli v Azerbaijan*, No. 2204/11, 22.10.15.

[2587] *Seyidzade v Azerbaijan*, No. 37700/05, 3.12.09. See also *Grosaru v Romania*, No. 78039/01, 2.3.10 (rules regulating the allocation of a parliamentary seat); *Dicle and Sadak v Turkey*, No. 48621/07, 16.6.15 (refusal to register parliamentary candidates based on convictions in criminal proceedings which were subsequently re-opened—law not adequately foreseeable—violation of Article 3 of Protocol No. 1).

[2588] *Ekoglasnost v Bulgaria*, No. 30386/05, 6.11.12.

[2589] Nos. 25144/94, 26149/95, 26154/95, 27100/95 and 27101/95, 11.6.02. See also *Kavakçı v Turkey*, No. 71907/01, 5.4.07; *Sobacı v Turkey*, No. 26733/02, 29.11.07; *Party for a Democratic Society (DTP) and others v Turkey*, No. 3840/10 et al, 12.1.16.

[2590] See, by contrast, *Etxeberria, Barrena Arza, Nafarroako Autodeterminazio Bilgunea and Aiarako and others v Spain*, Nos. 35579/03, 35613/03, 35626/03 and 35634/03, 30.6.09 and *Herritarren Zerrenda v Spain*, No. 43518/04, 30.6.09 (cancellation of candidacies due to links with terrorist organisation—no violation of Article 3 of Protocol No. 1).

[2591] No. 46726/99, 9.4.02.

and it was acknowledged that requiring a candidate to elections to a national parliament to have sufficient knowledge of the official language pursued a legitimate aim. However, any such eligibility criteria must be assessed by an impartial body whose discretion cannot be 'exorbitantly wide', but must be sufficiently prescribed by domestic law and the procedure for ruling on a prospective candidate's inclusion should ensure a fair and objective decision. Article 3 of Protocol No. 1 was found to have been violated in *Podkolzina* because of the decision to require the applicant to take an extra language test, which decision was taken by a single civil servant who was allowed a very wide discretion. It was also decisive that the applicant was questioned about the reasons for her political orientation.

6.826 At issue in *Kovach* v *Ukraine*[2592] was the way in which the outcome of an election was reviewed by the domestic authorities. The applicant stood as a parliamentary candidate and the votes he received in four electoral divisions were invalidated due to alleged voting irregularities, resulting in victory for his opponent. The irregularities had been reported by observers acting on behalf of the applicant's main opponent. The Parliamentary Elections Act provided that the vote in electoral divisions could be declared invalid on the basis of multiple voting by one person, or, on the basis of 'other circumstances' that made the establishment of the voters' wishes impossible. The Court was critical of the ambiguity of this law, and noted that neither the decisions of the electoral commission nor of the Supreme Court had provided clarification, and there had been no discussion of the credibility of the various actors in the elections. Accordingly, the Court held that the decision to annul the vote in the four electoral divisions was arbitrary and was not proportionate to any legitimate aim, in violation of Article 3 of Protocol No. 1. Following the 'Rose Revolution' in Georgia in 2003, the annulment of election results by the electoral commission in two districts, as a result of voting irregularities, led to the finding of a violation of Article 3 of Protocol No. 1 in *Georgian Labour Party* v *Georgia*.[2593] The decisions, which led to the de facto disfranchisement of a significant section of the population, had not been transparent or consistent. Sufficient reasons had not been given, and there was an absence of adequate safeguards to prevent abuse of power. By contrast, the violation that arose in *Namat Aliyev* v *Azerbaijan*[2594] resulted from the failure of the authorities (the electoral commissions and the courts) to respond adequately to the applicant's detailed and serious complaints about numerous election irregularities (including, for example, interference by local executive authorities, the stuffing of ballot boxes and the harassment of observers).

6.827 There was a violation of this provision in *Paschalidis, Koutmeridis and Zaharakis* v *Greece*[2595] where the applicants, elected parliamentarians, were deprived of their seats as a result of an unforeseeable departure by the Special Supreme Court from its settled case law concerning the method for calculating the electoral quotient (by taking blank ballot papers into consideration). The effect of that decision was to impair the essence of the rights

---

[2592] No. 39424/02, 7.2.08. See also *Kerimova* v *Azerbaijan*, No. 20799/06, 30.9.10; *Riza and others* v *Bulgaria*, Nos. 48555/10 and 48377/10, 13.10.15.

[2593] No. 9103/04, 8.7.08.

[2594] No. 18705/06, 8.4.10. See also *Karimov* v *Azerbaijan*, No. 12535/06, 25.9.14 (use of special polling stations for the military which breached relevant domestic regulations—violation of Article 3 of Protocol No. 1); *Annagi Hajibeyli* v *Azerbaijan*, No. 2204/11, 22.10.15 (irregularities as regards the registration of election candidates—violation of Article 3 of Protocol No. 1) and *Gahramanli and others* v *Azerbaijan*, No. 36503/11, 8.10.15 (ineffective examination of complaints concerning election irregularities—violation of Article 3 of Protocol No. 1).

[2595] Nos. 27863/05, 28422/05 and 28028/05, 10.4.08.

guaranteed under Article 3 of Protocol No. 1. The case of *Russian Conservative Party of Entrepreneurs and others v Russia*[2596] concerned the disqualification of the entire party from the electoral list for the 1999 elections to the *Duma* (the lower chamber of Parliament), because some individual candidates were found to have provided incorrect information about their income and property to the electoral commission. Article 3 of Protocol No. 1 was violated both because the principle of legal certainty was breached (a final judgment in the domestic proceedings was reopened through 'supervisory review' proceedings) and on the basis that it was disproportionate. However, a complaint brought by the third applicant, a party supporter, was rejected. While the free expression of the opinion of the people necessitated a plurality of political parties representing different shades of opinion, the right to vote did not guarantee that every voter should be able to vote for a particular candidate or the party that he had intended to vote for. Having reviewed the available evidence about the 1999 elections, which were considered to be 'competitive and pluralistic', there was no basis for finding that the third applicant's right to take part in free elections had been unduly restricted.

6.828 In *Ždanoka v Latvia*,[2597] a majority of the Grand Chamber found no violation of Article 3 of Protocol No. 1 resulting from the indefinite ban on the applicant from standing for election to Parliament, because of her previous political activity within the Communist Party of Latvia (a party which had been involved in unsuccessful attempted coups after the declaration of Latvia's independence in 1990). The ban was found to pursue aims that were compatible with the principle of the rule of law and the general objectives of the Convention: the protection of the state's independence, democratic order and national security. The Court found that the relevant legislation was clear as to the definition of the category of persons affected by it, and it was also sufficiently flexible to allow the domestic courts to examine whether or not a particular person belonged to that category. Taking into account the 'very special historico-political context', the ban on those who had 'actively participated' in the party's activities was not found to be arbitrary or disproportionate. The Court was prepared to grant the Latvian authorities a very wide margin of appreciation:[2598]

> ... the national authorities of Latvia, both legislative and judicial, are better placed to assess the difficulties faced in establishing and safeguarding the democratic order. Those authorities should therefore be left sufficient latitude to assess the needs of their society in building confidence in the new democratic institutions, including the national parliament ...

6.829 By contrast, there was a violation of Article 3 of Protocol No. 1 in *Paksas v Lithuania*.[2599] The applicant was a former President of Lithuania who had been impeached, and who was prevented from standing as an MP (or for other public office) by a decision of the Constitutional Court which imposed a lifetime ban on anyone who had been removed from office as president for a gross violation of the Constitution or a breach of the constitutional oath. Such a permanent and irreversible ban, which was unique within Council of Europe states, was considered disproportionate. The case of *Adamsons v Latvia*[2600] concerned the ineligibility

---

[2596] Nos. 55066/00 and 55638/00, 11.1.07. See also *Krasnov and Skuratov v Russia*, Nos. 17864/04 and 21396/04, 19.7.07.

[2597] No. 58278/00, 16.3.06.

[2598] *Ibid.*, para. 134. The Court did, however, stipulate that 'the Latvian parliament must keep the statutory restriction under constant review, with a view to bringing it to an early end' (para. 135).

[2599] No. 34932/04, 6.1.11.

[2600] No. 3669/03, 24.6.08.

of the applicant, as a former member of a military unit affiliated to the KGB, to stand for election. The applicant was disqualified as a result of a statutory restriction that was found by the Court to be too broad, in applying to any former member of the KGB, without consideration of their actual conduct. The applicant had not been accused of having been involved in the misdeeds of the former totalitarian regime and there was no evidence to suggest that he had been hostile to Latvia's independence or its democratic order. This requirement to 'individualise' measures was also relevant in *Tănase v Moldova*,[2601] which concerned the effect of a domestic law that prevented anyone with multiple nationalities from standing in parliamentary elections. Having been elected as an MP in the 2009 elections, the applicant was required to renounce his Romanian nationality in order to have his mandate confirmed by the Constitutional Court. Taking account of the consensus in Council of Europe states that, where multiple nationalities are permitted, the holding of more than one nationality is not a ground for ineligibility to stand as an MP, the Grand Chamber found the restriction to be disproportionate, and in violation of Article 3 of Protocol No. 1. The Court rejected arguments that the policy was necessary to protect the security and independence of Moldova, noting that the ban was not introduced on independence, in 1991, but only in 2008, and the Government had failed to explain why concerns about the loyalty of citizens with dual nationality had emerged recently. The Court also noted the introduction of the measure shortly before the elections, and that it operated solely, or principally, to the disadvantage of the opposition.

6.830 The Court has held that it may be justifiable for stricter requirements to be imposed on the eligibility to stand for election to parliament than for eligibility to vote. Therefore a condition such as a five-year continuous residency requirement for potential parliamentary candidates may be acceptable.[2602] However, in *Melnychenko v Ukraine*[2603] the Court laid down that any eligibility criteria must contain sufficient safeguards in order to prevent arbitrary decisions. The requirement for a candidate to pay an electoral deposit will not violate Article 3 of Protocol No. 1 unless it is excessive or creates an insurmountable administrative or financial barrier.[2604] In *Lykourezos v Greece*,[2605] there was a breach of Article 3 of Protocol No. 1 because the applicant, a lawyer, lost his parliamentary seat as a result of a revision to the Constitution which made all professional activity incompatible with the duties of a member of parliament, and which therefore deprived his constituents of the candidate whom they had chosen to represent them in Parliament. In *Mihaela Mihai Neagu v Romania*[2606] the Court did not find disproportionate the eligibility requirement for an independent candidate standing for the European Parliament to obtain 100,000 signatures.

6.831 Allegations of biased media coverage of parliamentary elections have been raised (unsuccessfully, to date) before the European Court, which has acknowledged the real difficulties in establishing a causal link between media coverage and voting patterns.[2607] In *Oran v*

[2601] No. 7/08, 27.4.10.
[2602] *Melnychenko v Ukraine*, No. 17707/02, 19.10.04, para. 57.
[2603] No. 17707/02, 19.10.04, para. 59.
[2604] *Sukhovetskyy v Ukraine*, No. 13716/02, 28.3.06.
[2605] No. 33554/03, 15.6.06.
[2606] No. 66345/09, dec. 6.3.14.
[2607] *Partija Jaunie Demokrāti and Partija Mūsu Zeme v Latvia*, Nos. 10547/07 and 34049/07, dec. 29.11.07; *Communist Party of Russia and others v Russia*, No. 29400/05, 19.6.12.

Turkey,[2608] the Court found no violation of Article 3 of Protocol No. 1 (by four votes to three) because of the ban on independent candidates from campaigning on national radio or television, unlike candidates standing for political parties.

Article 1 of Protocol No. 4: Prohibition of Imprisonment for Debt

6.832 Article 1 of Protocol No. 4 states:

> No one shall be deprived of his liberty merely on the ground of inability to fulfil a contractual obligation.

Although Protocol No. 4 came into force in 1968, there have been very few cases in which complaints of violations of this provision have been made, and consequently there is very little case law. Four of the 47 Council of Europe states have not yet ratified this Protocol (Greece, Switzerland, Turkey and the United Kingdom).[2609] Of those states that have ratified it, nine have entered declarations or reservations.[2610]

6.833 A number of applications have been rejected by the Strasbourg organs on the basis that the deprivation of liberty complained of resulted not from the inability to fulfil a contractual obligation, but in fact from some other measure, such as a sentence of imprisonment following a criminal conviction.[2611]

6.834 In *Göktan v France*[2612] the applicant complained (under Article 4 of Protocol No. 7— at 6.893 below) of being imprisoned for failing to pay customs fines, in addition to his sentence of imprisonment for drug trafficking. Whilst the Court was critical of the imprisonment in default system (as being 'an archaic custodial measure available only to the Treasury'), Article 1 of Protocol No. 4 was found not to be applicable, on the basis that it prohibits imprisonment for debt solely when the debt arises under a contractual obligation.

6.835 A deprivation of liberty would have the same meaning as in Article 5 of the Convention, and is to be contrasted with restrictions on freedom of movement which are subject to Article 2 of Protocol No. 4 (see 6.836 below).

Article 2 of Protocol No. 4: Freedom of Movement

6.836 Article 2 of Protocol No. 4 states:

> 1. Everyone lawfully within the territory of a State shall, within that territory, have the right to liberty of movement and freedom to choose his residence.
> 2. Everyone shall be free to leave any country, including his own.
> 3. No restrictions shall be placed on the exercise of these rights other than such as are in accordance with law and are necessary in a democratic society in the interests of national security or public safety, for the maintenance of *ordre public*, for the prevention of crime,

---

[2608] Nos. 28881/07 and 37920/07, 15.4.14.
[2609] As at the time of writing.
[2610] Austria, Azerbaijan, Cyprus, France, Ireland, Monaco, Netherlands, Spain and Ukraine.
[2611] See, e.g. *Bitti v France*, No. 28645/95, dec. 15.5.96; *Ninin v France*, No. 27373/95, dec. 15.5.96.
[2612] No. 33402/96, 2.7.02.

for the protection of health or morals, or for the protection of the rights and freedoms of others.

4. The rights set forth in paragraph 1 may also be subject, in particular areas, to restrictions imposed in accordance with law and justified by the public interest in a democratic society.

The right of freedom of movement in Article 2 of Protocol No. 4 incorporates three aspects: **6.837**

- liberty of movement within the state;
- freedom to choose a residence within the state; and
- the right to leave a country.

Any measure taken that interferes with these rights must be 'in accordance with the law' and **6.838** must be 'necessary in a democratic society' for one or more of the legitimate aims set out in Article 2(3) (conditions which are similar to those in Articles 8–11 of the Convention). Furthermore, in accordance with Article 2(4), lawful restrictions on freedom of movement and residence (but not on the right to leave a country) may be imposed in particular areas where it is 'justified by the public interest in a democratic society'.

The right to freedom of movement should be distinguished from the right to liberty and **6.839** security of the person under Article 5.[2613] The distinction may not always be obvious and will depend on various criteria, such as the nature of the restriction in question, its duration and purpose. In *Raimondo v Italy*,[2614] the applicant, a suspected member of a mafia-type organisation, was placed under 'special police supervision', including: a prohibition on leaving home without informing the police; an obligation to report to the police on certain days; and an obligation to return to his home by 9 pm and not to leave it before 7 am (unless he had valid reasons for doing so and had first informed the relevant authorities). These measures were found not to amount to a 'deprivation of liberty' under Article 5, but fell to be considered under Article 2 of Protocol No. 4 as an interference with the applicant's right to freedom of movement. The restrictions were held, 'in view of the threat posed by the Mafia to "democratic society"', to be proportionate to the aims of maintaining the *ordre public* and for the prevention of crime. Nevertheless, for a particular period there was a violation of the Article because of the failure to comply with domestic law requirements. Similar restrictive measures imposed on another mafia suspect were found to be disproportionate in *Labita v Italy*,[2615] not least because they were not rescinded even after the applicant's acquittal.[2616] In *De Tommaso v Italy*[2617] the applicant was made subject to special police supervision together with a compulsory residence order for a two-year period, because of his persistent criminal conduct. There was a violation of Article 2 of Protocol No. 4 because of the lack of precision and foreseeability of the domestic law, in particular as to what types of behaviour were to be regarded as posing a danger to society.

There was an interference with the right to freedom of movement in *Van Den Dungen* v **6.840** *Netherlands*[2618] where the applicant, an anti-abortion campaigner, was prevented by an

---

[2613] See *Guzzardi* v *Italy*, No. 7367/76, 6.11.80, para. 92 (applicant's detention on an island).
[2614] No. 12954/87, 22.02.94.
[2615] No. 26772/95, 6.4.00. See also *Santoro* v *Italy*, No. 36681/97, 1.7.04.
[2616] However, 'an acquittal does not necessarily deprive such measures of all foundation, as concrete evidence gathered at trial, though insufficient to secure a conviction, may nonetheless justify reasonable fears that the person concerned may in the future commit criminal offences' (para. 195).
[2617] No. 43395/09, 23.2.17.
[2618] No. 22838/93, dec. 22.2.95.

injunction from going within 250 metres of a particular abortion clinic. However, the measure was found to be justified in order to protect the rights of others, namely the clinic, and its visitors and employees.

6.841 The rights of freedom of movement, and of residence, require, as a pre-condition, lawful presence in the state concerned. In *Piermont* v *France*,[2619] the applicant MEP, an antinuclear campaigner, complained of a violation of Article 2 of Protocol No. 4 because of her expulsion from French Polynesia. The European Court held, however, that once the expulsion order had been served on the applicant, she was no longer lawfully on Polynesian territory and therefore did not suffer any interference with the exercise of her right to liberty of movement. She then travelled on to New Caledonia, where she was served at the airport with an exclusion order. Therefore, she was not considered to have been lawfully present on that territory, and so Article 2 of Protocol No. 4 again had no application. Foreign nationals who are provisionally admitted to the territory of a state pending proceedings to determine whether or not they are entitled to a residence permit under domestic law will only be 'lawfully' in the territory provided that they comply with any conditions imposed.[2620] In *Tatishvili* v *Russia*,[2621] the Court rejected the Government's arguments that the applicant had not been 'lawfully present' in Russia. The applicant was born in Georgia, and had been a citizen of the former USSR until 31 December 2000, when she became stateless. The Court found that under the domestic law, as a 'citizen of the former USSR', she was lawfully present in Russia. She complained about the system of residence registration—that her application for registration of her flat in Moscow had not been accepted. The Court found a violation of Article 2 of Protocol No. 4 because there had been no reason not to grant her application.

6.842 Article 2(2) has been interpreted as implying a right to leave for any other country of the person's choice to which they may be admitted.[2622] In *Pini and Bertani, Manera and Atripaldi* v *Romania*,[2623] the Court declared admissible the applicants' complaint that, as the authorities had failed to implement a final decision allowing for the adoption of children from a residential home in Romania, the children were being prevented from leaving Romania, in violation of Article 2(2).

6.843 The confiscation or seizure of an identity document, including a passport, will amount to an interference with the right to freedom of movement.[2624] In *Sissanis* v *Romania*,[2625] the applicant, a Greek national, had his passport marked to prevent him from leaving the country, in connection with criminal proceedings brought against him. This was found to violate Article 2 of Protocol No. 4 because the domestic law did not stipulate with sufficient precision the conditions in which such a measure could be imposed. In *Napijalo* v *Croatia*[2626] the applicant's passport was seized at the border by a customs officer because he refused to pay the fine for a customs offence. The refusal to return the applicant's passport over a prolonged

---

[2619] Nos. 15773/89 and 15774/89, 27.4.95.
[2620] *Omwenyeke* v *Germany*, No. 44294/04, dec. 20.11.07.
[2621] No. 1509/02, 22.2.07.
[2622] *Peltonen* v *Finland*, No. 19583/92, dec. 20.2.95.
[2623] Nos. 78028/01 and 78030/01, dec. 25.11.03. There was, however, found to be no violation on the merits: judgment of 22.6.04.
[2624] See, e.g. *Baumann* v *France*, No. 33592/96, 22.5.01. It may also raise issues under Article 8—see *İletmiş* v *Turkey*, No. 29871/96, 6.12.05.
[2625] No. 23468/02, 25.1.07.
[2626] No. 66485/01, 13.11.03.

period was found to be disproportionate as he was never charged with any customs offence. Similarly, in *Riener* v *Bulgaria*,[2627] a travel ban imposed on the applicant because of unpaid taxes was held to violate Article 2(2) of Protocol No. 4. The Court noted that the ban was imposed, in effect, automatically and lasted for nine years, without the authorities assessing whether it remained justified and proportionate throughout its duration. In *Battista* v *Italy*[2628] the refusal of a guardianship judge to issue the applicant with a new passport, because of his failure to pay full child maintenance, was held to violate Article 2 of Protocol No. 4. The measure had been applied automatically, without proper regard to the applicant's personal situation, and was unlimited either as to scope or duration. There was a violation of Article 2 of Protocol No. 4 in *Stamose* v *Bulgaria*[2629] as a result of the imposition of a two year ban on travelling abroad imposed by the Bulgarian authorities after the applicant was deported from the US for having breached its immigration rules. The Court found it was clearly disproportionate to automatically prohibit the applicant from travelling to any and every foreign country because he had breached the immigration laws of one particular country, and also without considering his particular circumstances. The applicant in *Nalbantski* v *Bulgaria*[2630] was the subject of a travel ban imposed during criminal proceedings. This was held to be disproportionate because he was given no reasons for the confiscation of his passport and the authorities failed to assess his particular situation. In *Bartik* v *Russia*,[2631] the authorities refused to issue the applicant a document to enable him to travel abroad because of his previous access to 'state secrets' during the course of his work within the aerospace industry. In assessing the proportionality of the interference with the applicant's rights, the Court noted that he had given up all his classified material at the termination of his contract and that his reason to travel abroad was personal—to visit his sick father. Furthermore, he had been prevented from travelling abroad for a period of 24 years. The Court therefore concluded that there had been a violation of Article 2 of Protocol No. 4. By contrast, in *Peltonen* v *Finland*[2632] the refusal to issue the applicant with a ten-year passport because of his failure to do military service was found to be proportionate to the aims of maintaining *ordre public* and of ensuring national security.

6.844 There was a violation of Article 2 of Protocol No. 4 in *Denizci and others* v *Cyprus*,[2633] arising from the absence of any lawful basis for various restrictions placed on the applicants: the Cypriot authorities closely monitored their movements between northern and south Cyprus, and within the south; nor were they allowed to move freely in the south, and they had to report to the police if they wanted to go to the north to visit their families or friends or upon their entry into the south. In *Timishev* v *Russia*[2634] the decision of the traffic police to refuse to allow the applicant Chechen to cross from Ingushetia into Kabardino-Balkaria was found not to be 'in accordance with the law' as its basis was merely an oral order by a Ministry of Interior official, which had not been properly formalised or recorded. As the order had been not to admit 'Chechens', the Court also found the applicant had been

---

[2627] No. 46343/99, 23.5.06. See also *Földes and Földesné Hajlik* v *Hungary*, No. 41463/02, 31.10.06; *Gochev* v *Bulgaria*, No. 34383/03, 26.11.09; *Khlyustov* v *Russia*, No. 28975/05, 11.7.13.
[2628] No. 43978/09, 2.12.14.
[2629] No. 29713/05, 27.11.12.
[2630] No. 30943/04, 10.2.11.
[2631] No. 55565/00, 21.12.06. See also *Soltysyak* v *Russia*, No. 4663/05, 10.2.11.
[2632] No. 19583/92, dec. 20.2.95. See also *Marangos* v *Cyprus*, No. 31106/96, dec. 20.5.97.
[2633] Nos. 25316/94, 25317/94, 25318/94, 25319/94, 25320/94. 25321/94 and 27207/95, 23.5.01.
[2634] Nos. 55762/00 and 55974/00, 13.12.05.

the victim of racial discrimination, in violation of Article 14 taken together with Article 2 of Protocol No. 4. In *Bolat* v *Russia*,[2635] the obligation on the applicant, a Turkish national, to register changes in residence with the police within three days was found not to be in accordance with the law, and in violation of Article 2 of Protocol No. 4. The Supreme Court had acknowledged that a fine imposed by the police had been unlawful and that the courts had shifted the burden of proof onto the applicant in breach of the principle of the presumption of innocence.

6.845 In *Olivieira* v *Netherlands*[2636] the applicant was the subject of a prohibition order made by the Burgomaster of Amsterdam, which barred him from an area of the city centre for 14 days. This was in response to police reports of the applicant's use of hard drugs in the area. Before the European Court it was undisputed that there was a restriction on the applicant's rights under Article 2 of Protocol No. 4. Whilst the majority Court found the domestic law (the Municipality Act) to be 'rather general', it did not fall foul of the 'in accordance with the law' test as the circumstances in which the Burgomaster might issue orders for the maintenance of public order were so diverse 'that it would scarcely be possible to formulate a law to cover every eventuality'.[2637] Moreover, the applicant had in fact been repeatedly warned to leave the area and accordingly he was considered to have been able to foresee the consequences of his actions. Nor was the prohibition order disproportionate, taking into account the fact that he neither lived nor worked in the area in question.

6.846 In a series of cases brought against Italy, applicants who have been the subject of bankruptcy proceedings, or compulsory company liquidation proceedings, have successfully complained about the requirement during the course of the proceedings to remain at their place of residence. Similar cases have been brought by applicants complaining of residence requirements imposed during and after criminal proceedings.[2638] Such obligations have been found by the Court to be a disproportionate burden where the proceedings lasted for several years.[2639] There was a violation of the right of the applicant to choose his place of residence in *Karpacheva and Karpachev* v *Russia*[2640] because of the authorities' refusal to grant the applicant a right of permanent residence in the 'closed city' of Ozersk, which decision had been found to breach the national law by the domestic judicial authorities.

[2635] No. 14139/03, 5.10.06.

[2636] No. 33129/96, 4.6.02. See also *Landvreugd* v *Netherlands*, No. 37331/97, 4.6.02. In *Garib* v *Netherlands*, No. 43494/09, 23.2.16 a majority of the Court found no violation of Article 2 of Protocol No. 4 due to the imposition of length of residence and income conditions in relation to anyone wanting to live in inner-city Rotterdam.

[2637] However, the three dissenting Judges (Judges Jörundsson, Türmen and Maruste) argued that the measures were neither sufficiently accessible nor foreseeable as they were based on instructions (delegated legislation) which were not publicly available.

[2638] See, e.g. *Rosengren* v *Romania*, No. 70786/01, 24.4.08 (prohibition on the applicant's leaving Bucharest in force for six years and three months—violation).

[2639] *Luordo* v *Italy*, No. 32190/96, 17.7.03 (14 years); *Bottaro* v *Italy*, No. 56298/00, 17.7.03 (12 years); *Peroni* v *Italy*, No. 44521/98, 6.11.03 (15 years); *Bassani* v *Italy*, No. 47778/99, 11.12.03 (24 years and five months); *Vadalà* v *Italy*, No. 51703/99, 20.4.04 (16 years and nine months); *Neroni* v *Italy*, No. 7503/02, 22.4.04 (19 years and six months); *Prescher* v *Bulgaria*, No. 6767/04, 7.6.11 (five years and three months); *Miażdżyk* v *Poland*, No. 23592/07, 24.1.12 (five years and two months—however, the duration of time was not the only relevant factor). But there was no violation in *Fedorov and Fedorova* v *Russia*, No. 31008/02, 13.10.05 (four years and three months) or in *Antonenkov and others* v *Ukraine*, No. 14183/02, 22.11.05 (four years and ten months).

[2640] No. 34861/04, 27.1.11.

In *Roldan Texeira and others* v *Italy*,[2641] domestic court orders preventing the Spanish applicant from taking her children on holiday with her to Spain were found to be a proportionate interference with her rights under this provision. Her applications were opposed by the children's Italian father and were dismissed by the domestic courts on the basis that, on the facts, there was a real risk of the children being removed from the jurisdiction permanently.

6.847

Article 3 of Protocol No. 4: Prohibition of Expulsion of Nationals

Article 3 of Protocol No. 4 states:

6.848

1. No one shall be expelled, by means either of an individual or of a collective measure, from the territory of the State of which he is a national.
2. No one shall be deprived of the right to enter the territory of the state of which he is a national.

Article 3 of Protocol No. 4 provides an absolute and unconditional freedom from expulsion of a national. The Court has held that the question of 'nationality' should be decided, in principle, by reference to the national law, on the basis that the Convention does not guarantee a right to nationality (although an arbitrary denial of nationality may engage Article 8 of the Convention).[2642] In *Slivenko and others* v *Latvia*,[2643] two applicants (a mother and daughter) invoked Article 3 of Protocol No. 4 in respect of their expulsion from Latvia. The mother was of Russian origin and had moved to Latvia at the age of one month. Her daughter had been born there. They were expelled from Latvia following the conclusion of a treaty in 1994 concerning the withdrawal of Russian troops, and their families, from Latvia. Both had been citizens of the Latvian Soviet Socialist Republic until 1991, while it was part of the USSR, but neither had been nationals of the independent Latvian state at any time since 1997 when the Convention entered into force in respect of Latvia. Accordingly, as they were not Latvian 'nationals', they could not claim the protection of Article 3 of Protocol No. 4 and their complaints were declared inadmissible *ratione materiae*.[2644]

6.849

In *Victor Emmanuel de Savoie* v *Italy*[2645] the applicant was the son of Umberto II, the last King of Italy. He had left Italy in 1946 when his father went into exile following the proclamation of the Italian Republic. He complained of a violation of Article 3(2) of Protocol No. 4 because he was banned from entering and staying in Italy by the Italian Constitution. The case was settled in 2003 after the Constitution was amended and the applicant was permitted to return to Italy.[2646]

6.850

This provision has no application to the process of extradition, as opposed to expulsion.[2647]

6.851

[2641] No. 40655/98, dec. 26.10.00.
[2642] *Slivenko and others* v *Latvia*, No. 48321/99, dec. 23.1.02, para. 77.
[2643] No. 48321/99, dec. 23.1.02.
[2644] See also, *Maikoe and Baboelal* v *Netherlands*, No. 22791/93, dec. 30.11.94; *LA* v *Sweden*, No. 23253/94, dec. 10.3.94; *Karassev and family* v *Sweden*, No. 31414/96, dec. 14.4.98; *Gribenko and others* v *Latvia*, No. 76878/01, dec. 15.5.03. The Court has noted that the revocation of citizenship followed by expulsion could raise problems under Article 3 of Protocol No. 4 (see, e.g. *Naumov* v *Albania*, No. 10513/03, dec. 4.1.05).
[2645] No. 53360/99, dec. 13.9.01. See also *Habsburg-Lothingen* v *Austria*, No. 5344/89, dec. 14.12.89 (complaint by the son of the last Austrian Emperor about a ban on his entering Austria—declared inadmissible because of a valid Austrian reservation).
[2646] No. 53360/99, 24.4.03.
[2647] *IB* v *Germany*, No. 6242/73, dec. 24.5.74.

Further provisions concerning the expulsion of *aliens*, as opposed to nationals, are contained in Article 4 of Protocol No. 4 (see 6.852, below) and in Article 1 of Protocol No. 7 (see 6.864, below).

Article 4 of Protocol No. 4: Prohibition of Collective Expulsion of Aliens

6.852   Article 4 of Protocol No. 4 states:

> Collective expulsion of aliens is prohibited.

6.853   The Court has defined the term 'collective expulsion' as being 'any measure compelling aliens, as a group, to leave a country, except where such a measure is taken on the basis of a reasonable and objective examination of the particular case of each individual alien of the group'.[2648] The authorities must therefore be able to demonstrate that personal circumstances have been 'genuinely and individually taken into account'.[2649] Furthermore, even where there has been an adequate assessment of individual cases, the Court has stated that the background to the execution of expulsion orders will nevertheless be relevant to the determination as to whether there has been compliance with Article 4 of Protocol No. 4. In *Andric* v *Sweden*,[2650] the Court emphasised that:

> the fact that a number of aliens receive similar decisions does not lead to the conclusion that there is a collective expulsion when each person concerned has been given the opportunity to put arguments against his expulsion to the competent authorities on an individual basis.

6.854   There was a violation of Article 4 of Protocol No. 4 in the case of *Conka* v *Belgium*,[2651] which concerned the expulsion of Slovakian nationals of Roma origin, who had sought asylum in Belgium after having been the victims of serious attacks by skinheads in Slovakia. At the end of September 1999 the police sent a notice to a number of Slovakian Roma families requiring them to attend a police station on 1 October 1999. The notice stated that their attendance was required in order to complete their asylum application files. However, at the police station, the applicants were served with an order to leave the country, as well as a decision for their removal to Slovakia and their detention for that purpose. Within a few hours the Roma families were taken to a closed transit centre near Brussels Airport. Four days later about 70 people were flown from a military airport to Slovakia. The Court held that whilst the decisions rejecting the applicants' asylum applications had been made following an assessment of the particular circumstances of each case, that was not the case in respect of the order for their expulsion. The only reference to the personal circumstances of the applicants in the expulsion order was that their stay in Belgium had exceeded three months; there was no reference to their asylum claims. The wider context was also noted by the Court: the authorities had

---

[2648] *Andric* v *Sweden*, No. 45917/99, dec. 23.2.99; *Conka* v *Belgium*, No. 51564/99, 5.2.02, para. 59; *Khlaifia and others* v *Italy*, No. 16483/12, 15.12.16, para. 237. See also *Becker* v *Denmark*, No. 7011/75, dec. 3.10.75, Yearbook 19, pp. 416, 454.

[2649] *Conka* v *Belgium*, No. 51564/99, 5.2.02, para. 63.

[2650] No. 45917/99, dec. 23.2.99. See also *A and others* v *Netherlands*, No. 14209/88, dec. 16.12.88, DR 59, p. 274; *Berisha and Haljiti* v *former Yugoslav Republic of Macedonia*, No. 18670/03, dec. 16.6.05.

[2651] No. 51564/99, 5.2.02. See, by contrast, *M.A.* v *Cyprus*, No. 41872/10, 23.7.13 (arrest of 149 Syrian Kurd protestors—assessment of immigration status was subject to individual examination of personal circumstances—no violation of Article 4 of Protocol No. 4).

previously announced that there would be operations of this kind; all of the people deported had been required to attend the police station at the same time; the arrest and expulsion orders were written in identical terms; it had been very difficult for them to contact a lawyer; and the asylum procedure had not been completed. The Court's rather circumspect conclusion (by four votes to three) was that the procedure followed by the Belgian authorities did not 'enable it to eliminate all doubt that the expulsion might have been collective'.[2652] The dissenting judges (Judges Velaers, Jungwiert and Kuris) were critical of the majority's overly formalistic approach in considering the order for expulsion independently of the decisions in respect of the asylum applications (which, it was acknowledged, had taken proper account of individual circumstances).

6.855 The applicants in *Hirst Jamaa and others* v *Italy*[2653] were Somali and Eritrean nationals on board boats travelling from Libya to Italy, which were intercepted by the Italian revenue police and coastguard. They were then transferred onto Italian military ships and returned to Tripoli. The Grand Chamber found that this amounted to an 'expulsion' within the meaning of Article 4 of Protocol No. 4, even though the applicants had not been on Italian territory, noting that the Italian authorities' intention had been to prevent irregular migrants disembarking on Italian soil. The transfer of the applicants to Libya had been carried out without any form of examination of each applicant's individual situation, and accordingly there was a violation of Article 4 of Protocol No. 4. When the applicants in *Sharifi and others* v *Italy and Greece*[2654] arrived by boat in Italy from Afghanistan, they were immediately deported by the border police to Greece. This practice was held to amount to collective and indiscriminate expulsion in violation of Article 4 of Protocol No. 4. The Court was critical of the authorities' failure to provide essential information in a comprehensible language during the identification process at the port, which would have prevented any of the intercepted immigrants from claiming asylum in Italy. The Court reached a different conclusion in *Khlaifia and others* v *Italy*[2655] which concerned the authorities' interception at sea of applicants who were travelling by boat from Tunisia to Italy, and their subsequent return to Tunisia. Although the three applicants were expelled almost simultaneously, this was not considered by the Grand Chamber to amount to a 'collective' decision, as they had undergone identification procedures on two occasions, their nationality had been established, and they were provided with the effective possibility of submitting arguments against their expulsion.

6.856 In 2007 Georgia brought inter-state proceedings against Russia as a result of a series of arrests, detentions and deportations of Georgians in 2006–2007 (which followed the arrest in Tbilisi of a number of Russian service personnel on espionage charges). The Court found Russia to be responsible for an administrative practice of the detention and collective expulsion of Georgian nationals, in breach of Article 4 of Protocol No. 4 (as well as Articles 3, 5(1), 5(4) and 13).[2656] The Court found that the Russian courts had made thousands of expulsion orders in circumstances which 'made it impossible to carry out a reasonable and objective examination of the particular case of each individual'.[2657]

[2652] *Conka* v *Belgium*, No. 51564/99, 5.2.02, para. 61.

[2653] No. 27765/09, 23.2.12.

[2654] No. 16643/09, 21.10.14.

[2655] No. 16483/12, 15.12.16 (in marked contrast to the earlier chamber judgment which had found a violation of Article 4 of Protocol No. 4 because the applicants' expulsion was deemed to be 'collective').

[2656] *Georgia* v *Russia (I)*, No. 13255/07, 3.7.14. See also *Berdzenishvili and others* v *Russia*, No. 14594/07, 20.12.16; *Dzidzava* v *Russia*, No. 16363/07, 20.12.16.

[2657] *Ibid.*, para. 175.

6.857   The applicant in *Andric v Sweden*[2658] claimed that he faced being collectively expelled to Croatia together with other Bosnian Croats. He alleged that the Swedish Government and immigration authorities had treated him as belonging to a group of Bosnian Croats and had failed to examine properly his individual claims. However, the Court found that the authorities had taken into account both the general situation in Croatia, as well as the applicant's statements concerning his own background and the risks allegedly facing him upon return. The Court was satisfied that the Swedish authorities had issued individual decisions concerning the applicant's situation and therefore there had been no collective expulsion.[2659]

6.858   In *Sulejmanovic and others and Sejdovic and Sulejmanovic v Italy*,[2660] the applicants were former Yugoslav nationals of gypsy origin who complained of being held in an immigration camp and then being collectively expelled with a group of gypsies to Bosnia and Herzegovina. The Court declared this aspect of the cases admissible in March 2002. However, in November 2002 the cases were struck out after the conclusion of a friendly settlement according to which the respondent government revoked the expulsion orders, allowed the applicants and their families to return to Italy and paid total compensation of more than €161,000.

As to restrictions on the political activity of aliens (Article 16 of the Convention), see 5.25 above.

Articles 1 and 2 of Protocol No. 6; Article 1 of Protocol No. 13: Abolition of the Death Penalty

6.859   Articles 1 and 2 of Protocol No. 6; Article 1 of Protocol No. 13 state:

> Article 1 of Protocol No. 6
>
> The death penalty shall be abolished. No one shall be condemned to such penalty or executed.
>
> Article 2 of Protocol No. 6
>
> A state may make provision in its law for the death penalty in respect of acts committed in time of war or of imminent threat of war; such penalty shall be applied only in the instances laid down in the law and in accordance with its provisions. The state shall communicate to the Secretary-General of the Council of Europe the relevant provisions of that law.
>
> Article 1 of Protocol No. 13
>
> The death penalty shall be abolished. No one shall be condemned to such penalty or executed.

6.860   Protocol No. 6 provides for the abolition of the death penalty in peacetime, but allows a state to maintain the death penalty in respect of acts of war or during imminent threat of war. Protocol No. 13, which came into force on 1 July 2003, also prohibits the death penalty absolutely (including in times of war and imminent threat of war). Article 1 (of Protocol Nos. 6 and 13, which are identical) prevent states from either passing the death sentence or

---

[2658] No. 45917/99, dec. 23.2.99.

[2659] See also: *Alibaks and others v Netherlands*, No. 14209/88, dec. 16.12.88; *B and others v Netherlands*, No. 14457/88, dec. 16.12.88; *Tahiri v Sweden*, No. 25129/94, dec. 11.1.95; *Majic v Sweden*, No. 45918/99, dec. 23.2.99; *Pavlovic v Sweden*, No. 45920/99, dec. 23.2.99; *Pranjko v Sweden*, No. 45925/99, dec. 23.2.99; *Juric v Sweden*, No. 45924/99, dec. 23.2.99; *Andrijic v Sweden*, No. 45923/99, dec. 23.2.99; *Maric v Sweden*, No. 45922/99, dec. 23.2.99. A similar conclusion was reached in *Sultani v France*, No. 45223/05, 20.9.07 (risk of deportation to Afghanistan).

[2660] Nos. 57574/00 and 57575/00, 8.11.02.

carrying out executions. Protocol No. 6 has been ratified by all member states except Russia. Protocol No. 13 has been ratified by 44 member states; only Armenia, Azerbaijan and Russia have not ratified it.[2661]

Articles 3 and 4 of Protocol No. 6, and Articles 2 and 3 of Protocol No. 13, provide that **6.861** there may be no derogation from the Protocol (under Article 15) and no reservation (under Article 57). Under Article 5 of Protocol No. 6, and under Article 4 of Protocol No. 13, a state may specify, on ratification or signature of the Protocol, to which territories the Protocol will apply. The Protocols may subsequently be extended to other territories, or their application in relation to particular territories may be withdrawn, by notification to the Secretary-General of the Council of Europe. Applicants who are under threat of deportation or expulsion to a country where they may face the death penalty will be able to argue before the Court that their expulsion would be in violation of Article 1 of Protocol No. 6 and/or Protocol No. 13. (As to the application of Article 3 in such cases, see above at 6.161.)

In *Nivette v France*[2662] the Court confirmed that it was possible that a state's responsibility **6.862** might be engaged under Article 1 of Protocol No. 6 if a person were extradited to a state in which there was a serious risk of their being sentenced to death and executed. The applicant in *Nivette*, an American national suspected of murder, was under threat of extradition back to the United States. However, the Californian Criminal Code provided that the death sentence could not be imposed unless the prosecuting attorney pleaded special circumstances. The prosecuting attorney had twice formally undertaken not to do so—such assurances were considered to eliminate the danger of the death penalty being imposed. In the 'extraordinary rendition' case of *Al Nashiri v Poland*,[2663] the Court found a violation of Articles 2 and 3, taken together with Article 1 of Protocol No. 6 to the Convention. As a result of the applicant's transfer from Poland, there was a substantial and foreseeable risk that he could be subjected to the death penalty following a trial before a US military commission (in the course of which he risked being subjected to a 'flagrant denial of justice').

The existence of a serious risk of being subjected to capital punishment in the event of **6.863** extradition must be supported by prima facie evidence; accordingly, the case of *Ismaili v Germany*[2664] was declared inadmissible as the Moroccan authorities had declared to the German authorities that the offence for which the applicant was wanted did not carry the death sentence and that the death sentence would therefore not be requested or carried out.

Article 1 of Protocol No. 7: Procedural Safeguards Relating to Expulsion of Aliens

Article 1 of Protocol No. 7 states: **6.864**

1. An alien lawfully resident in the territory of a state shall not be expelled therefrom except in pursuance of a decision reached in accordance with law and shall be allowed:

[2661] As at the time of writing.
[2662] No. 44190/98, dec. 14.12.00. See also *Jin v Hungary*, No. 58073/00, dec. 11.1.01 (extradition to China); *Einhorn v France*, No. 71555/01, dec. 16.10.01 (extradition to USA re Article 3).
[2663] No. 28761/11, 24.7.14. See also the discussion of *Al-Saadoon and Mufdhi v UK*, No. 61498/08, 2.3.10 at 6.163 above.
[2664] No. 58128/00, dec. 15.3.01.

a to submit reasons against his expulsion,

b to have his case reviewed, and

c to be represented for these purposes before the competent authority or a person or persons designated by that authority.

2. An alien may be expelled before the exercise of his rights under paragraph 1.a, b and c of this Article, when such expulsion is necessary in the interests of public order or is grounded on reasons of national security.

6.865 Article 1 of Protocol No. 7 provides the following procedural rights in respect of decisions to expel aliens:

- a right to submit reasons against expulsion;
- a right of review;
- a right to be represented; and
- the decision must have been reached 'in accordance with the law'.[2665]

6.866 As an article that provides for certain procedural rights only, Article 1 of Protocol No. 7 will usually be invoked together with other provisions of the Convention, which may have a bearing on the consequences of being expelled, such as Article 3, where the applicant alleges that expulsion would lead to torture or inhuman or degrading treatment or punishment (see 6.164 above), or Article 8, where the effects are allegedly to disrupt existing family life (see 6.509 above). Furthermore, Article 4 of Protocol No. 4 provides an absolute prohibition on the *collective* expulsion of aliens (see 6.852 above), whereas Article 3 of Protocol No. 4 prohibits the expulsion of *nationals* (see 6.848 above).

6.867 Although Article 6 of the Convention provides for various procedural rights in certain types of civil proceedings (see 6.297 above), the Court has confirmed that Article 6 does not apply to proceedings relating to expulsion decisions. In *Maaouia* v *France*,[2666] the Grand Chamber of the Court confirmed previous Commission decisions to the effect that proceedings for the rescission of an exclusion order do not concern the determination of a 'civil right' (nor a criminal charge, being special preventive measures for the purpose of immigration control). Accordingly, Article 6 cannot be invoked in such cases.

6.868 For Article 1 of Protocol No. 7 to apply, the person in question must be 'lawfully resident' in the state in question. The Explanatory Report to Protocol No. 7 states that the word resident:

> is intended to exclude from the application of the article any alien who has arrived at a port or other point of entry but has not yet passed through the immigration control or who has been admitted to the territory for the purpose only of transit or for a limited period for a non-residential purpose.

It also excludes 'the period pending a decision on a request for a residence permit'.[2667] Furthermore, the Explanatory Report states that the provision applies 'not only to aliens who have entered lawfully but also to aliens who have entered unlawfully and whose position has been subsequently regularised'.[2668] The Court has interpreted the phrase 'lawfully resident' 'to refer basically to lawfulness of the presence according to national law', and therefore an

---

[2665] See, e.g. *Bolat* v *Russia*, No. 14139/03, dec. 8.7.04.

[2666] No. 39652/98, 5.10.00.

[2667] Explanatory Report, para. 9.

[2668] *Ibid.*

alien whose visa or residence permit has expired cannot usually be regarded as being 'lawfully resident' in the country.[2669] Accordingly, the applicants in *Voulfovitch and Oulianova v Sweden*[2670] were found not to be entitled to rely on Article 1 of Protocol No. 7 as they had only had a transit visa for a one-day visit to Sweden and they had remained in the country, after the expiry of the visa, merely in order to obtain a decision on their request for political asylum or residence permits and to await the enforcement of the expulsion decision. In *T.A. v Sweden*[2671] where the applicant had been found to have entered Sweden illegally, using a false visa, the provision was also not applicable.

6.869 The Explanatory Report states that expulsion is an autonomous concept, and is used in a generic sense as meaning 'any measure compelling the departure of an alien from the territory'. It does not, however, include extradition.[2672]

6.870 The requirement that the expulsion decision must have been reached 'in accordance with law' uses a phrase which is seen elsewhere in the Convention, such as Article 8 (the right to respect for private and family life, home and correspondence) and Article 2 of Protocol No. 4 (the right to freedom of movement). Like the term 'prescribed by law' (see, for example, Article 5, and Article 2 of Protocol No. 7), this phrase not only requires that the decision was taken in compliance with domestic law, but also that the domestic law itself is sufficiently accessible and foreseeable. In *Bolat v Russia*,[2673] there was accordingly a violation of this provision because of the expulsion of the applicant, a Turkish national, without having obtained prior judicial authority, as was required by the domestic law.

6.871 Similarly, there was a violation of Article 1 of Protocol No. 7 in *Nolan and K. v Russia*,[2674] because of the exclusion from Russia of a member of the Unification Church, ostensibly on grounds of national security, but which was found to have no legal or factual justification. The exclusion decision was not sent to him for three months and he was not given the opportunity to challenge it.

6.872 The right of review will not necessarily require a two-stage procedure before different authorities. It is sufficient for the 'competent authority' (which may be judicial or administrative) to review the case in the light of the reasons against expulsion submitted by the person concerned. The form that the review should take is otherwise left to domestic law.[2675] The procedure may be oral or written; there is no necessity to hold an oral hearing.[2676]

6.873 In *BH, TH, RH and RH v Switzerland*,[2677] the European Commission rejected a complaint under Article 1 of Protocol No. 7 on the basis that the Swiss authorities had given 'reasoned

---

[2669] *Voulfovitch and Oulianova v Sweden*, No. 19373/92, dec. 13.1.93. See also *ST v France*, No. 20649/92, dec. 8.2.93; *Sejdovic and Sulejmanovic v Italy*, No. 57575/00, 14.3.02; *Yildirim v Romania*, No. 21186/02, dec. 20.9.07.

[2670] No. 19373/92, dec. 13.1.93. Contrast their situation with that of the applicants in *Bolat v Russia*, No. 14139/03, 5.10.06 and *Nolan and K. v Russia*, No. 2512/04, 12.2.09, who had been lawfully admitted onto Russian territory for residence purposes.

[2671] No. 23211/94, dec. 5.7.94.

[2672] Explanatory Report, para. 10.

[2673] No. 14139/03, 5.10.06. See also *C.G. and others v Bulgaria*, No. 1365/07, 24.4.08.

[2674] No. 2512/04, 12.2.09.

[2675] Explanatory Report, paras. 13.2 and 13.3.

[2676] Explanatory Report, para. 14.

[2677] No. 23810/94, dec. 11.5.94.

decisions' and found that there was no indication that 'the applicants could not properly explain their own point of view'. Similarly, a complaint under Article 1 of Protocol No. 7 was declared inadmissible in *Sadaghi v Sweden*,[2678] where the expulsion decision had been reviewed at three levels: the District Court, the Court of Appeal and the Supreme Court.

6.874 A number of cases initiated relying on this provision (and other Convention provisions) have been settled following the respondent state's revocation of its decision. For example, in *K.D. v Finland*[2679] the applicant was a Kosovo-Albanian Muslim who complained of the Finnish authorities' decision to deny her a residence permit, which prevented her from being reunited with her family. However, the application was struck out after having been settled following the Government's decision to issue the applicant with a residence permit.

6.875 Article 1(2) of Protocol No. 7 permits expulsion of an alien before the exercise of the rights under paragraphs 1(1)(a)–(c), when it is necessary in the interests of 'public order' (a phrase also seen for example in Article 9—the right to freedom of thought, conscience and religion) or is based on reasons of 'national security' (a term also to be seen, for example, in Article 10—the right to freedom of expression). Such a measure is subject to the principle of proportionality. If a person is expelled before being able to exercise these rights, they must be able to do so after the expulsion.[2680] Article 1 of Protocol No. 7 was found to have been violated in *C.G. and others v Bulgaria*[2681] as the applicant's expulsion had not been based on genuine reasons of national security. It had also not been established that it was necessary for public order reasons, or that it had been necessary to expel him before he had had an opportunity to challenge the decision.

Article 2 of Protocol No. 7: Right of Appeal in Criminal Matters

6.876 Article 2 of Protocol No. 7 states:

1. Everyone convicted of a criminal offence by a tribunal shall have the right to have his conviction or sentence reviewed by a higher tribunal. The exercise of this right, including the grounds on which it may be exercised, shall be governed by law.
2. This right may be subject to exceptions in regard to offences of a minor character, as prescribed by law, or in cases in which the person concerned was tried in the first instance by the highest tribunal or was convicted following an appeal against acquittal.

6.877 Article 2 of Protocol No. 7 provides for a right of review or appeal against both a criminal conviction, and against sentence. The concept of 'criminal offence' in the first paragraph of the Article corresponds to that of 'criminal charge' in Article 6(1).[2682] Article 2(2) expressly provides for three exceptions:

- in relation to minor offences, as prescribed by law;
- where the highest tribunal has tried the case in the first instance; and
- where the conviction followed an appeal against an acquittal.

[2678] No. 27794/95, dec. 14.10.96. See also *B v France*, No. 18412/91, dec. 1.4.92 (two levels of jurisdiction).
[2679] No. 23065/93, dec. 10.3.94.
[2680] Explanatory Report, para. 14.
[2681] No. 1365/07, 24.4.08.
[2682] *Gurepka v Ukraine*, No. 61406/00, 6.9.05, para. 55.

The Court permits states a wide margin of appreciation in principle to determine how the **6.878** right of review as set out in Article 2 of Protocol No. 7 may be exercised.[2683] The Court has expressly stated that the review by a higher court of a conviction or sentence may relate to the facts and the law, or it may be legitimately limited to points of law only.[2684] Article 2(1) makes express reference to 'grounds' on which the rights may be dependent. Indeed, the Court has confirmed that there may legitimately be an obligation in the domestic law to seek permission to appeal.[2685]

Both the right of review, and any grounds on which it is exercised, must be 'governed by law'. **6.879** It is suggested that by analogy with the requirements elsewhere in the Convention for restrictions on rights to be 'prescribed by law' or 'in accordance with the law', this will require that the relevant domestic law is both sufficiently accessible and foreseeable.

Furthermore, any restrictions in domestic legislation on the right to a review must pursue **6.880** a legitimate aim and not infringe the very essence of the right.[2686] These conditions mirror those relating to the right of access to court under Article 6(1) of the Convention.

There was a violation of Article 2 of Protocol No. 7 in *Krombach v France*[2687] where the appli- **6.881** cant, a German national, was convicted in absentia by the Paris Assize Court of voluntary assault of his stepdaughter unintentionally causing her death, and was sentenced to 15 years' imprisonment. However, because the proceedings had been conducted in absentia, the Code of Criminal Procedure did not permit an appeal in those circumstances to the Court of Cassation. The Government argued that the requirement for the accused to purge his contempt before being able to appeal to the Court of Cassation did not infringe the essence of the right contained in Article 2 of Protocol No. 7. However, the Court rejected that argument, noting that as a defendant in absentia he could neither be legally represented at his trial, nor did he have a right of review by a higher court: he therefore had no real possibility of being defended at first instance or of having his conviction reviewed by a higher court. Article 2 was also violated in *Zaicevs v Latvia*[2688] because there was no right of appeal to challenge a finding that the applicant lawyer had committed the regulatory offence of contempt of court, for which he was sentenced to three days' administrative detention. In *Galstyan v Armenia*,[2689] the power of review by a chairman of a superior court of a decision to impose administrative detention (which had no defined procedure, time limits or consistency of application in practice) was not considered to amount to a right of appeal compatible with Article 2 of Protocol No. 7. This provision was also breached in *Shvydka v Ukraine*,[2690] where

---

[2683] *Krombach v France*, No. 27731/96, 13.2.01, para. 96.

[2684] See *Nielsen v Denmark*, No. 19028/91, dec. 9.9.92, DR 73, p. 239; *NW v Luxembourg*, No. 19715/92, dec. 8.12.92; *Altieri v France, Cyprus and Switzerland*, No. 28140/95, dec. 15.5.96; *Saussier v France*, No. 35884/97, dec. 20.5.98; *Pesti and Frodl v Austria*, Nos. 27618/95 and 27619/95, dec. 18.1.00; *Loewenguth v France*, No. 53183/99, dec. 30.5.00; *Deperrois v France*, No. 48203/99, dec. 22.6.00; *Dorado Baúlde v Spain*, No. 23486/12, dec. 1.9.15.

[2685] *Peterson Sarpsborg AS and others v Norway*, No. 25944/94, dec. 27.11.96; *Krombach v France*, No. 27731/96, 13.2.01, para. 96; *Sawalha v Sweden*, No. 64299/01, dec. 13.1.04.

[2686] *Haser v Switzerland*, No. 33050/96, dec. 27.4.00.

[2687] No. 27731/96, 13.2.01.

[2688] No. 65022/01, 31.7.07.

[2689] No. 26986/03, 15.11.07.

[2690] No. 17888/12, 30.10.14. See also *Ruslan Yakovenko v Ukraine*, No. 5425/11, 4.6.15 (applicant effectively dissuaded from lodging appeal against conviction as an appeal would have delayed his release—violation of Article 2 of Protocol No. 7).

the applicant, an opposition politician, was sentenced to ten days' detention for publicly detaching part of a ribbon from a wreath laid by the Ukrainian President at a commemorative ceremony. She appealed immediately, but her appeal was not heard until after she had served her full sentence.

6.882   Article 2 of Protocol No. 7 does not include a right to have criminal proceedings reopened.[2691] In *Natsvlishvili and Togonidze* v *Georgia*,[2692] the Court found no violation of Article 2 of Protocol No. 7 (or of Article 6(1)) as a result of plea bargaining. This amounted to a waiver of the first applicant's right to appellate review, which had been agreed to on a voluntary basis, without any duress or false promises by the prosecution, and which was accompanied by adequate safeguards against possible abuse of process. If an offence is punishable by imprisonment it will not be considered an offence of a 'minor character', and therefore the Article 2(2) exception will not apply.[2693]

Article 3 of Protocol No. 7: Compensation for Wrongful Conviction

6.883   Article 3 of Protocol No. 7 states:

> When a person has by a final decision been convicted of a criminal offence and when subsequently his conviction has been reversed, or he has been pardoned, on the ground that a new or newly discovered fact shows conclusively that there has been a miscarriage of justice, the person who has suffered punishment as a result of such conviction shall be compensated according to the law or the practice of the state concerned, unless it is proved that the nondisclosure of the unknown fact in time is wholly or partly attributable to him.

6.884   Article 3 of Protocol No. 7 provides for a right to compensation for miscarriages of justice: 'some serious failure in the judicial process involving grave prejudice to the convicted person'.[2694] The Court has held that the purpose of Article 3 of Protocol No. 7 is not only to recover pecuniary losses caused by a wrongful conviction, but also to provide compensation for any non-pecuniary damage, such as distress, anxiety, inconvenience and loss of enjoyment of life.[2695] Article 3 does not, however, specify the procedure to be applied to establish a miscarriage of justice. It is applicable where an applicant has been convicted of a criminal offence by a final decision and suffered consequential punishment. As to the definition of a 'final decision', the Explanatory Report to Protocol No. 7 refers to the definition contained in the explanatory report of the European Convention on the International Validity of Criminal Judgments: a decision is final[2696]

> if ... it has acquired the force of *res judicata*. This is the case when it is irrevocable, that is to say when no further ordinary remedies are available or when the parties have exhausted such remedies or have permitted the time limit to expire without availing themselves of them.

6.885   The applicant in *Poghosyan and Baghdasaryan* v *Armenia*[2697] had his conviction for murder and rape quashed. Two police officers were subsequently found by the domestic courts to

---

[2691] *Kalashnikov* v *Russia*, No. 47095/99, dec. 18.9.01.

[2692] No. 9043/05, 29.4.14.

[2693] *Zaicevs* v *Latvia*, No. 65022/01, 31.7.07; *Galstyan* v *Armenia*, No. 26986/03, 15.11.07. See also Explanatory Report, para. 21.

[2694] Explanatory Report, para. 23.

[2695] *Poghosyan and Baghdasaryan* v *Armenia*, No. 22999/06, 12.6.12, para. 51.

[2696] Explanatory Report, para. 22.

[2697] No. 22999/06, 12.6.12.

have ill-treated the applicant in order to obtain a confession. As the Armenian Civil Code did not provide for a claim for non-pecuniary damages in such circumstances, the Court found a violation of Article 3 of Protocol No. 7.

The Article does not apply where an accused is acquitted by a higher court on appeal,[2698] or in other circumstances where a conviction is *not* quashed as a result of 'a new or newly discovered fact'.[2699] Nor will it enable an applicant to claim compensation in respect of a period on remand, where there has been no *conviction*.[2700]

In *Stamoulakatos* v *Greece*,[2701] the applicant was found guilty at first instance, but on appeal **6.886** the Court of Appeal discontinued the proceedings as being time-barred. The Court found that the applicant had not been convicted by a 'final decision' that was subsequently reversed, and therefore he could not claim a right to compensation under this article.

If the domestic law offers a right to claim compensation in such circumstances, then if such **6.887** a remedy has not been pursued by the applicant, the application is likely to be declared inadmissible for failing to exhaust domestic remedies, as was the position in *Saukaitis* v *Lithuania*,[2702] where the applicant had had the possibility of claiming reparation under the Criminal Damages Act.

Article 4 of Protocol No. 7: Right not to be Tried or Punished Twice

Article 4 of Protocol No. 7 states: **6.888**

1. No one shall be liable to be tried or punished again in criminal proceedings under the jurisdiction of the same state for an offence for which he has already been finally acquitted or convicted in accordance with the law and penal procedure of that state.
2. The provisions of the preceding paragraph shall not prevent the reopening of the case in accordance with the law and penal procedure of the state concerned, if there is evidence of new or newly discovered facts, or if there has been a fundamental defect in the previous proceedings, which could affect the outcome of the case.
3. No derogation from this Article shall be made under Article 15 of the Convention.

Reflecting the criminal law rule, *non bis in idem*, the aim of Article 4 of Protocol No. 7 **6.889** is to prevent a person being tried or punished twice for the same aspect of one criminal act.[2703] The principle is also reflected in Article 50 of the Charter of Fundamental Rights of the European Union and in Article 14(7) of the International Covenant on Civil and Political Rights. It applies not only to cases where a defendant is convicted twice, but also to cases where a defendant is prosecuted twice (regardless of whether there has been a conviction).[2704] A case may, however, justifiably be reopened in two circumstances: if there is evidence of new or newly discovered facts, or if there has been a fundamental defect in

---

[2698] *Georgiou* v *Greece*, No. 45138/98, dec. 13.1.00.
[2699] See, e.g. *Matveyev* v *Russia*, No. 26601/02, 3.7.08; *Bachowski* v *Poland*, No. 32463/06, dec. 2.11.10.
[2700] *Nakov* v *former Yugoslav Republic of Macedonia*, No. 68286/01, dec. 24.10.02.
[2701] No. 42155/98, dec. 9.11.99.
[2702] No. 41774/98, dec. 14.11.00.
[2703] *WF* v *Austria*, No. 38275/97, 30.5.02, para. 23.
[2704] *Sergey Zolotukhin* v *Russia*, No. 14939/03, 10.2.09. See also, e.g. *Zigarella* v *Italy*, No. 48154/99, dec. 3.10.02.

the proceedings that could affect its outcome. A state may not derogate from Article 4 of Protocol No. 7.

6.890 The fact that an offence is classified as 'administrative' by the domestic authorities, rather than criminal, may not exclude the application of Article 4 of Protocol No. 7. In such circumstances, the Court will make its assessment applying the three conditions known as the '*Engel* criteria' (discussed further in relation to Article 6, at 6.293 above) to decide whether the proceedings amounted to a criminal charge: the legal classification of the offence under national law; the very nature of the offence; and the degree of severity of the penalty that the person risks incurring.[2705]

6.891 Article 4 has been applied notably in a series of cases from Austria and Switzerland concerning road traffic accidents where separate criminal proceedings have been brought against drivers for alcohol-related driving offences. The Court had adopted different approaches in applying Article 4 in these cases, which are discussed below, before the Grand Chamber issued its judgment in the case of *Sergey Zolotukhin* v *Russia*[2706] in 2009, which sought to clarify and harmonise the legal position.

6.892 There was a violation of Article 4 of Protocol No. 7 in *Gradinger* v *Austria*,[2707] where the applicant was convicted by the Regional Court of causing death by negligence (following a traffic accident), but the Regional Court found that the aggravating factor of driving under the influence of alcohol (under the Criminal Code) was not made out against the applicant. Nevertheless, the district authority subsequently issued a 'sentence order' and fined the applicant for driving whilst under the influence of alcohol under the Road Traffic Act. The European Court noted that the two provisions differed both in respect of the designation of the offences and also as regards their nature and purpose.

6.893 Nevertheless, the provision was found to be violated because both decisions were based on the same conduct. In *Oliveira* v *Switzerland*,[2708] the applicant argued that the same traffic accident had led to her convictions for failing to control her vehicle and, subsequently, for negligently causing physical injury, in violation of Article 4 of Protocol No. 7. However, the Court concluded that there had been a single criminal act constituting two separate offences, which did not breach the provision. The Court did comment that it would have been 'more consistent with the principles governing the proper administration of justice' for sentence in respect of both offences to have been passed by the same court in a single set of proceedings. However, the fact that such a procedure was not followed was held to be irrelevant to the question of compliance with Article 4 of Protocol No. 7, particularly in view of the fact that the penalties imposed were not cumulative. The applicant in *Göktan* v *France*[2709] argued that there had been a violation of Article 4 of Protocol No. 7 because he was imprisoned for failing to pay customs fines in addition to his sentence of imprisonment for drug trafficking,

---

[2705] *Sergey Zolotukhin* v *Russia*, No. 14939/03, 10.2.09. Applying that test in *Palmén* v *Sweden*, No. 38292/15, dec. 22.3.16 the Court found that the revocation of a firearms licence (following a conviction for assault) did not amount to a criminal sanction for the purposes of Article 4 of Protocol No. 7.

[2706] No. 14939/03, 10.2.09.

[2707] No. 15963/90, 23.10.95. As a result of this decision, Austrian law was amended by a decision of the Austrian Constitutional Court in 1996: see *Franz Fischer* v *Austria*, No. 37950/97, 29.5.01, para. 31.

[2708] No. 25711/94, 30.7.98.

[2709] No. 33402/96, 2.7.02. See also *Gauthier* v *France*, No. 61178/00, dec. 24.6.03 and *Öngün* v *Turkey*, No. 15737/02, dec. 10.10.06.

which he argued amounted to two consecutive terms of imprisonment for the same offence. However, there was no violation of the provision as the Court found that a single criminal court had tried the applicant for the same criminal conduct, namely dealing in illegally imported drugs: a single criminal act had constituted two separate offences (as in *Oliveira*), under the general criminal law and under the customs law. Nevertheless, the Court was critical of the imprisonment in default system, as 'an archaic custodial measure available only to the Treasury'.[2710]

In the subsequent judgment in *Franz Fischer* v *Austria*,[2711] the Court acknowledged that the two approaches in *Gradinger* and *Oliveira* might appear to be contradictory, but it clarified that where different offences are prosecuted consecutively as a result of a single act, the key question is whether or not the offences have the 'same essential elements'.[2712] That test therefore necessitated a close examination of the elements of what may nominally be different offences. *Franz Fischer* concerned similar facts to *Gradinger*, except that the applicant in *Franz Fischer* was convicted by both the district authority and then the Regional Court. These differences were not, however, decisive: there was a violation of Article 4 of Protocol No. 7, as both offences had the same essential element, namely driving whilst under the influence of alcohol. Applying that test in *Manasson* v *Sweden*,[2713] the Court found that the applicant's convictions for a bookkeeping offence and the imposition of tax surcharges, did not involve the same essential elements. In the former, the applicant had breached a general obligation to enter income and salary payments in the books of his taxi firm, whereas the tax surcharges resulted from his supplying incorrect information to the tax authorities. The applicant also complained about a third matter, the revocation of his traffic licence, but this was held not to amount to a penal sanction and accordingly Article 4 of Protocol No. 7 was not applicable to it. **6.894**

In *Sergey Zolotukhin* v *Russia*[2714] the Grand Chamber revisited these cases and confirmed the applicable test, in order to harmonise the position. The applicant was convicted in administrative proceedings of a public order offence (for 'minor disorderly acts'), and was subsequently the subject of separate criminal proceedings (for 'disorderly acts') based on the same facts. Having reviewed the application of the *non bis in idem* principle internationally, the Court concluded that an approach that emphasised the *legal characterisation* of two offences would be too restrictive on the rights of the individual. Accordingly, it held that Article 4 of Protocol No. 7 prohibits the prosecution or trial of a second 'offence' in so far as it arises from identical facts or facts that are substantially the same. **6.895**

Applying that test to the particular circumstances of the case, the Court found that the facts of the two offences were substantially the same for the purposes of Article 4 of Protocol No. 7. There was accordingly a violation of the Article, even though the applicant was acquitted in the second set of proceedings—as Article 4 extends to the right not to be prosecuted or **6.896**

[2710] *Ibid.*, para. 51.

[2711] No. 37950/97, 29.5.01. See also *WF* v *Austria*, No. 38275/97, 30.5.02; *Sailer* v *Austria*, No. 38237/97, 6.6.02.

[2712] *Ibid.*, para. 25. See also *Ponsetti and Chesnel* v *France*, Nos. 36855/97 and 41731/98, 14.9.99; *Isaksen* v *Norway*, No. 13596/02, dec. 2.10.03.

[2713] No. 41265/98, dec. 8.4.03. For other examples of the application of the 'same essential elements test', see also *Mjelde* v *Norway*, No. 11143/04, dec. 1.2.07 and *Storbråten* v *Norway*, No. 12277/04, dec. 1.2.07.

[2714] No. 14939/03, 10.2.09.

tried twice. Applying the same test, the Court found a violation of Article 4 of Protocol No. 7 in *Ruotsalainen v Finland*[2715] where the applicant's conviction for petty tax fraud and a subsequent fuel-fee debit were found to be based on substantially the same facts, and also in *Lucky Dev v Sweden*[2716] where the applicant was subject to both criminal proceedings and tax surcharge proceedings in relation to the same facts (the failure to declare business proceeds and VAT). Article 4 of Protocol No. 7 was violated in *Kapetanios and others v Greece*,[2717] where the applicants were acquitted in criminal proceedings on contraband charges, after which they were fined in administrative proceedings in relation to the same conduct. There was also a breach of this provision in *Grand Stevens and others v Italy*[2718] where the applicants were the subject of administrative proceedings before the National Companies and Stock Exchange Commission (considered to be 'criminal' in nature by the Court) and subsequently of criminal proceedings, relating to the same conduct (the dissemination of false information to prevent market manipulation). However, the Grand Chamber has recently clarified in *A and B v Norway* that Article 4 of Protocol No. 7 will not prevent states from applying 'dual proceedings', in which a combination of proceedings are integrated to form a coherent whole—which may involve parallel stages of a legal response to the wrongdoing in question by different authorities and for different purposes.[2719] Accordingly, there was held to be no violation of Article 4 of Protocol No. 7 in *A and B v Norway* where the applicants were the subject of both an administrative penalty (a tax surcharge) and a criminal conviction as a result of their failure to declare all of their income on their tax returns.

6.897   Article 4 of Protocol No. 7 will usually only apply where new proceedings are brought in the knowledge that the defendant has already been tried in previous proceedings. Thus the complaint in *Zigarella v Italy*[2720] was declared inadmissible on this basis where the Italian courts had terminated the second set of proceedings against the applicant (relating to town planning law) as soon as they were informed that there had been a breach of the *non bis in idem* principle.

6.898   As Article 4(1) refers to 'criminal proceedings under the jurisdiction of the same state', it does not apply where a person has been tried, or is due to be tried or punished, by the courts of different states.[2721]

6.899   Article 4 of Protocol No. 7 does not apply where criminal proceedings are discontinued (because, as a result, there is neither a conviction nor an acquittal).[2722] In *Nikitin v Russia*[2723]

[2715] No. 13079/03, 16.6.09.

[2716] No. 7356/10, 27.11.14.

[2717] Nos. 3453/12, 42941/12 and 9028/13, 30.4.15. There was also a breach of the applicants' right to be presumed innocent under Article 6(2).

[2718] No. 18640/10 et al, 4.3.14.

[2719] The appropriate test is whether the measure 'entails, in substance or in effect, double jeopardy to the detriment of the individual or whether, in contrast, it is the product of an integrated system enabling different aspects of the wrongdoing to be addressed in a foreseeable and proportionate manner forming a coherent whole, so that the individual concerned is not thereby subjected to injustice'. See *A and B v Norway*, Nos. 24130/11 and 29758/11, 15.11.16, para. 122. The dual proceedings must also be 'sufficiently closely connected in substance and in time' (para. 128).

[2720] No. 48154/99, 20.7.04.

[2721] See, e.g. *Ipsilanti v Greece*, No. 56599/00, dec. 29.3.01; *Amrollahi v Denmark*, No. 56811/00, dec. 28.6.01; *SR v Sweden*, No. 62806/00, dec. 23.4.02; *Manoussos v Czech Republic and Germany*, No. 46468/99, 9.7.02.

[2722] See, e.g. *Smirnova and Smirnova v Russia*, Nos. 46133/99 and 48183/99, dec. 3.10.02; *Harutyunyan v Armenia*, No. 34334/04, dec. 7.12.06; *Marguš v Croatia*, No. 4455/10, 27.5.14.

[2723] No. 50178/99, 20.7.04. See also *Bratyakin v Russia*, No. 72776/01, dec. 9.3.06.

the applicant complained under Article 4 of Protocol No. 7 about the process of 'supervisory review' following his final acquittal. The applicant, an environmentalist, was prosecuted for treason for allegedly passing classified information to a foreign organisation. He was acquitted on all charges by the City Court, which decision was upheld (and thereby made final) by the Supreme Court. However, the prosecutor-general then lodged a request for a 'supervisory review' of the acquittal. That request was subsequently rejected by the Presidium of the Supreme Court. Nevertheless, the applicant argued that he was effectively prosecuted twice for the same offence, and that the review process could not be justified under either of the two conditions set out in Article 4(2) of Protocol No. 7. On the merits, the Court found no violation of Article 4 on the basis that the applicant was not 'tried again' and was not liable to be 'tried' twice. The supervisory review process amounted to a reopening of a finally decided criminal case, on the grounds of new or newly discovered evidence, or a fundamental defect.

In *Horciag* v *Romania*,[2724] the applicant confessed to a murder, but the prosecution found **6.900** that there was no case to answer as psychiatric assessments had shown that he had committed the offence at a time when his powers of discernment had been destroyed, so he could not be held criminally responsible. As a security measure, however, his provisional internment was ordered until he was cured. Subsequently, doctors expressed doubts as to the applicant's lack of criminal responsibility and so the proceedings were resumed. The applicant was found guilty and sentenced to a term of imprisonment. The applicant argued that he had been prosecuted and tried twice for the same offence. However, the Court found that Article 4 of Protocol No. 7 did not apply as he had initially been subject to a preventive measure, not an 'acquittal' within the meaning of this article. The resumption of the criminal proceedings had merely amounted to a continuation of the initial proceedings.

The case of *Marguš* v *Croatia*[2725] concerned the prosecution for war crimes of a former soldier **6.901** for killing civilians in 1991 during the war in Croatia. He had previously been granted an amnesty in respect of the same offences, and accordingly claimed that he had been prosecuted twice for the same offences, in violation of Article 4 of Protocol No. 7. However, the Grand Chamber found that the provision was not applicable. The applicant had been granted an amnesty for acts which amounted to grave breaches of fundamental human rights, something which was increasingly viewed as being unacceptable in international law. Furthermore, there was no process of reconciliation or compensation scheme for the victims which could have justified an amnesty in the applicant's case. The Court concluded that by bringing fresh proceedings against the applicant and convicting him of war crimes against the civilian population, the authorities had acted in compliance with Articles 2 and 3 of the Convention and consistently with international mechanisms and instruments.

Article 5 of Protocol No. 7: Equality Between Spouses

Article 5 of Protocol No. 7 states: **6.902**

> Spouses shall enjoy equality of rights and responsibilities of a private law character between them, and in their relations with their children, as to marriage, during marriage and in the

---

[2724] No. 70982/01, dec. 15.3.05.
[2725] No. 4455/10, 27.5.14.

event of its dissolution. This Article shall not prevent states from taking such measures as are necessary in the interests of children.

6.903 The Court has described the obligation under Article 5 of Protocol No. 7 as involving 'essentially a positive obligation to provide a satisfactory legal framework under which spouses have equal rights and obligations concerning such matters as their relations with their children'.[2726] An applicant invoking this provision should also consider utilising Article 8 (right to respect for private and family life) and Article 14 (prohibition of discrimination).

6.904 Article 5 of Protocol No. 7 applies only to 'private law' rights and responsibilities. Thus the Explanatory Report to Protocol No. 7 states that the provision does not apply to other fields of law, such as administrative, fiscal, criminal, social, ecclesiastical or labour laws.[2727] Accordingly, complaints about exemption from the obligation to pay social insurance contributions in Switzerland have been declared inadmissible on the basis they they were not of a private law character.[2728]

6.905 The provision only applies to 'spouses' and therefore cannot be relied on by someone who has never been married to their partner.[2729]

6.906 The final sentence of Article 5 of Protocol No. 7 provides that the Article shall not prevent states from taking such measures as are necessary in the interests of children. The term 'necessary' is to be interpreted in the same way as the term has been interpreted in respect of other parts of the Convention, such as Article 8.[2730] Accordingly, any interference with Article 5 must correspond to a 'pressing social need', and it must be proportionate to the legitimate aim pursued. This is essentially a matter that will often be for the national authorities to evaluate, unless the decision in question is unreasonable and therefore falls outside the authorities' legitimate margin of appreciation.[2731]

6.907 Article 5 of Protocol No. 7 does not prevent the national authorities from 'taking due account of all relevant factors when reaching decisions with regard to use of marital property pending its division in the event of dissolution of marriage'.[2732]

6.908 In *Cernecki* v *Austria*[2733] the parties raised conflicting arguments as to whether Article 5 of Protocol No. 7 only prohibits a difference in the treatment of spouses based on gender, or whether it contains a more general obligation to treat spouses equally in their family law relations. In that case the Court noted that section 177 of the Austrian Civil Code interfered with the right to equality between spouses because it attributed different legal positions to spouses in relation to their children after divorce. This was because under Article 177 an award of joint custody after divorce was excluded except in the case where the former spouses continued to live in a common household. The Court found this provision to fall within the state's margin of appreciation, noting the access and information rights that were made available to the parent not having custody.

[2726] *Purtonen* v *Finland*, No. 32700/96, dec. 9.9.98.
[2727] Explanatory Report, para. 35.
[2728] *Klöpper* v *Switzerland*, No. 25053/94, dec. 18.1.96; *Frischknecht* v *Switzerland*, No. 28334/95, dec. 18.1.96.
[2729] *Kaijalainen* v *Finland*, No. 24671/94, dec. 12.4.96.
[2730] See *Cernecki* v *Austria*, No. 31061/96, dec. 11.7.00; *Degrace* v *France*, No. 64910/01, dec. 7.1.03.
[2731] See, e.g. *Purtonen* v *Finland*, No. 32700/96, dec. 9.9.98.
[2732] *EP* v *Slovak Republic*, No. 33706/96, dec. 9.9.98.
[2733] No. 31061/96, dec. 11.7.00.

Article 1 of Protocol No. 12: General Prohibition of Discrimination

Article 1 of Protocol No. 12 states:

6.909

1. The enjoyment of any right set forth by law shall be secured without discrimination on any ground such as sex, race, colour, language, religion, political or other opinion, national or social origin, association with a national minority, property, birth or other status.
2. No one shall be discriminated against by any public authority on any ground such as those mentioned in paragraph 1.

The widely acknowledged limitations of the existing prohibition of discrimination in Article 14 of the Convention led to proposals within the Council of Europe to strengthen the provision.[2734] The main problem with Article 14 is that it does not provide a freestanding right to non-discrimination, but must be invoked in conjunction with another substantive Convention right (see above at 6.701 on Article 14). The only other provision in the Protocols to the Convention bearing on discrimination is Article 5 of Protocol No. 7 concerning equality between spouses (see 6.902). It is also accepted that discriminatory treatment may amount to degrading treatment in violation of Article 3 (see above at 6.181).

6.910

The introduction of an additional protocol dealing with equality and non-discrimination had been debated within the Council of Europe since the 1960s, but received greater impetus in the 1990s in view of the recognition of the importance of countering discrimination on grounds of sex and race in particular. The Steering Committee for Equality between Women and Men (CDEG) considered the inclusion of a substantive right of women and men to equality. A new expert body, the European Commission Against Racism and Intolerance (ECRI), focused on concerns about racism, xenophobia, antisemitism and intolerance. Accordingly, Protocol No. 12 to the Convention creates a freestanding anti-discrimination provision. The text of the protocol was adopted by the Committee of Ministers of the Council of Europe in June 2000, and entered into force on 1 April 2005.[2735] It has been ratified by only 20 of the 47 Convention states.[2736]

6.911

[2734] See G. Moon, 'The Draft Discrimination Protocol to the European Convention on Human Rights' [2000] EHRLR 49.

[2735] The United Kingdom has neither signed nor ratified Protocol No. 12. Its reasoning is as follows: 'a) The Government agrees in principle that the ECHR should contain a provision against discrimination that is freestanding and not parasitic on the other Convention rights. However the Government felt unable to accept the text of the provision eventually proposed by a majority of the Council of Europe. b) The Government has reviewed its position but, in the absence of any case law from the European Court of Human Rights, considers that there remain unacceptable uncertainties regarding the impact of Protocol 12 if it were incorporated into UK law:

—The drafting of the Protocol is very wide, covering any difference in treatment. It would apply to everything done by a public authority, and its application to 'rights set forth by law' would cover many, perhaps almost all, provisions in statute or common law. This could lead to an explosion of litigation as people sought to clarify the extent of the new law.

—Moreover, the coverage of "rights set forth by law" as cited in the Protocol may have the unintended effect of including other international instruments to which the United Kingdom is a party.

—Finally, until the European Court of Human Rights addresses the new Protocol, there cannot be complete certainty that it permits a defence of objective and reasonable justification on the same basis as under Article 14 ECHR.' See Report on the Outcome of an Inter-Departmental Review conducted by the Department of Constitutional Affairs, Department for Constitutional Affairs, July 2004.

[2736] As at the time of writing.

6.912 The first paragraph of Article 1 prohibits discrimination in relation to 'any right set forth by law' rather than 'the rights and freedoms set forth in this Convention' as set out in Article 14. This may include international law.[2737] The term 'discrimination' has the same meaning as in Article 14.[2738] It is important that the two paragraphs of Article 1 are read together, as they are intended to be complementary. The Explanatory Report to Protocol No. 12 suggests that the combined effect of the two paragraphs is to provide protection against discrimination in four situations:

(1) in the enjoyment of any right specifically granted to an individual under national law;

(2) in the enjoyment of a right that may be inferred from a clear obligation of a public authority under national law, i.e. where a public authority is under an obligation under national law to behave in a particular manner;

(3) by a public authority in the exercise of discretionary power (e.g. granting certain subsidies);

(4) by any other act or omission by a public authority (e.g. behaviour of law enforcement officers when controlling a riot).

6.913 The list of grounds in Protocol No. 12 is identical to the grounds listed in Article 14. It was decided not to include other grounds such as disability, sexual orientation and age expressly, on the basis that the list of grounds is in any event open-ended and that to include some additional grounds might be prejudicial to the consideration of other grounds that were not included. Be that as it may, the adoption by the Council of Europe of an additional anti-discrimination measure that expressly lists certain grounds, but omits disability, sexual orientation and age, is regrettable. The Parliamentary Assembly had recommended that non-discrimination based on sexual orientation and the principle of equality of rights between women and men should be explicitly included.[2739]

6.914 The Explanatory Report acknowledges that the Protocol may create certain positive obligations, but suggests that as between private persons, this will be limited to relations in the public sphere normally regulated by law, for which the state has a certain responsibility (such as employment contracts).

6.915 The preamble to the Protocol refers to the fundamental principle of equality before the law and equal protection of the law. It also reaffirms that the principle of non-discrimination does not prevent states from taking measures in order to promote full and effective equality, provided that there is an objective and reasonable justification. Accordingly, positive discrimination may be permissible.

6.916 The Grand Chamber found a violation of Article 1 of Protocol No. 12 in *Sejdić and Finci v Bosnia and Herzegovina*,[2740] which concerned the applicants' ineligibility to stand for elections to the Presidency of Bosnia and Herzegovina. According to the Constitution, in order to be eligible to stand for election, a candidate was required to declare affiliation with

---

[2737] See the Explanatory Report to Protocol No. 12, para. 29.

[2738] *Sejdić and Finci v Bosnia and Herzegovina*, Nos. 27996/06 and 34836/06, 22.12.09, para. 55.

[2739] Opinion No. 216 (2000) of 26.1.00.

[2740] Nos. 27996/06 and 34836/06, 22.12.09. See also *Zornić v Bosnia and Herzegovina*, No. 3681/06, 15.7.14 (violations of Article 1 of Protocol No. 12, as well as Article 14 together with Article 3 of Protocol No. 1); *Pilav v Bosnia and Herzegovina*, No. 41939/07, 9.6.16 (applicant barred from standing for election by a combination of his ethnic origin and place of residence—violation of Article 1 of Protocol No. 12).

a 'constituent people' (Bosniacs, Croats and Serbs).[2741] However, the applicants described themselves to be of Roma and Jewish origin, respectively, and accordingly objected to declaring such affiliation. They were therefore excluded from standing on a basis that lacked any objective and reasonable justification. The Court took note of the Opinion of the Venice Commission that there were mechanisms of power-sharing that did not automatically lead to the total exclusion of representatives of particular communities. For the same reasons, there was also a violation of Article 14 taken together with Article 3 of Protocol No. 1 as regards eligibility to stand for the House of Peoples (the second chamber of the state Parliament).

6.917 In the case of *Savez crkava 'Riječ života' and others* v *Croatia*,[2742] which concerned the authorities' unjustifiable refusal to conclude agreements relating to the legal status of a number of Reformist churches, the Court found a violation of Article 14 in conjunction with Article 9. Accordingly, it did not find it necessary also to consider the applicants' complaint under Article 1 of Protocol No. 12.

[2741] These provisions had been incorporated into the Constitution in order to end a brutal conflict marked by genocide and 'ethnic cleansing', and achieve peace.

[2742] No. 7798/08, 9.12.10.

7

DEROGATION AND RESERVATION

Derogation

7.01 Derogation enables a state to 'opt out' of limited aspects of the Convention, in particular, prescribed circumstances. It has only relatively rarely been invoked.[1] The right of a state to derogate is set out in Article 15, which provides as follows:

(1) In time of war or other public emergency threatening the life of the nation any High Contracting Party may take measures derogating from its obligations under this Convention to the extent strictly required by the exigencies of the situation, provided that such measures are not inconsistent with its other obligations under international law.

(2) No derogation from Article 2, except in respect of deaths resulting from lawful acts of war, or from Articles 3, 4 (paragraph 1) and 7 shall be made under this provision.

(3) Any High Contracting Party availing itself of this right of derogation shall keep the Secretary-General of the Council of Europe fully informed of the measures that it has taken and the reasons therefor. It shall also inform the Secretary-General of the Council of Europe when such measures have ceased to operate and the provisions of the Convention are again being fully executed.

7.02 Article 15(2) permits no derogation in relation to Article 3 (prohibition of torture and inhuman and degrading treatment or punishment), Article 4(1) (prohibition of slavery and servitude), Article 7 (prohibition of retrospective criminal penalties) and in relation to Article 2 (the right to life) other than in respect of acts of war. In addition there may be no derogation from either Protocols No. 6 or No. 13 (abolition of the death penalty)[2] or from Article 4 of Protocol No. 7 (right not to be tried or punished twice). However, derogation, for example,

---

[1] At the time of writing nine states had invoked the derogation provisions: Albania, Armenia, France, Georgia, Greece, Ireland, Turkey, Ukraine and the UK. See: European Court, Factsheet, Derogation in time of emergency, p. 2, available at: http://www.echr.coe.int/Documents/FS_Derogation_ENG.pdf. See also M. O'Boyle, 'Emergency Government and Derogation under the ECHR' [2016] 4 E.H.R.L.R. 331.

[2] See Article 3 of Protocol No. 6 and Article 2 of Protocol No. 13.

from Article 6 (the right to a fair hearing) is in theory possible, which it is suggested, must be extremely difficult to justify.

test: derogation

Article 15 lays down a threefold test for a valid derogation. First, the state must satisfy the **7.03** Court of the existence of 'war or a public emergency threatening the life of the nation'. If that condition is satisfied, the state must then establish, secondly, that the measures it has taken were 'strictly required by the exigencies of the situation'. Finally, such measures must also comply with the state's international law obligations. In addition, there must be compliance with the procedural requirements. Each of these conditions is considered below.

The Court acknowledges that the state is in a better position to make judgements about the **7.04** extent of an emergency and the measures necessary to deal with it. Accordingly, the respondent state is allowed a wide margin of appreciation in relation to Article 15,[3] although the discretion is not unlimited. The Court will take into account factors such as the nature of the rights affected by the derogation, the circumstances leading to the emergency situation, and how long it lasts.

Procedural requirements

For a derogation to be effective, there must be some formal, public act of derogation, such as **7.05** a declaration of martial law or state of emergency. Article 15 will not apply if no such declaration is made, unless it is prevented by special circumstances.[4] A governmental proclamation[5] will suffice, as will a ministerial statement in Parliament.[6]

States invoking the derogation provision are also required (by Article 15(3)) to keep the **7.06** Secretary-General of the Council of Europe fully informed of the measures which it has taken and the reasons for doing so.[7] Undue delay in doing so might be prejudicial.[8]

Public emergency threatening the life of the nation

During peacetime, a derogation can only apply in circumstances where there is a *public* **7.07** *emergency threatening the life of the nation*. This has been interpreted as meaning 'an exceptional situation of crisis or emergency that affects the whole population and constitutes a threat to the organised life of the community of which the state is composed'.[9] In the *Greek Case*, the European Commission of Human Rights found that the emergency (1) must be actual or imminent; (2) that its affects must involve the whole nation; (3) that the continuance of the organised life of the community must be threatened; and (4) that the crisis or danger must be exceptional, in that the normal measures or restrictions, permitted by the Convention for the maintenance of public safety, health and order, were plainly inadequate.[10]

---

[3] *Ireland* v *UK*, No. 5310/71, 18.1.78, para. 207.
[4] See, e.g. *Cyprus* v *Turkey*, No. 8007/77, Comm. Rep. 4.10.83.
[5] *Lawless* v *Ireland*, Series A, No. 3, 1.7.61.
[6] *Brannigan and McBride* v *UK*, Nos. 14553/89 and 14554/89, Series A, No. 258-B, 26.5.93.
[7] This provision was found to be violated in the *Greek Case*, Nos. 3321–3/67 and 3344/67, 5.11.69, *Yearbook of the European Convention on Human Rights*, Vol. 12, 1969, 1.
[8] *Lawless* v *Ireland*, Series A, No. 3, 1.7.61, para. 47.
[9] *Ibid.*, para. 28.
[10] Nos. 3321–3/67 and 3344/67, 5.11.69, *Yearbook of the European Convention on Human Rights*, Vol. 12, 1969, 1, para. 113.

7.08 In *Lawless* v *Ireland*,[11] which concerned the applicant's detention without trial for five months, the Court found it was reasonable to have claimed the existence of a public emergency in the late 1950s because of the increasing threat of the IRA both within and outside Ireland. In *Ireland* v *UK*,[12] in the context of the early 1970s when there had been numerous attacks by the IRA including bombings and shootings, it was undisputed that a public emergency existed. Allowing the state a wide margin of appreciation, the Grand Chamber of the Court acknowledged the existence of a public emergency in the United Kingdom following the terrorist attacks on the United States in 2001, in its 2009 judgment in *A and others* v *UK*[13] (discussed at 7.13 below), given the evidence adduced of a threat of serious terrorist attacks planned against the United Kingdom:[14]

> While it is striking that the United Kingdom was the only Convention State to have lodged a derogation in response to the danger from al'Qaeda, although other States were also the subject of threats, the Court accepts that it was for each Government, as the guardian of their own people's safety, to make their own assessment on the basis of the facts known to them.

7.09 In *Aksoy* v *Turkey*[15] the Court found that a public emergency existed in south-east Turkey as a result of the particular extent and impact of PKK terrorist activity in the region in the mid-1990s. In *Sakik* v *Turkey*, the Court stipulated that:

> Even where the existence of a public emergency is undisputed, the Court will nevertheless have to make its own assessment, but the state will be allowed a wide margin of appreciation. An 'emergency' in only part of a state may affect the whole population and therefore may threaten 'the life of the nation'. A derogation will only be valid in respect of those parts of a state's territory that are explicitly referred to in the notice of derogation.[16]

7.10 The European Commission of Human Rights rejected the Greek Government's claim of a public emergency in the *Greek case*.[17] The Government relied on the breakdown of public order, the constitutional crisis and the alleged threat of a communist takeover, but the Commission found no evidence for this, and so found Article 15 inapplicable.

Measures strictly required by the exigencies of the situation

7.11 Where the Court is satisfied that 'a public emergency threatening the life of the nation' is in existence, the respondent state may only take such measures as are 'strictly required by the exigencies of the situation'. For example, detention without trial of terrorist suspects in the context of the activities of the IRA in Ireland in the late 1950s was found to meet such criteria in *Lawless*.[18] There, the Court took into account the dangerousness of the situation, which the ordinary criminal law had been unable to check, and the available safeguards,

---

[11] Series A, No. 3, 1.7.61.

[12] *Ireland* v *UK*, Series A, No. 25, 18.1.78

[13] No. 3455/05, 19.2.09. See also Opinion 1/2002 of the Commissioner for Human Rights, Mr Alvaro Gil-Robles on certain aspects of the UK 2001 derogation from Article 5 para. 1 of the European Convention on Human Rights, CommDH(2002)8, 28.8.02.

[14] *Ibid.*, para. 180.

[15] No. 21987/93, 18.12.96. See also *Demir and others* v *Turkey*, Nos. 21380/93, 21381/93, 21383/93, 23.9.98, para. 45.

[16] *Sakik* v *Turkey*, Nos. 23878/94 to 23883/94, 26.11.97.

[17] Nos. 3321–3/67 and 3344/67, 5.11.69, *Yearbook of the European Convention on Human Rights*, Vol. 12, 1969, 1.

[18] Series A, No. 3, 1.7.61.

including parliamentary supervision of the detention regime and a 'Detention Commission' with binding powers to order release.

The respondent government will be allowed a wide margin of appreciation in assessing a **7.12** situation and deciding what measures are necessary, on the basis that it is in a better position to do so than the European Court.[19] The Court will consider various factors, including to what extent the ordinary law is inadequate; whether the continuance of the measures can be justified; and the proportionality of the measures introduced (is there another alternative?). Because of the difficulties faced by a state during an emergency, it will be allowed some leeway in introducing sufficient safeguards over time, rather than all at once.[20] The fact that a particular measure may be compliant with domestic law will not in itself be sufficient to justify measures derogating from the Convention.[21] In practice, the power of derogation has most frequently been raised in relation to powers of detention, as to which the Court has held that:

> where a derogating measure encroaches upon a fundamental Convention right, such as the right to liberty, the Court must be satisfied that it was a genuine response to the emergency situation, that it was fully justified by the special circumstances of the emergency and that adequate safeguards were provided against abuse.[22]

Following the judgment in *Brogan and others* v *UK*[23] in 1988, in which detention for **7.13** more than four days without judicial sanction was found to violate Article 5(3), the UK Government entered into a derogation in relation to Northern Ireland to permit detention without charge for up to seven days. The lawfulness of the UK derogation was upheld in *Brannigan and McBride* v *UK*[24] as the detention of terrorist suspects for up to seven days was considered not to exceed the state's margin of appreciation. The derogation was withdrawn with effect from 26 February 2001, following the introduction of the Terrorism Act 2000, which introduced judicial authorisation of extended periods of detention. In *Aksoy* v *Turkey*,[25] a 14-day detention period was considered too long. The Turkish Government failed to explain why the fight against terrorism made judicial intervention impracticable. The Court found that there were insufficient safeguards: 'in particular, the denial of access to a lawyer, doctor, relative or friend and the absence of any realistic possibility of being brought before the court to test the legality of the detention meant that he was left completely at the mercy of those holding him'.[26] In *Elçi and others* v *Turkey*,[27] the Court found that the Government failed to show how the applicant lawyers' detention without adequate prior authorisation could have been strictly required by the exigencies of the situation, in accordance with Article 15(1). Following the terrorist attacks on the United States on 11 September 2001, the United Kingdom entered into a derogation on 18 December 2001, in respect of Article 5(1) of the Convention, to permit the detention of foreign nationals

---

[19] See, e.g. *A and others* v *UK*, No. 3455/05, 19.2.09, para. 184.
[20] *Ireland* v *UK*, Series A, No. 25, 18.1.78.
[21] *Demir and others* v *Turkey*, Nos. 21380/93, 21381/93, 21383/93, 23.9.98, para. 52.
[22] *A and others* v *UK*, No. 3455/05, 19.2.09, para. 184.
[23] Nos. 11209/84, 11266/84 and 11365/85, Series A, No. 145-B, 29.11.88.
[24] Nos. 14553/89 and 14554/89, Series A, No. 258-B, 26.5.93. See also *Marshall* v *UK*, No. 41571/98, dec. 10.7.01.
[25] No. 21987/93, 18.12.96.
[26] *Aksoy* v *Turkey*, No. 21987/93, 18.12.96, para. 83.
[27] Nos. 23145/93 and 25091/94, 13.11.03, para. 684.

who were suspected of involvement in international terrorism (under the Anti-Terrorism, Crime and Security Act 2001).[28] Its purpose was to permit the extended detention of such individuals where, for example, they could not be deported because of an established risk that the person might be subject to ill-treatment in violation of Article 3 of the Convention. This is because Article 5(1)(f) only permits detention with a view to deportation, where 'action is being taken with a view to deportation'. The UK Government sought to rely on the derogation in the case of *A and others* v *UK*.[29] The applicants were foreign nationals who were detained under the 2001 Anti-Terrorism Act on suspicion of being involved in international terrorism. The Government would have deported them had it been possible to find a state to receive them where they would not face a real risk of being subjected to treatment contrary to Article 3 of the Convention. The authorities considered their detention was necessary because their presence in the country was a threat to national security. Nevertheless, as the authorities had accepted that they could not be deported or removed 'for the time being', Article 5 was breached because, as regards nine of the applicants, it could not be said that they were persons against whom action was being taken with a view to deportation or extradition. The Grand Chamber of the Court accepted that there had been a public emergency threatening the life of the nation, but it concluded that the measures taken were disproportionate as they discriminated unjustifiably between nationals and non-nationals.[30]

Other obligations under international law

7.14   Any derogation must also be consistent with a state's other obligations under international law, including treaty obligations (e.g. the Geneva Conventions in relation to armed conflict), or customary international law. There is a similar general obligation under Article 53 which provides that the Convention should not be construed as limiting or derogating from the human rights protected by a state's laws or by any agreement to which it is a party.

International armed conflict

7.15   The case of *Hassan* v *UK*[31] concerned the British army's arrest of Tarek Hassan in Basrah in Iraq in 2003 on suspicion of being a combatant, and it therefore raised questions about the applicability of international humanitarian law, in addition to international human rights law. The Court noted that it was not the practice of states parties to derogate from their Article 5 obligations in order to detain persons on the basis of the Third and Fourth Geneva Conventions during international armed conflicts. Accordingly, the Court accepted the UK Government's argument that the lack of a formal derogation under Article 15 did not prevent the Court from taking account of international humanitarian law when interpreting and applying Article 5 (see further the discussion of this case at 6.225).

Recent derogations

7.16   As a result of the armed conflict in eastern Ukraine, in June 2015, Ukraine notified the Council of Europe of a derogation from its obligations under Articles 5, 6, 8 and 13 in

---

[28]   The derogation was withdrawn with effect from 14 March 2005, following the House of Lords' judgment in the case of *A. and Others* v *Secretary of State for the Home Department* [2004] UKHL 56.

[29]   No. 3455/05, 19.2.09.

[30]   As had the House of Lords: *A. and Others* v *Secretary of State for the Home Department* [2004] UKHL 56.

[31]   No. 29750/09, 16.9.14.

relation to the 'anti-terrorist operations' being conducted in the Donetsk and Luhansk regions.[32] In November 2015, France introduced a state of emergency, and sent a notice of derogation to the Council of Europe, in response to the terrorist attacks in Paris in the same month and in view of the 'lasting nature' of the terrorist threat.[33] In July 2016, following an attempted coup, the Turkish Government declared a state of emergency and issued a notice of derogation under the Convention.[34] The validity and legality of these derogations will only be assessed by the Court as and when cases are brought to the Court in which the governments invoke their derogations.

Reservation

The Convention allows states, at the point of signature or ratification, to make express reservations from particular provisions. Article 57 (formerly Article 64) provides as follows: **7.17**

1. Any state may, when signing this Convention or when depositing its instrument of ratification, make a reservation in respect of any particular provision of the Convention to the extent that any law then in force in its territory is not in conformity with the provision. Reservations of a general character shall not be permitted under this Article.
2. Any reservation made under this Article shall contain a brief statement of the law concerned.

There are therefore four requirements for a reservation to be valid: (1) it must have been made when the Convention was signed or ratified; (2) it must relate to specific laws in force at the time of ratification; (3) it must not be a reservation 'of a general character'; and (4) it must contain a brief statement of the relevant law. For example, the Estonian reservation excluding from the scope of Article 1 of Protocol No. 1 a series of property laws regulating the restoration of property nationalised during the Soviet era has been found to meet these requirements,[35] and a Russian reservation relating to the power of detention by a public prosecutor, without there being any requirement for judicial supervision, has also been found valid.[36] **7.18**

As noted above, a reservation applies to the law in force at the time the reservation is made,[37] but a reservation may also extend to include a new law replacing an old law, provided that it does not extend beyond the scope of the reservation. A reservation must be interpreted in the language in which it was made. **7.19**

A reservation must be specifically pleaded by the respondent government for the Court to be able to consider it in a particular case.[38] If a reservation is upheld in relation to a **7.20**

---

[32] Derogation contained in a Note verbale from the Permanent Representation of Ukraine, 9.6.15. See also: European Court of Human Rights, Press Release, *European Court of Human Rights communicates to Russia new inter-State case concerning events in Crimea and Eastern Ukraine*, 1.10.15.

[33] Declaration contained in a Note verbale from the Permanent Representation of France, 24.11.15. The notice stated that some of the measures introduced by decrees 'may involve a derogation from the obligations under the Convention'.

[34] Declaration contained in a letter from the Permanent Representative of Turkey, 21.7.16 and Communication transmitted by the Permanent Representative of Turkey and registered by the Secretariat General on 5 August 2016, 5.8.16.

[35] *Shestjorkin* v *Estonia*, No. 49450/99, dec. 15.6.00.

[36] *Labzov* v *Russia*, No. 62208/00, dec. 28.2.02. See also *Boris Popov* v *Russia*, No. 23284/04, dec. 28.10.10.

[37] See, e.g. *Fischer* v *Austria*, No. 16922/90, Series A, No. 312, 26.4.95, para. 41.

[38] See, e.g. *Göktan* v *France*, No. 33402/96, 2.7.02, para. 51.

particular application, then the application will be declared inadmissible under Article 35[39] (see chapter 4).

Under Article 57(1), a state may not make a general reservation, which has been defined as 'a reservation couched in terms that are too vague or broad for it to be possible to determine their exact meaning and scope'.[40] In *Belilos v Switzerland*[41] this requirement was found to be breached by a reservation lodged by the respondent government in relation to Article 6. A territorial exclusion is also not permissible under Article 57[42] (although statements may be made in respect of dependent territories under Article 56—see 1.34 above). In *Ilașcu, Lesco, Ivantoc and Petrov-Popa v Moldova and Russia*,[43] the Court found that a 'declaration' made by the Moldovan Government concerning the Moldovan authorities' lack of control over Transdniestrian territory could not be equated to a reservation as it did not refer to any specific provision of either the Convention or of the domestic law. The Grand Chamber reached a similar decision in *Sargsyan v Azerbaijan*[44] as regards a declaration made by Azerbaijan that 'it was unable to guarantee the application of the Convention in territories occupied by the Republic of Armenia'.

7.21 The purpose of Article 57(2) is to ensure that the reservation does not go beyond the provisions expressly excluded by the state. The requirement to provide a brief statement of the law is considered to be both an evidential factor and contributes to legal certainty. A reservation may be invalidated on this ground alone. This requirement was found to have been breached in *Belilos v Switzerland*[45] where the Government conceded that no statement of law had been included with the reservation, and also in *Grande Stevens and others v Italy*.[46] In *Chorherr v Austria*,[47] by contrast, a reservation relating to Article 5 was found to be sufficiently specific as it included a limited number of laws which, taken together, amounted to 'a well-defined and coherent body of substantive and procedural administrative provisions'. In *Helle v Finland*,[48] a reservation aimed at relieving certain specified courts from holding oral hearings was found to be sufficiently specific to be valid. Similarly, Liechtenstein's reservation concerning the right to a hearing and public pronouncement of judgment was found to be valid in *Steck-Risch and others v Liechtenstein*.[49] In *Jécius v Lithuania*,[50] a reservation permitting a public prosecutor to authorise detention on remand was found to be valid as it referred with sufficient clarity to both Article 5(3) and the relevant domestic law.

7.22 A state is required to enter a reservation in respect of any provisions of any international treaties that it has concluded prior to ratification of the Convention which might not comply with it, such as the Austrian reservation to Article 1 of Protocol No. 1 in respect of the 1955 State Treaty. In *Slivenko and others v Latvia*,[51] the Latvian Government argued that its

---

[39] *Steck-Risch and others v Liechtenstein*, No. 63151/00, dec. 12.2.04.
[40] *Belilos v Switzerland*, No. 10328/83, Series A, No. 132, 29.4.88, para. 55.
[41] No. 10328/83, Series A, No. 132, 29.4.88.
[42] *Matthews v UK*, No. 24833/94, 18.2.99, para. 29; *Assanidze v Georgia*, No. 71503/01, 8.4.04, para. 140.
[43] No. 48787/99, dec. 4.7.01.
[44] No. 40167/06, dec. 14.12.11.
[45] No. 10328/83, Series A, No. 132, 29.4.88.
[46] No. 18640/10 et al, 4.3.14. See also *Weber v Switzerland*, No. 11034/84, 22.5.90 and *Eisenstecken v Austria*, No. 29477/95, 3.10.00.
[47] No. 13308/87, Series A, No. 266-B, 25.8.93.
[48] No. 20772/92, 19.12.97. See also *Laukkanen and Manninen v Finland*, No. 50230/99, 3.2.04.
[49] No. 63151/00, dec. 12.2.04.
[50] No. 34578/97, 31.7.00.
[51] No. 48321/99, dec. 23.1.02.

ratification of the European Convention was subject to its prior treaty with Russia concerning the expulsion of Russian military officers.[52] However, no reservation had been made and accordingly the Court decided that, contrary to the Government's submissions, it did have jurisdiction to consider the applicants' arguments concerning their deportation from Latvia to Russia. However, in *Kozlova and Smirnova v Latvia*,[53] the Latvian reservation precluding the application of Article 1 of Protocol No. 1 to national laws on restitution of real property was held to be valid, as covering a strictly limited number of laws and being sufficiently accessible to the public.

The UK Government has made a reservation in respect of the right to education in Article 2 **7.23** of Protocol No. 1, to the effect that the principle that education and teaching should be in conformity with parents' religious and philosophical convictions is accepted only so far as it is compatible with the provision of efficient instruction and training and the avoidance of unreasonable expenditure. The European Commission of Human Rights raised questions about the validity of the UK reservation in *SP v UK*[54] concerning the failure to provide adequate schooling for a dyslexic boy, on the basis that the relevant provisions of domestic law had come into force after the reservation had been made. However, the case was declared inadmissible for other reasons.

---

[52] The treaty was concluded in 1994 and Latvia ratified the European Convention on Human Rights on 27 June 1997.

[53] No. 57381/00, dec. 23.10.01. See also *Liepajnieks v Latvia*, No. 37586/06, dec. 2.11.10.

[54] No. 28915/95, dec. 17.1.97.

8

JUST SATISFACTION (ARTICLE 41)

Introduction

8.01 This chapter considers the redress that is available from the European Court. The usual form of remedy is an award of damages (together with the award of legal costs and expenses), but the Court is also able to stipulate other non-pecuniary measures of redress, which are also discussed.

8.02 The European Court's primary remedy is a declaration that there has been a violation of the Convention. In addition, where the Court finds that there has been a violation of the Convention, the judgment may include an award for 'just satisfaction' under Article 41 (previously under Article 50, prior to November 1998), if the question of compensation is ready for decision.[1] Article 41 states:

> If the Court finds that there has been a violation of the Convention or the protocols thereto, and if the internal law of the High Contracting Party concerned allows only partial reparation to be made, the Court shall, if necessary, afford just satisfaction to the injured party.

8.03 The award of just satisfaction is therefore not automatic, but discretionary.[2] The exhaustion of domestic remedies rule does *not* apply to just satisfaction claims.[3] Just satisfaction under Article 41 may include compensation for both pecuniary and non-pecuniary loss and legal costs and expenses.[4]

8.04 A Practice Direction on just satisfaction claims was issued by the Court in 2007.[5] The Practice Direction stipulates that the Court may be guided by domestic standards (although it is not bound by them) and that the Court will normally take account of 'the local economic circumstances'.[6]

---

[1] Judgments and their enforcement are discussed further in chapter 3.
[2] See *De Wilde, Ooms & Versyp* v *Belgium*, Nos. 2832/66, 2835/66 and 2899/66, 18.6.71. See also Practice Direction: *Just Satisfaction Claims*, paras. 1–2.
[3] See, e.g. *De Wilde, Ooms & Versyp* v *Belgium*, Nos. 2832/66, 2835/66 and 2899/66, 18.6.71, para. 15.
[4] This was established in the Court's early case law. See, e.g. *Neumeister* v *Austria*, No. 1936/63, 7.5.74.
[5] Practice Direction: *Just Satisfaction Claims*.
[6] Practice Direction: *Just Satisfaction Claims*, paras. 2 and 3.

A claim for just satisfaction should be lodged within the time limit fixed for the submission of the applicant's observations on the merits (unless the President of the Chamber directs otherwise).[7] Claims lodged out of time will usually be dismissed, although the Court may exercise its discretion to accept late claims in some cases.[8] The importance of obtaining adequate information and evidence about potential compensation claims, and of adequately recording legal costs, from the outset of a case, are also discussed above at 2.12–2.13 and 2.25 respectively.

Applicants may specify a bank account into which they wish any sums awarded to be paid.[9] **8.05**
Awards are usually made in euros, although awards in other currencies can also be made.[10] The time limit for the payment of any award will usually be three months from the date when the judgment becomes final and binding.[11] Interest will be payable in default of payment—normally at a rate equal to the marginal lending rate of the European Central bank, plus three percentage points.[12] The Court may require the Government to pay damages awarded to a legally incapacitated applicant to their guardian.[13] Exceptionally, in cases where the applicant is no longer within the jurisdiction of the respondent state, the Court may stipulate that the just satisfaction award is to be held by the applicant's representative in trust for the applicant.[14] The Court may exceptionally exercise its discretion to stipulate that a domestic body should not claim back from an applicant a sum awarded by the Court against the respondent state in respect of non-pecuniary damage.[15]

The Court will almost invariably adjudicate on a just satisfaction claim in the judgment **8.06**
on the merits of the case, but, exceptionally, it may produce a principal judgment on the merits, and reserve the question of Article 41 to be dealt with in a subsequent judgment. In those circumstances, it is open to the respondent government to seek the resolution of the issue of just satisfaction through the unilateral declaration procedure (see chapter 2).[16]

The applicant state in an inter-state application may be entitled to claim compensation **8.07**
pursuant to Article 41 of the Convention. In *Cyprus* v *Turkey*[17] the Grand Chamber found that the Cypriot Government was entitled to make a just satisfaction claim on behalf of 1,456 missing people and the Greek Cypriot residents of the Karpas peninsula. By way of non-pecuniary damages the Court awarded the surviving relatives of the missing persons €30 million and the Karpas residents €60 million. These sums were to be distributed by the applicant Government to the individual victims.

---

[7] Rule 60(2) and Practice Direction: *Just Satisfaction Claims*, para. 5.

[8] See, e.g. *Sufi and Elmi* v *UK*, Nos. 8319/07 and 11449/07, 28.6.11, paras. 315–17.

[9] Practice Direction: *Just Satisfaction Claims*, para. 22.

[10] Practice Direction: *Just Satisfaction Claims*, para. 24.

[11] The circumstances in which a judgment becomes final and binding are discussed further in chapter 3. For example, a request for the referral of a Chamber judgment to the Grand Chamber (under Article 43) will have the effect of delaying this process.

[12] Practice Direction: *Just Satisfaction Claims*, para. 25. See, e.g. *Krone Verlag GmbH & Co KG* v *Austria*, No. 39069/97, 11.12.03, para. 48.

[13] *Lashin* v *Russia*, No. 33117/02, 22.1.13.

[14] See, e.g. *Savriddin Dzhurayev* v *Russia*, No. 71386/10, 25.4.13.

[15] See, e.g. *Trévalec* v *Belgium*, No. 30812/07, 25.6.13 (the order related to a French compensation fund, as the applicant was a French national).

[16] *Megadat.com SRL* v *Moldova*, No. 21151/04, 17.5.11.

[17] No. 25781/94, 12.5.14.

8.08 Just satisfaction in the form of compensation is discussed at 8.09 below. Other, less common (non-monetary) remedies provided by the Court are discussed at 8.33.

Pecuniary and Non-pecuniary Compensation

8.09 In order to succeed in claiming damages, the applicant must establish a clear causal link or connection between the violation of the Convention in question and the losses claimed. The Practice Direction on *Just satisfaction claims* states:

> A clear causal link must be established between the damage claimed and the violation alleged. The Court will not be satisfied by a merely tenuous connection between the alleged violation and the damage, nor by mere speculation as to what might have been.
>
> Compensation for damage can be awarded in so far as the damage is the result of a violation found. No award can be made for damage caused by events or situations that have not been found to constitute a violation of the Convention, or for damage related to complaints declared inadmissible at an earlier stage of the proceedings.[18]

8.10 For example, in *Akkoç v Turkey*,[19] concerning the killing of the applicant's husband, the authorities were found to be liable under Article 2 of the Convention for failing to protect his life. Accordingly, there was a causal link between the violation of Article 2 and the widow's and children's loss of financial support.[20] However, in many cases, applicants have failed this test of causation. For example, in *Tele 1 Privatfernsehgesellschaft MBH v Austria*,[21] the applicant's claim for pecuniary damages was based on an assumption that the applicant would have obtained a television broadcasting licence if Austrian legislation had complied with Article 10. This, however, was found to be too speculative and no award was made. Similarly there was no causal link in *Oldham v UK*[22] where the Court found that any financial losses incurred by the applicant resulted from his recall to prison, rather than the delay in the review of the legality of his detention that was the reason for a finding of a violation of Article 5 of the Convention. The Court also found that any deterioration in the applicant's physical or mental condition was also not caused by the delay. Nevertheless, the Court found that the applicant 'must have suffered feelings of frustration, uncertainty and anxiety' and awarded him £1,000.

8.11 In general, awards of damages are relatively low compared with damages awarded by the domestic courts of some Council of Europe states. This is probably due to a prevailing view that the primary remedy in Strasbourg is the finding of a violation of the Convention itself. It may also reflect the fact that the Court's function, as set out in Article 19 of the Convention, is 'to ensure the observance of the engagements undertaken by the High Contracting Parties in the Convention and the Protocols thereto…'. Indeed in many cases, the Court will decline to award any damages on the basis that its finding of a violation of the Convention is 'sufficient' just satisfaction.[23] At the other end of the spectrum are a number of commercial

---

[18] Practice Direction: *Just Satisfaction Claims*, paras. 7 and 8.

[19] Nos. 22947/93 and 22948/93, 10.10.00. See also, e.g. *Çakıcı v Turkey*, No. 23657/94, 8.7.99, para. 127.

[20] Pecuniary damages of £35,000 were awarded, together with £15,000 non-pecuniary damages to the applicant as the surviving spouse and £25,000 non-pecuniary damages to the applicant in her personal capacity.

[21] No. 32240/96, 21.9.00, para. 46.

[22] No. 36273/97, 26.9.00.

[23] For criticism of this approach, see the partly dissenting opinion of Judge Bonello in *Aquilina v Malta*, No. 25642/94, 29.4.99, where he argued that it is 'inadequate and unacceptable that a court of justice should 'satisfy' the victim of a breach of fundamental rights with a mere handout of legal idiom'. See also his partly

cases in which huge damages awards were made by the Court. The case of *OAO Neftyanaya Kompaniya Yukos* v *Russia*[24] concerned tax and enforcement proceedings brought in 2004 against Yukos, the Russian oil company, which led to its liquidation in 2007 and which were found to breach Articles 6(1), 6(3)(b) and Article 1 of Protocol No. 1. The Court awarded total pecuniary damages of more than €1.866 billion, as a consequence of the unlawful retroactive imposition of tax penalties and an enforcement fee. In considering awards for just satisfaction, the Court is unlikely to take account of principles or scales of assessment used by domestic courts.[25] The practice of the Court is now to award non-pecuniary damages on a tax exempt basis. In the case of pecuniary damages, it will depend on the nature of the damage whether compensation is awarded tax exempt or not.

Rather than lay down specific means of calculating damages awards (such as an hourly rate for **8.12** unlawful detention), the Court applies general principles in assessing just satisfaction. The legal effect of a judgment is to place a duty on the respondent state to make reparation for its consequences in such a way as to restore as far as possible the situation existing before the breach (*restitutio in integrum*). On many occasions, the Court states that its award is made 'on an equitable basis'.[26] The Court has explained its approach in this way:

> As regards the claim for monetary compensation, the Court recalls that it is not its role under Article 41 to function akin to a domestic tort mechanism court in apportioning fault and compensatory damages between civil parties. Its guiding principle is equity, which above all involves flexibility and an objective consideration of what is just, fair and reasonable in all the circumstances of the case, including not only the position of the applicant but the overall context in which the breach occurred. Its non-pecuniary awards serve to give recognition to the fact that moral damage occurred as a result of a breach of a fundamental human right and reflect in the broadest of terms the severity of the damage ...[27]

Accordingly, in many cases it is extremely difficult, if not impossible, to discern how the Court has arrived at the sum awarded.[28] The Court utilises a set of internal guidelines, which it has not published.[29] Clearly, in calculating awards of damages, the Court will take account of the gravity of a Convention violation and its duration.[30] The Court may take a state's economic situation into account when assessing damages awards,[31] and, it would appear, an applicant's 'status'.[32]

---

dissenting opinion in *Maronek* v *Slovakia*, No. 32686/96, 19.4.01. See further *Vinter and others* v *UK*, Nos. 66069/09, 130/10 and 3896/10, 9.7.13 (concurring opinion of Judge Ziemele).

[24] No. 14902/04, 31.7.14.

[25] *Osman* v *UK*, No. 23452/94, 28.2.98, para. 164.

[26] Practice Direction: *Just Satisfaction Claims*, para. 14. See, e.g. *Scoppola* v *Italy (No. 2)*, No. 10249/03, 17.9.09.

[27] *Al-Skeini and others* v *UK*, No. 55721/07, 7.7.11, para. 182.

[28] See also the very interesting analysis of the Court's approach to damages in Szilvia Altwicker-Hàmori, Tilmann Altwicker and Anne Peters, *Measuring Violations of Human Rights—An Empirical Analysis of Awards in Respect of Non-Pecuniary Damage under the European Convention on Human Rights*, Zeitschrift für ausländisches öffentliches Recht und Völkerrecht (ZaöRV)/Heidelberg Journal of International Law (HJIL) 76 (2016), 1–51.

[29] See European Court of Human Rights, Comment from the Court on the report of the CDDH on the longer-term future of the Convention system, February 2016, para. 9.

[30] See, e.g. *W* v *Slovenia*, No. 24125/06, 23.1.14, para. 92; *N.D.* v *Slovenia*, No. 16605/09, 15.1.15, para. 85.

[31] *Basarba OOD* v *Bulgaria*, No. 77660/01, 20.1.11, para. 26. See also Practice Direction: *Just Satisfaction Claims*, para. 2.

[32] *Petrova and Chornobryvets* v *Ukraine*, Nos. 6360/04 and 16820/04, 15.5.08, para. 25 (taking account of the applicants' 'important judicial status').

8.13 The Court will frequently comment that it is unable to speculate on the outcome of the applicant's domestic proceedings, had there not been a violation of the Convention. This is often the position, for example, in cases where there has been a violation of the right to a fair hearing in civil or criminal proceedings.[33] In *Findlay* v *UK*,[34] for example, the applicant's claim for loss of income of £440,200 following his conviction and sentence by a court-martial that violated Article 6(1) was rejected for this reason by the Court. In fact, where a violation of Article 6 arises from failures of objective or structural independence and impartiality, the Court will not award monetary compensation in respect of loss of procedural opportunity or any distress, loss or damage allegedly caused by the outcome in the domestic proceedings.[35] It is arguable, however, that such speculation is not necessary and that the finding of a procedural error leading to a violation of Article 6 justifies the payment of monetary compensation. In *Kingsley* v *UK*,[36] where a ten-judge majority in the Grand Chamber found that a finding of a violation of Article 6 constituted sufficient just satisfaction, Judge Casadevall dissenting (joined by Judge Kovler) argued that 'applicants are entitled to something more than a mere moral victory or the satisfaction of having contributed to enriching the Court's case law'. They argued that, on the contrary, it would be possible to make an award in such circumstances for 'loss of opportunity' or uncertainty, anxiety, feelings of helplessness and frustration, or damage to reputation. It has also been suggested that where Article 6 has been violated in criminal proceedings, the principle of *restitutio in integrum* requires that there should be a full retrial in the domestic proceedings.[37] Indeed, it is increasingly common for the Court to *recommend*,[38] and even occasionally *require*, that the domestic proceedings be reopened (in states where re-opening is possible)[39] (see further at 3.69 above).

8.14 The Court has frequently reiterated how difficult it can be to quantify pecuniary claims:[40]

> A precise calculation of the sums necessary to make reparation (*restitutio in integrum*) in respect of the pecuniary losses suffered by an applicant may be prevented by the inherently uncertain character of the damage flowing from the violation.

It has also said that:[41]

> An award may still be made notwithstanding the large number of imponderables involved in the assessment of future losses, though the greater the lapse of time involved the more uncertain the link between the breach and the damage becomes.

8.15 This problem is illustrated by the case of *E and others* v *UK*[42] in which the Court found a violation of Article 3 as a result of the social services department's failure to respond

---

[33] See, e.g. *Hood* v *UK*, No. 27267/95, 18.2.99, para. 86.
[34] No. 22107/93, 25.2.97.
[35] See, e.g. *Hauschildt* v *Denmark*, No. 10486/83, Series A, No. 154, 24.5.89, para. 58; *Holm* v *Sweden*, No. 14191/88, Series A, No. 279-A, 25.11.93, para. 36; *Findlay* v *UK*, No. 22107/93, 25.2.97, para. 88; *Kingsley* v *UK*, No. 35605/97, 28.5.02, para. 43.
[36] No. 35605/97, 28.5.02. See also *Nikolova* v *Bulgaria*, No. 31195/96, 25.3.99.
[37] See, e.g. Judge Zupancic's partly concurring opinion in *Lucà* v *Italy*, No. 33354/96, 27.2.01.
[38] See, e.g. *Navalnyy and Ofitserov* v *Russia*, Nos. 46632/13 and 28671/14, 23.2.16.
[39] See *Maksimov* v *Azerbaijan*, No. 38228/05, 8.10.09 (operative provision 3).
[40] See, e.g. *Young, James and Webster* v *UK*, Nos. 7601/76 and 7807/77, Series A, No. 55, 18.10.82, para. 11; *Karandja* v *Bulgaria*, No. 69180/01, 7.10.10, para. 76.
[41] *Tanlı* v *Turkey*, No. 26129/95, 10.4.01, para. 182.
[42] No. 33218/96, 26.11.02.

adequately to the applicant children's allegations of physical and sexual abuse by their stepfather. The applicants claimed sums for loss of earnings since 1977, the date from which the Court found the authorities ought to have taken action. However, as the abuse had occurred for several years prior to 1977, the Court found that it was not possible to assess what additional damage occurred after that date. Accordingly, the Court made a 'global' assessment, awarding €16,000 to each of three applicants and €32,000 to the fourth applicant. In *Kurić and others v Slovenia*[43] the Grand Chamber found violations of Articles 8 and 13 because of the authorities' failure to regularise the applicants' residence status following their unlawful 'erasure' from the Register of Permanent Residents. In its separate just satisfaction judgment,[44] the Court acknowledged that there had been significant material consequences for the applicants, including the loss of access to a range of social and political rights and legal benefits, such as identity documents, driving licences, health insurance and education, and the loss of job and other opportunities. However, a precise calculation of the ensuing damages was prevented by the 'inherently uncertain character of the damage flowing from the violation'.[45]

It is vital that particularised claims for just satisfaction are made by the applicant. Where **8.16** an applicant fails to make such a claim, the Court will not consider an award of its own motion,[46] other than in very exceptional circumstances.[47] The Court is unlikely to make awards higher than the sums claimed by applicants, as it applies the principle of *ne ultra petita*.[48] A failure to back up claims for pecuniary damages with reliable documentary evidence may also lead to no award (the Court's usual practice), or a reduced award, being made.[49] However, where applicants are unable to provide evidence due to circumstances beyond their control, the Court may take this into account when deciding any claim for non-pecuniary damages.[50] Awards made in comparable domestic cases may be relevant, but will not be decisive.[51] In *Z and others v UK*,[52] the Court relied on medical reports in deciding on awards for future medical costs and loss of employment opportunities. In cases such as *Tanlı v Turkey*,[53] the Court has relied on actuarial calculations in assessing an appropriate capital sum to compensate applicants for the loss of income as a result of

---

[43] No. 26828/06, 26.6.12.

[44] No. 26828/06, 12.3.14.

[45] *Ibid.*, para. 88.

[46] See, e.g. *Moore and Gordon v UK*, Nos. 36529/97 and 37393/97, 29.9.99, para. 28; *Birutis and others v Lithuania*, Nos. 47698/99 and 48115/99, 28.3.02, paras. 36–8.

[47] See, e.g. *Chember v Russia*, No. 7188/03, 3.7.08, para. 77; *X v Croatia*, No. 12233/04, 17.7.08, para. 63; *Borodin v Russia*, No. 41867/04, 6.11.12 (apparently because the case concerned inhuman and degrading treatment—and therefore the violation of an absolute right (see para. 166)); *Nagmetov v Russia*, No. 35589/08, 30.3.17.

[48] See, e.g. *Mateescu v Romania*, No. 1944/10, 14.1.14, para. 39; *Kavaklıoğlu and others v Turkey*, No. 15397/02, 6.10.15, para. 301.

[49] See, e.g. *Bilgin v Turkey*, No. 23819/94, 16.11.00, para. 140 (where the Court stressed the absence of 'independent and conclusive evidence').

[50] See, e.g. *Hasan and Chaush v Bulgaria*, No. 30985/96, 26.10.00, para. 118.

[51] See, e.g. *Z and others v UK*, No. 29392/95, 10.5.01, para. 120; *Malhous v Czech Republic*, No. 33071/96, 12.7.01, para. 74.

[52] No. 29392/95, 10.5.01.

[53] No. 26129/95, 10.4.01. Indeed, the failure to apply actuarial methods in the calculation of lost future earnings and future expenses may result in a reduced award: *Mikheyev v Russia*, No. 77617/01, 26.1.06, paras. 160–1.

the death of a relative (£38,754.77 in *Tanlı*). In *Akdeniz v Turkey*,[54] a total of more than £380,000 was awarded as pecuniary damages in respect of the disappearance of 11 relatives (plus more than £200,000 in non-pecuniary damages). In *Aslakhanova and others v Russia*,[55] the Court awarded the applicants a total of €480,00 by way of non-pecuniary damages in respect of the enforced disappearances of their eight relatives in Chechnya in the early 2000s.

8.17 Claims for punitive, exemplary or aggravated damages have been rejected by the Court, without ruling out the possibility of making such awards.[56] Nevertheless, in the 'disappearance' case of *Çiçek v Turkey*,[57] it is arguably possible to discern that the authorities' conduct was an aggravating factor in the award of damages, as it was expressly noted by the Court that 'the authorities have not assisted the applicant in her search for the truth about the whereabouts of her sons'.

8.18 Unusually, in the case of *Anguelova v Bulgaria*,[58] concerning the death of a 17-year-old Roma man in police custody, the Court awarded the claim for non-pecuniary damages in full (€19,050) having regard, inter alia, to its similar previous judgments against Bulgaria.

8.19 One of the highest awards for damages, inter alia, for personal injury, in recent years was the award of 500,000 French francs in *Selmouni v France*[59] following the torture of the applicant by French police. In *Tomasi v France*,[60] the applicant, who was also ill-treated in police custody, was awarded 700,000 French francs for both pecuniary and non-pecuniary loss. In *Ilaşcu and others v Moldova and Russia*,[61] each applicant was awarded €180,000 as pecuniary and non-pecuniary damages in respect of violations of Articles 3 and 5 of the Convention. The applicants in *Oyal v Turkey*[62] were awarded pecuniary damages of €300,000 to cover the first applicant's past medical costs—as a new-born baby, he had contracted the HIV virus as a result of a blood transfusion carried out in hospital. In addition, it ordered the Government to provide free and full medical cover for the first applicant during his lifetime. The applicant in *Mikheyev v Russia*,[63] who was found to have been tortured in police custody, was awarded pecuniary damages of €130,000 in view of the seriousness of his condition, his need for specialised and continuous medical treatment and his complete inability to work in the future (together with €120,000 in non-pecuniary damages). The first applicant in *Maslova and Nalbandov v Russia*[64] was repeatedly raped by police officers and subjected to other forms of ill-treatment, including beatings, suffocation and electro-cution, amounting to torture. She was awarded non-pecuniary damages of €70,000. The

---

[54] No. 23954/94, 31.5.01.
[55] No. 2944/06 et al, 18.12.12.
[56] Practice Direction: *Just Satisfaction Claims*, para. 9. See, e.g. *Selçuk and Asker v Turkey*, Nos. 23184/94 and 23185/94, 24.4.98, para. 119 and *Hood v UK*, No. 27267/95, 18.2.99, para. 89; *Cable and others v UK*, Nos. 24436/94 et al, 18.2.99; *Orhan v Turkey*, No. 25656/94, 18.6.02; *Varnava and others v Turkey*, No. 16064/90, 18.9.09, para. 223.
[57] No. 25704/94, 27.2.01, para. 205.
[58] No. 38361/97, 13.6.02.
[59] No. 25803/94, 28.7.99.
[60] No. 12850/87, Series A, No. 241-A, 27.8.92.
[61] No. 48787/99, 8.7.04.
[62] No. 4864/05, 23.3.10.
[63] No. 77617/01, 26.1.06.
[64] No. 839/02, 24.1.08.

authorities in *Iribarren Pinillos v Spain*,[65] were found to have failed to comply with their positive obligations under Article 3 because of the inadequacies in the investigation of the applicant's serious injuries that were caused by a smoke bomb fired by the riot police during violent clashes in Pamplona. They were found to have failed to carry out a proper assessment of the damage he had sustained. He was awarded pecuniary damages of €100,000 (together with non-pecuniary damages of €40,000).

The conduct of the applicant may also be a factor in assessing damages awards. No award was made in *McCann and others v UK*[66] 'having regard to the fact that the three terrorist suspects who were killed had been intending to plant a bomb in Gibraltar'. Similarly in *Messina (No. 2) v Italy*,[67] the applicant, who had been found to be a mafia member and drug trafficker, was given no award, with the Court giving no reasons and relying on its 'mantra' that the finding of a violation constituted sufficient just satisfaction. The position of the applicants in *A and others v UK*[68] (foreign nationals detained on suspicion of their involvement in international terrorism following the terrorist attacks on the United States in 2001) was distinguished from *McCann* on the basis that it had not been established that any of the applicants had engaged, or attempted to engage, in any act of terrorist violence. Nevertheless, given the context, the Court made substantially lower damages awards in comparison with other unlawful detention cases. Where applicants are considered to be 'overly litigious', for example, by bringing applications concerning principles which are very well-established by the Court (such as the length of proceedings), but which relate, for example, to small monetary sums, this is likely to impact on the application of Article 41.[69] In *Piper v UK*[70] the Court had found a violation of Article 6(1) because of the length of the criminal proceedings brought against the applicant, who had been convicted of drug-trafficking offences and sentenced to fourteen years' imprisonment. However, the Court made no award for non-pecuniary damages having regard to the extent to which the applicant was himself responsible for delaying the proceedings. **8.20**

Awards for pecuniary damages may include the following: **8.21**

- loss of earnings (past and future);[71]
- loss of means of earning a living;[72]
- loss of pension scheme and/or social security benefits;[73]
- fines and taxes imposed;[74]
- the value of confiscation orders imposed[75] or sums of money confiscated;[76]

---

[65] No. 36777/03, 8.1.09.

[66] No. 18984/91, Series A, No. 324, 27.9.95. See also, e.g. *Sabanchiyeva and others v Russia*, No. 38450/05, 6.6.13.

[67] No. 25498/94, 28.9.00. See also, e.g. *Wenner v Germany*, No. 62303/13, 1.9.16.

[68] No. 3455/05, 19.2.09.

[69] See, e.g. *Ioannis Anastasiadis and others v Greece*, No. 45823/08, 18.4.13.

[70] No. 44547/10, 21.4.15.

[71] See, e.g. *Iatridis v Greece*, No. 31107/96, 19.10.00; *Elçi and others v Turkey*, Nos. 23145/93 and 25091/94, 13.11.03 (lawyers' loss of earnings during detention which violated Article 5); *Ivanova v Bulgaria*, No. 52435/99, 12.4.07; *Soare and others v Romania*, No. 24329/02, 22.2.11.

[72] *Lallement v France*, No. 46044/99, 12.6.03 (€150,000 pecuniary damages awarded as a result of the expropriation of part of the applicant farmer's land).

[73] See, e.g. *Willis v UK*, No. 36042/97, 11.06.02.

[74] See e.g. *Lopes Gomes de Silva v Portugal*, No. 37698/97, 28.9.00; *Association Les Témoins de Jéhovah v France*, No. 8916/05, 5.7.12.

[75] See, e.g. *Geerings v Netherlands*, No. 30810/03, 1.3.07.

[76] *Ismayilov v Russia*, No. 30352/03, 6.11.08.

- loss of company profits;[77]
- damages paid;[78]
- domestic costs incurred;[79]
- domestic court fees;[80]
- loss of inheritance;[81]
- medical expenses;[82]
- the value of a dissolved association's assets;[83] and
- the loss of the value of land.[84]

Interest may also be claimed as a pecuniary loss, from the dates on which each recoverable element of past pecuniary damage accrued.[85]

8.22 The value of an inheritance was awarded to the applicants in *Camp and Bourimi v Netherlands*.[86] The pecuniary loss awarded was to amount to the value of the father's estate that the applicant would have obtained if his relationship with his father had been legally recognised. Furthermore, this was to be valued as at the time it was distributed amongst his heirs.

8.23 Calculating the losses incurred in respect of land may pose particular problems, and the Court may order an expert valuation to be carried out in order for it to do so.[87] The case of *Iatridis v Greece*[88] concerned the eviction of an open air cinema manager, which was found to violate Article 1 of Protocol No. 1. The Court found that this interference had been 'manifestly' in breach of domestic law, which would justify awarding the applicant full compensation, to cover the loss of earnings which he would have derived from the cinema until the end of the current lease. Prohibitions on building and attempted expropriations of a plot of land were in issue in *Pialopoulos and Alexiou v Greece*,[89] which meant that it was impossible for the applicants to exploit their plot. As to damages, the Court refused to speculate as to what the use of the property, and its proceeds, would have been, and so damages were awarded corresponding to the income that would have been received annually, had they deposited into a bank account the sum of compensation which had been awarded by the first instance court in the domestic proceedings. Accordingly, the applicants were awarded pecuniary damages of €3,850,000, plus €40,000 non-pecuniary damages. In *Malamma v Greece*,[90] the Court was faced with a complaint concerning the expropriation of

---

[77] See, e.g. *Dacia S.R.L. v Moldova*, No. 3052/04, 19.2.09.

[78] See, e.g. *Lopes Gomes de Silva v Portugal*, No. 37698/97, 28.9.00, *Nikula v Finland*, No. 31611/96, 21.3.02; *Lombardo and others v Malta*, No. 7333/06, 24.4.07; *Björk Eiðsdóttir v Iceland*, No. 46443/09, 10.7.12.

[79] See, e.g. *Lopes Gomes de Silva v Portugal*, No. 37698/97, 28.9.00, *Nikula v Finland*, No. 31611/96, 21.3.02, *MGN Limited v UK*, No. 39401/04, 12.6.12.

[80] See, e.g. *Krone Verlag GmbH & Co KG v Austria*, No. 34315/96, 26.2.02.

[81] See, e.g. *Camp and Bourimi v Netherlands*, No. 28369/95, 3.10.00.

[82] See, e.g. *Pitkanen v Finland*, No. 30508/96, 9.3.04.

[83] *Association Rhino and others v Switzerland*, No. 48848/07, 11.10.11.

[84] See, e.g. *Gelsomini Sigeri SRL v Italy*, No. 63417/00, 18.12.03.

[85] *Lustig-Prean and Beckett v UK*, No. 31417/96 and 32377/96, 27.7.00, para. 28.

[86] No. 28369/95, 3.10.00.

[87] See, e.g. *Carbonara and Ventura v Italy*, No. 24638/94, 11.12.03 (in respect of agricultural land expropriated by the state: an award of €1,385,394.60 as pecuniary damages, €200,000 as non-pecuniary damages and €40,000 for costs and expenses).

[88] No. 31107/96, 19.10.00.

[89] No. 37095/97, 27.6.02. See also, e.g. *Motais de Narbonne v France*, No. 48161/99, 27.5.03 (€3,286,765.70 awarded in respect of expropriation of land).

[90] No. 43622/98, 18.4.02.

land in 1923. Domestic proceedings had begun in 1928 and led to a payment of compensation in 1999. The European Court awarded pecuniary damages of €487,060, plus €10,000 non-pecuniary damages. In the *Former King of Greece and others* v *Greece*,[91] the Court held that as the lack of any compensation, rather than the inherent illegality of the expropriation of land, had been the basis of the finding of a violation of Article 1 of Protocol No. 1, the compensation need not necessarily reflect the full value of the properties in question. Drawing parallels with the 'public interest' objectives in *James* v *UK*,[92] the Court found that less than full compensation could be justified where the taking of property had been intended to complete 'such fundamental changes of a country's constitutional system as the transition from monarchy to republic'.[93] The applicants were awarded pecuniary damages of €13,200,000 (plus €500,000 as legal costs).

In *Guiso-Gallisay* v *Italy*,[94] the Court changed its method for calculating compensation **8.24** for the illegal expropriation of land (to avoid potential anomalies). The new method was based on the market value of the property on the date when the right of ownership to the property had been lost, rather than the market value of the land increased by the value of any buildings erected on it by the local authority. In *Vistiņš and Perepjolkins* v *Latvia*[95] the Court found that the applicants had been insufficiently compensated for the expropriation of their land used by the port of Riga. The applicants' damages award was limited to the payment of appropriate compensation which should have been awarded at the time of the expropriation—they could not also justifiably claim loss of income in respect of the period subsequent to the expropriation.[96] Thus the Court was required to designate sums that were 'reasonably related' to the market value of the plots of land—in other words, sums that the Court would itself have found acceptable under Article 1 of Protocol No. 1 if the state had compensated the applicants. This involved a 'general assessment' of the consequences of the expropriation, and a calculation of the value of the land at the time the applicants lost their ownership of it. The Court has recognised that corporate bodies may suffer both pecuniary[97] and non-pecuniary damages.[98] As regards compensation for a company's non-pecuniary damages, the Court has stipulated that this:

> may include heads of claim that are to a greater or lesser extent 'objective' or 'subjective'. Among these, account should be taken of the company's reputation, uncertainty in planning and decision making, disruption in the management of the company and lastly, albeit to a lesser degree, anxiety and inconvenience caused to the members of the management team ...[99]

---

[91] No. 25701/94, 28.11.02.

[92] No. 8793/79, Series A, No. 98, 21.2.86.

[93] See also, *Broniowski* v *Poland*, No. 31443/96, 22.6.04, para. 149 (as regards 'transition from a totalitarian regime to a democratic form of government').

[94] No. 58858/00, 21.10.08 and 22.12.09.

[95] No. 71243/01, 25.10.12.

[96] *Vistiņš and Perepjolkins* v *Latvia*, No. 71243/01, 25.3.14, para. 34.

[97] *Comingersoll SA* v *Portugal*, No. 35382/97, 6.4.00.

[98] See, e.g. *Sovtransavto Holding* v *Ukraine*, No. 48553/99, 2.10.03; *Dacia S.R.L.* v *Moldova*, No. 3052/04, 19.2.09. But see *Krone Verlag GmbH & Co KG* v *Austria*, No. 34315/96, 26.2.02 where the Court left open the question whether the corporate applicant could claim *non-pecuniary* damages in respect of future losses in newspaper circulation or fines.

[99] *Microintelect OOD* v *Bulgaria*, No. 34129/03, 4.3.14, para. 59.

8.25 If the Court finds that an award of damages would constitute adequate compensation for a violation of the Convention, and if the applicant has an opportunity to claim damages through the domestic courts, the Court may exceptionally make no award of pecuniary damages.[100]

Awards for non-pecuniary damage may include elements in respect of the following:

- pain and suffering;[101]
- anguish and distress,[102] and disruption to life;[103]
- trauma;[104]
- uncertainty, anxiety, stress and feelings of injustice;[105]
- embarrassment;[106]
- frustration;[107]
- inconvenience;[108]
- feelings of isolation and helplessness;[109]
- loss of opportunity;[110]
- loss of reputation;[111] and
- loss of relationship.[112]

In relation to the level of non-pecuniary damages, it will often be productive to rely on 'appropriate comparators'—awards previously made by the Court in similar circumstances.[113] However, it should be noted that previous awards *may* have been limited by the amounts that the applicants had claimed. It may be useful in support of a claim for non-pecuniary damages for applicants to submit a statement which sets out why they have experienced anguish, distress or any of the 'heads' of damage mentioned above; however, the Court is very clear that there is no requirement as such for applicants to furnish any proof of the non-pecuniary damage which they sustained.[114] It also acknowledges that some forms of non-pecuniary damage (such as emotional distress) cannot always be the object of concrete proof.[115]

8.26 In cases concerning fatal incidents, it is possible for the Court to award non-pecuniary damages to the applicants to be held for the deceased's heirs (if they are not the same). For example, in *Taş v Turkey*,[116] a 'disappearance' case in which the Court found violations of

---

[100] See, e.g. *Clooth v Belgium*, No. 12718/87, 5.3.98; *Paudicio v Italy*, No. 77606/01, 24.5.07, para. 59. See also *Salah v Netherlands*, No. 8196/02, 6.7.06.

[101] See, e.g. *KA v Finland*, No. 22751/95, 14.1.03, para. 151.

[102] See, e.g. *Werner v Poland*, No. 26760/95, 15.11.01, para. 53.

[103] See, e.g. *Steel and Morris v UK*, No. 68416/01, 15.2.05, para. 109.

[104] See, e.g. *MC v Bulgaria*, No. 39272/98, 4.12.03.

[105] See, e.g. *Oldham v UK*, No. 36273/97, 26.9.00; *C v Finland*, No. 18249/02, 9.5.06.

[106] See, e.g. *Peck v UK*, No. 44647/98, 28.1.03.

[107] See, e.g. *RD v Poland*, Nos. 29692/96 and 34612/97, 18.12.01, para. 57; *Oldham v UK*, No. 36273/97, 26.9.00.

[108] See, e.g. *Stretch v UK*, No. 44277/98, 24.6.03.

[109] See, e.g. *Djavit An v Turkey*, No. 20652/92, 20.2.03.

[110] See, e.g. *Sadak and others v Turkey*, Nos. 29900/96, 29901/96, 29902/96 and 29903/96, 17.07.01; *Ezeh and Connors v UK*, Nos. 39665/98 and 40086/98, 9.10.03; *Basarba OOD v Bulgaria*, No. 77660/01, 20.1.11.

[111] See, e.g. *Kyprianou v Cyprus*, No. 73797/01, 15.12.05.

[112] See, e.g. *Kutzner v Germany*, No. 46544/99, 26.02.02.

[113] See, e.g. *A.D. and O.D. v UK*, No. 28680/06, 16.3.10, para. 110.

[114] *Gridin v Russia*, No. 4171/04, 1.6.06, para. 20; *Firstov v Russia*, No. 42119/04, 20.2.14, para. 49.

[115] *Peck v UK*, No. 44647/98, 28.1.03, para. 118.

[116] No. 24396/94, 14.11.00.

Articles 2, 3 and 13, the Court awarded non-pecuniary damages of £20,000 to be paid to the applicant (the father of the victim), which was to be held for his son's heirs. *Önen v Turkey*[117] concerned the killing of the applicant's brother and parents. The Court there held that it was empowered under Article 41 to make a non-pecuniary award not only to the applicant, but also to other members of the family who were victims of the violations found by the Court, and on whose behalf the applicant had brought the application and sought satisfaction.

In *Öneryildiz v Turkey*,[118] the applicant and his three sons were awarded non-pecuniary **8.27** damages of €135,000 following the loss of nine members of their family resulting from a methane gas explosion at a municipal rubbish tip where a shanty town had developed, taking into account their suffering as a result of the incident. The applicant in *Mikheyev v Russia*,[119] who was tortured in police custody, was awarded non-pecuniary damages of €120,000 (plus pecuniary damages of €130,000). The incident caused him severe mental and physical suffering. He then underwent several operations on his spine, and he had lost his mobility and sexual and pelvic function, and was unable to work or have children. The judgment in *Abuyeva and others v Russia*[120] concerned a series of fatalities caused by the shelling of the village of Katr-Yurt in Chechnya in 2000 by the Russian armed forces. As a result of the attack, 24 of the applicants' relatives were killed and a number of applicants sustained injuries. The Court awarded total non-pecuniary damages of €1.72 million. In *Finogenov and others v Russia*,[121] the case concerning the Moscow theatre siege, in which many of the hostages died, the 64 applicants were awarded a total of €1,254,000 as non-pecuniary damages.

A high award of €200,000 as non-pecuniary damages was made in *Dicle on behalf of the* **8.28** *Democratic Party (DEP) of Turkey v Turkey*[122] following the dissolution of the Democratic Party by the Turkish Constitutional Court, having regard to the party's active participation in Turkish political life (it had had 13 Members of Parliament at the date of its dissolution) and that it represented the primary political movement for a certain part of the population in Turkey. Thus the Court acknowledged the profound feelings of frustration that had arisen as a result of the party's dissolution.

In *L and V v Austria*, a case concerning the discriminatory criminalisation of homosexual **8.29** conduct, the Court awarded the applicants non-pecuniary damages of €15,000 each, taking into account that:[123]

> the criminal proceedings and … the trial during which details of the applicant's most intimate private life were laid open in public, have to be considered as profoundly destabilising events in the applicants' lives which had and, it cannot be excluded, continue to have a significant emotional and psychological impact on each of them.

---

[117] No. 22876/93, 14.5.02, para. 112. See also: *Ergi v Turkey*, No. 23818/94, 28.7.98, para. 110; *Kaya v Turkey*, No. 22729/93, 19.2.98, para. 122.

[118] No. 48939/99, 30.11.04.

[119] No. 77617/01, 26.1.06.

[120] No. 27065/05, 2.12.10. See further *Abakarova v Russia*, No. 16664/07, 15.10.15 (a case relating to the same incident as *Abuyeva*—€300,000 non-pecuniary damages awarded to the applicant in respect of the death of her five relatives). See also, e.g. *Esmukhambetov and others v Russia*, No. 23445/03, 29.3.11 (total damages awarded of €1,491,000 in respect of aerial attack on village by Russian armed forces).

[121] Nos. 18299/03 and 27311/03, 20.12.11. See also *Tagayeva and others v Russia*, No. 26562/07, 13.4.17.

[122] No. 25141/94, 10.12.02.

[123] Nos 39392/98 and 39829/98, 9.1.03, para. 60.

8.30 In *Arvanitaki-Roboti and others* v *Greece*,[124] and *Kakamoukas and others* v *Greece*,[125] the Grand Chamber was called on to make awards of non-pecuniary damages for excessive length of domestic proceedings to large numbers of joint claimants. The number of participants was found to have a bearing on the levels of damages to be awarded: 'Membership of a group of people who have resolved to apply to a court on the same factual or legal basis means that both the advantages and disadvantages of common proceedings will be shared.'[126]

8.31 The Court noted that the costs and fees of joint proceedings would usually be lower and the grouping of cases may mean their speedier resolution. It acknowledged, however, that joining proceedings may create an expectation that the state would act diligently in dealing with a case, and thus unjustified delay might exacerbate any prejudice sustained. Furthermore, the more each applicant's personal interests were at stake in the proceedings, the greater the inconvenience and uncertainty to which they would be subjected. The application of some of these factors could result in a reduction, and others in an increase, in the level of an award of damages.

8.32 In *L* v *Lithuania*,[127] the Court found a violation of Article 8 of the Convention as a result of the 'legislative gap' in the domestic law which prevented the applicant transsexual from undergoing gender reassignment surgery. In order to realise the applicant's claim for pecuniary damages the Court ordered the Government to pass the requisite subsidiary legislation within three months, or, alternatively, pay damages of €40,000.

Non-pecuniary Measures of Redress

8.33 As discussed above, the Court's standard form of redress is an award of damages (and costs). The Court's stock position is that it is a matter for the state to decide what measures, if any, need to be taken in response to a judgment (beyond the payment of damages):

> … a judgment in which the Court finds a violation of the Convention or its Protocols imposes on the respondent State a legal obligation not just to pay those concerned the sums awarded by way of just satisfaction, but also to choose, subject to supervision by the Committee of Ministers, the general and/or, if appropriate, individual measures to be adopted in its domestic legal order to put an end to the violation found by the Court and to redress the effects in such a way as to restore as far as possible the situation existing before the breach …[128]

However, exceptionally, invoking Article 46 and/or Article 41, the Court may stipulate that the state should provide other, individual non-pecuniary measures of redress. These have included the following: the release of a person unlawfully detained; the maintenance of effective family contact; the reinstatement of a person to their former occupation; the disclosure of information; the conduct of criminal investigations; the protection of witnesses; and the reopening of domestic proceedings following a finding of a violation of the Convention.

---

[124] No. 27278/03, 15.2.08.

[125] No. 38311/02, 15.2.08.

[126] *Arvanitaki-Roboti and others* v *Greece*, No. 27278/03, 15.2.08, para. 29. See also *Selahattin Çetinkaya and others* v *Turkey*, No. 31504/02, 20.10.09.

[127] No. 27527/03, 11.9.07.

[128] See, e.g. *Begheluri and others* v *Georgia*, No. 28490/02, 7.10.14, para. 187 (a case concerning religious violence perpetrated against Jehovah's Witnesses, in which the Court rejected the applicants' request to order the state to disseminate the judgment to the relevant authorities).

These measures are discussed in chapter 3. This chapter discusses non-pecuniary redress in two other areas: the non-implementation of domestic court judgments, and the restitution of property.

Non-implementation of Domestic Court Judgments

In cases concerning the failure of the domestic authorities to implement a judgment debt vis-à-vis the state (under Article 6), the Court's standard practice has been to award as pecuniary damages a sum equivalent to the entire amount awarded by the national court.[129] However, the Court's more recent practice in such cases is to acknowledge the applicant's right to recover the judgment debt in the domestic proceedings and to find that the government should secure, by appropriate means, the enforcement of the award made by the domestic courts (rather than make an award of damages equivalent to the value of the debt).[130] However, this may depend on whether the defendant against whom the judgment is to be enforced is the state, or a state-controlled entity, as opposed to a private company, for example, which might have gone out of business in the meantime.   **8.34**

Restitution of Property

As noted above, it is well established that the finding of a Convention violation imposes a legal obligation on the state to put an end to the breach and 'make reparation for its consequences in such a way as to restore as far as possible the situation existing before the breach'.[131]   **8.35**

In principle, the state is free to choose the means as to how it will comply with the judgment. But the state must effect *restitutio in integrum* if the nature of the breach allows it. Compensation will be payable if, as in the vast majority of cases, national law does not allow either full or partial reparation to be made for the consequences of the breach. Accordingly, the Court in some cases has required the state to return land and/or buildings which had been unlawfully and unjustifiably expropriated. In *Papamichalopoulos and others* v *Greece*,[132] the Court held that the unlawfulness of an expropriation would affect the criteria for determining the reparation owed, taking inspiration from the judgment of the International Court of Justice in the *Chorzów Factory Case* (of 13 September 1928) and referring to the principle of restitution in kind. A similar decision was made in *Brumarescu* v *Romania*,[133] reflecting the final domestic court order that had not been enforced. Failing such restitution, the Court required the state to pay damages equivalent to the current value of the property (more than $136,000). In *Gladysheva* v *Russia*[134] the Court found that the revocation of the   **8.36**

---

[129] See, e.g. *Qufaj Co. Sh.p.k.* v *Albania*, No. 54268, 18.11.04, para. 60.

[130] See, e.g. *Poznakhirina* v *Russia*, No. 25964/02, 24.2.05, para. 33; *Makarova and others* v *Russia*, No. 7023/03, 24.2.05, para. 37; *Fedotov* v *Russia*, No. 5140, 25.10.05, para. 101; *Apostol* v *Georgia*, No. 40765/02, 28.11.06, para. 73; *Karanović* v *Bosnia and Herzegovina*, No. 39462/03, 20.11.07, para. 30; *Niţescu* v *Romania*, No. 26004/03, 24.3.09, para. 48.

[131] See, e.g. *Brumarescu* v *Romania*, No. 28342/95, 23.1.01, para. 19; *Vasiliu* v *Romania*, No. 29407/95, 21.5.02; *Hodos and others* v *Romania*, No. 29968/96, 21.5.02.

[132] No. 14556/89, Series A, No. 330-B, 31.10.95.

[133] No. 28342/95, 23.1.01. See also *Zwierzynski* v *Poland*, No. 34049/96, 2.7.02; *Hirschhorn* v *Romania*, No. 29294/02, 26.7.07; *Mutishev and others* v *Bulgaria*, No. 18967/03, 28.2.12.

[134] No. 7097/10, 6.12.11. See also, e.g. *Stolyarova* v *Russia*, No. 15711/13, 29.1.15.

applicant's title to her flat (without compensation), in proceedings brought by the Moscow city authorities, violated both Article 1 of Protocol No. 1 and Article 8. The applicant was a bona fide purchaser of the flat which had been fraudulently acquired from the state by a previous owner. Accordingly, the Court directed the state (within three months) to ensure the full restitution of the applicant's title to the flat, and to annul an eviction order. The case of *Dacia S.R.L.* v *Moldova*[135] concerned the unlawful deprivation of the applicant company's hotel, in violation of Article 1 of Protocol No. 1 and Article 6. Under Article 41, the Court held that the most appropriate form of *restitutio in integrum* would be for the hotel and underlying land to be returned to the applicant company, and for compensation to be paid for any additional losses sustained. In case that were to prove impossible, the Court went on to determine the monetary value of the hotel to be paid in lieu of the return of the hotel (about €7.6 million, as the current market value), less sums already paid back to the applicant company, so as to avoid any unjust enrichment. A decision to similar effect was made in *Saghinadze and others* v *Georgia*,[136] which concerned the unlawful eviction of an Abkhazian IDP from a cottage belonging to the Georgian Ministry of Interior, after ten years' right of occupation. Under Article 41, the Court found[137] that:

> … the most appropriate form of redress would be *restitutio in integrum* under the IDPs Act, that is, to have the cottage restored to the first applicant's possession pending the establishment of conditions which would allow his return, in safety and with dignity, to his place of habitual residence in Abkhazia, Georgia. Alternatively, should the return of the cottage prove impossible, the Court is of the view that the first applicant's claim could also be satisfied by providing him, as an internally displaced person, with other proper accommodation or paying him reasonable compensation for the loss of the right to use the cottage …

8.37 In *Zafranis* v *Greece*,[138] legal proceedings concerning compensation which had been awarded to the applicants for the expropriation of their land were held to violate Article 1 of Protocol No. 1. As the applicants faced the risk of having to repay the compensation to the authorities, the Court directed the authorities (applying Article 41 and Article 46) to refrain from claiming back the compensation. In *Bozcaada Kimisis Teodoku Rum Ortodoks Kilisesi Vakfı* v *Turkey (No. 2)*,[139] the Court found a violation of Article 1 of Protocol No. 1 because the authorities refused to enter the applicant, a Greek Orthodox Church foundation, in the land register as the owner of property it had held for more than 20 years. Consequently, the Court required the property to be registered in the applicant foundation's name, or failing that the foundation was to be paid €100,000 by way of pecuniary damages.

8.38 These cases can be distinguished from cases in which property has been destroyed. In cases such as *Yöyler* v *Turkey*[140] and *Orhan* v *Turkey*,[141] where the applicants' houses were deliberately destroyed by the Turkish security forces, the Court rejected applicants' requests for restitution, on the basis in *Orhan* that restitution was 'in practice impossible'. The Court may also be mindful of the difficulties of enforcing orders of property restitution, a task which would fall to the Committee of Ministers. Nevertheless, the Court could be criticised in such

---

[135] No. 3052/04, 19.2.09.
[136] No. 18768/05, 27.5.10.
[137] *Ibid.*, para. 160.
[138] No. 4056/08, 4.10.11.
[139] Nos. 37639/03, 37655/03, 26736/04 and 42670/04, 3.3.09.
[140] No. 26973/95, 24.7.03.
[141] No. 25656/94, 18.6.02.

cases for failing to test the practicability or otherwise of restitution, by taking the issue up with the government and requiring the state to justify why restitution, at least to the land, if not the building themselves, would not be possible. The expropriation of the Van Gogh painting *Portrait of a Young Peasant*, was the subject of the application in *Beyeler* v *Italy*.[142] There, the Court found a violation of Article 1 of Protocol No. 1, but found that the nature of the breach did not allow for the restitution of the property and instead damages of €1,300,000 were awarded. In the *Former King of Greece and others* v *Greece*,[143] the Court found a violation of Article 1 of Protocol No. 1, not as a result of the state's expropriation, as such, of the applicants' property, but as a result of the failure to pay compensation. Accordingly, in view of the distinction which the Court made between lawful and unlawful expropriations, it was held that it was not appropriate to order *restitutio in integrum*, although the state was said to be free to decide to return some or all of the property to the applicants.

Costs and Expenses

The Court may award applicants their legal costs and expenses, provided that each of the **8.39** following conditions is satisfied:

(1) that the costs are *actually* incurred; and
(2) that they are *necessarily* incurred in order to prevent, or obtain redress for, the matter found to violate the Convention;[144] and
(3) that they are *reasonable as to quantum*.[145]

In addition to the costs of the European Court proceedings, a successful applicant may seek **8.40** to recover from the Court costs incurred in domestic proceedings that were aimed at preventing the violation from occurring or obtaining redress in respect of the Convention violation,[146] whether or not they were recoverable at the domestic level.[147] In *Papon* v *France*,[148] the only Convention violation related to the domestic cassation proceedings, and so the Court refused to reimburse the applicant's legal costs incurred during the investigation and trial phase of the domestic proceedings. In *Peck* v *UK*,[149] the applicant's award of legal costs included costs incurred in relation to his complaints to various domestic media commissions, on the basis that such bodies formed part of the legal regime for the protection of privacy in the United Kingdom.

Domestic fee scales may be relevant, but they are not binding on the Court.[150] In order to **8.41** attempt to recoup as much as possible of the costs and expenses actually and necessarily

---

[142] No. 33202/96, 28.5.02.
[143] No. 25701/94, 28.11.02.
[144] See, e.g. *Nilsen and Johnsen* v *Norway*, No. 23118/93, 25.11.99, para. 62.
[145] Practice Direction: *Just Satisfaction Claims*, paras. 18–20.
[146] Practice Direction: *Just Satisfaction Claims*, para. 16. See, e.g. *Lustig-Prean and Beckett* v *UK*, Nos. 31417/96 and 32377/96, 25.7.00, paras. 30–3; *Kingsley* v *UK*, No. 35605/97, 28.5.02, para. 50; *Wilson, NUJ and others* v *UK*, Nos. 30668/96, 30671/96 and 30678/96, 2.7.02, para. 67; *Roche* v *UK*, No. 32555/96, 19.10.05, para. 183; *Paksas* v *Lithuania*, No. 34932/04, 6.1.11, para. 122.
[147] See, e.g. *Associated Society of Locomotive Engineers & Firemen (ASLEF)* v *UK*, No. 11002/05, 27.2.07, para. 59.
[148] No. 54210/00, 25.7.02, para. 115.
[149] No. 44647/98, 28.1.03, para. 128.
[150] See also *Adam* v *Romania*, No. 45890/05, 3.11.09 in which the Court rejected a claim for costs as a percentage (20 per cent) of the damages awarded by the Court.

incurred, it is essential to submit to the Court a detailed bill of costs setting out the tasks carried out, the hours worked,[151] the hourly rates[152] and details of all expenses (see also chapters 2 and 3).[153] There is, however, no prescribed format for a 'bill of costs' as such. Where possible, copies of invoices relating to expenses incurred should be provided to the Court (see also Rule 60(2)). It should be noted that the Court very rarely awards all of the costs and expenses claimed by the applicant's representatives, especially where the respondent government disputes the amount claimed. In many cases, costs awarded by the Court are significantly lower than the amounts claimed. The costs incurred by several lawyers may be recoverable,[154] but not if the Court considers that there has been duplication of work.[155] Costs may also be reduced by the Court where several applicants in one case raise the same issue. This is due to the similarity of the cases, and the need for 'efficient co-ordination among the applicants' legal representatives'.[156]

8.42 Costs will not be deemed to have been incurred where a legal representative has acted free of charge and therefore they cannot in those circumstances be claimed under Article 41.[157] The Court may also consider whether legal aid has been granted in domestic proceedings to cover the costs incurred before the Strasbourg Court.[158]

8.43 If the applicant has not succeeded in establishing a violation of the Convention in respect of part of their case, this may be a factor in the Court reducing the costs sought.[159]

8.44 When an application is struck out under Article 37, the Court has a discretion to award an applicant's costs (under Rule 43(4)), as the Grand Chamber did, for example, in *Pisano v Italy*.[160] The award is made applying essentially the same principles as are applied under Article 41.[161]

Applicants may specify a bank account into which they wish any sums awarded to be paid.[162]

8.45 Costs awards may be expressed to be inclusive or exclusive of VAT and any sums previously paid by the Court as legal aid will be deductible.[163] The Court has adopted the practice of specifying that any sums payable in respect of costs and expenses should be exempt from tax payable by the applicant.[164] There is no provision in the Convention for costs to be awarded against an unsuccessful applicant.

---

[151] See, e.g. *Yazar and others v Turkey*, Nos. 22723–5/93, 9.4.02, para. 79.
[152] See, e.g. *C v Finland*, No. 18249/02, 9.5.06, para. 74.
[153] Practice Direction: *Just Satisfaction Claims*, para. 21.
[154] See, e.g. *Tysiąc v Poland*, No. 5410/03, 20.3.07, para. 160.
[155] See, e.g. *Roche v UK*, No. 32555/96, 19.10.05, para. 184.
[156] *IJL, GMR and AKP v UK*, Nos. 29522/95, 30056/96 and 30574/96, 25.9.01, para. 19.
[157] See, e.g. *McCann and others v UK*, No. 18984/91, Series A, No. 324, 27.9.95, para. 221; *Kondrulin v Russia*, No. 12987/15, 20.9.16, paras. 65–7.
[158] See *Geerings v Netherlands*, No. 30810/03, 14.2.08.
[159] See, e.g. *IJL, GMR and AKP v UK*, Nos. 29522/95, 30056/95 and 30574/96, 19.9.00, para. 151.
[160] No. 3673/97, 24.10.02 (applying former Rule 44).
[161] See *El Majjaoui & Stichting Touba Moskee v Netherlands*, No. 25525/03, 20.12.07, para. 39.
[162] Practice Direction: *Just Satisfaction Claims*, para. 22.
[163] Practice Direction: *Just Satisfaction Claims*, para. 18.
[164] See, e.g. *Kurić and others v Slovenia*, No. 26828/06, 12.3.14, para. 127.

INDEX